Data Analysis and Decision Making with Microsoft Excel

www.duxbury.com

Valuable resources @ no additional charge

Duxbury Titles of Related Interest

Data Analysis and Decision Making with Microsoft Excel

S. Christian Albright

School of Business, Indiana University

Wayne L. Winston

School of Business, Indiana University

Christopher Zappe

Bucknell University

With Case Studies by

Mark Broadie

Graduate School of Business, Columbia University

Peter Kolesar

Graduate School of Business, Columbia University

DUXBURY PRESS

An Imprint of Brooks/Cole Publishing Company

I(T)P® An International Thomson Publishing Company

Pacific Grove • Albany • Belmont • Boston • Cincinnati • Johannesburg • London • Madrid
Melbourne • Mexico City • New York • Scottsdale • Singapore • Tokyo • Toronto

Sponsoring Editor: *Curt Hinrichs*
Marketing Manager: *Laura Hubrich*
Assistant Editor: *Bryon Granmo*
Editorial Assistant: *Carrie Izant*
Production Editor: *Janet Hill*
Production Service/Manuscript Editor:
  Susan Reiland
Marketing Interns: *Christopher Fisher, Tami Cueny*

Cover Design: *Craig Hanson*
Interior Design: *John Edeen*
Photo Editor: *Terry Powell*
Composition: *Eigentype* and *SuperScript*
Cover Printing: *Phoenix Color Corporation*
Interior Printing and Binding: *The Courier
  Company, Inc.*

For more information, contact Duxbury Press at Brooks/Cole Publishing Company:

BROOKS/COLE PUBLISHING COMPANY
511 Forest Lodge Road
Pacific Grove, CA 93950
USA

International Thomson Publishing Europe
Berkshire House 168-173
High Holborn
London WC1V 7AA
England

Thomas Nelson Australia
102 Dodds Street
South Melbourne, 3205
Victoria, Australia

Nelson Canada
1120 Birchmount Road
Scarborough, Ontario
Canada M1K 5G4

International Thomson Editores
Seneca 53
Col. Polanco
11560 México, D.F., México

International Thomson Publishing GmbH
Königswinterer Strasse 418
53227 Bonn
Germany

International Thomson Publishing Asia
60 Albert St.
#15-01 Albert Complex
Singapore 189969

International Thomson Publishing Japan
Hirakawacho Kyowa Building, 3F
2-2-1 Hirakawacho
Chiyoda-ku, Tokyo 102
Japan

Printed in the United States of America

10 9 8 7 6 5 4 3 2 1

Library of Congress Cataloging-in-Publication Data

Albright, S. Christian.
    Data analysis and decision making with Microsoft Excel /
  S. Christian Albright, Wayne L. Winston, Christopher Zappe ; with case
  studies by Mark Broadie, Peter Kolesar.
      p.   cm.
  Includes bibliographical references and index.
  ISBN 0-534-26124-8
    1. Industrial management–Statistical methods–Computer programs.
  2. Decision making–Computer programs.   3. Microsoft Excel (Computer file)
  I. Winston, Wayne L.   II. Zappe, Christopher.   III. Title.
  HD30.215.A37   1999
  658.4'03'002855369–dc21
                                    98-48547

Photo Credits
Chapter 1 © Phil Schermeister/Corbis; **Chapter 2** © Gerald Davis/PNI; **Chapter 3** © John Maher/Stock Boston/PNI; **Chapter 4** © Ria-Novosti/Sovfoto/Eastfoto/PNI; **Chapter 5** © Myrleen Ferguson Cate/Photo Edit/PNI; **Chapter 6** © Dan Habib/Impact Visuals/PNI; **Chapter 7** © Joseph Nettis/Stock Boston/PNI; **Chapter 8** © Joel Gordon Photography; **Chapter 9** © Michael Thomas/Stock South/PNI; **Chapter 10** © Jasmine/PNI; **Chapter 11** © Kenneth Jarecke/Contact Press Images/PNI; **Chapter 12** © Herman J. Kokojan/ Black Star/PNI; **Chapter 13** © Mark Richards/Photo Edit/PNI; **Chapter 14** © Erica Lansner/Black Star/PNI; **Chapter 15** © Bruce Forster/Allstock/PNI; **Chapter 16** © Steve Winter/Black Star/PNI.

About the Authors

S. Christian Albright

Chris Albright got his B.S. degree in Mathematics from Stanford in 1968 and his Ph.D. in Operations Research from Stanford in 1972. Since then he has been teaching in the Operations & Decision Technologies Department in the Kelley School of Business at Indiana University. He has taught courses in management science, computer simulation, and statistics to all levels of business students: undergraduates, MBAs, and doctoral students. He has published over 20 articles in leading operations research journals in the area of applied probability, and he has authored the books *Statistics for Business and Economics*, *Student Execustat 3.0 MiniGuide*, and the spreadsheet-based *Practical Management Science*. His current interest is in spreadsheet modeling, including development of VBA applications in Excel.

On the personal side, Chris has been married to Mary for 27 years and has one son, Sam, who is about to begin his career as a jazz musician. Chris has many interests outside the academic area. They include activities with his family (especially traveling with Mary), going to cultural events at Indiana University, playing golf and tennis, running and power walking, and reading. And although he earns his livelihood from statistics and management science, his real passion is for playing the piano and listening to classical music.

Wayne Winston

Wayne L. Winston is Professor of Operations & Decision Technologies in the Kelley School of Business at Indiana University, where he has taught since 1975. Wayne received his B.S. degree in mathematics from MIT and his Ph.D. degree in operations research from Yale. He has written the successful textbooks *Operations Research: Applications and Algorithms*, *Mathematical Programming: Applications and Algorithms*, *Simulation Modeling with @RISK*, *Practical Management Science*, and *Financial Models Using Simulation and Optimization*. Wayne has published over 20 articles in leading journals and has won many teaching awards, including the school-wide MBA award four times. His current interest is in showing how spreadsheet models can be used to solve business problems in all disciplines, particularly in finance and marketing.

Wayne enjoys swimming and basketball, and his passion for trivia won him an appearance several years ago on the television game show *Jeopardy*, where he won two games. He is married to the lovely and talented Vivian. They have two children, Gregory and Jennifer.

Christopher J. Zappe

Chris earned his B.A. in mathematics from DePauw University in 1983 and his M.B.A. and Ph.D. in decision sciences from Indiana University in 1987 and 1988, respectively. Between 1988 and 1993, he performed research and taught various courses in the decision sciences area at the University of Florida in the College of Business Administration. Since 1993, Chris has been serving as an associate professor in the Department of Management at Bucknell University. He currently teaches undergraduate courses in business statistics, decision analysis, and computer simulation. Moreover, Chris teaches a graduate seminar in applied game theory. He has published articles in various journals including *Managerial and Decision Economics*, *OMEGA*, *Naval Research Logistics*, and *Interfaces*. His current scholarly interests focus on mathematical programming models of performance appraisal processes and innovative pedagogies in operations research/management science.

Chris has been married to his wonderful wife, Jeannie, for nearly four years now. Recently, Chris and Jeannie were blessed with the birth of their first child, Matthew. Beyond spending many long days with his students and colleagues at Bucknell, Chris enjoys playing with his new son, traveling to exciting faraway locations with his wife, reading great books of American history, watching major league baseball and college basketball games, and serving on the board of the local community center in Lewisburg, PA.

To my main supporters: *Mary, Sam, Tami, Ruth, and, of course, Charlie. And to Sam Senior, who is up there watching it all.*

S.C.A.

To my wonderful family: *Vivian, Jennifer, Gregory*

W.L.W.

To my wonderful family: *Jeannie and Matthew*

C.J.Z.

Brief Contents

Contents

12 Regression Analysis: Statistical Inference   628

13 Time Series Analysis and Forecasting   702

14 Introduction to Optimization Modeling   772

Preface

With today's technology, companies are able to *collect* tremendous amounts of data with relative ease. Indeed, many companies now have more data than they know what to do with. However, the data are usually meaningless until they are analyzed for trends, patterns, relationships, and other useful *information*. This book illustrates in a practical way a variety of statistical methods, from simple to complex, to help you analyze data sets and uncover important information. In many business contexts, data analysis is only the first step in the solution of a problem. Acting on the solution and the information it provides to make good decisions is a critical next step. Therefore, there is a heavy emphasis throughout this book on analytical methods that are useful in decision making. Again, the methods vary considerably, but the objective is always the same—to equip you with decision-making tools you can really *apply* in your business careers.

We take a very practical approach to teaching this material. We recognize that the vast majority of students in this type of course are *not* majoring in a quantitative area. They are typically *business* majors in finance, marketing, operations management, or some other business discipline who will need to analyze data and make quantitative-based decisions in their jobs. These students are not likely to learn, remember, or use material that is oriented primarily toward theory or formula-based calculations. In contrast, we offer a hands-on, example-based approach that provides value students will appreciate. Our vehicle is spreadsheet software, something with which most students are already familiar and will undoubtedly use in their careers. Our MBA students at Indiana University are so turned on by the required course that is based on this book that *well over 50%* of them (mostly finance and marketing majors) take our follow-up *elective* course in spreadsheet modeling (our management science course). We believe that students see value in statistics and quantitative analysis when the course is taught in a practical and example-based approach.

Rationale for Writing This Book

Data Analysis & Decision Making is different from the many fine textbooks written for statistics and management science. Our rationale for writing this book is based on three fundamental objectives:

1   We want the book to unify the student's ability to approach business-related problems by *integrating* methods and applications that have been traditionally taught in *separate* courses.

2 We want the emphasis to be placed on *realistic business examples* and the process by which a manager might analyze a problem—not on abstract theory or computational methods.

3 We want the book to provide students with the *skills to analyze* business problems with tools they have access to and will use in their careers. To this end, we have adopted Excel and commercial spreadsheet add-ins.

Integrative

In the past, many business schools, including ours at Indiana University, have had a required statistics course, a required decision making under uncertainty course, and a required management science course—or some subset of these. The current trend, however, is to have only one required course that covers the basics of statistics, some regression analysis, some decision making under uncertainty, some linear programming, some simulation, and possibly others. Essentially, we faculty in the quantitative area get one shot at teaching the business students, so we attempt to cover a *variety* of useful analytical methods. We cannot call this course a statistics course, a management science course, or any of the traditional labels because it cuts across a number of areas. We are not necessarily arguing that this trend is ideal, but rather that it is a reflection of the reality at our university and, we suspect, at many others.

We wrote this book for a very practical and selfish reason—to help us teach this integrated course. We found no other textbooks on the market that integrate all of the topics we want to include. After several years of teaching this course, we have found it to be a great opportunity to turn students on to the subject and to more advanced study.

Actually, this book is integrative in another important aspect. It not only integrates a number of analytical methods, but it applies them to a wide variety of business problems—that is, it integrates realistic examples from many business disciplines. We include examples, problems, and cases dealing with portfolio optimization, workforce scheduling, market share analysis, capital budgeting, new product analysis, and many others. We know our audience is comprised of *business* students, the majority of whom are typically in finance and marketing, and we have made every attempt to expose them to realistic, interesting, and challenging problems in their areas of interest.

Example-Based

Taking a cue from our *Practical Management Science* book, we wanted this book to be very example-based. We strongly believe that students learn best by working through examples, and they appreciate the material most when the examples are realistic and interesting business examples. Therefore, our approach in this book differs from traditional textbooks (particularly those in statistics) in two important ways. First, there is very little up-front discussion of the "theory" behind the methods. There is some, but just enough to give students an appreciation for the issues raised in the examples. This is not to say that we have thrown rigor out the window; we certainly have *not*. However, we often introduce important concepts (such as multicollinearity in regression) in the context of examples, rather than discussing them in the abstract. Our experience is that students gain greater intuition and understanding of the concepts and applications though this approach.

Second, we place virtually no emphasis on hand (or hand calculator) calculations. We believe it is more important for students to understand why they are conducting an analysis and what it means than to emphasize the tedious calculations associated with the mathematics of many analytical techniques. Therefore, we illustrate how good software can be used to create graphical and numerical outputs in a matter of seconds, freeing the rest of the time for in-depth interpretation of the output, sensitivity analysis, and alternative modeling approaches. Statistics and management science are already difficult topics for the majority of students, and we see no reason to make them *more* difficult—and less appealing—by making the students memorize complex formulas and perform tedious calculations. In our own courses, we move directly into a discussion of examples, where we focus almost exclusively on interpretation and modeling issues and let the computer software perform the number crunching.

Spreadsheet-Based

As we demonstrated in our *Practical Management Science* book, we are strongly committed to teaching spreadsheet-based, example-driven courses, regardless of whether the basic area is statistics or management science. We have found tremendous enthusiasm for this approach, both from students and from faculty around the world who have used the book. The students learn (and remember) more, and they *appreciate* the material more. The instructors typically enjoy teaching more, and they usually receive immediate reinforcement through better teaching evaluations.

When we wrote the *Practical Management Science* book, we had to retool ourselves for the move from traditional management science algebraic formulations to spreadsheet models. The move wasn't always easy, but as we climbed the learning curve, the benefits became increasingly obvious. In a similar way, we have had to retool ourselves for the move from non-spreadsheet statistics packages (Minitab, SPSS, JMP, Statgraphics, and so on) to doing it in Excel. This was a somewhat more difficult move, due to the lack of inherent statistical capabilities of Excel. However, as we describe below, we have addressed this problem by including the necessary tools to make the transition fairly easy—and fun.

What We Hope to Accomplish in This Book

Condensing the ideas in the above paragraphs, we hope to:

- Reverse negative student attitudes about statistics and quantitative methods by making them real, accessible, and interesting.

- Give students lots of hands-on experience with real problems and challenge them to develop their intuition, logic, and problem-solving skills.

- Expose students to real problems in many business disciplines and show them how these problems can be attacked with analytical methods.

- Develop spreadsheet skills, including experience with powerful spreadsheet add-ins, that will add immediate value in other courses and in their future careers.

Software

This book is based entirely on Microsoft Excel, the spreadsheet package that has become the standard analytical tool in business. Excel is an extremely powerful package, and one of our goals is to convert casual users into power users who can take full advantage of its features. If we accomplish no more than this, we will be imparting a valuable skill for the business world. However, Excel has many specific analytical limitations. Therefore, this book includes several Excel add-ins that greatly enhance Excel's capabilities. As a group, these add-ins comprise what is arguably the most impressive assortment of spreadsheet-based software in any book on the market.

When we began teaching this course in Excel, it quickly became obvious that Excel's inherent statistical capabilities were limited. Therefore, we provide an Excel add-in, StatPro™, that accompanies this book. We think you will find it to be quite powerful and extremely easy to use. (StatPro™ and the RandFns and SolverTable add-ins discussed below are marketed commercially by the Spreadsheet Solutions Corporation.) StatPro™ does not attempt to do what Excel already does well (pivot tables, for example), but it performs most statistical analyses, even those as complex as stepwise regression, in a matter of seconds. (To see a summary of its capabilities, see the file StatProHelp.htm on the CD-ROM.) If you have been using Excel's built-in Analysis ToolPak, we think you will be very pleasantly surprised with the functionality of StatPro™. Our students master it in no time at all.

A subset of StatPro™, RandFns, is also included and can be used separately. RandFns is a collection of functions for simulating random numbers from a variety of probability distributions, including the common distributions (normal, binomial, uniform, and so on) and some not so common (multivariate normal and multinomial, for example).

The CD-ROM accompanying this book contains the powerful DecisionTools™ Suite by Palisade Corporation—the first time this software has been included in a textbook. This suite includes five separate Excel add-ins:

- @Risk, the popular add-in for simulation

- PrecisionTree, a graphical-based add-in for creating and analyzing decision trees

- TopRank, a powerful add-in for performing what-if analyses

- BestFit, an add-in for fitting probability distributions to observed data

- RiskView, a graphical add-in for drawing probability distributions

The DecisionTools™ Suite included in this book is a special version for students only. It is only slightly scaled down from the professional version that sells for hundreds of dollars and is used by many leading companies. We make extensive use of @Risk and PrecisionTree in the chapters on simulation and decision making under uncertainty. We place less emphasis on TopRank, BestFit, and RiskView, but we illustrate them in several examples.

The final add-in we have included is SolverTable, a supplement to Excel's built-in Solver for optimization. If you have ever had difficulty trying to understand Solver's sensitivity reports, then SolverTable is right for you. It works like Excel's data tables, except that for each input (or pair of inputs), the add-in runs Solver and reports the optimal output values.

Together with Excel, these add-ins provide a tremendous amount of power for solving statistical, optimization, and simulation problems. They are easy to learn, and students will be able to carry their knowledge of these tools directly into the workplace. Excel and its add-ins show no signs of losing their prominent place in business in the foreseeable future.

Possible Sequences of Topics

Although we intend to use this book for our own required one-semester course, we admit that there is more material than can be covered adequately in one semester. We have tried to make the book as modular as possible, allowing an instructor to cover, say, simulation before linear programming or vice versa, or to omit either of these topics. The one exception is statistics. Due to the natural progression of statistical topics, the basic topics in the early chapters must be covered before the more advanced topics (regression, time series analysis, and statistical process control) in the later chapters. With this in mind, here are several possible ways to cover the topics.

- A one-semester required course, with no statistics prerequisite (or where MBA students have forgotten whatever statistics they might have learned years ago). If statistics is the primary focus of the course, then Chapters 2–5, 7–9, and 11–12 (all statistical topics) should be covered. Depending on the time remaining, any of the topics in Chapters 6 (decision making under uncertainty), 10 (statistical process control), 13 (time series analysis), 14–15 (optimization), or 16 (simulation) can be covered in practically any order.

- A one-semester required course, with a statistics prerequisite. Assuming students know the basic elements of statistics (up through hypothesis testing, say), then the material in Chapters 2–5 and 7–9 can be reviewed *quickly*, primarily to illustrate how Excel and add-ins can be used to advantage. Then the instructor can choose among any of the topics in Chapters 6, 10, 11–12, 13, 14–15, or 16 (in practically any order) to fill up the remainder of the course.

- A two-semester required sequence. Given the luxury of spreading the topics over two semesters, the entire book can be covered. The statistics topics in Chapters 2–5 and 7–9 should be covered in chronological order before other statistical topics (regression, time series analysis, and statistical process control), but the remaining chapters can be covered in practically any order.

Ancillaries for Adopting Faculty

The CD-ROM that accompanies this book contains:

- Excel add-ins from Spreadsheet Solutions and Palisade described earlier
- Excel files (usually data only—not the analyses) for examples in the chapters
- Data files required for the problems and cases
- A file TUTORIAL.HTM that contains a brief tutorial in the basic elements of Excel
- A file INSTALL.HTM that contains instructions for installing the add-ins

In addition, adopting instructors may obtain *Instructors Suite for Microsoft Office* CD-ROM, which includes:

- Solution files (in Excel and Word formats) for all of the problems and cases in the book
- PowerPoint presentation files for all of the examples in the book
- Completed Excel files for all of the examples in the book

Finally, adopting instructors will have access to the following:

- The AWZ (authors' initials) Web Resource Center that includes software updates, errata, additional problems and solutions, and additional resources for both students and faculty (accessible through www.duxbury.com by a password available to adopters)
- A Test Bank and the Thomson World Class Testing Service
- A Study Guide for students

Acknowledgments

The authors would like to thank several people who helped make this book a reality. First, the authors are indebted to Peter Kolesar and Mark Broadie of the Columbia Business School for contributing many excellent case studies that appear throughout the book. In addition, the manuscript went through several stages of review, where many valuable ideas emerged. We thank the following reviewers for their comments and suggestions:

Abe Feinberg, California State University, Northridge
Soumen Ghosh, Georgia Institute of Technology
Irwin Greenberg, George Mason University
Ching-Chung Kuo, Pennsylvania State University at Harrisburg
John Leschke, University of Virginia
Leslie Marx, University of Rochester
Jerrold May, University of Pittsburgh
Mike Middleton, University of San Francisco
Tyra Anne Mitchell, Georgia Institute of Technology
Richard Morris, Winthrop University
Herbert Moskowitz, Purdue University
Tom Obremski, University of Denver
Paul Paschke, Oregon State University
David W. Pentico, Duquesne University
William E. Stein, Texas A & M University
Donald N. Stengel, California State University, Fresno
Ralph E. Steuer, University of Georgia
Stan Taylor, California State University, Sacramento
Mustafa Yilmaz, Northeastern University
David Zalkind, George Washington University

There are more people who helped to produce this book than we can list here. However, there are a few special people whom we were happy (and lucky) to have on our team. To make a book with this many details look good on the page and be (relatively) free of errors requires meticulous compositors. We thank Peter Vacek and William Baxter for suffering through occasional corrupted graphics files, last-minute changes, and other headaches to produce a fine-looking product. There may be a few remaining errors, but they are certainly not the fault of our copy editor, Susan Reiland. Susan is a perfectionist, and her influence clearly shows throughout the book. Not only did she capture the typos, but she helped us improve our writing styles immeasurably. If you want to learn how to write well, write a book with Susan! The driving force behind this project from day one has been our editor, Curt Hinrichs. There were nights and weekends when we were in no mood to thank Curt, but even when he pushed us to our limits, we knew that he was one hundred percent behind us. No author can ask for more than an editor who knows the market and really cares about a project. We got that consistently from Curt. Any success this book has in the market is due largely to his efforts.

We are also grateful to many of the professionals at Duxbury who worked behind the scenes to make this book a success: Laura Hubrich, Marketing Manager; Janet Hill, Production Editor; Bryon Granmo, Assistant Editor; and Carrie Izant, Editorial Assistant.

Finally, we'd like to make one plug. There is a lot of software out there, but seldom does a package deliver exactly what a user needs. An exception is the HyperSnap screen capture shareware package developed by Greg Kochaniak (www.hyperionics.com). We don't know Greg personally, but we thank him for his excellent program. It helped make our lives so much easier!

S. Christian Albright
Wayne L. Winston
Christopher Zappe

Data Analysis and Decision Making with Microsoft Excel

1

Introduction to Data Analysis and Decision Making

Successful Applications

As you embark on your study of data analysis and decision making, you might question the usefulness of quantitative methods to the "real world." A front-page article in the December 31, 1997 edition of *USA Today* entitled "Higher Math Delivers Formula for Success" provides some convincing evidence of the applicability of the methods you will be learning. The subheading of the article, "Businesses turn to algorithms to solve complex problems," says it all. Today's business problems tend to be very complex. In the past, many managers and executives used a "seat of the pants" approach to solve problems—that is, they used their business experience, their intuition, and some thoughtful guesswork to obtain solutions. But common sense and intuition go only so far in the solution of the complex problems businesses now face. This is where data analysis and decision making—and the algorithms mentioned in the title of the article—are so useful. When the methods in this book are implemented in user-friendly computer software packages and are then applied to complex problems, the results can be amazing. Robert Cross, whose company, DFI Aeronomics, sells algorithm-based systems to airlines, states it succinctly: "It's like taking raw information and spinning money out of it."

The power of the methods in this book is that they are applicable to so many problems and environments. The article mentions the following "success stories" where quantitative analysis has been applied; others will be discussed throughout this book. (1) United Airlines installed one of DFI's systems, which cost between $10 million and $20 million. United expects the system to add $50 million to $100 million *annually* to its revenues. (2) The Gap clothing chain uses quantitative analysis to determine exactly how many employees should staff each store during the holiday rush. (3) Quantitative analysis has helped medical researchers test potentially dangerous drugs on fewer people with better results. (4) IBM obtained a $93 million contract to build a computer system for the Department of Energy that would do a once-impossible task: make exact real-time models of atomic blasts. It won the contract—and convinced the DOE that its system was cost-effective—only by developing quantitative methods that would cut the processing time by half. (5) Hotels, airlines, and television broadcasters all use quantitative analysis to implement a new method called "yield management." In this method, different prices are charged to different customers, depending on their willingness to pay. The effect is that more customers are attracted, and revenues increase.

The article concludes by stating that Microsoft's Excel spreadsheet software has a mini-optimization program inside called Solver. This is a key statement. Many of the algorithms that enable the successes discussed in the article are very complex mathematically. They are well beyond the grasp of the typical user, including most readers of this book. However, users no longer need to understand all of the details behind the algorithms. They need only to know how to model business problems so that appropriate algorithms can be applied and then how to apply them with user-friendly software. For example, we will see in Chapters 14 and 15 how to apply Excel's Solver to a variety of complex problems. You will not learn the intricacies of how Solver does its optimization, but you *will* learn how to use Solver very productively. The same statement applies to the other methods discussed in this book. You might not understand exactly what is happening in the computer's "black box" as it performs its calculations, but you will learn how to become very effective problem solvers by taking advantage of powerful software. ■

1.1 Introduction

We are living in the age of technology. This has two important implications for everyone entering the business world. First, technology has made it possible to collect huge amounts of data. Retailers collect point-of-sale data on products and customers every time a transaction occurs; credit agencies have all sorts of data on people who have or would like to obtain credit; investment companies have a limitless supply of data on the historical patterns of stocks, bonds, and other securities; and government agencies have data on economic trends, the environment, social welfare, consumer product safety, and virtually everything else we can imagine. It has become relatively *easy* to collect the data. As a result, data are plentiful. However, as many organizations are now beginning to discover, it is quite a challenge to analyze and make sense of all the data they have collected.

A second important implication of technology is that it has given many more people the power and responsibility to analyze data and make decisions on the basis of quantitative analysis. Those entering the business world can no longer push all of the quantitative analysis to the "quant jocks," the technical specialists who have traditionally done the number crunching. Virtually everyone now has a desktop or laptop computer at their disposal, they have access to relevant data, and they have been trained in easy-to-use software, particularly spreadsheet and database software. For these employees, statistics and other quantitative methods are no longer forgotten topics they once learned in college. Quantitative analysis is now an integral part of their daily jobs.

Huge quantities of data already exist, and they are only going to expand in the future. Many companies already complain of swimming in a sea of data. However, enlightened companies are seeing this expansion as a source of competitive advantage. By using quantitative methods to uncover the *information* in the data and then acting on this information— again guided by quantitative analysis—they are able to gain advantages that their less enlightened competitors are not able to gain. Several pertinent examples of this follow.

- Direct marketers analyze enormous customer databases to see which customers are likely to respond to various products and types of promotions. This allows them to target different classes of customers in different ways to maximize profits—and gives their customers what the customers want.

- Hotels and airlines also analyze enormous customer databases to see what their customers want and are willing to pay for. By doing this, they have been able to devise very clever pricing strategies, where not everyone pays the same price for the same accommodations. For example, a business traveler typically makes a plane reservation closer to the time of travel than a vacationer. The airlines know this. Therefore, they reserve seats for these business travelers and charge them a higher price (for the same seats). The airlines profit, and the customers are happy.

- Financial planning services have a virtually unlimited supply of data about security prices, and they have customers with widely differing preferences for various types of investments. Trying to find a match of investments to customers is a very challenging problem. However, customers can easily take their business elsewhere if good decisions are not made on their behalf. Therefore, financial planners are under extreme competitive pressure to analyze masses of data so that they can make informed decisions for their customers.

- We all know about the pressures U.S. manufacturing companies have faced from foreign competition in the past couple of decades. The automobile companies, for example, have had to change the way they produce and market automobiles to stay in business. They have had to improve quality and cut costs by orders of magnitude. Although the struggle continues, much of the success they have had can be attributed to data analysis and wise decision making. Starting on the shop floor and moving up through the organization, they now measure almost everything they do, they analyze these measurements, and then they act on the information from these measurements.

We talk about companies analyzing data and making decisions. However, *companies* don't really do this; *people* do it. And who will these people be in the future? They will be *you*! We know from experience that students in all areas of business, at both the undergraduate and graduate level, will soon be *required* to describe large complex data sets, run regression analyses, make quantitative forecasts, create optimization models, and run simulations. You are the people who will soon be analyzing data and making important decisions to help gain your companies a competitive advantage. And if you are *not* willing or able to do so, there will be plenty of other technically trained people who will be more than happy to replace you.

Our goal in this book is to teach you how to use a variety of quantitative methods to analyze data and make decisions. We plan to do so in a very hands-on way. We will discuss a number of quantitative methods and illustrate their use in a large variety of realistic business problems. As you will see, this book is very "example driven," with examples from finance, marketing, operations, accounting, and other areas of business. To analyze these examples, we will take advantage of the Microsoft Excel spreadsheet package, together with a number of powerful Excel add-ins. In each example we will provide step-by-step details of the method and its implementation in Excel.

This is *not* a "theory" book. It is also not a book where you can lean comfortably back in your chair, prop your legs up on a table, and read about how *other* people use quantitative methods. It is a "get your hands dirty" book, where you will learn best by actively following the examples throughout the book at your own PC. In short, you will learn by doing. By the time you've finished, you will have acquired some very useful skills for today's business world.

An Overview of the Book

This book is packed with quantitative methods and examples, probably more than can be covered in any single course. Therefore, we purposely intend to keep this introductory chapter brief so that you can get on with the analysis. Nevertheless, it is useful to get some feel for the methods you will be learning and the tools you will be using. In this section we will provide an overview of the methods covered in this book and the software that will be used to implement them. Then in the next section we will preview some of the examples we will cover in much more detail in later chapters. Finally, we will present a brief discussion of models and the modeling process. Our primary purpose at this point is to stimulate your interest in what is to follow.

1.2.1   The Methods

This book is rather unique in that it combines topics from two separate fields: statistics and management science. In a nutshell, statistics is the study of data analysis, whereas management science is the study of model building, optimization, and decision making. In the academic arena there has traditionally been a separation between the two fields, sometimes a wide separation. Indeed, they are often housed in separate academic departments. However, from a user's standpoint it makes little sense to separate them. Both are useful in accomplishing what the title of this book promises: data analysis and decision making.

Therefore, we don't distinguish between the "statistics" and "management science" parts of this book. Instead, we view the entire book as a collection of useful quantitative methods that can be used to analyze data and help make business decisions. In addition, our choice of software helps to integrate the various topics. By using a single package, Excel, together with a number of add-ins, we see that the methods of statistics and management science are similar in many important respects. Most importantly, their combination gives us the power and flexibility to solve a wide range of business problems.

Three important themes run through this book. Two of them are in the title: **data analysis** and **decision making**. The third is **dealing with uncertainty**.[1] Each of these themes has subthemes. Data analysis includes data **description**, data **inference**, and the search for **relationships** in data. Decision making includes **optimization** techniques for problems with no uncertainty, **decision analysis** for problems with uncertainty, and structured **sensitivity analysis**. Dealing with uncertainty includes **measuring** uncertainty and **modeling** uncertainty explicitly into the analysis. There are obvious overlaps between these themes and subthemes. When we make inferences from data and search for relationships in data, we must deal with uncertainty. When we use decision trees to help make decisions, we must deal with uncertainty. When we use simulation models to help make decisions, we must deal with uncertainty, and we often must make inferences from the simulated data.

Figure 1.1 shows where you will find these themes and subthemes in the remaining chapters of this book. In the next few paragraphs we will discuss the book's contents in more detail.

---

[1]The fact that the uncertainty theme didn't find its way into the title does not detract from its importance. We just wanted to keep the title reasonably short!

FIGURE 1.1   Themes and Subthemes

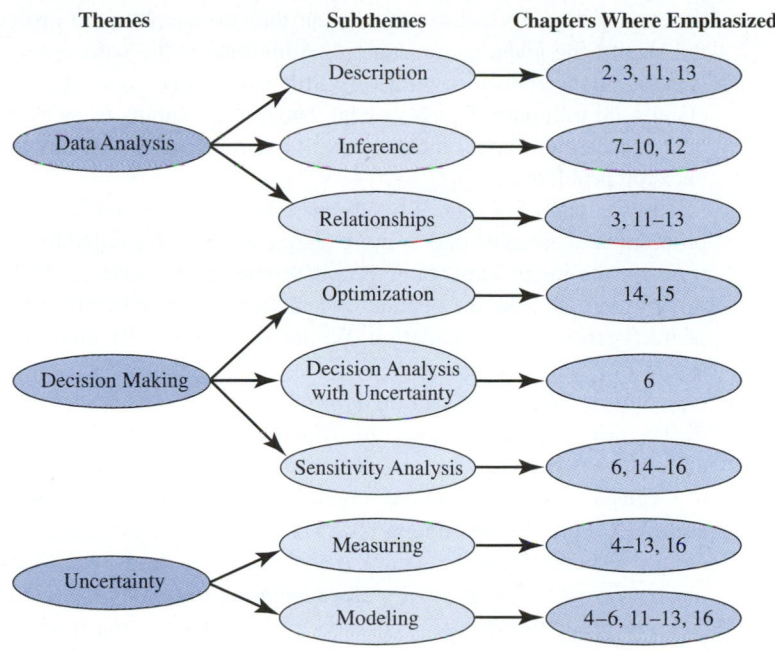

We begin in Chapters 2 and 3 by illustrating a number of ways to summarize the information in data sets. These include graphical and tabular summaries, as well as numerical summary measures such as means, medians, and standard deviations. The material in these two chapters is elementary from a mathematical point of view, but it is extremely important. As we stated at the beginning of this chapter, organizations are now able to collect huge amounts of raw data. The question then becomes, What does it all mean? Although there are very sophisticated methods for analyzing data sets, some of which we will cover in later chapters, the "simple" methods in Chapters 2 and 3 are crucial for obtaining an initial understanding of the data. Fortunately, Excel and available add-ins now make what was once a very tedious task quite easy. For example, Excel's pivot table tool for "slicing and dicing" data is an analyst's dream come true. You'll be amazed at the complex analysis it will enable you to perform—with almost no effort!

Uncertainty is a key aspect of most business problems. To deal with uncertainty, we need a basic understanding of probability. We provide this understanding in Chapters 4 and 5. Chapter 4 covers basic rules of probability and then discusses the extremely important concept of probability distributions in some generality. Chapter 5 follows up this discussion by focusing on two of the most important probability distributions, the normal and binomial distributions. It also briefly discusses the Poisson distribution, which finds many applications in probability models but is not used as extensively in this book.

We have found that one of the best ways to make probabilistic concepts "come alive" and easier to understand is by using computer simulation. Therefore, simulation is a common theme that runs through this book, beginning in Chapter 4. Although the final chapter of the book is devoted entirely to simulation, we do not hesitate to use it early and often to illustrate difficult probabilistic and statistical concepts.

In Chapter 6 we apply our knowledge of probability to decision making under uncertainty. These types of problems—faced by all companies on a continual basis—are characterized by the need to make a decision *now*, even though important information (such as demand for a product or returns from investments) will not be known until later.

The material in Chapter 6 provides a rational basis for making such decisions. The methods we illustrate do not guarantee perfect outcomes—the future could unluckily turn out differently than we had expected—but they do enable us to proceed rationally and make the best of the given circumstances. Additionally, the software we will use to implement these methods allows us, with very little extra work, to see how sensitive the optimal decisions are to inputs. This is crucial, because the inputs to many business problems are at best educated guesses. Finally, we will examine the role of risk aversion in these types of decision problems.

In Chapters 7, 8, and 9 we discuss sampling and statistical inference. Here the basic problem is to estimate one or more characteristics of a population. If it is too expensive or time-consuming to learn about the *entire* population—and it usually is—we instead select a random sample from the population and then use the information in the sample to *infer* the characteristics of the population. We see this continually on news shows that describe the results of this or that survey. We also see it in many business contexts. For example, auditors typically sample only a fraction of a company's records. Then they infer the characteristics of the entire population of records from the results of the sample to conclude whether the company has been following acceptable accounting standards.

Chapter 10 presents an introduction to statistical process control, also known as quality control. Quality has become a buzzword in many companies, in both manufacturing and service industries, for the simple reason that it is almost impossible to survive in today's business world without paying close attention to quality. As we discuss in Chapter 10, a "quality program" requires a number of initiatives, some quantitative and some not. For example, most quality advocates argue that lasting quality will not occur unless management takes an active role in helping workers to do their best work, including extensive job training. These are management issues that fall outside of the scope of this book. However, an important part of any quality program involves gathering data on company processes and using statistical techniques to analyze these data. We will focus on some of these statistical techniques in Chapter 10. Specifically, we will discuss control charts for checking whether a process is "in control," and we will discuss methods for checking whether a process is capable of producing outputs that meet specifications.

In Chapters 11 and 12 we discuss the extremely important topic of regression analysis, which is used to study relationships between variables. Its power is its generality. Every part of a business has variables that are related to one another, and regression can often be used to estimate possible relationships between these variables. In managerial accounting, regression is used to estimate how overhead costs depend on direct labor hours and production volume. In marketing, regression is used to estimate how sales volume depends on advertising and other marketing variables. In finance, regression is used to estimate how the return of a stock depends on the "market" return. In real estate studies, regression is used to estimate how the selling price of a house depends on the assessed valuation of the house and characteristics such as the number of bedrooms and square footage. Regression analysis finds perhaps as many uses in the business world as any method in this book.

From regression, we move to times series analysis and forecasting in Chapter 13. This topic is particularly important for providing inputs into business decision problems. For example, manufacturing companies must forecast demand for their product to make sensible decisions about order quantities from their suppliers. As another example, fast-food restaurants must forecast customer arrivals, sometimes down to the level of 15-minute intervals, so that they can staff their restaurants appropriately.

There are many approaches to forecasting, ranging from simple to complex. Some involve regression-based methods, in which one or more time series variables are used to forecast the variable of interest, whereas other methods are based on extrapolation. These latter methods are the primary focus of Chapter 13. In an extrapolation method the historical patterns of a time series variable, such as product demand or customer arrivals, are studied carefully and are then "extrapolated" into the future to obtain forecasts. A number of extrapolation methods are available. We will focus on the methods that have proved most successful in the business world.

Chapters 14 and 15 are devoted to spreadsheet optimization, with emphasis on linear programming. Here we assume a company must make several decisions, and there are constraints that limit the possible decisions. The job of the decision maker is to choose the decisions such that all of the constraints are satisfied and an objective such as total profit or total cost is optimized. The solution process consists of two steps. First, we build a spreadsheet model that relates the decision variables to other relevant quantities by means of logical formulas. In this first step there is no attempt to find the *optimal* solution; all we want to do is relate all relevant quantities in a logical way. The second step is then to find the optimal solution. Fortunately, Excel has a "Solver" add-in that performs this step. All we need to do is specify the objective, the decision variables, and the constraints; Solver then uses powerful algorithms to find the optimal solution. As with regression, the power of this approach is its generality. An enormous variety of problems can be solved by spreadsheet optimization.

Finally, Chapter 16 illustrates a number of computer simulation models. This will not be our first exposure to simulation—it is used in a number of previous chapters to illustrate probabilistic and statistical concepts—but here it will be studied in its own right. As we have discussed earlier, most business problems have some degree of uncertainty. The demand for a product is unknown, future interest rates are unknown, the delivery leadtime from a supplier is unknown, and so on. Simulation allows us to build this uncertainty *explicitly* into spreadsheet models. Essentially, some cells in the model contain random values with given probability distributions. Every time the spreadsheet recalculates, these random values change, which causes "bottom-line" output cells to change as well. The trick then is to force the spreadsheet to recalculate many times and keep track of interesting outputs. In this way we can see which output values are most likely, and we can see best-case and worst-case results.

Complex spreadsheet simulations can be performed entirely with Excel's built-in tools. However, this can be quite tedious. Therefore, we will show how spreadsheet add-ins streamline the process. In particular, we will learn how the @Risk add-in can be used to run replications of a simulation, keep track of outputs, create useful charts, and perform sensitivity analyses. With the inherent power of spreadsheets and the ease-of-use of such add-ins as @Risk, spreadsheet simulation is becoming one of the most frequently used quantitative tools in the business world.

1.2.2 The Software

The topics we have just discussed are very important. Together, they can be used to solve a wide variety of business problems. However, they are not of much practical use unless we have the software to do the number crunching. Very few business problems are small enough to be solved with pencil and paper. They require powerful software.

The software included in this book, together with Microsoft Excel, provides you with a powerful software combination that you will not use for one course and then discard. It is software that is being used—and will continue to be used—by leading companies all over the world to solve large, complex problems. We firmly believe that the experience you obtain with this software, through working the examples and problems in this book, will give you a key competitive advantage in the marketplace.

It all begins with Excel. All of the quantitative methods that we discuss are implemented in Excel. It is obviously impossible to forecast the state of computer software into the long-term or even medium-term future, but as we are writing this book, Excel is *the* most heavily used spreadsheet package on the market, and there is every reason to believe that this state will persist for at least several years. Most companies use Excel, most employees and most students have been trained in Excel, and Excel is a *very* powerful, flexible, and easy-to-use package.

Built-in Excel Features   Virtually everyone in the business world knows the basic features of Excel, but relatively few know many of its more powerful features. In short, relatively few people are the "power users" we expect you will become by working through this book. To get you started, the file TUTORIAL.HTM on the CD-ROM explains some of the "intermediate" features of Excel—features that we expect you to be able to use. These include the SUMPRODUCT, VLOOKUP, IF, NPV, and COUNTIF functions. They also include range names, the Data Table command, the Paste Special command, the Goal Seek command, and a few others. Finally, although we assume you can perform routine spreadsheet tasks such as copying and pasting, we include a few tips to help you perform these tasks more efficiently.

In the body of the book we describe several of Excel's advanced features in more detail. In Chapters 2 and 3 we introduce pivot tables, the Excel tool that enables you to summarize data sets in an almost endless variety of ways. (Excel has a lot of useful tools, but we personally believe that pivot tables are the most ingenious and powerful of all. We won't be surprised if you agree.) Beginning in Chapter 4, we introduce Excel's RAND function for generating random numbers. This function is used in all spreadsheet simulations (at least those that don't take advantage of an add-in).

Solver Add-in   In Chapters 14 and 15 we make heavy use of Excel's Solver add-in. This add-in, developed by Frontline Systems (not Microsoft), uses powerful algorithms—all behind the scenes—to perform spreadsheet optimization. Before this type of spreadsheet optimization add-in was available, we needed specialized (non-spreadsheet) software to solve optimization problems. Now we can do it all within a familiar spreadsheet environment.

StatPro Add-in   Much of this book discusses basic statistical analysis. Here we were in a quandary as we developed the book. There are a number of excellent statistical software packages on the market, including Minitab, SPSS, SAS, StatGraphics, and others. Although there are now user-friendly Windows versions of these packages, they are *not* spreadsheet-based. We have found through our own experience that students resist the use of non-spreadsheet packages, regardless of their inherent quality, so we wanted to use Excel as our "statistics package." Unfortunately, Excel's built-in statistical tools are rather limited, and the Analysis ToolPak (developed by a third party) that ships with Excel also has significant limitations.

Therefore, we provide an add-in called StatPro that accompanies this book.[2] The file INSTALL.HTM on the CD-ROM describes how to install StatPro, how to use it, and how to obtain online help. StatPro is powerful, easy-to-use, and capable of generating output quickly in an easily interpretable form. We do *not* believe you should have to spend hours each time you want to produce some statistical output. This might be a good learning experience the first time through, but after that it acts as a strong incentive not to perform the analysis at all! We believe you should be able to generate output quickly and easily. This gives you the time to *interpret* the output—and possibly redo the analysis if it didn't turn out right the first time.

A good illustration involves the construction of histograms, scatterplots, and time series plots, discussed in Chapter 2. All of these extremely useful graphs can be created in a straightforward way with Excel's built-in tools. But by the time you perform all the

---

[2]StatPro is also being marketed as a separate product by Duxbury Press.

necessary steps and "dress up" the charts exactly as you want them, you're not going to very anxious to repeat the whole process again. StatPro does it all quickly and easily. (You still might want to "dress up" the resulting charts, but that's up to you.) Therefore, if we advise you in a later chapter, say, to look at several scatterplots as a prelude to a regression analysis, you can do so in a matter of seconds.

RandFns Add-in   We have also included a set of functions in StatPro that are useful in developing simulation models. Each of these functions generates a random value from one of the well-known probability distributions we discuss in the book. For example, the NORMAL_ function simulates a normally distributed random value. Sometimes you might want to have these functions available *without* loading the entire StatPro add-in. Therefore, we have included them in a separate (small) add-in called RandFns. We will discuss the functions available from this add-in in several chapters, particularly in Chapter 16.

SolverTable Add-in   An important theme that runs throughout this book is sensitivity analysis: How do outputs change when inputs change? This is typically done in spreadsheets with a data table, a built-in Excel tool. However, data tables don't work in optimization models, where we would like to see how the *optimal* solution changes when certain inputs change. Therefore, we include an Excel add-in called SolverTable to perform this type of sensitivity analysis. It works almost exactly like Excel's data tables, and it is included with this book. In Chapters 14 and 15 we will explain how to use SolverTable.

Decision Tools Suite   Besides StatPro, RandFns, SolverTable, and built-in Excel add-ins, we have also contracted with Palisade Corporation to include a slightly scaled-down version of its powerful Decision Tools suite in this book. All items in this suite are Excel add-ins— so the learning curve isn't very steep. We describe how to install the suite and give some general guidelines for its use in the INSTALL.HTM file on the CD-ROM. There are five separate add-ins in this suite: @Risk, PrecisionTree, TopRank, BestFit, and RiskView. The first two are the most important for our purposes, but all are useful for certain tasks.

@Risk   The simulation add-in @Risk enables us to run as many replications of a spreadsheet simulation as we like. As the simulation runs, @Risk automatically keeps track of the outputs we select, and it then displays the results in a number of tabular and graphical forms. It also enables us to perform a sensitivity analysis, so that we can see which inputs have the most effect on the outputs.

PrecisionTree   The PrecisionTree add-in is used in Chapter 6 to analyze decision problems with uncertainty. The primary method for performing this type of analysis is to draw a decision tree. Decision trees are inherently graphical, and they were always difficult to implement in spreadsheets, which are based on rows and columns. However, PrecisionTree does this in a very clever and intuitive way. Equally important, once the basic decision tree has been built, it is easy to use PrecisionTree to perform a sensitivity analysis on the model inputs.

TopRank   Although we will not use the other Palisade add-ins as extensively as @Risk and PrecisionTree, they are all worth investigating. TopRank is the most general of them. It starts with any spreadsheet model, where a set of inputs are used, along with a number of spreadsheet formulas, to produce an output. TopRank then performs a sensitivity analysis to see which inputs have the largest effect on the output. For example, it might tell us which affects after-tax profit the most: the tax rate, the risk-free rate for investing, the inflation rate, or the price charged by a competitor. Unlike @Risk, TopRank is used when uncertainty is not *explicitly* built into a spreadsheet model. However, it considers uncertainty implicitly by performing sensitivity analysis on the important model inputs.

BestFit   BestFit is used to determine the most appropriate probability distribution for a spreadsheet model when we have data on some uncertain quantity. For example, a simulation might model each week's demand for a product as a random variable. What probability distribution should we use for weekly demand: the well-known normal distribution or possibly some skewed distribution? If we have historical data on weekly demands for the product, we can feed them into BestFit and let it recommend the distribution that best fits the data. This is a very useful tool in real applications. Instead of guessing a distribution that we think might be relevant, we can let BestFit point us to a distribution that fits historical data well. We discuss one application of BestFit in Chapter 5.

RiskView   Finally, RiskView is a drawing tool that complements @Risk. A number of probability distributions are available with @Risk and can be used in simulations. Each has an associated @Risk function, such as RiskNormal, RiskBinomial, and so on. Before selecting any of these distributions, however, it is useful (especially for beginners) to see what these distributions look like. RiskView performs this task easily. For any selected probability distribution (and any selected parameters of this distribution), it creates a graph of the distribution. We show how this can be done in Chapter 16.

Software Guide   Figure 1.2 provides a guide to where these various add-ins appear throughout the book. We don't show Excel explicitly in this figure for the simple reason that Excel is used extensively in *all* chapters.

FIGURE 1.2   **Software Guide**

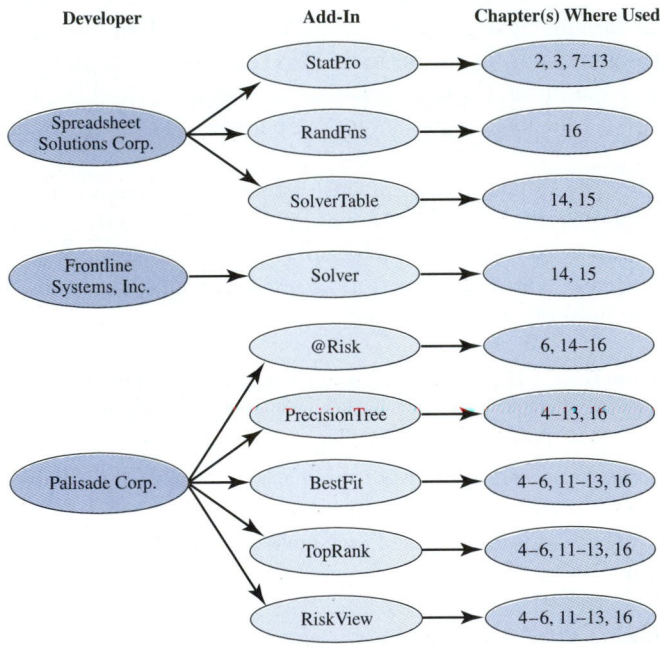

Together with Excel and the add-ins included in this book, you have a wealth of software at your disposal. The examples and step-by-step instructions throughout this book will help you to become a power user of this software. Admittedly, this takes plenty of practice and a willingness to experiment, but it is certainly within your grasp. When you are finished, we won't be surprised if you rate improved software skills as the most valuable thing you've learned from this book.

A Sampling of Examples

Perhaps the best way to illustrate what you'll be learning in this book is to preview a few examples from later chapters. Our intention here is not to teach you any methods; that will come later. We only want to indicate the types of problems you'll learn how to solve. Each example below is numbered as in the chapter where it appears.

E X A M P L E 3 . 9

The Spring Mills Company produces and distributes a wide variety of manufactured goods. Because of its variety, it has a large number of customers. It classifies these customers as small, medium, and large, depending on the volume of business each does with Spring Mills. Recently, Spring Mills has noticed a problem with its accounts receivable. It is not getting paid back by its customers in as timely a manner as it would like. This obviously costs Spring Mills money. If a customer delays a payment of $300 for 20 days, say, then the company loses potential interest on this amount. The company has gathered data on 280 customer accounts. For each of these accounts, the data set lists three variables: Size, the size of the customer (coded 1 for small, 2 for medium, 3 for large); Days, the number of days since the customer was billed; and Amount, the amount the customer owes. What information can we obtain from these data?

Solution

This example from Chapter 3 is a typical example of trying to make sense out of a large data set. Spring Mills has 280 observations on each of three variables. By realistic standards, this is not a huge data set, but it still presents a challenge. We examine the data from a number of angles and present several tables and charts. For example, the scatterplots in Figures 1.3 through 1.5 clearly indicate that there is a *positive* relationship between the amount owed and the number of days since billing for the medium-sized and large customers, but that no such relationship exists for the small customers. As we will see, graphs such as these are very easy to construct in Excel, regardless of the size of the data set.

F I G U R E 1 . 3   **Scatterplot of Amount versus Days for Small Customers**

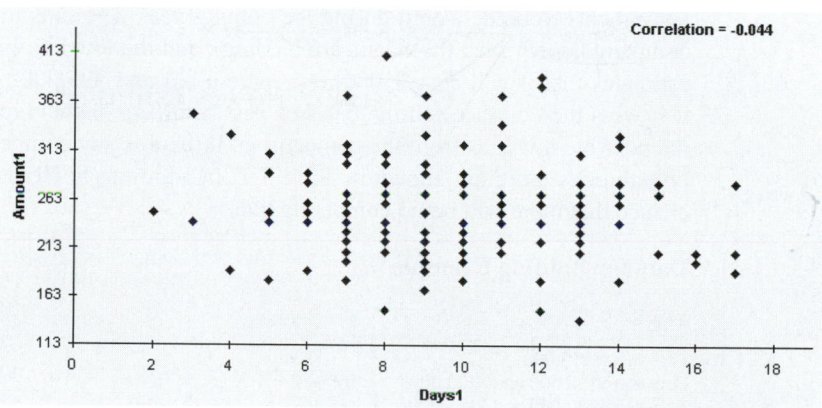

FIGURE 1.4 **Scatterplot of Amount versus Days for Medium Customers**

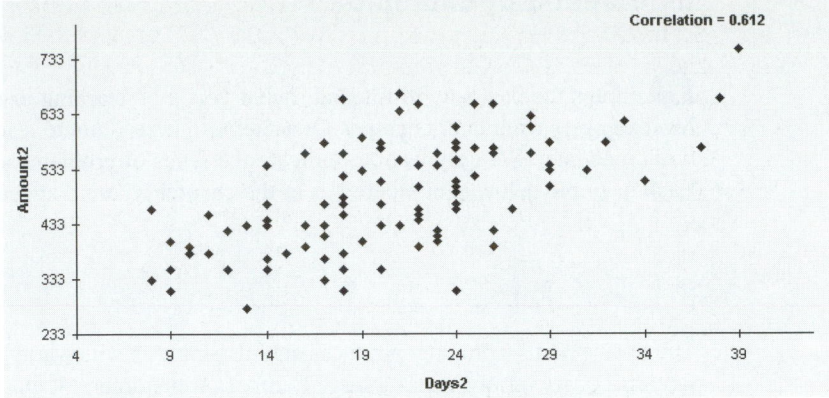

FIGURE 1.5 **Scatterplot of Amount versus Days for Large Customers**

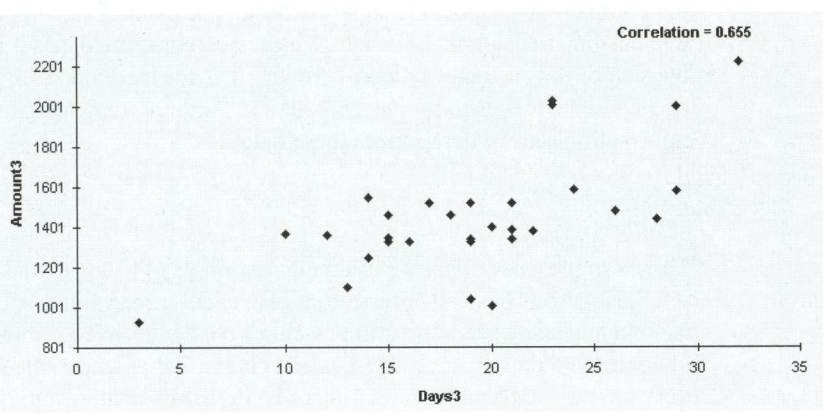

EXAMPLE 6.1

SciTools Incorporated, a company that specializes in scientific instruments, has been invited to make a bid on a government contract. The contract calls for a specific number of these instruments to be delivered during the coming year. The bids must be sealed (so that no company knows what the others are bidding), and the low bid wins the contract. SciTools estimates that it will cost $5000 to prepare a bid and $95,000 to supply the instruments if it wins the contract. On the basis of past contracts of this type, SciTools believes that the possible low bids from the competition, if there is any competition, and the associated probabilities are those shown in Table 1.1. In addition, SciTools believes there is a 30% chance that there will be no competing bids.

TABLE 1.1 **Data for Bidding Example**

Low Bid	Probability
Less than $115,000	0.2
Between $115,000 and $120,000	0.4
Between $120,000 and $125,000	0.3
Greater than $125,000	0.1

Solution

This is a typical example of decision making under uncertainty, the topic of Chapter 6. SciTools has to make decisions *now* (whether to bid and if so, how much to bid), without knowing what the competition is going to do. The company can't *assure* itself of a perfect outcome, but it can make a rational decision in light of the uncertainty it faces. We will see how decision trees, produced easily with the PrecisionTree add-in to Excel, not only lay out all of the elements of the problem in a logical manner, but also indicate the best solution. The completed tree for this problem appears in Figure 1.6. It indicates that SciTools should indeed prepare a bid, for the amount $115,000.

FIGURE 1.6   **Decision Tree for SciTools**

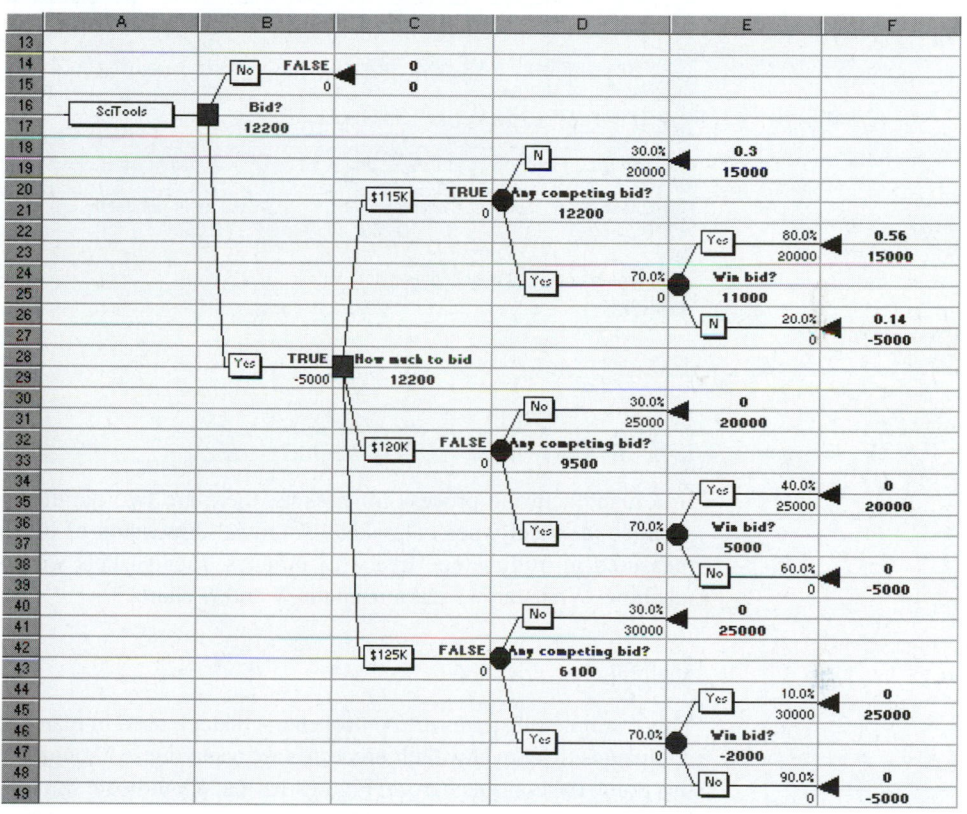

E X A M P L E   8 . 4

An auditor wants to determine the proportion of invoices that contain price errors—that is, prices that do not agree with those on an authorized price list. He checks 93 randomly sampled invoices and finds that two of them include price errors. What can he conclude, in terms of a 95% one-sided confidence interval, about the proportion of *all* invoices with price errors?

Solution

This is an important application of statistical inference in the auditing profession. Auditors try to determine what is true about a population (in this case, all of a company's invoices) by examining a relatively small sample from the population. Here the auditor wants an upper limit so that he is 95% confident that the overall proportion of invoices with errors is no greater than this upper limit. We show the spreadsheet solution in Figure 1.7. This shows that the auditor can be 95% confident that the overall proportion of invoices with errors is no greater than 6.6%.

FIGURE 1.7   **Analysis of Auditing Example**

	A	B	C	D	E	F
1	Auditing example for an exact one-sided confidence interval					
2				Range names		
3	Confidence level	95%		ConfLev: B3		
4	Number of errors	2		NErrors: B4		
5	Sample size	93		SampProp: B7		
6				SampSize: B5		
7	Sample proportion	0.0215		UpLimit: B10		
8						
9	Exact upper confidence limit for p			Goal seek condition		
10	Upper	0.066		0.050	=	0.05
11						
12	Large-sample upper confidence limit for p					
13	Upper	0.046				

EXAMPLE 10.3

In a manufacturing process for gaskets, there are two parallel production machines that produce identical types of gaskets. A crucial dimension of the gaskets is their thickness, measured in millimeters. Every 15 minutes, four gaskets were sampled, two from each machine. What can we learn from the $\overline{X}$ and R charts?

Solution

This example illustrates the control charts that are used in many manufacturing and service companies to learn how their processes are behaving. Although it is probably not obvious at this point, the control charts in Figures 1.8 and 1.9 indicate some rather suspicious behavior. Upon closer examination, we discover that the two machines are producing quite different outputs—the average thickness of one is well above the average for the other. Armed with this knowledge, a machine operator can take immediate action to bring the machines back into line with one another. Fortunately, the StatPro add-in makes it easy to produce these types of control charts in Excel.

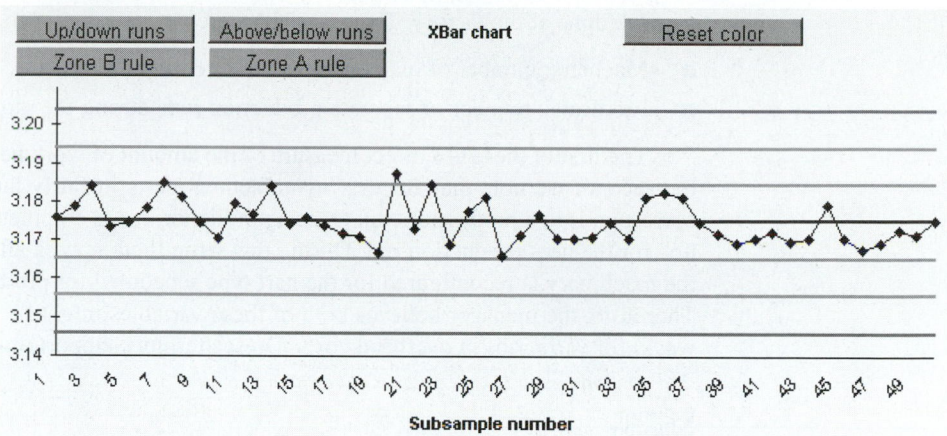

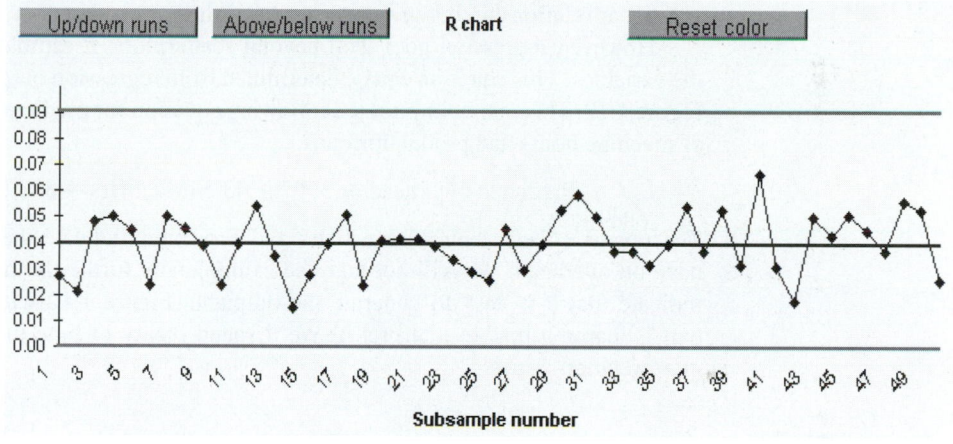

EXAMPLE 11.2

The Bendrix Company manufactures various types of parts for automobiles. The manager of the factory wants to get a better understanding of overhead costs. These overhead costs include supervision, indirect labor, supplies, payroll taxes, overtime premiums, depreciation, and a number of miscellaneous items such as charges for building depreciation, insurance, utilities, and janitorial and maintenance expenses. Some of these overhead costs are "fixed" in the sense that they don't vary appreciably with the volume of work being done, whereas others are "variable" and do vary directly with the volume of work. The fixed overhead costs tend to come from the supervision, depreciation, and miscellaneous categories, whereas the variable overhead costs tend to come from the indirect labor, supplies, payroll taxes, and overtime premiums categories. However, it is not easy to draw a clear line between the fixed and variable overhead components.

The Bendrix manager has tracked total overhead costs over the past 36 months. To help "explain" these, he has also collected data on two variables that are related to the amount of work done at the factory. These variables are:

- MachHrs: number of machine hours used during the month
- ProdRuns: number of separate production runs during the month

The first of these is a direct measure of the amount of work being done. To understand the second, we note that Bendrix manufactures parts in fairly large batches. Each batch corresponds to a production run. Once a production run is completed, the factory must "set up" for the next production run. During this setup there is typically some downtime while the machinery is reconfigured for the part type scheduled for production in the next batch. Therefore, the manager believes both of these variables might be responsible (in different ways) for variations in overhead costs. Do scatterplots support this belief?

Solution

This is a typical regression example, here in a cost accounting setting. The manager is trying to see what type of relationship, if any, there is between overhead costs and the two explanatory variables, number of machine hours and number of production runs. The scatterplots requested appear in Figures 1.10 and 1.11. They do indeed indicate a positive and linear relationship between overhead and the two explanatory variables.

However, regression goes well beyond scatterplots. It estimates an equation relating the variables. This equation can be determined from regression output such as that shown in Figure 1.12. This output implies the following equation for predicted overhead as a function of machine hours and production runs:

$$\text{Predicted Overhead} = 3997 + 43.54\text{MachHrs} + 883.62\text{ProdRuns}$$

The positive coefficients of MachHrs and ProdRuns indicate the effects these variables have on overhead. We will not take the example any further at this point but will simply indicate that it is easy to generate the output in Figure 1.12 with StatPro. The difficult part is learning how to interpret it. We'll spend plenty of time in Chapters 11 and 12 on interpretation issues.

FIGURE 1.10 **Scatterplot of Overhead versus Machine Hours**

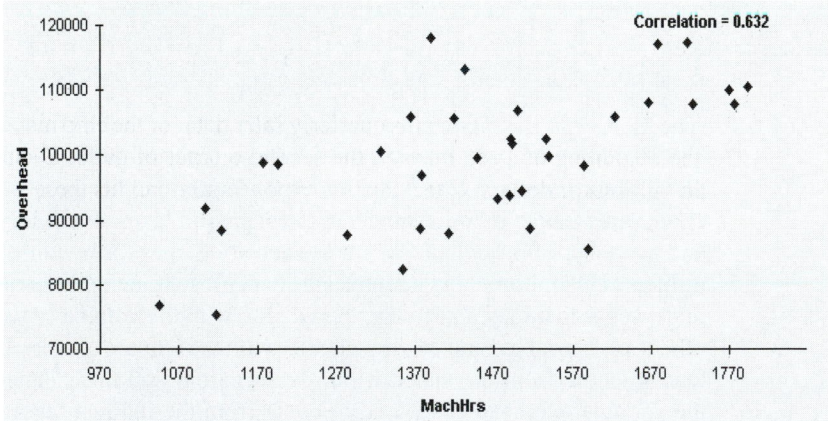

FIGURE 1.11 **Scatterplot of Overhead versus Production Runs**

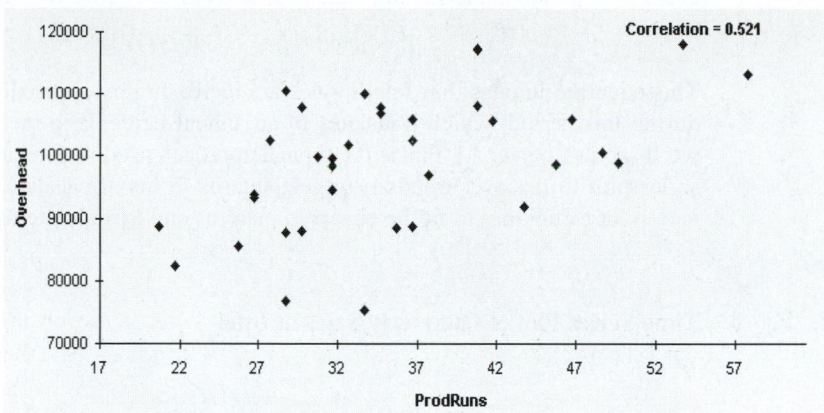

FIGURE 1.12 **Multiple Regression Output for Bendrix Example**

	A	B	C	D	E	F	G
1	*Results of multiple regression for Overhead*						
2							
3	*Summary measures*						
4		Multiple R	0.9308				
5		R-Square	0.8664				
6		Adj R-Square	0.8583				
7		StErr of Est	4108.9932				
8							
9	*ANOVA Table*						
10		Source	df	SS	MS	F	p-value
11		Explained	2	3614020652.0000	1807010326.0000	107.0261	0.0000
12		Unexplained	33	557166208.0000	16883824.4848		
13							
14	*Regression coefficients*						
15			Coefficient	Std Err	t-value	p-value	
16		Constant	3996.6782	6603.6509	0.6052	0.5492	
17		MachHrs	43.5364	3.5895	12.1289	0.0000	
18		ProdRuns	883.6179	82.2514	10.7429	0.0000	

EXAMPLE 13.7

The file INTEL.XLS contains quarterly sales data for the chip manufacturing firm Intel from the beginning of 1986 through the second quarter of 1996. Each sales value is expressed in millions of dollars. Check that an exponential trend fits these sales data reasonably well. Then estimate the relationship and interpret it.

Solution

This example illustrates a regression-based trend curve, one of several possible forecasting techniques for a time series variable. A time series plot of Intel's quarterly sales appears in Figure 1.13. It indicates that sales have been increasing steadily at an increasing rate. This is basically what an exponential trend curve implies. To estimate this curve we use regression analysis to obtain the following equation for predicted quarterly sales as a function of time:

$$\text{Predicted Sales} = 295.377e^{0.0657\text{Time}}$$

This equation implies that Intel's sales are increasing by approximately 6.6% per quarter during this period, which translates to an annual percentage increase of about 29%! As we'll see in Chapter 13, this is the typical approach used in forecasting. We look at a time series plot to discover trends or other patterns in historical data, and then use one of a variety of techniques to fit the observed patterns and extrapolate them into the future.

FIGURE 1.13 **Time Series Plot of Quarterly Sales at Intel**

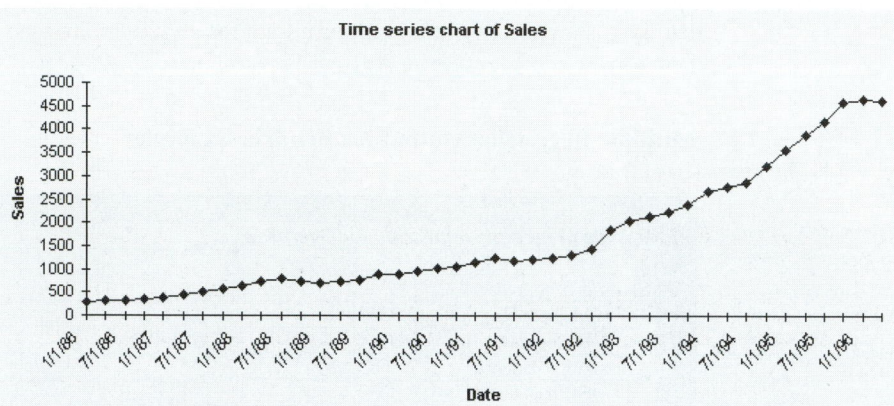

EXAMPLE 15.6

A small toy store, Tyco, projects the monthly cash inflows listed in Table 1.2 (in thousands of dollars) during the year 2000. A negative cash flow means that cash outflows exceed cash inflows to the business—bills exceed revenues. Tyco begins the year with a cash balance of $6500. To pay its bills, Tyco will need to borrow money early in the year. The company can borrow money in two ways. First, it can obtain a long-term 1-year loan and receive the total amount in January. Beginning in February 2000, 1% interest will be charged each month on this loan. The loan must be paid back by the beginning of January 2001. Second, Tyco can borrow money each month from a short-term bank line of credit with a monthly interest rate of 1.5%. All short-term loans must be paid back by the beginning of January 2001. At the end of each month, excess cash earns Tyco 0.4% interest. Tyco wants to maximize its cash on hand at the beginning of January 2001, after paying back all loans. Also, Tyco's policy is to have a cash balance of at least $5000 at the end of each month.

TABLE 1.2 **Cash Inflows for Tyco**

	Cash Inflow		Cash Inflow
January	−12	July	−7
February	−10	August	−2
March	−8	September	15
April	−10	October	12
May	−4	November	−7
June	5	December	45

Solution

This is one of many optimization examples we present in Chapters 14 and 15. The typical situation is that a company such as Tyco must make several decisions, subject to certain constraints, that optimize some objective. In this case Tyco needs to decide the amounts to borrow, short-term and long-term, to meet its cash balance constraints and maximize the amount of cash it has on hand a year from now. Our job is to formulate a spreadsheet model, similar to the one shown in Figure 1.14, that relates the various elements of the problem.

The loan amounts in rows 20 and 21 are the decision variables, called "changing cells" in Excel's terminology. When we formulate the model, we can enter *any* values in these changing cells; we do not need to guess "good" values. Then we turn it over to Excel's Solver add-in. The Solver uses a powerful algorithm to find the optimal values in the changing cells—that is, the values that optimize the objective while satisfying the constraints. The values shown in Figure 1.14 are actually the optimal values. They imply that Tyco should take out a long-term loan for slightly more than $30,000 in January and then borrow short-term from April to September.

FIGURE 1.14   Cash Balance Model

Tyco cash balance example

Assumptions:
At the beginning of any month, loans are received and loans are paid back with interest - the balance must be nonnegative
At the end of each month, after bills or revenues occur, the balance must be at least some minimal amount
The objective is to minimize total interest paid

Inputs

Monthly rates

Long-term loan	1.0%
Short-term loan	1.5%
Excess cash	0.4%

Minimal required cash balance at the end of each month	$5,000
Cash carried over from December 1999 (with interest)	$6,500

Range names:
BalAfterLoan: B26:N26
EndBal: B31:M31
FinalBal: B39
InitCash: D15
IntRate: B12
LTLoan: B20
LTRate: B10
MinBal: B33:M33
MinCashBal: D14
STLoan: B21:M21
STRate: B11

Financial section

	Jan	Feb	Mar	Apr	May	Jun	Jul	Aug	Sep	Oct	Nov	Dec	Jan
Beginning balance	$6,500	$24,944	$14,699	$6,421	$5,020	$5,020	$5,020	$5,020	$5,020	$15,060	$12,303	$5,020	$49,915
Long-term loan	$30,344												
Short-term loan	$0	$0	$0	$8,882	$13,299	$8,782	$16,197	$18,724	$14,288	$0	$0	$0	
Interest on long-term loan	$303	$303	$303	$303	$303	$303	$303	$303	$303	$303	$303	$303	
Interest on short-term loan	$0	$0	$0	$133	$199	$132	$243	$281	$214	$0	$0	$0	
Long-term interest/payback		$303	$303	$303	$303	$303	$303	$303	$303	$303	$303	$303	$30,648
Short-term interest/payback		$0	$0	$0	$9,016	$13,498	$8,914	$16,440	$19,004	$14,502	$0	$0	$0
Balance after loan activities	$36,844	$24,640	$14,396	$15,000	$9,000	($0)	$12,000	$7,000	($0)	$254	$12,000	$4,717	$19,267
	>=	>=	>=	>=	>=	>=	>=	>=	>=	>=	>=	>=	>=
Must be nonnegative	$0	$0	$0	$0	$0	$0	$0	$0	$0	$0	$0	$0	$0
Cash inflow/outflow	-$12,000	-$10,000	-$8,000	-$10,000	-$4,000	$5,000	-$7,000	-$2,000	$15,000	$12,000	-$7,000	$45,000	
Balance at end of month	$24,844	$14,640	$6,396	$5,000	$5,000	$5,000	$5,000	$5,000	$15,000	$12,254	$5,000	$49,717	
	>=	>=	>=	>=	>=	>=	>=	>=	>=	>=	>=	>=	
Minimal balance	$5,000	$5,000	$5,000	$5,000	$5,000	$5,000	$5,000	$5,000	$5,000	$5,000	$5,000	$5,000	
Interest on excess cash	$99	$59	$26	$20	$20	$20	$20	$20	$60	$49	$20	$199	

Summary data

Total interest paid	$4,844
Cash balance in Jan 2001	$19,267

EXAMPLE 16.9

Sweetness and IceT are the two dominant companies in the bottled iced tea market. Each currently possesses 49% of the total iced tea market, with three smaller companies splitting the remaining 2%. At the beginning of any year, a random number of new small companies enter the iced tea market. The actual number of new entries is assumed to be Poisson distributed with mean 1. After the new entries enter the market, there is a random shift in market share among all competitors. Essentially, all competitors lose a random percentage of their market share to other competitors. We will assume that each of these percentages is triangularly distributed with the parameters given in Table 1.3. For example, the percentage of Sweetness's market share lost to IceT has a triangular distribution with minimum value 1%, most likely value 5%, and maximum value 10%. Similarly, the percentage of market share Sweetness will lose to *each* of the small companies has parameters 0.5%, 1%, and 3%. Therefore, the more small companies there are in the market, the more of its market share Sweetness will tend to lose to them.

TABLE 1.3 **Parameters of Lost Market Share Percentages**

	Minimum	Most Likely	Maximum
From Sweetness			
To IceT	1.0%	5%	10%
To each small company	0.5%	1%	3%
From IceT			
To Sweetness	1.0%	5%	10%
To each small company	0.5%	1%	3%
From small companies			
To Sweetness	5.0%	10%	15%
To IceT	5.0%	10%	15%

At the end of each year, each of the small companies has a 50% chance of exiting the iced tea market. Each small company that exits will lose its market share to Sweetness or IceT. The percentage of this market share that goes to Sweetness is triangularly distributed with parameters 40%, 50%, and 60%; the rest goes to IceT.

The dominant companies, Sweetness and IceT, want to use simulation to see how their market share is likely to change over the next 10 years.

Solution

This is a typical example of computer simulation. We make a number of assumptions, build a spreadsheet model around these assumptions, explicitly incorporate uncertainty into some of the cells, and see how this uncertainty affects "bottom-line" outputs. The simulation model appears in Figure 1.15. Several cells in this model are random, including all of the numerical values in rows 50 through 57. Therefore, the numbers you see in this figure represent just one possible scenario of how market shares might evolve through time. By generating new random values, we see different scenarios.

Our job is to build the logic and randomness into the spreadsheet model. Then we can use Excel's built-in tools or an add-in such as @Risk to replicate the model and keep track of selected outputs. A typical result from @Risk appears in Figure 1.16. It shows a histogram of Sweetness's market share at the end of year 10, where this histogram is based on the 500 replications we ran. It shows that the most likely ending market share is about 49%—right where it started in year 1—but under worst-case and best-case scenarios, Sweetness's market share could be slightly less than 41% or slightly greater than 57%.

FIGURE 1.15 Spreadsheet Simulation for Iced Tea Example

	A	B	C	D	E	F	G	H	I	J	K
36	**Simulation section**										
37		Year 1	Year 2	Year 3	Year 4	Year 5	Year 6	Year 7	Year 8	Year 9	Year 10
38	Beginning market shares										
39	Sweetness	0.49	0.4813	0.48779	0.4878	0.4878	0.4878	0.4878	0.4878	0.4878	0.4878
40	IceT	0.49	0.4813	0.48779	0.4878	0.4878	0.4878	0.4878	0.4878	0.4878	0.4878
41	Small companies (combined)	0.02	0.0374	0.02441	0.0244	0.02439	0.02439	0.02439	0.02439	0.02439	0.02439
42											
43	Small companies before and after new entries										
44	Number of smalls before entries	3	2	1	1	1	1	1	1	1	1
45	Number entering at beginning	1	1	1	1	1	1	1	1	1	1
46	Total number of smalls	4	3	2	2	2	2	2	2	2	2
47											
48	Market shares lost during year										
49	Sweetness										
50	to IceT	0.02613	0.02567	0.02602	0.02602	0.02602	0.02602	0.02602	0.02602	0.02602	0.02602
51	to smalls (combined)	0.0294	0.02166	0.01463	0.01463	0.01463	0.01463	0.01463	0.01463	0.01463	0.01463
52	IceT										
53	to Sweetness	0.02613	0.02567	0.02602	0.02602	0.02602	0.02602	0.02602	0.02602	0.02602	0.02602
54	to smalls (combined)	0.0294	0.02166	0.01463	0.01463	0.01463	0.01463	0.01463	0.01463	0.01463	0.01463
55	Small companies										
56	to Sweetness	0.002	0.00374	0.00244	0.00244	0.00244	0.00244	0.00244	0.00244	0.00244	0.00244
57	to IceT	0.002	0.00374	0.00244	0.00244	0.00244	0.00244	0.00244	0.00244	0.00244	0.00244
58											
59	Information on exiters										
60	Market share of smalls before exit	0.0748	0.07324	0.0488	0.04879	0.04878	0.04878	0.04878	0.04878	0.04878	0.04878
61	Number of smalls exiting at end	2	2	1	1	1	1	1	1	1	1
62	Number of smalls remaining	2	1	1	1	1	1	1	1	1	1
63	Combined market share of exiters	0.0374	0.04882	0.0244	0.02439	0.02439	0.02439	0.02439	0.02439	0.02439	0.02439
64											
65	Market shares gained from exiters										
66	to Sweetness	0.0187	0.02441	0.0122	0.0122	0.0122	0.0122	0.0122	0.0122	0.0122	0.0122
67	to IceT	0.0187	0.02441	0.0122	0.0122	0.0122	0.0122	0.0122	0.0122	0.0122	0.0122
68											
69	Market shares at end										
70	Sweetness	0.4813	0.48779	0.4878	0.4878	0.4878	0.4878	0.4878	0.4878	0.4878	0.4878
71	IceT	0.4813	0.48779	0.4878	0.4878	0.4878	0.4878	0.4878	0.4878	0.4878	0.4878
72	Small companies (combined)	0.0374	0.02441	0.0244	0.02439	0.02439	0.02439	0.02439	0.02439	0.02439	0.02439

FIGURE 1.16 Histogram for Sweetness's Ending Year 10 Market Share

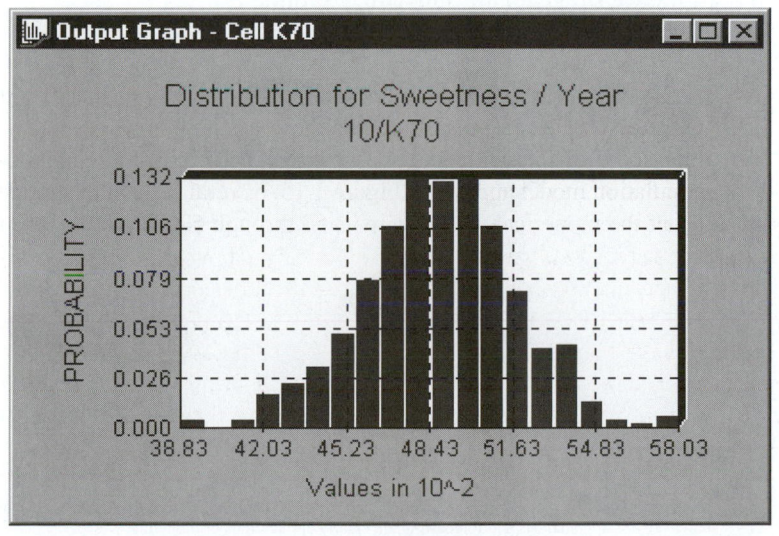

Modeling and Models

We have already used the term "model" several times in this chapter. In fact, we have shown several spreadsheet models in the previous section. Models and the modeling process are key elements throughout this book, so we explain them in more detail in this section.[3]

A model is an abstraction of a real problem. It is an abstraction that tries to capture the essence and key features of the problem without getting bogged down in relatively unimportant details. There are different types of models, and, depending on an analyst's preferences and skills, each can be a valuable aid in solving a real problem. We describe three types of models here: (1) graphical models, (2) algebraic models, and (3) spreadsheet models.

1.4.1 Graphical Models

Graphical models are probably the most intuitive and least quantitative type of model. They attempt to portray graphically how different elements of a problem are related— what affects what. A very simple graphical model appears in Figure 1.17. It is called an "influence diagram" and can be constructed easily with the Precision Tree add-in discussed in Chapter 6.

This particular influence diagram is for a company that is trying to decide how many souvenirs to order for the upcoming Olympics. The essence of the problem is that the company will order a certain supply, customers will request a certain demand, and the combination of supply and demand will yield a certain payoff for the company. The diagram indicates fairly intuitively what affects what. As it stands, the diagram does not provide enough quantitative details to enable us to "solve" the company's problem. But this is usually not the purpose of a graphical model. Instead, its purpose is simply to show the important elements of a problem and how they are related. For complex problems this can be very helpful and enlightening information.

F I G U R E   1 . 1 7   **Influence Diagram for Souvenir Example**

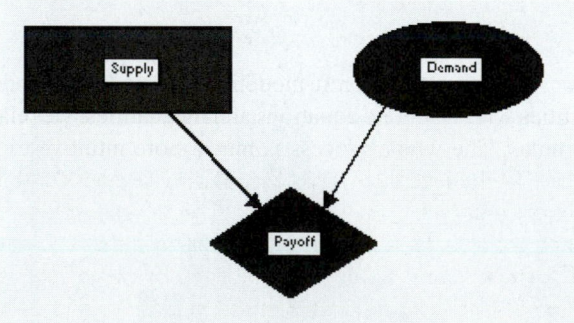

---

[3]Management scientists tend to use the terms "model" and "modeling" more than statisticians. Many traditional statistics topics such as regression analysis and forecasting are clearly applications of modeling.

1.4.2 Algebraic Models

Algebraic models are at the opposite end of the spectrum. By means of algebraic equations and inequalities, they specify a set of relationships in a very precise way, and their preciseness and lack of ambiguity are very appealing to people with a mathematical background. In addition, they can usually be stated concisely and with great generality.

A typical example is the "product mix" problem we discuss in Chapter 14. Here a company can make several products, each of which contributes a certain amount to profit and consumes certain amounts of several scarce resources. The problem is to select the product mix that maximizes profit subject to the limited availability of the resources. *All* product mix problems can be stated algebraically as follows:

$$\max \sum_{j=1}^{n} p_j x_j \tag{1.1}$$

$$\text{subject to } \sum_{j=1}^{n} a_{ij} x_j \leq b_i, \quad 1 \leq i \leq m \tag{1.2}$$

$$0 \leq x_j \leq u_j, \quad 1 \leq j \leq n \tag{1.3}$$

Here x_j is the amount of product j produced, u_j is an upper limit on the amount of product j that can be produced, p_j is the unit profit margin for product j, a_{ij} is the amount of resource i consumed by each unit of product j, b_i is the amount of resource i available, n is the number of products, and m is the number of scarce resources. This algebraic model states very concisely that we should maximize total profit [expression (1.1)], subject to consuming no more of the resources than is available [inequalities (1.2)], and all production quantities should be between 0 and the upper limits [inequalities (1.3)].

Algebraic models such as this appeal to mathematically trained analysts. They are concise, they spell out exactly which data are required (we would need to estimate the u_j's, the p_j's, the a_{ij}'s, and the b_i's from company data), they scale well (a problem with 500 products and 100 resource constraints is just as easy to state as one with only 5 products and 3 resource constraints), and many software packages accept algebraic models in essentially the same form as given above, so that no "translation" is required. Indeed, algebraic models were the preferred type of model for years—and still are by many people. Their main drawback is that they require an ability to work with abstract mathematical symbols. Some people have this ability, but many perfectly intelligent people do not have it.

1.4.3 Spreadsheet Models

A fairly recent alternative to algebraic modeling is spreadsheet modeling. Instead of relating various quantities with algebraic equations and inequalities, we relate them in a spreadsheet with cell formulas. The whole process is much more intuitive to most people (at least in our experience). We believe that one of the primary reasons for this is the instant feedback available from spreadsheets. If you enter a formula incorrectly, it is often immediately obvious (from error messages or unrealistic numbers) that you have made an error, which you can then go back and fix. Algebraic models provide no such immediate feedback.

A specific comparison might help at this point. We already saw a general algebraic model of the product mix problem. Figure 1.18 (page 26), taken from Chapter 14, illustrates a spreadsheet model for a specific example of this problem. The spreadsheet model should be fairly self-explanatory. All quantities in shaded cells are inputs to the model, the quantities in row 16 are the decision variables (they correspond to the x_j's in the algebraic model), and all other quantities are created through appropriate Excel formulas. To indicate constraints, we enter inequality signs in appropriate cells.

While a well-designed and well-documented spreadsheet model such as the one in Figure 1.18 is undoubtedly more intuitive for most people than its algebraic counterpart, the art of developing good spreadsheet models is not easy. Obviously, they must be *correct*. The formulas relating the various quantities must have the correct syntax, the correct cell references, and the correct logic. In complex models this can be quite a challenge.

However, correctness is not enough. If spreadsheet models are to be used in the business world, they must also be well designed and well documented. Otherwise, no one other than you (and maybe not even you after a few weeks have passed) will be able to understand what your models do or how they work. The strength of spreadsheets is their flexibility—you are limited only by your imagination. However, this flexibility can be a liability in spreadsheet modeling unless you plan the design of your models carefully.

Note the clear design in Figure 1.18. Most of the inputs are grouped at the top of the spreadsheet. All of the financial calculations are done at the bottom. When there are constraints, the two sides of the constraints are placed next to each other (as in the range B21:D23). Borders, colors (which appear on the screen but not in this book), and shading are used for added clarity. Descriptive labels are used liberally. Excel itself imposes none of these "rules," but you should impose them on yourself.

FIGURE 1.18 **Optimal Solution for Product Mix Example**

	A	B	C	D	E	F	G	H
1	Product Mix Problem							
2								
3	Input data							
4	Hourly wage rate	$8.00						
5	Cost per oz of metal	$0.50						
6	Cost per oz of glass	$0.75						
7								
8	Frame type	1	2	3	4	Range names:		
9	Labor hours per frame	2	1	3	2	Available: D21:D23		
10	Metal (oz.) per frame	4	2	1	2	MaxSales: B18:E18		
11	Glass (oz.) per frame	6	2	1	2	Produced: B16:E16		
12	Unit selling price	$28.50	$12.50	$29.25	$21.50	TotProfit: F32		
13						Used: B21:B23		
14	Production plan							
15	Frame type	1	2	3	4			
16	Frames produced	1000	800	400	0			
17		<=	<=	<=	<=			
18	Maximum sales	1000	2000	500	1000			
19								
20	Constraints on inputs	Used		Available				
21	Labor hours	4000	<=	4000				
22	Metal (oz.)	6000	<=	6000				
23	Glass (oz.)	8000	<=	10000				
24								
25	Revenue, cost summary							
26	Frame type	1	2	3	4	Totals		
27	Revenue	$28,500	$10,000	$11,700	$0	$50,200		
28	Costs of inputs							
29	Labor	$16,000	$6,400	$9,600	$0	$32,000		
30	Metal	$2,000	$800	$200	$0	$3,000		
31	Glass	$4,500	$1,200	$300	$0	$6,000		
32	Profit	$6,000	$1,600	$1,600	$0	$9,200		

We have made a conscious effort to establish good habits for you to follow throughout this book. We have designed and redesigned our spreadsheet models so that they are as clear as possible. This doesn't mean that you have to copy everything we do—everyone tends to develop their own spreadsheet style—but our models should give you something to emulate. Just remember that you typically start with a *blank* spreadsheet. It is then up to you to develop a model that is not only correct but also intelligible to you and to others. This takes a lot of practicing and a lot of editing, but it is a skill well worth developing.

1.4.4 The Seven-Step Modeling Process

Most of the modeling you will do in this book is only part of the overall modeling process typically done in the business world. We portray it as a seven-step process, as discussed below. Of course, not all problems require all seven steps. For example, the analysis of survey data might entail primarily steps 2 (data analysis) and 5 (decision making), without the formal model building discussed in steps 3 and 4.

1 **Define the problem.** Typically, a company does not develop a model unless it believes it has a problem. Therefore, the modeling process really begins by identifying an underlying problem. Perhaps the company is losing money, perhaps its market share is declining, or perhaps its customers are waiting too long for service. Any number of problems might be evident. However, as several people have warned [see Miser (1993) and Volkema (1995), for example], this step is not always as straightforward as it might appear. The company must be sure that it has identified the *right* problem before it spends time, effort, and money trying to solve it.

   For example, Miser cites the experience of an analyst who was hired by the military to investigate overly long turnaround times between fighter planes landing and taking off again to rejoin the battle. The military was convinced that the problem was caused by inefficient ground crews; if they were sped up, turnaround times would decrease. The analyst nearly accepted this statement of the problem and was about to do classical time-and-motion studies on the ground crew to pinpoint the sources of their inefficiency. However, by snooping around he found that the problem obviously lay elsewhere. The trucks that refueled the planes were frequently late, which in turn was due to the inefficient way they were refilled from storage tanks at another location. Once this latter problem was solved—and its solution was embarrassingly simple—the turnaround times decreased to an acceptable level without any changes on the part of the ground crews. If the analyst had accepted the military's statement of the problem, the *real* problem might never have been located or solved.

2 **Collect and summarize data.** This crucial step in the process is often the most tedious. All organizations keep track of various data on their operations, but these data might not be in the form an analyst requires. They also might be scattered in different places throughout the organization, in all kinds of different formats. Therefore, one of the first jobs of an analyst is to gather exactly the right data and summarize the data appropriately—as we discuss in detail in Chapters 2 and 3—for use in the model. Collecting the data typically requires asking questions of key people (such as the accountants) throughout the organization, studying existing organizational databases, and performing time-consuming observational studies of the organization's processes. In short, it entails a lot of leg work.

3 **Formulate a model.** This is the step we emphasize throughout much of this book. The form of the model varies from one situation to another. It could be a graphical model, an algebraic model, or a spreadsheet model. The key is that the model should capture the key elements of the business problem in such a way that it is understandable

by all parties involved. This latter requirement is why we favor spreadsheet models, especially when they are well designed and well documented.

4   **Verify the model.** Here the analyst tries to determine whether the model developed in the previous step is an accurate representation of reality. A first step in determining how well the model fits reality is to check whether the model is valid for the current situation. This verification might take several forms. For example, the analyst could use the model with the company's current values of the input parameters. If the model's outputs are then in line with the outputs currently observed by the company, the analyst has at least shown that the model can duplicate the current situation.

A second way to verify a model is to enter a number of sets of input parameters (even if they are not the company's current inputs) and see whether the outputs from the model are reasonable. One common approach is to use extreme values of the inputs to see whether the outputs behave as they should. If they do, then we have another piece of evidence that the model is reasonable.

If certain inputs are entered in the model, and the model's outputs are *not* as expected, there could be two causes. First, the model could simply be a poor representation of the actual situation. In this case it is up to the analyst to refine the model until it provides reasonably accurate predictions. The second possible cause is that the model is fine but our intuition is not very good. In this case the fault lies with us, not the model.

A typical example of this occurs with random sequences of 0's and 1's, such as might occur with successive flips of a fair coin. Most people expect that heads and tails will alternate and that there will be very few sequences of, say, four or more heads (or tails) in a row. However, a perfectly accurate simulation model of these flips will show, contrary to what most people expect, that fairly long runs of heads or tails are not at all uncommon. In fact, one or two long runs should be *expected* if there are enough flips.

The fact that outcomes sometimes defy intuition is an important reason why mathematical models are important. Such models prove that our ability to predict outcomes in complex environments is often not very good.

5   **Select one or more suitable decisions**. Many, but not all, models are decision models. For any specific decisions the model indicates the amount of profit obtained, the amount of cost incurred, the level of risk, and so on. If we believe the model is working correctly (as discussed in step 4), then we can use the model to see which decisions produce the *best* outputs.

6   **Present the results to the organization.** In a classroom setting you are typically finished when you have developed a model that correctly solves a particular problem. In the business world a correct model, even a useful one, is not always enough. An analyst typically has to "sell" the model to management. Unfortunately, the people in management are sometimes not as well trained in quantitative methods as the analyst, so they are not always inclined to trust complex models.

There are two ways to mitigate this problem. First, it is helpful to include relevant people throughout the company in the modeling process—from beginning to end—so that everyone has an understanding of the model and feels an ownership for it. Second, it helps to use a *spreadsheet* model whenever possible, especially if it is designed and documented properly. Almost everyone in today's business world is comfortable with spreadsheets, so spreadsheet models are more likely to be accepted.

7   **Implement the model and update it through time.** Again, there is a big difference between a classroom situation and a business situation. When you turn in a classroom assignment, you are typically finished with that assignment and can await the next one. In contrast, an analyst who develops a model for a company can usually not pack up his bags and leave. If the model is accepted by management, the company will then

need to implement it company-wide. This can be very time-consuming and politically difficult, especially if the model's prescriptions represent a significant change from the past. At the very least, employees must be trained how to use the model on a day-to-day basis.

In addition, the model will probably need to be updated over time, either because of changing conditions or because the company sees more potential uses for the model as it gains experience using it. This presents one of the greatest challenges for a model developer, namely, the ability to develop a model that *can* be modified easily as the need arises. Keep this in mind as you develop models throughout this book. Always try to make them as general as possible.

Conclusion

In this chapter we've tried to convince you that the skills in this book are important for *you* to know as you enter the business world. The methods we discuss are no longer the sole province of the "quant jocks." By having a PC on your desk that is loaded with powerful software, you incur a responsibility to use this software to solve business problems. We have described the types of problems you will learn to solve in this book, along with the software you will use to solve these problems. We have also discussed the modeling process, a theme that runs throughout this book. Now it's time for you to get started!

Cruise ship traveling has become big business. Many cruise lines are now competing for customers of all age groups and socioeconomic status levels. They offer all types of cruises, from relatively inexpensive 3–4-day cruises in the Caribbean, to 12–15-day cruises in the Mediterranean, to several-month around-the-world cruises. Cruises have several features that attract customers, many of whom book 6 months or more in advance: (1) they offer a relaxing, everything-done-for-you way to travel, (2) they serve food that is plentiful, usually excellent, and included in the price of the cruise, (3) they stop at a number of interesting ports and offer travelers a way to see the world, and (4) they provide a wide variety of entertainment, particularly in the evening.

This last feature, the entertainment, presents a difficult problem for a ship's staff. A typical cruise might have well over a thousand customers, including elderly singles and couples, middle-aged people with or without children, and young people, often honeymooners. These different types of passengers have varied tastes in terms of their after-dinner preferences in entertainment. Some want traditional dance music, some want comedians, some want rock music, some want movies, some want to go back to their cabins and read, and so on. Obviously, cruise entertainment directors want to provide the variety of entertainment their customers desire—within a reasonable budget—because satisfied customers tend to be repeat customers. The question is how to provide the right mix of entertainment.

On a cruise one of the authors and his wife recently took, the entertainment was of high quality and there was plenty of variety. A seven-piece show band played dance music nightly in the largest lounge, two other small musical combos played nightly at two smaller lounges, a pianist played nightly at a piano bar in an intimate lounge, a group of professional singers and dancers played Broadway–type shows about twice weekly, and various professional singers and comedians played occasional single-night performances.[4] Although this entertainment was free to all of the passengers, much of it had embarrassingly low attendance. The nightly show band and musical combos, who were contracted to play nightly until midnight, often had less than a half dozen people in the audience—sometimes literally none. The professional singers, dancers, and comedians attracted larger audiences, but there were still plenty of empty seats. In spite of this, the cruise staff posted a weekly schedule, and they stuck to it regardless of attendance. In a short-term financial sense, it didn't make much difference. The performers got paid the same whether anyone was in the audience or not, the passengers had already paid (indirectly) for the entertainment as part of the cost of the cruise, and the only possible opportunity cost to the cruise line (in the short run) was the loss of liquor sales from the lack of passengers in the entertainment lounges. The morale of the entertainers was not great—entertainers love packed houses—but they usually argued, philosophically, that their hours were relatively short and they were still getting paid to see the world.

If you were in charge of entertainment on this ship, how would you describe the problem with entertainment: Is it a problem with deadbeat passengers, low-quality entertainment, or a mismatch between the entertainment offered and the entertainment desired? How might you try to solve the problem? What constraints might you have to work within? Would you keep a strict schedule such as the one followed by this cruise director, or would you play it more "by ear"? Would you gather data to help solve the problem? What data would you gather? How much would financial considerations dictate your decisions? Would they be long-term or short-term considerations?

---

[4] There was also a moderately large onboard casino, but it tended to attract the same people every night, and it was always closed when the ship was in port.

2

Describing Data: Graphs and Tables

Applications

On the morning of January 28, 1986, the U.S. space shuttle *Challenger* exploded a few minutes after takeoff, killing all seven crew members. The physical cause of this tragic accident was found to be a failure in one of the O-rings located in a joint on the right-hand-side solid rocket booster. The Presidential Commission investigating the disaster concluded that the decision-making process leading up to the launch of *Challenger* was seriously flawed. Prior to the *Challenger* disaster, engineers from NASA and Morton Thiokol (the manufacturer of the shuttle's solid rocket motors) had observed evidence of in-flight damage to these O-rings. In spite of this evidence and the cold weather that adversely affected the performance of the O-ring seals, the *Challenger* was launched—and the outcome was disastrous.

This tragedy provides a dramatic example of how well-chosen graphs can make—or could have made—a huge difference. Data were available from previous shuttle flights on the ambient temperature of the solid rocket motor joints at launch and the number of joints observed to have suffered some form of damage. (These are included for your interest in the file CHALLENGER.XLS.) One set of data lists this information only for those 7 previous flights where at least one joint suffered damage. Another set lists this information for all 23 previous flights. A scatterplot—one of the graph types we will examine in this chapter—of the first set shows how 2 previous flights, one with a relatively cool temperature and one with a relatively warm temperature, each had two joints damaged. The other 5 flights, all with intermediate temperatures, each had a single joint damaged. This scatterplot appears in Figure 2.1. (Two of the points are identical, which explains why there appear to be only 6 points.) It contains virtually no evidence that damage is related to temperature. Perhaps the decision makers referred to this plot on launch day to confirm their go-ahead decision.

However, a scatterplot of the data from all 23 previous flights, shown in Figure 2.2, tells a somewhat different story. (Again, several points are identical, so there appear to be fewer than 23 points.) Note that the extra 16 points on this plot are all on the horizontal axis—that is, they all correspond to flights with no damage—and all correspond to relatively warm temperatures. In addition, it now becomes apparent that *most* of the flights with some damage occurred at relatively cool temperatures. The only exception is the point marked as a possible "outlier"—that is, a point outside the general pattern. If we ignore this potential outlier, a fairly clear

FIGURE 2.1 **Scatterplot for Flights with Some Damage**

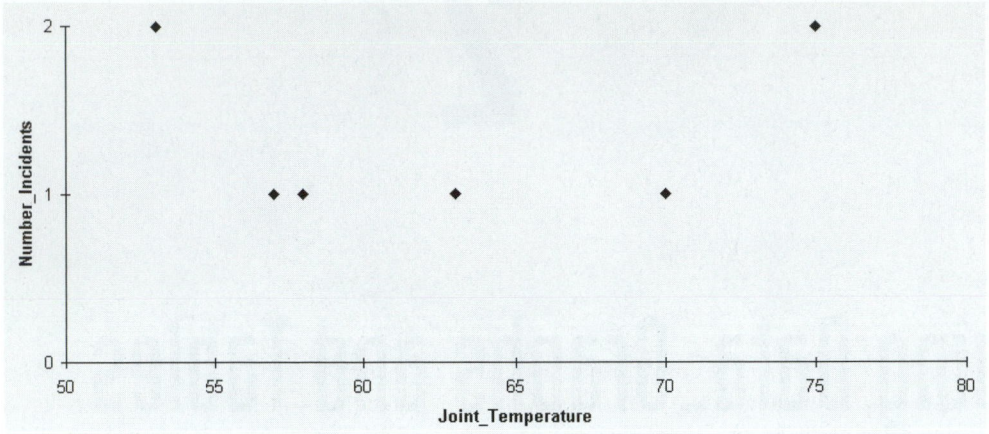

FIGURE 2.2 **Scatterplot for All Previous Flights**

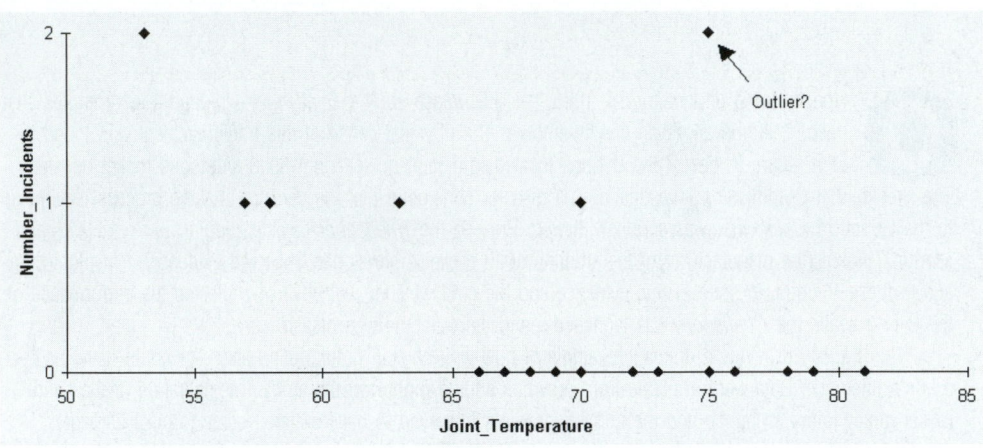

pattern emerges: More damage tends to occur at low temperatures. Of course, this plot does not provide conclusive evidence that a shuttle launched at near-freezing temperatures, which the fateful launch experienced, was doomed to disaster. However, it provides a clear warning. If you had observed this plot and the freezing temperature on that January morning, would you have decided to go ahead with the launch? ■

2.1 Introduction

T he goal of this chapter and the next is very simple—to make sense out of data by constructing appropriate summary measures, tables, and graphs. Our purpose here is to take a set of data that at first glance has little meaning, and to present the data in a form that makes sense to people. There are numerous ways to do this, limited only by our imagination, but there are several tools used most often: (1) a variety of graphs, including bar charts, pie charts, histograms, scatterplots, and time series plots, (2) tables of summary measures grouped by categories, and (3) numerical summary measures such as counts, percentages, averages, and measures of variability. These terms might not all be familiar at this point, but you've undoubtedly seen examples of them in newspapers, magazine articles, and books.

The material in these two chapters is *simple*, *complex*, and *important*. It is simple because there are no difficult mathematical concepts. With the possible exception of variance, covariance, and correlation, all of the numerical measures, tables, and graphs are natural and easy to understand. It used to be a tedious chore to produce them, but with the advances in statistical software, including add-ins for spreadsheet packages such as Excel, they can now be produced easily and quickly.

If it's so easy, why do we also claim that the material in this chapter is complex? The data sets available to companies in today's computerized world tend to be extremely large and filled with "unstructured" data. As we will see, even in data sets that are quite small in comparison to those real companies face, it is a challenge to summarize the data in such a way that the important *information* stands out clearly. It is easy to produce summary measures, tables, and graphs, but the issue is one of producing the most *appropriate* measures, tables, and graphs.

The typical employees of today—not just the managers and technical specialists—have a wealth of easy-to-use tools at their disposal, and it is frequently up to them to summarize data in a way that is both meaningful and useful to their constituents: people within their company, their company's suppliers, and their company's customers. It takes some training and practice to do this effectively.

Because today's companies are inundated with data, and because virtually every employee in the company must summarize data to some extent, the material in this chapter is arguably the most important material in this book. There has sometimes been a tendency to race through the "descriptive statistics" chapter to get to the more "interesting" material in later chapters as quickly as possible. We want to resist this tendency. The material covered in these two chapters deserves close examination, and this takes some time.

Most of the material in this chapter and the next could be covered in any order. However, we have structured the material so that most of this chapter involves graphs and tables. In the next chapter we then discuss numerical summary measures and one further type of graph, the boxplot, that utilizes several of the summary measures. We conclude the next chapter with several examples that put all of the descriptive tools from both chapters to good use.

2.2

Basic Concepts

We begin with a short discussion of several important concepts: populations and samples, variables and observations, and types of data.

2.2.1 Populations and Samples

First, we distinguish between a population and a sample. A **population** includes all of the objects of interest, whether they be people, households, machines, or whatever. The following are three typical populations:

- All potential voters in a presidential election
- All subscribers to cable television
- All invoices submitted for Medicare reimbursement by a nursing home

In these situations and many others it is virtually impossible to obtain information about all members of the population. For example, it is far too costly to ask all potential voters which presidential candidates they prefer. Therefore, we often try to gain insights into the characteristics of a population by examining a **sample**, or subset, of the population. In later chapters we will examine populations and samples in some depth, but for now, it is enough to know that we typically want samples to be *representative* of the population so that observed characteristics of the sample can be generalized to the population as a whole.

An example where this was *not* the case is the *Literary Digest* fiasco of 1936. In the 1936 presidential election, subscribers to the *Literary Digest*, a highbrow literary magazine, were asked to mail in a ballot with their preference for president. Overwhelmingly, these ballots favored the Republican candidate, Alf Landon, over the Democratic candidate, Franklin D. Roosevelt. Despite this, FDR was a landslide winner. The reason for the discrepancy was that the readers of the *Literary Digest* were not at all representative of most voters in 1936. Most voters in 1936 could barely make ends meet, let alone subscribe to a literary magazine. Thus the typical lower-middle-income voter had almost no chance of being chosen in this sample.

Today, Gallup, Harris, and other pollsters make a conscious effort to ensure that their samples—which usually include about 1500 people—are representative of the population. (It is truly remarkable, for example, that a sample of 1500 voters can almost surely predict a candidate's actual percentage of votes correct to within 3%. We will explain why this is possible in Chapters 7 and 8.) The important point is that a representative sample of reasonable size can give us a lot of important information about the population of interest.

We will use the terms *population* and *sample* a few times in this chapter, which is why we have defined them here. However, the distinction is not too important until later chapters. Our intent in this chapter is to focus entirely on the data in a given data set, not to generalize beyond it. Therefore, the given data set could be a population or a sample from a population. At this point, the distinction is largely irrelevant.

2.2.2 Variables and Observations

To standardize data analysis, especially on a computer, it is customary to present the data in rows and columns. Each column represents a **variable**, and each row corresponds to an **observation**, that is, a member of the population or sample. The numbers of variables and observations vary widely from one data set to another, but they can all be put in this row–column format.

The terms *variables* and *observations* are fairly standard. However, you might hear alternative terms. First, many people refer to **cases** instead of observations; that is, each row is a case. Second, if the data are stored in database packages such as Microsoft Access, the terms **fields** and **records** are typically used. Fields are the same as variables; each column corresponds to a field. Records are the same as observations (or cases); each row corresponds to a record.

EXAMPLE 2.1

The data set shown in Figure 2.3 represents 30 responses from a questionnaire concerning the president's environmental policies. (See the file CODING.XLS.) Identify the variables and observations.

FIGURE 2.3   **Data from Environmental Survey**

	A	B	C	D	E	F
1	Data from a questionnaire on environmental policy					
2						
3	Age	Gender	State	Children	Salary	Opinion
4	35	Male	Minnesota	1	$65,400	5
5	61	Female	Texas	2	$62,000	1
6	35	Male	Ohio	0	$63,200	3
7	37	Male	Florida	2	$52,000	5
8	32	Female	California	3	$81,400	1
9	33	Female	New York	3	$46,300	5
10	65	Female	Minnesota	2	$49,600	1
11	45	Male	New York	1	$45,900	5
12	40	Male	Texas	3	$47,700	4
13	32	Female	Texas	1	$59,900	4
14	57	Male	New York	1	$48,100	4
15	38	Female	Virginia	0	$58,100	3
16	37	Female	Illinois	2	$56,000	1
17	42	Female	Virginia	2	$53,400	1
18	38	Female	New York	2	$39,000	2
19	48	Male	Michigan	1	$61,500	2
20	40	Male	Ohio	0	$37,700	1
21	57	Female	Michigan	2	$36,700	4
22	44	Male	Florida	2	$45,200	3
23	40	Male	Michigan	0	$59,000	4
24	21	Female	Minnesota	2	$54,300	2
25	49	Male	New York	1	$62,100	4
26	34	Male	New York	0	$78,000	3
27	49	Male	Arizona	0	$43,200	5
28	40	Male	Arizona	1	$44,500	3
29	38	Male	Ohio	1	$43,300	1
30	27	Male	Illinois	3	$45,400	2
31	63	Male	Michigan	2	$53,900	1
32	52	Male	California	1	$44,100	3
33	48	Female	New York	2	$31,000	4

Solution

This data set includes data on 30 people who responded to the questionnaire. Each person represents an observation. Each observation lists the person's age, gender, state of residence, number of children, annual salary, and opinion of the president's environmental policies. These six pieces of information represent the variables. It is customary to include a row (row 3) that gives variable names. These variable names should obviously be meaningful—and no longer than necessary.   ■

2.2.3 Types of Data

There are several ways to categorize data, as we will explain in the context of Example 2.1. One way is **numerical** versus **categorical**. The basic distinction here is whether we intend to do any arithmetic on the data. It makes sense to do arithmetic on numerical data, but not on categorical data. Clearly, the Gender and State variables are categorical, and the Children and Salary variables are numerical. The Age and Opinion variables are more difficult to categorize. Age is expressed numerically, and we *might* want to perform some arithmetic on age (such as calculating the average age of the respondents). However, age might be treated as a categorical variable, as we will see shortly.

The Opinion variable is expressed numerically, on a 1-to-5 **Likert** scale. These numbers are only "codes" for the categories "strongly disagree," "disagree," "neutral," "agree," and "strongly agree." We never intend to perform arithmetic on these numbers; in fact, it is not really appropriate to do so.[1] Therefore, it is best to treat the Opinion variable as categorical. In addition, we note that there is a definite ordering of its categories, whereas there is no natural ordering of the categories for the Gender or State variables. When there is a natural ordering of categories, we classify the variable as **ordinal**. If there is no natural ordering, as with the Gender and State variables, we classify the variables as **nominal**. However, both ordinal and nominal variables are categorical.

Excel Tip   *How do you remember, for example, that 1 stands for "strongly disagree" in the Opinion variable? You can enter a note—a reminder to yourself and others—in any cell. This feature appears under the Insert menu. A small red tag appears in any cell with a note. Moving the cursor over that cell causes the note to appear. You will see numerous notes in the files that accompany this book. (Notes are called "comments" as of Excel 97.)*

When variables are categorical, they can be *coded* numerically or be left in uncoded form. In Figure 2.3, Gender has not been coded, whereas Opinion has been coded. This is largely a matter of taste—so long as you realize that coding a truly categorical variable doesn't make it numerical and open to arithmetic operations. An alternative way to represent this data set is shown in Figure 2.4. Now Gender has been coded (1 for males, 2 for females), and Opinion has not been coded. In addition, we have categorized the Age variable as "young" (34 or younger), "middle-aged" (from 35 to 59), and "elderly" (60 or older). The purpose of the study dictates whether age should be treated numerically or categorically; there is no right or wrong way.

We can also subdivide numerical variables into two types—**discrete** and **continuous**. The basic distinction is whether the data arise from counts or continuous measurements. The Children variable is clearly discrete, whereas the Salary variable is best treated as continuous. This distinction between discrete and continuous variables is sometimes important, as it dictates the type of analysis that is most natural.

Finally, data can be categorized as **cross-sectional** or **time series**. The opinion data in Example 2.1 are cross-sectional. A pollster evidently sampled a cross section of people at one particular point in time. In contrast, time series data occur when we track one or more variables through time. A typical example of a time series variable is the series of daily closing values of the Dow Jones Index. Very different types of analysis are appropriate for cross-sectional and time series data, as will become apparent in this and later chapters.

---

[1]Some people do take averages, for example, of numbers such as these, but there are conceptual reasons for *not* doing so; the resulting averages can be misleading.

Environmental Data Using a Different Coding

	A	B	C	D	E	F
1	Data from a questionnaire on environmental policy					
2						
3	Age	Gender	State	Children	Salary	Opinion
4	Middle-aged	1	Minnesota	1	$65,400	Strongly agree
5	Middle-aged	2	Texas	2	$62,000	Strongly disagree
6	Elderly	1	Ohio	0	$63,200	Neutral
7	Middle-aged	1	Florida	2	$52,000	Strongly agree
8	Young	2	California	3	$81,400	Strongly disagree
9	Young	2	New York	3	$46,300	Strongly agree
10	Elderly	2	Minnesota	2	$49,600	Strongly disagree
11	Middle-aged	1	New York	1	$45,900	Strongly agree
12	Middle-aged	1	Texas	3	$47,700	Agree
13	Young	2	Texas	1	$59,900	Agree
14	Middle-aged	1	New York	1	$48,100	Agree
15	Middle-aged	2	Virginia	0	$58,100	Neutral
16	Middle-aged	2	Illinois	2	$56,000	Strongly disagree
17	Middle-aged	2	Virginia	2	$53,400	Strongly disagree
18	Middle-aged	2	New York	2	$39,000	Disagree
19	Middle-aged	1	Michigan	1	$61,500	Disagree
20	Middle-aged	1	Ohio	0	$37,700	Strongly disagree
21	Middle-aged	2	Michigan	2	$36,700	Agree
22	Middle-aged	1	Florida	2	$45,200	Neutral
23	Middle-aged	1	Michigan	0	$59,000	Agree
24	Young	2	Minnesota	2	$54,300	Disagree
25	Middle-aged	1	New York	1	$62,100	Agree
26	Young	1	New York	0	$78,000	Neutral
27	Middle-aged	1	Arizona	0	$43,200	Strongly agree
28	Middle-aged	1	Arizona	1	$44,500	Neutral
29	Middle-aged	1	Ohio	1	$43,300	Strongly disagree
30	Young	1	Illinois	3	$45,400	Disagree
31	Elderly	1	Michigan	2	$53,900	Strongly disagree
32	Middle-aged	1	California	1	$44,100	Neutral
33	Middle-aged	2	New York	2	$31,000	Agree

2.3

Frequency Tables and Histograms

A good place to start building a "toolkit" of descriptive methods is with **frequency tables** and their graphical analog, **histograms**. A frequency table indicates how many observations fall in various categories. A histogram shows this same information graphically. We'll construct a frequency table and a histogram in the following example.

E X A M P L E   2 . 2

The file ACTORS.XLS contains information on 66 movie stars. (See Figure 2.5 on page 40.) This data set contains the name of each actor and the following four variables:

- Gender
- DomesticGross: average domestic gross of star's last few movies (in $ millions)

FIGURE 2.5   Data on Famous Actors and Actresses

	A	B	C	D	E
1	**Famous actors and actresses**				
2					
3	Note: All monetary values are in $ millions.				
4					
5	Name	Gender	DomesticGross	ForeignGross	Salary
6	Angela Bassett	F	32	17	2.5
7	Jessica Lange	F	21	27	2.5
8	Winona Ryder	F	36	30	4
9	Michelle Pfeiffer	F	66	31	10
10	Whoopi Goldberg	F	32	33	10
11	Emma Thompson	F	26	44	3
12	Julia Roberts	F	57	47	12
13	Sharon Stone	F	32	47	6
14	Meryl Streep	F	34	47	4.5
15	Susan Sarandon	F	38	49	3
16	Nicole Kidman	F	55	51	4
17	Holly Hunter	F	51	53	2.5
18	Meg Ryan	F	43	55	8.5
19	Andie Macdowell	F	26	75	2
59	Clint Eastwood	M	55	94	12.5
60	Mel Gibson	M	91	95	19
61	Bruce Willis	M	55	99	16.5
62	Bill Pullman	M	38	103	6
63	Liam Neeson	M	29	108	3
64	Samuel Jackson	M	40	122	4.5
65	Jim Carrey	M	122	123	15
66	Morgan Freeman	M	77	123	6
67	Arnold Scharz	M	108	124	20
68	Brad Pitt	M	57	124	10
69	Michael Douglas	M	68	137	18
70	Robin Williams	M	92	180	15
71	Tom Hanks	M	166	182	17.5

■ ForeignGross: average foreign gross of star's last few movies (in $ millions)

■ Salary: current amount the star asks for a movie (in $ millions)[2]

We are interested in summarizing the 66 salaries in a frequency table and a histogram.

Solution

To obtain a frequency table for data that are essentially continuous, such as the Salary variable, we must first choose appropriate categories. There is no set rule here. We want to have enough categories so that we can see a meaningful distribution, but we don't want so many categories that there are only a few observations per category. A good rule of thumb is to divide the range of values into 8 to 15 equally spaced categories, plus a possible open-ended category at either end of the range. For this data set we choose the categories 0–2, 2–4, 4–6, 6–8, 8–10, 10–12, 12–14, 14–16, 16–18, 18–20, and over 20. (All of these are in millions of dollars, and 2–4, for example, means greater than 2 and less than or equal to 4.)

---

[2] We realize that this quantity is not a salary in the usual sense of the term, but we'll use the word *salary* throughout this example.

To create the histogram in Excel, we use the StatPro add-in that accompanies this book. (See the file INSTALL.HTM on the CD-ROM for more discussion of the add-in, including how to load it.) Assuming the add-in is loaded, the steps for creating a histogram and the associated frequency table are as follows:

1   Place the cursor anywhere within the data set. This is a common first step in the StatPro add-in. If you can imagine a big rectangular range that contains the data set, including the variable names at the top, the cursor should be somewhere—anywhere—within this range. If you forget to place it there, the add-in will prompt you to do so before continuing.

2   Select the StatPro/Charts/Histogram(s) menu item.

3   A list of *numerical* variables in the data set appears. You should select one of these to obtain a frequency table and histogram for the variable you select. For now, select the Salary variable.

4   The histogram is placed on a separate "chart" sheet. Enter a name for this sheet, such as SalHist. If a sheet with this name already exists, it is replaced.

5   A sheet with the name you enter, plus the appendix "Data" (such as SalHistData), is added to capture the frequency table.[3] Click on OK to add this sheet.

6   Now comes the important part, where you specify the categories. (See Figure 2.6.) You need to enter (1) the upper limit of the first (leftmost) category, (2) the total number of categories, and (3) the typical length of a category. For this example, enter 2, 11, and 2.

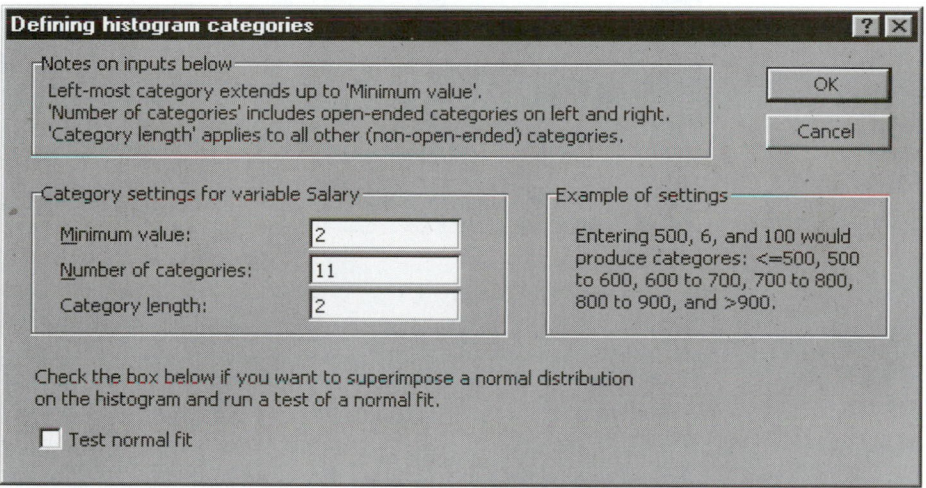

FIGURE 2.6   **Histogram Dialog Box in StatPro Add-In**

The resulting histogram and frequency table for the Salary variable appear in Figures 2.7 and 2.8. It is clear that most salaries are in the $2 to $10 million range, but a few are considerably larger. If you aren't satisfied with this histogram (you want fewer categories, for example), just repeat the procedure. If you use the same sheet names, you'll overwrite the previous output.

---

[3]Actually, it is added as a "hidden" sheet. To unhide it, use the Format/Sheet/Unhide menu item.

FIGURE 2.7   **Histogram of Actor and Actress Salaries**

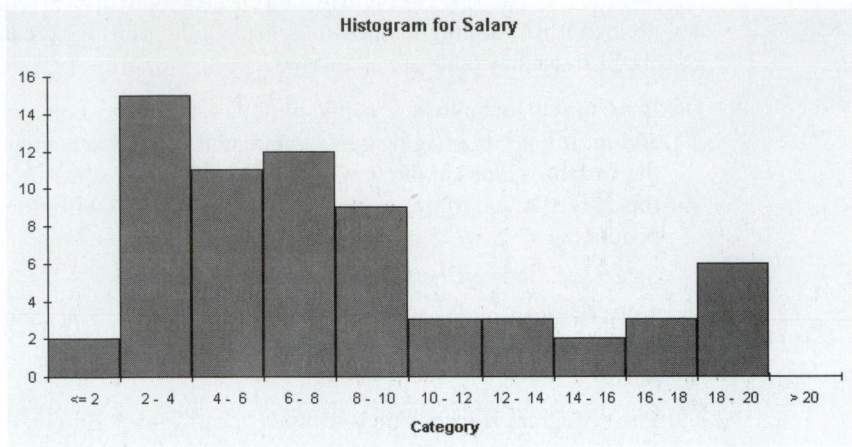

FIGURE 2.8   **Frequency Table for Actor and Actress Salaries**

	A	B	C
1	**Frequency table for Salary**		
2			
3	Upper limit	Category	Frequency
4	2	<= 2	2
5	4	2 - 4	15
6	6	4 - 6	11
7	8	6 - 8	12
8	10	8 - 10	9
9	12	10 - 12	3
10	14	12 - 14	3
11	16	14 - 16	2
12	18	16 - 18	3
13	20	18 - 20	6
14		> 20	0

Excel Tip   *StatPro automatically puts all charts on separate "chart sheets." If you would rather have a chart on the same sheet as the data, it is easy to move it. Go to the chart sheet, use the Chart/Location menu item, and select the "As object in" option, with the desired data sheet selected in the box. The chart sheet will no longer exist, and the chart will automatically appear in the data sheet. This process can also be reversed by selecting the "As new sheet" option under the Chart/Location menu item.*

Creating a histogram can be a tedious task, but an add-in such as StatPro makes it relatively easy. However, you must be prepared to fill in the dialog box in Figure 2.6—that is, you must be ready to specify the categories. This might take some trial and error. Several guidelines should be helpful:

■ Usually, choose about 8–15 categories. The more observations you have, the more categories you can afford to have.

- Try to select categories that "fill" the range of data. For example, it wouldn't make sense to have 10 categories of length $1000, starting with the category "less than $30,000," if most of the observations are in the $20,000 to $50,000 range. In this case all of the data would fall in the first few categories, virtually no data would fall in the higher categories, and the histogram would not tell a very interesting story.

- It is customary to plan the categories so that the "breakpoints" between categories are nice round numbers.

- The leftmost and rightmost categories are usually open-ended categories such as "less than or equal to $20,000" and "greater than $100,000." (In this case, the first entry in the dialog box in Figure 2.6 would be 20000.) The "category length" requested in the dialog box is for the middle categories, not these open-ended categories. If a typical middle category is from $30,000 to $40,000, then 10000 should be entered as the category length.

- Above all, remember that there is not a single "right answer." If your initial entries in the dialog box don't produce a very interesting histogram, try it again with new entries. If you get to the dialog box and have no idea what to enter, don't be afraid to click on the Cancel button. Then you can look at the data (how small are the smallest observations, how large are the largest?) to get an idea of what categories would produce an interesting histogram.

Alternative Methods for Creating Histograms in Excel   In case the StatPro add-in is not available, there are two alternative methods for creating frequency tables and histograms. We describe them briefly here. The first method creates a frequency table directly with Excel's FREQUENCY function and then uses the Chart Wizard in a straightforward way to form a histogram from this table. The steps are as follows.

1   Define the categories as in column A of Figure 2.8. That is, specify the *upper limit* of each category: 2 through 20. Excel refers to this range of upper limits (A4:A13 in the figure) as the "bin range," so we suggest giving it the range name Bins. The "greater than 20" is then treated as an implied extra category.

2   Enter *labels* to describe the categories in column B, again as in Figure 2.8. (This step is not necessary, but it will make the histogram more readable.)

3   Select the range C4:C14 (one cell longer than the Bins range), type the formula

$$=FREQUENCY(Salary,Bins)$$

and press Ctrl-Shift-Enter. That is, press all three keys at once. Here, Salary is the range name for the Salary variable data (E6:E71 in Figure 2.5).

Excel Tip   *The FREQUENCY function is an **array** function in Excel, which means that it fills a whole range in one step. If you look at the formula bar, you'll notice curly brackets around this formula. You should **not** type these curly brackets. They appear automatically when you press Ctrl-Shift-Enter, and they indicate that this is an array formula. Note that the value in the "extra" cell, C14, is the number of observations greater than the last bin value, 20. For this example it just happens that there are no such observations.*

4   Form the histogram from columns B and C by using the Chart Wizard with the column chart type. You should obtain a chart essentially like the one shown in Figure 2.7, which can then be modified to your taste with Excel's many chart options.

A second alternative method is to use the Analysis ToolPak add-in that comes with Excel. This add-in accomplishes many statistical tasks with a minimum of effort. For histograms, you must first enter the upper limits of the categories as above in a "bins" range. Then select the Tools/Data Analysis menu item, select the Histogram option, and fill out the dialog box in the obvious way. (Make sure to check the Labels box if the ranges you specify include variable names, and check the Chart Output box to obtain a histogram.)

Although this tool is quick and easy, it does have one serious drawback. The frequency table and corresponding histogram are not linked to the data. That is, if you change any of the data after using this tool, the outputs do not change. In contrast, the outputs from the StatPro add-in *are* linked to the data.

Excel Tip *Before you can use Excel's Analysis ToolPak, you must make sure it is available. Click on the Tools menu. If there is a Data Analysis menu item near the bottom, you're all set. Otherwise, click on the Tools/Add-ins menu item. If there is an unchecked Analysis ToolPak option, check it and click on OK. This will load the Analysis ToolPak. If there is no Analysis ToolPak option, this means that it was not installed as part of the original Excel installation. In this case you must rerun the Excel (or MSOffice) setup program and install this option.*

In summary, we have provided three methods for creating frequency tables and histograms in Excel. Again keep in mind that each of these methods requires you to define the categories. To do this sensibly, you should first take a look at the data—how many observations are there, and how small and large are the data values? Of course, if you create a histogram and it doesn't appear to provide much information, you can always redefine the categories and try again.

2.3.1 Shapes of Histograms

Four different shapes of histograms are commonly observed: symmetric, positively skewed, negatively skewed, and bimodal. A histogram is **symmetric** if it has a single peak and looks approximately the same to the left and right of the peak. For reasons that will become apparent in a later chapter, symmetric histograms are very common. One is illustrated in the following example.

E X A M P L E   2 . 3

Otis Elevator has measured the diameter (in inches) of 400 elevator rails. (See the file OTIS1.XLS.) The diameters range from a low of approximately 0.449 inch to a high of approximately 0.548 inch. Check that these diameters follow a symmetric distribution.

Solution

To create a histogram, we must first decide on categories. Given the range of the diameters, we choose the categories "less than 0.455," "0.455 to 0.465," and so on, up to "greater than 0.545." Of course, other choices are certainly possible. Then we use StatPro's Histogram procedure to create the histogram in Figure 2.9. [The settings required to obtain these categories are: (1) upper limit of first category: 0.455; (2) number of categories: 11; and (3) length of typical category: 0.01.]

Clearly, the most likely diameters are between 0.495 and 0.505. Also, we see that the distribution of diameters is fairly symmetric. For example, 70 rails have diameters between 0.485 and 0.495, while nearly the same number (67) have diameters between 0.505 and 0.515. Actually, the diameters appear to follow the bell-shaped "normal" distribution. We will discuss the normal distribution in detail in Chapter 5.

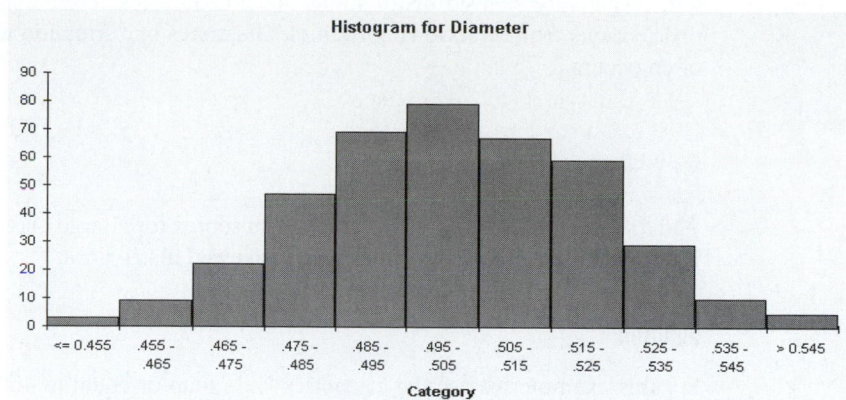

A histogram is **skewed to the right** (or **positively** skewed) if it has a single peak and the values of the distribution extend much farther to the right of the peak than to the left of the peak. One common example of positively skewed data is the following.

E X A M P L E   2 . 4

The file BANK.XLS lists the time between customer arrivals—called interarrival times—for all customers arriving at a bank on a given day. Do these interarrival times appear to be positively skewed?

Solution

For this data set we choose the categories "0 to 2.5," "2.5 to 5.0," and so on, up to "greater than 27.5." The resulting histogram appears in Figure 2.10. It is clear that these interarrival times are positively skewed. There is a "longer tail" to the right of the peak than to the left of the peak. We also see that values over 15 minutes are quite unlikely. Evidently, there is usually very little time between consecutive customer arrivals. Now and then, however, there is a fairly large gap between arrivals.

F I G U R E   2 . 1 0   **Positively Skewed Distribution of Interarrival Times**

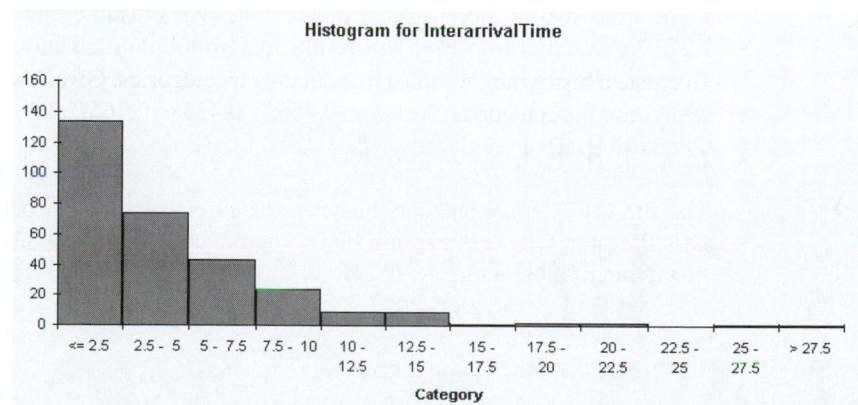

A histogram is **skewed to the left** (or **negatively** skewed) if its longer tail is on the left. Negatively skewed distributions are probably less common than positively skewed distributions, but the following example illustrates one situation where negative skewness often occurs.

EXAMPLE 2.5

The file MIDTERM.XLS lists the midterm scores for a large class of accounting students. Does the histogram indicate a negatively skewed distribution?

Solution

For this example we use the categories "less than or equal to 45," "45 to 50," and so on, up to "greater than 95" to create the histogram in Figure 2.11. This histogram shows that the most likely score is between 85 and 90. Clearly, the right tail can extend only to 100, while the left tail tapers off gradually. This leads to the obvious negative skewness. You've probably been in such classes, where most students do reasonably well but a few pull down the class average.

FIGURE 2.11   **Negatively Skewed Distribution of Midterm Scores**

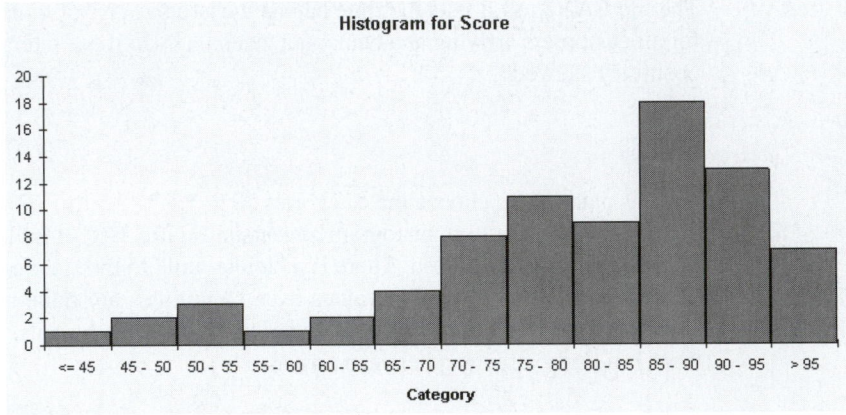

Some histograms have two or more peaks. This is often an indication that the data come from two or more distinct populations. We illustrate one possible situation where there are exactly *two* peaks. This results in a **bimodal** distribution.

EXAMPLE 2.6

The file OTIS2.XLS lists the diameters of all elevator rails produced on a single day at Otis Elevator. Otis uses two machines to produce elevator rails. What do we learn from a histogram of these data?

Solution

The diameters from the individual machines are listed in columns A and B of the OTIS2.XLS file. We merge these into a single variable in column C. Figure 2.12 shows the histogram on the merged data in column C. This is an obvious bimodal distribution, and it provides clear evidence of two distinct populations. Evidently, rails from one machine average about 0.5 inch in diameter, while rails from the other average about 0.6 inch in diameter. (A closer look at the data confirms this.) In such a case it is better to construct a single histogram for each machine's production, as in Figures 2.13 and 2.14. (These are based on the data in columns A and B, respectively.) These show that each machine's distribution is reasonably symmetric, although the scales on their horizontal axes are quite different.

FIGURE 2.12   **Bimodal Distribution of Diameters from Both Machines**

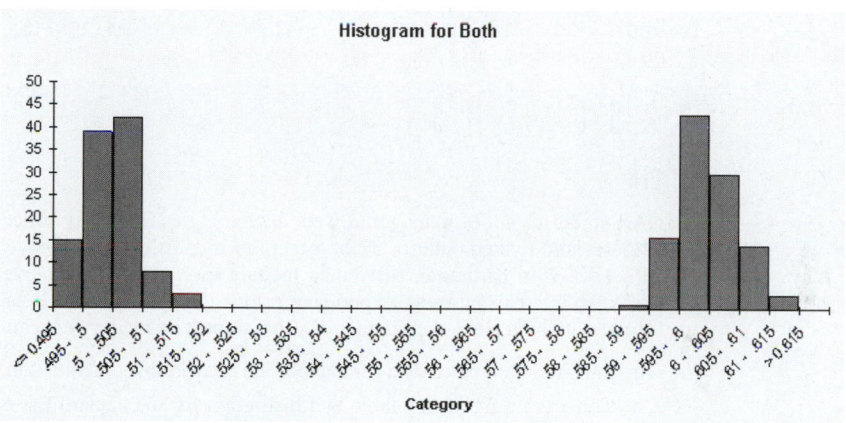

FIGURE 2.13   **Distribution of Diameters from Machine 1**

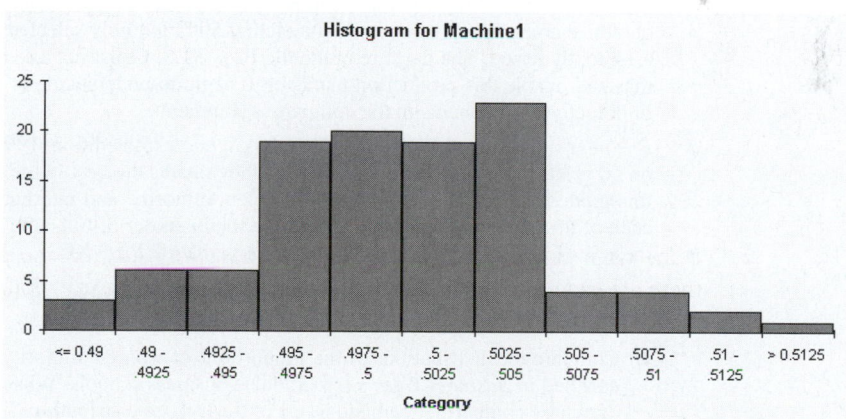

FIGURE 2.14   **Distribution of Diameters from Machine 2**

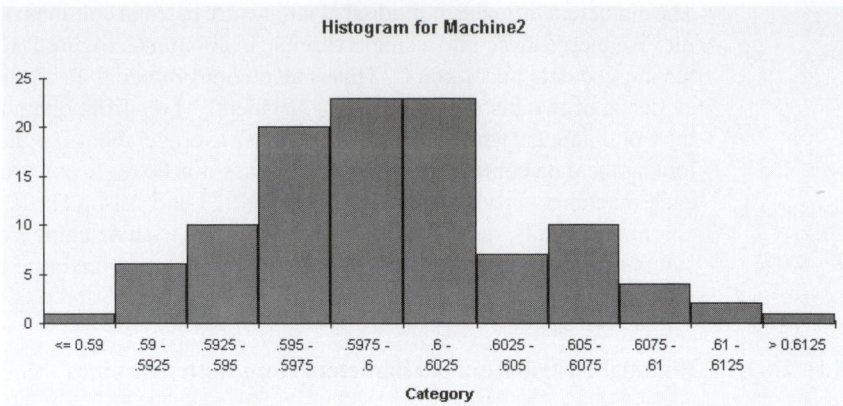

PROBLEMS
Level A

1   A human resources manager at Beta Technologies, Inc., has collected current annual salary figures and related data for 52 of the company's full-time employees. The data are in the file P2_1.XLS. In particular, these data include each selected employee's gender, age, number of years of relevant work experience prior to employment at Beta, the number of years of employment at Beta, the number of years of post-secondary education, and annual salary.

   a Indicate the type of data for each of the six variables included in this set.

   b Construct a frequency table and histogram for the ages of the employees included in this sample. How would you characterize the age distribution in this case?

   c Construct a frequency table and histogram for the salaries of the employees included in this sample. How would you characterize the salary distribution in this case?

2   A production manager is interested in determining the proportion of defective items in a typical shipment of one of the computer components that her company manufactures. The proportion of defective components is recorded for each of 500 randomly selected shipments collected during a 1-month period. The data are in the file P2_2.XLS. Construct a frequency table and histogram that will enable this production manager to begin to understand the variation of the proportion of defective components in the company's shipments.

3   *Business Week's Guide to the Best Business Schools* (5th edition, 1997) provides enrollment data on 50 graduate business programs which they rate as the best in the United States. Specifically, this guide reports the percentages of women, minority, and international students enrolled in each of the top 50 programs, as well as the total number of full-time students enrolled in each of these distinguished programs. The data are in the file P2_3.XLS.

   a Generate frequency tables and histograms for the distributions of each of the four variables included in this data set.

   b Compare the distributions of the proportions of women, minority, and international students enrolled in *Business Week's* top graduate business schools. What general conclusions can be drawn by comparing the histograms of these three distributions?

4   The manager of a local fast-food restaurant is interested in improving the service provided to customers who use the restaurant's drive-up window. As a first step in this process, the manager asks his assistant to record the time (in minutes) it takes to serve 200 different customers at the final window in the facility's drive-up system. The given 200 customer service times are all observed during the busiest hour of the day for this fast-food operation. The data are in the file P2_4.XLS.

a Construct a frequency table and histogram for the distribution of observed customer service times.

b Are shorter or longer service times more likely in this case?

5 A finance professor has just given a midterm examination in her corporate finance course. In particular, she is interested in learning how her class of 100 students performed on this exam. The data are in the file P2_5.XLS. Generate a histogram of this distribution of exam scores (where the maximum possible score is 100). Based on the histogram and associated frequency table, how would you characterize the group's performance on this test?

6 Five hundred households in a middle-class neighborhood were recently surveyed as a part of an economic development study conducted by the local government. Specifically, for each of the 500 randomly selected households, the survey requested information on the following variables: family size, approximate location of the household within the neighborhood, an indication of whether those surveyed owned or rented their home, gross annual income of the first household wage earner, gross annual income of the second household wage earner (if applicable), monthly home mortgage or rent payment, average monthly expenditure on utilities, and the total indebtedness (excluding the value of a home mortgage) of the household. The data are in the file P2_6.XLS.

a Indicate the type of data for each of the eight variables included in this survey.

b For each of the categorical variables in this survey, indicate whether the identified variable is *nominal* or *ordinal*. Explain your reasoning in each case.

c Construct a frequency table and histogram for each of the numerical variables in this data set. Indicate whether each of these distributions is approximately symmetric or skewed. Which, if any, of these distributions are skewed to the right? Which, if any, of these distributions are skewed to the left?

7 A real estate agent has gathered data on 150 houses that were recently sold in a suburban community. Included in this data set are observations for each of the following variables: the appraised value of each house (in thousands of dollars), the selling price of each house (in thousands of dollars), the size of each house (in hundreds of square feet), and the number of bedrooms in each house. The data are in the file P2_7.XLS.

a Indicate whether each of these four variables is *continuous* or *discrete*.

b Generate frequency tables and histograms for both the appraised values and selling prices of the 150 houses included in the given sample. In what ways are these two distributions similar? In what ways are they different?

8 In a recent ranking of top graduate business schools in the United States published by *U.S. News & World Report* (March 10, 1997), data were provided on a number of attributes of 25 recognized graduate programs. Specifically, the following variables were considered by *U.S. News & World Report* in establishing its overall ranking: each program's reputation rank by academics, each program's reputation rank by recruiters, each program's student selectivity rank, each program's placement success rate, the average GMAT score for students enrolled in each program, the average undergraduate grade-point average for students enrolled in each program, each program's recent acceptance rate, the typical starting base salary for recent graduates from each program, the proportion of recent graduates from each program who were employed within 3 months of completing their graduate studies, and the out-of-state tuition paid by affected full-time students in each program. The data are in the file P2_8.XLS.

a Indicate the type of data for each of the ten variables considered in the formulation of the overall ranking.

b For each of the categorical variables in this set, indicate whether the identified variable is *nominal* or *ordinal*. Explain your reasoning in each case.

c Construct a frequency table and histogram for each of the numerical variables in this data set. Indicate whether each of these distributions is approximately symmetric or skewed. Which, if any, of these distributions are skewed to the right? Which, if any, of these distributions are skewed to the left?

9 The operations manager of a toll booth, located at a major exit of a state turnpike, is trying to estimate the average number of vehicles that arrive at the toll booth during a 1-minute period during the peak of rush-hour traffic. In an effort to estimate this average throughput value, he records the number of vehicles that arrive at the toll booth over a 1-minute interval commencing at the same time for each of 365 normal weekdays. The data are in the file P2_9.XLS.

a Generate a histogram of the number of vehicles that arrive at this toll booth over the period of this study.

b Characterize this observed arrival distribution. Specifically, is it equally likely for smaller and larger numbers of vehicles to arrive during the chosen 1-minute period?

10 The SAT test score includes both verbal and mathematical components. The average scores on both the verbal and mathematical portions of the SAT have been computed for students taking this standardized test in each of the 50 states and the District of Columbia. Also, the proportion of high school graduates taking the test in each of the 50 states and the District of Columbia is recorded. The data are in the file P2_10.XLS.

a Construct a histogram for each of these three distributions of numerical values. Are these distributions essentially symmetric or are they skewed?

b Compare the distributions of the mean verbal scores and mean mathematical scores. In what ways are these two distributions similar and in what ways are they different?

11 In ranking 325 metropolitan areas in the United States, David Savageau and Geoffrey Loftus, the authors of *Places Rated Almanac* (published in 1997 by Macmillan) consider the average time (in minutes) it takes a citizen of each metropolitan area to travel to work and back home each day. The data are in the file P2_11.XLS. Generate a histogram for this distribution of daily commute times. Are shorter or longer average daily commute times generally more likely for citizens residing in these metropolitan areas?

12 The U.S. Department of Transportation regularly publishes the *Air Travel Consumer Report,* which provides a variety of performance measures of major U.S. commercial airlines. One dimension of performance reported is each airline's percentage of domestic flights arriving within 15 minutes of the scheduled arrival time at major reporting airports throughout the country. The data are in the file P2_12.XLS.

a Construct a frequency table and histogram for each airline's distribution of percentage of on-time arrivals at the reporting airports. Indicate whether each distribution is skewed or not.

b Visually compare the histograms you constructed in part **a**. What general conclusions emerge from your visual comparisons regarding the on-time performance of these major U.S. air carriers?

13 According to a survey conducted by New York compensation consultants William M. Mercer Inc. and published recently in *The Wall Street Journal* (April 9, 1998), chief executive officers from 350 of the nation's biggest businesses gained an 11.7% increase in salaries and bonuses in 1997. The data are in the file P2_13.XLS. This dramatic increase came on the heels of an 8.9% jump in corporate profit. Construct frequency tables and histograms to gain a clearer understanding of both the distributions of annual base salaries and of bonuses earned by the surveyed CEOs in fiscal 1997. ■

2.4

Analyzing Relationships with Scatterplots

We are often interested in the relationship between two variables. A useful way to picture this relationship is to plot a point for each observation, where the coordinates of the point represent the values of the two variables. The resulting graph is called a **scatterplot**. By examining the scatter of points, we can usually see whether there is any relationship between the two variables, and if so, what type of relationship it is. We illustrate this method in the following example.

EXAMPLE 2.7

Referring again to the data set in the ACTORS.XLS file, we might guess that stars whose movies gross large amounts have the largest salaries. Is this actually true?

Solution

To analyze this, we plot each star's salary on the vertical axis and the corresponding domestic gross on the horizontal axis. The resulting scatterplot appears in Figure 2.15. This graph can be obtained with StatPro add-in. To do so, use the StatPro/Charts/Scatterplot menu item, select Salary as the *Y* variable, select DomesticGross as the *X* variable, and give the chart sheet a name such as Scatter.

FIGURE 2.15   **Scatterplot of Salary versus DomesticGross**

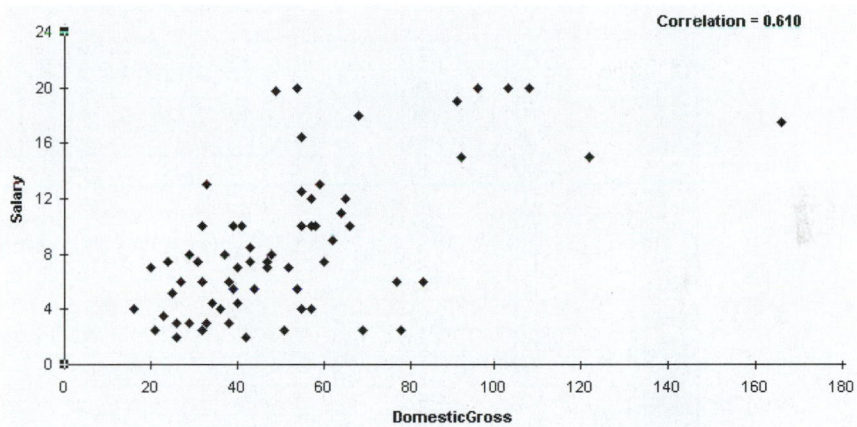

An alternative way to create the graph is to use Excel's Chart Wizard directly, using an "X-Y" type of chart. However, this method has a drawback. When you select the ranges for the two variables, say, the variables in columns B and E, Excel *automatically* puts the variable in the leftmost column (here column B) on the horizontal axis. You can't get around this Excel convention except by physically moving the data in column B to the right of the data in column E (or by doing something clever we haven't yet discovered!). There is no such limitation in the StatPro add-in.

The message from Figure 2.15 is fairly clear. First, the points tend to move up and to the right. This means that stars in films with large domestic grosses tend to make the largest salaries. The correlation of 0.61 shown in the chart supports this conclusion. As we'll see in the next chapter, this implies a reasonably strong positive *linear* relationship between the two variables. ■

For the sake of contrast, we now consider a relationship that is quite different.

EXAMPLE 2.8

Suppose we are interested in the relationship between sales productivity and the number of years a salesperson has worked the territory. We collect the data in Figure 2.16. (See the file SALES.XLS.) Describe the relationship between sales and experience.

FIGURE 2.16 **Sales versus Experience Data**

	A	B	C	D	E
1	**Sales productivity versus years of experience**				
2					
3	Note: All monetary values are in $ thousands.				
4					
5	YrsExper	Sales			
6	24	54			
7	8	57			
8	2	45			
9	12	61			
10	8	57			
11	4	50			
12	6	54			
13	6	54			
14	11	60			
15	10	60			
16	11	60			
17	16	62			
18	14	62			
19	10	60			
20	18	61			
21	22	57			
22	20	60			

Solution

Using StatPro's Scatterplot procedure, we construct the scatterplot shown in Figure 2.17. Note that as experience increases to around 14 years, sales increases, but at a decreasing rate. This indicates that there is a *nonlinear* relationship between sales and experience. Then beyond 14 years, additional experience appears to result in a sales decrease. Can you think of a reason why this might be the case? In Chapter 11 we will learn how to estimate nonlinear relationships.

FIGURE 2.17 **Scatterplot Illustrating a Nonlinear Relationship**

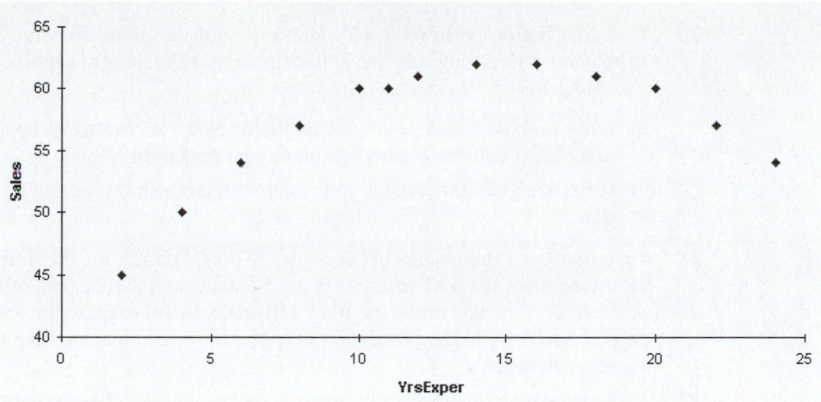

PROBLEMS

Level A

14 Explore the relationship between the selling prices and the appraised values of the 150 homes in the file P2_7.XLS by generating a scatterplot.

    a Is there evidence of a *linear* relationship between the selling price and appraised value in this case? If so, characterize the relationship (i.e., indicate whether the relationship is a positive or negative one).

    b For which of the two remaining variables, the size of the home and the number of bedrooms in the home, is the relationship with the home's selling price *stronger*? Justify your choice.

15 A human resources manager at Beta Technologies, Inc., is trying to determine the variable that best explains the variation of employee salaries using the previously gathered sample of 52 full-time employees in the file P2_1.XLS. Generate scatterplots to help this manager identify whether the employee's (a) gender, (b) age, (c) number of years of relevant work experience prior to employment at Beta, (d) the number of years of employment at Beta, or (e) the number of years of post-secondary education has the *strongest* linear relationship with annual salary.

16 Consider the enrollment data for *Business Week*'s top 50 U.S. graduate business programs in the file P2_3.XLS. Specifically, generate scatterplots to assess whether there is a systematic relationship between the total number of full-time students and each of the following: (a) the proportion of female students, (b) the proportion of minority students, and (c) the proportion of international students enrolled at these distinguished business schools.

17 What is the relationship between the number of short-term general hospitals and the number of general or family physicians in metropolitan areas? Explore this question by producing a scatterplot for these two variables using the data in the file P2_17.XLS. Interpret your computer-generated result.

18 Motorco produces electric motors for use in home appliances. One of the company's production managers is interested in examining the relationship between the dollars spent per month in inspecting finished motor products and the number of motors produced during that month that were returned by dissatisfied customers. He has collected the data in the file P2_18.XLS to explore this relationship for the past 36 months. Produce a scatterplot for these two variables and interpret it for this production manager.

19 The *ACCRA Cost of Living Index* provides a useful and reasonably accurate measure of cost of living differences among 321 urban areas. Items on which the index is based have been carefully chosen to reflect the different categories of consumer expenditures. The data are in the file P2_19.XLS. Generate scatterplots to explore the relationship between the composite index and each of the various expenditure components.

a Which expenditure component has the *strongest* relationship with the composite index?

b Which expenditure component has the *weakest* relationship with the composite index?

20 Consider the proportions of U.S. domestic airline flights arriving within 15 minutes of the scheduled arrival times at the Philadelphia and Pittsburgh airports. The data are in the file P2_20.XLS.

a Do you expect these two sets of performance measures to be *positively* or *negatively* associated with each other? Explain your reasoning.

b Compare your expectation to the actual relationship revealed by a scatterplot of the given data.

21 Examine the relationship between the average scores on the verbal and mathematical components of the SAT test across the 50 states and the District of Columbia by generating a scatterplot. The data are in the file P2_10.XLS. Also, explore the relationship between each of these variables and the proportion of high school graduates taking the SAT. Interpret each of these scatterplots.

22 Is there a strong relationship between a chief executive officer's annual compensation and her or his organization's recent profitability? Explore this question by generating relevant scatterplots for the survey data in the file P2_13.XLS. In particular, generate and interpret scatterplots for the change in the company's net income from 1996 to 1997 (see *Comp_NetInc96* column) and the CEO's 1997 base salary, as well as for the change in the company's net income from 1996 to 1997 and the CEO's 1997 bonus. Summarize your findings.

23 In response to a recent ranking of top graduate business schools in the United States published by *U.S. News & World Report* (March 10, 1997), the director of one of the recognized programs would like to know which variables are most strongly associated with a school's overall score. Ideally, she hopes to use an enhanced understanding of the ranking scheme to improve her program's score in the forthcoming years and thus please both external and internal constituents. The data are in the file P2_8.XLS.

a Use scatterplots to provide her with an indication of the measures that are most strongly related to the overall score in the *U.S. News & World Report* ranking.

b Generally, how can she and her administrative colleagues proceed to improve their program's ranking in forthcoming publications?

24 Consider the relationship between the size of the population and the average household income level for residents of U.S. towns. What do you expect the relationship between these two variables to be? Using the data in the file P2_24.XLS, produce and interpret the scatterplot for these two variables.

25 Based on the data in the file P2_25.XLS from the U.S. Department of Agriculture, explore the relationship between the number of farms and the average size of a farm in the United States between 1950 and 1997. Specifically, generate a scatterplot and interpret it. ■

2.5

Time Series Plots

When we are interested in forecasting future values of a time series, it is helpful to create a time series plot. This is essentially a scatterplot, with the time series variable on the vertical axis and time itself on the horizontal axis. Also, to make patterns in the data more apparent, the points are usually connected with lines.

When we look at a time series plot, we usually look for two things:

■ Is there an observable trend? That is, do the values of the series tend to increase (an upward trend) or decrease (a downward trend) over time?

- Is there a seasonal pattern? For example, do the peaks or valleys for quarterly data tend to occur every fourth observation? Or do soft drink sales peak in the summer months?

The following example illustrates the construction and interpretation of a time series plot.

EXAMPLE 2.9

The file TOYS.XLS lists quarterly sales revenues (in $ millions) for Toys "R" Us during the years 1992–1995. The data are shown in Figure 2.18. Display these sales data in a time series plot and comment on whether trend and/or seasonality is present.

FIGURE 2.18   **Revenue Data for Toys "R" Us**

	A	B	C	D
1	Toys "R" Us revenues			
2				
3	Note: All monetary values are in $ millions.			
4				
5	Quarter	Revenue		
6	Q1-92	1026		
7	Q2-92	1056		
8	Q3-92	1182		
9	Q4-92	2861		
10	Q1-93	1172		
11	Q2-93	1249		
12	Q3-93	1346		
13	Q4-93	3402		
14	Q1-94	1286		
15	Q2-94	1317		
16	Q3-94	1449		
17	Q4-94	3893		
18	Q1-95	1462		
19	Q2-95	1452		
20	Q3-95	1631		
21	Q4-95	4200		

Solution

To obtain the time series plot, as shown in Figure 2.19, we use the StatPro/Charts/Time Series Plot menu item. This procedure allows us to plot either one or more times series variables (on the same chart). In this example there is only one variable, Revenue, to plot. We also have the option of selecting a "date" variable for labeling the horizontal axis. Here we select Quarter (in column A) as the date variable. (If there were no date variable, the horizontal axis would be labeled with consecutive integers, starting with 1.)

The time series plot exhibits an obvious seasonal pattern. Fourth quarter sales each year are much larger than the sales for the first three quarters. Of course, this is due to holiday sales. Also, focusing on the first three quarters of each successive year, we see a small upward trend in sales. This upward trend is also visible in the pattern of fourth quarters. The lesson from this graph is that if we want to forecast future quarterly sales for Toys "R" Us, we need to estimate the upward trend and seasonality of quarterly sales.

FIGURE 2.19   Time Series Plot of Revenue

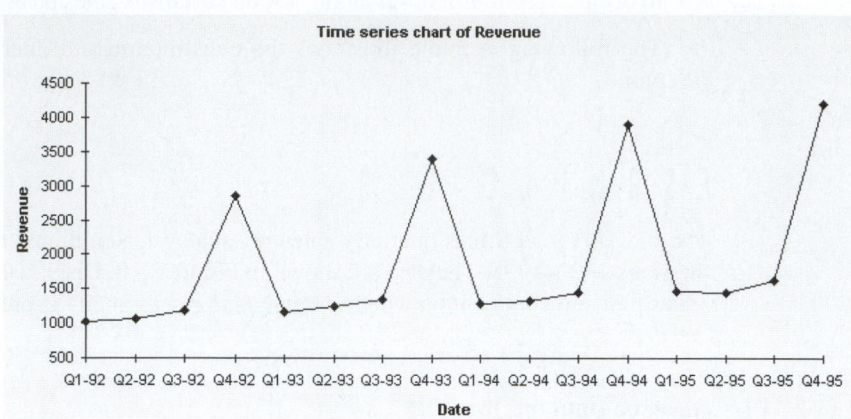

Sometimes it is useful to plot two time series variables on the same chart to compare their time series behavior. This is simple to do in StatPro by selecting *two* time series variables to plot. However, if the data for these two variables are of completely different magnitudes, the graph will be dominated by the variable with the largest data; the graph of the other variable will barely be visible. Therefore, StatPro provides the option of using the *same* vertical scale for both variables or using *different* vertical scales. The following example illustrates the second option. (Note that this latter option is not available if you select to plot *more* than two series on the same chart.)

EXAMPLE 2.10

Consider a company that sells two products. Product 1, however, is a much better seller than product 2. (See the file TWOVARS.XLS.) The monthly revenues from product 1 are typically above $100,000, whereas the revenues from product 2 are typically around $5000. How can the time series behavior of these revenues be shown on a single chart in a meaningful way?

Solution

The desired graph is shown in Figure 2.20. Note that it has two vertical scales. The scale on the left is appropriate for product 1, and the scale on the right is appropriate for product 2. We produced this chart in StatPro by filling in the key dialog box in the Time Series Plot procedure as shown in Figure 2.21. (There is no "date" variable in this file, which explains why the second box is not checked.)

FIGURE 2.20 **Plotting Time Series Variables on Two Different Scales**

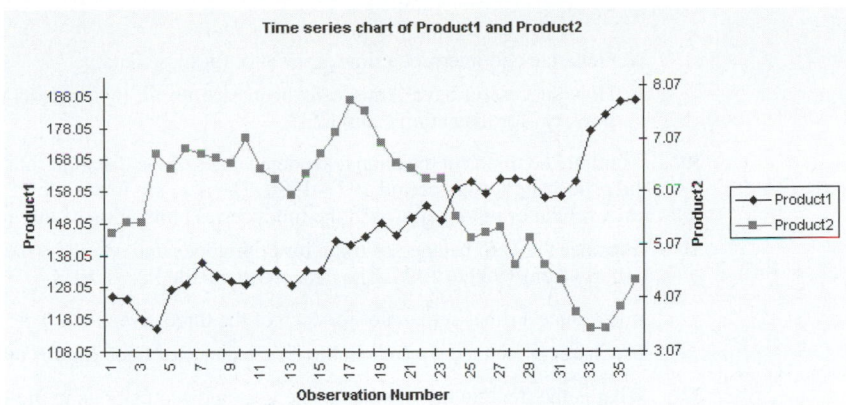

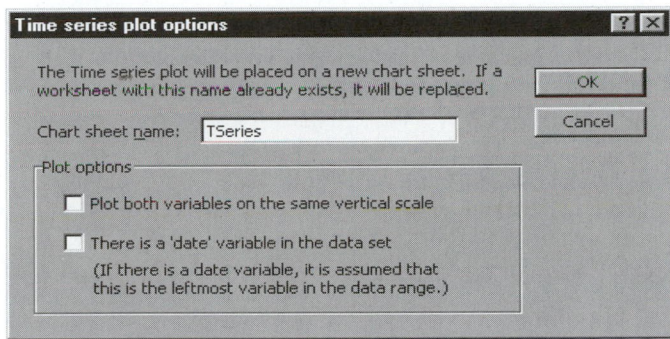

PROBLEMS

Level A

26 Consider the Consumer Price Index, which provides the annual percentage change in consumer prices, for the period from 1914 through 1996. The data are in the file P2_26.XLS.

 a Construct a time series plot for these data.

 b What, if any, trend do you see in the CPI for the given time period?

27 Compare the trends of the percentage changes of annual new orders for all manufacturing, durable goods, and nondurable goods industries in the United States for the years 1987–1996. The data are in the file P2_27.XLS.

 a Are the trends in these three times series similar?

 b Can you explain the variation in each of these series over the given time period?

28 The Consumer Confidence Index attempts to measure people's feelings about general business conditions, employment opportunities, and their own income prospects.

 a Generate a time series plot for the annual average values of the CCI for the period 1967–1996. The data are in the file P2_28.XLS.

 b Is it possible to say that U.S. consumers are more or less confident as we move out of the present decade?

 c How would you explain recent variations in the overall trend of the CCI?

29   Consider the proportion of Americans under the age of 18 living below the poverty level for each of the years beginning in 1959 and proceeding through 1996. The data are in the file P2_29.XLS.

   a Generate and interpret a time series plot for these data.

   b How successful have Americans been recently in their efforts to win "the war against poverty" for the nation's children?

30   Examine the trends in the annual average values of the discount rate, the federal funds rate, and the prime rate for the period 1977–1996. The data are in the file P2_30.XLS. Can you discern any cyclical or other patterns in the times series plots of these three key interest rates?

31   Consider the U.S. balance of trade for both goods and services (measured in millions of U.S. dollars) from 1980 to 1996. The data are in the file P2_31.XLS.

   a Produce a times series plot for each of the three given time series.

   b Characterize recent trends in the U.S. balance of trade figures using your time series plots.

32   What is the trend in the number of mergers and acquisitions in the United States over the past decade? Confirm your knowledge of this feature of U.S. business activity by generating a time series plot for the data in the file P2_32.XLS from the years 1985 through 1996.

33   The Federal Deposit Insurance Corporation provides annual data on the number of insured commercial banks and the number of commercial failures in the United States. The file P2_33.XLS contains these data for the period 1980–1996.

   a Explore the relationship between these two time series by first producing and interpreting a scatterplot. Is the revealed relationship consistent with your expectations?

   b Next, generate time series plots for each of these variables and comment on recent trends in their behavior.

34   Is cigar consumption in the United States on the rise? Explore this question by producing time series plots for each of the variables in the file P2_34.XLS. Comment on any observed trends in annual cigar consumption of the general U.S. population and of the U.S. male population over the given period (i.e., 1920 through 1996).

35   Examine the trend of average annual interest rates on 30-year fixed mortgages in the United States over the past 25 years. The data are in the file P2_35.XLS. What conclusion(s) can be drawn from an analysis of the time series plot generated with the given data?

36   What has happened to the total *number* and average *size* of farms in the United States during the second half of the 20th century? Respond to this question by producing a time series plot of the data from the U.S. Department of Agriculture in the file P2_36.XLS. Is the observed result consistent with your knowledge of the structural changes within the U.S. farming economy?

37   Consider the file P2_37.XLS, which contains total monthly U.S. retail sales data for the years 1993–1996.

   a Generate a plot of this time series and comment on any observable trends, including a possible seasonal pattern, in the data.

   b Based on your time series plot, make a qualitative projection about the total retail sales levels for the months of 1997. Specifically, in which months of the subsequent year do you expect retail sales levels to be *highest*? In which months of the subsequent year do you expect retail sales levels to be *lowest*?

38   Are there certain times of the year at which Americans typically purchase greater quantities of liquor? Investigate this question by generating a time series plot for the monthly retail sales data from U.S. liquor stores listed in the file P2_38.XLS. Interpret the seasonal pattern revealed by your graph.

39   Examine the provided monthly time series data for total U.S. retail sales of building materials (which includes retail sales of building materials, hardware and garden supply stores, and mobile home dealers). The data are in the file P2_39.XLS.

   a Is there an observable trend in these data? That is, do the values of the series tend to increase or decrease over time?

   b Is there a seasonal pattern in these data? If so, how do you explain this seasonal pattern?

40 In which months of the calendar year do U.S. gasoline service stations typically have their *lowest* retail sales levels? In which months of the calendar year do U.S. gasoline service stations typically have their *highest* retail sales levels? Produce a time series plot for the monthly data in the file P2_40.XLS to respond to these two questions. ■

Exploring Data with Pivot Tables

We now look at one of Excel's most powerful—and easy-to-use—tools, **pivot tables**. This tool provides an incredible amount of useful information about a data set. Pivot tables allow us to "slice and dice" the data in a variety of ways. That is, they break the data down into subpopulations so that we can, for example, see average salaries for male actors and female actresses separately. Statisticians often refer to the resulting tables as **contingency tables** or **crosstabs**. However, Excel provides more variety and flexibility with its pivot table tool than most other statistical software packages provide with their "crosstab" options.

It is easiest to understand pivot tables by means of examples, so we will illustrate several possibilities with the data in the ACTORS.XLS file. However, these only begin to show the power of pivot tables. The examples in Section 3.9 will show their real power.

E X A M P L E   2 . 1 1

Female actresses claim they are being underpaid relative to male actors. Do the data support this claim?

Solution

We first determine the male–female breakdown in the data set. Although there are other ways to count the number of males and females, the following steps show how it can be done with a pivot table.

1 Position the cursor anywhere in the data range. (Pivot tables are similar to the StatPro add-in in expecting you to perform this step first.)

2 Select the Data/PivotTable Report menu item. This takes you to a four-step PivotTable Wizard that leads you through the process.

3 In the first step, click on Next to indicate that the data for the pivot table are in an Excel spreadsheet.

4 In the second step, specify the range of the data set. Assuming that you placed the cursor somewhere in the data set, the Wizard correctly guesses the range of the data, so click on Next.

5 The third step is the crucial one, where you specify the variables you want in the pivot table. To put any field in one of the four areas (page, row, column, or data), just click on the variable's button and drag it to the appropriate area. Essentially, the page, row, and column areas allow you to break the data down by the categories of the variables in these areas. The "data" area specifies the data you want to calculate. For this example drag Gender to the row area and Gender to the data area. The screen should appear as shown in Figure 2.22 (page 60). Then click on Next.

FIGURE 2.22   Pivot Table Dialog Box

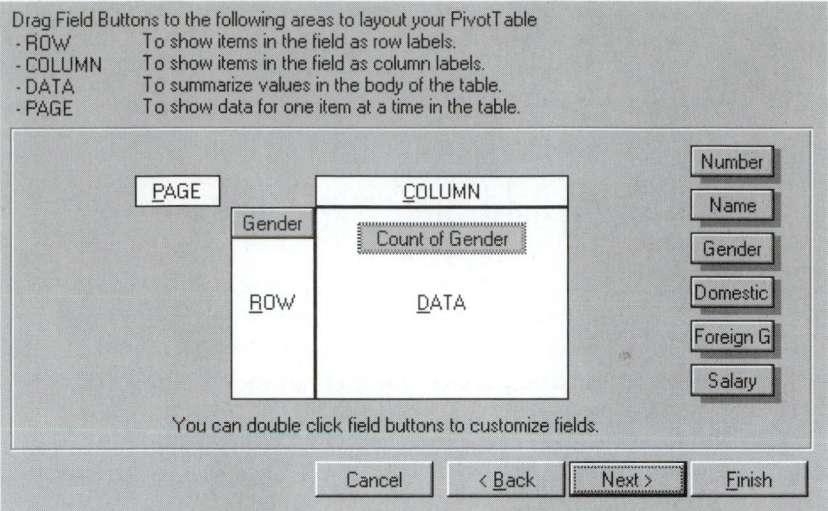

FIGURE 2.23   Pivot Table of Gender Counts

Excel Tip   *In this example we want **counts**, the number of men and the number of women. To get these we place Gender in the row area (it could instead be in the column area), and we place **any nonnumerical** variable in the data area. When we want counts from a pivot table, the variable in the data area is irrelevant as long as it provides counts. When a nonnumerical variable is placed in the data area, we get counts by default.*

6   The last step of the Wizard allows you to specify the location of the pivot table (in the topmost box). If you leave this blank, the pivot table is automatically placed on a new sheet. You can also specify other settings, such as whether you want row or column totals. For now, click on Finish to accept the defaults. This produces the pivot table in Figure 2.23.

	A	B
1	Count of Gender	
2	Gender	Total
3	F	18
4	M	48
5	Grand Total	66

This table shows that there are 66 stars; 48 are male and 18 are female. When we create this pivot table, a pivot table toolbar appears on the screen. This toolbar allows us to modify the pivot table in various ways. For example, suppose we want to express these counts as percentages of the total. To do so, put the cursor anywhere in the pivot table, say, cell B3, and click on the leftmost button of the new toolbar. This takes us back to step 3 of the Pivot Table Wizard. Now do the following.

1   Double-click on the variable in the data area (the Count of Gender button) to bring up a dialog box. Click on the Options button.

2   In the "Show Data as" area, click on the down arrow, and click on the "% of column" option.

3   Click on OK to close the dialog box, and click on Finish to see the modified pivot table.

The new pivot table is shown in Figure 2.24. It still contains the same information, but expressed differently. To show this information graphically, we also created the 3-D pie chart (from the range A3:B4) shown in the figure. The point here is that pivot table data are like any other data in Excel—we can use them to create a variety of charts.

FIGURE 2.24   **Pivot Table with Counts Expressed as Percentages**

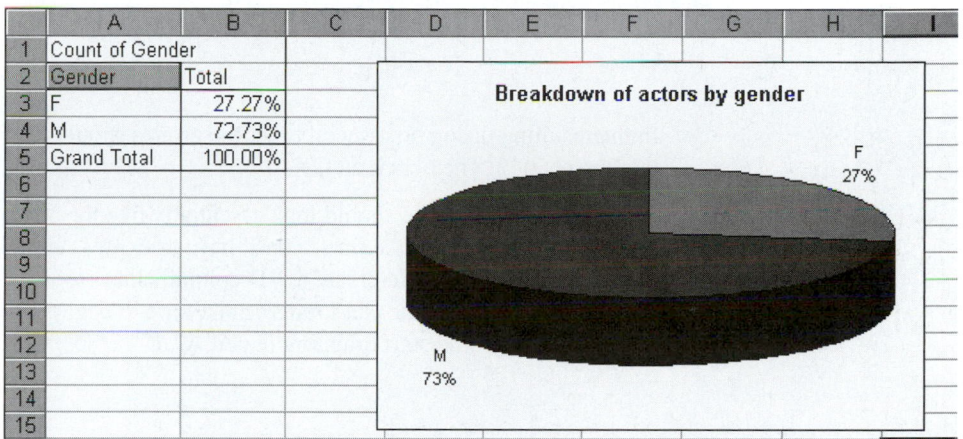

We still don't know whether women are underpaid, so we will create other pivot tables to examine the distribution of salaries, classified by gender. The following steps accomplish this.

1   Place the cursor anywhere in the data range (on the Data sheet).

2   Select the Data/PivotTable menu item, and click on Next in the first two steps to accept the defaults.

3   Drag the Salary variable to the Row area, drag Gender to the column area, drag Gender to the data area, and click on Next. (Again, we want to create counts in the pivot table, so *any* nonnumerical variable could be placed in the data area.)

4   Click on Finish to accept the defaults on the final screen.

The completed pivot table appears in Figure 2.25 (page 62). It shows the number of men and women making each possible salary. (It also shows row and column totals.) This is a bit too much detail, although it is already apparent that men typically earn more than women. It would be better to show these counts for broader categories.

We can easily "group" the Salary categories as follows.

1   Click on any cell in the Salary column of the pivot table, such as cell A3.

2   Click on the right arrow button (the Group button) of the Pivot Table toolbar. This allows us to group the categories. (As you might guess, the left arrow button allows us to ungroup them.)

FIGURE 2.25 **Pivot Table Showing Distribution of Salary by Gender**

	A	B	C	D
1	Count of Gender	Gender		
2	Salary	F	M	Grand Total
3	2	1	1	2
4	2.5	4	1	5
5	3	2	2	4
6	3.5	0	1	1
7	4	2	3	5
22	15	0	2	2
23	16.5	0	1	1
24	17.5	0	1	1
25	18	0	1	1
26	19	0	1	1
27	19.8	0	1	1
28	20	0	4	4
29	Grand Total	18	48	66

3 In the resulting dialog box, specify that the groups should start at 2, end at 20, and use increments of 3. Then click on OK.

The modified pivot table should look essentially like the one in Figure 2.26. Actually, to make yours look exactly like ours, you'll have to express counts as percentages (as we did earlier), and you'll have to create a 3-D column chart from the range A2:C8. (To drag this range when specifying the chart range, make sure to begin dragging in cell C8, *not* cell A2. You'll see why if you start dragging in cell A2.)

FIGURE 2.26 **Using the Pivot Table Group Option**

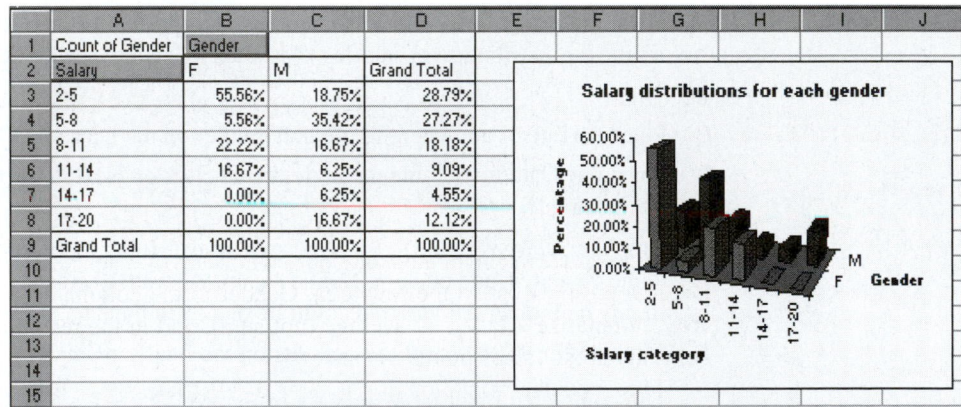

Figure 2.26 makes it clear that over half the women are in the lowest salary category, whereas only 19% of the men are in this category. Also, no women are in the highest two salary categories, whereas 23% of the men are in these categories. Evidently, male actors make considerably more money from movies than female actresses.

Another way to compare salaries of men and women is to look at the *average* salary by gender. We can also do this with a pivot table using the following steps.

1 Proceed as before to get to the third step of the Pivot Table Wizard.

2 Drag Gender to the row area and Salary to the data area. Note that the data area now shows "Sum of Salary." When a *numerical* variable is dragged to the data area, the default is to show its sum in the pivot table. Therefore, if we finished now, we'd see the sum of all male salaries and the sum of all female salaries. However, we want averages, not sums. Therefore, go to step 3.

3 Double-click on the Sum of Salary button in the data area. In the "Summary by" box, click on Average. (While you're here, look at the other "summarizing" options available.) Then click on OK to close the dialog box, and click on Finish to create the pivot table.

The result appears in Figure 2.27. Clearly, the male actors make considerably more on average than the female actresses. The corresponding 3-D column chart of the average salaries shows this discrepancy graphically.

FIGURE 2.27 **Pivot Table of Average Salary by Gender**

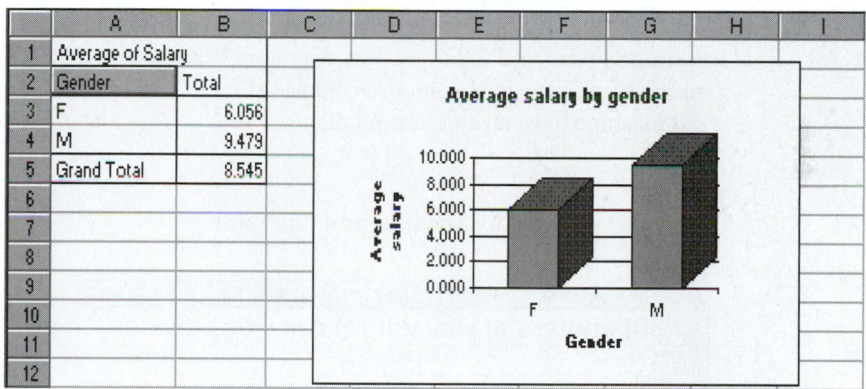

The analysis so far appears to indicate that the movie industry discriminates against women. However, it is possible that women are paid less because movies with female leads gross less money than movies with male leads. To analyze this further, we look at the average salary of men and women for each domestic gross level. (We could also take into account the influence of foreign grosses, but we won't do so here.)

The pivot table for doing this appears in Figure 2.28 (page 64). By this time you should be able to create the pivot table on your own. But if you need help, here are the basic steps: Drag DomesticGross to the row area, Gender to the column area, and Salary to the data area; summarize salaries by average (not sum); and in the resulting pivot table group the domestic gross values in increments of 20.

First, note the "#DIV/0!" in four of the cells. The reason is that no movies with female leads had domestic grosses in these highest four categories, so it is impossible to calculate averages for them. (Essentially, we are trying to divide by 0.) Now it's fair to ask whether men average more than women, after controlling for the domestic gross. Clearly, they do so in the two lowest domestic gross categories, but only barely in the third. Beyond the third category, it is hard to tell because no females were leads in the real blockbusters. In any case, we can now say with more assurance that the industry *does* appear to discriminate against women in terms of salary.

FIGURE 2.28 **Pivot Table of Average Salary by Domestic Gross and Gender**

	A	B	C	D
1	Average of Salary	Gender		
2	Domestic Gross	F	M	Grand Total
3	16-36	4.357	6.155	5.456
4	36-56	4.400	8.990	8.072
5	56-76	9.417	9.500	9.462
6	76-96	#DIV/0!	9.700	9.700
7	96-116	#DIV/0!	20.000	20.000
8	116-136	#DIV/0!	15.000	15.000
9	156-176	#DIV/0!	17.500	17.500
10	Grand Total	6.056	9.479	8.545

The next example provides further illustration of the possibilities of pivot tables.

EXAMPLE 2.12

The file OTIS3.XLS lists the diameters (in inches) of elevator rails produced by Otis Elevator's two machines and two operators. Each diameter corresponds to a particular machine/operator combination, as shown in Figure 2.29. What effects, if any, do the operator and machine have on elevator rail diameters?

FIGURE 2.29 **Diameters at Otis by Machine and Operator**

	A	B	C	D	E
1	**Diameters of elevator rails at Otis Elevator**				
2					
3	Note: All diameters are expressed in fractions of inches.				
4					
5	Machine	Operator	Diameter		
6	2	1	0.5184		
7	2	2	0.5357		
8	1	2	0.5290		
9	1	2	0.5298		
10	2	1	0.5423		
11	1	1	0.5188		
12	2	2	0.5387		
13	1	1	0.5207		
14	2	1	0.5095		
15	2	2	0.5438		
16	2	1	0.5187		
17	1	1	0.5179		
131	1	1	0.5169		
132	2	1	0.5458		
133	1	1	0.5419		
134	1	1	0.5160		
135	2	2	0.5413		

Solution

The relevant pivot table and an associated 3-D column chart appear in Figure 2.30. Here we dragged Machine to the row area, Operator to the column area, and Diameter (expressed as an average) to the data area. The numbers and graph indicate several interesting results:

- On average, the diameters for machine 2 are about 0.01 inch larger than those for machine 1 (see column D). This pattern is approximately the same whether operator 1 or operator 2 is operating the machines (see columns B and C).

- On average, the diameters for operator 2 are about 0.01 inch larger than those for operator 1 (see row 5). This pattern is approximately the same whether operators are operating machine 1 or machine 2 (see rows 3 and 4).

FIGURE 2.30 **Diameters by Operator and Machine**

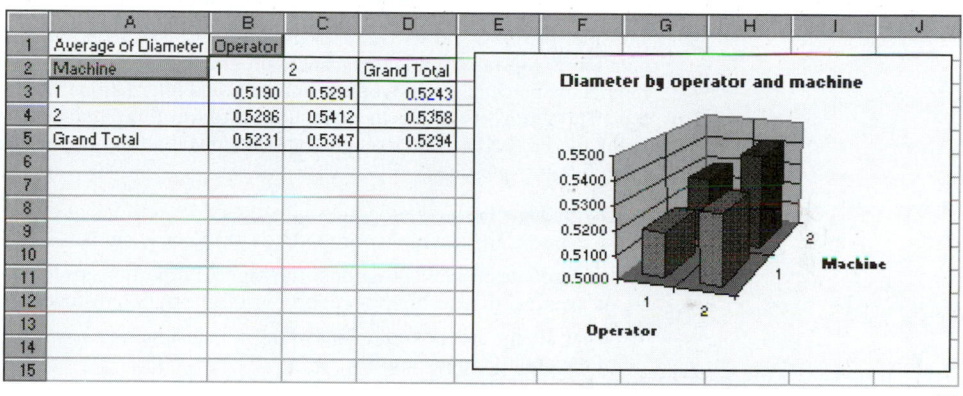

Final Remarks on Pivot Tables We have just begun to see the power and flexibility of pivot tables. Other available options include the following.

- The data used to create a pivot table can come from an external database (such as Microsoft Access) as well as a database within an Excel spreadsheet.

- We can use a "page" field for added flexibility. For example, if we drag Gender to the page field, we can then see three separate pivot tables with a click of the mouse: one for all people, one for males only, and one for females only. We'll explore this option in the next chapter.

- We can drag multiple fields to any of the areas (row, column, page, or data) of a pivot table. Also, once the pivot table is visible, we can drag any row, column, or page area to another area—without going back to the Wizard—and the pivot table automatically readjusts itself.

- By double-clicking on any pivot table entry, we see all of the data that were used to compute that entry. For example, by double-clicking on cell B3 in Figure 2.30, we see the diameters of all rods that were produced on machine 1 by operator 1.

- The pivot table retains a link to the original data, so that if the original data change, the pivot table recalculates automatically. To get it to do so, click on the exclamation point button (the rightmost button) of the Pivot Table toolbar.

We encourage you to experiment with pivot tables. They are extremely powerful, intuitive, and easy to use. Many people claim they represent one of Excel's best features.

P R O B L E M S

Level A

41 A human resources manager at Beta Technologies, Inc., has collected current annual salary figures and related data for 52 of the company's full-time employees. In particular, these data include each selected employee's gender, age, number of years of relevant work experience prior to employment at Beta, the number of years of employment at Beta, the number of years of post-secondary education, and annual salary. The data are in the file P2_1.XLS. Use Excel to construct pivot tables or other descriptive graphs to answer the following questions:

    a What proportion of these full-time Beta employees are female?

    b Is there evidence of salary discrimination against women at Beta Technologies? What are the limitations of the conclusion that you have drawn in answering this question?

    c Is additional post-secondary education positively associated with higher average salaries at Beta?

    d Is there evidence of salary discrimination against older employees at Beta Technologies? What are the limitations of the conclusion that you have drawn in answering this question?

42 Consider *Business Week's Guide to the Best Business Schools* (5th edition, 1997) enrollment data for 50 top-rated graduate business programs in the United States. Specifically, this guide reports the percentages of women, minority, and international students enrolled in each of the top 50 programs, as well as the total number of full-time students enrolled in each. The data are in the file P2_3.XLS. Use Excel to construct pivot tables or other descriptive graphs to answer the following questions:

    a Do graduate business programs with higher proportions of female student enrollments tend, on average, to have higher proportions of minority student enrollments?

    b Do graduate business programs with higher proportions of female student enrollments tend, on average, to have higher proportions of international student enrollments?

    c What, if any, are the limitations of the conclusions you have reached in responding to each of the previous questions?

43 Who is most likely to access the Internet today? Consider the survey data collected from 1000 randomly selected Internet users, given in the file P2_43.XLS. Construct pivot tables to answer each of the following questions.

    a What proportion of these Internet users are men under the age of 30?

    b What proportion of these Internet users are single with no formal education beyond high school?

    c What proportion of these Internet users are currently employed? What is the average salary of the employed Internet users in this sample?

44 Is there a relationship between a state's number of classroom teachers and the average salary of classroom teachers in the state? Generate one or more pivot tables using Excel to answer this question for the data from 1996 in the file P2_44.XLS. In addition to exploring the relationship between a state's total number of classroom teachers and their average annual salary, consider the same relationships for both elementary and secondary teachers.

45 Using the first given data set in file P2_45.XLS, which was collected in 1994, construct a single pivot table that breaks down the 1000 randomly selected U.S. workers by sex *and* race. Develop a similar breakdown for those workers randomly selected in 1982. How have the proportions of U.S. workers in these various cross sections changed between 1982 and 1994?

46 Given data in the file P2_13.XLS from a recent survey of chief executive officers from 350 of the nation's biggest businesses, generate pivot tables using Excel to determine whether the levels of the 1997 annual salaries and bonuses earned by CEOs are related somewhat to the *types* of companies in which they serve.

47 Consider the data in the file P2_12.XLS on various performance measures for the largest U.S. airlines in 1996. In particular, employ a pivot table and/or descriptive graphs to determine whether the level of consumer complaints about an airline is associated with the number of reports of mishandled baggage filed by the airline's passengers in 1996. Summarize your findings.

48 What influences a metropolitan area's vulnerability to recession? Construct pivot tables or other descriptive graphs to explore this issue using the given job statistics for selected towns in the United States in the file P2_48.XLS. Be sure to consider the relative mix of new blue-collar jobs versus new white-collar jobs in attempting the explain an area's unemployment threat level.

49 As a part of an economic development study conducted by the local government, 500 households in a middle-class neighborhood were recently surveyed. In particular, for each of the randomly selected households, the survey requested information on the following variables: family size, approximate location of the household within the neighborhood, an indication of whether those surveyed owned or rented their home, gross annual income of the first household wage earner, gross annual income of the second household wage earner (if applicable), monthly home mortgage or rent payment, average monthly expenditure on utilities, and the total indebtedness (excluding the value of a home mortgage) of the household. The data are in the file P2_6.XLS. Use Excel to construct pivot tables or other descriptive graphs to answer the following questions:

a What proportion of households in each of the four locations within this neighborhood own their homes?

b What relationship, if any, exists between the primary household income level and family size?

c What relationship, if any, exists between the primary household income level and the household's location within the neighborhood?

d What relationship, if any, exists between the primary household income level and whether the household owns or rents their home?

50 Consider the relationship between the population size of selected metropolitan areas in the United States and the location's average annual rates for various forms of violent crime, including murder, rape, robbery, and aggravated assault. The data are in the file P2_50.XLS. Use pivot tables or other descriptive methods to explore the relationship between a metro area's size and the area's level of violent criminal acts. Summarize your findings.

51 Using cost-of-living data from the *ACCRA Cost of Living Index* in the file P2_19.XLS, examine the relationship between the geographical *location* of an urban area within the United States (e.g., northeast, southeast, midwest, northwest, or southwest) and its *composite* cost-of-living index. In other words, is the overall cost of living higher or lower for urban areas in particular geographical regions of the country? You will need to assign the given urban areas to one of any number of such geographical regions before you can produce pivot tables or other graphical tools in responding to this question.

52 Consider the relationship between the size of the population and the average time (in minutes) it takes citizens of selected American communities to travel to work and back home each day. Using the data in the file P2_11.XLS, produce a pivot table with Excel to determine whether the population size is useful in explaining the variation of average commute times.

53 In a recent ranking of top graduate business schools in the United States published by *U.S. News & World Report* (March 10, 1997), data were provided on numerous attributes of 25 recognized graduate programs. Specifically, we are now interested in understanding the variation of the average starting base salaries for recent graduates from these programs. The data are in the file P2_8.XLS. Use Excel to construct pivot tables or other descriptive graphs to answer the following questions:

a Are higher average GMAT scores for enrolled students associated with higher average starting base salaries for recent graduates from these programs?

b Are higher average undergraduate grade-point averages for enrolled students associated with higher average starting base salaries for recent graduates from these programs?

c Are lower program acceptance rates associated with higher starting base salaries for recent graduates from these programs?

d What are the limitations of the conclusions you have reached in answering these three questions? ■

Conclusion

The graphs and tables we have discussed in this chapter are extremely useful for describing data sets. The graphs show at a glance how a single variable is distributed, how two variables are related, or how a variable varies over time. The tables are also useful, not only in their own right, but for providing the data needed to create graphs. We have paid special attention to the pivot table feature available in Excel. Pivot tables allow us to see relationships in a data set that would be very difficult to see in any other way. In fact, they might be the best kept secret in Excel, but their popularity will surely grow as business managers learn to take advantage of their power and flexibility.

PROBLEMS

Level A

54 An economic development researcher wants to understand the relationship between the size of the monthly home mortgage or rent payment for households in a particular middle-class neighborhood and each of the following household variables: family size, approximate location of the household within the neighborhood, an indication of whether those surveyed owned or rented their home, gross annual income of the first household wage earner, gross annual income of the second household wage earner (if applicable), average monthly expenditure on utilities, and the total indebtedness (excluding the value of a home mortgage) of the household. The data are in the file P2_54.XLS.

    a Use a computer to generate a scatterplot for each pairing of variables with the size of the household's monthly home mortgage or rent payment.

    b Which of the aforementioned variables have a *positive* linear relationship with the size of the household's monthly home mortgage or rent payment?

    c Which of the aforementioned variables have a *negative* linear relationship with the size of the household's monthly home mortgage or rent payment?

    d Which of the aforementioned variables have essentially *no* linear relationship with the size of the household's monthly home mortgage or rent payment?

55 David Savageau and Geoffrey Loftus, the authors of *Places Rated Almanac* (published in 1997 by Macmillan) have ranked 325 metropolitan areas in the United States with consideration of the following aspects of life in each area: cost of living, transportation, jobs, education, climate, crime, arts, health, and recreation. The data are in the file P2_55.XLS.

    a Generate scatterplots to discern the relationship between the metropolitan area's overall score and each of these numerical factors.

    b Are the relationships revealed by the scatterplots consistent with your expectations? If not, can you explain any discrepancies between your findings and expectations?

56 The U.S. Bureau of Labor Statistics provides data on the year-to-year percentage changes in the wages and salaries of workers in private industries, including both "white-collar" and "blue-collar" occupations. Here we consider these data for the years 1980–1996 in the file P2_56.XLS.

    a Is there evidence of a strong relationship between the yearly changes in the wages and salaries of "white-collar" and "blue-collar" workers in the United States over the given time period? Describe the nature of any observed systematic relationship between these two variables.

    b Construct graphs for each of the three given time series and comment on any observed trends in these data.

57 The file P2_57.XLS contains three years (1991–1993) of sales data for the Sky's the Limit Women's Apparel store. Each observation represents sales during a 4-week period. Thus the first observation is sales during the first 4 weeks of 1991, and so on.

a Does there appear to be any trend in sales?

b Do sales appear to be seasonal? If so, discuss the nature of the seasonality.

58 For approximately 170 companies, the file P2_58.XLS contains two pieces of information: a measure of the strength of the corporate culture (from 1 = High to 5 = Low), and the percentage net income growth from 1977 to 1988. Do these data indicate that a strong corporate culture is associated with financial success or weakness?

59 The file P2_59.XLS contains quarterly sales revenues for Wal-Mart for the years 1992–1995. Construct a time series plot and discuss the trend and seasonal characteristics of Wal-Mart's sales.

60 Consider the data in the file P2_60.XLS. In particular, columns C–E contain the following information about a sample of Bloomington residents: education level (completed high school only or completed college), income level (low or high), and whether the last purchased car was financed.

a Using the data in columns C–E, determine how education and income influence the likelihood that a family finances a car.

b Column A of this file contains the exact salaries of these Bloomington residents. Using categories of length $10,000, construct a histogram of these salaries. (You can experiment with the appropriate leftmost and rightmost categories.) Does the histogram appear to be bell shaped?

61 The file P2_61.XLS contains the following information about a sample of Bloomington families: family size (large or small), number of cars owned by family (1, 2, 3, or 4), and whether family owns a foreign car.

a Use these data to determine how family size and number of cars influence the likelihood that a family owns a foreign car.

b Construct a histogram with four bars, using the obvious categories, for the number of cars owned by a family. Interpret the height of the second bar.

62 The file P2_62.XLS contains monthly returns on Barnes and Noble stock. Do monthly stock returns appear to be skewed or symmetric?

63 The file P2_63.XLS contains annual returns for firms grouped by size. For example, in 1926, firms that ranked in the top 10% by size of sales returned an average of 14.9%, whereas firms that ranked in the bottom 10% by size returned an average of −6.1%. What do these data tell you about the relationship between firm size and average stock return? What are possible investment implications of this information?

64 The file P2_64.XLS contains monthly returns on Mattel stock for the years 1990–1994. Plot a histogram of these data and summarize what you learn from it.

65 It has been hypothesized that a reduction in the average length of the workweek in a country will reduce the unemployment rate. The theory is that of job-sharing—if everybody works 5% less, the unemployed workers can pick up the reduced hours. Table 2.1 gives the percentage decrease in annual working hours per employee from 1975 to 1994 as well as the increase in unemployment rate for nine countries. Do these data support the hypothesis that job-sharing reduces unemployment? (Source: *The Economist*, November 25, 1995)

TABLE 2.1 **Data on Workweeks and Unemployment**

Country	% Decrease in Annual Working Hours per Employee	% Increase in Unemployment
U.S.	3.0%	−2.0%
Italy	5.3	5.0
Japan	7.0	0.0
Canada	6.6	5.0
Britain	9.4	5.0
Spain	10.8	15.0
Holland	12.5	0.5
Germany	12.5	3.0
France	12.8	9.0

66 Do countries with high rates of home ownership have higher or lower unemployment rates? The file P2_66.XLS lists the 1996 home ownership percentage and unemployment rate for various countries. Discuss the relationship between home ownership and unemployment. Do you have any explanation for this relationship? (Source: *The Economist*, June 14, 1997)

67 During the first four games played by the Mudville All-Stars, the number of points scored and the number of times they punted were as shown in Table 2.2. Announcer Frank Albert has just taken a statistics course and observes that there is a negative relationship between points scored and punts. He reasons that a decrease in punts will lead to an increase in points scored; therefore, a football team should never punt. What is wrong with this logic?

TABLE 2.2 **Data for Mudville All-Stars**

Points	Punts
28	2
42	1
14	4
7	5

68 The file P2_68.XLS contains data on the average 1988 automobile insurance premium and the fraction of uninsured motorists for each state in the United States. (This fraction is categorized as less than 5%, 5%–10%, 10%–15%,15%–25%, greater than 25%.) How is the fraction of uninsured motorists related to auto insurance premiums?

69 You are a local Coca-Cola bottler. You want to determine whether sales of Coke and Diet Coke are more sensitive than the competition to changes in price. The file P2_69.XLS contains weekly data on the price per can of Coke, Diet Coke, Pepsi, and Diet Pepsi, and the number of cans (in hundreds) sold of each product. Which of these products exhibits more price sensitivity?

70 Use the data in the file P2_70.XLS to determine how the type of school (public or Catholic) that students attend affects their chance of graduating from high school. (Source: Based on *The Economist*, April 5, 1997)

71 It is well known that stock prices are a leading indicator of a recession. This means that several months before a recession begins, stock prices usually drop (foreshadowing a drop in the economy), and several months before a recession ends, stock prices usually increase (foreshadowing the end of the recession). Use the data in the file P2_71.XLS to argue that the Dow Jones Index was a leading indicator for both the April 1960–February 1961 recession and the December 1969–November 1970 recession.

72 The file P2_72.XLS contains information on daily stock prices and trading volume for Wal-Mart. The data include date, low price for the day, high price for the day, closing price for the day, and number of shares traded during the day.

a Create a time series plot of High, Low, and Close, all on the same graph. Are there any obvious time series patterns?

b Create a time series plot of Volume. Are there any obvious time series patterns?

c Create a scatterplot of Volume versus Close. Does there appear to be any relationship between these two variables?

73 The file P2_73.XLS contains expense account data on your company's seven sales representatives for the past 4 months. Each row in the database includes a single expense record, which contains the rep's name, the month, the category (trip, entertaining client, or miscellaneous supplies), the amount claimed, and the amount reimbursed. (Only "legitimate" expenses are reimbursed.)

a Create a pivot table to tabulate the number of expense records of each category by each representative for the entire 4-month period. (For example, it will list the number of trips taken by Smith.) Use the data in the resulting pivot table to construct an appropriate bar chart. (You can decide on the exact form of the chart.)

b Create a pivot table to show the total amount spent each month by each rep. Use the resulting pivot table to create time series plots, one for each rep.

c Create a histogram of reimbursed amounts, for the entertaining clients and miscellaneous supplies categories only.

Level B

74 The annual base salaries for 200 students graduating from a reputable MBA program this year are of interest to those in the admissions office who are responsible for marketing the program to prospective students. The data are in the file P2_74.XLS.

a Generate a frequency table and histogram for the given distribution of starting salaries. What does the histogram suggest about this distribution of starting salaries?

b Is it possible to separate these salaries into two or more subgroups? If so, generate a frequency distribution and histogram for each subset of starting salaries. Also, characterize the shape of each subgroup's distribution.

c As an admissions officer of this MBA program, how would you proceed to use these findings to market the program to prospective students?

75 The percentage of private-industry jobs that are managerial has steadily declined in recent years as companies have found middle management a ripe area for cutting costs. How have women and various minority groups fared in gaining management positions during this period of corporate downsizing of the management ranks? Relevant data are listed in the file P2_75.XLS. Generate scatterplots and/or time series plots using these data to make general comparisons across the various groups included in the set.

76 Chandler Enterprises produces Pentium chips. Five types of defects (labeled 1–5) have been known to occur. Chips are manufactured by two operators (A and B). Four machines (1–4) are used to manufacture chips. The file P2_76.XLS contains data for a sample of defective chips including the type of defect, operator, machine, and day of the week. Use the data in this file to chart a course of action that would lead, as quickly as possible, to improved product quality. You should use the Pivot Table Wizard to "stratify" the defects with respect to type of defect, day of the week, machine used, and operator working. You might even want to break the data down by machine and operator (or in some other way). Assume that each operator and machine made an equal number of products.

77 You own a local McDonald's and have done some market research in an attempt to better understand your customers. For a random sample of Bloomington residents, the file P2_77.XLS contains the income, gender, and number of days per week the resident goes to McDonald's. Use this information to determine how gender and income influence the frequency with which Bloomington residents attend McDonald's.

78 Students at Faber College apply to study either English or science. You have been assigned to determine whether Faber College discriminates against women in admitting students to the school of their choice. The file P2_78.XLS contains the following data on Faber's students: gender, major applied for (English or science), and admission decision (yes or no). Assuming that women and men are equally qualified for each major, do the data indicate that the college discriminates against women? Make sure you use all available information.

79 You have been assigned to evaluate the quality of care given to heart attack patients at Emergency Room (ER) and Chicago Hope (CH). For the last month the file P2_79.XLS contains the following patient data: hospital where patient was admitted (ER or CH), risk category (high or low, where high-risk people are less likely to survive than low-risk people), and patient's outcome (lived or died). Use the data to determine which hospital is doing a better job of caring for heart attack patients. Use all of the data.

80 The file P2_80.XLS contains the monthly level of the Dow Jones Index for the years 1947–1992. Do these data indicate any unusual seasonal patterns in stock returns? [*Hint*: You can extract the month (January, February, etc.) with the formula =TEXT(A4,"mmm") copied down any column.]

81 You sell station wagons and want to know how family size and salary influence the likelihood that a family will purchase a station wagon. You have surveyed some local families and found out whether they own a station wagon, the size of the family (Large means at least five people, Small means no more than four people), and the family's salary (High means at least $80,000, Low means less than $80,000). The data are in the file P2_81.XLS. Analyze these data to determine how salary and family size influence the likelihood that a family will purchase a station wagon.

82 The file P2_82.XLS contains data on the diameter of an elevator rail, the operator who built the elevator rail, and the machine used to build the elevator rail. What can you learn from these data?

83 The file P2_83.XLS contains daily returns and the daily level of the Standard and Poor's 500 stock index. Describe what you learn from these data.

84 Viscerex, a small chemical company, wants to determine how viscosity of liquid supplied to the company influences the level of impurities. The file P2_84.XLS contains the following information: firm supplying the liquid to Viscerex, viscosity level of the liquid, and level of impurities in the liquid. Describe how viscosity affects the level of impurities.

85 Two major awards are given to daytime soap operas and their actors and actresses: the Daytime Emmys and the Soap Opera Digest Awards. The Daytime Emmys are voted on by members of the TV industry. The Soap Opera Digest Awards are voted on by soap opera viewers who are readers of *Soap Opera Digest*. The file P2_85.XLS contains the number of awards of each type won by each daytime soap. Use these data to determine whether voters for Daytime Emmys and Soap Opera Digest Awards appear to be looking for the same qualities when they vote for awards. (Source: *Soap Opera Digest*, April 16, 1998)

86 In recent years economists and others have debated whether investment in information technology is good or bad for employment growth. Table 2.3 contains information technology (IT) investment as a percentage of total investment for eight countries during the 1980s. It also contains the average annual percentage change in employment during the 1980s. Explain how these data shed light on the question of whether IT investment creates or costs jobs. (Source: *The Economist*, September 28, 1996)

87 Do countries with more income inequality have lower unemployment rates? Table 2.4 contains the following information for ten countries during the 1980–1995 time period: change from 1980 to 1995 in ratio of the average wage of the top 10% of all wage earners to the median wage, and change from 1980 to 1995 in unemployment rate. (Source: *The Economist*, August 17, 1996)

TABLE 2.3 **Data on IT Investment**

Country	IT Investment as % of Total Investment (1980s)	Annual Average % Change in Employment (1980–1989)
Netherlands	2.0%	1.3%
Italy	3.6	1.9
Germany	4.0	1.7
France	5.6	1.5
Canada	7.8	2.4
Japan	7.8	2.4
Britain	7.8	3.0
U.S.	11.9	3.4

TABLE 2.4 **Data on Income Inequality**

Country	Change in Wage Inequality Ratio	Change in Unemployment Rate
Germany	−6.0%	6.0%
France	−3.5	5.6
Italy	1.0	5.2
Japan	0.0	0.6
Australia	5.0	2.4
Sweden	4.0	5.9
Canada	5.5	2.0
New Zealand	9.5	4.0
Britain	15.6	2.5
U.S.	15.8	−1.8

a Explain why the ratio of the average wage of the top 10% of all wage earners to the median measures income inequality.

b Do these data help to confirm or contradict the hypothesis that increased wage inequality leads to lower unemployment levels?

c What other data would you need to be more confident that increased income inequality leads to lower unemployment?

88 One magazine reported that a man's weight at birth has a significant impact on the chance that the man will suffer a heart attack during his life. Analyze the data in the file P2_88.XLS to determine how birth weight influences the chances that a man will have a heart attack. (Source: *Newsweek*, August 11, 1997)

89 When Staples and Office Depot proposed merging in 1997, the Federal Trade Commission (FTC) rejected the merger. In analyzing the impact of the merger, the FTC looked at the prices of the following quantities:

■ A Pentium 166 computer with 16 meg of RAM, 10-speed CD-ROM, and 2g hard drive (labeled Computer)

■ A desk, filing cabinet, 10 reams of computer paper, and a laser printer (labeled Office)

■ 10 notebooks, 5 boxes of pencils, a book bag, 10 boxes of crayons (labeled School)

The file P2_89.XLS contains data on these variables for several cities. For example, the first city had both a Staples and an Office Depot, and a computer cost $1979.31. The second city had only a Staples, and the school supplies cost $179.86. Based on these data, can you explain why the FTC rejected the merger? (*Note*: The data in this file are fictitious but are consistent with the conclusions of the article.) (Source: Based on *The Economist*, May 3, 1998)

90 An important question in finance is whether the stock market is efficient. The market is efficient if knowledge of past changes in a stock's price tells us nothing about future changes in the stock's price. Here you'll check whether daily price changes in IBM stock during 1994 are consistent with efficient markets, using the data in the file P2_90.XLS. Define an "up" day for IBM as a day when the return is greater than 0. A "down" day is when the return is less than or equal to 0. Does it appear that knowledge of whether IBM went up or down yesterday can help us predict whether it will go up or down today?

91 You work for a small travel agency and are about to do a mass mailing of a travel brochure. Your funds are limited, so you want to mail to the people who spend the most money on travel. The file P2_91.XLS contains data for a random sample of 925 residents. These data include their gender, age, and amount spent on travel last year. Use these data to determine how gender and age influence a person's travel expenditures. Also make recommendations on the type of person to whom you should mail your brochure.

92 A question of great interest is how the distribution of family income has changed in the United States during the last 20 years. The file P2_92.XLS contains data for a sample of 499 family incomes (in real 1995 dollars). For each family, the 1975 and 1995 incomes are listed. (Although these data are fictitious, they are consistent with what has actually happened to U.S. family income during these years.) Based on these data, discuss as completely as possible how the distribution of family income in the United States changed from 1975 to 1995. ■

2.1 Customer Arrivals at Bank98

Bank98 operates a main location and three branch locations in a medium-sized city. All four locations perform similar services, and customers typically do business at the location nearest them. The bank has recently had more congestion—long waiting lines—than it (or its customers) would like. As part of a study to learn the causes of these long lines and to suggest possible solutions, all locations have kept track of customer arrivals during 1-hour intervals for the past 10 weeks. All branches are open Monday through Friday from 9 A.M. until 5 P.M. and on Saturday from 9 A.M. until noon. For each location, the file BANK98.XLS contains the number of customer arrivals during each hour of a 10-week period. The manager of Bank98 has hired you to make some sense out of these data. Specifically, your task is to present charts and/or tables that indicate how customer traffic into the bank locations varies by day of week and hour of day. There is also interest in whether any daily or hourly patterns you observe are stable across weeks. Although you don't have full information about the way the bank currently runs its operations—you know only its customer arrival pattern and the fact that it is currently experiencing long lines—you are encouraged to append any suggestions for improving operations, based on your analysis of the data.

2.2 Automobile Production and Purchases

Are people in the United States buying more cars than in the past? Are they buying more foreign cars relative to domestic cars? Are auto sales seasonal, with more sales occurring during some months than others? Does automobile production mirror sales very closely? These are some questions you have been asked to answer, using the data in the file AUTOS.XLS. This file contains monthly data on U.S. sales of domestic and foreign cars since 1967. It also shows monthly production of domestic cars since 1993. The data are shown in two forms: not seasonally adjusted—the raw data—and seasonally adjusted. (Although you will learn more about seasonal adjustment of time series data in Chapter 13, the basic idea is that this is a method for smoothing out seasonal ups and downs so that underlying trends can be seen more clearly.) You have been asked to prepare a report that explains any important patterns you observe in these data. Of course, your report should contain relevant charts and/or tables. Make sure your report indicates whether you are using seasonally adjusted data or raw data (or both) and why.

2.3 Saving, Spending, and Social Climbing

The recent best-selling book *The Millionaire Next Door* by Thomas J. Stanley and William D. Danko (Longstreet Press, 1996) presents some very interesting data on the characteristics of millionaires. We tend to believe that people with expensive houses, expensive cars, expensive clothes, country club memberships, and other outward indications of wealth are the millionaires. The authors define wealth, however, in terms of savings and investments, not consumer items. In this sense, they argue that people with a lot of expensive *things* and even large incomes often have surprisingly little wealth. These people tend to spend much of what they make on consumer items, often trying to keep up with, or impress, their peers. In contrast, the real millionaires, in terms of savings and investments, frequently come from "unglamorous" professions (particularly teaching!), own unpretentious homes and cars, dress in inexpensive clothes, and otherwise lead rather ordinary lives.

Consider the (hypothetical) data in the file SOCIAL_CLIMBERS.XLS. For several hundred couples, it lists their education level, their annual combined salary, the market value of their home and cars, the amount of savings they have accumulated (in savings accounts, stocks, retirement accounts, and so on), and a self-reported "social climber index" on a scale of 1 to 10 (with 1 being very unconcerned about social status and material items and 10 being very concerned about these). Prepare a report based on these data, supported by relevant charts and/or tables, that might be used in a book such as *The Millionaire Next Door*. Although your report might be used in such a book, your conclusions can either support or contradict those of Stanley and Danko.

WARNING!
Platinum Edition
U.S. BANK
JCPenney
Bank
American Road
Valid Thru

3

Describing Data: Summary Measures

Successful Applications

The types of data analysis we discuss in this and other chapters of this book are crucial to the success of most companies in today's data-driven business world. However, the sheer volume of available data often defies traditional methods of data analysis. Therefore, a whole new set of methods—and accompanying software—have recently been developed under the name of **data mining**. Data mining attempts to discover the patterns, trends, and relationships among data, especially nonobvious and unexpected patterns. For example, the analysis might discover that people who purchase skim milk also tend to purchase whole wheat bread, or that cars built on Mondays before 10 A.M. on production line #5 using parts from suppliers ABC and XYZ have significantly more defects than average. This new knowledge can then be used for more effective management of a business.

A good introductory account of data mining appears in the article by Pass (1997). As he states, the place to start is with a **data warehouse**. This is typically a huge database that is designed specifically to study patterns in data and is *not* the same as the databases companies use for their day-to-day operational activities. A data warehouse should (1) combine data from multiple sources to discover as many interrelationships as possible, (2) contain accurate and consistent data, (3) be structured to enable quick and accurate responses to a variety of queries, and (4) allow follow-up responses to specific, newly-relevant questions. In short, a data warehouse represents a relatively new type of database, one that is specifically structured to enable data mining.

Once a data warehouse is in place, analysts can begin to mine the data with a collection of methodologies, techniques, and accompanying software. Some of the primary methodologies are **cluster analysis**, **linkage analysis**, **time series analysis**, and **categorization analysis**. Cluster analysis is used to identify associations among data points. For example, data mining software might search through credit card purchases to discover that meals charged on business-issued Gold Cards are typically purchased on weekdays and have an average value of more than $200. Linkage analysis is used to link two or more events together. It attempts to find items that are typically purchased together as part of a "market basket," such as beer and pretzels, yogurt and skim milk, or less obvious pairs. Time series analysis is used to relate events in time. Financial analysts, for example, might try to relate interest rate fluctuations or stock performance to a series of preceding events. Categorization analysis contains elements of the preceding three methodologies and is probably the most broadly applicable to different types of business problems. It attempts to explain the influence that numerous factors have on one specific outcome. For example, given all information on a loan applicant, categorization analysis might attempt to predict whether the applicant will pay back a loan promptly.

A number of evolving technologies and algorithms are available to perform data mining. These include neural networks, decision trees (*not* the same as those we will study in Chapter 6), genetic algorithms, fuzzy logic, hybrid approaches, and traditional statistical methods. Except for the latter, these techniques are not as well known or as widely available as the methods we will discuss in this book. However, they are becoming more popular, and easy-to-use software is quickly becoming available to support them.

In his article, Pass describes one successful application of data mining at Allders International, a company that operates duty-free outlets throughout Europe. Like many companies, Allders was deluged by paper-based reports and spreadsheets of data. In fact, meaningful information was usually obtained too late to be useful for day-to-day decision making. The introduction of data mining made an immediate impact, both on the bottom line and on employee morale. As one manager stated, "In one store we've been able to move the margin up by four points, by being able to identify why it wasn't performing as well as other outlets. We took out the lower margin lines, even though they might sell well, substituting them or adjusting their positioning." Data mining has enabled Allders to fine-tune its product line by identifying and eliminating the low-performing SKUs (stock keeping units). However, it has also identified apparently unprofitable items that still have an important role in pulling shoppers into the stores. The data warehouse is continually being made available to new users, and existing users expect to find new ways to exploit its power for competitive advantage. ■

3.1 Introduction

In the previous chapter we summarized data mainly with tables and graphs. It is often useful to summarize data even further with a few well-chosen numbers. In this chapter we will learn the most frequently used numerical summary measures. These include measures for describing a single variable, such as the mean, median, and standard deviation, plus a couple of measures, correlation and covariance, for describing the potential relationship between two variables. Using these numerical summary measures, we will then discuss an additional graph called a boxplot. Boxplots are useful for describing a single variable or comparing two or more related variables.

We conclude this chapter—and our study of descriptive measures—by examining three relatively complex examples. Here we are able to put all of the descriptive tools we have learned to good use. These examples are typical of the large-scale data sets business managers face on a continual basis. Only by looking at the data from a number of points of view can we discover the information and patterns hidden in the data.

3.2 Measures of Central Location

Most of the numerical summary measures we will discuss are for a single variable. Each describes some aspect of the distribution of the variable. That is, it describes one feature of the distribution that we see graphically in a histogram. We begin with measures of central location. The three most commonly used measures are the mean, median, and mode. Each of these gives a slightly different interpretation to the term "central location."

3.2.1 The Mean

The mean, usually denoted as $\overline{X}$, is the average of all values of a variable. If the data represent a sample from some larger population, we call this measure the **sample mean**. If the data represent the entire population, we call it the **population mean**. This distinction is not important in this chapter, but it will become relevant in later chapters when we discuss statistical inference. In either case the formula for the mean is

$$\overline{X} = \frac{\sum_{i=1}^{n} X_i}{n} \tag{3.1}$$

Here n is the number of observations and X_i is the value of observation i. Equation (3.1) simply says to add all the observations and divide by n, the number of observations.

To obtain the mean in Excel, we use the AVERAGE function on the appropriate range, as illustrated in the following example.

EXAMPLE 3.1

The file SALARY.XLS lists starting salaries for 190 graduates from an undergraduate school of business. The data are in the range named Salary on a sheet called Data. Figure 3.1 includes a number of summary measures produced by Excel's built-in functions. In particular, we calculate the mean salary by entering the formula

=AVERAGE(Salary)

in cell B6. It is nearly $30,000.

FIGURE 3.1   **Selected Summary Measures of Salary Data**

	A	B	C
1	**Summary measures using Excel functions**		
2			
3	Count	190	
4	Minimum	$17,100	
5	Maximum	$38,200	
6	Average	$29,762	
7	Median	$29,850	
8	Lower quartile	$27,325	
9	Upper quartile	$32,300	
10	5-percentile	$23,690	
11	95-percentile	$35,810	
12	Range	$21,100	
13	Standard deviation	$3,707	
14	Variance	13743424	

The mean in Example 3.1 is a "representative" measure because the distribution of salaries is nearly symmetric. (You can check this statement by constructing a histogram of salaries.) However, the mean is often misleading because of skewness. For example, if a few of the undergraduates got abnormally high salaries (over $100,000, say), these large values would tend to inflate the mean and make it unrepresentative of the majority of the salaries. In this case, we might want to report the next summary measure instead, the median.

3.2.2 The Median

The **median** is the "middle" observation when the data are listed from smallest to largest. If there is an odd number of observations, the median is the middle observation. For example, if there are nine observations, the median is the fifth smallest (or fifth largest) observation. If there is an even number of observations, we take the median to be the average of the two middle observations. For example, if there are ten observations, the median is the average of the fifth and sixth smallest values.

We calculate the median salary in Example 3.1 by entering the formula

=MEDIAN(Salary)

in cell B7. (See Figure 3.1.) Its value is again approximately $30,000, almost the same as the mean. This is typical of symmetric distributions, but it is not true for skewed distributions. For example, if a few graduates received abnormally large salaries, the mean would be affected by them, but the median would not be affected at all. It would still represent the "middle" of the distribution.

3.2.3 The Mode

The **mode** is the most frequently occurring value. If the values are essentially continuous, as with the salaries in Example 3.1, then the mode is essentially irrelevant. There is typically no *single* value that occurs more than once, or there are at best a few ties for the most frequently occurring value. In either case the mode is not likely to provide much information. However, the following example provides an illustration where the mode is useful.

E X A M P L E   3 . 2

The file SHOES.XLS lists shoe sizes purchased at a shoe store. What is the store's best-seller?

Solution

Shoe sizes come in discrete increments, rather than a continuum, so it makes sense to find the mode, the size that is requested most often. This can be done with Excel's MODE function. It shows that size 11 is the most frequently purchased size. This is also apparent from the histogram in Figure 3.2, where the category 10.5–11 corresponds to the highest bar. (Recall that a category such as "10.5–11" means greater than 10.5 and less than or equal to 11, so in this case it means "exactly 11.") ■

3.3

Quartiles and Percentiles

The median splits the data in half. It is sometimes called the 50th **percentile** because (approximately) half of the data are below the median. It is also called the second **quartile**, because if we divide the data into four parts, then the median separates the lower two parts from the upper two. We can also find other percentiles and quartiles. Some of these appear in Figure 3.1, which summarizes the salary data from Example 3.1.

FIGURE 3.2   Distribution of Shoe Sizes for Example 3.2

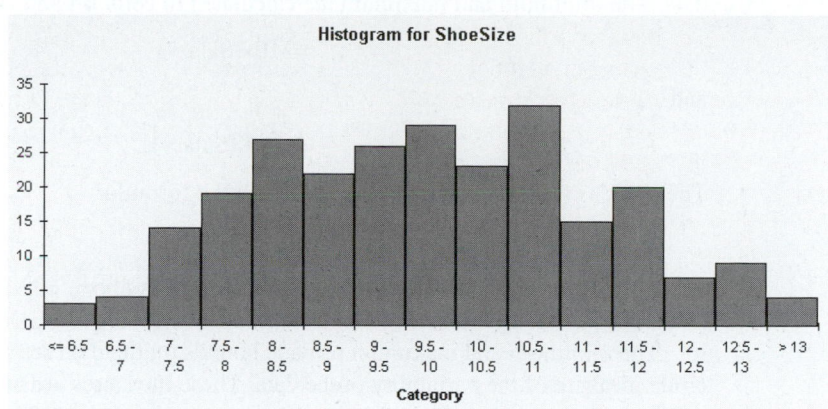

For example, the 5th and 95th percentiles appear in cells B10 and B11. They are calculated with the formulas

=PERCENTILE(Salary,.05)

and

=PERCENTILE(Salary,.95)

They say that 5% of all salaries are below $23,690 (so that 95% are above $23,690), and 95% of all salaries are below $35,810 (so that 5% are above $35,810). These two percentiles (and sometimes others) are frequently quoted.

Similarly, Figure 3.1 lists the lower and upper quartiles in cells B8 and B9. These are the 25th and 75th percentiles, so they can be calculated with the PERCENTILE function. They can also be calculated with the formulas

=QUARTILE(Salary,1)

and

=QUARTILE(Salary,3)

That is, they are the first and third quartiles. (The median is the second quartile.) In short, 25% of the salaries are below $27,325, 25% are above $32,300, and the other 50% are in between.

The difference between the first and third quartiles is called the **interquartile range** (IQR). It measures the spread between the largest and smallest of the middle half of the data. In the salary example the IQR is $4,975 (= $32,300 − $27,325). We will come back to the IQR when we discuss boxplots later in this chapter.

3.4

Minimum, Maximum, and Range

T hree other descriptive measures of a variable are its minimum, maximum, and range. The minimum is the smallest value, the maximum is the largest value, and the range is the difference between the maximum and minimum. These are listed in Figure 3.1 for the salary data. The minimum and maximum are calculated in cells B4 and B5 with the formulas

$$=\text{MIN(Salary)}$$

and

$$=\text{MAX(Salary)}$$

The range is then calculated in cell B12 with the formula

$$=\text{B5-B4}$$

We see that no salary is below \$17,100, no salary is above \$38,200, and all salaries are contained within an interval of length \$21,100.

The minimum and maximum provide bounds on the data set, and the range provides a crude measure of the variability of the data. These measures are often worth reporting, but they can obviously be affected by one or two extreme values. The range, in particular, is usually not as good a measure of variability as the measures discussed next.

3.5

Measures of Variability: Variance and Standard Deviation

To really understand a data set, we need to know more than measures of central location; we also need measures of variability. To see this, consider the following example.

EXAMPLE 3.3

Suppose Otis Elevator is going to stop manufacturing elevator rails. Instead, it is going to buy them from an outside supplier. Otis would like each rail to have a diameter of 1 inch. The company has obtained samples of ten elevator rails from each supplier. These are listed in columns A and B of Figure 3.3. (See the file OTIS4.XLS.) Which supplier should Otis prefer?

FIGURE 3.3   **Two Samples with Different Amounts of Variability**

	A	B	C	D	E	F
1	Diameters from two suppliers					
2						
3	Data			Summary measures		
4	Supplier1	Supplier2			Supplier1	Supplier2
5	1.00	0.96		Mean	1	1
6	0.98	1.05		Median	1	1
7	1.02	1.00		Mode	1	1
8	1.01	0.97		Variance	0.000133	0.001200
9	1.00	1.00		Standard Deviation	0.0115	0.0346
10	0.99	1.03				
11	0.99	0.98		**Range names**		
12	1.00	1.02		Supplier1: A4:A14		
13	1.01	0.95		Supplier2: B4:B14		
14	1.00	1.04				

Solution

Observe that the mean, median, and mode are all exactly 1 inch for each supplier. Based on these measures, the two suppliers are equally good and both are right on the mark. It is clear from a glance at the data, however, that supplier 1 is somewhat better than supplier 2. The reason is that supplier 2's rails exhibit more variability about the mean than supplier 1's rails. If we want rails to have a diameter of 1 inch, then variability around the mean is bad! ■

The most commonly used measures of variability are the **variance** and **standard deviation**. The variance is essentially the average of the squared deviations from the mean. We say "essentially" because there are two versions of variance: the **population variance**, usually denoted by σ^2, and the **sample variance**, usually denoted by s^2. The formulas for them are

$$\sigma^2 = \frac{\sum_{i=1}^{n}(X_i - \overline{X})^2}{n} \tag{3.2}$$

and

$$s^2 = \frac{\sum_{i=1}^{n}(X_i - \overline{X})^2}{n-1} \tag{3.3}$$

These formulas are very similar, differing only in their denominators. Also, their numerical values are practically the same when n, the number of observations, is large.

As their names imply, σ^2 is relevant if the data set includes the entire population, whereas s^2 is relevant for a sample from a population. Excel has a built-in function for each. To obtain σ^2 we use the VARP function; to obtain s^2 we use the VAR function. In this chapter we will illustrate only the sample variance s^2.

The important part about either variance formula is that the variance tends to increase when there is more variability around the mean. Indeed, large deviations from the mean contribute heavily to the variance because they are *squared*. One consequence of this is that the variance is expressed in squared units (squared dollars, for example) rather than original units. Therefore, a more intuitive measure is the **standard deviation**, defined as the square root of the variance. It is measured in original units, such as dollars, and, as we will discuss shortly, it is much easier to interpret.

$$\text{Standard deviation} = \sqrt{\text{Variance}} \tag{3.4}$$

Of course, depending on which variance measure we use, we obtain the corresponding standard deviation, either σ (population) or s (sample). Excel has built-in functions for each of these; we use STDEVP for σ and STDEV for s. In this chapter we will illustrate only s.

The variances and standard deviations of the diameters from the two suppliers in Example 3.3 appear in Figure 3.3. To obtain them, enter the formulas

$$=\text{VAR(Supplier1)}$$

and

$$=\text{STDEV(Supplier1)}$$

in cells E8 and E9, and enter similar formulas for Supplier 2 in cells F8 and F9. Because of the relationship between variance and standard deviation, we could also have used the formula

$$=\text{SQRT(E8)}$$

in cell E9, but we instead took advantage of the STDEV function.

As we mentioned above, it is difficult to interpret these variances numerically because they are expressed in squared inches, not inches. All we can say is that the variance from supplier 2 is considerably larger than the variance from supplier 1. The standard deviations, on the other hand, are expressed in inches. The standard deviation for supplier 1 is approximately 0.012 inch, and supplier 2's standard deviation is approximately three times this large. This is quite a disparity, as we explain next.

3.5.1 Interpretation of the Standard Deviation: Rules of Thumb

Many data sets follow certain "rules of thumb." In particular, suppose that a histogram of the data is approximately symmetric and "bell shaped." That is, heights of the bars rise to some peak and then decline. Such behavior is quite common, and it allows us to interpret the standard deviation intuitively. Specifically, we can state that

- Approximately 68% of the observations are within one standard deviation of the mean, that is, within the interval $\overline{X} \pm s$;
- Approximately 95% of the observations are within two standard deviations of the mean, that is, within the interval $\overline{X} \pm 2s$; and
- Approximately 99.7%—almost all—of the observations are within three standard deviations of the mean, that is, within the interval $\overline{X} \pm 3s$.

We illustrate these rules of thumb with the following example.

E X A M P L E   3 . 4

The file DOW.XLS contains monthly closing prices for the Dow Jones index from January 1947 through January 1993. The monthly returns from the index are also shown, starting with the February 1947 value. Each return is the monthly percentage change (expressed as a decimal) in the index. How well do the rules of thumb work for these data?

Solution

Figures 3.4 and 3.5 show time series plots of the index itself and the monthly returns. Clearly, the index has been increasing fairly steadily over the period, whereas the returns exhibit no obvious trend. Whenever a series indicates a clear trend, most of the measures we have been discussing are less relevant. For example, the mean closing index for this period has at most historical interest. We are probably more interested in predicting the *future* of the Dow, and the historical mean (or standard deviation or variance) has little relevance for predicting the future.

In contrast, the measures we have been discussing are relevant for the series of returns, which fluctuates around a stable mean. In Figure 3.6 (page 86) we first calculate the mean and standard deviation of returns with the AVERAGE and STDEV functions in cells B4 and B5. These indicate an average return of about 0.59% and a standard deviation of about 3.37%. Therefore, the rules of thumb (if they apply) imply, for example, that about 2/3 of all returns are within the interval 0.59% ± 3.37%, that is, from −2.78% to 3.95%.

We can use a frequency table to check whether the rules of thumb apply to these returns. We first enter the upper limits of suitable categories in the range A8:A15. Although any categories could be chosen, it is convenient to choose values of the form $\overline{X} \pm ks$ as breakpoints for the categories, where the open-ended categories on either end are "more than 3 standard deviations from the mean." Then the upper limits of the categories can be calculated in column B by entering the formulas

$$=B4-3*B5$$

and

$$=B8+B5$$

in cells B8 and B9, and then copying this latter formula to the range B10:B14. In words, each breakpoint is one standard deviation higher than the previous one.

Next, we use the FREQUENCY function to fill in column C. Specifically, we highlight the range C8:C15, type the formula

$$=FREQUENCY(Return,Bins)$$

and press Ctrl-Shift-Enter. (Here, Return is the range name for the Returns variable, and Bins is the range name of the range B8:B14.)

FIGURE 3.4 **Time Series Plot of Dow Closing Index**

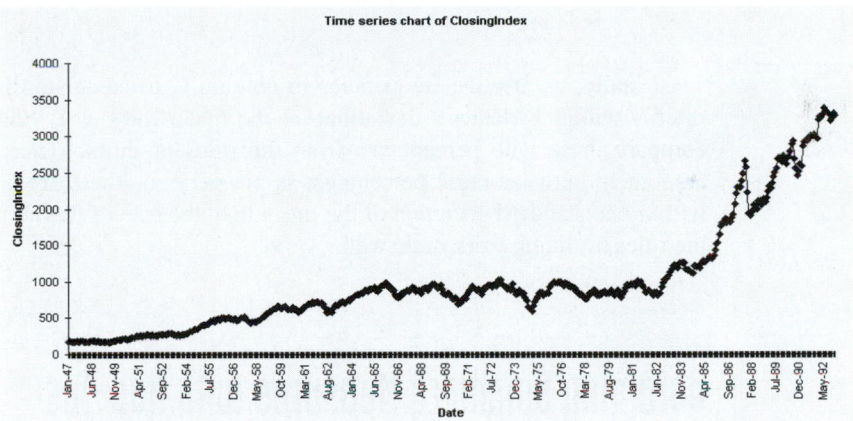

FIGURE 3.5 **Time Series Plot of Dow Returns**

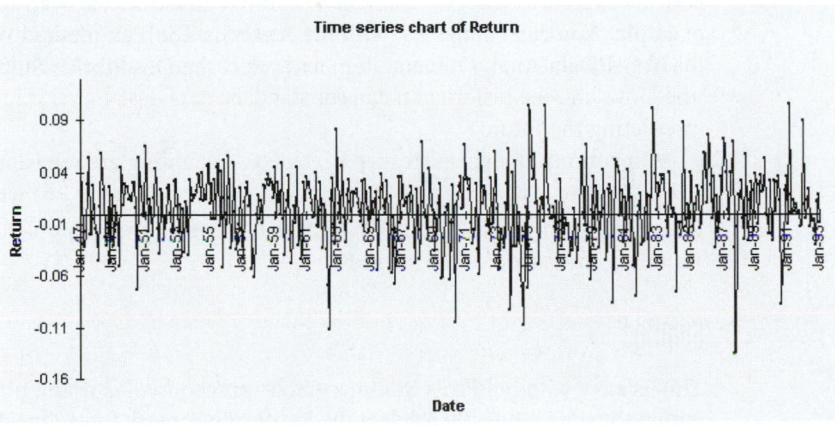

FIGURE 3.6   Rules of Thumb for Dow Jones Data

	A	B	C	D
1	**Checking rule of thumb for returns**			
2				
3	Summary measures of returns			
4	Mean	0.0059		
5	Stdev	0.0337		
6				
7	Category	Upper limit	Frequency	
8	More than 3 stdevs below mean	-0.0951	5	
9	Between 2 and 3 stdevs below mean	-0.0614	13	
10	Between 1 and 2 stdevs below mean	-0.0278	57	
11	Between mean and 1 stdev below mean	0.0059	194	
12	Between mean and 1 stdev above mean	0.0395	217	
13	Between 1 and 2 stdevs above mean	0.0732	55	
14	Between 2 and 3 stdevs above mean	0.1069	11	
15	More than 3 stdevs above mean		0	
16				
17	Percentages within k stdevs of mean			
18	k	1	2	3
19	Actual	74.5%	94.7%	99.1%
20	Rule of thumb	68.0%	95.0%	99.7%

Finally, we use the frequencies in column C to calculate the actual percentages of returns within k standard deviations of the mean for $k = 1$, $k = 2$, and $k = 3$, and we compare these with percentages from the rules of thumb. (See rows 19 and 20.) The agreement between these percentages is not perfect—there are a few more observations within one standard deviation of the mean than the rule of thumb predicts—but in general the rules of thumb work quite well.   ■

3.6   Obtaining Summary Measures with Add-Ins

In the past few sections we have used Excel's built-in functions (AVERAGE, STDEV, and so on) to calculate a number of summary measures. A quicker way is to use the StatPro add-in or Excel's Analysis ToolPak add-in. We illustrate the StatPro add-in in the following example. You can compare it with the Analysis ToolPak method if you like. To do so, use the Tools/Data Analysis menu item and select the Descriptive Statistics option.

EXAMPLE 3.5

Referring again to the SALARY.XLS data set used in Example 3.1, find a set of useful summary measures for the salaries.

Solution

This is easy with StatPro's Summary Stats procedure. As usual, place the cursor anywhere within the data range, then select the StatPro/Summary Stats/One-Variable Summary Stats menu item, select all variables you want to summarize, and select the summary measures you want from the dialog box shown in Figure 3.7. Note that four common measures (mean,

FIGURE 3.7 **Summary Stats Dialog Box**

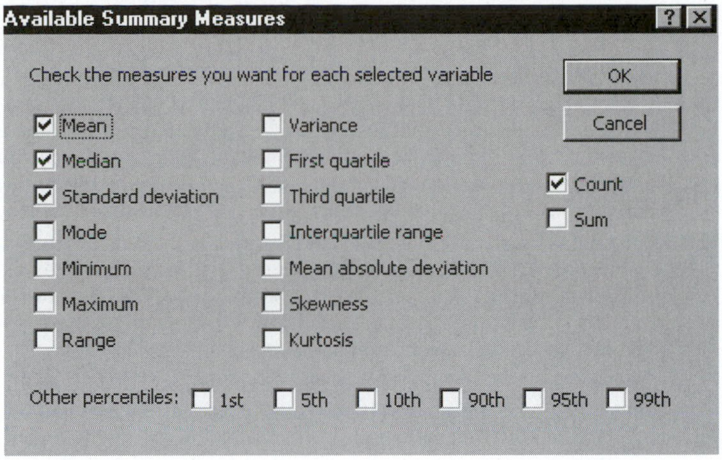

median, standard deviation, and count) are checked by default, but you can override these defaults.

A typical output appears in Figure 3.8. It includes many of the summary measures we have discussed, plus a few more. The mean absolute deviation is similar to the variance, except that it is an average of the *absolute* (not squared) deviations from the mean. The kurtosis and skewness indicate the relative peakedness of the distribution and its skewness. These are relatively technical measures that we won't discuss here.

By clicking on any of the cells in column B of Figure 3.8, you'll see that StatPro provides *formulas* for the outputs. (Excel's Analysis ToolPak does not do so.) The effect is that if any of the original data change, the summary measures we just produced change automatically. Finally, note that all outputs are formatted as "numerical" to three decimal places by default. You might want to reformat them in a more appropriate manner.

FIGURE 3.8 **Selected Summary Measures Using StatPro Add-In**

	A	B	C
1		*Summary measures for selected variables*	
2			Salary
3		Count	190.000
4		Mean	29762.105
5		Median	29850.000
6		Standard deviation	3707.212
7		Minimum	17100.000
8		Maximum	38200.000
9		Range	21100.000
10		Variance	13743424.116
11		First quartile	27325.000
12		Third quartile	32300.000
13		Interquartile range	4975.000
14		Mean absolute deviation	2967.767
15		Skewness	-0.166
16		Kurtosis	-0.071
17		5th percentile	23690.000
18		95th percentile	35810.000

PROBLEMS

Level A

1 A human resources manager at Beta Technologies, Inc., is interested in compiling some statistics on the *typical* full-time Beta employee. In particular, she is interested in finding the typical age, number of years of relevant full-time work experience prior to coming to Beta, number of years of full-time work experience at Beta, number of years of post-secondary education, and salary based on the given representative sample of 52 of the company's full-time employees. Describe the typical Beta employee with regard to each of these factors in the file P2_1.XLS.

2 A production manager is interested in determining the typical proportion of defective items in a shipment of one of the computer components that her company manufactures. The spreadsheet provided in the file P2_2.XLS contains the proportion of defective components for each of 500 randomly selected shipments collected during a 1-month period. Is the mean, median, or mode the most appropriate measure of central location in this case?

3 *Business Week's Guide to the Best Business Schools* (5th edition, 1997) provides enrollment data on 50 graduate business programs that it rates as the best in the United States. Specifically, this guide reports the percentages of women, minority, and international students enrolled in each of the top 50 programs, as well as the total number of full-time students enrolled in each program. Use the most appropriate measure(s) of central location to find the typical percentage of women, minority, and international students enrolled in these elite programs. These data are contained in the file P2_3.XLS.

4 The manager of a local fast-food restaurant is interested in improving the service provided to customers who use the restaurant's drive-up window. As a first step in this process, the manager asks his assistant to record the time (in minutes) it takes to serve 200 different customers at the final window in the facility's drive-up system. The given 200 customer service times in the file P2_4.XLS are all observed during the busiest hour of the day for this fast-food operation.

   a Compute the mean, median, and mode of this sample of customer service times.

   b Which of these measures do you believe is the most appropriate one in describing this distribution? Explain the reasoning behind your choice.

5 A finance professor has just given a midterm examination in her corporate finance course. In particular, she is interested in learning how her class of 100 students performed on this exam. The 100 exam scores are given in the file P2_5.XLS.

   a What are the mean and median scores (out of 100 possible points) on this exam?

   b Explain why the mean and median values are different in this case.

6 Compute the mean, median, and mode of the given set of average annual household income levels of citizens from selected U.S. metropolitan areas in the file P3_6.XLS. What can you infer about the shape of this particular income distribution from the computed measures of central location?

7 The operations manager of a toll booth, located at a major exit of a state turnpike, is trying to estimate the typical number of vehicles that arrive at the toll booth during a 1-minute period during the peak of rush-hour traffic. In an effort to estimate this typical throughput value, he records the number of vehicles that arrive at the toll booth over a 1-minute interval commencing at the same time for each of 365 normal weekdays. These data are contained in the file P2_9.XLS.

   a Find the most appropriate measure of the given distribution's central location.

   b Is this distribution of arrivals *skewed* somewhat? Explain.

8 The proportions of high school graduates annually taking the SAT test in each of the 50 states and the District of Columbia are provided in the file P2_10.XLS.

   a Compute the mean, median, and mode of this set of proportions.

   b Which of these measures do you believe is the most appropriate one in describing this distribution? Explain the reasoning behind your choice.

9 Consider the average time (in minutes) it takes a citizen of each metropolitan area to travel to work and back home each day. Refer to the data given in the file P2_11.XLS.

   a Find the most representative average commute time across this distribution.

   b Does it appear that this distribution of average commute times is *approximately* symmetric? Explain why or why not.

10 Five hundred households in a middle-class neighborhood were recently surveyed as a part of an economic development study conducted by the local government. Specifically, for each of the 500 randomly selected households, the survey requested information on several variables, including the household's level of indebtedness (excluding the value of any home mortgage). These data are provided in the file P2_6.XLS.

   a Find the maximum and minimum debt levels for the households in this sample.

   b Find the indebtedness levels at each of the 25th, 50th, and 75th percentiles.

   c Compute and interpret the interquartile range in this case.

11 A real estate agent has gathered data on 150 houses that were recently sold in a suburban community. Included in this data set are observations for each of the following variables: the appraised value of each house (in thousands of dollars), the selling price of each house (in thousands of dollars), the size of each house (in hundreds of square feet), and the number of bedrooms in each house. Refer to the file P2_7.XLS in answering the following questions.

   a Find the house(s) at the 80th percentile of all sample houses with respect to *appraised value.*

   b Find the house(s) at the 80th percentile of all sample houses with respect to *selling price.*

   c Find the maximum and minimum sizes (measured in *square footage*) of all sample houses.

   d What is the typical number of bedrooms in a recently sold house in this suburban community?

12 The U.S. Department of Transportation regularly publishes the *Air Travel Consumer Report,* which provides a variety of performance measures of major U.S. commercial airlines. One dimension of performance reported is each airline's percentage of domestic flights arriving within 15 minutes of the scheduled arrival time at major reporting airports throughout the country. Use these data, given in the file P2_12.XLS, to answer the following questions:

   a Which major U.S. airline has the *highest* third quartile on-time arrival percentage?

   b Which major U.S. airline has the *lowest* first quartile on-time arrival percentage?

   c Which major U.S. airline has the *largest* range of on-time arrival percentages?

   d Which major U.S. airline has the *smallest* range of on-time arrival percentages?

13 Having computed measures of central location for various numerical attributes of full-time employees, a human resources manager at Beta Technologies, Inc., is now interested in compiling some statistics on the variability of sample data values about their respective means. Using the data provided in the file P2_1.XLS, assist this manager by computing sample standard deviations for each of the following numerical variables: age, number of years of relevant full-time work experience prior to coming to Beta, number of years of full-time work experience at Beta, number of years of post-secondary education, and salary. Do the rules of thumb apply for any of these variables? In each case explain why the rules of thumb apply or do not apply.

14 A production manager is interested in determining the variability of the proportion of defective items in a shipment of one of the computer components that her company manufactures. The spreadsheet provided in the file P2_2.XLS contains the proportion of defective components for each of 500 randomly selected shipments collected during a 1-month period. Compute the sample standard deviation of these data and use this value in interpreting the rules of thumb in this case.

15 In an effort to provide more consistent customer service, the manager of a local fast-food restaurant would like to know the dispersion of customer service times about their average value for the facility's drive-up window. The file P2_4.XLS contains 200 customer service times, all of which were observed during the busiest hour of the day for this fast-food operation.

   a Find and interpret the variance and standard deviation of these sample values.

   b Are the rules of thumb applicable in this case? If so, apply the rules of thumb and interpret your results. If not, explain why the rules of thumb are not applicable here.

16 Compute the standard deviation of the given set of average annual household income levels of citizens from selected U.S. metropolitan areas in the file P3_6.XLS. Is it appropriate to apply the rules of thumb in this case? Explain.

17 The file P2_26.XLS contains annual percentage changes in consumer prices for the years 1914–1996. Are the rules of thumb applicable in this case? If so, apply these rules and interpret your results.

18 The diameters of 100 rods produced by Rodco are listed in the file P3_18.XLS. Based on these data, you can be approximately 99.7% sure that the diameter of a typical rod will be between what two numbers?

19 The file P3_19.XLS contains the thickness (in centimeters) of some mica pieces. A piece meets specifications if it is between 7 and 15 centimeters in thickness.

   a What fraction of mica pieces meet specifications?

   b Do the rules of thumb appear to be valid for this data set?

Level B

20 A finance professor has just given a midterm examination in her corporate finance course. In particular, she is now interested in assigning letter grades to the scores earned by her 100 students who took this exam. The top 10% of all ordered scores should receive a grade of A. The next 10% of all ordered scores should be assigned a grade of B. The third 10% of all ordered scores should receive a grade of C. The next 10% of all ordered scores should be assigned a grade of D. All subsequent scores should be considered to be failing (i.e., equivalent to F grades). The100 exam scores are given in the file P2_5.XLS. Assist this instructor in assigning letter grades to each of the given finance exam scores.

21 The operations manager of a toll booth, located at a major exit of a state turnpike, is trying to estimate the variability of the number of vehicles that arrive at the toll booth during a 1-minute period during the peak of rush-hour traffic. In an effort to estimate this measure of dispersion, he records the number of vehicles that arrive at the toll booth over a 1-minute interval commencing at the same time for each of 365 normal weekdays. These data are contained in the file P2_9.XLS.

   a Is the sample variance (or sample standard deviation) a reliable measure of dispersion in this case? Explain why or why not.

   b If the sample variance (or sample standard deviation) is not a reliable measure of dispersion in this case, how can this operations manager most appropriately measure the variability of the values in the given sample?

22 The file P2_10.XLS contains the proportions of high school graduates annually taking the SAT test in each of the 50 states and the District of Columbia. Approximately 95% of these proportions fall between what two fractions?

23 The file P3_23.XLS contains the salaries of all Indiana University business school professors.

   a If you increased every professor's salary by $1000, what would happen to the mean and median salary?

   b If you increased every professor's salary by $1000, what would happen to the sample standard deviation of the salaries?

   c If you increased everybody's salary by 5%, what would happen to the sample standard deviation of the salaries?

24 The file P3_24.XLS contains a sample of family incomes (in thousands of 1980 dollars) for a set of families sampled in 1980 and 1990. Assume that these families are representative of the whole United States. The Republicans claim that the country was better off in 1990 than 1980, because average income increased. Do you agree?

25 According to the Educational Testing Service, the scores of people taking the SAT in 1980 were as listed in Table 3.1.

   a Estimate the average and standard deviation of SAT scores for students whose families made at least $18,000 and for those whose families made no more than $6000. (*Hint*: Assume all scores in a group are concentrated at the group's midpoint.)

   b Do these results have any implications for college admissions?

26 The file P3_26.XLS lists the fraction of U.S. men and women of various heights. Use these data to estimate the mean and standard deviation of the height of American men and women. (*Hint*: Assume all heights in a group are concentrated at the group's midpoint.)

27 The file P3_27.XLS lists the fraction of U.S. men and women of various weights. Use these data to estimate the mean and standard deviation of the weights of U.S. men and women. ■

TABLE 3.1 **Data on SAT Scores**

Range	Number Having Family Income ≥$18,000	Number Having Family Income ≤$6000
200–250	325	1638
251–300	4,212	7980
301–350	13,896	9622
351–400	26,175	8973
401–450	37,213	8054
451–500	41,412	6663
501–550	37,400	4983
551–600	28,151	3119
601–650	17,992	1626
651–700	9,284	686
701–750	3,252	239
751–800	415	17

3.7

Measures of Association: Covariance and Correlation

All of the summary measures to this point involve a single variable. It is also useful to summarize the relationship between two variables. Specifically, we would like to summarize the type of behavior often observed in a scatterplot. Two such measures are **covariance** and **correlation**. We will discuss them briefly here and in more depth in later chapters. Each measures the strength (and direction) of a *linear* relationship between two numerical variables. Intuitively, the relationship is "strong" if the points in a scatterplot cluster tightly around some straight line. If this straight line rises from left to right, then the relationship is "positive" and the measures are positive numbers. If it falls from left to right, then the relationship is "negative" and the measures are negative numbers.

First, it is important to realize that if we want to measure the covariance or correlation between two variables X and Y—indeed, even if we just want to form a scatterplot of X versus Y— then X and Y must be "paired" variables. That is, they must have the same number of observations, and the X and Y values for any observation should be naturally paired. For example, each observation could be the height and weight for a particular person, the time in a store and the amount purchased for a particular customer, and so on.

With this in mind, let X_i and Y_i be the paired values for observation i, and let n be the number of observations. Then the covariance between X and Y, denoted by $\text{Cov}(X, Y)$, is given by the formula

$$\text{Cov}(X, Y) = \frac{\sum_{i=1}^{n}(X_i - \overline{X})(Y_i - \overline{Y})}{n - 1} \tag{3.5}$$

You probably won't ever have to use this formula directly—Excel has a built-in COVAR function that does it for you—but the formula does indicate what covariance is all about. It is essentially an average of products of deviations from means. If X and Y vary in the *same* direction, then when X is above (or below) its mean, Y will also tend to be above (or below) its mean. In either case, the product of deviations will be positive—a positive times a positive or a negative times a negative—so the covariance will be positive. The opposite is true when X and Y vary in *opposite* directions. Then the covariance will be negative.

The limitation of covariance as a descriptive measure is that it is affected by the *units* in which X and Y are measured. For example, we can inflate the covariance by a factor of 1000 simply by measuring X in dollars rather than in thousands of dollars.

The correlation, denoted by Corr(X, Y), remedies this problem. It is a *unitless* quantity defined by

$$\text{Corr}(X, Y) = \frac{\text{Cov}(X, Y)}{\text{Stdev}(X) \times \text{Stdev}(Y)} \tag{3.6}$$

where Stdev(X) and Stdev(Y) denote the standard deviations of X and Y. Again, you'll probably never have to use this formula for calculations—Excel does it for you with the built-in CORREL function—but it does show that to produce a unitless quantity, we need to divide the covariance by the product of the standard deviations.

The correlation is *always* between -1 and $+1$. The closer it is to either of these two extremes, the closer the points in a scatterplot are to some straight line, either in the negative or positive direction. On the other hand, if the correlation is close to 0, then the scatterplot is typically a "cloud" of points with no apparent relationship. However, it is also possible that the points are close to a *curve* and have a correlation close to 0. This is because correlation is relevant only for measuring linear relationships.

When there are more than two variables in a data set, it is often useful to create a table of covariances and/or correlations. Each value in the table then corresponds to a particular pair of variables. The StatPro add-in allows you to do this easily, as illustrated in the following example.

EXAMPLE 3.6

A survey questions members of 100 households about their spending habits. The data in the file EXPENSES.XLS represent the salary, expenses for cultural activities, expenses for sports-related activities, and expenses for dining out for each household over the past year. Do these variables appear to be related linearly?

Solution

Scatterplots of each variable versus each other variable answer the question quite nicely, but six scatterplots are required, one for each pair. To get a quick indication of possible linear relationships, we can use StatPro to obtain a table of correlations and/or covariances. To do so, place the cursor anywhere in the data range, use the StatPro/Summary Stats/Correlations, Covariances menu item, and proceed in the obvious way. The tables of correlations and covariances appear in Figure 3.9.

The only relationships that stand out are the positive relationships between salary and cultural expenses and between salary and dining expenses, and the negative relationship between cultural and sports-related expenses. To confirm these graphically, we show scatterplots of Salary versus Culture and Culture versus Sports in Figures 3.10 and 3.11. These indicate more intuitively what a correlation of approximately ± 0.5 really means.

In general, we point out the following properties that are evident from Figure 3.9:

- The correlation between a variable and itself is always 1.

- The correlation between X and Y is the same as the correlation between Y and X. Therefore, it is sufficient to list the correlations below (or above) the diagonal in the table. (The same is true for covariances.) StatPro provides these options.

- The covariance between a variable and itself is the *variance* of that variable. We indicate this in the heading of the covariance table.

- It is difficult to interpret the magnitudes of the covariances. These depend on the fact that the data are measured in dollars rather than, say, thousands of dollars. It is much easier to interpret the magnitudes of the correlations because they are scaled to be between -1 and $+1$.

FIGURE 3.9 **Table of Correlations and Covariances**

	A	B	C	D	E	F
1	*Table of correlations*					
2			Salary	Culture	Sports	Dining
3		Salary	1.000			
4		Culture	0.506	1.000		
5		Sports	-0.081	-0.520	1.000	
6		Dining	0.558	0.170	0.266	1.000
7						
8	*Table of covariances (variances on the diagonal)*					
9			Salary	Culture	Sports	Dining
10		Salary	91130278.788			
11		Culture	1094786.800	52315.394		
12		Sports	-219026.400	-33607.520	81427.232	
13		Dining	2564694.800	18748.640	36461.280	236187.667

FIGURE 3.10 **Scatterplot Indicating a Positive Relationship**

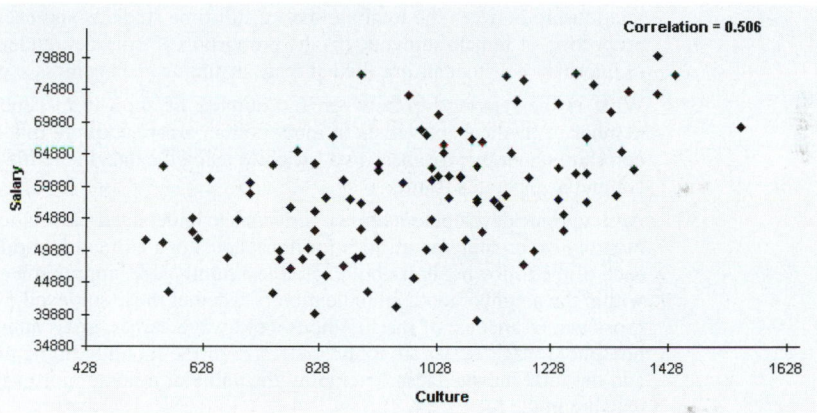

FIGURE 3.11 **Scatterplot Indicating a Negative Relationship**

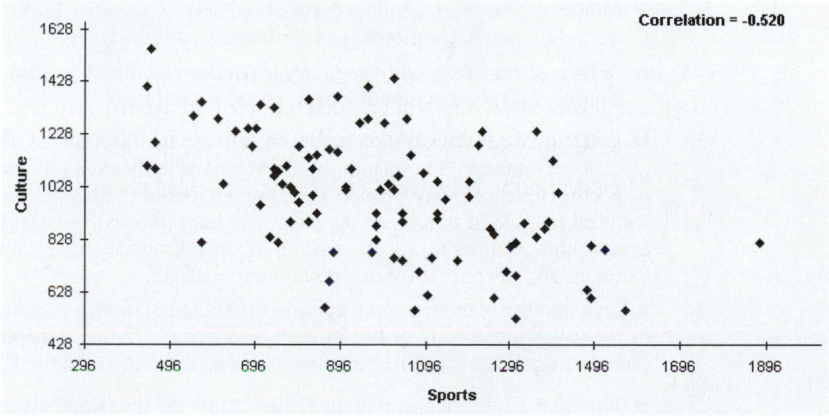

PROBLEMS

Level A

28 Explore the relationship between the selling prices and the appraised values of the 150 homes in the file P2_7.XLS by computing a correlation.

   a Is there evidence of a *linear* relationship between the selling price and appraised value in this case? If so, characterize the relationship (i.e., indicate whether the relationship is a positive or negative one).

   b For which of the two remaining variables, the size of the home and the number of bedrooms in the home, is the relationship with the home's appraised value *stronger*? Justify your choice.

29 A human resources manager at Beta Technologies, Inc., is trying to determine the variable that best explains the variation of employee salaries using the previously gathered sample of 52 full-time employees in the file P2_1.XLS. Generate a table of correlations to help this manager identify whether the employee's (a) gender, (b) age, (c) number of years of relevant work experience prior to employment at Beta, (d) the number of years of employment at Beta, or (e) the number of years of post-secondary education has the *strongest* linear relationship with annual salary.

30 Consider the enrollment data for *Business Week*'s top 50 U.S. graduate business programs in the file P2_3.XLS. Specifically, compute correlations to assess whether there is a linear relationship between the total number of full-time students and each of the following: (a) the proportion of female students, (b) the proportion of minority students, and (c) the proportion of international students enrolled at these distinguished business schools.

31 What is the relationship between the number of short-term general hospitals and the number of medical specialists in metropolitan areas? Explore this question by producing a correlation measure for these two variables using the data in the file P2_17.XLS. Interpret your computer-generated result.

32 An economic development researcher wants to understand the relationship between the average monthly expenditure on utilities for households in a particular middle-class neighborhood and each of the following household variables: family size, approximate location of the household within the neighborhood, an indication of whether those surveyed owned or rented their home, gross annual income of the first household wage earner, gross annual income of the second household wage earner (if applicable), size of the monthly home mortgage or rent payment, and the total indebtedness (excluding the value of a home mortgage) of the household. The data are in the file P2_54.XLS.

   a Use a computer to generate a correlation for each pairing of variables with the household's average monthly expenditure on utilities.

   b Which of the aforementioned variables have a *positive* linear relationship with the household's average monthly expenditure on utilities?

   c Which of the aforementioned variables have a *negative* linear relationship with the household's average monthly expenditure on utilities?

   d Which of the aforementioned variables have essentially *no* linear relationship with the household's average monthly expenditure on utilities?

33 Motorco produces electric motors for use in home appliances. One of the company's production managers is interested in examining the relationship between the dollars spent per month in inspecting finished motor products and the number of motors produced during that month that were returned by dissatisfied customers. He has collected the data in the file P2_18.XLS to explore this relationship for the past 36 months. Produce a correlation measure for these two variables and interpret it for this production manager.

34 A large number of metropolitan areas in the United States have been ranked with consideration of the following aspects of life in each area: cost of living, transportation, jobs, education, climate, crime, arts, health, and recreation. The data are in the file P2_55.XLS.

   a Generate a table of correlations to discern the relationship between the metropolitan area's overall score and each of these numerical factors.

   b Which variables are most strongly associated with the overall score? Are you surprised by any of the results here?

35 The *ACCRA Cost of Living Index* provides a useful and reasonably accurate measure of cost-of-living differences among 321 urban areas. Items on which the index is based have been carefully chosen to reflect the different categories of consumer expenditures. The data are in the file P2_19.XLS. Compute correlation measures to explore the relationship between the composite index and each of the various expenditure components.

    a Which expenditure component has the *strongest* linear relationship with the composite index?

    b Which expenditure component has the *weakest* linear relationship with the composite index?

36 Based on the data in the file P2_25.XLS from the U.S. Department of Agriculture, determine whether a linear relationship exists between the number of farms and the average size of a farm in the United States between 1950 and 1997. Specifically, generate a correlation measure and interpret it. ■

3.8 Describing Data Sets with Boxplots

The final tool we discuss is the boxplot, a very useful graphical method for summarizing data. We saved boxplots for this chapter because they are based on a number of summary measures we discussed in Section 3.2. Boxplots can be used in two ways: either to describe a single variable in a data set or to compare two (or more) variables. We illustrate these uses in the following examples.

E X A M P L E 3 . 7

Recall that the DOW.XLS file lists the monthly returns on the Dow from February 1947 through January 1993. Use a boxplot to summarize the distribution of these returns.

Solution

Excel has no boxplot option, but we have included this option in the StatPro add-in. To create a boxplot, place the cursor anywhere within the data set, use the StatPro/Charts/Boxplot(s) menu item, and proceed in the obvious way. Eventually, two sheets will be added. One has the boxplot chart, while the other contains summary measures used to form the boxplot, as explained below.[1] The resulting boxplot appears in Figure 3.12 and the summary measure sheet appears in Figure 3.13 (page 96).

The keys to understanding a boxplot are the following.

■ The right and left of the box are at the third and first quartiles. Therefore, the length of the box equals the interquartile range (IQR), and the box itself represents the middle 50% of the observations. The height of the box has no significance.

■ The vertical line inside the box indicates the location of the median. The point inside the box indicates the location of the mean.

■ Horizontal lines are drawn from each side of the box. They extend to the most extreme observations that are no farther than 1.5 IQRs from the box. They are useful for indicating variability and skewness.

---

[1]The second sheet, which includes the summary data for the boxplot, is actually hidden by StatPro.

FIGURE 3.12   **Boxplot of Dow Returns**

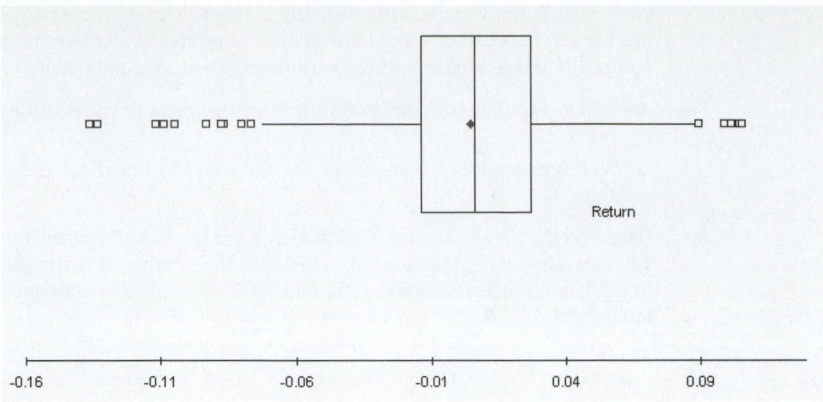

FIGURE 3.13   **Summary Measures for Boxplot**

	A	B
1	**Summary measures for boxplots**	
2		Return
3	Mean	0.00588
4	Median	0.007417
5	Q1	-0.012566
6	Q3	0.02836
7	IQR	0.040926
8		
9	Outer lower fence	-0.135342
10	Outer upper fence	0.151137
11		
12	Inner lower fence	-0.073954
13	Inner upper fence	0.089748
14		
15	Lower adjacent value	-0.071125
16	Upper adjacent value	0.089421
17		
18	# of extreme outliers	0
19	# of mild outliers	16
20		
21	# of low outliers	10
22	# of high outliers	6

■ Observations farther than 1.5 IQRs from the box are shown as individual points. If they are between 1.5 IQRs and 3 IQRs from the box, they are called **mild outliers** and are hollow. Otherwise, they are called **extreme outliers** and are solid.[2]

The boxplot implies that the Dow returns are approximately symmetric on each side of the median, although the mean is a bit below the median. In addition, there are a few mild outliers but no extreme outliers.   ■

---

[2] These conventions, along with the rather quaint terminology of fences and adjacent values listed in the summary table, are due to the statistician John Tukey.

Boxplots are probably most useful for comparing two populations graphically, as we illustrate in the following example.

EXAMPLE 3.8

Recall that the salaries of famous actors and actresses are listed in the file ACTORS.XLS. Use side-by-side boxplots to compare the salaries of male and female actors and actresses.

Solution

The data setup for this type of "comparison" problem can be in one of two forms: stacked or unstacked. The data are stacked if there is a "code" variable such as Gender that designates which gender each observation is in, and there is a single "measurement" variable Salary that lists the salaries for both genders. The data are unstacked if there is a *separate* Salary column for each gender (one for males and one for females). As Figure 3.14 indicates, the data in the ACTORS.XLS file are in stacked form. Therefore, to obtain side-by-side boxplots of male and female salaries, use the StatPro/Charts/Boxplot(s) menu item, and, after the opening dialog box, check the "stacked" option. Then choose Gender as the code variable and Salary as the measurement variable.

FIGURE 3.14   **Actor Data in Stacked Form**

	A	B	C	D	E
1	**Famous actors and actresses**				
2					
3	Note: All monetary values are in $ millions.				
4					
5	Name	Gender	DomesticGross	ForeignGross	Salary
6	Angela Bassett	F	32	17	2.5
7	Jessica Lange	F	21	27	2.5
8	Winona Ryder	F	36	30	4
9	Michelle Pfeiffer	F	66	31	10
10	Whoopi Goldberg	F	32	33	10
11	Emma Thompson	F	26	44	3
12	Julia Roberts	F	57	47	12
13	Sharon Stone	F	32	47	6
14	Meryl Streep	F	34	47	4.5
15	Susan Sarandon	F	38	49	3
16	Nicole Kidman	F	55	51	4
17	Holly Hunter	F	51	53	2.5
18	Meg Ryan	F	43	55	8.5
19	Andie Macdowell	F	26	75	2
20	Jodie Foster	F	62	85	9
21	Rene Russo	F	69	85	2.5
22	Sandra Bullock	F	64	104	11
23	Demi Moore	F	65	125	12
24	Danny Glover	M	42	4	2
25	Billy Crystal	M	52	14	7

The resulting side-by-side boxplots appear in Figure 3.15 (page 98). It is clear that the female salary box is considerably to the left of the male salary box, although both have about the same IQR. Each boxplot has three indications that the salary distributions are skewed to the right: (1) the means are larger than the medians, (2) the medians are closer to the left sides of the boxes than to the right sides, and (3) the horizontal lines extend farther to the right than to the left of the boxes. However, there are no outliers—not even the big stars like Harrison Ford or Sylvester Stallone!

FIGURE 3.15   Side-by-side Boxplots of Female and Male Salaries

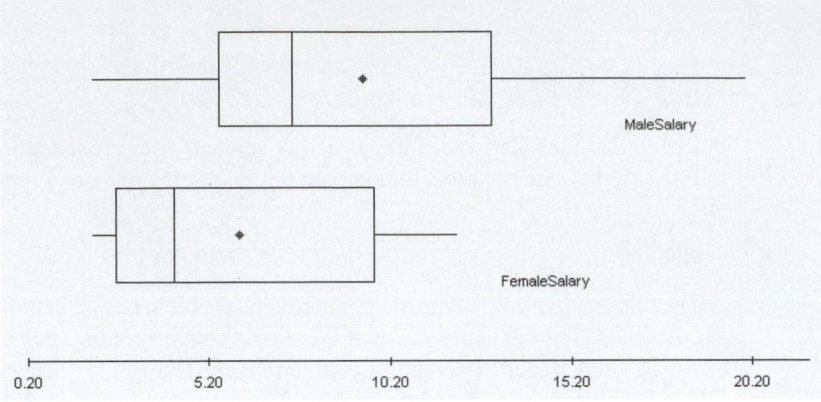

PROBLEMS

Level A

37 Consider the data in the file P3_37.XLS on various performance measures for the largest U.S. airlines in 1996. In particular, generate boxplots to summarize each of the given measures of airline performance. Are these four performance measures linearly associated with one another? Explain your findings.

38 In a recent ranking of top graduate business schools in the United States published by *U.S. News & World Report*, the average starting base salaries for recent graduates from 25 recognized graduate programs were provided. These data are given in the file P2_8.XLS. Construct a boxplot to characterize this distribution of average starting MBA salaries. In particular, is this distribution essentially symmetric or skewed?

39 Consider the average annual rates for various forms of violent crime (including murder, rape, robbery, and aggravated assault) and the average annual rates for various forms of property-related crime (including burglary, larceny-theft, and motor vehicle theft) in selected U.S. metropolitan areas. The data are provided in the file P2_50.XLS. Use side-by-side boxplots to compare the rates of these two general classes of crimes. Summarize your findings.

40 The annual average values of the Consumer Confidence Index for the years 1967–1996 are given in the file P2_28.XLS. Construct a boxplot to find the middle 50% of this distribution of values. Characterize the nature and amount of the variability about the interquartile range in this case.

41 Consider the given set of average annual household income levels of citizens from selected U.S. metropolitan areas in P3_6.XLS. What can you infer about the shape of this particular income distribution from a computer-generated boxplot of the given data? If applicable, note the presence of any outliers in this data set.

42 Using cost-of-living data from the *ACCRA Cost of Living Index* in the file P2_19.XLS, generate a boxplot to summarize the *composite* cost-of-living index values.

Level B

43 In 1970 a lottery was held to determine who would be drafted (and sent to Vietnam). For each date of the year, a ball was put into an urn. For instance, January 1 was number 305 and February 14 was number 4. Thus a person born on February 14 would be drafted before a person born on January 1. The file P3_43.XLS contains the "draft number" for each date for the 1970 and 1971 lotteries. Do you notice anything unusual about the results of either lottery? What do you think might have caused this result? (*Hint*: Use a boxplot for each month's numbers.) ■

Applying the Tools

Now that we're equipped with a collection of tools for describing data, it's time to apply these tools to some serious data analysis. We will examine three data sets in this section. Each of these is rather small by comparison with the data sets real companies often face, but they are large enough to make the analysis far from trivial. In each example we will illustrate some of the output that might be obtained by the company involved, but you should realize that we're never really finished. With data sets as rich as these, there are always more numbers that could be calculated, more tables that could be formed, and more charts that could be created. We encourage you to take each analysis a few steps beyond what we present there.

Each example has a decision problem lurking behind it. If these data belonged to real companies, the companies would not only want to describe the data, but they would want to use the information from their data analysis as a springboard for decision making. We are not yet in a position to perform this decision making, but you should appreciate that the data analysis we perform here is really just the first step in an overall business analysis.

EXAMPLE 3.9

The Spring Mills Company produces and distributes a wide variety of manufactured goods. Due to its variety, it has a large number of customers. It classifies these customers as small, medium, and large, depending on the volume of business each does with Spring Mills. Recently, Spring Mills has noticed a problem with its accounts receivable. It is not getting paid back by its customers in as timely a manner as it would like. This obviously costs Spring Mills money. If a customer delays a payment of $300 for 20 days, say, then the company loses potential interest on this amount. The company has gathered data on 280 customer accounts. For each of these accounts, the data set lists three variables: Size, the size of the customer (coded 1 for small, 2 for medium, 3 for large); Days, the number of days since the customer was billed; and Amount, the amount the customer owes. (See the file RECEIVE.XLS.) What information can we obtain from these data?

Solution

It is always a good idea to get a rough sense of the data first. We do this by calculating several summary measures for Days and Amount, a histogram of Amount, and a scatterplot of Amount versus Days in Figures 3.16, 3.17, and 3.18 (page 100). Figure 3.16 indicates positive skewness in the Amount variable—the mean is considerably larger than the median, probably because of some large amounts due. Also, the standard deviation of Amount is quite large. This positive skewness is confirmed by the histogram. The scatterplot suggests some suspicious behavior, with two distinct groups of points.

The next logical step is to see whether the different customer sizes have any effect on either Days, Amount, or the relationship between Days and Amount. To do this, it is useful to "unstack" the Days and Amount variables—that is, to create a new Days and Amount variable for *each* group of customer sizes. For example, the Days and Amount variables for customers of size 1 are named Days1 and Amount1. (We used StatPro's Unstack procedure, which is quite straightforward, to accomplish this, but copying and pasting also works.) Summary measures and a variety of charts based on these unstacked variables appear in Figures 3.19 through 3.27 (pages 101–103).

FIGURE 3.16   **Summary Measures for the Combined Data**

	A	B	C	D
1	*Summary measures for selected variables*			
2			Days	Amount
3		Count	280.000	280.000
4		Sum	4102.000	130000.000
5		Mean	14.650	464.286
6		Median	13.000	320.000
7		Standard deviation	7.221	378.055
8		Minimum	2.000	140.000
9		Maximum	39.000	2220.000

FIGURE 3.17   **Histogram of All Amounts Owed**

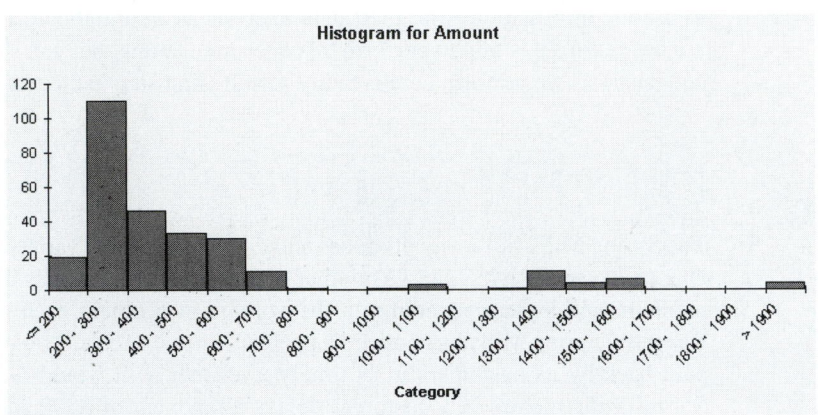

FIGURE 3.18   **Scatterplot of Amount versus Days for All Customers**

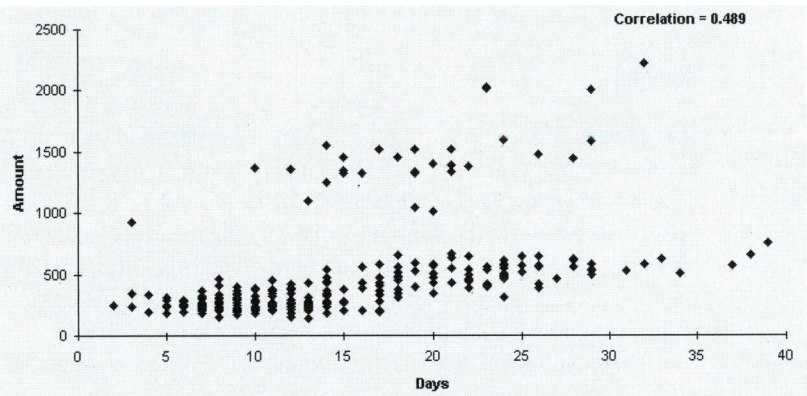

FIGURE 3.19 **Summary Measures Broken Down by Size**

	A	B	C	D	E	F	G	H
1	*Summary measures for selected variables*							
2			Days1	Amount1	Days2	Amount2	Days3	Amount3
3		Count	150.000	150.000	100.000	100.000	30.000	30.000
4		Sum	1470.000	38180.000	2055.000	48190.000	577.000	43630.000
5		Mean	9.800	254.533	20.550	481.900	19.233	1454.333
6		Median	10.000	250.000	20.000	470.000	19.000	1395.000
7		Standard deviation	3.128	49.285	6.622	99.155	6.191	293.888
8		Minimum	2.000	140.000	8.000	280.000	3.000	930.000
9		Maximum	17.000	410.000	39.000	750.000	32.000	2220.000

FIGURE 3.20 **Histogram of Amount for Small Customers**

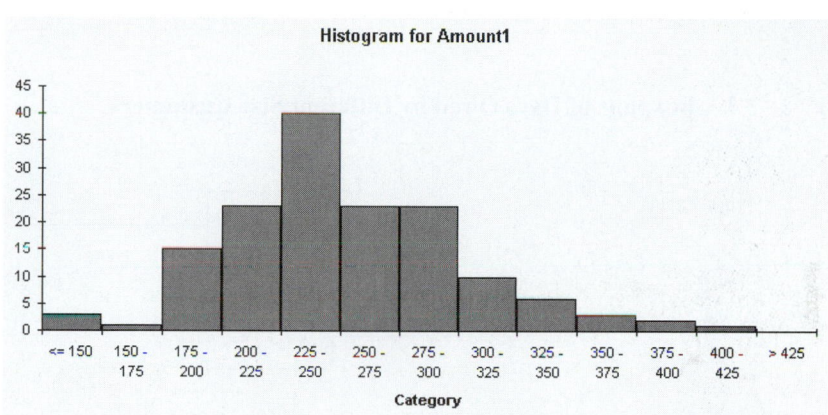

FIGURE 3.21 **Histogram of Amount for Medium Customers**

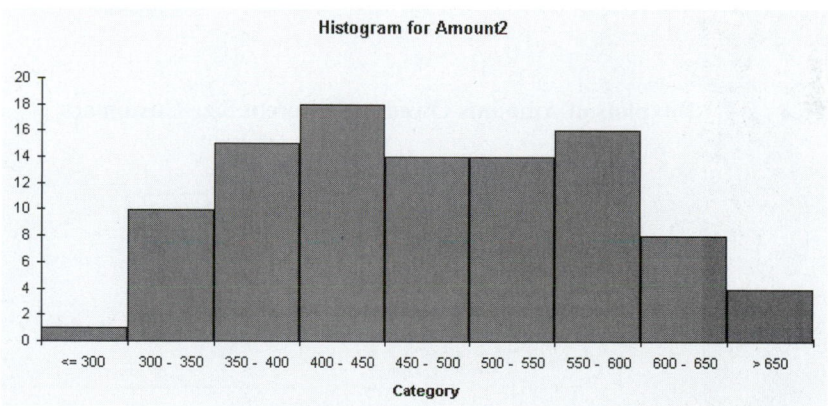

FIGURE 3.22   Histogram of Amount for Large Customers

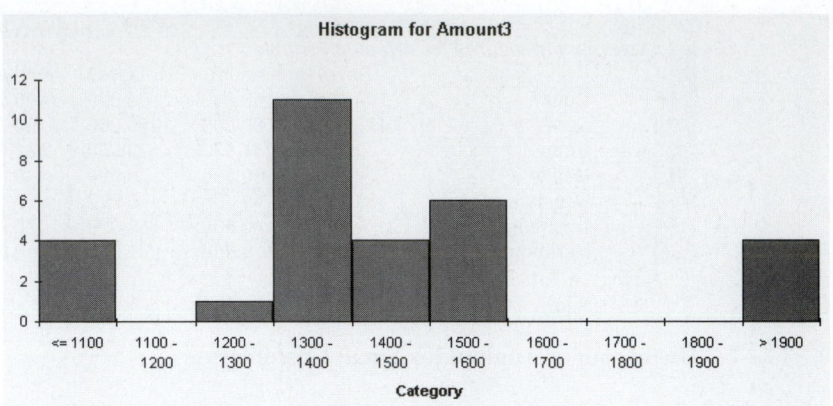

FIGURE 3.23   Boxplots of Days Owed by Different Size Customers

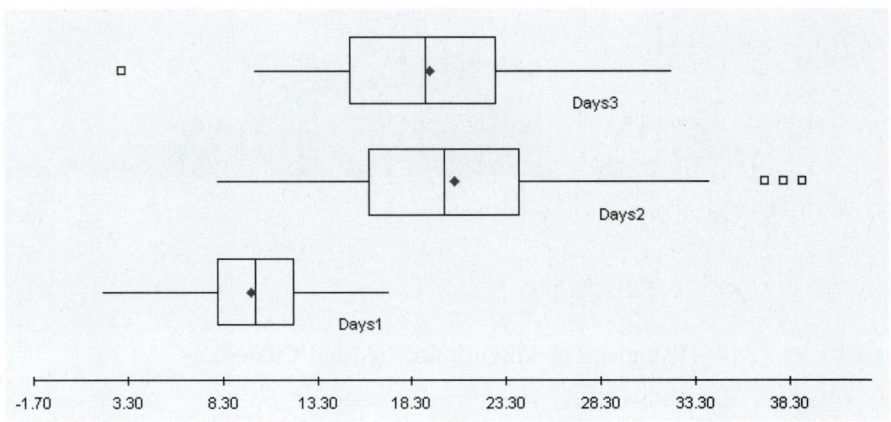

FIGURE 3.24   Boxplots of Amounts Owed by Different Size Customers

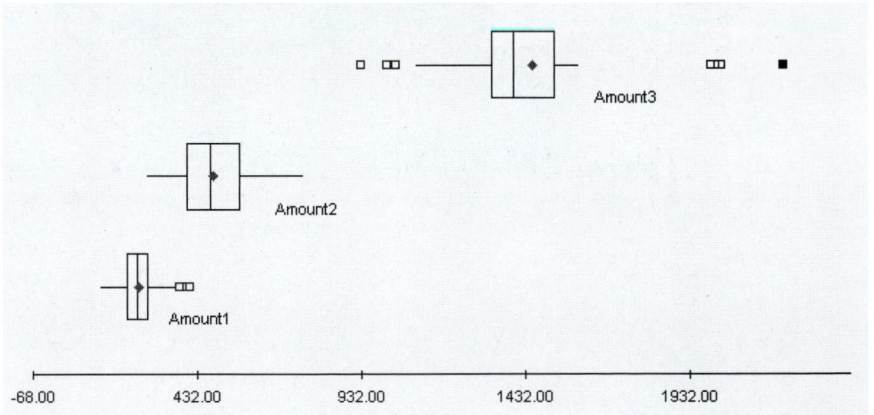

FIGURE 3.25 Scatterplot of Amount versus Days for Small Customers

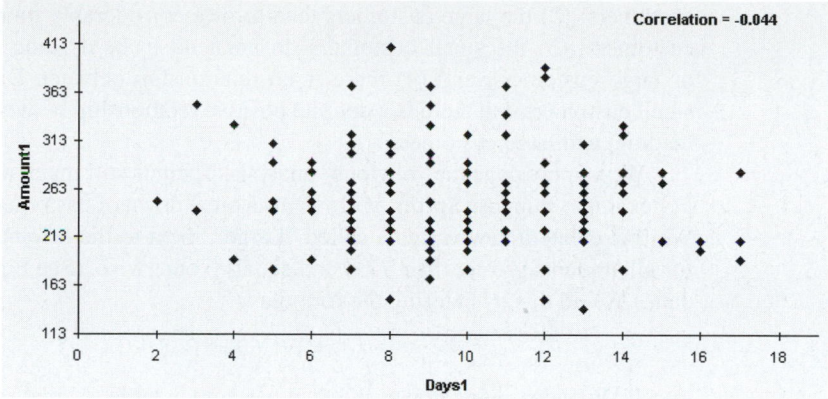

FIGURE 3.26 Scatterplot of Amount versus Days for Medium Customers

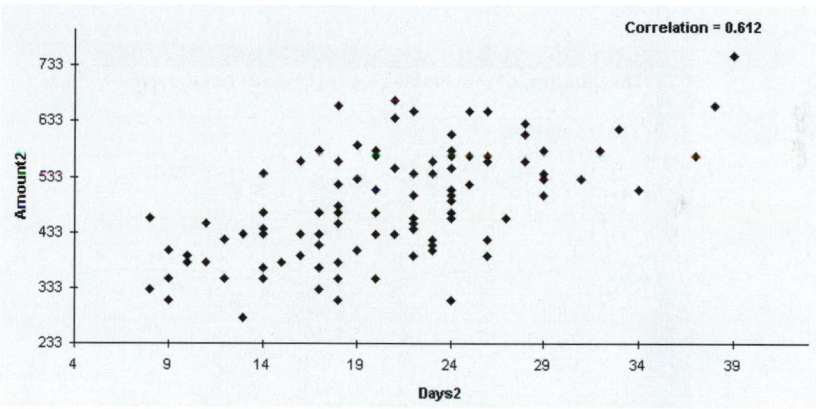

FIGURE 3.27 Scatterplot of Amount versus Days for Large Customers

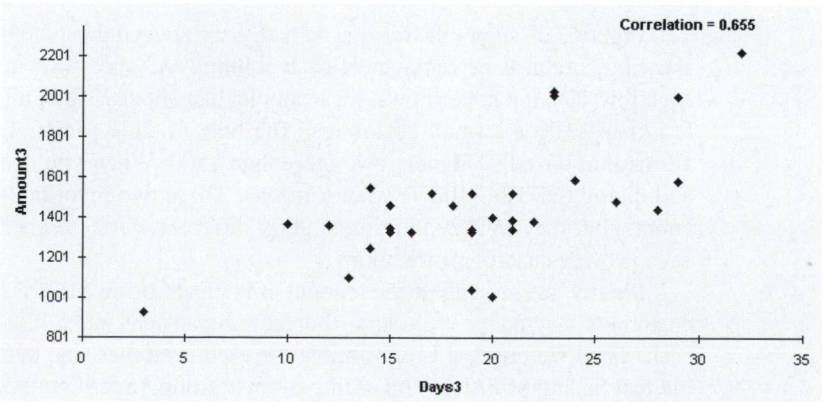

There is obviously a lot going on here, and most of it is clear from the figures. We point out the following: (1) there are many fewer large customers than small or medium customers; (2) the large customers tend to owe considerably more than small or medium customers; (3) the small customers do not tend to be as long overdue as the medium or large customers; and (4) there is no relationship between Days and Amount for the small customers, but there is a definite positive relationship between these variables for the medium and large customers.

We've now done the "obvious" analysis. There is still much more we can do, however. For example, suppose Spring Mills wants a breakdown of customers who owe at least $500. We first create a new variable called "Large?" next to the original variables that equals 1 for all amounts greater than $500 and equals 0 otherwise. (See Figure 3.28 for some of the data.) We do this by entering the formula

$$=IF(C6>=\$B\$3,1,0)$$

in cell D6 and copying down. We then use a pivot table to create a *count* of the number of 1's in this new variable for each value of the Size variable.

FIGURE 3.28   **Checking for Amounts Greater than $500**

	A	B	C	D	E
1	Distribution of receivables - checking for large values				
2					
3	Value to check for	$500			
4					
5		Size	Days	Amount	Large?
6		1	7	$180	0
7		1	8	$210	0
8		1	10	$210	0
9		1	8	$150	0
10		1	9	$300	0
11		1	5	$240	0
12		1	4	$330	0
13		1	10	$290	0
14		1	5	$240	0
15		1	13	$270	0
16		1	12	$220	0
17		1	11	$260	0

Figure 3.29 shows the results. Actually, we created this pivot table twice, once (on top) showing counts as percentages of each column, and once showing them as percentages of each row. The top table shows, for example, that about 73% of all customers with amounts less than $500 are small customers. The bottom table shows, for example, that 45% of all medium-sized customers owe more than $500. When you hear the expression "slicing and dicing the data," this is what it means. These two pivot tables are based on the *same* counts, but they portray them in slightly different ways. Neither is better than the other; each provides useful information.

Finally, we investigate the amount of interest Spring Mills is losing by the delays in its customers' payments. We assume that the company can make 12% annual interest on excess cash. Then we create a Lost variable for each customer size that indicates the amount of interest Spring Mills loses on each customer group. (See Figure 3.30.) The typical formula for lost interest in cell C10 is

$$=B10*A10*\$C\$7/365$$

FIGURE 3.29 **Pivot Tables for Counts of Customers Who Owe More Than $500**

	A	B	C	D
1				
2	Count of Large?	Large?		
3	Size	0	1	Grand Total
4	1	73.17%	0.00%	53.57%
5	2	26.83%	60.00%	35.71%
6	3	0.00%	40.00%	10.71%
7	Grand Total	100.00%	100.00%	100.00%
8				
9	Count of Large?	Large?		
10	Size	0	1	Grand Total
11	1	100.00%	0.00%	100.00%
12	2	55.00%	45.00%	100.00%
13	3	0.00%	100.00%	100.00%
14	Grand Total	73.21%	26.79%	100.00%

FIGURE 3.30 **Summary Measures of Lost Interest**

	A	B	C	D	E	F	G	H	I
1	Interest lost								
2									
3	Summary measures for selected variables								
4		Lost1	Lost2	Lost3					
5	Sum	$122.68	$338.65	$287.25					
6									
7	Annual interest rate		12%						
8									
9	Days1	Amount1	Lost1	Days2	Amount2	Lost2	Days3	Amount3	Lost3
10	7	$180	$0.41	17	$470	$2.63	19	$1,330	$8.31
11	8	$210	$0.55	22	$540	$3.91	20	$1,400	$9.21
12	10	$210	$0.69	28	$560	$5.16	14	$1,550	$7.13
13	8	$150	$0.39	24	$470	$3.71	15	$1,460	$7.20
14	9	$300	$0.89	26	$650	$5.56	23	$2,030	$15.35
15	5	$240	$0.39	29	$530	$5.05	19	$1,520	$9.49
16	4	$330	$0.43	21	$550	$3.80	15	$1,330	$6.56
17	10	$290	$0.95	33	$620	$6.73	17	$1,520	$8.50
18	5	$240	$0.39	16	$430	$2.26	21	$1,390	$9.60
19	13	$270	$1.15	27	$460	$4.08	24	$1,590	$12.55

This is the amount owed multiplied by the number of days owed multiplied by the interest rate, divided by the number of days in a year. Then we calculate sums of these amounts in row 5. Although Spring Mills is losing more per customer from the large customers, it is losing more in *total* from the medium-sized customers—because there are more of them. This is shown graphically in Figure 3.31 by a pie chart of the sums in row 5. This pie chart shows, for example, that 46% of the lost interest is due to the medium-sized customers.

If Spring Mills really wants to decrease its receivables, it might want to target the medium-sized customer group, from which it is losing the most interest. Or it could target the large customers because they owe the most on average. The most appropriate action depends on the cost and effectiveness of targeting any particular customer group. However, the analysis presented here gives the company a much better picture of what's currently going on.

FIGURE 3.31 **Pie Chart of Lost Interest by Customer Size**

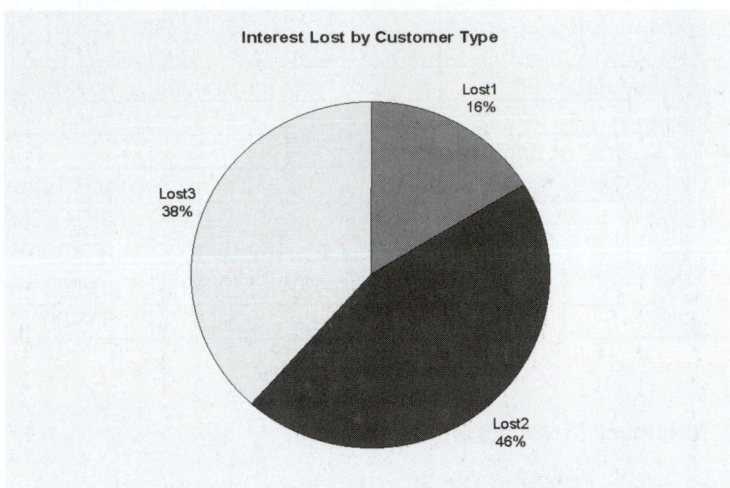

Interest Lost by Customer Type

■

EXAMPLE 3.10

The R&P Supermarket is open 24 hours a day, 7 days a week. Lately, it has been receiving a lot of complaints from its customers about excessive waiting in line for checking out. R&P has decided to investigate this situation by gathering data on arrivals, departures, and line lengths at the checkout stations. It has collected data in half-hour increments for an entire week—336 observations—starting at 8 A.M. on Monday morning and ending at 8 A.M. the following Monday.

Specifically, it has collected data on the following variables: InitialWaiting, the number waiting or being checked out at the beginning of a half-hour period; Arrivals, the number of arrivals to the checkout stations during a period; Departures, the number finishing the checkout process during a period; and Checkers, the number of checkout stations open during a period. (See the file CHECKOUT.XLS.)

The data set also includes time variables: Day, day of week; StartTime, clock time at the beginning of each half-hour period; and TimeInterval, a descriptive term for the time of day, such as Lunch rush for 11:30 A.M. to 1:30 P.M. (The note in cell C4 of the Data sheet spells these out.) Finally, the data set includes the *calculated* variable EndWaiting, the number waiting or being checked out at the end of a half-hour period. For any time period, it equals InitialWaiting plus Arrivals minus Departures; it also equals InitialWaiting for the *next* period. A partial listing of the data appears in Figure 3.32.

The manager of R&P wants to analyze these data to discover any trends, particularly in the pattern of arrivals throughout a day or across the entire week. Also, the store currently uses a "seat-of-the-pants" approach to opening and closing checkout stations each half hour. The manager would like to see how well the current approach is working. Of course, she would love to know the "best" strategy for opening and closing checkout stations—but this is beyond her (and our) capabilities at this point.

FIGURE 3.32 **A Partial Listing of the Supermarket Checkout Data**

	A	B	C	D	E	F	G	H	I
1	Supermarket checkout efficiency								
2									
3	Day	StartTime	TimeInterval	InitialWaiting	Arrivals	Departures	EndWaiting	Checkers	TotalCustomers
4	Mon	8:00 AM	Morning rush	2	21	22	1	3	23
5	Mon	8:30 AM	Morning rush	1	25	18	8	3	26
6	Mon	9:00 AM	Morning	8	27	28	7	3	35
7	Mon	9:30 AM	Morning	7	21	23	5	3	28
8	Mon	10:00 AM	Morning	5	20	23	2	5	25
9	Mon	10:30 AM	Morning	2	36	31	7	5	38
10	Mon	11:00 AM	Morning	7	30	36	1	5	37
11	Mon	11:30 AM	Lunch rush	1	34	29	6	5	35
12	Mon	12:00 PM	Lunch rush	6	56	48	14	7	62
13	Mon	12:30 PM	Lunch rush	14	58	64	8	7	72
14	Mon	1:00 PM	Lunch rush	8	53	52	9	7	61
15	Mon	1:30 PM	Afternoon	9	30	36	3	5	39
16	Mon	2:00 PM	Afternoon	3	34	31	6	5	37
17	Mon	2:30 PM	Afternoon	6	36	37	5	5	42
18	Mon	3:00 PM	Afternoon	5	30	28	7	5	35
19	Mon	3:30 PM	Afternoon	7	29	34	2	5	36
20	Mon	4:00 PM	Afternoon	2	35	33	4	5	37
21	Mon	4:30 PM	Afternoon rush	4	32	25	11	5	36

Solution

Obviously, time plays a crucial role in this example, so a good place to start is to create one or more time series plots. The graph in Figure 3.33 shows the time series behavior of InitialWaiting (the lower line) and Arrivals during the entire week. (This looks much better on a PC monitor, where the two lines are in different colors.) There is almost *too* much clutter in this graph to see exactly what's happening, but it is clear that (1) Fridays and Saturdays are the busiest days; (2) the time pattern of arrivals is somewhat different—more spread out—during the weekends than during the weekdays; (3) there are fairly regular peak arrival periods during the weekdays; and (4) the number waiting is sometimes as large as 10 or 20, and the largest of these tend to be around the peak arrival times.

FIGURE 3.33 **Time Series Plot of InitialWaiting and Arrivals Variables**

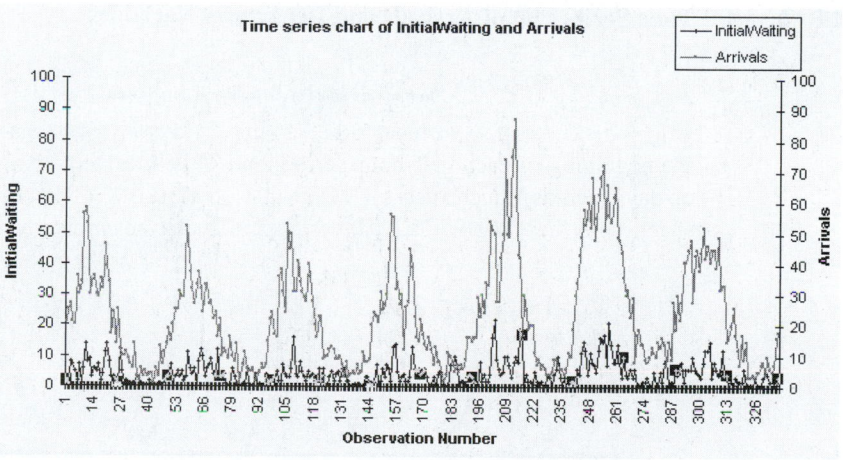

A similar time series plot appears in Figure 3.34. This shows Arrivals and Departures, although it is difficult to separate the two time series—they are practically on top of one another. Perhaps this is not so bad. It means that for the most part, the store is checking out customers approximately as quickly as they are arriving.

A somewhat more efficient way to obtain this time series behavior is with pivot tables. Figure 3.35 shows one possibility. To create this pivot table, we drag the InitialWaiting variable to the Data area, express it as an average, drag the StartTime variable to the Row area, and drag the Day variable to the Page area. (We could also condense the information from half-hour periods to hour-long periods by using the grouping option on the Pivot Table toolbar.) Finally, we create a time series plot from the data in the pivot table. Note how the variable in the Page area works. For example, we obtain the graph in Figure 3.35 if we choose Monday in the Page area (the dropdown list in cell B1). However, if we choose another day in cell B1, the data in the pivot table and the graph change automatically. So we can make comparisons across the days of the week with a couple of clicks of the mouse!

Similarly, the pivot table and corresponding column chart in Figure 3.36 indicate the average number of arrivals per half-hour period for each interval in the day. To obtain this output, we drag the Arrival variable to the Data area, express it as an average, drag the TimeInterval variable to the Row area, and drag the Day variable to the Page area. You can check that the pattern shown here for Friday is a bit different than for the other days—it has a significant bulge during the afternoon rush period.

Excel Tip *If you try to create this pivot table on your own, you'll no doubt wonder how we got the time intervals in column A in the correct chronological order. The trick is to create a* **custom sort list**. *To do so, use the Tools/Options menu item, and select the Custom Lists tab. Then type a list of items in the List Entries box in the order you want them, and click on the Add button. To sort in this list order in the pivot table, place the cursor on any item in column A, select the Data/Sort menu item, click on Options, and select the new list from the dropdown list. This custom list will then be available in this or any other workbook you develop.*

The manager of R&P is ultimately interested in whether the "right" number of checkout stations are available throughout the day. Figures 3.37 and 3.38 (page 110) provide some evidence. The first of these is a scatterplot of Checkers versus TotalCustomers. (We

FIGURE 3.34 Time Series Plot of Arrivals and Departures Variables

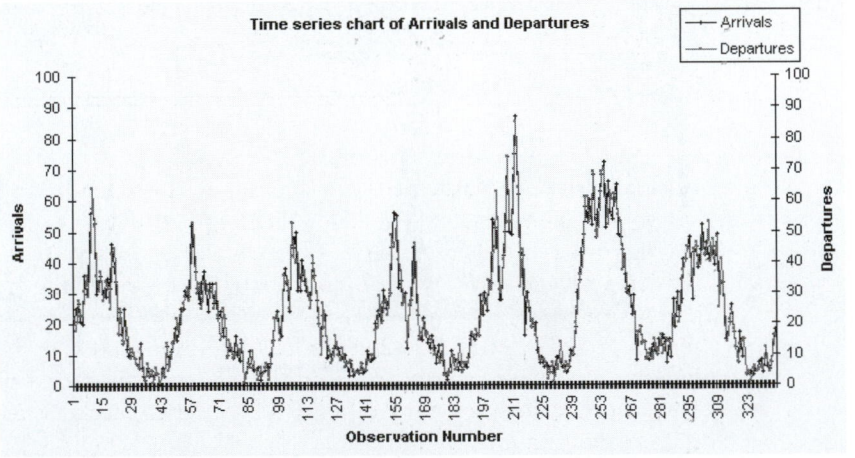

FIGURE 3.35 **Average InitialWaiting by Hour of Day**

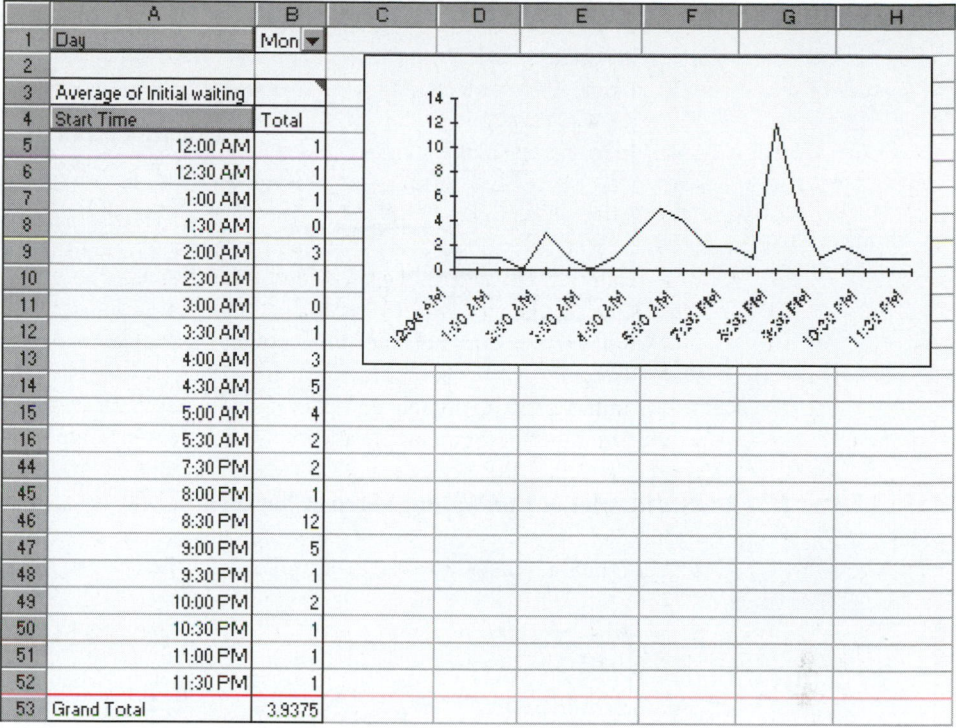

	A	B	C	D	E	F	G	H
1	Day	Mon ▼						
2								
3	Average of Initial waiting							
4	Start Time	Total						
5	12:00 AM	1						
6	12:30 AM	1						
7	1:00 AM	1						
8	1:30 AM	0						
9	2:00 AM	3						
10	2:30 AM	1						
11	3:00 AM	0						
12	3:30 AM	1						
13	4:00 AM	3						
14	4:30 AM	5						
15	5:00 AM	4						
16	5:30 AM	2						
44	7:30 PM	2						
45	8:00 PM	1						
46	8:30 PM	12						
47	9:00 PM	5						
48	9:30 PM	1						
49	10:00 PM	2						
50	10:30 PM	1						
51	11:00 PM	1						
52	11:30 PM	1						
53	Grand Total	3.9375						

FIGURE 3.36 **Average Arrivals by TimeInterval of Day**

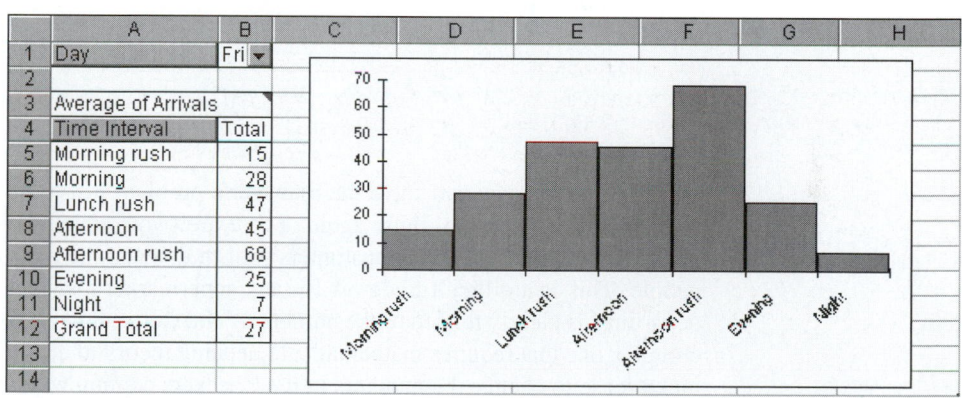

	A	B	C	D	E	F	G	H
1	Day	Fri ▼						
2								
3	Average of Arrivals							
4	Time Interval	Total						
5	Morning rush	15						
6	Morning	28						
7	Lunch rush	47						
8	Afternoon	45						
9	Afternoon rush	68						
10	Evening	25						
11	Night	7						
12	Grand Total	27						
13								
14								

calculated the TotalCustomers variable as the sum of the InitialWaiting and the Arrivals variables to measure the total amount of work presented to the checkout stations in any half-hour period.) There is an obvious positive relationship between these two variables. Evidently, management is reacting as it should—it is opening more checkout stations when there is more traffic. The second scatterplot shows EndWaiting versus Checkers. There is again a definite upward trend. Periods when more checkout stations are open tend to be associated with periods where more customers still remain in the checkout process. Presumably, management is reacting with more open checkout stations in busy periods, but it is not reacting strongly enough.

FIGURE 3.37 Scatterplot of Checkers versus TotalCustomers

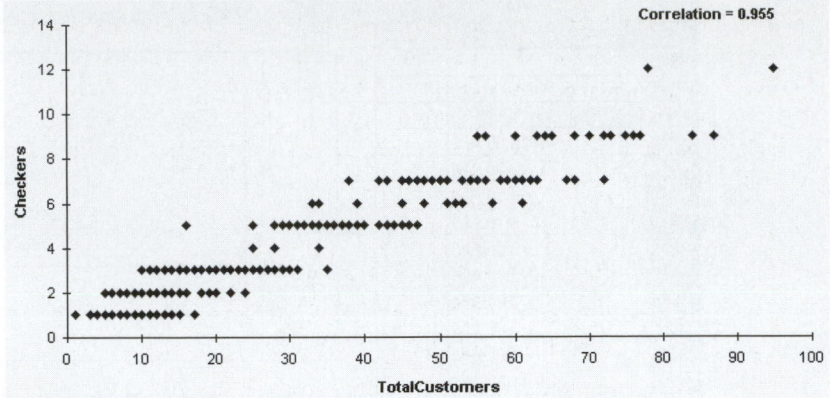

FIGURE 3.38 Scatterplot of EndWaiting versus Checkers

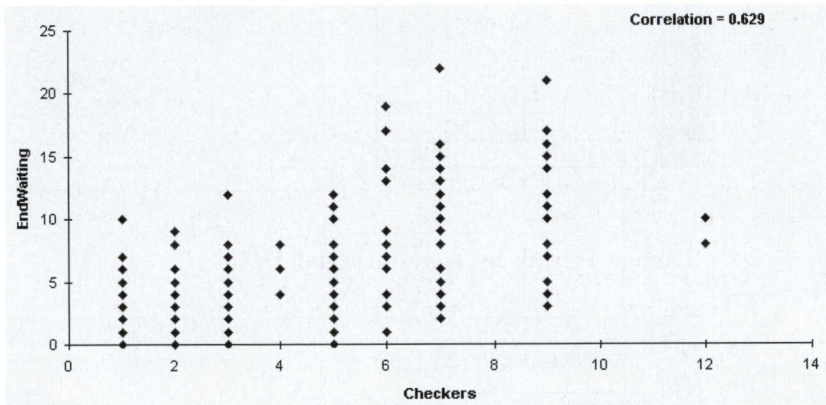

If you think you can solve the manager's problem just by fiddling with the numbers in the Checkers column, think again. There are two problems. First, there is a trade-off between the "cost" of having customers wait in line and the cost of paying extra checkout people. This is a difficult trade-off for any supermarket manager. Second, the number of departures is clearly related to the number of checkout stations open. (The relationship is a complex one that requires mathematical queueing theory to quantify.) Therefore, it doesn't make sense to change the numbers in the Checkers column without changing the numbers in the Departures (and hence the InitialWaiting and EndWaiting) columns in an appropriate way. This is *not* an easy problem! ■

EXAMPLE 3.11

The HyTex Company is a direct marketer of stereophonic equipment, personal computers, and other electronic products. HyTex advertises entirely by mailing catalogs to its customers, and all of its orders are taken over the telephone. The company spends a great deal of money on its catalog mailings, and it wants to be sure that this is paying off in sales. Therefore, it has collected data on 1000 customers at the end of the current year. (See the file CATALOGS.XLS.) For each customer it has data on the following variables:

- Age: coded as 1 for 30 or younger, 2 for 31 to 55, 3 for 56 or older
- Gender: coded as 1 for males, 2 for females
- OwnHome: coded as 1 if customer owns a home, 2 otherwise
- Married: coded as 1 if customer is currently married, 2 otherwise
- Close: coded as 1 if customer lives reasonably close to a shopping area that sells similar merchandise, 2 otherwise
- Salary: combined annual salary of customer and spouse (if any)
- Children: number of children living with customer
- History: coded as "NA" if customer had no dealings with the company before this year, 1 if customer was a low-spending customer last year, 2 if medium-spending, 3 if high-spending
- Catalogs: Number of catalogs sent to the customer this year
- AmountSpent: Total amount of purchases made by the customer this year

HyTex wants to analyze these data carefully to understand its customers better. Also, it wants to see whether it is sending the catalogs to the right customers. Currently, each customer receives either 6, 12, 18, or 24 catalogs through the mail each year. However, who receives how many has not really been thought out carefully. Is the current distribution of catalogs effective? Is there room for improvement?

Solution

This is the most difficult example we've faced so far, but it pales in comparison to the difficulty *real* direct marketing companies face. They have all sorts of data on millions of customers. How can they make sense of all these data? Using our relatively small data set, we will get the ball rolling. We'll let you discover additional patterns in the data that might exist. Furthermore, we'll only see an indication of whether the current distribution of catalog mailings is effective. It is well beyond our abilities at this point to find a more effective catalog distribution policy.

HyTex is obviously interested in the AmountSpent variable. Therefore, it makes sense to create scatterplots of AmountSpent versus selected "explanatory" variables. We do this in Figures 3.39 through 3.41 (page 112). Figure 3.39 shows AmountSpent versus Salary. It is clear that customers with higher salaries tend to spend more, although the variability in amounts spent increases significantly as salary increases. Figure 3.40 shows that there is some tendency toward higher spending among customers who receive more catalogs. But do the catalogs *cause* more spending, or are more catalogs sent to customers who would tend to spend more anyway? There is no way to answer this question with the data the company has collected. Figure 3.41 shows the interesting tendency of customers with more children to spend less. Perhaps customers with more children are already spending so much on $100-plus athletic shoes that they have little left to spend on electronic equipment!

FIGURE 3.39 Scatterplot of AmountSpent versus Salary

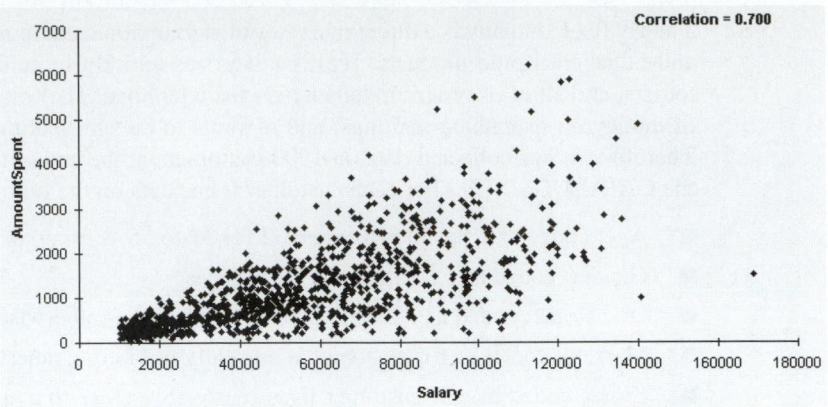

FIGURE 3.40 Scatterplot of AmountSpent versus Catalogs

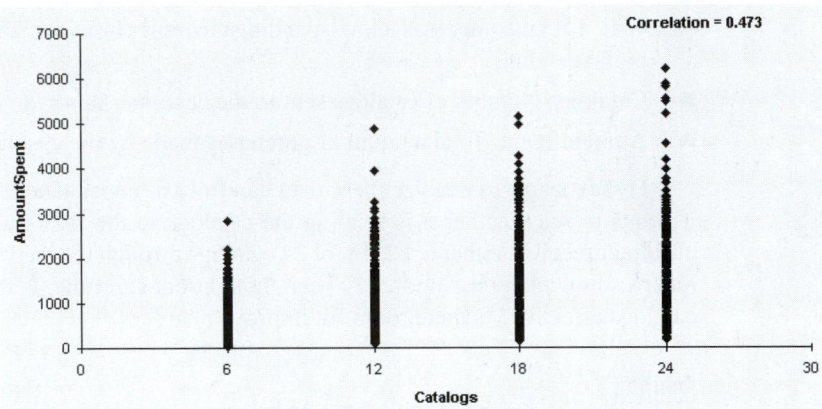

FIGURE 3.41 Scatterplot of AmountSpent versus Children

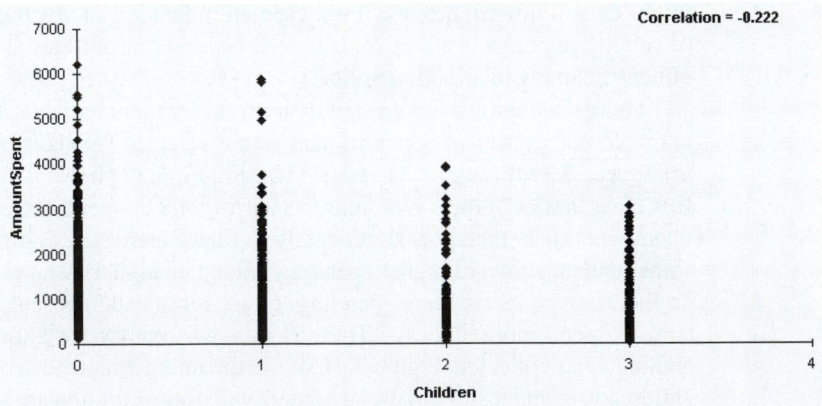

Pivot tables and accompanying charts are very useful in this type of situation. We show several. First, Figures 3.42 and 3.43 can be used to better understand the demographics of the customers. Each row of Figure 3.42 shows the percentages of an age group who own homes. By changing the page variables Gender and Married in cells B1 and B2, we can see how these percentages change for married women, unmarried men, and so on. You can check that these percentages remain relatively stable for the various groups. Specifically, a small percentage of the younger people own their own home, regardless of marital status or gender.

FIGURE 3.42 **Percent Home Owners versus Age, Married, and Gender**

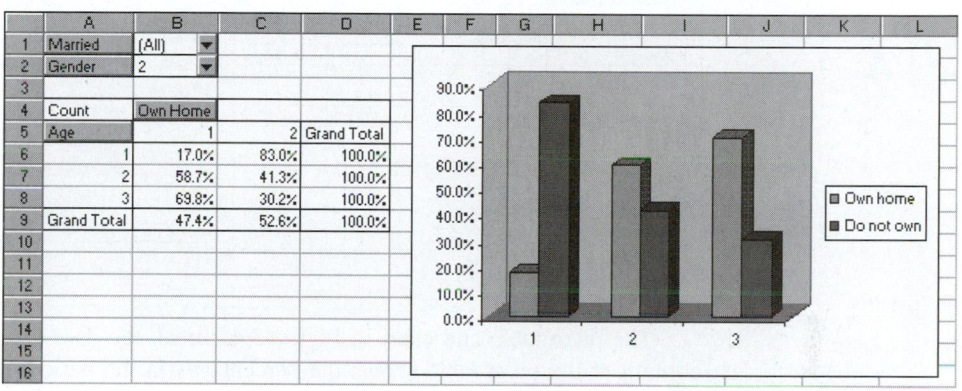

Figure 3.43 is similar. It shows the percentages of each age group who are married, for any combination of the Gender and OwnHome variables. Here the percentages change considerably for different settings of the page variables. For example, you can check that the married/unmarried split is quite different for women who don't own a home than for the male home owners shown in the figure. (By the way, we can just about create Figure 3.43 from Figure 3.42 by dragging the Married variable down to the column area and the OwnHome variable up to the page area—right on the sheet with the pivot table. Try it! The only problem is that the legend in the chart doesn't change.)

FIGURE 3.43 **Percent Married versus Age, OwnHome, and Gender**

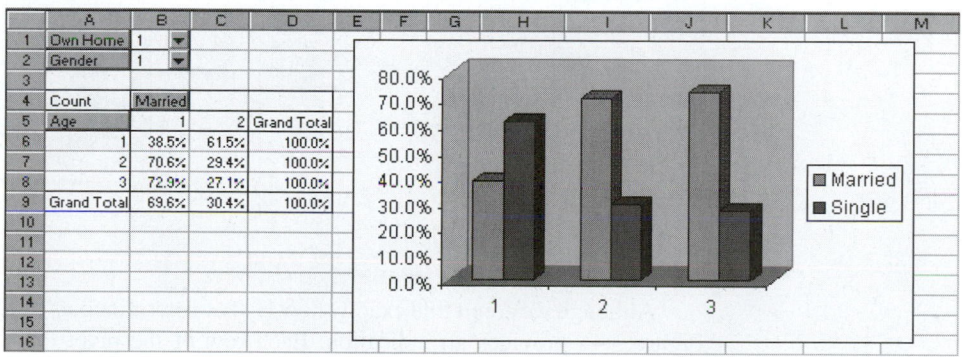

Figure 3.44 provides more demographic information. Now we show the average Salary broken down by Age and Gender, with page variables for OwnHome and Married. You can check that the *shape* of the resulting chart is practically the same for any combination of the page variables. However, the heights of the bars change appreciably. For example, the average salaries are considerably larger for the married home owners shown in the figure than for unmarried customers who are not home owners.

FIGURE 3.44 **Average Salary versus Age, Gender, Married, and OwnHome**

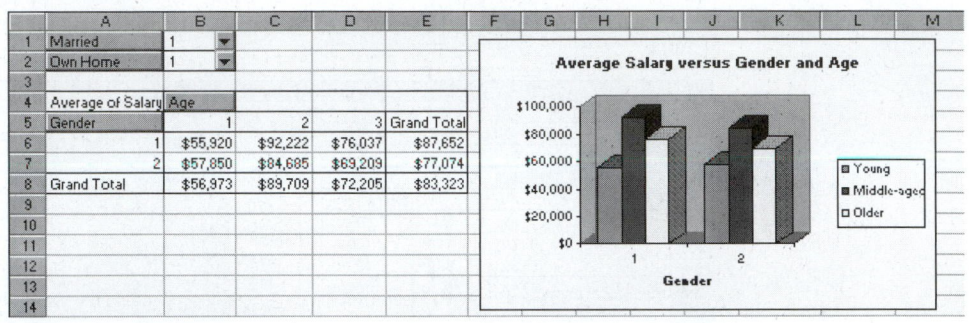

The pivot table and chart in Figure 3.45 break the data down in another way. Each column in the pivot table shows the percentages in the various History categories for a particular number of children. Each of these columns corresponds to one of the bars in the "stacked" bar chart. Also, we have used Close as a page variable. Two interesting points emerge. First, customers with more children tend to be more heavily represented in the low-spending History category (and less heavily represented in the high-spending category). Also, as you can check by changing the setting of the Close variable from 1 to 2, the percentage of high-spenders among customers who live far from electronics stores is much higher than for those who live close to such stores.

FIGURE 3.45 **Percentages in History Categories versus Children and Close**

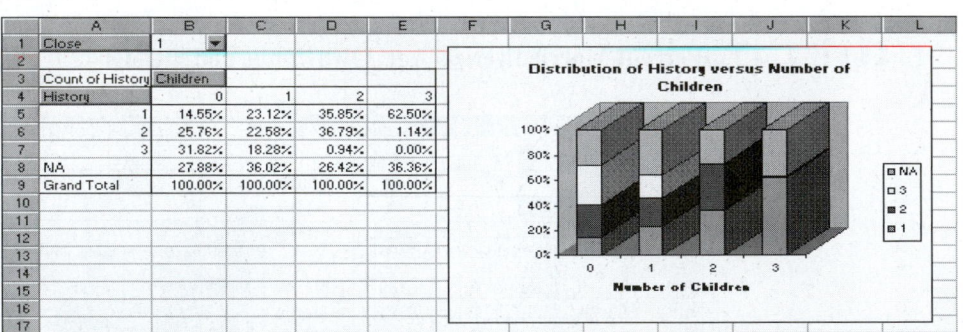

Although we aren't told exactly how HyTex determined its catalog mailing distribution, Figure 3.46 provides an indication. Each row of the pivot table shows the percentages of a particular History category that were sent 6, 12, 18, or 24 catalogs. The company's distribution policy is still somewhat unclear—and there is probably hope for improvement—but it *did* evidently send more catalogs to high-spending customers and fewer to low-spending customers.

FIGURE 3.46 **Catalog Distribution versus History**

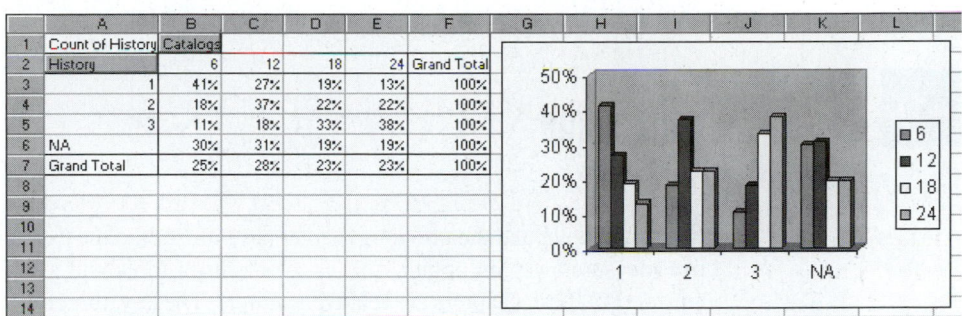

Count of History	Catalogs				
History	6	12	18	24	Grand Total
1	41%	27%	19%	13%	100%
2	18%	37%	22%	22%	100%
3	11%	18%	33%	38%	100%
NA	30%	31%	19%	19%	100%
Grand Total	25%	28%	23%	23%	100%

Finally, Figure 3.47 shows the average AmountSpent versus History and Catalogs, with a variety of demographic variables in the page area. There are so many possible combinations that it is difficult to discover all the existing patterns. However, one thing stands out loud and clear from the graph: the more catalogs customers receive, the more they tend to spend. In addition, if they were large spenders last year, they tend to be large spenders this year.

FIGURE 3.47 **Average AmountSpent versus History, Catalogs, and Demographic Variables**

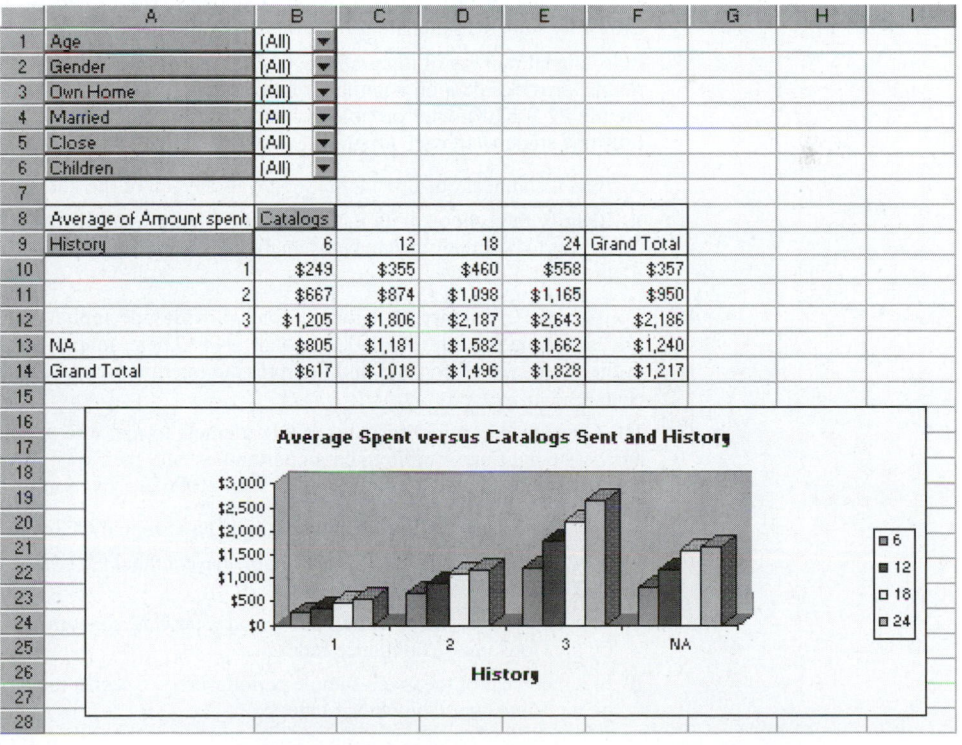

Age	(All)
Gender	(All)
Own Home	(All)
Married	(All)
Close	(All)
Children	(All)

Average of Amount spent	Catalogs				
History	6	12	18	24	Grand Total
1	$249	$355	$460	$558	$357
2	$667	$874	$1,098	$1,165	$950
3	$1,205	$1,806	$2,187	$2,643	$2,186
NA	$805	$1,181	$1,582	$1,662	$1,240
Grand Total	$617	$1,018	$1,496	$1,828	$1,217

In a pivot table with this many combinations, there will almost certainly be some combinations with no observations. For example, it turns out that there are no young married males who were low-spenders last year and received 18 catalogs. In this case you'll see #DIV/0! in the corresponding pivot table cell. (Excel tried to divide by 0 to obtain an average.) Worse yet, there are no young married male home owners who received 12 catalogs. If you try this combination, the whole "12" column of the pivot table will disappear—which will mess up the graph. Even Excel can't anticipate every possibility! ■

3.10

Conclusion

This chapter and the previous chapter have illustrated the tremendous variety of descriptive measures we can obtain with Excel's built-in tools and add-ins such as StatPro. The *concepts* in these chapters are relatively simple. The key, therefore, is to have simple-to-use tools available to produce tables, graphs, and numerical summary measures in a matter of minutes. This is now possible, not only with statistical software packages but with spreadsheet packages, particularly Excel. It allows us to concentrate on presenting the data in the most appropriate way, so that interesting information hidden in the data is brought to the surface.

PROBLEMS

Level A

44 The annual base salaries for 200 students graduating from a reputable MBA program this year (see the file P2_74.XLS) are of interest to those in the admissions office who are responsible for marketing the program to prospective students. What salary level is *most* indicative of those earned by students graduating from this MBA program this year?

45 In its annual ranking of top graduate business schools in the United States, *U.S. News & World Report* provides data on a number of attributes of 25 recognized graduate programs (refer to the file P2_8.XLS). One variable of interest is the annual out-of-state tuition paid by affected full-time students in each program.

    a Find the annual out-of-state tuition levels at each of the 25th, 50th, and 75th percentiles.

    b Identify the schools with the largest and smallest annual out-of-state tuitions. Does there appear to be a relationship between the program's overall ranking and its out-of-state tuition level?

46 Consider the Consumer Price Index, which provides the annual percentage change in consumer prices, for the period from 1914 through 1996. These annual percentage changes are given in the file P2_26.XLS. Find and interpret the interquartile range of these annual percentage changes.

47 The Consumer Confidence Index (CCI) attempts to measure people's feelings about general business conditions, employment opportunities. and their own income prospects. The annual average values of the CCI for the years 1967–1996 are given in the file P2_28.XLS.

    a Fifteen percent of all years in this sample have annual CCI values that exceed what value?

    b Forty percent of all years in this sample have annual CCI values that are less than or equal to what value?

    c In which year of the given sample period were U.S. consumers *most* confident, as measured by the Consumer Confidence Index?

    d In which year of the given sample period were U.S. consumers *least* confident, as measured by the Consumer Confidence Index?

48 Consider the proportion of Americans under the age of 18 living below the poverty level for each of the years 1959 through 1996. The data are in the file P2_29.XLS.

    a In which years of the sample has the poverty rate for American children exceeded the rate that defines the third quartile of these data?

    b In which years of the sample has the poverty rate for American children fallen below the rate that defines the first quartile of these data?

    c What is the typical poverty rate for American children during the period from 1959 through 1996?

49 The annual averages of the discount rate, federal funds rate, and the prime rate for the years 1977–1996 are given in the file P2_30.XLS. For each of these three key interest rates, determine the following:

    a Thirty percent of all years in the sample period have annual average rates that exceed what value?

    b Twenty-five percent of all years in the sample period have annual average rates that are less than or equal to what value?

    c What is the most typical annual average rate over the given sample period?

50 Given data in the file P2_13.XLS from a recent survey of chief executive officers from 350 of the nation's biggest businesses, respond to the following questions.

    a Find the annual salary below which 75% of all given CEO salaries fall.

    b Find the annual bonus above which 55% of all given CEO bonuses fall.

    c Determine the range of the middle 50% of all given total annual compensation figures (i.e., of the amounts found in column *Sum97*).

51 The file P2_44.XLS contains the number of classroom teachers and the average salary of classroom teachers for each of the 50 states and the District of Columbia in 1996. Which of the states paid their teachers average salaries that exceeded approximately 90% of all average salaries in 1996? Which of the states paid their teachers average salaries that exceeded only about 10% of all average salaries in 1996?

52 The annual base salaries for 200 students graduating from a reputable MBA program this year are given in the file P2_74.XLS.

    a Is it appropriate to apply the rules of thumb in this case? Explain.

    b If it is appropriate to apply the rules of thumb here, between what two numbers can we be about 68% sure that the salary of any one of these 200 students will fall?

53 Refer to the data given in the file P2_11.XLS. Consider the average time (in minutes) it takes a citizen of each metropolitan area to travel to work and back home each day.

    a Find a reliable measure of the dispersion of these average commute times around the overall sample mean.

    b Between what two numbers can we be approximately 99.7% sure that any one of these average travel times will fall?

54 Is there a strong relationship between a chief executive officer's annual compensation and her or his organization's recent profitability? Explore this question by generating correlations for the survey data in the file P2_13.XLS. In particular, compute and interpret correlation measures for the change in the company's net income from 1996 to 1997 (see *Comp_NetInc96* column) and the CEO's 1997 base salary, as well as for the change in the company's net income from 1996 to 1997 and the CEO's 1997 bonus. Summarize your findings here.

55 Construct boxplots to compare recent job growth rates with forecasted job growth rates for selected towns in the United States. These growth rates are all provided in the file P3_55.XLS. Do you detect the presence of any outliers in either of these two distributions? Also, compute a correlation measure for these two sets of job growth rates and interpret it.

56 The percentage of private-industry jobs that are managerial has steadily declined in recent years as companies have found middle management a ripe area for cutting costs. How have women and various minority groups fared in gaining management positions during this period of corporate downsizing of the management ranks? Relevant data are given in the file P2_75.XLS. Generate boxplots using these data to make general comparisons across the various groups included in the set.

57 The U.S. Bureau of Labor Statistics provides data on the year-to-year percentage changes in the wages and salaries of workers in private industries, including both "white-collar" and "blue-collar" occupations. Here we consider these data for the years 1980–1996. The percentage changes of interest are in the file P2_56.XLS. Develop side-by-side boxplots to summarize these distributions of annual percentage changes. In particular, state and interpret the interquartile range for each of three given distributions.

58 Explore the given distribution of the numbers of beds in short-term general hospitals in selected U.S. metropolitan areas by producing a boxplot (refer to the data in the file P2_17.XLS). In particular, use your computer-generated boxplot to answer the following questions:

a Is it more likely for these metropolitan areas to have larger or smaller numbers of hospital beds?

b Is the mean or median the more accurate measure of central location in this case? Explain.

c Characterize the variation of these values around the center of the data.

d Do you detect the presence of any *extreme* outliers in this case?

59 The file P3_59.XLS contains the proportion of annual revenue spent on research and development (R&D) activities for each of 200 randomly selected high-technology firms. Characterize this distribution by computing numerical summary measures and constructing a boxplot diagram. In particular, comment on the typical proportion of revenue dollars spent on R&D by these firms and the variation about the typical proportion value.

60 Consider various characteristics of the U.S. civilian labor force provided in the file P3_60.XLS. In particular, examine the given unemployment rates taken across the United States.

a Characterize the distribution of total unemployment rates. What is the most typical value? How are the other total unemployment rates distributed about the typical rate?

b Compare the total unemployment rate distribution to those of the male unemployment rate and the female unemployment rate. How are these distributions similar? How are they different?

c Which is more strongly associated with the total unemployment rate in the United States—the male unemployment rate or the female unemployment rate?

61 The file P3_61.XLS contains the sale price of gasoline in each of the 50 states for the years 1987–1996.

a Compare these ten distributions of gasoline sale price data. Specifically, do you find the mean and standard deviation of these distributions to be changing over time? If so, how do you explain the trends?

b In which regions of the country have gasoline prices changed the most?

c In which regions of the country have gasoline prices remained relatively stable?

62 Examine life expectations (in years) at birth for various countries across the world. These data can be found in the file P3_62.XLS.

a Generate an estimate of the *typical* human's life span at birth using the 1997 data. What are the limitations of the method you have employed in estimating this world population parameter?

b Characterize the *variability* of the life spans at birth using the 1997 data. Is this distribution fairly symmetric or skewed? How do you know?

c How strongly are the 1997 life expectations associated with projections for births in 2000 and 2010? Explain why the degree of linear association between the 1997 data and each set of projections diminishes somewhat over time.

63 This problem focuses on the per capita circulation of daily newspapers in the United States during the period from 1991 to 1996. The file P3_63.XLS contains these data.

a Compare the yearly distributions of daily newspaper per capita circulation over the period.

b Note any clear trends, both nationally and regionally, in the average value of and variability of per capita newspaper circulation during the given six years.

64 Have the proportions of Americans receiving public aid changed in recent years? Explore this question through a careful examination of the data provided in the file P3_64.XLS. In particular, generate numerical summary measures to respond to each of the following.

a Report any observed changes in the overall mean or median rates during the given time period.

b Can you find evidence of regional changes in the proportions of Americans receiving public aid? If so, summarize your specific findings.

65 The file P3_65.XLS contains the measured weight (in ounces) of a particular brand of ready-to-eat breakfast cereal placed in each of 500 randomly selected boxes by one of five different filling machine operators. Quality assurance personnel at this company are interested in determining how well these five operators are performing their assigned task of *consistently* placing 15 ounces of cereal in each box.

a Employ descriptive graphs and summary measures to ascertain whether some or all of these operators are consistently missing the target weight of 15 ounces per box.

b If you were charged with selecting the "Outstanding Employee of the Month" from this set of filling machine operators, which operator would you select based on the given data? Defend your choice.

66 Electro produces voltage-regulating equipment in New York and ships the equipment to Chicago. The voltage held is measured in New York before each unit is shipped to Chicago. The voltage held by each unit is also measured when the unit arrives in Chicago. The file P3_66.XLS contains a sample of voltage measurements at each city. A voltage regulator is considered acceptable if it can hold a voltage of between 25 and 75 volts.

a Using boxplots and descriptive statistics, what can you learn about the voltage held by units before shipment and after shipment?

b What percentage of units are acceptable before and after shipping?

c Do you have any suggestions about how to improve the quality of Electro's regulators?

d Ten percent of all New York regulators have a voltage exceeding what value?

e Five percent of all New York regulators have a voltage less than or equal to what value?

67 The file P3_67.XLS contains the individual scores of students in two different accounting sections who took the same exam. Comment on the differences between exam scores in the two sections.

68 The file P3_68.XLS contains the monthly interest rates (from 1985 to 1995) on 3-month government T-bills. For example, in January 1985, 3-month T-bills yielded 7.76% annual interest. To succeed in investments, it is important to understand the characteristics of the monthly changes in T-bill rates.

a Construct a histogram of the monthly changes in interest rates. Try to choose categories so that you get an "interesting" histogram.

b Do the rules of thumb hold for changes in monthly interest rates?

c Based on the given data, there is a 5% chance that during a given month T-bill rates will increase by less than what value? (A negative number is allowed here.)

d Based on the given data, there is a 10% chance that during a given month T-bill rates will increase by at least what number?

e Based on the given data, estimate the chances that T-bill rates during a given month will increase by more than 0.5%.

Level B

69 Data on the numbers of insured commercial banks in the United States during the period 1990–1996 are given in the file P3_69.XLS.

a Compare these seven distributions of the numbers of U.S. commercial banks. Do you find the mean and standard deviation of these numbers to be changing over time? If so, how do you explain the trends?

b What trends do you notice in the numbers of commercial banks *by region*? For example, how do the numbers of commercial banks appear to be changing in the northeastern United States over the given period? Summarize your findings for each region of the country.

70 Educational attainment in the United States is the focus of this problem. Employ descriptive methods with the data provided in the file P3_70.XLS to characterize the educational achievements of Americans in the given year. Do your findings surprise you in some way?

71 U.S. home ownership rate data are given in the file P3_71.XLS.

    a Employ numerical summary measures to characterize the changes in home ownership rates across the country from 1984 to 1996.

    b Do the trends appear to be uniform across the United States or are they unique to certain regions of the country? Explain.

72 Community hospital average daily cost data for the years 1980–1995 are provided in the file P3_72.XLS. Do the yearly distributions of average cost figures tend to become more or less variable over the given time period? Justify your answer with descriptive graphs and/or relevant summary measures.

73 The median sales price of existing one-family homes in selected metropolitan areas is the variable of interest in this exercise. Using the data contained in the file P3_73.XLS, characterize the distribution of median sales prices of existing single-family homes in 1996. How is this distribution different from that for the median sales prices of such homes in 1992? Carefully summarize the essential differences here.

74 Are U.S. traffic fatalities related to the speed limit and/or road type? Consider the data found in the file P3_74.XLS.

    a Do the average number and/or variability in the number of traffic fatalities occurring on interstate highways tend to increase as the speed limit is raised above 55 miles per hour? Explain your answer.

    b Do the average number and/or variability in the number of traffic fatalities occurring on non-interstate roads tend to increase as the speed limit rises above 35 miles per hour? Explain your answer.

    c Do the average number and/or variability in the number of traffic fatalities occurring on a road with a posted speed limit of 55 miles per hour tend to change with the road type (i.e., interstate versus non-interstate highway)? Explain your answer.

    d Based on these data, which combination of speed limit and road type appears to be most lethal for U.S. drivers?

    e Based on these data, which combination of speed limit and road type appears to be safest for U.S. drivers?

75 Have greater or lesser proportions of Americans joined labor unions during the past decade? Respond to this question by applying descriptive summary measures and graphical tools to the data provided in the file P3_75.XLS. Interpret your computer-generated output. What conclusions can you draw from an analysis of these data?

76 Consider the percent of the U.S. population without health insurance coverage. The file P3_76.XLS contains such percentages by state for both 1994 and 1995.

    a Describe the distribution of state percentages of Americans without health insurance coverage in 1995. Be sure to employ both measures of central location and dispersion in developing your characerization of this sample.

    b Compare the 1995 distribution with the corresponding set of percentages taken in 1994. How are these two sets of figures similar? In what ways are they different?

    c Compute a correlation measure for the two given sets of percentages. What does the correlation coefficient tell you in this case?

    d Based on your answers in parts **b** and **c** above, what would you expect to find upon analyzing similar data for 1996?

77 Given data in the file P2_13.XLS from a recent survey of 350 chief executive officers of the nation's biggest businesses, apply your knowledge of numerical summary measures to determine whether the typical levels and variances of the 1997 annual salaries and bonuses earned by CEOs depend in part on the *types* of companies in which they serve.

78 Consider survey data collected from 1000 randomly selected Internet users, given in the file P2_43.XLS.

    a Use these data to formulate a profile of the typical *female* Internet user. Consider such attributes as age, education level, marital status, annual income, and family size in formulating your profile.

b Use these data to formulate a profile of the typical *married* Internet user. Consider such attributes as gender, age, education level, annual income, and family size in formulating your profile.

c Use these data to formulate a profile of the typical *high-income* (say, with an annual income in excess of $80,000) Internet user. Consider such attributes as gender, age, education level, marital status, and family size in formulating your profile.

79 As a part of an economic development study conducted by the local government, 500 households in a middle-class neighborhood were recently surveyed. In particular, for each of the randomly selected households, the survey requested information on the following variables: family size, approximate location of the household within the neighborhood, an indication of whether those surveyed owned or rented their home, gross annual income of the first household wage earner, gross annual income of the second household wage earner (if applicable), monthly home mortgage or rent payment, average monthly expenditure on utilities, and the total indebtedness (excluding the value of a home mortgage) of the household. These data are provided in the file P2_6.XLS. Compute and interpret relevant numerical summary measures to complete the following.

a Use these data to formulate a profile of the typical household residing within each of the four neighborhood locations. Consider such attributes as family size, home ownership status, gross annual income(s) of household wage earner(s), monthly home mortgage or rent payment, average monthly expenditure on utilities, and the total indebtedness (excluding the value of a home mortgage) of the household in formulating your profile.

b Do differences arise in the mean or median income levels of those wage earners from households located in different quadrants of this neighborhood? If so, summarize these differences.

c Do differences arise in the mean or median monthly home mortgage or rent payment paid by households located in different quadrants of this neighborhood? If so, summarize these differences.

d Do differences arise in the mean or median debt levels of households located in different quadrants of this neighborhood? If so, summarize these differences.

80 A human resources manager at Beta Technologies, Inc., is interested in developing a profile of the highest-paid full-time Beta employees based on the given representative sample of 52 of the company's full-time workers in the file P2_1.XLS. In particular, she is interested in determining the typical age, number of years of relevant full-time work experience prior to coming to Beta, number of years of full-time work experience at Beta, and number of years of post-secondary education for those employees in the *highest quartile* with respect to annual salary. Employ appropriate descriptive methods to help the human resources manager develop this desired profile.

81 Using cost-of-living data from the *ACCRA Cost of Living Index* (see the file P2_19.XLS), examine the relationship between the geographical *location* of an urban area within the United States (e.g., northeast, southeast, midwest, northwest, or southwest) and its *composite* cost-of-living index. In other words, is the overall cost of living higher or lower and more or less variable for urban areas in particular geographical regions of the country? You will need to assign the given urban areas systematically to one of several geographical regions before you can apply appropriate summary measures in responding to this question. Summarize your findings in detail.

82 The file P3_82.XLS contains monthly interest rates on bonds that pay money a year after the day they are bought. It is often suggested that interest rates are more volatile (tend to change more) when interest rates are high. Do these data support this statement?

83 The file P3_83.XLS contains data on 1000 of Marvak's best customers. Marvak is a direct-marketing firm that sells electronic items. It has collected these data to learn more about its customers. The variables are self-explanatory, although a few cell notes have been added in row 3. Your boss at Marvak would like you, the Excel guru, to do the following.

a She wants a breakdown of gender by age group. That is, she wants a pivot table that lists, for each age group, the percentages of females and males. She wants to be able to access this information easily (with a couple of clicks) for any subcategories of Home and Married.

b She guesses that customers with larger salaries tend to spend more at Marvak. To check this, she wants you to append a new variable called SalaryCat to the data set that contains the four category labels in column J. A customer with salary below $30,000 is categorized as "LowSal"; between $30,000 and $70,000 as "MedSal"; between $70,000 and $120,000 as "HighSal"; and over $120,000 as "HugeSal." (By the way, no incomes are exactly equal to $30,000, $70,000, or $120,000.) You can use the lookup table in columns I and J to form this new *SalaryCat* column. Then create a pivot table that shows the average amount spent for each of the four salary categories, and comment briefly (on that sheet) whether your boss's conjecture appears to be correct.

84 The file P3_84.TXT contains the largest 100 public companies in the world, as listed in *The Wall Street Journal* on September 24, 1992, ranked by market value. The rankings are shown for 1992, as well as for 1991. The following variables are included:

- Company: name of company
- Location: 1 for U.S., 2 for Japan/Australia, 3 for Europe
- Bank: 1 if bank (or savings institution), 0 otherwise
- Rank92: rank according to market value in 1992
- Rank91: rank according to market value in 1991
- MarketVal: market value in millions of U.S. dollars (12/31/91 exchange rates used)
- Sales91: sales in 1991 in millions of U.S. dollars
- PctChSales: percent change in sales from 1990, based on home currency
- Profit91: profit in 1991 in millions of U.S. dollars
- PctChProfit: percent change in profit from 1990, based on home currency

a This file is in ASCII (text) form, with blanks between the items and names (nonnumerical data) in double quotes. Open this file in Excel. (There is no "import" command; you simply open the file.) Excel will recognize that this is a text file, and a "wizard" will lead you through the steps to open it properly into Excel format. The key is that it is "delimited" with blanks. Once the file is opened, look at it to make sure everything is lined up correctly. Then use the Save As command to save the file as an .XLS file. (Once you do this, the .TXT version is no longer needed.)

b Note that percentage changes from 1990 to 1991 are given for sales and profits. Use formulas to create variables Sales90 and Profit90, the sales and profits for 1990. [*Hint*: For example, the formula for Sales90 is given by 100*Sales91/(100+PctChSales).]

c Create a scattergram of Profit91 (vertical axis) versus Profit90. Most of the points lie close to a line. For this problem, consider an outlier to be any point that is obviously not very close to this line. Which companies are the worst outliers in this sense? In business terms, what makes these companies outliers?

d The companies designated "banks" are clearly different from the other companies in that their sales figures are much larger. For this question, consider only the subset of *nonbanks*. Define an outlier with respect to any variable as an observation that is at least 1.5 IQRs above the third quartile or below the first quartile. (This is the boxplot definition of outliers.) How many outliers are there with respect to Sales91?

e Notice that there is a variable that codes the location of the company: 1 for U.S., 2 for Japan/Australia, 3 for Europe. With regard to Profit91, are there any obvious differences among these? (Use summary statistics and/or charts.)

85 The file P3_85.XLS contains 1993 compensation data on the top 200 CEOs. The data include the CEO's name, company, total compensation, and the company's 5-year total return to shareholders (expressed as an annual rate). The data are sorted in descending order according to the 5-year return. (Source: *Fortune*, July 25, 1994)

a How large must a total compensation be to qualify as an outlier on the high side according to the boxplot definition of outliers? In column A of the spreadsheet, highlight the names of all CEOs whose total compensations are outliers. (You can highlight them by making them boldface, italicizing them, or painting them a different color, for example.)

b Form a scatterplot of total compensation versus 5-year return. (Put total compensation on the horizontal axis.) Do the CEOs in this database appear to be worth their pay?

86 The file P3_86.WK1 contains data on over 1000 professional football players as of the beginning of the 1990 season. (In case you are not a pro football fan, there are two conferences in the NFL—the NFC and the AFC. The variable NFC is 1 for players in the NFC and 0 for players in the AFC.) The data for each player include years of professional football before

1990 season, professional games played before 1990 season, whether the player is on an NFC or AFC team, team the player belongs to at beginning of 1990 season, whether the player plays offense or defense, position played, and beginning 1990 salary (in $1000s).

a Open this file into Excel. (You'll notice that when you use the Open command, a box at the bottom of the screen allows you to specify a .WK1 format. This feature allows you to "import" a file in Lotus 1-2-3 format into Excel, just by opening the file.) Then use the File/Save As menu item to save the file as an .XLS file. For the remaining parts, use pivot tables or any other methods you think appropriate.

b Create histograms of the salaries for (i) all of the players, (ii) all of the NFC players, and (iii) all of the AFC players. Create tables of summary statistics for these three groups.

c Proceed as in part **b**, but now make the distinction between offensive and defensive players (not which conference they are in).

d Repeat parts **b** and **c**, this time eliminating all quarterbacks (since they make the highest salaries in general). Do your summary statistics and charts change very much?

e Create scattergrams of Salary versus Games and Salary versus Years. Are there any obvious relationships?

f Think of other ways to summarize the data, assuming that your primary objective is to understand the salary structure in the NFL as of 1990.

87 The file P3_87.XLS contains questionnaire data from a random sample of 200 TV viewers. (The variable name headings actually begin in row 25.) The questionnaire was taken by the local station XYZ, an affiliate of one of the three main networks. Like the local affiliates of the other two networks, XYZ's local dinnertime news program follows the national news program. The purpose of the questionnaire was to discover characteristics of the viewing public, presumably with the intention of doing something to increase XYZ's ratings. Your assignment is very open-ended—purposely so. Summarize any aspects of the data that you think are relevant—find means, proportions, scatterplots, pivot tables, whatever—to help XYZ management understand these viewers. (All 200 people watch both national and local news.) ■

The Dow Jones Industrial Average (DJIA) is a composite index of 30 of the largest "blue-chip" companies in the United States. It is probably the most quoted index from Wall Street, partly because it is old enough that many generations of investors have become accustomed to quoting it, and partly because the U.S. stock market is the world's largest. Besides longevity, two other factors play a role in the Dow's widespread popularity: It is understandable to most people, and it reliably indicates the market's basic trend. As this book was going to press, the Dow had just passed the 9300 mark for the first time, one of many milestones it had reached in the past few years in the booming economy.[3] (Perhaps it has reached the magical 10,000 mark as you are now reading.)

Unlike most other market indexes that are weighted indexes (usually by market capitalization, that is, price times shares outstanding), the DJIA is an unweighted index. It was originally an average, namely, the sum of the stock prices divided by the number of stocks. In fact, the very first average price of industrial stocks, on May 26, 1896, was 40.94. However, because of stock splits, the DJIA is now calculated somewhat differently to preserve historical continuity. To calculate the DJIA, the prices of the 30 stocks in the index are summed, and this sum is divided by the "divisor," which is currently slightly greater than 0.33. The effect is to multiply the sum by approximately 3. Therefore, if the combined price of the 30 stocks rises by $10, say, the DJIA rises by about 30 points.

The Dow originally consisted of 12 stocks in 1896 and increased to 20 in 1916. The 30-stock average made its debut in 1928, and the number has remained constant ever since. However, the 30 stocks comprising the Dow do not remain the same. The most recent change occurred in March 1997, when Woolworth Corp., Westinghouse Electric, Texaco Inc., and Bethlehem Steel were replaced by Hewlett-Packard Co., Johnson & Johnson, Traveler's Group Inc., and Wal-Mart Stores Inc. The editors of *The Wall Street Journal* select the components of the DJIA. They take a broad view of what "industrial" means. In essence, it is almost any company that isn't in the transportation business and isn't a utility. In choosing a new company for the DJIA, they look among substantial industrial companies with a history of successful growth and wide interest among investors. The components of the DJIA are not changed often. It isn't a "hot stock" index, and the *Journal* editors believe that stability of composition enhances the trust that many people have in the averages. The most frequent reason for changing a stock is that something is happening to one of the components (for example, a company is being acquired).

Some people make predictions about where the stock market is headed based in part on their interpretation of DJIA movements, as well as movements of the transportation and utilities averages. But indexes don't predict anything. They are doing their job if they accurately reflect where the market has been. However, there is a great deal of common ground between the economy and the market. Stock investors try to anticipate future profits, and corporate profits are a prime fuel for the U.S. economy. So, not surprisingly, the market frequently rises ahead of economic expansion and falls prior to economic slowdown or contraction. The trouble is that this relationship isn't perfectly correlated; there are other factors that move markets and still others that affect the economy. Moreover, many people make the mistake of calibrating their economic expectations to the DJIA's movements. The result, as Nobel-laureate economist Paul A. Samuelson put it, "The market has predicted nine of the last five recessions."

---

[3] By a strange coincidence, we wrote this on the day when the Dow peaked. Like other investors, we had no idea it was about to descend from its lofty heights.

As indicated above, the DJIA is not the only market index. There are two other Dow Jones indexes, one for transportation (DJTA), consisting of 20 stocks, and one for utilities (DJUA), consisting of 15 stocks. An elaborate analytical system dubbed Dow Theory holds that the DJTA must "confirm" the movement of the industrial average for a market trend to have staying power. If the industrials reach a new high, the transportations would need to reach a new high to "confirm" the broad trend. The trend reverses when both averages experience sharp downturns at around the same time. If they diverge—for example, if the industrial average keeps climbing while the transportations decline—watch out! The underlying fundamentals of the Dow Theory hold that the industrials make and the transportations take. If the transportations aren't taking what the industrials are making, it portends economic weakness and market problems. Similarly, according to analysts who study the averages, a rise in utility stock prices indicates that investors anticipate falling interest rates, because utilities are big borrowers and their profits are enhanced by lower interest costs. But the utility average tends to decline when investors expect rising interest rates. Because of this interest-rate sensitivity, the utility average is regarded by some as a leading indicator for the stock market as a whole.

This information and other interesting facts about the Dow Jones averages are available at the www.dowjones.com web site. Other web sites have data on the averages themselves. We used one such site (www.quotecentral.com/iwatch.asp) to download a year's worth of daily data (from mid-July 1997 to mid-July 1998) for the DJIA, DJTA, and DJUA, as well as for the stocks comprising these averages. The data are in the files DJIA.XLS, DJTA.XLS, and DJUA.XLS. Each file contains a sheet for the Dow Jones average and a sheet for each stock in the average. (The sheet names for the latter are the ticker symbols for the stocks, such as HWP for Hewlett-Packard Co.)

Use the tools you've learned in the past two chapters to analyze these data sets (or more recent Dow Jones data sets if you can download them). Here are some suggested directions for analysis.

1   The return for any period is the percentage change in the price over that period. That is, the return is

$$\frac{p_{end} - p_{beg}}{p_{beg}} \times 100$$

where p_{end} is the ending price and p_{beg} is the beginning price. (The return also includes dividends, but you can ignore these here.) Are the daily returns for the 30 stocks in the DJIA highly correlated with each other? Are the daily returns correlated with the DJIA itself? What about weekly returns? What about monthly returns? Answer the same questions for the DJTA; for the DJUA.

2   How would you evaluate portfolios of any of these stocks over the 1-year period? How much better (or worse) are some portfolios?

3   As stated earlier, some analysts believe that the DJUA is a leading indicator of the market. Do the data bear this out, assuming we identify the DJIA as "the market"? One way to answer this is with "cross-correlations," such as the correlation between the DJIA today and the DJUA a week ago. Alternatively, we could compare a time series graph of the DJIA with a "shifted" version of the DJUA.

4   Similarly, is there any relationship between the DJIA and the DJTA?

5   Obviously, some very prominent companies are missing from these indexes. One in particular is Microsoft. Its daily data over the same period are listed in the file MICROSOFT.XLS. How do daily (or weekly or monthly) Microsoft returns correlate with returns from the companies in the DJIA (or with the DJIA itself)?

3.2 Other Market Indexes

Following up on Case Study 3.1, there are many market indexes other than the Dow Jones averages. These include broad U.S. indexes such as the Nasdaq Composite Index (mainly technology stocks), the NYSE Composite Index (an index of many stocks on the New York Stock Exchange), the S&P 500 index (an index of 500 of the largest U.S. companies), and others. There are also U.S. indexes for particular industries, such as the AMEX Biotechnology Index, and foreign indexes, such as the AMEX Japan Index. Daily data (from the same source as in the previous case) for several of these indexes are listed in the files US_MARKET_INDEXES.XLS, INDUSTRIAL_INDEXES.XLS, and FOREIGN_INDEXES.XLS. Formulate and answer any interesting questions relating to these data and the Dow Jones data. In particular, do all of these indexes tend to move together, or do they tend to move in opposite directions?

4

Probability and Probability Distributions

Successful Applications

Several years ago McDonald's ran a campaign in which it gave game cards to its customers. These game cards made it possible for customers to win hamburgers, french fries, soft drinks, and other fast-food items, as well as cash prizes. Each card had 10 covered spots that could be uncovered by rubbing them with a coin. Beneath three of these spots were "zaps." Beneath the other seven spots were names of prizes, two of which were identical. (Some cards had variations of this pattern, but we'll use this type of card for purposes of illustration.) For example, one card might have two pictures of a hamburger, one picture of a Coke, one of french fries, one of a milk shake, one of $5, one of $1000, and three zaps. For this card the customer could win a hamburger. To win on any card, the customer had to uncover the two matching spots (which showed the potential prize for that card) before uncovering a zap; any card with a zap uncovered was automatically void. Assuming that the two matches and the three zaps were arranged randomly on the cards, what is the probability of a customer winning?

We'll label the two matching spots M_1 and M_2, and the three zaps Z_1, Z_2, and Z_3. Then the probability of winning is the probability of uncovering M_1 *and* M_2 before uncovering Z_1, Z_2, *or* Z_3. In this case the relevant set of outcomes is the set of all orderings of M_1, M_2, Z_1, Z_2, and Z_3, shown in the order they are uncovered. As far as the outcome of the game is concerned, the other five spots on the card are irrelevant. Then an outcome such as M_2, M_1, Z_3, Z_1, Z_2 is a winner, whereas M_2, Z_2, Z_1, M_1, Z_3 is a loser. Actually, the first of these would be declared a winner as soon as M_1 were uncovered, and the second would be declared a loser as soon as Z_2 were uncovered. However, we show the whole sequence of M's and Z's so that we can count outcomes correctly. We then find the probability of winning by an equally-likely-probability argument. Specifically, we divide the number of outcomes that are winners by the total number of outcomes. It can be shown that the number of outcomes that are winners is 12, whereas the total number of outcomes is 120. Therefore, the probability of a winner is $12/120 = 0.1$.

This calculation was obviously important for McDonald's. It showed that on the average, 1 out of 10 cards would be winners. Actually, this provides only an upper bound on the fraction of cards where a prize was awarded. The fact is that many customers threw their cards away without playing the game, and even some of the winners neglected to claim their prizes. So, for example, McDonald's knew that if they made 50,000 cards where a milk shake was the winning prize, somewhat less than 5000 milk shakes would be given away. Knowing approximately what their expected "losses" would be from winning cards, McDonald's was able to design the game (how many cards of each type to print) so that the expected extra revenue (from customers attracted to the game) would cover the expected losses. ■

4.1

Introduction

A large part of the subject of statistics deals with uncertainty. Demands for products are uncertain, times between arrivals to a supermarket are uncertain, stock price returns are uncertain, changes in interest rates are uncertain, and so on. In these examples and many others, the uncertain quantity—demand, time between arrivals, stock price return, change in interest rate—is a numerical quantity. In the language of statistics and probability, such a numerical value is called a **random variable**. A random variable associates a numerical value with each possible random outcome.

Associated with each random variable is a **probability distribution** that lists all of the possible values of the random variable and their corresponding probabilities. A probability distribution provides very useful information. It not only tells us the possible values of the random variable, but also how likely they are. For example, it is useful to know that the possible demands for a product are, say, 100, 200, 300, and 400, but it is even more useful to know that the probabilities of these four values are 0.1, 0.2, 0.4, and 0.3. Now we know, for example, that there is a 70% chance that demand will be at least 300.

It is often useful to summarize the information from a probability distribution with several well-chosen numerical summary measures. These include the mean, variance, and standard deviation, and, for distributions of more than one random variable, the covariance and correlation. As their names imply, these summary measures are much like the summary measures in Chapter 3. However, they are not identical. The summary measures in this chapter are based on probability distributions, not an observed data set. We will use numerical examples to explain the difference between the two—and how they are related.

The purpose of this chapter is to explain the basic concepts and tools necessary to work with probability distributions and their summary measures. We will begin by briefly discussing the basic rules of probability, as these are needed in this chapter and in several later chapters. We will also introduce computer simulation, an extremely useful tool for illustrating important concepts in probability and statistics. Although an entire chapter, Chapter 16, will eventually be devoted to simulation models, the brief introduction given here will allow us to employ simulation for illustrative purposes right away.

We conclude this chapter with a discussion of weighted sums of random variables. These are particularly useful in investment analysis, where we want to analyze portfolios of stocks or other securities. In this case the weights are the relative amounts invested in the securities, and the weighted sum represents the portfolio return. Our goal is to investigate the probability distribution of a weighted sum, particularly its summary measures.

Probability Essentials

We begin with a brief discussion of probability. The concept of probability is one that we all encounter in everyday life. When a weather forecaster states that the chance of rain is 70%, she is making a probability statement. When we hear that the odds of the Chicago Bulls winning the NBA Championship are 2 to 1, this is also a probability statement. The *concept* of probability is quite intuitive. However, the *rules* of probability are not always as intuitive or easy to master. We will examine the most important of these rules in this section.

Mathematically, a probability is a number between 0 and 1 that measures the likelihood that some event will occur. An event with probability 0 cannot occur, whereas an event with probability 1 is certain to occur. An event with probability greater than 0 and less than 1 involves uncertainty, but the closer its probability is to 1, the more likely it is to occur. As the examples in the preceding paragraph illustrate, we often express probabilities as percentages or odds. However, these can easily be converted to probabilities on a 0–1 scale. If the chance of rain is 70%, then the probability of rain is 0.7. Similarly, if the odds of the Bulls winning are 2 to 1, then the probability of the Bulls winning is 2/3 (or 0.6667).

4.2.1 Rule of Complements

The simplest probability rule involves the **complement** of an event. If A is any event, then the complement of A, denoted by $\overline{A}$ (or in some books by A^c), is the event that A does *not* occur. For example, if A is the event that the Dow Jones Index will finish the year at or above the 9000 mark, then the complement of A is that the Dow will finish the year below 9000.

If the probability of A is $P(A)$, then the probability of its complement, $P(\overline{A})$, is

$$P(\overline{A}) = 1 - P(A) \qquad \textbf{(4.1)}$$

Equivalently, the probability of an event and the probability of its complement sum to 1. For example, if we believe that the probability of the Dow finishing at or above 9000 is 0.55, then the probability that it will finish the year below 9000 is $1 - 0.55 = 0.45$.

4.2.2 Addition Rule

We say that events are **mutually exclusive** if at most one of them can occur. That is, if one of them occurs, then none of the others can occur. For example, consider the following three events involving a company's annual revenue in 1999: (1) revenue is less than $1 million, (2) revenue is at least $1 million but less than $2 million, and (3) revenue is at least $2 million. Clearly, only one of these events can occur. Therefore, they are mutually exclusive. They are also **exhaustive**, which means that they exhaust all possibilities—one of these three events *must* occur.

Let A_1 through A_n be any n events. Then the **addition rule** of probability involves the probability that at least one of these events will occur. In general, this probability is quite complex, but it simplifies considerably when the events are mutually exclusive. In this case the probability that at least one of the events will occur is the sum of their individual probabilities:

$$P(\text{at least one of } A_1 \text{ through } A_n) = P(A_1) + P(A_2) + \cdots + P(A_n) \qquad \textbf{(Addition Rule)}$$

Of course, when the events are mutually exclusive, "at least one" is equivalent to "exactly one." In addition, if the events A_1 through A_n are exhaustive, then the probability above is 1. In this case we are certain that one of the events will occur.

In a typical application, the events A_1 through A_n are chosen to partition the set of all possible outcomes into a number of mutually exclusive events. For example, in terms of a company's annual revenue, define A_1 as "revenue is less than \$1 million," A_2 as "revenue is at least \$1 million but less than \$2 million," and A_3 as "revenue is at least \$2 million." As we discussed above, these three events are mutually exclusive and exhaustive. Therefore, their probabilities must sum to 1. Suppose these probabilities are $P(A_1) = 0.5$, $P(A_2) = 0.3$, and $P(A_3) = 0.2$. (Note that these probabilities *do* sum to 1.) Then the additive rule enables us to calculate other probabilities. For example, the event that revenue is at least \$1 million is the event that either A_2 or A_3 occurs. From the addition rule, its probability is

$$P(\text{revenue is at least \$1 million}) = P(A_2) + P(A_3) = 0.5$$

Similarly,

$$P(\text{revenue is less than \$2 million}) = P(A_1) + P(A_2) = 0.8$$

and

$$P(\text{revenue is less than \$1 million } or \text{ at least \$2 million}) = P(A_1) + P(A_3) = 0.7$$

4.2.3 Conditional Probability and the Multiplication Rule

Probabilities are always assessed relative to the information currently available. As new information becomes available, probabilities often change. For example, if you read that Michael Jordan pulled a hamstring muscle, your assessment of the probability that the Bulls will win the NBA Championship would obviously change. A formal way to revise probabilities on the basis of new information is to use **conditional probabilities**.

Let A and B be any events with probabilities $P(A)$ and $P(B)$. Typically, the probability $P(A)$ is assessed without knowledge of whether B does or does not occur. However, if we are *told* that B has occurred, then the probability of A might change. The new probability of A is called the conditional probability of A given B. It is denoted by $P(A|B)$. Note that there is still uncertainty involving the event to the left of the vertical bar in this notation; we do not know whether it will occur or not. However, there is no uncertainty involving the event to the right of the vertical bar; we *know* that it has occurred.

The following **conditional probability formula** enables us to calculate $P(A|B)$:

$$P(A|B) = \frac{P(A \text{ and } B)}{P(B)} \qquad \textbf{(Conditional Probability)}$$

The numerator in this formula is the probability that *both* A and B occur. This probability must be known to find $P(A|B)$. However, in some applications $P(A|B)$ and $P(B)$ are known. Then we can multiply both sides of the conditional probability formula by $P(B)$ to obtain the following **multiplication rule** for $P(A \text{ and } B)$:

$$P(A \text{ and } B) = P(A|B)P(B) \qquad \textbf{(Multiplication Rule)}$$

The conditional probability formula and the multiplication rule are both valid; in fact, they are equivalent. The one we use depends on which probabilities we know and which we want to calculate, as illustrated in the following example.

EXAMPLE 4.1

The Bendrix Company supplies contractors with materials for the construction of houses. The company currently has a contract with one of its customers to fill an order by the end of July. However, there is some uncertainty about whether this deadline can be met, due to uncertainty about whether Bendrix will receive the materials it needs from one of its suppliers by the middle of July. Right now it is July 1. How can the uncertainty in this situation be assessed?

Solution

Let A be the event that Bendrix meets its end-of-July deadline, and let B be the event that Bendrix receives the materials from its supplier by the middle of July. The probabilities Bendrix is best able to assess on July 1 are probably $P(B)$ and $P(A|B)$. At the beginning of July, Bendrix might estimate that the chances of getting the materials on time from its supplier are 2 out of 3, that is, $P(B) = 2/3$. Also, thinking ahead, Bendrix estimates that *if* it receives the required materials on time, the chances of meeting the end-of-July deadline are 3 out of 4. This is a conditional probability statement, namely, that $P(A|B) = 3/4$. Then we can use the multiplication rule to obtain

$$P(A \text{ and } B) = P(A|B)P(B) = (3/4)(2/3) = 0.5$$

That is, there is a 50–50 chance that Bendrix will get its materials on time *and* meet its end-of-July deadline.

There are several other probabilities of interest in this example. First, let $\overline{B}$ be the complement of B; it is the event that the materials from the supplier do *not* arrive on time. We know that $P(\overline{B}) = 1 - P(B) = 1/3$ from the rule of complements. However, we do not yet know the conditional probability $P(A|\overline{B})$, the probability that Bendrix will meet its end-of-July deadline, given that it does not receive the materials from the supplier on time. In particular, $P(A|\overline{B})$ is *not* equal to $1 - P(A|B)$. (Can you see why?) Suppose Bendrix estimates that the chances of meeting the end-of-July deadline are 1 out of 5 if the materials do not arrive on time, that is, $P(A|\overline{B}) = 1/5$. Then a second use of the multiplication rule gives

$$P(A \text{ and } \overline{B}) = P(A|\overline{B})P(\overline{B}) = (1/5)(1/3) = 0.0667$$

In words, there is only 1 chance out of 15 that the materials will not arrive on time *and* Bendrix will meet its end-of-July deadline.

The bottom line for Bendrix is whether it will meet its end-of-July deadline. After mid-July, this probability is either $P(A|B) = 3/4$ or $P(A|\overline{B}) = 1/5$ because by this time, Bendrix will *know* whether the materials arrived on time. But on July 1, the relevant probability is $P(A)$—there is still uncertainty about whether B or $\overline{B}$ will occur. Fortunately, we can calculate $P(A)$ from the probabilities we already know. The logic is that A consists of the two mutually exclusive events $(A \text{ and } B)$ and $(A \text{ and } \overline{B})$. That is, if A is to occur, it must occur with B or with $\overline{B}$. Therefore, using the *additive* rule for mutually exclusive events, we obtain

$$P(A) = P(A \text{ and } B) + P(A \text{ and } \overline{B}) = 1/2 + 1/15 = 17/30 = 0.5667$$

In words, the chances are 17 out of 30 that Bendrix will meet its end-of-July deadline, given the information it has at the beginning of July. ■

4.2.4 Probabilistic Independence

A concept that is closely tied to conditional probability is **probabilistic independence**. We just saw how the probability of an event A can depend on whether another event B has or has not occurred. Typically, the probabilities $P(A)$, $P(A|B)$, and $P(A|\overline{B})$ are all different, as in Example 4.1. However, there are situations where all of these probabilities are equal. In this case we say that the events A and B are independent. This does *not* mean they are mutually exclusive; it means that knowledge of one of the events is of no value when assessing the probability of the other event.

The main advantage to knowing that two events are independent is that the multiplication rule simplifies to

$$P(A \text{ and } B) = P(A)P(B) \qquad \textbf{(Independence)}$$

This follows by substituting $P(A)$ for $P(A|B)$ in the multiplication rule, which we are allowed to do because of independence. In words, the probability that both events occur is the product of their individual probabilities.

An important issue is whether events *are* probabilistically independent. Unfortunately, this issue usually cannot be settled with mathematical arguments; typically, we must use empirical data to decide whether independence is reasonable. As an example, let A be the event that a family's first child is male, and let B be the event that its second child is male. Are A and B independent? We would argue that they aren't independent if we believe, say, that a boy is more likely to be followed by another boy than by a girl. We would argue that they are independent if we believe the chances of the second child being a boy are the same, regardless of the gender of the first child. (Note that neither argument has anything to do with boys and girls being equally likely.)

In any case, the only way to settle the argument is to observe many families with at least two children and see what occurs. If we observe, say, that 55% of all families with first child male also have the second child male, and only 45% of all families with first child female have the second child male, then we can make a good case for *nonindependence* of A and B.

4.2.5 Equally Likely Events

Much of what you know about probability is probably based on situations where outcomes are equally likely. These include flipping coins, throwing dice, drawing balls from urns, and other random mechanisms that are often discussed in books on probability. For example, suppose an urn contains 20 red marbles and 10 blue marbles. We plan to randomly select 5 marbles from the urn, and we are interested, say, in the probability of selecting at least 3 red marbles. To find this probability, we argue that because of randomness, every possible group of 5 marbles is equally likely to be chosen. Then we *count* the number of groups of 5 marbles that contain at least 3 red marbles, we count the total number of groups of 5 marbles that could be selected, and we set the desired probability equal to the ratio of these two counts.

Our only purpose in this section is to put this method of calculating probabilities into proper perspective. It is true that many probabilities, particularly in games of chance, *can* be calculated by using an equally likely argument. It is also true that probabilities calculated in this way satisfy all of the rules of probability, including the rules we have discussed above. However, many probabilities, especially those in business situations, *cannot* be calculated by equally likely arguments, simply because the possible outcomes are not equally likely. For example, just because we are able to identify five possible scenarios for a company's future, there is probably no reason whatsoever to conclude that each scenario has probability 1/5.

The bottom line is that we will have almost no need in this book to discuss counting rules for equally likely outcomes. If you feared that probability is all about balls and urns, you can rest assured that this is definitely *not* the case!

PROBLEMS

Level A

1 In a particular suburb, 30% of the households have installed electronic security systems.

   a If a household is chosen at random from this suburb, what is the probability that this household has not installed an electronic security system?

   b If two households are chosen at random from this suburb, what is the probability that *neither* has installed an electronic security system?

2 Several major automobile producers are competing to have the largest market share for sport utility vehicles in the coming quarter. A professional automobile market analyst assesses that the odds of General Motors *not* being the market leader are 6 to 1. The odds against Chrysler and Ford having the largest market share in the coming quarter are similarly assessed to be 12 to 5 and 8 to 3, respectively.

   a Find the probability that General Motors will have the largest market share for sport utility vehicles in the coming quarter.

   b Find the probability that Chrysler will have the largest market share for sport utility vehicles in the coming quarter.

   c Find the probability that Ford will have the largest market share for sport utility vehicles in the coming quarter.

   d Find the probability that some other automobile manufacturer will have the largest market share for sport utility vehicles in the coming quarter.

3 The publisher of a popular financial periodical has decided to undertake a campaign in an effort to attract new subscribers. Market research analysts in this company believe that there is a 1 in 4 chance that the increase in the number of new subscriptions resulting from this campaign will be less than 3000, and there is a 1 in 3 chance that the increase in the number of new subscriptions resulting from this campaign will be between 3000 and 5000. What is the probability that the increase in the number of new subscriptions resulting from this campaign will be less than 3000 *or* more than 5000?

4 Suppose that 18% of the employees of a given corporation engage in physical exercise activities during the lunch hour. Moreover, assume that 57% of all employees are male, and 12% of all employees are males who engage in physical exercise activities during the lunch hour.

   a If we choose an employee at random from this corporation, what is the probability that this person is a female who engages in physical exercise activities during the lunch hour?

   b If we choose an employee at random from this corporation, what is the probability that this person is a female who does not engage in physical exercise activities during the lunch hour?

5 In a study designed to gauge married women's participation in the workplace today, the data provided in the file P4_5.XLS are obtained from a sample of 750 randomly selected married women. Consider a woman selected at random from this sample in answering each of the following questions.

   a What is the probability that this randomly selected woman has a job outside the home?

   b What is the probability that this randomly selected woman has at least one child?

   c What is the probability that this randomly selected woman has a full-time job and no more than one child?

   d What is the probability that this randomly selected woman has a part-time job or at least one child but not both?

6 Suppose that we draw a single card from a standard deck of 52 playing cards.

a What is the probability that a diamond *or* club is drawn?

b What is the probability that the drawn card is not a 4?

c Given that a black card has been drawn, what is the probability that a spade has been drawn?

d Let E_1 be the event that a black card is drawn. Let E_2 be the event that a spade is drawn. Are E_1 and E_2 independent events? Why or why not?

e Let E_3 be the event that a heart is drawn. Let E_4 be the event that a 3 is drawn. Are E_3 and E_4 independent events? Why or why not?

Level B

7 In a large accounting firm, the proportion of accountants with MBA degrees and at least 5 years of professional experience is 75% as large as the proportion of accountants with no MBA degree and less than 5 years of professional experience. Furthermore, 35% of the accountants in this firm have MBA degrees, and 45% have less than 5 years of professional experience. If one of the firm's accountants is selected at random, what is the probability that this accountant has an MBA degree or at least 5 years of professional experience but not both?

8 A local beer producer sells two types of beer, a regular brand and a light brand with 30% fewer calories. The company's marketing department wants to verify that its traditional approach of appealing to local white-collar workers with light beer commercials and appealing to local blue-collar workers with regular beer commercials is indeed a good strategy. A randomly selected group of 400 local workers are questioned about their beer-drinking preferences, and the data shown in the file P4_8.XLS are obtained.

a If a blue-collar worker is chosen at random from this group, what is the probability that she or he prefers light beer (to regular beer or no beer at all)?

b If a white-collar worker is chosen at random from this group, what is the probability that she or he prefers light beer (to regular beer or no beer at all)?

c If we restrict our attention to workers who like to drink beer, what is the probability that a randomly selected blue-collar worker prefers to drink light beer?

d If we restrict our attention to workers who like to drink beer, what is the probability that a randomly selected white-collar worker prefers to drink light beer?

e Does the company's marketing strategy appear to be appropriate? Explain why or why not.

9 Suppose that two dice are tossed. For each die, it is equally likely that 1, 2, 3, 4, 5, or 6 dots will show.

a What is the probability that the sum of the dots on the uppermost faces of the two dice will be 5 or 7?

b What is the probability that the sum of the dots on the uppermost faces of the two dice will be some number other than 4 or 8?

c Let E_1 be the event that the first die shows a 3. Let E_2 be the event that the sum of the dots on the uppermost faces of the two dice is 6. Are E_1 and E_2 independent events?

d Again, let E_1 be the event that the first die shows a 3. Let E_3 be the event that the sum of the dots on the uppermost faces of the two dice is 7. Are E_1 and E_3 independent events?

e Given that the sum of the dots on the uppermost faces of the two dice is 7, what is the probability that the first die showed 4 dots?

f Given that the first die shows a 3, what is the probability that the sum of the dots on the uppermost faces of the two dice is an even number? ■

Distribution of a Single Random Variable

We now discuss the topic of most interest in this chapter, probability distributions. In this section we examine the probability distribution of a single random variable. In later sections we will discuss probability distributions of two or more related random variables.

There are really two types of random variables: **discrete** and **continuous**. A discrete random variable has only a finite number of possible values, whereas a continuous random variable has a continuum of possible values.[1] As an example, consider demand for televisions. Is this discrete or continuous? Strictly speaking, it is discrete because the number of televisions demanded must be an integer. However, because the number of possible demand values is probably quite large—all integers between 1000 and 5000, say—it might be easier to treat demand as a continuous random variable. On the other hand, for reasons of simplicity we might go the other direction and treat demand as discrete with only a few possible values, such as 1000, 2000, 3000, 4000, and 5000. This is obviously an approximation to reality, but it might suffice for all practical purposes.

Mathematically, there is an important difference between discrete and continuous probability distributions. Specifically, a proper treatment of continuous distributions, analogous to the treatment we will provide in this chapter, requires calculus—which we do not presume for this book. Therefore, we will discuss only discrete distributions in this chapter. In later chapters we will often *use* continuous distributions, particularly the bell-shaped normal distribution, but we will simply state their properties, without trying to derive them mathematically.

The essential properties of a discrete random variable and its associated probability distribution are quite simple. We will discuss them in general and then analyze a numerical example. Let X be a random variable. (Usually, capital letters toward the end of the alphabet, such as X, Y, and Z, are used to denote random variables.)

To specify the probability distribution of X, we need to specify its possible values and their probabilities. We assume that there are k possible values, denoted $v_1, v_2, \ldots, v_k$. The probability of a typical value v_i is denoted in one of two ways, either $P(X = v_i)$ or $p(v_i)$. The first reminds us that this is a probability involving the random variable X, whereas the second is a simpler "shorthand" notation. There are two restrictions on the probabilities: (1) they must be nonnegative, and (2) they must sum to 1. In symbols, we must have

$$\sum_{i=1}^{k} p(v_i) = 1, \quad p(v_i) \geq 0$$

This is basically all there is to it—a list of possible values and a list of associated probabilities that sum to 1. Although this list of probabilities completely determines a probability distribution, it is sometimes useful to calculate **cumulative** probabilities. A cumulative probability is the probability that the random variable is *less than or equal to* some particular value. For example, assume that 10, 20, 30, and 40 are the possible values of a random variable X, with corresponding probabilities 0.15, 0.25, 0.35, and 0.25. Then a typical cumulative probability is $P(X \leq 30)$. From the addition rule it can be calculated as

$$P(X \leq 30) = P(X = 10) + P(X = 20) + P(X = 30) = 0.75$$

In addition, it is often convenient to summarize a probability distribution with two or three well-chosen numbers. The first of these is the **mean**, usually denoted μ. It is often

---

[1] Actually, a more rigorous discussion allows a discrete random variable to have an infinite number of possible values, such as all the positive integers. The only time this occurs in this book is when we discuss the Poisson distribution in Chapter 5.

called the **expected value** of X and denoted $E(X)$ (for *expected* X). The mean is a weighted sum of the possible values, weighted by their probabilities:

$$\mu = E(X) = \sum_{i=1}^{k} v_i p(v_i) \tag{4.2}$$

In much the same way that an average of a set of numbers indicates "central location," the mean indicates the center of the probability distribution. We will see this more clearly when we analyze a numerical example.

To measure the variability in a distribution, we calculate its **variance** or **standard deviation**. The variance, denoted by σ^2 or $\text{Var}(X)$, is a weighted sum of the squared deviations of the possible values from the mean, where the weights are again the probabilities:

$$\sigma^2 = \text{Var}(X) = \sum_{i=1}^{k} \left(v_i - E(X)\right)^2 p(v_i) \tag{4.3}$$

As in the previous chapter, the variance is expressed in the *square* of the units of X, such as dollars squared. Therefore, a more natural measure of variability is the standard deviation, denoted by σ or $\text{Stdev}(X)$. It is the square root of the variance:

$$\sigma = \text{Stdev}(X) = \sqrt{\text{Var}(X)} \tag{4.4}$$

We now consider a typical example.

EXAMPLE 4.2

An investor is concerned with the market return for the coming year, where the market return is defined as the percentage gain (or loss, if negative) over the year. The investor believes there are five possible scenarios for the national economy in the coming year: rapid expansion, moderate expansion, no growth, moderate contraction, and serious contraction. Furthermore, she has used all of the information available to her to estimate that the market returns for these scenarios are, respectively, 0.23, 0.18, 0.15, 0.09, and 0.03. That is, the possible returns vary from a high of 23% to a low of 3%. Also, she has assessed that the probabilities of these outcomes are 0.12, 0.40, 0.25, 0.15, and 0.08. Use this information to describe the probability distribution of the market return.

Solution

To make the connection between the general notation and this particular example, we let X denote the market return for the coming year. Then each possible economic scenario leads to a possible value of X. For example, the first possible value is $v_1 = 0.23$, and its probability is $p(v_1) = 0.12$. These values and probabilities appear in columns B and C of Figure 4.1.[2] (See the Market sheet in the file MRETURN.XLS.) Note that the five probabilities sum to 1, as they should. This probability distribution implies, for example, that the probability of a market return at least as large as 0.18 is $0.12 + 0.40 = 0.52$, because it could occur as a result of rapid or moderate expansion of the economy. Similarly, the probability that the market return is 0.09 or less is $0.15 + 0.08 = 0.23$, because this could occur as a result of moderate or serious contraction of the economy.

[2]From here on, we will often color the given inputs in the spreadsheet figures gray. This way you can see which values are given and which are calculated. We will also box in the range names used.

FIGURE 4.1 **Probability Distribution of Market Returns**

	A	B	C	D
1	**Mean, variance, and standard deviation of a random variable**			
2				
3	Economic outcome	Probability	Market	Sq dev from mean
4	Rapid Expansion	0.12	0.23	0.005929
5	Moderate Expansion	0.40	0.18	0.000729
6	No Growth	0.25	0.15	0.000009
7	Moderate Contraction	0.15	0.09	0.003969
8	Serious Contraction	0.08	0.03	0.015129
9				
10	Mean return	0.153		
11	Variance of return	0.002811	**Range names**	
12	Stdev of return	0.053	Mean: B10	
13			Probs: B4:B8	
14			Returns: C4:C8	
15			SqDevs: D4:D8	
16			Var: B11	

The summary measures of this probability distribution appear in the range B10:B12. They can be calculated with the following steps.

1   Mean return. Calculate the mean return in cell B10 with the formula

$$\text{=SUMPRODUCT(Returns,Probs)}$$

This formula illustrates the general rule in equation (4.2): The mean is the sum of products of possible values and probabilities.

2   Squared deviations. To get ready to compute the variance, calculate the squared deviations from the mean by entering the formula

$$\text{=(C4-Mean)\textasciicircum2}$$

in cell D4 and copying it down through cell D8.

3   Variance. Calculate the variance of the market return in cell B11 with the formula

$$\text{=SUMPRODUCT(SqDevs,Probs)}$$

This illustrates the general formula for variance in equation (4.3): It is always a sum of products of squared deviations from the mean and probabilities.

4   Standard deviation. Calculate the standard deviation of the market return in cell B12 with the formula

$$\text{=SQRT(Var)}$$

We see that the mean return is 15.3% and the standard deviation is 5.3%. What do these measures really mean? First, the mean, or *expected*, return does not imply that the most likely return is 15.3%, nor is this the value that the investor "expects" to occur. In fact, the value 15.3% is not even a possible market return (at least not according to the model). We can understand these measures better in terms of long-run averages. That is, if we could imagine the coming year being repeated many times, each time using the probability distribution in columns B and C to generate a market return, then the average of these market returns would be close to 15.3%, and their standard deviation—calculated as in the *previous* chapter—would be close to 5.3%. ∎

PROBLEMS

Level A

10 A fair coin (i.e., heads and tails are equally likely) is tossed three times. Let X be the number of heads observed in three tosses of this fair coin.

   a Find the probability distribution of X.

   b Compute the probability that two or fewer heads are observed in three tosses.

   c Compute the probability that at least one head is observed in three tosses.

   d Find the expected value of X.

   e Find the standard deviation of X.

11 Consider a random variable with the following probability distribution: $P(X = 0) = 0.1$, $P(X = 1) = 0.2$, $P(X = 2) = 0.3$, $P(X = 3) = 0.3$, and $P(X = 4) = 0.1$.

   a Find $P(X \leq 2)$.

   b Find $P(1 < X \leq 3)$.

   c Find $P(X > 0)$.

   d Find $P(X > 3 \mid X > 2)$.

   e Find the expected value of X.

   f Find the standard deviation of X.

12 A study has shown that the probability distribution of X, the number of customers in line (including the one being served, if any) at a checkout counter in a department store, is given by $P(X = 0) = 0.25$, $P(X = 1) = 0.25$, $P(X = 2) = 0.20$, $P(X = 3) = 0.20$, and $P(X \geq 4) = 0.10$. Consider a newly arriving customer to the checkout line.

   a What is the probability that this customer will not have to wait behind anyone?

   b What is the probability that this customer will have to wait behind at least one customer?

   c On average, behind how many other customers will the newly arriving customer have to wait?

13 A construction company has to complete a project no later than 3 months from now or there will be significant cost overruns. The manager of the construction company believes that there are four possible values for the random variable X, the number of months from now it will take to complete this project: 2, 2.5, 3, and 3.5. It is currently believed that the probabilities of these four possibilities are in the ratio 1 to 2 to 4 to 2. That is, $X = 2.5$ is twice as likely as $X = 2$, $X = 3$ is twice as likely as $X = 2.5$, and $X = 3.5$ is half as likely as $X = 3$.

   a Find the probability distribution of X.

   b What is the probability that this project will be completed in less than 3 months from now?

   c What is the probability that this project will *not* be completed on time?

   d What is the expected completion time (in months) of this project from now?

   e How much variability (in months) exists around the expected value you found in part **d**?

14 A corporate executive officer is attempting to arrange a meeting of his three vice presidents for tomorrow morning. He believes that each of these three busy individuals, independently of the others, has about a 60% chance of being able to attend the meeting.

   a Find the probability distribution of X, the number of vice presidents who can attend the meeting.

   b What is the probability that none of the three vice presidents can attend the meeting?

   c If the meeting will be held tomorrow morning only if everyone can attend, what is the probability that the meeting will take place at that time?

   d How many of the vice presidents should the CEO expect to be available for tomorrow morning's meeting?

15 Several students enrolled in a finance course subscribe to *Money* magazine. If two students are selected at random from this class, the probability that neither of the chosen students subscribes to *Money* is 0.81. Furthermore, the probability of selecting one student who subscribes and one student who does not subscribe to this magazine is 0.18. Finally, the probability of selecting two students who subscribe to *Money* is 0.01. Let X be the number of students who subscribe to *Money* magazine from the two selected at random. Find the mean and standard deviation of X.

16 The "house edge" in any game of chance is defined as

$$\frac{E(\text{player's loss on a bet})}{\text{Size of player's loss on a bet}}$$

For example, if a player wins \$10 with probability 0.48 and loses \$10 with probability 0.52 on any bet, then the house edge is

$$\frac{-(10(0.48) - 10(0.52))}{10} = 0.04$$

Give an interpretation to the house edge that relates to how much money the house is likely to win on average. Which do you think has a larger house edge: roulette or sports gambling? Why? ■

4.4 An Introduction to Simulation

In the previous section we asked you to "imagine" many repetitions of an event, with each repetition resulting in a different random outcome. Fortunately, we can do more than *imagine*; we can make it happen with computer **simulation**. Simulation is an extremely useful tool that can be used to incorporate uncertainty explicitly into spreadsheet models. As we will see, a simulation model is the same as a regular spreadsheet model except that some cells include random quantities. Each time the spreadsheet recalculates, new values of the random quantities occur, and these typically lead to different "bottom-line" results. By forcing the spreadsheet to recalculate many times, a business manager is able to discover the results that are most likely to occur, those that are least likely to occur, and best-case and worst-case results. We will devote an entire chapter, Chapter 16, to developing simulation models for a variety of business problems. However, in the intervening chapters we can also use simulation to help explain difficult concepts in probability and statistics. We begin in this section by using simulation to explain the connection between summary measures of probability distributions and the corresponding summary measures from the previous chapter.

We continue to use the market return distribution in Figure 4.1 from Example 4.2. Because this is our first discussion of computer simulation in Excel, we proceed in some detail. Our goal is to simulate many returns (we arbitrarily choose 400) from this distribution and analyze the resulting returns. We want each simulated return to have probability 0.12 of being 0.23, probability 0.40 of being 0.18, and so on. Then, using the methods for summarizing data from the previous chapter, we will calculate the average and standard deviation of the 400 simulated returns.

The method for simulating many market returns is straightforward once we know how to simulate a *single* market return. The key to this is Excel's RAND function, which generates a random number between 0 and 1. The RAND function has no arguments, so every time we call it, we enter RAND(). (Although there is nothing inside the parentheses next to RAND, the parentheses cannot be omitted.) That is, to generate a random number between 0 and 1 in any cell, we enter the formula

$$=RAND()$$

in that cell. The RAND function can also be used as part of another function. For example, we can simulate the result of a single flip of a fair coin by entering the formula

$$=IF(RAND()<=0.5,``Heads",``Tails")$$

Random numbers generated with Excel's RAND function are said to be **uniformly distributed** between 0 and 1 because all decimal values between 0 and 1 are equally likely. These uniformly distributed random numbers can then be used to generate numbers from any discrete distribution such as the market return distribution in Figure 4.1. To see how this is done, note first that there are five possible values in this distribution. Therefore, we divide the interval from 0 to 1 into five parts with lengths equal to the probabilities in the probability distribution. Then we see which of these parts the random number from RAND falls into and generate the associated market return. If the random number is between 0 and 0.12 (of length 0.12), we generate 0.23 as the market return; if the random number is between 0.12 and 0.52 (of length 0.40), we generate 0.18 as the market return; and so on. See Figure 4.2.

FIGURE 4.2 **Associating RAND Values with Market Returns**

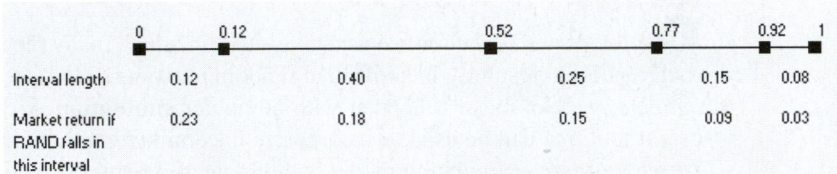

This procedure is accomplished most easily in Excel with a VLOOKUP function, as explained in the following steps. (Refer to Figure 4.3 and the Simulation sheet in the MRETURN.XLS file.)

1   **Lookup table.** Copy the possible returns to the range E13:E17. Then enter the **cumulative** probabilities next to them in the range D13:D17. To do this, enter the value 0 in cell D13. Then enter the formula

$$=D13+Market!B4$$

in cell D14 and copy it down through cell D17. (Note that the Market!B4 in this formula refers to cell B4 in the Market sheet, that is, cell B4 in Figure 4.1.) Each value in column D is the current probability plus the previous value. The table in this range, D13:E17, becomes the lookup range. For convenience, we have named this range LTable.

2   **Random numbers.** Enter random numbers in the range A13:A412. An easy way to do this is to highlight the range, then type the formula

$$=RAND()$$

and finally press Ctrl-Enter. Note that these random numbers are "live." That is, each time you do any calculation in Excel or press the recalculation key (the F9 key), these random numbers change.

FIGURE 4.3 Simulation of Market Returns

	A	B	C	D	E
1	Simulating market returns				
2					
3	Summary statistics from simulation below				
4	Average return	0.154			
5	Stdev of returns	0.053			
6					
7	Exact values from previous sheet (for comparison)				
8	Average return	0.153			
9	Stdev of returns	0.053			
10					
11	Simulation			Lookup table	
12	Random #	Market return		CumProb	Return
13	0.367667	0.18		0	0.23
14	0.067166	0.23		0.12	0.18
15	0.844740	0.09		0.52	0.15
16	0.400211	0.18		0.77	0.09
17	0.679358	0.15		0.92	0.03
18	0.186991	0.18			
19	0.650088	0.15		Range names	
20	0.728323	0.15		Ltable: D13:E17	
21	0.070214	0.23		SimReturns: B13:B412	
22	0.782275	0.09			
410	0.832221	0.09			
411	0.455817	0.18			
412	0.786873	0.09			

3 Market returns. Generate the random market returns by referring the random numbers in column A to the lookup table. Specifically, enter the formula

$$=VLOOKUP(A13,LTable,2)$$

in cell B13 and copy it down through cell B412. This formula compares the random number in cell A13 to the cumulative probabilities in the first column of the lookup table and sees where it "fits," as illustrated in Figure 4.2. Then it returns the corresponding market return in the second column of the lookup table. (It uses the *second* column because the third argument of the VLOOKUP function is 2.)

4 Summary statistics. Summarize the 400 market returns by entering the formulas

$$=AVERAGE(SimReturns)$$

and

$$=STDEV(SimReturns)$$

in cells B4 and B5. For comparison, copy the average and standard deviation from the Market sheet in Figure 4.1 to cells B8 and B9.

Now let's step back and see what we've accomplished. The following points are relevant.

■ Simulations such as this are very common, and we will continue to use them to illustrate concepts in probability and statistics.

- The numbers you obtain will be different from the ones in Figure 4.3. This is the nature of simulation. The results depend on the particular random numbers that happen to be generated.

- The way we entered cumulative probabilities and then used a lookup table is generally the best way to generate random numbers from a discrete probability distribution. However, there is an easier way if a simulation add-in is available. We will discuss this possibility in Chapter 16.

- Each generated market return in the SimReturns range is one of the five possible market returns. If you count the number of times each return appears and then divide by 400, the number of simulated values, you'll see that the resulting fractions are *approximately* equal to the original probabilities. For example, the fraction of times the highest return 0.23 appears is about 0.12. This is the essence of what it means to simulate from a given probability distribution.

- The average and standard deviation in cells B4 and B5, calculated from the formulas in the previous chapter, are very close to the mean and standard deviation of the probability distribution in cells B8 and B9. Note, however, that these measures are calculated in entirely different ways. For example, the average in cell B4 is a simple average of 400 numbers, whereas the mean in cell B8 is a weighted sum of the possible market returns, weighted by their probabilities.

This last point allows us to interpret the summary measures of a probability distribution. Specifically, the mean and standard deviation of a probability distribution are approximately what we would obtain if we calculated the average and standard deviation, using the formulas from the *previous* chapter, of many simulated values from this distribution. In other words, the mean is the long-run average of the simulated values. Similarly, the standard deviation measures their variability.

You might ask whether this long-run average interpretation of the mean is relevant if the situation is going to occur only once. For example, the market return in the example is for "the coming year," and the coming year is going to occur only once. So what is the use of a long-run average? In this type of situation, the long-run average interpretation is probably *not* very relevant, but fortunately, there is another use of the expected value that we will exploit in Chapter 6—namely, when a decision maker must choose among several actions that have uncertain outcomes, the preferred decision is often the one with the largest expected (monetary) value. This makes the expected value of a probability distribution extremely important in decision-making contexts.

PROBLEMS

Level A

17 A personnel manager of a large manufacturing plant is investigating the number of reported on-the-job accidents at the facility over the past several years. Let X be the number of such accidents reported during a 1-month period. Based on past records, the manager has established the probability distribution for X as shown in Table 4.1.

    a Generate 400 values of this random variable X with the given probability distribution using computer simulation.

    b Compare the distribution of simulated values to the given probability distribution. Is the simulated distribution indicative of the given probability distribution? Explain why or why not.

18 A quality inspector picks a sample of 15 items at random from a manufacturing process known to produce 10% defective items. Let X be the number of defective items found in the random sample of 15 items. Assume that the condition of each item is independent of that of each of the other items in the sample. The probability distribution of X is provided in Table 4.2.

TABLE 4.1 Reported On-the-Job Accidents

Number of Accidents Reported	Probability
0	0.50
1	0.25
2	0.10
3	0.05
4	0.05
5	0.02
6	0.01
7	0.01
8	0.01
9 or more	0.00

TABLE 4.2 Number of Defective Items in a Random Sample of 15 Items

Number of Defective Items	Probability
0	0.0874
1	0.2312
2	0.2856
3	0.2184
4	0.1156
5	0.0449
6	0.0132
7	0.0030
8	0.0005
9	0.0001
10 or more	0.0000

a Generate 500 values of this random variable with the given probability distribution using computer simulation.

b Compute the mean and standard deviation of the distribution of simulated values. How do these summary measures compare to the mean and standard deviation of the given probability distribution?

19 Table 4.3 gives the probability distribution for the number of job applications processed at a small employment agency during a typical week.

TABLE 4.3 Weekly Number of Job Applications Processed

Number of Job Applications Processed	Probability
5	0.05
6	0.10
7	0.15
8	0.20
9	0.20
10	0.15
11	0.10
12	0.05

a Generate 400 values of this random variable with the given probability distribution using computer simulation.

b Compute the mean and standard deviation of the distribution of simulated values. How do these summary measures compare to the mean and standard deviation of the given probability distribution?

c Use your simulated distribution to find the probability that the weekly number of job applications processed will be within two standard deviations of the mean.

20 Consider a random variable with the following probability distribution: $P(X = 0) = 0.1$, $P(X = 1) = 0.2$, $P(X = 2) = 0.3$, $P(X = 3) = 0.3$, and $P(X = 4) = 0.1$.

a Generate 400 values of this random variable with the given probability distribution using computer simulation.

b Compare the distribution of simulated values to the given probability distribution. Is the simulated distribution indicative of the given probability distribution? Explain why or why not.

c Compute the mean and standard deviation of the distribution of simulated values. How do these summary measures compare to the mean and standard deviation of the given probability distribution?

21 The probability distribution of X, the number of customers in line (including the one being served, if any) at a checkout counter in a department store, is given by $P(X = 0) = 0.25$, $P(X = 1) = 0.25$, $P(X = 2) = 0.20$, $P(X = 3) = 0.20$, and $P(X = 4) = 0.10$.

a Generate 500 values of this random variable with the given probability distribution using computer simulation.

b Compare the distribution of simulated values to the given probability distribution. Is the simulated distribution indicative of the given probability distribution? Explain why or why not.

c Compute the mean and standard deviation of the distribution of simulated values. How do these summary measures compare to the mean and standard deviation of the given probability distribution?

Level B

22 Betting on a football point spread works as follows. Suppose Michigan is favored by 17.5 points over Indiana. If you bet a "unit" on Indiana and Indiana loses by 17 or less, you win $10. If Indiana loses by 18 or more points, you lose $11. Find the mean and standard deviation of your winnings on a single bet. Assume that there is a 0.5 probability that you will win your bet and a 0.5 probability that you will lose your bet. Also simulate 1600 "bets" to estimate the average loss per bet. [*Note*: Do not be too disappointed if you are off by up to 50 cents. It takes many, say 10,000, simulated bets to get a really good estimate of the mean loss per bet because there is a lot of variability on each bet.] ■

4.5

Subjective Versus Objective Probabilities

In this section we ask an even more basic question. Where do the probabilities in a probability distribution come from? For example, where did the investor get the probabilities in column B of Figure 4.1? A complete answer to this question could lead to a chapter by itself, so we will only briefly discuss the issues involved. There are essentially two distinct ways to assess probabilities, objectively and subjectively. **Objective probabilities** are those that can be estimated from long-run proportions, whereas **subjective probabilities** cannot be estimated from long-run proportions. Some examples will make this distinction clearer.

Consider throwing two dice and observing the sum of the two sides that face up. What is the probability that the sum of these two sides is 7? We might argue as follows. Because there are $6 \times 6 = 36$ ways the two dice can fall, and because exactly 6 of these result in a sum of 7, the probability of a 7 is $6/36 = 1/6$. This is the equally likely argument we discussed in Section 4.2 that reduces probability to counting. However, there is a more important and general principle involved.

What if the dice are weighted in some way? Then the equally likely argument is no longer valid. We can, however, toss the dice many times and record the proportion of tosses that result in a sum of 7. A famous result called the **law of large numbers** states that this proportion, in the long run, will get closer and closer to the "true" probability of a 7. This is exactly what we mean by an objective probability. It is a probability that can be estimated as the long-run proportion of times an event occurs in a sequence of many identical experiments.

When it comes to flipping coins, throwing dice, and spinning roulette wheels, objective probabilities are certainly relevant. We don't need a person's *opinion* of the probability that a roulette wheel, say, will end up pointing to a red number; we can simply spin it many times and keep track of the proportion of times it points to a red number. However, there are many situations, particularly in business, that cannot be repeated many times—or even more than once—under identical conditions. In these situations objective probabilities make no sense (and equally likely arguments usually make no sense either), so we must resort to subjective probabilities. A subjective probability is one person's assessment of the likelihood that a certain event will occur. We assume that the person making the assessment uses all of the information available to make the most rational assessment possible.

This definition of subjective probability implies that one person's assessment of a certain probability might differ from another person's assessment of the *same* probability. For example, consider the probability that the Dallas Cowboys will win the next Super Bowl. If we ask a casual football observer to assess this probability, we'll get one answer, but if we ask a person with a lot of inside information about injuries, team cohesiveness, and so on, we might get a very different answer. There is nothing inconsistent about this. As the name implies, these probabilities are *subjective*, so that people with different information and even different "gut" feelings typically assess probabilities in different ways.

Subjective probabilities are usually relevant for unique, one-time situations. However, most situations are not completely unique; we usually have some history to guide us. Therefore, subjective probabilities usually combine some amount of subjectivity with historical frequencies. For example, suppose a company is about to market a new product. This product might be quite different in some ways than any products the company has marketed before, but it might also share some features with the company's previous products. If the company wants to assess the probability that the new product will be a success, it will certainly analyze the unique features of this product and the current state of the market to obtain a subjective assessment. However, it will also look at its past series of successes and failures with reasonably similar products. If the proportion of successes with past products was 40%, then this value might be a starting point in the search for a subjective estimate of *this* product's probability of success.

All of the "given" probabilities in this chapter and later chapters can be placed somewhere on the objective-to-subjective continuum, usually closer to the subjective end. An important implication of this is that these probabilities are not cast in stone; they are only educated guesses. Therefore, it is always a good idea to run a **sensitivity analysis** (especially on a spreadsheet, where this is easy to do) to see how any "bottom-line" answers depend on the "given" probabilities. Sensitivity analysis is especially important in Chapter 6, when we study decision making under uncertainty.

Derived Probability Distributions

F requently, we begin with the probability distribution of one random variable X, and we want to obtain the probability distribution or summary measures of a random variable Y that is a function of X. The following example illustrates the methods involved.

EXAMPLE 4.3

A bookstore is planning to order a shipment of special edition Christmas calendars. The bookstore will then sell these calendars for $15 apiece. It will place only one order. If the demand for the calendar is less than the order quantity, the excess calendars will be given to a paper recycling company (since they are essentially worthless to the bookstore). On the other hand, if the demand is greater than the order quantity, the excess demand will be lost; customers will take their business elsewhere. The bookstore estimates that the demand for calendars will be anywhere from 250 to 400. Using subjective estimates and some historical data from previous years as guides, it estimates that demand for calendars follows the probability distribution shown in the range B10:C16 of Figure 4.4. (See the file

FIGURE 4.4 **Derived Distributions of Units Sold and Revenue**

	A	B	C	D	E	F	G
1	**A derived probability distribution - revenue from demand**						
2							
3	Assumption: Excess demand (over amount on hand) is lost						
4					**Selected range names**		
5	Units on hand	350			DerivedProbs: D20:D26		
6	Unit selling price	$15			Onhand: B5		
7					Revenues: C20:C26		
8	Probability distribution of demand				UnitPrice: B6		
9		Demand (D)	Pr(D)	Sq devs from mean			
10		250	0.05	7014.06			
11		275	0.10	3451.56			
12		300	0.15	1139.06			
13		325	0.20	76.56			
14		350	0.25	264.06			
15		375	0.15	1701.56			
16		400	0.10	4389.06			
17							
18	Probability distribution of sales				Squared devs from means		
19		Units sold (S)	Revenue (R)	Pr(S) or Pr(R)	Units sold	Revenue	
20		250	$3,750	0.05	5625	1265625	
21		275	$4,125	0.10	2500	562500	
22		300	$4,500	0.15	625	140625	
23		325	$4,875	0.20	0	0	
24		350	$5,250	0.25	625	140625	
25		350	$5,250	0.15	625	140625	
26		350	$5,250	0.10	625	140625	
27							
28		Demand	Units sold	Revenue			
29	Means	333.75	325	$4,875			
30	Variances	1642.19	937.5	210937.5			
31	Stdevs	40.52	30.62	$459.28			

DERIVED.XLS.) If the bookstore decides to order 350 calendars, what is the probability distribution of units sold? What is the probability distribution of revenue?

Solution

Let D, S, and R denote demand, units sold, and revenue. The key to the solution is that each value of D directly determines the value of S, which in turn determines the value of R. Specifically, S is the smaller of D and the number of units ordered, 350, and R is $15 multiplied by the value of S. Therefore, we can derive the probability distributions of S and R with the following steps.

1 **Units sold.** To calculate the number of units sold for each possible demand, enter the formula

$$= \text{MIN(B10,Onhand)}$$

in cell B20 and copy it down through cell B26.

2 **Revenue.** To calculate the revenue for each value of units sold, enter the formula

$$= \text{UnitPrice*B20}$$

in cell C20 and copy it down through cell C26.

3 **Derived probabilities.** Transfer the *same* probabilities for demand down to the range D20:D26. That is, enter the formula

$$= \text{C10}$$

in cell D20 and copy it down through cell D26.

4 **Means.** Calculate the means of demand, units sold, and revenue in the same way as before. For example, calculate the mean revenue in cell D29 with the formula

$$= \text{SUMPRODUCT(Revenues,DerivedProbs)}$$

5 **Variances and standard deviations.** Calculate the variances and standard deviations of demand, units sold, and revenue in the same way as before. For example, first calculate the squared deviations of revenues from their mean in column F and then calculate the sum of products of these squared deviations and the revenue probabilities to obtain the variance of revenue. Finally, calculate the standard deviation as the square root of the variance.

Note that each value of demand leads directly to a value of units sold, which leads to a value of revenue, and the list of probabilities doesn't change. You might be bothered, however, by the fact that some values of units sold and revenue are repeated. For example, the value 350 appears in cells B24 through B26. The reason is that with an order quantity of 350, there are only five distinct possible values of units sold: 250, 275, 300, 325, and 350. The probability of this last value, 350, is the sum of the associated probabilities in column D, namely, $0.25 + 0.15 + 0.10 = 0.50$. This is the probability that demand is *at least* 350 (which is also the probability that revenue equals $5250). ∎

Summary Measures for Linear Functions   When one random variable Y is a **linear** function of another random variable X, there is a particularly simple way to calculate the summary measures of Y from the summary measures of X. (Actually, the shortcut formulas in this subsection are special cases of more general formulas that we will discuss in Section 4.10.) Suppose that Y can be written as

$$Y = a + bX$$

for some constants a and b. Then the mean, variance, and standard deviation of Y can be calculated from the similar quantities for X with the formulas

$$E(Y) = a + bE(X) \qquad \textbf{(4.5)}$$

$$\text{Var}(Y) = b^2 \, \text{Var}(X) \qquad \textbf{(4.6)}$$

and

$$\text{Stdev}(Y) = b \, \text{Stdev}(X) \qquad \textbf{(4.7)}$$

In particular, note that if Y is a constant multiple of X, that is, $a = 0$, then the mean and standard deviation of Y are this same multiple of the mean and standard deviation of X.

For example, letting revenue R and units sold S in Example 4.3 play the roles of Y and X, we have $R = 15S$, so that R is a linear function of S with $a = 0$ and $b = 15$. Therefore, after calculating the summary measures of S in cells B29 through B31 of Figure 4.4, we could calculate the summary measures of R with the formulas

$$E(R) = bE(S) = 15(325) = \$4875$$

$$\text{Var}(R) = b^2 \, \text{Var}(S) = 15^2(937.5) = 210,937.5$$

and

$$\text{Stdev}(R) = b \, \text{Stdev}(S) = 15(30.62) = \$459.30$$

The point is that we don't need to go back to the *distribution* of R (and SUMPRODUCT functions) to calculate these values. It is easier to use these shortcut formulas instead.

PROBLEMS

Level A

23 A typical consumer buys a random number (X) of polo shirts when he shops at a men's clothing store. The distribution of X is given by the following probability distribution: $P(X = 0) = 0.30$, $P(X = 1) = 0.30$, $P(X = 2) = 0.20$, $P(X = 3) = 0.10$, and $P(X = 4) = 0.10$.

   a Find the mean and standard deviation of X.

   b Assuming that each shirt costs $35, let Y be the total amount of money (in dollars) spent by a customer when he visits this clothing store. Find the mean and standard deviation of Y.

   c Compute the probability that a customer's expenditure will be more than one standard deviation above the mean expenditure level.

24 Based on past experience, the number of customers who arrive at a local gasoline station during the noon hour to purchase fuel is best described by the probability distribution given in the file P4_24.XLS.

   a Find the mean, variance, and standard deviation of this random variable.

   b Find the probability that the number of arrivals during the noon hour will be within one standard deviation of the mean number of arrivals.

   c Suppose that the typical customer spends $15 on fuel upon stopping at this gasoline station during the noon hour. Compute the mean and standard deviation of the total gasoline revenue earned by this gas station during the noon hour.

   d What is the probability that the total gasoline revenue will be less than the mean value found in part c?

   e What is the probability that the total gasoline revenue will be more than two standard deviations above the mean value found in part c?

25 Let X be the number of defective items found by a quality inspector in a random batch of 15 items from a particular manufacturing process. The probability distribution of X is provided in

Table 4.4. This firm earns $500 profit from the sale of each *acceptable* item in a given batch. In the event that an item is found to be *defective*, it must be reworked at a cost of $100 before it can be sold, thus reducing its per-unit profitability to $400.

TABLE 4.4 **Number of Defective Items in a Random Sample of 15 Items**

Number of Defective Items	Probability
0	0.0874
1	0.2312
2	0.2856
3	0.2184
4	0.1156
5	0.0449
6	0.0132
7	0.0030
8	0.0005
9	0.0001
10 or more	0.0000

a Find the mean and standard deviation of the profit earned from the sale of all items in a given batch.

b What is the probability that the profit earned from the sale of all items in a given batch is within two standard deviations of the mean profit level? Is this result consistent with the rule of thumb we learned earlier? Explain.

26 The probability distribution for the number of job applications processed at a small employment agency during a typical week is given in Table 4.5.

TABLE 4.5 **Weekly Number of Job Applications Processed**

Number of Job Applications Processed	Probability
5	0.05
6	0.10
7	0.15
8	0.20
9	0.20
10	0.15
11	0.10
12	0.05

a Assuming that it takes the agency's administrative assistant 2 hours to process a submitted job application, on average how many hours in a typical week will the administrative assistant spend processing incoming job applications?

b Find an interval with the property that the administrative assistant can be approximately 99.7% sure that the total amount of time he spends each week processing incoming job applications will be in this interval.

Level B

27 The weekly demand function for one of a given firm's products can be represented by $Q = 200 - 5p$, for $p = 1, 2, ..., 40$, where Q is the number of units purchased (in hundreds) at a sales price of p (in dollars). Assume that the probability distribution of the sales price is given by $P(p = k) = .025$, for $k = 1, 2, ..., 40$. (In words, each price is equally likely.)

a Find the mean and standard deviation of p. Interpret these measures in this case.

b Find the mean and standard deviation of Q. Interpret these measures in this case.

c Assuming that it costs this firm $10 to manufacture and sell each unit of the given product, define π to be the firm's weekly contribution to profit from the sale of this product (measured in dollars). Express π as a function of the quantity purchased, Q.

d Find the expected weekly contribution to the firm's profit from the sale of this product. Also, compute the standard deviation of the weekly contribution to the firm's profit from the sale of this product.

28 A retailer purchases a batch of 1000 fluorescent lightbulbs from a wholesaler at a cost of $2 per bulb. The wholesaler agrees to replace each defective bulb with one that is guaranteed to function properly for a charge of $.20 per bulb. The retailer sells the bulbs at a price of $2.50 per bulb and gives his customers free replacements if they bring defective bulbs back to the store. Let X be the number of defective bulbs in a typical batch, and assume that the mean and standard deviation of X are 50 and 10, respectively.

a Find the mean and standard deviation of the profit (in dollars) the retailer makes from selling a batch of lightbulbs.

b Find an interval with the property that the retailer can be approximately 95% sure that his profit will be in this interval. ■

4.7 Distribution of Two Random Variables: Scenario Approach

We now turn to the distribution of two related random variables. In this section we discuss the situation where the two random variables are related in the sense that they both depend on which of several possible scenarios occurs. In the next section we will discuss a second way of relating two random variables probabilistically. These two methods differ slightly in the way they assign probabilities to different outcomes. However, for both methods there are two summary measures, **covariance** and **correlation**, that measure the relationship between the two random variables. We begin with a discussion of these summary measures.

As with the mean, variance, and standard deviation, covariance and correlation are similar to the measures with the same names from the previous chapter, but they are conceptually different. In the previous chapter, correlation and covariance were calculated from data; here they are calculated from a probability distribution. If the random variables are X and Y, then we denote the covariance and correlation between X and Y by $\mathrm{Cov}(X, Y)$ and $\mathrm{Corr}(X, Y)$. These are defined by the formulas

$$\mathrm{Cov}(X, Y) = \sum_{i=1}^{k}(x_i - E(X))(y_i - E(Y))p(x_i, y_i) \tag{4.8}$$

and

$$\mathrm{Corr}(X, Y) = \frac{\mathrm{Cov}(X, Y)}{\mathrm{Stdev}(X) \times \mathrm{Stdev}(Y)} \tag{4.9}$$

Here, $p(x_i, y_i)$ is the probability that X and Y equal the values x_i and y_i. It is called a **joint probability**.

Although they are calculated differently, the interpretation of covariance and correlation is essentially the same as we discussed in the previous chapter. Each indicates the strength of a linear relationship between X and Y. That is, if X and Y tend to vary in the *same* direction, then both measures are positive. If they vary in *opposite* directions, both measures are negative. As before, the magnitude of the covariance is more difficult to interpret because it depends on the units of measurement of X and Y. However, the correlation is always between -1 and $+1$.

The following example illustrates the scenario approach, as well as covariance and correlation. It again employs simulation to explain the relationship between the covariance and correlation as defined here and the similar measures from the previous chapter.

EXAMPLE 4.4

An investor plans to invest in General Motors (GM) stock and in gold. He assumes that the returns on these investments over the next year depend on the general state of the economy during the year. To keep things simple, he identifies four possible states of the economy: depression, recession, normal, and boom. Also, given the most up-to-date information he can obtain, he assumes that these four states have probabilities 0.05, 0.30, 0.50, and 0.15. For each state of the economy, he estimates the resulting return on GM stock and the return on gold. These appear in the shaded section of Figure 4.5. (See the file GMGOLD.XLS.) For example, if there is a depression, the investor estimates that GM stock will decrease by 20% and the price of gold will increase by 5%. The investor wants to analyze the joint distribution of returns on these two investments. He also wants to analyze the distribution of a portfolio of investments in GM stock and gold.

FIGURE 4.5 **Distribution of GM and Gold Returns**

	A	B	C	D	E	F	G	H
1	Calculating covariance and correlation between two random variables							
2								
3	Economic outcome	Probability	GM Return	Gold Return		Selected range names		
4	Depression	0.05	-0.20	0.05		Covar: B23		
5	Recession	0.30	0.10	0.20		GMDevs: B14:B17		
6	Normal	0.50	0.30	-0.12		GMMean: B10		
7	Boom	0.15	0.50	0.09		GMReturns: C4:C7		
8						GMSqDevs: D14:D17		
9		GM	Gold			GMStdev: B21		
10	Means	0.245	0.016			GoldDevs: C14:C17		
11						GoldMean: C10		
12		Deviations from means		Sq devs from means		GoldReturns: D4:D7		
13		GM	Gold	GM	Gold	GoldSqDevs: E14:E17		
14	Depression	-0.45	0.03	0.1980	0.0012	GoldStdev: C21		
15	Recession	-0.15	0.18	0.0210	0.0339	Probs: B4:B7		
16	Normal	0.06	-0.14	0.0030	0.0185			
17	Boom	0.26	0.07	0.0650	0.0055			
18								
19		GM	Gold					
20	Variances	0.0275	0.0203					
21	Stdevs	0.166	0.142					
22								
23	Covariance	-0.0097						
24	Correlation	-0.410						

Solution

To obtain the joint distribution, note that the distribution of GM return is defined by columns B and C of the shaded region in Figure 4.5, and the distribution of gold return is defined by columns B and D. The essence of the scenario approach is that a given state of the economy determines *both* GM and gold returns, so that only four pairs of returns are possible. For example, −0.20 is a possible GM return and 0.09 is a possible gold return, but they cannot occur simultaneously. The only possible *pairs* of returns are −0.20 and 0.05, 0.10 and 0.20,

0.30 and −0.12, and 0.50 and 0.09. These possible pairs have the joint probabilities shown in column B.

To calculate means, variances, and standard deviations, we treat GM and gold returns separately. For example, the formula for the mean GM return in cell B10 is

=SUMPRODUCT(GMReturns,Probs)

The only new calculations in Figure 4.5 involve the covariance and correlation between GM and gold returns. To obtain these, we use the following steps.

1   **Deviations between means.** The formula for covariance [equation (4.8)] is a weighted sum of deviations from means (not squared deviations), so we first need to calculate these deviations. To do this, enter the formula

=C4-GMMean

in cell B14 and copy it down through cell B17. Calculate the deviations for gold similarly in column C.

2   **Covariance.** Calculate the covariance between GM and gold returns in cell B23 with the formula

=SUMPRODUCT(GMDevs,GoldDevs,Probs)

Note the use of the SUMPRODUCT function in this formula. It usually takes two range arguments, but it is allowed to take more than two, all of which must have exactly the same size and shape. This function multiplies corresponding elements from each of the three ranges and sums these products—exactly as prescribed by equation (4.8).

3   **Correlation.** Calculate the correlation between GM and gold returns in cell B24 with the formula

=Covar/(GMStdev*GoldStdev)

as prescribed by equation (4.9).

The negative covariance indicates that GM and gold returns tend to vary in opposite directions, although it is difficult to judge the strength of the relationship between them by the magnitude of the covariance. The correlation of −0.410, on the other hand, is also negative and indicates a moderately strong relationship. We can't rely too much on this correlation, however, because the relationship between GM and gold returns is *not* linear. From the values in the range C4:D7, we see that GM does better and better as the economy improves, whereas gold does better, then worse, then better.

A simulation of GM and gold returns helps to explain the covariance and correlation measures. This simulation appears in Figure 4.6. There are two keys to this simulation. First, we simulate the states of the economy, not—at least not directly—the GM and gold returns. For example, any random number between 0.05 and 0.35 implies a recession. The returns for GM and gold from a recession are then known to be 0.10 and 0.20. We implement this idea by entering a RAND function in cell A21 and then entering the formulas

=VLOOKUP(A21,LTable,2)

and

=VLOOKUP(A21,LTable,3)

in cells B21 and C21. These formulas are then copied down through row 420. This way, the *same* random number—hence the same scenario—is used to generate both returns in a given row, and the effect is that only four *pairs* of returns are possible.

FIGURE 4.6 **Simulation of GM and Gold Returns**

	A	B	C	D	E	F	G
1	Simulating GM and Gold returns						
2							
3	Summary measures from simulation below						
4		GM	Gold				
5	Means	0.253	0.015		Selected range names		
6	Stdevs	0.176	0.139		LTable: E21:G24		
7					SimGM: B21:B420		
8	Covariance	-0.0082			SimGold: C21:C420		
9	Correlation	-0.338					
10							
11	Exact results from previous sheet (for comparison)						
12		GM	Gold				
13	Means	0.245	0.016				
14	Stdevs	0.166	0.142				
15							
16	Covariance	-0.0097					
17	Correlation	-0.410					
18							
19	Simulation results				Lookup table for generating returns		
20	Random #	GM return	Gold return		CumProb	GM return	Gold return
21	0.8160631	0.30	-0.12		0.00	-0.20	0.05
22	0.7669436	0.30	-0.12		0.05	0.10	0.20
23	0.3641895	0.30	-0.12		0.35	0.30	-0.12
24	0.9164001	0.50	0.09		0.85	0.50	0.09
25	0.1769629	0.10	0.20				
26	0.1642849	0.10	0.20				
418	0.0021624	-0.20	0.05				
419	0.4483744	0.30	-0.12				
420	0.6959186	0.30	-0.12				

Second, once we have the simulated returns in the range B21:C420, we can calculate the covariance and correlation of these numbers in cells B8 and B9 with the formulas

$$=\text{COVAR(SimGM,SimGold)}$$

and

$$=\text{CORREL(SimGM,SimGold)}$$

Here, COVAR and CORREL are the built-in Excel functions discussed in the previous chapter for calculating the covariance and correlation between pairs of numbers. A comparison of cells B8 and B9 with B16 and B17 shows that there is a reasonably good agreement between the covariance and correlation of the probability distribution [from equations (4.8) and (4.9)] and the measures based on the simulated values. This agreement is not perfect, but it typically improves as we simulate more pairs.

The final question in this example involves a portfolio consisting of GM stock and gold. The analysis appears in Figure 4.7 (page 156). We assume that the investor has $10,000 to invest. He puts some fraction of this in GM stock (see cell B6) and the rest in gold. Of course, these fractions determine the total dollar values invested in row 7. The key to the analysis is the following. Because there are only four possible scenarios, there are only four possible portfolio returns. For example, if there is a recession, the GM and gold returns are 0.10 and 0.20, so the portfolio return (per dollar) is a weighted average of these returns, weighted by the fractions invested:

$$\text{Portfolio return in recession} = 0.6(0.10) + 0.4(0.20) = 0.14$$

FIGURE 4.7 Distribution of Portfolio Return

	A	B	C	D	E	F	G	H	I	J
1	Analyzing a portfolio of GM and Gold									
2										
3	Total to invest	$10,000								
4										
5	Investments	GM	Gold							
6	Fraction of total	0.60	0.40							
7	Dollar value	$6,000	$4,000							
8										
9	Distribution of portfolio returns				Sq devs from means					
10	Economic outcom	Per dollar	Total		Per dollar	Total				
11	Depression	-0.1	($1,000)		0.064212	6421156				
12	Recession	0.14	$1,400		0.00018	17956				
13	Normal	0.132	$1,320		0.000458	45796				
14	Boom	0.336	$3,360		0.033343	3334276				
15										
16	Summary measures of portfolio returns									
17		Per dollar	Total							
18	Mean return	0.153	$1,534.00							
19	Variance of return	0.008495	849484							
20	Stdev of return	0.092167	$921.67							
21										
22	Data table for mean and stdev of portfolio return as a function of GM investment									
23	GM investment	Mean	StDev							
24		$1,534.00	$921.67							
25	0.0	$160.00	$1,424.22							
26	0.1	$389.00	$1,223.28							
27	0.2	$618.00	$1,048.16							
28	0.3	$847.00	$913.81							
29	0.4	$1,076.00	$840.04							
30	0.5	$1,305.00	$842.90							
31	0.6	$1,534.00	$921.67							
32	0.7	$1,763.00	$1,059.57							
33	0.8	$1,992.00	$1,236.97							
34	0.9	$2,221.00	$1,439.34							
35	1.0	$2,450.00	$1,657.56							

Mean and StDev of Portfolio Return

In this way, we can calculate the entire portfolio return distribution—either per dollar or total dollars—and then calculate its summary measures in the usual way. The details, which are similar to other spreadsheet calculations in this chapter, can be found in the GMGOLD.XLS file. In particular, the possible returns are listed in the ranges B11:B14 and C11:C14 of Figure 4.7, and the associated probabilities are the same as those used earlier in this example. These lead to the summary measures in the range B18:C20. In particular, the investor's expected return per dollar invested is 0.153 and the standard deviation is 0.092. Based on a $10,000 investment, these translate to an expected total dollar return of $1534 and a standard deviation of $921.67.

It is interesting to see how the expected portfolio return and the standard deviation of portfolio return change as the amount the investor puts into GM stock changes. To do this, we make sure that the value in cell B6 is a constant and that *formulas* are entered in cells C6, B7, and C7. In this way, these last three cells update automatically when the value in cell B6 changes—and the total investment amount remains $10,000. Then we form a data table in the range A24:C35 that calculates the mean and standard deviation of the total dollar portfolio return for each of several GM investment proportions in column A. (To do this, enter the formulas =C18 and =C20 in cells B24 and C24, highlight the range A24:C35, select the Data/Table command, and enter cell B6 as the column input cell. No row input cell is necessary.)

The graph of the means and standard deviations from this data table appears in Figure 4.7. It shows that the expected portfolio return steadily increases as more and more is put into GM (and less is put into gold). However, the standard deviation, often used as a measure of risk, first decreases, then increases. This means there is a trade-off between expected return and risk as measured by the standard deviation. The investor could obtain a higher expected return by putting more of his money into GM, but past a fraction of approximately 0.4, the risk also increases. ∎

PROBLEMS

Level A

29 The quarterly sales levels (in millions of dollars) of two U.S. retail giants are dependent on the general state of the national economy in the forthcoming months. Table 4.6 provides the probability distribution for the projected sales volume of each of these two retailers in the forthcoming quarter.

TABLE 4.6 Quarterly Sales Volume of Two U.S. Retail Giants

State of the National Economy	Probability of State	Sears Sales	Kmart Sales
Strong growth	0.15	10.5	8.8
Moderate growth	0.35	9.7	7.9
Weak growth	0.25	8.2	7.5
No growth	0.25	7.5	7.0

a Find the mean and standard deviation of the quarterly sales volume for each of these two retailers. Compare these two sets of summary measures.

b Compute covariance and correlation measures for the given quarterly sales volumes. Interpret your numerical findings.

30 The possible annual percentage returns of the stocks of Alpha, Inc. and Beta, Inc. share a common probability distribution, given in Table 4.7.

TABLE 4.7 Annual Stock Returns of Alpha and Beta

Probability	Annual Return of Alpha, Inc.	Annual Return of Beta, Inc.
0.05	40.3	−18.8
0.15	37.9	−9.5
0.30	30.1	1.3
0.22	24.6	6.9
0.13	19.7	13.0
0.09	7.5	22.6
0.06	−2.3	35.8

a What is the expected annual return of Alpha's stock? What is the expected annual return of Beta's stock?

b What is the standard deviation of the annual return of Alpha's stock? What is the standard deviation of the annual return of Beta's stock?

c On the basis of your answers to the questions in parts **a** and **b**, which of these two stocks would you prefer to buy? Defend your choice.

d Are the annual returns of these two stocks positively or negatively associated with each other? How might the answer to this question influence your decision to purchase shares of one or both of these companies?

31 The annual bonuses awarded to members of the management team and assembly line workers of an automobile manufacturer depend largely on the corporation's sales performance during the preceding year. Table 4.8 contains the probability distribution associated with possible bonuses awarded (measured in hundreds of dollars) to white-collar and blue-collar employees at the end of the company's fiscal year.

Annual Bonuses Awarded to White- and Blue-Collar Employees

Characterization of Sales Performance	Probability	White-Collar Bonus	Blue-Collar Bonus
Outstanding	0.11	50.5	7.9
Strong	0.24	33.7	6.3
Good	0.26	26.8	5.5
Fair	0.25	13.3	3.4
Weak	0.09	4.1	1.2
Poor	0.05	0.0	0.0

   a How much do a manager and an assembly line worker expect to receive in their bonus check at the end of a typical year?

   b For which group of employees within this organization does there appear to be more variability in the distribution of possible annual bonuses?

   c How strongly associated are the bonuses awarded to the white-collar and blue-collar employees of this company at the end of the year? What are some possible implications of this result for the relations between members of the management team and the assembly line workers in the future?

32 Consumer demand for small, economical automobiles depends somewhat on recent trends in the average price of unleaded gasoline. For example, consider the information given in Table 4.9 on the distributions of average annual sales of the Honda Civic and the Saturn SL in relation to the trend of the average price of unleaded fuel over the past 2 years.

Annual Sales of Compact Cars in Relation to Average Price of Unleaded Gasoline

Trend in Average Price of Unleaded Gasoline	Probability	Honda Civic Sales	Saturn SL Sales
Large increase	0.07	268,407	276,796
Moderate increase	0.19	277,129	278,438
Slight increase	0.31	285,002	282,950
No change	0.24	286,350	284,574
Slight decrease	0.12	289,435	286,636
Moderate decrease	0.06	291,044	287,674
Large decrease	0.01	292,787	288,369

   a Find the annual mean sales levels of the Honda Civic and the Saturn SL.

   b For which of these two models are sales levels more sensitive to recent changes in the average price of unleaded gasoline?

   c Given the available information, how strongly associated are the typical annual sales volumes of these two popular compact cars? Provide a qualitative explanation of your quantitative measure here.

Level B

33 Upon completing their respective homework assignments, marketing majors and accounting majors at a large state university enjoy hanging out at the local tavern in the evenings. Table 4.10 contains the distribution of number of hours spent by these students at the tavern in a typical week, along with typical cumulative grade-point averages (on a 4-point scale) for marketing and accounting students with common social habits.

TABLE 4.10 **Hours Spent at the Local Tavern Each Week by Marketing and Accounting Majors**

Hours Spent at the Tavern in a Typical Week	Probability	Average GPA of Marketing Majors	Average GPA of Accounting Majors
0	0.19	3.43	3.23
1–3	0.12	3.28	3.17
4–6	0.19	3.14	3.11
7–9	0.23	3.00	3.05
10–12	0.18	2.81	2.98
13–15	0.06	2.65	2.84
15 or more	0.03	2.49	2.69

a Compare the means and standard deviations of the grade-point averages of the two groups of students. Does one of the two groups consistently perform better academically than the other? Explain.

b Does academic performance, as measured by cumulative GPA, seem to be associated with the amount of time students typically spend at the local tavern? If so, characterize the observed relationship.

c Compute the covariance and correlation between the typical grade-point averages earned by the two subgroups of students. What do these measures of association indicate in this case? ■

4.8 Distribution of Two Random Variables: Joint Probability Approach

The previous section illustrated one method for specifying the joint distribution of two random variables. We first identify several possible scenarios, next specify the value of each random variable that will occur under each scenario, and then assess the probability of each scenario. For people who think in terms of scenarios—and this includes many business managers—this is a very appealing approach.

In this section we illustrate an alternative method for specifying the probability distribution of two random variables X and Y. We first identify the possible values of X and the possible values of Y. Let x and y be any two such values. Then we *directly* assess the joint probability of the pair (x, y) and denote it by $P(X = x$ and $Y = y)$ or more simply by $p(x, y)$. This is the probability of the joint event that $X = x$ and $Y = y$ both occur. As always, the joint probabilities must be nonnegative and sum to 1.

A joint probability distribution, specified by all probabilities of the form $p(x, y)$, provides a tremendous amount of information. It indicates not only how X and Y are related, but also how each of X and Y is distributed in its own right. In probability terms, the joint distribution of X and Y determines the **marginal distributions** of both X and Y, where each marginal distribution is the probability distribution of a *single* random variable. The joint distribution also determines the **conditional distributions** of X given Y, and of Y given X. The conditional distribution of X given Y, for example, is the distribution of X, given that Y is known to equal a certain value.

These concepts are best explained by means of an example, as we do next.

EXAMPLE 4.5

A company sells two products, product 1 and product 2, that tend to be substitutes for one another. That is, if a customer buys product 1, she tends not to buy product 2, and vice versa. The company assesses the joint probability distribution of demand for the two products during the coming month. This joint distribution appears in the shaded region of Figure 4.8. (See the Demand sheet of the file SUBS.XLS.) The left and top margins of this table show the possible values of demand for the two products. Specifically, the company assumes that demand for product 1 can be from 100 to 400 (in increments of 100) and demand for product 2 can be from 50 to 250 (in increments of 50). Furthermore, each possible value of demand 1 can occur with each possible value of demand 2, with the joint probability given in the table. For example, the joint probability that demand 1 is 200 *and* demand 2 is 100 is 0.08. Given this joint probability distribution, describe more fully the probabilistic structure of demands for the two products.

FIGURE 4.8 **Joint Probability Distribution of Demands**

	A	B	C	D	E	F
1	Probability distribution of demands for substitute products					
2						
3				Demand for product 1		
4			100	200	300	400
5		50	0.015	0.040	0.050	0.035
6	Demand	100	0.030	0.080	0.075	0.025
7	for	150	0.050	0.100	0.100	0.020
8	product 2	200	0.045	0.100	0.050	0.010
9		250	0.060	0.080	0.025	0.010

Solution

Let D_1 and D_2 denote the demands for products 1 and 2. We first find the marginal distributions of D_1 and D_2. These are the row and column sums of the joint probabilities in Figure 4.9. An example of the reasoning is as follows. Consider the probability $P(D_1 = 200)$. If demand for product 1 is to be 200, it must be accompanied by *some* value of D_2; that is, exactly one of the joint events ($D_1 = 200$ and $D_2 = 50$) through ($D_1 = 200$ and $D_2 = 250$) must occur. Using the addition rule for probability, we find the total probability of these joint events by summing the corresponding joint probabilities. The result is $P(D_1 = 200) = 0.40$, the column sum corresponding to $D_1 = 200$. Similarly, marginal probabilities for D_2 such as $P(D_2 = 150) = 0.27$ are the row sums in column G. Note that the marginal probabilities, either those in row 10 or those in column G, sum to 1, as they should. They indicate how the demand for either product behaves in its own right, aside from any considerations of the *other* product.

The marginal distributions indicate that "in-between" values of D_1 or of D_2 are most likely, whereas extreme values in either direction are less likely. However, these marginal distributions tell us nothing about the *relationship* between D_1 and D_2. After all, products 1 and 2 are supposedly substitute products. The joint probabilities spell out this relationship, but they are rather difficult to interpret. A better way is to calculate the conditional distributions of D_1 given D_2, or of D_2 given D_1. We do this in rows 12 through 29 of Figure 4.9.

We first focus on the conditional distribution of D_1 given D_2, shown in rows 12 through 19. In each row of this table (rows 15 through 19), we fix the value of D_2 at the value in column B and calculate the conditional probabilities of D_1 given this fixed value

FIGURE 4.9   **Marginal and Conditional Distributions and Summary Measures**

	A	B	C	D	E	F	G	H	I	J	K
1	Probability distribution of demands for substitute products										
2											
3				Demand for product 1							
4			100	200	300	400			Selected range names		
5		50	0.015	0.040	0.050	0.035	0.14		CovDem: B47		
6	Demand	100	0.030	0.080	0.075	0.025	0.21		Demands1: C4:F4		
7	for	150	0.050	0.100	0.100	0.020	0.27		Demands2: B5:B9		
8	product 2	200	0.045	0.100	0.050	0.010	0.21		JtProbs: C5:F9		
9		250	0.060	0.080	0.025	0.010	0.18		MeanDem1: B32		
10			0.20	0.40	0.30	0.10			MeanDem2: C32		
11									Probs1: C10:F10		
12	Conditional distribution of demand for product 1, given demand for product 2								Probs2: G5:G9		
13				Demand for product 1					ProdDevsDem: C37:F41		
14			100	200	300	400			SqDevsDem1: C36:F36		
15		50	0.11	0.29	0.36	0.25	1		SqDevsDem2: B37:B41		
16	Demand	100	0.14	0.38	0.36	0.12	1		StdevDem1: B45		
17	for	150	0.19	0.37	0.37	0.07	1		StdevDem2: C45		
18	product 2	200	0.22	0.49	0.24	0.05	1				
19		250	0.34	0.46	0.14	0.06	1				
20											
21	Conditional distribution of demand for product 2, given demand for product 1										
22				Demand for product 1							
23			100	200	300	400					
24		50	0.08	0.10	0.17	0.35					
25	Demand	100	0.15	0.20	0.25	0.25					
26	for	150	0.25	0.25	0.33	0.20					
27	product 2	200	0.23	0.25	0.17	0.10					
28		250	0.30	0.20	0.08	0.10					
29			1	1	1	1					
30											
31		Product 1	Product 2								
32	Means	230.00	153.25								
33											
34	Squared deviations from means (along left and top)										
35	and products of deviations from mean (in body)										
36			16900.0	900.0	4900.0	28900.0					
37		10660.6	13422.5	3097.5	-7227.5	-17552.5					
38		2835.6	6922.5	1597.5	-3727.5	-9052.5					
39		10.6	422.5	97.5	-227.5	-552.5					
40		2185.6	-6077.5	-1402.5	3272.5	7947.5					
41		9360.6	-12577.5	-2902.5	6772.5	16447.5					
42											
43		Product 1	Product 2								
44	Variances	8100.00	4176.94								
45	Stdevs	90.00	64.63								
46											
47	Covariance	-1647.50									
48	Correlation	-0.283									

of D_2. From the conditional probability formula, this is the joint probability divided by the marginal probability of D_2. For example, the conditional probability that D_1 equals 200, given that D_2 equals 150, is

$$P(D_1 = 200|D_2 = 150) = \frac{P(D_1 = 200 \text{ and } D_2 = 150)}{P(D_2 = 150)} = \frac{0.10}{0.27} = 0.37$$

These conditional probabilities can be calculated all at once by entering the formula

$$=C5/\$G5$$

in cell C15 and copying it to the range C15:F19. (Make sure you see why only column G, not row 5, is held absolute in this formula.) We can also check that each row of this table is a probability distribution in its own right by summing across rows. The row sums shown in column G are all equal to 1, as they should be.

Similarly, the conditional distribution of D_2 given D_1 appears in rows 21 through 29. Here, each column represents the conditional probability distribution of D_2 given the fixed value of D_1 in row 23. These probabilities can be calculated by entering the formula

$$=C5/C\$10$$

in cell C24 and copying it to the range C24:F28. Now the column sums shown in row 29 are 1, indicating that each column of the table represents a probability distribution.

Various summary measures can now be calculated. We show some of them in Figure 4.9. The following steps present the details.

1   **Expected values.** The expected demands in cells B32 and C32 follow from the marginal distributions. To calculate these, enter the formulas

$$=SUMPRODUCT(Demands1,Probs1)$$

and

$$=SUMPRODUCT(Demands2,Probs2)$$

in these two cells. Note that each of these is the usual formula for an expected value, that is, a sum of products of possible values and their (marginal) probabilities.

2   **Variances and standard deviations.** These measures of variability are also calculated from the marginal distributions in the usual way. We first find squared deviations from the means, then calculate the weighted sum of these squared deviations, weighted by the corresponding marginal probabilities. For example, to find the variance of D_1, enter the formula

$$=(C4-MeanDem1)^2$$

in cell C36 and copy it across to cell F36. Then enter the formula

$$=SUMPRODUCT(SqDevsDem1,Probs1)$$

in cell B44, and take its square root in cell B45.

3   **Covariance and correlation.** The formulas for covariance and correlation are the same as before [see equations (4.8) and (4.9)]. However, we proceed somewhat differently than in Example 4.4. Now we form a complete table of products of deviations from means in the range C37:F41. To do so, enter the formula

$$=(C\$4-MeanDem1)*(\$B5-MeanDem2)$$

in cell C37 and copy it to the range C37:F41. Then calculate the covariance in cell B47 with the formula

$$=SUMPRODUCT(ProdDevsDem,JtProbs)$$

Finally, calculate the correlation in cell B48 with the formula

$$=CovarDem/(StdevDem1*StdevDem2)$$

Now let's step back and see what we have. If we are interested in the behavior of a single demand only, say D_1, then the relevant quantities are the marginal probabilities in row 10 and the mean and standard deviation of D_1 in cells B32 and B45. However, we are often more interested in the joint behavior of D_1 and D_2. The best way to see this behavior is in the conditional probability tables. For example, compare the probability distributions in rows 15 through 19. As the value of D_2 increases, the probabilities for D_1 tend to shift to the left. That is, as demand for product 2 increases, demand for product 1 tends to decrease. This is only a *tendency*. When D_2 equals its largest value, there is still some chance that D_1 will be large, but this probability is fairly small.

This behavior can be seen more clearly from the graph in Figure 4.10. Each line in this graph corresponds to one of the rows 15 through 19. The legend represents the different values of D_2. We see that when D_2 is large, D_1 tends to be small, although again, this is only a tendency, not a perfect relationship. When we say that the two products are substitutes for one another, this is the type of behavior we imply.

By symmetry, the conditional distribution of D_2 given D_1 shows the same type of behavior. This is illustrated in Figure 4.11, where each line represents one of the columns C through F in the range C24:F28 and the legend represents the different values of D_1.

FIGURE 4.10 **Conditional Distributions of Demand 1 Given Demand 2**

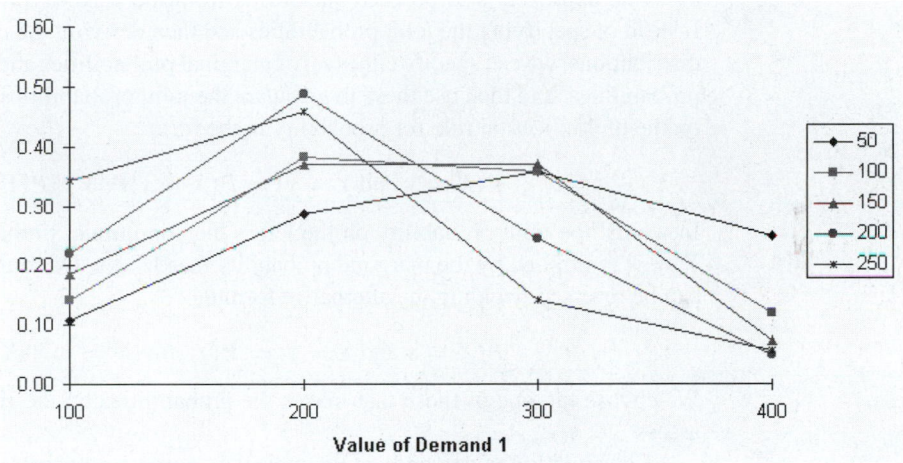

FIGURE 4.11 **Conditional Distributions of Demand 2 Given Demand 1**

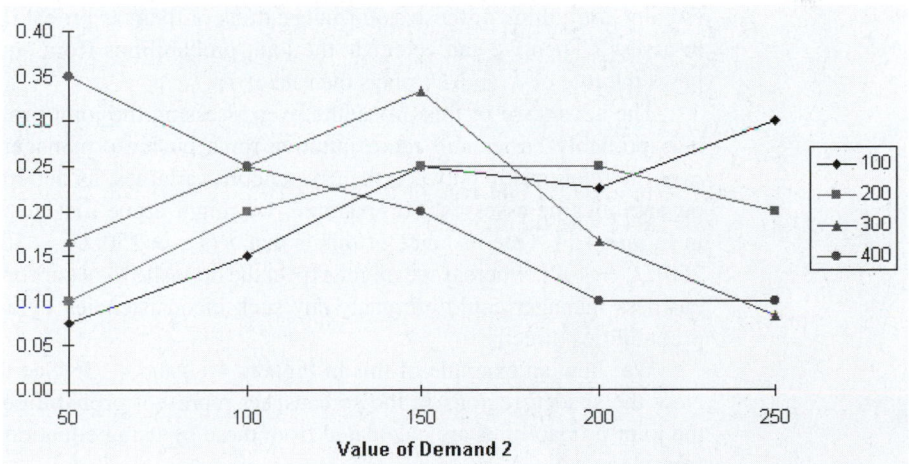

The information in these graphs is confirmed—to some extent, at least—by the co-variance and correlation between D_1 and D_2. In particular, their negative values indicate that demands for the two products tend to move in opposite directions. Also, the rather small magnitude of the correlation, -0.283, indicates that the relationship between these demands is far from perfect. When D_1 is large, there is still a reasonably good chance that D_2 will be large, and when D_1 is small, there is still a reasonably good chance that D_2 will be small. ■

How to Assess Joint Probability Distributions   In the scenario approach from Section 4.7, only one probability for each scenario has to be assessed. In the joint probability approach, a whole table of joint probabilities must be assessed. This can be quite difficult, especially when there are many possible values for each of the random variables. In the above example it requires $4 \times 5 = 20$ joint probabilities that not only sum to 1 but imply the "substitute product" behavior we want.

One approach is to proceed *backwards* from the way we proceeded in the example. Instead of specifying the joint probabilities and then deriving the marginal and conditional distributions, we can specify either set of marginal probabilities and either set of conditional probabilities, and then use these to *calculate* the joint probabilities. The reasoning is based on the multiplication rule for probability in the form

$$P(X = x \text{ and } Y = y) = P(X = x|Y = y)P(Y = y) \qquad \textbf{(4.10)}$$

In words, the joint probability on the left is the conditional probability that $X = x$ given $Y = y$, multiplied by the marginal probability that $Y = y$. Of course, the roles of X and Y can be reversed, yielding the alternative formula

$$P(X = x \text{ and } Y = y) = P(Y = y|X = x)P(X = x) \qquad \textbf{(4.11)}$$

We choose the one of these that makes the probabilities on the right-hand side easiest to assess.

Referring to the demands in Example 4.5, suppose a business manager can assess the marginal distribution of D_1 shown in row 10 of Figure 4.9. (Don't think of these as column sums any more; think of them as probabilities of demand for product 1 that the manager assesses, possibly using historical data.) Also, suppose that for each possible value of D_1, the manager is able to assess the conditional distributions of D_2 shown in the range C24:F28. (Again, don't think of these as formulas; think of them as probabilities the manager is able to assess.) Then we can calculate the joint probabilities from equation (4.10), where D_2 plays the role of X and D_1 plays the role of Y.

The advantage of this procedure over assessing the joint probabilities directly is that it is probably easier and more intuitive for a business manager. He gets more control over the relationship between the two random variables, as determined by the conditional probabilities he assesses. For example, we might argue that there is some inconsistency in Figure 4.11. One instance of this is that $P(D_2 = 250|D_1 = 300)$ is *less than* $P(D_2 = 250|D_1 = 400)$, whereas we might expect the opposite to occur for substitute products. The business manager could eliminate any such inconsistencies by assessing the conditional probabilities directly.

We show an example of this in Figures 4.12 and 4.13. (See the file JTPROBS.XLS.) Now the shaded regions in the spreadsheet represent probabilities assessed *directly*, and the joint probabilities are calculated from these by using equation (4.10). Specifically, the formula in cell C20 is

$$=C11*C\$6$$

which is then copied to the range C20:F24. The associated graph of the conditional probabilities now appears to be consistent with the meaning of substitute products.

FIGURE 4.12 **Indirect Method for Assessing Joint Probabilities**

	A	B	C	D	E	F	G
1	**An indirect assessment of joint probabilities**						
2							
3	Marginal distribution of demand for product 1						
4				Demand 1			
5		Values	100	200	300	400	
6		Probabilities	0.20	0.40	0.30	0.10	
7							
8	Conditional distributions of demand for product 2 given demand for product 1						
9				Demand 1			
10			100	200	300	400	
11	Demand	50	0.025	0.050	0.150	0.350	
12		100	0.075	0.150	0.250	0.250	
13		150	0.250	0.300	0.300	0.200	
14		200	0.300	0.250	0.200	0.150	
15		250	0.350	0.250	0.100	0.050	
16							
17	Calculated joint probability distribution of demands						
18				Demand 1			
19			100	200	300	400	
20	Demand	50	0.005	0.020	0.045	0.035	
21		100	0.015	0.060	0.075	0.025	
22		150	0.050	0.120	0.090	0.020	
23		200	0.060	0.100	0.060	0.015	
24		250	0.070	0.100	0.030	0.005	

FIGURE 4.13 **Conditional Distributions of Demand 2 Given Demand 1**

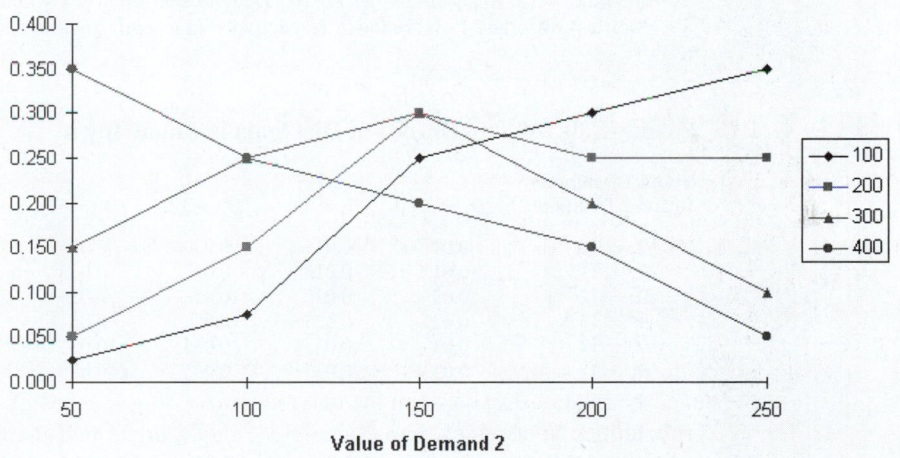

PROBLEMS

Level A

34 Let X and Y represent the number of Dell and Compaq desktop computers, respectively, sold per month at a local computer store. Table 4.11 contains the probabilities of various combinations of monthly sales volumes of these competitors.

TABLE 4.11 **Local Monthly Sales of Dell and Compaq Desktop Computers**

Dell Sales/Compaq Sales	$Y = 25$	$Y = 30$	$Y = 35$	$Y = 40$	$Y = 45$
$X = 25$	0.01	0.01	0.03	0.02	0.01
$X = 30$	0.02	0.03	0.04	0.05	0.01
$X = 35$	0.04	0.04	0.08	0.08	0.03
$X = 40$	0.04	0.04	0.08	0.08	0.03
$X = 45$	0.02	0.03	0.04	0.05	0.01
$X = 50$	0.01	0.01	0.03	0.02	0.01

a Find the marginal distributions of X and Y. Interpret your findings.

b Calculate the expected monthly desktop computer sales volumes for Dell and Compaq at this computer store.

c Calculate the standard deviations of the monthly desktop computer sales volumes for Dell and Compaq at this computer store.

d Construct and interpret the conditional distribution of X given Y.

e Construct and interpret the conditional distribution of Y given X.

f Find and interpret the correlation between X and Y.

35 The joint probability distribution of the weekly demand for two brands of diet soda is provided in Table 4.12. In particular, let D_1 and D_2 represent the weekly demand (in hundreds of 2-liter bottles) for brand 1 and brand 2, respectively, in a small town in central Pennsylvania.

TABLE 4.12 **Weekly Sales of Two Brands of Diet Soda in Small Town**

Brand 1 Demand/ Brand 2 Demand	$D_2 = 10$	$D_2 = 11$	$D_2 = 12$	$D_2 = 13$	$D_2 = 14$	$D_2 = 15$
$D_1 = 10$	0.01	0.015	0.03	0.035	0.035	0.03
$D_1 = 11$	0.01	0.015	0.03	0.035	0.035	0.03
$D_1 = 12$	0.02	0.025	0.05	0.05	0.025	0.02
$D_1 = 13$	0.02	0.025	0.05	0.05	0.025	0.02
$D_1 = 14$	0.03	0.035	0.035	0.03	0.015	0.01
$D_1 = 15$	0.03	0.035	0.035	0.03	0.015	0.01

a Find the mean and standard deviation of this community's weekly demand for each brand of diet soda.

b What is the probability that the weekly demand for each brand will be at least one standard deviation above its mean?

c What is the probability that at least one of the two weekly demands will be at least one standard deviation above its mean?

d What is the correlation between the weekly demands for these two brands of diet soda? What does this measure of association tell you about the relationship between these two products?

36 A local pharmacy has two checkout stations available to its customers: a regular checkout station and an express checkout station. Customers with six or fewer items are assumed to join the express line. Let X and Y be the numbers of customers in the regular checkout line and the express checkout line, respectively, at the busiest time of a typical day. Note that these numbers include the customer(s) being served, if any. The joint distribution for X and Y is given in Table 4.13.

TABLE 4.13 **Numbers of Customers in Checkout Lines at a Local Pharmacy**

Number in Regular Line/ Number in Express Line	$Y = 0$	$Y = 1$	$Y = 2$	$Y = 3$ or more
$X = 0$	0.05	0.05	0.04	0.16
$X = 1$	0.10	0.05	0.02	0.03
$X = 2$	0.09	0.05	0.01	0.11
$X = 3$ or more	0.06	0.05	0.03	0.10

a Find the marginal distributions of X and Y. What does each of these distributions tell you?

b Calculate the conditional distribution of X given Y. What is the practical benefit of knowing this conditional distribution?

c What is the probability that no one is waiting or being served in the regular checkout line?

d What is the probability that no one is waiting or being served in the express checkout line?

e What is the probability that no more than two customers are waiting in both lines combined?

f On average, how many customers would we expect to see in each of these two lines during the busiest time of day at the pharmacy?

37 Suppose that the manufacturer of a particular product assesses the joint distribution of price P per unit and demand D for its product in the upcoming quarter as provided in Table 4.14.

TABLE 4.14 **Quarterly Price and Quantity Demanded for a Given Product**

Price per Unit/Demand	$D = 2000$	$D = 2500$	$D = 3000$	$D = 3500$
$P = \$30$	0.025	0.05	0.05	0.175
$P = \$35$	0.045	0.06	0.095	0.05
$P = \$40$	0.075	0.10	0.05	0.025
$P = \$45$	0.10	0.05	0.025	0.025

a Find the expected price and demand level in the upcoming quarter.

b What is the probability that the price of this product will be above its mean in the upcoming quarter?

c What is the probability that the demand for this product will be below its mean in the upcoming quarter?

d What is the probability that demand for this product will exceed 2500 units during the upcoming quarter, given that its price will be less than $40?

e What is the probability that demand for this product will be less than 3500 units during the upcoming quarter, given that its price will be greater than $30?

f Compute the correlation between price and demand. Is the result consistent with your expectations? Explain.

38 The recent weekly trends of two particular stock prices, P_1 and P_2, can best be described by the joint probability distribution shown in Table 4.15.

TABLE 4.15 **Weekly Trends in Two Stock Prices**

Stock 1/Stock 2	P_2 Increases	P_2 Remains Constant	P_2 Decreases
P_1 Increases	0.05	0.05	0.10
P_1 Remains Constant	0.05	0.20	0.25
P_1 Decreases	0.10	0.05	0.15

   a What is the probability that the price of stock 1 will not increase in the upcoming week?

   b What is the probability that the price of stock 2 will change in the upcoming week?

   c What is the probability that the price of stock 1 will not decrease, given that the price of stock 2 will remain constant in the upcoming week?

   d What is the probability that the price of stock 2 will change, given that the price of stock 1 will change in the upcoming week?

   e Why is it impossible to find the correlation between the typical weekly movements of these two stock prices from the information given? Nevertheless, does it appear that they are positively or negatively related? Why? What are the implications of this result for choosing an investment portfolio that may or may not include these two particular stocks?

39 Two service elevators are used in parallel by employees of a three-story hotel building. At any point in time when both elevators are stationary, let X_1 and X_2 be the floor numbers at which elevators 1 and 2, respectively, are currently located. The joint probability distribution of X_1 and X_2 is given in Table 4.16.

TABLE 4.16 **Locations of Two Service Elevators**

Location of Elevator 1/ Location of Elevator 2	$X_2 = 1$	$X_2 = 2$	$X_2 = 3$
$X_1 = 1$	0.25	0.08	0.14
$X_1 = 2$	0.07	0.10	0.07
$X_1 = 3$	0.16	0.08	0.05

   a What is the probability that these two elevators are not stationed on the same floor?

   b What is the probability that elevator 2 is located on the third floor?

   c What is the probability that elevator 1 is not located on the first floor?

   d What is the probability that elevator 2 is located on the first floor, given that elevator 1 is not stationed on the first floor?

   e What is the probability that a hotel employee approaching the first-floor elevators will find at least one available for service?

   f Repeat part **e** for a hotel employee approaching each of the second- and third-floor elevators.

   g How might this hotel's operations manager respond to your findings for each of the previous questions? ■

Independent Random Variables

A very important special case of joint distributions is when the random variables are **independent**. Intuitively, this means that any information about the values of any of the random variables is worthless in terms of predicting any of the others. In particular, if there are only two random variables X and Y, then information about X is worthless in terms of predicting Y, and vice versa. Usually, random variables in real applications are *not* independent; they are usually related in some way, in which case we say they are **dependent**. However, we often make an assumption of independence in mathematical models to simplify the analysis.

The most intuitive way to express independence of X and Y is to say that their conditional distributions are equal to their marginals. For example, the conditional probability that X equals any value x, given that Y equals some value y, equals the marginal probability that X equals x—and this statement is true for *all* values of x and y. In words, knowledge of the value of Y has no effect on probabilities involving X. Similarly, knowledge of the value of X has no effect on probabilities involving Y.

An equivalent way of stating the independence property is that for all values x and y, the events $X = x$ and $Y = y$ are probabilistically independent in the sense of Section 4.2.4. This leads to the important property that joint probabilities equal the product of the marginals, that is,

$$P(X = x \text{ and } Y = y) = P(X = x)P(Y = y) \tag{4.12}$$

This follows from equation (4.10) and the fact that conditionals equal marginals under independence. Equation (4.12) might not be as intuitive, but it is very useful, as illustrated in the following example.

E X A M P L E   4 . 6

A distributor of parts keeps track of the inventory of each part type at the end of every week. If the inventory of a given part type is at or below a certain value called the **reorder point**, the distributor places an order for that part. The amount ordered is a constant called the **order quantity**. We make several assumptions: (1) the ordering lead time is negligible, so that orders placed at the end of one week arrive at the beginning of the next week; (2) sales are lost if customer demand during any week is greater than that week's beginning inventory, that is, there is no backlogging of demand; (3) customer demands for a given part type in different weeks are independent random variables; and (4) the marginal distribution of weekly demand for a given part type is the same each week. The plant manager has estimated the data shown in the shaded regions of Figure 4.14 (page 170) for a particular part type. (See the file INVNTORY.XLS.) She wants to calculate the mean revenue in each of the first two weeks, given that the initial inventory at the beginning of week 1 is 250, the value shown in cell B12.

Solution

This example is both simpler and more complex than the previous example. The simpler part is the probabilistic structure. Due to the assumptions that weekly demands are independent and have the same distribution, all the manager needs to assess is a *single* weekly distribution of demand, as shown in the range D12:E16 of Figure 4.14. Then we can use equation (4.12)

FIGURE 4.14 Input Data for Inventory Example

	A	B	C	D	E	F	G	H
1	**Distribution of two-period revenue with independent demands**							
2								
3	**Assumptions:**							
4	Demands in each of two periods are independent random variables with the same distribution							
5	Sales are lost if demand is greater than on-hand inventory (no backlogging)							
6	Ordering policy at end of period 1 is a reorder point/order quantity policy							
7	Lead time for order delivery is zero							
8	Unit selling price is the same in each period							
9								
10	**Input parameters**			Probability distribution of demand in each period				
11				Demand	Probability			
12	Initial inventory	250		100	0.10			
13	Reorder point	100		200	0.25			
14	Order quantity	400		300	0.25			
15	Unit selling price	$5		400	0.30			
16				500	0.10			

to obtain the joint distribution of demands in weeks 1 and 2. These appear in the range C21:G25 of Figure 4.15. To obtain these joint probabilities, we calculate products of marginals by entering the formula

$$=VLOOKUP(C\$20,DistTable,2)*VLOOKUP(\$B21,DistTable,2)$$

in cell C21 and copying it to the range C21:G25. (This formula is not as bad as it looks. It simply multiplies the two marginal probabilities corresponding to the demands in the top and left margins of the joint probability table.) As a check, we calculate the row sums (in

FIGURE 4.15 Calculations for Inventory Example

	A	B	C	D	E	F	G	H	I	J	K
10	**Input parameters**			Probability distribution of demand in each week					**Selected range names**		
11				Demand	Probability				DistTable: D12:E16		
12	Initial inventory	250		100	0.10				InitInv: B12		
13	Reorder point	100		200	0.25				JtProbs: C21:G25		
14	Order quantity	400		300	0.25				OrderQuan: B14		
15	Unit selling price	$5		400	0.30				Probs1: C26:G26		
16				500	0.10				ReorderPt: B13		
17									Revenues1: C30:G30		
18	Joint distribution of demands in two weeks								Revenues2: C37:G41		
19				Demand in week 1					UnitPrice: B15		
20			100	200	300	400	500	Check			
21	Demand in	100	0.010	0.025	0.025	0.030	0.010	0.10			
22	week 2	200	0.025	0.063	0.063	0.075	0.025	0.25			
23		300	0.025	0.063	0.063	0.075	0.025	0.25			
24		400	0.030	0.075	0.075	0.090	0.030	0.30			
25		500	0.010	0.025	0.025	0.030	0.010	0.10			
26		Check	0.10	0.25	0.25	0.30	0.10				
27											
28	Table of revenues in week 1 for each value of demand in week 1										
29		Demand	100	200	300	400	500				
30		Revenue	$500	$1,000	$1,250	$1,250	$1,250				
31											
32	Mean revenue in week 1	$1,113									
33											
34	Table of revenues in week 2 for each combination of demands										
35				Demand in week 1							
36			100	200	300	400	500				
37	Demand in	100	$500	$500	$500	$500	$500				
38	week 2	200	$750	$1,000	$1,000	$1,000	$1,000				
39		300	$750	$1,500	$1,500	$1,500	$1,500				
40		400	$750	$2,000	$2,000	$2,000	$2,000				
41		500	$750	$2,250	$2,000	$2,000	$2,000				
42											
43	Mean revenue in week 2	$1,406.25									

row 26) and column sums (in column H) of the joint probabilities. These are the marginal probabilities of demands in weeks 1 and 2, and they agree with the probabilities in the range E12:E16, as they should.

The more complex part of this example involves the random variables of interest, the revenues in weeks 1 and 2. This is especially true for the revenue in week 2 because it depends on the demands in *both* periods. (Do you see why?) We begin with the revenue in week 1. This revenue is the unit price multiplied by the smaller of on-hand inventory and demand in week 1. We use this fact to calculate the revenue in week 1 for each week 1 demand listed in row 29. Specifically, enter the formula

$$=UnitPrice*MIN(C29,InitInv)$$

in cell C30 and copy it across row 30. Given these values, we can then calculate the mean revenue in week 1 by entering the formula

$$=SUMPRODUCT(Revenues1,Probs1)$$

in cell B32.

Now we turn to revenue in week 2. It is the unit price multiplied by the number of units sold in week 2, and this latter quantity is the smaller of the beginning inventory in week 2 and the demand in week 2. Furthermore, the beginning inventory in week 2 depends on the demand in week 1 because this demand determines how much (if any) is left at the end of week 1 and whether an order is placed. The analysis breaks down into three cases. To describe these, let I_0, D_1, and RP denote the beginning inventory in week 1, the demand in week 1, and the reorder point. Then exactly one of the following occurs.

- If $I_0 - D_1 \leq 0$, the ending inventory in week 1 is 0, and an order is placed. This brings the beginning inventory in week 2 up to 400 units (the order quantity).

- If $0 < I_0 - D_1 \leq RP$, then positive inventory is on hand at the end of week 1, but demand in week 1 is large enough to trigger an order. Therefore, beginning inventory in week 2 is $I_0 - D_1$ plus the order quantity.

- If $I_0 - D_1 > RP$, no order is triggered, so the beginning inventory in week 2 equals the ending inventory in week 1, $I_0 - D_1$.

Putting all of this together, we can calculate the revenue in week 2 for each combination of week 1 and week 2 demands. We do this in the range C37:G41 by entering the formula

$$= UnitPrice*MIN(\$B37,IF(InitInv-C\$36<=0,OrderQuan,IF(InitInv-C\$36<=$$

$$ReorderPt,InitInv-C\$36+OrderQuan,InitInv-C\$36)))$$

in cell C37 and copying it to the range C37:G41. Although this formula is complex, it simply implements the logic in the above discussion with nested IF functions. The rest is straightforward. We calculate the mean revenue in week 2 in the usual way, as a sum of products of possible revenues and their probabilities. This is done in cell B43 with the formula

$$=SUMPRODUCT(Revenues2,JtProbs)$$

The advantage of doing all this work is that we can now change any of the inputs in the shaded cells and the mean revenues will be recalculated automatically. For example, you can check that if the initial inventory, reorder point, and order quantity are changed to 300, 50, and 350, the mean revenues in weeks 1 and 2 become $1275 and $1113.75. You can also check that if *only* the reorder point and the order quantity change, the mean revenue in week 1 remains the same. This should come as no surprise. The revenue in week 1 doesn't depend on the ordering policy at the *end* of week 1. ■

PROBLEMS

Level A

40 Table 4.17 shows the conditional distribution of the daily number of accidents at a given intersection during the winter months, X_2, given the amount of snowfall (in inches) for the day, X_1. The marginal distribution of X_1 is provided in the bottom row of the table.

TABLE 4.17 **Daily Snowfall and Number of Accidents at a Given Intersection**

Daily Number of Accidents, Given Daily Snowfall	$X_1 = 0$	$X_1 = 1$	$X_1 = 2$	$X_1 = 3$	$X_1 = 4$ or more
$X_2 = 0$	0.85	0.70	0.66	0.57	0.50
$X_2 = 1$	0.12	0.23	0.25	0.30	0.27
$X_2 = 2$	0.02	0.05	0.06	0.07	0.13
$X_2 = 3$ or more	0.01	0.02	0.03	0.06	0.10
Marginal Distribution of X_1	**0.50**	**0.20**	**0.12**	**0.10**	**0.08**

   a Are X_1 and X_2 independent random variables? Explain why or why not.

   b What is the probability of observing no accidents at this intersection on a winter day with no snowfall?

   c What is the probability of observing no accidents at this intersection on a randomly selected winter day?

   d What is the probability of observing at least two accidents at this intersection on a randomly selected winter day on which the snowfall is at least 3 inches?

   e What is the probability of observing less than 4 inches of snowfall on a randomly selected day in this area?

41 A sporting goods store sells two competing brands of exercise bicycles. Let X_1 and X_2 be the numbers of the two brands sold on a typical day at this store. Based on available historical data, the conditional probability distribution of X_1 given X_2 is assessed and provided in Table 4.18. The marginal distribution of X_2 is given in the bottom row of this table.

TABLE 4.18 **Daily Sales of Two Competing Brands of Bicycles**

Sales of Brand 1, Given Sales of Brand 2	$X_2 = 0$	$X_2 = 1$	$X_2 = 2$	$X_2 = 3$
$X_1 = 0$	0.05	0.10	0.25	0.30
$X_1 = 1$	0.15	0.30	0.50	0.58
$X_1 = 2$	0.60	0.45	0.20	0.10
$X_1 = 3$	0.20	0.15	0.05	0.02
Marginal Distribution of X_2	**0.20**	**0.30**	**0.30**	**0.20**

   a Are X_1 and X_2 independent random variables? Explain why or why not.

   b What is the probability of observing the sale of one brand 1 bicycle and one brand 2 bicycle on the same day at this sporting goods store?

   c What is the probability of observing the sale of at least one brand 1 bicycle on a given day at this sporting goods store?

   d What is the probability of observing no more than two brand 2 bicycles on a given day at this sporting goods store?

   e Given that no brand 2 bicycles are sold on a given day, what is the likelihood of observing the sale of at least one brand 1 bicycle at this sporting goods store?

42 Table 4.19 contains the probabilities of various combinations of monthly sales volumes of Dell (X) and Compaq (Y) desktop computers at a local computer store. Are the monthly sales of these two competitors independent of each other? Explain your answer.

TABLE 4.19 **Local Monthly Sales of Dell and Compaq Desktop Computers**

Dell Sales/Compaq Sales	$Y = 25$	$Y = 30$	$Y = 35$	$Y = 40$	$Y = 45$
$X = 25$	0.01	0.01	0.03	0.02	0.01
$X = 30$	0.02	0.03	0.04	0.05	0.01
$X = 35$	0.04	0.04	0.08	0.08	0.03
$X = 40$	0.04	0.04	0.08	0.08	0.03
$X = 45$	0.02	0.03	0.04	0.05	0.01
$X = 50$	0.01	0.01	0.03	0.02	0.01

43 Let D_1 and D_2 represent the weekly demand (in hundreds of 2-liter bottles) for brand 1 diet soda and brand 2 diet soda, respectively, in a small central Pennsylvania town. The joint probability distribution of the weekly demand for these two brands of diet soda is provided in Table 4.20. Are D_1 and D_2 independent random variables in this case? Explain why or why not.

TABLE 4.20 **Weekly Sales of Two Brands of Diet Soda in Small Town**

Brand 1 Demand/ Brand 2 Demand	$D_2 = 10$	$D_2 = 11$	$D_2 = 12$	$D_2 = 13$	$D_2 = 14$	$D_2 = 15$
$D_1 = 10$	0.01	0.015	0.03	0.035	0.035	0.03
$D_1 = 11$	0.01	0.015	0.03	0.035	0.035	0.03
$D_1 = 12$	0.02	0.025	0.05	0.05	0.025	0.02
$D_1 = 13$	0.02	0.025	0.05	0.05	0.025	0.02
$D_1 = 14$	0.03	0.035	0.035	0.03	0.015	0.01
$D_1 = 15$	0.03	0.035	0.035	0.03	0.015	0.01

44 Table 4.21 contains the joint probability distribution of price P per unit and demand D for a particular product in the upcoming quarter.

TABLE 4.21 **Quarterly Price and Quantity Demanded for a Given Product**

Price per Unit/Demand	$D = 2000$	$D = 2500$	$D = 3000$	$D = 3500$
$P = \$30$	0.025	0.05	0.05	0.175
$P = \$35$	0.045	0.06	0.095	0.05
$P = \$40$	0.075	0.10	0.05	0.025
$P = \$45$	0.10	0.05	0.025	0.025

a Are P and D independent random variables? Explain your answer.

b If P and D are *not* independent random variables, which joint probabilities result in the same *marginal* probabilities for P and D as given in Table 4.21 but make P and D independent of each other?

Level B

45 You know that in 1 year you are going to buy a house. (In fact, you've already selected the neighborhood, but right now you're finishing your graduate degree, and you're engaged to be married this summer, so you're delaying the purchase for a year.) Right now, the annual interest rate for fixed-rate 30-year mortgages is 7.00%, and the price of the type of house you're considering is $120,000. However, things may change. Using your knowledge of the economy (and a crystal ball), you estimate that the interest rate may increase or decrease by as much as 1 percentage point. Also, the price of the house may increase by as much as $10,000—it certainly won't decrease! You assess the probability distribution of the interest rate change as shown in Table 4.22. The probability distribution of the increase in the price of the house is as shown in Table 4.23. Finally, you assume that the two random events (change in interest rate, change in house price) are probabilistically independent. This means that the probability of any joint event, such as an interest increase of 0.50% and a price increase of $5000, is the product of the individual probabilities.

TABLE 4.22 **Interest Rate Change**

Change in Annual Rate	Probability
Down 1.0%	0.02
Down 0.75%	0.03
Down 0.5%	0.05
Down 0.25%	0.10
No change	0.40
Up 0.25%	0.20
Up 0.5%	0.10
Up 0.75%	0.07
Up 1.0%	0.03

TABLE 4.23 **Price Increase**

Increase in house price	Probability
No increase	0.20
Up $5000	0.50
Up $10,000	0.30

a Use a spreadsheet and the PMT function to find the expected monthly house payment (using a 30-year fixed-rate mortgage) if there is no down payment. Find the variance and standard deviation of this monthly payment.

b Repeat part **a**, but assume that the down payment is 10% of the price of the house (so that you finance only 90%). ■

Weighted Sums of Random Variables

I n this final section we will analyze summary measures of weighted sums of random variables. An extremely important application of this topic is in financial investments. The example in this section illustrates such an application. However, there are many other applications of weighted sums of random variables, both in business and elsewhere. It is a topic well worth learning.

Before proceeding to the example, we lay out the main concepts and results. Let $X_1, X_2, \ldots, X_n$ be any n random variables (which could be independent or dependent), and let $a_1, a_2, \ldots, a_n$ be any n constants. We form a new random variable Y that is the weighted sum of the X's:

$$Y = a_1 X_1 + a_2 X_2 + \cdots + a_n X_n$$

In general, it is too difficult to obtain the complete probability distribution of Y, so we will be content to obtain its summary measures, namely, the mean $E(Y)$ and the variance $Var(Y)$. Of course, we can then calculate $Stdev(Y)$ as the square root of $Var(Y)$.

The mean is the easy part. We substitute the mean of each X into the formula for Y to obtain $E(Y)$:

$$E(Y) = a_1 E(X_1) + a_2 E(X_2) + \cdots + a_n E(X_n) \tag{4.13}$$

Using summation notation, we can write this more compactly as

$$E(Y) = \sum_{i=1}^{n} a_i E(X_i)$$

The variance is not as straightforward. It depends on whether the X's are independent or dependent. If they are independent, then $Var(Y)$ is a weighted sum of the variances of the X's, using the *squares* of the a's as weights:

$$Var(Y) = a_1^2 Var(X_1) + a_2^2\, Var(X_2) + \cdots + a_n^2 Var(X_n) \tag{4.14}$$

Using summation notation, this becomes

$$Var(Y) = \sum_{i=1}^{n} a_i^2 Var(X_i)$$

If the X's are not independent, the variance of Y is more complex and requires covariance terms. In particular, for every pair X_i and X_j, there is an extra term in equation (4.14): $2a_i a_j Cov(X_i, X_j)$. The general result is best written in summation notation:

$$Var(Y) = \sum_{i=1}^{n} a_i^2 Var(X_i) + \sum_{i,j} 2a_i a_j Cov(X_i, X_j) \tag{4.15}$$

The first summation is the variance when the X's are independent. The second summation indicates that we should add the covariance term for all pairs of X's that have nonzero covariances. Actually, this equation is *always* valid, regardless of independence, because the covariance terms are all zero when the X's are independent.

There are several important special cases of the above formulas.

- **Sum of independent random variables.** Here we assume the X's are independent and the weights are all 1, that is,

$$Y = X_1 + X_2 + \cdots + X_n$$

Then the mean of the sum is the sum of the means, and the variance of the sum is the sum of the variances:

$$E(Y) = E(X_1) + E(X_2) + \cdots + E(X_n)$$

$$Var(Y) = Var(X_1) + Var(X_2) + \cdots + Var(X_n)$$

- **Difference between two independent random variables.** Here we assume X_1 and X_2 are independent and the weights are $a_1 = 1$ and $a_2 = -1$, so that we can write Y as

$$Y = X_1 - X_2$$

Then the mean of the difference is the difference between means, but the variance of the difference is the *sum* of the variances (because $a_2^2 = (-1)^2 = 1$):

$$E(Y) = E(X_1) - E(X_2)$$

$$Var(Y) = Var(X_1) + Var(X_2)$$

- **Sum of two dependent random variables.** Here we make no independence assumption and set the weights equal to 1, so that $Y = X_1 + X_2$. Then the mean of the sum is again the sum of the means, but the variance of the sum includes a covariance term:

$$E(Y) = E(X_1) + E(X_2)$$

$$\text{Var}(Y) = \text{Var}(X_1) + \text{Var}(X_2) + 2\text{Cov}(X_1, X_2)$$

- **Difference between two dependent random variables.** This is the same as the second case above, except that the X's are no longer independent. Again, the mean of the difference is the difference between means, but the variance of the difference now includes a covariance term, and because of the negative weight $a_2 = -1$, the sign of this covariance term is negative:

$$E(Y) = E(X_1) - E(X_2)$$

$$\text{Var}(Y) = \text{Var}(X_1) + \text{Var}(X_2) - 2\text{Cov}(X_1, X_2)$$

We now put these concepts to use in an investment example.

EXAMPLE 4.7

An investor has $100,000 to invest, and she would like to invest it in a portfolio of eight stocks. She has gathered historical data on the returns of these stocks and has used the historical data to estimate means, standard deviations, and correlations for the stock returns. These summary measures appear in rows 12, 13, and 17–24 of Figure 4.16. (See the file INVEST.XLS.)

FIGURE 4.16 **Input Data for Investment Example**

	A	B	C	D	E	F	G	H	I	J
1	Calculating mean, variance, and stdev for a weighted sum of random variables									
2										
3	Random variables are one-year returns from various stocks									
4	Weights are amounts invested in stocks									
5	Weighted sum is return from portfolio									
6										
7	Given quantities									
8		Stock1	Stock2	Stock3	Stock4	Stock5	Stock6	Stock7	Stock8	Total
9	Weights	$10,500	$16,300	$9,600	$9,300	$9,500	$15,400	$14,300	$15,100	$100,000
10										
11		Stock1	Stock2	Stock3	Stock4	Stock5	Stock6	Stock7	Stock8	
12	Means	0.101	0.073	0.118	0.099	0.118	0.091	0.096	0.123	
13	Stdevs	0.124	0.119	0.134	0.141	0.158	0.159	0.113	0.174	
14										
15	Correlations between stock returns									
16		Stock1	Stock2	Stock3	Stock4	Stock5	Stock6	Stock7	Stock8	
17	Stock1	1.000	0.320	0.370	0.610	0.800	0.610	0.550	0.560	
18	Stock2	0.320	1.000	0.410	0.780	0.430	0.800	0.950	0.480	
19	Stock3	0.370	0.410	1.000	0.330	0.860	0.380	0.340	0.700	
20	Stock4	0.610	0.780	0.330	1.000	0.680	0.500	0.500	0.670	
21	Stock5	0.800	0.430	0.860	0.680	1.000	0.580	0.420	0.540	
22	Stock6	0.610	0.800	0.380	0.500	0.580	1.000	0.920	0.340	
23	Stock7	0.550	0.950	0.340	0.500	0.420	0.920	1.000	0.650	
24	Stock8	0.560	0.480	0.700	0.670	0.540	0.340	0.650	1.000	

For example, the mean and standard deviation of stock 1 are 0.101 and 0.124. These imply that the historical annual returns of stock 1 averaged 10.1% and the standard deviation of the annual returns was 12.4%. Also, the correlation between the annual returns on stocks 1 and 2, for example, is 0.32 (see either cell C17 or B18, which necessarily contain the same value). This value, 0.32, indicates a moderate positive correlation between the historical annual returns of these stocks. (In fact, all of the correlations are positive, which probably indicates that each stock tends to vary in the same direction as some underlying economic indicator. Also, the diagonal entries in the correlation matrix are all 1 because any stock return is perfectly correlated with itself.)

Although these summary measures have been obtained from historical data, the investor believes they are relevant for *future* returns. Now she would like to analyze a portfolio of these stocks, using the investment amounts shown in row 9. What is the mean annual return from this portfolio? What are its variance and standard deviation?

Solution

This is a typical weighted sum model. The random variables, the X's, are the annual returns from the stocks; the weights, the a's, are the dollar amounts invested in the stocks; and the summary measures of the X's are given in rows 12, 13, and 17–24 of Figure 4.16. Be careful about units, however. Each X_i represents the return on a *single* dollar invested in stock i, whereas Y, the weighted sum of the X's, represents the *total* dollar return. So a typical value of an X might be 0.105, whereas a typical value of Y might be $10,500.

We can immediately apply equation (4.13) to obtain the mean return from the portfolio. This appears in cell B49 of Figure 4.17 (page 178), using the formula

$$=\text{SUMPRODUCT(Weights,Means)}$$

We are not quite ready to calculate the variance of the portfolio return. The reason is that the input data include standard deviations and correlations for the X's, not the variances and covariances required in equation (4.15) for Var(Y).[3] But the variances and covariances are related to standard deviations and correlations by

$$\text{Var}(X_i) = (\text{Stdev}(X_i))^2 \qquad \textbf{(4.16)}$$

and

$$\text{Cov}(X_i, X_j) = \text{Stdev}(X_i) \times \text{Stdev}(X_j) \times \text{Corr}(X_i, X_j) \qquad \textbf{(4.17)}$$

To calculate these in Excel, it is useful first to create a *column* of standard deviations in column L by using Excel's TRANSPOSE function. To do this, highlight the range L12:L19, type the formula

$$=\text{TRANSPOSE(Stdevs)}$$

and press Ctrl-Shift-Enter—all three keys at once. (This is a useful procedure any time you want to transform a row into a column or vice versa. But don't forget to highlight the range where the transpose will go *before* you type the formula.)

Next, we form a table of variances and covariances of the X's in the range B28:I35, using equations (4.16) and (4.17). Actually, we can do this all at once by entering the formula

$$=\$L12*B\$13*B17$$

in cell B28 and copying it to the range B28:I35. Each diagonal element of this range is a

---

[3]This was intentional. It is often easier for an investor to assess standard deviations and correlations because they are more intuitive measures.

FIGURE 4.17 Calculations for Investment Example

	A	B	C	D	E	F	G	H	I	J	K	L
1	Calculating mean, variance, and stdev for a weighted sum of random variables											
2												
3	Random variables are one-year returns from various stocks											
4	Weights are amounts invested in stocks											
5	Weighted sum is return from portfolio											
6												
7	Given quantities											
8		Stock1	Stock2	Stock3	Stock4	Stock5	Stock6	Stock7	Stock8	Total		
9	Weights	$10,500	$16,300	$9,600	$9,300	$9,500	$15,400	$14,300	$15,100	$100,000		
10												
11		Stock1	Stock2	Stock3	Stock4	Stock5	Stock6	Stock7	Stock8		Standard deviations	
12	Means	0.101	0.073	0.118	0.099	0.118	0.091	0.096	0.123		Stock1	0.124
13	Stdevs	0.124	0.119	0.134	0.141	0.158	0.159	0.113	0.174		Stock2	0.119
14											Stock3	0.134
15	Correlations between stock returns										Stock4	0.141
16		Stock1	Stock2	Stock3	Stock4	Stock5	Stock6	Stock7	Stock8		Stock5	0.158
17	Stock1	1.000	0.320	0.370	0.610	0.800	0.610	0.550	0.560		Stock6	0.159
18	Stock2	0.320	1.000	0.410	0.780	0.430	0.800	0.950	0.480		Stock7	0.113
19	Stock3	0.370	0.410	1.000	0.330	0.860	0.380	0.340	0.700		Stock8	0.174
20	Stock4	0.610	0.780	0.330	1.000	0.680	0.500	0.500	0.670			
21	Stock5	0.800	0.430	0.860	0.680	1.000	0.580	0.420	0.540			
22	Stock6	0.610	0.800	0.380	0.500	0.580	1.000	0.920	0.340			
23	Stock7	0.550	0.950	0.340	0.500	0.420	0.920	1.000	0.650			
24	Stock8	0.560	0.480	0.700	0.670	0.540	0.340	0.650	1.000			
25												
26	Covariances between stock returns (variances of stock returns are on the diagonal)											
27		Stock1	Stock2	Stock3	Stock4	Stock5	Stock6	Stock7	Stock8			
28	Stock1	0.0154	0.0047	0.0061	0.0107	0.0157	0.0120	0.0077	0.0121			
29	Stock2	0.0047	0.0142	0.0065	0.0131	0.0081	0.0151	0.0128	0.0099			
30	Stock3	0.0061	0.0065	0.0180	0.0062	0.0182	0.0081	0.0051	0.0163			
31	Stock4	0.0107	0.0131	0.0062	0.0199	0.0151	0.0112	0.0080	0.0164			
32	Stock5	0.0157	0.0081	0.0182	0.0151	0.0250	0.0146	0.0075	0.0148			
33	Stock6	0.0120	0.0151	0.0081	0.0112	0.0146	0.0253	0.0165	0.0094			
34	Stock7	0.0077	0.0128	0.0051	0.0080	0.0075	0.0165	0.0128	0.0128			
35	Stock8	0.0121	0.0099	0.0163	0.0164	0.0148	0.0094	0.0128	0.0303			
36												
37	Weights (top row, left column) and terms for calculating portfolio variance											
38		10500	16300	9600	9300	9500	15400	14300	15100			
39	10500	1695204	808156.6	619710.3	1041461	1563442	1944727	1157146	1915690			
40	16300	808156.61	3762436	1023044	1983952	1251941	3799640	2977643	2446257			
41	9600	619710.34	1023044	1654825	556662.6	1660562	1196954	706755.9	2365921			
42	9300	1041460.7	1983952	556662.6	1719508	1338418	1605425	1059465	2308357			
43	9500	1563441.6	1251941	1660562	1338418	2253001	2131702	1018696	2129613			
44	15400	1944727.1	3799640	1196954	1605425	2131702	5995642	3640157	2187374			
45	14300	1157146	2977643	706755.9	1059465	1018696	3640157	2611133	2759650			
46	15100	1915689.9	2446257	2365921	2308357	2129613	2187374	2759650	6903231			
47												
48	Summary measures of portfolio											
49	Mean	$10,056.40										
50	Variance	124992021										
51	Stdev	$11,179.98										

Range names
Corrs: B17:I24
Covar: B28:I35
Means: B12:I12
PortVarTerms: B39:I46
Stdevs: B13:I13
Var: B50
Weights: B9:I9

variance, and the other elements off the diagonal are covariances. (As usual, make sure you understand the effect of the mixed references $L12 and B$13.)

Finally, we use equation (4.15) for $Var(Y)$ to calculate the portfolio variance in cell B50. To do so, we form a table of the terms needed in equation (4.15) and then sum these terms, as in the following steps.

1 **Row of weights.** Enter the weights in row 38 by highlighting the range B38:I38, typing the formula

$$=Weights$$

and pressing Ctrl-Enter.

2 **Column of weights.** Enter these same weights as a *column* in the range A39:A46 by highlighting this range, typing the formula

$$=TRANSPOSE(Weights)$$

and pressing Ctrl-Shift-Enter.

3 Table of terms. Now use these weights and the covariances to fill in the table of terms required for the portfolio variance. To do so, enter the formula

$$=\$A39*B28*B\$38$$

in cell B39 and copy it to the range B39:I46. The terms on the diagonal of this table are squares of weights multiplied by variances. These are the terms in the first summation in equation (4.15). Each term off the diagonal is the product of two weights and a covariance. These are the terms needed in the second summation in equation (4.15).

4 Portfolio variance and standard deviation. Calculate the portfolio variance in cell B50 with the formula

$$=SUM(PortVarTerms)$$

Then calculate the standard deviation of the portfolio return in cell B51 as the square root of the variance.

The results in Figure 4.17 indicate that the investor has an expected return of slightly more than $10,000 (or 10%) from this portfolio. However, the standard deviation of approximately $11,200 is sizable. This standard deviation is a measure of the portfolio's risk. Investors always want a large mean return, but they also want low risk. Moreover, they realize that the only way to obtain a higher mean return is usually to accept more risk. You can experiment with the spreadsheet for this example to see how the mean and standard deviation of portfolio return vary with the investment amounts. Just enter new weights in row 9 (keeping the sum equal to $100,000) and see how the values in B49 through B51 change. ■

PROBLEMS

Level A

46   Consider a financial services salesperson whose annual salary consists of both a fixed portion of $25,000 and a variable portion that is a commission based on her sales performance. In particular, she estimates that her monthly sales commission can be represented by a random variable with mean $5000 and standard deviation $700.

  a What annual salary can this salesperson expect to earn?

  b Assuming that her sales commissions in different months are independent random variables, what is the standard deviation of her annual salary?

  c Between what two annual salary levels can this salesperson be approximately 95% sure that her true total earnings will fall?

47   A film processing shop charges its customers 18 cents per print, but customers may refuse to accept one or more of the prints for various reasons. Assume that this shop does not charge its customers for refused prints. The number of prints refused per 24-print roll is a random variable with mean 1.5 and standard deviation 0.5.

  a What are the mean and standard deviation of the amount that customers pay for the development of a typical 24-print roll?

  b Assume that this shop processes 250 24-print rolls of film in a given week. If the numbers of refused prints on these rolls are independent random variables, what are the mean and standard deviation of the weekly film processing revenue of this shop?

  c Find an interval such that the manager of this film shop can be approximately 99.7% sure that the weekly processing revenue will be contained within the interval.

48   Suppose the monthly demand for Thompson televisions has a mean of 40,000 and a standard deviation of 20,000. Determine the mean and standard deviation of the annual demand for Thompson TVs. Assume that demand in any month is probabilistically independent of demand in any other month. (Is this assumption realistic?)

49 Suppose there are five stocks available for investment and each has an annual mean return of 10% and a standard deviation of 4%. Assume the returns on the stocks are independent random variables.

    a If you invest 20% of your money in each stock, determine the mean, standard deviation, and variance of the annual dollar return on your investments.

    b If you invest $100 in a single stock, determine the mean, standard deviation, and variance of the annual return on your investment.

    c How do the answers to parts **a** and **b** relate to the phrase, "Don't put all your eggs in one basket"?

50 An investor puts $10,000 into each of four stocks, labeled A, B, C, and D. Table 4.24 contains the means and standard deviations of the annual returns of these four stocks. Assuming that the returns of these four stocks are independent of each other, find the mean and standard deviation of the total amount that this investor earns in 1 year from these four investments.

TABLE 4.24 **Means and Standard Deviations of Annual Returns for Stocks A-D**

Stock	Mean Annual Return	Standard Deviation of Annual Return
A	0.13	0.04
B	0.16	0.06
C	0.12	0.02
D	0.15	0.05

Level B

51 Consider again the investment problem described in Problem 50. Now, assume that the returns of the four stocks are no longer independent of one another. Specifically, the correlations between all pairs of stock returns are given in Table 4.25.

TABLE 4.25 **Correlations of Annual Returns for Stocks A, B, C, and D**

Correlations	Stock A	Stock B	Stock C	Stock D
Stock A	1.00	0.45	0.75	−0.60
Stock B	0.45	1.00	0.55	−0.35
Stock C	0.75	0.55	1.00	−0.80
Stock D	−0.60	−0.35	−0.80	1.00

    a Find the mean and standard deviation of the total amount that this investor earns in 1 year from these four investments. Compare these results to those you found in the previous problem. Explain the differences in your answers.

    b Suppose that this investor now decides to place $15,000 each in stocks B and D, and $5000 each in stocks A and C. How do the mean and standard deviation of the total amount that this investor earns in 1 year change as the $40,000 in cash available is reallocated for investment? Provide an intuitive explanation for the changes you observe here.

52 A supermarket chain operates five stores of varying sizes in Harrisburg, Pennsylvania. Profits (represented as a percentage of sales volume) earned by these five stores are 2.75%, 3%, 3.5%, 4.25%, and 5%, respectively. The means and standard deviations of the daily sales volumes at these five stores are given in Table 4.26. Assuming that the daily sales volumes are independent of each other, find the mean and standard deviation of the total *profit* that this supermarket chain earns in 1 day from the operation of its five stores in Harrisburg.

53 A manufacturing company constructs a 1-cm assembly by snapping together four parts that average 0.25 cm in length. The company would like the standard deviation of the length of the assembly to be 0.01 cm. Its engineer, Peter Purdue, believes that the assembly will meet

TABLE 4.26 **Means and Standard Deviations of Daily Sales Volumes for Five Supermarkets**

Store	Mean Daily Sales Volume	Standard Deviation of Daily Sales
1	$75,000	$7,500
2	$82,500	$8,500
3	$90,100	$9,200
4	$98,400	$10,000
5	$106,000	$11,100

the desired level of variability if each part has a standard deviation of $0.01/4 = 0.0025$ cm. Instead, show Peter that you can do the job by making each part have a standard deviation of $0.01/\sqrt{4} = 0.005$ cm. This could save the company a lot of money, because not as much precision is needed for each part. ■

4.11 Conclusion

This chapter has introduced some very important concepts, including the basic rules of probability, random variables, probability distributions, and summary measures of probability distributions. We have also shown how computer simulation can be used to help explain some of these concepts. Much of the material in this chapter will be used in later chapters, so it is important to learn it now. In particular, we will rely heavily on probability distributions in Chapter 6 when we discuss decision making under uncertainty. There we will learn how the expected value of a probability distribution is the primary criterion for making decisions. We will also continue to use computer simulation in later chapters to help explain complex statistical concepts.

PROBLEMS

Level A

54 A business manager who needs to make many phone calls has estimated that when she calls a client, the probability that she will reach the client right away is 60%. If she does not reach the client on the first call, the probability that she will reach the client with a subsequent call in the next hour is 20%.

  a Find the probability that the manager will reach her client in two or fewer calls.

  b Find the probability that the manager will reach her client on the second call but not on the first call.

  c Find the probability that the manager will be unsuccessful on two consecutive calls.

55 Suppose that a marketing research firm sends questionnaires to two different companies. Based on historical evidence, the marketing research firm believes that each company, independently of the other, will return the questionnaire with probability 0.40.

  a What is the probability that *both* questionnaires will be returned?

  b What is the probability that *neither* of the questionnaires will be returned?

  c Now, suppose that this marketing research firm sends questionnaires to *ten* different companies. Assuming that each company, independently of the others, returns its completed questionnaire with probability 0.40, how do your answers to parts **a** and **b** change?

56 Based on past sales experience, an appliance store stocks five window air conditioner units for the coming week. No orders for additional air conditioners will be made until next week. The weekly consumer demand for this type of appliance has the probability distribution given in Table 4.27.

TABLE 4.27 **Weekly Air Conditioner Demand**

Number Demanded	Probability
0	0.05
1	0.05
2	0.08
3	0.16
4	0.30
5	0.16
6	0.10
7	0.05
8	0.05
9 or more	0.00

    a Let X be the number of window air conditioner units left at the end of the week (if any), and let Y be the number of special stockout orders required (if any), assuming that a special stockout order is required each time there is a demand and no unit is available in stock. Find the probability distributions of X and Y.

    b Find the expected value of X and the expected value of Y.

    c Assume that this appliance store makes a $40 profit on each air conditioner sold from the weekly available stock, but the store loses $10 for each unit sold on a special stockout order basis. Let Z be the profit that the store earns in the upcoming week from the sale of window air conditioners. Find the probability distribution of Z.

    d Find the expected value of Z.

57 Simulate 400 weekly consumer demands for window air conditioner units with the probability distribution given in Table 4.27. How does your simulated distribution compare to the given probability distribution? Explain any differences between these two distributions.

58 The probability distribution of the weekly demand (in hundreds of reams) of copier paper used in the duplicating center of a corporation is provided in Table 4.28.

TABLE 4.28 **Weekly Copier Paper Demand**

Demand	Probability
10	0.05
11	0.10
12	0.14
13	0.16
14	0.21
15	0.13
16	0.11
17	0.04
18	0.03
19	0.02
20	0.01

    a Find the mean and standard deviation of this distribution.

    b Find the probability that weekly copier paper demand will be at least one standard deviation above the mean.

    c Find the probability that weekly copier paper demand will be within one standard deviation of the mean.

59 Consider the probability distribution of the weekly demand (in hundreds of reams) of copier paper used in a corporation's duplicating center, as shown in Table 4.28.

   a Generate 500 values of this random variable with the given probability distribution using computer simulation.

   b Compute the mean and standard deviation of the simulated values.

   c Use your simulated distribution to find the probability that weekly copier paper demand will be within one standard deviation of the mean.

60 The probability distribution of the weekly demand (in hundreds of reams) of copier paper used in the duplicating center of a corporation is provided in Table 4.28. Assuming that it costs the duplicating center $5 to purchase a ream of paper, find the mean and standard deviation of the weekly copier paper cost for this corporation.

61 The instructor of an introductory organizational behavior course believes that there might be a relationship between the number of writing assignments (X) she makes in the course and the final grades (Y) earned by students enrolled in this class. She has taught this course with varying numbers of writing assignments for many semesters now. She has compiled relevant historical data in Table 4.29 for you to review.

TABLE 4.29 **Number of Writing Assignments Given and Final Grades Earned in an OB Course**

Number of Writing Assignments/ Final Course Grade	$Y = 4$ (A)	$Y = 3$ (B)	$Y = 2$ (C)	$Y = 1$ (D)	$Y = 0$ (F)
$X = 1$	10	40	40	5	5
$X = 2$	15	45	33	4	3
$X = 3$	20	50	25	4	1
$X = 4$	18	52	27	3	0

   a Convert the given frequency table to a table of conditional probabilities of final grades (Y) earned by students enrolled in this class, given the number of writing assignments (X) made in the course. Comment on your constructed table of conditional probabilities. Generally speaking, what does this table tell you?

   b Given that this instructor makes only one writing assignment in the course, what is the expected final grade earned by the typical student?

   c How much variability exists around the conditional mean grade you found in part **b**? Furthermore, what proportion of all relevant students earn final grades within two standard deviations of this conditional mean?

   d Given that this instructor makes more than one writing assignment in the course, what is the expected final grade earned by the typical student?

   e How much variability exists around the conditional mean grade you found in part **d**? Moreover, what proportion of all relevant students earn final grades within two standard deviations of this conditional mean?

   f Compute the covariance and correlation of X and Y in this case. What does each of these measures tell you? In particular, is this organizational behavior instructor correct in believing that there is a systematic relationship between the number of writing assignments made and final grades earned in her classes?

62 Table 4.30 contains the joint probability distribution of recent weekly trends of two particular stock prices, P_1 and P_2.

TABLE 4.30 **Weekly Trends in Two Stock Prices**

Stock 1/Stock 2	P_2 Increases	P_2 Remains Constant	P_2 Decreases
P_1 Increases	0.05	0.05	0.10
P_1 Remains Constant	0.05	0.20	0.25
P_1 Decreases	0.10	0.05	0.15

a Are P_1 and P_2 independent random variables? Explain why or why not.

b If P_1 and P_2 are *not* independent random variables, which joint probabilities result in the same *marginal* probabilities for P_1 and P_2 as given in Table 4.30 but make P_1 and P_2 independent of each other?

63 Consider two service elevators used in parallel by employees of a three-story hotel building. At any point in time when both elevators are stationary, let X_1 and X_2 be the floor numbers at which elevators 1 and 2, respectively, are currently located. Table 4.31 contains the joint probability distribution of X_1 and X_2.

TABLE 4.31   **Locations of Two Service Elevators**

Location of Elevator 1/ Location of Elevator 2	$X_2 = 1$	$X_2 = 2$	$X_2 = 3$
$X_1 = 1$	0.25	0.08	0.14
$X_1 = 2$	0.07	0.10	0.07
$X_1 = 3$	0.16	0.08	0.05

a Are X_1 and X_2 independent random variables? Explain your answer.

b If X_1 and X_2 are *not* independent random variables, which joint probabilities result in the same *marginal* probabilities for X_1 and X_2 as given in Table 4.31 but make X_1 and X_2 independent of each other?

64 A roulette wheel contains the numbers 0, 00, and 1, 2, . . . , 36. If you bet \$1 on a single number coming up, you earn \$35 if the number comes up and lose \$1 if the number does not come up. Find the mean and standard deviation of your winnings on a single bet.

65 Assume that there are four equally likely states of the economy: boom, low growth, recession, and depression. Also, assume that the percentage annual return you obtain when you invest a dollar in gold or the stock market is shown in Table 4.32.

TABLE 4.32   **Returns on Gold and the Market**

State of Economy	Market	Gold
Boom	25%	−30%
Low growth	20%	−9%
Recession	5%	35%
Depression	−14%	50%

a Find the covariance and correlation between the annual return on the market and the annual return on gold. Interpret your answers.

b Suppose you invest 40% of your money in the market and 60% of your money in gold. Determine the mean and standard deviation of the annual return on your portfolio.

c Obtain your part **b** answer by determining the actual return on your portfolio in each state of the economy and determining the mean and variance directly without using any formulas involving covariances or correlations.

d Suppose you invested 70% of your money in the market and 30% in gold. Without doing any calculations, determine whether the mean and standard deviation of your portfolio would increase or decrease from your answer in part **b**. Give intuition to support your answers.

66 You are considering buying a share of Ford stock with the possible returns for the next year as shown in Table 4.33. Determine the mean, variance, and standard deviation of the annual return on Ford stock.

TABLE 4.33 **Stock Returns**

Business Conditions	Probability	Annual Return
Normal growth	1/3	10%
Rapid growth	1/3	30%
Recession	1/3	−10%

67 Suppose there are three states of the economy: boom, moderate growth, and recession. The annual return on GM and Ford stock in each state of the economy is shown in Table 4.34.

TABLE 4.34 **GM and Ford Stock Returns**

State of the Economy	GM Return	Ford Return
Boom	25%	32%
Moderate growth	22%	18%
Recession	1%	4%

a Calculate the mean, standard deviation, and variance of the annual return on each stock assuming the probability of each state is 1/3.

b Calculate the mean, standard deviation, and variance of the annual return on each stock assuming the probabilities of the three states are 1/4, 1/4, and 1/2.

c Calculate the covariance and correlation between the annual return on GM and Ford stocks assuming the probability of each state is 1/3.

d Calculate the covariance and correlation between the annual return on GM and Ford stocks assuming the probabilities of the three states are 1/4, 1/4, and 1/2.

e You have invested 25% of your money in GM and 75% in Ford. Assuming that each state is equally likely, determine the mean and variance of your portfolio's return.

f Now check your answer to part **e** by directly computing for each state the return on your portfolio and use the formulas for mean and variance of a random variable. For example, in the Boom state, your portfolio earns 0.25(0.25) + 0.75(0.32).

68 You have placed 30% of your money in investment A and 70% of your money in investment B. The annual returns on investments A and B depend on the state of the economy as shown in Table 4.35. Determine the mean and standard deviation of the annual return on your investments.

TABLE 4.35 **Stock Returns**

State	Probability	A Return	B Return
Boom	0.40	0.30	0.05
Bust	0.60	−0.20	0.15

69 There are three possible states of the economy during the next year (states 1, 2, and 3). The probability of each state of the economy, as well as the percentage annual return on IBM and Disney stocks, are as shown in Table 4.36.

TABLE 4.36 **Returns on IBM and Disney Stocks**

State	Probability	IBM Return	Disney Return
1	0.40	0.20	0.24
2	0.30	0.14	0.16
3	0.30	0.12	0.06

a Find the correlation between the annual return on IBM and Disney. Interpret this correlation.

b If you put 80% of your money in IBM and 20% in Disney, find the mean and standard deviation of your annual return.

70 There are three possible states of the economy during the next year (states 1, 2, and 3). The probability of each state of the economy, as well as the percentage annual return on P&G and US Steel, are as shown in Table 4.37.

TABLE 4.37 **Returns on Stocks**

State	Probability	P&G Return	US Steel Return
1	0.40	0.08	0.20
2	0.30	0.14	0.19
3	0.30	0.12	0.18

a Find the correlation between the annual return on P&G and US Steel. Interpret this correlation.

b If you put 80% of your money in P&G and 20% in US Steel, find the mean and standard deviation of your annual return.

71 The return on a portfolio during a period is defined by

$$\frac{PV_{end} - PV_{beg}}{PV_{beg}}$$

where PV_{beg} is the portfolio value at the beginning of a period and PV_{end} is the portfolio value at the end of the period. Suppose there are two stocks in which we can invest, stock 1 and stock 2. During each year there is a 50% chance that each dollar invested in stock 1 will turn into $2 and a 50% chance that each dollar invested in stock 1 will turn into $0.50. During each year there is a 50% chance that each dollar invested in stock 2 will turn into $2 and a 50% chance that each dollar invested in stock 2 will turn into $0.50.

a If you invest all your money in stock 1, determine the expected value, variance, and standard deviation of your 1-year return.

b Assume the returns on stocks 1 and 2 are independent random variables. If you put half your money into each stock, determine the expected value, variance, and standard deviation of your 1-year return.

c Can you give an intuitive explanation of why the variance and standard deviation in part **b** are smaller than the variance and standard deviation in part **a**?

d Use simulation to check your answers to part **b**. Use at least 1000 trials.

72 Each year the employees at Zipco receive either a $0, $2000, or $4500 salary increase. They also receive a merit rating of 0, 1, 2, or 3, with 3 indicating outstanding performance and 0 indicating poor performance. The joint probability distribution of salary increase and merit rating is listed in the file P4_72.XLS. For example, 20% of all employees receive a $2000 increase and have a merit rating of 1. Find the correlation between salary increase and merit rating. Then interpret this correlation.

73 Suppose X and Y are independent random variables. The possible values of X are -1, 0, and 1; the possible values of Y are 10, 20, and 30. You are given that $P(X = -1 \text{ and } Y = 10) = 0.05$, $P(X = 0 \text{ and } Y = 30) = 0.20$, $P(Y = 10) = 0.20$, and $P(X = 0) = 0.50$. Determine the joint probability distribution of X and Y.

74 You are involved in a risky business venture where three outcomes are possible: (1) you will lose not only your initial investment ($5000) but an additional $3000, (2) you will just make back your initial investment (for a net gain of $0), or (3) you will make back your initial investment plus an extra $10,000. The probability of (1) is half as large as the probability of (2), and the probability of (3) is one-third as large as the probability of (2).

a Find the individual probabilities of (1), (2), and (3). (They should add to 1.)

b Find the expected value of your net gain (or loss) from this venture. Find its variance and standard deviation.

Level B

75 Consider an individual selected at random from a sample of 750 married women (see the data in the file P4_5.XLS) in answering each of the following questions.

  a What is the probability that this woman does not work outside the home, given that she has at least one child?

  b What is the probability that this woman has no children, given that she works part-time?

  c What is the probability that this woman has at least two children, given that she does not work full-time?

76 Suppose that 8% of all managers in a given company are African-American, 13% are women, and 17% have earned an MBA degree from a top-10 graduate business school. Let A, B, and C be, respectively, the events that a randomly selected individual from this population is African-American, is a woman, and has earned an MBA from a top-10 graduate business school.

  a Would you expect A, B, and C to be independent events? Explain why or why not.

  b Assuming that A, B, and C *are* independent events, compute the probability that a randomly selected manager from this company is a white male and has an earned an MBA degree from a top-10 graduate business school.

  c If A, B, and C are *not* independent events, could you calculate the probability requested in part **b** from the information given? What further information would you need?

77 Consider again the supermarket chain described in Problem 52. Now, assume that the daily sales of the five stores are no longer independent of one another. In particular, Table 4.38 contains the correlations between all pairs of daily sales volumes.

TABLE 4.38 **Correlations of Daily Sales Volumes for Five Supermarket Stores**

Correlations	Store 1	Store 2	Store 3	Store 4	Store 5
Store 1	1.00	0.80	0.65	0.52	0.38
Store 2	0.80	1.00	0.86	0.67	0.50
Store 3	0.65	0.86	1.00	0.75	0.61
Store 4	0.52	0.67	0.75	1.00	0.78
Store 5	0.38	0.50	0.61	0.78	1.00

  a Find the mean and standard deviation of the total profit that this supermarket chain earns in 1 day from the operation of its five stores in Harrisburg. Compare these results to those you found in Problem 52. Explain the differences in your answers.

  b Find an interval such that the regional sales manager of this supermarket chain can be approximately 95% sure that the total daily profit earned by its stores in Harrisburg will be contained within the interval.

78 A manufacturing plant produces two distinct products, X and Y. The cost of producing one unit of X is $18 and that of Y is $22. Assume that this plant incurs a weekly setup cost of $24,000 regardless of the number of units of X or Y produced. The means and standard deviations of the weekly production levels of X and Y are given in Table 4.39.

TABLE 4.39 **Means and Standard Deviations of Weekly Production of Two Products**

Product	Mean Weekly Production	Standard Deviation of Weekly Production
X	22,500 units	2,500 units
Y	30,000 units	3,350 units

a Assuming that the weekly production levels of X and Y are independent, compute the mean and standard deviation of this plant's total weekly production cost. Between what two total cost figures can we be about 68% sure that this plant's actual total weekly production cost will fall?

b How do your answers in part **a** change when you discover that the correlation between the weekly production levels of X and Y is actually 0.29? Explain the differences in the two sets of results.

79 The typical standard deviation of the annual return on a stock is 20% and the typical mean return is about 12%. The typical correlation between the annual returns of two stocks is about 0.25. Mutual funds often put an equal percentage of their money in a given number of stocks. By choosing a large number of stocks, they hope to diversify away the risk involved with choosing particular stocks. How many stocks does an investor need to own to diversify away the risk associated with individual stocks? To answer this question, use the above information about "typical" stocks to determine the mean and standard deviation for the following portfolios:

- Portfolio 1: Half your money in each of two stocks
- Portfolio 2: 20% of your money in each of 5 stocks
- Portfolio 3: 10% of your money in each of 10 stocks
- Portfolio 4: 5% of your money in each of 20 stocks
- Portfolio 5: 1% of your money in each of 100 stocks

What do your answers tell you about the number of stocks a mutual fund needs to invest in to diversify? (*Hint*: You will need to consider a square range. For portfolio 2, for example, it will be a square range with 25 cells, 5 on the diagonal and 20 off the diagonal. Each diagonal term makes the same contribution to the variance and each off-diagonal term makes the same contribution to the variance.)

80 You are ordering milk for Mr. D's and are determined to please! Milk is delivered once a week (at midnight Sunday). The mean and standard deviation of the number of gallons of milk demanded each day are given in Table 4.40. Determine the mean and standard deviation of the weekly demand for milk. What assumption must you make to determine the weekly standard deviation? Presently you are ordering 1000 gallons per week. Is this a sensible order quantity? Assume all milk spoils after 1 week.

T A B L E   4 . 4 0   **Daily Demand for Milk**

Day	Mean	Standard Deviation
Mon.	100	24
Tues.	120	34
Wed.	80	18
Thurs.	90	12
Fri.	40	16
Sat.	10	19
Sun.	30	12

81 At the end of 1995, Wall Street's best estimates of the means, standard deviations, and correlations for the 1996 returns on stocks, bonds, and T-bills were as shown in the file P4_81.XLS. Stocks have the highest average return and the most risk, whereas T-bills have the lowest average return and the least risk. Find the mean and standard deviation for the return on your 1996 investments for the three asset allocations listed in Table 4.41. For example, portfolio 1 allocates 53% of all assets to stocks, 6% to bonds, and 41% to T-bills. (This is what most Wall Street firms did.) Based on your results, can you explain why nobody in 1996 should have allocated all their assets to bonds? (*Note*: T-bills are 90-day government issues; the bonds are 10-year government bonds.)

TABLE 4.41   Portfolio Distributions

Portfolio	Stocks	Bonds	T-Bills
1	53%	6%	41%
2	15%	80%	5%
3	20%	0%	80%

82   The annual returns on stocks 1 and 2 for three possible states of the economy are given in Table 4.42.

TABLE 4.42   Returns for Stocks 1 and 2

State	Probability	Stock 1	Stock 2
Good	0.50	0.40	0.20
Average	0.30	0.20	0.40
Bad	0.20	0.10	0.08

     a   Find and interpret the correlation between stocks 1 and 2.

     b   Consider another stock (stock 3) that always yields an annual return of 10%. Suppose you invest 60% of your money in stock 1, 10% in stock 2, and 30% in stock 3. Determine the standard deviation of the annual return on your portfolio. (*Hint*: You do not need Excel to compute the variance of stock 3 and the covariance of stock 3 with the other two stocks!)

83   The application at the beginning of this chapter describes the campaign McDonald's used several years ago, where customers could win various prizes.

     a   Verify the figures that are given in the description. That is, argue why there are 10 winning outcomes and 120 total outcomes.

     b   Suppose McDonald's had designed the cards so that each card had 2 zaps and 3 pictures of the winning prize (and again 5 pictures of other irrelevant prizes). The rules are the same as before: To win, the customer must uncover all 3 pictures of the winning prize before uncovering a zap. Would there be more or fewer winners with this design? Argue by calculating the probability that a card is a winner.

     c   Going back to the original game (as in part **a**), suppose McDonald's printed 1 million cards, each of which was eventually given to a customer. Assume that the (potential) winning prizes on these were: 500,000 Cokes worth $.40 each, 250,000 french fries worth $.50 each, 150,000 milk shakes worth $.75 each, 75,000 hamburgers worth $1.50 each, 20,000 cards with $1 cash as the winning prize, 4000 cards with $10 cash as the winning prize, 800 cards with $100 cash as the winning prize, and 200 cards with $1000 cash as the winning prize. Find the expected amount (the dollar equivalent) that McDonald's gave away in winning prizes, assuming everyone played the game and claimed the prize if they won. Find the standard deviation of this amount. ∎

4.1 Simpson's Paradox

The results we obtain when we work with conditional probabilities can be quite unintuitive, even paradoxical. This case is similar to one described in an article by Blyth (1972) and is usually referred to as Simpson's paradox. [Two other examples of Simpson's paradox are described in the articles by Westbrooke (1998) and Appleton et al. (1996).] Essentially, Simpson's paradox says that even if one treatment has a better effect than another on *each* of two separate subpopulations, it can have a *worse* effect on the population as a whole.

Suppose that the population is the set of managers in a large company. We categorize the managers as those with an MBA degree (the *B*'s) and those without an MBA degree (the $\overline{B}$'s). These categories are the two "treatment groups." We also categorize the managers as those who were hired directly out of school by this company (the *C*'s) and those who worked with another company first (the $\overline{C}$'s). These two categories form the two "subpopulations." Finally, we use as a measure of effectiveness those managers who have been promoted within the past year (the *A*'s).

Assume the following conditional probabilities are given:

$$P(A|B \text{ and } C) = 0.10, \quad P(A|\overline{B} \text{ and } C) = 0.05 \tag{4.18}$$

$$P(A|B \text{ and } \overline{C}) = 0.35, \quad P(A|\overline{B} \text{ and } \overline{C}) = 0.20 \tag{4.19}$$

$$P(C|B) = 0.90, \quad P(C|\overline{B}) = 0.30 \tag{4.20}$$

Each of these can be interpreted as a proportion. For example, the probability $P(A|B$ and $C)$ implies that 10% of all managers who have an MBA degree and were hired by the company directly out of school were promoted last year. Similar explanations hold for the other probabilities.

Joan Seymour, the head of personnel at this company, is trying to understand these figures. From the probabilities in equation (4.18), she sees that among the subpopulation of workers hired directly out of school, those with an MBA degree are twice as likely to be promoted as those without an MBA degree. Similarly, from the probabilities in equation (4.19), she sees that among the subpopulation of workers hired after working with another company, those with an MBA degree are *almost* twice as likely to be promoted as those without an MBA degree. The information provided by the probabilities in equation (4.20) is somewhat different. From these, she sees that employees with MBA degrees are three times as likely as those without MBA degrees to have been hired directly out of school.

Joan can hardly believe it when a whiz-kid analyst uses these probabilities to show— correctly—that

$$P(A|B) = 0.125, \quad P(A|\overline{B}) = 0.155 \tag{4.21}$$

In words, those employees *without* MBA degrees are more likely to be promoted than those with MBA degrees. This appears to go directly against the evidence in equations (4.18) and (4.19), both of which imply that MBAs have an advantage in being promoted. Can you derive the probabilities in equation (4.21)? Can you shed any light on this "paradox"?

5

Normal, Binomial, and Poisson Distributions

Successful Applications

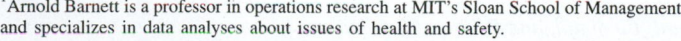

One of the most controversial books of the past decade is *The Bell Curve* (Herrnstein and Murray, 1994). The authors are the late Richard Herrnstein, a psychologist, and Charles Murray, an economist, both of whom had extensive training in statistics. The book is a scholarly treatment of differences in intelligence, measured by IQ, and its effect on socioeconomic status (SES). The authors argue, by appealing to many past studies and presenting many statistics and graphs, that there are significant differences in IQ among different groups of people, and that these differences are at least partially responsible for differences in SES. Specifically, their basic claims are that (1) there is a quantity, intelligence, that can be measured by an IQ test, (2) IQ scores are normally distributed, (3) IQ scores are highly correlated with various indicators of success, (4) IQ is determined predominantly by genetic factors and less so by environmental factors, and (5) African-Americans score significantly lower—about 15 points lower—on IQ than whites.

Although the discussion of this latter point takes up a relatively small part of the book, it has generated by far the most controversy. Many criticisms of the authors' racial thesis have been based on emotional arguments. However, it can also be criticized on entirely statistical grounds, as Barnett (1995) has done.[1] Barnett never states that the analysis by Herrnstein and Murray is *wrong*. He merely states that (1) the assumptions behind some of the analysis are at best questionable, and (2) some of the crucial details are not made as explicit as they should have been. As he states, "The issue is not that *The Bell Curve* is demonstrably wrong, but that it falls so far short of being demonstrably right. The book does not meet the burden of proof we might reasonably expect of it."

For example, Barnett takes issue with the claim that the genetic component of IQ is, in the words of Herrnstein and Murray, "unlikely to be smaller than 40 percent or higher than 80 percent." Barnett asks what it would mean if

[1]Arnold Barnett is a professor in operations research at MIT's Sloan School of Management and specializes in data analyses about issues of health and safety.

genetics made up, say, 60 percent of IQ. His only clue from the book is in an endnote, which implies this definition: If a large population of genetically identical newborns grew up in randomly chosen environments, and their IQs were measured once they reached adulthood, then the variance of these IQs would be 60 percent less than the variance for the entire population. The key word is *variance*. As Barnett notes, however, this statement implies that the corresponding drop in *standard deviation* is only 37 percent. That is, even if all members of the population were exactly the same genetically, differing environments would create a standard deviation of IQs 63 percent as large as the standard deviation that exists today. If this is true, it is hard to argue, as Herrnstein and Murray have done, that environment plays a minor role in determining IQ.

Because the effects of different racial environments are so difficult to disentangle from genetic effects, Herrnstein and Murray try at one point to bypass environmental influences on IQ by matching blacks and whites from similar environments. They report that blacks in the top decile of SES have an average IQ of 104, but that whites within that decile have an IQ one standard deviation higher. Even assuming that they have their facts straight, Barnett criticizes the vagueness of their claim. What standard deviation are they referring to—the standard deviation of the entire population or only the standard deviation of the people in the upper decile of SES? The latter is certainly much smaller than the former. Should we assume that the "top-decile blacks" are in the top decile of the black population or of the overall population? If the latter, then the matched comparison between blacks and whites is flawed because the wealthiest 10 percent of whites have far more wealth than the wealthiest 10 percent of blacks. Moreover, even if the reference is to the pooled national population, the matching is imperfect. It is possible that the blacks in this pool could average around the ninth percentile, whereas the whites could average around the fourth percentile, with a significant difference in income between the two groups.

The problem is that Herrnstein and Murray never state these details explicitly. Therefore, we have no way of knowing—without collecting and analyzing all of the data ourselves—whether their results are essentially correct. As Barnett concludes his article, "I believe that *The Bell Curve*'s statements about race would have been better left unsaid even if they were definitely true. And they are surely better left unsaid when, as we have seen, their meaning and accuracy [are] in doubt." ■

5.1 Introduction

In the previous chapter we discussed probability distributions in general. In this chapter we investigate three specific distributions that occur constantly throughout the study of statistics. They also occur in a variety of management science applications. The first of these is a continuous distribution called the **normal** distribution. It is characterized by a symmetric, bell-shaped curve and is the cornerstone of statistical theory. The other two distributions are discrete distributions called the **binomial** and **Poisson** distributions. The binomial distribution is relevant when we sample from a population with only two types of members or when we perform a series of independent, identical experiments with only two possible outcomes. The Poisson distribution is usually relevant when we are interested in the number of events that occur over a given interval of time, such as arrivals to a bank or calls to a telephone switchboard.

The main goals in this chapter are to present the properties of these three distributions, give some examples of when they apply, and see how to perform calculations involving them. Regarding this last objective, special tables have been the traditional means of looking up probabilities or values for the distributions in this chapter. However, we will see how these tasks can be simplified with the statistical functions available in Excel. Given the availability of these Excel functions, the traditional tables are no longer necessary.

We cannot overemphasize the importance of these distributions. Almost all of the statistical results we will learn in later chapters are based on either the normal distribution or the binomial distribution. The Poisson distribution plays a less important role in this book, but it is nevertheless extremely important in many management science applications. Therefore, it is essential that you become thoroughly familiar with these distributions before proceeding.

5.2

The Normal Distribution

The single most important distribution in statistics is the normal distribution. It is a *continuous* distribution and is associated with the familiar symmetric, bell-shaped curve. The normal distribution is defined by its mean and standard deviation. By changing the mean, we can shift the normal curve to the right or left. By changing the standard deviation, we can make the curve more or less spread out. Therefore, there are really many normal distributions, not just a single normal distribution.

5.2.1 Continuous Distributions and Density Functions

We first take a moment to discuss continuous probability distributions in general. In the previous chapter we dealt entirely with discrete distributions, characterized by a list of possible values and their probabilities. The same idea holds for continuous distributions such as the normal distribution, but the mathematics becomes more complex. Now instead of a list of possible values, there is a *continuum* of possible values, such as all values between 0 and 100 or all values greater than 0. Instead of assigning probabilities to each individual value in the continuum, we "spread" the total probability of 1 over this continuum. The key to this spreading is called a probability **density** function, which acts like a histogram. The higher the value of the density function, the more likely is this region of the continuum.

As an example, consider the density function—*not* a normal density function—shown in Figure 5.1. It indicates that all values in the continuum from 25 to 100 are possible, but that the values near 70 are most likely. (This density function might correspond to scores on

FIGURE 5.1 **A Skewed Density Function**

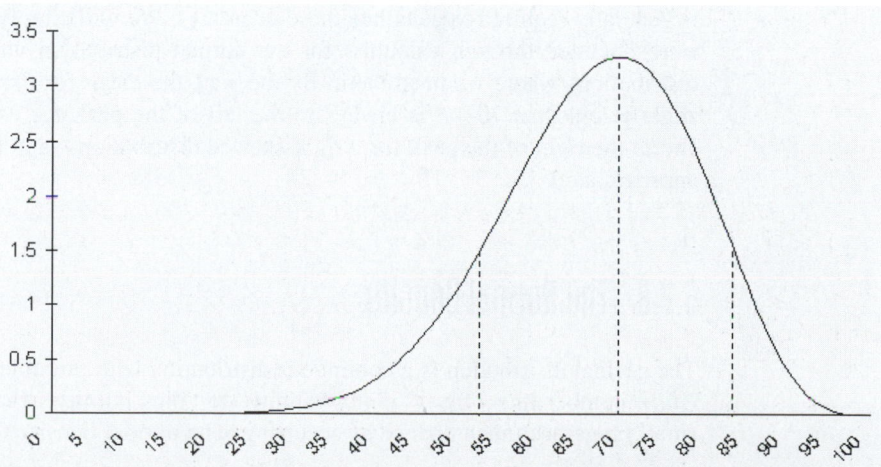

an exam.) To be a bit more specific, because the height of the density at 70 is approximately twice the height of the curve at 84 or 53, a value near 70 is approximately twice as likely as a value near 84 or a value near 53. In this sense, the height of the density function indicates *relative* likelihoods.

To find probabilities from a density function, we need to calculate areas under the curve. For example, the area of the designated region in Figure 5.2 represents the probability of a score between 65 and 75. Also, the area under the *entire* curve is 1, because the total probability of all possible values is always 1. Unfortunately, this is about as much as we can say without calculus. The problem is that integral calculus is necessary to find areas under curves. Fortunately, statistical tables have been constructed to find such areas for a number of well-known density functions, including the normal. Even better, special Excel functions have been developed to find these areas—without the need for bulky tables. We will take advantage of these Excel functions as we study the normal distribution (and other distributions).

FIGURE 5.2 **Probability as the Area Under the Density**

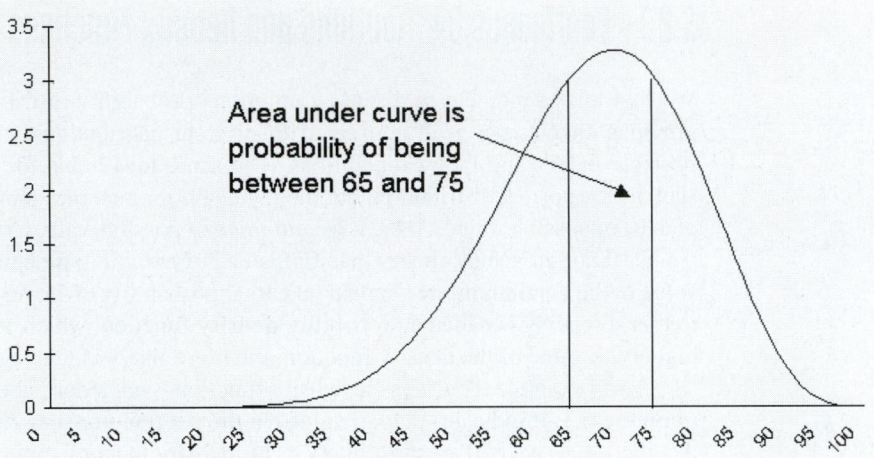

What about the mean and standard deviation (or variance) of a continuous distribution? As before, the mean is a measure of central tendency of the distribution, and the standard deviation (or variance) measures the variability of the distribution. Again, however, calculus is generally required to calculate these quantities. We will simply list their values (which *were* obtained through calculus) for the normal distribution and any other continuous distributions where we need them. By the way, the mean for the density in Figure 5.1 is slightly *less* than 70—it is always to the left of the peak for a left-skewed distribution and to the right of the peak for a right-skewed distribution—and the standard deviation is approximately 15.

5.2.2 The Normal Density

The normal distribution is a continuous distribution with possible values ranging over the *entire* number line—from "minus infinity" to "plus infinity." However, only a relatively small range has much chance of occurring. The normal density function is actually quite complex, in spite of its "nice" bell-shaped appearance. For the sake of completeness, we list the formula for the normal density function below:

$$f(x) = \frac{1}{\sqrt{2\pi}\sigma} e^{-(x-\mu)^2/(2\sigma^2)} \quad \text{for } -\infty < x < +\infty$$

Here, μ and σ are the mean and standard deviation of the distribution.

The curves in Figure 5.3 illustrate several normal density functions for different values of μ and σ. As we see, the effect of increasing or decreasing the mean μ is to shift the curve to the right or the left. Actually, μ can be any number: negative, positive, or zero. On the other hand, the standard deviation σ must be a *positive* number. It controls the spread of the normal curve. When σ is small, the curve is more peaked; when σ is large, the curve is more spread out. For shorthand, we use the notation $N(\mu, \sigma)$ to refer to the normal distribution with mean μ and standard deviation σ. For example, $N(-2, 1)$ refers to the normal distribution with mean -2 and standard deviation 1.

FIGURE 5.3 **Several Normal Density Functions**

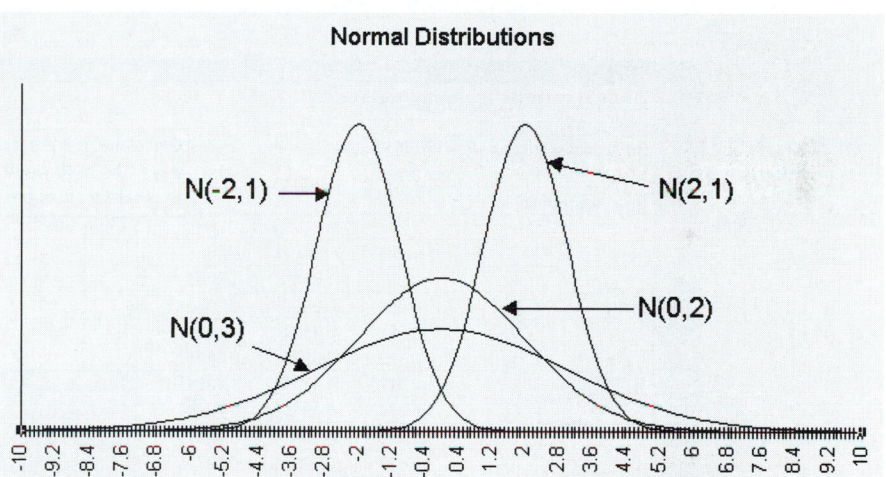

5.2.3 Standardizing: Z-Values

There are infinitely many normal distributions, one for each pair μ and σ. However, we single out one of these for special attention, the **standard normal** distribution. The standard normal distribution has mean 0 and standard deviation 1, so we can denote it by $N(0, 1)$. It is also referred to as the Z distribution. Suppose the random variable X is normally distributed with mean μ and standard deviation σ. We define the random variable Z by

$$Z = \frac{X - \mu}{\sigma}$$

This operation is called **standardizing**. That is, to standardize a variable, we subtract its mean and then divide the difference by the standard deviation. When X is normally distributed, the standardized variable is $N(0, 1)$.

One reason for standardizing is to measure variables with different means and/or standard deviations on a single scale. For example, suppose several sections of a college course are taught by different instructors. Because of differences in teaching methods and grading procedures, the distributions of scores in these sections might differ, possibly by a wide margin. However, if each instructor calculates his or her mean and standard deviation and then calculates a Z-value for each student, the distributions of the Z-values should be approximately the same in each section.

It is also easy to interpret a Z-value. It is the number of standard deviations to the right or the left of the mean. If Z is positive, the original score is to the *right* of the mean; if Z is negative, the original score is to the *left* of the mean. For example, if the Z-value for some student is 2, then this student's score is two standard deviations above the mean. If the Z-value for another student is -0.5, then this student's score is one-half standard deviation below the mean. We illustrate Z-values in the following example.

EXAMPLE 5.1

The annual returns for 30 mutual funds appear in Figure 5.4. (See the file FUNDS.XLS.) Find and interpret the Z-values of these returns.

FIGURE 5.4   **Mutual Fund Returns and Z-Values**

	A	B	C	D	E	F	G
1	**Annual returns from mutual funds**						
2							
3	Summary statistics from returns below				Calculated two different		
4	Mean return	0.091	0		ways - the second with the		
5	Stdev of returns	0.047	1		Standardize function		
6							
7	Fund	Annual return	Z value	Z value			
8	1	0.007	-1.8047	-1.8047			
9	2	0.080	-0.2363	-0.2363			
10	3	0.082	-0.1934	-0.1934			
11	4	0.123	0.6875	0.6875			
12	5	0.022	-1.4824	-1.4824		**Range names:**	
13	6	0.054	-0.7949	-0.7949		MeanReturn: B4	
14	7	0.109	0.3867	0.3867		StdevReturn: B5	
15	8	0.097	0.1289	0.1289		Returns: B8:B37	
16	9	0.047	-0.9453	-0.9453		ZValues: C8:C37	
17	10	0.021	-1.5039	-1.5039			
18	11	0.111	0.4297	0.4297			
19	12	0.180	1.9121	1.9121			
20	13	0.157	1.4180	1.4180			
21	14	0.134	0.9238	0.9238			
22	15	0.140	1.0528	1.0528			
23	16	0.107	0.3438	0.3438			
24	17	0.193	2.1914	2.1914			
25	18	0.156	1.3965	1.3965			
26	19	0.095	0.0859	0.0859			
27	20	0.039	-1.1172	-1.1172			
28	21	0.034	-1.2246	-1.2246			
29	22	0.064	-0.5801	-0.5801			
30	23	0.071	-0.4297	-0.4297			
31	24	0.079	-0.2578	-0.2578			
32	25	0.088	-0.0645	-0.0645			
33	26	0.077	-0.3008	-0.3008			
34	27	0.125	0.7305	0.7305			
35	28	0.094	0.0645	0.0645			
36	29	0.078	-0.2793	-0.2793			
37	30	0.066	-0.5371	-0.5371			

Solution

The 30 annual returns appear in column B. Their mean and standard deviation are calculated in cells B4 and B5 with the AVERAGE and STDEV functions. The corresponding Z-values are calculated in column C by entering the formula

$$=(B8-MeanReturn)/StdevReturn$$

in cell C8 and copying it down column C.

There is an equivalent way to calculate these Z-values in Excel. We do this in column D, using Excel's STANDARDIZE function directly. To use this function, enter the formula

$$=STANDARDIZE(B8,MeanReturn,StdevReturn)$$

in cell D8 and copy it down column D.

The Z-values in Figure 5.4 range from a low of -1.80 to a high of 2.19. Specifically, the return for stock 1 is about 1.80 standard deviations below the mean, whereas the return for fund 17 is about 2.19 standard deviations above the mean. As we will see shortly, these values are typical; Z-values are usually in the range from -2 to $+2$; values beyond -3 or $+3$ are very uncommon. Also, the Z-values automatically have mean 0 and standard deviation 1, as we see in cells C5 and C6 by using the AVERAGE and STDEV functions on the Z-values in column C (or D). ■

5.2.4 Normal Tables and Z-Values

A common use for Z-values and the standard normal distribution is in calculating probabilities and percentiles by the "traditional" method.[2] This method is based on a table of the standard normal distribution found in most statistics textbooks. Such a table is given in Figure 5.5 (page 200). The body of the table contains probabilities. The left and top margins contain possible values. Specifically, suppose we want to find the probability that a standard normal random variable is less than 1.35. We locate 1.3 along the left and .05—for the second decimal in 1.35—along the top, and then read into the table to find the probability 0.9115. In words, the probability is about 0.91 that a standard normal random variable is less than 1.35.

Alternatively, if we are given a probability, we can use the table to find the value with this much probability to the left of it under the standard normal curve. We call this a **percentile** calculation. For example, if the probability is 0.75, we can find the 75th percentile by locating the probability in the table closest to 0.75 and then reading to the left and up. With interpolation, the required value is approximately 0.675. In words, the probability of being to the left of 0.675 under the standard normal curve is approximately 0.75.

We can perform the same kind of calculations for *any* normal distribution if we first standardize. As an example, suppose that X is normally distributed with mean 100 and standard deviation 10. We will find the probability that X is less than 115 and the 85th percentile of this normal distribution. To find the probability that X is less than 115, we first standardize the value 115. The corresponding Z-value is

$$Z = (115 - 100)/10 = 1.5$$

Now we look up 1.5 in the table (1.5 row, .00 column) to obtain the probability 0.9332. For the percentile question we first find the 85th percentile of the standard normal distribution.

---

[2] If you intend to rely on Excel functions for normal calculations, you can omit this subsection.

FIGURE 5.5 Normal Probabilities

z	.00	.01	.02	.03	.04	.05	.06	.07	.08	.09
0.0	0.5000	0.5040	0.5080	0.5120	0.5160	0.5199	0.5239	0.5279	0.5319	0.5359
0.1	0.5398	0.5438	0.5478	0.5517	0.5557	0.5596	0.5636	0.5675	0.5714	0.5753
0.2	0.5793	0.5832	0.5871	0.5910	0.5948	0.5987	0.6026	0.6064	0.6103	0.6141
0.3	0.6179	0.6217	0.6255	0.6293	0.6331	0.6368	0.6406	0.6443	0.6480	0.6517
0.4	0.6554	0.6591	0.6628	0.6664	0.6700	0.6736	0.6772	0.6808	0.6844	0.6879
0.5	0.6915	0.6950	0.6985	0.7019	0.7054	0.7088	0.7123	0.7157	0.7190	0.7224
0.6	0.7257	0.7291	0.7324	0.7357	0.7389	0.7422	0.7454	0.7486	0.7517	0.7549
0.7	0.7580	0.7611	0.7642	0.7673	0.7704	0.7734	0.7764	0.7794	0.7823	0.7852
0.8	0.7881	0.7910	0.7939	0.7967	0.7995	0.8023	0.8051	0.8078	0.8106	0.8133
0.9	0.8159	0.8186	0.8212	0.8238	0.8264	0.8289	0.8315	0.8340	0.8365	0.8389
1.0	0.8413	0.8438	0.8461	0.8485	0.8508	0.8531	0.8554	0.8577	0.8599	0.8621
1.1	0.8643	0.8665	0.8686	0.8708	0.8729	0.8749	0.8770	0.8790	0.8810	0.8830
1.2	0.8849	0.8869	0.8888	0.8907	0.8925	0.8944	0.8962	0.8980	0.8997	0.9015
1.3	0.9032	0.9049	0.9066	0.9082	0.9099	0.9115	0.9131	0.9147	0.9162	0.9177
1.4	0.9192	0.9207	0.9222	0.9236	0.9251	0.9265	0.9279	0.9292	0.9306	0.9319
1.5	0.9332	0.9345	0.9357	0.9370	0.9382	0.9394	0.9406	0.9418	0.9429	0.9441
1.6	0.9452	0.9463	0.9474	0.9484	0.9495	0.9505	0.9515	0.9525	0.9535	0.9545
1.7	0.9554	0.9564	0.9573	0.9582	0.9591	0.9599	0.9608	0.9616	0.9625	0.9633
1.8	0.9641	0.9649	0.9656	0.9664	0.9671	0.9678	0.9686	0.9693	0.9699	0.9706
1.9	0.9713	0.9719	0.9726	0.9732	0.9738	0.9744	0.9750	0.9756	0.9761	0.9767
2.0	0.9772	0.9778	0.9783	0.9788	0.9793	0.9798	0.9803	0.9808	0.9812	0.9817
2.1	0.9821	0.9826	0.9830	0.9834	0.9838	0.9842	0.9846	0.9850	0.9854	0.9857
2.2	0.9861	0.9864	0.9868	0.9871	0.9875	0.9878	0.9881	0.9884	0.9887	0.9890
2.3	0.9893	0.9896	0.9898	0.9901	0.9904	0.9906	0.9909	0.9911	0.9913	0.9916
2.4	0.9918	0.9920	0.9922	0.9925	0.9927	0.9929	0.9931	0.9932	0.9934	0.9936
2.5	0.9938	0.9940	0.9941	0.9943	0.9945	0.9946	0.9948	0.9949	0.9951	0.9952
2.6	0.9953	0.9955	0.9956	0.9957	0.9959	0.9960	0.9961	0.9962	0.9963	0.9964
2.7	0.9965	0.9966	0.9967	0.9968	0.9969	0.9970	0.9971	0.9972	0.9973	0.9974
2.8	0.9974	0.9975	0.9976	0.9977	0.9977	0.9978	0.9979	0.9979	0.9980	0.9981
2.9	0.9981	0.9982	0.9982	0.9983	0.9984	0.9984	0.9985	0.9985	0.9986	0.9986
3.0	0.9987	0.9987	0.9987	0.9988	0.9988	0.9989	0.9989	0.9989	0.9990	0.9990
3.1	0.9990	0.9991	0.9991	0.9991	0.9992	0.9992	0.9992	0.9992	0.9993	0.9993
3.2	0.9993	0.9993	0.9994	0.9994	0.9994	0.9994	0.9994	0.9995	0.9995	0.9995
3.3	0.9995	0.9995	0.9995	0.9996	0.9996	0.9996	0.9996	0.9996	0.9996	0.9997
3.4	0.9997	0.9997	0.9997	0.9997	0.9997	0.9997	0.9997	0.9997	0.9997	0.9998

Interpolating, we obtain a value of approximately 1.037. Then we set this value equal to a standardized value:

$$Z = 1.037 = (X - 100)/10$$

Finally, we solve for X to obtain 110.37. In words, there is a probability 0.85 of being to the left of 110.37 in the $N(100, 10)$ distribution.

There are some obvious drawbacks to using the standard normal table for probability calculations. The first is that there are holes in the table—we often have to interpolate. A second drawback is that the standard normal table takes different forms in different textbooks. These differences are rather minor, but they can easily cause errors. Finally, the table requires us to perform calculations. For example, we might have to standardize. More importantly, we often have to use the symmetry of the normal distribution to find probabilities that are not in the table. As an example, to find the probability that Z is less than -1.5, we must go through some mental gymnastics. First, by symmetry this is the same as the probability that Z is greater than 1.5. Then since only left-tail probabilities are tabulated, we must find the probability that Z is less than 1.5 and subtract this probability from 1. The chain of reasoning is:

$$P(Z < -1.5) = P(Z > 1.5) = 1 - P(Z < 1.5) = 1 - .9332 = .0668$$

This is not too difficult, given a bit of practice, but it is easy to make a mistake. Spreadsheet functions make the whole procedure much easier and less prone to errors.

5.2.5 Normal Calculations in Excel

There are two types of calculations we typically make with normal distributions: finding probabilities and finding percentiles. Excel makes each of these fairly simple. The functions used for normal probability calculations are NORMDIST and NORMSDIST. The main difference between these is that the one with the "S" (for standardized) applies only to $N(0, 1)$ calculations, whereas NORMDIST applies to *any* normal distribution. On the other hand, percentile calculations, where we supply a probability and require a value, are often called **inverse** calculations. Therefore, the Excel functions for these are named NORMINV and NORMSINV. Again, the "S" in the second of these indicates that it applies only to the standard normal distribution.

The NORMDIST and NORMSDIST functions give left-tail probabilities, such as the probability that a normally distributed variable is *less than* 35. The syntax for these functions is

$$=\text{NORMDIST}(x,\mu,\sigma,1)$$

and

$$=\text{NORMSDIST}(x)$$

Here, x is a number we supply, and μ and σ are the mean and standard deviation of the normal distribution. The last argument "1" in the NORMDIST function is used to obtain the *cumulative* normal probability, the only kind we'll ever need. (This 1 is a bit of a nuisance to remember, but it's necessary.) Note that NORMSDIST takes only one argument, so it is easier to use—when it applies.

The NORMINV and NORMSINV functions return values for user-supplied probabilities. For example, if we supply the probability 0.95, these functions return the 95th percentile. Their syntax is

$$=\text{NORMINV}(p,\mu,\sigma)$$

and

$$=\text{NORMSINV}(p)$$

where p is a probability we supply. These are analogous to the NORMDIST and NORMSDIST functions (except there is no fourth argument "1" necessary in the NORMINV function).

We illustrate these Excel functions in the following example.[3]

---

[3]Actually, we already illustrated the NORMSDIST function; it was used to create the body of Figure 5.5.

E X A M P L E   5 . 2

Use Excel to calculate the following probabilities and percentiles for the standard normal distribution: (i) $P(Z < -2)$, (ii) $P(Z > 1)$, (iii) $P(-0.4 < Z < 1.6)$, (iv) the 5th percentile, (v) the 75th percentile, and (vi) the 99th percentile. Then for the $N(75, 8)$ distribution, find the following probabilities and percentiles: (i) $P(X < 70)$, (ii) $P(X > 73)$, (iii) $P(75 < X < 85)$, (iv) the 5th percentile, (v) the 60th percentile, and (vi) the 97th percentile.

Solution

The solution appears in Figure 5.6. (See the file NORMFNS.XLS.) The $N(0, 1)$ calculations appear in rows 7 through 14; the $N(75, 8)$ calculations appear in rows 23 through 30. For your convenience, the formulas used in column B are spelled out in column D. Note that the standard normal calculations use the normal functions with the "S" in the middle; the rest use the normal functions without the "S"—and require more arguments.

FIGURE 5.6   **Normal Calculations with Excel Functions**

	A	B	C	D	E	F	G	H	I
1	**Using Excel's normal functions**								
2									
3	**Examples with standard normal**								
4									
5	**Probability calculations**								
6	Range	Probability		Formula					
7	Less than -2	0.0228		NORMSDIST(-2)					
8	Greater than 1	0.1587		1-NORMSDIST(1)					
9	Between -.4 and 1.6	0.6006		NORMSDIST(1.6)-NORMSDIST(-0.4)					
10									
11	**Percentiles**								
12	5th	-1.645		NORMSINV(0.05)					
13	75th	0.674		NORMSINV(0.75)					
14	99th	2.326		NORMSINV(0.99)					
15									
16	**Examples with nonstandard normal**								
17				**Range names**					
18	Mean	75		Mean: B18					
19	Stdev	8		Stdev: B19					
20									
21	**Probability calculations**								
22	Range	Probability		Formula					
23	Less than 70	0.2660		NORMDIST(70,Mean,Stdev,1)					
24	Greater than 73	0.5987		1-NORMDIST(73,Mean,Stdev,1)					
25	Between 75 and 85	0.3944		NORMDIST(85,Mean,Stdev,1)-NORMDIST(75,Mean,Stdev,1)					
26									
27	**Percentiles**								
28	5th	61.841		NORMINV(0.05,Mean,Stdev)					
29	60th	77.027		NORMINV(0.6,Mean,Stdev)					
30	97th	90.046		NORMINV(0.97,Mean,Stdev)					

Note the following for normal *probability* calculations:

■ For "less than" probabilities, use NORMDIST or NORMSDIST directly. (See rows 7 and 23.)

- For "greater than" probabilities, subtract the NORMDIST or NORMSDIST function from 1. (See rows 8 and 24.)

- For "between" probabilities, subtract the two NORMDIST or NORMSDIST functions. For example, in row 9 the probability of being between -0.4 and 1.6 is the probability of being less than 1.6 minus the probability of being less than -0.4.

The percentile calculations are even more straightforward. In most percentile problems we want to find the value with a certain probability to the *left* of it. In this case we use the NORMINV or NORMSINV function with the specified probability as the first argument. See rows 12 through 14 and 28 through 30. ■

There are a couple of variations of percentile calculations. First, suppose we want the value with probability 0.05 to the *right* of it. This is the same as the value with probability 0.95 to the left of it, so we use NORMINV or NORMSINV with probability argument 0.95. For example, the value with probability 0.4 to the right of it in the $N(75, 8)$ distribution is 77.027 (see cell B29 in Figure 5.6).

As a second variation, suppose we want to find an interval of the form $-x$ to x, for some positive number x, with (1) probability 0.025 to the left of $-x$, (2) probability 0.025 to the right of x, and (3) probability 0.95 between $-x$ and x. This is a very common problem in statistical inference. In general, we want a probability such as 0.95 to be in the middle of the interval and half of the remaining probability (0.025) to be in each of the tails. (See Figure 5.7.) Then the required x can be found with NORMINV or NORMSINV, using probability argument 0.975, because there must be a total probability of 0.975 to the left of x.

For example, if the relevant distribution is the standard normal, then the required value of x is 1.96, found with the function NORMSINV(0.975). Similarly, if we want probability 0.90 in the middle and probability 0.05 in each tail, the required x is 1.645, found with the function NORMSINV(0.95). Remember these two numbers, 1.96 and 1.645. They occur frequently in statistical applications.

FIGURE 5.7 **Typical Normal Probabilities**

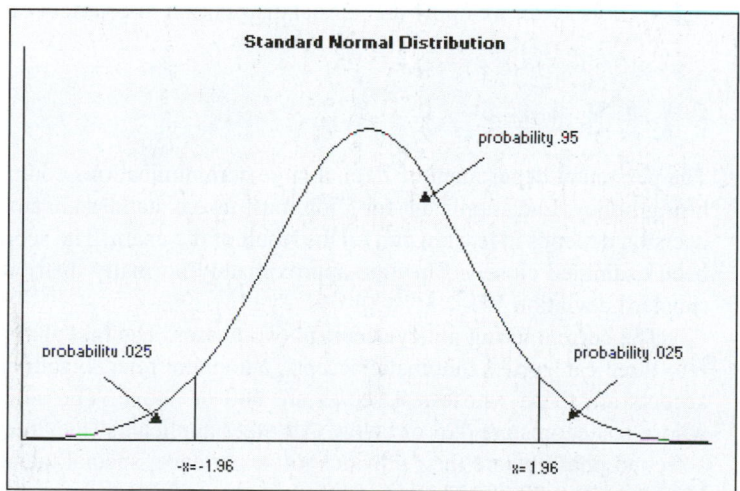

Standard Normal Distribution

probability .95

probability .025

probability .025

$-x = -1.96$

$x = 1.96$

5.2.6 Rules of Thumb Revisited

In Chapter 3 we discussed rules of thumb that apply to many data sets. Namely, about 68% of the data fall within one standard deviation of the mean, about 95% fall within two standard deviations of the mean, and almost all fall within three standard deviations of the mean. These rules of thumb are actually based on the normal distribution, as we will now see. So for them to hold with real data, the distribution of the data must be at least approximately symmetric and bell shaped.

Let X be normally distributed with mean μ and standard deviation σ. To perform a probability calculation on X, we can first standardize X and then perform the calculation on the standardized variable Z. Specifically, we will find the probability that X is within k standard deviations of the mean for $k = 1$, $k = 2$, and $k = 3$. In general, this probability is $P(\mu - k\sigma < X < \mu + k\sigma)$. But by standardizing the values $\mu - k\sigma$ and $\mu + k\sigma$, we obtain the equivalent probability $P(-k < Z < k)$, where Z has a $N(0, 1)$ distribution. This latter probability can be calculated in Excel with the formula

$$=\text{NORMSDIST}(k)\text{-NORMSDIST}(-k)$$

By substituting the values 1, 2, and 3 for k, we find the following probabilities:

$$P(-1 < Z < 1) = .6827$$

$$P(-2 < Z < 2) = .9545$$

$$P(-3 < Z < 3) = .9973$$

As we see, there is virtually no chance of being beyond three standard deviations from the mean, the chances are about 19 out of 20 of being within two standard deviations of the mean, and the chances are about 2 out of 3 of being within one standard deviation of the mean.

Applications of the Normal Distribution

In this section we apply the normal distribution to a variety of business problems.

EXAMPLE 5.3

The personnel department of ZTel, a large communications company, is reconsidering its hiring policy. Each applicant for a job must take a standard exam, and the hire or no-hire decision depends at least in part on the result of the exam. The scores of all applicants have been examined closely. They are approximately normally distributed with mean 525 and standard deviation 55.

The current hiring policy occurs in two phases. The first phase separates all applicants into three categories: automatic accepts, automatic rejects, and "maybes." The automatic accepts are those whose test scores are 600 or above. The automatic rejects are those whose test scores are 425 or below. All other applicants (the "maybes") are passed on to a second phase where their previous job experience, special talents, and other factors are used as hiring criteria. The personnel manager at ZTel wants to calculate the percentage of applicants who are automatic accepts or rejects, given the current standards. She also wants to know how to change the standards in order to automatically reject 10% of all applicants and automatically accept 15% of all applicants.

Solution

Let X be the test score of a typical applicant. Then the distribution of X is $N(525, 55)$. If we find a probability such as $P(X \leq 425)$, we can interpret this as the probability that a typical applicant is an automatic reject, or we can interpret it as the percentage of *all* applicants who are automatic rejects. Given this observation, the solution to ZTel's problem appears in Figure 5.8. (See the file PERSONNL.XLS.) The probability that a typical applicant is automatically accepted is 0.0863, found in cell B10 with the formula

$$=1\text{-NORMDIST(B7,Mean,Stdev,1)}$$

Similarly, the probability that a typical applicant is automatically rejected is .0345, found in cell B11 with the formula

$$=\text{NORMDIST(B8,Mean,Stdev,1)}$$

Therefore, ZTel automatically accepts about 8.6% and rejects about 3.5% of all applicants under the current policy.

FIGURE 5.8 **Calculations for Personnel Example**

	A	B	C	D	E	F
1	Personnel Accept/Reject Example					
2						
3	Mean of test scores	525		Range		
4	Stdev of test scores	55		names		
5				Mean: B3		
6	Current Policy			Stdev: B4		
7	Automatic accept point	600				
8	Automatic reject point	425				
9						
10	Percent accepted	8.63%		1-NORMDIST(B7,Mean,Stdev,1)		
11	Percent rejected	3.45%		NORMDIST(B8,Mean,Stdev,1)		
12						
13	New Policy					
14	Percent accepted	15%				
15	Percent rejected	10%				
16						
17	Automatic accept point	582		NORMINV(1-B14,Mean,Stdev)		
18	Automatic reject point	455		NORMINV(B15,Mean,Stdev)		

To find new cutoff values that reject 10% and accept 15% of the applicants, we need the 10th and 85th percentiles of the $N(525, 55)$ distribution. These are 455 and 582 (rounded to the nearest integer), found in cells B17 and B18 with the formulas

$$=\text{NORMINV(1-B14,Mean,Stdev)}$$

and

$$=\text{NORMINV(B15,Mean,Stdev)}$$

To accomplish its objective, ZTel needs to raise the automatic rejection point from 425 to 455 and lower the automatic acceptance point from 600 to 582. ■

EXAMPLE 5.4

The PaperStock Company runs a manufacturing facility that produces a paper product. The fiber content of this product is supposed to be 20 pounds per 1000 square feet. (This is typical for the type of paper used in grocery bags, for example.) Because of random variations in the inputs to the process, however, the fiber content of a typical 1000-square-foot roll varies according to a $N(\mu, \sigma)$ distribution. The value of μ can be set to any desired level by adjusting an instrument on the machine. The value of σ is 0.1 pound when the process is "good," but it sometimes increases to 0.15 pound when the machine goes "bad." A given roll of this product must be rejected if its actual fiber content is less than 19.8 pounds or greater than 20.3 pounds. Calculate the probability that a given roll is rejected, for a setting of $\mu = 20$, when the machine is "good" and when it is "bad."

Solution

Let X be the content of a typical roll. Then the distribution of X is either $N(20, 0.1)$ or $N(20, 0.15)$, depending on the status of the machine. In either case, the probability that the roll must be rejected can be calculated as shown in Figure 5.9. (See the file PAPER.XLS.) The formula for rejection in the "good" case appears in cell B12:

$$\text{=NORMDIST(B8,Mean,Stdev1,1)+(1-NORMDIST(B9,Mean,Stdev1,1))}$$

It is the sum of two probabilities: the probability of being to the left of the lower limit and the probability of being to the right of the upper limit. A similar formula for the "bad" case appears in cell B13, using Stdev2 in place of Stdev1.

FIGURE 5.9   **Calculations for Paper Quality Example**

	A	B	C	D	E	F	G	H	I
1	Paper Machine Setting Problem								
2									
3	Mean	20							
4	Stdev in good case	0.1		Range names					
5	Stdev in bad case	0.15		Mean: B3					
6				Stdev1: B4					
7	Reject region			Stdev2: B5					
8	Lower limit	19.8							
9	Upper limit	20.3							
10									
11	Probability of reject								
12	in good case	0.024		NORMDIST(B8,Mean,Stdev1,1)+(1-NORMDIST(B9,Mean,Stdev1,1))					
13	in bad case	0.114		NORMDIST(B8,Mean,Stdev2,1)+(1-NORMDIST(B9,Mean,Stdev2,1))					
14									
15	Data table of rejection probability as a function of the mean and good standard deviation								
16					Standard deviation				
17		0.024	0.1	0.11	0.12	0.13	0.14	0.15	
18		19.7	0.841	0.818	0.798	0.779	0.762	0.748	
19		19.8	0.500	0.500	0.500	0.500	0.500	0.500	
20		19.9	0.159	0.182	0.203	0.222	0.240	0.256	
21	Mean	20	0.024	0.038	0.054	0.072	0.093	0.114	
22		20.1	0.024	0.038	0.054	0.072	0.093	0.114	
23		20.2	0.159	0.182	0.203	0.222	0.240	0.256	
24		20.3	0.500	0.500	0.500	0.500	0.500	0.500	
25		20.4	0.841	0.818	0.798	0.779	0.762	0.748	

We see that the probability of a rejected roll in the "good" case is 0.024; in the "bad" case it is 0.114. That is, when the standard deviation increases by 50% from 0.1 to 0.15, the percentage of rolls rejected more than quadruples, from 2.4% to 11.4%.

It is certainly possible that the true process mean and "good" standard deviation are not exactly equal to the values we've assumed in cells B3 and B4. Therefore, it is useful to see how sensitive the rejection probability is to these two parameters. We do this with a two-way data table, as shown in Figure 5.9. (To form this data table, enter the formula =B12 in cell B17, highlight the range B17:H25, and use the Data/Table menu item with row input cell B4 and column input cell B3.) The tabulated values show that the probability of rejection varies greatly even for small changes in the key inputs. In particular, a combination of a badly centered mean and a large standard deviation can make the probability of rejection very large. ■

EXAMPLE 5.5

Howard Davis invests $10,000 of his money in a certain stock on January 1, 1998. By examining past movements of this stock and consulting with his broker, Howard estimates that the annual return from this stock, X, is normally distributed with mean 10% and standard deviation 4%. Here X (when expressed as a decimal) is the amount of profit Howard receives per dollar invested. It means that on December 31, 1998, his $10,000 will have grown to $10,000(1 + X)$ dollars. Because Howard is in the 33% tax bracket, he will then have to pay the Internal Revenue Service 33% of his profit. Calculate the probability that Howard will have to pay the IRS at least $400. Also, calculate the dollar amount such that Howard's after-tax profit is 90% certain to be less than this amount, that is, calculate the 90th percentile of his after-tax profit.

Solution

Howard's before-tax profit is $10,000X$ dollars, so the amount he pays the IRS is $0.33(10,000X)$, or $3300X$ dollars. We want the probability that this is at least $400. But $3300X > 400$ is the same as $X > 4/33$, so the probability of this outcome can be found as in Figure 5.10. (See the file STOCKTAX.XLS.) It is calculated with the formula

$$=1\text{-NORMDIST}(400/(\text{InvestAmt*TaxRate}),\text{Mean},\text{Stdev},1)$$

in cell D8. As we see, Howard has about a 30% chance of paying at least $400 in taxes.

FIGURE 5.10 Calculations for Taxable Returns Example

	A	B	C	D	E	F	G	H	I	J
1	**Tax on Stock Return Problem**									
2				**Range names**						
3	Amount invested	$10,000		InvestAmt: B3						
4	Mean return	10%		Mean: B4						
5	StDev of return	4%		Stdev: B5						
6	Tax rate	33%		TaxRate: B6						
7										
8	Probability he pays at least $400 in taxes			0.298		1-NORMDIST(400/(InvestAmt*TaxRate),Mean,Stdev,1)				
9										
10	90th percentile of stock return			15.13%		NORMINV(0.9,Mean,Stdev)				
11	90th percentile of after-tax return			$1,013		(1-TaxRate)*InvestAmt*D10				

To answer the second question, note that the after-tax profit is 67% of the before-tax profit, or $6700X$ dollars, and we want its 90th percentile. If this percentile is x, then we know that $P(6700X < x) = 0.90$, which is the same as $P(X < x/6700) = 0.90$. In words, we want the 90th percentile of the X distribution to be $x/6700$. From cell D10 of Figure 5.10, we see that the 90th percentile is 15.13%, so the required value of x is $1,013. Note that the *mean* after-tax profit is $670 (67% of the mean before-tax profit of 0.10 multiplied by $10,000). Of course, Howard might get lucky and make more than this, but he is 90% certain that his after-tax profit will be no greater than $1,013. ■

It is sometimes tempting to model every continuous random variable with a normal distribution. This can be dangerous for at least two reasons. First, not all random variables have a *symmetric* distribution. Some are skewed to the left or the right, and for these the normal distribution can be a poor approximation. The second problem is that many random variables in real applications must be *nonnegative*, and the normal distribution allows the possibility of negative values. The following example shows how this can get us into trouble if we aren't careful.

EXAMPLE 5.6

The Highland Company is a retailer that sells microwave ovens. The company wants to model its demand for microwaves over the next 12 years. Using historical data as a guide, it assumes that demand in year 1 is normally distributed with mean 5000 and standard deviation 1500. It assumes that demand in every subsequent year is normally distributed with mean equal to the *actual* demand from the previous year and standard deviation 1500. For example, if demand in year 1 turns out to be 4500, then the *mean* demand in year 2 is 4500. This assumption appears plausible because it leads to correlated demands. For example, if demand is high one year, it will tend to be high the next year. Investigate the ramifications of this model, and suggest models that might be more realistic.

Solution

The best way to analyze this model is with simulation, much as we did in Chapter 4. To do this, we must be able to simulate normally distributed random numbers in Excel. We can do this with the NORMINV function. Specifically, to generate a normally distributed number with mean μ and standard deviation σ, we use the formula

$$=NORMINV(RAND(),\mu,\sigma)$$

Because this formula uses the RAND function, it generates a *different* random number each time it is used—and each time the spreadsheet recalculates.[4]

The spreadsheet in Figure 5.11 shows a simulation of yearly demands over a 12-year period. (See the Model1 sheet in the DEMMODS.XLS file.) To simulate the demands in row 15, we enter the formula

$$=NORMINV(RAND(),B6,B7)$$

in cell B15. Then we enter the formula

$$=NORMINV(RAND(),B15,\$B\$11)$$

---

[4] To see why this formula makes sense, note that the RAND function in the first argument generates a uniformly distributed random value between 0 and 1. Therefore, the effect of the function is to generate a random *percentile* from the normal distribution.

FIGURE 5.11   One Set of Demands for Model 1 in the Microwave Example

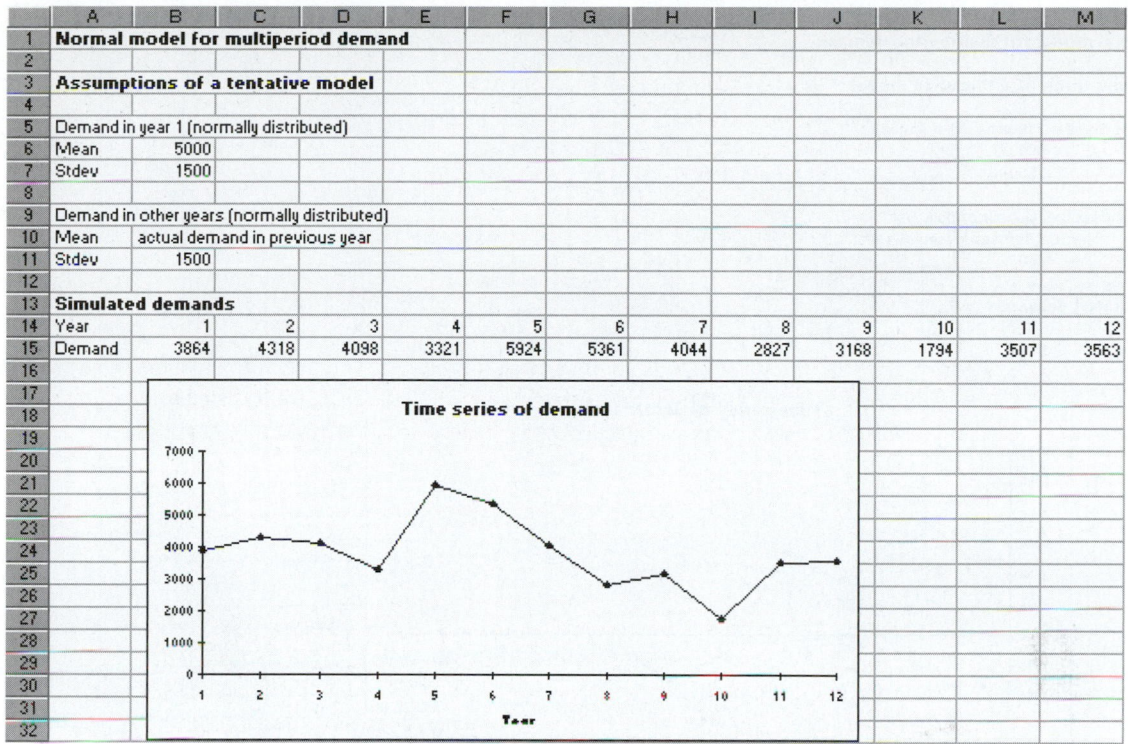

in cell C15 and copy it across row 15. As the accompanying time series graph of these demands indicates, the model seems to be performing well.

However, the simulated demands in Figure 5.11 are only one set of possible demands. Remember that each time the spreadsheet recalculates, all of the random numbers change.[5] Figure 5.12 shows a different set of random numbers generated by the *same* formulas. Clearly, the model is not working well in this case—some demands are negative, which makes no sense. The problem is that if the actual demand is low in one year, there is a fair chance that the next normally distributed demand will be negative. You can check (by recalculating many times) that the demand sequence is *usually* all positive, but every now and then you'll get a nonsense sequence as in Figure 5.12 (page 210). We need a new model!

One way to modify the model is to let the standard deviation and mean move together. That is, if the mean is low, then the standard deviation will also be low. This minimizes the chance that the *next* random demand will become negative. Besides, this type of model is probably more realistic. If demand in one year is low, there is likely to be less variability in next year's demand. Figure 5.13 (page 211) illustrates one way to model this changing standard deviation. (See the Model2 sheet of the DEMMODS.XLS file.)

We let the standard deviation of demand in any year (after year 1) be the original standard deviation, 1500, multiplied by the ratio of the expected demand for this year to the expected demand in year 1. For example, if demand in some year is 500, then the expected demand next year is 500, and the standard deviation of next year's demand is reduced to

---

[5]The usual way to get Excel to recalculate is to press the F9 key. However, this makes all of the data tables in the workbook recalculate, which can take forever. Because there is a data table in another sheet of the DEMMODS.XLS file, we suggest a different way to recalculate. Simply position the cursor on any blank cell and press the Delete key.

FIGURE 5.12   Another Set of Demands for Model 1 in the Microwave Example

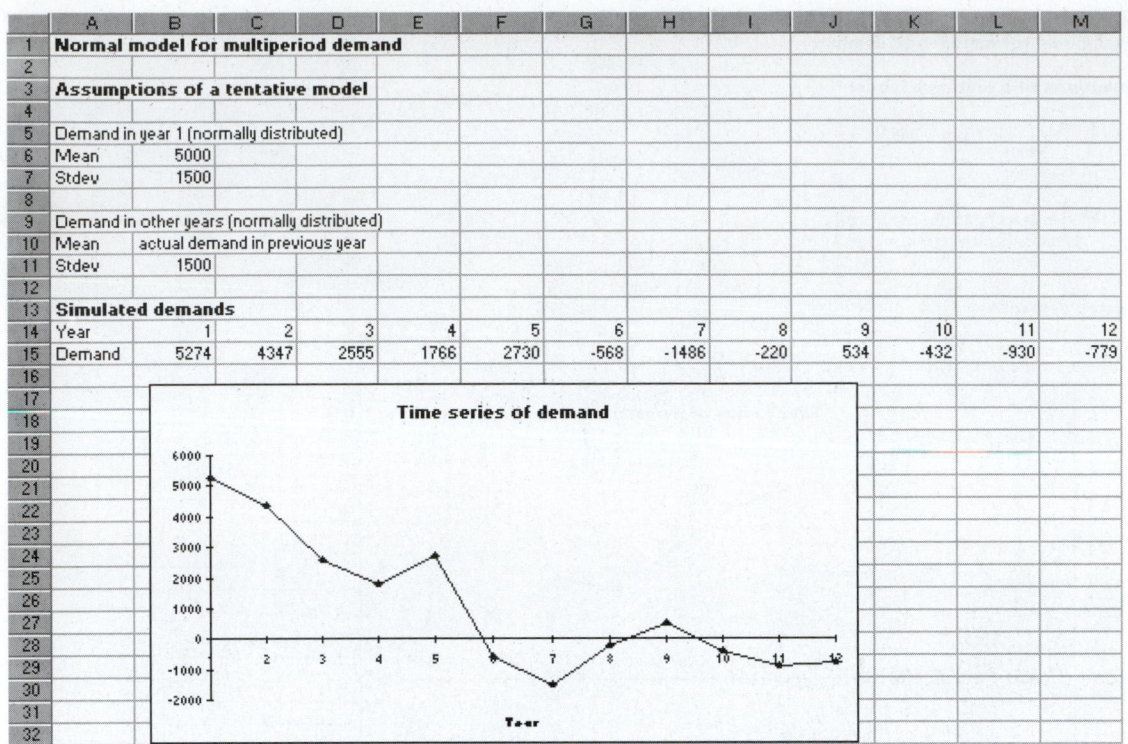

$1500(500/5000) = 150$. The only change to the spreadsheet model is in row 15, where we enter

$$=NORMINV(RAND(),B15,\$B\$7*B15/\$B\$6)$$

in cell C15 and copy it across row 15. Now the chance of a negative demand is practically negligible because this would require a value more than three standard deviations below the mean.

The model in Figure 5.13 is still not foolproof. By recalculating many times, we can still generate a negative demand now and then. To be even safer, we can "truncate" the demand distribution at some nonnegative value such as 250, as shown in Figure 5.14. Now we generate a random demand as in the previous model, but if this randomly generated value is below 250, we set the demand equal to 250. This is done by entering the formulas

$$=MAX(NORMINV(RAND(),B8,B9),D5)$$

and

$$=MAX(RAND(),B17,\$B\$9*B17/\$B\$8),\$D\$5)$$

in cells B17 and C17 and copying this latter formula across row 17. Whether this is the way the demand process works for Highland's microwaves is an open question, but at least we have prevented demands from ever becoming negative—or even falling below 250. Moreover, this type of truncation is a common way of modeling when we want to use a normal distribution but for physical reasons cannot allow the random quantities to become negative.

FIGURE 5.13 Generated Demands for Model 2 in Microwave Example

	A	B	C	D	E	F	G	H	I	J	K	L	M
1	Normal model for multiperiod demand												
2													
3	Assumptions of a "safer" model												
4													
5	Demand in year 1 (normally distributed)												
6	Mean	5000											
7	Stdev	1500											
8													
9	Demand in other years (normally distributed)												
10	Mean	actual demand in previous year											
11	Stdev	1500 times ratio of previous year's actual demand to year 1's mean demand											
12													
13	Simulated demands												
14	Year	1	2	3	4	5	6	7	8	9	10	11	12
15	Demand	1960	2425	2509	1643	1847	2169	1673	1920	1101	914	848	648

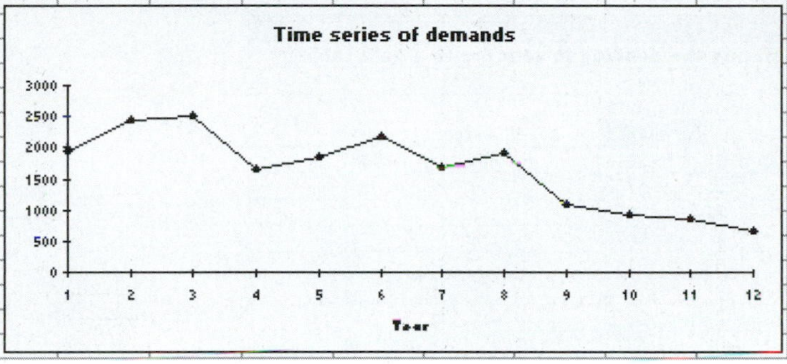

Time series of demands

FIGURE 5.14 Generated Demands for a Truncated Model in Microwave Example

	A	B	C	D	E	F	G	H	I	J	K	L	M
1	Normal model for multiperiod demand												
2													
3	Assumptions of an even "safer" model												
4													
5	Minimum demand in any year		250										
6													
7	Demand in year 1 (truncated normal)												
8	Mean	5000											
9	Stdev	1500											
10													
11	Demand in other years (truncated normal)												
12	Mean	actual demand in previous year											
13	Stdev	1500 times ratio of previous year's actual demand to year 1's mean demand											
14													
15	Simulated demands												
16	Year	1	2	3	4	5	6	7	8	9	10	11	12
17	Demand	3716	3836	2928	3212	3307	1586	2231	2056	3215	2416	2434	2334

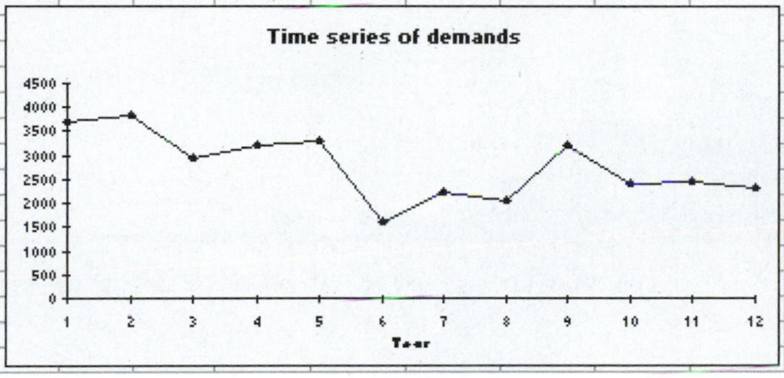

Time series of demands

Before leaving this example, we challenge your intuition. In the final model in Figure 5.14, the demand in any year (say, year 6) is, aside from the truncation, normally distributed with a mean and standard deviation that depend on the previous year's demand. Does this mean that if we recalculate many times and keep track of the year 6 demand each time, the resulting histogram of these year 6 demands will be normally distributed? Perhaps surprisingly, the answer is a clear "no." We show the evidence in Figures 5.15 and 5.16. In Figure 5.15 we use a data table to obtain 400 replications of demand in year 6 (in column B). Then we use StatPro's histogram procedure to create a histogram of these simulated demands in Figure 5.16. It is clearly skewed to the right and *nonnormal*.

FIGURE 5.15 **Replication of Demand in Year 6**

	A	B	C	D	E	F
34	Simulating the demand in year 6 with a data table					
35						
36	Replication	Demand 6				
37		11846		Average	4801	
38	1	3043		Stdev	3538	
39	2	5732				
40	3	15942				
41	4	5614				
42	5	3162				
43	6	1302				
44	7	3316				
45	8	5310				
46	9	2877				
47	10	4965				
48	11	4344				
49	12	2066				
50	13	7710				
51	14	8789				
52	15	5007				
53	16	4592				
54	17	14978				
55	18	381				
56	19	377				
433	396	2307				
434	397	1385				
435	398	3611				
436	399	5017				
437	400	1711				

FIGURE 5.16 **Histogram of Year 6 Demands**

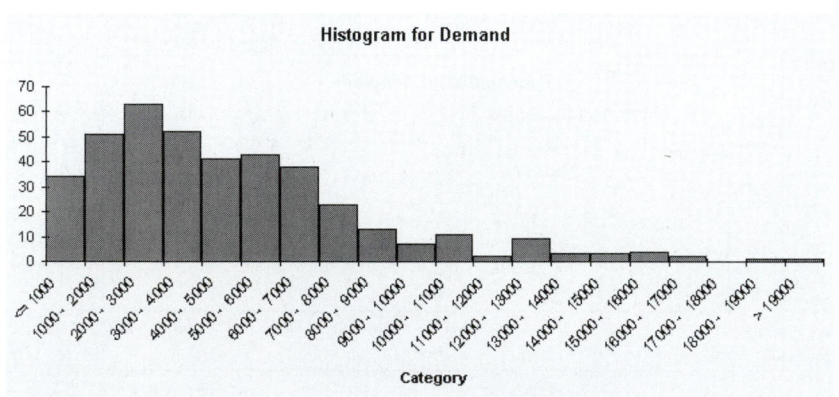

What causes this distribution to be nonnormal? It is *not* the truncation. This has a relatively minor effect because most of the demands don't need to be truncated anyway. The real reason is that the distribution of year 6 demand is only normal *conditional* on the demand in year 5. That is, if we fix the demand in year 5 at any level and then replicate year 6 demand many times, the resulting histogram *is* normally shaped. But we don't fix the year 5 demand. It varies from replication to replication, and this variation causes the skewness in Figure 5.16. Admittedly, the reason for this skewness is not obvious from an intuitive standpoint, but simulation makes it easy to demonstrate. ∎

PROBLEMS

Level A

1   The grades on the midterm examination given in a large managerial statistics class are normally distributed with mean 75 and standard deviation 9. The instructor of this class wants to assign an A grade to the top 10% of the scores, a B grade to the next 10% of the scores, a C grade to the next 10% of the scores, a D grade to the next 10% of the scores, and an F grade to all scores below the 60th percentile of this distribution. For each possible letter grade, find the lowest acceptable score within the established range. For example, the lowest acceptable score for an A is the score at the 90th percentile of this normal distribution.

2   Suppose it is known that the distribution of purchase amounts by customers entering a popular retail store is approximately normal with mean $25 and standard deviation $8.

   a   What is the probability that a randomly selected customer spends less than $35 at this store?

   b   What is the probability that a randomly selected customer spends between $15 and $35 at this store?

   c   What is the probability that a randomly selected customer spends more than $10 at this store?

   d   Find the dollar amount such that 75% of all customers spend no more than this amount.

   e   Find the dollar amount such that 80% of all customers spend at least this amount.

   f   Find two dollars amounts, equidistant from the mean of $25, such that 90% of all customer purchases are between these values.

3   A machine used to regulate the amount of a certain chemical dispensed in the production of a particular type of cough syrup can be set so that it discharges an average of μ milliliters (ml) of the chemical in each bottle of cough syrup. The amount of chemical placed into each bottle of cough syrup is known to have a normal distribution with a standard deviation of 0.250 ml. If this machine discharges more than 2 ml of the chemical when preparing a given bottle of this cough syrup, the bottle is considered to be unacceptable by industry standards. Determine the setting for μ so that no more than 1% of the bottles of cough syrup prepared through the use of this machine will be rejected.

4   The weekly demand for Ford car sales follows a normal distribution with mean 50,000 cars and standard deviation 14,000 cars.

   a   There is a 1% chance that Ford will sell more than what number of cars during the next year?

   b   What is the probability that Ford will sell between 2.4 and 2.7 million cars during the next year?

5   Warren Dinner has invested in nine different investments. The returns on the different investments are probabilistically independent, and each return follows a normal distribution with mean $500 and standard deviation $100.

   a   There is a 1% chance that the total return on the nine investments is less than what value? (Use the fact that the sum of independent normal random variables is normally distributed, with mean equal to the sum of the individual means, and variance equal to the sum of the individual variances.)

   b   What is the probability that Warren's total return is between $4000 and $5200?

6   Scores on an exam appear to follow a normal distribution with $\mu = 60$ and $\sigma = 20$. The instructor wishes to give a grade of D to students scoring between the 10th and 30th percentiles on the exam. For what range of scores should a D be given?

7 Suppose the weight of a typical American male follows a normal distribution with $\mu = 180$ lb and $\sigma = 30$ lb. Also, suppose 91.92% of all American males weigh more than I weigh.

a What fraction of American males weigh more than 225 pounds?

b How much do I weigh?

8 Assume that the length of a typical televised baseball game, including all the commercial timeouts, is normally distributed with mean 2.45 hours and standard deviation 0.37 hour. Consider a televised baseball game that begins at 2:00 in the afternoon. The next regularly scheduled broadcast is at 5:00.

a What is the probability that the game will cut into the next show, that is, go past 5:00?

b If the game is over before 4:30, another half-hour show can be inserted into the 4:30–5:00 slot. What is the probability of this occurring?

9 The amount of a soft drink that goes into a typical 12-ounce can varies from can to can. It is normally distributed with an adjustable mean μ and a fixed standard deviation of 0.05 ounce. (The adjustment is made to the filling machine.)

a If regulations require that cans have at least 11.9 ounces, what is the smallest mean μ that can be used so that at least 99.5% of all cans meet the regulation?

b If the mean setting from part **a** is used, what is the probability that a typical can has at least 12 ounces?

Level B

10 The manufacturer of a particular bicycle model has the following costs associated with the management of this product's inventory. In particular, the company currently maintains an inventory of 1000 units of this bicycle model at the beginning of each year. If X units are demanded each year and X is less than 1000, the excess supply, $1000 - X$ units, must be stored until next year at a cost of $50 per unit. If X is greater than 1000 units, the excess demand, $X - 1000$ units, must be produced separately at an extra cost of $80 per unit. Assume that the annual demand (X) for this bicycle model is normally distributed with mean 1000 and standard deviation 75.

a Find the expected annual cost associated with managing potential shortages or surpluses of this product.

b Find two annual total cost levels, equidistant from the expected value found in part **a**, such that 95% of all costs associated with managing potential shortages or surpluses of this product are between these values.

c Comment on this manufacturer's annual production policy for this bicycle model in light of your findings in part **b**.

11 Matthew's Bakery prepares peanut butter cookies for sale every morning. It costs the bakery $.25 to bake each peanut butter cookie, and each cookie is sold for $.50. At the end of the day, leftover cookies are discounted and sold the following day at $.10 per cookie. The daily demand (in dozens) for peanut butter cookies at this bakery is known to be normally distributed with mean 50 and standard deviation 15. The manager of Matthew's Bakery is trying to determine how many dozen peanut butter cookies to make each morning to maximize the product's contribution to bakery profits. Use computer simulation to find a very good, if not optimal, production plan in this case.

12 Suppose that a particular production process fills detergent in boxes of a given size. Specifically, this process fills the boxes with an amount of detergent (in ounces) that is adequately described by a normal distribution with mean 50 and standard deviation 0.5.

a Simulate this production process for the filling of 500 boxes of detergent. Compute the mean and standard deviation of your computer-generated sample weights. How do your sample statistics compare to the theoretical population parameters in this case? How well do the rules of thumb apply in describing the variation in the weights of the detergent in your simulated detergent boxes?

b A box of detergent is rejected by quality control personnel if it is found to contain less than 49 ounces or more than 51 ounces of detergent. Given these quality standards, what proportion of all boxes are rejected? What step(s) could the supervisor of this production process take to reduce this proportion to 1%?

13 It is widely known that many drivers on interstate highways in the United States do not observe the posted speed limit. Assume that the actual rates of speed driven by U.S. motorists are normally distributed with mean μ mph and standard deviation 5 mph. Given this information, answer each of the following independent questions:

a If 40% of all U.S. drivers are observed traveling at 65 mph or more, what is the mean μ?

b If 25% of all U.S. drivers are observed traveling at 50 mph or less, what is the mean μ?

c Suppose now that the mean μ and standard deviation σ of this distribution are both unknown. Furthermore, it is observed that 40% of all U.S. drivers travel at less than 55 mph and 10% of all U.S. drivers travel at more than 70 mph. What must μ and σ be?

14 The lifetime of a washing machine is normally distributed with mean 4 years. Only 15% of all washing machines last at least 5 years. What is the standard deviation of the lifetime of a washing machine?

15 You have been told that the distribution of regular unleaded gasoline prices over all gas stations in Indiana is normally distributed with mean $1.25 and standard deviation $.075, and you have been asked to find two dollar values such that 95% of all gas stations charge somewhere between these two values. Why are each of the following acceptable answers: between $1.076 and $1.381, or between $1.103 and $1.397? Can you find any other acceptable answers? Which of the many possible answers would you prefer if you are asked to obtain the *shortest* such interval?

16 When we create boxplots, we place the sides of the "box" at the first and third quartiles, and the difference between these (the length of the box) is called the interquartile range (IQR). A mild outlier is then defined as an observation that is between 1.5 and 3 IQRs from the box, and an extreme outlier is defined as an observation that is more than 3 IQRs from the box.

a If the data are normally distributed, what percentage of values will be mild outliers? What percentage will be extreme outliers? Why don't the answers depend on the mean and/or standard deviation of the distribution?

b Check out your answers in part **a** with simulation. Simulate a large number of normal random numbers (you can choose any mean and standard deviation), and count the number of mild and extreme outliers with appropriate IF functions. Do these match, at least approximately, your answers to part **a**?

17 A fast-food restaurant sells hamburgers and chicken sandwiches. On a typical weekday the demand for hamburgers is normally distributed with mean 313 and standard deviation 57; the demand for chicken sandwiches is normally distributed with mean 93 and standard deviation 22.

a How many hamburgers must the restaurant stock to be 98% sure of not running out on a given day?

b Answer part **a** for chicken sandwiches.

c If the restaurant stocks 400 hamburgers and 150 chicken sandwiches for a given day, what is the probability that it will run out of hamburgers or chicken sandwiches (or both) that day? Assume that the demand for hamburgers and the demand for chicken sandwiches are probabilistically independent.

d Why is the independence assumption in part **c** probably not realistic? Using a more realistic assumption, do you think the probability requested in part **c** would increase or decrease?

18 Suppose that the demands for a company's product in weeks 1, 2, and 3 are each normally distributed. The means are 50, 45, and 65. The standard deviations are 10, 5, and 15. Assume that these three demands are probabilistically independent. This means that if you observe one of them, it doesn't help you to predict the others. Then it turns out that total demand for the 3 weeks is also normally distributed. Its mean is the sum of the individual means, and its variance is the sum of the individual variances. (Its standard deviation, however, is not the sum of the individual standard deviations; square roots don't work that way.)

a Suppose that the company currently has 180 units in stock, and it will not be receiving any further shipments from its supplier for at least 3 weeks. What is the probability that it will stock out during this 3-week period?

b How many units should the company currently have in stock so that it can be 98% certain of not stocking out during this 3-week period? Again assume that it won't receive any further shipments during this period. ■

The Binomial Distribution

The normal distribution is undoubtedly the most important probability distribution in statistics. Not far behind in order of importance, however, is the **binomial** distribution. The binomial distribution is a discrete distribution that can occur in two situations: (1) whenever we sample from a population with only two types of members (males and females, for example), and (2) whenever we perform a sequence of identical experiments, each of which has only two possible outcomes.

Imagine any experiment that can be repeated many times under identical conditions. It is common to refer to each repetition of the experiment as a **trial**. We assume that the outcomes of successive trials are probabilistically independent of one another and that each trial has only two possible outcomes. We label these two possibilities generically as success and failure. In any particular application the outcomes might be Democrat/Republican, defective/nondefective, went bankrupt/remained solvent, and so on. The probability of a success on each trial is p, and the probability of a failure is $1 - p$. The number of trials is n.

In this setup, where there are n independent, identical trials, each with probability of success p, we let X be the random number of successes. Then X has a binomial distribution with parameters n and p. For example, the binomial distribution with parameters 100 and 0.3 is the distribution of the number of successes in 100 trials when the probability of success is 0.3 on each trial. A simple example that you can keep in mind throughout this section is the number of heads you would see if you flipped a coin n times. Assuming the coin is well balanced, the relevant distribution is binomial with parameters n and $p = 0.5$. This coin-flipping example is often used to illustrate the binomial distribution because of its simplicity, but we will see that the binomial distribution also applies to many important business situations.

To understand how the binomial distribution works, consider the coin-flipping example with $n = 3$. If X represents the number of heads in three flips of the coin, then the possible values of X are 0, 1, 2, and 3. We can find the probabilities of these values by considering the eight possible outcomes of the three flips: (T,T,T), (T,T,H), (T,H,T), (H,T,T), (T,H,H), (H,T,H), (H,H,T), and (H,H,H). Because of symmetry (the well-balanced property of the coin), each of these eight possible outcomes must have the same probability, so each must have probability 1/8. Next, note that one of the outcomes has $X = 0$, three outcomes have $X = 1$, three outcomes have $X = 2$, and one outcome has $X = 3$. Therefore, the probability distribution of X is

$$P(X = 0) = 1/8, \quad P(X = 1) = 3/8, \quad P(X = 2) = 3/8, \quad P(X = 3) = 1/8$$

This is a special case of the binomial distribution, with $n = 3$ and $p = 0.5$. In general, where n can be any positive integer and p can be any probability between 0 and 1, there is a rather complex formula for calculating $P(X = k)$ for any integer k from 0 to n. Instead of presenting this formula, we will discuss how to calculate binomial probabilities in Excel. We do this with the BINOMDIST function. The general form of this function is

$$=\text{BINOMDIST}(k, n, p, cum)$$

The middle two arguments are as above: the number of trials n and the probability of success p on each trial. The first parameter k is an integer number of successes that we specify. The last parameter, *cum*, is either 0 or 1. It is 1 if we want the probability of *less than or equal to* k successes, and it is 0 if we want the probability of *exactly* k successes. We illustrate typical binomial calculations in the following example.

E X A M P L E 5 . 7

Suppose 100 identical batteries are inserted in identical flashlights. Each flashlight takes a single battery. After 8 hours of continuous use, we assume that a given battery is still operating with probability 0.6 and has failed with probability 0.4. Let X be the number of successes in these 100 trials, where a success means that the battery is still functioning. Find the probabilities of the following events: (i) exactly 58 successes, (ii) no more than 65 successes, (iii) less than 70 successes, (iv) at least 59 successes, (v) greater than 65 successes, (vi) between 55 and 65 successes (inclusive), (vii) exactly 40 failures, (viii) at least 35 failures, and (ix) less than 42 failures. Then find the 95th percentile of the distribution of X.

Solution

Figure 5.17 shows the solution to all of these problems. (See the file BINOMDST.XLS.) The probabilities requested in parts (i)–(vi) all involve the number of successes X. The key to these is the wording of phrases such as "no more than," "greater than," and so on. In particular, we have to be careful to distinguish between probabilities such as $P(X < k)$ and $P(X \leq k)$. The latter includes the possibility of having $X = k$ and the former does not.

FIGURE 5.17 **Typical Binomial Calculations**

	A	B	C	D	E	F	G	H	I
1	**Binomial Probability Calculations**								
2				**Range names**					
3	Number of trials	100		NTrials: B3					
4	Probability of success on each trial	0.6		PSucc: B4					
5									
6	**Event**	**Probability**		**Formula**					
7	Exactly 58 successes	0.0742		BINOMDIST(58,NTrials,PSucc,0)					
8	No more than 65 successes	0.8697		BINOMDIST(65,NTrials,PSucc,1)					
9	Less than 70 successes	0.9752		BINOMDIST(69,NTrials,PSucc,1)					
10	At least 59 successes	0.6225		1-BINOMDIST(58,NTrials,PSucc,1)					
11	Greater than 65 successes	0.1303		1-BINOMDIST(65,NTrials,PSucc,1)					
12	Between 55 and 65 successes (inclusive)	0.7386		BINOMDIST(65,NTrials,PSucc,1)-BINOMDIST(54,NTrials,PSucc,1)					
13									
14	Exactly 40 failures	0.0812		BINOMDIST(40,NTrials,1-PSucc,0)					
15	At least 35 failures	0.8697		1-BINOMDIST(34,NTrials,1-PSucc,1)					
16	Less than 42 failures	0.6225		BINOMDIST(41,NTrials,1-PSucc,1)					
17									
18	**Finding the 95th percentile (trial and error)**								
19	Trial values	CumProb							
20	65	0.8697		BINOMDIST(A20,NTrials,PSucc,1)					
21	66	0.9087		(Copy down)					
22	67	0.9385							
23	68	0.9602							
24	69	0.9752							
25	70	0.9852							
26				Formula in cell A27:					
27	68	0.95		CRITBINOM(NTrials,PSucc,B27)					

With this in mind, we can translate the probabilities requested in (i) – (vi) to the following:

(i) $P(X = 58)$

(ii) $P(X \leq 65)$

(iii) $P(X < 70) = P(X \leq 69)$

(iv) $P(X \geq 59) = 1 - P(X < 59) = 1 - P(X \leq 58)$

(v) $\quad P(X > 65) = 1 - P(X \le 65)$

(vi) $\quad P(55 \le X \le 65) = P(X \le 65) - P(X < 55) = P(X \le 65) - P(X \le 54)$

Note how we have converted each of these so that it includes only terms of the form $P(X = k)$ or $P(X \le k)$ (for suitable values of k). These are the types of probabilities that can be handled directly by the BINOMDIST function. The answers appear in the range B7:B12, and the corresponding formulas are shown in column D.

The probabilities requested in (vii)–(ix) involve *failures* rather than successes. But because each trial results in either a success or a failure, the number of failures is also binomially distributed, with parameters n and $1 - p = 0.4$. So in rows 14 through 16, we calculate the requested probabilities in exactly the same way, except that we substitute 1-PSucc for PSucc in the third argument of the BINOMDIST function.

Finally, to calculate the 95th percentile of the distribution of X, we proceed by trial and error. For each value k from 65 to 70, we have calculated the probability $P(X \le k)$ in column B with the BINOMDIST function. Note that there is no value k such that $P(X \le k) = 0.95$ exactly. We see that $P(X \le 67)$ is slightly less than 0.95, and $P(X \le 68)$ is slightly greater than 0.95. Therefore, the meaning of the "95th percentile" is a bit ambiguous. If we want the largest value k such that $P(X \le k) \le 0.95$, then this k is 67. If instead we want the smallest value k such that $P(X \le k) \ge 0.95$, then this value is 68. The latter interpretation is the one usually accepted for binomial percentiles.

In fact, Excel has another built-in function, CRITBINOM, for finding this value of k. We illustrate it in row 27 of Figure 5.17. Now we enter the requested probability, 0.95, in cell B27 and the formula

$$=\text{CRITBINOM(NTrials,PSucc,B27)}$$

in cell A27. It returns 68, the smallest value k such that $P(X \le k) \ge 0.95$ for this binomial distribution. ∎

5.4.1 Mean and Standard Deviation of the Binomial Distribution

It can be shown that the mean and standard deviation of a binomial distribution with parameters n and p are

$$E(X) = np$$

$$\text{Stdev}(X) = \sqrt{np(1 - p)}$$

The formula for the mean is quite intuitive. For example, if you observe 100 trials, each with probability of success 0.6, what is your best guess for the number of successes? It is clearly $100(0.6) = 60$. The standard deviation is less obvious but still very useful. It indicates how far the actual number of successes might deviate from the mean. In this case the standard deviation is $\sqrt{100(0.6)(0.4)} = 4.90$.

Fortunately, the rules of thumb discussed in Section 3.5 apply, at least approximately. That is, there is about a 95% chance that the actual number of successes will be within two standard deviations of the mean, and there is almost no chance that the number of successes will be more than three standard deviations from the mean. So for this example, it is very likely that the number of successes will be in the range of approximately 50 to 70, and it is very unlikely that there will be fewer than 45 or more than 75 successes.

This reasoning is extremely useful. It gives us a rough estimate of the number of successes we are likely to observe. Suppose we randomly sample 1000 parts from an assembly line and, based on historical performance, we know that the percentage of parts with some type of defect is about 5%. Translated into a binomial model, we assume that each of the 1000 parts, independently of the others, has some type of defect with probability 0.05. Would we be surprised to see, say, 75 parts with a defect? The mean is $1000(0.05) = 50$ and the standard deviation is $\sqrt{1000(0.05)(0.95)} = 6.89$. Therefore, the number of parts with defects is 95% certain to be within $50 \pm 2(6.89)$, or approximately from 35 to 65. Because 75 is slightly beyond three standard deviations from the mean, it is highly unlikely that we would observe 75 parts with defects.

5.4.2 The Binomial Distribution in the Context of Sampling

Before we look at applications of the binomial distribution, we discuss how this distribution applies to sampling from a population with two types of members. For now, we'll call these two types men and women, although in applications they might be Democrats versus Republicans, users of our product versus nonusers, and so on. We will assume that the population has N members, of whom N_M are men and N_W are women (where $N_M + N_W = N$). If we sample n of these randomly, we are typically interested in the composition of the sample. The question is whether the number of men in the sample is binomially distributed with parameters n and $p = N_M/N$, the fraction of men in the population.

The answer depends on how the sampling is performed. If sampling is done **without replacement**, then each member of the population can be sampled only once. That is, once a person is sampled, his or her name is struck from the list and cannot be sampled again. If sampling is done **with replacement**, then it is possible, although maybe not likely, to select a given member of the population any number of times. Most real-world sampling is performed *without* replacement. There is no point in obtaining information from the same person more than once. However, the binomial model applies only to sampling with replacement. It is only an approximation if sampling is done without replacement. The reason is that the composition of the remaining population keeps changing as the sampling progresses. This means that the value of p, the proportion of men, does not stay constant, a requirement of the binomial model. It turns out that the appropriate distribution for sampling without replacement is the **hypergeometric** distribution, a distribution we will not discuss here.

That's the bad news. The good news is that if n is small relative to N, then the binomial model is a very good approximation to the hypergeometric model, so it works well when sampling is without replacement. A rule of thumb is that if n is no greater than 10% of N, that is, no more than 10% of the population is sampled, then the binomial model can be used safely. Of course, as you probably know, many national polls sample considerably less than 10% of the population. In fact, they often sample only a few thousand people from the hundreds of millions in the entire population. The bottom line is that in most real-world sampling contexts, the binomial model is perfectly adequate.

5.4.3 The Normal Approximation to the Binomial

If we graph the binomial probabilities, we see an interesting phenomenon—namely, the graph begins to look symmetric and bell shaped when n is fairly large and p is not too close to 0 or 1. An example is illustrated in Figure 5.18 (page 220) with the parameters $n = 30$ and $p = 0.4$. Generally, if $np > 5$ and $n(1 - p) > 5$, the binomial distribution can be approximated well by a normal distribution with mean np and standard deviation $\sqrt{np(1 - p)}$.

One practical use of the normal approximation to the binomial is that it allows us to use the rules of thumb discussed earlier. That is, because the binomial distribution is approximately symmetric and bell shaped, we know the chances are about 2 out of 3 that

FIGURE 5.18 Bell-shaped Binomial Distribution

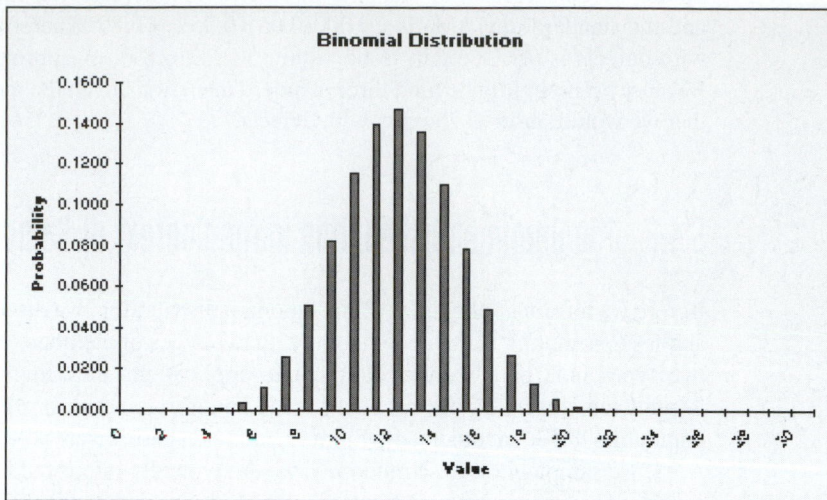

the number of successes will be within one standard deviation of the mean. Similarly, there is about a 95% chance that the number of successes will be within two standard deviations of the mean, and the number of successes will almost surely be within three standard deviations of the mean. Here, the mean is np and the standard deviation is $\sqrt{np(1-p)}$.

5.5

Applications of the Binomial Distribution

The binomial distribution finds many applications in the business world and elsewhere. We discuss a few such applications in this section.

EXAMPLE 5.8

An investment broker at the Michaels & Dodson Company claims that he has found a real winner. He has tracked a mutual fund that has beaten a standard market index in 37 of the past 52 weeks. Could this be due to chance, or has he *really* found a winner?

Solution

The broker is no doubt tracking a lot of mutual funds, and he is probably reporting on the best of these. Therefore, we will check whether the best of *many* mutual funds could do at least this well purely by chance. To do this, we first specify what we mean by the term "purely by chance." This means that each week, a given fund has a 50–50 chance of beating the market index, independently of performance in other weeks. In other words, the number of weeks where a given fund outperforms the market index is binomially distributed with $n = 52$ and $p = 0.5$. With this in mind, cell B6 of Figure 5.19 shows the probability that a given fund does at least as well—beats the market index at least 37 out of 52 weeks—as

FIGURE 5.19 Binomial Calculations for Investment Example

	A	B	C	D	E	F	G	H	I
1	**Michaels & Dodson mutual fund problem**								
2									
3	Weeks beating market index	37							
4	Total number of weeks	52							
5									
6	Probability of doing at least this well by chance	0.00159		1-BINOMDIST(NBeatMkt-1,NWeeks,0.5,1)					
7									
8	Number of mutual funds	400							
9	Probability of at least one doing at least this well	0.471		1-BINOMDIST(0,NFunds,PAtLeast37,1)					
10									
11	Two-way data table of the probability in B9 as a function of values in B3 and B8								
12			Number of weeks beating the market index						
13		0.471	36	37	38	39	40		
14	Number of mutual funds	200	0.542	0.273	0.113	0.040	0.013		
15		300	0.690	0.380	0.164	0.060	0.019		
16		400	0.790	0.471	0.213	0.079	0.025		
17		500	0.858	0.549	0.258	0.097	0.031		
18		600	0.904	0.616	0.301	0.116	0.038		

Range names
NBeatMkt: B3
NFunds: B8
NWeeks: B4
PAtLeast37: B6
PStar: B9

the reported fund. (See the MUTFUND.XLS file.) Because $P(X \geq 37) = 1 - P(X \leq 36)$, the relevant formula is

$$=1\text{-BINOMDIST(NBeatMkt-1,NWeeks,0.5,1)}$$

Obviously, this probability, 0.00159, is quite small. A single fund isn't likely to beat the market this often purely by chance.

However, the probability that the *best* of many mutual funds does at least this well is much larger. To calculate this probability, let's assume that there are 400 funds being tracked, and let Y be the number of these that beat the market at least 37 of 52 weeks. Then Y is also binomially distributed, with parameters $n = 400$ and $p = 0.00159$, the probability calculated above. We want to know whether *any* of the 400 funds beats the market at least 37 of 52 weeks, so we calculate $P(Y \geq 1) = 1 - P(Y = 0)$. We do this in cell B9 with the formula

$$=1\text{-BINOMDIST(0,NFunds,PAtLeast37,1)}$$

(Can you see why the fourth argument could be 0 *or* 1?) The resulting probability is nearly 0.5—that is, there is nearly a 50–50 chance that at least one of 400 funds will do as well as the reported fund. This certainly casts doubt on the broker's claim that he found a real winner. Perhaps his star fund just got lucky and will perform no better than average in succeeding weeks.

It is interesting to see how this probability in cell B9 depends on the level of success of the reported fund (the value in cell B3) and the number of mutual funds being tracked (in cell B8). We do this by creating a two-way data table in the range B13:G18. (The formula in cell B13 is =PStar, the row input cell is B3, and the column input cell is B8.) As we saw, beating the market 37 times out of 52 is no big deal with 400 funds, but beating it 40 times out of 52, even with 600 funds, is something worth reporting. The probability of this happening purely by chance is only 0.038, or less than 1 out of 25. ■

The next example requires a normal calculation to find a probability p, which is then used in a binomial calculation.

EXAMPLE 5.9

Customers at the Diggly Wiggly Supermarket spend varying amounts. Historical data show that the amount spent per customer is normally distributed with mean $85 and standard deviation $30. If 500 customers shop in a given day, calculate the mean and standard deviation of the number who spend at least $100. Then calculate the probability that at least 30% of these customers spend at least $100.

Solution

Both questions involve the number of customers who spend at least $100. Because the amounts spent are normally distributed, the probability that a typical customer spends at least $100 is found with the NORMDIST function. This probability, 0.309, appears in cell B8 of Figure 5.20. (See the file SUPERMKT.XLS.) We calculate it with the formula

$$=1\text{-NORMDIST}(100,\text{NormMean},\text{NormStdev},1)$$

This probability is then used as the parameter p in a binomial model. The mean and standard deviation of the number who spend at least $100 are calculated in cells B13 and B14 as np and $\sqrt{np(1-p)}$, using $n = 500$, the number of shoppers, and $p = 0.309$. The expected number who spend at least $100 is slightly greater than 154, and the standard deviation of this number is slightly greater than 10.

FIGURE 5.20 **Calculations for Supermarket Example**

	A	B	C	D	E	F	G
1	**Supermarket problem**						
2					**Range names**		
3	Amount spent per customer (normally distributed)				NCusts: B10		
4	Mean	$85			NormMean: B4		
5	StDev	$30			NormStdev: B5		
6					PAtLeast100: B8		
7	Probability that a customer spends at least $100						
8		0.309		1-NORMDIST(100,NormMean,NormStdev,1)			
9							
10	Number of customers	500					
11							
12	Mean and stdev of number who spend at least $100						
13	Mean	154.27		NCusts*PAtLeast100			
14	StDev	10.33		SQRT(NCusts*PAtLeast100*(1-PAtLeast100))			
15							
16	Probability at least 30% spend at least $100						
17		0.676		1-BINOMDIST(0.3*NCusts-1,NCusts,PAtLeast100,1)			

To answer the second question, note that 30% of 500 customers is 150 customers. Then the probability that at least 30% of the customers spend at least $100 is the probability that a binomially distributed random variable, with $n = 500$ and $p = 0.309$, is at least 150. We calculate this binomial probability, which turns out to be about 2/3, in cell B17 with the formula

$$=1\text{-BINOMDIST}(0.3*\text{NCusts}-1,\text{NCusts},\text{PAtLeast100},1)$$

Note that the first argument calculates to 149. This is because the probability of *at least* 150 customers is 1.0 minus the probability of less than or equal to 149 customers. ∎

EXAMPLE 5.10

This example presents a simplified version of calculations used by airlines when they over-book flights. They realize that a certain percentage of ticketed passengers will cancel at the last minute. Therefore, to avoid empty seats, they sell more tickets than there are seats, hoping that just about the right number of passengers show up. We will assume that the no-show rate is 5%. In binomial terms, we are assuming that each ticketed passenger, independently of the others, shows up with probability 0.95 and cancels with probability 0.05.

For a flight with 200 seats, the airline wants to find how sensitive various probabilities are to the number of tickets it issues. In particular, it wants to calculate (i) the probability that more than 205 passengers show up, (ii) the probability that more than 200 passengers show up, (iii) the probability that at least 195 seats will be filled, and (iv) the probability that at least 190 seats will be filled. The first two of these are "bad" events from the airline's perspective; they mean that some customers will be bumped from the flight. The last two events are "good" in the sense that the airline wants most of the seats to be occupied.

Solution

To solve the airline's problem, we use the BINOMDIST function and a data table. The solution appears in Figure 5.21. (See the file OVERBOOK.XLS.) We first enter a possible

FIGURE 5.21   **Binomial Calculations for Overbooking Example**

	A	B	C	D	E
1	**Airline Overbooking Problem**				
2					
3	Number of seats	200			
4	Probability of no-show	0.1	**Range names**		
5			NTickets: B6		
6	Number of tickets issued	215	PNoShow: B4		
7					
8	**Required probabilities**				
9		More than 205 show up	More than 200 show up	At least 195 seats filled	At least 190 seats filled
10		0.001	0.050	0.421	0.820
11					
12	**Data table showing sensitivity of probabilities to number of tickets issued**				
13	Number of tickets issued	More than 205 show up	More than 200 show up	At least 195 seats filled	At least 190 seats filled
14		0.001	0.050	0.421	0.820
15	206	0.000	0.000	0.012	0.171
16	209	0.000	0.001	0.064	0.384
17	212	0.000	0.009	0.201	0.628
18	215	0.001	0.050	0.421	0.820
19	218	0.013	0.166	0.659	0.931
20	221	0.064	0.370	0.839	0.978
21	224	0.194	0.607	0.939	0.995
22	227	0.406	0.802	0.981	0.999
23	230	0.639	0.920	0.995	1.000
24	233	0.822	0.974	0.999	1.000

number of tickets issued in cell B6 and, for this number, calculate the required probabilities in row 10. For example, the formulas in cells B10 and D10 are

=1-BINOMDIST(205,NTickets,1-PNoShow,1)

and

$$=1\text{-BINOMDIST}(194,\text{NTickets},1\text{-PNoShow},1)$$

Note how the wording "more than" is slightly different from "at least." The probability of more than 205 is 1.0 minus the probability of less than or equal to 205, whereas the probability of at least 195 is 1.0 minus the probability of less than or equal to 194. Also, note that we are treating a "success" as a passenger who shows up. Therefore, the third argument of each BINOMDIST function is 1.0 minus the no-show probability.

To see how sensitive these probabilities are to the number of tickets issued, we create a one-way data table at the bottom of the spreadsheet. It is *one-way* because there is only one *input*, the number tickets issued, even though there are four output probabilities tabulated. (To create the data table, list several possible numbers of tickets issued along the side in column A and transfer the probabilities from row 10 to row 14. That is, enter the formula =B10 in cell B14 and copy it across row 14. Then form a data table using the range A14:E24, no row input cell, and column input cell B6.)

The results are as expected. As the airline issues more tickets, there is a larger chance of having to bump passengers from the flight, but there is also a larger chance of filling most seats. In reality, the airline has to make a trade-off between these two, taking its various costs and revenues into account. ■

The following example is another simplified version of a real problem. It occurs every time we watch election returns on TV. The basic question is how soon the networks can declare one of the candidates the winner, based on early voting returns. This version is somewhat unrealistic because it ignores the fact that early tabulations might be biased one way or the other. For example, the earliest reporting precincts might be known to be more heavily in favor of the Democrat than the population in general. Nevertheless, the essence of this example is valid. It explains why the networks are able to make conclusions based on such seemingly small amounts of data.

E X A M P L E   5 . 1 1

We assume that there are N voters in the population, of whom N_R will vote for the Republican and N_D will vote for the Democrat. The eventual winner will be the Republican if $N_R > N_D$, and will be the Democrat otherwise, but we won't know which until all of the votes are tabulated. (To simplify the example, we assume there are only two candidates and that the election will *not* end in a tie.) Let's suppose that a small percentage of the votes have been counted and the Republican is currently ahead 540 to 460. On what basis can the networks declare the Republican the winner?

Solution

Let $n = 1000$ be the total number of votes that have been tabulated. If X is the number of Republican votes so far, we are told that $X = 540$. Now we pose the following question. If the Democrat were going to be the eventual winner, that is, $N_D > N_R$, and we randomly sampled 1000 voters from the population, how likely is it that we would see at least 540 of these in favor of the Republican? If the answer is that this is very *unlikely*, then the only reasonable conclusion is that the Democrat will *not* be the eventual winner. This is the reasoning the networks use to declare the Republican the winner.

We use a binomial model to see how unlikely is the event "at least 540 out of 1000," assuming that the Democrat will be the eventual winner. The value of n is 1000. What about the value of p, the probability that a typical vote is for the Republican? This probability should be the proportion of voters in the entire population who favor the Republican. All we know is that this probability is less than 0.5, because we have assumed that the Democrat will win. In Figure 5.22, we show how the probability of at least 540 out of 1000 varies with values of p less than, but close to, 0.5. (See the file VOTING.XLS.)

We enter a trial value of 0.49 for p in cell B3 and then calculate the required probability in cell B9 with the formula

$$=1-BINOMDIST(NVotesRepub-1,NVotes,PRepub,1)$$

Then we use this to create the data table at the bottom of the spreadsheet. This data table tabulates the probability of the given lead (at least 540 out of 1000) for various values of p less than 0.5. As shown in the last few rows, even if the eventual outcome were going to be a virtual tie—with the Democrat slightly ahead—there would still be very little chance of the Republican being at least 80 votes ahead so far. But because the Republican *is* currently ahead by 80 votes, the networks feel safe in declaring the Republican the winner.

FIGURE 5.22   **Binomial Calculations for Voting Example**

	A	B	C	D	E
1	Election Voting Example				
2					
3	Population proportion for Republican	0.49	**Range names**		
4			PRepub: B3		
5	Votes tabulated so far	1000	NVotes: B5		
6	Votes for Republican so far	540	NVoteRepub: B6		
7					
8	Binomial probability of at least this many votes for Republican				
9		0.0009			
10					
11	Data table showing sensitivity of this probability to population proportion for Republican				
12	Population proportion for Republican	Probability			
13		0.0009			
14	0.490	0.0009			
15	0.492	0.0013			
16	0.494	0.0020			
17	0.496	0.0030			
18	0.498	0.0043			
19	0.499	0.0052			

The final example in this section challenges the two assumptions of the binomial model. So far, we have assumed that the outcomes of successive trials (1) have the same probability p of success and (2) are probabilistically independent. There are many situations where either or both of these assumptions are questionable. For example, consider successive items from a production line, where each item either meets specifications (a success) or doesn't (a failure). If the process deteriorates over time, at least until it receives maintenance, then the probability p of success could slowly decrease. Even if p remains constant, defective items could come in bunches (because of momentary inattentiveness on the part of a worker, say), which would invalidate the independence assumption.

If an analyst believes that the binomial assumptions are invalid, then an alternative model must be specified that reflects reality more closely. This is not easy—all kinds of *nonbinomial* assumptions can be imagined. Furthermore, even when we make such assumptions, there are probably no simple formulas to use, such as the BINOMDIST formulas we have been using. Simulation might be the only alternative, as we illustrate in the following example.

EXAMPLE 5.12

Do basketball players shoot in streaks? This question has been debated by thousands of basketball fans, and it has even been studied statistically by several academic researchers. Most fans believe the answer is "yes," arguing that players clearly alternate between hot streaks where they can't miss and cold streaks where they can't hit the broad side of a barn. This is quite different from a belief in a binomial model where, say, a "450 shooter" makes each shot with probability 0.450 and misses each with probability 0.550, independently of other shots. If this binomial model is *not* correct, what model might be appropriate, and how could it be used to calculate a probability such as the probability of making at least 13 shots out of 25 attempts?[6]

Solution

This problem is quite open-ended. There are numerous alternatives to the binomial model that could capture the "streakiness" most fans believe in, and the one we suggest here is by no means definitive. We challenge you to develop others.

The model we propose assumes that this shooter makes 45% of his shots in the long run. The probability that he makes his first shot in a game is 0.45. In general, consider his nth shot. If he has made his last k shots, then the probability of making shot n is $0.45 + kd_1$. On the other hand, if he has missed his last k shots, the probability of making shot n is $0.45 - kd_2$. Here, d_1 and d_2 are small values (0.01 and 0.02, for example) that indicate how much the shooter's probability of success increases or decreases depending on his current streak. The model implies that the shooter gets better the more he makes and worse the more he misses.

To implement this model, we use simulation as shown in Figure 5.23. (See the file BBALL.XLS.) Actually, we first do a "baseline" binomial calculation in cell B9, using the parameters $n = 25$ and $p = 0.450$. The formula in cell B9 is

$$=1-\text{BINOMDIST}(12,\text{NShots},\text{PMake},1)$$

If the player makes each shot with probability 0.45, independently of the other shots, then the probability that he will make over half of his 25 shots is 0.306—about a 30% chance.

The simulation in the range A17:D41 shows the results of 25 random shots according to the *nonbinomial* model we have assumed. Column B indicates the length of the current streak, where a negative value indicates a streak of misses and a positive value indicates a streak of makes. Column C indicates the probability of a make on the current shot, and column D contains 1's for makes and 0's for misses. Here are step-by-step instructions for developing this range.

1 **First shot.** Enter the formulas

$$=\text{PMake}$$

and

$$=\text{IF}(\text{RAND}()<\text{C17},1,0)$$

in cells C17 and D17 to determine the outcome of the first shot.

---

[6] There are obviously a lot of extenuating circumstances surrounding any shot: the type of shot (layup versus jump shot), the type of defense, the score, the time left in the game, and so on. For this example we focus on a pure jump shooter who is more or less unaffected by the various circumstances in the game.

FIGURE 5.23 Simulation of Basketball Shooting Model

	A	B	C	D	E	F	G	H	I
1	Basketball shooting example								
2									
3	Long-run average	0.45		Range names					
4	Increment d1 after a make	0.015		AtLeast13: B13					
5	Increment d2 after a miss	0.015		Inc_d1: B4					
6				Inc_d2: B5					
7	Number of shots	25		NMakes: B12					
8				NShots: B7					
9	Binomial probability of at least 13 out of 25	0.306		PMake: B3					
10									
11	Summary statistics from simulation below			Compare these		Fraction of reps with at least 13 from table below			
12	Number of makes	14				0.268			
13	At least 13 makes?	1							
14									
15	Simulation of makes and misses using nonbinomial model					Data table to replicate 25 shots many times			
16		Shot	Streak	P(make)	Make?		Rep	At least 13?	
17		1	NA	0.45	1			1	
18		2	1	0.465	0		1	0	
19		3	-1	0.435	0		2	0	
20		4	-2	0.42	0		3	0	
21		5	-3	0.405	0		4	0	
22		6	-4	0.39	1		5	1	
23		7	1	0.465	0		6	0	
24		8	-1	0.435	1		7	0	
25		9	1	0.465	0		8	0	
26		10	-1	0.435	1		9	0	
27		11	1	0.465	1		10	0	
28		12	2	0.48	0		11	1	
29		13	-1	0.435	0		12	0	
30		14	-2	0.42	1		13	0	
31		15	1	0.465	0		14	0	
32		16	-1	0.435	1		15	0	
33		17	1	0.465	1		16	0	
34		18	2	0.48	0		17	0	
35		19	-1	0.435	1		18	1	
36		20	1	0.465	0		19	0	
37		21	-1	0.435	1		20	0	
38		22	1	0.465	1		21	0	
39		23	2	0.48	1		22	0	
40		24	3	0.495	1		23	1	
41		25	4	0.51	1		24	0	
42							25	0	
43							26	0	
265							248	0	
266							249	1	
267							250	0	

2 **Second shot.** Enter the formulas

$$=IF(D17=0,-1,1)$$

$$=IF(B18<0,PMake+B18*Inc\_d2,PMake+B18*Inc\_d1)$$

and

$$=IF(RAND()<C18,1,0)$$

in cells B18, C18, and D18. The first of these indicates that by the second shot, the shooter will have a streak of one make or one miss. The second formula is the important one. It indicates how the probability of a make changes depending on the current streak. The third formula simulates a make or a miss, using the probability in cell C18.

3 **Length of streak on third (and succeeding) shots.** Enter the formula

$$=IF(AND(B18<0,D18=0),B18-1, IF(AND(B18<0,D18=1),1,$$

$$IF(AND(B18>0,D18=0),-1,B18+1)))$$

in cell B19 and copy it down column B. This nested IF formula checks for all four combinations of the previous streak (negative or positive, indicated in cell B18) and the most recent shot (make or miss, indicated in cell D18) to see whether the current streak continues by one or a new streak starts.

4 **Results of remaining shots.** The logic for the formulas in columns C and D is the same for the remaining shots as for shot 2, so copy the formulas in cells C18 and D18 down their respective columns.

5 **Summary of 25 shots.** Enter the formulas

$$=SUM(D17:D41)$$

and

$$=IF(NMakes>=13,1,0)$$

in cells B12 and B13 to summarize the results of the 25 simulated shots. In particular, the value in cell B13 is 1 only if at least half of the shots are successes.

What about the *probability* of making at least 13 shots with this nonbinomial model? So far, we have simulated one set of 25 shots and have reported whether at least half of the shots are successes. We need to replicate this simulation many times and report the fraction of the replications where at least half of the shots are successes. We do this with a data table in columns F and G.

To create this table, enter the replication numbers 1 through 250 (you could use any number of replications) in column F, using the Edit/Fill/Series menu item. Then transfer the value in B13 to cell G17 by entering =AtLeast13 in this cell. Essentially, we are recalculating this value 250 times, each with different random numbers. To do this, highlight the range F17:G267, use the Data/Table menu item, leave the row input cell blank, and enter *any blank cell* (such as H17) as the column input cell. This causes Excel to recalculate the basic simulation 250 times, each time with different random numbers. Finally, enter the formula

$$=AVERAGE(G18:G267)$$

in cell F12 to calculate the fraction of the replications with at least 13 makes out of 25 shots.

After finishing all of this, you'll note that the spreadsheet is "live" in the sense that if you press the F9 recalculation key, all of the simulated quantities change—new random numbers. In particular, the estimate in cell F12 of the probability of at least 13 makes out of 25 shots changes. It is sometimes less than the binomial probability in cell B9 and sometimes greater. In general, the two probabilities are roughly the same. The bottom line? Even if the world doesn't behave exactly as the binomial model indicates, probabilities of various events can often be approximated fairly well by binomial probabilities—which saves us the trouble of developing and working with more complex models! ■

PROBLEMS

Level A

19 In a typical month, an insurance agent presents life insurance plans to 40 potential customers. Historically, one in four such customers chooses to buy life insurance from this agent. Based on the relevant binomial distribution, answer the following questions:

a What is the probability that exactly 5 customers will buy life insurance from this agent in the coming month?

b What is the probability that no more than 10 customers will buy life insurance from this agent in the coming month?

c What is the probability that at least 20 customers will buy life insurance from this agent in the coming month?

d Determine the mean and standard deviation of the number of customers who will buy life insurance from this agent in the coming month.

e What is the probability that the number of customers who buy life insurance from this agent in the coming month will lie within two standard deviations of the mean?

f What is the probability that the number of customers who buy life insurance from this agent in the coming month will lie within three standard deviations of the mean?

20 Continuing the previous exercise, use the normal approximation to the binomial to answer each of the questions posed in parts **a–f** above. How well does the normal approximation perform in this case? Explain.

21 Many vehicles used in space travel are constructed with redundant systems to protect flight crews and their valuable equipment. In other words, backup systems are included within many vehicle components so that if one or more systems fail, backup systems will assure the safe operation of the given component and thus the entire vehicle. For example, consider one particular component of the U.S. space shuttle that has n duplicated systems (i.e., one original system and $n - 1$ backup systems). Each of these systems functions, independently of the others, with probability 0.98. This shuttle component functions successfully provided that *at least* one of the n systems functions properly.

a Find the probability that this shuttle component functions successfully if $n = 2$.

b Find the probability that this shuttle component functions successfully if $n = 4$.

c What is the minimum number n of duplicated systems that must be incorporated into this shuttle component to ensure at least a 0.9999 probability of successful operation?

22 Suppose that a popular hotel for vacationers in Orlando, Florida, has a total of 300 identical rooms. Like many major airline companies, this hotel has adopted an overbooking policy in an effort to maximize the usage of its available lodging capacity. Assume that each potential hotel customer holding a room reservation, independently of other customers, cancels the reservation or simply does not show up at the hotel on a given night with probability 0.15.

a Find the largest number of room reservations that this hotel can book and still be at least 95% sure that everyone who shows up at the hotel will have a room on a given night.

b Given that the hotel books the number of reservations found in answering part **a**, find the probability that at least 90% of the available rooms will be occupied on a given night.

c Given that the hotel books the number of reservations found in answering part **a**, find the probability that at most 80% of the available rooms will be occupied on a given night.

d How does your answer to part **a** change as the required assurance rate increases from 95% to 97%? How does your answer to part **a** change as the required assurance rate increases from 95% to 99%?

e How does your answer to part **a** change as the cancellation rate varies between 5% and 25% (in increments of 5%)? Assume now that the required assurance rate is held fixed at 95%.

23 A production process manufactures items with weights that are normally distributed with mean 15 pounds and standard deviation 0.1 pound. An item is considered to be defective if its weight is less than 14.8 pounds or greater than 15.2 pounds. Suppose that these items are currently produced in batches of 1000 units.

a Find the probability that at most 5% of the items in a given batch will be defective.

b Find the probability that at least 90% of the items in a given batch will be acceptable.

c How many items would have to be produced in a batch to guarantee that a batch consists of no more than 1% defective items?

24 Past experience indicates that 30% of all individuals entering a certain store decide to make a purchase. Using (i) the binomial distribution and (ii) the normal approximation to the binomial, find that probability that 10 or more of the 30 individuals entering the store in a given hour will decide to make a purchase. Compare the results obtained using the two different approaches. Under what conditions will the normal approximation to this binomial probability become even more accurate?

25 Suppose that the number of ounces of soda put into a Pepsi can is normally distributed with $\mu = 12.05$ ounces and $\sigma = 0.03$ ounce.

a Legally, a can must contain at least 12 ounces of soda. What fraction of cans will contain at least 12 ounces of soda?

b What fraction of cans will contain less than 11.9 ounces of soda?

c What fraction of cans will contain between 12 and 12.08 ounces of soda?

d One percent of all cans will weigh more than what value?

e Ten percent of all cans will weigh less than what value?

f Pepsi controls the mean weight in a can by setting a timer. For what mean should the timer be set so that only 1 in 1000 cans will be underweight?

g Every day Pepsi produces 10,000 cans. The government inspects 10 randomly chosen cans each day. If at least two are underweight, Pepsi is fined $10,000. Given that $\mu = 12.05$ ounces and $\sigma = 0.03$ ounce, what is the probability that Pepsi will be fined on a given day?

26 Suppose that 52% of all registered voters prefer Bill Clinton to Bob Dole. (You may substitute the names of the current presidential candidates!)

a In a random sample of 100 voters, what is the probability that the sample will indicate that Clinton will win the election (that is, there will be more votes in the sample for Clinton)?

b In a random sample of 100 voters, what is the probability that the sample will indicate that Dole will win the election?

c In a random sample of 100 voters, what is the probability that the sample will indicate a dead heat (50–50)?

d In a random sample of 100 voters, what is the probability that between 40 and 60 (inclusive) voters will prefer Clinton?

27 Assume that, on average, 95% of all ticket-holders show up for a flight. If a plane seats 200 people, how many tickets should be sold to make the chance of an overbooked flight as close as possible to 5%?

28 Suppose that 60% of all people prefer Coke to Pepsi. We randomly choose 500 people and ask them if they prefer Coke to Pepsi. What is the probability that our survey will (erroneously) indicate that Pepsi is preferred by more people than Coke?

29 A firm's office contains 150 PCs. The probability that a given PC will not work on a given day is 0.05.

a On a given day what is the probability that exactly one computer will not be working?

b On a given day what is the probability that at least two computers will not be working?

c What assumptions do your answers in parts **a** and **b** require?

30 Suppose that 4% of all tax returns are audited. In a group of n tax returns, consider the probability that at most two returns are audited. How large must n be before this probability will be less than 0.01?

31 The height of a typical American female is normally distributed with $\mu = 64$ inches and $\sigma = 4$ inches. We observe the height of 10 American females.

a What is the probability that exactly half the women will be under 58 inches tall?

b Let X be the number of the 10 women who are under 58 inches tall. Determine the mean and standard deviation of X.

32 Consider a large population of shoppers, each of whom spends a certain amount during their current shopping trip; the distribution of these amounts is normally distributed with mean $55 and standard deviation $15. We randomly choose 25 of these shoppers. What is the probability that at least 15 of them spend between $45 and $75?

Level B

33 Many firms utilize sampling plans to control the quality of manufactured items ready for shipment. To illustrate the use of a sampling plan, suppose that a particular company produces and ships electronic computer chips in lots, each consisting of 1000 chips. This company's sampling plan specifies that quality control personnel will randomly sample 50 chips from each lot and accept the lot for shipping if the number of defective chips is less than 5. Of course, the given lot will be rejected if the number of defective chips is found to be 5 or more.

a Find the probability of accepting a lot as a function of the actual fraction of defective chips. In particular, let the actual fraction of defective chips in a given lot equal 0.1, 0.2, ..., 0.8, 0.9. Then compute the lot acceptance probability for each of these lot defective fractions.

b Construct a graph showing the probability of lot acceptance for each of the 9 lot defective fractions. Interpret your graph.

34 Continuing the previous exercise, repeat parts **a** and **b** under a revised sampling plan that calls for accepting a given lot if the number of defective chips found in the random sample of 50 chips is *not greater than* 5. Summarize any notable differences between the two graphs you have constructed in completing part **b** of this and the previous exercise.

35 Dell Computer receives computer chips from Chipco. Each batch sent by Chipco is inspected as follows: 35 chips are tested and the batch passes inspection if at most one defective chip is found in the set of 35 tested chips. Past history indicates an average of 1% of all chips produced by Chipco are defective. Dell has received 10 batches this week. What is the probability that at least 9 of the batches will pass inspection?

36 A standardized test consists entirely of multiple-choice questions, each with 5 possible choices. You want to ensure that a student who randomly guesses on each question will obtain an expected score of zero. How would you accomplish this?

37 In the current tax year, suppose that 5% of the millions of individual tax returns are fraudulent. That is, they contain errors that were purposely made to cheat the government. Although these errors are often well concealed, let's suppose that a thorough IRS audit will uncover them.

a If a random 250 tax returns are audited, what is the probability that the IRS will uncover at least 15 fraudulent returns?

b Answer the same question as in part **a**, but this time assume there is only a 90% chance that a given fraudulent return will be spotted as such if it is audited.

38 Suppose you work for a survey research company. In a typical survey, you mail questionnaires to 150 companies. Of course, some of these companies might decide not to respond. We'll assume that the nonresponse rate is 45%; that is, each company's probability of not responding, independently of the others, is 0.45. If your company requires at least 90 responses for a "valid" survey, what is the chance that it will get this many? Use a data table to see how your answer varies as a function of the nonresponse rate (for a reasonable range of response rates surrounding 45%).

39 Continuing the previous problem, suppose your company does this survey in two "waves." It mails the 150 questionnaires and waits a certain period for the responses. As above, we assume that the nonresponse rate is 45%. However, after this initial period, your company follows up (by telephone, say) on the nonrespondents, asking them to please respond. Suppose that the nonresponse rate on this second "wave" is 70%; that is, each original nonrespondent now responds with probability 0.3, independently of the others. Your company now wants to find the probability of obtaining at least 110 responses total. It turns out that this is a very difficult probability to calculate directly. So instead, approximate it with simulation.

40 A person claims that she is a fortune teller. Specifically, she claims that she can predict the direction of the change (up or down) in the Dow Jones Industrial Average for the next 10 days (such as U, U, D, U, D, U, U, D, D, D). (You can assume that she makes all 10 predictions right now, although that won't affect your answer to the question below.) Obviously, you're skeptical, thinking that she's just guessing, so you'll be surprised if her predictions are accurate. Which would surprise you more: (1) she predicts at least 8 out of 10 correctly, or (2) she predicts at least 6 out of 10 correctly on each of 4 separate occasions? Answer by assuming that (1) she really is guessing and (2) each day the Dow is equally likely to go up or down. ■

5.6 The Poisson Distribution

The final distribution in this chapter is called the **Poisson** distribution. In most statistical applications, including those in the rest of this book, the Poisson distribution plays a much less important role than either the normal or the binomial distribution. For this reason we will not analyze it in as much detail. However, in many applied management science models, the Poisson distribution is as important as any other distribution, discrete or continuous. For example, much of the study of probabilistic inventory models, queueing models, and reliability models relies heavily on the Poisson distribution.

The Poisson distribution is a discrete distribution. Its possible values are all of the nonnegative integers: 0, 1, 2, and so on—there is no upper limit. Even though there is an infinite number of possible values, this causes no real problems because the probabilities of all sufficiently large values are essentially 0.

The Poisson distribution is characterized by a single parameter, usually labeled λ (Greek lambda), which must be positive. By adjusting the value of λ, we are able to produce different Poisson distributions, all of which have the same basic shape as in Figure 5.24. That is, they first increase, then decrease. It turns out that λ is easy to interpret. It is both the mean and the variance of the Poisson distribution. Therefore, the standard deviation is $\sqrt{\lambda}$.

FIGURE 5.24   **Typical Poisson Distribution**

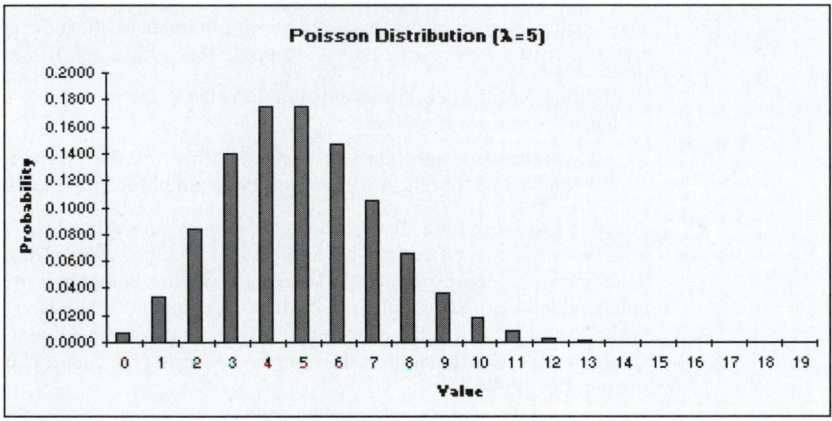

The usual situation where the Poisson distribution arises is when we are interested in the number of events that occur in some amount of time or space. Here are several typical examples.

1   A bank manager is studying the arrival pattern to the bank. Then the events are customer arrivals, the number of arrivals in an hour is Poisson distributed, and λ represents the expected number of arrivals per hour.

2   An engineer is interested in the lifetime of a type of battery. A device that uses this type of battery is operated continuously. When the first battery fails, it is replaced by a second; when the second fails, it is replaced by a third, and so on. The events are battery failures, the number of failures that occur in a month is Poisson distributed, and λ represents the expected number of failures per month.

3 A retailer is interested in the number of units of a product demanded in a particular unit of time such as a week. Then the events are customer demands, the number of units demanded in a week is Poisson distributed, and λ is the expected number of units demanded per week.

4 In a quality control setting, the Poisson distribution is often relevant for describing the number of defects in some unit of space. For example, when paint is applied to the body of a new car, any minor blemish is considered a defect. Then the number of defects on the hood, say, might be Poisson distributed. In this case, λ is the expected number of defects per hood.

These examples are representative of the many situations where the Poisson distribution has been applied. For the obvious reason, the parameter λ is often called a rate—arrivals per hour, failures per month, and so on. If we change the unit of time, we simply modify the rate accordingly. For example, if the number of arrivals to a bank in a single hour is Poisson distributed with rate $\lambda = 30$, then the number of arrivals in a half-hour period is Poisson distributed with rate $\lambda = 15$.

We can use Excel to calculate Poisson probabilities much as we did with binomial probabilities. The relevant function is the POISSON function. It takes the form

$$=\text{POISSON}(k, \lambda, cum)$$

The third argument *cum* works exactly as in the binomial case. If it is 0, the function returns $P(X = k)$; if it is 1, the function returns $P(X \leq k)$. As examples, if $\lambda = 5$, POISSON(7,5,0) returns the probability of exactly 7, POISSON(7,5,1) returns the probability of less than or equal to 7, and 1-POISSON(3,5,1) returns the probability of greater than 3.

The following example shows how a manager or consultant might use the Poisson distribution.

EXAMPLE 5.13

Kriegland is a department store that sells various brands of color television sets. One of the manager's biggest problems is to decide on an appropriate inventory policy for stocking television sets. On the one hand, he wants to have enough in stock so that customers receive their requests right away, but on the other hand, he does not want to tie up too much money in inventory that sits on the storeroom floor.

Most of the difficulty results from the unpredictability of customer demand. If this demand were constant and known, the manager could decide on an appropriate inventory policy fairly easily. But the demand varies widely from month to month in a random manner. All the manager knows is that the historical average demand per month is approximately 17. Therefore, he decides to call in a consultant. The consultant immediately suggests using a probability model. Specifically, she attempts to find the probability distribution of demand in a typical month. How might she proceed?

Solution

Let X be the demand in a typical month. The consultant knows that there are many possible values of X. For example, if historical records show that monthly demands have always been between 0 and 40, the consultant knows that almost all of the probability should be assigned to the values 0 through 40. However, she does not relish the thought of finding 41 probabilities, $P(X = 0)$ through $P(X = 40)$, that sum to 1 and reflect historical frequencies. Instead, she discovers from the manager that the histogram of demands from previous months is shaped much like the graph in Figure 5.24. That is, it rises to some peak, then falls.

FIGURE 5.25 Poisson Calculations for Television Example

	A	B	C	D	E	F	G	H	I	J	K
1	Poisson distribution for department store example										
2											
3	Mean monthly demand (λ)	17		Range names:							
4				MeanDem: B3							
5	Representative probability calculations										
6	Less than or equal to 20	0.805		=POISSON(20,MeanDem,1)							
7	Between 10 and 15 (inclusive)	0.345		=POISSON(15,MeanDem,1)-POISSON(9,MeanDem,1)							
8											
9	Individual probabilities										
10	Value	Prob									
11	0	0.000		=POISSON(A11,MeanDem,0)							
12	1	0.000									
13	2	0.000									
14	3	0.000									
15	4	0.000									
16	5	0.000									
17	6	0.001									
18	7	0.003									
19	8	0.007									
20	9	0.014									
21	10	0.023									
22	11	0.036									
23	12	0.050									
24	13	0.066									
25	14	0.080									
26	15	0.091									
27	16	0.096									
28	17	0.096									
29	18	0.091									
30	19	0.081									
31	20	0.069									
32	21	0.056									
33	22	0.043									
34	23	0.032									
35	24	0.023									
36	25	0.015									
37	26	0.010									
38	27	0.006									
39	28	0.004									
40	29	0.002									
41	30	0.001									
42	31	0.001									
43	32	0.000									
44	33	0.000									
45	34	0.000									
46	35	0.000									
47	36	0.000									
48	37	0.000									
49	38	0.000									
50	39	0.000									
51	40	0.000									

Poisson Distribution with λ=17

Knowing that a Poisson distribution has this same basic shape, the consultant decides to model the monthly demand with a Poisson distribution. To choose a particular Poisson distribution, all she has to do is choose a value of λ, the mean demand per month. Because the historical average is approximately 17, she chooses λ = 17. Now she can test the Poisson model by calculating probabilities of various events and asking the manager whether these probabilities are a reasonable approximation to reality.

For example, the Poisson probability that monthly demand is less than or equal to 20, $P(X \leq 20)$, is 0.806 (using the Excel function POISSON(20,17,1)), and the probability that demand is between 10 and 15 inclusive, $P(10 \leq X \leq 15)$, is 0.345 (using POISSON(15,17,1)-POISSON(9,17,1)). Figure 5.25 illustrates various probability calculations and shows the graph of the individual Poisson probabilities. (See the file DPT-STORE.XLS.)

If the manager believes that these probabilities and other similar probabilities are reasonable, then the *statistical* part of the consultant's job is finished. Otherwise, she must try a different Poisson distribution—a different value of λ—or perhaps a different type of distribution altogether. ■

PROBLEMS

Level A

41 The annual number of industrial accidents occurring in a particular manufacturing plant is known to follow a Poisson distribution with mean 12.

a What is the probability of observing exactly 12 accidents at this plant during the upcoming year?

b What is the probability of observing no more than 12 accidents at this plant during the upcoming year?

c What is the probability of observing at least 15 accidents at this plant during the upcoming year?

d What is the probability of observing between 10 and 15 accidents (inclusive) at this plant during the upcoming year?

e Find the smallest integer k such that we can be at least 99% sure that the annual number of accidents occurring at this plant will be less than k.

42 Suppose that the number of customers arriving each hour at the only checkout counter in a local pharmacy is approximately Poisson distributed with an expected arrival rate of 20 customers per hour.

a Find the probability that exactly 10 customers arrive at this checkout counter in a given hour.

b Find the probability that at least 5 customers arrive at this checkout counter in a given hour.

c Find the probability that no more than 25 customers arrive at this checkout counter in a given hour.

d Find the probability that between 10 and 30 customers (inclusive) arrive at this checkout counter in a given hour.

e Find the largest integer k such that we can be at least 95% sure that the number of customers arriving at this checkout counter in a given hour will be greater than k.

43 Suppose the number of points scored by the Indiana University basketball team in 1 minute follows a Poisson distribution with $\lambda = 1.5$. In a 10-minute span of time, what is the probability that Indiana University scores exactly 20 points? (Use the fact that if the rate per minute is λ, then the rate in t minutes is λt.)

44 The average number of misprints on a page of the *Pleasant Valley Gazette* is 3. Assuming that the Poisson distribution is appropriate for describing the incidence of misprints on a page, what is the probability that an 8-page paper has at least 20 misprints? Exactly 12 misprints? (Use the fact that if the rate per page is λ, then the rate in t pages is λt.)

Level B

45 Consider a Poisson random variable X with parameter $\lambda = 2$.

a Find the probability that X is within one standard deviation of its mean.

b Find the probability that X is within two standard deviations of its mean.

c Find the probability that X is within three standard deviations of its mean.

d Do the rules of thumb we learned earlier seem to be applicable in working with the Poisson distribution where $\lambda = 2$? Explain why or why not.

e Repeat parts **a–d** for the case of a Poisson random variable where $\lambda = 20$.

46 Based on historical data, the probability that a major league pitcher pitches a no-hitter in a game is about 1/1300.

a Use the binomial distribution to determine the probability that in 650 games 0, 1, 2, or 3 no-hitters will be pitched. (Find the separate probabilities of these four events.)

b Repeat part **a** using the Poisson approximation to the binomial. This approximation says that if n is large and p is small, a binomial distribution with parameters n and p is approximately Poisson with $\lambda = np$. ■

5.7

Fitting a Probability Distribution to Data: BestFit

The normal, binomial, and Poisson distributions are three of the most commonly used distributions in real applications. However, many other discrete and continuous distributions are also used. These include the uniform, triangular, exponential, Erlang, lognormal, and many others. How do we know which to choose for any particular application? Often we can answer this by seeing which of several potential distributions fits a given set of data most closely. Essentially, we compare a histogram of the data with the theoretical probability distributions available and see which gives the best fit.

BestFit, one of the add-ins in the Decision Tools suite, makes this fairly easy. We illustrate the procedure in the following example.

EXAMPLE 5.14

A supermarket has collected checkout times on over 100 customers. (See the file TIMES.XLS.) As shown in Figure 5.26, the times vary from 40 seconds to 279 seconds, with the mean and median right around 2 minutes.

The supermarket manager would like to check whether these data are normally distributed or whether some other distribution fits them better. How can he tell?

Solution

We will take advantage of the BestFit add-in. There are several ways to open this add-in. Perhaps the easiest is to do so directly from the Windows Start button in the usual way. Once BestFit is open, a small spreadsheet appears. To fill it with data, get into Excel, copy the range B4:B116 of checkout times, and then go back into BestFit and paste these times into its spreadsheet. BestFit will build a histogram of these times and try fitting a number of distributions to it. Because we have over 100 observations, we can afford to have 15 categories in the histogram, so change the #Classes box to 15, as shown in Figure 5.27.

The easiest way to do the fitting is to use BestFit's Wizard. Click on the Wizard button on BestFit's toolbar, and fill in the dialog boxes as follows: Choose the Continuous option, choose the Open option for both upper and lower limits, and accept the defaults in the other dialog boxes. BestFit then does goodness-of-fit calculations for several distributions. When it is finished, we see a ranking, from best to worst, of the distributions it tried. In this case Normal is at the top of the list. With Normal highlighted, click on the Graph

FIGURE 5.26 Supermarket Checkout Times

	A	B	C	D	E	F	G
1	Checkout times (seconds) at a supermarket						
2							
3	Customer	Time			Summary measures for selected variables		
4	1	131				Time	
5	2	101			Count	113.000	
6	3	178			Mean	159.239	
7	4	246			Median	155.000	
8	5	207			Standard deviation	52.609	
9	6	155			Minimum	40.000	
10	7	95			Maximum	279.000	
11	8	105					
12	9	168					
109	106	145					
110	107	225					
111	108	202					
112	109	133					
113	110	138					
114	111	279					
115	112	90					
116	113	155					

FIGURE 5.27 Data in BestFit Window

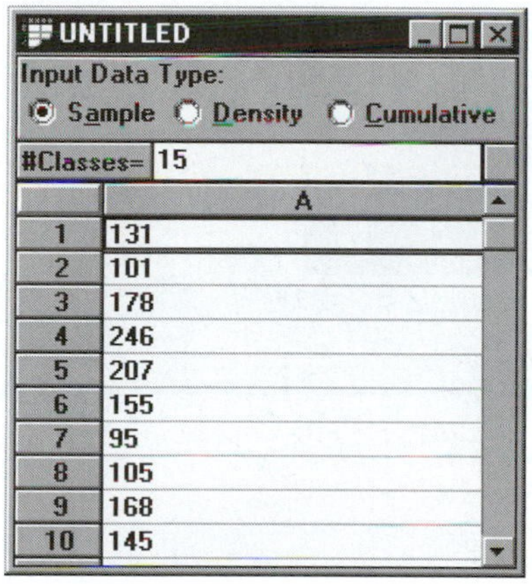

button to see the chart in Figure 5.28 (page 238). It shows the histogram of the data with the best-fitting normal curve superimposed. By clicking on the Stats button on the toolbar, we see a number of numerical measures of the goodness of fit. However, unless you know the theory behind the fitting process, the chart is probably much more meaningful.

In the second dialog box of the Wizard, we might want to specify a lower bound of 0. After all, checkout times cannot be negative. If we do so, we rule out the normal distribution—it allows negative values—and we open the competition to a number of positively skewed distributions. The winner in this case happens to be the Weibull distribution, as shown in Figure 5.29. (The Weibull distribution, while not nearly as well known as the normal, is used in many reliability studies to model times to failure.) However, a visual check of the two charts indicates essentially equally good fits. The supermarket manager can feel safe in concluding that the normal distribution provides a reasonably good fit.

FIGURE 5.28   Normal Fit to Checkout Times

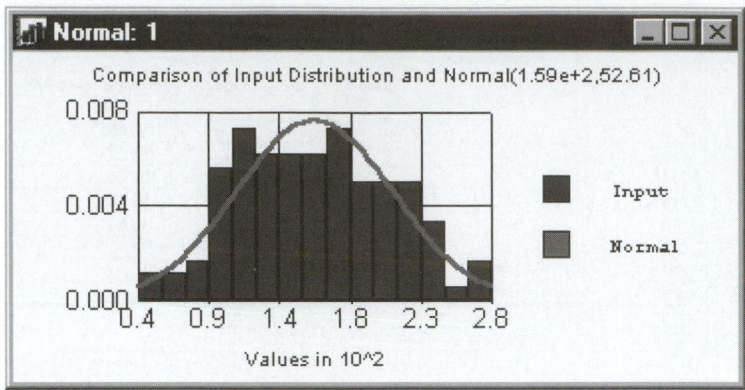

FIGURE 5.29   Weibull Fit of Checkout Times

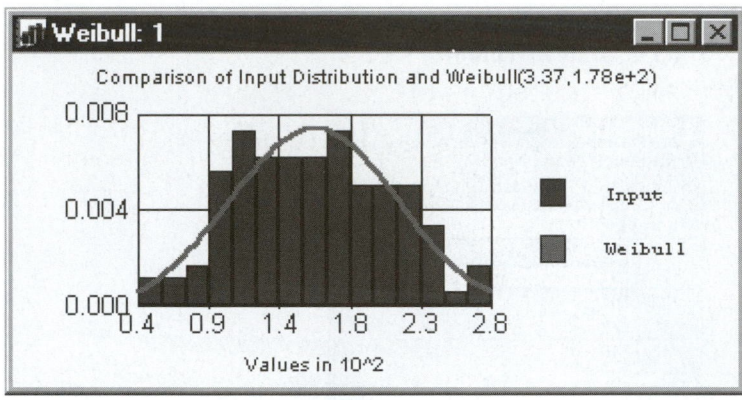

PROBLEMS

Level A

47 A production manager is interested in determining the proportion of defective items in a typical shipment of one of the computer components that her company manufactures. The proportion of defective components is recorded for each of 500 randomly selected shipments collected during a 1-month period. The data are in the file P5_47.XLS. Use the BestFit add-in to determine which probability distribution best fits these data.

48 The manager of a local fast-food restaurant is interested in improving the service provided to customers who use the restaurant's drive-up window. As a first step in this process, the manager asks his assistant to record the time (in minutes) it takes to serve 200 different customers at the final window in the facility's drive-up system. The given 200 customer service times are all observed during the busiest hour of the day for this fast-food operation. The data are in the file P5_48.XLS. Use the BestFit add-in to determine which probability distribution best fits these data.

49 The operations manager of a toll booth, located at a major exit of a state turnpike, is trying to estimate the average number of vehicles that arrive at the toll booth during a 1-minute period during the peak of rush-hour traffic. In an effort to estimate this average throughput value, he records the number of vehicles that arrive at the toll booth over a 1-minute interval commencing at the same time for each of 365 normal weekdays. The data are in the file P5_49.XLS. Use the BestFit add-in to determine which probability distribution best fits these data.

50 A finance professor has just given a midterm examination in her corporate finance course and is interested in learning how her class of 100 students performed on this exam. The data are in the file P5_50.XLS. Use the BestFit add-in to determine which probability distribution best fits these data. ■

Conclusion

e have covered a lot of ground in this chapter, and much of the material, especially the material regarding the normal distribution, will be used in later chapters. The normal distribution is the cornerstone for much of statistical theory. As we will see when we study statistical inference and regression, an assumption of normality is behind most of the procedures we use. Therefore, it is important to understand the properties of the normal distribution and how to work with it in Excel. The binomial and Poisson distributions, while not used as frequently as the normal distribution in this book, are also extremely important. The examples we have discussed indicate how these distributions can be used in a variety of business situations.

Although we have attempted to stress *concepts* in this chapter, we have also described the details necessary to work with these distributions in Excel. Fortunately, these details are not too difficult to master once you understand Excel's built-in functions such as NORMDIST, NORMINV, and BINOMDIST. Figures 5.6 and 5.17 provide typical examples of these functions. We suggest that you keep a copy of these figures handy.

PROBLEMS

Level A

51 Suppose the annual return on XYZ stock follows a normal distribution with mean 0.12 and standard deviation 0.30.

a What is the probability that XYZ's value will decrease during a year?

b What is the probability that the return on XYZ during a year will be at least 20%?

c What is the probability that the return on XYZ during a year will be between −6% and 9%?

d There is a 5% chance that the return on XYZ during a year will be greater than or equal to what value?

e There is a 1% chance that the return on XYZ during a year will be less than what value?

f There is a 95% chance that the return on XYZ during a year will be between what two values (equidistant from the mean)?

52 The annual mean return on Walt Disney stock is around 15% and the annual standard deviation is around 25%. Assume the annual and daily returns on Disney stock are normally distributed.

a What is the probability that Disney will lose money during a year?

b There is a 5% chance that Disney will earn a return of at least what value during a year?

c There is a 10% chance that Disney will earn a return of less than or equal to what value during a year?

d What is the probability that Disney will earn at least 35% during a year?

e Assume there are 252 trading days in a year. What is the probability that Disney will lose money on a given day? [*Hint*: Let Y be the annual return on Disney and X_i be the return on Disney on day i. Then (approximately) $Y = X_1 + X_2 + \cdots + X_{252}$. Also, use the fact that the sum of independent normal random variables is normally distributed, with mean equal to the sum of the individual means, and variance equal to the sum of the individual variances.]

53 Suppose Dell Computer receives its disk drives from Diskco. On average, 4% of all floppy disk drives received by Dell are defective.

   a Dell has adopted the following policy. It samples 50 disk drives in each shipment and accepts the shipment if all disk drives in the sample are nondefective. What fraction of batches will Dell accept?

   b Suppose instead that the batch is accepted if at most 1 disk drive in the sample is defective. What fraction of batches will Dell accept?

   c What is the probability that a sample of size 50 will contain at least 10 defectives?

54 A family is considering a move from a midwestern city to a city in California. The distribution of housing costs where the family currently lives is normal with mean $105,000 and standard deviation $18,200. The distribution of housing costs in the California city is normal with mean $135,000 and standard deviation $20,400. The family's current house is valued at $110,000.

   a What percentage of houses in the family's current city cost less than theirs?

   b If the family buys a $110,000 house in the new city, what percentage of houses there will cost less than theirs?

   c What price house will the family need to buy to be in the same percentile (of housing costs) in the new city as they are in the current city?

55 The number of traffic fatalities in a typical month in a given state has a normal distribution with mean 125 and standard deviation 31.

   a If a person in the highway department claims that there will be at least m fatalities in the next month with probability 0.95, what value of m makes this claim true?

   b If the claim is that there will be no more than n fatalities in the next month with probability 0.98, what value of n makes this claim true?

56 It can be shown that a sum of independent normally distributed random variables is also normally distributed. Do all functions of normal random variables lead to normal random variables? Consider the following.

   SuperDrugs is a chain of drugstores with three similar-sized stores in a given city. The sales in a given week for any of these stores is normally distributed with mean $15,000 and standard deviation $3000. At the end of each week, the sales figure for the store with the largest sales among the three stores is recorded. Is this maximum value normally distributed? Find out with simulation. Simulate a weekly sales figure at each of the three stores and calculate the maximum. Then replicate this maximum 500 times with a data table and create a histogram of the 500 maximum values. Does it appear to be normally shaped? Whatever this distribution looks like, use your simulated values to estimate its mean and standard deviation.

Level B

57 When we sum 30 or more independent random variables, the sum of the random variables will usually be approximately normally distributed, even if each individual random variable is not normally distributed. Use this fact to estimate the probability that a casino will be behind after 90,000 roulette bets, given that it wins $1 or loses $35 on each bet with probabilities 37/38 and 1/38.

58 The daily demand for six-packs of Coke at Mr. D's follows a normal distribution with mean 120 and standard deviation 30. Every Monday the Coke delivery driver delivers Coke to Mr. D's. If Mr. D's wants to have only a 1% chance of running out of Coke by the end of the week, how many should Mr. D's order for the week? Assume orders are placed Sunday at midnight. (Assume also that demands on different days are probabilistically independent. Use the fact that the sum of independent normal random variables is normally distributed, with mean equal to the sum of the individual means, and variance equal to the sum of the individual variances.)

59 Many companies use sampling to determine whether a batch should be accepted. An (n, c) sampling plan consists of inspecting n randomly chosen items from a batch and accepting the batch if c or fewer sampled items are defective. Suppose a company uses a (100, 5) sampling plan to determine whether a batch of 10,000 computer chips is acceptable.

a The "producer's risk" of a sampling plan is the probability that an acceptable batch will be rejected by a sampling plan. Suppose the customer considers a batch with 3% defectives acceptable. What is the producer's risk for this sampling plan?

b The "consumer's risk" of a sampling plan is the probability that an unacceptable batch will be accepted by a sampling plan. Our customer says that a batch with 9% defectives is unacceptable. What is the consumer's risk for this sampling plan?

60 Suppose that if a presidential election were held today, 52% of all voters would vote for Clinton over Dole. (You may substitute the names of the current presidential candidates!) This problem shows that even if there are 100 million voters, a sample of several thousand is enough to determine the outcome, even in a fairly close election.

a If we were to randomly sample 1500 voters, what is the chance that the sample would indicate (correctly) that Clinton is preferred to Dole?

b If we were to randomly sample 6000 voters, what is the chance that the sample would indicate (correctly) that Clinton is preferred to Dole?

61 The Coke factory fills bottles of soda by setting a timer on a filling machine. It has generally been observed that the distribution of the number of ounces the machine puts into a bottle is normal with standard deviation 0.05 oz. The company wants 99.9% of all its bottles to have at least 16 oz of soda. To what amount should the mean amount put in each bottle be set? (The company does not want to put in any more than is necessary!)

62 The time it takes me to swim 100 yards in a race is normally distributed with mean 62 seconds and standard deviation 2 seconds. In my next five races, what is the chance I will swim under a minute exactly twice?

63 We assemble a large part by joining two smaller parts together. In the past, the smaller parts we have produced have a mean length of 1 inch and a standard deviation of 0.01 inch. Assume that the lengths of the smaller parts are normally distributed.

a What fraction of the larger parts are longer than 2.05 inches? (Use the fact that the sum of independent normal random variables is normally distributed, with mean equal to the sum of the individual means, and variance equal to the sum of the individual variances.)

b What fraction of the larger parts are between 1.96 inches and 2.02 inches long?

64 (Suggested by Sam Kaufmann, Indiana University MBA who runs Harrah's Lake Tahoe Casino) A high roller has come to the casino to play 300 games of craps. For each game of craps played there is a 0.493 probability that the high roller will win $1 and a 0.507 probability that the high roller will lose $1. After 300 games of craps, what is the probability that the casino will be behind more than $10?

65 (Suggested by Sam Kaufmann, Indiana University MBA who runs Harrah's Lake Tahoe Casino) A high roller comes to the casino intending to play 500 hands of blackjack for $1 a hand. On each hand, the high roller will win $1 with probability 0.48 and lose $1 with probability 0.52. After the 500 hands, what is the probability that the casino has lost more than $40?

66 Bottleco produces 100,000 12-oz bottles of soda per year. By adjusting a timer, Bottleco can adjust the mean number of ounces placed in a bottle. No matter what the mean, the standard deviation of the number of ounces in a bottle is 0.05. Soda costs $0.05 per ounce. Any bottle weighing less than 12 ounces will incur a $10 fine for being underweight. Determine a setting for the mean number of ounces per bottle of soda that will minimize the expected cost per year of producing soda. Your answer should be accurate within 0.001 ounce. Does the number of bottles produced per year influence your answer?

67 The weekly demand for televisions at Lowland Appliance is normally distributed with mean 400 and standard deviation 100. Each time an order for TVs is placed, it arrives exactly 4 weeks later. That is, TV orders have a 4-week lead time. Lowland doesn't want to run out of TVs during any more than 1% of all lead times. How low should Lowland let its TV inventory drop before it places an order for more TVs? (*Hint*: How many standard deviations above the mean lead-time demand must the reorder point be for there to be a 1% chance of a stockout during the lead time? Also, use the fact that the sum of independent normal random variables is normally distributed, with mean equal to the sum of the individual means, and variance equal to the sum of the individual variances.)

68 An elevator rail is assumed to meet specifications if its diameter is between 0.98 and 1.01 inches. Each year we make 100,000 elevator rails. For a cost of $10/\sigma^2$ per year we can rent a machine that produces elevator rails whose diameters have a standard deviation of σ. Any machine will produce rails having a mean diameter of 1 inch. Any rail that does not meet specifications must be reworked (at a cost of $12) to meet specifications. Assume that the diameter of an elevator rail follows a normal distribution.

a What standard deviation (within 0.001 inch) will minimize our annual cost of producing elevator rails? You need not try standard deviations in excess of 0.02 inch.

b For your answer in part **a**, one elevator rail in 1000 will be at least how many inches in diameter?

69 A 20-question true–false examination is given. Each correct answer is worth 5 points. Consider an unprepared student who randomly guesses on each question.

a If no points are deducted for incorrect answers, what is the probability that the student will score at least 60 points?

b If 5 points are deducted for each incorrect answer, what is the probability that the student will score at least 60 points?

c If 5 points are deducted for each incorrect answer, what is the probability that the student will receive a negative score?

70 The percentage of examinees who took the GMAT (Graduate Management Admission) exam from June 1992 to March 1995 and scored below each total score is given in the file P5_70.XLS. For example, 96% of all examinees scored 690 or below. The mean GMAT score for this time period was 497 and the standard deviation was 105. Does it appear that GMAT scores can accurately be approximated by a normal distribution? (Source: 1995 GMAT Examinee Interpretation Guide)

71 Do we really know what happened to TWA Flight 800? Physics Professors Hailey and Helfand of Columbia University believe there is a reasonable possibility that a meteor hit Flight 800. They reason as follows. On a given day, 3000 meteors of a size large enough to destroy an airplane hit the earth's atmosphere. Around 50,000 flights per day, averaging 2 hours in length, have been flown from 1950 to1996. (Flight 800 flew in 1996.) This means that at any given point in time, planes in flight cover approximately two-billionths of the world's atmosphere. Determine the probability that at least one plane in the last 47 years has been downed by a meteor. (*Hint*: Use the Poisson approximation to the binomial. This approximation says that if n is large and p is small, a binomial distribution with parameters n and p is approximately Poisson with $\lambda = np$.)

72 In the decade 1982–1991, ten employees working at the Amoco Company chemical research center were stricken with brain tumors. The average employment at the center was 2000 employees. Nationwide, the average incidence of brain tumors in a single year is 20 per 100,000 people. If the incidence of brain tumors at the Amoco chemical research center were the same as the nationwide incidence, what is the probability that at least 10 brain tumors would be observed among Amoco workers during the decade 1982–1991? What do you conclude from your analysis? (Source: AP wire service report, March 12, 1994)

73 Claims arrive at random times to an insurance company. The daily amount of claims is normally distributed with mean $1570 and standard deviation $450. Total claims on different days each have this distribution, and they are probabilistically independent of one another.

a Find the probability that the amount of total claims over a period of 100 days is at least $150,000. (Use the fact that the sum of independent normally distributed random variables is normally distributed, with mean equal to the sum of the individual means and variance equal to the sum of the individual variances.)

b If the company receives premiums totaling $165,000, find the probability that the company will net at least $10,000 for the 100-day period.

74 A popular model for stock prices is the following. If p_0 is the current stock price, then the price, p_k, k periods from now (where a period could be a day, week, or any other convenient unit of time, and k is any positive integer) is given by

$$p_k = p_0 \exp\left((\mu - 0.5\sigma^2)k + sZ\sqrt{k}\right)$$

where exp is the exponential function (EXP in Excel), μ is the mean percentage growth rate per period of the stock, σ is the standard deviation of the growth rate per period, and Z is a normally distributed random variable with mean 0 and standard deviation 1. Both μ and σ are typically estimated from actual stock price data, and they are typically expressed in decimal form, such as $\mu = 0.01$ for a 1% mean growth rate. Suppose a period is defined as a month, the current price of the stock (as of the end of December 1997) is $75, $\mu = 0.006$, and $\sigma = 0.028$. Use simulation to simulate 500 possible stock price changes from the end of December 1997 to the end of December 2000. (Note that you can simulate a given change in one line and then copy it down.) Draw a histogram of these changes to see whether the stock price change is at least approximately normally distributed. Also, use the simulated data to estimate the mean price change and the standard deviation of the change.

75 Continuing the previous problem (with the same parameters), use simulation to generate the ending stock prices for each month in 1998. (Use $k = 1$ to get January's price from December's, use $k = 1$ again to get February's price from January's, and so on.) Then use a data table to replicate the ending December 1998 stock price 500 times. Draw a histogram of these 500 values. Do they appear to resemble a normal distribution?

76 Your company is running an audit on the Sleaze Company. Since Sleaze has a bad habit of overcharging its customers, the focus of your audit is on checking whether the billing amounts on its invoices are correct. We'll assume that each invoice is for too high an amount with probability 0.06 and for too low an amount with probability 0.01 (so that the probability of a correct billing is 0.93). Also, we assume that the outcome for any invoice is probabilistically independent of the outcomes for other invoices.

   a If you randomly sample 200 of Sleaze's invoices, what is the probability that you will find at least 15 invoices that overcharge the customer? What is the probability you won't find any that undercharge the customer?

   b Find an integer k such that the probability is at least 0.99 that you will find at least k invoices that overcharge the customer. (*Hint*: Use trial and error with the BINOMDIST function to find k.)

77 Continuing the previous problem, suppose that when Sleaze overcharges a customer, the distribution of the amount overcharged (expressed as a percentage of the correct billing amount) is normally distributed with mean 15% and standard deviation 4%.

   a What percentage of overbilled customers are charged at least 10% more than they should pay?

   b What percentage of *all* customers are charged at least 10% more than they should pay?

   c If your auditing company samples 200 randomly chosen invoices, what is the probability that it will find at least 5 where the customer was overcharged by at least 10%?

78 Let X be normally distributed with a given mean and standard deviation. Sometimes you want to find two values a and b such that $P(a < X < b)$ is equal to some specific probability such as 0.90 or 0.95. There are many answers to this problem, depending on how much probability you put in each of the two tails. For this question, assume the mean and standard deviation are $\mu = 100$ and $\sigma = 10$, and that we want to find a and b such that $P(a < X < b) = 0.90$.

   a Find a and b so that there is probability 0.05 in each tail.

   b Find a and b so that there is probability 0.025 in the left tail and 0.075 in the right tail.

   c The "usual" answer to the general problem is the answer from part **a**, that is, where you put equal probability in the two tails. It turns out that this is the answer that minimizes the length of the interval from a to b. That is, if you solve the problem: $\min(b - a)$, subject to $P(a < X < b) = 0.90$, you'll get the same answer as in part **a**. Verify this using Excel's Solver.

79 Your manufacturing process makes parts such that each part meets specifications with probability 0.98. You need a batch of 250 parts that meet specifications. How many parts must you produce to be at least 99% certain of producing at least 250 parts that meet specifications?

80 The Excel functions discussed in this chapter are useful for solving a lot of probability problems, but there are other problems that, even though they are similar to normal or binomial problems, cannot be solved with these functions. In cases like this, computer simulation can often be used. Here are a couple of such problems for you to simulate. For each example, use 500 replications of the experiment.

   a You observe a sequence of parts from a manufacturing line. These parts use a component that is supplied by one of two suppliers. The probability that a given part uses a component supplied by supplier 1 is 0.6; it is supplied by supplier 2 with probability 0.4. Each part made with a component from supplier 1 works properly with probability 0.95, and each part made with a component from supplier 2 works properly with probability 0.98. Assuming that 30 of these parts are made, we want the probability that at least 29 of them work properly.

b Here we look at a more generic example such as coin flipping. That is, there is a sequence of trials where each trial is a success with probability p and a failure with probability $1 - p$. A "run" is a sequence of consecutive successes or failures. For most of us, intuition says that there should not be "long" runs. Test this by finding the probability that there is at least 1 run of length at least 6 in a sequence of 15 trials. (The run could be of 0's or 1's.) You can use any value of p you like—or try different values of p.

81 As any credit-granting agency knows, there are always some customers who default on credit charges. Typically, customers are grouped into relatively homogeneous categories, so that customers within any category have approximately the same chance of defaulting on their credit charges. Here we'll look at one particular group of customers. We'll assume each of these customers has (1) probability 0.07 of defaulting on his or her current credit charges, and (2) total credit charges that are normally distributed with mean $350 and standard deviation $100. We'll also assume that if a customer defaults, 20% of his or her charges can be recovered. The other 80% are written off as bad debt.

a What is the probability that a typical customer in this group will default and produce a write-off of more than $250 in bad debt?

b If there are 500 customers in this group, what are the mean and standard deviation of the number of customers who will meet the description in part **a**?

c Again assuming there are 500 customers in this group, what is the probability that at least 25 of them will meet the description in part **a**?

d Suppose now that nothing is recovered from a default—the whole amount is written off as bad debt. Show how to simulate the total amount of bad debt from 500 customers in just two cells, one with a binomial calculation, the other with a normal calculation. ■

5.1   EuroWatch Company

The EuroWatch Company assembles expensive wristwatches and then sells them to retailers throughout Europe. The watches are assembled at a plant with two assembly lines. These lines are intended to be identical, but line 1 uses somewhat older equipment than line 2 and is typically less reliable. Historical data have shown that each watch coming off line 1, independently of the others, is free of defects with probability 0.98. The similar probability for line 2 is 0.99. Each line produces 500 watches per hour. The production manager has asked you to answer the following questions.

1   She wants to know how many defect-free watches each line is likely to produce in a given hour. Specifically, find the smallest integer k (for each line separately) such that you can be 99% sure that the line will not produce more than k defective watches in a given hour.

2   EuroWatch currently has an order for 500 watches from an important customer. The company plans to fill this order by packing slightly more than 500 watches, all from line 2, and sending this package off to the customer. Obviously, EuroWatch wants to send as few watches as possible, but it wants to be 99% sure that when the customer opens the package, there are at least 500 defect-free watches. How many watches should be packed?

3   EuroWatch has another order for 1000 watches. Now it plans to fill this order by packing slightly more than one hour's production from each line. This package will contain the *same* number of watches from each line. As in the previous question, EuroWatch wants to send as few watches as possible, but it again wants to be 99% sure that when the customer opens the package, there are at least 1000 defect-free watches. The question of how many watches to pack is unfortunately quite difficult because the total number of defect-free watches is *not* binomially distributed. (Why not?) Therefore, the manager asks you to solve the problem with simulation (and some trial and error). (*Hint*: It turns out that it's much faster to simulate small numbers than large numbers, so simulate the number of watches with defects, not the number without defects.)

4   Finally, EuroWatch has a third order for 100 watches. The customer has agreed to pay $50,000 for the order—that is, $500 per watch. If EuroWatch sends more than 100 watches to the customer, its revenue doesn't increase; it can never exceed $50,000. Its unit cost of producing a watch is $450, regardless of which line it is assembled on. The order will be filled entirely from a single line, and EuroWatch plans to send slightly more than 100 watches to the customer.

   If the customer opens the shipment and finds that there are fewer than 100 defect-free watches (which we'll assume the customer has the ability to do), then he'll pay only for the defect-free watches—EuroWatch's revenue will decrease by $500 per watch short of the 100 required—and on top of this, EuroWatch will be required to make up the difference at an expedited cost of $1000 per watch. The customer won't pay a dime for these expedited watches. (If expediting is required, EuroWatch will make sure that the expedited watches are defect-free. It doesn't want to lose this customer entirely!)

   You have been asked to develop a spreadsheet model to find EuroWatch's expected profit for any number of watches it sends to the customer. You should develop it so that it responds correctly, regardless of which assembly line is used to fill the order and what the shipment quantity is. (*Hints*: Use the BINOMDIST function, with last argument 0, to fill up a column of probabilities for each possible number of defective watches. Next to each of these, calculate EuroWatch's profit. Then use a SUMPRODUCT to obtain the expected profit. Finally, you can assume that EuroWatch will never send more than 110 watches. It turns out that this large a shipment is not even close to optimal.)

5.2   Cashing in on the Lottery

Many states supplement their tax revenues with state-sponsored lotteries. Most of them do so with a game called lotto. Although there are various versions of this game, they are all basically as follows. People purchase tickets that contain r distinct numbers from 1 to m, where r is generally 5 or 6 and m is generally around 50. For example, in Virginia, the state discussed in this case, $r = 6$ and $m = 44$. Each ticket costs $1, about 39 cents of which is allocated to the total jackpot.[7] There is eventually a drawing of $r = 6$ distinct numbers from the $m = 44$ possible numbers. Any ticket that matches these 6 numbers wins the jackpot.

There are two interesting aspects of this game. First, the current jackpot includes not only the revenue from this round of ticket purchases but any jackpots carried over from previous drawings because of no winning tickets. Therefore, the jackpot can build from one drawing to the next, and in celebrated cases it has become huge. Second, if there is more than one winning ticket—a distinct possibility—the winners share the jackpot equally. (This is called the "pari-mutuel" effect.) So, for example, if the current jackpot is $9 million and there are three winning tickets, then each winner receives $3 million.

It can be shown that for Virginia's choice of r and m, there are approximately 7 million possible tickets (7,059,052 to be exact). Therefore, any ticket has about one chance out of 7 million of being a winner. That is, the probability of winning with a single ticket is $p = 1/7,059,052$—not very good odds! If n people purchase tickets, then the number of winners is binomially distributed with parameters n and p. Because n is typically very large and p is small, the number of winners has approximately a Poisson distribution with rate $\lambda = np$. (This makes ensuing calculations somewhat easier.) For example, if 1 million tickets are purchased, then the number of winning tickets is approximately Poisson distributed with $\lambda = 1/7$.

In 1992, an Australian syndicate purchased a huge number of tickets in the Virginia lottery in an attempt to assure itself of purchasing a winner. It worked! Although the syndicate wasn't able to purchase all 7 million possible tickets (it was about 1.5 million shy of this), it did purchase a winning ticket, and there were no other winners. Therefore, the syndicate won a 20-year income stream worth approximately $27 million, with a net present value of approximately $14 million. This easily covered the cost of the tickets it purchased. The questions are: (1) Is this "hogging" of tickets unfair to the rest of the public? and (2) Is it a wise strategy on the part of the syndicate (or did it just get lucky)?

To answer the first question, consider how the lottery changes for the general public with the addition of the syndicate. To be specific, suppose the syndicate can invest $7 million and obtain *all* of the possible tickets, making itself a sure winner. Also, suppose n people from the general public purchase tickets, each of which has 1 chance out of 7 million

---

[7]Of the remaining 61 cents, the state takes about 50 cents. The other 11 cents is used to pay off lesser prize winners whose tickets match some, but not all, of the winning 6 numbers. To keep this case relatively simple, however, we will ignore these lesser prizes and concentrate only on the jackpot.

of being a winner. Finally, let R be the jackpot carried over from any previous lotteries. Then the total jackpot on this round will be $[R + 0.39(7,000,000 + n)]$, because 39 cents from every ticket goes toward the jackpot. The number of winning tickets for the public will be Poisson distributed with $\lambda = n/7,000,000$. However, any member of the public who wins will *necessarily* have to share the jackpot with the syndicate, which is a sure winner. Use this information to calculate the expected amount the public will win. Then do the same calculation when the syndicate does *not* play. (In this case the jackpot will be smaller, but the public won't have to share any winnings with the syndicate.) For values of n and R that you can select, is the public better off with or without the syndicate? Would you, as a general member of the public, support a move to outlaw syndicates from "hogging" the tickets?

The second question is whether the syndicate is wise to buy so many tickets. Again assume that the syndicate can spend $7 million and purchase each possible ticket. (Would this be possible in reality?) Also, assume that n members of the general public purchase tickets, and that the carryover from the previous jackpot is R. The syndicate is thus assured of having a winning ticket, but is it assured of covering its costs? Calculate the expected net benefit (in terms of net present value) to the syndicate, using any reasonable values of n and R, to see whether the syndicate can expect to come out ahead.

Actually, the analysis suggested in the previous paragraph is not complete. There are at least two complications to consider. The first is the effect of taxes. Fortunately for the Australian syndicate, it did not have to pay federal or state taxes on its winnings, but a U.S. syndicate wouldn't be so lucky. Second, the jackpot from a 20-million-dollar jackpot, say, is actually paid in 20 annual 1-million-dollar payments. The Lottery Commission pays the winner 1 million dollars immediately and then purchases 19 "strips" (bonds with the interest not included) maturing at 1-year intervals with face value of 1 million dollars each. Unfortunately, the lottery prize does not offer the liquidity of the Treasury issues that back up the payments. This lack of liquidity could make the lottery less attractive to the syndicate.

6

Decision Making Under Uncertainty

Successful Applications

Formal decision analysis in the face of uncertainty frequently occurs at the most strategic levels of a company's planning process and typically involves teams of high-level managers from all areas of the company. This is certainly the case with Du Pont, as reported by two internal decision analysis experts, Krumm and Rolle (1992), in their article "Management and Application of Decision and Risk Analysis in Du Pont." Du Pont's formal use of decision analysis began in the 1960s, but because of a lack of computing power and distrust of the method by senior-level management, it never really got a foothold. However, by the mid-1980s things had changed considerably. The company was involved in a faster-moving, more uncertain environment, more people throughout the company were empowered to make decisions, and these decisions had to be made more quickly. In addition, the computing power had arrived to make large-scale quantitative analysis feasible. Since that time, Du Pont has embraced formal decision-making analysis in all of its businesses, and the trend is almost certain to continue.

The article describes a typical example of decision analysis within the company. One of Du Pont's businesses, Business Z (so-called for reasons of confidentiality), was stagnating. It was not set up to respond quickly to changing customer demands, and its financial position was declining due to lower prices and market share. A decision board and a project team were empowered to turn things around. The project team developed a detailed timetable to accomplish three basic steps: frame the problem, assess uncertainties and perform the analysis, and implement the recommended decision. The first step involved setting up a "strategy table" to list the possible strategies and the factors that would affect or be affected by them. The three basic strategies were (1) a base-case strategy (continue operating as is), (2) a product differentiation strategy (develop new products), and (3) a cost leadership strategy (shut down the plant and streamline the product line).

In the second step the team asked a variety of experts throughout the company for their assessments of the likelihood of key uncertain events. In the analysis step they then used all of the information gained to determine the strategy with the largest expected net present value. Two important aspects of this analysis step were the extensive use of sensitivity analysis (many what-if questions) and the emergence of new "hybrid" strategies that dominated the strategies that had been considered to that point. In particular, the team finally decided on a product differentiation strategy that also decreased costs by shutting down some facilities in each plant.

By the time of the third step, implementation, the decision board needed little convincing. Since all of the key people had been given the opportunity to provide input to the process, everyone was convinced that the right strategy had been selected. All that was left was to put the plan in motion and monitor its results. The results were impressive. Business Z made a complete turnaround, and its net present value increased by close to $200 million. Besides this tangible benefit, there were definite intangible benefits from the overall process. As Du Pont's vice president for finance said, "The D&RA [decision and risk analysis] process improved communication within the business team as well as between the team and corporate management, resulting in rapid approval and execution. As a decision maker, I highly value such a clear and logical approach to making choices under uncertainty and will continue to use D&RA whenever possible." ■

6.1 Introduction

In this chapter we will provide a formal framework for analyzing decision problems that include uncertainty. We will discuss the most frequently used criteria for choosing among alternative decisions, how probabilities are used in the decision-making process, how decisions made at an early stage are dependent on decisions made at a later stage, how a decision maker can quantify the value of information, and how attitudes toward risk can affect the analysis. Throughout, we will employ two graphical tools—decision trees and influence diagrams—to guide the analysis. Each of these enables the decision maker to view all important aspects of the problem at once: the decision alternatives, the uncertain outcomes and their probabilities, the economic consequences, and the chronological order of events. We will show how to implement these graphical tools in Excel by taking advantage of a very powerful and flexible add-in from Palisade called PrecisionTree.

Many examples of decision making under uncertainty exist in the business world. Here are several examples.

1   Companies routinely place bids for contracts to complete a certain project within a fixed time frame. Often these are sealed bids, where each of several companies presents in a sealed envelope a bid for completing the project; then the envelopes are opened, and the low bidder is awarded the bid amount to complete the project. Any particular company in the bidding competition must deal with the possible uncertainty of its *actual* cost of completing the project (should it win the bid), as well as the uncertainty involved in what the other companies will bid. The trade-off is between bidding low in order to win the bid and bidding high in order to make a profit.

2   Whenever a company contemplates introducing a new product into the market, there are a number of uncertainties that affect the decision, probably the most important being the customers' reaction to this product. If the product generates high customer demand, then the company will make a large profit. But if demand is low (and, after all, the vast majority of new products do poorly), then the company might not even recoup its development costs. Because the level of customer demand is critical, the company might try to gauge this level by test marketing the product in one region of the country. If this test market is a success, the company can then be more optimistic that a full-scale national marketing of the product will also be successful. But if the test market is a failure, the company can cut its losses by abandoning the product.

3   Should athletes be required to undergo drug testing? And if drug testing is required, should an athlete who tests positive be banned from the sport? Several sources of

uncertainty, as well as several "costs," are relevant here. The uncertainties involve the proportion of the total athlete population who use drugs and the reliability of the tests. The costs include the obvious cost of the tests, but also the less obvious "costs" of invading an athlete's privacy and of declaring an athlete a drug user when in fact he or she is not (because of a faulty test).

4   A recent *Interfaces* article (Borison, 1995) describes an application of formal decision analysis by Oglethorpe Power Corporation (OPC), a Georgia-based electricity supplier. The basic decision OPC faced was whether to build a new transmission line to supply large amounts of electricity to parts of Florida and, if they decided to build it, how to finance this project. OPC had to deal with several sources of uncertainty: the cost of building new facilities, the demand for power in Florida, and various market conditions, such as the spot price of electricity.

5   Another *Interfaces* article (Ulvila, 1987) describes the decision analysis performed by the U.S. Postal Service regarding the purchase of automation equipment. One of the investment decisions was which type of OCR (optical character recognition) equipment the Postal Service should purchase (or convert) for reading single- and/or multiple-line addresses on packages. An important factor in this decision was the level of use by businesses of the "zip+4" (nine-digit zip codes). Zip+4 usage had been recommended for some time but was used only sporadically. The Postal Service was uncertain about the future level of business zip+4 usage. If businesses used the nine-digit codes heavily in the future, then a certain type of (expensive) OCR equipment would be most economical. If business use of zip+4 did not increase, then purchasing this equipment would be a waste of money. The decision was an extremely important one, given the expense of the proposed equipment and the fact that the Postal Service would have to live with whatever equipment it purchased for a number of years.

6   Utility companies must make many decisions that have significant environmental and economic consequences. [A good discussion of such consequences appears in an *Interfaces* article by Balson et al. (1992).] For these companies it is not necessarily enough to conform to federal or state environmental regulations. Recent court decisions have found companies liable—for huge settlements—when accidents occurred, even though the companies followed all existing regulations. Therefore, when utility companies decide, say, whether to replace equipment or mitigate the effects of environmental pollution, they must take into account the possible environmental consequences (such as injuries to people) as well as economic consequences (such as lawsuits). An aspect of these situations that makes decision analysis particularly difficult is that the potential "disasters" are often extremely improbable; hence, their likelihoods are very difficult to assess accurately.

6.2

Elements of a Decision Analysis

Although decision making under uncertainty occurs in a wide variety of contexts, all problems have three elements in common: (1) the set of decisions (or strategies) available to the decision maker, (2) the set of possible outcomes and the probabilities of these outcomes, and (3) a value model that prescribes results, usually monetary values, for the various combinations of decisions and outcomes. Once these elements are known, the decision maker can find an "optimal" decision, depending on the optimality criterion chosen. The following example illustrates these concepts.

EXAMPLE 6.1

SciTools Incorporated, a company that specializes in scientific instruments, has been invited to make a bid on a government contract. The contract calls for a specific number of these instruments to be delivered during the coming year. The bids must be sealed (so that no company knows what the others are bidding), and the low bid wins the contract. SciTools estimates that it will cost $5000 to prepare a bid and $95,000 to supply the instruments if it wins the contract. On the basis of past contracts of this type, SciTools believes that the possible low bids from the competition, if there is any competition, and the associated probabilities are those shown in Table 6.1. In addition, SciTools believes there is a 30% chance that there will be *no* competing bids.

TABLE 6.1 **Data for Bidding Example**

Low Bid	Probability
Less than $115,000	0.2
Between $115,000 and $120,000	0.4
Between $120,000 and $125,000	0.3
Greater than $125,000	0.1

Solution

Let's discuss the three elements of SciTools' problem. First, SciTools has two basic strategies: submit a bid or do not submit a bid. If SciTools submits a bid, then it must decide how much to bid. Based on SciTools' cost to prepare the bid and its cost to supply the instruments, there is obviously no point in bidding less than $100,000—SciTools wouldn't make a profit even if it won the bid. Although any bid amount over $100,000 might be considered, the data in Table 6.1 might persuade SciTools to limit its choices to $115,000, $120,000, and $125,000.[1]

The next element of the problem involves the uncertain outcomes and their probabilities. We have assumed that SciTools knows exactly how much it will cost to prepare a bid and how much it will cost to supply the instruments if it wins the bid. (In reality, these are probably estimates of the actual costs.) Therefore, the only source of uncertainty is the behavior of the competitors—will they bid, and if so, how much? From SciTools' standpoint, this is difficult information to obtain. The behavior of the competitors depends on (1) how many competitors are likely to bid and (2) how the competitors assess *their* costs of supplying the instruments. However, we will assume that SciTools has been involved in similar bidding contests in the past and can, therefore, predict competitor behavior from past competitor behavior. The result of such prediction is the assessed probability distribution in Table 6.1 and the 30% estimate of the probability of no competing bids.

The last element of the problem is the value model that transforms decisions and outcomes into monetary values for SciTools. The value model is straightforward in this example, but it can become quite complex in other applications, especially when the time value of money is involved and some quantities (such as the costs of environmental pollution) are difficult to quantify. If SciTools decides right now not to bid, then its monetary value is $0—no gain, no loss. If it makes a bid and is underbid by a competitor, then it loses $5000, the cost of preparing the bid. If it bids B dollars and wins the contract, then it makes a profit of $B - \$100,000$, that is, B dollars for winning the bid, less $5000 for preparing

---

[1]The problem with a bid such as $117,000 is that the data in Table 6.1 make it impossible to calculate the probability of SciTools winning the contract if it bids this amount. Other than this, however, there is nothing that rules out such an "in-between" bid.

the bid, less $95,000 for supplying the instruments. For example, if it bids $115,000 and the lowest competing bid, if any, is greater than $115,000, then SciTools makes a profit of $15,000.

It is often convenient to list the monetary outcomes in a **payoff table**, as shown in Table 6.2. For each possible decision and each possible outcome, the payoff table lists the monetary value to SciTools, where a positive value represents a profit and a negative value represents a loss. At the bottom of the table, we list the probabilities of the various outcomes. For example, the probability that the competitors' low bid is less than $115,000 is 0.7 (the probability of at least one competing bid) multiplied by 0.2 (the probability that the lowest competing bid is less than $115,000, given that there is at least one competing bid).

TABLE 6.2   Payoff Table for SciTools Bidding Example

			Competitors' Low Bid ($1000s)			
		No Bid	**<115**	**>115, <120**	**>120, <125**	**>125**
SciTools' Bid ($1000s)	No Bid	0	0	0	0	0
	115	15	−5	15	15	15
	120	20	−5	−5	20	20
	125	25	−5	−5	−5	25
	Probability	0.3	0.7(0.2)	0.7(0.4)	0.7(0.3)	0.7(0.1)

It is sometimes possible to simplify payoff tables to better understand the essence of the problem. In the present example, if SciTools bids, then the only necessary information about the competitors' bid is whether it is lower or higher than SciTools' bid. That is, SciTools cares only whether it wins the contract or not. Therefore, an alternative way of presenting the payoff table is shown in Table 6.3.

TABLE 6.3   Alternative Payoff Table for SciTools Bidding Example

		Monetary value		Probability That
		SciTools Wins	**SciTools Loses**	**SciTools Wins**
SciTools' Bid ($1000s)	No bid	NA	0	0.00
	115	15	−5	0.86
	120	20	−5	0.58
	125	25	−5	0.37

The third and fourth columns of this table indicate the payoffs to SciTools, depending on whether it wins or loses the bid. The rightmost column shows the probability that SciTools wins the bid for each possible decision. For example, if SciTools bids $120,000, then it wins the bid if there are no competing bids (probability 0.3) or if there are competing bids but the lowest of these is greater than $120,000 (probability 0.7(0.3 + 0.1)). In this case the total probability that SciTools wins the bid is 0.3 + 0.28 = 0.58. ∎

6.2.1 Risk Profiles

From Table 6.3 we can obtain **risk profiles** for each of SciTools' decisions. A risk profile simply lists all possible monetary values and their corresponding probabilities. For example, if SciTools bids $120,000, there are two monetary values possible, a profit of $20,000 or a loss of $5000, and their probabilities are 0.58 and 0.42, respectively. On the other hand, if SciTools decides not to bid, there is a sure monetary value of $0—no profit, no loss.

A risk profile can also be illustrated graphically as a bar chart. There is a bar above each possible monetary value with height proportional to the probability of that value. For example, the risk profile for a $120,000 bid decision is a bar chart with two bars, one above −$5000 with height 0.42 and one above $20,000 with height 0.58. The risk profile for the "no bid" decision is even simpler. It has a single bar above $0 with height 1. We don't show these bar charts for this example because they are so simple, but in more complex examples they can provide insight.

6.2.2 Expected Monetary Value (EMV)

From the information we have discussed so far, it is not at all obvious which decision SciTools should make. The "no bid" decision is certainly safe, but it is certain to make zero profit. If SciTools decides to bid, the probability that it will lose $5000 is smallest with the $115,000 bid, but this bid has the smallest potential profit. Of course, if SciTools knew what the competitors were going to do, its decision would be easy. However, this uncertainty is the defining aspect of the problems in this chapter. The decision must be made *before* the uncertainty is resolved.

The most common way to make the choice is to calculate the **expected monetary value** (EMV) of each alternative and then choose the alternative with the largest EMV. The EMV is a weighted average of the possible monetary values, weighted by their probabilities. Formally, if v_i is the monetary value corresponding to outcome i and p_i is its probability, then EMV is defined as

$$\text{EMV} = \sum v_i p_i$$

Actually, this is nothing new. It is the mean of the probability distribution of possible monetary outcomes, as defined in Chapter 4.

The EMVs for SciTools' problem are listed in Table 6.4. They indicate that if SciTools uses the EMV criterion for making its decision, it should bid $115,000, as this yields the largest EMV.

TABLE 6.4 **EMVs for SciTools Bidding Example**

Alternative	EMV Calculation	EMV
No bid	0(1)	$0
Bid $115,000	15,000(0.86) + (−5000)(0.14)	$12,200
Bid $120,000	20,000(0.58) + (−5000)(0.42)	$9,500
Bid $125,000	25,000(0.37) + (−5000)(0.63)	$6,100

It is very important to understand what an EMV implies and what it does not imply. If SciTools bids $115,000, then its EMV is $12,200. However, SciTools will certainly *not* earn a profit of $12,200. It will earn $15,000 or it will lose $5000. So what does the EMV of $12,200 really mean? It means that if SciTools could enter many "gambles" like this, where on each gamble it would win $15,000 with probability 0.86 or lose $5000 with probability 0.14, then *on average* it would win $12,200 per gamble. In other words, the EMV can be interpreted as a long-term average.

It might seem peculiar, then, to base a one-time decision on EMV, which represents a long-term average. There are two ways to explain this apparent inconsistency. First, most companies make frequent decisions under uncertainty. Although each decision might have its own unique characteristics, it seems reasonable that if the company plans to make many such decisions, it should be willing to "play the averages," as it does when it uses EMV as the decision criterion. Second, even if this is the only such decision the company is *ever* going to make, decision theorists have proven that under certain conditions, maximizing EMV is a rational basis for making this decision. These "certain conditions" relate to the decision maker's attitude toward risk. As we will discuss later in this chapter, if the decision maker is risk averse and the possible monetary payoffs or losses are large relative to her wealth, then EMV is *not* the appropriate decision criterion to use. However, the EMV criterion has proved useful in the vast majority of decision-making applications, so we will use it throughout most of this chapter.

6.2.3 Decision Trees

By now, we have gone through most of the steps of solving SciTools' problem. We have listed the decision alternatives, the uncertain outcomes and their probabilities, and the profits and losses from all combinations of decisions and outcomes. We have then calculated the EMV for each alternative and have chosen the alternative with the largest EMV. All of this can be done efficiently using a graphical tool called a **decision tree**. The decision tree that corresponds to SciTools' problem appears in Figure 6.1 on page 256. (This figure is actually part of an Excel spreadsheet and was created with the PrecisionTree add-in. We'll explain how it was created shortly.)

To understand Figure 6.1, we need to know the following conventions that have been established for decision trees.

1 Decision trees are composed of **nodes** (circles, squares, and triangles) and **branches** (lines).

2 The nodes represent points in time. A **decision node** (a square) is a time when the decision maker makes a decision. A **probability node** (a circle) is a time when the result of an uncertain event becomes known. An **end node** (a triangle) indicates that the problem is completed—all decisions have been made, all uncertainty has been resolved, and all payoffs/costs have been incurred.

3 Time proceeds *from left to right*. This means that any branches leading into a node (from the left) have already occurred. Any branches leading out of a node (to the right) have not yet occurred.

4 Branches leading out of a decision node represent the possible decisions; the decision maker can choose the preferred branch. Branches leading out of probability nodes represent the possible outcomes of uncertain events; the decision maker has no control over which of these will occur.

5 Probabilities are listed on probability branches. These probabilities are *conditional* on the events that have already been observed (those to the left). Also, the probabilities on branches leading out of any particular probability node must sum to 1.

6 Individual monetary values are shown on the branches where they occur, and cumulative monetary values are shown to the right of the end nodes. (Actually, PrecisionTree shows two values to the right of each end node. The top one is the probability of getting to that end node, and the bottom one is the associated monetary value.)

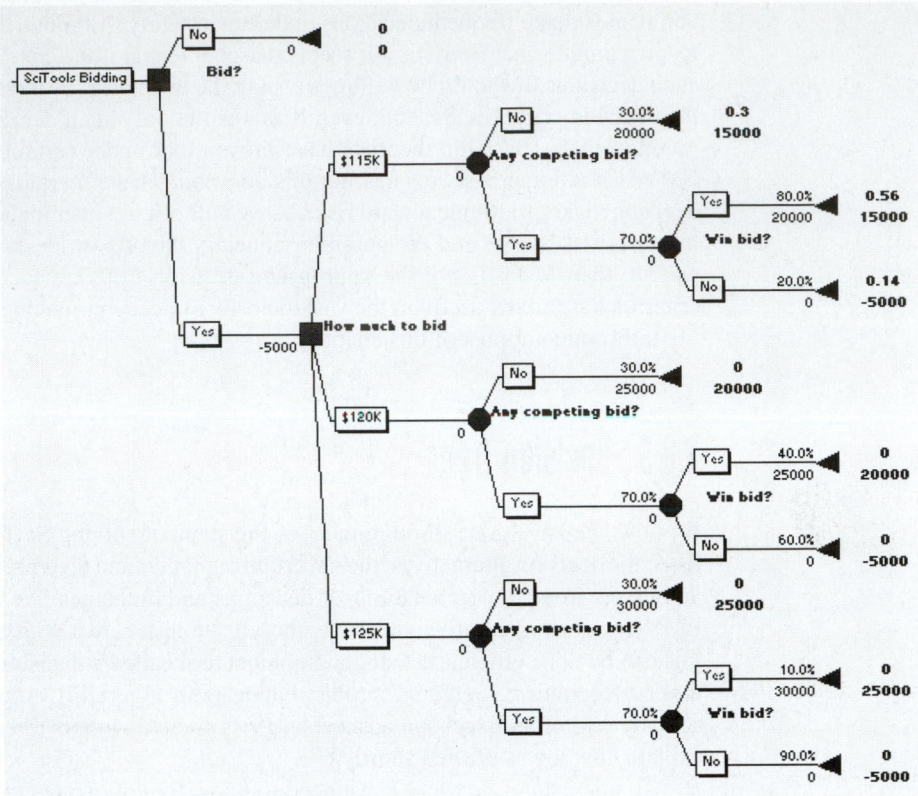

The decision tree in Figure 6.1 illustrates these conventions for a **single-stage** decision problem, the simplest type of decision problem. In a single-stage problem all decisions are made *first*, and then all uncertainty is resolved. Later in this chapter we will see **multistage** decision problems, where decisions and outcomes alternate. That is, a decision maker makes a decision, then some uncertainty is resolved, then the decision maker makes a second decision, then some further uncertainty is resolved, and so on. Because these multistage decisions problems are inherently more complex, we will focus initially on single-stage problems.

Once a decision tree has been drawn and labeled with probabilities and monetary values, it can be solved easily. The solution for the decision tree in Figure 6.1 is shown in Figure 6.2. Among other things, it shows that the decision to bid $115,000 is optimal (follow the decision branches with "True" above them), with a corresponding EMV of $12,200 (the value under "Bid?" at the left of the tree). This is consistent with what we saw earlier for this example.

The solution procedure used to develop Figure 6.2 is called **folding back** on the tree. Starting at the right of the tree and working back to the left, the procedure consists of two types of calculations.

1   At each probability node, we calculate the EMV (sum of monetary values times probabilities) and write it below the name of the node. For example, consider the node (top right) after SciTools' decision to bid $115,000 and after it learns that there will be

FIGURE 6.2   Result of Folding Back to Obtain Optimal Decision

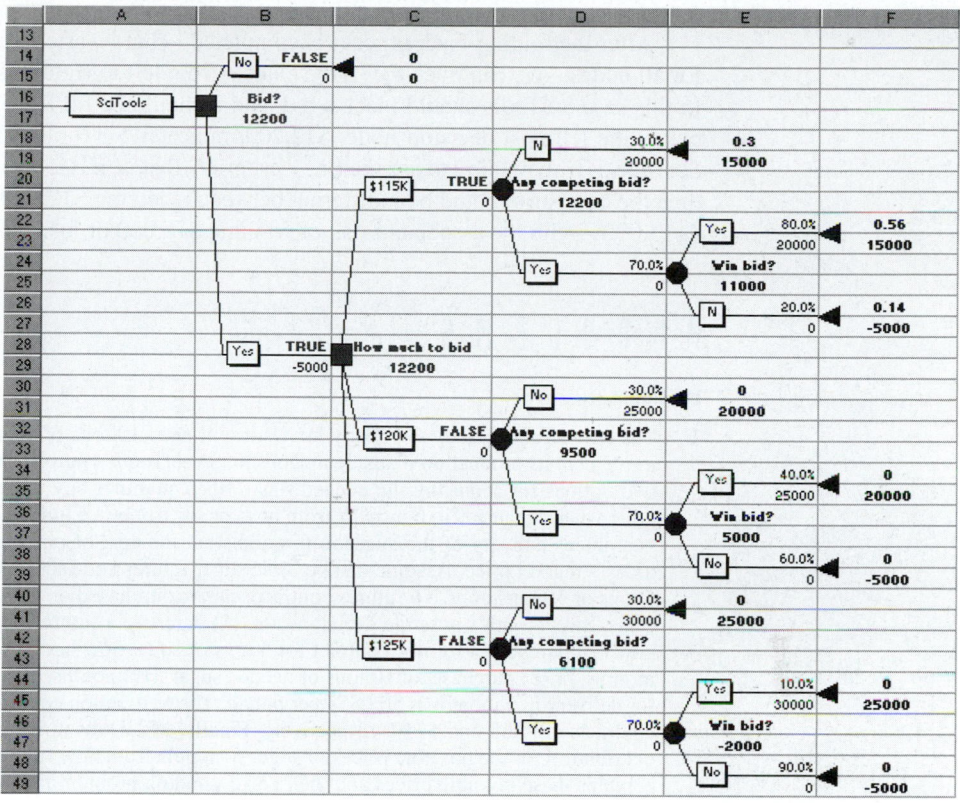

a competing bid. From that point, SciTools will either win $15,000 with probability 0.8 or lose $5000 with probability 0.2. The corresponding EMV is

$$0.8(15,000) + 0.2(-5000) = 11,000$$

and this value is entered below the node name "Win bid?".

Now, back up a step and consider the preceding probability node (the one to the left of the "Win bid?" node). At this point, SciTools has bid $115,000 and is about to discover whether there will be a competing bid. If there is none, with probability 0.3, then SciTools will win $15,000. But if there is a competing bid, with probability 0.7, the EMV from that point on is the $11,000 we just calculated. Essentially, this $11,000 summarizes the consequences of being at the "Win bid?" node, and SciTools acts the same as if it were going to receive $11,000 *for certain*. Therefore, the EMV for the "Any competing bid?" node is

$$0.3(15,000) + 0.7(11,000) = 12,200$$

This EMV is written below the node name.

2   Decision nodes are much easier. At each decision node we find the maximum of the EMVs and write it below the node name. PrecisionTree indicates the winner by placing "True" on the decision branch with the maximum EMV and "False" on all other branches emanating from this node. For example, consider the node where SciTools is deciding how much to bid (after having already decided to place a bid). The EMVs under the three succeeding *probability* nodes are $12,200, $9500, and

$6100. Since the maximum of these is $12,200, the EMV for the "How much to bid" node is $12,200 and is written below the node name.

After the folding-back process is completed—that is, after we have calculated EMVs for all nodes—we can trace the "True" labels from left to right to see the optimal strategy. In this case SciTools should place a bid, and it should be for $115,000. The EMV written below the leftmost decision node, $12,200, indicates SciTools' EMV for this strategy. If SciTools is truly willing to use the EMV criterion, that is, if it is willing to play the averages, then the company should be indifferent between receiving $12,200 *for certain* and bidding $115,000—with the associated risk of winning $15,000 or losing $5000.

PROBLEMS

Level A

1 The SweetTooth Candy Company knows it will need 10 tons of sugar 6 months from now to implement its production plans. Jean Dobson, SweetTooth's purchasing manager, has essentially two options for acquiring the needed sugar. She can either buy the sugar at the going market price when she needs it, 6 months from now, or she can buy a futures contract now. The contract guarantees delivery of the sugar in 6 months but the cost of purchasing it will be based on today's market price. Assume that possible sugar futures contracts available for purchase are for 5 tons or 10 tons only. No futures contracts can be purchased or sold in the intervening months. Thus, SweetTooth's possible decisions are: (1) purchase a futures contract for 10 tons of sugar now, (2) purchase a futures contract for 5 tons of sugar now and purchase 5 tons of sugar in 6 months, or (3) purchase all 10 tons of needed sugar in 6 months. The price of sugar bought now for delivery in 6 months is $0.0851 per pound. The transaction costs for 5-ton and 10-ton futures contracts are $65 and $110, respectively. Finally, Ms. Dobson has assessed the probability distribution for the possible prices of sugar 6 months from now (in dollars per pound). Table 6.5 contains these possible prices and their corresponding probabilities.

TABLE 6.5 **Distribution of Possible Sugar Prices**

Possible Sugar Prices in 6 Months ($/pound)	Probability
0.078	0.05
0.083	0.25
0.087	0.35
0.091	0.20
0.096	0.15

a Given that SweetTooth wants to acquire the needed sugar in the least-cost way, formulate a payoff table that specifies the cost (in dollars) associated with each possible decision and possible sugar price in the future.

b Generate a risk profile for each of SweetTooth's possible decisions in this problem.

c Construct a decision tree to identify the course of action that minimizes SweetTooth's *expected* cost of meeting its sugar demand.

2 Carlisle Tire and Rubber, Inc. is considering expanding production to meet potential increases in the demand for one of its tire products. Carlisle's alternatives are to construct a new plant, expand the existing plant, or do nothing in the short run. The market for this particular tire product may expand, remain stable, or contract. Carlisle's marketing department estimates the probabilities of these market outcomes as 0.25, 0.35, and 0.40, respectively. Table 6.6 contains Carlisle's estimated payoff (in dollars) table.

a Generate a risk profile for each of Carlisle's possible decisions in this problem.

b Construct a decision tree to identify the course of action that maximizes Carlisle's expected profit.

TABLE 6.6 **Payoff Table for Carlisle's Decision Problem**

Decision/Market Outcome	Market Expands	Market Stable	Market Contracts
Construct a New Plant	400,000	−100,000	−200,000
Expand Existing Plant	250,000	−50,000	−75,000
Do Nothing	50,000	0	−30,000

3   A local energy provider offers a landowner $180,000 for the exploration rights to natural gas on a certain site and the option for future development. This option, if exercised, is worth an additional $1,800,000 to the landowner, but this will occur only if natural gas is discovered during the exploration phase. The landowner, believing that the energy company's interest in the site is a good indication that gas is present, is tempted to develop the field herself. To do so, she must contract with local experts in natural gas exploration and development. The initial cost for such a contract is $300,000, which is lost forever if no gas is found on the site. If gas is discovered, however, the landowner expects to earn a net profit of $6,000,000. Finally, the landowner estimates the probability of finding gas on this site to be 60%.

   a   Formulate a payoff table that specifies the landowner's payoff (in dollars) associated with each possible decision and each outcome with respect to finding natural gas on the site.

   b   Generate a risk profile for each of the landowner's possible decisions in this problem.

   c   Construct a decision tree to identify the course of action that maximizes the landowner's expected gain (in dollars) from this opportunity.

4   Techware Incorporated is considering the introduction of two new software products to the market. In particular, the company has four options regarding these two proposed products: introduce neither product, introduce product 1 only, introduce product 2 only, or introduce both products. Research and development costs for products 1 and 2 are $180,000 and $150,000, respectively. Note that the first option entails no costs because research and development efforts have not yet begun. The success of these software products depends on the trend of the national economy in the coming year and on the consumers' reaction to these products. The company's revenues earned by introducing product 1 only, product 2 only, or both products in various states of the national economy are given in Table 6.7. The probabilities of observing a strong, fair, and weak trend in the national economy in the coming year are 0.30, 0.50, and 0.20, respectively.

TABLE 6.7 **Revenue Table for Techware's Decision Problem**

Decision/Trend in National Economy	Strong	Fair	Weak
Introduce Neither Product	$0	$0	$0
Introduce Product1 Only	$500,000	$260,000	$120,000
Introduce Product2 Only	$420,000	$230,000	$110,000
Introduce Both Products	$820,000	$390,000	$200,000

   a   Formulate a payoff table that specifies Techware's net revenue (in dollars) for each possible decision and each outcome with respect to the trend in the national economy.

   b   Generate a risk profile for each of Techware's possible decisions in this problem.

   c   Construct a decision tree to identify the course of action that maximizes Techware's expected profit (in dollars) from these marketing opportunities.

5   Consider an investor with $10,000 available to invest. He has the following options regarding the allocation of his available funds: (1) he can invest in a risk-free savings account with a guaranteed 3% annual rate of return; (2) he can invest in a fairly safe stock, where the possible annual rates of return are 6%, 8%, or 10%; or (3) he can invest in a more risky stock where the possible annual rates of return are 1%, 9%, or 17%. Note that the investor can place all of his available funds in any one of these options, or he can split his $10,000 into two $5000 investments in any two of these options. The joint probability distribution of the possible return rates for the two aforementioned stocks is given in Table 6.8 (page 260).

TABLE 6.8 **Joint Probability Distribution of Safe and Risky Stock Return Rates**

Safe Stock Return Rates (S)/ Risky Stock Return Rates (R)	$R = 1\%$	$R = 9\%$	$R = 17\%$
$S = 6\%$	0.10	0.05	0.10
$S = 8\%$	0.25	0.05	0.20
$S = 10\%$	0.10	0.05	0.10

a Formulate a payoff table that specifies this investor's return (in dollars) in one year for each possible decision and each outcome with respect to the two stock returns.

b Generate a risk profile for each of this investor's possible decisions in this problem.

c Construct a decision tree to identify the course of action that maximizes this investor's expected earnings (in dollars) in one year from these investment opportunities.

6 A buyer for a large department store chain must place orders with an athletic shoe manufacturer 6 months prior to the time the shoes will be sold in the department stores. In particular, the buyer must decide on November 1 how many pairs of the manufacturer's newest model of tennis shoes to order for sale during the upcoming summer season. Assume that the each pair of this new brand of tennis shoes costs the department store chain $45. Furthermore, assume that each pair of these shoes can then be sold to the chain's customers for $70. Any pairs of these shoes remaining unsold at the end of the summer season will be sold in a closeout sale next fall for $35 each. The probability distribution of consumer demand for these tennis shoes (in hundreds of pairs) during the upcoming summer season has been assessed by market research specialists and is provided in Table 6.9. Finally, assume that the department store chain must purchase these tennis shoes from the manufacturer in lots of 100 pairs.

TABLE 6.9 **Distribution of Consumer Demand for Tennis Shoes**

Consumer Demand	Probability
1	0.025
2	0.05
3	0.075
4	0.10
5	0.15
6	0.20
7	0.175
8	0.10
9	0.075
10	0.05

a Formulate a payoff table that specifies the contribution to profit (in dollars) from the sale of the tennis shoes by this department store chain for each possible purchase decision (in hundreds of pairs) and each outcome with respect to consumer demand.

b Generate a risk profile for each of the buyer's possible decisions in this problem.

c Construct a decision tree to identify the buyer's course of action that maximizes the expected profit (in dollars) earned by the department store chain from the purchase and subsequent sale of tennis shoes in the coming year.

Level B

7 In designing a new space vehicle, NASA needs to decide whether to provide 0, 1, or 2 backup systems for a crucial component of the vehicle. The first backup system, if included, comes into use only if the original system fails. The second backup system, if included, comes into use only if the original system and the first backup system both fail. NASA engineers claim that each system, independently of the others, has a 1% chance of failing if called into use. Each backup system costs $70,000 to produce and install within the vehicle. Once the vehicle is in flight, the mission will be scrubbed only if the original system and all backups fail. The cost of a scrubbed mission, in addition to production costs, is assessed to be $8,000,000.

a Generate a risk profile for each of NASA's possible decisions in this problem.

b Construct a decision tree to identify the course of action that minimizes NASA's expected total cost in this case.

8 Mr. Maloy has just bought a new $30,000 sport utility vehicle. As a reasonably safe driver, he believes that there is only about a 5% chance of being in an accident in the forthcoming year. If he is involved in an accident, the damage to his new vehicle depends on the severity of the accident. The probability distribution for the range of possible accidents and the corresponding damage amounts (in dollars) are given in Table 6.10. Mr. Maloy is trying to decide whether he is willing to pay $170 each year for collision insurance with a $300 deductible. Note that with this type of insurance, he pays the *first* $300 in damages if he causes an accident and the insurance company pays the remainder.

TABLE 6.10 **Distribution of Accident Types and Corresponding Damage Amounts**

Type of Accident	Conditional Probability	Damage to Vehicle
Minor	0.60	$200
Moderate	0.20	$1,000
Serious	0.10	$4,000
Catastrophic	0.10	$30,000

a Formulate a payoff table that specifies the cost (in dollars) associated with each possible decision and type of accident.

b Generate a risk profile for each of Mr. Maloy's possible decisions in this problem.

c Construct a decision tree to identify the course of action that minimizes Mr. Maloy's annual expected total cost, including the possible insurance premium, deductible payment, and damage payment.

9 The purchasing agent for a microcomputer manufacturer is currently negotiating a purchase agreement for a particular electronic component with a given supplier. This component is produced in lots of 1000, and the cost of purchasing a lot is $30,000. Unfortunately, past experience indicates that this supplier has occasionally shipped defective components to its customers. Specifically, the proportion of defective components supplied by this supplier is well described by the probability distribution given in Table 6.11. While the microcomputer manufacturer can repair a defective component at a cost of $20 each, the purchasing agent is intrigued to learn that this supplier will now assume the cost of replacing defective components in excess of the first 100 faulty items found in a given lot. This guarantee may be purchased by the microcomputer manufacturer prior to the receipt of a given lot at a cost of $1000 per lot. The purchasing agent is interested in determining whether it is worthwhile for her company to purchase the supplier's guarantee policy.

TABLE 6.11 **Distribution of Defective Components in a Lot**

Proportion of Defective Components	Probability
0.05	0.50
0.10	0.25
0.25	0.15
0.50	0.10

a Formulate a payoff table that specifies the microcomputer manufacturer's total cost (in dollars) of purchasing and repairing (if necessary) a complete lot of components for each possible decision and each outcome with respect to the proportion of defective items.

b Generate a risk profile for each of the purchasing agent's possible decisions in this problem.

c Construct a decision tree to identify the purchasing agent's course of action that minimizes the expected total cost (in dollars) of achieving a complete lot of satisfactory components. ■

The PrecisionTree Add-In

Decision trees present a challenge for Excel. We must somehow take advantage of Excel's calculating capabilities (to calculate EMVs, for example) and its graphical capabilities (to depict the decision tree). Fortunately, there is now a powerful add-in, PrecisionTree developed by Palisade Corporation, that makes the process relatively straightforward. This add-in not only enables us to build and label a decision tree, but it performs the folding-back procedure automatically and then allows us to perform sensitivity analysis on key input parameters.

The first thing you must do to use PrecisionTree is to "add it in." We describe this procedure in the file INSTALL.HTM on the CD-ROM that accompanies this book. You'll know that PrecisionTree is ready for use when you see its toolbar (shown in Figure 6.3) and a PrecisionTree menu to the left of the Help menu. (You'll probably also see a "DTools" toolbar that allows you to switch between any of the add-ins in the Palisade suite.)

FIGURE 6.3 **PrecisionTree Toolbar**

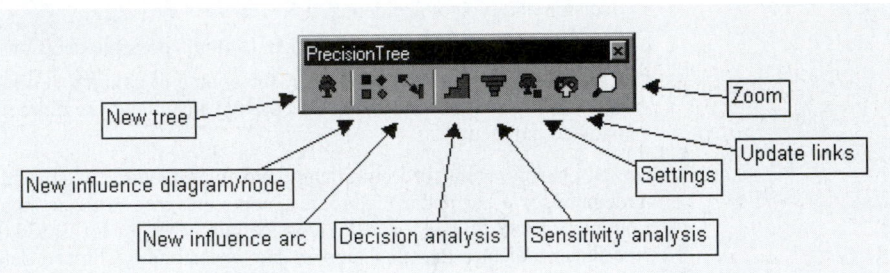

PrecisionTree is quite easy to use—at least its most basic items are—but it can be confusing at first. We'll lead you through the steps for the SciTools example. (The file SCITOOLS.XLS lists the inputs. You should work through the following steps on your own.

1   Inputs. Check that the inputs are as shown in columns A and B of Figure 6.4.

FIGURE 6.4   **Inputs for SciTools Bidding Example**

	A	B	C
1	**SciTools Bidding Example**		
2			
3	**Inputs**		
4	Cost to prepare a bid	$5,000	
5	Cost to supply instruments	$95,000	
6			**Range names**
7	Probability of no competing bid	0.3	BidCost: B4
8	Comp bid distribution (if they bid)		PrNoBid: B7
9	<$115K	0.2	ProdCost: B5
10	$115K to $120K	0.4	
11	$120K to $125K	0.3	
12	>$125K	0.1	

2   New tree. Click on the new tree button (the far left button) on the PrecisionTree toolbar, and then click on any cell (say, cell A14) below the input section to start a new tree. Click on the name box of this new tree (it probably says "tree #1") to open a dialog box. Type in a descriptive name for the tree, such as SciTools Bidding, and click on OK. You should now see the beginnings of a tree, as shown in Figure 6.5.

F I G U R E   6 . 5   **Beginnings of a New Tree**

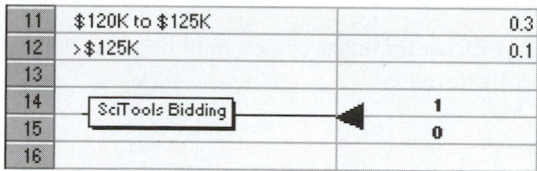

3   Decision nodes and branches. From here on, keep the finished tree in Figure 6.2 in mind. This is the finished product toward which we're building. To obtain decision nodes and branches, click on the (only) triangle end node to open the dialog box in Figure 6.6. Click on the green square to indicate that this is a decision node, and fill in

F I G U R E   6 . 6   **Dialog Box for Adding a New Decision Node and Branches**

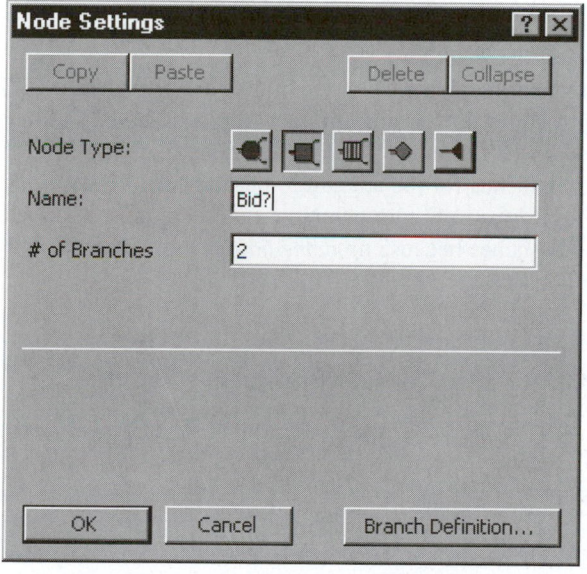

the dialog box as shown. We're calling this decision "Bid?" and specifying that there are two possible decisions. The tree expands as shown in Figure 6.7 (page 264). The boxes that say "branch" show the default labels for these branches. Click on either of them to open another dialog box where you can provide a more descriptive name for the branch. Do this to label the two branches "No" and "Yes." Also, you can enter the

FIGURE 6.7   Tree with Initial Decision Node and Branches

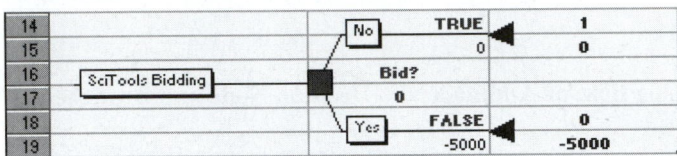

immediate payoff/cost for either branch right below it. Since there is a $5000 cost of bidding, enter the formula

=-BidCost

right below the "Yes" branch in cell B19. (It is negative to reflect a *cost*.) The tree should now appear as in Figure 6.8.

FIGURE 6.8   Decision Tree with Decision Branches Labeled

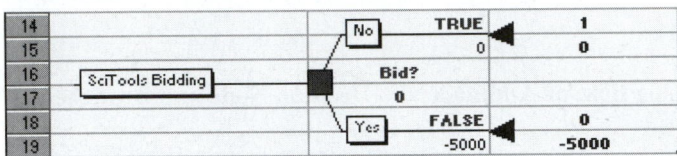

4   **More decision branches.** The top branch is completed; if SciTools does not bid, there is nothing left to do. So click on the bottom end node, following SciTools' decision to bid, and proceed as in the previous step to add and label the decision node and three decision branches for the amount to bid. (Refer to Figure 6.2.) The tree to this point should appear as in Figure 6.9. Note that there are no monetary values below these decision branches because no *immediate* payoffs or costs are associated with the bid amount decision.

FIGURE 6.9   Tree with All Decision Nodes and Branches

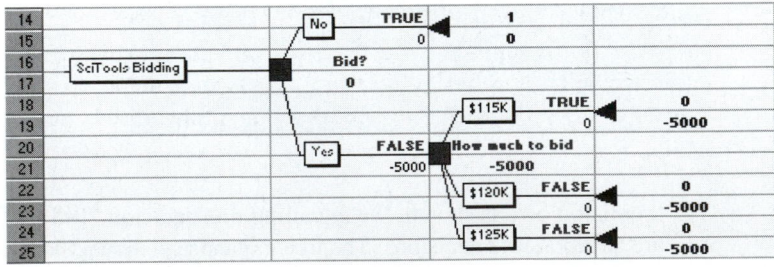

5   **Probability nodes and branches.** We now need a probability node and branches from the rightmost end nodes to capture whether the competition bids. Click on the top one of these end nodes to bring up the same dialog box as in Figure 6.6. Now, however,

click on the red circle box to indicate that this is a probability node. Label it "Any competing bid?", specify two branches, and click on OK. Then label the two branches "No" and "Yes." Next, repeat this procedure to form another probability node (with two branches) following the "Yes" branch, call it "Win bid?", and label its branches as shown in Figure 6.10.

FIGURE 6.10 **Decision Tree with One Set of Probability Nodes and Branches**

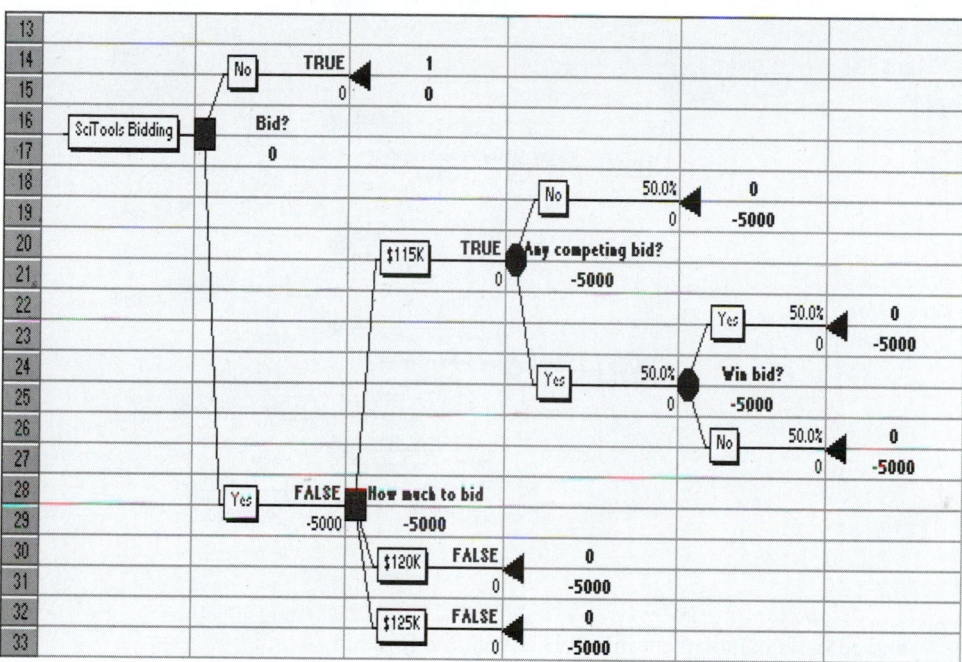

6 **Copying probability nodes and branches.** You could now repeat the same procedure from the previous step to build probability nodes and branches following the other bid amount decisions, but because they're structurally equivalent, you can save a lot of work by using PrecisionTree's copy and paste feature. Click on the leftmost probability node to open a dialog box and click on Copy. Then click on either end node to bring up the same dialog box and click on Paste. Do this again with the other end node. Decision trees can get very "bushy," but this copy and paste feature can make them much less tedious to construct.

7 **Labeling probability branches.** You should now have the decision tree shown in Figure 6.11. It is structurally the same as the completed tree in Figure 6.2, but the probabilities and monetary values on the probability branches are not correct. Note that each probability branch has a value above and below the branch. The value above is the probability (the default values make the branches equally likely), and the value below is the monetary value (the default values are 0). We can enter any values or formulas in these cells, exactly as we do in typical Excel worksheets. As usual, it is a good practice to refer to input cells in these formulas whenever possible. We'll get you started with the probability branches following the decision to bid $115,000. First, enter the probability of no competing bid in cell D18 with the formula

=PrNoBid

FIGURE 6.11 **Structure of Completed Tree**

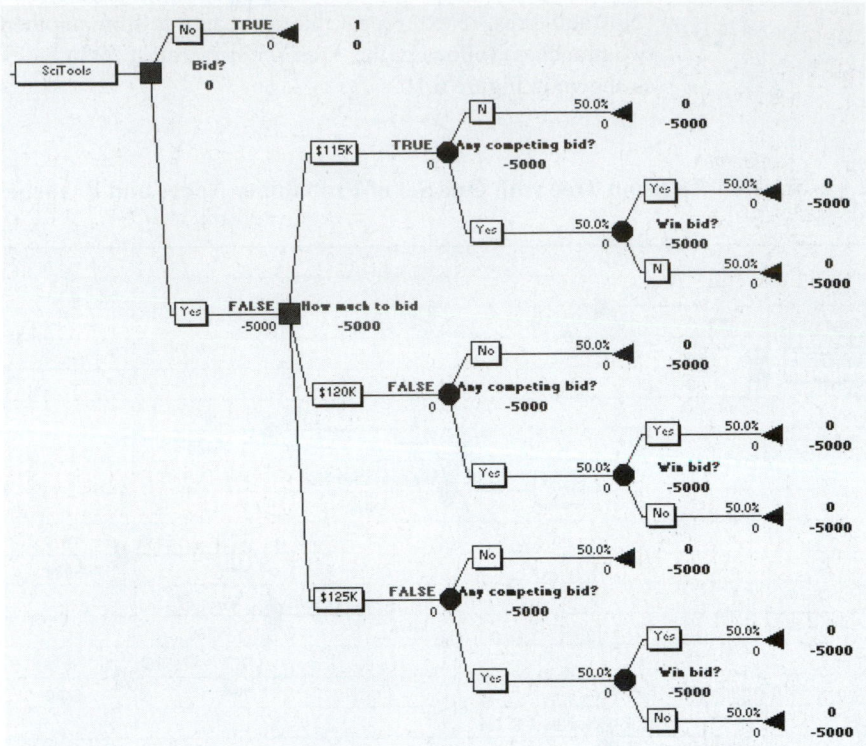

and enter its complement in cell D24 with the formula

$$=1\text{-}D18$$

Next, enter the probability that SciTools wins the bid in cell E22 with the formula

$$=\text{SUM(B10:B12)}$$

and enter its complement in cell E26 with the formula

$$=1\text{-}E22$$

(Remember that SciTools wins the bid only if the competitor bids higher, and in this part of the tree, SciTools is bidding $115,000.) For the monetary values, enter the formula

$$=115000\text{-ProdCost}$$

in the two cells, D19 and E23, where SciTools wins the contract. Note that we already subtracted the cost of the bid (cell B29), so we shouldn't do so again. This would be double-counting, and it should always be avoided in decision problems.

8 **Enter the other formulas on probability branches.** Using the previous step and Figure 6.2 as a guide, enter formulas for the probabilities and monetary values on the other probability branches, that is, those following the decision to bid $120,000 or $125,000.

We're finished! The completed tree in Figure 6.2 shows the best strategy and its associated EMV, as we discussed earlier. Note that we never have to perform the folding-back procedure manually. PrecisionTree does it for us. In fact, the tree is completed as soon as we finish entering the relevant inputs. In addition, if we change any of the inputs, the tree reacts automatically. For example, try changing the bid cost in cell B4 from $5000 to some large value such as $20,000. You'll see that the tree calculations update automatically, and the best decision is then *not* to bid, with an associated EMV of $0.

6.3.1 Risk Profile of Optimal Strategy

Once the decision tree is completed, PrecisionTree has several tools we can use to gain more information about the decision analysis. First, we can see a risk profile and other information about the *optimal* decision. To do so, click on the fourth button from the left on the PrecisionTree toolbar (it looks like a staircase) and fill in the resulting dialog box as shown in Figure 6.12. (You can experiment with other options.) The Policy Suggestion

FIGURE 6.12 **Dialog Box for Information About Optimal Decision**

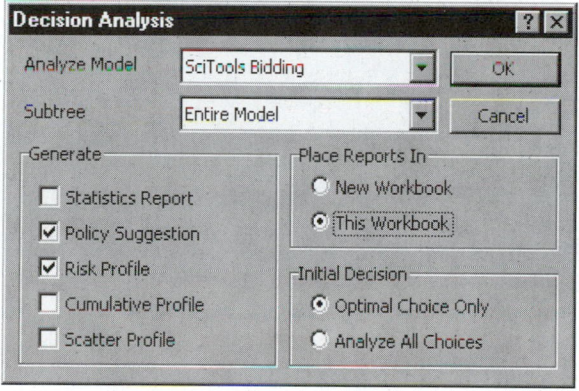

option allows us to see only that part of the tree that corresponds to the best decision, as shown in Figure 6.13 (page 268).

The Risk Profile option allows us to see a graphical risk profile of the optimal decision. (If we checked the Statistics Report box, we would also see this information numerically.) As the risk profile in Figure 6.14 shows, there are only two possible monetary outcomes if SciTools bids $115,000. It either wins $15,000 or loses $5000, and the former is much more likely. (The associated probabilities are 0.86 and 0.14.) This graphical information is even more useful when there are a larger number of possible monetary outcomes. We can see what they are and how likely they are.

6.3.2 Sensitivity Analysis

We have already stressed the importance of a follow-up sensitivity analysis for any decision problem, and PrecisionTree makes this relatively easy to perform. First, we can enter any values into the input cells and watch how the tree changes. But we can get more systematic

FIGURE 6.13   Subtree for Optimal Decision

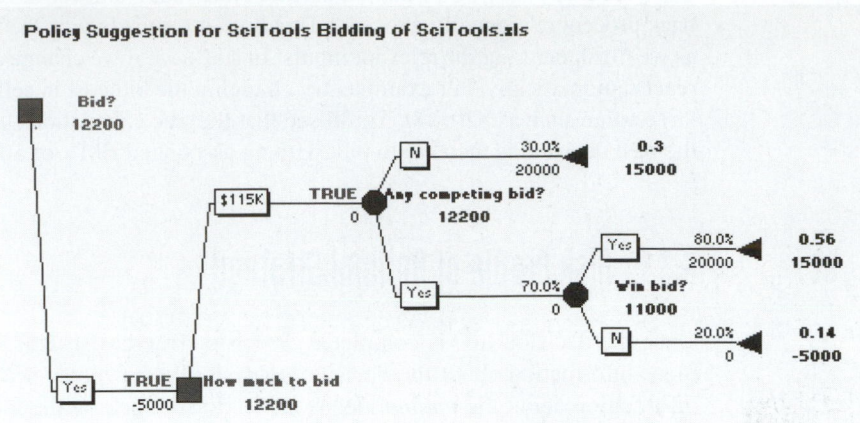

FIGURE 6.14   Risk Profile of Optimal Decision

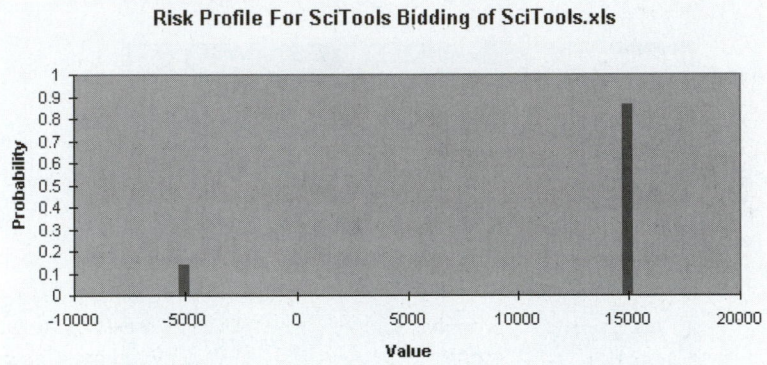

information by clicking on PrecisionTree's sensitivity button, the fifth from the left on the toolbar (it looks like a tornado). This brings up the dialog box in Figure 6.15. It requires an EMV cell (and an optional descriptive name) to analyze at the top and one or more input cells in the middle. The specifications for these input cells are actually entered at the bottom of the dialog box.

The cell to analyze (at the top) is usually the EMV cell at the far left of the decision tree—this is the cell shown in the figure—but it can be any EMV cell. For example, if we *assume* SciTools will prepare a bid and we want to see how sensitive the EMV from that point on is to inputs, we could select cell C29 (refer to Figure 6.2) to analyze. Next, for any input cell such as the production cost cell (B5), we enter a minimum value, a maximum value, a base value (probably the original value in the model), and a step size. For example, to specify these for the production cost, we clicked on the Suggest Values button. This default setting varies the production cost by as much as 10% from the original value in either direction in a series of 10 steps. We can also enter our own desired values. We did so for the probability of no competing bids, varying its value from 0 to 0.6 in a sequence of 12 steps.

FIGURE 6.15 **Sensitivity Analysis Dialog Box**

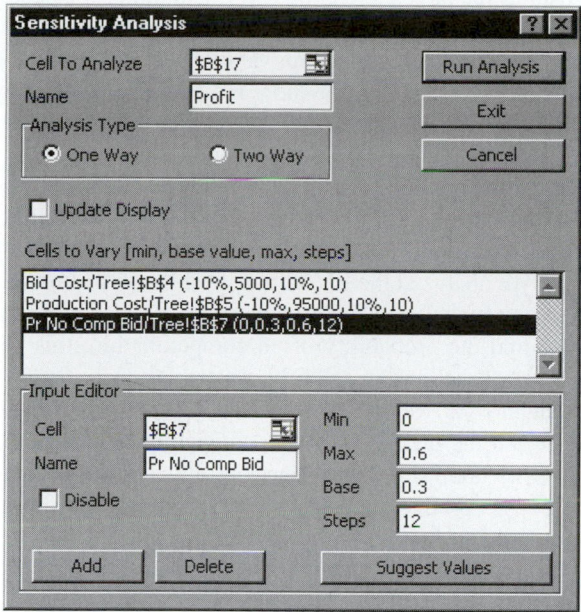

When we click on Run Analysis, PrecisionTree varies each of the specified inputs (one at a time if we select the One Way option) and presents the results in several ways in a *new* Excel file with Sensitivity, Tornado, and Spider Graph sheets. The Sensitivity sheet includes several charts, a typical one of which appears in Figure 6.16. This shows how the EMV varies with the production cost for *both* of the original decisions (bid or don't bid). This type of graph is useful for seeing whether the optimal decision *changes* over the range of the input variable. It does so only if the two lines cross. In this particular graph it is clear that the "Bid" decision dominates the "No bid" decision over the production cost range we selected.

The Tornado sheet shows how sensitive the EMV of the *optimal* decision is to each of the selected inputs over the ranges selected. (See Figure 6.17, page 270.) The length of each bar shows the percentage change in the EMV in either direction, so the longer the bar, the more sensitive this EMV is to the particular input. The bars are always arranged from

FIGURE 6.16 **EMV versus Production Cost for Each of Two Decisions**

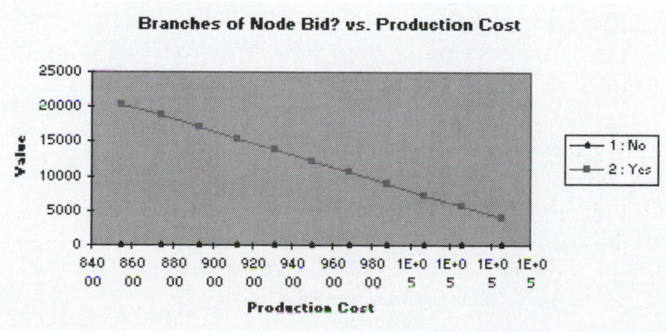

longest on top to shortest on the bottom—hence the name *tornado* chart. Here we see that production cost has the largest effect on EMV, and bid cost has the smallest effect.

Finally, the Spider Chart sheet contains the chart in Figure 6.18. It shows how much the optimal EMV varies in magnitude for various percentage changes in the input variables. The steeper the slope of the line, the more the EMV is affected by a particular input. We again see that the production cost has a relatively large effect, whereas the other two inputs have relatively small effects.

Each time we click on the sensitivity button, we can run a different sensitivity analysis. An interesting option is to run a two-way analysis (by clicking on the Two Way button in Figure 6.15). Then we see how the selected EMV varies as each *pair* of inputs vary simultaneously. We analyzed the EMV in cell C29 with this option, using the same inputs as before. A typical result is shown in Figure 6.19. For each of the possible values of production cost and the probability of no competitor bid, this chart indicates which bid amount is optimal. (By choosing cell C29, we are assuming SciTools will bid; the question is only how much.) As we see, the optimal bid amount remains $115,000 unless the production cost *and* the probability of no competing bid are both large. Then it becomes optimal to bid $125,000. This makes sense intuitively. As the chance of no competing bid increases and a larger production cost must be recovered, it seems reasonable that SciTools will increase its bid.

FIGURE 6.17 **Tornado Chart for SciTools Example**

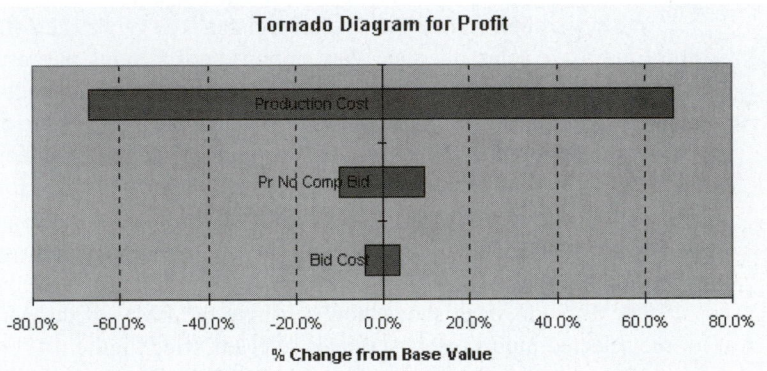

FIGURE 6.18 **Spider Chart for SciTools Example**

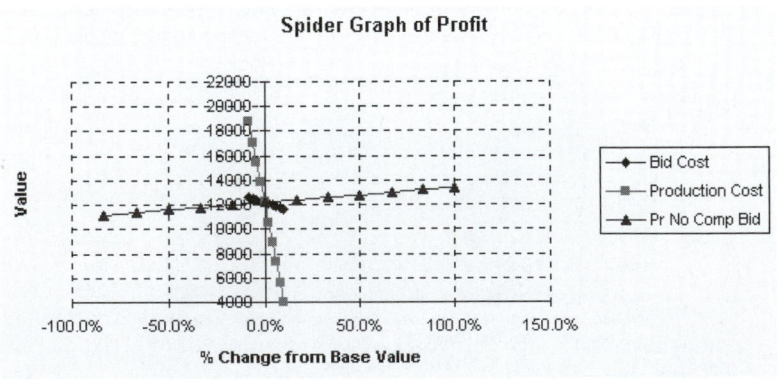

FIGURE 6.19   Two-Way Sensitivity Analysis

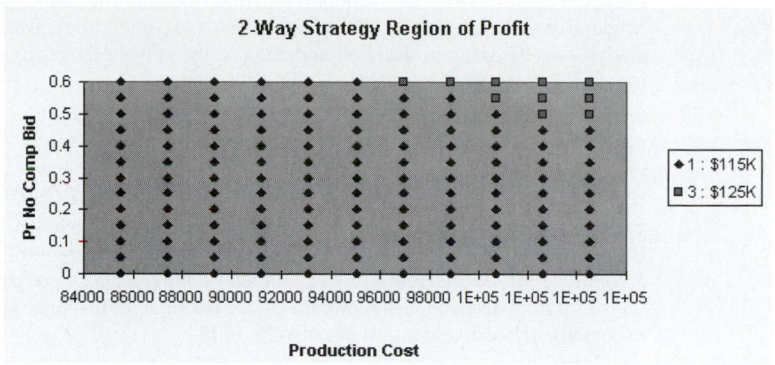

We reiterate that a sensitivity analysis is always an important aspect in real decision analyses. If we had to construct decision trees by hand—with paper and pencil—a sensitivity analysis would be virtually out of the question. We would have to recompute everything each time through. Therefore, one of the most valuable features of the PrecisionTree add-in is that it enables us to perform sensitivity analyses in a matter of seconds.

PROBLEMS

Level A

10   Consider again SweetTooth Candy Company's decision problem described in Problem 1. Use the PrecisionTree add-in to identify the strategy that minimizes SweetTooth's expected cost of meeting its sugar demand. Also, perform sensitivity analysis on the optimal decision and summarize your findings. In response to which model inputs is the expected cost value most sensitive?

11   Consider again Carlisle Tire and Rubber's decision problem described in Problem 2. Use the PrecisionTree add-in to identify the strategy that maximizes this tire manufacturer's expected profit. Also, perform sensitivity analysis on the optimal decision and summarize your findings. In response to which model inputs is the expected profit value most sensitive?

12   Consider again the landowner's decision problem described in Problem 3. Use the PrecisionTree add-in to identify the strategy that maximizes the landowner's expected net earnings from this opportunity. Also, perform sensitivity analysis on the optimal decision and summarize your findings. In response to which model inputs is the expected net earnings value most sensitive?

13   Consider again Techware's decision problem described in Problem 4. Use the PrecisionTree add-in to identify the strategy that maximizes Techware's expected net revenue from the given marketing opportunities. Also, perform sensitivity analysis on the optimal decision and summarize your findings. In response to which model inputs is the expected net revenue value most sensitive?

14   Consider again the investor's decision problem described in Problem 5. Use the PrecisionTree add-in to identify the strategy that maximizes the investor's expected earnings in one year from the given investment opportunities. Also, perform sensitivity analysis on the optimal decision and summarize your findings. In response to which model inputs is the expected earnings value most sensitive?

15   Consider again the department store buyer's decision problem described in Problem 6. Use the PrecisionTree add-in to identify the strategy that maximizes the department store chain's expected profit earned by purchasing and subsequently selling pairs of the new tennis shoes. Also, perform sensitivity analysis on the optimal decision and summarize your findings. In response to which model inputs is the expected profit value most sensitive?

16 Consider again NASA's decision problem described in Problem 7. Use the PrecisionTree add-in to identify the strategy that minimizes NASA's expected total cost. Also, perform sensitivity analysis on the optimal decision and summarize your findings. In response to which model inputs is the expected total cost value most sensitive?

17 Consider again Mr. Maloy's decision problem described in Problem 8. Use the PrecisionTree add-in to identify the strategy that minimizes Mr. Maloy's annual expected total cost. Also, perform sensitivity analysis on the optimal decision and summarize your findings. In response to which model inputs is the expected total cost value most sensitive?

18 Consider again the purchasing agent's decision problem described in Problem 9. Use the PrecisionTree add-in to identify the strategy that minimizes the expected total cost of achieving a complete lot of satisfactory microcomputer components. Also, perform sensitivity analysis on the optimal decision and summarize your findings. In response to which model inputs is the expected total cost value most sensitive? ■

6.4

Introduction to Influence Diagrams[2]

Decision trees show all the elements of a decision problem, including the solution, in a straightforward manner. The only real drawback to decision trees is that they get very large for problems of even moderate size. In particular, decision trees in a spreadsheet quickly outgrow the screen and become difficult to visualize all at once. An alternative way of depicting a decision problem is to use an **influence diagram**. These diagrams also have their drawbacks—their conventions vary from one software implementation to another and are rather difficult to master—but they definitely provide a more compact representation of a problem. Furthermore, a well-drawn influence diagram is easier to explain to a nontechnical manager than a big bushy decision tree.

Before we explain the details of influence diagrams and how they are implemented in PrecisionTree, it is important to realize that influence diagrams can be used on two levels. On one level they can be used simply as *diagrams* to illustrate the key elements and relationships in decision problems. Once these key elements and relationships are understood, it might be easier to solve the problem with a full-blown decision tree. On another level an influence diagram can capture *all* of the information—the timing, the structure, and the numerical information—that is captured in a decision tree. That is, an influence diagram can be developed so that it is *equivalent* to a decision tree. This is the difficult part. All we see in an influence diagram are a few shapes connected with arcs. Most of the information from the problem is stored "behind the scenes," and it takes some practice to see how this is done.

We illustrate influence diagrams with the following simple example.

EXAMPLE 6.2

Souvenirs, Inc. is in charge of manufacturing and distributing various types of souvenirs for the upcoming Olympic Games. The company is undecided about the quantity of each item to produce. On the one hand, a profit can be made for each souvenir produced and sold. On the other hand, Olympics souvenirs that are not sold before or during the Olympics can

---

[2]This section is optional. We believe that influence diagrams are more difficult to master than decision trees, so we will stick to decision trees in the rest of this chapter.

be sold for only half price afterward. For one particular souvenir, the total cost per unit of producing and marketing is $10. Each unit will then be sold for $15. The uncertainty arises because the demand for this souvenir (before the Olympics are over) is unknown. The company assumes that this demand has a discrete distribution with possible values 5000, 6000, 7000, 8000, 9000, and 10,000, and corresponding probabilities 0.1, 0.2, 0.3, 0.2, 0.1, and 0.1. Assuming that the company must produce this souvenir in batches of 1000 units, how many batches should it produce to maximize its expected profit?

Solution

A possible influence diagram for this problem appears in Figure 6.20. (It is actually part of a spreadsheet; we have just hidden the gridlines.) The convention for influence diagrams, at least in PrecisionTree, is that there are several specific shapes:

- Green rectangles represent decisions.
- Red ovals represent uncertain outcomes.
- Blue rounded rectangles represent intermediate calculations.
- Blue diamonds represent the ultimate payoff (or cost).

FIGURE 6.20   **Influence Diagram for Souvenir Example**

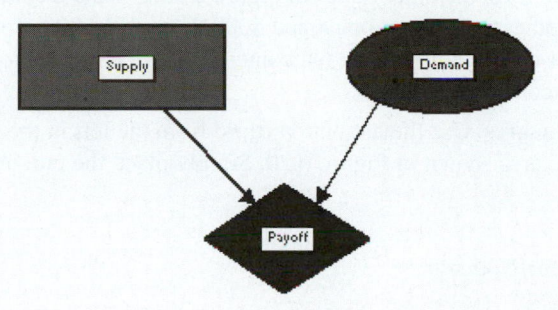

In this case the diagram makes the structure of the problem evident. The company first decides how many souvenirs to supply. Independently of this decision, the potential demand is generated randomly. Then the supply and demand jointly determine the company's payoff. Although the arcs in an influence diagram can signify various types of relationships, in the present case they all signify "value" and "timing." This means that if an arc leads from node A to node B, then node A occurs first, and the values at node B are affected by what happens at node A. In this case the supply decision and the demand outcome both occur *before* the eventual payoff and they determine its value. Hence, both are "value" and "timing" arcs.

We could stop right here with influence diagrams, using them only to illustrate the basic structure of the problem, and proceed directly to a decision tree. But we can build all of the required information directly into the influence diagram itself. The procedure is explained in the following steps. (See the file SOUVENIR.XLS.)

1   **Input values.** Enter the input parameters in the upper left corner of a spreadsheet, as in Figure 6.21 on page 274. (Note that we begin in row 7. PrecisionTree reserves the higher rows for its own summary information in an influence diagram.)

2   **Draw the nodes.** To draw the nodes in Figure 6.20, click on the shape button (second from the left in the PrecisionTree toolbar). The cursor changes to a crosshair, and

FIGURE 6.21 Inputs for Souvenir Example

	A	B	C	D
7	**Inputs for souvenir example**			
8	Unit selling price	$15		
9	Unit variable cost	$10		
10	Unit salvage value	$7		
11				
12	Distribution of demand			
13	Demand	Probability		
14	5000	0.1		
15	6000	0.2		
16	7000	0.3		
17	8000	0.2		
18	9000	0.1		
19	10000	0.1		

Range names
SellingPrice: B8
VarCost: B9
SalvageVal: B10

you can drag out a shape anywhere on the spreadsheet. (Don't worry about its size or position; these can be changed easily later on.) Then click on the name box inside the new shape to open the dialog box shown in Figure 6.22.

First, click on the appropriate shape. Then you can name the node and its possible outcomes. Here we have designated that this is a decision node named Supply with possible outcomes 5000 through 10,000. (We assume the company will not consider any production amounts other than these.) Later we will return to this dialog box and click on the Values button, but for now, click on OK.

Then form the other nodes in Figure 6.20. For the Demand node, you'll also need six outcomes, which can be named 5000 through 10,000. For the payoff node, you'll note that it does not have an Outcomes option. Only decision and probability nodes have outcomes.

3 **Draw the arcs.** Use the arc button (third from the left in the PrecisionTree toolbar) to draw the arcs shown in Figure 6.20. Simply place the cursor inside the "from" node

FIGURE 6.22 Dialog Box for Nodes

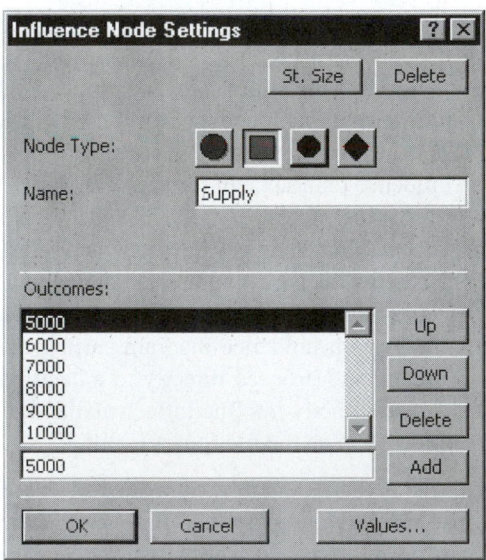

and drag it inside the "to" node. Each time you create a new arc, the dialog box in Figure 6.23 appears. Each of the arcs in this example should have the first two options, Value and Timing, checked (as we explained above). Actually, you have no choice for arcs that lead to blue (calculation or payoff) nodes; they are automatically value and timing arcs.

4   **Enter node values.** We now link the values of the nodes in the influence diagram to the inputs in Figure 6.21. This is analogous to entering monetary values and probabilities in a decision tree. To get started, click on the Demand name box to open a dialog box analogous to the one in Figure 6.22, and click on the Values button. This opens a miniature spreadsheet that works essentially like a regular Excel spreadsheet. (See Figure 6.24.) Because this is a probability node, we need to enter the probability distribution of demand in its cells—values on the left and probabilities on the right. To do so, enter an equals sign in any "cell" and then click (actually, it takes two clicks) on the appropriate cell of the input section of the *original* spreadsheet. (We named this sheet Influence; hence the "Influence!" prefix in each formula.) Then you can copy and paste as usual to fill in the other cells. The values for the Supply node are even simpler to enter. In its miniature spreadsheet, just enter the values (not formulas) 5000 through 10,000.

The Payoff node is a bit trickier. We fill in its dialog box as shown in Figure 6.25 (page 276). The trick here is to realize that the formulas are entered in column B (starting in row 4) of this miniature spreadsheet, and the values of preceding nodes are

FIGURE 6.23   **Dialog Box for Arcs**

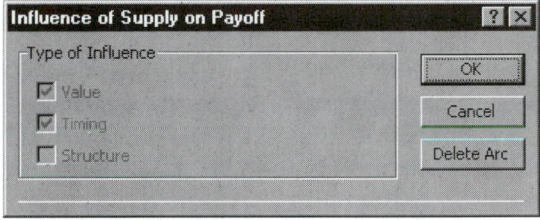

FIGURE 6.24   **Value Dialog Box for Probability Node**

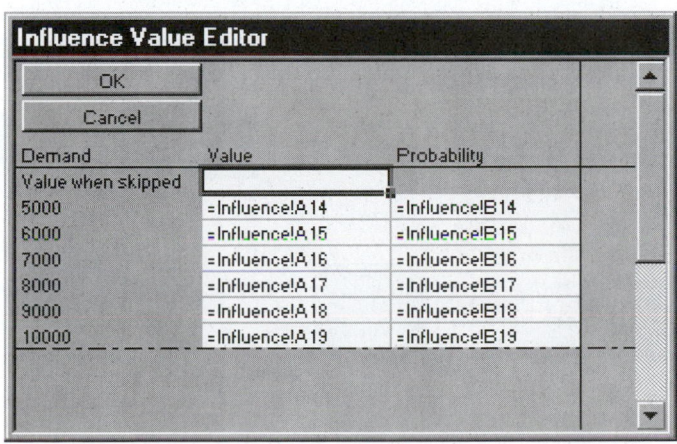

FIGURE 6.25   Value Dialog Box for Profit Node

Influence Value Editor

| OK |
| Cancel |

Payoff	Value	Demand	Supply
	=-VarCost*E4+SellingPrice*MIN(D4,E4)+SalvageVal*MAX(E4-D4,0)	5000	5000
	=-VarCost*E5+SellingPrice*MIN(D5,E5)+SalvageVal*MAX(E5-D5,0)	6000	5000
	=-VarCost*E6+SellingPrice*MIN(D6,E6)+SalvageVal*MAX(E6-D6,0)	7000	5000
	=-VarCost*E7+SellingPrice*MIN(D7,E7)+SalvageVal*MAX(E7-D7,0)	8000	5000
	=-VarCost*E8+SellingPrice*MIN(D8,E8)+SalvageVal*MAX(E8-D8,0)	9000	5000
	=-VarCost*E9+SellingPrice*MIN(D9,E9)+SalvageVal*MAX(E9-D9,0)	10000	5000
	=-VarCost*E10+SellingPrice*MIN(D10,E10)+SalvageVal*MAX(E10-D10,	5000	6000
	=-VarCost*E11+SellingPrice*MIN(D11,E11)+SalvageVal*MAX(E11-D11,	6000	6000
	=-VarCost*E12+SellingPrice*MIN(D12,E12)+SalvageVal*MAX(E12-D12,	7000	6000

stored to the right in columns D and E. We can refer to these values in the formulas. For example, the first formula is

$$\text{=-VarCost*E4+SellingPrice*MIN(D4,E4)+SalvageVal*MAX(E4-D4,0)}$$

This says that the profit is the selling price multiplied by the number sold, plus the salvage value (half the selling price) multiplied by the number left over, minus the variable cost multiplied by the number produced.

This completes the influence diagram. We believe that the conventions are more difficult to master than the conventions for a decision tree. However, we also believe that once the conventions are mastered, influence diagrams are easier and quicker to develop than decision trees. In addition, we can form the equivalent decision tree from an influence diagram—and check that we created it correctly—very easily. When we form an influence diagram, PrecisionTree puts summary measures of the profit distribution in the upper left corner of the spreadsheet. (See Figure 6.26.) By clicking on the name box in this summary section, we obtain a dialog box (not shown here) where we can click on a Convert to Tree button. This automatically forms the equivalent tree on another sheet. For the souvenir example this equivalent tree appears in Figure 6.27. (We have used the Collapse option—see the dialog

FIGURE 6.26   Influence Diagram with Summary Measures

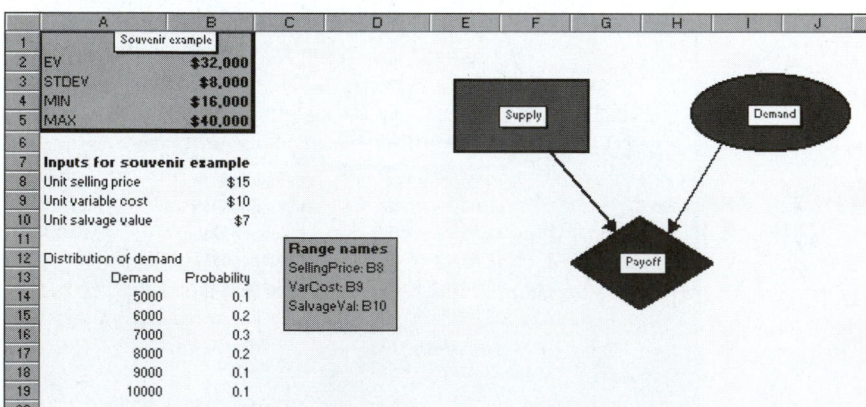

FIGURE 6.27 **Equivalent Decision Tree for Souvenir Example**

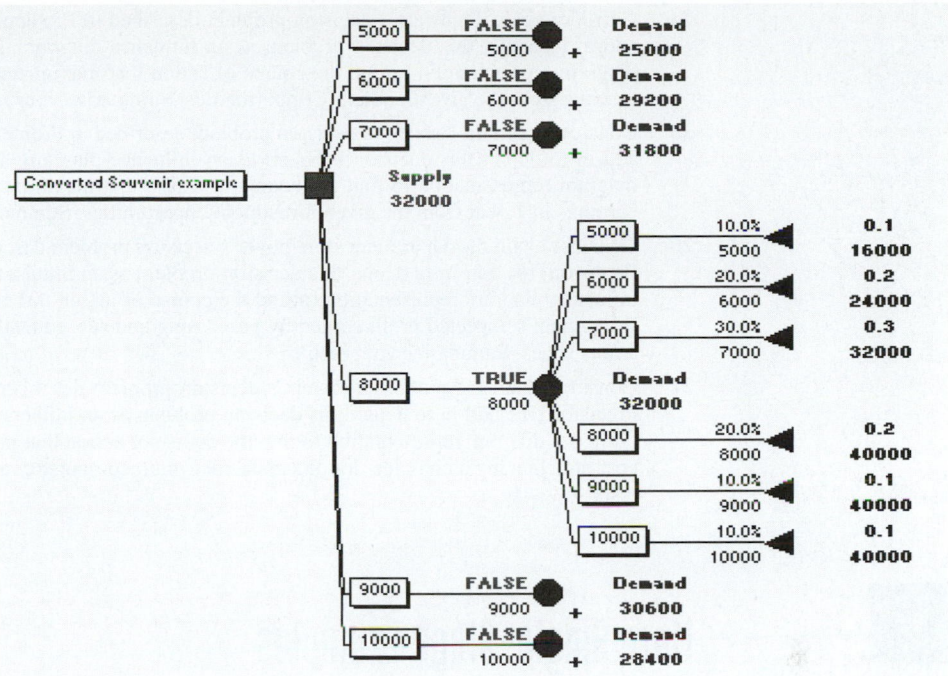

box in Figure 6.6—to "collapse" all of the probability branches except for the optimal one. This example illustrates how decision trees for even simple problems can become very bushy, very quickly!) This tree shows that the optimal decision is to produce 8000 units with an expected profit of $32,000. ■

PROBLEMS

Level B

19 Consider again SweetTooth Candy Company's decision problem described in Problem 1. Use the PrecisionTree add-in to depict this decision problem as an influence diagram. Then use your influence diagram representation to find the course of action that minimizes SweetTooth's expected cost of meeting its sugar demand. Summarize your results.

20 Consider again Carlisle Tire and Rubber's decision problem described in Problem 2. Use the PrecisionTree add-in to depict this decision problem as an influence diagram. Then use your influence diagram representation to find the course of action that maximizes this tire manufacturer's expected profit. Summarize your results.

21 Consider again NASA's decision problem described in Problem 7. Use the PrecisionTree add-in to depict this decision problem as an influence diagram. Then use your influence diagram representation to find the course of action that minimizes NASA's expected total cost. Summarize your results.

22 Consider again Mr. Maloy's decision problem described in Problem 8. Use the PrecisionTree add-in to depict this decision problem as an influence diagram. Then use your influence diagram representation to find the course of action that minimizes Mr. Maloy's annual expected total cost. Summarize your results.

23 Consider again the landowner's decision problem described in Problem 3. Use the PrecisionTree add-in to depict this decision problem as an influence diagram. Then use your influence diagram representation to find the course of action that maximizes the landowner's expected net earnings from this opportunity. Summarize your results.

24 Consider again Techware's decision problem described in Problem 4. Use the PrecisionTree add-in to depict this decision problem as an influence diagram. Then use your influence diagram representation to find the course of action that maximizes Techware's expected net revenue from the given marketing opportunities. Summarize your results.

25 Consider again the investor's decision problem described in Problem 5. Use the PrecisionTree add-in to depict this decision problem as an influence diagram. Then use your influence diagram representation to find the course of action that maximizes the investor's expected earnings in 1 year from the given investment opportunities. Summarize your results.

26 Consider again the department store buyer's decision problem described in Problem 6. Use the PrecisionTree add-in to depict this decision problem as an influence diagram. Then use your influence diagram representation to find the course of action that maximizes the department store chain's expected profit earned by purchasing and subsequently selling pairs of the new tennis shoes. Summarize your results.

27 Consider again the purchasing agent's decision problem described in Problem 9. Use the PrecisionTree add-in to depict this decision problem as an influence diagram. Then use your influence diagram representation to find the course of action that minimizes the expected total cost of achieving a complete lot of satisfactory microcomputer components. Summarize your results. ∎

6.5 More Single-Stage Examples

All applications of decision making under uncertainty follow the procedures discussed so far. We first identify the possible decision alternatives, assess relevant probabilities, and calculate monetary values. Then we use a decision tree (or influence diagram) to identify the alternative with the largest EMV and follow this up with a thorough sensitivity analysis. We can also examine the risk profiles for the various alternatives. This is particularly useful if criteria other than straight EMV maximization are considered, as we will discuss in Section 6.8. In this section we will illustrate the process with several single-stage examples, where the decision maker makes one decision and then learns which of several uncertain outcomes occurs. In this next section we will examine multistage examples, where two or more sequential decisions must be made.

The following example illustrates a decision problem most of us face on an annual basis, although most of us probably don't go to the trouble of analyzing it formally.

EXAMPLE 6.3

Each year employees at State University are asked to decide on one of three health care plans. The terms of these are as follows:[3]

Plan 1: The monthly cost is $24. There is a $500 deductible. The participant pays all expenses until payments for the year equal $500. After that, 90% of remaining expenses are paid by the insurer.

Plan 2: This is the same as plan 1, except that the monthly cost is $1 and the deductible amount is $1000.

Plan 3: The monthly cost is $20. There is no deductible. The employee pays 30% of all medical expenses. The rest is paid by the insurer.

---

[3]We assume that these terms apply only to the employee; that is, these are not family plans.

Which of these three plans should an employee choose?

Solution

Clearly, the solution will vary from one employee to another, depending on the assessed probability distribution of medical expenses. To illustrate, however, we will consider an employee who assesses the distribution of yearly medical expenses shown in Table 6.12. These expenses include hospital visits, surgery, office visits, and prescriptions, all of which are covered under the terms of the plans. As in the previous example, this distribution is only an approximation of the real distribution, which would contain a continuum of expenses. However, it is probably adequate for making a decision among the three plans.

TABLE 6.12 **Distribution of Medical Expenses for Insurance Example**

Total Medical Expense	Probability
$200	0.30
$600	0.50
$1000	0.15
$5000	0.03
$15,000	0.02

The next step is to determine the employee's cost for each plan and each outcome. For example, suppose that the employee chooses plan 1 and incurs $600 in expenses. Then the total cost is the cost of the insurance plus the full amount of the first $500 in expenses plus 10% of the last $100 in expenses, that is,

$$24(12) + 500 + 0.1(100) = \$798$$

However, if this employee's medical expenses are only $200, then the cost is

$$24(12) + 200 = \$488$$

The costs for the other plans and other outcomes can be calculated in a similar manner. We list all of the costs in Table 6.13.

TABLE 6.13 **Employee Cost Table for Insurance Example**

Medical Expense	Plan 1	Plan 2	Plan 3
$200	$488	$212	$300
$600	$798	$612	$420
$1000	$838	$1012	$540
$5000	$1238	$1412	$1740
$15,000	$2238	$2412	$4740

The choice is certainly not clear from this table. The plan with the lowest premium, plan 2, looks good if the year's medical expenses are low. This is also true for the no-deductible plan, plan 3, although its cost is quite large in case of a disaster. For moderate medical expenses, plan 1 is obviously inferior, but it is the best for guarding against a disaster. These trade-offs could be illustrated by risk profiles, which you might want to examine. Instead, we turn directly to the decision tree.

Using PrecisionTree

1 **Inputs.** Enter the inputs for the three plans and the probabilities from Table 6.12 in the top left portion of the spreadsheet (down to row 15). (See Figure 6.28 and the file MEDICAL.XLS.)

FIGURE 6.28 Inputs and Cost Table for Medical Example

	A	B	C	D
1	**Medical insurance problem**			
2				
3	Inputs for plans			
4		Plan1	Plan2	Plan3
5	Monthly cost	$24	$1	$20
6	Deductible	$500	$1,000	$0
7	Copay Pct	10%	10%	30%
8				
9	Distribution of medical expenses			
10		Expense	Prob	
11		$200	0.3	
12		$600	0.5	
13		$1,000	0.15	
14		$5,000	0.03	
15		$15,000	0.02	
16				
17	Out of pocket cost table (plan along top, expense along side), not including premiums			
18		Plan1	Plan2	Plan3
19	$200	$200	$200	$60
20	$600	$510	$600	$180
21	$1,000	$550	$1,000	$300
22	$5,000	$950	$1,400	$1,500
23	$15,000	$1,950	$2,400	$4,500

2 **Cost table.** For later use in the decision tree, calculate the costs to the employee (not counting insurance premiums) in the range B19:D23. To do this, enter the formula

$$=IF(\$A19<=B\$6,\$A19,B\$6+B\$7*(\$A19-B\$6))$$

in cell B19 and copy this to the range B19:D23. This IF function says that if the medical expense is less than the deductible, the employee pays it all. Otherwise, the employee pays the deductible amount plus a percentage of the remainder.

3 **Decision tree.** Use PrecisionTree to create the decision tree shown in Figure 6.29. Here are some tips. First, create the decision node and decision branches, and enter formulas for their values as 12 times the relevant monthly premiums. Then create a single probability node and its branches, label the branches, and enter formulas for the probabilities with *absolute* references. For example, enter the formula

$$=\$C\$11$$

for the probability of the top branch. Next, copy the probability node to the end nodes below it. (Do you see the effect of the absolute references?) Finally, link the values for all of the probability branches to the cells in the cost table. (We know of no quick way to do this. We entered 15 separate formulas, one for each branch. However, it is much easier to create a cost table and link branch formulas to it than to create the branch formulas directly from input values.)

FIGURE 6.29   Decision Tree for Medical Insurance Example

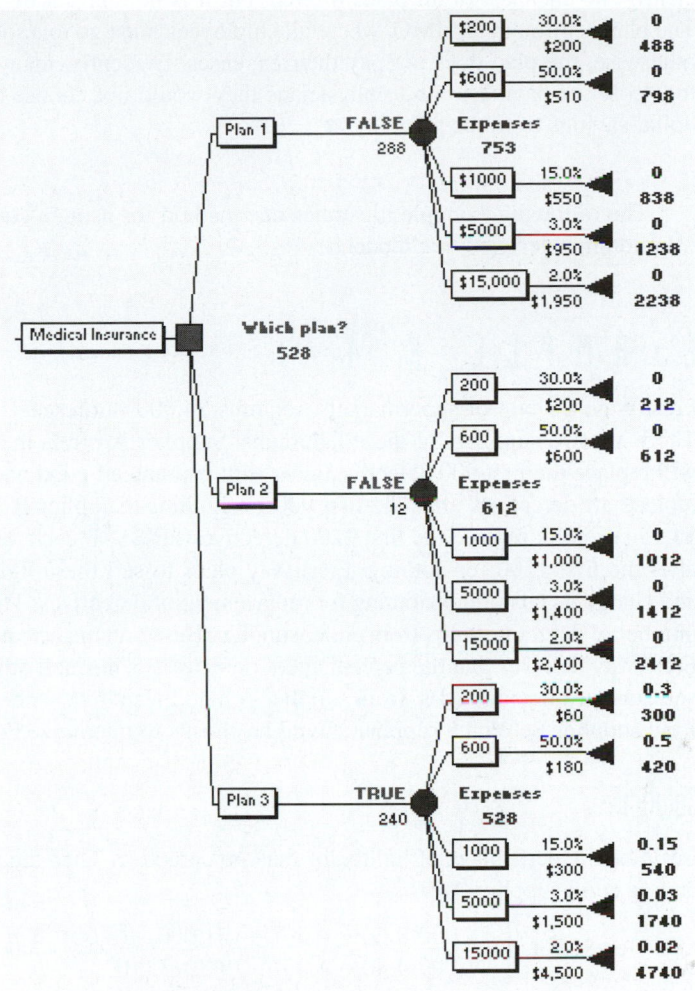

4   Minimize costs. If we quit here, we would mistakenly choose the *worst* of the three plans. This is because PrecisionTree *maximizes* EMV by default, and in this problem we want to *minimize* the EMV of the costs. However, this is simple to change. Click on the name box at the far left in the decision tree. This brings up a dialog box (not shown here) where we can select the Minimize option.

As we see from Figure 6.29, the optimal plan is plan 3. Its EMV—an expected *cost*—is $528. The EMVs for plans 1 and 2 are $753 and $612. Evidently, this employee's chances of large medical expenses where plan 3 is at its worst are not large enough to outweigh plan 3's no-deductible benefit. However, we might want to experiment with various inputs, either the properties of the plans or the employee's medical expense distribution, to see whether plan 3 continues to be the preferred plan. For example, if the probabilities in Table 6.12 change to 0.30, 0.40, 0.15, 0.10, and 0.05, so that large expenses are much more probable, the EMVs for the three plans become $827, $722, and $750. Now plan 2 is preferred, although the difference in EMV between plans 2 and 3 is quite small.

We can use this insurance example to illustrate one *nonmonetary* aspect of decision problems that is difficult to incorporate into a decision tree. At the university where we teach, there is another insurance plan in addition to the types in the example. Its premiums are low, and there are *no* copayments—the insurer pays all medical expenses. This plan is clearly the cheapest of all plans offered, but it is not chosen by many employees. Why? The plan is through an HMO, where all employees must go to a specified set of physicians; otherwise, the plan does not pay their expenses. Evidently, many employees believe that the "cost" of having to go to physicians they would not choose otherwise outweighs the dollar savings from the plan. ∎

The following example illustrates one method for using a *continuous* probability distribution in a decision tree model.

EXAMPLE 6.4

FreshWay, a chain of supermarkets, requires 24,000 fluorescent lightbulbs for its stores. There are two suppliers of these lightbulbs. Supplier A offers them at $4.00 per bulb and will replace the first 900 defective bulbs with guaranteed good ones for $3.00 each. It will replace all defectives after the first 900 for nothing. Supplier B is similar. It will charge $4.15 per bulb, replace the first 1200 defectives for $1.00 each, and replace all defectives after the first 1200 for nothing. FreshWay plans to sell these lightbulbs for $4.40 apiece and charge its customers nothing for replacement of defectives. The only uncertainty is the number of defective bulbs from either supplier. Based on historical data from each supplier, FreshWay believes that the percentage of defectives is normally distributed with mean 4% and standard deviation 1% from supplier A, and mean 4.2% and standard deviation 1.2% from supplier B. Which supplier should be chosen to maximize FreshWay's EMV?

Solution

Let p be the percentage of lightbulbs that are defective. Then the profit to FreshWay from buying from supplier A is

$$\text{Profit} = \begin{cases} 24{,}000(4.40 - 4.00) - (24{,}000p)(3.00) & \text{if } p \leq 900/24{,}000 \\ 24{,}000(4.40 - 4.00) - (900)(3.00) & \text{if } p > 900/24{,}000 \end{cases}$$

A similar expression holds for supplier B. The only random quantity in this expression is p, which is normally distributed. The question is how we can model the *continuous* distribution of p in a *discrete* decision tree—that is, a tree with a discrete number of probability branches. The method usually used is to approximate the continuous normal distribution by a discrete distribution with a relatively small, say 5, number of equally likely values.

The idea is to divide the normal distribution into an equal number of equal probability regions and take the midpoint (in a probability sense) of each region as a value for the decision tree. For example, if we use five points, then each region has probability 0.2. The probability halfway between 0 and 0.2 is 0.1, so the first point on the tree is the 10th percentile of the normal distribution. Similarly, the next point is the 30th percentile, the next is the 50th, the next is the 70th, and the last is the 90th.

Figure 6.30 illustrates the calculations. (See the file LIGHTBULB.XLS.) Through row 13 we enter the given inputs for the problem. Then in rows 17–26 we enter the information we'll use in the decision tree regarding the percentage defective for each supplier. This information is based on the five-point approximation to the normal distribution. For example, the 10th percentile of the normal distribution for supplier A is found in cell C17 with the formula

=NORMINV(B17,$B$12,$C$12)

and this is copied down to cell C21. Then the cost to FreshWay from defectives, assuming the value in C17 is the percentage of defectives, is calculated in cell D17 with the formula

$$=\$C\$7*IF(C17<=\$D\$7/Quantity,Quantity*C17,\$D\$7)$$

and it is copied down to cell D21. Similar formulas are used for supplier B.

It is then straightforward to construct the decision tree shown in Figure 6.31 (page 294). We have entered the revenue from selling the bulbs and the cost of purchasing them in cells B33 and B47. For example, the formula in cell B33 is

$$=Quantity*(SellingPrice-B7)$$

Then we have linked the monetary values below the probability branches to the relevant cells in the D17:D26 range.

The EMVs for suppliers A and B are $7088 and $5027, so supplier A is the clear choice. Evidently, the higher price charged by supplier B and its slightly higher mean percentage of defects outweigh its better deal on replacing defectives. Of course, if supplier B really wants to get FreshWay's business, it could attempt to sweeten its deal in a number of ways. Sensitivity analysis is useful to see how the EMV for supplier B (in cell C47) is affected by the various input parameters. We tried this, varying the inputs in cells B8, C8, D8, and B13 by PrecisionTree's default values (10% in either direction) and keeping track of the change in the EMV for supplier B. The tornado chart in Figure 6.32 makes it very clear that the most important input is the unit purchase cost. The effects of the other three inputs are practically negligible in comparison. If supplier B wants FreshWay's business, it will have to lower its unit purchase cost.

FIGURE 6.30 **Inputs and Calculations for Lightbulb Example**

	A	B	C	D
1	FreshWay lightbulb purchasing example			
2			Range names	
3	Quantity	24000	Quantity: B3	
4	Selling price	$4.40	SellingPrice: B4	
5				
6		UnitCost	ReplaceCost	Charge for first:
7	Supplier A	$4.00	$3.00	900
8	Supplier B	$4.15	$1.00	1200
9				
10	Distribution of percent defective: normal			
11		Mean	Stdev	
12	Supplier A	4.0%	1.0%	
13	Supplier B	4.2%	1.2%	
14				
15	Percentages to use on decision tree			
16		Midpoint probability	Percentile	FreshWay's cost
17	Supplier A	0.1	2.72%	$1,957.28
18		0.3	3.48%	$2,502.43
19		0.5	4.00%	$2,700.00
20		0.7	4.52%	$2,700.00
21		0.9	5.28%	$2,700.00
22	Supplier B	0.1	2.66%	$638.91
23		0.3	3.57%	$856.97
24		0.5	4.20%	$1,008.00
25		0.7	4.83%	$1,159.03
26		0.9	5.74%	$1,200.00

FIGURE 6.31 **Decision Tree for Lightbulb Example**

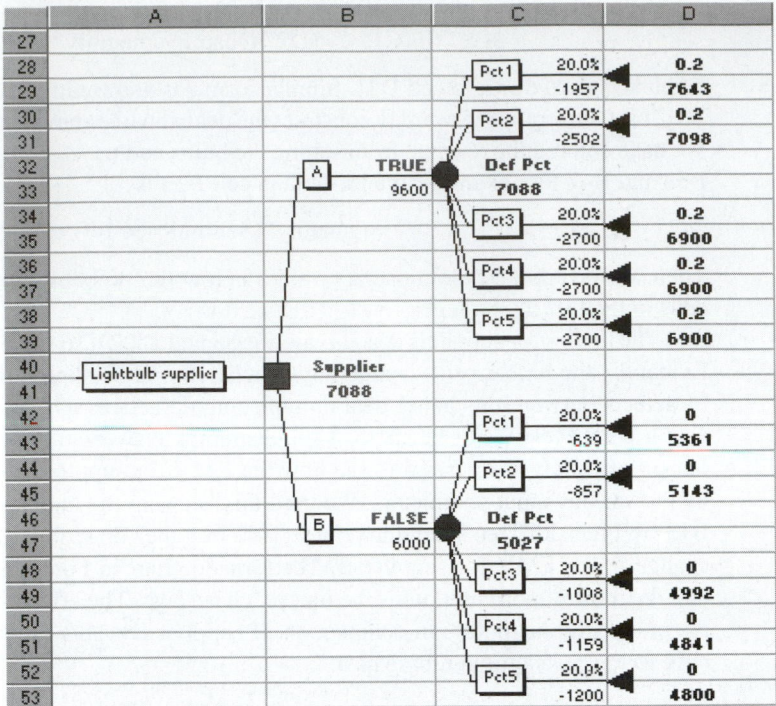

FIGURE 6.32 **Tornado Chart to Analyze the EMV for Supplier B**

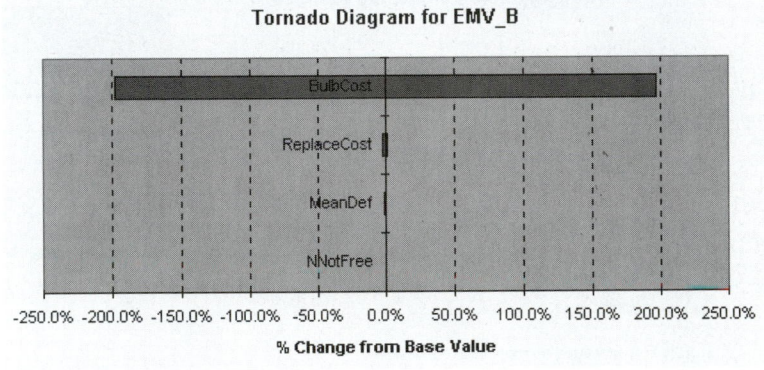

Modeling Issue The discrete approximation used in Example 6.4 can be used in *any* decision tree with continuous probability distributions, regardless of whether they are normal. We first need to decide how many values to have in the discrete approximation. The usual choices are 5 or 3. (Surprisingly, a three-point approximation does an adequate job in many situations.) Then we need to use the "inverse" function—in the previous example it was the NORMINV function—to find the values to use in the decision tree. The appropriate inverse function is available in Excel for a number of widely used continuous distributions.

PROBLEMS

Level A

28   Each day the manager of a local bookstore must decide how many copies of the community newspaper to order for sale in her shop. She pays the newspaper's publisher $0.40 for each copy and sells the newspapers to local residents for $0.50 each. Newspapers that are unsold at the end of day are considered worthless. The probability distribution of the number of copies of the newspaper purchased daily at her shop is provided in Table 6.14. Employ a decision tree to find the book store manager's profit-maximizing daily order quantity.

TABLE 6.14   **Distribution of Daily Local Newspaper Demand**

Daily Demand for Local Newspaper	Probability
10	0.10
11	0.15
12	0.30
13	0.20
14	0.15
15	0.10

29   Two construction companies are bidding against one another for the right to construct a new community center building in Lewisburg, Pennsylvania. The first construction company, Fine Line Homes, believes that its competitor, Buffalo Valley Construction, will place a bid for this project according to the distribution shown in Table 6.15. Furthermore, Fine Line Homes estimates that it will cost $160,000 for its own company to construct this building. Given its fine reputation and long-standing service within the local community, Fine Line Homes believes that it will likely be awarded the project in the event that it and Buffalo Valley Construction submit exactly the same bids. Employ a decision tree to identify Fine Line Homes' profit-maximizing bid for the new community center building.

TABLE 6.15   **Distribution of Possible Competing Bids for Construction Project**

Buffalo Valley Construction's Bid	Probability
$160,000	0.40
$165,000	0.30
$170,000	0.20
$175,000	0.10

30   Suppose that you have sued your employer for damages suffered when you recently slipped and fell on an icy surface that should have been treated by your company's physical plant department. Specifically, your injury resulting from this accident was sufficiently serious that you, in consultation with your attorney, decided to sue your company for $500,000. Your company's insurance provider has offered to settle this suit with you out of court. If you decide to reject the settlement and go to court, your attorney is confident that you will win the case but is uncertain about the amount the court will award you in damages. He has provided his assessment of the probability distribution of the court's award to you in Table 6.16 (page 286). Let S be the insurance provider's proposed out-of-court settlement (in dollars). For which values of S will you decide to accept the settlement? For which values of S will you choose to take your chances in court? Of course, you are seeking to maximize the expected payoff from this litigation.

31   Suppose that one of your colleagues has $2000 available to invest. Assume that all of this money must be placed in one of three investments: a particular money market fund, a certain stock, or gold. Each dollar your colleague invests in the money market fund earns a virtually guaranteed 12% annual return. Each dollar he invests in the stock earns an annual return characterized by the probability distribution provided in Table 6.17. Finally, each dollar he invests in gold earns an annual return characterized by the probability distribution given in Table 6.18.

TABLE 6.16 **Distribution of Possible Court Award Amounts**

Amount of Court Award	Probability
$0	0.025
$50,000	0.075
$100,000	0.10
$200,000	0.125
$300,000	0.175
$400,000	0.20
$500,000	0.30

TABLE 6.17 **Distribution of Annual Returns for Given Stock**

Annual Returns for Given Stock	Probability
0%	0.10
6%	0.20
12%	0.40
18%	0.20
24%	0.10

TABLE 6.18 **Distribution of Annual Returns for Gold**

Annual Returns for Gold	Probability
−36%	0.10
−12%	0.20
12%	0.40
36%	0.20
60%	0.10

a If your colleague must place all of his available funds in a single investment, which investment should he choose to maximize his expected earnings over the next year?

b Suppose now that your colleague can place all of his available funds in one of these three investments as before, or he can invest $1000 in one alternative and $1000 in another. Assuming that he seeks to maximize his expected total earnings in 1 year, how should he allocate his $2000?

Level B

32 A home appliance company is interested in marketing an innovative new product. The company must decide whether to manufacture this product essentially on its own or employ a subcontractor to manufacture it. Table 6.19 contains the estimated probability distribution of the cost of manufacturing one unit of this new product (in dollars) under the alternative that the home appliance company produces the item on its own. Table 6.20 contains the estimated probability distribution of the cost of purchasing one unit of this new product (in dollars) under the alternative that the home appliance company commissions a subcontractor to produce the item.

a Assuming that the home appliance company seeks to minimize the expected unit cost of manufacturing or buying the new product, should the company make the new product or buy it from a subcontractor?

TABLE 6.19 Distribution of Unit Production Cost under "Make" Alternative

Cost Per Unit	Probability
$50	0.20
$53	0.25
$55	0.30
$57	0.20
$59	0.05

TABLE 6.20 Distribution of Unit Production Cost under "Buy" Alternative

Cost Per Unit	Probability
$50	0.10
$53	0.20
$55	0.40
$57	0.20
$59	0.10

b Perform sensitivity analysis on the optimal expected cost. Under what conditions, if any, would the home appliance company select an alternative different from the one you identified in part **a**?

33 A grapefruit farmer in central Florida is trying to decide whether to take protective action to limit damage to his crop in the event that the overnight temperature falls to a level well below freezing. He is concerned that if the temperature falls sufficiently low and he fails to make an effort to protect his grapefruit trees, he runs the risk of losing his entire crop, which is worth approximately $75,000. Based on the latest forecast issued by the National Weather Service, the farmer estimates that there is a 60% that he will lose his entire crop if it is left unprotected. Alternatively, the farmer can insulate his fruit by spraying water on all of the trees in his orchards. This action, which would likely cost the farmer C dollars, would prevent total devastation but might not completely protect the grapefruit trees from incurring some damage as a result of the unusually cold overnight temperatures. Table 6.21 contains the assessed distribution of possible damages (in dollars) to the insulated fruit in light of the cold weather forecast. Of course, this farmer seeks to minimize the expected total cost of coping with the threatening weather.

TABLE 6.21 Distribution of Damages to Insulated Grapefruit Crop

Damage to Grapefruit Crop	Probability
$0	0.30
$5000	0.15
$10,000	0.10
$15,000	0.15
$20,000	0.30

a Find the maximum value of C below which the farmer will choose to insulate his crop in hopes of limiting damage as result of the unusually cold weather.

b Set C equal to the value identified in part **a**. Perform sensitivity analysis to determine under what conditions, if any, the farmer might be better off not spraying his grapefruit trees and taking his chances in spite of the threat to his crop.

34 Consider again the department store buyer's decision problem described in Problem 6. Assume now that consumer demand for the new tennis shoe model (in hundreds of pairs) during the upcoming summer season is *normally* distributed with mean 6 and standard deviation 1.5.

a Formulate a payoff table that specifies the contribution to profit (in dollars) from the sale of the tennis shoes by this department store chain for each possible purchase decision (in hundreds of pairs) and each outcome with respect to consumer demand. Use an appropriate discrete approximation of the given normal demand distribution.

b Construct a decision tree to identify the buyer's course of action that maximizes the expected profit (in dollars) earned by the department store chain from the purchase and subsequent sale of tennis shoes in the coming year.

35 Consider again the purchasing agent's decision problem described in Problem 9. Assume now that the proportion of defective components supplied by this supplier is well described by the *triangular* distribution with parameters 0, 0, and 1. (This is called the **right triangular** distribution with range 1.)

a Formulate a payoff table that specifies the microcomputer manufacturer's total cost (in dollars) of purchasing and repairing (if necessary) a complete lot of components for each possible decision and each outcome with respect to the proportion of defective items. Use an appropriate discrete approximation of the given triangular distribution for the proportion of defective items.

b Construct a decision tree to identify the purchasing agent's course of action that minimizes the expected total cost (in dollars) of achieving a complete lot of satisfactory components.

36 A retired partner from Goldman Sachs has 1 million dollars available to invest in particular stocks or bonds. Each investment's annual rate of return depends on the state of the economy in the forthcoming year. Table 6.22 contains the distribution of returns for these stocks and bonds as a function of the economy's state in the coming year. This investor wants to allocate her \$1 million to maximize her expected total return 1 year from now.

TABLE 6.22 **Distribution of Annual Returns for Given Stocks and Bonds**

State of the Economy	Probability	Annual Returns for Given Stocks	Annual Returns for Given Bonds
Very strong	0.20	25%	20%
Moderately strong	0.40	20%	17.5%
Fair	0.25	$X\%$	$Y\%$
Moderately weak	0.10	10%	12.5%
Very weak	0.05	5%	10%

a If $X = Y = 15\%$, find the optimal investment strategy for this investor.

b For which values of X (where $10\% < X < 20\%$) and Y (where $12.5\% < Y < 17.5\%$), if any, will this investor prefer to place all of her available funds in the given stocks to maximize her expected total return 1 year from now?

c For which values of X (where $10\% < X < 20\%$) and Y (where $12.5\% < Y < 17.5\%$), if any, will this investor prefer to place all of her available funds in the given bonds to maximize her expected total return one year from now? ■

6.6

Multistage Decision Problems

S o far, all of the examples have required a single decision. We now examine a problem where the decision maker must make at least two decisions that are separated in time, such as when a company must decide whether to buy information that will help it make a second decision. The following example illustrates the typical situation.

EXAMPLE 6.5

The Acme Company is trying to decide whether to market a new product. As in many new-product situations, there is considerable uncertainty about whether the new product will eventually "catch on." Acme believes that it might be prudent to introduce the product in a regional test market before introducing it nationally. Therefore, the company's first decision is whether to conduct the test market. Acme estimates that the fixed cost of the test market is $3 million. If it decides to conduct the test market, it must then wait for the results. Based on the results of the test market, it can then decide whether to market the product nationally, in which case it will incur a fixed cost of $90 million. On the other hand, if the original decision is *not* to run a test market, then the final decision—whether to market the product nationally—can be made without further delay. Acme's unit margin, the difference between its selling price and its unit variable cost, is $18 (in the test market and in the national market).

Acme classifies the results in either the test market or the national market as great, fair, or awful. Each of these is accompanied by a forecast of total units sold. These sales volumes (in 1000s of units) are 200, 100, and 30 for the test market and 6000, 3000, and 900 for the national market. Based on previous test markets for similar products, Acme estimates that probabilities of the three test market outcomes are 0.3, 0.6, and 0.1. Then, based on historical data from previous products that were test marketed and eventually marketed nationally, it assesses the probabilities of the national market outcomes given each possible test market outcome. If the test market is great, the probabilities for the national market outcomes are 0.8, 0.15, and 0.05. If the test market is fair, these probabilities are 0.3, 0.5, and 0.2. If the test market is awful, they are 0.05, 0.25, and 0.7. (Note how the probabilities of the national market outcomes tend to mirror the test market outcomes.)

The company wants to use a decision tree approach to find the best strategy.

Solution

We begin by discussing the three basic elements of this decision problem: the possible strategies, the possible outcomes and their probabilities, and the value model. The possible strategies are clear. Acme must first decide whether to conduct a test market. Then it must decide whether to introduce the product nationally. However, it is important to realize that if Acme decides to conduct a test market, it can base the national market decision on the results of the test market. In this case its final strategy will be a **contingency plan**, where it conducts the test market, then introduces the product nationally if it receives sufficiently positive test market results and abandons the product if it receives sufficiently negative test market results. The optimal strategies from many multistage decision problems involve similar contingency plans.

Regarding the uncertain outcomes and their probabilities, we note that the given probabilities—probabilities of test market outcomes and *conditional* probabilities of national market outcomes given test market outcomes—are exactly the ones we need in the decision tree. This is because the test market outcome is known *before* the national market outcome will occur. However, suppose Acme decides not to run a test market and then decides to market nationally. Then what are the probabilities of the national market outcomes?

It is important to realize that we cannot simply assess three *new* probabilities for this situation. These probabilities are *implied* by the given probabilities. This follows from the rules of conditional probability. If we let T_1, T_2, and T_3 be the test market outcomes, and N be any of the national market outcomes, then by the addition rule for probability and the conditional probability formula,

$$P(N) = P(N \text{ and } T_1) + P(N \text{ and } T_2) + P(N \text{ and } T_3) \tag{6.1}$$

$$= P(N|T_1)P(T_1) + P(N|T_2)P(T_2) + P(N|T_3)P(T_3) \tag{6.2}$$

(This is sometimes called the **law of total probability**.) For example, if N_1 represents a great national market, then from equation (6.1),

$$P(N_1) = (0.8)(0.3) + (0.3)(0.6) + (0.05)(0.1) = 0.425$$

Similarly, we find that $P(N_2) = 0.37$ and $P(N_3) = 0.205$. These are the probabilities we need to use for the probability branches when no test market is used.

Finally, the monetary values in the tree are straightforward. There are fixed costs of test marketing or marketing nationally, and these are incurred as soon as these "go ahead" decisions are made. From that point, we observe the sales volumes and multiply them by the unit margin to obtain the profits.

The inputs for the decision tree appear in Figure 6.33. (See the file ACME.XLS.) The only calculated values in this part of the spreadsheet are in row 28, which follow from equation (6.1). Specifically, the formula in cell B28 is

$$=\text{SUMPRODUCT(B22:B24,\$B\$16:\$B\$18)}$$

which is copied across row 28. The tree is then straightforward to build and label, as shown in Figure 6.34. Note how the fixed costs of test marketing and marketing nationally appear on the decision branches where they occur, so that only the selling profits need to be placed on the probability branches. Also, the probabilities on the various probability branches are exactly those listed in Figure 6.33.

FIGURE 6.33 Inputs for Acme Marketing Example

	A	B	C	D
1	**Acme marketing example**			
2				
3	Fixed costs ($1000s)		Range names:	
4	Test mkt	$3,000	NatlMktCost: B5	
5	National mkt	$90,000	TestMktCost: B4	
6			UnitMargin: B18	
7	Unit margin	$18		
8				
9	Possible quantities sold (1000s)			
10		Test mkt	Natl mkt	
11	Great	200	6000	
12	Fair	100	3000	
13	Awful	30	900	
14				
15	Probabilities of test outcomes			
16	Great	0.30		
17	Fair	0.60		
18	Awful	0.10		
19				
20	Probabilities of test mkt outcomes, given natl mkt outcomes			
21		Natl great	Natl fair	Natl awful
22	Test great	0.80	0.15	0.05
23	Test fair	0.30	0.50	0.20
24	Test awful	0.05	0.25	0.70
25				
26	Probabilities of natl mkt outcomes without test mkt (calculated from above inputs)			
27		Natl great	Natl fair	Natl awful
28		0.425	0.370	0.205

The interpretation of this tree is fairly straightforward if we realize that each value just below each node name is an EMV. For example, the 807 in cell B43 is the EMV for the entire decision problem. It means that Acme's best EMV is $807,000. As another example, the 5910 in cell D47 means that if Acme ever gets to that point—the test market has been conducted and it has been great—the EMV for ACME is $5,910,000. Each of these EMVs

FIGURE 6.34   **Decision Tree for Acme Marketing Example**

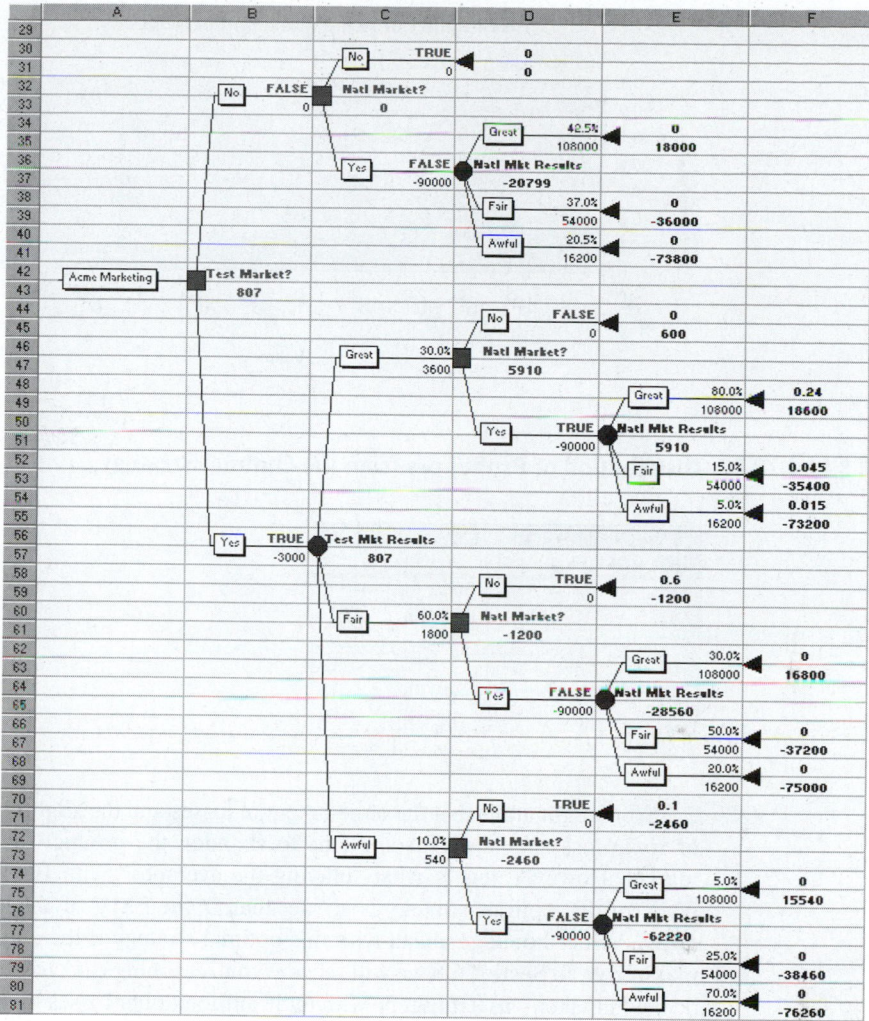

has been calculated by the folding-back procedure we discussed earlier, starting from the right and working back toward the left. PrecisionTree takes EMVs at probability nodes and maximums at decision nodes.

We can also see Acme's optimal strategy by following the "TRUE" branches from left to right. Acme should first run a test market. If the test market results are great, then the product should be marketed nationally. However, if the test market results are only fair or awful, the product should be abandoned. In these cases the prospects from a national market look bleak, so Acme should cut its losses. (And there *are* losses. In these latter two cases, Acme has spent $3,000,000 on the test market and has recouped only $1,800,000 or $540,000 on test market sales.)

The risk profile from the optimal strategy appears in Figure 6.35 (page 292). It is based on the data in Figure 6.36. (These were obtained by clicking on PrecisionTree's "staircase" button and selecting the Statistics and Risk Profile options.) We see that there is a small chance of two possible large losses (approximately $73 million and $35 million), there is a 70% chance of a moderate loss of about $1 or $2 million, and there is a 24% chance of an $18.6 million profit. Of course, the net effect is an EMV of $807,000.

FIGURE 6.35   Risk Profile of Optimal Strategy

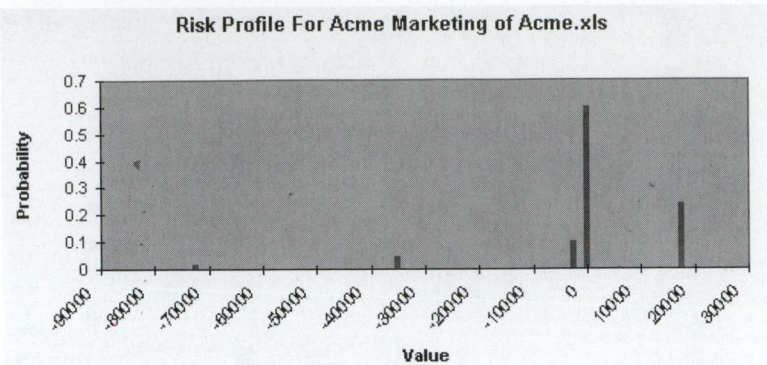

FIGURE 6.36   Distribution of Profit/Loss from the Optimal Strategy

	A	B	C
16	PROFILE:		
17	#	X	P
18	1	-73200	0.015
19	2	-35400	0.045
20	3	-2460	0.1
21	4	-1200	0.6
22	5	18600	0.24

You might argue that the large potential losses and the slightly higher than 70% chance of *some* loss should persuade Acme to abandon the product right away—without a test market. However, this is what "playing the averages" with EMV is all about. Since the EMV of this optimal strategy is greater than 0, the EMV of abandoning the product right away, Acme should go ahead with this optimal strategy if the company is indeed an EMV maximizer. In Section 6.8 we will see how this reasoning can change if Acme is a risk-averse decision maker—as it might be with multimillion dollar losses looming in the future!   ■

6.6.1 Expected Value of Sample Information

The role of the test market in the Acme marketing example is to provide information in the form of more accurate probabilities of national market results. Information usually costs something, as it does in Acme's problem. Currently, the fixed cost of the test market is $3 million, which is evidently not too much to pay because Acme's best strategy is to conduct the test market. However, we might ask how much this test market is worth. This is easy to answer. From the decision tree in Figure 6.34, we see that the EMV from test marketing is $807,000 better than the decision *not* to test market (and then abandon the product). Therefore, if the fixed cost of test marketing were any more than $807,000 above its current value, Acme would be better not to run a test market. Equivalently, the most Acme would be willing to pay for the test market (as a fixed cost) is $3.807 million.

This value is called the **expected value of sample information**, or **EVSI**. In general, we can write the following expression for EVSI:

$$\text{EVSI} = \text{EMV with } \textit{free} \text{ information} - \text{EMV without information}$$

In Acme's problem, the EMV with free information is $3.807 million (just don't charge for the test market fixed cost), and the EMV without any test market information is $0 (because Acme abandons the product when there is no test market available). Therefore,

$$\text{EVSI} = \$3.807 - \$0 = \$3.807 \text{ million}$$

6.6.2 Expected Value of Perfect Information

The reason for the term *sample* is that the information does not remove all uncertainty about the future. That is, even after the test market results are in, there is still uncertainty about the national market results. Therefore, we might go one step further and ask how much *perfect* information is worth. We can imagine perfect information as an envelope that contains the true final outcome (of the national market). That is, either "the national market will be great," "the national market will be fair," or "the national market will be awful" is written inside the envelope. Admittedly, no such envelope exists, but if it did, how much would Acme be willing to pay for it?

We can answer this question with the simple decision tree in Figure 6.37. Now the probability node on the left corresponds to opening the envelope. Its probabilities are the same as before (when there is no test market available). Note the reasoning here. Acme doesn't know what the contents of the envelope will be, so we need a probability node. However, once the envelope is opened, the true national market outcome will be revealed. At that point Acme's decision is fairly obvious. If it learns that a national market will be great, it knows the product will be profitable and will market it. Otherwise, if it learns that the national market will be fair or poor, it knows that there will be a loss from marketing nationally, so it will abandon the product. Folding back in the usual way produces an EMV of $7.65 million.

FIGURE 6.37 **EVPI for Acme Marketing Example**

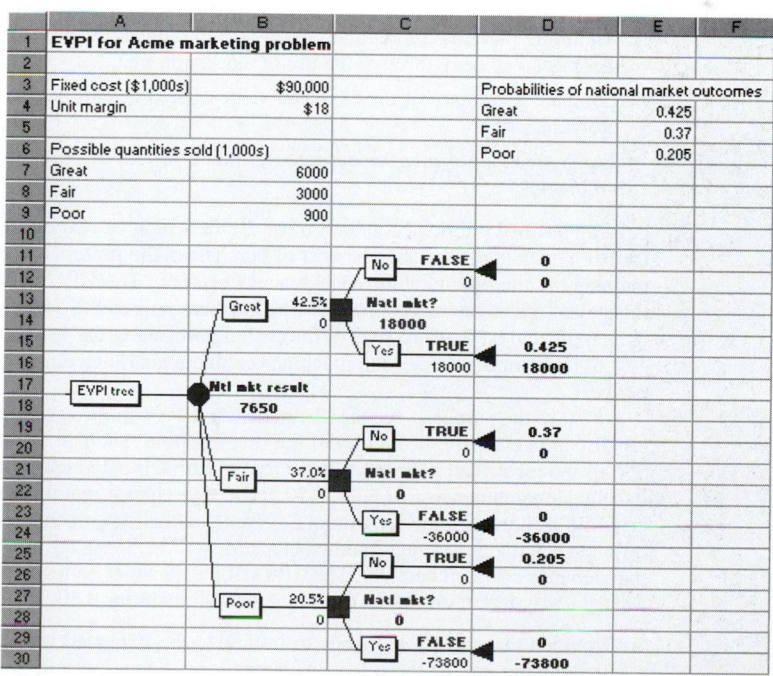

Now compare this $7.65 million with the EMV in the top part of Figure 6.34 that results from no test market, namely, $0. The difference, $7.65 million, is called the **expected value of perfect information**, or **EVPI**. It represents the maximum amount the company would pay for perfect information about the final outcome (of the national market). In general, the expression for EVPI is

$$\text{EVPI} = \text{EMV with } \textit{free} \text{ perfect information} - \text{EMV with no information}$$

In Acme's case this expression becomes

$$\text{EVPI} = \$7.65 - \$0 = \$7.65 \text{ million}$$

The EVPI may appear to be an irrelevant concept since perfect information is almost never available—at *any* price. However, it is often useful because it represents an *upper bound* on the EVSI for any potential sample information. That is, no sample information can ever be worth more than the EVPI. For example, if Acme is contemplating an expensive test market with an anticipated fixed cost of more than $8 million, then there is really no point in pursuing it any further. The information gained from this test market, no matter how reliable it is, cannot possibly justify its cost because its cost is greater than the EVPI.

PROBLEMS

Level A

37 The senior executives of an oil company are trying to decide whether to drill for oil in a particular field in the Gulf of Mexico. It costs the company $300,000 to drill in the selected field. Company executives believe that if oil is found in this field its estimated value will be $1,800,000. At present, this oil company believes that there is a 50% chance that the selected field actually contains oil. Before drilling, the company can hire a geologist at a cost of $30,000 to prepare a report that contains a recommendation regarding drilling in the selected field. There is a 55% chance that the geologist will issue a favorable recommendation and a 45% chance that the geologist will issue an unfavorable recommendation. Given a favorable recommendation from the geologist, there is a 75% chance that the field actually contains oil. Given an unfavorable recommendation from the geologist, there is a 15% chance that the field actually contains oil.

a Assuming that this oil company wishes to maximize its expected net earnings, determine its optimal strategy through the use of a decision tree.

b Compute and interpret the expected value of sample information (EVSI) in this decision problem.

c Compute and interpret the expected value of perfect information (EVPI) in this decision problem.

38 A local certified public accountant must decide which of two copying machines to purchase for her expanding business. The cost of purchasing the first machine is $4500, and the cost of maintaining the first machine each year is uncertain. The CPA's office manager believes that the annual maintenance cost for the first machine will be $0, $150, or $300 with probabilities 0.35, 0.35, and 0.30, respectively. The cost of purchasing the second machine is $3000, and the cost of maintaining the second machine through a guaranteed maintenance agreement is $225 per year.
   Before the purchase decision is made, the CPA can hire an experienced copying machine repairman to evaluate the quality of the first machine. Such an evaluation would cost the CPA $60. If the repairman believes that the first machine is satisfactory, there is a 65% chance that its annual maintenance cost will be $0 and a 35% chance that its annual maintenance cost will be $150. If, however, the repairman believes that the first machine is unsatisfactory, there is a 60% chance that its annual maintenance cost will be $150 and a 40% chance that its annual maintenance cost will be $300. The CPA's office manager believes that the repairman will issue a satisfactory report on the first machine with probability 0.50.

a Provided that the CPA wishes to minimize the expected total cost of purchasing and maintaining one of these two machines for a 1-year period, which machine should she purchase? When, if ever, would it be worthwhile for the CPA to obtain the repairman's review of the first machine?

b Compute and interpret the expected value of sample information (EVSI) in this decision problem.

c Compute and interpret the expected value of perfect information (EVPI) in this decision problem.

39 Upjohn is developing a new product to promote hair growth in cases of male pattern baldness. If Upjohn markets the new product and it is successful, the company will earn $500,000 in additional profit. If the marketing of this new product proves to be unsuccessful, the company will lose $350,000 in development and marketing costs. In the past, similar products have been successful 60% of the time. At a cost of $50,000, the effectiveness of the new restoration product can be thoroughly tested. If the results of such testing are favorable, there is an 80% chance that the marketing efforts of this new product will be successful. If the results of such testing are not favorable, there is a mere 30% chance that the marketing efforts of this new product will be successful. Upjohn currently believes that the probability of receiving favorable test results is 0.60.

a Identify the strategy that maximizes Upjohn's expected net earnings in this situation.

b Compute and interpret the expected value of sample information (EVSI) in this decision problem.

c Compute and interpret the expected value of perfect information (EVPI) in this decision problem.

40 Hank is considering placing a bet on the upcoming showdown between the Penn State and Michigan football teams in State College. The winner of this contest will represent the Big Ten Conference in the Rose Bowl on New Year's Day. Without any additional information, Hank believes that each team has an equal chance of winning this big game. If he wins the bet, he will win $500; if he loses the bet, he will lose $550. Before placing his bet, he may decide to pay his friend Al, who happens to be a football sportswriter for the *Philadelphia Enquirer*, $50 for Al's expert prediction on the game. Assume that Al predicts that Penn State will win similar games 55% of the time, and that Michigan will win similar games 45% of the time. Furthermore, Hank knows that when Al predicts that Penn State will win, there is a 70% chance that Penn State will indeed win the football game. Finally, when Al predicts that Michigan will win, there is a 20% chance that Penn State will proceed to win the upcoming game.

a To maximize his expected profit from this betting opportunity, how should Hank proceed in this situation?

b Compute and interpret the expected value of sample information (EVSI) in this decision problem.

c Compute and interpret the expected value of perfect information (EVPI) in this decision problem.

41 A product manager at Procter & Gamble seeks to determine whether her company should market a new brand of toothpaste. If this new product succeeds in the marketplace, P&G estimates that it could earn $1,800,000 in future profits from the sale of the new toothpaste. If this new product fails, however, the company expects that it could lose approximately $750,000. If P&G chooses not to market this new brand, the product manager believes that there would be little, if any, impact on the profits earned through sales of P&G's other products. The manager has estimated that the new toothpaste brand will succeed with probability 0.55. Before making her decision regarding this toothpaste product, the manager can spend $75,000 on a market research study. Such a study of consumer preferences will yield either a positive recommendation with probability 0.50 or a negative recommendation with probability 0.50. Given a positive recommendation to market the new product, the new brand will eventually succeed in the marketplace with probability 0.75. Given a negative recommendation regarding the marketing of the new product, the new brand will eventually succeed in the marketplace with probability 0.25.

a To maximize expected profit in this case, what course of action should the P&G product manager take?

b Compute and interpret the expected value of sample information (EVSI) in this decision problem.

c Compute and interpret the expected value of perfect information (EVPI) in this decision problem.

42 A publishing company is trying to decide whether to publish a new business law textbook. Based on a careful reading of the latest draft of the manuscript, the publisher's senior editor in the business textbook division assesses the distribution of possible payoffs earned by publishing this new book. Table 6.23 contains this probability distribution. Before making a final decision regarding the publication of the book, the editor may learn more about the text's potential for success by thoroughly surveying business law instructors teaching at universities across the country. Historical frequencies based on similar surveys administered in the past are provided in Table 6.24.

TABLE 6.23 **Distribution of Payoffs for New Business Law Textbook**

Textbook Performance	Probability	Estimated Payoff (if published)
Very strong	0.20	$100,000
Moderately strong	0.20	$50,000
Fair	0.20	$0
Poor	0.40	−$50,000

TABLE 6.24 **Historical Frequencies of Combinations of Past Survey Results and Actual Outcomes**

Survey Indication/Actual Performance	Very Strong	Moderately Strong	Fair	Poor
Very strong	13	12	2	3
Moderately strong	10	20	6	4
Fair	5	12	15	8
Poor	1	3	9	22

a Find the strategy that maximizes the publisher's expected payoff (in dollars).

b What is the most (in dollars) that the publisher should be willing to pay to conduct a new survey of business law instructors?

c If the actual cost of conducting the given survey is less than the amount identified in part **a**, what should the publisher do?

d Assuming that a survey could be constructed that provides "perfect information" to the publisher, how much should the company be willing to pay to acquire and implement such a survey?

43 Land's End Direct Merchants is trying to decide whether to ship some customer orders now via UPS or wait until after the threat of another UPS strike is over. If Land's End decides to ship the requested merchandise now and the UPS strike takes place, the company will incur $60,000 in delay and shipping costs. If Land's End decides to ship the customer orders via UPS and no strike occurs, the company will incur $4000 in shipping costs. If Land's End decides to postpone shipping its customer orders via UPS, the company will incur $10,000 in delay costs regardless of whether or not UPS goes on strike. Let p represent the probability that UPS will go on strike and affect Land End's shipments.

a For which values of p, if any, does Land's End minimize its expected total cost by choosing to postpone shipping its customer orders via UPS?

b Suppose now that at a cost of $1000, Land's End can purchase information regarding the likelihood of a UPS strike in the near future. Based on similar strike threats in the past, the probability that this information indicates the occurrence of a UPS strike is 27.5%. If the purchased information indicates the occurrence of a UPS strike, the chance of a strike actually occurring is 0.105/0.275. If the purchased information does not indicate the occurrence of a UPS strike, the chance of a strike actually occurring is 0.680/0.725. Provided that $p = 0.15$, what strategy should Land's End pursue to minimize their expected total cost?

c Continuing part **b**, compute and interpret the expected value of sample information (EVSI) when $p = 0.15$.

d Continuing part **b**, compute and interpret the expected value of perfect information (EVPI) when $p = 0.15$. ■

Bayes' Rule

In multistage decision problems we typically have alternating sets of decision nodes and probability nodes. The decision maker makes a decision, some uncertain outcomes are observed, the decision maker makes another decision, more uncertain outcomes are observed, and so on. In the resulting decision tree, all probability branches at the *right* of the tree are conditional on outcomes that have occurred earlier, to their left. Therefore, the probabilities on these branches are of the form $P(A|B)$, where B is an event that occurs *before* event A in time. However, it is sometimes more natural to assess conditional probabilities in the opposite order, that is, $P(B|A)$. Whenever this is the case, we require **Bayes' rule** to obtain the probabilities we need on the tree. Essentially, Bayes' rule is a mechanism for updating probabilities as new information becomes available. We illustrate the mechanics of Bayes' rule in the following example. [See Feinstein (1990) for a real application of this example.]

E X A M P L E 6 . 6

If an athlete is tested for a certain type of drug usage (steroids, say), then the test will come out either positive or negative. However, these tests are never perfect. Some athletes who are drug free test positive, and some who are drug users test negative. The former are called false positives; the latter are called false negatives. We will assume that 5% of all athletes use drugs, 8% of all tests on drug-free athletes yield false positives, and 3% of all tests on drug users yield false negatives. The question then is what we can conclude from a positive or negative test result.

Solution

Let D and ND denote that a randomly chosen athlete is or is not a drug user, and let $T+$ and $T-$ indicate a positive or negative test result. We are given the following probabilities. First, since 5% of all athletes are drug users, we know that $P(D) = 0.05$ and $P(ND) = 0.95$. These are called **prior probabilities** because they represent the chance that an athlete is or is not a drug user *prior* to the results of a drug test. Second, from the information on drug test accuracy, we know the conditional probabilities $P(T+|ND) = 0.08$ and $P(T-|D) = 0.03$. But a drug-free athlete either tests positive or negative, and the same is true for a drug user. Therefore, we also have the probabilities $P(T-|ND) = 0.92$ and $P(T+|D) = 0.97$. These four conditional probabilities of test results given drug user status are often called the **likelihoods** of the test results.

Given these priors and likelihoods, we want **posterior** probabilities such as $P(D|T+)$, the probability that an athlete who tested positive is a drug user, or $P(ND|T-)$, the probability that an athlete who tested negative is drug free. They are called posterior probabilities because they are assessed *after* the drug test results. This is where Bayes' rule enters. We will develop Bayes' rule in some generality and then apply it to the present example.

Let A be any "information" event, such as the result of a drug test, and let $B_1, B_2, \ldots, B_n$ be any mutually exclusive and exhaustive set of events. That is, exactly one of the B_i's must occur. To apply Bayes' rule, we assume that the prior probabilities $P(B_1), P(B_2), \ldots,$ $P(B_n)$ are given, as are the likelihoods $P(A|B_i)$ for each i. Then we want the posterior probabilities $P(B_i|A)$ for each i. Bayes' rule shows how to find these. For any i, we have

$$P(B_i|A) = \frac{P(A|B_i)P(B_i)}{P(A|B_1)P(B_1) + \cdots + P(A|B_n)P(B_n)} \qquad \textbf{(Bayes' rule)}$$

This formula says that a typical posterior probability is a ratio. The numerator is a likelihood times a prior, and the denominator is the sum of likelihoods times priors.

Before illustrating Bayes' rule numerically, we make two other observations about the terms in Bayes' rule. First, we can use the multiplication rule of probability to write any product of a likelihood and a prior as

$$P(A|B_i)P(B_i) = P(A \text{ and } B_i)$$

The probability on the right, that *both* A and B_i occur, is called a **joint** probability. Second, we can use the definition of conditional probability directly to write

$$P(B_i|A) = \frac{P(A \text{ and } B_i)}{P(A)}$$

Therefore, the probability in the denominator of Bayes' rule is really just the probability of A:

$$P(A) = P(A|B_1)P(B_1) + \cdots + P(A|B_n)P(B_n)$$

As we will see shortly, this natural by-product of Bayes' rule will come in very handy in decision trees.

It is fairly easy to implement Bayes' rule in a spreadsheet, as illustrated in Figure 6.38 for the drug example. Here A corresponds to either test result, and B_1 and B_2 correspond to D and ND. (See the file DRUGBAYES.XLS.[4]) In words, we want to see how the chances of D and ND change after seeing the results of the drug test.

FIGURE 6.38   **Bayes' Rule for Drug Testing Example**

	A	B	C	D
1	**Illustration of Bayes' rule using drug example**			
2				
3	Prior probabilities of drug user status			
4		User	Non-user	
5		0.05	0.95	1
6				
7	Likelihoods of test results, given drug user status			
8		User	Non-user	
9	Test positive	0.92	0.03	
10	Test negative	0.08	0.97	
11		1	1	
12				
13	Joint probabilities of drug user status and test results			
14		User	Non-user	Unconditional
15	Test positive	0.046	0.0285	0.075
16	Test negative	0.004	0.9215	0.926
17				1
18				
19	Posterior probabilities of drug user status			
20		User	Non-user	
21	Test positive	0.617	0.383	1
22	Test negative	0.004	0.996	1

[4]The Bayes2 sheet in this file illustrates how Bayes' rule can be used when there are more than two possible test results and/or drug user categories.

The given priors and likelihoods are listed in the ranges B5:C5 and B9:C10. We then calculate the products of likelihoods and priors in the range B15:C16. The formula in cell B15 is

$$=B\$5*B9$$

and this is copied to the rest of the B15:C16 range. Their row sums are calculated in the range D15:D16. These represent the unconditional probabilities of the two possible results. They are also (as we saw above) the denominators of Bayes' rule. Finally, we calculate the posterior probabilities in the range B21:C22. The formula in cell B21 is

$$=B15/\$D15$$

and this is copied to the rest of the B21:C22 range. The various 1's in the margins of Figure 6.38 are row sums or column sums that must equal 1. We show them only as checks of our logic.

Note that a negative test result leaves little doubt that the athlete is drug free. The posterior probability that the athlete is drug free, given a negative test result, is 0.996. However, there is still a lot of doubt about an athlete who tests positive. The posterior probability that the athlete uses drugs, given a positive test result, is only 0.617. This asymmetry occurs because of the prior probabilities. We are fairly certain that a randomly selected athlete is drug free because only 5% of all athletes use drugs. It takes a lot of evidence to convince us otherwise. This initial bias, plus the fact that the test produces a few false positives, means that athletes with positive test results still have a decent chance (probability 0.383) of being drug free. Is this a valid argument for not requiring drug testing of athletes? We explore this question in the following continuation of the drug-testing example. It all depends on the "costs." (It might also depend on whether there is a second type of test that could help confirm the findings of the first test. However, we won't consider such a test.) ■

EXAMPLE 6.7

The administrators at State University are trying to decide whether to institute mandatory drug testing for the athletes. They have the same information about priors and likelihoods as in the previous example, but now they want to use a decision tree approach to see whether the benefits outweigh the costs.[5]

Solution

We have already discussed the uncertain outcomes and their probabilities. Now we need to discuss the decision alternatives and the monetary values—the other two elements of a decision analysis. We will assume that there are only two alternatives: perform drug testing on all athletes or don't perform any drug testing. In the former case we assume that if an athlete tests positive, this athlete is barred from sports.

The "monetary" values are more difficult to assess. They include

- the benefit B from correctly identifying a drug user and barring him or her from sports
- the cost C_1 of the test itself for a single athlete (materials and labor)
- the cost C_2 of falsely accusing a nonuser (and barring him or her from sports)

[5]Again, see Feinstein (1990) for an enlightening discussion of this drug-testing problem at a real university.

- the cost C_3 of not identifying a drug user (either by not testing at all or by obtaining a false negative)
- the cost C_4 of violating a nonuser's privacy by performing the test

It is clear that only C_1 is a direct monetary cost that is easy to measure. However, the other "costs" and the benefit B are real, and they must be compared on some scale to enable administrators to make a rational decision. We will do so by comparing everything to the cost C_1, to which we will assign value 1. (This does not mean that the cost of testing an athlete is necessarily \$1; it just means that we will express all other costs as multiples of C_1.) Clearly, there is a lot of subjectivity involved in making these comparisons, so sensitivity analysis on the final decision tree is a must.

Before developing this decision tree, it is useful to form a benefit–cost table for both alternatives and all possible outcomes. Because we will eventually maximize expected net *benefit*, all benefits in this table have a positive sign and all costs have a negative sign. These net benefits appear in Table 6.25. The first two columns are relevant if no tests are performed; the last four are relevant when testing is performed. For example, if a positive test is obtained for a nonuser, there are three costs: the cost of the test (C_1), the cost of falsely accusing the athlete (C_2), and the cost of violating the nonuser's privacy (C_4). The other entries are obtained similarly.

TABLE 6.25   **Net Benefit for Drug-Testing Example**

Don't Test		Perform Test			
D	ND	D and $T+$	ND and $T+$	D and $T-$	ND and $T-$
$-C_3$	0	$B - C_1$	$-(C_1 + C_2 + C_4)$	$-(C_1 + C_3)$	$-(C_1 + C_4)$

The solution with PrecisionTree shown in Figure 6.39 is now fairly straightforward. (See the file DRUG.XLS.) We first enter all of the benefits and costs in an input section. These, together with the Bayes' rule calculations from before, appear at the top of the spreadsheet. Then we use PrecisionTree in the usual way to build the tree and enter the links to the values and probabilities.

Before we interpret this solution, we discuss the timing (from left to right). If drug testing is performed, the result of the drug test is observed first (a probability node). Each test result leads to an action (bar from sports or don't), and then the eventual benefit or cost depends on whether the athlete uses drugs (again a probability node). You might argue that the university never knows for certain whether the athlete uses drugs, but we must include this information in the tree to get the benefits and costs correct. If no drug testing is performed, then there is no intermediate test result node or branches.

Now to the interpretation. First, we discuss the benefits and costs shown in Figure 6.39. These were chosen fairly arbitrarily, but with some hope of reflecting reality. They say that the largest cost is falsely accusing (and barring) a nonuser. This is 50 times as large as the cost of the test. The benefit of identifying a drug user is only half this large, and the cost of not identifying a user is 40% as large as barring a nonuser. The violation of privacy of a nonuser is twice as large as the cost of the test. Based on these values, the decision tree implies that drug testing should *not* be performed. The EMVs for testing and for not testing are both negative, indicating that the costs outweigh the benefits for each, but the EMV for not testing is slightly *less* negative.[6]

---

[6] The university in the Feinstein (1990) study came to the same conclusion.

FIGURE 6.39 Decision Tree for Drug-Testing Example

	A	B	C	D	E	F	G
1	Drug testing decision tree						
2							
3	Benefits			Given probabilities			
4	Identifying user	25		Prior probabilities			
5						User	Non-user
6	Costs					0.05	0.95
7	Test cost	1					
8	Barring non-user	50		Conditional probabilities of test results			
9	Not identifying user	20				User	Non-user
10	Violation of privacy	2		Positive		0.93	0.03
11				Negative		0.07	0.97
12	Key probabilities						
13	PrUser	0.05		Bayesian revision			
14	PrFalseNegative	0.07		Joint probabilities			
15	PrFalsePositive	0.03				User	Non-user	Sums
16				Positive		0.047	0.029	0.075
17				Negative		0.004	0.922	0.925
18							
19				Posterior probabilities			
20						User	Non-user
21				Positive		0.620	0.380
22				Negative		0.004	0.996

Range names
BarNonUser: B8
IdentUser: B4
NotIdentUser: B9
PrFalseNeg: B14
PrFalsePos: B15
PrUser: B13
TestCost: B7
ViolPrivacy: B10

Decision tree (cells 23–45):

- Drug testing — Test? -1
  - Yes — FALSE -1 — Test results -3.233
    - Positive 7.5% 0 — User? -5.26
      - Yes 62.0% 0 → 25 → 24
      - No 38.0% 0 → -52 → -53
    - Negative 92.5% 0 — User? -3.068
      - Yes 0.4% 0 → -20 → -21
      - No 99.6% 0 → -2 → -3
  - No — TRUE 0 — User? -1
    - Yes 5.0% -20 → 0.05 → -20
    - No 95.0% 0 → 0.95 → 0

What would it take to change this decision? We'll start with the assumption, probably accepted by most people in our society, that the cost of falsely accusing a nonuser (C_2) ought to be the largest of the benefits or costs in the range B4:B10. In fact, because of possible legal costs, we might argue that C_2 should be *more* than 50 times the cost of the test. But if we increase C_2, the scales are tipped even farther in the direction of not testing. On the other hand, if the benefit B from identifying a user and/or the cost C_3 for not identifying a user increase, then testing might be the preferred alternative. We tried this, keeping C_2 constant at 50. When B and C_3 both had value 45, no testing was still optimal, but when they both increased to 50—the same magnitude as C_2—then testing won out by a small margin. However, it would be difficult to argue that B and C_3 should be of the same magnitude as C_2.

Other than the benefits and costs, the only other thing we might vary is the accuracy of the test, measured by the error probabilities in cells B14 and B15. Presumably, if the test makes fewer false positives and false negatives, testing might be a more attractive alternative. We tried this, keeping the benefits and costs the same as those shown in Figure 6.39 but changing the error probabilities. Even when each error probability was decreased to 0.01, however, the no-testing alternative was still optimal—by a fairly wide margin.

In summary, based on a number of reasonable assumptions and parameter settings, this example has shown that it is difficult to make a case for mandatory drug testing. ∎

PROBLEMS

Level A

44 Consider a population of 2000 individuals, 800 of whom are women. Assume that 300 of the women in this population earn at least $60,000 per year, and 200 of the men earn at least $60,000 per year.

  a What is the probability that a randomly selected individual from this population earns less than $60,000 per year?

  b If a randomly selected individual is observed to earn less than $60,000 per year, what is the probability that this person is a man?

  c If a randomly selected individual is observed to earn at least $60,000 per year, what is the probability that this person is a woman?

45 Yearly automobile inspections are required for residents of the state of Pennsylvania. Suppose that 18% of all inspected cars in Pennsylvania have problems that need to be corrected. Unfortunately, Pennsylvania state inspections fail to detect these problems 12% of the time. Consider a car that is inspected and is found to be free of problems. What is the probability that there is indeed something wrong that the inspection has failed to uncover?

46 Consider again the landowner's decision problem described in Problem 3. Suppose now that, at a cost of $90,000, the landowner can request that a soundings test be performed on the site where natural gas is believed to be present. The company that conducts the soundings concedes that 30% of the time the test will indicate that no gas is present when it actually is. When natural gas is not present in a particular site, the soundings test is accurate 90% of the time.

  a Given that the landowner pays for the soundings test and the test indicates that gas is present, what is the landowner's revised estimate of the probability of finding gas on this site?

  b Given that the landowner pays for the soundings test and the test indicates that gas is not present, what is the landowner's revised estimate of the probability of not finding gas on this site?

  c Should the landowner request the given soundings test at a cost of $90,000? Explain why or why not. If not, when (if ever) would the landowner choose to obtain the soundings test?

47 The chief executive officer of a firm in a highly competitive industry believes that one of her key employees is providing confidential information to the competition. She is 90% certain that this informer is the vice president of finance, whose contacts have been extremely valuable in obtaining financing for the company. If she decides to fire this vice president and he is the informer, she estimates that the company will gain $500,000. If she decides to fire this vice president but he is not the informer, the company will lose his expertise and still have an informer within the staff; the CEO estimates that this outcome would cost her company about $2.5 million. If she decides not to fire this vice president, she estimates that the firm will lose $1.5 million whether or not he actually is the informer (because in either case the informer is still with the company).

  Before deciding whether to fire the vice president for finance, the CEO could order lie detector tests. To avoid possible lawsuits, the lie detector tests would have to be administered to all company employees, at a total cost of $150,000. Another problem she must consider is that the available lie detector tests are not perfectly reliable. In particular, if a person is lying, the test will reveal that the person is lying 95% of the time. Moreover, if a person is not lying, the test will indicate that the person is not lying 85% of the time.

  a To minimize the expected total cost of managing this difficult situation, what strategy should the CEO adopt?

  b Should the CEO order the lie detector tests for all of her employees? Explain why or why not.

c Determine the maximum amount of money that the CEO should be willing to pay to administer lie detector tests.

48 A customer has approached a bank for a $10,000 1-year loan at a 12% interest rate. If the bank does not approve this loan application, the $10,000 will be invested in bonds that earn a 6% annual return. Without additional information, the bank believes that there is a 4% chance that this customer will default on the loan, assuming that the loan is approved. If the customer defaults on the loan, the bank will lose $10,000. At a cost of $100, the bank can thoroughly investigate the customer's credit record and supply a favorable or unfavorable recommendation. Past experience indicates that in cases where the customer did not default on the approved loan, the probability of receiving a favorable recommendation on the basis of the credit investigation was 77/96. Furthermore, in cases where the customer defaulted on the approved loan, the probability of receiving a favorable recommendation on the basis of the credit investigation was 1/4.

a What course of action should the bank take to maximize its expected profit?

b Compute and interpret the expected value of sample information (EVSI) in this decision problem.

c Compute and interpret the expected value of perfect information (EVPI) in this decision problem.

49 A company is considering whether to market a new product. Assume, for simplicity, that if this product is marketed, there are only two possible outcomes: success or failure. The company assesses that the probabilities of these two outcomes are p and $1 - p$, respectively. If the product is marketed and it proves to be a failure, the company will lose $450,000. If the product is marketed and it proves to be a success, the company will gain $750,000. Choosing not to market the product results in no gain or loss for the company.

The company is also considering whether to survey prospective buyers of this new product. The results of the consumer survey can be classified as favorable, neutral, or unfavorable. In similar cases where proposed products proved to be market successes, the likelihoods that the survey results were favorable, neutral, and unfavorable were 0.6, 0.3, and 0.1, respectively. In similar cases where proposed products proved to be market failures, the likelihoods that the survey results were favorable, neutral, and unfavorable were 0.1, 0.2, and 0.7, respectively. The total cost of administering this survey is C dollars.

a Let $p = 0.4$. For which values of C, if any, would this company choose to conduct the consumer survey?

b Let $p = 0.4$. What is the largest amount that this company would be willing to pay for perfect information about the potential success or failure of the new product?

c Let $p = 0.5$ and $C = \$15,000$. Find the strategy that maximizes the company's expected earnings in this situation. Does the optimal strategy involve conducting the consumer survey? Explain why or why not.

50 The U.S. government is attempting to determine whether immigrants should be tested for a contagious disease. Let's assume that the decision will be made on a financial basis. Furthermore, assume that each immigrant who is allowed to enter the United States and has the disease costs the country $100,000. Also, each immigrant who is allowed to enter the United States and does not have the disease will contribute $10,000 to the national economy. Finally, assume that x percent of all potential immigrants have the disease. The U.S. government can choose to admit all immigrants, admit no immigrants, or test immigrants for the disease before determining whether they should be admitted. It costs T dollars to test a person for the disease; the test result is either positive or negative. A person who does not have the disease *always* tests negative. However, 20% of all people who *do* have the disease test negative. The government's goal is to maximize the expected net financial benefits per potential immigrant.

a Let $x = 10$ (i.e., 10%). What is the largest value of T at which the U.S. government will choose to test potential immigrants for the disease?

b How does your answer to the question in part **a** change when x increases to 15?

c Let $x = 10$ and $T = \$100$. Find the government's optimal strategy in this case.

d Let $x = 10$ and $T = \$100$. Compute and interpret the expected value of perfect information (EVPI) in this decision problem.

51 A city in Ohio is considering replacing its fleet of gasoline-powered automobiles with electric cars. The manufacturer of the electric cars claims that this municipality will experience significant cost savings over the life of the fleet if it chooses to pursue the conversion. If the manufacturer is correct, the city will save about $1.5 million dollars. If the new technology employed within the electric cars is faulty, as some critics suggest, the conversion to electric cars will cost the city $675,000. A third possibility is that less serious problems will arise and the city will break even with the conversion. A consultant hired by the city estimates that the probabilities of these three outcomes are 0.30, 0.30, and 0.40, respectively.

The city has an opportunity to implement a pilot program that would indicate the potential cost or savings resulting from a switch to electric cars. The pilot program involves renting a small number of electric cars for 3 months and running them under typical conditions. This program would cost the city $75,000. The city's consultant believes that the results of the pilot program would be significant but not conclusive; she submits Table 6.26, a compilation of probabilities based on the experience of other cities, to support her contention. For example, the first row of her table indicates that given that a conversion to electric cars actually results in a savings of $1.5 million, the conditional probabilities that the pilot program will indicate that the city saves money, loses money, and breaks even are 0.6, 0.1, and 0.3, respectively.

TABLE 6.26 **Likelihoods of Pilot Program Outcomes Given Actual Conversion Outcomes**

Actual Outcome of Conversion/ Pilot Program Indication	Savings	Loss	Break Even
Savings	0.6	0.1	0.3
Loss	0.1	0.4	0.5
Break Even	0.4	0.2	0.4

a What actions should this city take to maximize the expected savings?

b Should the city implement the pilot program at a cost of $75,000?

c Compute and interpret the expected value of sample information (EVSI) in this decision problem.

52 A manufacturer must decide whether to extend credit to a retailer who would like to open an account with the firm. Past experience with new accounts indicates that 45% are high-risk customers, 35% are moderate-risk customers, and 20% are low-risk customers. If credit is extended, the manufacturer can expect to lose $60,000 with a high-risk customer, make $50,000 with a moderate-risk customer, and make $100,000 with a low-risk customer. If the manufacturer decides not to extend credit to a customer, the manufacturer neither makes nor loses any money.

Prior to making a credit extension decision, the manufacturer can obtain a credit rating report on the retailer at a cost of $2000. The credit agency concedes that its rating procedure is not completely reliable. In particular, the credit rating procedure will rate a low-risk customer as a moderate-risk customer with probability 0.10 and as a high-risk customer with probability 0.05. Furthermore, the given rating procedure will rate a moderate-risk customer as a low-risk customer with probability 0.06 and as a high-risk customer with probability 0.07. Finally, the rating procedure will rate a high-risk customer as a low-risk customer with probability 0.01 and as a moderate-risk customer with probability 0.05.

a Find the strategy that maximizes the manufacturer's expected net earnings.

b Should the manufacturer routinely obtain credit rating reports on those retailers who seek credit approval? Why or why not?

c Compute and interpret the expected value of sample information (EVSI) in this decision problem.

53 A television network earns an average of $1.6 million each season from a hit program and loses an average of $400,000 each season on a program that turns out to be a flop. Of all programs picked up by this network in recent years, 25% turn out to be hits and 75% turn out to be flops. At a cost of C dollars, a market research firm will analyze a pilot episode of a prospective program and issue a report predicting whether the given program will end up being a hit. If the program is actually going to be a hit, there is a 90% chance that the market researchers will predict the program to be a hit. If the program is actually going to be a flop, there is a 20% chance that the market researchers will predict the program to be a hit.

a Assuming that $C = \$160,000$, identify the strategy that maximizes this television network's expected profit in responding to a newly proposed television program.

b What is the maximum value of C that this television network should be willing to incur in choosing to hire the market research firm?

c Compute and interpret the expected value of perfect information (EVPI) in this decision problem. ∎

Incorporating Attitudes Toward Risk

R ational decision makers are sometimes willing to violate the EMV maximization criterion when large amounts of money are at stake. These decision makers are willing to sacrifice some EMV to reduce risk. Are you ever willing to do so personally? Consider the following scenarios.

1 You have a chance to enter a lottery where you will win $100,000 with probability 0.1 or win nothing with probability 0.9. Alternatively, you can receive $5000 for certain. How many of you—truthfully—would take the certain $5000, even though the EMV of the lottery is $10,000? Or change the $100,000 to $1,000,000 and the $5000 to $50,000 and ask yourself whether you'd prefer the sure $50,000!

2 You can either buy collision insurance on your expensive new car or not buy it, where the insurance costs a certain premium and carries some deductible provision. If you decide to pay the premium, then you are essentially paying a certain amount to avoid a gamble—the possibility of wrecking your car and not having it insured. You can be sure that the premium is greater than the expected cost of damage; otherwise, the insurance company would not stay in business. Therefore, from an EMV standpoint you should not purchase the insurance. But how many of you drive without this type of insurance?

These examples, the second of which is certainly realistic, illustrate situations where rational people do not behave as EMV maximizers. Then how do they act? This question has been studied extensively by many researchers, both mathematically and behaviorally. Although the answer is still not agreed upon universally, most researchers believe that if certain basic behavioral assumptions hold, people are **expected utility** maximizers—that is, they choose the alternative with the largest expected utility. Although we will not go deeply into the subject of expected utility maximization, the discussion in this section will acquaint you with the main ideas.

6.8.1 Utility Functions

We begin by discussing an individual's **utility function**. This is a mathematical function that transforms monetary values—payoffs and costs—into **utility values**. Essentially, an individual's utility function specifies the individual's preferences for various monetary payoffs and costs and, in doing so, it automatically encodes the individual's attitudes toward risk. Most individuals are **risk averse**, which means intuitively that they are willing to sacrifice some EMV to avoid risky gambles. In terms of the utility function, this means that every extra dollar of payoff is worth slightly less to the individual than the previous dollar, and every extra dollar of cost is considered slightly more costly (in terms of utility) than the previous dollar. The resulting utility functions are shaped as shown in Figure 6.40. Mathematically, these functions are said to be **increasing** and **concave**. The increasing part means that they go uphill—everyone prefers more money to less money. The concave part means that they increase at a decreasing rate. This is the risk-averse behavior.

F I G U R E   6 . 4 0   **Risk-Averse Utility Function**

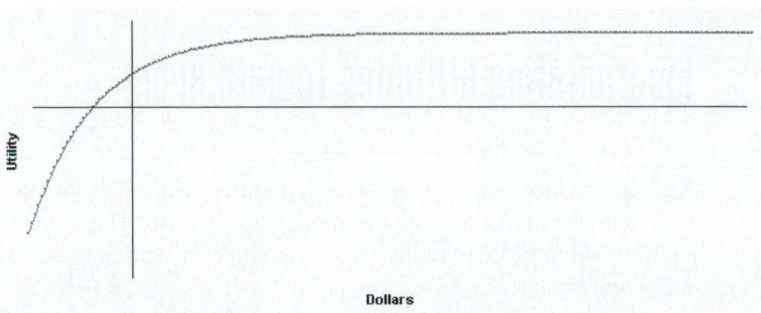

There are two problems involved in implementing utility maximization in a real decision analysis. The first is obtaining an individual's (or company's) utility function; we will discuss this below. The second is using the resulting utility function to find the best decision. This second step is actually quite straightforward. We simply substitute utility values for monetary values in the decision tree and then fold back as usual. That is, we calculate expected *utilities* at probability branches and take maximums (of expected utilities) at decision branches. We will look at a numerical example later in this section. So the real work involves finding an individual's (or company's) utility function in the first place.

6.8.2 Assessing a Utility Function

We will outline a method that can be used to estimate a person's utility function. There are two things we must understand about this method. First, it asks the person to make a series of trade-offs. Because each of us has different attitudes toward risk, we will not all make the trade-offs in the same way. Therefore, each of us will obtain our own utility function. Second, even a particular person's utility function is not unique. If $U(x)$ represents a person's utility function, then it turns out that $aU(x) + b$ also describes that person's utility function, for any constants a and b with $a > 0$. They are equivalent in the sense that they lead to exactly the same decisions.

We take advantage of this nonuniqueness by specifying two points on the utility function. Specifically, we begin by asking the person for two monetary values that represent the worst possible loss and the best possible gain imaginable. Let's say these values are $-A$ and B. Then we *arbitrarily* assign utility values 0 and 1 to these two monetary values, that is, $U(-A) = 0$ and $U(B) = 1$. Don't worry about the absolute magnitudes, 0 and 1, we've assigned—we could assign any other values, such as 14 and 320. The important thing is to use these as "anchors" and then obtain other utility values in terms of them.

The procedure is as follows. Given any two known utility values, say, $U(x)$ and $U(y)$, where x and y are monetary values, we present the person with a choice between the following two options:

- Option 1: Obtain a certain payoff of z.
- Option 2: Obtain a payoff of either x or y, depending on the flip of a fair coin.

Then we ask the person to select the monetary value z in option 1 so that he or she is *indifferent* between the two options. If the person is indifferent, then the expected utilities from the two options must be equal. We will call the resulting value of z the **indifference value**. This leads to the equation for $U(z)$:

$$U(z) = 0.5U(x) + 0.5U(y) \qquad \textbf{(6.3)}$$

In words, we have generated a new utility value from two known utility values. This process continues until we have enough utility values to approximate a utility curve. (Note that if any of x, y, and z are negative, then "payoff" really means "cost.") We'll illustrate this procedure with an example.

EXAMPLE 6.8

John Jacobs owns his own business. Because he is about to make an important decision where large losses or large gains are at stake, he wants to use the expected utility criterion to make his decision. He knows that he must first assess his own utility function, so he hires a decision analysis expert, Susan Schilling, to help him out. How might the session between John and Susan proceed?

Solution

Susan first asks John for the largest loss and largest gain he can imagine. He answers with the values $200,000 and $300,000, so she assigns utility values $U(-200000) = 0$ and $U(300000) = 1$ as anchors for the utility function. Now she presents John with the choice between two options:

- Option 1: Obtain a payoff of z (really a loss if z is negative).
- Option 2: Obtain a loss of $200,000 or a payoff of $300,000, depending on the flip of a fair coin.

Susan reminds John that the EMV of option 2 is $50,000 (halfway between −$200,000 and $300,000). He realizes this, but because he is quite risk averse, he would far rather have $50,000 for certain than take the gamble in option 2. Therefore, the indifference value of z must be less than $50,000. Susan then poses several values of z to John. Would he rather have $10,000 for sure or take option 2? He says he'd rather take the $10,000. Would he rather *pay* $5000 for sure or take the gamble in option 2? (This is like an insurance premium.) He says he'd rather take option 2. By this time, we know the indifference value of z must be less than $10,000 and greater than −$5000. With a few more questions of this type, John finally decides on $z = \$5000$ as his indifference value. He is indifferent between obtaining $5000 for sure and taking the gamble in option 2. We can substitute these values into equation (6.3):

$$U(5000) = 0.5U(-200000) + 0.5U(300000) = 0.5(0) + 0.5(1) = 0.5$$

Note that John is giving up $45,000 in EMV because of his risk aversion. The EMV of the gamble in option 2 is $50,000, and he is willing to accept a *sure* $5000 in its place.

The process would then continue. For example, since she now knows $U(5000)$ and $U(300000)$, Susan could ask John to choose between these options:

- Option 1: Obtain a payoff of z.
- Option 2: Obtain a payoff of $5000 or a payoff of $300,000, depending on the flip of a fair coin.

If John decides that his indifference value is now $z = \$130,000$, then with equation (6.3) we know that

$$U(130000) = 0.5U(5000) + 0.5U(300000) = 0.5(0.5) + 0.5(1) = 0.75$$

Note that John is now giving up $22,500 in EMV because the EMV of the gamble in option 2 is $152,500. By continuing in this manner, Susan can help John assess enough utility values to approximate a continuous utility curve. ■

As this example illustrates, utility assessment is tedious. Even in the best of circumstances, when a trained consultant attempts to assess the utility function of a single person, the process requires the person to make a series of choices between hypothetical alternatives involving uncertain outcomes. Unless the person has some training in probability, these choices can be difficult to understand, let alone make, and it is unlikely that the person will answer *consistently* as the questioning proceeds. The process is even more difficult when a company's utility function is being assessed. Because company executives involved typically have different attitudes toward risk, it is difficult for these people to reach a consensus on a common utility function.

6.8.3 Exponential Utility

For these reasons there are classes of "ready-made" utility functions that have been developed. One important class is called **exponential utility** and has been used in many financial investment analyses. An exponential utility function has only one adjustable numerical parameter, and there are straightforward ways to discover the most appropriate value of this parameter for a particular individual or company. So the advantage of using an exponential utility function is that it is relatively easy to assess. The drawback is that exponential utility functions do not capture all types of attitudes toward risk. Nevertheless, their ease of use has made them popular.

An exponential utility function has the following form:

$$U(x) = 1 - e^{-x/R} \tag{6.4}$$

Here x is a monetary value (a payoff if positive, a cost if negative), $U(x)$ is the utility of this value, and $R > 0$ is an adjustable parameter called the **risk tolerance**. Basically, the risk tolerance measures how much risk the decision maker will tolerate. The larger the value of R, the less risk averse the decision maker is. That is, a person with a large value of R is more willing to take risks than a person with a small value of R.

To assess a person's (or company's) exponential utility function, we need only to assess the value of R. There are a couple of tips for doing this. First, it has been shown that the risk tolerance is approximately equal to that dollar amount R such that the decision maker is indifferent between the following two options:

- Option 1: Obtain no payoff at all.
- Option 2: Obtain a payoff of R dollars or a loss of $R/2$ dollars, depending on the flip of a fair coin.

For example, if you are indifferent between a bet where you win $1000 or lose $500, with probability 0.5 each, and not betting at all, then your R is approximately $1000. From this criterion it certainly makes intuitive sense that a wealthier person (or company) ought to have a larger value of R. This has been found in practice.

A second tip for finding R is based on empirical evidence found by Ronald Howard, a prominent decision analyst. Through his consulting experience with several large companies, he discovered tentative relationships between risk tolerance and several financial variables—net sales, net income, and equity. [See Howard (1992).] Specifically, he found that R was approximately 6.4% of net sales, 124% of net income, and 15.7% of equity for the companies he studied. For example, according to this prescription, a company with net sales of $30 million should have a risk tolerance of approximately $1.92 million. Howard admits that these percentages are only guidelines. However, they do indicate that larger and more profitable companies tend to have larger values of R, which means that they are more willing to take risks involving given dollar amounts.

We illustrate the use of the expected utility criterion, and exponential utility in particular, with the following example.

EXAMPLE 6.9

Venture Limited is a company with net sales of $30 million. The company currently must decide whether to enter one of two risky ventures or do nothing. The possible outcomes of the less risky venture are a $0.5 million loss, a $0.1 million gain, and a $1 million gain. The probabilities of these outcomes are 0.25, 0.50, and 0.25. The possible outcomes of the more risky venture are a $1 million loss, a $1 million gain, and a $3 million gain. The probabilities of these outcomes are 0.35, 0.60, and 0.05. If Venture Limited can enter at most one of the two risky ventures, what should it do?

Solution

We will assume that Venture Limited has an exponential utility function. Also, based on Howard's guidelines, we will assume that the company's risk tolerance is 6.4% of its net sales, or $1.92 million. (We'll do a sensitivity analysis on this parameter later on.) We can substitute into the exponential utility formula (6.4) to find the utility of any monetary outcome. For example, the gain from doing nothing is $0, and its utility is

$$U(0) = 1 - e^{-0/1.92} = 1 - 1 = 0$$

As another example, the utility of a $1 million loss is

$$U(-1) = 1 - e^{-(-1)/1.92} = 1 - 1.683 = -0.683$$

These are the values we use (instead of monetary values) in the decision tree.

Fortunately, PrecisionTree takes care of all the details. After we build a decision tree and label it (with monetary values) in the usual way, we click on the name of the tree (the box on the far left of the tree) to open the dialog box in Figure 6.41 (page 310). We then fill in the utility function information as shown in the upper right section of the dialog box. This says to use an exponential utility function with risk tolerance 1.92. It also indicates that we want expected utilities (as opposed to EMVs) to appear in the decision tree.

The completed tree for this example appears in Figure 6.42. (See the file VENTURE.XLS.) We build it in exactly the same way as usual and link probabilities and monetary values to its branches in the usual way. For example, there is a link in cell C22 to the monetary value in cell A10. However, the expected values shown in the tree (those shown in color on your screen) are expected *utilities*, and the optimal decision is the

FIGURE 6.41 **Dialog Box for Specifying the Exponential Utility Criterion**

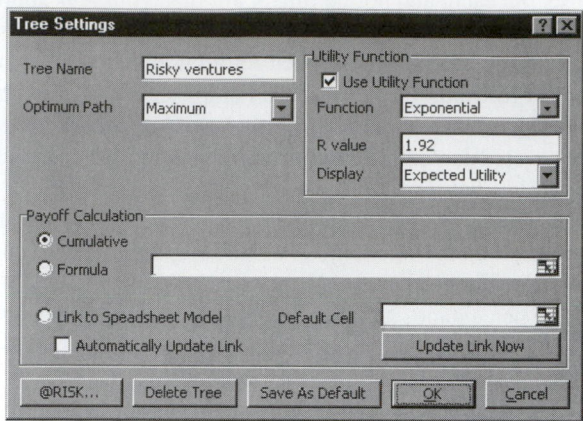

FIGURE 6.42 **Decision Tree for Risky Venture Example**

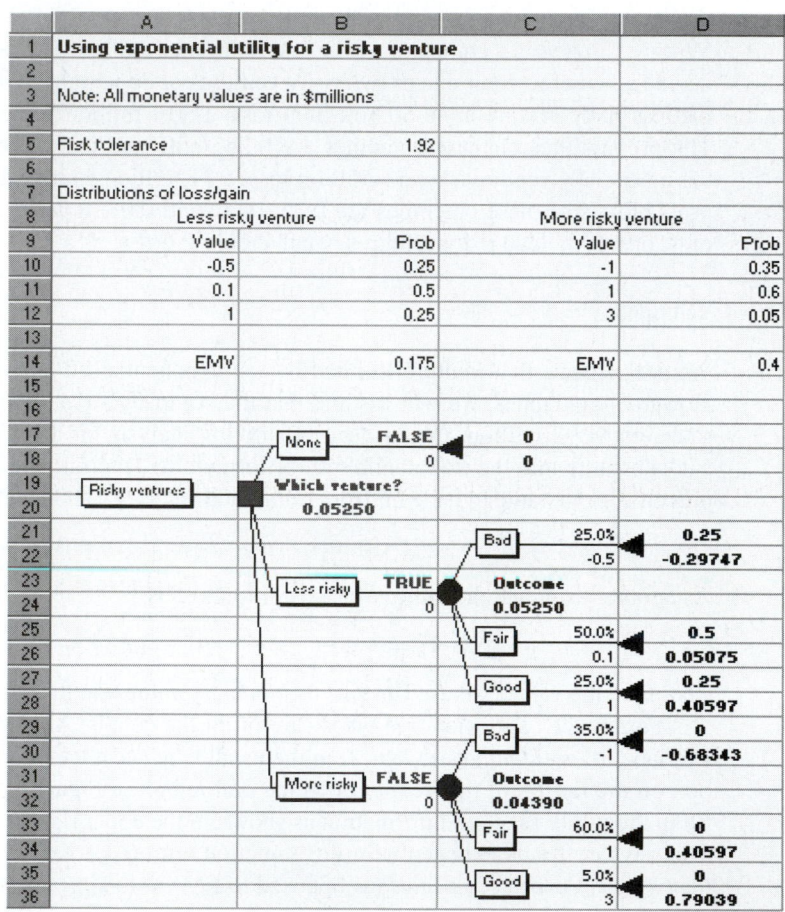

one with the largest expected utility. In this case the expected utilities for doing nothing, investing in the less risky venture, and investing in the more risky venture are 0, 0.0525, and 0.0439. Therefore, the optimal decision is to invest in the less risky venture.

Note that the EMVs of the three decisions are $0, $0.175 million, and $0.4 million. The latter two of these are calculated in row 14 as the usual "sumproduct" of monetary values and probabilities. So from an EMV point of view, the more risky venture is definitely best. However, Venture Limited is sufficiently risk averse, and the monetary values are sufficiently large, that the company is willing to sacrifice EMV to reduce its risk.

How sensitive is the optimal decision to the key parameter, the risk tolerance? We can answer this by changing the risk tolerance (through the dialog box in Figure 6.41) and watching how the decision tree changes.[7] You can check that when the company becomes *more* risk tolerant, the more risky venture eventually becomes optimal. In fact, this occurs when the risk tolerance increases to approximately $2.075 million. In the other direction, when the company becomes *less* risk tolerant, the "do nothing" decision eventually becomes optimal. This occurs when the risk tolerance decreases to approximately $0.715 million. So the "optimal" decision depends heavily on the attitudes toward risk of Venture Limited's top management. ∎

6.8.4 Certainty Equivalents

Now suppose that Venture Limited has only two options. It can either enter the less risky venture or receive a *certain* dollar amount x and avoid the gamble altogether. We want to find the dollar amount x such that the company is indifferent between these two options. If it enters the risky venture, its expected utility is 0.0525, calculated above. If it receives x dollars for certain, its (expected) utility is

$$U(x) = 1 - e^{-x/1.92}$$

To find the value x where it is indifferent between the two options, we set $1 - e^{-x/1.92}$ equal to 0.0525, or $e^{-x/1.92} = 0.9475$, and solve for x. Taking natural logarithms of both sides and multiplying by -1.92, we obtain

$$x = -1.92 \ln(0.9475) \simeq \$0.104 \text{ million}$$

This value is called the **certainty equivalent** of the risky venture. The company is indifferent between entering the less risky venture and receiving $0.104 million to avoid it. Although the EMV of the less risky venture is $0.175 million, the company acts as if it is equivalent to a sure $0.104 million. In this sense, the company is willing to give up the difference in EMV, $71,000, to avoid a gamble.

By a similar calculation, the certainty equivalent of the more risky venture is approximately $0.086 million. That is, the company acts as if this more risky venture is equivalent to a sure $0.086 million, when in fact its EMV is a hefty $0.4 million! So in this case it is willing to give up the difference in EMV, $314,000, to avoid this particular gamble. Again, the reason is that the company dislikes risk. We can see these certainty equivalents in PrecisionTree by adjusting the Display box in Figure 6.41 to show Certainty Equivalent. The tree then looks as in Figure 6.43. The certainty equivalents we just discussed appear in cells C24 and C32.

---

[7]We show the risk tolerance in cell B5, but the values in the decision tree are not linked to that cell. We need to go through the dialog box to change the risk tolerance.

FIGURE 6.43 **Decision Tree with Certainty Equivalents**

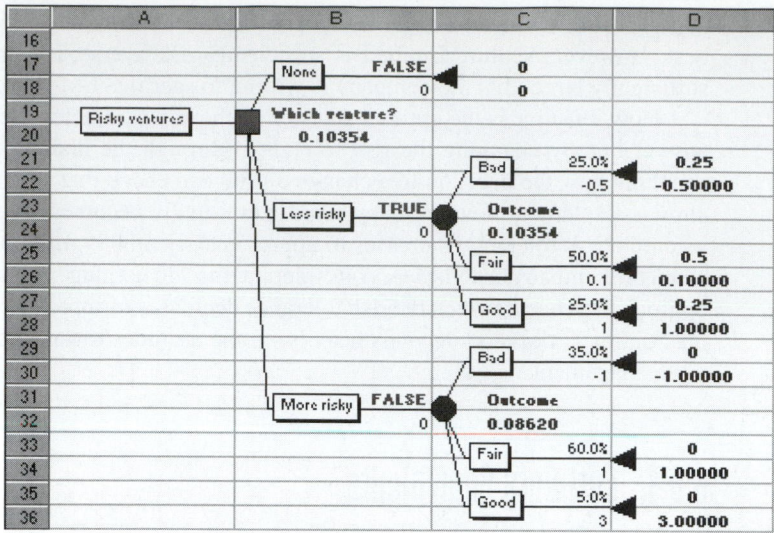

6.8.5 Is Expected Utility Maximization Used?

The above discussion indicates that utility maximization is a fairly involved task. The bottom line, then, is whether the difficulty is worth the trouble. Theoretically, expected utility maximization might be interesting to researchers, but is it really used? The answer appears to be: not very often. For example, one recent article on the practice of decision making [see Kirkwood (1992)] quotes Ronald Howard—the same person we quoted earlier—as having found risk aversion to be of practical concern in only 5% to 10% of business decision analyses. This same article quotes the president of a Fortune 500 company as saying, "Most of the decisions we analyze are for a few million dollars. It is adequate to use expected value (EMV) for these."

With these comments in mind, it is clear that knowledge of expected utility maximization is an important requirement for anyone intending to specialize in the field. In some of the greatest success stories, expected utility maximization was indeed implemented. For nonspecialists, however, a passing knowledge of the concepts is sufficient.

PROBLEMS

Level A

54 Suppose that a decision maker's utility as a function of his wealth, x, is given by $U(x) = \ln x$ (the natural logarithm of x).

    a Is this decision maker risk averse? Explain why or why not.

    b The decision maker now has $10,000 and two possible decisions. For decision 1, he loses $500 for certain. For decision 2, he loses $0 with probability 0.9 and loses $5000 with probability 0.1. Which decision maximizes the expected utility of his net wealth?

55 An investor has $10,000 in assets and can choose between two different investments. If she invests in the first investment opportunity there is an 80% chance that she will increase her assets by $590,000 and a 20% chance that she will increase her assets by $190,000. If she invests in the second investment opportunity there is a 50% chance that she will increase her assets by $1.19 million and a 50% chance that she will increase her assets by $1000. This investor has an exponential utility function for final assets with a risk tolerance parameter equal to $600,000. Which investment opportunity will she prefer?

56 Consider again FreshWay's decision problem described in Example 6.4. Suppose now that FreshWay's utility function of profit π, earned from the acquisition and sale of the 24,000 fluorescent lightbulbs, is $U(\pi) = \ln(\pi)$. Find the course of action that maximizes FreshWay's expected utility. How does this optimal decision compare to the optimal decision with an EMV criterion? Explain any difference between the two decisions.

57 Consider again the landowner's decision problem described in Problem 3. Suppose now that the landowner's utility function of financial gain x is $U(x) = x^2$. Find the course of action that maximizes the landowner's expected utility. How does this optimal decision compare to the optimal decision with an EMV criterion? Explain any difference between the two decisions.

58 Consider again Techware's decision problem described in Problem 4. Suppose now that Techware's utility function of net revenue r (measured in dollars), earned from the given marketing opportunities, is $U(r) = 1 - e^{-r/350,000}$.

    a Find the course of action that maximizes Techware's expected utility. How does this optimal decision compare to the optimal decision with an EMV criterion? Explain any difference between the two optimal decisions.

    b Repeat part **a** when Techware's utility function is $U(r) = 1 - e^{-r/50,000}$.

59 Consider again the bank's customer loan decision problem in Problem 48. Suppose now that the bank's utility function of profit π (in dollars) is $U(\pi) = 1 - e^{-\pi/10,000}$. Find the strategy that maximizes the bank's expected utility in this case. How does this optimal strategy compare to the optimal decision with an EMV criterion? Explain any difference between two optimal strategies.

Level B

60 Suppose that a decision maker has a utility function for monetary gains x given by $U(x) = (x + 10000)^{0.5}$.

    a Show that this decision maker is indifferent between gaining nothing (i.e., $0) and entering a risky situation where she gains $80,000 with probability 1/3 and loses $10,000 with probability 2/3.

    b If there is a 10% chance that one of the decision maker's family heirlooms, valued at $5000, will be stolen during the next year, what is the most that she would be willing to pay each year for an insurance policy that completely covers the potential loss of her cherished item?

61 A decision maker is going to invest $2000 for a period of 6 months. Two potential investments are available to him: U.S. Treasury bills and gold. If this decision maker invests the $2000 in T-bills, he is sure to end the 6-month period with $2592. If this decision maker invests in gold, there is a 75% chance that he will end the 6-month period with $800 and a 25% chance that he will end up with $20,000. The decision maker's utility function of ending up with x dollars is $U(x) = x^{0.5}$.

    a Should this decision maker invest in gold or T-bills?

    b Suppose the decision maker invests a proportion y of his $2000 in T-bills and the remaining fraction $(1 - y)$ of his available funds in gold. In this case his gain or loss from either investment is reduced proportionally. For example, if he invests half of his money in gold, he will either lose $600 with probability 0.75 or gain $9000 with probability 0.25. Given the same utility function $U(x) = x^{0.5}$, find the investor's optimal choice of y. ∎

Conclusion

I n this chapter we have discussed methods that can be used in decision-making problems in which future uncertainty is a key element. Perhaps the most important skill we can gain from this chapter is the ability to approach decision problems that include uncertainty in a systematic manner. This systematic approach requires the decision maker to list all possible decisions or strategies, list all possible uncertain outcomes, assess the probabilities of these outcomes (possibly with the aid of Bayes' rule), calculate all necessary monetary values, and finally do the calculations necessary to obtain the best decision. If large dollar amounts are at stake, it might also be necessary to perform a utility analysis, where the decision maker's feelings toward risk are taken into account. Once the basic analysis has been completed, using "best guesses" for the various parameters of the problem, a sensitivity analysis should be conducted to see whether the best decision continues to be best within a range of problem parameters.

PROBLEMS

Level A

62 Ford is going to produce a new vehicle, the Pioneer, and wants to determine the amount of annual capacity it should build. Ford's goal is to maximize the profit from this vehicle over the next 10 years. Each vehicle will sell for $13,000 and incur a variable production cost of $10,000. Building one unit of annual capacity will cost $3000. Each unit of capacity will also cost $1000 per year to maintain, even if the capacity is unused. Demand for the Pioneer is unknown but marketing estimates the distribution of annual demand to be as shown in Table 6.27. Assume that unit sales during a year is the minimum of capacity and annual demand.

TABLE 6.27 **Distribution of Annual Demand**

Annual Demand	Probability
400,000	0.25
900,000	0.50
1,300,000	0.25

    a Explain why a capacity of 1,300,000 is not a good choice.

    b Which capacity level should Ford choose?

63 You are CEO of the venture capital firm D&D. Billy comes to you with an investment proposition. You estimate that your distribution of cash flows from this investment is as shown in Table 6.28.

TABLE 6.28 **Distribution of Cash Flow**

Cash Flow	Probability
−1,000,000	0.35
500,000	0.60
3,000,000	0.05

    a If you are trying to maximize the expected value of the firm's cash flows, should you take the project?

    b Suppose you assess your firm to be risk averse, with an exponential utility function. You also use the rule of thumb that the firm's risk tolerance is about 6.4% of its annual revenues, which are $30 million. Determine whether D&D should enter the venture.

64 Pizza King (PK) and Noble Greek (NG) are competitive pizza chains. Pizza King believes there is a 25% chance that NG will charge $6 per pizza, a 50% chance that NG will charge $8 per pizza, and a 25% chance that NG will charge $10 per pizza. If PK charges price p_1 and NG charges price p_2, PK will sell $100 + 25(p_2 - p_1)$ pizzas. It costs PK $4 to make a pizza. PK is considering charging $5, $6, $7, $8, or $9 per pizza. To maximize its expected profit, what price should PK charge for a pizza?

65 Sodaco is considering producing a new product: Chocovan soda. Sodaco estimates that the annual demand for Chocovan, D (in thousands of cases), has the following probability distribution: $P(D = 30) = 0.30$, $P(D = 50) = 0.40$, $P(D = 80) = 0.30$. Each case of Chocovan sells for $5 and incurs a variable cost of $3. It costs $800,000 to build a plant to produce Chocovan. Assume that if $1 is received every year (forever), this is equivalent to receiving $10 at the present time. If Sodaco decides to build the plant and produce Chocovan, find the expected net present value of its profit.

66 Many decision problems have the following simple structure. A decision maker has two possible decisions, 1 and 2. If decision 1 is made, a *sure* cost of c is incurred. If decision 2 is made, there are two possible outcomes, with costs c_1 and c_2 and probabilities p and $1 - p$. We assume that $c_1 < c < c_2$. The idea is that decision 1, the riskless decision, has a "moderate" cost, whereas decision 2, the risky decision, has a "low" cost c_1 or a "high" cost c_2.

  a Find the decision maker's cost table—that is, the cost for each possible decision and each possible outcome.

  b Calculate the expected cost from the risky decision.

  c List as many scenarios as you can think of that have this structure. (Here'a an example to get you started. Think of insurance, where you pay a sure premium to avoid a large possible loss.)

67 During the summer, Olympic swimmer Adam Johnson swims every day. On sunny summer days he goes to an outdoor pool, where he may swim for no charge. On rainy days he must go to a domed pool. At the beginning of the summer, he has the option of purchasing a $15 season pass to the domed pool, which allows him use for the entire summer. If he doesn't buy the season pass, he must pay $1 each time he goes there. Past meteorological records indicate that there is a 60% chance that the summer will be sunny (an average of 6 rainy days during the summer) and a 40% chance the summer will be rainy (an average of 30 rainy days during the summer).

  Before the summer begins, Adam has the option of purchasing a long-range weather forecast for $1. The forecast predicts a sunny summer 80% of the time and a rainy summer 20% of the time. If the forecast predicts a sunny summer, there is a 70% chance that the summer will actually be sunny. If the forecast predicts a rainy summer, there is an 80% chance that the summer will actually be rainy. Assuming that Adam's goal is to minimize his total expected cost for the summer, what should he do? Also find the EVSI and the EVPI.

68 Erica is going to fly to London on August 5 and return home on August 20. It is now July 1. On July 1, she may buy a one-way ticket (for $350) or a round-trip ticket (for $660). She may also wait until August 1 to buy a ticket. On August 1, a one-way ticket will cost $370, and a round-trip ticket will cost $730. It is possible that between July 1 and August 1, her sister (who works for the airline) will be able to obtain a free one-way ticket for Erica. The probability that her sister will obtain the free ticket is 0.30. If Erica has bought a round-trip ticket on July 1 and her sister has obtained a free ticket, she may return "half" of her round-trip to the airline. In this case, her total cost will be $330 plus a $50 penalty. Use a decision tree approach to determine how to minimize Erica's expected cost of obtaining round-trip transportation to London.

69 A nuclear power company is deciding whether to build a nuclear power plant at Diablo Canyon or at Roy Rogers City. The cost of building the power plant is $10 million at Diablo and $20 at Roy Rogers City. If the company builds at Diablo, however, and an earthquake occurs at Diablo during the next 5 years, construction will be terminated and the company will lose $10 million (and will still have to build a power plant at Roy Rogers City). Without further information, the company believes there is a 20% chance that an earthquake will occur at Diablo during the next 5 years. For $1 million, a geologist can be hired to analyze the fault structure at Diablo Canyon. She will either predict that an earthquake will occur or that an earthquake will not occur. The geologist's past record indicates that she will predict an earthquake on 95% of the occasions for which an earthquake will occur and no earthquake on 90% of the occasions for which an earthquake will not occur. Should the power company hire the geologist? Also find the EVSI and the EVPI.

70 Joan's utility function for her asset position x (for x between 0 and $160,000) is given by $U(x) = \sqrt{x}/400$.

  a Is Joan risk averse? Explain.

b Currently, Joan's assets consist of $10,000 in cash and a $90,000 home. During a given year, there is a 0.001 probability that Joan's home will be destroyed by fire or other causes. How much should Joan be willing to pay for insurance that covers her home completely from this type of destruction?

71 My current annual income is $40,000. I believe that I owe $8000 in taxes. For $500, I can hire a CPA to review my tax return. There is a 20% chance she will save me $4000 in taxes and an 80% chance she won't save me anything. If x is my disposable income for the current year, my utility function is given by $U(x) = \sqrt{x}/200$.

    a Am I risk averse or risk seeking?

    b Should I hire the accountant?

Level B

72 City officials in Ft. Lauderdale, Florida, are trying to decide whether to evacuate coastal residents in anticipation of a major hurricane that may make landfall near their city within the next 48 hours. Based on previous studies, it is estimated that it will cost approximately 1 million dollars to evacuate the residents living along the coast of this major metropolitan area. However, if city officials choose not to evacuate their residents and the storm strikes Fort Lauderdale, there would likely be some deaths as a result of the hurricane's storm surge along the coast. While city officials are reluctant to place an economic value on the loss of human life resulting from such a storm, they realize that it may ultimately be necessary to do so to make a sound judgment in this situation. Prior to making the evacuation decision, city officials consult hurricane experts at the National Hurricane Center in Coral Gables regarding the accuracy of past predictions. They learn that in similar past cases, hurricanes that were *predicted* to make landfall near a particular coastal location actually did so 60% of the time. Moreover, they learn that in past similar cases hurricanes that were predicted *not* to make landfall near a particular coastal location actually did so 20% of the time. Finally, in response to similar threats in the past, weather forecasters have issued predictions of a major hurricane making landfall near a particular coastal location 40% of the time.

    a Let L be the economic valuation of the loss of human life resulting from a coastal strike by the hurricane in this case. Employ a decision tree to help these city officials make a decision that minimizes the expected cost of responding to the threat of the impending storm as a function of L. To proceed, you might begin by choosing an initial value of L and then perform sensitivity analysis on the optimal decision by varying this model parameter. Summarize your findings.

    b For which values of L will these city officials *always* choose to evacuate the coastal residents, regardless of the Hurricane Center's prediction?

73 A homeowner wants to decide whether he should install an electronic heat pump in his home. Given that the cost of installing a new heat pump is fairly large, the homeowner would like to do so only if he can count on being able to recover the initial expense over *five* consecutive years of cold winter weather. Upon reviewing historical data on the operation of heat pumps in various kinds of winter weather, he computes the expected annual costs of heating his home during the winter months with and without a heat pump in operation. These cost figures are shown in Table 6.29. The probabilities of experiencing a mild, normal, colder than normal, and severe winter are $0.2(1 - x)$, $0.5(1 - x)$, $0.3(1 - x)$, and x, respectively.

TABLE 6.29 **Expected Winter Heating Costs for Homeowner's Decision Problem**

Decision Alternatives	Mild	Normal	Colder than Normal	Severe
Purchase Pump	$420	$590	$720	$900
Don't Purchase Pump	$358	$503	$612	$765

    a Given that $x = 0.1$, what is the most that the homeowner is willing to pay for the heat pump?

    b If the heat pump costs $500, how large must x be before the homeowner decides it is economically worthwhile to install the heat pump?

c Given that $x = 0.1$, compute and interpret the expected value of perfect information (EVPI) when the heat pump costs $500.

d Repeat part **c** when $x = 0.15$.

74 Consider a company that manufactures computer memory chips in lots of ten chips. From past experience, the company knows that 80% of all lots contain 10% defective chips, and 20% of all lots contain 50% defective chips. If an *acceptable* (that is, 10% defective) batch of chips is sent on to the next stage of production, processing costs of $10,000 are incurred. If an *unacceptable* (that is, 50% defective) batch is sent on to the next stage of production, processing costs of $40,000 are incurred. This company also has the option of reworking a batch of chips at a cost of $10,000. A reworked batch is guaranteed to be acceptable. Alternatively, at a cost of $1000, the company can test one memory chip from each batch in an attempt to determine whether the given batch is unacceptable. If a randomly selected chip is found to be defective, the batch from which the chip came is acceptable with probability 8/18. If a randomly selected chip is found *not* to be defective, the batch from which the chip came is acceptable with probability 72/82.

a Determine how this company can minimize the expected total cost per batch of computer memory chips.

b Compute and interpret the expected value of sample information (EVSI) in this decision problem.

c Compute and interpret the expected value of perfect information (EVPI) in this decision problem.

d Suppose now that this manufacturer's utility function of cost c per batch is $U(c) = -(c)^{0.5}$. Find the strategy that maximizes the manufacturer's expected utility. How does this optimal strategy compare to the optimal decision with an EMV criterion? Explain any difference between the two optimal strategies.

75 Patty is trying to determine whether to take management science or statistics. If she takes management science, she believes there is a 10% chance she will receive an A, a 40% chance she will receive a B, and a 50% chance she will receive a C. If Patty takes statistics, she has a 70% chance of receiving a B, a 25% chance of a C, and a 5% chance of a D. Patty is indifferent between the following two options:

- Option 1: Receiving a B for certain
- Option 2: A 70% chance at an A and a 30% chance at a D

    Patty is also indifferent between the following two options:

- Option 3: Receiving a C for certain
- Option 4: A 25% chance at an A and a 75% chance at a D

To maximize the expected utility associated with her final grade, which course should Patty take?

76 Many men over 50 take the PSA blood test. The purpose of the PSA test is to catch prostate cancer early. Dr. Rene Labrie of Quebec conducted a study to determine whether the PSA test can actually prevent cancer deaths. In 1989 Dr. Labrie randomly divided all male registered voters between 45 and 80 in Quebec City into two groups. Two-thirds of the men were asked to be tested for prostate cancer and one-third were not asked. Eventually, 8137 men were screened for prostate cancer (PSA plus digital rectal exam) in 1989; 38,056 men were not screened. By 1997 only 5 of the screened men had died of prostate cancer while 137 of the men who were not screened had died of prostate cancer. (Source: *New York Times*, May 19,1998)

a Discuss why this study seems to indicate that screening for prostate cancer saves lives.

b Despite the results of this study, many doctors are not convinced that early screening for prostate cancer saves lives. Can you see why they doubt the conclusions of the study?

77 You have just been chosen to appear on *Hoosier Millionaire*! The rules are as follows: There are four hidden cards. One says "STOP" and the other three have dollar amounts of $150,000, $200,000, and $1,000,000. You get to choose a card. If the card says "STOP," you win no money. At any time you may quit and keep the largest amount of money that has appeared on any card you have chosen, or you may continue. If you continue and choose the STOP card, however, you win no money. As an example, you might first choose the $150,000 card, then the $200,000 card, and then choose to quit and receive $200,000.

a If your goal is to maximize your expected payoff, what strategy should you follow?

b Suppose your utility function for an increase in cash satisfies $U(0) = 0$, $U(\$40,000) = 0.25$, $U(\$120,000) = 0.50$, $U(\$400,000) = 0.75$, and $U(\$1,000,000) = 1$. Are you risk averse? Explain.

c After drawing a curve through the points in part **b**, determine a strategy that maximizes your expected utility. (Alternatively, you might want to assess and use your *actual* utility function.)

78 You are trying to determine how much money to put in your Tax Saver Benefit (TSB) plan. At the beginning of the calendar year, a TSB allows you to put money into an account. The money in the account can be used to pay for medical expenses incurred during the year. Once the TSB is exhausted, you must pay the medical expenses out of pocket. The benefit of the TSB is that money placed in the TSM is not subject to federal taxes. The catch is that any money left in the TSB at the end of the year is lost to you. Suppose the federal tax rate is 40% and your current annual salary is $50,000. You believe that it is equally likely that your medical expenses during the current year will be $3000, $4000, $5000, $6000, or $7000.

a If you are risk neutral and want to maximize your expected disposable income, how much should you put in your TSB?

b Suppose you assess a utility function for disposable income given by $U(x) = 0.000443x^{0.713595}$. (Who said they all have to have nice round numbers!) Are you risk averse? How much should you put in the TSB?

79 Peter is thinking of purchasing an advertising company from Amanda. At present, only Amanda (not Peter) knows the current value of the company. Peter knows, however, that there is an equal chance that the company is worth 10, 20, 30, 40, 50, 60, 70, 80, 90, or 100 million dollars. Amanda will accept an offer from Peter only if Peter bids at least the value of the company. For example, if Amanda knows the company is worth $20 million, she will accept any bid of $20 million or higher. As soon as Peter purchases the company, his reputation as a skilled businessman immediately increases the actual value of the company by 80%.

a Suppose Peter is risk neutral and is considering bidding 10, 20, 30, 40, 50, 60, 70, 80, 90, or 100 million dollars. What should he bid?

b Suppose Peter's utility function for financial gains or losses (in millions of dollars) is given by $U(x) = ((x + 82)/144)^{1.7}$. Determine whether Peter is risk averse or risk seeking and determine Peter's optimal decision.

80 Sarah Chang is the owner of a small electronics company. In 6 months a proposal is due for an electronic timing system for the 1998 Olympic Games. For several years, Chang's company has been developing a new microprocessor, a critical component in a timing system that would be superior to any product currently on the market. However, progress in research and development has been slow, and Chang is unsure about whether her staff can produce the microprocessor in time. If they succeed in developing the microprocessor (probability p_1), there is an excellent chance (probability p_2) that Chang's company will win the $1 million Olympic contract. If they do not, there is a small chance (probability p_3) that she will still be able to win the same contract with an alternative, inferior timing system that has already been developed.

   If she continues the project, Chang must invest $200,000 in research and development. In addition, making a proposal (which she will decide whether to do after seeing whether the R&D is successful or not) requires developing a prototype timing system at an additional cost of $50,000. Finally, if Chang wins the contract, the finished product will cost an additional $150,000 to produce.

a Develop a decision tree that can be used to solve Chang's problem. You can assume in this part that she is using EMV (of her net profit) as a decision criterion. Build the tree so that she can enter any values for p_1, p_2, and p_3 (in input cells) and automatically see her optimal EMV and optimal strategy from the tree.

b If $p_2 = 0.8$ and $p_3 = 0.1$, what value of p_1 makes Chang indifferent between abandoning the project and going ahead with it?

c How much would Chang be willing to pay the Olympic organization (now) to guarantee her the contract in the case where her company is successful in developing the contract? (This guarantee is in force only if she is successful in developing the product.) Assume $p_1 = 0.4$, $p_2 = 0.8$, and $p_3 = 0.1$.

d Suppose now that this a "big" project for Chang. Therefore, she decides to use expected utility as her criterion, with an exponential utility function. Using some trial and error, see which risk tolerance changes her initial decision from "go ahead" to "abandon" when $p_1 = 0.4$, $p_2 = 0.8$, and $p_3 = 0.1$.

81 Suppose an investor has the opportunity to buy the following contract, a stock call option, on March 1. The contract allows him to buy 100 shares of ABC stock at the end of March, April, or May at a guaranteed price of $50 per share. He can "exercise" this option at most once. For example, if he purchases the stock at the end of March, he cannot purchase more in April or May at the guaranteed price. The current price of the stock is $50. Each month, we assume the stock price either goes up by a dollar (with probability 0.6) or down by a dollar (with probability 0.4). If the investor buys the contract, he is hoping that the stock price will go up. The reasoning is that if he buys the contract, the price goes up to $51, and he buys the stock (that is, he exercises his option) for $50, he can turn around and sell the stock for $51 and make a profit of $1 per share. On the other hand, if the stock price goes down, he doesn't have to exercise his option; he can just throw the contract away.

a Use a decision tree to find the investor's optimal strategy (that is, when he should exercise the option), *assuming* he purchases the contract.

b How much should he be willing to pay for such a contract?

82 The Ventron Engineering Company has just been awarded a $2 million development contract by the U.S. Army Aviation Systems Command to develop a blade spar for its Heavy Lift Helicopter program. The blade spar is a metal tube that runs the length of and provides strength to the helicopter blade. Due to the unusual length and size of the Heavy Lift Helicopter blade, Ventron is unable to produce a single-piece blade spar of the required dimensions, using existing extrusion equipment and material.

The engineering department has prepared two alternatives for developing the blade spar: (1) sectioning or (2) an improved extrusion process. Ventron must decide which process to use. (Backing out of the contract at any point is not an option.) The risk report has been prepared by the engineering department. The information from it is explained below.

The sectioning option involves joining several shorter lengths of extruded metal into a blade spar of sufficient length. This work will require extensive testing and rework over a 12-month period at a total cost of $1.8 million. Although this process will definitely produce an adequate blade spar, it merely represents an extension of existing technology.

To improve the extrusion process, on the other hand, it will be necessary to perform two steps: (1) improve the material used, at a cost of $300,000, and (2) modify the extrusion press, at a cost of $960,000. The first step will require 6 months of work, and if this first step is successful, the second step will require another 6 months of work. If both steps are successful, the blade spar will be available at that time—that is, 1 year from now. The engineers estimate that the probabilities of succeeding in steps 1 and 2 are 0.9 and 0.75, respectively. However, if either step is unsuccessful (which will be known only in 6 months for step 1 and in 1 year for step 2), Ventron will have no alternative but to switch to the sectioning process – and incur the sectioning cost on top of any costs already incurred.

Development of the blade spar must be completed within 18 months to avoid holding up the rest of the contract. If necessary, the sectioning work can be done on an accelerated basis in a 6-month period, but the cost of sectioning will then increase from $1.8 million to $2.4 million.

Frankly, the Director of Engineering, Dr. Smith, wants to try developing the improved extrusion process. This is not only cheaper (if successful) for the current project, but its expected side benefits for future projects could be sizable. Although these side benefits are difficult to gauge, Dr. Smith's best guess is an additional $2 million. (Of course, these side benefits are obtained only if both steps of the modified extrusion process are completed successfully.)

a Develop a decision tree to maximize Ventron's EMV. This includes the revenue from this project, the side benefits (if applicable) from an improved extrusion process, and relevant costs. You don't need to worry about the time value of money—that is, no discounting or NPVs are required. Summarize your findings in words in the spreadsheet.

b What value of side benefits would make Ventron indifferent between the two alternatives?

c How much would Ventron be willing to pay, right now, for perfect information about both steps of the improved extrusion process? (This information would tell Ventron, right now, the ultimate success/failure outcomes of both steps.)

83 Ligature, Inc. is a company that does contract work for publishing companies. It specializes in writing textbooks for secondary schools. Because states such as Texas and California typically adopt only about four to eight textbooks for any given subject and grade level (from which individual schools can choose), the potential for large profits is great.

Ligature is currently negotiating a contract with Brockway and Coates (B&C), a large publishing company, to write a Social Studies series for grades 9–12. Actually, the development of the books is already well under way, and the only details not yet worked out concern the fee B&C will pay Ligature. Ligature has always operated on a fixed-fee basis. Under this arrangement, B&C would pay Ligature its costs, in this case $4.15 million, plus 25%. Ligature would receive this payment in 6 months, at the beginning of year 1. Although this is still an option, the companies have also been discussing a royalty arrangement as an alternative.

Under the royalty plan, B&C would still pay Ligature its $4.15 million costs at the beginning of year 1, but Ligature would then receive yearly royalty payments at the ends of years 1 through 5. These payments would depend on (1) total sales over the 5 years, (2) the timing of sales, and (3) the negotiated royalty rate—that is, Ligature's percentage of each sales dollar. As for timing, both parties agree that 10% of total sales will be in year 1, 20% will be in each of years 2 and 3, 30% will be in year 4, and 20% will be in year 5. They also estimate that the probability distribution of total sales is discrete, with possible values $25 million, $30 million, $50 million, and $70 million, and corresponding probabilities 0.10, 0.45, 0.30, and 0.15.

To guard its interests, B&C has imposed the following restriction to any royalty agreement. It places a cap on the amount Ligature can earn through the royalty scheme. Specifically, the royalties, discounted back to the beginning of year 1 at a 10% discount rate, cannot exceed 33% of Ligature's $4.15 million costs. Obviously, this limits B&C's downside exposure, regardless of the negotiated royalty rate or how well the books sell.

Ligature is interested in maximizing the NPV of its profit from this project (discounted back to the beginning of year 1), using a 10% discount rate. The following steps lead you through the required calculations to "solve" the problem. No decision tree is required for this problem.

a The file P6_83.XLS supplies the inputs in an input section (blue border), and it has a calculation section (red border). First, calculate the upper part of the calculation section. To do so, enter any trial value for total sales in cell G8 and do the necessary calculations to eventually find (in cell G17) the NPV to Ligature from the royalty agreement. At this point, you can use any royalty rate in the RoyRate cell (C28).

b Using the calculations from part **a**, complete the data table in the middle part of the calculation section. It should show the NPV to Ligature for any potential value of total sales. Then use these NPVs to calculate the expected NPV to Ligature in the ExpNPV cell (G27).

c Suppose the current "offer on the table" is a 3% royalty rate. In the bottom part of the calculation section, use IF comparisons to see which arrangement, fixed fee or royalty, each party would favor.

d Continuing part **c** (with the 3% offer on the table), what do you think the two parties will eventually agree upon? That is, will they stick with the 3% royalty rate, move to a different royalty rate, or settle on the fixed-fee arrangement? Answer below cell B36.

84 The American chess master Jonathan Meller is playing the Soviet expert Yuri Gasparov in a two-game exhibition match. Each win earns a player one point, and each draw earns half a point. The player who has the most points after two games wins the match. If the players are tied after two games, they play until one wins a game; then the first player to win a game wins the match. During each game, Meller has two possible strategies: to play a daring strategy or to play a conservative strategy. His probabilities of winning, losing, and drawing when he follows each strategy are shown in Table 6.30. To maximize his probability of winning the match, what should the American do?

TABLE 6.30 **Probabilities for Chess Problem**

Strategy	Win	Loss	Draw
Daring	0.45	0.55	0.00
Conservative	0.00	0.10	0.90

85 [Based on Balston et al. (1992)] An electric utility company is trying to decide whether to replace its PCB transformer in a generating station with a new and safer transformer. To evaluate this decision, the utility needs information about the likelihood of an incident, such as a fire, the cost of such an incident, and the cost of replacing the unit. Suppose that the total cost of replacement as a present value is $75,000. If the transformer is replaced, there is virtually no chance of a fire. However, if the current transformer is retained, the probability of a fire is assessed to be 0.0025. If a fire occurs, then the cleanup cost could be high ($80 million) or low ($20 million). The probability of a high cleanup cost, given that a fire occurs, is assessed at 0.2.

    a If the company uses EMV as its decision criterion, should it replace the transformer?

    b Perform a sensitivity analysis on the key parameters of the problem that are difficult to assess, namely, the probability of a fire, the probability of a high cleanup cost, and the high and low cleanup costs. Does the optimal decision from part **a** remain optimal for a "wide" range of these parameters?

    c Do you believe EMV is the correct criterion to use in this type of problem involving environmental accidents?

86 [Based on Mellichamp et al. (1993)] Construction equipment managers typically have many large pools of engines, transmissions, and other equipment units to maintain. One approach to this maintenance is to use oil analysis, where the oil from any of these is subjected periodically to an inspection. These inspections can sometimes signal an impending failure (for example, too much iron in the oil), and preventive maintenance is then performed (at a relatively low cost), eliminating the risk of failure (failure would result in a relatively high cost). However, oil analysis costs money, and it is not perfect. That is, it can indicate that a unit is defective when in fact it is not about to fail, and it can indicate that a unit is nondefective when in fact it is about to fail. As a possible substitute for oil analysis, the company could simply change the oil periodically, thereby reducing the probability of a failure.

    Suppose the company has four alternatives: (1) do nothing, (2) use oil analysis only, (3) replace oil only, or (4) replace oil and do oil analysis. For option (1) the probability of a failure is p_1, and the cost of a failure is C_1. For option (2), the probability of a failure remains at p_1. If the unit is about to fail, the oil analysis will indicate this with probability $1 - \alpha$; if the unit is not about to fail, the oil analysis will indicate this with probability $1 - \beta$. (Therefore, α and β are the error probabilities of the oil analysis.) The oil analysis itself costs C_2, and if it indicates that a failure is about to occur, the oil will be changed, at cost C_3, and preventive maintenance will be performed. The cost of maintenance to restore a unit that is about to fail is C_4, whereas the cost of maintenance for a unit that is not about to fail is C_5. The only difference between options (3) and (4) is that the probability of a failure decreases to p_2 after changing the oil. The values of these parameters for a particular class of units (engines in light trucks, say) appear in Table 6.31.

TABLE 6.31   **Parameters for Oil Analysis Problem**

Parameter	Value
p_1	0.10
p_2	0.04
α	0.30
β	0.20
C_1	$1200.00
C_2	$20.00
C_3	$14.80
C_4	$500.00
C_5	$250.00

    a For these parameters, develop a decision tree to find the company's best decision and the corresponding expected cost.

    b If the company has 500 units, what should it do? What is the expected cost for the entire fleet?

    c Suppose that the company has different types of units. For example, the cost of an oil change might be higher for some, or the cost of a failure might be higher or lower. Run a sensitivity analysis on any of the parameters you believe might be "key" parameters and see whether the optimal decision changes in ways you would anticipate.

87 [Based on Hess (1993)] A company that is heavily involved in R&D projects believes it might have the potential to develop a very lucrative commercial product that would (if successful) reduce pulp mill water pollution. At the current stage, however, everything is quite uncertain, and the company is trying to decide whether to go ahead with its R&D or abandon the product. The following are the primary risks:

■ Would market tests confirm that there is a significant market for the product?

■ Could the company develop a new process for making this product—that is, is it technically feasible?

■ Even if there is a significant market and the process is technically feasible, would the company's board sanction the new plant capital necessary to produce the product on a commercial scale?

■ Assuming the answers to the above questions are all yes and the plant is built, would the venture turn out to be successful?

We assume that each of these questions has a yes or no answer. The probabilities of yes answers are shown in Table 6.32. The plus-or-minus value indicates the company's uncertainty about the true probabilities.

TABLE 6.32 **Probabilities for Water Pollution Problem**

Event	Probability
Significant market	0.6 ± 0.15
Technically feasible	0.6 ± 0.15
Board sanctions plant expenditures	0.8 ± 0.2
Commercial success	0.8 ± 0.2

The primary economic factors are the following:

■ the research expenses to identify a new production process for the product

■ the marketing development cost to determine whether there is a significant market

■ the process development costs, including presanction engineering

■ the commercial development costs, both before and after the board's sanction

■ the venture value (net present value) if successful

The estimates of these values are shown in Table 6.33. Again, the plus-or-minus values indicate the company's considerable uncertainty about the values. All dollar values are in millions of dollars.

TABLE 6.33 **Monetary Estimates for Water Pollution Problem**

Expense or Gain	Net Present Value
Research expense	$0.8 \pm 25\%$
Market development expense	$0.2 \pm 25\%$
Process development expense (presanction)	$3.0 \pm 25\%$
Commercial development expense (presanction)	$0.5 \pm 25\%$
Commercial development expense (postsanction)	$1.0 \pm 25\%$
Value if successful	$25.0 \pm 50\%$

The timing of events is as follows:

■ Decide whether to abandon product now. (This is really the only nontrivial decision the company will make.) If not, then:

- Spend on research and marketing development. If marketing development indicates an insignificant market for the product *or* research indicates that the process is technically infeasible, cut expenses and quit. Otherwise:

- Spend on process and commercial development. If company board then declines to sanction money for plant, cut expenses and quit. Otherwise:

- Spend on further commercial development. By this time, the company has made all of its decisions. If the venture turns out to be a commercial success, then it gains the venture value for a success (less expenses so far). Otherwise, the company has lost the money spent so far, but that is all.

Analyze the company's problem. Obviously, with the high degree of uncertainty, sensitivity analysis is the key. Note that there are many uncertainties about the input parameters in Tables 6.32 and 6.33. In fact, there are far too many to allow you to try every combination. Therefore, just try a few combinations that you believe might be the most important. ■

6.1 Jogger Shoe Company

The Jogger Shoe Company is trying to decide whether to make a change in its most popular brand of running shoes. The new style would cost the same to produce, and it would be priced the same, but it would incorporate a new kind of lacing system that (according to its marketing research people) would make it more popular. There is a fixed cost of $300,000 of changing over to the new style. The unit contribution to before-tax profit for either style is $8. The tax rate is 35%. Also, because the fixed cost can be depreciated and will therefore affect the after-tax cash flow, we need a depreciation method. We assume it is straight-line depreciation.

The current demand for these shoes is 190,000 pairs annually. The company assumes this demand will continue for the next 3 years if the current style is retained. However, there is uncertainty about demand for the new style, if it is introduced. The company models this uncertainty by assuming a normal distribution in year 1, with mean 220,000 and standard deviation 20,000. The company also assumes that this demand, whatever it is, will remain constant for the next 3 years. However, if demand in year 1 for the new style is sufficiently low, the company can always switch back to the current style and realize an annual demand of 190,000. The company wants a strategy that will maximize the expected net present value (NPV) of total cash flow for the next 3 years, where a 15% interest rate is used for the purpose of calculating NPV.

6.2 Westhouser Paper Company

The Westhouser Paper Company in the state of Washington currently has an option to purchase a piece of land with good timber forest on it. It is now May 1, and the current price of the land is $2.2 million. Westhouser does not actually need the timber from this land until the beginning of July, but its top executives fear that another company might buy the land between now and the beginning of July. They assess that there is 1 chance out of 20 that a competitor will buy the land during May. If this does not occur, they assess that there is 1 chance out of 10 that the competitor will buy the land during June. If Westhouser does not take advantage of its current option, it can attempt to buy the land at the beginning of June or the beginning of July, provided that it is still available.

Westhouser's incentive for delaying the purchase is that its financial experts believe there is a good chance that the price of the land will fall significantly in one or both of the next two months. They assess the possible price decreases and their probabilities in Tables 6.34 and 6.35. Table 6.34 shows the probabilities of the possible price decreases during May. Table 6.35 shows the *conditional* probabilities of the possible price decreases in June, *given* the price decrease in May. For example, if the price decrease in May is $60,000, then the possible price decreases in June are $0, $30,000, and $60,000 with respective probabilities 0.6, 0.2, and 0.2.

If Westhouser purchases the land, it believes that it can gross $3 million. (This does not count the cost of purchasing the land.) But if it does not purchase the land, it believes that it can make $650,000 from alternative investments. What should the company do?

TABLE 6.34 Distribution of Price Decrease in May

Price Decrease	Probability
$0	0.5
$60,000	0.3
$120,000	0.2

TABLE 6.35 Distribution of Price Decrease in June

Price Decrease in May					
$0		$60,000		$120,000	
June Decrease	Probability	June Decrease	Probability	June Decrease	Probability
$0	0.3	$0	0.6	$0	0.7
$60,000	0.6	$30,000	0.2	$20,000	0.2
$120,000	0.1	$60,000	0.2	$40,000	0.1

7

Sampling and Sampling Distributions

Successful Applications

In the first half of this chapter, we discuss methods for selecting random samples. The purpose of these samples is to discover characteristics of a population, such as the proportion who favor the President's economic policy. By selecting a *random* sample of perhaps 1000 people out of a population of millions, we can make fairly accurate inferences about the population as a whole, at savings of much time and money.

A different type of sample has recently become the focus of many direct response marketers, companies that mail advertisements for their products directly to prospective customers. The experience of one such company, the Franklin Mint (FM) of Philadelphia, is described in Zahavi (1995). The FM markets expensive collectibles, ranging from famous Precision Car models to the Sword of Francis Drake, to a relatively small, but avid, collector population. The FM relies entirely on its mailings to prospective customers for sales. However, it is important for the company to mail ads for any particular products to the right customers; otherwise, mailing costs can seriously erode profits. This is especially the case when, on average, the response rate to products in this type of market is less than one-half percent—that is, no more than 1 person out of every 200 who receive a mailing actually purchases a product.

Until recently, companies such as the FM used relatively subjective rules to choose the sample of customers to receive mailings. However, these companies now have an abundance of data about their customers, and they are beginning to use sophisticated statistical methods to locate the samples of customers who are most likely to purchase any particular type of product. In essence, they build a probability model that relates the probability of purchasing to (1) the customer's purchase history; (2) demographic variables (many of which can be acquired from outside vendors and appended to the customer's record); and (3) the product attributes, such as theme, material, artist, sponsor, and product code.[1] The most challenging part of the model is to identify the best predictor variables from the hundreds available, but techniques (and software) are now available to perform this task efficiently.

Direct marketers such as the FM have found that this is a situation where even a small amount of explanatory power from a statistical model can

---

[1]This is actually an application of regression analysis, which we will study in Chapters 11 and 12, but it is a special case in that the variable of interest is binary—a customer either purchases or doesn't purchase. Regression methods for binary dependent variables are available but fall outside the scope of this book.

make a big difference in the bottom line. No model can correctly identify *exactly* who will respond positively to an ad and who will not, but if the model can identify customer samples where the response rate to mailings is even a *little* higher than it was, the ratio of mailing costs to eventual sales can decrease significantly. For example, the FM installed its system (called AMOS) in 1992 and realized an increase in profit of approximately 7.5% in 3 years; undoubtedly, it has increased even more since then. As Zahavi states, "Looking beyond the FM, the implications of using AMOS-like systems to support the decision-making process in the database marketing industry are likely to be quite substantial, which, given the size of the industry, could run well in excess of several hundred million dollars a year!" ■

7.1 Introduction

In a typical statistical inference problem we want to discover one or more characteristics of a given population. For example, we might want to know the proportion of toothpaste customers who have tried, or intend to try, a particular brand. Or we might want to know the average amount owed on credit card accounts for a population of customers at a shopping mall. Generally, the population is large and/or spread out, and it is difficult, maybe even impossible, to contact each member. Therefore, we identify a sample of the population and then obtain information from the members of the sample.

There are two main objectives of this chapter. The first is to discuss the sampling schemes that are generally used in real sampling applications. We will focus on several types of *random* samples and see why these are preferable to nonrandom samples. The second objective is to see how the information from a sample of the population—for example, 1% of the population—can be used to infer the properties of the entire population. The key here is the concept of sampling distributions. We will focus on the sampling distribution of the sample mean, and we will see how a famous mathematical result called the central limit theorem is the key to the analysis.

7.2 Sampling Terminology

We begin by introducing some of the terminology that is used in sampling. In any sampling problem there is a relevant **population**. It is the set of all members about which a study intends to make inferences. It is important to realize that a population is defined in relationship to any particular study. Any analyst planning a survey should first decide which population the conclusions of the study will concern, so that a sample can be chosen from this population.

For example, if a marketing researcher plans to use a questionnaire to infer consumers' reactions to a new product, she must first decide which population of consumers is of interest—all consumers, consumers over 21 years old, consumers who do most of their shopping in shopping malls, or others. Once the relevant consumer population has been designated, a sample from this population can then be surveyed. However, inferences made from the study pertain only to this *particular* population.

Before we can choose a sample from a given population, we typically need a list of all members of the population. This list is called a **frame**, and the potential sample members are called **sampling units**. Depending on the context, sampling units could be individual people, households, companies, cities, or others.

In this chapter we will assume that the population is finite and consists of N sampling units. We also assume that a frame of these N sampling units is available. Unfortunately, there are situations where a complete frame is practically impossible to obtain. For example, if we want to survey the attitudes of all unemployed teenagers in Chicago, it is practically impossible to obtain a complete frame of them. In this situation all we can hope to obtain is a partial frame, from which the sample can be selected. If the partial frame omits any significant segments of the population—which a complete frame would include—then the resulting sample could be biased. For instance, if we use the Yellow Pages of a Los Angeles telephone book to choose a sample of restaurants, we automatically omit all restaurants that do not advertise in the Yellow Pages. Depending on the purposes of the study, this might or might not be a serious omission.

There are two basic types of samples, probability samples and judgmental samples. A **probability sample** is a sample in which the sampling units are chosen from the population by means of a random mechanism such as a random number table. In contrast, no formal random mechanism is used to select a **judgmental sample**. In this case the sampling units are chosen according to the sampler's judgment.

We will not discuss judgmental samples. The reason is very simple—there is no way to measure the accuracy of judgmental samples because the rules of probability do not apply to them. In other words, if we estimate some population characteristic from the observations in a judgmental sample, there is no way to tell how accurate this estimate is. In addition, it is very difficult to choose a representative sample from a population *without* using some random mechanism. Because our judgment is usually not as good as we think, judgmental samples are likely to contain our own built-in biases. Therefore, we will focus exclusively on probability samples from here on.

7.3 Methods for Selecting Random Samples

In this section we discuss the types of random samples that are used in real sampling applications. Different types of sampling schemes have different properties. There is typically a trade-off between cost and accuracy. Some sampling schemes are cheaper and easier to administer, whereas others cost a bit more but provide more accurate information. We will discuss some of these issues, but anyone who intends to make a living in survey sampling needs to learn much more about the topic than we can cover here.

7.3.1 Simple Random Sampling

The simplest type of sampling scheme is appropriately called **simple random sampling**. Consider a population of size N and suppose we want to sample n units from this population. Then a simple random sample of size n has the property that every possible sample of size n has the same probability of being chosen. Simple random samples are the easiest to understand, and their statistical properties are fairly straightforward. Therefore, we will focus primarily on simple random samples in the rest of this book. However, as we will discuss shortly, simple random samples are typically *not* used in real applications.

The defining property of a simple random sample is that every sample has the same chance of being chosen. We illustrate what this means for a small population. Suppose the population size is $N = 5$, and we label the five members of the population as a, b, c, d, and e. Also, suppose we want to sample $n = 2$ of these members. Then the possible samples are (a, b), (a, c), (a, d), (a, e), (b, c), (b, d), (b, e), (c, d), (c, e), and (d, e). That is, there are 10 possible samples—the number of ways two members can be chosen from five members. Then a *simple* random sample of size $n = 2$ has the property that each of these 10 possible samples has an equal probability, 1/10, of being chosen.

One other property of simple random samples can be seen from this example. If we focus on any member of the population, say, member b, we note that b is a member of 4 of the 10 samples. Therefore, the probability that b is chosen in a simple random sample is 4/10, or 2/5. In general, any member has probability n/N of being chosen in a simple random sample. If you are one of 100,000 members of a population, then the probability that you will be selected in a simple random sample of size 100 is 100/100,000, or 1 out of 1000.

There are several ways simple random samples can be chosen, all of which involve random numbers. One approach that works well for our small example with $N = 5$ and $n = 2$ is to generate a single random number with the RAND function in Excel. We divide the interval from 0 to 1 into 10 equal subintervals of length 1/10 each and see which of these subintervals the random number falls into. We then choose the corresponding sample. For example, suppose the random number is 0.465. This is in the fifth subinterval, that is, the interval from 0.4 to 0.5, so we choose the fifth sample, (b, c).

Clearly, this method is consistent with simple random sampling—each of the samples has the same chance of being chosen—but it is prohibitive when n and N are large. In this case there are too many possible samples to list. Fortunately, there is another method that can be used. We illustrate it in the following example.

EXAMPLE 7.1

Consider the frame of 40 families with annual incomes shown in column B of Figure 7.1. (See the file RANDSAMP.XLS.) We want to choose a simple random sample of size 10 from this frame. How can this be done? And how do summary statistics of the chosen families compare to the corresponding summary statistics of the population?

FIGURE 7.1 **Population Income Data**

	A	B	C	D
1	Illustration of simple random sampling			
2				
3	Summary statistics			
4		Mean	Median	Stdev
5	Population	$39,985	$38,500	$7,377
6	Sample			
7				
8	Population			
9	Family	Income		
10	1	$43,300		
11	2	$44,300		
12	3	$34,600		
13	4	$38,000		
14	5	$44,700		
15	6	$45,600		
16	7	$42,700		
17	8	$36,900		
18	9	$38,400		
19	10	$33,700		
20	11	$44,100		
21	12	$51,500		
22	13	$35,900		
23	14	$35,600		
24	15	$43,000		
47	38	$46,900		
48	39	$37,300		
49	40	$41,000		

Solution

The idea is very simple. We first generate a column of random numbers in column C. Then we sort the rows according to the random numbers and choose the first 10 families in the sorted rows. The following procedure produces the results in Figure 7.2. (See the Manual sheet in the file RANDSAMP.XLS.)

1   **Random numbers.** Enter the formula

$$=RAND()$$

in cell C10 and copy it down column C.

FIGURE 7.2   **Selecting a Simple Random Sample**

	A	B	C	D	E	F	G
1	Illustration of simple random sampling						
2							
3	Summary statistics						
4		Mean	Median	Stdev		Range names	
5	Population	$39,985	$38,500	$7,377		PopInc: B10:B49	
6	Sample	$38,750	$38,200	$5,922		SampInc: F10:F19	
7							
8	Population				Random sample		
9	Family	Income	Random #		Family	Income	Random #
10	1	$43,300	0.6835		32	$31,700	0.0513
11	2	$44,300	0.5237		34	$39,300	0.0742
12	3	$34,600	0.8313		4	$38,000	0.0814
13	4	$38,000	0.0814		14	$35,600	0.0922
14	5	$44,700	0.1955		22	$33,600	0.1162
15	6	$45,600	0.2007		40	$41,000	0.1219
16	7	$42,700	0.8300		12	$51,500	0.1231
17	8	$36,900	0.8036		10	$33,700	0.1677
18	9	$38,400	0.1788		9	$38,400	0.1788
19	10	$33,700	0.1677		5	$44,700	0.1955
20	11	$44,100	0.2638		6	$45,600	0.2007
21	12	$51,500	0.1231		16	$38,600	0.2316
22	13	$35,900	0.7965		21	$56,400	0.2571
23	14	$35,600	0.0922		36	$36,300	0.2585
24	15	$43,000	0.6672		11	$44,100	0.2638
47	38	$46,900	0.7248		31	$33,000	0.9277
48	39	$37,300	0.3655		20	$31,900	0.9489
49	40	$41,000	0.1219		37	$28,400	0.9491

2   **Replace with values.** To enable sorting we must first "freeze" the random numbers—that is, replace their formulas with values. To do this, select the range C10:C49, use Edit/Copy menu item, and then use the Edit/Paste Special menu item with the Values option.

3   **Copy to a new range.** Copy the range A10:C49 to the range E10:G49.

4   **Sort.** Select the range E10:G49 and use the Data/Sort menu item. Sort according to the Random # column (column G) in ascending order. Then the 10 families with the 10 smallest random numbers are the ones in the sample. (These are enclosed in a border.)

5   **Means.** Use the AVERAGE, MEDIAN, and STDEV functions in row 6 to calculate summary statistics of the first 10 incomes in column F. These similar summary statistics for the population have already been calculated in row 5.

To obtain more random samples of size 10 (for comparison), we would need to go through this process repeatedly. To save you the trouble of doing so, we wrote a macro to automate the process. (See the Automated sheet in the RANDSAMP.XLS file.) This sheet looks essentially the same as the sheet in Figure 7.2, except that there is a button to run the macro and only the required data remain on the spreadsheet. Try clicking on this button. Each time you do so, you'll get a different random sample—and different summary measures in row 6. By doing this many times and keeping track of the sample summary data, you can see how the summary measures vary from sample to sample. We will have much more to say about this type of variation later in this chapter. ■

The procedure described in Example 7.1 can be used in Excel to select a simple random sample of any size from any population. All we need is a frame—a list of the population values. Then it's just a matter of inserting random numbers, freezing them, and sorting on the random numbers.

Perhaps surprisingly, simple random samples are almost never used in real applications. There are several reasons for this.

■ Because each sampling unit has the same chance of being sampled, simple random sampling can result in samples that are spread over a large geographical region. This can make sampling extremely expensive, especially if personal interviews are used.

■ Simple random sampling requires that all sampling units be identified prior to sampling. Sometimes this is infeasible.

■ Simple random sampling can result in underrepresentation or overrepresentation of certain segments of the population. For example, if the primary—but not sole—interest is in the graduate student subpopulation of university students, a simple random sample of *all* university students might not provide enough information about the graduate students.

In the next several subsections we will describe sampling plans that are often used. These plans differ from simple random sampling both in the way the samples are chosen and in the way the data analysis is performed. However, we will barely touch on this latter issue. The details are quite complicated and are better left to a book devoted entirely to sampling. [See, for example, the excellent book by Levy and Lemeshow (1991).]

7.3.2 Using StatPro to Generate Simple Random Samples

The method described in Example 7.1 is simple but somewhat tedious, especially if we want to generate more than one random sample. (Even the macro described at the end of the example works only for that particular file.) Therefore, we developed a more general method as part of StatPro. It generates any number of simple random samples of any specified sample size from a given data set. It can be found under the StatPro/Statistical Inference/Generate Random Samples menu item.

Actually, this procedure returns only the *indexes* of the members selected in the samples. For example, from a data set with 500 members, one random sample of size 5 might have the indexes 413, 22, 310, 156, and 209. This indicates that these particular members are included in the sample. To get the *data* for these members, we can use a lookup command, as illustrated in the following example.

EXAMPLE 7.2

The file RECEIVE.XLS contains 280 accounts receivable for the Spring Mills Company (the same data we discussed in Example 3.9). There are three variables:

- Size: customer size (small, medium, large), depending on its volume of business with Spring Mills
- Days: number of days since the customer was billed
- Amount: amount of the bill

Generate 50 random samples of size 15 each from the small customers only, calculate the average amount owed in each random sample, and construct a histogram of these 50 averages.

Solution

The original file (from Chapter 3) contains only the Size, Days, and Amount variables, and the data are sorted by Size. We append an extra variable Account in column A that indexes the accounts: 1 to 280. (Use the Edit/Fill menu item to do this quickly.) To select small accounts only, insert a blank row after account 150 (the last small account). Then, with the cursor anywhere in the small account data set, use the StatPro/Statistical Inference/Generate

FIGURE 7.3 **Randomly Generated Samples**

	A	B	C	D	E	AV	AW	AX	AY	AZ	BA	BB
1	*Indices of members in samples*										Averages shown as a column	
2		Sample1	Sample2	Sample3	Sample4	Sample47	Sample48	Sample49	Sample50			
3		86	124	139	44	16	101	122	77		Averages	
4		124	84	81	91	76	104	84	111		250.67	
5		85	12	32	82	49	41	50	16		244.00	
6		42	28	46	142	120	103	71	20		238.67	
7		88	88	71	45	27	89	65	150		255.33	
8		30	50	148	47	119	102	12	66		242.67	
9		127	59	50	24	103	30	5	70		248.00	
10		128	136	132	17	88	21	35	99		261.33	
11		15	30	24	26	67	63	86	85		246.00	
12		2	43	29	7	74	12	108	94		251.33	
13		90	115	124	143	3	34	7	142		258.00	
14		108	94	88	68	32	14	133	1		252.67	
15		150	18	70	112	79	23	28	32		260.00	
16		61	142	143	16	48	95	139	68		246.67	
17		20	55	37	39	97	15	30	102		256.00	
18											259.33	
19	Amounts owed for accounts selected in samples										254.67	
20		Sample1	Sample2	Sample3	Sample4	Sample47	Sample48	Sample49	Sample50		251.33	
21		280	270	210	210	270	310	220	220		269.33	
22		270	280	300	320	270	320	280	240		258.67	
23		180	260	200	290	250	230	190	270		270.00	
24		280	240	230	240	240	240	240	250		246.67	
25		260	260	240	320	220	220	200	370		242.67	
26		140	190	240	270	250	280	260	280		260.00	
27		190	320	190	230	240	140	300	240		258.67	
28		300	170	260	260	260	240	200	320		267.33	
29		350	140	230	210	390	190	280	180		259.33	
30		210	310	260	330	370	260	260	240		260.00	
31		180	220	270	210	210	330	330	240		261.33	
32		260	240	260	260	200	320	290	180		239.33	
33		370	240	240	220	190	290	240	200		264.00	
34		240	240	210	270	240	260	210	260		258.00	
35		250	280	240	190	290	350	140	280		241.33	
36	Averages										263.33	
37		250.67	244.00	238.67	255.33	259.33	265.33	242.67	251.33		239.33	
38											232.00	

Random Samples menu item, enter 50 and 15 as the number of samples and the sample size, and put the results in a new sheet. The top part of Figure 7.3 should appear. (We have hidden many of the intermediate samples.)

To find the amounts owed for the sampled accounts, enter the formula

$$=VLOOKUP(B3,Data!Data,4)$$

in cell B21 and copy it to the range B21:AY35. (Note that Data is the range name StatPro automatically gives to the original data range in the Data sheet. We use this range here as the lookup table range.) Then calculate the averages in row 37 with the AVERAGE function, and transpose this *row* of averages to a *column* of averages in column BA by highlighting the range BA4:BA53, entering the formula

$$=TRANSPOSE(B37:AY37)$$

and pressing Ctrl-Shift-Enter. (A column is needed by StatPro to create the histogram.) Finally, use StatPro's histogram procedure with appropriate settings to create a histogram similar to that shown in Figure 7.4. (Yours might look different because the random numbers you use to generate the random samples will be different from ours.)

The histogram in Figure 7.4 indicates the variability of sample means we might obtain by selecting many *different* random samples of size 15 from this particular population of small customer accounts. We will come back to this important idea when we study sampling distributions in Section 7.4.

FIGURE 7.4   **Histogram of 50 Sample Averages**

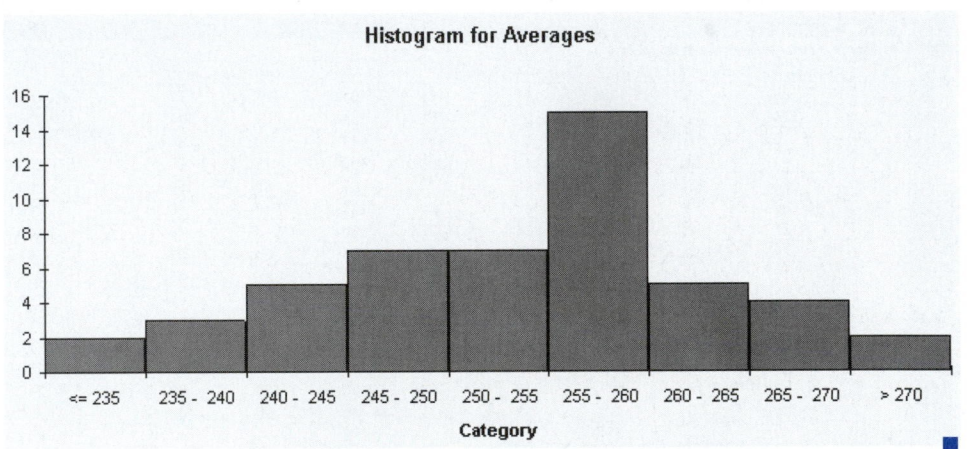

7.3.3 Systematic Sampling

Suppose you are asked to select a random sample of 250 names from the white pages of a telephone book. Let's also say that there are 55,000 names listed in the white pages. A **systematic sample** provides a convenient way to choose the sample. It works as follows. First, we calculate the **sampling interval** as the population size divided by the sample size: $55,000/250 = 220$. Conceptually, we can think of dividing the book into 250 "blocks" with 220 names per block. Next, we use a random mechanism to choose a number between 1 and 220. Say this number is 131. Then we choose the 131st name and every 220th name thereafter. So we would choose the 131st name, the 351st name, the 571st name, and so on. The result is a systematic sample of size $n = 250$.

Clearly, this is different from simple random sampling because not every sample of size 250 has a chance of being chosen. In fact, there are only 220 different samples possible (depending on the first number chosen), and each of these is equally likely. Nevertheless, systematic sampling is generally similar to simple random sampling in its statistical properties. The key is the relationship between the ordering of the sampling units in the frame (the white pages of the telephone book in this case) and the purpose of the study.

If the purpose of the study is to analyze personal incomes, say, then there is probably no relationship between the alphabetical ordering of names in the telephone book and personal income. However, there are situations where the ordering of the sampling units is not random, which can make systematic sampling more or less appealing. For example, suppose that a company wants to sample randomly from its customers, and its customer list is in decreasing order of order volumes. That is, the largest customers are at the top of the list and the smallest are at the bottom. Then systematic sampling might be more representative than simple random sampling because it guarantees a wide range of customers in terms of order volumes.

However, some type of cyclical ordering in the list of sampling units can lead to very *unrepresentative* samples. As an extreme, suppose a company has a list of daily transactions and it decides to draw a systematic sample with the sampling interval equal to 7. Then if the first sampled day is Monday, all other days in the sample will be Mondays! This could clearly bias the sample. Nevertheless, except for obvious examples like this one, systematic sampling can be an attractive alternative to simple random sampling and is often used because of its convenience.

7.3.4 Stratified Sampling

Suppose we can identify various subpopulations within the total population. We call these subpopulations **strata**. Then instead of taking a simple random sample from the entire population, it might make more sense to select a simple random sample from each stratum separately. This sampling method is called **stratified sampling**. It is a particularly useful approach when there is considerable variation *between* the various strata but relatively little variation *within* a given stratum.

There are several advantages to stratified sampling. One obvious advantage is that we obtain separate estimates within each stratum—which we would not obtain if we took a simple random sample from the entire population. Even if we eventually plan to pool the samples from the individual strata, it cannot hurt to have the total sample broken down into separate samples initially.

A more important advantage of stratified sampling is that the accuracy of the resulting population estimates can be increased by using appropriately defined strata. The trick is to define the strata so that there is less variability within the individual strata than in the population as a whole. We want strata such that there is relative homogeneity within the strata, but relative heterogeneity among the strata, with respect to the variable(s) being analyzed. By choosing the strata in this way, we can generally obtain more accuracy for a given sampling cost than we could obtain from a simple random sample at the same cost. Alternatively, we can achieve the same level of accuracy at a lower sampling cost.

The key to using stratified sampling effectively is selecting the appropriate strata. Suppose a company that advertises its product on television wants to estimate the reaction of viewers to the advertising. Here the population consists of all viewers who have seen the advertising. But what are the appropriate strata? The answer depends on the company's objectives and its product. The company could stratify the population by gender, by income, by amount of television watched, by the amount of the product class consumed, and probably others. Without knowing more specific information about the company's objectives, it is impossible to say which of these stratification schemes is most appropriate.

Suppose that we have identified I nonoverlapping strata in a given population. Let N be the total population size, and let N_i be the population size of stratum i, so that

$$N = N_1 + N_2 + \cdots + N_I$$

To obtain a stratified random sample, we must choose a total sample size n, and we must choose a sample size n_i from each stratum i, such that

$$n = n_1 + n_2 + \cdots + n_I$$

We can then select a simple random sample of the specified size from *each* stratum exactly as in Example 7.1.

However, how do we choose the individual sample sizes n_1 through n_I, given that the total sample size n has been chosen? For example, if we decide to sample 500 customers in total, how many should come from each stratum? There are many ways that we could choose numbers n_1 through n_I that sum to n, but probably the most popular method is to use **proportional sample sizes**. The idea is very simple. If one stratum has, say, 15% of the total population, then we select 15% of the total sample from this stratum. For example, if the total sample size is $n = 500$, we select $0.15(500) = 75$ members from this stratum.

The advantage of proportional sample sizes is that they are very easy to determine. The disadvantage is that they ignore differences in variability among the strata. To illustrate, suppose that we are attempting to estimate the population mean amount paid annually per student for textbooks at a large university. We identify three strata: undergraduates, masters students, and doctoral students. Their population sizes are 20,000, 4000, and 1000, respectively. Therefore, the proportions of students in these strata are $20{,}000/25{,}000 = 0.80$, $4000/25{,}000 = 0.16$, and $1000/25{,}000 = 0.04$. If the total sample size is $n = 150$, then the sample should include 120 undergraduates, 24 masters students, and 6 doctoral students if proportional sample sizes are used.

However, let σ_i be the standard deviation of annual textbook payments in stratum i, and suppose that $\sigma_1 = \$50$, $\sigma_2 = \$120$, and $\sigma_3 = \$180$. Thus, there is considerably more variation in the amounts paid by doctoral students than by undergraduates, with the masters students in the middle. If we are interested in estimating the mean amount spent per student, then despite its small sample size, the doctoral sample is likely to have a large effect on the accuracy of our estimate of the mean. This is because of its relatively large standard deviation. In contrast, we might not need to sample as heavily from the undergraduate population because of its relatively small standard deviation. In general, strata with less variability can afford to be sampled less heavily than proportional sampling calls for, and the opposite is true for strata with larger variability. In fact, there are *optimal* sample size formulas that take the σ_i's into account, but we will not present them here.

In the following example we illustrate how stratified sampling can be accomplished with Excel by using random numbers.

E X A M P L E   7 . 3

The file STRATIFIED.XLS contains a frame of all 1000 people in the city of Smalltown who have Sears credit cards. Sears is interested in estimating the average number of *other* credit cards these people own, as well as other information about their use of credit. The company decides to stratify these customers by age, select a stratified sample of size 100 with proportional sample sizes, and then contact these 100 people by phone. How might Sears proceed?

Solution

First, Sears has to decide exactly how to stratify by age. Their reasoning is that different age groups probably have different attitudes and behavior regarding credit. After some preliminary investigation, they decide to use three age categories: 18–30, 31–62, and 63–80. (No one in the population is younger than 18 or older than 80.)

Figure 7.5 shows how the calculations might then proceed. We begin with the following inputs: (1) the total sample size in cell C3, (2) the definitions of the strata in rows 6–8, and (3) the customer data in the range A11:B1010. To see which age category each customer is in, we enter the formula

$$=IF(B11<=\$D\$6,1,IF(B11<=\$D\$7,2,3))$$

in cell C11 and then copy it down column C.

FIGURE 7.5 **Selecting a Stratified Sample**

	A	B	C	D	E	F	G	H	I	J	K	L	M	N
1	Stratified sampling by Sears													
2														
3	Total sample size		100											
4									Range names:					
5	Strata based on age					Counts	SampSize		TotSampSize: C3					
6	Stratum 1	18	to	30		132	13							
7	Stratum 2	31	to	62		766	77							
8	Stratum 3	63	to	80		102	10							
9														
10	Cust	Age	Category		Cust_1	Age_1	Cust_2	Age_2	Cust_3	Age_3		Cust_1	Age_1	Rand #
11	1	49	2		11	23	1	49	4	66		835	24	0.002255
12	2	39	2		13	24	2	39	12	63		412	26	0.04736
13	3	55	2		15	30	3	55	38	75		67	27	0.054435
14	4	66	3		20	29	5	52	40	64		163	30	0.057802
15	5	52	2		26	30	6	37	42	71		874	23	0.063774
16	6	37	2		34	26	7	34	53	63		637	23	0.092121
17	7	34	2		43	25	8	34	64	71		513	28	0.092475
18	8	34	2		55	25	9	33	68	66		409	27	0.096296
19	9	33	2		56	28	10	36	95	64		56	28	0.098075
20	10	36	2		60	21	14	47	102	76		531	29	0.119406
21	11	23	1		62	28	16	59	117	63		250	29	0.133212
22	12	63	3		67	27	17	31	127	67		622	28	0.137265
23	13	24	1		79	30	18	34	128	71		215	30	0.147072
24	14	47	2		80	29	19	35	130	74		99	26	0.157176

Next, it is useful to "unstack" the data into three groups, one for each age category, as shown in columns E–J. For example, columns E and F list the customer numbers and ages for all customers in the first age category. It is easy to unstack the data in columns A–C with StatPro. With the cursor anywhere in the A10:C1010 range, use the StatPro/Data Utilities/Unstack Variables menu item, select Category as the Code variable, select Cust and Age as the variables to unstack, and accept the default location for the unstacked variables. (With 1000 customers, don't be surprised if this takes a while.)

Once the variables are unstacked, we can calculate the information in the range F6:G8 by entering the formulas

$$=COUNT(E11:E142)$$

and

$$=ROUND(TotSampSize*F6/1000,0)$$

in cells F6 and G6, with similar formulas for the other two categories. In words, if Sears wants to use proportional sample sizes, then it should sample 13, 77, and 10 customers from the three age categories.

Finally, we can proceed as in Example 7.1 for each of the three categories separately. Figure 7.5 illustrates the selection of 13 customers from age category 1. We copy the data in columns E and F to columns L and M, append a column of random numbers with the RAND function in column N, freeze these random numbers (with the Copy and Paste Special/Values commands), sort on the random number column, and choose the first 13 customers. (The STRATIFIED.XLS file shows similar calculations for the other two age categories to the right of column N.) Note that if we wanted a *different* sample of 13 from age category 1, all we would need to do is generate new random numbers in column N with the RAND function, freeze them, and sort again. ■

Many of the sampling schemes used in real applications use some form of stratification. The following example describes one of these applications.

Stratified Sampling at the OTA

When congressional committees and other federal agencies in Washington contemplate changes in tax laws, they frequently ask the Office of Tax Analysis (OTA) to provide information on how the tax changes will affect various groups of taxpayers. The OTA finds this information by simulating the changes on a randomly selected representative sample of taxpayers. That is, it discovers how the tax returns for these sampled taxpayers would be affected by the proposed changes. This is a time-consuming process, and the OTA's job is made even more difficult because (1) the information is sought quickly, often within a day, and (2) the OTA has to run literally thousands of these simulations per year. Therefore, it is essential that the sample of taxpayers be as small as possible, in addition to being representative.

One researcher, John Mulvey, reported a methodology for choosing this sample. [See Mulvey (1980).] Actually, he explains that the OTA already had a representative subset of approximately 155,000 taxpayers. For each of these there was information on 192 attributes such as adjusted gross income, taxes paid, salary and wages, total tax credits, pensions, and so on. This represents an enormous amount of data, so the OTA wanted to reduce the sample size to about 75,000 without losing any of the representativeness of the original large sample.

One idea was to stratify the sample of 155,000 taxpayers in some way and then choose representative members from each stratum to be in the smaller sample. The question, though, was how to define the strata. For example, if the strata were based on only a single attribute, such as adjusted gross income, the smaller sample might resemble the larger sample very closely with respect to adjusted gross income, but the resemblance might not be very good for other important attributes.

Therefore, Mulvey decided to define strata in a more sophisticated manner. He used an intricate computer program to separate the 155,000 taxpayers into strata such that the taxpayers within each stratum were similar with respect to two attributes, adjusted gross income and taxes paid. His idea is shown graphically in Figure 7.6, where each point represents a single taxpayer. (For clarity, we show only ten taxpayers from the thousands available.) For the ten points shown, the four strata, or groupings, are shown by circles. Mulvey then chose representative taxpayers from each grouping so that the total sample size was approximately 75,000. As he reports, the resemblance between the original large sample and the newly created small sample was very good. In particular, the percentage differences between means and standard deviations for the two samples were less than 2% for most of the important attributes. This was good enough for the OTA, which began using the reduced sample in 1980. ■

7.3.5 Cluster Sampling

Suppose that a company is interested in various characteristics of households in a particular city. The sampling units are households. We could select a random sample of households by one of the sampling methods already discussed. However, it might be more convenient to proceed somewhat differently. We could first divide the city into city blocks and consider

FIGURE 7.6 **Clusters for Collecting Tax Information**

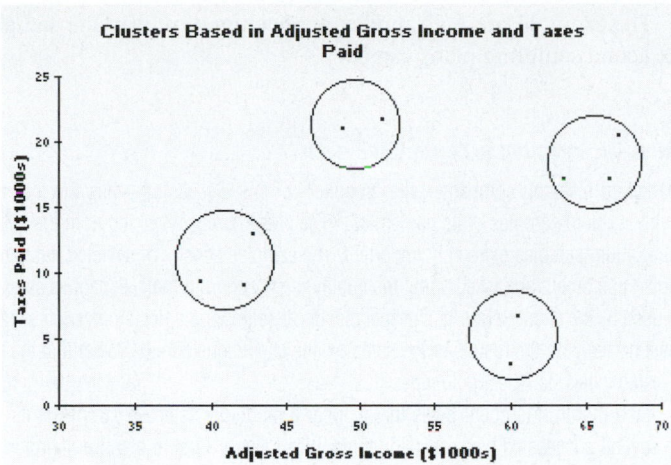

the city blocks as sampling units. We could then select a simple random sample of city blocks and then sample *all* of the households in the chosen blocks. In this case the city blocks are called **clusters** and the sampling scheme is called **cluster sampling**.

The primary advantage of cluster sampling is sampling convenience (and possibly less cost). If an agency is sending interviewers out to interview heads of household, say, it is much easier for them to concentrate on particular city blocks than to contact households throughout the city. The downside, however, is that the inferences drawn from a cluster sample can be less accurate, for a given sample size, than for other sampling plans.

Consider the following scenario. A nationwide company wants to survey its salespeople with regard to management practices. It decides to randomly select several sales districts (the clusters) and then interview all salespeople in the selected districts. It is likely that in any particular sales district the attitudes toward management are somewhat similar. This overlapping information means that the company is probably not getting the maximum amount of information per sampling dollar spent. Instead of sampling 20 salespeople from a given district who all have similar attitudes, it might be better to sample 20 salespeople from different districts who have a wider variety of attitudes. Nevertheless, the relative convenience of cluster sampling sometimes outweighs these statistical considerations.

It is straightforward to select a cluster sample. The key is to define the sampling units as the *clusters*—the city blocks, for example. Then we can select a simple random sample of clusters exactly as in Example 7.1. Once the clusters are selected, we typically sample all of the population members in each selected cluster.

7.3.6 Multistage Sampling Schemes

The cluster sampling scheme just described, where a sample of clusters is chosen and then all of the sampling units within each chosen cluster are taken, is called a **single-stage** sampling scheme. Real applications are often more complex than this, resulting in **multistage** sampling schemes. For example, the Gallup organization uses multistage sampling in its nationwide surveys. A random sample of approximately 300 locations is chosen in the first stage of the sampling process. City blocks or other geographical areas are then randomly sampled from the first-stage locations in the second stage of the process.

This is followed by a systematic sampling of households from each second-stage area. A total of about 1500 households comprise a typical Gallup poll.

The example presents another application of multistage sampling. It shows how complex actual sampling plans can be.

Multistage Sampling in Market Research

A marketing research company—the "supplier" in this discussion—has the job of supplying a large client with monthly random samples of its customers.[2] The client company, which is in the sales/service business, considers these random samples extremely important. The samples consist of selected customers from the entire nation. The sampled customers are asked about the quality of service from their respective salespeople, and this information is then used by the client to rate its salespeople. Because important decisions such as raises and promotions are based at least partially on the results of the samples, the client considers it crucial that the sampling be done according to well-established statistical guidelines.

Each month, the client gives the supplier a randomly selected sample of its customers. This list is chosen from several successive hierarchical (geographical) levels. First, the entire nation is divided into four areas: North, Central, South, and West. Then each of these areas is subdivided into several regions. For example, the Central area is subdivided into the Midwest, South Central, and Southwest regions. Then each region is subdivided into divisions, which are defined by states. For example, the Midwest region might include specified parts of Iowa, Minnesota, and Michigan. Finally, each division is subdivided into districts. A district is at the lowest end of the hierarchy.

The client randomly samples a certain number of its customers from each district and furnishes this list (one for each district) to the supplier. It also sets a target sample size for each district. The job of the supplier is to survey the specified number of customers from each list during a given month. For example, the list for one district might include 320 customers, from which the supplier is required to survey 10 customers.

Although the procedural details followed by the supplier are quite complex and will not be described here, the supplier basically selects a systematic sample from each district list that is about 5 times as large as the required number of contacts. So if the supplier needs 10 contacts from 320 customers, it chooses a systematic sample of about 50 customers from that district's list. It then "releases" the customers in this random sample to its phone-calling headquarters, and callers begin calling customers in the release sample until the required number of contacts is made.

Because of the importance of the sample information to the client, the client is understandably critical of all phases of the supplier's procedure. One particular cause of concern is the following. In each district the customers come from approximately 25 different calling zones, defined by their area code and the first three digits of their phone number. Some of these calling zones have up to 30 customers on the district list given to the supplier, whereas other zones have only one or two customers on the list. Now, the supplier is not instructed to stratify by calling zones, which would ensure proportional representation from the various calling zones among the release sample and/or the final contacts. However, the client *expects* that random sampling will guarantee such representativeness.

Unfortunately, it does not. For example, if one district list has 320 customers, 5% of whom come from a given calling zone, there is no guarantee that a random sample taken from these 320 customers will contain exactly 5% from that particular zone. In one month the sample might have more than 5%, and in another month it might have less than 5%. Neither the client nor the supplier understood exactly how much variation to expect. The client suspected that the procedure was producing too much variation (more than would be expected under a "valid" random sampling procedure), whereas the supplier defended its scheme as being valid.

This is where a consultant entered the picture. He was hired by the supplier to provide statistical evidence that the supplier's random sampling scheme was indeed valid and that the variation just described was within acceptable limits. The consultant agreed that the supplier was acting appropriately. He used computer simulation and appropriate probability models to illustrate the amount of variation that could be expected (between percentage available and percentage released/contacted in a given calling zone) under true random sampling and showed that the supplier's observed variation was of a similar magnitude. This demonstration satisfied both the supplier and the client that the sampling procedures being used were statistically valid. ■

---

[2] This example describes the consulting experience of one of the authors. For proprietary reasons, all company names are withheld in this discussion.

PROBLEMS

Level A

1   Consider the frame of 52 full-time employees of Beta Technologies, Inc. Beta's human resources manager has collected current annual salary figures and related data for these employees. The data are in the file P2_1.XLS. In particular, these data include each selected employee's gender, age, number of years of relevant work experience prior to employment at Beta, the number of years of employment at Beta, the number of years of post-secondary education, and annual salary.

a   Compute the mean, median, and standard deviation of the annual salaries for the 52 employees in the given frame.

b   Use Excel to choose a simple random sample of size 15 from this frame.

c   Compute the mean, median, and standard deviation of the annual salaries for the 15 employees included in your simple random sample. Compare these statistics with your computed descriptive measures for the frame obtained in part **a**. Is your simple random sample representative of the frame with respect to the annual salary variable?

2   A manufacturing company's quality control personnel have recorded the proportion of defective items for each of 500 monthly shipments of one of the computer components that the company produces. The data are in the file P2_2.XLS. The quality control department manager does not have sufficient time to review all of these data. Rather, she would like to examine the proportions of defective items for a simple random sample of 50 shipments.

a   Use Excel to generate such a random sample from the given frame.

b   What are the advantages and disadvantages of the sampling method requested by this quality control manager?

3   The manager of a local fast-food restaurant is interested in improving the service provided to customers who use the restaurant's drive-up window. As a first step in this process, the manager asks his assistant to record the time (in minutes) it takes to serve a large number of customers at the final window in the facility's drive-up system. The given frame of 200 customer service times are all observed during the busiest hour of the day for this fast-food operation. The data are in the file P2_4.XLS.

a   Compute the mean, median, and standard deviation of the customer service times in the given frame.

b   Use Excel to choose a simple random sample of size 20 from this frame.

c   Compute the mean, median, and standard deviation of the service times for the 20 customers included in your simple random sample. Compare these statistics with your computed descriptive measures for the frame obtained in part **a**.

4   A finance professor has just given a midterm examination in her corporate finance course. In particular, she is interested in learning how her large class of 100 students performed on this exam. The data are in the file P2_5.XLS.

a   Using these 100 students as the frame, generate a simple random sample of size 10 with Excel.

b   Compare the mean of the scores in the frame with that of the scores contained in the simple random sample.

5   Consider a frame consisting of 500 households in a middle-class neighborhood that was the recent focus of an economic development study conducted by the local government. Specifically, for each of the 500 households, information was gathered on each of the following variables: family size, location of the household within the neighborhood, an indication of whether those surveyed owned or rented their home, gross annual income of the first household wage earner, gross annual income of the second household wage earner (if applicable), monthly home mortgage or rent payment, average monthly expenditure on utilities, and the total indebtedness (excluding the value of a home mortgage) of the household. The data are in the file P2_6.XLS.

a   Compute the mean, median, and standard deviation of the monthly home mortgage or rent payments of all households in the given frame.

b Use Excel to choose a simple random sample of size 25 from this frame.

c Compute the mean, median, and standard deviation of the monthly home mortgage or rent payments for the 25 households included in your simple random sample. Compare these statistics with your computed descriptive measures for the frame obtained in part **a**.

6   A real estate agent has received data on 150 houses that were recently sold in a suburban community. Included in this data set are observations for each of the following variables: the appraised value of each house (in thousands of dollars), the selling price of each house (in thousands of dollars), the size of each house (in hundreds of square feet), and the number of bedrooms in each house. The data are in the file P2_7.XLS. Suppose that this real estate agent wishes to examine a representative subset of these 150 houses. Use Excel to assist her by finding a simple random sample of size 10 from this frame.

7   Consider the given set of average annual household income levels of citizens of selected U.S. metropolitan areas in the file P3_6.XLS. Use Excel to obtain a simple random sample of size 15 from this frame.

8   The operations manager of a toll booth located at a major exit of a state turnpike is trying to estimate the average number of vehicles that arrive at the toll booth during a 1-minute period during the peak of rush-hour traffic. In an effort to estimate this average throughput value, he records the number of vehicles that arrive at the toll booth over a 1-minute interval commencing at the same time for each of 365 normal weekdays. The data are provided in the file P2_9.XLS. Choose a simple random sample of size 20 from the given frame of 365 values to help the operations manager estimate the average throughput value.

9   In ranking 325 metropolitan areas in the United States, David Savageau and Geoffrey Loftus, the authors of *Places Rated Almanac* (published in 1997 by Macmillan, Inc.) consider the average time (in minutes) it takes a citizen of each metropolitan area to travel to work and back home each day. The data are in the file P2_11.XLS. Use Excel to obtain a simple random sample of 20 average commute times from the given set of 325 such values.

10 Given data in the file P2_13.XLS from a recent survey of chief executive officers from 350 of the nation's biggest businesses (*The Wall Street Journal*, April 9, 1998), choose a simple random sample of 25 executives and find the mean, median, and standard deviation of the bonuses awarded to them in 1997. How do these sample statistics compare to the mean, median, and standard deviation of the bonuses given to all executives included in the frame?

11 A lightbulb manufacturer wants to know the number of defective bulbs contained in a typical box shipped by the company. Production personnel at this company have recorded the number of defective bulbs found in each of the 1000 boxes shipped during the past week. These data are provided in P7_11.XLS. Using this shipment of boxes as a frame, select a simple random sample of 50 boxes and compute the mean number of defective bulbs found in a box.

12 Consider the frame of 52 full-time employees of Beta Technologies, Inc. Beta's human resources manager has collected current annual salary figures and related data for these employees. The data are in the file P2_1.XLS.

a Compute the mean, median, and standard deviation of the annual salaries for the 52 employees in the given frame.

b Use Excel to choose a systematic sample of size 13 from this frame.

c Compute the mean, median, and standard deviation of the annual salaries for the 13 employees included in your systematic sample. Compare these statistics with your computed descriptive measures for the frame obtained in part **a**. Is your systematic sample representative of the frame with respect to the annual salary variable?

13 A manufacturing company's quality control personnel have recorded the proportion of defective items for each of 500 monthly shipments of one of the computer components that the company produces. The data are in the file P2_2.XLS. The quality control department manager does not have sufficient time to review all of these data. Rather, she would like to examine the proportions of defective items for a systematic sample of 50 shipments.

a Use Excel to generate such a systematic sample from the given frame.

b What are the advantages and disadvantages of the sampling method requested by this quality control manager?

14 The manager of a local fast-food restaurant is interested in improving the service provided to customers who use the restaurant's drive-up window. As a first step in this process, the manager asks his assistant to record the time (in minutes) it takes to serve a large number of customers

at the final window in the facility's drive-up system. The given frame of 200 customer service times are all observed during the busiest hour of the day for this fast-food operation. The data are in the file P2_4.XLS.

  a Compute the mean, median, and standard deviation of the customer service times in the given frame.

  b Use Excel to choose a systematic sample of size 20 from this frame.

  c Compute the mean, median, and standard deviation of the service times for the 20 customers included in your systematic sample. Compare these statistics with your computed descriptive measures for the frame obtained in part **a**.

15 A finance professor has just given a midterm examination in her corporate finance course. In particular, she is interested in learning how her large class of 100 students performed on this exam. The data are in the file P2_5.XLS.

  a Using these 100 students as the frame, generate a systematic sample of size 10 with Excel.

  b Compare the mean of the scores in the frame with that of the scores included in the systematic sample.

16 Consider a frame consisting of 500 households in a middle-class neighborhood that was the recent focus of an economic development study conducted by the local government. The data are in the file P2_6.XLS.

  a Compute the mean, median, and standard deviation of the monthly home mortgage or rent payments of all households in the given frame.

  b Use Excel to choose a systematic sample of size 25 from this frame.

  c Compute the mean, median, and standard deviation of the monthly home mortgage or rent payments for the 25 households included in your systematic sample. Compare these statistics with your computed descriptive measures for the frame obtained in part **a**.

17 A real estate agent has received data on 150 houses that were recently sold in a suburban community. Included in this data set are observations for each of the following variables: the appraised value of each house (in thousands of dollars), the selling price of each house (in thousands of dollars), the size of each house (in hundreds of square feet), and the number of bedrooms in each house. The data are in the file P2_7.XLS. Suppose that this real estate agent wishes to examine a representative subset of these 150 houses. Use Excel to assist her by finding a systematic sample of size 10 from this frame.

18 Consider the given set of average annual household income levels of citizens of selected U.S. metropolitan areas in the file P3_6.XLS. Use Excel to obtain a systematic sample of size 25 from this frame.

19 The operations manager of a toll booth located at a major exit of a state turnpike is trying to estimate the average number of vehicles that arrive at the toll booth during a 1-minute period during the peak of rush-hour traffic. In an effort to estimate this average throughput value, he records the number of vehicles that arrive at the toll booth over a 1-minute interval commencing at the same time for each of 365 normal weekdays. The data are provided in the file P2_9.XLS. Choose a systematic sample of size 20 from the given frame of 365 values to help the operations manager estimate the average throughput value.

20 Consider the average time (in minutes) it takes citizens of each of 325 metropolitan areas across the United States to travel to work and back home each day. The data are in the file P2_11.XLS. Use Excel to obtain a systematic sample of 25 average commute times from the given set of 325 such values.

21 Consider the frame of 52 full-time employees of Beta Technologies, Inc. Beta's human resources manager has collected current annual salary figures and related data for these employees. The data are in the file P2_1.XLS.

  a Compute the mean, median, and standard deviation of the annual salaries for the 52 employees in the given frame.

  b Assuming that the human resources manager wishes to stratify these employees by the number of years of post-secondary education, select such a stratified sample of size 15 with approximately proportional sample sizes.

  c Compute the mean, median, and standard deviation of the annual salaries for the 15 employees included in your stratified sample. Compare these statistics with your computed descriptive measures for the frame obtained in part **a**. Is your stratified sample representative of the frame with respect to the annual salary variable?

22 Consider a frame consisting of 500 households in a middle-class neighborhood that was the recent focus of an economic development study conducted by the local government. Specifically, for each of the 500 households, information was gathered on each of the following variables: family size, location of the household within the neighborhood, an indication of whether those surveyed owned or rented their home, gross annual income of the first household wage earner, gross annual income of the second household wage earner (if applicable), monthly home mortgage or rent payment, average monthly expenditure on utilities, and the total indebtedness (excluding the value of a home mortgage) of the household. The data are in the file P2_6.XLS.

a Compute the mean, median, and standard deviation of the gross annual income of the first wage earner of all households in the given frame.

b Given that researchers have decided to stratify the given households by location within the neighborhood, choose a stratified sample of size 25 with proportional sample sizes.

c Compute the mean, median, and standard deviation of the gross annual income of the first wage earner of the 25 households included in your stratified sample. Compare these statistics with your computed descriptive measures for the frame obtained in part **a**.

d Explain how economic researchers could apply cluster sampling in selecting a sample of size 25 from this frame. What are the advantages and disadvantages of employing cluster sampling in this case?

23 A real estate agent has received data on 150 houses that were recently sold in a suburban community. Included in this data set are observations for each of the following variables: the appraised value of each house (in thousands of dollars), the selling price of each house (in thousands of dollars), the size of each house (in hundreds of square feet), and the number of bedrooms in each house. The data are in the file P2_7.XLS.

a Suppose that this real estate agent wishes to examine a representative subset of these 150 houses that has been stratified by the number of bedrooms. Use Excel to assist her by finding such a stratified sample of size 15 with proportional sample sizes.

b Explain how the real estate agent could apply cluster sampling in selecting a sample of size 15 from this frame. What are the advantages and disadvantages of employing cluster sampling in this case?

24 Given data in the file P2_13.XLS from a recent survey of chief executive officers from 350 of the nation's biggest businesses (*The Wall Street Journal*, April 9, 1998), choose a sample of 25 executives stratified by company type with proportional sample sizes. Next, find the mean, median, and standard deviation of the salaries awarded to them in 1997. How do these sample statistics compare to the mean, median, and standard deviation of the salaries given to all executives included in the frame?

Level B

25 The employee benefits manager of a small private university would like to know the proportion of its full-time employees who prefer adopting each of three available health care plans in the forthcoming annual enrollment period. A reliable frame of the university's employees and their tentative health care preferences are given in P7_25.XLS.

a Compute the proportion of the employees in the given frame who favor *each* of the three plans (i.e., plans A, B, and C).

b Use Excel to choose a sample of 45 employees stratified by employee classification with proportional sample sizes.

c Compute the proportion of the 45 employees in the stratified sample who favor each health plan. Compare these sample proportions to the corresponding values obtained in part **a**. Explain any differences between the corresponding values.

d What are the advantages and disadvantages of employing stratified sampling in this particular case?

e Explain how the benefits manager could apply cluster sampling in selecting a sample of size 30 from this frame. What are the advantages and disadvantages of employing cluster sampling in this case?

26 The file P2_17.XLS reports the number of short-term general hospitals in each of a large number of U.S. metropolitan areas. Suppose that you are a sales manager for a major pharmaceutical producer and are interested in estimating the average number of such hospitals in *all* metropolitan areas across the entire country. Assuming that you do not have access to the data for each metropolitan location, you decide to select a sample that will be representative of all such areas.

   a Choose a simple random sample of 30 metropolitan areas from the given frame. Compute the mean number of short-term general hospitals for the metropolitan areas included in your sample.

   b Do you believe that simple random sampling is the best approach to obtaining a representative subset of the metropolitan areas in the given frame? Explain. If not, how might you proceed to select a better sample of size 30 using the data provided in P2_17.XLS? Compute the mean number of short-term general hospitals for the metropolitan areas included in your revised sample. How does this sample mean compare to that computed from your simple random sample in part **a**?

27 As human resources manager of a manufacturing plant, you are quite concerned about recent reports of sexual and racial harassment from the production workers within the organization. In an effort to gain a better understanding of the apparent problems, you decide that it would be wise to interview a cross section of your employees about this and other issues in the workplace.

   a Using the frame of employees provided in the file P7_27.XLS, select a subset of 30 production workers stratified by sex with proportional sample sizes.

   b Next, select another subset of 30 workers stratified by race with proportional sample sizes.

   c Finally, select one more subset of 30 workers stratified by *both* sex and race (e.g., Black women, White men, Asian women, Hispanic men, etc.) with proportional sample sizes.

   d Explain how the human resources manager could apply cluster sampling in selecting a sample of size 30 from this frame. What are the advantages and disadvantages of employing cluster sampling in this case?

28 Is the overall cost of living higher or lower for urban areas in particular geographical regions of the United States?

   a Begin to answer this question by first selecting 40 urban areas from the given frame provided in the file P7_28.XLS (Source: *ACCRA Cost of Living Index*). The urban areas you select should be stratified by geographical location within the United States (e.g., northeast, southeast, midwest, northwest, or southwest) and should reflect proportional sample sizes. Note that you will need to assign the given urban areas to one of any number of such geographical regions before you can generate a stratified sample.

   b Explain how one could apply cluster sampling in selecting a sample of size 40 from this frame. What are the advantages and disadvantages of employing cluster sampling in this case? ■

7.4

An Introduction to Estimation

The purpose of any random sample is to estimate properties of a population from the data observed in the sample. The mathematical procedures appropriate for performing this estimation depend on which properties of the population are of interest and which type of random sampling scheme is used. Because the details are considerably more complex when a more complex sampling scheme such as multistage sampling is used, we will focus on *simple* random samples, where the mathematics is relatively straightforward. Details for other sampling schemes such as stratified sampling can be found in Levy and Lemeshow (1991). However, even for more complex sampling schemes, the *concepts* are the same as those we will discuss here; only the details change.

Throughout this section, we focus on the population mean of some variable such as household income. Our goal is to estimate this population mean by using the data in a randomly selected sample. We first discuss the types of errors that can occur in this estimation problem.

7.4.1 Sources of Estimation Error

There are two basic sources of errors that can occur when we sample randomly from a population: **sampling error** and all other sources, usually lumped together as **nonsampling error**. Sampling error results from "unlucky" samples. As such, the term *error* is somewhat misleading. Suppose we randomly sample 10 families as in Example 7.1 and use the sample mean from these 10 families to estimate the mean income of all 40 families in the population. Because any conceivable sample of size 10 could be chosen, it is possible, although not likely, that we could choose the 10 families with the 10 highest incomes. In this case the sample mean would seriously overestimate the population mean, and the error of estimation—caused entirely by *sampling* error—would be large. Similarly, a sample with, say, seven large incomes and three average incomes would also produce sampling error, although not as great.

We will see shortly how to measure the potential sampling error involved. The point here is that the resulting estimation error is not caused by anything we're doing wrong—we might just get unlucky.

Nonsampling error is quite different and can occur for a variety of reasons. We discuss a few of them.

- Perhaps the most serious type of nonsampling error is **nonresponse bias**. This occurs when a portion of the sample fails to respond to the survey. Anyone who has ever conducted a questionnaire, whether by mail, by phone, or any other method, knows that the percentage of nonrespondents can be quite large. The question is whether this introduces estimation error. If the nonrespondents *would* have responded similarly to the respondents, had they responded, we don't lose much by not hearing from them. However, because the nonrespondents don't respond, we typically have no way of knowing whether they differ in some important respect from the respondents. Therefore, unless we are able to persuade the nonrespondents to respond—through a follow-up phone call, for example—we must guess at the amount of nonresponse bias.

  By the way, it is interesting that we always learn (from statistics books!) to take *larger* samples to reduce sampling error. This makes intuitive sense. We can typically learn more about a population from a larger sample. However, if the potential for nonresponse bias is large, *smaller* samples might be preferable—they tend to decrease the amount of nonresponse bias.

- Another source of nonsampling error is **nontruthful responses**. This is particularly a problem when we ask sensitive questions in a questionnaire. For example, if the questions "Have you ever had an abortion?" or "Do you regularly use cocaine?" are asked, most people will answer "no," regardless of whether the true answer is "yes" or "no."

  There is a way of getting at such sensitive information, called the **randomized response** technique. Here the investigator presents each respondent with two questions, one of which is the sensitive question. The other is innocuous, such as, "Were you born in the summer?" The respondent is asked to decide randomly which of the two questions to answer—by flipping a coin, say—and then answer the chosen question truthfully. The investigator sees only the answer (yes or no), not the result of the coin flip. That is, the investigator doesn't know which question is being answered.

However, by using probability theory, it is possible for the investigator to infer from many such responses the percentage of the population whose truthful answer to the sensitive question is "yes."

■ Another type of nonsampling error is **measurement error**. This occurs when the responses to the questions do not reflect what the investigator had in mind. It might result from poorly worded questions, questions the respondents don't fully understand, questions that require the respondents to supply information they don't have, and so on. Undoubtedly, there have been times when you were filling out a questionnaire and said to yourself, "OK, I'll answer this as well as I can, but I know it's not what they want to know."

From this discussion and your own experience with questionnaires, you should realize that the potential for nonsampling error is enormous. However, unlike sampling error, it cannot be measured with probability theory. It can only be controlled by using appropriate sampling procedures and designing good survey instruments. We will not pursue this topic any further here. If you are interested, however, you can learn about methods for controlling nonsampling error, such as proper questionnaire design, from books on marketing research.

7.4.2 Sampling Distribution of the Sample Mean

We now focus on sampling error. Let's return to the population of 40 family incomes in Figure 7.1 of Example 7.1. Suppose we want to estimate the population mean. Of course, the population mean in the example is known—it is $39,985, in cell B5—because we have an entire list of the population incomes. However, in most realistic situations it is unknown. We typically estimate the population mean by the sample mean of the randomly chosen sample. In this case the sample mean is called a **point estimate** of the population mean. In general, a point estimate of *any* population parameter is a single-value estimate (or "best guess") of that parameter, based on observed sample data.

For the sample of size 10 shown in Figure 7.2, this point estimate is $38,750, in cell B6. Then the **sampling error** is the difference between the observed sample mean and the true population mean:

$$\text{Sampling error} = \$38,750 - \$39,985 = -\$1235$$

Because this is negative, the point estimate (the sample mean) *underestimates* the population mean by $1235.

Now we generalize. Let $\overline{X}$ be the observed sample mean, and let μ be the population mean. The value of μ is unknown; it is the parameter we want to estimate. The value of $\overline{X}$ can be calculated from the sample data; it is the point estimate of μ. We define the sampling error of this estimate as

$$\text{Sampling error} = \overline{X} - \mu$$

In words, the sampling error is the amount by which the point estimate $\overline{X}$ overestimates or underestimates the population parameter μ.

Clearly, the sampling error depends on which sample we happen to choose since each sample has its own value of $\overline{X}$. The crucial question is the following: Is there any way to gauge the magnitude of the sampling error for a "typical" random sample? For example, is a typical random sample likely to produce a sampling error greater than $2000 in magnitude?

The answer to this question depends on an extremely important concept in statistics—a sampling distribution. In this case we are interested in the **sampling distribution of the sample mean**. Imagine that we select numerous random samples from a given population and then calculate the resulting sample mean $\overline{X}$ for each sample. Obviously, these values of

$\overline{X}$ will vary. There will be a few low $\overline{X}$'s from samples with mostly low incomes, a few high $\overline{X}$'s from samples with mostly high incomes, and many $\overline{X}$'s in the middle. The distribution of these $\overline{X}$'s is called the sampling distribution of the sample mean. More precisely, the sampling distribution of the sample mean is the distribution of $\overline{X}$ values that would result from observing every conceivable sample (of a fixed sample size) from a population.

Because the sampling distribution of the sample mean is a specific type of probability distribution, it has a mean and a standard deviation. They are given below. The standard deviation of $\overline{X}$, which we denote by SE($\overline{X}$), is usually called the **standard error of the mean**.[3]

$$E(\overline{X}) = \mu \tag{7.1}$$

$$\hat{\text{S}}\text{tdev}(\overline{X}) = \text{SE}(\overline{X}) = \sigma/\sqrt{n} \tag{7.2}$$

Because our goal is to use $\overline{X}$ to estimate μ, these equations are very important. Equation (7.1) indicates that the sample mean is an **unbiased** estimate of the population mean. In words, this says that the $\overline{X}$'s from some samples will underestimate μ and others will overestimate μ, but on average they will be right on target. Therefore, there is no reason to suspect that the $\overline{X}$ from any *particular* sample is on the low side or the high side. This unbiased property is an attractive property of any estimate.

The standard error of the mean, given by equation (7.2), is also important. It provides a measure of the accuracy of $\overline{X}$ as an estimate of μ. The smaller this standard error is, the closer to μ the value of $\overline{X}$ will tend to be. Unfortunately, one piece of equation (7.2) is usually missing—we almost never know the population standard deviation σ. Therefore, we generally use the following approximate standard error, where the *sample* standard deviation s is used in place of the unknown population standard deviation σ.

$$\text{Approximate SE}(\overline{X}) = s/\sqrt{n} \tag{7.3}$$

The following example illustrates a typical use of sample information.

EXAMPLE 7.4

An internal auditor for a furniture retailer wants to estimate the average of all accounts receivable, where this average is taken over the population of all customer accounts. Because the company has approximately 10,000 accounts, an exhaustive enumeration of all accounts receivable is impossible. Therefore, the auditor randomly samples 100 of the accounts. The observed data appear in Figure 7.7. (See the file AUDIT.XLS.) What can the auditor conclude from this sample?

Solution

The receivables for the 100 sampled accounts appear in column E. This is the only information available to the auditor, so he must base all conclusions on these sample data. We calculate the sample mean and sample standard deviation in cells B7 and B8 with the formulas

=AVERAGE(Amounts)

and

=STDEV(Amounts)

---

[3] This formula for SE($\overline{X}$) assumes that the sample size n is small relative to the population size N. As a rule of thumb, we assume that n is no more than 5% of N. Later we will provide a "correction" to this formula when n is a larger percentage of N.

Then we use equation (7.3) to calculate the (approximate) standard error of the mean in cell B9 with the formula

$$\text{=SStdev/SQRT(SampSize)}$$

FIGURE 7.7 **Sampling in Auditing Example**

	A	B	C	D	E
1	**Random sample of accounts receivable**				
2					
3	Population size	10000		**Sample of receivables**	
4	Sample size	100		Account	Amount
5				1	$85
6	**Summary measures from sample**			2	$1,061
7	Sample mean	$279		3	$0
8	Sample stdev	$419		4	$1,260
9	Std Error of mean	$42		5	$924
10				6	$129
11	With fpc	$42		7	$0
12				8	$54
13				9	$101
14		Range names		10	$1,091
15		Amounts: B5:B104		11	$103
16		PopSize: B3		12	$0
17		SampSize: B4		13	$1,109
18		SStdev: B8		14	$87
19				15	$94
20				16	$1,090
21				17	$108
101				97	$1,097
102				98	$657
103				99	$86
104				100	$0

The auditor should interpret these values as follows. First, the sample mean $279 can be used to estimate the unknown population mean. It provides a best guess for the average of the receivables from all 10,000 accounts. In fact, because the sample mean is an unbiased estimate of the population mean, there is no reason to suspect that $279 either underestimates or overestimates the population mean. Second, the standard error $42 provides a measure of accuracy of the $279 estimate. Specifically, as we will see shortly, there is about a 95% chance that the estimate differs by no more than two standard errors ($84) from the true population mean. Therefore, the auditor can be 95% certain that the mean from all 10,000 accounts is within the interval $279 ± $84, that is, between $195 and $363. ■

It is important to distinguish between the sample standard deviation s and the standard error of the mean, approximated by $s/\sqrt{n}$. The sample standard deviation in the auditing example, $419, measures the variability in *individual* receivables in the sample (or in the population). By scrolling down column E, we see that there are some very low amounts (many zeros) and some fairly large amounts. This variability is indicated by the rather large sample standard deviation s. However, this value does not measure the accuracy of the sample mean as an estimate of the population mean. To judge *its* accuracy, we need to divide s by the square root of the sample size n. The resulting standard error, about $42, is much smaller than the sample standard deviation. It indicates that we can be about 95% certain that the sampling error is no greater than $84.

The Finite Population Correction We mentioned that equation (7.2) [or equation (7.3)] for the standard error of $\overline{X}$ is appropriate when the sample size n is small relative to the population size N. Generally, "small" means that n is no more than 5% of N. In most realistic samples this is certainly true. For example, political polls are typically based on samples of approximately 1000 people from the entire U.S. population.

There are situations, however, when we sample more than 5% of the population. In this case the formula for the standard error of the mean should be modified with a **finite population correction**, or fpc, factor. Then the modified standard error of the mean is

$$\text{SE}(\overline{X}) = fpc(s/\sqrt{n}) \tag{7.4}$$

where the fpc is

$$fpc = \sqrt{\frac{N-n}{N-1}}$$

Note that this factor is always less than 1 (when $n > 1$) and it decreases as n increases. Therefore, the standard error of the mean decreases—and the accuracy increases—as n increases.

To see how the fpc varies with n and N, consider the values in Table 7.1. Rather than listing n, we have listed the percentage of the population sampled, that is, $n/N \times 100\%$. It is clear that when 5% or less of the population is sampled, the fpc is very close to 1 and can safely be ignored. In this case we can use $s/\sqrt{n}$ as the standard error of the mean. Otherwise, we should use the modified formula in equation (7.4).

TABLE 7.1 **Finite Population Correction Factors**

N	% Sampled	fpc
100	5%	.980
100	10%	.953
10,000	1%	.995
10,000	5%	.975
10,000	10%	.949
1,000,000	1%	.995
1,000,000	5%	.975
1,000,000	10%	.949

In the auditing example, $n/N = 100/100,000 = 0.1\%$. This suggests that the fpc can safely be omitted. We illustrate this in cell B11 of Figure 7.7, which uses the formula from equation (7.4):

=SQRT((PopSize-SampSize)/(PopSize-1))*SStdev/SQRT(SampSize)

Clearly, it makes no practical difference in this example whether we use the fpc or not. The standard error, rounded to the nearest dollar, is $42 in either case.

Virtually all standard error formulas used in sampling include an fpc factor. However, because it is rarely necessary—the sample size is usually very small relative to the population size—we will omit it from here on.

7.4.3 The Central Limit Theorem

Our discussion to this point has concentrated primarily on the mean and standard deviation of the sampling distribution of the sample mean. In this section we discuss this sampling distribution in more detail. Because of an important theoretical result called the central limit theorem, we know that this distribution is approximately *normal* with mean μ and standard deviation $\sigma/\sqrt{n}$. This theorem is the reason why the normal distribution appears in so many statistical results. We can state the theorem as follows.

Central Limit Theorem

For any population distribution with mean μ and standard deviation σ, the sampling distribution of the sample mean $\overline{X}$ is approximately normal with mean μ and standard deviation $\sigma/\sqrt{n}$, and the approximation improves as n increases. ■

The important part of this result is the normality of the sampling distribution. We know, without any conditions placed upon n, that the mean and standard deviation are μ and $\sigma/\sqrt{n}$. However, the central limit theorem also implies normality, provided that n is reasonably large.

How large must n be for the approximation to be valid? Most analysts suggest $n \geq 30$ as a rule of thumb. However, this depends on the population distribution. If the population distribution is very *nonnormal*—extremely skewed or bimodal, say—then the normal approximation might not be accurate unless n is considerably greater than 30. On the other hand, if the population distribution is already approximately symmetric, then the normal approximation is quite good for n considerably less than 30. In fact, in the special case where the population distribution itself is normal, the sampling distribution of $\overline{X}$ is *exactly* normal for *any* value of n.

The central limit theorem is not a simple concept to grasp. To help explain it, we employ simulation in the following example.

E X A M P L E   7 . 5

Suppose you have the opportunity to play a game with a "wheel of fortune" (similar to a popular television game show). When you spin a large wheel, it is equally likely to stop in any position. Depending on where it stops, you win anywhere from $0 to $1000. Let's suppose your winnings are actually based on not one, but n spins of the wheel. For example, if $n = 2$, your winnings are based on the average of two spins. If the first spin results in $580 and the second spin results in $320, then you win the average, $450. How does the distribution of your winnings depend on n?

Solution

First, we need to discuss what this experiment has to do with random sampling. Here, the population is the set of all outcomes we could obtain from a *single* spin of the wheel—that is, all dollar values from $0 to $1000. Each spin results in one randomly sampled dollar value from this population. Furthermore, because we have assumed that the wheel is equally likely to land in any position, all possible values in the continuum from $0 to $1000 have the same chance of occurring. The resulting population distribution is called the **uniform**

distribution on the interval from $0 to $1000. (See Figure 7.8.) It can be shown (with calculus) that the mean and standard deviation of this uniform distribution are $\mu = \$500$ and $\sigma = \$289$.[4]

FIGURE 7.8 **Uniform Distribution**

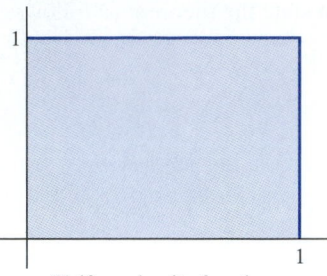

Uniform density function

Now we'll analyze the distribution of winnings based on the average of n spins. We do so by means of a sequence of simulations in Excel, for $n = 1, n = 2, n = 3, n = 6,$ and $n = 10$. (See the files SPIN1.XLS, SPIN2.XLS, SPIN3.XLS, SPIN6.XLS, and SPIN10.XLS.) For each simulation we consider 1000 replications of an experiment. The experiment simulates n spins of the wheel and calculates the average—that is, the winnings—from these n spins. Based on these 1000 replications, we can then calculate the average winnings, the standard deviation of winnings, and a histogram of winnings for each n. These will show clearly how the distribution of winnings depends on n.

The values in Figure 7.9 and the histogram in Figure 7.10 show the results for $n = 1$. Here there is no averaging—we spin the wheel once and win the amount shown. To replicate this experiment 1000 times and collect statistics, we proceed as follows.

1 **Random outcomes.** To generate outcomes uniformly distributed between $0 and $1000, enter the formula

$$=\$B\$3+RAND()*(\$B\$4-\$B\$3)$$

in cell B11 and copy it down column B. The effect of this formula, given the values in cells B3 and B4, is to generate a random number between 0 and 1 and multiply it by $1000.

2 **Summary measures.** Calculate the average and standard deviation of the 1000 winnings in column B with the AVERAGE and STDEV functions. These values appear in cells E4 and E5.

3 **Frequency table and histogram.** Use the StatPro histogram procedure to create a histogram of the values in column B.

Note the following from Figures 7.9 and 7.10.

■ The sample mean of the winnings (cell E4) is very close to the population mean, $500.

■ The standard deviation of the winnings (cell E5) is very close to the population standard deviation, $289.

■ The histogram is nearly flat.

---

[4] In general, if a distribution is uniform on the interval from a to b, then its mean is the midpoint $(a + b)/2$ and its standard deviation is $(b - a)/\sqrt{12}$.

Simulation of Winnings from a Single Spin

	A	B	C	D	E	F
1	**Wheel of fortune simulation**					
2						
3	Minimum winnings	$0		**Summary measures of winnings**		
4	Maximum winnings	$1,000		Mean	$502	
5				Stdev	$298	
6	Number of spins	1				
7						
8	**Simulation of spins**					
9						
10	Replication	Outcome				
11	1	$685				
12	2	$383				
13	3	$916				
14	4	$179				
15	5	$81				
16	6	$875				
17	7	$824				
18	8	$872				
19	9	$618				
20	10	$309				
21	11	$795				
1008	998	$619				
1009	999	$294				
1010	1000	$921				

F I G U R E   7 . 1 0   **Histogram of Simulated Winnings from a Single Spin**

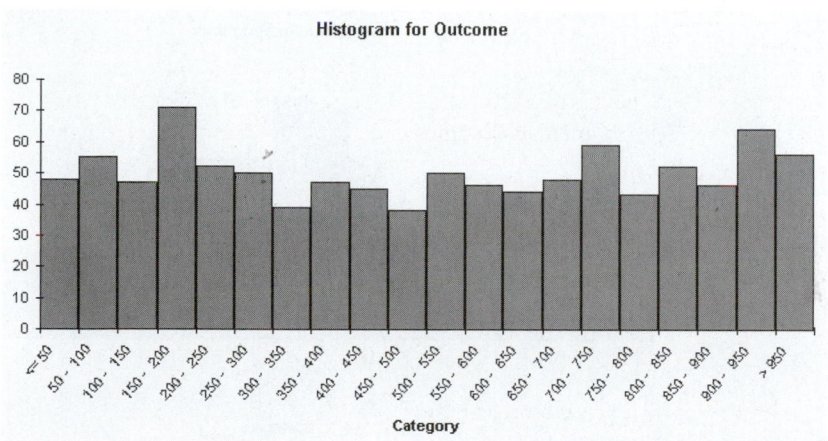

These properties should come as no surprise. When $n = 1$, the "sample mean" is a single observation—that is, no averaging takes place. Therefore, the sampling distribution of the sample mean is *equivalent* to the flat population distribution in Figure 7.8.

But what happens when $n > 1$? Figures 7.11 and 7.12 show the results for $n = 2$. Now we form a second column of outcomes in column C, corresponding to the second spin in each experiment, and we average the values in columns B and C to obtain each of the winnings in column D. None of the rest of the spreadsheet changes. The average winnings is again very close to $500, but the standard deviation of winnings is much lower. In fact, it is close to $\sigma/\sqrt{2} = 289/\sqrt{2} = \$204$, exactly as theory predicts. In addition, the histogram of winnings is no longer flat. It is triangularly shaped—symmetric, but not yet bell shaped.

FIGURE 7.11   Simulation of Winnings from Two Spins

	A	B	C	D	E	F	G	H
1	Wheel of fortune simulation							
2								
3	Minimum winnings	$0				Summary measures of winnings		
4	Maximum winnings	$1,000				Mean	$507	
5						Stdev	$199	
6	Number of spins	2						
7								
8	Simulation of spins							
9								
10	Replication	Outcome1	Outcome2	Winnings				
11	1	$396	$160	$278				
12	2	$693	$457	$575				
13	3	$910	$853	$881				
14	4	$673	$985	$829				
15	5	$661	$547	$604				
16	6	$84	$682	$383				
17	7	$518	$725	$621				
18	8	$303	$661	$482				
19	9	$204	$889	$546				
20	10	$728	$892	$810				
21	11	$52	$570	$311				
1008	998	$688	$430	$559				
1009	999	$590	$602	$596				
1010	1000	$985	$525	$755				

FIGURE 7.12   Histogram of Simulated Winnings from Two Spins

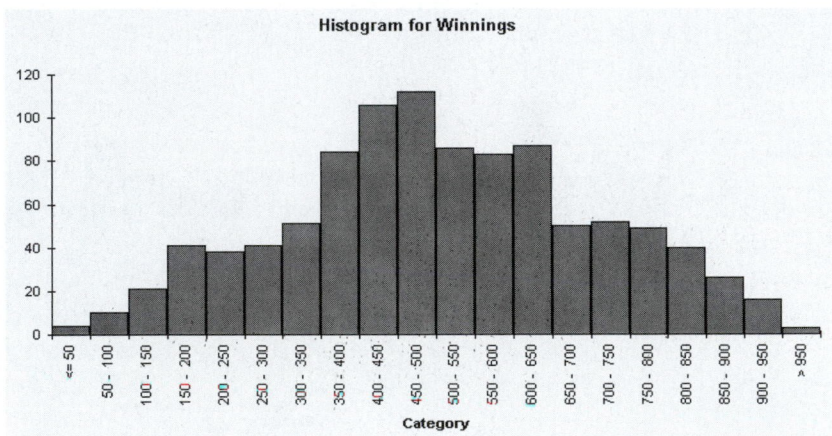

To develop similar simulations for $n = 3$, $n = 6$, $n = 10$, or any other n, we insert additional outcome columns and make sure that the AVERAGE formula in the Winnings column averages all n outcomes to its left. The resulting histograms appear in Figures 7.13, 7.14, and 7.15. They clearly show two effects of increasing n: (1) the histogram becomes more bell shaped, and (2) there is less variability. However, the mean stays right at $500. This behavior is exactly what the central limit theorem predicts. In fact, because the population distribution is symmetric in this example—it's flat—we see the effect of the central limit theorem for n much less than 30; it is already evident for n as low as 6.

FIGURE 7.13 Histogram of Simulated Winnings from Three Spins

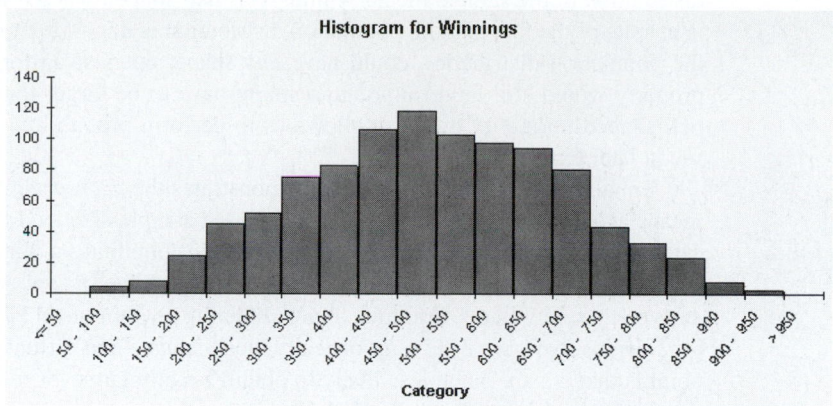

FIGURE 7.14 Histogram of Simulated Winnings from Six Spins

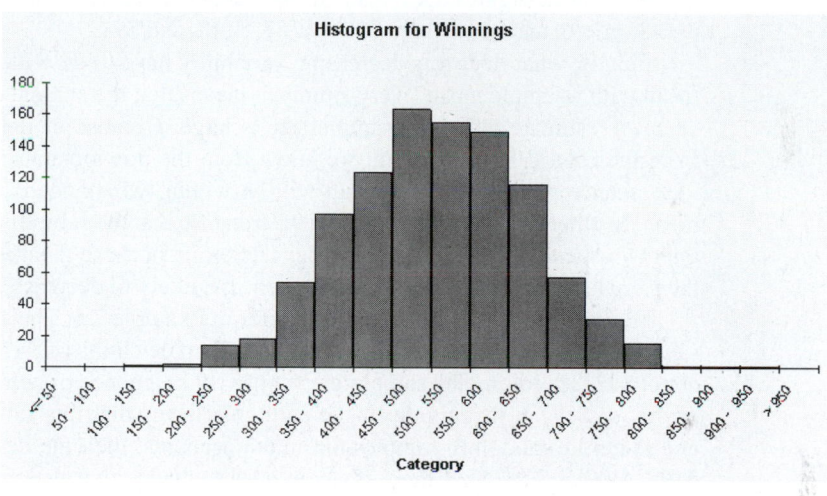

FIGURE 7.15 Histogram of Simulated Winnings from Ten Spins

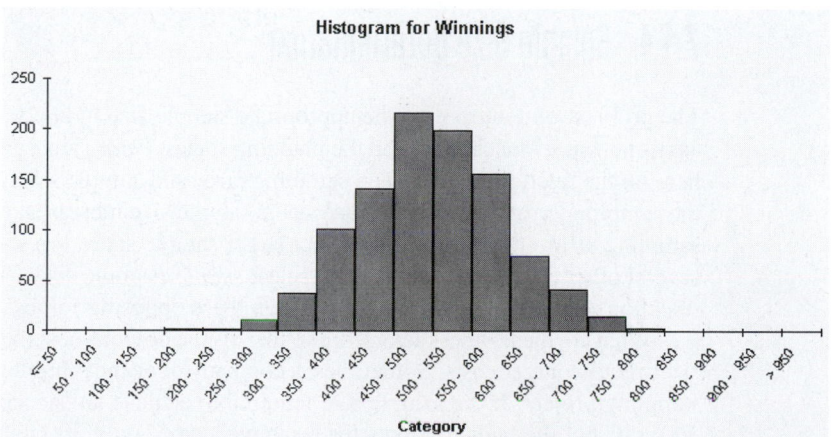

What are the main lessons from this example? For one, we see that the sampling distribution of the sample mean (winnings) is bell shaped when n is reasonably large. This is in spite of the fact that the population distribution is flat—far from bell shaped. Actually, the population distribution could have *any* shape, not just uniform, and the bell-shaped property would still hold (although n might have to be larger than in the example). This bell-shaped normality property allows us to perform probability calculations, as we will see in later examples.

Equally important, this example demonstrates the *decreased variability* in the sample means as n increases. Why should an increased sample size lead to decreased variability? The reason is the averaging process. Think about obtaining a winnings of $750 based on the average of two spins. All we need is two lucky spins. In fact, one really lucky spin and an average spin will do. But think about obtaining a winnings of $750 based on the average of *ten* spins. Now we need a *lot* of really lucky spins—and virtually no unlucky ones. The point is that we are much less likely to obtain a really large (or really small) sample mean when n is large than when n is small. This is exactly what it means to say that the variability of the sample means decreases with increasing sample size.

This decreasing variability is predicted by the formula for the standard error of the mean, $\sigma/\sqrt{n}$. As n increases, the standard error obviously decreases. This is what drives the behavior in Figures 7.12–7.15. In fact, using $\sigma = \$289$, the standard errors for $n = 2$, $n = 3$, $n = 6$, and $n = 10$ are $204, $167, $118, and $91.

Finally, what does this decreasing variability have to do with estimating a population mean with a sample mean? Very simply, it means that the sample mean tends to be a more *accurate* estimate when the sample size is large. Because of the approximate normality from the central limit theorem, we know from the previous chapter that there is about a 95% chance that the sample mean will be within two standard errors of the population mean. In other words, there is about a 95% chance that the sampling error will be no greater than two standard errors in magnitude. Therefore, because the standard error decreases as the sample size increases, the sampling error is likely to decrease as well.

To illustrate this, reconsider the auditor in Example 7.4. The standard error based on a sample of size $n = 100$ yielded a sample standard deviation of $419 and a standard error of about $42. Therefore, the sampling error has a 95% chance of being less than two standard errors, or $84, in magnitude. If the auditor believes that this sampling error is too large and therefore randomly samples 300 more accounts, then the new standard error will be $419/\sqrt{400} \simeq \$21$. Now there is about a 95% chance that the sampling error will be no more than $42. Note that because of the square root, small standard errors come at a high price. To halve the standard error, we must quadruple the sample size!

7.4.4 Sample Size Determination

The problem of determining the appropriate sample size in any sampling context is not an easy one, but it must be faced in the planning stages, *before* any sampling is done. We focus here on the relationship between sampling error and sample size. As we discussed earlier, the sampling error tends to decrease as the sample size increases, so the desire to minimize sampling error encourages us to select larger sample sizes. We should note, however, that several other factors encourage us to select *smaller* sample sizes. The ultimate sample size selection must achieve a trade-off between these opposing forces.

What are these other factors? First, there is the obvious cost of sampling. Larger sample sizes require larger costs. Sometimes, a company or agency might have a budget for a given sampling project. If the sample size required to achieve an "acceptable" sampling error is 500, say, but the budget allows for a sample size of only 300, budget considerations will probably prevail.

Another problem caused by large sample sizes is timely collection of the data. Suppose a retailer wants to collect sample data from its customers to decide whether to run an advertising blitz in the coming week. Obviously, the retailer needs to collect these data quickly if they are to be of any use, and a large sample could require too much time to collect.

Finally, a more subtle problem caused by large sample sizes is the increased chance of *nonsampling* error, such as nonresponse bias. As we discussed earlier in this chapter, there are many potential sources of nonsampling error, and they are usually very difficult to quantify. However, it is likely that they tend to increase as the sample size increases. Arguably, the potential increase in *sampling* error from a smaller sample could be more than offset by a decrease in nonsampling error, especially if the cost saved by the smaller sample size is used to reduce the sources of nonsampling error—more follow-up of nonrespondents, for example.

Nevertheless, the determination of sample size is usually driven by sampling error considerations. If we want to estimate a population mean with a sample mean, then the key is the standard error of the mean, given by

$$\text{SE}(\overline{X}) = \sigma/\sqrt{n}$$

We know from the central limit theorem that if n is reasonably large, there is about a 95% chance that the magnitude of the sampling error will be no more than two standard errors. Because σ is fixed in the formula for $\text{SE}(\overline{X})$, we can choose n to make $2\text{SE}(\overline{X})$ acceptably small.

The usual procedure is to select an acceptable sampling error B, called the **maximum probable absolute error**. Then we set $2\text{SE}(\overline{X})$ equal to B and solve for n. After doing the required algebra, we obtain

$$n = \frac{4\sigma^2}{B^2} \tag{7.5}$$

The implication is that if we randomly sample this many members from the population, then there is a 95% chance that the resulting sampling error will be no greater than B in magnitude.[5]

This formula makes sense intuitively. Specifically, when the variability in the population is large, as measured by σ^2, we need a large sample size to achieve a given level of accuracy. In an extreme case, if all household incomes in the population are within $100 dollars of one another—very little variability—we don't need to sample many households to get a good estimate of the mean household income. But if the household incomes vary from a low of, say, $10,000, to a high of over a million dollars, we might need to sample quite a few households to achieve an accurate estimate of the mean household income.

Similarly, it makes sense that n should vary inversely with B. The value of B indicates the level of accuracy we want. The lower the value of B, the less error we are willing to tolerate. Therefore, if we want really accurate estimates, we have to pay for them with large sample sizes.

From a practical point of view, the only problem in applying equation (7.5) is that we generally do not know σ, and we cannot simply approximate σ by the sample standard deviation s because we are still in the planning stages—we don't yet have a sample! The usual way to overcome this problem is to use a reasonable "guess" for σ, perhaps based on historical data or a pilot sample. We discuss this issue in the following example.

---

[5]The sample size formula given here assumes the eventual sample size will be "small" relative to the population size. When this isn't true, there are more precise formulas that take the population size into account. See Levy and Lemeshow (1991), for example.

EXAMPLE 7.6

A marketing researcher has been hired by a videocassette rental company to estimate the average number of videocassettes rented annually by households in a particular metropolitan area. The researcher decides to determine the sample size that makes the maximum probable absolute error approximately equal to 10. Discuss how she should proceed.

Solution

The solution appears in Figure 7.16. (See the file SAMPSIZE.XLS.) The researcher has chosen the maximum probable absolute error criterion, with $B = 10$, as the value she is willing to tolerate. Therefore, she should use equation (7.5). To use this equation, she must estimate a value for σ. Based on her knowledge of the industry and available historical data, she uses a best guess of $\sigma = 50$. She then uses these values (see cells C7 and C8 of Figure 7.16) to find the required sample size in cell C10 with the formula

$$\text{=4*PopStdev^2/MaxAbsErr^2}$$

FIGURE 7.16 **Sample Size Determination**

	A	B	C	D	E	F
1	Determining sample size for estimating a population mean					
2						
3	Assumption: Population size is very large					
4						
5					Sample results	
6	Inputs				Household	# of rentals
7		Pop stdev (guess)	50		1	44
8		Max absolute error	10		2	95
9					3	42
10		Resulting sample size	100.00		4	39
11					5	155
12	Outputs from sample				6	38
13		Sample mean	89.78		7	159
14		Sample stdev	59.31		8	86
15		Std Error	5.93		9	151
16		Absolute error	11.86		10	42
17					11	36
18		Range names			12	169
103		MaxAbsErr: B8			97	197
104		PopStdev: B7			98	26
105		Sample1: F7:F106			99	43
106					100	159

Finally, she takes a sample of size 100, as prescribed in cell C10. We assume she observes the sample values shown in column F. Based on this sample, we calculate summary measures in the usual way in the range C13:C16. Note that the value in cell C16 is 2 times the standard error in cell C15. It is slightly greater than the maximum absolute error she specified (10, in cell C8) because she observed a larger standard deviation than she guessed (59.31 versus 50). In other words, the fact that there is evidently more variation in the population than she thought makes her sample mean based on 100 households slightly less accurate than she intended. ■

Sample size determination is extremely important in real sampling applications. It is one of the few "levers" the researcher has for controlling the amount of sampling error. We will have more to say about sample size determination in the next chapter when we study confidence interval estimation.

7.4.5 Summary of Key Ideas for Simple Random Sampling

To this point, we have covered some very important concepts. Because we will build upon these concepts in later chapters, we summarize them here.

- To estimate a population mean with a simple random sample, we use the sample mean as a "best guess." This estimate is usually called a point estimate. That is, $\overline{X}$ is a point estimate for μ.

- The accuracy of the point estimate is measured by its standard error. It is the standard deviation of the sampling distribution of the point estimate. The standard error of $\overline{X}$ is approximately $s/\sqrt{n}$, where s is the sample standard deviation.

- From the central limit theorem, the sampling distribution of $\overline{X}$ is approximately normal when n is reasonably large.

- There is approximately a 95% chance that any particular $\overline{X}$ will be within two standard errors of the population mean μ.

- The sampling error can be reduced by increasing the sample size n. Appropriate sample size formulas are available for achieving an acceptable level of the maximum probable absolute error.

PROBLEMS

Level A

29 A manufacturing company's quality control personnel have recorded the proportion of defective items for each of 500 monthly shipments of one of the computer components that the company produces. The data are in the file P2_2.XLS. The quality control department manager does not have sufficient time to review all of these data. Rather, she would like to examine the proportions of defective items for a sample of these shipments.

   a Use Excel to generate a simple random sample of size 25 from the given frame.
   b Compute a point estimate of the population mean from the sample selected in part **a**. What is the sampling error in this case? Assume that the population consists of the proportion of defective items for each of the given 500 monthly shipments.
   c Determine a good approximation to the standard error of the mean in this case.
   d Repeat parts **b** and **c** after generating a simple random sample of size 50 from the given frame.

30 The manager of a local fast-food restaurant is interested in improving the service provided to customers who use the restaurant's drive-up window. As a first step in this process, the manager asks his assistant to record the time (in minutes) it takes to serve a large number of customers at the final window in the facility's drive-up system. The given frame of 200 customer service times are all observed during the busiest hour of the day for this fast-food operation. The data are in the file P2_4.XLS.

   a Use Excel to generate a simple random sample of size 10 from this frame.
   b Compute a point estimate of the population mean from the sample selected in part **a**. What is the sampling error in this case? Assume that the population consists of the given 200 customer service times.
   c Determine a good approximation to the standard error of the mean in this case.
   d Repeat parts **b** and **c** after generating a simple random sample of size 20 from the given frame.

31 Consider the given set of average annual household income levels of citizens of selected U.S. metropolitan areas in the file P3_6.XLS.

    a Use Excel to obtain a simple random sample of size 15 from this frame.

    b Compute a point estimate of the population mean from the sample selected in part **a**. What is the sampling error in this case? Assume that the population consists of all average annual household income levels in the given frame.

    c Determine a good approximation to the standard error of the mean in this case.

    d Repeat parts **b** and **c** after generating a simple random sample of size 30 from the given frame.

32 The operations manager of a toll booth located at a major exit of a state turnpike is trying to estimate the average number of vehicles that arrive at the toll booth during a 1-minute period during the peak of rush-hour traffic. In an effort to estimate this average throughput value, he records the number of vehicles that arrive at the toll booth over a 1-minute interval commencing at the same time for each of 365 normal weekdays. The data are provided in the file P2_9.XLS.

    a Choose a simple random sample of size 18 from the given frame to help the operations manager estimate the average throughput value.

    b Compute a point estimate of the population mean from the sample selected in part **a**. What is the sampling error in this case? Assume that the population consists of the numbers of vehicle arrivals over the 365 weekdays in the given frame.

    c Determine a good approximation to the standard error of the mean in this case.

    d Repeat parts **b** and **c** after generating a simple random sample of size 36 from the given frame.

33 The operations manager of a toll booth located at a major exit of a state turnpike is trying to estimate the average number of vehicles that arrive at the toll booth during a 1-minute period during the peak of rush-hour traffic. In an effort to estimate this average throughput value, he records the number of vehicles that arrive at the toll booth over a 1-minute interval commencing at the same time for each of many normal weekdays. The data are provided in the file P2_9.XLS.

    a What sample size would be required for the operations manager to be approximately 95% sure that his estimate of the average throughput value is within 1 unit of the true mean? Assume that his best estimate of the population standard deviation σ is 1.7 arrivals per minute.

    b How does the answer to part **a** change if the operations manager wants his estimate to be within 0.75 unit of the actual population mean? Explain the difference in your answers to parts **a** and **b**.

34 A lightbulb manufacturer wants to estimate the average number of defective bulbs contained in a box shipped by the company. Production personnel at this company have recorded the number of defective bulbs found in each of the 1000 boxes shipped during the past week. These data are provided in P7_11.XLS.

    a What sample size would be required for the production personnel to be approximately 95% sure that their estimate of the average number of defective bulbs per box is within 0.25 unit of the true mean? Assume that their best estimate of the population standard deviation σ is 0.9 defective bulb per box.

    b How does the answer to part **a** change if the production personnel want their estimate to be within 0.40 unit of the actual population mean? Explain the difference in your answers to parts **a** and **b**.

35 Senior management of a certain consulting services firm is concerned about a growing decline in the organization's productivity. In an effort to understand the depth and extent of this problem, management would like to estimate the average number of hours its employees spend on work-related activities in a typical week. The frame of virtually all of the firm's full-time employees, including the employees' self-reported amounts of time typically devoted to work activities each week, is provided in P7_35.XLS.

    a What sample size would be required for management to be approximately 95% sure that its estimate of the average number of hours the employees spend on work-related activities in a typical week is within 6 hours of the true mean? Assume that management's best estimate of the population standard deviation σ is 10 hours per week.

b How does the answer to part **a** change if management want its estimate to be within 3 hours of the actual population mean? Explain the difference in your answers to parts **a** and **b**.

36 Elected officials in a small Florida town are preparing the annual budget for their community. Specifically, they would like to estimate how much their constituents living in this town are typically paying each year in real estate taxes. Given that there are over 3000 homeowners in this small community, officials have decided to sample a representative subset of taxpayers and thoroughly study their tax payments. The latest frame of homeowners is given in P7_36.XLS.

    a What sample size would be required for elected officials to be approximately 95% sure that their estimate of the average annual real estate tax payment made by homeowners in their community is within $100 of the true mean? Assume that their best estimate of the population standard deviation σ is $535.

    b Choose a simple random sample of the size found in part **a**.

    c Compute the observed sampling error based on the sample you have drawn from the population given in P7_36.XLS. How does the actual sampling error compare to the maximum probable absolute error established in part **a**? Explain.

Level B

37 Continuing Problem 29, what proportion of the given 500 monthly shipments contain fractions of defective components within *one* standard error of the mean (based on the original simple random sample of size 25)? What proportion of the 500 monthly shipments contain fractions of defective components within *two* standard errors of the mean (again, based on the original simple random sample of size 25)?

38 Continuing Problem 30, what proportion of the given 200 customer service times are within *two* standard errors of the mean (based on the original simple random sample of size 10)? What proportion of the 200 customer service times are within *three* standard errors of the mean (again, based on the original simple random sample of size 10)?

39 Continuing Problem 31, what proportion of the given average annual household income levels are within *two* standard errors of the mean (based on the original simple random sample of size 15)? What proportion of the given average annual household income levels are within *two* standard errors of the mean (now, based on the second simple random sample of size 30)?

40 Continuing Problem 32, what proportion of the numbers of vehicle arrivals over the given 365 weekdays are within *two* standard errors of the mean (based on the original simple random sample of size 18)? What proportion of the given numbers of vehicle arrivals are within *two* standard errors of the mean (now, based on the second simple random sample of size 36)?

41 Wal-Mart buyers seek to purchase adequate supplies of various brands of toothpaste to meet the ongoing demands of its customers. In particular, Wal-Mart is interested in estimating the proportion of its customers who favor the country's leading brand of toothpaste, Crest. The file P7_41.XLS contains the toothpaste brand preferences of 2000 Wal-Mart customers, obtained recently through the administration of a customer survey.

    a Use Excel to choose a simple random sample of size 100 from the given frame.

    b Using the sample found in part **a**, compute a point estimate (called the sample proportion, $\hat{p}$) of the true proportion of Wal-Mart customers who prefer Crest toothpaste. What is the sampling error in this case? Assume that the population consists of the preferences of all customers in the given frame.

    c Given that the standard error of the sampling distribution of the sample proportion $\hat{p}$ is approximately $\sqrt{\hat{p}(1 - \hat{p})/n}$, compute a good approximation to the standard error of the sample proportion in this case.

    d Repeat parts **b** and **c** after generating a simple random sample of size 50 from the given frame. How do you explain the differences in your computed results?

42 A finance professor has just given a midterm examination in her corporate finance course. The 100 scores are provided in P2_5.XLS.

    a Generate an appropriate histogram for the given distribution of 100 examination scores. Characterize this distribution. Also, compute the mean and standard deviation of the given scores.

    b Repeatedly choose simple random samples of size 2 from the original distribution given in P2_5.XLS. Record the sample mean for each of 500 sampling repetitions and generate an appropriate histogram of the resulting sampling distribution. Characterize this sampling distribution and compute its mean and standard deviation.

c Repeatedly choose simple random samples of size 5 from the original distribution given in P2_5.XLS. Record the sample mean for each of 500 sampling repetitions and generate an appropriate histogram of the resulting sampling distribution. Characterize this sampling distribution and compute its mean and standard deviation.

d Repeatedly choose simple random samples of size 10 from the original distribution given in P2_5.XLS. Record the sample mean for each of 500 sampling repetitions and generate an appropriate histogram of the resulting sampling distribution. Characterize this sampling distribution and compute its mean and standard deviation.

e Explain the changes in your constructed sampling distributions as the sample size was increased from $n = 2$ to $n = 10$. In particular, how does the sampling distribution you constructed in part **d** compare to the original distribution (where $n = 1$) you described in part **a**?

43 The annual base salaries for 200 students graduating from a reputable MBA program this year are of interest to those in the admissions office who are responsible for marketing the program to prospective students. These salaries are given in the file P2_74.XLS.

a Generate an appropriate histogram for the given distribution of 200 annual salaries. Characterize this distribution. Also, compute the mean and standard deviation of the given salaries.

b Repeatedly choose simple random samples of size 3 from the original distribution given in P2_74.XLS. Record the sample mean for each of 500 sampling repetitions and generate an appropriate histogram of the resulting sampling distribution. Characterize this sampling distribution and compute its mean and standard deviation.

c Repeatedly choose simple random samples of size 6 from the original distribution given in P2_74.XLS. Record the sample mean for each of 500 sampling repetitions and generate an appropriate histogram of the resulting sampling distribution. Characterize this sampling distribution and compute its mean and standard deviation.

d Repeatedly choose simple random samples of size 12 from the original distribution given in P2_74.XLS. Record the sample mean for each of 500 sampling repetitions and generate an appropriate histogram of the resulting sampling distribution. Characterize this sampling distribution and compute its mean and standard deviation.

e Explain the changes in your constructed sampling distributions as the sample size was increased from $n = 3$ to $n = 12$. In particular, how does the sampling distribution you constructed in part **d** compare to the original distribution (where $n = 1$) you described in part **a**?

44 A market research consultant hired by the Pepsi-Cola Co. is interested in determining the proportion of consumers who favor Pepsi-Cola over Coke Classic in a particular urban location. A frame of customers from the market under investigation is provided in P7_44.XLS.

a What sample size would be required for the market research consultant to be approximately 95% sure that her estimate of the proportion of consumers who favor Pepsi-Cola in the given urban location is within 0.20 of the true proportion? Assume that her best estimate of the population proportion parameter p is 0.45. [*Hint:* The required sample size formula in this case is given by $n = 4p(1 - p)/B^2$, where p is the population proportion parameter and B is the familiar maximum probable absolute error.]

b How does the answer to part **a** change if the market research consultant wants her estimate to be within 0.15 of the actual population proportion? Explain the difference in your answers to parts **a** and **b**. ■

7.5 Conclusion

This chapter has provided the fundamental concepts behind statistical inference. We have discussed ways to obtain random samples from a population, how to calculate a point estimate of a particular population parameter, the population mean, and how to measure the accuracy of this point estimate. The key idea is the sampling distribution of the estimate and specifically its standard deviation, called the standard error of the estimate. From the central limit theorem, we have seen that the sampling distribution of the sample mean is approximately normal, which implies that the sample mean will be within two standard errors of the population mean in approximately 95% of all random samples. In the next two chapters we will build on these important concepts.

PROBLEMS

Level A

45 The annual base salaries for 200 students graduating from a reputable MBA program this year are of interest to those in the admissions office who are responsible for marketing the program to prospective students. The data are in the file P2_74.XLS. Use Excel to choose 10 simple random samples of size 15 from the given frame. For each simple random sample you obtain, compute the mean annual salary. Are these sample means equivalent? Explain why or why not.

46 A market research consultant hired by the Pepsi-Cola Co. is interested in determining who favors the Pepsi-Cola brand over Coke Classic in a particular urban location. A frame of customers from the market under investigation is provided in P7_44.XLS.

    a Compute the proportion of the customers in the given frame who favor Pepsi.

    b Use Excel to choose a simple random sample of size 30 from the given frame.

    c Compute the proportion of the 30 customers in the random sample who favor Pepsi. Compare this sample proportion to the value obtained in part **a**. Explain any difference between the two values.

    d What are the advantages and disadvantages of employing simple random sampling in this particular case?

47 The employee benefits manager of a small private university would like to know the proportion of its full-time employees who prefer adopting each of three available health care plans in the forthcoming annual enrollment period. A reliable frame of the university's employees and their tentative health care preferences are given in P7_25.XLS.

    a Compute the proportion of the employees in the given frame who favor *each* of the three plans (i.e., plans A, B, and C).

    b Use Excel to choose a simple random sample of size 45 from the given frame.

    c Compute the proportion of the 45 employees in the random sample who favor each health plan. Compare these sample proportions to the corresponding values obtained in part **a**. Explain any differences between the corresponding values.

    d What are the advantages and disadvantages of employing simple random sampling in this particular case?

48 Senior management of a certain consulting services firm is concerned about a growing decline in the organization's productivity. In an effort to understand the depth and extent of this problem, management would like to determine the average number of hours its employees spend on work-related activities in a typical week. The frame of virtually all of the firm's full-time employees, including the employees' self-reported amounts of time typically devoted to work activities each week, is provided in P7_48.XLS.

    a Select a simple random sample of size 100 from the given frame.

    b Compute the mean and standard deviation of the weekly number of hours worked by all employees in the frame. Also, compute the mean and standard deviation of the weekly number of hours worked by employees in the simple random sample. How do these two sets of descriptive measures compare?

49 Elected officials in a small Florida town are preparing the annual budget for their community. Specifically, they would like to know how much their constituents living in this town are typically paying each year in real estate taxes. Given that there are over 3000 homeowners in this small community, officials have decided to sample a representative subset of taxpayers and thoroughly study their tax payments. The latest frame of homeowners is given in P7_49.XLS. Note that this file contains the real estate tax payment made by each homeowner last year.

a Compute the average real estate tax payment made by the homeowners included in the frame. Is the overall mean a valid measure of central tendency in this case?

b Use Excel to choose a simple random sample of 150 homeowners from the given frame.

c Compute the average real estate tax payment for the 150 homeowners in the random sample. Compare this sample mean to the corresponding summary measure obtained in part **a**.

d Is the sample mean computed in part **c** a good estimate of the average real estate tax payment made by homeowners living in this small town? Explain why or why not.

50 Auditors of a particular bank are interested in comparing the reported value of customer savings account balances with their own findings regarding the actual value of such assets. Rather than reviewing the records of each savings account at the bank, the auditors decide to examine a representative sample of savings account balances. The frame from which they will sample is given in the file P7_50.XLS.

a Assist the bank's auditors by selecting a simple random sample of 100 savings accounts.

b Explain how the auditors might use the simple random sample identified in part **a** to estimate the value of *all* savings accounts balances within this bank.

51 The manager of a local supermarket wants to know the average amount (in dollars) customers spend at his store on Fridays. He would like to study the buying behavior of each customer who makes a purchase at the store on a typical Friday. However, the manager's assistant, who is currently enrolled in a managerial statistics course at a local college, urges the manager to save his scarce time and money by studying a sample of customer purchases. The available frame of relevant customer purchases is provided in file P7_51.XLS.

a Compute the average purchase amount made by the customers included in the given frame.

b Use Excel to choose a simple random sample of 25 customers from the given frame.

c Compute the average purchase amount made by the 25 customers in the random sample. Compare this sample mean to the corresponding summary measure obtained in part **a**.

d Is the sample mean a good estimate of the overall population mean in this case? Explain why or why not.

52 The annual base salaries for 200 students graduating from a reputable MBA program this year are of interest to those in the admissions office who are responsible for marketing the program to prospective students. The data are in the file P2_74.XLS. Use Excel to choose 15 systematic samples of size 10 from the given frame. For each systematic sample you obtain, compute the mean annual salary. Are these sample means equivalent? Explain why or why not.

53 Given data in the file P2_13.XLS from a recent survey of chief executive officers from 350 of the nation's biggest businesses (*The Wall Street Journal*, April 9, 1998), choose a systematic sample of 25 executives and find the mean, median, and standard deviation of the bonuses awarded to them in 1997. How do these sample statistics compare to the mean, median, and standard deviation of the bonuses given to all executives included in the frame?

54 A market research consultant hired by the Pepsi-Cola Co. is interested in determining who favors the Pepsi-Cola brand over Coke Classic in a particular urban location. A frame of customers from the market under investigation is provided in P7_44.XLS.

a Compute the proportion of the customers in the given frame who favor Pepsi.

b Use Excel to choose a systematic sample of size 30 from the given frame.

c Compute the proportion of the 30 customers in the systematic sample who favor Pepsi. Compare this sample proportion to the value obtained in part **a**. Explain any difference between the two values.

d What are the advantages and disadvantages of employing systematic sampling in this particular case?

55 A lightbulb manufacturer wants to know the number of defective bulbs contained in a typical box shipped by the company. Production personnel at this company have recorded the number of defective bulbs found in each of the 1000 boxes shipped during the past week. These data are provided in P7_11.XLS. Using this shipment of boxes as a frame, select a systematic sample of 50 boxes and compute the mean number of defective bulbs found in a box.

56 The employee benefits manager of a small private university would like to know the proportion of its full-time employees who prefer adopting each of three available health care plans in the forthcoming annual enrollment period. A reliable frame of the university's employees and their tentative health care preferences are given in P7_25.XLS.

a Compute the proportion of the employees in the given frame who favor *each* of the three plans (i.e., plans A, B, and C).

b Use Excel to choose a systematic sample of size 47 from the given frame.

c Compute the proportion of the 47 employees in the systematic sample who favor each health plan. Compare these sample proportions to the corresponding values obtained in part **a**. Explain any differences between the corresponding values.

d What are the advantages and disadvantages of employing systematic sampling in this particular case?

57 Senior management of a certain consulting services firm is concerned about a growing decline in the organization's productivity. In an effort to understand the depth and extent of this problem, management would like to determine the average number of hours their employees spend on work-related activities in a typical week. The frame of virtually all of the firm's full-time employees, including the employees' self-reported amounts of time typically devoted to work activities each week, is provided in P7_48.XLS.

a Select a systematic sample of size 100 from the given frame.

b Compute the mean and standard deviation of the weekly number of hours worked by all employees in the frame. Also, compute the mean and standard deviation of the weekly number of hours worked by employees in the systematic sample. How do these two sets of descriptive measures compare?

58 Elected officials in a small Florida town are preparing the annual budget for their community. Specifically, they would like to know how much their constituents living in this town are typically paying each year in real estate taxes. Given that there are over 3000 homeowners in this small community, officials have decided to sample a representative subset of taxpayers and thoroughly study their tax payments. The latest frame of homeowners is given in P7_49.XLS. Note that this file contains the real estate tax payment made by each homeowner last year.

a Use Excel to choose a systematic sample of 150 homeowners from the given frame.

b Compute the average real estate tax payment for the 150 homeowners in the systematic sample.

c Is the sample mean computed in part **b** a good estimate of the average real estate tax payment made by homeowners living in this small town? Explain why or why not.

59 Auditors of a particular bank are interested in comparing the reported value of customer savings account balances with their own findings regarding the actual value of such assets. Rather than reviewing the records of each savings account at the bank, the auditors decide to examine a representative sample of savings account balances. The frame from which they will sample is given in the file P7_50.XLS.

a Assist the bank's auditors by selecting a systematic sample of 151 savings accounts.

b Explain how the auditors might use the systematic sample identified in part **a** to estimate the value of *all* savings accounts balances within this bank.

60 The manager of a local supermarket wants to know the average amount (in dollars) customers spend at his store on Fridays. He would like to study the buying behavior of each customer who makes a purchase at the store on a typical Friday. However, the manager's assistant, who is currently enrolled in a managerial statistics course at a local college, urges the manager to save his scarce time and money by studying a sample of customer purchases. The available frame of relevant customer purchases is provided in file P7_51.XLS.

a Compute the average purchase amount made by the customers included in the given frame.

b Use Excel to choose a systematic sample of 43 customers from the given frame.

c Compute the average purchase amount made by the 43 customers in the systematic sample. Compare this sample mean to the corresponding summary measure obtained in part **a**.

d Is the sample mean a good estimate of the overall population mean in this case? Explain why or why not.

61 Elected officials in a small Florida town are preparing the annual budget for their community. Specifically, they would like to know how much their constituents living in this town are typically paying each year in real estate taxes. Given that there are over 3000 homeowners in this small community, officials have decided to sample a representative subset of taxpayers and thoroughly study their tax payments. The latest frame of homeowners is given in P7_49.XLS. Note that this file contains the real estate tax payment made by each homeowner last year.

a Compute the average real estate tax payment made by the homeowners included in the frame. Is the overall mean a valid measure of central tendency in this case?

b Use Excel to choose a sample of 150 homeowners stratified by neighborhood with proportional sample sizes.

c Compute the average real estate tax payment for the 150 homeowners in the stratified sample. Compare this sample mean to the corresponding summary measure obtained in part **a**.

d Is the sample mean computed in part **c** a good estimate of the average real estate tax payment made by homeowners living in this small town? Explain why or why not.

e Explain how the elected officials could apply cluster sampling in selecting a sample of size 150 from this frame. What are the advantages and disadvantages of employing cluster sampling in this case?

62 Auditors of a particular bank are interested in comparing the reported value of customer savings account balances with their own findings regarding the actual value of such assets. Rather than reviewing the records of each savings account at the bank, the auditors decide to examine a representative sample of savings account balances. The frame from which they will sample is given in the file P7_50.XLS.

a What sample size would be required for the auditors to be approximately 95% sure that their estimate of the average savings account balance at this bank is within $100 of the true mean? Assume that their best estimate of the population standard deviation σ is $500.

b Choose a simple random sample of the size found in part **a**.

c Compute the observed sampling error based on the sample you have drawn from the population given in P7_50.XLS. How does the actual sampling error compare to the maximum probable absolute error established in part **a**? Explain.

63 The manager of a local supermarket wants to estimate the average amount customers spend at his store on Fridays. He would like to study the buying behavior of each customer who makes a purchase at the store on a typical Friday. However, the manager's assistant, who is currently enrolled in a managerial statistics course at a local college, urges the manager to save his scarce time and money by studying a sample of customer purchases. The available frame of relevant customer purchases is provided in file P7_51.XLS.

a What sample size would be required for the supermarket manager to be approximately 95% sure that his estimate of the average customer expenditure on Fridays is within $25 of the true mean? Assume that his best estimate of the population standard deviation σ is $72.

b Choose a simple random sample of the size found in part **a**.

c Compute the observed sampling error based on the sample you have drawn from the population given in P7_51.XLS. How does the actual sampling error compare to the maximum probable absolute error established in part **a**? Explain.

64 *The Hite Report* was Sheri Hite's survey of the attitudes of American women toward sexuality. She sent out over 100,000 surveys; each contained multiple-choice and open-ended questions. These surveys were given to women's groups and announced in church newsletters. Ads were also placed in women's magazines. A total of 3019 surveys were returned. Sheri Hite's findings challenged much conventional wisdom about sexuality. She found that most women were unhappy in their romantic relationships (some for reasons that are too graphic for this book!). How would you criticize Hite's methodology? A later poll, by the way, contradicted many of her findings.

a Give two criticisms of Hite's sampling methodology.

b Despite these criticisms, what value might you see in Hite's results?

65 A market research consultant hired by the Pepsi-Cola Co. is interested in determining who favors the Pepsi-Cola brand over Coke Classic in a particular urban location. A frame of customers from the market under investigation is provided in P7_44.XLS.

a Compute the proportion of the consumers in the given frame who favor Pepsi.

b Use Excel to choose a sample of size 30 stratified by gender with proportional sample sizes.

c Compute the proportion of the 30 consumers in the stratified sample who favor Pepsi. Compare this sample proportion to the value obtained in part **a**. Explain any difference between the two values.

d What are the advantages and disadvantages of employing stratified sampling in this particular case?

Level B

66 Repeat Problem 65, but now stratify the consumers in the given frame by *age* rather than by gender. How does this modification affect your answers to the questions posed in parts **b** and **c**? Finally, stratify the consumers by both gender *and* age (e.g., all females over 60) with proportional sample sizes. How does this change affect your answers to the questions posed in parts **b** and **c**? Which approach to stratification appears to give the best results in estimating the actual proportion of the customers in the given frame who favor Pepsi?

67 Wal-Mart buyers seek to purchase adequate supplies of various brands of toothpaste to meet the ongoing demands of their customers. In particular, Wal-Mart is interested in knowing the proportion of its customers who favor such leading brands of toothpaste as Aquafresh, Colgate, Crest, and Mentadent. The file P7_41.XLS contains the toothpaste brand preferences of 2000 Wal-Mart customers, obtained recently through the administration of a customer survey.

a Determine the proportion of Wal-Mart customers who favor each major brand of toothpaste.

b Assuming that the given data constitute an appropriate frame, choose a simple random sample of 100 of these customers.

c Calculate the proportion of Wal-Mart customers in the random sample who favor each major brand of toothpaste. Compare these sample proportions to the corresponding values found in part **a**. How do you explain any disparities between corresponding proportions for customers included in the sample and those in the frame?

68 Wal-Mart buyers seek to purchase adequate supplies of various brands of toothpaste to meet the ongoing demands of their customers. In particular, Wal-Mart is interested in knowing the proportion of its customers who favor such leading brands of toothpaste as Aquafresh, Colgate, Crest, and Mentadent. The file P7_41.XLS contains the toothpaste brand preferences of 2000 Wal-Mart customers, obtained recently through the administration of a customer survey.

a Determine the proportion of Wal-Mart customers who favor each major brand of toothpaste.

b Assuming that the given data constitute an appropriate frame, choose a systematic sample of 100 of these customers.

c Calculate the proportion of Wal-Mart customers in the systematic sample who favor each major brand of toothpaste. Compare these sample proportions to the corresponding values found in part **a**. How do you explain any disparities between corresponding proportions for customers included in the sample and those in the frame?

69 Suppose that you are an entrepreneur interested in establishing a new Internet-based sports information service. Furthermore, suppose that you have gathered basic demographic information on a large number of Internet users. Assume that these 1000 individuals were carefully selected through stratified sampling. These data are stored in the file P2_43.XLS.

a To assess potential interest in your proposed enterprise, you would like to conduct telephone interviews with a representative subset of the 1000 Internet users you surveyed previously. How would you proceed to stratify the given frame of 1000 individuals to choose 50 for telephone interviews? Explain your approach and implement it to select a useful sample of size 50.

b Explain how the entrepreneur could apply cluster sampling to obtain a sample of size 50 from this frame. What are the advantages and disadvantages of employing cluster sampling in this case?

70 A market research consultant hired by the Pepsi-Cola Co. is interested in determining the proportion of consumers who favor Pepsi-Cola over Coke Classic in a particular urban location. A frame of customers from the market under investigation is provided in P7_44.XLS.

a Use Excel to choose a simple random sample of size 30 from the given frame.

b Using the sample found in part **a**, compute a point estimate (called the sample proportion, $\hat{p}$) of the true proportion of consumers who favor Pepsi-Cola in this market. What is the sampling error in this case? Assume that the population consists of the preferences of all consumers in the given frame.

c Given that the standard error of the sampling distribution of the sample proportion $\hat{p}$ is approximately $\sqrt{\hat{p}(1 - \hat{p})/n}$, compute a good approximation to the standard error of the sample proportion in this case.

d Repeat parts **b** and **c** after generating a simple random sample of size 15 from the given frame. How do you explain the differences in your computed results?

71 The employee benefits manager of a small private university would like to estimate the proportion of full-time employees who prefer adopting the first (i.e., plan A) of three available health care plans in the forthcoming annual enrollment period. A reliable frame of the university's employees and their tentative health care preferences are given in P7_47.XLS.

a Use Excel to choose a simple random sample of size 45 from the given frame.

b Using the sample found in part **a**, compute a point estimate (called the sample proportion, $\hat{p}$) of the true proportion of university employees who prefer plan A. What is the sampling error in this case? Assume that the population consists of the preferences of all employees in the given frame.

c Given that the standard error of the sampling distribution of the sample proportion p is approximately $\sqrt{\hat{p}(1 - \hat{p})/n}$, compute a good approximation to the standard error of the sample proportion in this case.

d Repeat parts **b** and **c** after generating a simple random sample of size 25 from the given frame. How do you explain the differences in your computed results?

72 Auditors of a particular bank are interested in comparing the reported value of customer savings account balances with their own findings regarding the actual value of such assets. Rather than reviewing the records of each savings account at the bank, the auditors decide to examine a representative sample of savings account balances. The frame from which they will sample is given in the file P7_50.XLS.

a Generate an appropriate histogram for the given distribution of 2265 savings account balances. Characterize this distribution. Also, compute the mean and standard deviation of the given account balances.

b Repeatedly choose simple random samples of size 2 from the original distribution given in P7_50.XLS. Record the sample mean for each of 500 sampling repetitions and generate an appropriate histogram of the resulting sampling distribution. Characterize this sampling distribution and compute its mean and standard deviation.

c Repeatedly choose simple random samples of size 5 from the original distribution given in P7_50.XLS. Record the sample mean for each of 500 sampling repetitions and generate an appropriate histogram of the resulting sampling distribution. Characterize this sampling distribution and compute its mean and standard deviation.

d Repeatedly choose simple random samples of size 10 from the original distribution given in P7_50.XLS. Record the sample mean for each of 500 sampling repetitions and generate an appropriate histogram of the resulting sampling distribution. Characterize this sampling distribution and compute its mean and standard deviation.

e Explain the changes in your constructed sampling distributions as the sample size was increased from $n = 2$ to $n = 10$. In particular, how does the sampling distribution you constructed in part **d** compare to the original distribution (where $n = 1$) you described in part **a**?

73 A lightbulb manufacturer wants to estimate the number of defective bulbs contained in a typical box shipped by the company. Production personnel at this company have recorded the number of defective bulbs found in each of the 1000 boxes shipped during the past week. These data are provided in P7_11.XLS.

a Generate an appropriate histogram for the given distribution of 1000 numbers of defective bulbs. Characterize this distribution. Also, compute the mean and standard deviation of the given numbers.

b Repeatedly choose simple random samples of size 3 from the original distribution given in P7_11.XLS. Record the sample mean for each of 500 sampling repetitions and generate an appropriate histogram of the resulting sampling distribution. Characterize this sampling distribution and compute its mean and standard deviation.

c Repeatedly choose simple random samples of size 6 from the original distribution given in P7_11.XLS. Record the sample mean for each of 500 sampling repetitions and generate an appropriate histogram of the resulting sampling distribution. Characterize this sampling distribution and compute its mean and standard deviation.

d Repeatedly choose simple random samples of size 12 from the original distribution given in P7_11.XLS. Record the sample mean for each of 500 sampling repetitions and generate an appropriate histogram of the resulting sampling distribution. Characterize this sampling distribution and compute its mean and standard deviation.

e Explain the changes in your constructed sampling distributions as the sample size was increased from $n = 3$ to $n = 12$. In particular, how does the sampling distribution you constructed in part **d** compare to the original distribution (where $n = 1$) you described in part **a**?

74 The employee benefits manager of a small private university would like to estimate the proportion of full-time employees who prefer adopting the first (i.e., plan A) of three available health care plans in the forthcoming annual enrollment period. A reliable frame of the university's employees and their tentative health care preferences are given in P7_25.XLS.

a What sample size would be required for the benefits manager to be approximately 95% sure that her estimate of the proportion of full-time university employees who prefer adopting plan A is within 0.15 of the true proportion? Assume that her best estimate of the population proportion parameter p is $1/3$. [*Hint:* The required sample size formula in this case is given by $n = 4p(1 - p)/B^2$, where π is the population proportion parameter and B is the familiar maximum probable absolute error.]

b How does the answer to part **a** change if the benefits manager wants her estimate to be within 0.25 of the actual population proportion? Explain the difference in your answers to parts **a** and **b**.

75 Suppose the monthly unpaid balance on a Citicorp Mastercard is normally distributed with a mean of \$1200 and standard deviation of \$240. We want to show that the sample mean $\overline{X}$ is an unbiased estimate of the population mean μ, and the sample variance s^2 is an unbiased estimate of the population variance σ^2. Note that you can generate observations from CITICORP accounts by using the formula =NORMINV(RAND(),1200,240). Develop a simulation as follows:

■ Generate 50 samples of five credit card balances each. Then freeze the random numbers.

■ Calculate $\overline{X}$ and s^2 for each sample.

■ Show that the $\overline{X}$'s average to a value near the actual mean of \$1200.

■ Show that the s^2's average to a value near the true value $\sigma^2 = 240^2$.

76 (Based on an actual case) Indiana audits nursing homes to see whether and how much the nursing home has overbilled Medicaid. Here is how they do it. Nurseco has 70 homes in Indiana. The state randomly samples one invoice per nursing home and determines Nurseco's liability as follows. Suppose nursing home 1 has billed Medicaid \$100,000. If the one surveyed invoice at nursing home 1 indicates Nurseco has overbilled by 40%, then Nurseco would have to return 40% (or \$40,000) that it has collected from the state. What is wrong with this approach? Assuming all nursing homes have overbilled at a similar rate, can you suggest a better plan to determine how much money should be returned to the state?

77 The central limit theorem states that when many independent random variables are summed, the result follows a normal distribution even if the individual random variables in the sum do not. To illustrate this idea, simulate 500 samples of size 15 from the uniform (0,1) distribution (generated with the RAND function). Are the 500 sums (where each is a sum of 15 values) normally distributed? Show by constructing a histogram and also by checking the rules of thumb.

78 Assume a very large normally distributed population of scores on a test with mean 70 and standard deviation 7.

a Find an interval that includes 95% of the population.

b Suppose you randomly sample a single member from this population. Find an interval so that you are 95% confident that this member's score will be in the interval.

c Now suppose you sample 30 members randomly from this population. Find an interval so that you are 95% confident that the average of these members' scores will be in the interval.

d Finally, suppose you sample 300 members randomly from this population. Find an interval so that you are 95% confident that the average of these members' scores will be in the interval.

e Explain intuitively why the answers to parts **a–d** are not all the same. ■

7.1   Sampling from Videocassette Renters

The file VIDEOS.XLS contains a large database on 10,000 customer transactions for a fictional chain of video stores in the United States. Each row corresponds to a different customer and lists (1) a customer ID number (1–10,000); (2) the state where the customer lives; (3) the city where the customer lives; (4) the customer's gender; (5) the customer's favorite type of movie (drama, comedy, science fiction, or action); (6) the customer's next favorite type of movie; (7) the number of times the customer has rented movies in the past year; and (8) the total dollar amount the customer has spent on movie rentals during the past year. The data are sorted by state, then city, then gender. We assume that this database represents the entire population of customers for this video chain. (Of course, national chains would have significantly larger customer populations, but this database is large enough to illustrate the ideas.)

Imagine that only the data in columns A–D are readily available for this population. The company is interested in summary statistics of the data in columns E–H, such as the percentage of customers whose favorite movie type is drama or the average amount spent annually per customer, but it will have to do some work to obtain the data in columns E–H for any particular customer. Therefore, the company wants to perform sampling. The question is: What form of sampling—simple random sampling, systematic sampling, stratified sampling, cluster sampling, or even some type of multistage sampling—is most appropriate?

Your job is to investigate the possibilities and to write up a report on your findings. For any sampling method, any sample size, and any quantity of interest (such as average dollar amount spent annually), you should be concerned with sampling cost and accuracy. One way to judge the latter is to generate several random samples from a particular method and calculate the mean and standard deviation of your point estimates from these samples. For example, you might generate 10 systematic samples, calculate the average amount spent (an $\overline{X}$) for each sample, and then calculate the mean and standard deviation of these 10 $\overline{X}$'s. If your sampling method is accurate, the mean of the $\overline{X}$'s should be close to the population average, and the standard deviation should be small. By doing this for several sampling methods and possibly several sample sizes, you can experiment to see what is most cost efficient for the company. You can make any reasonable assumptions about the cost of sampling with any particular method.

8

Confidence Interval Estimation

Successful Applications

I n Example 7.4 from the previous chapter, we illustrated how sampling can be used in auditing. We will see another illustration of sampling in auditing in Example 8.4 of this chapter. In both examples, the point of the sampling is to discover some property (such as a mean or a proportion) from a large population of a company's accounts by examining a small fraction of these accounts and projecting the results to the population. The article by Press (1995) offers an interesting variation on this problem. He poses the question of how a government revenue agency should assess a business taxpayer's income for tax purposes on the basis of a sample audit of the company's business transactions. A sample of the company's transactions will indicate a taxable income for each sampled transaction. The methods of this chapter will be applied to the sample information to obtain a confidence interval for the total taxable income owed by the company.

Suppose for the sake of illustration that this confidence interval extends from $1,000,000 to $2,200,000 and is centered at $1,600,000. In words, the government's best guess of the company's taxable income is $1,600,000, and it is fairly confident that the true taxable income is between $1,000,000 and $2,200,000. How much tax should it assess the company? Press argues that the agency would like to maximize its revenue while minimizing the risk that the company will be assessed more than it really owes. This last assumption, that the government does not want to *overassess* the company, is crucial. By making several reasonable assumptions, he is able to argue that the agency should base the tax on the *lower* limit of the confidence interval, in this case, $1,000,000.[1]

On the other hand, if the agency were indifferent between overcharging and undercharging, then it would base the tax on the midpoint, $1,600,000, of the confidence interval. Using this strategy, the agency would overcharge in about half the cases and undercharge in the other half. This would certainly be upsetting to companies—it would appear that the agency were flipping a coin to decide whether to overcharge or undercharge! (This strategy is currently in most common use by state agencies, but it is being challenged, and the courts will have to make a decision.)

[1] In case this sounds overly generous on the government's part, the result is based on two important assumptions: (1) the confidence interval is a 90% confidence interval, and (2) the agency is 19 times more concerned about overassessing than about underassessing. If it were, say, only 5 times more concerned about overassessing than about underassessing, then it would base the tax on a larger estimate—but still below the midpoint of the confidence interval.

If the government agency does indeed decide to base the tax on the *lower* limit of the confidence interval, Press argues that it can still increase its tax revenue—by increasing the sample size of the audit. When the sample size increases, the confidence interval shrinks in width, and the lower limit, which governs the agency's tax revenue, almost surely increases. But there is some point at which larger samples are not warranted, for the simple reason that larger samples cost more money to obtain. Therefore, there is an optimal size that will balance the cost of sampling with the desire to obtain more tax revenue. ■

8.1 Introduction

This chapter expands upon the ideas from the previous chapter. Given an observed data set, we want to make inferences to some larger population. Two typical examples are the following:

- A mail-order company has accounts with thousands of customers. It would like to infer the average time its customers take to pay their bills, so it randomly samples a relatively small number of its customers, sees how long these customers take to pay their bills, and draws inferences about the entire population of customers.

- A manufacturing company is considering several compensation schemes to implement for its workers. It believes that different compensation schemes might provide different incentives and hence result in different worker productivity. To see whether this is true, the company randomly assigns groups of workers to the different compensation schemes for a period of 3 months and observes their productivity. Then it attempts to infer whether any differences observed in the experiment can be generalized to the overall worker population.

The inferences we draw in this chapter are always based on an underlying probability model, which means that some type of random mechanism must generate the given data. Two random mechanisms are generally used. The first involves sampling randomly from a larger population, as we discussed in the previous chapter. This is the mechanism responsible for generating the sample of customers in the above mail-order example. Regardless of whether the sample is a simple random sample or a more complex random sample, such as a stratified sample, the fact that it is *random* allows us to use the rules of probability to make inferences about the population as a whole.

The second commonly used random mechanism is called a **randomized experiment**. The compensation scheme example just described is a typical randomized experiment. Here we select a set of subjects (employees), randomly assign them to different **treatment groups** (compensation schemes), and then compare some quantitative measure (productivity) across the groups. The fact that the subjects are *randomly* assigned to the various treatment groups is useful for two reasons. First, it allows us to rule out a number of factors that might have led to differences across groups. For example, assuming that males and females are randomly spread across groups, we can rule out gender as the cause of observed group differences. Second, the random selection allows us to use the rules of probability to infer whether observed differences can be generalized to all employees.

Generally, statistical inferences are of two types, **confidence interval estimation** and **hypothesis testing**. The first of these is the subject of the current chapter; we will study hypothesis testing in the next chapter. They differ primarily in their point of view. For example, the mail-order company might sample 100 customers and find that they average

15.5 days before paying their bills. In confidence interval estimation, we use the data to obtain a point estimate and a confidence interval around this point estimate. In this example the point estimate is 15.5 days. It is a best guess for the mean bill-paying time in the entire customer population. Then, using the methods in this chapter, the company might find that a 95% confidence interval for the mean bill-paying time in the population is from 13.2 days to 17.8 days. The company is now 95% certain that the true mean bill-paying time in the population is within this interval.

Hypothesis testing takes a different point of view. Here we wish to check whether the observed data provide support for a particular hypothesis. In the compensation scheme example, suppose the manager believes that workers will have higher productivity if they are paid by salary than by an hourly wage. He runs the 3-month randomized experiment described above and finds that the salaried workers produce on average eight more parts per day than the hourly workers. Now he must make one of two conclusions. Either salaried workers are in general no more productive than hourly workers and the ones in the experiment just got lucky, or salaried workers really *are* more productive. We will learn in the next chapter how to decide which of these conclusions is more reasonable.

There are only a few key ideas in this chapter, and the most important of these, sampling distributions, was introduced in Chapter 7. It is important to concentrate on these key ideas and not get bogged down in formulas or numerical calculations. Statistical software such as the StatPro add-in is generally available to take care of these calculations. The job of a business person is much more dependent on knowing which methods to use in which situations and how to interpret computer output than on memorizing and plugging into formulas.

8.2

Sampling Distributions

In the previous chapter we introduced the sampling distribution of the sample mean $\overline{X}$ and saw how it was related to the central limit theorem. In general, whenever we make inferences about one or more population parameters, such as a mean or the difference between two means, we always base this inference on the sampling distribution of a sample statistic, such as the sample mean. Although the *concepts* of sample statistics and sampling distributions are no different from those in the previous chapter, there are some new details we need to learn.

We again begin with the sample mean $\overline{X}$. We know that if the sample size n is reasonably large, then for *any* population distribution, the sampling distribution of $\overline{X}$ is approximately normally distributed with mean μ and standard deviation $\sigma/\sqrt{n}$, where μ and σ are the population mean and standard deviation. An equivalent statement is that the standardized quantity Z defined by

$$Z = \frac{\overline{X} - \mu}{\sigma/\sqrt{n}}$$

is approximately normal with mean 0 and standard deviation 1. We can make a stronger statement if the population distribution itself is normal. In this case Z is *exactly* normally distributed, regardless of the sample size n.

Typically, we use this fact to make inferences about an unknown population mean μ. There is one problem, however—we usually do not know the population standard deviation σ. This parameter, σ, is called a **nuisance parameter** because we need its value even though it is typically not the parameter of primary interest. The solution appears to be straightforward: Replace the nuisance parameter σ by its sample estimate s in the formula for Z and proceed from there. However, when we replace σ by the sample standard deviation s, we introduce a new source of variability, and the sampling distribution is no longer normal. It is instead called the t **distribution**, a close relative of the normal distribution that appears in a variety of statistical applications.

8.2.1 The t Distribution

We first set the stage for this new sampling distribution. We are interested in estimating a population mean μ with a sample of size n. We assume the population distribution is normal with unknown standard deviation σ. We intend to base inferences on the standardized value of $\overline{X}$, where σ is replaced by the sample standard deviation s. Then the standardized value

$$\frac{\overline{X} - \mu}{s/\sqrt{n}}$$

has a t **distribution with** $n - 1$ **degrees of freedom**.

The "degrees of freedom" is a numerical parameter of the t distribution that defines the precise shape of the distribution. Each time we encounter a t distribution, we will specify its degrees of freedom. In this particular sampling context, where we are basing inferences about μ on the sampling distribution of $\overline{X}$, the degrees of freedom turns out to be 1 less than the sample size n.

The t distribution looks very much like the standard normal distribution. It is bell shaped and is centered at 0. The only difference is that it is slightly more spread out, and this increase in spread is greater for *small* degrees of freedom. In fact, when n is large, so that the degrees of freedom is large, the t distribution and the standard normal distribution are practically indistinguishable. This is illustrated in Figure 8.1. With 5 degrees of freedom, it is possible to see the increased spread in the t distribution. With 30 degrees of freedom, the t and standard normal curves are practically the same curve.

In Chapter 5 we learned how to use Excel's NORMSDIST and NORMSINV functions to calculate probabilities or values from the standard normal distribution. There are similar Excel functions for the t distribution: TDIST and TINV. Unfortunately, these functions are somewhat trickier to master than their normal counterparts. To make the transition easier, it helps to know what these functions are usually used for. They are usually used to find (1) the probability beyond a certain value, either in one or both tails, or (2) the value that has a certain (usually small) probability beyond it, in either one or both tails.

FIGURE 8.1 **The t and Standard Normal Distributions**

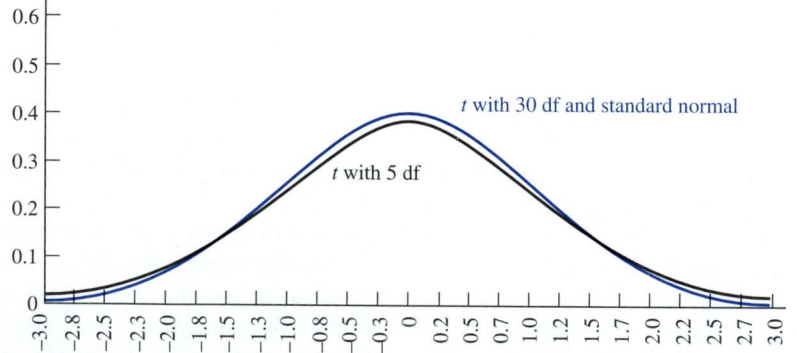

The sample calculations in Figure 8.2 illustrate these functions. (See the file TDIST.XLS.) For comparison, it also shows similar calculations based on the standard normal distribution. We first enter any degrees of freedom in cell B3. Then formulas involving the TDIST function appear in row 7. We see that the probability to the right of 1.5 for the *t* distribution with 30 degrees of freedom is 0.0720. By comparison, it is 0.0668 for the standard normal distribution. The formulas in cells B7 and C7 are

$$=TDIST(Value,df,1)$$

and

$$=1-NORMSDIST(Value)$$

FIGURE 8.2   **Excel Functions for the *t* Distribution**

	A	B	C	D
1	**Using the TDIST and TINV functions for the t distribution**			
2				
3	Degrees of freedom	30		
4				
5	Using TDIST to find probabilities to the right of given positive values			
6	Value	t probability	normal probability	
7	1.5	0.0720	0.0668	
8				
9	Using TINV to find values for given probabilities			
10	Probability	t value	normal value	
11	0.10	1.697	1.645	
12				
13		**Range names**		
14		df: B3		
15		Prob: A11		
16		Value: A7		
17				

Here are the technical details for using the TDIST function properly:

■ Its first argument must be nonnegative.

■ Unlike the NORMSDIST function, it returns the probability to the *right* of the first argument (if the third argument is 1). Note how we had to subtract the NORMSDIST function from 1 to obtain a comparable right-hand tail probability.

■ Its third argument is either 1 or 2 and indicates the number of tails. By using 1 for this argument, we get the probability in the right-hand tail only. If we use 2 for the third argument, we obtain the probability of greater than 1.5 or less than −1.5. Because of symmetry, the effect is to *double* the probability in cell B7.

Row 11 illustrates the inverse problem, where we want the value that "cuts off" a given probability in the tails. The value in cell B11 shows that there is a total probability of 0.10 to the right of 1.697 and to the left of −1.697 in the *t* distribution with 30 degrees of freedom. In other words, there is probability 0.05 in each tail. By contrast, the cutoff values for the standard normal distribution are 1.645 and −1.645. The formulas in cells B11 and C11 are

$$=TINV(Prob,df)$$

and

$$=NORMSINV(1-Prob/2)$$

The technical details for using the TINV function properly are as follows:

- The first argument is the total probability we want in both tails—half of this goes in the right-hand tail and half goes in the left-hand tail. By contrast, the NORMSINV is inherently a one-tailed function (the left-hand tail), which is why we had to base it on half the probability in cell A11.

- Unlike the TDIST function, there is no third argument for the TINV function.

We agree that these differences between the t distribution and normal distribution functions are more complex than they ought to be, but this is the way Microsoft decided to program them. Fortunately, the StatPro add-in simplifies the process for most statistical inference applications.

You might want to experiment with the degrees of freedom parameter in cell B3. You'll notice that if you decrease it, the differences between the t and normal outputs in columns B and C increase, whereas if you increase it to, say, 100, these differences practically disappear.

8.2.2 Other Sampling Distributions

We have seen that the t distribution, a close relative of the normal distribution, is used when we want to make inferences about a population mean and the population standard deviation is unknown. Throughout this chapter (and later chapters) we will see other contexts where the t distribution appears. The theme is always the same—one or more means are of interest, and one or more standard deviations are unknown.

The t (and normal) distributions are not the only sampling distributions we will encounter. Two other close relatives of the normal distribution that appear in various contexts are the **chi-square** and **F distributions**. These are used primarily to make inferences about variances (or standard deviations), as opposed to means. We omit the details of these distributions for now, but you can look forward to seeing them in the near future.

P R O B L E M S

Level A

1   Compute the following probabilities using Excel:

   a $P(t_{10} \geq 1.75)$, where t_{10} has a t distribution with 10 degrees of freedom.

   b $P(t_{100} \geq 1.75)$, where t_{100} has a t distribution with 100 degrees of freedom. How do you explain the difference between this result and the one obtained in part **a**?

   c $P(Z \geq 1.75)$, where Z is a standard normal random variable. Compare this result to the results obtained in parts **a** and **b**. How do you explain the differences in these probabilities?

   d $P(t_{20} \leq -0.80)$, where t_{20} has a t distribution with 20 degrees of freedom.

   e $P(t_3 \leq -0.80)$, where t_3 has a t distribution with 3 degrees of freedom. How do you explain the difference between this result and the result obtained in part **d**?

2   Determine the following quantities using Excel:

   a $P(-2.00 \leq t_{10} \leq 1.00)$, where t_{10} has a t distribution with 10 degrees of freedom.

   b $P(-2.00 \leq t_{100} \leq 1.00)$, where t_{100} has a t distribution with 100 degrees of freedom. How do you explain the difference between this result and the one obtained in part **a**?

   c $P(-2.00 \leq Z \leq 1.00)$, where Z is a standard normal random variable. Compare this result to the results obtained in parts **a** and **b**. How do you explain the differences in these probabilities?

d Find the 68th percentile of the t distribution with 20 degrees of freedom.

   e Find the 68th percentile of the t distribution with 3 degrees of freedom. How do you explain the difference between this result and the result obtained in part **d**?

3 Determine the following quantities using Excel:

   a Find the value of x such that $P(t_{10} > x) = 0.75$, where t_{10} has a t distribution with 10 degrees of freedom.

   b Find the value of y such that $P(t_{100} > y) = 0.75$, where t_{100} has a t distribution with 100 degrees of freedom. How do you explain the difference between this result and the result obtained in part **a**?

   c Find the value of z such that $P(Z > z) = 0.75$, where Z is a standard normal random variable. Compare this result to the results obtained in parts **a** and **b**. How do you explain the differences in the values of x, y, and z?

4 The NORMSDIST and NORMSINV functions in Excel give you probabilities and z-values, respectively, for the standard normal distribution. The analogous functions for the t distribution are TDIST and TINV. However, they do not work exactly the same as the normal functions. Try the following.

   a You have a t distribution with 15 df (degrees of freedom), and you want the probability to the right of the value 1.074. From t tables included in many statistics books, this probability is 0.15. Verify that you can get the answer in Excel with =TDIST(1.074,15,1), where the last "1" means one tail only.

   b This is the same as part **a**, but now you want the probability to the left of -1.074 or the right of 1.074, that is, the combined probability in both tails. Verify that you can get the answer in Excel with =TDIST(1.074,15,2), where the last "2" means two tails.

   c You have a t distribution with 15 df, and you want the t-value with probability 0.05 to the right of it. From t tables, this t-value is 1.753. Verify that you can get the answer in Excel with =TINV(.10,15). (The tricky part here is that the first argument, .10, is double the original probability you asked for. This is hard to remember!)

   d This is the same as part **c**, but now you want the t-value, call it t, such that probability 0.025 is to the right of t, and probability 0.025 is to the left of $-t$. The t tables show that t is 2.131. Verify that you can get the answer in Excel with =TINV(.05,15). (Here you can see the trick in part **c** better. You use the *combined* probability in both tails as the first argument in TINV.) ■

8.3

Confidence Interval for a Mean

W e now come to the focal point of this chapter: using results about sampling distributions to construct confidence intervals. As explained in the introduction to this chapter, we assume that data have been generated by some random mechanism, either by observing a random sample from some population or by performing a randomized experiment. We want to use these data to infer the values of one or more population parameters such as the mean or the standard deviation. For each such parameter we will use the data to calculate a point estimate, which can be considered a "best guess" for the unknown parameter. We will also calculate a confidence interval around the point estimate to gauge its accuracy. This is directly analogous to the way we went out two standard errors on either side of the point estimate to form intervals in the previous chapter. However, we'll expand on this procedure in this chapter.

We begin by deriving a confidence interval for a population mean μ, and we discuss its interpretation. Although the particular details pertain to a specific parameter, the mean, the same ideas carry over to estimation of other parameters as well, as we will see in later sections. As usual, we use $\overline{X}$, the sample mean, as the point estimate of μ.

To obtain a confidence interval for μ, we first specify a **confidence level**, usually 90%, 95%, or 99%. We then use the sampling distribution of the point estimate to determine the *multiple* of the standard error we need to go out on either side of the point estimate to achieve the given confidence level. If the confidence level is 95%, the value used most frequently in applications, then the multiple is approximately 2. More precisely, it is a t-value. That is, a typical confidence interval for μ is of the form

$$\overline{X} \pm t\text{-multiple} \times SE(\overline{X}) \tag{8.1}$$

where $SE(\overline{X}) = s/\sqrt{n}$.

To obtain the correct t-multiple, let α be 1 minus the confidence level (expressed as a decimal). For example, if the confidence level is 90%, then $\alpha = 0.10$. Then the appropriate t-multiple is the value that cuts off probability $\alpha/2$ in each tail of the t distribution with $n - 1$ degrees of freedom. For example, if $n = 31$ and the confidence level is 90%, we see from cell B11 of Figure 8.2 that the correct t-value is 1.697. The corresponding 90% confidence interval for μ is then

$$\overline{X} \pm 1.697(s/\sqrt{n})$$

If the confidence level is instead 95%, the appropriate t-value is 2.042 (to see this, change the probability in cell A11 to 0.05), and the resulting 95% confidence interval is

$$\overline{X} \pm 2.042(s/\sqrt{n})$$

If the confidence level is 99%, the appropriate t-value is 2.750 (to see this, change the probability in cell A11 to 0.01), and the resulting 99% confidence interval is

$$\overline{X} \pm 2.750(s/\sqrt{n})$$

Note that as the confidence level increases, the width of the confidence interval also increases. Since we naturally want confidence intervals to be as narrow as possible, this presents a trade-off. We can either have less confidence and a narrow interval, or we can have more confidence and a wide interval. However, we can also take a larger sample. As n increases, the standard error $s/\sqrt{n}$ decreases, and the length of the confidence interval tends to decrease for *any* confidence level. (Why won't it decrease for sure? The larger sample *might* result in a larger value of s that could offset the increase in n.)

The following example illustrates confidence interval estimation for a population mean. It uses the One-Sample procedure in the StatPro add-in to perform the calculations. However, by examining the resulting Excel formulas, you can check that all it is really doing is (1) calculating the sample mean, (2) calculating the standard error of the sample mean, $s/\sqrt{n}$, (3) finding the appropriate t-multiple with the TINV function, and (4) combining these to form the confidence interval via expression (8.1).

EXAMPLE 8.1

A fast-food restaurant recently added a new sandwich to its menu. To estimate the popularity of this sandwich, a random sample of 40 customers who ordered the sandwich were surveyed. Each of these customers was asked to rate the sandwich on a 1 to 10 scale, 10 being the best. The results of this survey appear in column B of Figure 8.3. (See the file SANDWICH1.XLS.) The manager wants to estimate the mean satisfaction rating over the entire population of customers by using a 95% confidence interval. How should she proceed?

FIGURE 8.3   Analysis of New Sandwich Data

	A	B	C	D	E	F	G	H
1	Customer satisfaction with new sandwich							
2								
3	Customer	Satisfaction			*Results for one-sample analysis*			
4	1	7						
5	2	5			*Confidence interval results for mean of Satisfaction*			
6	3	5			Confidence level	95.0%		
7	4	6			Sample mean	6.250		
8	5	8			Std error of mean	0.253		
9	6	7			Degrees of freedom	39		
10	7	6			Lower limit	5.739		
11	8	7			Upper limit	6.761		
12	9	10						
13	10	7			**Range names**			
14	11	9			ConfLev: F6			
15	12	5			df: F9			
16	13	5			SampMean: F7			
17	14	8			StErr: F8			
18	15	8			Satisfaction: B3:B43			
19	16	6						
20	17	7						
41	38	9						
42	39	5						
43	40	4						

Solution

We use StatPro's One-Sample procedure on the Satisfaction variable. Although this procedure is capable of doing more than we're asking here, it is the appropriate procedure when we want to estimate the mean from a single population. To use it, place the cursor anywhere in the data set (cell B4, say) and select the StatPro/Statistical Inference/One-Sample Analysis menu item. In the succeeding dialog boxes, select Satisfaction as the variable that you want to analyze and then accept the defaults from there on. You should obtain the output shown in Figure 8.3.

The principal results are that (1) the best guess for the population mean rating is 6.250, the sample average in cell F7, and (2) a 95% confidence interval for the population mean rating extends from 5.739 to 6.761, as seen in cells F10 and F11. The manager can be 95% confident that the true mean rating over all customers who might try the sandwich is within this confidence interval.

To make sure you understand where these numbers come from, take a look at the formulas in column F. Note that the standard error in cell F8 corresponds to $s/\sqrt{n}$. It is calculated with the formula

$$=\text{STDEV(Satisfaction)/SQRT(COUNT(Satisfaction))}$$

The degrees of freedom for the t distribution is 1 less than the sample size, as shown in cell F9. Finally, the t-multiple for the confidence interval, while not shown explicitly, is used in the formulas (via the TINV function) in cells F10 and F11. For example, the formula for the lower limit in cell F10 is[2]

$$=\text{SampMean-TINV(1-ConfLev,df)*StErr}$$

Before leaving this example, we discuss the assumptions that lead to the confidence interval. First, we might question whether the sample is really a *random* sample—or whether it matters. Perhaps the manager used some random mechanism to select the customers to be surveyed. More likely, however, she simply surveyed 40 consecutive customers who

---

[2]Although StatPro doesn't create the range names used in this (and succeeding) formulas, we've added them for clarity.

tried the sandwich on a given day. This is called a **convenience sample** and is not really a random sample. However, unless there is some reason to believe that these 40 customers differ in some relevant aspect from the entire population of customers, it is probably safe to treat them as a random sample.

A second assumption is that the population distribution is *normal*. We made this assumption when we discussed the t distribution. Obviously, the population distribution *cannot* be exactly normal because it is concentrated on the ten possible satisfaction ratings, and the normal distribution describes a continuum. However, this is probably not a problem for two reasons. First, confidence intervals based on the t distribution are **robust** to violations of normality. This means that the resulting confidence intervals are valid for any populations that are *approximately* normal. Second, the normal population assumption is less crucial for larger sample sizes because of the central limit theorem. For n as large as 40, the results should be valid. ■

In the sandwich example we said that the manager can be 95% confident that the true mean rating is between 5.739 and 6.761. What does this statement really mean? Contrary to what you might expect, it does *not* mean that the true mean lies between 5.739 and 6.761 with probability 0.95. Either the true mean is inside this interval or it is not. The true meaning of a 95% confidence interval is based on the *procedure* used to obtain it. Specifically, if we use this procedure on a large number of random samples, all from the same population, then approximately 95% of the resulting confidence intervals will be "good" ones that include the true mean, and the other 5% will be "bad" ones that do not include the true mean. Of course, when we have only a single sample, as in the sandwich example, we have no way of knowing whether our confidence interval is one of the good ones or one of the bad ones, but we can be 95% confident that we obtained one of the good intervals.

Because this is such an important concept, we illustrate it in Figure 8.4 with simulation. (See the file CONFINT.XLS.) The data in column B are generated randomly from a normal distribution with the *known* values of μ and σ in cells B3 and B4. Next, we invoke the One-Sample procedure to calculate a 95% confidence interval for the true value of μ, exactly as in the sandwich example. However, we now know whether the true value of μ is within the interval or not, so we record a 1 in cell F15 if it is and a 0 otherwise. This requires the formula

$$=IF(AND(B3>=F13,B3<=F14),1,0)$$

Finally, we use a data table to replicate the simulated results 1000 times.[3] Specifically, we enter the formula

$$=F15$$

in cell E22 and build a data table (only a few rows of which are shown) in the range D22:E1022, leaving the row input cell box empty and using any blank cell as the column input cell. Then we calculate the fraction of values in the range E23:E1022 that are 1's in cell E18 with the AVERAGE function.

We see that 949 of the simulated confidence intervals (each based on a *different* random sample of size 30) contain the true mean 100. In theory, we would expect 950 of the 1000 intervals to cover the true mean, and this is almost exactly what we obtained. Of course, in a particular application you might unluckily obtain the first sample (in row 23). However, without knowing that the true mean is 100, you would have no way of knowing that you obtained a "bad" interval!

---

[3] It takes quite awhile to simulate 1000 samples of size 30 in this data table. Therefore, it's definitely a good idea to use the Tools/Options menu item to set the recalculation mode to "automatic except tables." That way, the data table will recalculate only if you explicitly tell it to (by pressing the F9 key).

FIGURE 8.4 Simulation Demonstration of Confidence Intervals

	A	B	C	D	E	F	G	H	I	J
1	Interpretation of a "95% confidence interval"									
2										
3	Population mean	100								
4	Population stdev	20								
5										
6		Random sample			*Results for one-sample analysis*					
7		118.46								
8		148.93			*Confidence interval results for mean of Random_sample*					
9		91.94			Confidence level	95.0%				
10		106.03			Sample mean	102.914				
11		109.51			Std error of mean	4.037				
12		96.92			Degrees of freedom	29				
13		125.92			Lower limit	94.657				
14		121.79			Upper limit	111.170				
15		104.56			Mean captured?	1				
16		135.42								
17		93.18			**% of replications where mean is in confidence interval (from table below)**					
18		107.21			94.9%					
19		116.72								
20		139.11			**Data table used to replicate confidence intervals**					
21		78.84			Rep	Mean captured?				
22		86.64				1				
23		63.00			1	0				
24		71.84			2	1				
25		103.86			3	1				
26		105.27			4	1				
27		78.45			5	1				
28		120.67			6	1				
29		123.62			7	1				
30		118.21			8	1				
31		94.85			9	1				
32		96.57			10	1				
33		112.49			11	1				
34		67.22			12	1				
35		70.31			13	1				
36		79.86			14	1				

PROBLEMS

Level A

5 A manufacturing company's quality control personnel have recorded the proportion of defective items for each of 500 monthly shipments of one of the computer components that the company produces. The data are in the file P2_2.XLS. The quality control department manager does not have sufficient time to review all of these data. Rather, she would like to examine the proportions of defective items for a sample of these shipments.

   a Use Excel to generate a simple random sample of size 25 from the given frame.

   b Using the sample generated in part **a**, construct a 95% confidence interval for the mean proportion of defective items over all monthly shipments. Assume that the population consists of the proportion of defective items for each of the given 500 monthly shipments.

   c Interpret the 95% confidence interval constructed in part **b**.

   d Does the 95% confidence interval contain the actual population mean in this case? If not, explain why not. What proportion of many similarly constructed confidence intervals should include the true population mean value?

6 Consider the given set of average annual household income levels of citizens of selected U.S. metropolitan areas in the file P3_6.XLS.

   a Use Excel to obtain a simple random sample of size 15 from this frame.

   b Using the sample generated in part **a**, construct a 99% confidence interval for the mean average annual household income level of citizens in the selected U.S. metropolitan areas.

Assume that the population consists of all average annual household income levels in the given frame.

c Interpret the 99% confidence interval constructed in part **b**.

d Does the 99% confidence interval contain the actual population mean? If not, explain why not. What proportion of many similarly constructed confidence intervals should include the true population mean value?

7 The file P8_7.XLS contains data on all NFL players as of 1990. Because this file contains all players, you can calculate the *population* mean if we define "population" as all 1990 NFL salaries. However, proceed as in Chapter 7 to select a random sample of size 50 from this population. Based on this random sample, calculate a 95% confidence interval for the mean NFL salary in 1990. Does it contain the population mean? Repeat this procedure several times until you find a random sample where the population mean is *not* included in the confidence interval.

8 The file P8_8.XLS contains data on repetitive task times for each of two workers. John has been doing this task for months, whereas Fred has just started. Each time listed is the time (in seconds) to perform a routine task on an assembly line. The times shown are in chronological order.

a Find a 95% confidence interval for the mean time it takes John to perform the task. Do the same for Fred.

b Do you believe both of the confidence intervals in part **a** are valid and/or useful? Why or why not? Which of the two workers would you rather have (assuming time is the only issue)?

9 The manager of a local fast-food restaurant is interested in improving the service provided to customers who use the restaurant's drive-up window. As a first step in this process, the manager asks his assistant to record the time (in minutes) it takes to serve a large number of customers at the final window in the facility's drive-up system. The given frame of 200 customer service times are all observed during the busiest hour of the day for this fast-food operation. The data are in the file P2_4.XLS.

a Use Excel to generate a simple random sample of size 10 from this frame.

b Using the sample generated in part **a**, construct a 90% confidence interval for the mean service time of all customers arriving during the busiest hour of the day at this fast-food operation. Assume that the population consists of the given 200 customer service times.

c Interpret the 90% confidence interval constructed in part **b**.

Level B

10 Continuing the previous problem, use Excel to generate 100 simple random samples of size 10 from the frame given in P2_4.XLS. Then use each of these random samples to construct a 90% confidence interval for the mean service time of all customers arriving during the busiest hour of the day at this fast-food operation. How many of the 100 constructed confidence intervals actually contain the true value of the population mean in this case? Is this result consistent with your expectations? Explain. ■

Confidence Interval for a Total

T here are situations where a population mean is not the population parameter of most interest. A good example is the auditing example discussed in the previous chapter (Example 7.4). Rather than estimating the mean amount of receivables *per account*, the auditor might be more interested in the *total* amount of all receivables, summed over all accounts. In this section we will provide a point estimate and a confidence interval for a population total.

First, we introduce some notation. Let T be a population total we want to estimate, such as the total of all receivables, and let $\widehat{T}$ be a point estimate of T based on a simple random sample of size n from a population of size N. We need reasonable formulas for $\widehat{T}$; that is, we need to know how to calculate a point estimate of T. For the population total T, it is reasonable to sum all of the values in the sample, denoted T_S, and then "project" this total to the population with the formula

$$\widehat{T} = \frac{N}{n}T_S = N\overline{X} \tag{8.2}$$

where the second equality follows because the sample total T_S divided by the sample size n is the sample mean $\overline{X}$.

Actually, equation (8.2) is quite intuitive. Suppose there are 1000 accounts in the population, we sample 50 of them, and we observe a sample total of $5000. Then, because we sampled only 1/20 of the population, a natural estimate of the population total is $20 \times \$5000 = \$100,000$.

Like the sample mean $\overline{X}$, the estimate $\widehat{T}$ has a sampling distribution. The mean and standard deviation of this sampling distribution are

$$E(\widehat{T}) = T \tag{8.3}$$

and

$$SE(\widehat{T}) = N\sigma/\sqrt{n} \tag{8.4}$$

where σ is again the population standard deviation. If σ is unknown, we use s instead of σ to obtain the approximate standard error of $\widehat{T}$:

$$SE(\widehat{T}) = Ns/\sqrt{n} = N \times SE(\overline{X}) \tag{8.5}$$

The second equality follows because $s/\sqrt{n}$ is the standard error of $\overline{X}$.

Note from equation (8.3) that $\widehat{T}$ is an unbiased estimate of the population total T. Therefore, it shows no tendency to either overestimate or underestimate T.

From equations (8.2) and (8.5), we see that the point estimate of T is the point estimate of the mean multiplied by N, and that the standard error of this point estimate is the standard error of the sample mean multiplied by N. This has a very nice consequence. We can form a confidence interval for T simply by forming a confidence interval for the mean and then "scaling" it by a factor of N. We illustrate this in the following example.

EXAMPLE 8.2

Suppose the Internal Revenue Service would like to estimate the total net amount of refund due to a particular set of 10,000 taxpayers. Each taxpayer will either receive a refund, in which case the net refund is positive, or will have to pay an amount due, in which case the net refund is negative. Therefore the *total* net amount of refund is a natural quantity of interest; it is the total amount the IRS will have to pay out (or receive, if negative). Find a 95% confidence interval for this total using the refunds from a random sample of 500 taxpayers in the file IRS.XLS.

Solution

The solution appears in Figure 8.5 (page 386). Although there is no explicit StatPro procedure for dealing with population totals, we can take advantage of the close relationship between the confidence interval for a mean and the confidence interval for a total. That is, we first use StatPro to find a 95% confidence interval for the population mean. This output appears in rows 5–18. The average refund per taxpayer in the sample is slightly less than $300 (cell F14), and the standard error of this sample mean (in cell F15) is about $26. The

FIGURE 8.5 Confidence Interval for a Population Total

	A	B	C	D	E	F	G
1	IRS tax refunds & payments						
2					Range names:		
3	Population size	10000			PopSize: B3		
4							
5	Customer	Refund			Results for one-sample analysis for Refund		
6	1	$70					
7	2	$1,190			Summary measures		
8	3	$220			Sample size		500
9	4	($280)			Sample mean		294.980
10	5	$260			Sample standard deviation		581.312
11	6	$370					
12	7	$450			Confidence interval for mean		
13	8	$210			Confidence level		95.0%
14	9	$1,150			Sample mean		294.980
15	10	$270			Std error of mean		25.997
16	11	$470			Degrees of freedom		499
17	12	($10)			Lower limit		243.903
18	13	($160)			Upper limit		346.057
19	14	$2,430					
20	15	$140			Confidence interval for the population total		
21	16	($190)			Confidence level		95%
22	17	($810)			Point estimate		$2,949,800
23	18	($20)			Standard error		$259,970
24	19	$300			Lower limit		$2,439,029
25	20	($280)			Upper limit		$3,460,571
26	21	($300)					
502	497	$790					
503	498	$190					
504	499	$1,840					
505	500	($20)					

confidence interval for the mean (in cells F17 and F18) extends from $244 to $346. This part of the output analyzes the average refund for a single taxpayer.

Now all we need to do is project these results to the entire population. We do this in the range F22:F25 by multiplying each of the values in the previous paragraph by PopSize, the population size. The IRS can be 95% confident that it will need to pay out somewhere between 2.44 and 3.46 million dollars to these 10,000 taxpayers. ■

PROBLEMS

Level A

11 The operations manager of a toll booth located at a major exit of a state turnpike is trying to estimate the total number of vehicles that arrive at the toll booth during a 1-minute period during the peak of rush-hour traffic. In an effort to estimate this total throughput value, he records the number of vehicles that arrive at the toll booth over a 1-minute interval commencing at the same time for each of 50 normal weekdays. The data are provided in the file P8_11.XLS. Construct a 95% confidence interval for the total number of vehicles that arrive at the toll booth during a 1-minute period during the peak of rush-hour traffic for 1000 normal weekdays. What does this interval reveal about the actual throughput value of interest?

12 A lightbulb manufacturer wants to estimate the total number of defective bulbs contained in all of the boxes shipped by the company during the past week. Production personnel at this company have recorded the number of defective bulbs found in each of 50 randomly selected boxes shipped during the past week. These data are provided in the file P8_12.XLS. Construct a 99% confidence interval for the total number of defective bulbs contained in the

1000 boxes shipped by this company during the past week. Interpret this confidence interval for the production personnel at this company.

13 Auditors of a particular bank are interested in comparing the reported value of all 2265 customer savings account balances with their own findings regarding the actual value of such assets. Rather than reviewing the records of each savings account at the bank, the auditors decide to examine a representative sample of savings account balances. The frame from which they will sample is given in the file P7_50.XLS.

    a Select a simple random sample consisting of 100 savings account balances from the given frame.

    b Using the sample generated in part **a**, construct a 90% confidence interval for the total value of all savings account balances within this bank. Assume that the population consists of all savings account balances in the given frame.

    c Interpret the 90% confidence interval constructed in part **b**.

Level B

14 Continuing the previous problem, use Excel to generate 50 simple random samples of size 100 from the frame given in P7_50.XLS. Then use each of these random samples to construct a 90% confidence interval for the total value of all 2265 savings account balances within this bank. How many of the 50 constructed confidence intervals actually contain the true total value in this case? Is this result consistent with your expectations? Explain. ■

Confidence Interval for a Proportion

How often have you heard on the evening news a survey finding such as, "52% of the public agree with the President's handling of the economy, with a sampling error of plus or minus 3%"? Surveys are often used to estimate proportions, such as the proportion of the public that agree with the President's handling of the economy. We touched on this topic in the previous chapter, and we will expand on it here. In particular, we will see how to form a confidence interval for any population proportion p.

The basic procedure is very similar to what we described for a population mean. We find a point estimate, the standard error of this point estimate, and a multiple that depends on the confidence level. Then the confidence level has the form

$$\text{point estimate} \pm \text{multiple} \times \text{standard error}$$

In the news illustration the point estimate is 52% and the "multiple×standard error" is 3%. Therefore, the confidence interval extends from 49% to 55%. Although the news show doesn't state the confidence level explicitly, it is 95% by convention. In words, we can be 95% confident that the percentage of the public who agree with the President's handling of the economy is somewhere between 49% and 55%.

The theory that leads to this result is fairly straightforward. Let A be any property that members of a population either have or do not have. As examples, A might be the property that

- a person agrees with the President's handling of the economy;
- a person has purchased a company's product at least once within the past 3 months;
- the diameter of a part is with specification limits;
- a customer's account is at least 2 months overdue.

In each of these examples, we are interested in the proportion p of the population that have property A. We sample n members randomly and let $\widehat{p}$ be the sample proportion of members with property A. For example, if 10 out of 50 sampled members have property A, then $\widehat{p} = 10/50 = 0.2$. Then we use $\widehat{p}$ as a point estimate of p.

It can be shown that for sufficiently large n, the sampling distribution of $\widehat{p}$ is approximately normal with mean p and standard deviation $\sqrt{p(1-p)/n}$. Because p is the unknown parameter, we substitute $\widehat{p}$ for p in this standard deviation to obtain the following approximate standard error of $\widehat{p}$:

$$\text{SE}(\widehat{p}) = \sqrt{\frac{\widehat{p}(1-\widehat{p})}{n}}$$

Finally, the multiple we use to obtain a confidence interval for p is a z-value. It is the standard normal value that cuts off an appropriate probability in each tail. For example, the z-multiple for a 95% confidence interval is 1.96 because this value cuts off probability 0.025 in each tail of the standard normal distribution. In general, the confidence interval has the form

$$\widehat{p} \pm z\text{-multiple} \times \sqrt{\frac{\widehat{p}(1-\widehat{p})}{n}} \qquad \textbf{(8.6)}$$

This confidence interval is based on the assumption of a large sample size. A rule of thumb for checking the validity of this assumption is the following. Let p_L and p_U be the lower and upper limits of the confidence interval. Then the sample size is sufficiently large—and the confidence interval is valid—if $np_L > 5$, $n(1 - p_L) > 5$, $np_U > 5$, and $n(1 - p_U) > 5$.

We illustrate the procedure in the following example.

E X A M P L E   8 . 3

The fast-food manager from Example 8.1 has already sampled 40 customers to estimate the population mean rating of its new sandwich. Recall that each rating is on a 1 to 10 scale, 10 being the best. The manager would now like to use the same sample to estimate the proportion of customers who rate the sandwich at least 6. Her thinking is that these are the customers who are likely to purchase the sandwich on subsequent visits.

Solution

The solution appears in Figure 8.6. (See the file SANDWICH2.XLS.) To create this output, we first had to create the High_Rating variable in column C. (The original file includes only the data in columns A and B.) This High_Rating variable is 1 for all ratings 6 or larger and is 0 otherwise. We can create this variable with an IF function, or we can use the StatPro add-in. To use the latter, select the StatPro/Data Utilities/Create Dummy Variables menu item, which allows us to create a dummy (0–1) variable from the Satisfaction variable. Then check the "One dummy based on a numerical variable" option, select the Satisfaction variable, and finally specify "greater than or equal to" the cutoff value 6. A variable with default name Satisfaction_GE_P6 is created in column C. We changed this name to High_Rating.

The confidence interval is formed in rows 14–18. These use formula (8.6). Specifically, the formulas StatPro enters in cells G14–G18 are

=AVERAGE(High_Rating)

=SQRT(SampProp*(1-SampProp)/COUNT(High_Rating))

=NORMSINV(ConfLev+(1-ConfLev)/2)

=SampProp-zMult*StErr

and

$$=\text{SampProp}+\text{zMult}*\text{StErr}$$

Then using the confidence interval limits, $p_L = 0.475$ and $p_U = 0.775$, we can check the assumption of large sample size. With $n = 40$, you can check that np_L, $n(1 - p_L)$, np_U, and $n(1 - p_U)$ are all well above 5, so that the validity of this confidence interval is established.

FIGURE 8.6   **Analysis of a Proportion for New Sandwich Data**

	A	B	C	D	E	F	G	H	I	J
1	**Customer satisfaction with new sandwich**									
2										
3	Customer	Satisfaction	High Rating		*Results for one-sample analysis*					
4	1	7	1							
5	2	5	0		*Confidence interval results for mean of High_Rating*					
6	3	5	0			Confidence level	95.0%			
7	4	6	1			Sample mean	0.625			
8	5	8	1			Std error of mean	0.078			
9	6	7	1			Degrees of freedom	39			
10	7	6	1			Lower limit	0.468			
11	8	7	1			Upper limit	0.782			
12	9	10	1							
13	10	7	1		**Normal analysis (done manually)**					
14	11	9	1			Sample proportion	0.625			
15	12	5	0			Standard error	0.077			
16	13	5	0			z-mulitple	1.960			
17	14	8	1			Lower limit	0.475			
18	15	8	1			Upper limit	0.775			
19	16	6	1							
20	17	7	1		**Range names**					
21	18	8	1		ConfLev: G6					
22	19	7	1		High_Rating: C3:C43					
23	20	5	0		SampProp: G14					
24	21	5	0		StErr: G15					
25	22	5	0		zMult: G16					
26	23	5	0							
27	24	5	0							
42	39	5	0							
43	40	4	0							

For comparison, we also used the StatPro One-Sample procedure on the variable High_Rating. This output appears in rows 6–11. It is appropriate for a mean, but when a variable consists of 0's and 1's, a mean is really just the proportion of 1's. The confidence interval from this procedure is close to the one in rows 17 and 18, but it differs slightly. The difference is due mainly to using a t-multiple in rows 10 and 11 and a z-multiple in rows 17 and 18. This difference is negligible for larger sample sizes, which means that you can safely use the One-Sample procedure to obtain a confidence interval for a proportion when n is reasonably large.

The output is fairly good news for the manager. Based on this sample of size 40, she can be 95% confident that the percentage of all customers who would rate the sandwich 6 or higher is somewhere between 47.5% and 77.5%. Of course, she realizes that this is a very wide interval, so there is still a lot of uncertainty about the true population proportion. To reduce the length of this interval, she would need to sample more customers—quite a few more customers. Typically, confidence intervals for proportions are fairly wide unless n is quite large. ■

We explore this final statement a bit more. Referring again to news shows, you've probably noticed that they almost always quote a sampling error of plus or minus 3%. In words, the "plus or minus" part of their 95% confidence interval is 3%, or 0.03. How large a sample size must they use to achieve this? We know that the "plus or minus" part of the confidence interval is 1.96 times the standard error of $\widehat{p}$, so we must have

$$1.96 \times \sqrt{\widehat{p}(1 - \widehat{p})/n} = 0.03$$

Now, the quantity $\widehat{p}(1 - \widehat{p})$ is fairly constant for values of $\widehat{p}$ between 0 and 1, provided that $\widehat{p}$ isn't too close to 0 or 1. To get a reasonable estimate of the required n, we assume $\widehat{p} = 0.5$. Then we have

$$1.96 \times \sqrt{(0.5)(0.5)/n} = 0.03$$

Solving for n, we obtain $n = [(1.96)(0.5)/0.03]^2 \simeq 1067$.

This is a rather remarkable result. To obtain a 95% confidence interval of this length for a population proportion, where the population consists of millions of people, only about 1000 people need to be sampled. The remarkable fact is that this small a sample can provide such accurate information about such a large population.

One of many business applications of confidence intervals for proportions is in auditing. Auditors typically use **attribute sampling** to check whether certain procedures are being followed correctly. The term "attribute" implies that each item checked is done either correctly or incorrectly—there is no "in between." Examples of items not done correctly might include (1) an invoice copy that is not initialed by an accounting clerk, (2) an invoice quantity that does not agree with the quantity on the shipping document, (3) an invoice price that does not agree with the price on an authorized price list, and (4) an invoice with a clerical inaccuracy. Typically, an auditor focuses on one of these types of errors and then estimates the proportion of items with this type of error.

Because auditors are concerned primarily with how *large* the proportion of errors might be, they usually calculate 95% **one-sided** confidence intervals for proportions. Instead of using sample data to find lower and upper limits p_L and p_U of a confidence interval, they automatically use $p_L = 0$ and then determine an upper limit p_U such that the 95% confidence interval is from 0 to p_U. A simple modification of the confidence interval in formula (8.6) provides the result:

$$p_U = \widehat{p} + z\text{-multiple} \times \sqrt{\widehat{p}(1 - \widehat{p})/n} \tag{8.7}$$

where the z-multiple is chosen so that the entire probability (0.05 for a 95% interval) is in the right-hand tail. So for a 95% confidence level, the relevant z-multiple is 1.645.

One further complication occurs, however. This formula for p_U relies on the large-sample approximation of the normal distribution to the binomial distribution. Auditors typically use an *exact* procedure to find p_U that is based directly on the binomial distribution. We illustrate how this is done in the following example.

E X A M P L E   8 . 4

An auditor wants to check the proportion of invoices that contain price errors—that is, prices that do not agree with those on an authorized price list. He checks 93 randomly sampled invoices and finds that two of them include price errors. What can he conclude, in terms of a 95% one-sided confidence interval, about the proportion of all invoices with price errors?

Solution

The results appear in Figure 8.7. (See the file AUDIT.XLS.) The sample proportion is $\widehat{p} = 2/93 = 0.0215$ and the upper confidence limit based on the large-sample approximation is 0.046. This latter value is calculated in cell B13 with the formula

=SampProp+NORMSINV(ConfLev)*SQRT(SampProp*(1-SampProp)/SampSize)

However, the fact that $np_U = 93(0.046) = 4.278$ is less than 5 indicates that the large-sample approximation might not be very accurate.

FIGURE 8.7 **Analysis of Auditing Example**

	A	B	C	D	E	F
1	Auditing example for an exact one-sided confidence interval					
2				Range names		
3	Confidence level	95%		ConfLev: B3		
4	Number of errors	2		NErrors: B4		
5	Sample size	93		SampProp: B7		
6				SampSize: B5		
7	Sample proportion	0.0215		UpLimit: B10		
8						
9	Exact upper confidence limit for p			Goal seek condition		
10	Upper	0.066		0.050	=	0.05
11						
12	Large-sample upper confidence limit for p					
13	Upper	0.046				

A more accurate procedure, based on the binomial distribution, appears in row 10. It turns out that if p_U is the appropriate upper confidence limit, then p_U satisfies the equation

$$P(X \leq k) = \alpha \tag{8.8}$$

Here, X is binomially distributed with parameters n and p_U, k is the observed number of errors, and α is 1 minus the confidence level. There is no way to find p_U directly (by means of a formula) from equation (8.8). However, we can use Excel's Goal Seek tool. First, we enter *any* trial value of p_U in cell B10 and the binomial formula

=BINOMDIST(NErrors,SampSize,UpLimit,1)

in cell D10. (This formula calculates $P(X \leq k)$ from the trial value in cell B10.) Then we use the Tools/Goal Seek menu item, with cell B10 as the Set cell, 0.05 as the target value, and cell B10 as the Changing cell.

The resulting value of p_U is 0.066. This is considerably different (from the auditor's point of view) from the 0.046 value found from the large-sample approximation. It allows the auditor to state with 95% confidence that the percentage of invoices with price errors is no greater than 6.6%. ∎

PROBLEMS

Level A

15 Wal-Mart buyers seek to purchase adequate supplies of various brands of toothpaste to meet the ongoing demands of its customers. In particular, Wal-Mart is interested in estimating the proportion of its customers who favor the country's leading brand of toothpaste, Crest. The file P8_15.XLS contains the toothpaste brand preferences of 200 Wal-Mart customers, obtained recently through the administration of a customer survey. Construct a 95% confidence interval for the proportion of all Wal-Mart customers who prefer Crest toothpaste. Interpret this confidence interval for the buyers at Wal-Mart.

16 The employee benefits manager of a small private university would like to estimate the proportion of full-time employees who prefer adopting the first (i.e., plan A) of three available health care plans in the coming annual enrollment period. A reliable frame of the university's employees and their tentative health care preferences are given in the file P7_25.XLS.

   a Use Excel to choose a simple random sample of size 45 from the given frame.

   b Using the sample found in part **a**, construct a 99% confidence interval for the proportion of university employees who prefer plan A. Assume that the population consists of the preferences of all employees in the given frame.

   c Interpret the 99% confidence interval constructed in part **b**.

17 A market research consultant hired by the Pepsi-Cola Co. is interested in determining the proportion of consumers who favor Pepsi-Cola over Coke Classic in a particular urban location. A random sample of 250 consumers from the market under investigation is provided in P8_17.XLS. Construct a 90% confidence interval for the proportion of all consumers in this market who prefer Pepsi. Interpret this confidence interval for Pepsi-Cola's market researchers.

Level B

18 Continuing Problem 16, select simple random samples of 30 individuals from *each* of the given employee classifications (i.e., administrative staff, support staff, and faculty). Construct a 99% confidence interval for the proportion of employees who prefer adopting plan A for each of the three classifications. Do you see evidence of significant differences among these three interval estimates? Summarize your findings.

19 Continuing Problem 17, separate the given random sample of consumers (provided in the file P8_17.XLS) into two gender subgroups: *males* and *females*. Construct 90% confidence intervals for the proportion of male consumers who prefer Pepsi and the proportion of female consumers who prefer Pepsi. Do you see evidence of a significant difference between the preferences of males and females in this case? Repeat this same process with the *age* attribute of the given consumers. In other words, separate the given sample of consumers by age (i.e., *under 20, between 20 and 40, between 40 and 60,* and *over 60*). Construct a 90% confidence interval for the proportion of consumers in each age category favoring Pepsi. Summarize your findings. ■

8.6   Confidence Interval for a Standard Deviation

In Section 8.3 we focused primarily on estimation of a population *mean*. Our concern with the population standard deviation σ was in its role as a nuisance parameter. That is, we needed an estimate of σ to estimate the standard error of the sample mean. However, there are cases where the variability in the population, measured by σ, is of interest in its own right. We briefly describe a procedure for obtaining a confidence interval for σ in this section.

The theory is somewhat more complex than for the case of the mean. As you might expect, we use the sample standard deviation s as a point estimate of σ. However, the sampling distribution of s is not symmetric—in particular, it is not the normal distribution or the t distribution. Rather, the appropriate sampling distribution is a right-skewed distribution called the **chi-square** distribution. Like the t distribution, the chi-square distribution has a degrees of freedom parameter, which (for this procedure) is again $n - 1$.

Tables of the chi-square distribution, for selected degrees of freedom, appear in many statistics books, but the necessary information can be obtained more easily with Excel's CHIDIST and CHIINV functions. The CHIDIST function takes the form

$$=CHIDIST(v, df)$$

This function returns the probability to the right of value v when the degrees of freedom parameter is df. Similarly, the CHIINV function takes the form

$$=CHIINV(p, df)$$

It returns the value with probability p to the right of it when the degrees of freedom parameter is df.

We will not present the rather complex confidence interval formulas for σ. However, we point out that because of the skewness of the sampling distribution of s, a confidence interval for σ is not centered at s. That is, the confidence interval is *not* the point estimate plus or minus a multiple of a standard error. Instead, s is always closer to the left endpoint of the confidence interval than to the right endpoint, as indicated in Figure 8.8.

FIGURE 8.8 **Confidence Interval for a Standard Deviation**

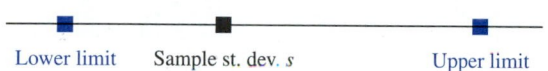

Lower limit   Sample st. dev. s Upper limit

The StatPro One-Sample procedure enables us to obtain a confidence interval for a population standard deviation as easily as for a mean. We illustrate this in the following example.

E X A M P L E   8 . 5

A machine produces parts that are supposed to have diameter 10 centimeters. However, due to inherent variability, some diameters are greater than 10 and some are less. The production supervisor is concerned about two things. First, he is concerned that the mean diameter might not be 10 centimeters. Second, he is worried about the extent of variability in the diameters. Even if the mean is on target, excessive variability implies that many of the parts will fail to meet specifications. To analyze the process, he randomly samples 50 parts during the course of a day and measures the diameter of each part to the nearest millimeter. The results are shown in columns A and B of Figure 8.9 on page 394. (See the file PARTS.XLS.) Should he be concerned about the results from this sample?

Solution

Because the manager is concerned about the mean *and* the standard deviation of diameters, we obtain 95% confidence intervals for both. This is easy to do with StatPro's One-Sample procedure. We go through the same dialog boxes as before, except that we now check the boxes for both confidence interval options—mean and standard deviation. The top part of the output in Figure 8.9 provides a 95% confidence interval for the mean. This confidence interval extends from 9.986 cm to 10.005 cm. Therefore, there is probably not too much cause for concern about the mean. The supervisor can be fairly confident that the mean diameter of all parts is close to 10 cm.

FIGURE 8.9 Analysis of Parts Data

	A	B	C	D	E	F	G	H	I	J
1	Measuring diameters of parts from a production process									
2										
3	Note: Each diameter is measured in cm									
4										
5	Part	Diameter			Results for one-sample analysis					
6	1	10.031								
7	2	10.011			Confidence interval results for mean of Diameter					
8	3	10.003			Confidence level	95.0%				
9	4	10.025			Sample mean	9.996				
10	5	10.048			Std error of mean	0.005				
11	6	10.014			Degrees of freedom	49				
12	7	10.030			Lower limit	9.986				
13	8	10.008			Upper limit	10.005				
14	9	10.049								
15	10	9.995			Confidence interval results for standard deviation of Diameter					
16	11	9.965			Confidence level	95.0%				
17	12	10.003			Sample standard deviation	0.034				
18	13	9.959			Degrees of freedom	49				
19	14	10.013			Lower limit	0.029				
20	15	10.012			Upper limit	0.043				
21	16	10.005								
22	17	9.921			Proportion of unusable parts					
23	18	9.930			Deviation for unusability	0.065		Range names		
24	19	9.990			Assumed mean	10		MaxDev: F23		
25	20	9.948			Assumed standard deviation	0.043		Mean: F24		
26	21	10.077			Proportion unusable	0.131		StDev: F25		
27	22	9.959								
28	23	10.000			Two-way data table for finding propotion unusable as a function of mean and stdev					
29	24	9.998					Assumed standard deviation			
30	25	9.983				0.131	0.029	0.034	0.043	
31	26	9.995			Assumed mean	9.986	0.041	0.080	0.149	
32	27	9.917				9.996	0.025	0.060	0.130	
33	28	9.934				10.005	0.026	0.061	0.131	
34	29	10.044								
35	30	10.023								
54	49	9.973								
55	50	9.970								

The bottom part of the output provides a 95% confidence interval for the standard deviation of diameters. This interval extends from 0.029 cm to 0.043 cm.[4] Is this good news or bad news? It depends. Let's say that a part is unusable if its diameter is more than 0.065 cm from the target. Let's also assume the true mean is right on target and that the standard deviation is at the *upper* end of the confidence interval, that is, $\sigma = 0.043$ cm. Finally, we assume that the population distribution of diameters is normal. Then the calculation in cell F26 shows that 13.1% of the parts will be unusable! The formula in cell F26 is

$$= \text{NORMDIST}(10\text{-MaxDev,Mean,StDev,1})$$

$$+(1\text{-NORMDIST}(10\text{+MaxDev,Mean,StDev,1}))$$

It adds the normal probabilities of being below or above the usable range.

To pursue this analysis one step further, we form a two-way data table in the range F30:I33. The assumed means we use in column F are the lower confidence limit, the sample mean, and the upper confidence limit. Similarly, the assumed standard deviations in row 30 are the lower confidence limit, the sample standard deviation, and the upper confidence limit. To form the table, enter the formula =F26 in cell F30, highlight the range F30:I33, use the Data/Table menu item, and enter F25 and F24 as the row and column input cells.

---

[4]You can check the spreadsheet formulas for the confidence interval limits to see how they use the CHIINV function.

Each value in the body of the data table is the resulting proportion of unusable parts. Obviously, a mean close to the target and a small standard deviation are best, but even this best-case scenario results in 2.5% unusable parts (see cell G32). However, a mean off target and a large standard deviation can lead to as many as 14.9% unusable parts (see cell I31). In any case, the message for the supervisor should be clear—he must work to reduce the underlying variability in the process. This variability is hurting him much more than an off-target mean. ■

PROBLEMS

Level A

20 Consider a frame consisting of 500 households in a middle-class neighborhood that was the recent focus of an economic development study conducted by the local government. Specifically, for each of the 500 households, information was gathered on the total indebtedness (excluding the value of a home mortgage) of the household and each of several other variables. The data are in the file P2_6.XLS.

   a Use Excel to choose a simple random sample of size 25 from this frame.

   b Using the sample generated in part **a**, construct a 95% confidence interval for the standard deviation of the total indebtedness of all households in the given neighborhood.

   c Interpret the 95% confidence interval constructed in part **b**.

   d Does the 90% confidence interval contain the actual value of the population standard deviation in this case? If not, explain why not. What proportion of many similarly constructed confidence intervals should include the true population standard deviation?

21 Senior management of a certain consulting services firm is concerned about a growing decline in the organization's weekly number of billable hours. Ideally, the organization expects each professional employee to spend *at least* 40 hours per week on work. In an effort to understand this problem better, management would like to estimate the standard deviation of the number of hours their employees spend on work-related activities in a typical week. The frame of virtually all of the firm's full-time employees, including the employees' self-reported amounts of time typically devoted to work activities each week, is provided in the file P7_48.XLS.

   a Select a simple random sample of size 100 from the given frame.

   b Using the sample generated in part **a**, construct a 99% confidence interval for the standard deviation of the number of hours this organization's employees spend on work-related activities in a typical week.

   c Given the target range of 40–60 hours of work per week, should senior management be concerned about the number of hours their employees are currently devoting to work? Explain why or why not.

Level B

22 A manufacturing company's quality control personnel have recorded the proportion of defective items for each of 500 randomly selected shipments of one of the computer components that the company produces. The data are in the file P8_22.XLS. The quality control department manager would like to use this random sample to estimate the mean and standard deviation of the proportion of defective items in the company's shipments. She is concerned that some shipments of this computer component contain an unacceptably high proportion of defective items. In particular, her company cannot tolerate a defective rate higher than 5% for any of its shipments.

   a Use the given random sample to construct 95% confidence intervals for the mean and standard deviation of the proportion of defective items in the company's shipments. Interpret each of these interval estimates.

   b Assuming the proportion of defective computer components in a given shipment is *normally* distributed, what is the probability that a randomly selected shipment will be unacceptable? Based on information derived from the confidence intervals constructed in part **a**, compute this probability for various combinations of the mean and standard deviation. You might want to generate a two-way data table to compute this probability for various combinations of the mean and standard deviation of the defective rate in the company's shipments. ■

Confidence Interval for the Difference Between Means

One of the most important applications of statistical inference is the comparison of two population means. There are many applications to business, including the following:

■ Men and women shop at a retail clothing store. The manager would like to know how much more (or less), on average, a woman spends on a typical purchase occasion than a man.

■ Two airline companies fly similar routes. A consumer organization would like to check how much the average delay differs between the two airlines, where delay is defined as the actual arrival time at the destination minus the scheduled arrival time.

■ A supermarket chain mails coupons for various products to its customers in one city. Its customers in another city receive no such coupons. The chain would like to check how much the average amount spent on these products differs between the two sets of customers over the next couple of months.

■ A computer company has a customer service center that responds to customers' questions and complaints. The center employs two types of people: those who have had a recent course in dealing with customers (but little actual experience) and those with a lot of experience dealing with customers (but no formal course). The company would like to know how these two types of employees differ with respect to the average number of customer complaints of poor service in the last 6 months.

■ A consulting company hires business students directly out of undergraduate school. The new hires all take a problem-solving test. They then go through an intensive 3-month training program, after which they take another similar problem-solving test. The company wants to know how much the average test score improves after the training program.

■ A car dealership often deals with husband–wife pairs shopping for cars. To check whether husbands react differently than their wives to the sales presentation, husbands and wives are asked (separately) to rate the quality of the sales presentation. The dealership wants to know how much husbands differ from their wives in terms of average ratings.

Each of these examples deals with a difference between means from two populations. However, the first four examples differ in one important respect from the last two. In the last two examples there is a natural *pairing* across the two samples. In the first of these, each employee takes a test before a course and then a test after the course, so that each employee is naturally paired with himself or herself. In the final example husbands and wives are naturally paired with one another. There is no such pairing in the first four examples. Instead, we assume that the samples in these examples are chosen *independently* of one another. For statistical reasons we need to distinguish these two cases, independent samples and paired samples, in the discussion that follows.

8.7.1 Independent Samples

The framework for this situation is the following. We are interested in some quantity, such as dollars spent or airplane delay, for each of two populations. The population means are μ_1 and μ_2, and the population standard deviations are σ_1 and σ_2. We take random samples of sizes n_1 and n_2 from the populations to estimate the difference between means, $\mu_1 - \mu_2$. A point estimate of this difference is the natural one, the difference between sample means, $\overline{X}_1 - \overline{X}_2$.

It turns out that the appropriate sampling distribution of this estimate is again the t distribution, now with $n_1 + n_2 - 2$ degrees of freedom.[5] Therefore, a confidence interval for $\mu_1 - \mu_2$ is

$$\overline{X}_1 - \overline{X}_2 \pm t\text{-multiple} \times \text{SE}(\overline{X}_1 - \overline{X}_2) \tag{8.9}$$

The t-multiple is found as usual with the TINV function. It is the value that cuts off the appropriate probability (depending on the confidence level) in each tail of the t distribution with $n_1 + n_2 - 2$ degrees of freedom. For example, if the confidence level is 95% and $n_1 = n_2 = 30$, then the appropriate t-multiple is 2.002, found in Excel with the function TINV(.05,58).

The standard error, $\text{SE}(\overline{X}_1 - \overline{X}_2)$, is more involved. We must first make the assumption that the population standard deviations are equal, that is, $\sigma_1 = \sigma_2$. Then an estimate of this common standard deviation is provided by the "pooled" estimate from both samples, labeled s_p:

$$s_p = \sqrt{\frac{(n_1 - 1)s_1^2 + (n_2 - 1)s_2^2}{n_1 + n_2 - 2}}$$

Here, s_1 and s_2 are the sample standard deviations from the two samples. This pooled estimate is somewhere between s_1 and s_2, with the relative sample sizes determining its exact value. Then the standard error of $\overline{X}_1 - \overline{X}_2$ is

$$\text{SE}(\overline{X}_1 - \overline{X}_2) = s_p \sqrt{\frac{1}{n_1} + \frac{1}{n_2}}$$

Fortunately, the StatPro Two-Sample procedure takes care of all these calculations, as illustrated in the following example.

E X A M P L E   8 . 6

The SureStep Company manufactures high-quality treadmills for use in exercise clubs. SureStep currently purchases its motors for these treadmills from supplier A. However, it is considering a change to supplier B, which offers a slightly lower cost. The only question is whether supplier B's motors are as reliable as supplier A's. To check this, SureStep installs motors from supplier A on 30 of its treadmills and motors from supplier B on another 30 of its treadmills. It then runs these treadmills under typical conditions and, for each treadmill, records the number of hours until the motor fails. The data from this experiment appear in Figure 8.10 (page 398). (See the file MOTORS.XLS.) What can SureStep conclude?

[5]This assumes that either the population distributions are normal or that the sample sizes are reasonably large, conditions that are at least approximately met in a wide variety of applications.

FIGURE 8.10 Analysis of Treadmill Motors Data

	A	B	C	D	E	F	G	H
1	Differences between treadmill motors							
2								
3	Sample data (hours until motor fails)							
4								
5		Supplier A	Supplier B			Two-sample analysis for Supplier_A minus Supplier_B		
6		1358	658					
7		793	404			Summary stats for two samples		
8		587	735				Supplier_A	Supplier_l
9		608	457			Sample sizes	30	3
10		472	431			Sample means	748.800	655.66
11		562	658			Sample standard deviations	283.881	259.98
12		879	453					
13		575	488			Confidence interval for difference between means		
14		1293	522			Confidence level	95.0%	
15		1457	1247			Sample mean difference	93.133	
16		705	1095			Pooled standard deviation	272.196	N.
17		623	430			Std error of difference	70.281	70.28
18		725	726			Degrees of freedom	58	5
19		569	793			Lower limit	-47.549	-47.54
20		424	498			Upper limit	233.815	233.81
21		436	502					
22		1250	589			Test of equality of variances		
23		493	975			Ratio of sample variances	1.192	
24		485	808			p-value	0.319	
25		462	456					
34		684	732					
35		666	507					

Solution

In any comparison problem it is a good idea to look initially at side-by-side boxplots of the two samples. These appear in Figure 8.11. These show that (1) the distributions of times until failure are skewed to the right for each supplier, (2) the mean for supplier A is somewhat greater than the mean for supplier B, and (3) there are several mild outliers. There seems to be little doubt that supplier A's motors will last longer on average than supplier B's—or is there? A confidence interval for the mean difference allows us to see whether the differences apparent in the boxplots can be generalized to *all* motors from the two suppliers.

We find this confidence interval by using the StatPro Two-Sample procedure. To do so, place the cursor anywhere in the data set, use the StatPro/Statistical Inference/Two-Sample Analysis menu item, select the Unstacked option, select Supplier_A and Supplier_B as the variables to analyze, and accept the defaults in all other dialog boxes. We obtain the output in Figure 8.10. The top part of the output summarizes the two samples. It shows that the sample means differ by approximately 93 hours and that the sample standard deviations are of roughly the same magnitude.

The confidence interval calculations appear in the range G14:G20. Here we see that the difference between sample means is 93.133 hours, the pooled estimate of the common population standard deviation is 272.196 hours, the standard error of the sample mean difference is 70.281 hours, and a 95% confidence interval for the mean difference extends from −47.549 to 233.815 hours. Not only is this interval quite wide, but it extends from a negative value to a positive value. If SureStep had to make a guess, it would say that supplier A's motors last longer on average than supplier B's. But because of the negative part of the confidence interval, there is still a possibility that the opposite is true.[6]

Should SureStep continue with supplier A? This depends on the trade-off between the cost of the motors and warranty costs (and any other relevant costs). Because the warranty probably depends on whether a motor lasts a certain amount of time, warranty costs probably depend on a proportion (the proportion that fail before 500 hours, say) rather than a mean. Therefore, we will postpone further discussion of this issue until we discuss differences between proportions.

FIGURE 8.11 **Boxplots for Treadmill Motors Data**

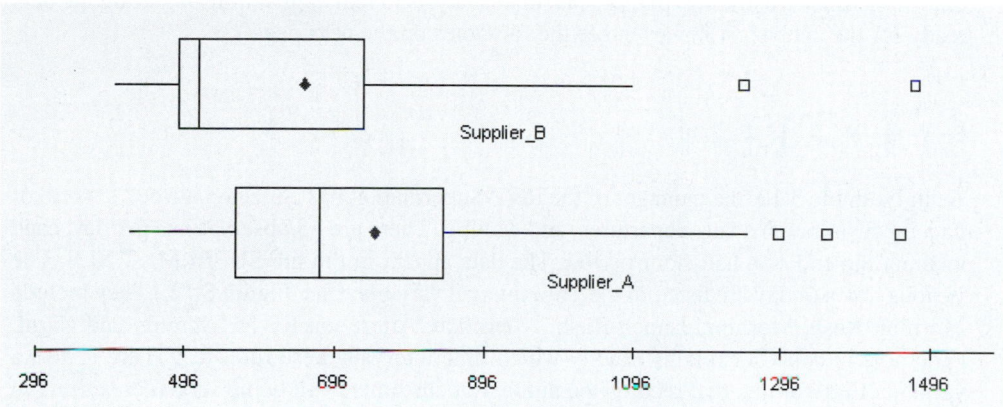

This two-sample analysis makes the strong assumption that the standard deviations (or variances) from the two populations are equal. How can we tell whether they are equal, and what do we do if they are not equal?

To check whether they are equal, we can obviously look at the two sample standard deviations. If they are of widely different magnitudes, this certainly casts doubt on the equal-variance assumption. The sample standard deviations in the treadmill example, 283.881 and 259.986, are of similar magnitudes and present no clear evidence of unequal population variances. A statistical test for equality of two population variances is automatically shown at the bottom of the StatPro Two-Sample output. Because we have not yet discussed hypothesis testing, however, we will postpone discussion of this test for now. Suffice it to say that it also presents no evidence of unequal variances for this example.

If we do have reason to believe that the population variances are unequal, then a slightly different procedure can be used to calculate a confidence interval for the difference between means. The appropriate standard error of $\overline{X}_1 - \overline{X}_2$ is now

$$\text{SE}(\overline{X}_1 - \overline{X}_2) = \sqrt{s_1^2/n_1 + s_2^2/n_2}$$

and the degrees of freedom used to find the t-multiple is given by a complex expression that we will not present here.

StatPro's Two-Sample procedure automatically calculates the confidence interval for this unequal-variance case. For the treadmill example you can see the results in the range H17:H20. In this example they are exactly the same as the results (in column G) when

---

[6]If there is any confusion about whether the quoted difference refers to "supplier A minus supplier B" or "supplier B minus supplier A," place the cursor over cell E5. The note in this cell confirms that the difference refers to "supplier A minus supplier B." StatPro's Two-Sample procedure automatically adds this note to prevent confusion.

we make the equal-variance assumption. This is a consequence of the equal sample sizes and roughly equal sample variances. In general, the two results will differ appreciably only when the sample sizes *and* the sample variances differ considerably across samples. In any case, the appropriate results to use are those on the right (column H) if we have reason to suspect unequal population variances and those on the left (column G) otherwise.

We next revisit the R&P Supermarket data in Example 3.10 from Chapter 3. We again make a comparison between two means, this time the mean number of customers left in line during rush times versus normal times. There are two objectives in this example. First, it provides one more illustration of the two-sample procedure, now with unequal sample sizes. Perhaps more importantly, it illustrates that not all data sets come "ready-made" for performing a particular analysis. We have to do some data manipulation before we can invoke StatPro's Two-Sample procedure. Indeed, this is often the most time-consuming (and sometimes frustrating) part of statistical analysis in real applications—getting the data ready for the analysis. (However, see the footnotes on the next page.)

EXAMPLE 8.7

As in Example 3.10, the manager of the R&P Supermarket has collected a week's worth of data on customer arrivals, departures, and waiting. There are 48 observations per day, each taken at the end of a half-hour period. The data appear in the file SUPERMKT.XLS. The various times of day are listed in the TimeInterval variable. (See Figure 8.12.) They include Morning Rush, Morning, Lunch Rush, Afternoon, Afternoon Rush, Evening, and Night. (The note in cell C3 explains exactly which time intervals these refer to.) There is also a variable, EndWaiting, that records the number of customers still being served or waiting in line at the end of each half-hour period.

The manager would like to check whether the average value of EndWaiting differs during rush periods from normal, non-night periods. She is concerned that there might be

FIGURE 8.12   Original Data for Supermarket Example

	A	B	C	D	E	F	G	H	I
1	Supermarket checkout efficiency								
2									
3	Day	StartTime	TimeInterval	InitialWaiting	Arrivals	Departures	EndWaiting	Checkers	TotalCustomers
4	Mon	8:00 AM	Morning rush	2	21	22	1	3	23
5	Mon	8:30 AM	Morning rush	1	25	18	8	3	26
6	Mon	9:00 AM	Morning	8	27	28	7	3	35
7	Mon	9:30 AM	Morning	7	21	23	5	3	28
8	Mon	10:00 AM	Morning	5	20	23	2	5	25
9	Mon	10:30 AM	Morning	2	36	31	7	5	38
10	Mon	11:00 AM	Morning	7	30	36	1	5	37
11	Mon	11:30 AM	Lunch rush	1	34	29	6	5	35
12	Mon	12:00 PM	Lunch rush	6	56	48	14	7	62
13	Mon	12:30 PM	Lunch rush	14	58	64	8	7	72
14	Mon	1:00 PM	Lunch rush	8	53	52	9	7	61
15	Mon	1:30 PM	Afternoon	9	30	36	3	5	39
16	Mon	2:00 PM	Afternoon	3	34	31	6	5	37
17	Mon	2:30 PM	Afternoon	6	36	37	5	5	42
18	Mon	3:00 PM	Afternoon	5	30	28	7	5	35
335	Mon	5:30 AM	Night	2	6	8	0	1	8
336	Mon	6:00 AM	Morning rush	0	5	4	1	2	5
337	Mon	6:30 AM	Morning rush	1	7	7	1	2	8
338	Mon	7:00 AM	Morning rush	1	16	14	3	3	17
339	Mon	7:30 AM	Morning rush	3	18	16	5	3	21

excessive waiting during rush periods, in which case she might need to add more checkout people during these times. She plans to exclude the night period from the analysis because she knows from experience that customers very seldom need to wait during the night.

Solution

Starting with the data set in its original form, we need to perform three main steps:

1 Rename the seven time intervals (Morning rush, Morning, and so on) so that there are only three: Rush, Normal, and Night.

2 "Unstack" the single EndWaiting variable so that there are three EndWaiting variables: one for Rush, one for Normal, and one for Night.[7]

3 Perform the statistical comparison between the EndWaiting variables for the Rush and Normal periods.

The SUPERMKT.XLS file contains the results of step 1 in the NewData sheet and the results of steps 2 and 3 in the Analysis sheet. If you want to follow along, hands-on, with the step-by-step procedure, you should delete all but the OriginalData sheet from the SUPERMKT.XLS file and perform the following steps.

1 **Copy sheet:** Create a copy of the OriginalData sheet by pressing the Ctrl key and dragging the OriginalData sheet tab to the right. Double-click on the new sheet tab and rename it NewData.

2 **Rename time intervals:** To rename the time intervals on the NewData sheet, use Excel's Find and Replace feature. Click on column C's tab to select the entire column, then select the Edit/Replace menu item. Type **Morning rush** in the "Find what:" box, type **Rush** in the "Replace with:" box, and click on the Replace All button. Repeat this for the other time intervals to be renamed. That is, replace Lunch rush and Afternoon rush by Rush, and replace Morning, Afternoon, and Evening by Normal. Figure 8.13 (page 402) shows some of the results.

3 **Unstack End Waiting variable:** Right now, there is one "long" EndWaiting variable. To use StatPro's Two-Sample procedure, we need three "short" EndWaiting variables, one for each time interval, which will be placed on a new sheet called Analysis. To do this, use StatPro's Unstack procedure. Place the cursor anywhere inside the data set in the NewData sheet and select the StatPro/Data Utilities/Unstack Variables menu item. In response to the dialog boxes, select TimeInterval as the code variable, EndWaiting as the single variable to unstack, and choose to put the results on a new sheet called Analysis. This produces three new variables: EndWaiting_Night, EndWaiting_Normal, and EndWaiting_Rush. (See Figure 8.14 for a partial listing of these variables.)

4 **Create boxplots:** Use StatPro's Boxplot procedure, using the *unstacked* variables on the Analysis sheet, to create side-by-side boxplots of the EndWaiting variables. You can do this for all three variables or only the two corresponding to Normal and Rush. We selected all three, as shown in Figure 8.15, to check whether the manager's assumption of low waiting lines at night is correct.[8]

5 **Perform Two-Sample Analysis:** With the cursor anywhere in the data set on the Analysis sheet, select the StatPro/Statistical Inference/Two-Sample Analysis menu

---

[7]Some software packages require variables to be in "stacked" form, as in Figure 8.12, for a two-sample procedure. Others require the variables to be unstacked. StatPro originally required the latter, and the procedure described below was written at that time. At the last minute, however, we revised StatPro to accommodate *either* form, unstacked or stacked. Therefore, the steps below will certainly work, but unstacking is not really necessary.

[8]StatPro's Boxplot procedure also accommodates data in stacked or unstacked form.

FIGURE 8.13 **Supermarket Data with Time Categories Renamed**

	A	B	C	D	E	F	G	H	I
1	Supermarket checkout efficiency								
2									
3	Day	StartTime	TimeInterval	InitialWaiting	Arrivals	Departures	EndWaiting	Checkers	TotalCustomers
4	Mon	8:00 AM	Rush	2	21	22	1	3	23
5	Mon	8:30 AM	Rush	1	25	18	8	3	26
6	Mon	9:00 AM	Normal	8	27	28	7	3	35
7	Mon	9:30 AM	Normal	7	21	23	5	3	28
8	Mon	10:00 AM	Normal	5	20	23	2	5	25
9	Mon	10:30 AM	Normal	2	36	31	7	5	38
10	Mon	11:00 AM	Normal	7	30	36	1	5	37
11	Mon	11:30 AM	Rush	1	34	29	6	5	35
12	Mon	12:00 PM	Rush	6	56	48	14	7	62
13	Mon	12:30 PM	Rush	14	58	64	8	7	72
14	Mon	1:00 PM	Rush	8	53	52	9	7	61
15	Mon	1:30 PM	Normal	9	30	36	3	5	39
16	Mon	2:00 PM	Normal	3	34	31	6	5	37
17	Mon	2:30 PM	Normal	6	36	37	5	5	42
18	Mon	3:00 PM	Normal	5	30	28	7	5	35
335	Mon	5:30 AM	Night	2	6	8	0	1	8
336	Mon	6:00 AM	Rush	0	5	4	1	2	5
337	Mon	6:30 AM	Rush	1	7	7	1	2	8
338	Mon	7:00 AM	Rush	1	16	14	3	3	17
339	Mon	7:30 AM	Rush	3	18	16	5	3	21

FIGURE 8.14 **Unstacked Variables for Supermarket Example**

	A	B	C
1	EndWaiting_Night	EndWaiting_Normal	EndWaiting_Rush
2	1	7	1
3	1	5	8
4	3	2	6
5	1	7	14
6	1	1	8
7	0	3	9
8	0	6	11
9	0	5	14
10	2	7	8
11	0	2	3
12	0	4	0
13	0	3	2
14	1	2	3
15	1	1	3
16	3	12	7
17	1	5	0
18	0	1	3

item. Select EndWaiting_Normal and EndWaiting_Rush as the variables to analyze, check the Confidence Interval option, and accept the defaults on the other dialog boxes.

The side-by-side boxplots in Figure 8.15 show that (1) the distribution of EndWaiting is definitely skewed to the right for each time interval, with a number of outliers, and (2) the mean value of EndWaiting is slightly larger for Rush than for Normal, with Night a distant third. Given the nature of the data, it should not really be surprising that the data are skewed to the right with a number of outliers. When the supermarket gets busy, waiting lines can really build. All it takes is one or two really long checkout times to produce an excessively large value of EndWaiting, and this is evidently what happened at R&P.

FIGURE 8.15

Boxplots for Supermarket Example

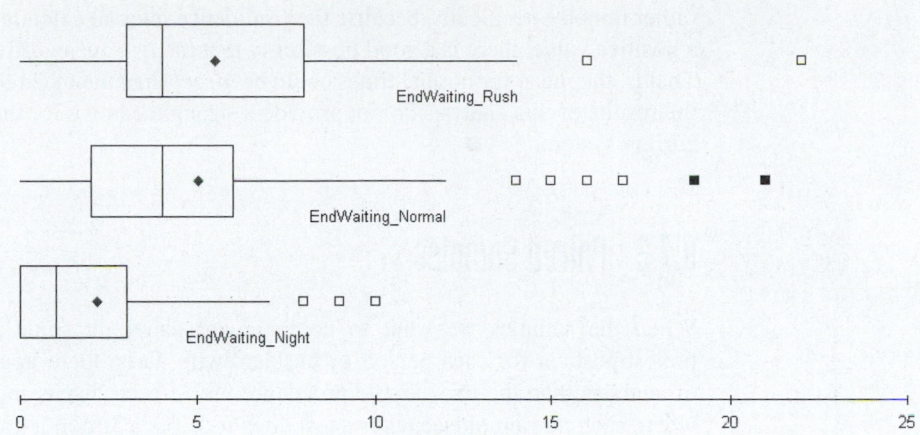

The output from the two-sample procedure appears in Figure 8.16. The sample means of EndWaiting are 5.480 and 5.014 for the Rush and Normal periods, the sample standard deviations are 4.284 and 4.293, and these are based on sample sizes of 98 and 140 half-hour periods. These summary statistics provide some evidence of a difference between population means but very little evidence of different population variances. This latter statement means that we can use the results in column G, not column H (although they are practically identical). We see that a point estimate for the mean difference (Normal minus Rush) is −0.465 and that a 95% confidence interval for this mean difference extends from −1.578 to 0.648.

What can the manager conclude from this analysis? Should she add extra checkout people during rush periods? This is difficult to answer because it obviously involves a trade-off between the cost of extra checkout people and the "cost" of making customers wait in line. Also, we have no way of knowing, at least not from the present analysis,

FIGURE 8.16 **Analysis of Supermarket Data**

	E	F	G	H	I
1		*Two-sample analysis for EndWaiting_Normal minus EndWaiting_Rush*			
2					
3		*Summary stats for two samples*			
4			EndWaiting_Normal	EndWaiting_Rush	
5		Sample sizes	140	98	
6		Sample means	5.014	5.480	
7		Sample standard deviations	4.293	4.284	
8					
9		*Confidence interval for difference between means*			
10		Confidence level	95.0%		
11		Sample mean difference	-0.465		
12		Pooled standard deviation	4.290	NA	
13		Std error of difference	0.565	0.565	
14		Degrees of freedom	236	209	
15		Lower limit	-1.578	-1.579	
16		Upper limit	0.648	0.648	
17					
18		*Test of equality of variances*			
19		Ratio of sample variances	1.004		
20		p-value	0.496		

how much effect extra checkout people would have on waiting. However, the manager does know from this analysis that the mean difference between rush and normal periods is rather minor. Specifically, because the confidence interval extends from a negative value to a positive value, there is a good possibility that the *true* mean difference could be *positive*. That is, the mean for normal times could be *larger* than the mean for rush times. Therefore, the results of this analysis do not provide a strong incentive for the manager to change the current system. ■

8.7.2 Paired Samples

When the samples we want to compare are paired in some natural way, such as a pretest/posttest for each person or husband/wife pairs, there is a more appropriate form of analysis than the two-sample procedure we've been discussing. Consider the example where each new employee takes a test, then receives a 3-month training course, and finally takes another similar test. There is likely to be a fairly strong correlation between the pretest and posttest scores. Employees who score relatively low on the first test are likely to score relatively low on the second test, and employees who score relatively high on the first test are likely to score relatively high on the second test. The two-sample procedure does not take this correlation into account and essentially ignores important information. The paired procedure described in this section, on the other hand, uses this information to advantage.

The procedure itself is very straightforward. We do not directly analyze two separate variables (pretest scores and posttest scores, say); we analyze their *differences*. For each pair in the sample, we calculate the difference between the two scores for the pair. Then we perform a *one*-sample analysis, as in Section 8.3, on these differences. Actually, Stat-Pro's Paired-Sample procedure does the differencing *and* the ensuing one-sample analysis automatically, as described in the following example.

E X A M P L E 8 . 8

The Stevens Honda–Olds automobile dealership often sells to husband/wife pairs. The manager would like to check whether the sales presentation is viewed any more or less favorably by the husbands than the wives. If it is, then some new training might be recommended for its salespeople. To check for differences, a random sample of husbands and wives are asked (separately) to rate the sales presentation on a 1 to 10 scale, 10 being the most favorable rating. The results appear in Figure 8.17. (See the AUTO.XLS file.) What can the manager conclude from these data?

Solution

We illustrate two ways to perform the analysis. Normally, we would only use the second of these, but the first sheds some light on the procedure. For the first method, make a copy of the Data sheet and call it OneSample. Then manually form a new variable in column D called Difference by entering the formula

$$=B4-C4$$

in cell D4 and copying it down column D. (See Figure 8.18.) Next, with the cursor anywhere in the resulting data set, select the StatPro/Statistical Inference/One-Sample Analysis menu item, select the variable Difference for analysis, and accept all the defaults in the other dialog boxes. This produces the output shown in Figure 8.18. We see that the sample mean Husband minus Wife difference is 1.629 and that a 95% confidence interval for this

FIGURE 8.17 Data for Sales Presentation Example

	A	B	C
1	Sales presentation ratings		
2			
3	Pair	Husband	Wife
4	1	6	3
5	2	7	8
6	3	8	5
7	4	6	4
8	5	8	5
9	6	7	6
10	7	8	5
11	8	6	7
12	9	7	8
33	30	7	3
34	31	7	5
35	32	5	1
36	33	7	5
37	34	7	4
38	35	10	5

FIGURE 8.18 One-Sample Analysis of Differences for Automobile Data

	A	B	C	D	E	F	G	H	I	J
1	Sales presentation ratings									
2										
3	Pair	Husband	Wife	Difference			Results for one-sample analysis			
4	1	6	3	3						
5	2	7	8	-1			Confidence interval results for mean of Difference			
6	3	8	5	3			Confidence level	95.0%		
7	4	6	4	2			Sample mean	1.629		
8	5	8	5	3			Std error of mean	0.281		
9	6	7	6	1			Degrees of freedom	34		
10	7	8	5	3			Lower limit	1.057		
11	8	6	7	-1			Upper limit	2.200		
12	9	7	8	-1						
13	10	7	5	2						
14	11	6	3	3						
15	12	5	4	1						
16	13	8	5	3						
36	33	7	5	2						
37	34	7	4	3						
38	35	10	5	5						

difference extends from 1.057 to 2.200. The standard error in cell H8, 0.281, refers to the standard error of the sample mean *difference*.

To perform this analysis more efficiently, again make a copy of the Data sheet and called it Paired. Then use the StatPro/Statistical Inference/Paired-Sample Analysis menu item, select the Husband and Wife variables for analysis, name the new difference variable Difference, and accept the defaults in the other dialog boxes. We obtain the output in Figure 8.19 (page 406). Obviously, the results are exactly the same as before. This is because StatPro's Paired-Sample procedure performs a one-sample analysis on the differences—and it saves you the work of creating the differences.

Figure 8.20 shows side-by-side boxplots of the husband and wife scores. These boxplots are not as useful here as in the two-sample procedure because we lose sight of which husbands are paired with which wives. A more useful boxplot is of the differences, shown in Figure 8.21. Here we see that the sample mean difference is positive, but even more importantly, we see that the vast majority of husband scores are greater than the corre-

FIGURE 8.19   Paired-Sample Analysis of Automobile Data

	A	B	C	D	E	F	G	H	I	J
1	Sales presentation ratings									
2										
3	Pair	Husband		Wife	Difference		*Results of paired-sample analysis*			
4	1	6		3	3					
5	2	7		8	-1		*Confidence interval results for mean of Difference*			
6	3	8		5	3		Confidence level	95.0%		
7	4	6		4	2		Sample mean	1.629		
8	5	8		5	3		Std error of mean	0.281		
9	6	7		6	1		Degrees of freedom	34		
10	7	8		5	3		Lower limit	1.057		
11	8	6		7	-1		Upper limit	2.200		
12	9	7		8	-1					
13	10	7		5	2					
14	11	6		3	3					
15	12	5		4	1					
16	13	8		5	3					
36	33	7		5	2					
37	34	7		4	3					
38	35	10		5	5					

FIGURE 8.20   Side-by-side Boxplots for Automobile Data

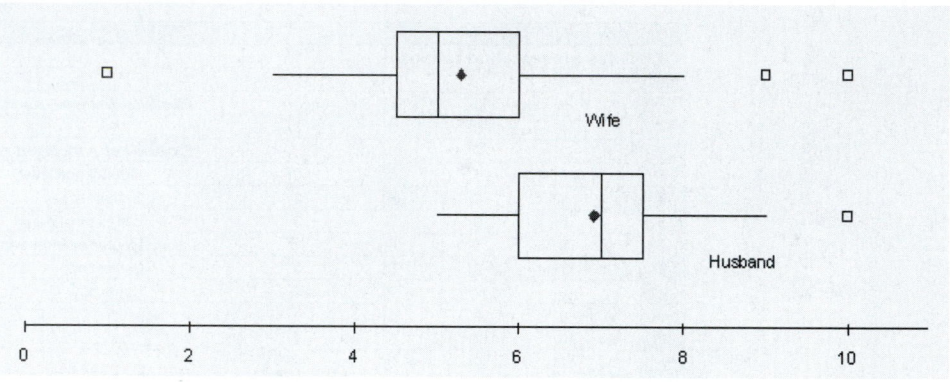

FIGURE 8.21   Single Boxplot of Differences for Automobile Data

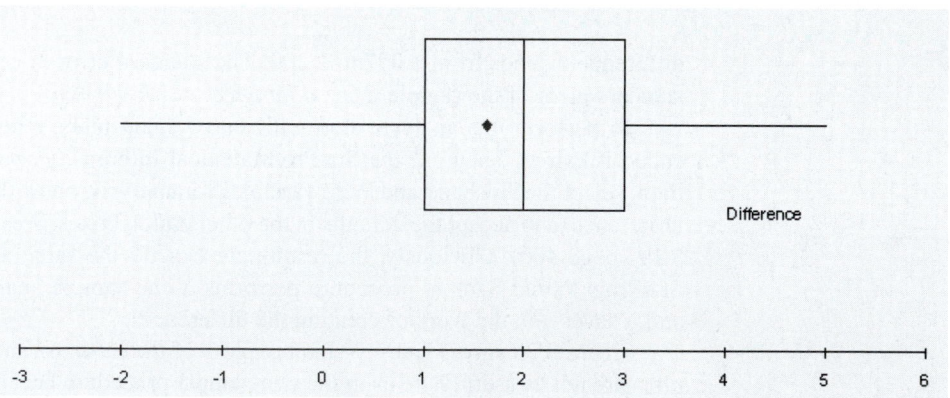

sponding wife scores. There is little doubt that most husbands tend to react more favorably to the sales presentations than their wives. Perhaps the salespeople need to be somewhat more sensitive to their female customers!

Before leaving this example, we check what would have happened if we had used the two-sample procedure on the Husband and Wife variables. The results appear in Figure 8.22. Because there is a considerable difference between the sample standard deviations, we should probably use the confidence interval output in column H, not column G, although there is not much difference between the two. The important point is that the resulting confidence interval for the mean difference extends from 0.895 to 2.362, which is somewhat *wider* than the confidence interval from the paired-sample procedure. This is typical. When we use the two-sample procedure in a situation where the paired-sample procedure is more appropriate, we do not use the data as efficiently. The effect is that the standard error of the difference tends to be larger, and the resulting confidence interval tends to be wider.

FIGURE 8.22   **Two-Sample Analysis of Automobile Data**

	A	B	C	D	E	F	G	H	I
1	Sales presentation ratings								
2									
3	Pair	Husband	Wife			Results of two-sample analysis			
4	1	6	3						
5	2	7	8			Summary stats for two samples			
6	3	8	5				Husband	Wife	
7	4	6	4			Sample sizes	35	35	
8	5	8	5			Sample means	6.914	5.286	
9	6	7	6			Sample standard deviations	1.222	1.792	
10	7	8	5						
11	8	6	7			Confidence interval results for difference between means			
12	9	7	8			Confidence level	95.0%		
13	10	7	5			Sample mean difference	1.629		
14	11	6	3			Pooled standard deviation	1.533	NA	
15	12	5	4			Std error of difference	0.367	0.367	
16	13	8	5			Degrees of freedom	68	60	
17	14	7	8			Lower limit	0.897	0.895	
18	15	7	5			Upper limit	2.360	2.362	
19	16	7	6						
20	17	6	5			Test of equality of variances			
21	18	5	4			Ratio of sample variances	2.151		
22	19	6	5			p value	0.014		
23	20	9	10						
37	34	7	4						
38	35	10	5						

Why is the paired-sample procedure appropriate here? It is *not* just because husbands and wives naturally come in pairs. It is because they tend to react similarly to one another. You can check that the correlation between the husbands' scores and their wives' scores is 0.442. (Use Excel's CORREL function on the Husband and Wife variables.) This is far from perfect correlation, but it is large enough to warrant using the paired-sample procedure. ■

In general, the paired-sample procedure is appropriate when the samples are naturally paired in some way *and* there is a reasonably large positive correlation between the pairs. In this case the paired-sample procedure makes more efficient use of the data and generally results in narrower confidence intervals.

PROBLEMS

Level A

23 The director of a university's career development center is interested in comparing the starting annual salaries of male and female students who recently graduated from the university and commenced full-time employment. The director has formed pairs of male and female graduates with the same major and similar grade-point averages. Specifically, she has collected a random sample of 50 such pairs and has recorded the starting annual salary of each person. These data are provided in the file P8_23.XLS. Construct a 99% confidence interval for the mean difference between similar male and female graduates of this university. Interpret your result.

24 A real estate agent has collected a random sample of 75 houses that were recently sold in a suburban community. She is particularly interested in comparing the appraised value and recent selling price of the houses in this particular market. The values of these two variables for each of the 75 randomly chosen houses are provided in the file P8_24.XLS. Using the sample data, generate a 95% confidence interval for the mean difference between the appraised values and selling prices of the houses sold in this suburban community. Interpret the constructed interval estimate for the real estate agent.

25 A company employs two shifts of workers. Each shift produces a type of gasket where the thickness is the critical dimension. The average thickness and the standard deviation of thickness for shift 1, based on a random sample of 30 gaskets, are 10.53 mm and 0.14 mm. The similar figures for shift 2, based on a random sample of 25 gaskets, are 10.55 mm and 0.17 mm. Let $\mu_1 - \mu_2$ be the mean difference in thickness between shifts 1 and 2.

   a Find a 95% confidence interval for $\mu_1 - \mu_2$.

   b Based on your answer to part **a**, are you convinced that the gaskets from shift 2 are, on average, wider than those from shift 1? Why or why not?

   c How would your answers to parts **a** and **b** change if the sample sizes were instead 300 and 250?

Level B

26 Consider a random sample of 100 households from a middle-class neighborhood that was the recent focus of an economic development study conducted by the local government. Specifically, for each of the 100 households, information was gathered on each of the following variables: family size, location of the household within the neighborhood, an indication of whether those surveyed owned or rented their home, gross annual income of the first household wage earner, gross annual income of the second household wage earner (if applicable), monthly home mortgage or rent payment, average monthly expenditure on utilities, and the total indebtedness (excluding the value of a home mortgage) of the household. The data are in the file P8_26.XLS.

   a Separate the households in the sample by the *location* of their residence within the given community. For each of the four locations, use the sample information to generate a 90% confidence interval for the mean annual income of all relevant first household wage earners. Compare these four interval estimates. You might also consider generating boxplots of the primary wage earner variable for households in each of the four given locations.

   b Generate a 90% confidence interval for the difference between the mean annual income levels of the first household wage earners in the first (i.e., SW) and second (i.e., NW) sectors of this community. Generate similar 90% confidence intervals for the differences between the mean annual income levels of primary wage earners from all other pairs of locations (i.e., first and third, first and fourth, second and third, second and fourth, and third and fourth). Summarize your findings.

27 Given data in the file P2_13.XLS from a recent survey of chief executive officers of the nation's 350 biggest businesses (*The Wall Street Journal*, April 9, 1998), construct 95% confidence intervals for the differences in the mean levels of 1997 salaries awarded to executives from *Technology* companies and each of the other seven company types. For instance, construct a 95% confidence interval for the difference in the mean 1997 salaries of executives from *Technology* and *Basic Materials* companies. What conclusions can you draw from the seven 95% confidence intervals you have generated? ■

Confidence Interval for the Difference Between Proportions

T he final confidence interval we examine is a confidence interval for the difference between two population proportions. As in the previous section, this "comparison" procedure finds many real applications. Several potential business applications are the following:

- When an appliance store is about to run a sale, it sometimes sends selected customers a mailing to notify them of the sale. On other occasions it includes a coupon for 5% off the sale price in these mailings. The store's manager would like to know whether the inclusion of coupons affects the proportion of customers who respond.

- A manufacturing company has two plants that produce identical products. The company wants to know how much the proportion of out-of-spec products differs across the two plants.

- A pharmaceutical company has developed a new over-the-counter sleeping pill. To judge its effectiveness, the company runs an experiment where one set of randomly chosen people takes the new pill and another set takes a placebo. (Neither set knows which type of pill they are taking.) The company judges the effectiveness of the new pill by comparing the proportions of people who fall asleep within a certain amount of time with the new pill and with the placebo.

- An advertising agency would like to check whether men are more likely than women to switch TV channels when a commercial comes on. It runs an experiment where the channel switching behavior of randomly chosen men and women can be monitored, and it collects data on the proportion of viewers who switch channels on at least half of the commercial times. It then compares these proportions across gender.

The basic form of analysis in each of these examples is the same as in the two-sample analysis for differences between means. However, instead of comparing two quantitative variables, we now compare two 0–1 variables. Each observation is 1 if that sample member has a certain property (buys an appliance or falls asleep within a half hour, say) and is 0 otherwise. We then compare the proportion of 1's across the two samples.

Formally, let p_1 and p_2 represent the two unknown population proportions, and let $\widehat{p}_1$ and $\widehat{p}_2$ be the two sample proportions, based on samples of sizes n_1 and n_2. Then the point estimate of the difference between proportions, $p_1 - p_2$, is the difference between sample proportions, $\widehat{p}_1 - \widehat{p}_2$. Assuming that the sample sizes are reasonably large, the sampling distribution of $\widehat{p}_1 - \widehat{p}_2$ is approximately normal.[9]

Therefore, a confidence interval for $p_1 - p_2$ is given by

$$\widehat{p}_1 - \widehat{p}_2 \pm z\text{-multiple} \times \text{SE}(\widehat{p}_1 - \widehat{p}_2) \tag{8.10}$$

Here, the z-multiple is the usual value from the normal distribution that cuts off the appropriate probability in each tail (1.96 for a 95% confidence interval, for example). Also, the standard error of $\widehat{p}_1 - \widehat{p}_2$ is given by

$$\text{SE}(\widehat{p}_1 - \widehat{p}_2) = \sqrt{\frac{\widehat{p}_1(1 - \widehat{p}_1)}{n_1} + \frac{\widehat{p}_2(1 - \widehat{p}_2)}{n_2}} \tag{8.11}$$

The following example illustrates this procedure in the case where we do not have the raw data (the 0's and 1's) but instead have only counts.

---

[9]This large-sample assumption is valid as long as $n_i \widehat{p}_i > 5$ and $n_i(1 - \widehat{p}_i) > 5$ for $i = 1$ and $i = 2$.

EXAMPLE 8.9

An appliance store is about to run a big sale. It selects 300 of its best customers and randomly divides them into two sets of 150 customers each. It then mails a notice of the sale to all 300 customers but includes a coupon for an extra 5% off the sale price to the second set of customers only. As the sale progresses, the store keeps track of which of these customers purchase appliances. The resulting data appear in Figure 8.23. (See the file COUPONS.XLS.) What can the store's manager conclude about the effectiveness of the coupons?

FIGURE 8.23   Analysis of Coupon Data

	A	B	C	D
1	Effectiveness of coupons in promoting a sale			
2				
3		Purchased	Didn't purchase	Total
4	Received coupon	55	95	150
5	Didn't receive coupon	35	115	150
6				
7	Sample proportions who purchased			
8	Received coupon	0.3667	Range names	
9	Didn't receive coupon	0.2333	ConfLev: B14	
10			Diff: B11	
11	Difference between sample proportions	0.1333	SampProp1: B8	
12	Standard error of difference	0.0524	SampProp2: B9	
13			SampSize1: D4	
14	Confidence level	95%	SampSize2: D5	
15	z-multiple	1.960	StErr: B12	
16			zMult: B15	
17	Confidence interval for difference between proportions			
18	Lower limit	0.0307		
19	Upper limit	0.2359		

Solution

First, note that the data have been arranged in a "contingency" table, much like the pivot tables we discussed in Chapters 2 and 3.[10] Of the 150 customers who received coupons, 55 purchased an appliance. Of the 150 who did not receive coupons, only 35 purchased an appliance. These translate to the sample proportions 0.3667 and 0.2333, calculated in cells B8 and B9 with the formulas

$$=B4/D4$$

and

$$=B5/D5$$

By subtraction, these lead directly to the sample difference between proportions, 0.1333, in cell B11. The standard error of this difference is calculated in cell B12 with the formula

$$= SQRT(SampProp1*(1-SampProp1)/SampSize1$$

$$+SampProp2*(1-SampProp2)/SampSize2)$$

---

[10] StatPro doesn't have a procedure for solving this problem when the data are in the form of a contingency table. However, the COUPONS.XLS file can be used as a "template" for all such problems.

Also, the z-multiple for the confidence interval is calculated in cell B15 with the formula

$$=\text{NORMSINV(ConfLev+(1-ConfLev)/2)}$$

Finally, the limits of the confidence interval for the difference are calculated in cells B18 and B19 with the formulas

$$=\text{Diff-zMult*StErr}$$

and

$$=\text{Diff+zMult*StErr}$$

Because the confidence limits are both positive, we can conclude that the effect of coupons is almost surely to *increase* the proportion of buyers. How can the store manager interpret this mean difference? He can use it to estimate the extra business he will receive by including coupons as opposed to not including them. The confidence interval implies that for every 100 customers, the coupons will probably induce an extra 3 to 23 customers to purchase an appliance who otherwise would not have made a purchase.

However, the difference between proportions does not directly indicate the difference in *profit* from including coupons. This is because the customers with coupons pay 5% less than the customers without them. Suppose the average purchase amount without a coupon is $400, $50 of which is profit for the store. For every 100 customers who receive a mailing with no coupon, the store can expect to make about

$$\$50(0.2333)(100) = \$1166.50$$

in profit. If these 100 customers receive coupons, the expected profit becomes

$$\$30(0.3667)(100) = \$1100.10$$

because these customers pay only $380 on average, $30 of which is profit to the store. Therefore, it appears that if the sample proportions in cells B8 and B9 are anywhere near the true proportions, the store will make *less* profit by including coupons than by not including them. ■

Recall that the one-sample procedure for a single 0–1 variable gives an approximate confidence interval for a proportion p. We illustrated this result in Example 8.3. In the same way, the two-sample procedure used on two 0–1 variables provides an approximate confidence interval for the difference between two proportions, $p_1 - p_2$. We illustrate this in the following example, a continuation of Example 8.6.

EXAMPLE 8.10

As before, the SureStep Company is trying to decide whether to switch from supplier A to supplier B for the motors in its treadmills. Let's suppose that each treadmill carries a 3-month warranty on the motor. If the motor fails within 3 months, SureStep will supply the customer with a new motor at no cost. This includes installation of the new motor at SureStep's expense. Based on the normal usage at most exercise clubs, SureStep translates the 3-month warranty period into approximately 500 hours of treadmill use. Therefore, using the data from Example 8.6 (in the MOTORS.XLS file), it would like to compare the proportion of motors failing before 500 hours across the two suppliers.

Solution

To analyze the proportions, we must first create 0–1 variables for each supplier to see which of the motors in the samples fail within the warranty period. To do this, make a copy of the Data sheet and name it Proportions. Then use StatPro's Dummy Variable procedure twice, once to create a 0–1 variable for supplier A and once for supplier B. Each creates the 0–1 variable by specifying the cutoff value 500 and the "less than" criterion. (We also changed the default 0–1 variable names to Warranty A and Warranty B.) The resulting data appear in Figure 8.24.[11]

FIGURE 8.24 **Analysis of Treadmill Warranty Data**

	A	B	C	D	E	F	G	H	I	J	K
1	Differences between treadmill motors										
2											
3	Sample data (hours until motor fails)										
4											
5		Supplier A	Supplier B	Warranty A	Warranty B		Results of two-sample analysis				
6		1358	658	0	0						
7		793	404	0	1		Summary stats for two samples				
8		587	735	0	0				Warranty_A	Warranty_B	
9		608	457	0	1		Sample sizes		30	30	
10		472	431	1	1		Sample means		0.200	0.367	
11		562	658	0	0		Sample standard deviations		0.407	0.490	
12		879	453	0	1						
13		575	488	0	1		Confidence interval results for difference between means				
14		1293	522	0	0		Confidence level		95.0%		
15		1457	1247	0	0		Sample mean difference		-0.167		
16		705	1095	0	0		Pooled standard deviation		0.450	NA	
17		623	430	0	1		Std error of difference		0.116	0.116	
18		725	726	0	0		Degrees of freedom		58	56	
19		569	793	0	0		Lower limit		-0.399	-0.400	
20		424	498	1	1		Upper limit		0.066	0.066	
21		436	502	1	0						
22		1250	589	0	0		Test of equality of variances				
23		493	975	1	0		Ratio of sample variances		1.451		
24		485	808	1	0		p value		0.161		
25		462	456	1	1						
26		765	731	0	0		Normal analysis (done manually)				
27		854	491	0	1		Sample proportion A		0.200		
28		634	487	0	1		Sample proportion B		0.367		
29		1109	503	0	0		Difference		-0.167		
30		800	465	0	1		Standard error		0.114		
31		883	1475	0	0		z-multiple		1.960		
32		522	508	0	0		Lower limit		-0.391		
33		791	846	0	0		Upper limit		0.057		
34		684	732	0	0						
35		666	507	0	0						

To obtain an approximate 95% confidence interval for the difference in proportions (where the difference refers to "Warranty A minus Warranty B"), we use StatPro's Two-Sample procedure on the two 0–1 Warranty columns. The results appear in the upper section of Figure 8.24. For comparison, we can also form this confidence interval, using formulas (8.10) and (8.11), in the range I27:I33.

By comparing the outputs, it clearly makes little difference whether we use the two-sample procedure or the (more exact) formulas from this section. Using the latter, we see that the point estimate for the difference in proportions is -0.167 and that a 95% confidence interval for this difference extends from -0.391 to 0.057.

---

[11]Of course, we could do this without StatPro by using IF functions.

This is fairly convincing, but not conclusive, evidence that a higher proportion of supplier B motors will fail under warranty. It says that if 100 motors from each supplier were tested, as many as 39 more B motors than A motors might fail before 500 hours—but as many as 5 or 6 more A motors than B motors might fail before 500 hours. In other words, there is still some uncertainty about which supplier makes the more reliable motors, even though the weight of the evidence favors supplier A.

What does this mean in terms of costs? And should SureStep change suppliers? As we just saw, the confidence interval implies that more motors are likely to fail under warranty if SureStep changes to supplier B, but B's motors cost less. A cost analysis might go along the following lines. Suppose that each motor from supplier A costs SureStep $500, whereas supplier B offers them for $475 apiece. Let's follow 100 motors sent to exercise clubs for a period of 3 months. If these are from supplier A, they cost $500 apiece, and approximately 20% (see cell I27) will fail within the warranty period. Of course, each failure costs SureStep another $500. Therefore, the expected cost to SureStep is

$$\$500(100) + \$500(20\%)(100) = \$60,000$$

On the other hand, if these 100 motors come from supplier B, the unit cost is only $475, but approximately 36.7% of them will fail within the warranty period. Therefore, the expected cost is

$$= \$475(100) + \$475(36.7\%)(100) = \$64,933$$

Based on this analysis, the cheaper motors from supplier B are likely to cost more in the long run, so SureStep should probably not switch suppliers. (By the way, we omitted the cost of installing the motors from the analysis. This would have made supplier A look even better.) ■

Before leaving this section, we discuss two related issues. First, we illustrate the caution you should take when interpreting confidence intervals. In the file CAUTION.XLS we randomly generated two normally distributed samples of size 30 each. The means and standard deviations of the two populations (known to enable us to simulate the data) are $\mu_1 = 1100$, $\mu_2 = 1000$, and $\sigma_1 = \sigma_2 = 300$. Therefore, the mean difference, 100, is *known* to be positive. To deal with proportions, we also calculated corresponding 0–1 variables for each sample, where 1's correspond to all values greater than 1050 and 0's correspond to values less than or equal to 1050. From the normal distribution we can calculate the population proportions greater than 1050; they are $p_1 = .566$ and $p_2 = .434$. So the difference, 0.132, is again *known* to be positive. These data appear in Figure 8.25.

Next, we used the two-sample procedure twice: once for the difference between means and once for the difference between proportions, each time obtaining a 95% confidence interval. Then we used a data table to replicate these confidence intervals 100 times, each time keeping track of which confidence limits are negative. We might expect *all* confidence limits to be positive. After all, we know that the population differences between means and between proportions are both positive, so we might expect the confidence intervals to confirm this by returning all positive values. This is *not* what happened in the simulation, as shown in Figure 8.26. Admittedly, none of the *upper* confidence limits are negative, but 72% of the lower confidence limits for means and 81% for proportions are negative. That is, a clear majority of the confidence intervals extend from a negative value to a positive value, leaving considerable doubt about which of the two population means or which of the two population proportions is larger.

You can probably guess why this happened—small sample sizes. Although many applications use sample sizes as small as 30, we can learn only so much from them. If we want to obtain "convincing" evidence in a comparison problem, then we might need to take considerably larger samples—if it is feasible from the standpoint of time and cost.

FIGURE 8.25 **Data for Confidence Interval Simulation**

	A	B	C	D	E
1	**Simulation of confidence intervals for differences**				
2					
3	Note: The samples are normally distributed with the parameters shown				
4					
5	Population parameters				
6		Population 1	Population 2	Difference	
7	Mean	1100	1000	100	
8	Stdev	300	300		
9	Proportion > 1050	0.566	0.434	0.132	
10					
11					
12	Sample 1	Sample 2	GT1050_1	GT1050_2	
13	1040.01	659.67	0	0	
14	1034.61	848.37	0	0	
15	1033.93	1054.07	0	1	
16	1312.65	524.13	1	0	
17	1557.89	1047.73	1	0	
18	1500.06	993.58	1	0	
40	1172.14	1022.88	1	0	
41	1370.50	840.51	1	0	
42	1471.60	1267.40	1	1	

FIGURE 8.26 **Results of Confidence Interval Simulation**

	P	Q	R	S	T	U
12	**Proportion of replications with confidence limits negative**					
13		Lower		Upper		
14		Means	Proportions	Means	Proportions	
15		72%	81%	0%	0%	
16						
17	**Data table of whether confidence limits are negative**					
18		Lower		Upper		
19	Replication	Means	Proportions	Means	Proportions	
20		0	1	0	0	
21	1	1	1	0	0	
22	2	0	0	0	0	
23	3	1	1	0	0	
24	4	1	1	0	0	
25	5	1	1	0	0	
26	6	1	1	0	0	
27	7	1	1	0	0	
28	8	1	1	0	0	
29	9	1	1	0	0	
30	10	0	0	0	0	
31	11	0	0	0	0	
118	98	1	1	0	0	
119	99	1	1	0	0	
120	100	1	1	0	0	

A second issue concerns the magnitude of a given difference between two proportions. Suppose the proportion in question is the proportion of a company's workers who are absent from work, and the company is adopting a new policy to decrease this proportion. Is a decrease from 0.10 to 0.075 the same as, say, a decrease from 0.05 to 0.025? In one sense they are the same; each represents a difference of 0.025. However, in another sense the latter decrease is "larger."

To see why, we introduce the concepts of **odds** and **odds ratios**. If p is any proportion (or probability), the corresponding odds, labeled w, is

$$w = \frac{p}{1 - p}$$

Algebraically, we can solve for p in terms of w:

$$p = \frac{w}{1 + w}$$

The odds of an event is a well-known concept, especially in sports. If the probability that a particular horse will win a race is $p = 1/3$, then the quoted odds in favor of the horse winning is $w = (1/3)/(2/3) = 1/2$, or "1 to 2." On the other hand, if the horse is a favorite with odds 3 to 1 to win, then the corresponding probability of winning is 3/4.

In the absentee illustration, a decrease in the proportion from 0.10 to 0.075 represents a decrease in odds from 1/9 (1 to 9) to 7.5/92.5 (about 1 to 12). The ratio of these, $(7.5/92.5)/(1/9) \simeq 0.73$, is called the odds ratio. In words, the odds decreases by about 27%. In contrast, a decrease in proportion from 0.05 to 0.025 represents an odds ratio of $(2.5/97.5)/(1/19) \simeq 0.487$. Here the odds decreases by over 51%. In this sense the latter decrease is "larger."

Although we will not pursue them here, there are confidence interval formulas for the odds ratio. [See, for example, Ramsey and Schafer (1997).] In some situations this confidence interval is more meaningful than a confidence interval for the difference between proportions.

PROBLEMS

Level A

28 A market research consultant hired by the Pepsi-Cola Co. is interested in estimating the difference between the proportions of female and male consumers who favor Pepsi-Cola over Coke Classic in a particular urban location. A random sample of 250 consumers from the market under investigation is provided in the file P8_17.XLS. After separating the 250 randomly selected consumers by *gender*, construct a 95% confidence interval for the difference between these two proportions. Of what value might this interval estimate be to marketing managers at the Pepsi-Cola Co.?

Level B

29 Continuing the previous problem, marketing managers at the Pepsi-Cola Co. have asked their market research consultant to explore further the difference between the proportions of women and men who prefer drinking Pepsi over Coke Classic. Specifically, Pepsi managers would like to know whether the difference between the proportions of female and male consumers who favor Pepsi varies by the *age* of the consumers. Use the random sample of 250 consumers provided in the file P8_17.XLS to assess whether estimates of this difference vary across the four given age categories: *under 20, between 20 and 40, between 40 and 60,* and *over 60.* Employ a 95% confidence level in generating each of the *six* required interval estimates. Summarize your findings in detail. Finally, what recommendations would you make to the marketing managers in light of your statistical findings?

30 The employee benefits manager of a small private university would like to estimate differences in the proportions of various groups of full-time employees who prefer adopting the third (i.e., plan C) of three available health care plans in the forthcoming annual enrollment period. A reliable frame of the university's employees and their tentative health care preferences are given in the file P7_25.XLS.

a First, select a simple random sample of 25 employees from *each* of three employee classifications: *administrative staff, support staff,* and *faculty.*

b Use the three simple random samples obtained in part **a** to generate three 90% confidence intervals for the differences in the proportions of employees within respective classifications who favor plan C in the coming year. For instance, the first such confidence interval should estimate the difference between the proportion of administrative employees who favor plan C and the proportion of the support staff who prefer plan C.

c Interpret each of your constructed confidence intervals. How might the benefits manager use the information you have derived from the three random samples of university employees?

31 Consider a random sample of 100 households from a middle-class neighborhood that was the recent focus of an economic development study conducted by the local government. Specifically, for each of the 100 randomly selected households, information was gathered on each of the following variables: family size, location of the household within the neighborhood, an indication of whether those surveyed owned or rented their home, gross annual income of the first household wage earner, gross annual income of the second household wage earner (if applicable), monthly home mortgage or rent payment, average monthly expenditure on utilities, and the total indebtedness (excluding the value of a home mortgage) of the household. The data are provided in the file P8_26.XLS.

Researchers would like to use the available sample information to discern whether home ownership rates vary by household *location*. For example, is there a nonzero difference between the proportions of individuals who own their homes (as opposed to those who rent their homes) in households located in the first (i.e., SW) and second (i.e., NW) sectors of this community? Use the given sample to construct a 99% confidence interval that estimates this potential difference in home ownership rates as well as those of other combinations of household locations. Interpret and summarize your results. (*Hint:* To be complete, you should construct and interpret a total of *six* 99% confidence intervals.) ∎

Controlling Confidence Interval Length

In this section we discuss the most widely used methods for achieving a confidence interval of a specified length. Confidence intervals are a function of three things: (1) the data in the sample, (2) the confidence level, and (3) the sample size(s). We briefly discuss the role of the first two in terms of their effect on confidence interval length and then discuss the effect of sample size in more depth.

The data in the sample directly affect the length of a confidence interval through their determination of the sample standard deviation(s). It might appear that because of *random* sampling, we have no control over the sample data, but this is not entirely true. In the case of surveys from a population, there are random sampling plans that can reduce the amount of variability in the sample and hence reduce confidence interval length. Indeed, this is the primary reason for using the stratified sampling procedure we discussed in the previous chapter.

Variance reduction is also possible in randomized experiments. There is a whole area of statistics called **experimental design** that suggests how to perform experiments to obtain the most information from a given amount of sample data. Although this is often aimed at scientific and medical research, it is also appropriate in business contexts. For example, the automobile dealership in Example 8.8 was wise to use *paired* husband–wife data rather two independent samples of men and women. The pairing leads to a potential reduction in variability and hence a narrower confidence interval.

The confidence level has a clear effect on confidence interval length. As the confidence level increases, the length of the confidence interval increases as well. For example, a 99% confidence interval is always longer than a 95% confidence interval, assuming that they are both based on the same data. However, we rarely use the confidence level to control the length of the confidence interval. Instead, we usually choose the confidence level based on convention, and 95% is by far the most commonly used value. For example, it is the default level built into most software packages, including the StatPro add-in. We can override this default (by choosing 90% or 99%, for example), but we don't usually do so simply to control the confidence interval length.

The most obvious way to control confidence interval length is to choose the sample size(s) appropriately. In the rest of this section, we will see how this can be done. For each parameter we discuss, our goal is to make the length of a confidence interval sufficiently narrow. Because each confidence interval we have discussed (with the exception of the confidence interval for a standard deviation) is a point estimate plus or minus some quantity, we will focus on the "plus or minus" part, called the *half-length* of the interval. (See Figure 8.27.) The usual approach is to specify the half-length B we would like to obtain. Then we find the sample size(s) necessary to achieve this half-length.

FIGURE 8.27 **Half-Length of a Confidence Interval**

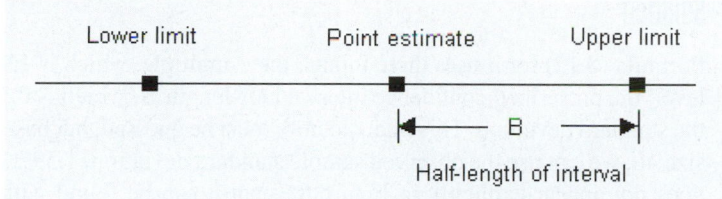

8.9.1 **Sample Size for Estimation of the Mean**

We begin with a confidence interval for the mean. From Section 8.3, we know that its formula is

$$\overline{X} \pm t\text{-multiple} \times s/\sqrt{n}$$

We want to make the half-length of this interval equal to some prescribed value B. For example, if we want the confidence interval to be of the form $\overline{X} \pm 5$, we use $B = 5$. Actually, we won't be able to achieve this half-length B exactly, but we will be able to approximate it.

By setting

$$t\text{-multiple} \times s/\sqrt{n} = B$$

and solving for n, we obtain

$$n = \left(\frac{t\text{-multiple} \times s}{B}\right)^2$$

Unfortunately, sample size selection must be done *before* a sample is observed. Therefore, no value of s is yet available. Also, because the t-multiple depends on n (through the degrees of freedom parameter), it is not clear which t-multiple to use.

The usual way out of this dilemma is to replace s by some reasonable estimate σ_{est} of the population standard deviation σ, and to replace the t-multiple with the corresponding z-multiple from the standard normal distribution. The latter replacement is justified because z-values and t-values are practically equal unless n is very small. The resulting sample size formula is then

$$n = \left(\frac{z\text{-multiple} \times \sigma_{\text{est}}}{B}\right)^2 \qquad \textbf{(8.12)}$$

This formula generally results in a noninteger value of n, in which case the practice is to round n *up* to the next larger integer.

The following example, an extension of Example 8.1, shows how to implement equation (8.12).

EXAMPLE 8.11

The fast-food manager in Example 8.1 surveyed 40 customers, each of whom rated a new sandwich on a 1 to 10 scale. Based on the data, a 95% confidence interval for the mean rating of all potential customers extended from 5.739 to 6.761, for a half-length of $(6.761 - 5.739)/2 = 0.511$. How large a sample would be needed to reduce this half-length to approximately 0.3?

Solution

Formula (8.12) for n uses three inputs: the z-multiple, which is 1.96 for a 95% confidence level; the prescribed confidence interval half-length B, which is 0.3; and an estimate σ_{est} of the standard deviation. This final quantity must be guessed, but based on the given sample of size 40, we can use the observed sample standard deviation, 1.597. (This standard deviation does not appear explicitly in Figure 8.3, but it can be found with the STDEV function.) Therefore, formula (8.12) yields

$$n = \left(\frac{1.96(1.597)}{0.3} \right)^2 = 108.86$$

which we round up to $n = 109$. The claim, then, is that if the manager surveys 109 customers, a 95% confidence interval will have approximate half-length 0.3. Its *exact* half-length will differ slightly from 0.3 because the sample standard deviation will not equal 1.597 exactly.

The StatPro add-in has a Sample Size Selection procedure that performs this sample size calculation. It can be used anywhere in a spreadsheet—the cursor doesn't have to be placed inside a data set. There doesn't even have to be a data set. Just select the StatPro/Statistical Inference/Sample Size Selection menu item, select the parameter to analyze (in this case the mean), and enter the requested values. In this case the requested values are the confidence level (95), the half-length of the interval (0.3), and an estimate of the standard deviation (1.597). This produces the message in Figure 8.28.

FIGURE 8.28 **Sample Size for a Mean**

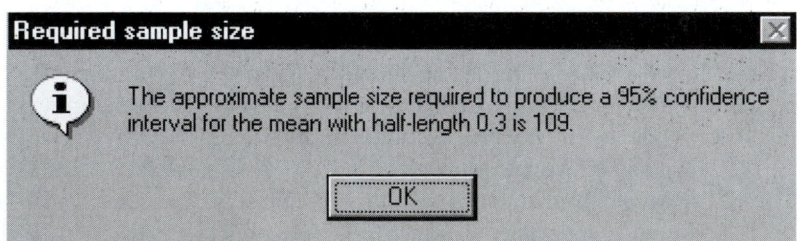

Required sample size

The approximate sample size required to produce a 95% confidence interval for the mean with half-length 0.3 is 109.

OK

What if the manager were at the planning stage and didn't have a "preliminary" sample of size 40? What standard deviation estimate should she use for σ_{est} (since the value 1.597 is no longer available)? This is not an easy question to answer, but because of the role of

σ_{est} in equation (8.12), it is crucial for the determination of n. The manager basically has three choices: (1) she can base her estimate of the standard deviation on historical data, assuming relevant historical data are available, (2) she can take a small preliminary sample (of size 20, say) just to get an estimate of the standard deviation, or (3) she can simply guess a value for the standard deviation. We do not recommend the third option, but there are cases where it is the only feasible option available. ■

We have demonstrated the use of equation (8.12) for a sample mean. In the same way, it can also be used in the paired-sample procedure. In this case the resulting value of n refers to the number of *pairs* that should be included in the sample, and σ_{est} refers to an estimate of the standard deviation of the *differences* (husband scores minus wife scores, for example).

8.9.2 Sample Size for Estimation of Other Parameters

The sample-size analysis for the mean carries over with very few changes to other parameters. We discuss three other parameters in this section: a proportion, the difference between two means, and the difference between two proportions. In each case the required confidence interval can be obtained by setting the half-length equal to a prescribed value B and solving for n.

There are two points worth mentioning. First, the confidence interval for the difference between means uses a t-multiple. As we did for the mean, we replace this by a z-multiple, which is perfectly acceptable in most situations. Second, the confidence intervals for differences between means or proportions require *two* sample sizes, one for each sample. The formulas below assume that each sample uses the *same* sample size, denoted by n.

The sample size formula for a proportion p is

$$n = \left(\frac{z\text{-multiple}}{B}\right)^2 p_{est}(1 - p_{est}) \tag{8.13}$$

Here, p_{est} is an estimate of the population proportion p. A *conservative* value of n can be obtained by using $p_{est} = 0.5$. It is conservative in the sense that the sample size obtained by using $p_{est} = 0.5$ guarantees a confidence interval half-length no greater than B, regardless of the true value of p.

The sample size formula for the difference between means is

$$n = 2\left(\frac{z\text{-multiple} \times \sigma_{est}}{B}\right)^2 \tag{8.14}$$

Here, σ_{est} is an estimate of the standard deviation of *each* population, where we again make the assumption (as in Section 8.7.1) that the two populations have a *common* standard deviation σ.

Finally, the sample size formula for the difference between proportions is

$$n = \left(\frac{z\text{-multiple}}{B}\right)^2 \left[p_{1est}(1 - p_{1est}) + p_{2est}(1 - p_{2est})\right] \tag{8.15}$$

Here, p_{1est} and p_{2est} are estimates of the two unknown population proportions p_1 and p_2. As in the case of a single proportion, we obtain a conservative value of n by using the estimates $p_{1est} = p_{2est} = 0.5$.

EXAMPLE 8.12

Suppose that the fast-food manager from the previous example wants to estimate the proportion of customers who have tried its new sandwich. It wants a 90% confidence interval for this proportion to have half-length 0.05. For example, if the sample proportion turns out to be 0.42, then a 90% confidence interval should be (approximately) 0.42 ± 0.05. How many customers need to be surveyed?

Solution

If the manager has "no idea" what the proportion is, then she can use $p_{est} = 0.5$ in equation (8.13) to obtain a conservative value of n. The appropriate z-multiple is now 1.645 because this value cuts off probability 0.05 in each tail of the standard normal distribution. Therefore, the required value of n is

$$n = \left(\frac{1.645}{0.05}\right)^2 (0.5)(1 - 0.5) \simeq 271$$

On the other hand, if the manager is "pretty sure" that the proportion who have tried the new sandwich is around 0.3, she can use $p_{est} = 0.3$ instead. This time we use the StatPro add-in and enter the values 90 (confidence level), 0.05 (desired half-length), and 0.3 (estimate of the proportion). We receive the message in Figure 8.29.

FIGURE 8.29   **Sample Size for a Proportion**

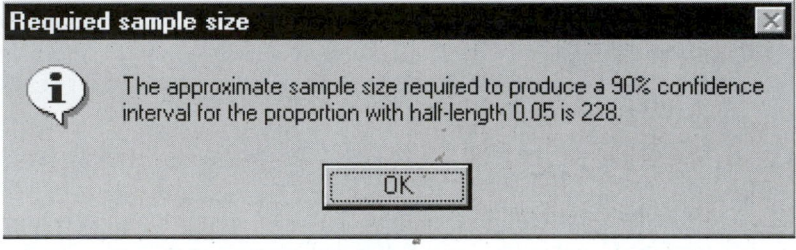

These calculations indicate that if we have more specific information about the unknown proportion, we can get by with a smaller sample size—in this case 228 rather than 271. Also, note that we selected a 90% confidence level rather than the usual 95% level. There is a trade-off here. Using 90% rather than 95% obviously gives us less confidence in the result, but it requires a smaller sample size. You can check that the required sample sizes for a 95% confidence level increase from 271 and 228 to 385 and 323. ■

EXAMPLE 8.13

A computer company has a customer service center that responds to customers' questions and complaints. The center employs two types of people: those who have had a recent course in dealing with customers (but little actual experience) and those with a lot of experience dealing with customers (but no formal course). The company wants to estimate the difference between these two types of employees in the average number of customer complaints regarding poor service in the last 6 months. The company plans to obtain information on a randomly selected sample of each type of employee, using equal sample sizes. How many employees should be in each sample to achieve a 95% confidence interval with approximate half-length 2?

Solution

We use equation (8.14) with z-multiple 1.96 and $B = 2$. However, this formula also requires a value for σ_{est}, an estimate of the (assumed) common standard deviation for each group of employees, and there is no obvious estimate available. The manager might use the following argument. Based on a brief look at complaint data, he believes that some employees receive as few as 6 complaints over a 6-month period, while others receive as many as 36 (about 6 per month). Now he can estimate σ_{est} by arguing that all observations are likely to be within three standard deviations of the mean, so that the range of data—minimum to maximum—is about six standard deviations. Therefore, he sets

$$6\sigma_{est} = 36 - 6 = 30$$

and obtains $\sigma_{est} = 5$. Using this value in equation (8.14), the required sample size is

$$n = 2\left(\frac{1.96(5)}{2}\right)^2 \simeq 49$$

The StatPro Sample Size Selection procedure confirms this value. Here, we enter the values 95 (confidence level), 2 (desired half-length), and 5 (estimated standard deviation). We receive message in Figure 8.30.

FIGURE 8.30   **Sample Size for a Difference Between Means**

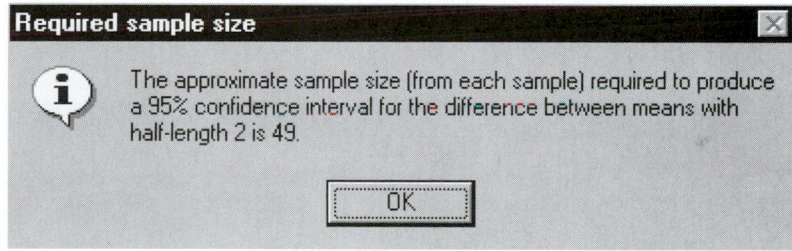

Some analysts prefer the estimate

$$4\sigma_{est} = 36 - 6 = 30$$

that is, $\sigma_{est} = 7.5$, arguing that the quoted range (6 to 36) might not include "extreme" values and hence might extend to only *two* standard deviations on either side of the mean. By using this estimate of the standard deviation, you can check that the required sample size increases from 49 to 109. The important point here is that the estimate of the standard deviation can have a dramatic effect on the required sample size. (And don't forget that this size sample must be taken from *each* group of employees.) ■

The final example in this section illustrates what can happen when we ask for extremely accurate confidence intervals.

EXAMPLE 8.14

A manufacturing company has two plants that produce identical products. The production supervisor wants to know how much the proportion of out-of-spec products differs across the two plants. He suspects that the proportion of out-of-spec products in each plant is in the range of 3% to 5%, and he wants a 99% confidence interval to have approximate half-length 0.005 (or 0.5%). How many items should he sample from each plant?

Solution

Here we use equation (8.15) with z-multiple 2.576 (the value that cuts off probability .005 in each tail of the standard normal distribution), $B = 0.005$, and $p_{1est} = p_{2est} = 0.05$. The reasoning for the latter is that the supervisor believes each proportion is around 3% to 5%, and we obtain the most conservative (largest) sample size by using the larger 5% figure. Then the required sample size is

$$n = \left(\frac{2.576}{0.005}\right)^2 [0.05(0.95) + 0.05(0.95)] \simeq 25,213$$

This sample size (from *each* sample) is almost certainly prohibitive, so the supervisor decides he must lower his goals. One way is to decrease the confidence level, say, from 99% to 95%. Another way is to increase the desired half-length from 0.005 to, say, 0.025. We implemented both of these changes in the StatPro Sample Size Selection procedure by entering the values 95 (confidence level), 0.025 (desired half-length), and 0.05 and 0.05 (estimates of the proportions). The resulting message is in Figure 8.31. Even now the required sample size is 584. Obviously, narrow confidence intervals for differences between proportions can require very large sample sizes.

FIGURE 8.31   **Sample Size for a Difference Between Proportions**

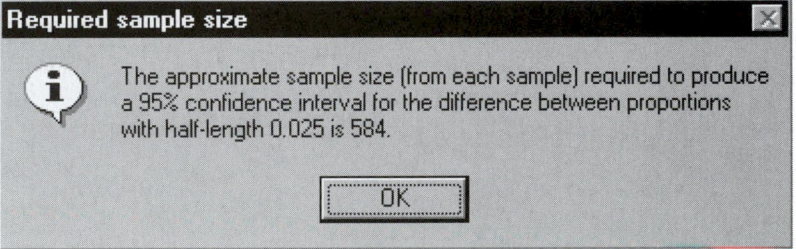

PROBLEMS

Level A

32   Elected officials in a small Florida town are preparing the annual budget for their community. Specifically, they would like to estimate how much their constituents living in this town are typically paying each year in real estate taxes. Given that there are over 3000 homeowners in this small community, officials have decided to sample a representative subset of taxpayers and thoroughly study their tax payments. The latest frame of homeowners is given in the file P7_49.XLS.

a What sample size would be required to generate a 95% confidence interval for the community's mean annual real estate tax payment with a half-length of $100? Assume that the best estimate of the population standard deviation σ is $535.

b Choose a simple random sample of the size found in part **a** from the frame in the file P7_49.XLS. Construct a 95% confidence interval for the population mean. What is the half-length of this interval estimate? Is the half-length consistent with your expectations? Explain.

c Now suppose that elected officials want to construct a 95% confidence interval with a half-length of $75. What sample size would be required to achieve this objective? Again, assume that the best estimate of the population standard deviation σ is $535. Explain the difference between your result here and the result you obtained in part **a**.

33 You have been assigned to determine whether more people prefer Coke or Pepsi. Assume that roughly half the population prefers Coke and half prefers Pepsi. How large a sample would you need to take to ensure that you could estimate, with 95% confidence, the fraction of people preferring Coke within 2% of the actual value?

34 You are trying to estimate the average amount a family spends on food during a year. In the past the standard deviation of the amount a family has spent on food during a year has been approximately $1000. If you want to be 99% sure that you have estimated average family food expenditures within $50, how many families do you need to survey?

35 In past years, approximately 20% of all U.S. families purchased potato chips at least once a month. We are interested in determining the fraction of all U.S. families that currently purchase potato chips at least once a month. How many families must we survey if we want to be 99% sure that our estimate of the fraction of U.S. families currently purchasing potato chips at least once is month is accurate within 2%?

36 Continuing Problem 32, suppose that elected officials in this community would like to estimate the proportion of taxpayers whose annual real estate tax payments exceed $2000.

a What sample size would be required to generate a 99% confidence interval for this proportion with a half-length of 0.10? Assume for now that the relevant population proportion p is close to 0.50.

b Assume now that officials discover old tax records that suggest that approximately 30% of all property owners in this community pay more than $2000 annually in real estate taxes. What sample size would now be required to generate a 99% confidence interval for this proportion with a half-length of 0.10?

c Explain the difference in your answers to parts **a** and **b**.

d Choose a simple random sample of the size found in part **b** from the frame given in the file P7_49.XLS. Use this sample to evaluate the revised assumption that approximately 30% of all property owners in this community pay more than $2000 annually in real estate taxes.

Level B

37 Continuing the previous problem, suppose that elected officials in this town would like to estimate the difference between the proportions, labeled p_2 and p_6, of taxpayers living in the *second* neighborhood whose annual real estate tax payments exceed $2000 and those living in the *sixth* neighborhood whose annual real estate tax payments exceed $2000.

a What sample size (randomly selected from a frame of all taxpayers residing in each neighborhood) would be required to generate a 90% confidence interval for this difference between proportions with a half-length of 0.10? Assume for now that p_2 and p_6 are both close to 0.5.

b Choose a simple random sample of the size found in part **a** from the frame of all taxpayers residing in the second neighborhood. Also, choose a simple random sample of the size found in part **a** from the frame of all taxpayers residing in the sixth neighborhood. Use these samples to evaluate the assumption that p_2 and p_6 are both close to 0.5.

c Use the samples obtained in part **b** to generate revised estimates of p_2 and p_6. Repeat part **a** with these revised estimates of p_2 and p_6. Explain the difference between your original and revised responses to the question posed in part **a**. ∎

Conclusion

When we want to estimate a population parameter from sample data, one of the most useful ways to do so is to report a point estimate and a corresponding confidence interval. This confidence interval gives us a quick sense of where the true parameter lies. It essentially quantifies the amount of uncertainty in the point estimate. Obviously, we prefer narrow confidence intervals. We have seen that the length of a confidence interval is determined by the variability in the data, the confidence level, usually set at 95%, and the sample size(s). We have also seen how sample size formulas can be used at the planning stage to achieve confidence intervals that are sufficiently narrow. Finally, we have seen how confidence intervals can be calculated from mathematical formulas or with statistical software such as the StatPro add-in. The advantage of software is that it enables us to concentrate on the important issues for business applications: which confidence intervals are appropriate, how to interpret them, and how to control their length.

PROBLEMS

Level A

38   A sample of 9 quality control managers with over 20 years experience have an average salary of $68,000 and a sample standard deviation of $19,000.

   a   You can be 95% confident that the mean salary for all quality managers with at least 20 years of experience is between what two numbers? What assumption are you making about the distribution of salaries?

   b   What size sample would be needed to ensure that we could estimate the true mean salary of all quality managers with more than 20 years of experience and have only 1 chance in 100 of being off by more than $500?

39   According to *The New York Times*, in October 1996, a random sample of 1281 registered voters showed that 720 preferred Clinton and 561 preferred Dole.

   a   Based on these data, you can be 95% confident that the actual percentage of voters preferring Clinton to Dole is between what two values?

   b   If we wanted to be 99% sure that we could estimate the actual percentage preferring Clinton to Dole within 1%, how large a sample would we need?

40   To illustrate the meaning of a confidence interval for a proportion, suppose that 60% of all voters actually prefer Clinton to Dole. Use simulation to construct 50 samples of 20 voters each. Use each sample to construct a 90% confidence interval for the true proportion of voters who prefer Clinton to Dole. What percentage of your confidence intervals contain the true value of 0.60? How does this compare to what you would expect?

41   The widths of 100 elevator rails have been measured. The sample mean and standard deviation of the elevator rails are 2.05 inches and 0.01 inch.

   a   Construct a 95% confidence interval for the average width of an elevator rail. Do you need to assume that the width of elevator rails follows a normal distribution?

   b   How large a sample of elevator rails would we have to measure to ensure that we could estimate, with 95% confidence, the average diameter of an elevator rail within 0.01 inch?

42   We want to determine the percentage of Fortune 500 CEOs who think Indiana University deserves its current *Business Week* rating. We mail a questionnaire to all 500 CEOs and 100 respond. Exactly half of the respondents believe IU does deserve its ranking.

   a   Construct a 99% confidence interval for the fraction of Fortune 500 CEOs who believe IU deserves its ranking.

b Suppose again that we want to estimate the fraction of Fortune 500 CEOs who believe IU deserves its ranking. Our goal is to have only a 5% chance of having our estimate be in error by more than 0.02. What size sample do we need to take?

43 The SEC requires companies to file annual reports concerning their financial status. It is impossible to audit every account receivable. Suppose we audit a random sample of 49 accounts receivable invoices and find a sample average of $128 and a sample standard deviation of $53.

a Find a 99% confidence interval for the mean size of an accounts receivable invoice. Does your answer require that the sizes of the accounts receivable invoices follow a normal distribution?

b How large a sample do we need if we want to be 99% sure that we can estimate the mean invoice size within $5?

44 An opinion poll surveyed 900 people and reported that 52% believe the White House broke campaign financing laws.

a Compute a 95% confidence interval for the true proportion of people who believe the White House broke campaign financing laws. Does the result of the poll convince you that a *majority* of citizens favor that viewpoint?

b Suppose 10,000 (not 900) people are surveyed and 52% believe that the White House broke campaign financing laws. Would you now be convinced that a majority of citizens believe the White House broke campaign financing laws? Why might your answer be different than in part **a**?

c How many people would you have to survey to be 99% confident that you can estimate the fraction of people who believe the White House has broken a campaign financing law to within 1%?

45 Sometimes you are given summary data, not the original data, and are asked for a confidence interval. In this case it is probably easier to calculate it by hand calculator. Try it in the following examples.

a A sample of 35 jazz CD recordings has been examined. The average playing time of these 35 recordings is 54.7 minutes, and the standard deviation is 6.8 minutes. Find a 95% confidence interval for the mean playing time of all jazz recordings in the population from which this was a sample.

b You are told that a random sample of 130 people from Indiana has been given cholesterol tests, and 47 of these people had levels over the "safe" count of 180. Find a 95% confidence interval for the population proportion of people with cholesterol levels over 180.

Level B

46 We know that IQs are normally distributed with a mean of 100 and standard deviation of 15. Suppose we did not know this, and we took 100 random samples of 4 people's IQs and, for each sample, constructed a 95% confidence interval for the mean IQ. We expect that approximately 95 of these intervals would contain the true mean IQ (100) and approximately 5 of these intervals would not contain the true mean. Use simulation in Excel to see whether this is the case.

47 In Section 8.9, we gave a sample size formula for confidence interval estimation of a mean. If the confidence level is 95%, then (because the z-multiple is about 2), this formula is essentially

$$n = \frac{4\sigma^2}{B^2}$$

However, this formula is based on the assumption that the sample size n will be small relative to the population size N. If this is *not* the case, the appropriate formula is

$$n = \frac{N\sigma^2}{\sigma^2 + (N - 1)B^2/4}$$

Now suppose we want to find a 95% confidence interval for a population mean. Based on preliminary (or historical) data, we believe that the population standard deviation is approximately 15. We want the confidence interval to have length 4. That is, we want the confidence interval to be of the form $\overline{X} \pm 2$. What sample size is required if $N = 400$; if

$N = 800$; if $N = 10,000$; if $N = 100,000,000$? How would you summarize these findings in words?

48 The Ritter Manufacturing Company has kept track of machine hours and overhead costs at its main manufacturing plant for the past 52 weeks. The data appear in the file P8_48.XLS. Ritter has studied these data to understand the relationship between machine hours and overhead costs. Although the relationship is far from perfect, Ritter believes it can obtain a fairly accurate prediction of overhead costs from machine hours through the equation

$$\text{Estimated Overhead} = 746.5 + 3.32\text{MachHrs}$$

By substituting any observed value of MachHrs into this equation, Ritter obtains an estimated value of Overhead, which is always somewhat different from the true value of Overhead. The difference is called the prediction error.

a Find a 95% confidence interval for the mean prediction error. Do the same for the *absolute* prediction error. (*Hint*: For example, the prediction error in week 1, actual overhead minus predicted overhead, is −94.5. The absolute prediction error is the absolute value, 94.5.)

b A close examination of the data suggests that week 45 is a possible outlier. Illustrate this by creating a boxplot of the prediction errors. In what sense would you say week 45 is an outlier? See whether week 45 has much effect on the confidence intervals from part **a** by recalculating these confidence intervals, this time with week 45 deleted. Discuss your findings briefly.

Problems 49–58 are related to the data in the file P8_49.XLS. This file contains data on 400 customers' orders from ElecMart, a company that sells electronic appliances by mail order. The variables are:

- Date: date of order
- Day: day (Monday through Sunday) of order
- Time: time of day (morning, afternoon, evening) order was placed
- Region: region of customer (Northeast, Midwest, South, West) customer is from
- CardType: whether order is paid for by ElecMart's own credit card or another type of credit card
- Gender: gender of customer
- BuyCategory: level of customer's previous order volume from ElecMart (high, medium, low)
- ItemsOrdered: number of items ordered on this order
- TotalCost: total cost of this order
- HighItem: cost of most expensive item on this order

You can consider the data as a random sample from all of ElecMart's orders.

49 Find a 95% confidence interval for the mean total cost of all customer orders. Then do this separately for each of the four regions. Create side-by-side boxplots of total cost for the four regions. Does the positive skewness in these boxplots invalidate the confidence interval procedure used?

50 Find a 95% confidence interval for the proportion of all customers whose order is for more than $100. Then do this separately for each of three times of day.

51 Find a 95% confidence interval for the proportion of all customers whose orders contain at least 3 items *and* cost at least $100 total.

52 Find a 95% confidence interval for the difference between the mean amount of the highest-cost item purchased for the High customer category and the similar mean for the Medium customer category. Do the same for the difference between the Medium and Low customer categories. Because of the way these customer categories are defined, you would probably expect these mean differences to be positive. Is this what the data indicate?

53 Find a 95% confidence interval for the difference between the proportion of customers who are female and order during the morning or afternoon and the proportion of customers who are male and order during these times. Do the same for the evening times.

54 Find a 95% confidence interval for the difference between the proportion of female customers who order during the evening and the proportion of male customers who order during the evening. Explain how this is different from the question in Problem 53.

55 Find a 95% confidence interval for the difference between the mean total order cost for West customers and Northeast customers. Do the same for the other combinations: West versus Midwest, West versus South, Northeast versus South, Northeast versus Midwest, and South versus Midwest.

56 Find a 95% confidence interval for the difference between the mean cost per item for female orders and the similar mean for males.

57 Let $p_{E,F}$ be the proportion of female orders that are paid for with the ElecMart credit card, and let $p_{E,M}$ be the similar proportion for male orders.

    a Find a 95% confidence interval for $p_{E,F}$; for $p_{E,M}$; for the difference $p_{E,F} - p_{E,M}$.

    b Let $p_{E,F,Wd}$ be the proportion of female orders on weekdays that are paid for with the ElecMart credit card, and let $p_{E,F,We}$ be the similar proportion for weekends. Define $p_{E,M,Wd}$ and $p_{E,M,We}$ similarly for males. Find a 95% confidence interval for the difference $(p_{E,F,Wd} - p_{E,M,Wd}) - (p_{E,F,We} - p_{E,M,We})$. Interpret this difference in words. Might it be of any interest to ElecMart?

58 Suppose these 400 orders are a sample of the 4295 orders made during this time period, and suppose 2531 of these orders were placed by females. Find a 95% confidence interval for the total paid for all 4295 orders. Do the same for all 2531 orders placed by females. Do the same for all 1764 orders placed by males.

      Problems 59–64 are related to the data in the file P8_59.XLS. This file contains data on 91 billings from Rebco, a company that sells plumbing supplies to retailers. The three variables in the file are:

    ■ CustSize: small, medium, or large, depending on the volume of business the customer does with Rebco

    ■ Days: number of days from when Rebco billed the customer until Rebco got paid

    ■ Amount: amount of the bill

    You can consider the data as a random sample from all of Rebco's billings.

59 Find a 95% confidence interval for the mean amount of all Rebco's bills. Do the same for each customer size separately.

60 Find a 95% confidence interval for the mean number of days it takes Rebco's customers (as a combined group) to pay their bills. Do the same for each customer size separately. Create a boxplot for the variable Days, based on all 91 billings. Also, create side-by-side boxplots for Days for the three separate customer sizes. Do any of these suggest problems with the validity of the confidence intervals?

61 Find a 95% confidence interval for the proportion of all large customers who pay bills of at least $1000 at least 15 days after they are billed.

62 Find a 95% confidence interval for the proportion of all bills paid within 15 days. Find a 95% confidence interval for the difference between the proportion of large customers who pay within 15 days and the similar proportion of medium-sized customers. Find a 95% confidence interval for the difference between the proportion of medium-sized customers who pay within 15 days and the similar proportion of small customers.

63 Suppose a bill is considered late if it is paid after 20 days. In this case its "lateness" is the number of days over 20. For example, a bill paid 23 days after billing has a lateness of 3, whereas a bill paid 18 days after billing has a lateness of 0. Find a 95% confidence interval for the mean amount of lateness for all customers. Find similar confidence intervals for each customer size separately.

64 Suppose Rebco can earn interest at the rate of 0.011% daily on excess cash. The company realizes that it could earn extra interest if its customers would pay their bills more promptly.

    a Find a 95% confidence interval for the mean amount of interest it could gain if each of its customers would pay exactly 1 day more promptly. Find similar confidence intervals for each customer class separately.

    b Suppose these 91 billings represent a random sample of the 965 billings Rebco generates during the year. Find a 95% confidence interval for the total amount of extra interest it could gain by getting each of these 965 billings to be paid 2 days more promptly.

65 The file P8_65.XLS contains data on the first 100 customers who entered a two-teller bank on Friday. All variables in this file are times, measured in minutes. These variables are:

- ArriveTime: arrival time of customer (measured from the time the bank's doors opened)
- ServiceTime: amount of time customer spent with a teller
- WaitTime: amount of time customer spent waiting in line
- BankTime: amount of time customer spent in the bank (waiting plus in service)

a Find a 95% confidence interval for the mean amount of time a customer spends in service with a teller.

b The bank is most interested in mean waiting times because customers get upset when they have to spend a lot of time waiting in line. Use the usual procedure to calculate a 95% confidence interval for the mean waiting time per customer.

c Your answer in part **b** is not valid! (It is much too narrow. It makes you believe you have a much more accurate estimate of the mean waiting time than you really have.) We made two implicit assumptions when we stated the confidence interval procedure for a mean: (1) The individual observations all come from the same distribution, and (2) the individual observations are probabilistically independent. Why are both of these, particularly (2), violated for the customer waiting times? [*Hint*: For (1), how do the first few customers differ from "typical" customers? For (2), if you are behind someone in line who has to wait a long time, what about your own waiting time?]

d Following up on (2) of part **c**, you might expect waiting times of successive customers to be "autocorrelated," that is, correlated with each other. Large waiting times tend to be followed by large waiting times, and small by small. Check this with StatPro's Autocorrelation procedure, under the StatPro/Summary Stats/Autocorrelations menu item. An autocorrelation of a certain lag, say, lag 2, is the correlation in waiting times between a customer and the customer two behind her. Do these successive waiting times appear to be autocorrelated? (A *valid* confidence interval for the mean waiting time takes autocorrelations into account—but it is considerably more difficult to calculate.)

Problems 66–68 are related to the data in the file P8_66.XLS. The SoftBus Company sells PC equipment and customized software to small companies to help them manage their day-to-day business activities. Although SoftBus spends time with all customers to understand their needs, the customers are eventually on their own to use the equipment and software intelligently. To understand its customers better, SoftBus recently sent questionnaires to a large number of prospective customers. Key personnel—those who would be using the software—were asked to fill out the questionnaire. SoftBus received 82 usable responses, as shown in the file. The variables are:

- Gender: gender of key person
- YrsExper: years of experience of key person with this company
- Education: level of education of key person
- OwnPC: whether key person owns his or her own home PC
- PCKnowledge: key person's self-reported level of computer knowledge

You can assume that these employees represent a random sample of all of SoftBus's prospective customers.

66 Construct a histogram of the PCKnowledge variable. (Since there are only five possible responses (1–5), this histogram should have only five bars.) Repeat this separately for those who own a PC and those who do not. Then find a 95% confidence interval for the mean value of PCKnowledge for all of SoftBus's prospective customers; of all its prospective customers who own PCs; of all its prospective customers who do not own PCs. The PCKnowledge variable obviously can't be exactly normally distributed because it has only five possible values. Do you think this invalidates the confidence intervals?

67 SoftBus believes it can afford to spend much less time with customers who own PCs and score at least 4 on PCKnowledge. We'll call these the "PC-savvy" customers. On the other hand, SoftBus believes it will have to spend a lot of time with customers who do not own a PC and score 2 or less on PCKnowledge. We'll call these the "PC-illiterate" customers.

a Find a 95% confidence interval for the proportion of all prospective customers who are PC-savvy. Find a similar interval for the proportion who are PC-illiterate.

b Repeat part **a** twice, once for the subpopulation of customers who have at least 12 years of experience, and once for the subpopulation who have less than 12 years of experience.

c Again repeat part **a** twice, once for the subpopulation of customers who have no more than a high school diploma, and once for the subpopulation who have more than a high school diploma.

d Find a 95% confidence interval for the difference between the proportion of all customers with some college education who are PC-savvy and the similar proportion of all customers with no college education. Repeat this, substituting "PC-savvy" with "PC-illiterate."

e Discuss any insights you gain from parts **a–c** that might be of interest to SoftBus.

68 Following up on the previous problem, SoftBus believes its profit from each prospective customer depends on the customer's level of PC knowledge. It divides the customers into three classes: PC-savvy, PC-illiterate, and all others (where the first two classes are as defined in the previous problem). As a rough guide, SoftBus figures it can gain profit P_1 from each PC-savvy customer, profit P_3 from each PC-illiterate company, and profit P_2 from each of the others.

a What values of P_1, P_2, and P_3 seem "reasonable"? For example, would you expect $P_1 < P_2 < P_3$ or the opposite?

b Using any reasonable values for P_1, P_2, and P_3, find a 95% confidence interval for the mean profit per customer that SoftBus can expect to obtain.

Problems 69–72 are related to the data in the file P8_69.XLS. The Comfy Company sells medium-priced patio furniture through a mail-order catalog. It has operated primarily in the East but is now expanding to the Southwest. To get off to a good start, it plans to send potential customers a catalog with a discount coupon. However, Comfy is not sure how large a discount is needed to entice customers to buy. It experiments by sending catalogs to selected residents in six cities. Tucson and San Diego receive coupons for 5% off any furniture within the next 2 months, Phoenix and Santa Fe receive coupons for 10% off, and Riverside and Albuquerque receive coupons for 15% off. The variables are:

- City: city where customer lives
- Discount: discount offered (5%, 10%, 15%)
- ItemsPurch: number of items purchased with the discount
- TotPaid: total paid (after subtracting the discount) for the items

69 Find a 95% confidence interval for the proportion of customers who will purchase at least one item if they receive a coupon for 5% off. Repeat for 10% off; for 15% off.

70 Find a 95% confidence interval for the proportion of customers who will purchase at least one item and pay at least $500 total if they receive a coupon for 5% off. Repeat for 10% off; for 15% off.

71 Comfy wonders whether the customers who receive larger discounts are buying more expensive items. Recalling that the value in the TotPaid column is *after* the discount, find a 95% confidence interval for the difference between the mean *original price per item* for customers who purchase something with the 5% coupon and the similar mean for customers who purchase something with the 10% coupon. Repeat with 5% and 10% replaced by 10% and 15%. What can you conclude?

72 Comfy wonders whether there are differences across cities that receive the *same* discount.

a Find a 95% confidence interval for the difference between the mean amount spent in Tucson and the similar mean in San Diego. (These means should include the "0 purchases.") Repeat this for the difference between Phoenix and Santa Fe; between Riverside and Albuquerque. Does city appear to make a difference?

b Repeat part **a**, but instead of analyzing differences between means, analyze differences between proportions of customers who purchase something. Does city appear to make a difference?

Problems 73–76 are related to the data in the files P8_73a.XLS and P8_73b.XLS. The Niyaki Company sells VCRs through a number of retail stores. On one popular model, there is a standard warranty that covers parts for the first 6 months and labor for the first year. Customers are always asked whether they wish to purchase an extended service plan for $25 that extends the original warranty 2 more years—that is, to 30 months on parts and 36 months on service. To get a better understanding of warranty costs, the company has gathered data on 70 VCRs purchased. The variables in the P8_73a.XLS file are:

- ExtendedPlan: whether customer purchased the extended service plan

- FailureTime: time (months) until the *first* failure of the unit
- PartsCost: cost of parts to repair the unit
- LaborCost: cost of labor to repair the unit

The latter two costs are tracked only for repairs covered by warranty. [Otherwise, the customer bears the cost(s).] The variables in the P8_73b.XLS file are similar, but they also include information of *subsequent* failures of the units (that occur during the warranty period).

73 Construct a histogram of the time until first failure for this type of VCR. Then find a 95% confidence interval for the mean time until failure for this type of VCR. Does the shape of the histogram invalidate the confidence interval? Why or why not?

74 Find a 95% confidence interval for the proportion of customers who purchase the extended service plan. Find a 95% confidence interval for the proportion of all customers who would benefit by purchasing the extended service plan.

75 Find a 95% confidence interval for Niyaki's mean net warranty cost per unit sold (net of the $25 paid for the plan for those who purchase it). You can assume that this mean is for the *first* failure only; subsequent failures of the same units are ignored here.

76 This problem follows up on the previous two problems with the data in the P8_73b.XLS file. Here Niyaki did more investigation on the same 70 customers. It tracked subsequent failures and costs (if any) that occurred within the warranty period. (Note that only two customers had three failures within the warranty period, and parts weren't covered for either on the third failure. Also, no one had more than three failures within the warranty period.)

a With these data, find the confidence intervals requested in the previous two problems.

b Suppose that Niyaki sold this VCR model to 12,450 customers during the year. Find a 95% confidence interval for its total net cost due to warranties from all of these sales. ■

8.1   Harrigan University Admissions

Harrigan University is a liberal arts university in the Midwest that attempts to attract the highest-quality students, especially from its region of the country. It has gathered data on 178 applicants who were accepted by Harrigan (a random sample from all acceptable applicants over the past several years). The data are in the file HARRIGAN.XLS. The variables are:

- Accepted: whether the applicant accepts Harrigan's offer to enroll
- MainRival: whether the applicant enrolls at Harrigan's main rival university
- HSClubs: number of high school clubs applicant served as an officer
- HSSports: number of varsity letters applicant earned
- HSGPA: applicant's high school GPA
- HSPctile: applicant's percentile (in terms of GPA) in his or her graduating class
- HSSize: number of students in applicant's graduating class
- SAT: applicant's combined SAT score
- CombinedScore: a combined score for the applicant used by Harrigan to rank applicants

The derivation of the combined score is a closely kept secret by Harrigan, but it is basically a weighted average of the various components of high school performance and SAT. Harrigan is concerned that it is not getting enough of the best students, and worse yet, it is concerned that many of these best students are going to Harrigan's main rival. Solve the following problems and then, based on your analysis, comment on whether Harrigan appears to have a legitimate concern.

1   Find a 95% confidence interval for the proportion of all acceptable applicants who accept Harrigan's invitation to enroll. Do the same for all acceptable applicants with a combined score less than 330; with a combined score between 330 and 375; with a combined score greater than 375. (Note that 330 and 375 are approximately the first and third quartiles of the Score variable.)

2   Find a 95% confidence interval for the proportion of all acceptable students with a combined score less than the median (356) who choose Harrigan's rival over Harrigan. Do the same for those with a combined score greater than the median.

3   Find 95% confidence intervals for the mean combined score, the mean high school GPA, and the mean SAT score of all acceptable students who accept Harrigan's invitation to enroll. Do the same for all acceptable students who choose to enroll elsewhere. Then find 95% confidence intervals for the differences between these means, where each difference is a mean for students enrolling at Harrigan minus the similar mean for students enrolling elsewhere.

4   Harrigan is interested (as are most schools) in getting students who are involved in extracurricular activities (clubs and sports). Does it appear to be doing so? Find a 95% confidence interval for the proportion of all students who decide to enroll at Harrigan who have been officers of at least two clubs. Find a similar confidence interval for those who have earned at least four varsity letters in sports.

5   The combined score Harrigan calculates for each student gives some advantage to students who rank highly in a *large* high school relative to those who rank highly in a

small high school. Therefore, Harrigan wonders whether it is relatively more successful in attracting students from large high schools than from small high schools. Develop one or more confidence intervals for relevant parameters to shed some light on this issue.

8.2 Employee Retention at D&Y

Demand for systems analysts in the consulting industry is greater than ever. Graduates with a combination of business and computer knowledge—some even from liberal arts programs—are getting great offers from consulting companies. Once these people are hired, they frequently switch from one company to another as competing companies lure them away with even better offers. One consulting company, D&Y, has collected data on a sample of systems analysts they hired with an undergraduate degree several years ago. The data are in the file D&Y.XLS. The variables are:

- StartSal: employee's starting salary at D&Y
- OnRoadPct: percentage of time employee has spent on the road with clients
- StateU: whether the employee graduated from State University (D&Y's principal source of recruits)
- CISDegree: whether the employee majored in Computer Information Systems (CIS) or a similar computer-related area
- Stayed3Yrs: whether the employee stayed at least 3 years with D&Y
- Tenure: tenure of employee at D&Y (months) if he or she moved before 3 years

D&Y is trying to learn everything it can about retention of these valuable employees. You can help by solving the following problems and then, based on your analysis, presenting a report to D&Y.

1 Although starting salaries are in a fairly narrow band, D&Y wonders whether they have anything to do with retention.

   a Find a 95% confidence interval for the mean starting salary of all employees who stay at least 3 years with D&Y. Do the same for those who leave before 3 years. Then find a 95% confidence interval for the difference between these means.

   b Among all employees whose starting salary is above the median ($37,750), find a 95% confidence interval for the proportion who stay with D&Y for at least 3 years. Do the same for the employees with starting salaries above the median. Then find a 95% confidence interval for the difference between these proportions.

2 D&Y wonders whether the percentage of time on the road might influence who stays and who leaves. Repeat the previous problem, but now do the analysis in terms of percentage of time on the road rather than starting salary. (The median percentage of time on the road is 54%.)

3 Find a 95% confidence interval for the mean tenure (in months) of all employees who leave D&Y within 3 years of being hired. Why is it not possible with the given data to find a confidence interval for the mean tenure at D&Y among *all* systems analysts hired by D&Y?

4   State University's students, particularly those in its nationally acclaimed CIS area, have traditionally been among the best of D&Y's recruits. But are they relatively hard to retain? Find one or more relevant confidence intervals to help you make an argument one way or the other.

8.3   Delivery Times at SnowPea Restaurant

The SnowPea Restaurant is a Chinese carryout/delivery restaurant. Most of SnowPea's deliveries are within a 10-mile radius, but it occasionally delivers to customers more than 10 miles away. SnowPea employs a number of delivery people, four of whom are relatively new hires. The restaurant has recently been receiving customer complaints about excessively long delivery times. Therefore, SnowPea has collected data on a random sample of deliveries by its four new delivery people during the peak dinner time. The data are in the file SNOWPEA.XLS. The variables are:

■   Deliverer: which person made the delivery

■   PrepTime: time from when order was placed until delivery person started driving it to the customer

■   TravelTime: time to drive from SnowPea to customer

■   Distance: distance (miles) from SnowPea to customer

Solve the following problems and then, based on your analysis, write a report that makes reasonable recommendations to SnowPea management.

1   SnowPea is concerned that one or more of the new delivery people might be slower than others.

a   Let μ_{Di} and μ_{Ti} be the mean delivery time and mean total time for delivery person i, where the total time is the sum of the delivery and prep times. Find 95% confidence intervals for each of these means for each delivery person. Although these might be interesting, give two reasons why they are not really fair measures for comparing the efficiency of the delivery people.

b   Responding to the criticisms in part a, find a 95% confidence interval for the mean speed of delivery for each delivery person, where speed is measured as miles per hour during the trip from SnowPea to the customer. Then find 95% confidence intervals for the mean difference in speed between each pair of delivery people.

2   SnowPea would like to advertise that it can achieve a total delivery time of no more than M minutes for all customers within a 10-mile radius. On all orders that take more than M minutes, SnowPea will give the customers a $10 certificate on their next purchase.

a   Assuming for now that the delivery people in the sample are representative of all of SnowPea's delivery people, find a 95% confidence interval for the proportion of deliveries (within the 10-mile limit) that will be on time if $M = 25$ minutes; if $M = 30$ minutes; if $M = 35$ minutes.

b Suppose SnowPea makes 1000 deliveries within the 10-mile limit. For each of the values of M in part **a**, find a 95% confidence interval for the total dollar amount of certificates it will have to give out for being late.

3 The policy in the previous problem is simple to state and simple to administer. However, it is somewhat unfair to customers who live close to SnowPea—they will never get $10 certificates! A fairer, but more complex, policy is the following. SnowPea first analyzes the data and finds that total delivery times can be predicted fairly well with the equation

$$\text{Predicted DeliveryTime} = 14.8 + 2.06\text{Distance}$$

(This is based on regression analysis, the topic of Chapters 11 and 12.) Also, most of these predictions are within 5 minutes of the actual delivery times. Therefore, whenever SnowPea receives an order over the phone, it looks up the customer's address in its computerized geographical database to find distance, calculates the predicted delivery time based on this equation, rounds this to the nearest minute, adds 5 minutes, and guarantees this delivery time or else a $10 certificate. It does this for *all* customers, even those beyond the 10-mile limit.

a Assuming again that the delivery people in the sample are representative of all of SnowPea's delivery people, find a 95% confidence interval for the proportion of all deliveries that will be within the guaranteed total delivery time.

b Suppose SnowPea makes 1000 deliveries. Find a 95% confidence interval for the total dollar amount of certificates it will have to give out for being late.

CASE STUDY 8.4 **The Bodfish Lot Cruise**[12]

Ralph Butts, Manager of Woodland Operations for Intergalactica Papelco's Southeastern Region, had to decide this morning whether to approve the Bodfish Lot logging contract that was sitting on his desk. Accompanying the contract was a cruise report that gave Mr. Butts the results of a sample survey of the timber on the Bodfish Lot. Was there enough timber to make logging operations worthwhile?

The Pluto Mill of Intergalactica Papelco is located on the River Styxx in Median, Michigan. The scale of operations at Pluto is enormous. Just one of its several $500 million, football-field-long, 4-story-high paper machines has the capability to produce a 20-mile-long, 16-foot-wide, 20-ton reel of paper every hour. Such a machine is run nonstop 24 hours a day for as many of the 365 days in the year that mill maintenance can keep it up and producing paper within specified quality levels. In total, the Pluto Mill produces about 400,000 tons of white paper a year, and because it takes about a ton of wood to produce a ton of paper, a huge quantity of cordwood logs suitable for chipping and pulping must be supplied continually to keep the mill operating. Intergalactica Papelco runs a large-scale logistics, planning, and procurement operation to provide the Pluto Mill with the requisite species, quantity, and quality of wood in a timely fashion.

[12]This case was contributed by Peter Kolesar from Columbia University.

The Pluto Mill sits on 500 acres of land in the midst of a region in which the huge Intergalactica Papelco owns over a quarter of a million acres of forest. While this wholly-owned forest is the single largest supplier of wood to the mill, more than 60% of the wood used at Pluto is purchased from independent landowners and loggers under contract. Supplying contract wood dependably on such an enormous scale involves frequent purchasing decisions by the Intergalactica Woodlands Operations as to which independent woodlots have sufficient wood volume and quality to support economical logging operations. A prospective seller enters into a tentative agreement with Intergalactica on the basis of market price and a visual scan of the woodlot. The final decision about whether to proceed with the logging is usually based on sampling estimates of the total wood volume on the lot.

A recent case in point was the Bodfish Lot in Henryville, Arkansas, whose owner approached Intergalactica with a proposal for logging during the 1991–1992 season. Aerial photographs indicated that the land was sufficiently promising to warrant a "cruise" to estimate the total volume of wood. (Cruising is a term used in the forestry industry to describe a systematic procedure for estimating the quantity, quality, variety, and value of the wood on a plot of land. Indeed, standard cruising methods have been developed and disseminated by the U.S. Department of Agriculture and Forestry Service.) Estimation based on limited sampling is essential. Even for the modest sized Bodfish Lot, with 586 acres of forested land, it would be practically impossible to measure every tree on the lot.

For the Bodfish Lot cruise it was decided to sample 89 distinct 1/7th-acre plots for actual measurement. Although the plots were chosen "systematically," the sample was, Intergalactica hoped, still effectively "random." Indeed, *no* consistent attempt was made to select the plots from areas of heavy tree growth, large-diameter trees, heavy spruce concentration, and so on. In fact, the opposite was true—the regular spacing of the sampling grid more or less guaranteed a good cross section of the entire lot. This was what is called in forestry industry jargon a "standard line plot cruise." The total lot was 700 acres in area. The plots were spaced at 8-chain intervals apart on a rectangular grid drawn in advance at the Intergalactica Woodlands Field Office at One Rootmean Square in the town of Covariance, Illinois. The aerial photographs showed that, of the Bodfish Lot's 700 total acres, 586 acres were forested. The total volume estimate was to be based on the average for the 89 sampled plots on these 586 acres, and was also to be done separately for each species.

A circular area two-person cruise was then initiated. Typically, about ten plots could be cruised in one day. The foresters counted the entire number of cordwood trees over 6 inches in diameter within each 1/7-acre circle. Then, back in the office in Covariance, the number of trees on each plot was entered into a computer according to species, diameter, and possible end product. The file BODFISH.XLS contains this tabulation from the cruise notes of the counts for spruce, hard maple, and beech of the number of cordwood trees on the 89 sampled plots. (In the actual database, 13 different species of tree were recorded, and Intergalactica would have decided which trees were more suitable for lumber, plywood, or pulping applications.)

With these data, Intergalactica now had to decide whether to contract to log the Lot. Ralph Butts, manager of Woodlands Operations, knew that even though Intergalactica would pay on the basis of the weight received at the mill, he needed at least 31,000 cordwood size trees on the lot to make operations economical. More detailed knowledge of the amount of timber by species would help the Pluto Mill make the crucial blending decisions that affect the cost and quality of the resulting wood pulp.

This was just one of several hundred similiar contracts to be made over the coming year. Butts was concerned with the rising cost of cruising in the Southeastern Region. Was the Bodfish Lot cruise excessive, he wondered? Could he get by in the future with considerably smaller samples? Suppose that only a half or a quarter of the plots on Bodfish had been cruised?

Hypothesis Testing

Successful Applications

Hypothesis testing is one of the most frequently used tools in academic research, including research in the area of business. Many studies pose interesting questions, stated as hypotheses, and then test these with appropriate statistical analysis of experimental data. One such study is reported in McDaniel and Kinney (1996). They investigate the effectiveness of "ambush marketing" in prominent sports events such as the Olympic Games. Many companies pay significant amounts of money, perhaps $10 million, to become official sponsors of the Olympics. Ambushers are their competitors who pay no such fees but nevertheless advertise heavily during the Olympics, with the intention of linking their own brand image to the event in the minds of consumers. The question McDaniel and Kinney investigate is whether consumers are confused into thinking that the ambushers are the official sponsors.

At the time of the 1994 Winter Olympics in Lillehammer, Norway, the researchers ran a controlled experiment using 215 subjects ranging in age from 19 to 49 years old. Approximately half of the subjects—the "control group"—viewed a 20-minute tape of a women's skiing event in which several actual commercials for official sponsors in four product categories were interspersed. (The categories were fast food, automobile, credit card, and insurance; the official sponsors were McDonald's, Chrysler, VISA, and John Hancock.) The other half—the "treatment group"—watched the same tape but with commercials for competing ambushers. (The ambushers were Wendy's, Ford, American Express, and Northwestern Mutual, all of which advertised during the 1994 Olympics.) After watching the tape, each subject was asked to fill out a questionnaire. This questionnaire asked subjects to recall the official Olympics sponsors in each product category, to rate their attitudes toward the products, and to state their intentions to purchase the products.

McDaniel and Kinney tested several hypotheses. First, they tested the null hypothesis that there would be no difference between the control and treatment groups in terms of which products they would recall as official Olympics sponsors. The experimental evidence allowed them to reject this hypothesis decisively. For example, the vast majority of the control group, who watched the McDonald's commercial, recalled McDonald's as being the official sponsor in the fast-food category. But a clear majority of the treatment group, who watched the Wendy's commercial, recalled Wendy's as being the official sponsor in this category. Evidently, Wendy's commercial was compelling.[1]

Because the ultimate objective of commercials is to increase purchases of a company's brand, the researchers also tested the hypothesis that viewers of official sponsor commercials would rate their intent to purchase that brand *higher* than viewers of ambusher commercials would rate their intent to purchase the ambusher brand. After all, isn't this why the official sponsors were paying large fees to be "official" sponsors? However, except for the credit card category, the data did *not* support this hypothesis. VISA viewers did indeed rate their intent to use VISA higher than American Express viewers rated their intent to use American Express. But in the other three product categories, the ambusher brand came out ahead of the official brand in terms of intent to purchase (although the differences were not statistically significant).

There are at least two important messages this research should convey to business. First, if a company is going to spend a lot of money to become an official sponsor of an event such as the Olympic Games, it needs to create a more vivid link in the mind of consumers between its product and the event. Otherwise, it might be wasting its money. Second, ambush marketing is very possibly a wise strategy. By seeing enough of the ambushers' commercials during the event, consumers get confused into thinking that the ambusher is an "official" sponsor. In addition, previous research in the area suggests that consumers do not view ambushers negatively for using an ambushing strategy. ■

9.1 Introduction

Hypothesis testing is the second side of a two-sided statistical inference coin, confidence interval estimation being the first side. When we want to make inferences to a population on the basis of sample data, we can perform the analysis in either of two ways. We can proceed as in the previous chapter, where we calculate a point estimate of a population parameter and then form a confidence interval around this point estimate. In this way we bring no preconceived ideas to the analysis but instead let the data "speak for themselves" in telling us where the true parameter is likely to be.

In contrast, an analyst often has a particular theory, or hypothesis, that he or she would like to test. This hypothesis might be that a new packaging design will produce more sales than the current design, that a new drug will have a higher cure rate for a given disease than any drug currently on the market, that people who smoke cigarettes are more susceptible to heart disease than nonsmokers, and so on. In this case the analyst typically collects sample data and checks whether the data provide enough evidence to support the hypothesis.

The hypothesis that the analyst is attempting to prove is called the **alternative hypothesis**. It is also frequently called the **research hypothesis**. The opposite of the alternative hypothesis is called the **null hypothesis**. It usually represents the current thinking or status quo. That is, the null hypothesis is usually the accepted theory that the analyst is trying to *disprove*. In the above examples the null hypotheses are:

■ The new packaging design is no better than the current design.

■ The new drug has a cure rate no higher than other drugs on the market.

■ Smokers are no more susceptible to heart disease than nonsmokers.

---

[1]Whereas the McDonald's commercial featured the five-ringed Olympics logo and had an Olympics theme, the Wendy's commercial used a humorous approach built around the company's founder, Dave Thomas, and his dream of winning gold in Olympics bobsled competition.

The burden of proof is traditionally on the alternative hypothesis. It is up to the analyst to provide enough evidence in support of the alternative; otherwise, the null hypothesis will continue to be accepted. A slight amount of evidence in favor of the alternative is usually not enough. For example, if a slightly higher percentage of people are cured with a new drug in a sequence of clinical tests, this still might not be enough evidence to warrant introducing the new drug to the market. In general, we reject the null hypothesis—and accept the alternative—only if the results of a hypothesis test are "statistically significant," a concept we will explain in this chapter.

As we will see in this chapter, confidence interval estimation and hypothesis testing use data in much the same way and they often report basically the same results, only from different points of view. There continues to be a debate (largely among academic researchers) over which of these two procedures is more useful. We believe that in a business context, confidence interval estimation is more useful and enlightening than hypothesis testing. However, hypothesis testing continues to be a key aspect of statistical analysis. Indeed, statistical software packages routinely include the elements of standard hypothesis tests in their outputs. We will see this, for example, when we study regression analysis in Chapters 11 and 12. Therefore, it is essential to understand the fundamentals of hypothesis testing so that we can interpret this output intelligently.

Concepts in Hypothesis Testing

Before we plunge into the details of specific hypothesis tests, it is useful to discuss the *concepts* behind hypothesis testing. There are a number of concepts and statistical terms involved, all of which lead eventually to the key concept of statistical significance. To make this discussion somewhat less abstract, we place it in the context of the following example.

EXAMPLE 9.1

The manager of the Pepperoni Pizza Restaurant has recently begun experimenting with a new method of baking its pepperoni pizzas. He personally believes that the new method produces a better-tasting pizza, but he would like to base a decision on whether to switch from the old method to the new method on customer reactions. Therefore, he performs an experiment. For 100 randomly selected customers who order a pepperoni pizza for home delivery, he includes both an old-style and a free new-style pizza in the order. All he asks is that these customers rate the *difference* between pizzas on a −10 to +10 scale, where −10 means that they strongly favor the old style, +10 means they strongly favor the new style, and 0 means they are indifferent between the two styles. Once he gets the ratings from the customers, how should he proceed?

We begin by stating that Example 9.1 is used primarily to explain hypothesis-testing concepts. We do *not* want to imply that the manager would, or should, use a hypothesis-testing procedure to decide whether to switch from the old method to the new method. First, hypothesis testing does not take costs into account. If the new method of making pizzas uses more expensive cheese, for example, then hypothesis testing would ignore this important aspect of the decision problem. Second, even if the costs of the two pizza-making methods are equivalent, the manager might base his decision on a simple point estimate and possibly a confidence interval. For example, if the sample mean rating is 1.8 and a

95% confidence interval for the mean rating extends from 0.3 to 3.3, this in itself might be enough evidence to make the manager switch to the new method.

We will come back to these ideas—basically, that hypothesis testing is not necessarily the best procedure to use in a business decision-making context—throughout this chapter. However, with these caveats in mind, we discuss how the manager *might* proceed by using hypothesis testing. ■

9.2.1 Null and Alternative Hypotheses

As we stated in the introduction to this chapter, the hypothesis the manager is trying to prove is called the alternative, or research, hypothesis, whereas the "status quo" is called the null hypothesis. In this example the manager would personally like to prove that the new method provides better-tasting pizza, so this becomes the alternative hypothesis. The opposite, that the old-style pizzas are at least as good as the new-style pizzas, becomes the null hypothesis. We'll assume he judges which of these is true on the basis of the mean rating over the entire customer population, labeled μ. If it turns out that $\mu \leq 0$, then the null hypothesis is true. Otherwise, if $\mu > 0$, the alternative hypothesis is true.

Usually, the null hypothesis is labeled H_0 and the alternative hypothesis is labeled H_a. Therefore, in our example we can specify these as $H_0: \mu \leq 0$ and $H_a: \mu > 0$. This is typical. The null and alternative hypotheses divide all possibilities into two nonoverlapping sets, exactly one of which must be true. In our case either the mean rating is less than or equal to 0, or it is positive. Exactly one of these possibilities *must* be true, and the manager intends to use sample data to learn which of them is true.

Traditionally, hypothesis testing has been phrased as a decision-making problem, where an analyst decides either to accept the null hypothesis or reject it, based on the sample evidence. In our example, accepting the null hypothesis means deciding that the new-style pizza is not really better than the old-style pizza and presumably discontinuing the new style. In contrast, rejecting the null hypothesis means deciding that the new-style pizza is indeed better than the old-style pizza and presumably switching to the new style.

9.2.2 One-Tailed Versus Two-Tailed Tests

The form of the alternative hypothesis can be either **one-tailed** or **two-tailed**, depending on what the analyst is trying to prove. The pizza manager's alternative hypothesis is one-tailed because he is hoping to prove that the customers' ratings are, on average, greater than 0. The only sample results that can lead to rejection of the null hypothesis are those in a particular direction, namely, those where the sample mean rating is *positive*. Of course, if the manager sets up his rating scale in the reversed order, so that *negative* ratings favor the new-style pizza, then the test is still one-tailed, but now only negative sample means lead to rejection of the null hypothesis.

In contrast, a two-tailed test is one where results in either of two directions can lead to rejection of the null hypothesis. A slight modification of the pizza example where a two-tailed alternative might be appropriate is the following. Suppose the manager currently uses two methods for producing pepperoni pizzas. He is thinking of discontinuing one of these methods if it appears that customers, on average, favor one method over the other. Therefore, he runs the same experiment as before, but now the hypotheses he tests are $H_0: \mu = 0$ versus $H_a: \mu \neq 0$, where μ is again the mean rating across the customer population. In this case *either* a large positive sample mean or a large negative sample mean will lead to rejection of the null hypothesis—and presumably to discontinuing one of the production methods.

Once the hypotheses are set up, it is easy to detect whether the test is one-tailed or two-tailed. One-tailed alternatives are phrased in terms of ">" or "<" whereas two-tailed alternatives are phrased in terms of "≠". The real question is whether to set up hypotheses for a particular problem as one-tailed or two-tailed. There is no *statistical* answer to this question. It depends entirely on what we are trying to prove. If the pizza manager is trying to prove that the new-style pizza is better than the old-style pizza—only results on "one side" will lead to a switch—a one-tailed alternative is appropriate. However, if he is trying to decide whether to discontinue either of two existing production methods—where results on "either side" will lead to a switch—then a two-tailed alternative is appropriate.

9.2.3 Types of Errors

Regardless of whether the manager decides to accept or reject the null hypothesis, it *might* be the wrong decision. He might incorrectly reject the null hypothesis when it is true ($\mu \leq 0$), and he might incorrectly accept the null hypothesis when it is false ($\mu > 0$). In the tradition of hypothesis testing, these two types of errors have acquired the names **type I** and **type II errors**. In general, we commit a type I error when we incorrectly *reject* a null hypothesis that is true. We commit a type II error when we incorrectly *accept* a null hypothesis that is false. These ideas appear graphically in Figure 9.1.

FIGURE 9.1 **Types of Errors in Hypothesis Testing**

	Truth	
	H_0 is true	H_a is true
Reject H_0	Type I error	No error
Do not reject H_0	No error	Type II error

Decision

The pizza manager commits a type I error if he concludes, based on sample evidence, that the new-style pizza is better (and switches to it) when in fact the entire customer population would, on average, favor the old-style pizza. In contrast, he commits a type II error if he concludes, again based on sample evidence, that the new-style is no better (and discontinues it) when in fact the entire customer population would, on average, favor the new style.

Although we might be inclined to regard these two types of errors as equally serious or costly, type I errors have traditionally been regarded as the more serious of the two. Therefore, the hypothesis-testing procedure favors caution in terms of rejecting the null hypothesis. The thinking is that if we reject the null hypothesis and it is really true, then we commit a type I error—which is bad. Given this rather conservative way of thinking, we are inclined to accept the null hypothesis unless the sample evidence provides strong support for the alternative hypothesis. Unfortunately, we can't have it both ways. By accepting the null hypothesis, we risk committing a type II error.

This is exactly the dilemma the pizza manager faces. If he wants to avoid a type I error (where he switches to the new style but really shouldn't), then he will require fairly convincing evidence from the survey that he *should* switch. If he observes *some* evidence to this effect, such as a sample mean rating of +1.5 and a 95% confidence interval that extends from −0.3 to +3.3, say, this evidence might not be strong enough to make him switch. However, if he decides not to switch, he risks committing a type II error.

9.2.4 Significance Level and Rejection Region

The real question, then, is how strong the evidence in favor of the alternative hypothesis must be to reject the null hypothesis. Two approaches to this problem are commonly used. In the first, the analyst prescribes the probability of a type I error that he is willing to tolerate. This type I error probability is usually denoted by α and is most commonly set equal to 0.05, although $\alpha = 0.01$ and $\alpha = 0.10$ are also frequently used. The value of α is called the **significance level** of the test. Then, given the value of α, we use statistical theory to determine a **rejection region**. If the sample evidence falls into the rejection region, we reject the null hypothesis; otherwise, we accept it. The rejection region is chosen precisely so that the probability of a type I error is at most α. Sample evidence that falls into the rejection region is called **statistically significant at the α level**. For example, if $\alpha = 0.05$, we say that the evidence is statistically significant at the 5% level.

9.2.5 Significance from p-values

A second approach, and one that is currently more popular, is to avoid the use of an α level and instead simply report "how significant" the sample evidence is. We do this by means of a **p-value**. The idea is quite simple—and very important. Suppose in the pizza example that the true mean rating (if it could be observed) is $\mu = 0$. In other words, the customer population, on average, judges the two styles of pizza to be about equal. Now suppose that the sample mean rating is $+2.5$. The manager has two options at this point. (Remember that he doesn't know that $\mu = 0$; he only observes the sample.) He can conclude that (1) the null hypothesis is true—the new-style pizza is not preferred over the old style—and he just observed an unusual sample, or (2) the null hypothesis is *not* true—customers do prefer the new-style pizza—and the sample he observed is a typical one.

The p-value of the sample quantifies this. It is the probability of seeing a random sample at least as extreme as the sample observed, given that the null hypothesis is true. Here, "extreme" is relative to the null hypothesis. For example, a sample mean rating of $+3.5$ from the pizza customers is more extreme evidence than a sample mean rating of $+2.5$. Each provides some evidence against the null hypothesis, but the former provides stronger, more extreme evidence.

Let's suppose that the pizza manager collects data from the 100 sampled customers and finds that the p-value for the sample is 0.03. This means that *if* the entire customer population, on average, judges the two types of pizza to be approximately equal, then only 3 random samples out of 100 would provide as much evidence in support of the new style as the observed sample. So should he conclude that the null hypothesis is true and he just happened to observe an unusual sample, or should he conclude that the null hypothesis is *not* true? There is no clear statistical answer to this question; it depends on how convinced the manager needs to be before switching. But we can say in general that smaller p-values indicate more evidence in support of the alternative hypothesis. If a p-value is sufficiently small, almost any decision maker will conclude that rejecting the null hypothesis (and accepting the alternative) is the most "reasonable" decision.

How small is a "small" p-value? This is largely a matter of semantics, but Figure 9.2 indicates the attitude of many analysts. If a p-value is less than 0.01, it provides "convincing" evidence that the alternative hypothesis is true. After all, fewer than 1 sample out of 100 would provide such support for the alternative hypothesis if it weren't true. If the p-value is between 0.01 and 0.05, there is "strong" evidence in favor of the alternative hypothesis. Unless the consequences of making a type I error are really serious, we are likely to reject the null hypothesis in this case.

FIGURE 9.2 **Evidence in Favor of the Alternative Hypothesis**

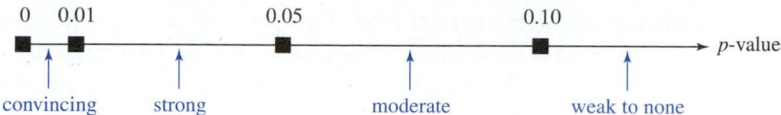

The interval between 0.05 and 0.10 is a "gray area." If a scientific researcher were trying to prove a research hypothesis and observed a p-value between 0.05 and 0.10, she would probably be reluctant to publish her results as "proof" of the alternative hypothesis, but she would probably be encouraged to continue her research and collect more sample evidence. Finally, p-values larger than 0.10 are generally interpreted as weak or no evidence in support of the alternative.

There is a strong connection between the α-level approach and the p-value approach. Namely, we can reject the null hypothesis at a specified level of significance α only if the p-value from the sample is less than or equal to α. Equivalently, the sample evidence is statistically significant at a given α level only if its p-value is less than or equal to α. For example, if the p-value from a sample is 0.03, then we can reject the null hypothesis at the 10% and the 5% significance levels, but we cannot reject it at the 1% level. The p-value essentially states *how* significant a given sample is.

The advantage of the p-value approach is that the analyst doesn't have to choose a significance value α ahead of time. Since it is far from obvious what value of α we should choose in any particular situation, this is certainly an advantage. Another compelling advantage is that p-values for standard hypothesis tests are routinely included in most statistical software output. In addition, all p-values can be interpreted in basically the same way: a small p-value provides support for the alternative hypothesis.

9.2.6 Hypothesis Tests and Confidence Intervals

When we present the results of hypothesis tests, we often include confidence intervals in the output. This gives us two complementary ways to interpret the data. However, there is a more formal connection between the two, at least for two-tailed tests. Let α be the stated significance level of the test. We will state the connection for the most commonly used level, $\alpha = 0.05$, although it extends to any α value. The connection is that we can reject the null hypothesis at the 5% significance level if and only if a 95% confidence interval does *not* include the hypothesized value of the parameter.

As an example, consider the test of $H_0: \mu = 0$ versus $H_a: \mu \neq 0$. Suppose a 95% confidence interval for μ extends from 1.35 to 3.42; that is, it does *not* include the hypothesized value 0. Then we can reject H_0 at the 5% significance level, and we know that the p-value from the sample must be less than 0.05. On the other hand, if a 95% confidence interval for μ extends, say, from -1.25 to 2.31 (negative to positive), then we can't reject the null hypothesis at the 5% significance level, and the p-value must be greater than 0.05.

9.2.7 Practical versus Statistical Significance

We have stated that statistically significant results are those that produce sufficiently small p-values. In other words, statistically significant results are those that provide strong evidence in support of the alternative hypothesis. We frequently hear about studies, particularly in the medical sciences, that produce statistically significant results. For example, we might hear that mice injected with one kind of drug develop "significantly more" cancer cells than mice injected with a second kind of drug.

The point of this section is that such results are not necessarily significant in the sense of being *important*. They might be significant only in the statistical sense. An example of what could happen is the following. An education researcher wants to see whether quantitative SAT scores differ, on average, across gender. He sets up the hypotheses $H_0: \mu_M = \mu_F$ versus $H_a: \mu_M \neq \mu_F$, where μ_M and μ_F are the mean quantitative SAT scores for males and females. He then randomly samples scores from 4000 males and 4000 females and finds the male and female sample averages to be 521 and 524. The sample standard deviation for each group is about 50. Based on these numbers, the *p*-value for the sample data is approximately 0.007. (We'll see how to make this calculation later in this chapter.) Therefore, he claims that the results are "significant proof" that males do score differently (lower) than females.

If you read these results in a newspaper, your immediate reaction might be, "Who cares?" After all, the difference between 521 and 524 is certainly not very large from a practical point of view. So why does the education researcher get to make his claim? Here's what's going on. The chances are that the means μ_M and μ_F are not *exactly* equal. There is bound to be some difference between genders over the entire population. If the researcher takes large enough samples—and 4000 is plenty large—he is almost certain to obtain enough evidence to "prove" that the means are not equal. That is, he will almost surely obtain *statistically* significant results. However, the difference he finds, as in the numbers we quoted, might be of little *practical* significance. No one really cares whether females score 3 points higher or lower than males. If the difference were on the order of 30 to 40 points, then we might be interested.

As this example illustrates, there is always a possibility of statistical significance but not practical significance with large sample sizes. To be fair, we should also mention the opposite case, which typically occurs with small sample sizes. Here we fail to obtain statistical significance even though the truth about the population(s), if it were known, would be of practical significance. Let's assume that a medical researcher wants to test whether a new form of treatment produces a higher cure rate for a deadly disease than the best treatment currently on the market. Due to expenses, the researcher is able to run a controlled experiment on only a relatively small number of patients with the disease. Unfortunately, the results of the experiment are inconclusive. They show some evidence that the new treatment works better, but the *p*-value for the test is only 0.25.

In the scientific community these results would not be enough to warrant a switch to the new treatment. However, it is certainly possible that the new treatment, if it were used on a large number of patients, would provide a "significant" improvement in the cure rate—where "significant" now implies *practical* significance. In this type of situation, we could easily fail to discover practical significance because the sample sizes are not large enough to detect it statistically.

From here on, when we use the term "significant," we mean *statistically* significant. However, you should always keep the ideas in this section in mind. A statistically significant result is not necessarily of practical importance. Conversely, a result that fails to meet the criterion for statistical significance is not necessarily one that should be ignored.

Hypothesis Tests for a Population Mean

Now that we have covered the general concepts behind hypothesis testing and the principal sampling distributions, the mechanics of hypothesis testing are fairly straightforward. We will discuss in some detail how the procedure works for a population mean. Then in later sections we will illustrate similar hypothesis tests for other parameters.

As with confidence intervals, the key to the analysis is the sampling distribution of the sample mean. We know that if we subtract the true mean μ from the sample mean and divide the difference by the standard error $s/\sqrt{n}$, the result has a t distribution with $n-1$ degrees of freedom. In a hypothesis-testing context, the true mean to use is the null hypothesis value, specifically, the borderline value between the null and alternative hypotheses. This value is usually labeled μ_0, where the subscript reminds us that it is based on the null hypothesis.

To run the test, we calculate the following "test statistic":

$$t\text{-value} = \frac{\overline{X} - \mu_0}{s/\sqrt{n}}$$

If the null hypothesis is true, or more specifically, if $\mu = \mu_0$, this test statistic has a t distribution with $n-1$ degrees of freedom. The p-value for the test is the probability beyond the test statistic in both tails (for a two-tailed alternative) or in a single tail (for a one-tailed alternative) of the t distribution.

We illustrate the procedure by continuing the pizza manager's problem in Example 9.1.

EXAMPLE 9.1 [CONTINUED]

Recall that the manager of the Pepperoni Pizza Restaurant is running an experiment to test the hypotheses $H_0: \mu \leq 0$ versus $H_a: \mu > 0$, where μ is the mean rating in the entire customer population. Here, each customer rates the difference between an old-style pizza and a new-style pizza on a -10 to $+10$ scale, where negative ratings favor the old style and positive ratings favor the new style. The ratings for 40 randomly selected customers and several summary statistics appear in Figure 9.3 on page 446. (See the file PIZZA1.XLS.) Is there sufficient evidence from these sample data for the manager to reject H_0?

Solution

From the summary statistics, we see that the sample mean is $\overline{X} = 2.10$ and the sample standard deviation is $s = 4.717$. This positive sample mean provides some evidence in favor of the alternative hypothesis, but given the rather large value of s and the boxplot of ratings shown in Figure 9.4, which indicates a lot of negative ratings, does it provide *enough* evidence to reject H_0?

To run the test, we calculate the test statistic, using the borderline null hypothesis value $\mu_0 = 0$, and report how much probability is beyond it in the right tail of the appropriate t distribution. We use the *right* tail because the alternative is one-tailed of the "greater than" variety. The test statistic is

$$t\text{-value} = \frac{2.10 - 0}{4.717/\sqrt{40}} = 2.816$$

The probability beyond this value in the right tail of a t distribution with $n - 1 = 39$

FIGURE 9.3   Data and Summary Measures for Pizza Example

	A	B	C	D	E	F	G
1	Testing the pizza manager's one-tailed hypothesis						
2							
3	Customer	Rating		Summary measures for selected variables			
4	1	-7				Rating	
5	2	7			Count	40.000	
6	3	-2			Mean	2.100	
7	4	4			Median	2.000	
8	5	7			Standard deviation	4.717	
9	6	6					
10	7	0					
11	8	2					
40	37	7					
41	38	3					
42	39	5					
43	40	-6					

FIGURE 9.4   Boxplot for Pizza Data

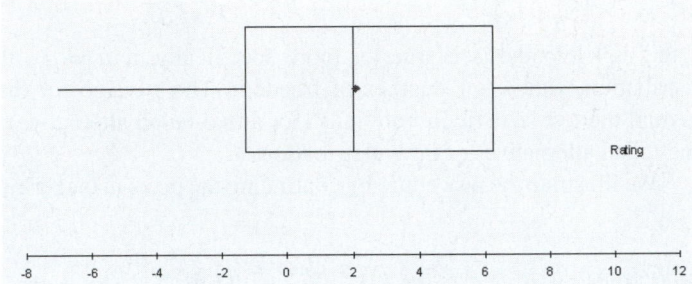

degrees of freedom is approximately 0.004, which can be found in Excel with the function TDIST(2.816,39,1). (Recall that the first argument is the *t*-value, the second is the degrees of freedom, and the third is the number of tails.)

This probability, 0.004, is the *p*-value for the test. It indicates that these sample results would be *very* unlikely if the null hypothesis is true. The manager has two choices at this point. He can conclude that the null hypothesis is true and he obtained a very unlikely sample, or he can conclude that the alternative hypothesis is true—and presumably switch to the new-style pizza. This second conclusion certainly appears to be the more reasonable of the two.

Another way of interpreting the results of the test is in terms of traditional significance levels. We can reject H_0 at the 1% significance level because the *p*-value is less than 0.01. Of course, we can also reject H_0 at the 5% level or the 10% level because the *p*-value is also less than 0.05 and 0.10. But as we discussed earlier, the *p*-value is a preferred way of reporting the results because it indicates exactly *how* significant these sample results are.

The StatPro One-Sample procedure can be used to perform this analysis easily, with the results shown in Figure 9.5. To use it, select the StatPro/Statistical Inference/One-Sample Analysis menu item, and choose the Rating variable as the variable to analyze. Then fill out the next two dialog boxes as shown in Figures 9.6 and 9.7.

Most of the output in Figure 9.5 should be familiar. It mirrors the calculations we did above, and you can check the formulas in the output cells to ensure that you understand the procedure. We note the following. First, the value in cell F6, 0, is the null hypothesis value μ_0 at the borderline between H_0 and H_a; it is the value specified in the dialog box in Figure 9.7. Second, take a look at the notes entered in cells D5 and F11. (These notes

FIGURE 9.5 Hypothesis Test for the Mean for the Pizza Example

FIGURE 9.5   Hypothesis Test for the Mean for the Pizza Example

	D	E	F	G	H
3	*Results for one-sample analysis*				
4					
5	*Test of mean<=0 versus one-tailed alternative for Rating*				
6		Hypothesized mean	0.000		
7		Sample mean	2.100		
8		Std error of mean	0.746		
9		Degrees of freedom	39		
10		t test statistic	2.816		
11		p value	0.004		

FIGURE 9.6   One-Sample Options Dialog Box

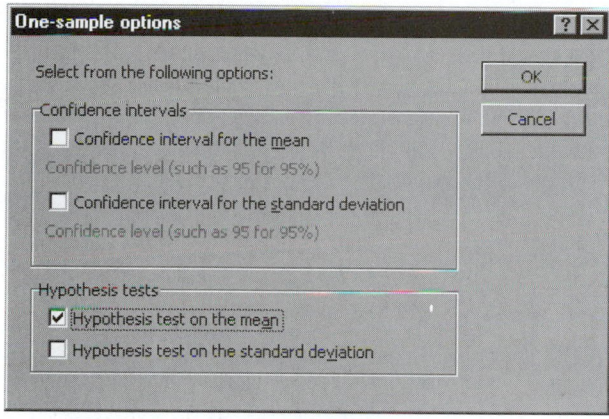

FIGURE 9.7   Hypothesis Test Dialog Box

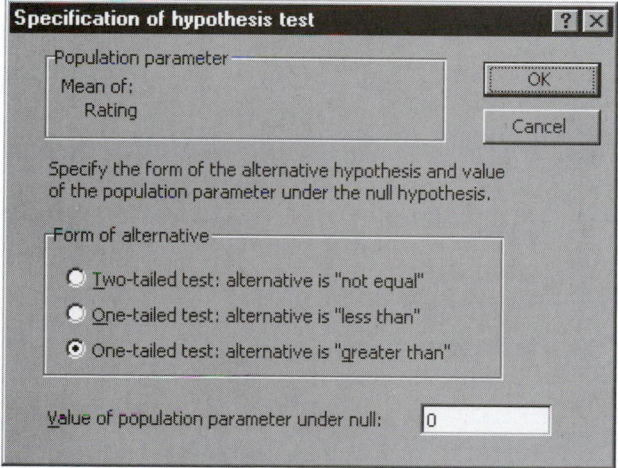

aren't visible in Figure 9.5, but they can be seen in the completed file.) The note in cell D5 reminds us that this test is based on normality of the underlying population distribution and/or a sufficiently large sample size. If these conditions are not satisfied (which is not a problem for this example), then other more appropriate tests are available. The note in cell

F11 indicates that the results are significant at the 1% level. In general, StatPro compares the *p*-value to the three traditional significance levels, 1%, 5%, and 10%, and interprets significance in terms of these.

Before leaving this example, we ask one last question. Should the manager switch to the new-style pizza on the basis of these sample results? We would probably recommend "yes." There is no indication that the new-style pizza costs any more to make than the old-style pizza, and the sample evidence is fairly convincing that customers, on average, will prefer the new-style pizza. Therefore, unless there are reasons for not switching that we haven't mentioned here, we recommend the switch. However, if it costs more to make the new-style pizza, hypothesis testing is *not* the best way to perform a decision analysis. We will come back to this theme throughout this chapter. ∎

Example 9.1 illustrates how to run and interpret any one-tailed hypothesis for the mean, assuming the alternative is of the "greater than" variety. If the alternative is still one-tailed but of the "less than" variety, there is virtually no change. We illustrate this in Figure 9.8, where the ratings have been reversed in sign. That is, we multiplied each rating by -1, so that negative ratings now favor the new-style pizza. The hypotheses are now $H_0: \mu \geq 0$ versus $H_a: \mu < 0$. We obtain the negative of the previous test statistic, -2.816, and exactly the same *p*-value, 0.004. This is now the probability in the *left* tail of the *t* distribution, but the interpretation of the results is exactly the same as before.

FIGURE 9.8 **Hypothesis Test with Reverse Coding**

	A	B	C	D	E	F	G	H
1	Testing the pizza manager's one-tailed hypothesis with reverse coding							
2								
3	Customer	Rating			Results for one-sample analysis			
4	1	7						
5	2	-7			Test of mean>=0 versus one-tailed alternative for Rating			
6	3	2			Hypothesized mean	0.000		
7	4	-4			Sample mean	-2.100		
8	5	-7			Std error of mean	0.746		
9	6	-6			Degrees of freedom	39		
10	7	0			t test statistic	-2.816		
11	8	-2			p value	0.004		
12	9	-8						
40	37	-7						
41	38	-3						
42	39	-5						
43	40	6						

The analysis of two-tailed tests for the mean is also quite similar to the analysis in Example 9.1. We illustrate a typical two-tailed test in the following modification of the pizza example.

EXAMPLE 9.2

Assume that the manager of the Pepperoni Pizza Restaurant currently uses two methods of producing pepperoni pizzas. He plans to discontinue one of these methods if the results of a survey indicate that customers favor one of the methods by a "significant" margin. The survey is conducted exactly as in Example 9.1. Each of 40 randomly selected customers receives two pizzas, one made by each method. These customers are asked to rate the pizzas on a -10 to $+10$ scale, where negative ratings favor the first method and positive ratings favor the second method. The results of the survey appear in Figure 9.9. (See the file PIZZA2.XLS.) Is there enough evidence in these sample data to persuade the manager to discontinue one of the methods?

FIGURE 9.9 **Analysis for Comparing Two Pizza-Making Methods**

	A	B	C	D	E	F	G	H
1	Testing the pizza manager's two-tailed hypothesis							
2								
3	Customer	Rating			Results for one-sample analysis			
4	1	2						
5	2	-8			Test of mean=0 versus two-tailed alternative for Rating			
6	3	-2			Hypothesized mean	0.000		
7	4	0			Sample mean	-1.325		
8	5	4			Std error of mean	0.488		
9	6	-5			Degrees of freedom	39		
10	7	-9			t test statistic	-2.718		
11	8	-3			p value	0.010		
12	9	-3						
13	10	-4						
40	37	0						
41	38	2						
42	39	-3						
43	40	0						

Solution

We now write the hypotheses as $H_0: \mu = 0$ versus $H_a: \mu \neq 0$, where μ is the mean rating over the entire customer population. A two-tailed alternative is appropriate here because the manager has no idea, before the sample is taken, which method (if either) will be favored. Note that it is *not* appropriate to observe the sample, see that the sample mean is, say, negative (as in this data set), and then conclude that the alternative should be of the one-tailed "less than" variety. The hypotheses should always be formulated *before* the sample data are observed.

The test is run (and the StatPro One-Sample procedure can be used) almost exactly as in a one-tailed test. We calculate the t-distributed test statistic in the same way as before:

$$t\text{-value} = \frac{\overline{X} - 0}{s/\sqrt{n}} = \frac{-1.325}{0.488} = -2.718$$

We now see how much probability is beyond -2.718 in the left tail *and* beyond $+2.718$ in the right tail in a t distribution with $n - 1 = 39$ degrees of freedom. The effect is to double the one-tailed p-value. From the output, we see that the two-tailed p-value is 0.010 (in cell F11). It results from the Excel function TINV(ABS(-2.718),39,2). The absolute value function ABS is used because the first argument of the TINV function must always be nonnegative. The third argument is 2 because this is a two-tailed test.

This small p-value provides convincing evidence for the manager that there *is* a difference, on average, between customers' reactions to the two methods of making pizzas. On average, customers appear to favor the first method.

We conclude this example by again asking whether the manager should discontinue the (evidently) less popular second method on the basis on this hypothesis test. The answer almost certainly depends on costs that have not been mentioned. The primary reason for discontinuing one of the methods is presumably to save costs by using only one production method instead of two. However, in spite of the fact that the customer population, on average, appears to favor the first method, the data show that a good-sized minority favors the second method. So why not continue to use the second method if the cost is not prohibitive? The company could very easily achieve a *greater* overall profit by continuing to make pizzas by both methods than by discontinuing the slightly less popular method. Here again we see that hypothesis testing provides useful information, but the ultimate decision should be based on a careful cost analysis. ∎

In the following example, we illustrate the danger of relying too much on *p*-values from a hypothesis test.

EXAMPLE 9.3

John Jacobs works for the Fresh Toothpaste Company and has recently been assigned to investigate a new type of toothpaste dispenser. The traditional tube of toothpaste uses a screw-off cap. The new dispenser uses the same type of tube, but there is now a flip-top cap on a hinge. John believes this new cap is easier to use, although it is a bit messier than the screw-off cap—toothpaste tends to accumulate around the new cap. So far, the positive aspects appear to outweigh the negatives. In informal tests, consumers reacted favorably to the new cap. The next step was to introduce the new cap in a regional test market. The company has just conducted this test market for a 6-month period in 85 stores in the Cincinnati region. The results, in units sold per store, appear in Figure 9.10. (See the file TPASTE.XLS.)

FIGURE 9.10 **Toothpaste Dispenser Data from Cincinnati Region**

	A	B	C	D	E	F	G
1	Sales volumes in Cincinnati regional test market for 6 months						
2							
3	Store	Units sold					
4	1	4106					
5	2	2786					
6	3	3858					
7	4	3015					
8	5	3900					
9	6	3572					
10	7	4633					
11	8	4128					
12	9	3044					
13	10	2585					
85	82	1889					
86	83	6436					
87	84	4179					
88	85	3539					

John has done his homework on the financial side. Figure 9.11 shows a break-even analysis for the new dispenser relative to the current dispenser. The analysis is over the entire U.S. market, which consists of 9530 stores (of roughly similar size) that stock the product. Based on several assumptions that we'll soon discuss, John figures that to break even with the new dispenser, the sales volume per store per 6-month period must be 3622

FIGURE 9.11 **Break-even Analysis for Toothpaste Example**

	A	B	C	D	E	F
1	**Breakeven analysis for Stripe Toothpaste**					
2						
3	**Assumptions:**					
4	The planning horizon is 4 years					
5	Sales volume is expected to remain constant over the 4 years					
6	Unit selling prices and unit costs will remain constant over the 4 years					
7	Straight-line depreciation is used to depreciate the initial investment for the new dispenser					
8	Breakeven analysis is based on NPV for the four-year period					
9					**Range names**	
10	**Given data**				AfterTaxProfit: C33:F33	
11	Current volume (millions of units) using current dispenser		65.317		BeforeTaxContrib: C31:F31	
12	Initial investment ($ millions) for new dispenser		1.5		CashFlow: C34:F34	
13	Unit selling price (either dispenser)		$1.79		Deprec: C32:F32	
14	Unit cost (current dispenser)		$1.25		DiscRate: C17	
15	Unit cost (new dispenser)		$1.27		Invest: B34	
16	Tax rate		35%		TaxRate: C16	
17	Discount rate		16%			
18						
19	**Note:** From here on, all sales volumes are in millions of units, monetary values are in $ millions.					
20						
21	**Analysis of current dispenser**		Year 1	Year 2	Year 3	Year 4
22	Sales volume		65.317	65.317	65.317	65.317
23	Before-tax contribution		35.27	35.27	35.27	35.27
24	After-tax profit		22.926	22.926	22.926	22.926
25	Cash flow		22.926	22.926	22.926	22.926
26	NPV	$64.152				
27						
28	**Analysis of new dispenser**		Year 1	Year 2	Year 3	Year 4
29	Initial investment	$1.5				
30	Sales volume		69.027	69.027	69.027	69.027
31	Before-tax contribution		35.89	35.89	35.89	35.89
32	Depreciation		0.38	0.38	0.38	0.38
33	After-tax profit		23.087	23.087	23.087	23.087
34	Cash flow	($1.50)	23.462	23.462	23.462	23.462
35	NPV	$64.152				
36						
37	Number of stores nationally	9530				
38	Breakeven sales volume per store per 6 months	3622				

units. The question is whether the test market data support a decision to abandon the current dispenser and market the new dispenser nationally.

Solution

We first discuss the break-even analysis in Figure 9.11. The assumptions are listed in rows 4–8 and relevant inputs are listed in rows 11–17. In particular, the new dispenser involves an up-front investment of $1.5 million, and its unit cost is 2 cents higher than the unit cost for the current dispenser. However, the company doesn't plan to raise the selling price. Rows 21–26 calculate the net present value (NPV) for the next 4 years, assuming that the company does not switch to the new dispenser. Starting with *any* first-year sales volume in cell C30, rows 28–35 calculate the NPV for the next 4 years, assuming that the company does switch to the new dispenser. The goal of the break-even analysis is to find a value in cell C30 that makes the two NPVs (in cells B26 and B35) equal.

The trickiest part of the analysis concerns the depreciation calculations for the new dispenser. We find the before-tax contribution from sales in row 31 and subtract the depreciation each year (one-quarter of the investment) to figure the after-tax profit. For example, the formula in cell C33 is

$$=(BeforeTaxContrib-Deprec)*(1-TaxRate)$$

Then the depreciation is added back to obtain the cash flow, so that the formula in cell C34 is

$$=AfterTaxProfit+Deprec$$

Finally, we calculate the NPV for the new dispenser in cell B35 with the formula

$$=Invest+NPV(DiscRate,CashFlow)$$

Note that the initial investment, which is assumed to occur at the *beginning* of year 1, is not part of the NPV function, which includes only *end-of-year* cash flows.

We then use Excel's Goal Seek tool to force the NPVs in cells B26 and B35 to be equal. Again, we begin by entering *any* value for first-year sales volume with the new dispenser in cell C30. Then we use the Tools/Goal Seek menu item and fill out the dialog box as shown in Figure 9.12. This drives the value in cell C30 to 69.027 millions of units, which translates (in cell B38) to 3622 units per store per 6-month period. (Divide 69.027 million by 9530 stores. Then divide by 2 to obtain the 6-month value.) The new dispenser must increase overall U.S. sales volume by about 5.7% to achieve a higher NPV than the current dispenser.

FIGURE 9.12 **Goal Seek Dialog Box**

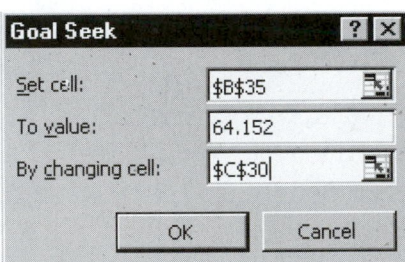

Because John is hoping to further his career with a successful new dispenser, he is hoping to prove the hypothesis that the mean 6-month sales volume per store over all U.S. stores is greater than the break even value 3622. He therefore sets up the hypotheses $H_0: \mu \leq 3622$ versus $H_a: \mu > 3622$ and runs the test on the Cincinnati data. The results appear in Figure 9.13. Note that the borderline value μ_0 is now nonzero—it is 3622—but other than this, the test is run exactly as in the previous two examples.

John is somewhat disappointed by the results. On the one hand, the sample mean sales volume per store is about 3773, well above the required break-even level. But the standard error of the mean is quite large, and this results in a *p*-value of 0.191, which is *not* the overwhelming evidence he hoped to obtain. It means that if the true mean volume (in all U.S. stores) were really only 3622, there would be a 19.1% chance of seeing an average sales volume this high in the test market purely by chance. So John is worried that the new dispenser might not be better after all and that he might simply have obtained a lucky test-market sample.

FIGURE 9.13   Hypothesis Test for Toothpaste Example

	D	E	F	G	H	I
3	Results for one-sample analysis					
4						
5	Test of mean<=3622 versus one-tailed alternative for Units_sold					
6		Hypothesized mean	3622.000			
7		Sample mean	3773.129			
8		Std error of mean	171.649			
9		Degrees of freedom	84			
10		t test statistic	0.880			
11		p value	0.191			

This is certainly one way to analyze the problem, and a conservative manager at this point might decide that the new dispenser is not worth the risk. In this case "risk" means making a type I error, that is, switching to the new dispenser when it is no better—and may be worse—than the current dispenser. But the decision *not* to switch to the new dispenser also carries a risk, the risk of a type II error. This is the risk of losing profit by not switching to a potentially better product. Traditional hypothesis testing treats type I errors as more "serious" than type II errors. Indeed, many analyses based on hypothesis testing never even consider type II errors, at least not explicitly. In this problem, however, we see no reason to take the traditional hypothesis-testing point of view. A more compelling decision analysis might proceed as follows.

We know that the NPV from the entire U.S. market is $64.152 million if the company continues with the current dispenser. If it switches, the NPV depends on the new sales volume, which is currently uncertain. However, based on the Cincinnati sample, the company's *best guess* is that the national first-year sales volume will be 71.916 million units [$= 3773.129 \times 9530 \times 2/1{,}000{,}000$]. By entering this value in cell C30 of Figure 9.11, we obtain an NPV of $66.884 million. The difference, $66.884 - 64.152 = \$2.732$ million, is the *expected* NPV the company stands to gain by switching to the new dispenser.

Admittedly, the 71.916 sales volume is an expected value. The observed value could be more or less, and it could be low enough to result in a loss relative to not switching. However, this is exactly the issue we dealt with throughout Chapter 6. If the company is an EMV maximizer, then the Cincinnati data provide plenty of support for making the switch to the new dispenser.

We briefly discuss two other potentially relevant issues. First, is it appropriate to base results on a sample of stores that are all from the same (Cincinnati) region? This is certainly not a simple random sample, as discussed in Chapter 7. It is more likely to be a cluster sample, where one region of the country is sampled randomly and then all of the stores in this region are sampled. This type of sampling has obvious logistical benefits for the company, and if there is no reason to believe that the chosen region differs from other regions with respect to its consumer behavior, then our analysis is probably valid.

Second, what if the company is *not* an EMV maximizer but is instead a risk-averse expected utility maximizer? In this case we would need to estimate a utility function for the company, and we would need to postulate a distribution (normal?) of the first-year sales volume with the new dispenser. The decision analysis would be more complex, but it would still go along the lines that we discussed in Chapter 6. In particular, it would not be appropriate to base the decision solely on a *p*-value from a hypothesis test. We suspect that unless the company is extremely risk averse, the best decision would still be to switch to the new dispenser.

In summary, this example has illustrated a situation where a decision should not be based on the results of a hypothesis test. The reason is not that the hypothesis test fails to take financial data into consideration. Indeed, the borderline value between the null and alternative hypotheses was based on a detailed financial analysis. The problem is that hypothesis testing gives unequal weights to type I and type II errors. If a type II error is potentially just as costly as a type I error, as it is here, then the decision analysis should instead be based on the methods from Chapter 6. ▪

PROBLEMS

Level A

1   Suppose a firm producing lightbulbs wants to know whether it can claim that its lightbulbs typically last more than 1000 burning hours. Hoping to find support for this claim, the firm collects a random sample of 100 lightbulbs and records the lifetime (in hours) of each. The sample data are contained in the file P9_1.XLS.

  a Using a 5% significance level, can this lightbulb manufacturer claim that its bulbs typically last more than 1000 hours? Explain your answer.

  b Using a 1% significance level, can this lightbulb manufacturer claim that its bulbs typically last more than 1000 hours? Explain your answer.

2   A manufacturer is interested in determining whether it can claim that the boxes of detergent it sells contain, on average, more than 500 grams of detergent. From past experience the manufacturer knows that the amount of detergent in the boxes is approximately normally distributed. The firm selects a random sample of 100 boxes and records the amount of detergent (in grams) in each box. These data are provided in the file P9_2.XLS. Formulate an appropriate hypothesis test and report a p-value. Do you find statistical support for the manufacturer's claim? Explain.

3   A producer of steel cables wants to know whether the steel cables it produces have an average breaking strength of 5000 pounds. An average breaking strength of less than 5000 pounds would not be adequate, and to produce steel cables with an average breaking strength in excess of 5000 pounds would unnecessarily increase production costs. The producer collects a random sample of 64 steel cable pieces. The breaking strength for each of these cable pieces is recorded in the file P9_3.XLS.

  a Using a 5% significance level, what statistical conclusion can the producer reach regarding the average breaking strength of its steel cables? Explain your answer.

  b Using a 1% significance level, what statistical conclusion can the producer reach regarding the average breaking strength of its steel cables? Explain your answer.

4   A U.S. Navy recruiting center knows from past experience that the heights of its recruits are normally distributed with mean 68 inches. The recruiting center wants to test the claim that the average height of this year's recruits is greater than 68 inches. To do this, recruiting personnel take a random sample of 64 recruits from this year and record their heights (in inches). The data are provided in the file P9_4.XLS.

  a On the basis of the available sample information, do the recruiters find support for the given claim at the 1% significance level? Explain.

  b Use the sample data to construct a 95% confidence interval for the average height of this year's recruits. Based on this confidence interval, what conclusion should recruiting personnel reach regarding the given claim?

5   Suppose that we wish to test $H_0: \mu = 10$ versus $H_a: \mu > 10$ at the $\alpha = 0.05$ significance level. Furthermore, suppose that we observe values of the sample mean and sample standard deviation when $n = 40$ that do *not* lead to the rejection of H_0. Is it true that we might reject H_0 if we observed the same values of the sample mean and sample standard deviation from a sample with $n > 40$? Why or why not?

Level B

6   A study is performed in a large southern town to determine whether the average weekly grocery bill per four-person family in the town is significantly different from the national average. A random sample of the weekly grocery bills of four-person families in this town appears in the file P9_6.XLS.

a Assume that the national average weekly grocery bill for a four-person family is $100. Is the sample evidence statistically significant? If so, at what significance levels can you reject the null hypothesis?

b For which values of the sample mean (i.e., average weekly grocery bill) would you decide to reject the null hypothesis at the $\alpha = 0.01$ significance level? For which values of the sample mean would you decide to reject the null hypothesis at the $\alpha = 0.10$ level?

7 An aircraft manufacturer needs to buy aluminum sheets with an average thickness of 0.05 inch. The manufacturer knows that significantly thinner sheets would be unsafe and considerably thicker sheets would be too heavy. A random sample of 100 sheets from a potential supplier is collected. The thickness of each sheet in this sample is measured (in inches) and recorded in the file P9_7.XLS.

a Based on the results of an appropriate hypothesis test, should the aircraft manufacturer buy aluminum sheets from this supplier? Explain why or why not.

b For which values of the sample mean (i.e., average thickness) would the aircraft manufacturer decide to buy sheets from this supplier? Assume that $\alpha = 0.05$ in answering this question.

8 Suppose that we observe a random sample of size n from a normally distributed population. If we are able to reject $H_0: \mu = \mu_0$ in favor of a two-tailed alternative hypothesis at the 10% significance level, is it true that we can definitely reject H_0 in favor of the appropriate one-tailed alternative at the 5% significance level? Why or why not? ■

Hypothesis Tests for Other Parameters

Just as we developed confidence intervals for a variety of parameters, we can develop hypothesis tests for other parameters. They are based on the same sampling distributions we discussed in the previous chapter, and they are run and interpreted exactly as the tests for the mean in the previous section. In each case we use sample data to calculate a test statistic that has a well-known sampling distribution. Then we calculate a corresponding p-value to measure the support for the alternative hypothesis. Beyond this, only the details change, as we illustrate in this section.

9.4.1 Hypothesis Tests for a Population Proportion

To test a population proportion p, recall that the sample proportion $\widehat{p}$ has a sampling distribution that is approximately normal when the sample size is reasonably large. Specifically, the standardized value

$$\frac{\widehat{p} - p}{\sqrt{p(1 - p)/n}}$$

is approximately distributed as a standard normal random variable Z.

Let p_0 be the borderline value of p between the null and alternative hypotheses. Then we substitute p_0 for p to obtain the following test statistic:

$$z\text{-value} = \frac{\widehat{p} - p_0}{\sqrt{p_0(1 - p_0)/n}}$$

The p-value of the test is found by seeing how much probability is beyond this test statistic in the tail (or tails) of the standard normal distribution.[2] A rule of thumb for checking the large-sample assumption of this test is to check whether $np_0 > 5$ and $n(1 - p_0) > 5$.

We illustrate this test in the following example.

E X A M P L E   9 . 4

The Walpole Appliance Company has a customer service department that handles customer questions and complaints. This department's processes are set up to respond quickly and accurately to customers who phone in their concerns. However, there is a sizable minority of customers who prefer to write letters. Traditionally, the customer service department has not been very efficient in responding to these customers.

Letter writers first receive a mail-gram asking them to call customer service (which is exactly what letter writers wanted to avoid in the first place!), and when they do call, the customer service representative who answers the phone typically has no knowledge of the customer's problem. As a result, the department manager estimates that 15% of letter writers have not obtained a satisfactory response within 30 days of the time their letters were first received. The manager's goal is to reduce this value by at least half, that is, to 7.5% or less.

To do so, she changes the process for responding to letter writers. Under the new process, these customers now receive a prompt and courteous form letter that responds to their problem. (This is possible because the vast majority of concerns can be addressed by one of several form letters.) Each form letter states that if the customer still has problems, he or she can call the department. The manager also files the original letters so that if customers do call back, the representative who answers will be able to find their letters quickly and respond intelligently. With this new process in place, the manager has tracked 400 letter writers and has found that only 23 of them are classified as "unsatisfied" after a 30-day period. Does it appear that the manager has achieved her goal?

Solution

The manager's goal is to reduce the proportion of unsatisfied customers after 30 days from 0.15 to 0.075 or less. Because the burden of proof is on her to "prove" that she has accomplished this goal, we set up the hypotheses as $H_0: p \geq 0.075$ versus $H_a: p < 0.075$, where p is the proportion of all letter writers who are still unsatisfied after 30 days. The sample proportion she has observed is $\hat{p} = 23/400 = 0.0575$. This is obviously less than 0.075, but is it *enough* less to reject the null hypothesis?

The test statistic for the data, using the borderline value $p_0 = 0.075$, is

$$z\text{-value} = \frac{0.0575 - 0.075}{\sqrt{0.075(1 - 0.075)/400}} = -1.329$$

This value appears in cell B10 of Figure 9.14. (See the file LETTERS.XLS.) Note that we first find the denominator (the standard error of $\hat{p}$) in cell B8 with the formula

=SQRT(HypProp*(1-HypProp)/SampSize)

The corresponding p-value, 0.092, is found with the formula

=NORMSDIST(TestStat)

---

[2] Do not confuse the unknown proportion p with the p-value of the test. They are logically different concepts and just happen to share the same letter p.

in cell B11. It is the probability to the *left* of -1.329 in the standard normal distribution. Also, because $np_0 = 400(0.075) = 30 > 5$ and $n(1 - p_0) = 400(0.925) > 5$, this test is valid; that is, the sample size is large enough for the normal approximation to hold.

FIGURE 9.14 **Analysis of New Process for Letter Writers**

	A	B	C	D
1	Test of a proportion: responding to letter writers			
2				
3	Target proportion with new procedure	0.075		
4				
5	Number of unsatisfied customers after 30 days	23		
6	Number of customers sampled	400	**Range names**	
7	Sample proportion	0.0575	HypProp: B3	
8	Standard error of sample proportion	0.01317	SampProp: B7	
9			SampSize: B6	
10	z test statistic	-1.329	StErr: B8	
11	p value for a one-tailed test	0.092	TestStat: B10	
12				
13	95% confidence interval for true proportion			
14	Lower limit	0.035		
15	Upper limit	0.080		

The *p*-value in cell B11 might not be as low as you expected—or as low as the manager would like. In spite of the fact that the sample proportion appears to be well below the target proportion of 0.075, the evidence in support of the alternative hypothesis is not overwhelming. In statistical terminology, the results are significant at the 10% level, but not at the 5% or 1% levels.

We also show a 95% confidence interval for the unknown proportion *p* in Figure 9.14. For example, the formula in cell B14 is

$$\text{=SampProp-1.96*SQRT(SampProp*(1-SampProp)/SampSize)}$$

This confidence interval extends from 0.035 to 0.080. It includes the target value, 0.075, but just barely. In this sense it also supports the argument that the manager has indeed achieved her goal.[3]

Analysts might disagree on whether a hypothesis test or a confidence interval is the more appropriate way to present these results. However, we see them as complementary and do not necessarily favor one over the other. The bottom line is that they both provide strong, but not totally conclusive, evidence that the manager has achieved her goal. ■

9.4.2 Hypothesis Tests for Differences Between Population Means

We now discuss the comparison problem, where we test the difference between two population means. As in the previous chapter, the form of the analysis depends on whether the two samples are independent or paired. If they are paired, then the test proceeds exactly as

---

[3] Note that the standard error in cell B8 for the hypothesis test uses the target proportion 0.075. In contrast, the standard error for the confidence interval uses the sample proportion 0.0575. The sampling distribution for a hypothesis test always uses the borderline value between H_0 and H_a. But because confidence intervals aren't connected to any hypotheses, their standard errors must rely on sample data. In most cases the two standard errors are practically the same.

in Section 9.3, using the differences as the single variable of analysis. That is, if $\overline{D}$ is the sample mean difference between n pairs, D_0 is the hypothesized difference (the borderline value between H_0 and H_a), and s_D is the sample standard deviation of the differences, then the test is based on the test statistic

$$t\text{-value} = \frac{\overline{D} - D_0}{s_D/\sqrt{n}}$$

If D_0 is the true mean difference, then this test statistic has a t distribution with $n - 1$ degrees of freedom. The validity of the test also requires that n be reasonably large and/or the population of *differences* be approximately normally distributed.

If the samples are independent and the population standard deviations are equal, then the two-sample theory discussed in Section 8.6.1 is relevant. It leads to the test statistic

$$t\text{-value} = \frac{(\overline{X}_1 - \overline{X}_2) - D_0}{s_p\sqrt{1/n_1 + 1/n_2}}$$

Here, $\overline{X}_1$ and $\overline{X}_2$ are the two sample means, D_0 is the hypothesized difference, n_1 and n_2 are the sample sizes, and s_p is the pooled estimate of the common population standard deviation, based on the sample standard deviations s_1 and s_2:

$$s_p = \sqrt{\frac{(n_1 - 1)s_1^2 + (n_2 - 1)s_2^2}{n_1 + n_2 - 2}}$$

If D_0 is the true mean difference, then this test statistic has a t distribution with $n_1 + n_2 - 2$ degrees of freedom. The validity of this test again requires that the sample sizes be reasonably large and/or the populations be approximately normally distributed.

We begin with an example of the paired-sample t test.

EXAMPLE 9.5

Beer and soft-drink companies have recently become very concerned about the style of their cans. There are cans with fluted and embossed sides and cans with six-color graphics and holograms. Coca-Cola is even experimenting with a contoured can, shaped like the old-fashioned Coke bottle minus the neck. Evidently, these companies believe the style of the can makes a difference to consumers, which presumably translates into higher sales.

Assume that a soft-drink company is considering a style change to its current can, which has been the company's trademark for many years. To determine whether this new style is popular with consumers, the company runs a number of focus group sessions around the country. At each of these sessions, randomly selected consumers are allowed to examine the new and traditional styles, exchange ideas, and offer their opinions. Eventually, they fill out a form where, among other items, they are asked to respond to the following items, each on a 1 to 7 scale, 7 being the best:

■ Rate the attractiveness of the traditional-style can.

■ Rate the attractiveness of the new-style can.

■ Rate the likelihood that you would buy the product with the traditional-style can.

■ Rate the likelihood that you would buy the product with the new-style can.

The results over all focus groups are shown in Figures 9.15 and 9.16. (See the file CANS.XLS.) What can the company conclude from these data? Are hypothesis tests appropriate?

FIGURE 9.15 Data on Soft-Drink Cans

	A	B	C	D	E
1	Focus group results on can styles				
2					
3	Consumer	Attractive Old	Attractive New	Will Buy Old	Will Buy New
4	1	5	7	4	1
5	2	7	7	6	6
6	3	6	7	7	6
7	4	1	3	1	1
8	5	3	4	1	1
9	6	7	7	7	7
10	7	5	7	4	6
11	8	6	7	6	7
12	9	5	7	6	6
13	10	5	4	4	6
175	172	2	4	1	1
176	173	1	1	1	1
177	174	3	1	3	4
178	175	3	3	3	5
179	176	6	7	5	7
180	177	6	7	6	7
181	178	5	4	4	3
182	179	3	4	1	3
183	180	3	5	6	7
184					
185	Averages	4.41	4.95	3.86	4.34

FIGURE 9.16 Correlations for Soft-Drink Can Data

	G	H	I	J	K	L
3	Table of correlations					
4			Attractive_Old	Attractive_New	Will_Buy_Old	Will_Buy_New
5		Attractive_Old	1.000			
6		Attractive_New	0.740	1.000		
7		Will_Buy_Old	0.746	0.595	1.000	
8		Will_Buy_New	0.594	0.401	0.774	1.000

Solution

First, it is a good idea to examine summary statistics for the data. The averages from each survey item are shown at the bottom of Figure 9.15. They indicate some support for the new-style can. Also, we might expect the ratings for a given consumer to be correlated. This turns out to be the case, as shown by the relatively large positive correlations in Figure 9.16. These large positive correlations indicate that if we want to examine differences between survey items, a paired-sample procedure will make the most efficient use of the data. Of course, a paired-sample procedure also makes sense because each consumer answers each item on the form. (If this is confusing, think about the following alternative setup. We have four *separate* groups of consumers. The first group responds to item 1 only, the second group responds to item 2 only, and so on. Then the responses to the various items are in no way paired, and an *independent-sample* procedure would be used instead.)

There are several differences of interest. The two most obvious are the difference between the attractiveness ratings of the two styles and the difference between the likelihoods of buying the two styles—that is, column B minus column C and column D minus column E. A third difference of interest is the difference between the attractiveness ratings of the new style and the likelihoods of buying the new can—that is, column C minus column E. This difference indicates whether perceptions of the new-style can are likely to translate into sales. Finally, a fourth difference that might be of interest is the difference between the third difference (column C minus column E) and the similar difference for the old style (column B minus column D). This checks whether the translation of perceptions into sales is any different for the two styles of cans.

All of these differences appear next to the original data in Figure 9.17. In terms of the original data, they are defined as:

- Diff1: Column B − Column C
- Diff2: Column D − Column E
- Diff3: Column C − Column E
- Diff4: Column B − Column D
- Diff5: Column H − Column I = (Column C − Column E) − (Column B − Column D)

We generate all of them automatically (except for Diff4) with the StatPro/Statistical Inference/Paired-Sample Analysis menu item. (We generate the variable Diff4 manually because we have no particular interest in testing it; it is used only to form Diff5.)

FIGURE 9.17 **Original and Difference Variables for Soft-Drink Can Data**

	A	B	C	D	E	F	G	H	I	J
1	Focus group results on can styles									
2										
3	Consumer	Attractive Old	Attractive New	Will Buy Old	Will Buy New	Diff1	Diff2	Diff3	Diff4	Diff5
4	1	5	7	4	1	-2	3	6	1	5
5	2	7	7	6	6	0	0	1	1	0
6	3	6	7	7	6	-1	1	1	-1	2
7	4	1	3	1	1	-2	0	2	0	2
8	5	3	4	1	1	-1	0	3	2	1
9	6	7	7	7	7	0	0	0	0	0
10	7	5	7	4	6	-2	-2	1	1	0
11	8	6	7	6	7	-1	-1	0	0	0
12	9	5	7	6	6	-2	0	1	-1	2
13	10	5	4	4	6	1	-2	-2	1	-3
14	11	1	3	1	1	-2	0	2	0	2
15	12	2	1	1	3	1	-2	-2	1	-3
16	13	6	6	6	6	0	0	0	0	0
17	14	4	5	3	3	-1	0	2	1	1
18	15	2	5	1	1	-3	0	4	1	3
19	16	6	7	7	7	-1	0	0	-1	1
20	17	4	5	2	1	-1	1	4	2	2
178	175	3	3	3	5	0	-2	-2	0	-2
179	176	6	7	5	7	-1	-2	0	1	-1
180	177	6	7	6	7	-1	-1	0	0	0
181	178	5	4	4	3	1	1	1	1	0
182	179	3	4	1	3	-1	-2	1	2	-1
183	180	3	5	6	7	-2	-1	-2	-3	1

For each of the differences, Diff1, Diff2, Diff3, and Diff5, we test the mean difference over all potential consumers with a paired-sample analysis. Exactly as in the previous chapter, we treat each difference variable as a *single* sample and run the same *t* test as in Section 9.3 on this sample. In each case the hypothesized difference, D_0, is 0. The only question is whether to run one-tailed or two-tailed tests. We propose that the tests for Diff1, Diff2, and Diff5 be two-tailed tests and that the test on Diff3 be a one-tailed test with the alternative of the "greater than" variety. The reasoning is that the company probably has little idea which way the differences Diff1, Diff2, and Diff5 will go (positive or negative), whereas it expects that Diff3 will be positive on average. That is, it expects that consumers' ratings of the attractiveness of the new design will, on average, be larger than their likelihoods of purchasing the product. However, any of these hypotheses could be run as one-tailed or two-tailed tests. It depends on the prior beliefs of the company. In any case, to change a one-tailed p-value to a two-tailed p-value, all we need to do is multiply by 2. Similarly, we can change two-tailed p-values to one-tailed p-values by dividing by 2.

The results from the four tests appear in Figures 9.18 and 9.19. These outputs also include 99% confidence intervals for the corresponding mean differences. We obtained each output for Diff1, Diff2, and Diff3 with the StatPro/Statistical Inference/Paired-Sample Analysis menu item, used on the appropriate pair of original variables (those in columns B–E in Figure 9.15). The output for Diff5 was based on the Diff3 and Diff4 variables.

FIGURE 9.18 **Analysis of Diff1 and Diff2 Variables**

	T	U	V	W	X	Y	Z	AA	AB
3	*Results of paired-sample analysis*				*Results of paired-sample analysis*				
4									
5	*Confidence interval results for mean of Diff2*				*Confidence interval results for mean of Diff1*				
6		Confidence level	99.0%			Confidence level	99.0%		
7		Sample mean	-0.478			Sample mean	-0.539		
8		Std error of mean	0.100			Std error of mean	0.101		
9		Degrees of freedom	179			Degrees of freedom	179		
10		Lower limit	-0.739			Lower limit	-0.801		
11		Upper limit	-0.216			Upper limit	-0.277		
12									
13	*Test of mean=0 versus two-tailed alternative for Diff2*				*Test of mean=0 versus two-tailed alternative for Diff1*				
14		Hypothesized mean	0.000			Hypothesized mean	0.000		
15		Sample mean	-0.478			Sample mean	-0.539		
16		Std error of mean	0.100			Std error of mean	0.101		
17		Degrees of freedom	179			Degrees of freedom	179		
18		t test statistic	-4.758			t test statistic	-5.351		
19		p value	0.000			p value	0.000		

FIGURE 9.19 **Analysis of Diff3 and Diff5 Variables**

	L	M	N	O	P	Q	R	S
3	*Results of paired-sample analysis*				*Results of paired-sample analysis*			
4								
5	*Confidence interval results for mean of Diff5*				*Confidence interval results for mean of Diff3*			
6		Confidence level	99.0%			Confidence level	99.0%	
7		Sample mean	0.061			Sample mean	0.611	
8		Std error of mean	0.152			Std error of mean	0.165	
9		Degrees of freedom	179			Degrees of freedom	179	
10		Lower limit	-0.336			Lower limit	0.182	
11		Upper limit	0.458			Upper limit	1.041	
12								
13	*Test of mean=0 versus two-tailed alternative for Diff5*				*Test of mean=0 versus one-tailed alternative for Diff3*			
14		Hypothesized mean	0.000			Hypothesized mean	0.000	
15		Sample mean	0.061			Sample mean	0.611	
16		Std error of mean	0.152			Std error of mean	0.165	
17		Degrees of freedom	179			Degrees of freedom	179	
18		t test statistic	0.401			t test statistic	3.705	
19		p value	0.689			p value	0.000	

The results can be summarized as follows.

■ From the output for the Diff1 variable in Figure 9.18, there is overwhelming evidence that consumers, on average, rate the attractiveness of the new design higher than the attractiveness of the current design. The t-distributed test statistic is -5.351, calculated as

$$\frac{-0.539 - 0}{0.101} = -5.351$$

and the corresponding p-value for a two-tailed test of the mean difference is (to three decimal places) 0.000. A 99% confidence interval for the mean difference extends from -0.801 to -0.277. Note that this 99% confidence interval does *not* include the hypothesized value 0. We know this must be the case because the two-tailed p-value is less than 0.01. (Recall the relationship between confidence intervals and two-tailed hypothesis tests from Section 9.2.6.)

■ The results are basically the same for the difference between consumers' likelihoods of buying the product with the two styles. (See the output for the Diff2 variable in Figure 9.18.) Again, consumers are definitely more likely, on average, to buy the product with the new-style can. A 99% confidence interval for the mean difference extends from -0.739 to -0.216.

■ The company's hypothesis that consumers' ratings of attractiveness of the new-style can are greater, on average, than their likelihoods of buying the product with this style can is confirmed. (See the output for the Diff3 variable in Figure 9.19.) The test statistic for this one-tailed test is 3.705 and the corresponding p-value is 0.000. A 99% confidence interval for the mean difference extends from 0.182 to 1.041.

■ There is no evidence that the difference between attractiveness ratings and the likelihood of buying is any different for the new-style can than for the current-style can. (See the output for the Diff5 variable in Figure 9.19.) The test statistic for a two-tailed test of this difference is 0.401 and the corresponding p-value, 0.689, isn't close to any of the traditional significance levels. Furthermore, a 99% confidence interval for the mean difference extends from a negative value, -0.336, to a positive value, 0.458.

These results are further confirmed by histograms of the difference variables such as those shown in Figures 9.20 and 9.21.[4] (Boxplots could be used, but we prefer histograms when the variables include only a few possible integer values.) The histogram of the Diff1 variable in Figure 9.20 shows many more negative differences than positive differences. This leads to the large negative test statistic and the all-negative confidence interval. In contrast, the histogram of the Diff5 variable in Figure 9.21 is almost perfectly symmetric around 0 and hence provides no evidence that the mean difference is nonzero.

FIGURE 9.20 **Histogram of the Diff1 Variable**

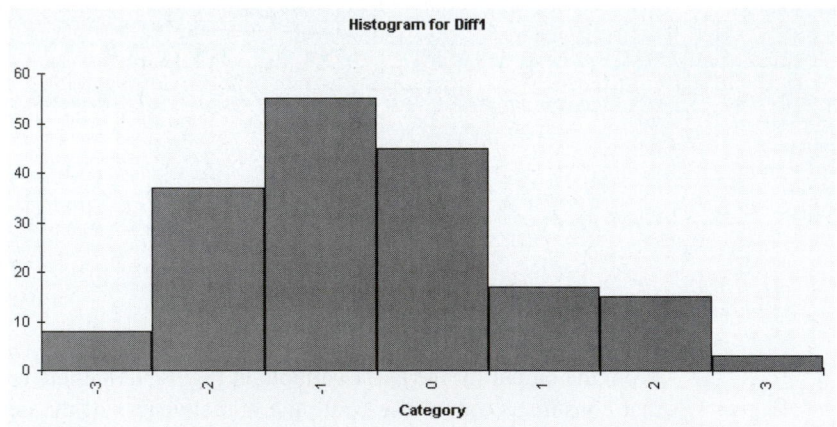

[4] To obtain the simplified horizontal axis labels (-3 instead of ≤ -3, for example), we simply change the labels in column B of the corresponding (hidden) "Data" sheets produced by StatPro's Histogram procedure.

FIGURE 9.21 **Histogram of the Diff5 Variable**

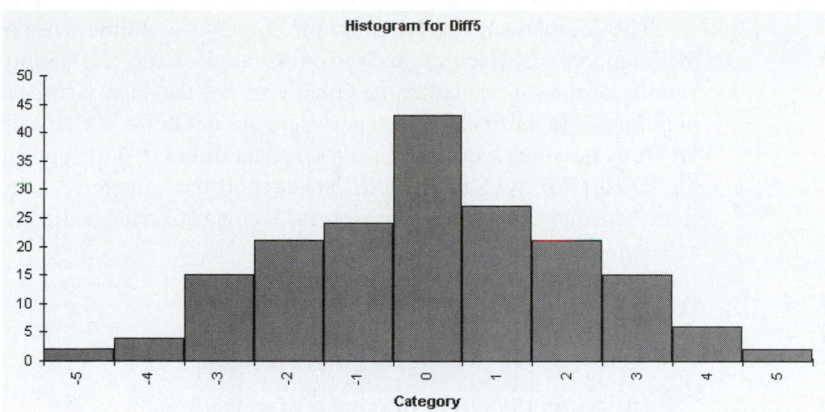

This example illustrates once again how hypothesis tests and confidence intervals provide complementary information, although the confidence intervals are arguably the more useful of the two here. The hypothesis test for the first difference, for example, shows that the average rating for the new style is undoubtedly larger than for the current style. This is useful information, but it might be even more useful to know *how much* larger the average for the new style is. A confidence interval provides this information.

We conclude this example by recalling the distinction between practical significance and statistical significance. Due to the extremely low *p*-values, the results in Figure 9.18, for example, leave no doubt as to statistical significance. But this could be due to the large sample size. That is, if the true mean differences are even slightly different from 0, large samples will almost surely discover this and report small *p*-values. The soft-drink company, on the other hand, is more interested in knowing whether the observed differences are of any practical importance. This is not a statistical question. It is a question of what differences are important for the *business*. We suspect that the company would indeed be quite impressed with the observed differences in the sample—and might very well switch to the new-style can. ■

The following example illustrates the independent two-sample *t* test. We can tell that a paired-sample procedure is not appropriate because there is no attempt to match the observations in the two samples in any way. Indeed, this would be impossible because the sample sizes are not equal.

EXAMPLE 9.6

Many companies are now installing exercise facilities at their plants. The goal is not only to provide a bonus (free use of exercise equipment) for their employees, but to make the employees more productive by getting them in better shape. One such company, the Informatrix Software Company, installed exercise equipment on site a year ago. To check whether it is having a beneficial effect on employee productivity, the company has gathered data on a sample of 80 randomly chosen employees, all between the ages of 30 and 40 and all with similar job titles and duties. The company observed which of these employees use the exercise facility regularly (at least three times per week on average). This group included 23 of the 80 employees in the sample. The other 57 employees were asked whether they exercise regularly elsewhere, and six of them replied that they do. The remaining 51, who admitted to being nonexercisers, were then compared to the combined group of 29 exercisers.

The comparison was based on the employees' productivity over the year, as rated by their supervisors. Each rating was on a 1 to 25 scale, 25 being the best. To increase the validity of the study, neither the employees nor the supervisors were told that a study was in progress. In particular, the supervisors did not know which employees were involved in the study or which were exercisers. The data from the study appear in Figure 9.22. (See the file EXERCISE.XLS.) Do these data support the company's (alternative) hypothesis that exercisers outperform nonexercisers on average? Can the company infer that any difference between the two groups is due to exercise?

F I G U R E   9 . 2 2   **Data for Study on Effectiveness of Exercise**

	A	B	C	D
1	Study on the effect of regular exercise			
2				
3	Employee	Exercise	Rating	
4	1	1	15	
5	2	1	17	
6	3	1	16	
7	4	1	20	
8	5	1	20	
9	6	1	14	
10	7	1	14	
11	8	1	16	
12	9	1	24	
13	10	1	10	
73	70	0	20	
74	71	0	10	
75	72	0	13	
76	73	0	9	
77	74	0	15	
78	75	0	19	
79	76	0	18	
80	77	0	13	
81	78	0	6	
82	79	0	19	
83	80	0	11	

Solution

The data in Figure 9.22 are "stacked." That is, there is a code variable Exercise that indicates which employees are exercisers (the 1's) and which aren't (the 0's), and there is a single Rating variable for the entire group of employees. Although some statistical software packages expect the data for the two-sample procedure to be in this format, the StatPro add-in requires unstacked data—that is, a separate Rating variable for each sample.[5] Therefore, we first use StatPro's Unstack procedure to create the separate variables Rating_0 and Rating_1 shown in Figure 9.23. (To create these variables, use the StatPro/Data Utilities/Unstack Variables menu item, select Exercise as the code variable, and select Rating as the variable to unstack.) Although the portion of the spreadsheet in the figure does not show it, the Rating_0 and Rating_1 variables have different numbers of observations: 51 and 29, respectively.

---

[5] As we stated in Chapter 8, this is no longer true. StatPro now accepts the data in stacked or unstacked form. However, the instructions given here still work.

FIGURE 9.23   Unstacked Rating Variables in Exercise Study

	A	B	C	D	E	F
1	Study on the effect of regular exercise					
2						
3	Employee	Exercise	Rating		Rating_0	Rating_1
4	1	1	15		6	15
5	2	1	17		19	17
6	3	1	16		19	16
7	4	1	20		14	20
8	5	1	20		20	20
9	6	1	14		12	14
10	7	1	14		15	14
11	8	1	16		16	16
12	9	1	24		16	24
13	10	1	10		14	10
14	11	1	23		10	23
15	12	1	22		24	22
16	13	1	15		15	15
17	14	1	13		9	13
18	15	1	14		14	14
19	16	1	15		13	15
20	17	1	14		11	14
21	18	1	8		12	8
22	19	1	15		14	15
23	20	1	23		11	23
24	21	1	20		11	20
25	22	1	12		15	12
26	23	1	23		9	23
27	24	1	19		20	19
28	25	1	20		22	20
29	26	1	19		12	19
30	27	1	19		22	19
31	28	1	16		23	16
81	78	0	6			
82	79	0	19			
83	80	0	11			

To see whether there is any indication of a difference between the two groups, we create side-by-side boxplots of the unstacked variables. These appear in Figure 9.24. Although there is a great deal of overlap between the two distributions, the distribution for the exercisers is somewhat to the right of that for the nonexercisers. Also, the variances of the two distributions appear to be roughly the same, although there is a bit more variation in the nonexerciser distribution.

FIGURE 9.24   Boxplots for Exercise Data

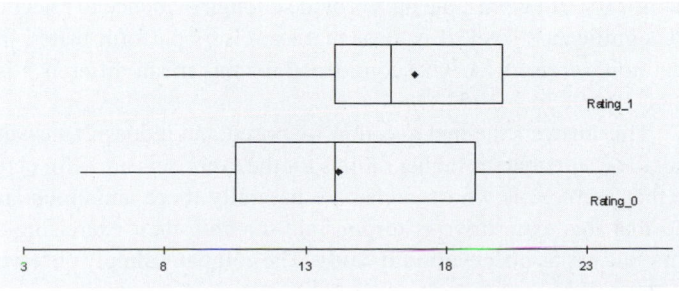

A formal test on the mean difference uses the hypotheses $H_0: \mu_1 - \mu_2 \geq 0$ versus $H_a: \mu_1 - \mu_2 < 0$, where μ_1 and μ_2 are the mean ratings for the nonexerciser and exerciser populations. We use a one-tailed test, with the alternative of the "greater than" variety, because the company expects higher ratings, on average, for the exercisers. The output for this test, along with a 95% confidence interval for $\mu_1 - \mu_2$, appears in Figure 9.25. We obtain it by using the StatPro/Statistical Inference/Two-Sample Analysis menu item and filling out the dialog boxes in the obvious way.

FIGURE 9.25   **Analysis of Exercise Data**

	H	I	J	K	L
3	*Results of two-sample analysis*				
4					
5	*Summary stats for two samples*				
6			Rating_0	Rating_1	
7		Sample sizes	51	29	
8		Sample means	14.137	16.862	
9		Sample standard deviations	5.307	4.103	
10					
11	*Confidence interval results for difference between means*				
12		Confidence level	95.0%		
13		Sample mean difference	-2.725		
14		Pooled standard deviation	4.909	NA	
15		Std error of difference	1.142	1.064	
16		Degrees of freedom	78	71	
17		Lower limit	-4.998	-4.847	
18		Upper limit	-0.452	-0.603	
19					
20	*Test of difference>=0 versus one-tailed alternative*				
21		Hypothesized mean difference	0.000		
22		Sample mean difference	-2.725		
23		Pooled standard deviation	4.909	NA	
24		Std error of difference	1.142	1.064	
25		Degrees of freedom	78	71	
26		t test statistic	-2.387	-2.560	
27		p value	0.010	0.006	
28					
29	*Test of equality of variances*				
30		Ratio of sample variances	1.673		
31		p value	0.073		

If we can assume that the population standard deviations are equal (and the values in cells J9 and K9 suggest that this assumption is plausible), then the output in the range J21:J27 is relevant. It shows that the observed sample mean difference, -2.725, is indeed negative. That is, the exercisers in the sample outperformed the nonexercisers by 2.725 rating points on average. The output also shows that (1) the standard error of the sample mean difference is 1.142, (2) the test statistic is -2.387, and (3) the p-value for a one-tailed test is 0.010. In words, the data provide enough evidence to reject the null hypothesis at the 1% significance level. It is clear that exercisers perform better, in terms of mean ratings, than nonexercisers. A 95% confidence for this mean difference is all negative; it extends from -4.998 to -0.452.

This answers the first question we posed, but it doesn't answer the second. There is no way to be sure that the higher ratings for the exercisers are a direct result of exercise. It could be that employees who exercise are naturally more ambitious and hard-working people, and that this extra drive is responsible for *both* their exercising and their higher ratings. This study is an **observational study**. The company simply observes two randomly selected groups of employees and analyzes the results. It does not explicitly control for other factors, such as personality, that might be responsible for differences in ratings. Therefore, it can never be sure that there is a cause–effect relationship between exercise and performance ratings. All it can state is that exercisers appear, on average, to be more productive than nonexercisers—for whatever reason.

We are almost finished with this example, but not quite. What about the output in column K, and the test in rows 29–31? The test we just performed and the confidence interval we reported are based on the assumption of equal population standard deviations (or variances). As we discussed in Section 8.7.1, if this assumption is violated, then a slightly different form of analysis should be performed, and its results are reported in column K. As we see, the results are very similar to those in column J, although the p-value is slightly lower and the confidence interval is slightly narrower.

The test reported in rows 29 and 31 is a formal test of the hypothesis $H_0: \sigma_1^2/\sigma_2^2 = 1$ versus $H_a: \sigma_1^2/\sigma_2^2 \neq 1$, where the parameter being tested is the *ratio* of the two population variances. (The details behind this test are explained in the following subsection.) If we can reject this null hypothesis on the basis of a low p-value in cell J31, then we are fairly certain that the equal-variance assumption is *not* valid and that we should use the output in column K. Otherwise, we can use the output in column J. The p-value in cell J31, 0.073, suggests that the two population variances might not be equal, but the evidence is not overwhelming. Of course, the similarity of the outputs in columns J and K implies, especially from a practical point of view, that it doesn't really make much difference. In other examples it could be more critical. ■

9.4.3 Hypothesis Test for Equal Population Variances

As we just saw, the two-sample procedure for a difference between population means depends on whether we can assume equal population variances.[6] Therefore, it is natural to test first for equal variances. We phrase this latter test in terms of the *ratio* of population variances, σ_1^2/σ_2^2. The null hypothesis is that this ratio is 1 (equal variances), whereas the alternative is that it is not 1 (unequal variances). The test statistic for this test is the ratio of sample variances:

$$F\text{-value} = s_1^2/s_2^2$$

Assuming that the population variances are equal, this test statistic has an F distribution with $n_1 - 1$ and $n_2 - 1$ degrees of freedom.

The F distribution, named after the famous statistician R. A. Fisher, is another sampling distribution that arises frequently in statistical studies. (We will see it again when we study regression analysis in Chapters 11 and 12.) Because it always describes a ratio, there are two degrees of freedom parameters, one for the numerator and one for the denominator, and the numerator degrees of freedom is always quoted first.

Tables of the F distribution, for selected degrees of freedom, appear in many statistics books, but the necessary information can be obtained more easily with Excel's FDIST and FINV functions. The FDIST function takes the form

$$=\text{FDIST}(v, df1, df2)$$

---

[6] The test in this section is traditionally stated in terms of variances, as we do here. It could also be stated in terms of standard deviations because equal variances imply equal standard deviations.

This function returns the probability to the right of value v when the degrees of freedom are $df1$ and $df2$. Similarly, the FINV function takes the form

$$=\text{FINV}(p, df1, df2)$$

It returns the value with probability p to the right of it when the degrees of freedom are $df1$ and $df2$.

The F test for equal variances is performed as follows. We first create the test statistic by putting the *larger* of the two sample variances in the numerator. Hence, the test statistic is always greater than or equal to 1. Then we find the corresponding p-value with the FDIST function. For example, the formulas in cells J30 and J31 of Figure 9.25 are

$$=(\text{J9/K9})^2$$

and

$$=\text{FDIST(J30,J7-1,K7-1)}$$

The StatPro Two-Sample procedure first checks that the larger sample standard deviation is in cell J9, so it puts the corresponding variance in the numerator of the test statistic. Then it finds the probability to the right of this test statistic with the FDIST function, where the degrees of freedom are $51 - 1$ and $29 - 1$. If the larger sample standard deviation had been in cell K9, then these formulas would have been

$$=(\text{K9/J9})^2$$

and

$$=\text{FDIST(J30,K7-1,J7-1)}$$

That is, the degrees of freedom would have been reversed.

For our purposes, the most important thing is the conclusion we draw from the test. If the p-value is small, we can conclude that the population variances are *not* equal. Otherwise, we can accept an equal-variance assumption. The p-value for the exercise data, 0.073, is in the "gray area." It provides some evidence of unequal variances, but the evidence is not overwhelming.

9.4.4 Hypothesis Tests for Differences Between Population Proportions

One of the most common uses of hypothesis testing is to test whether two population proportions are equal. The theory is as follows. Let p_1 and p_2 be the two population proportions, and let $\widehat{p}_1$ and $\widehat{p}_2$ be the corresponding sample proportions, based on sample sizes n_1 and n_2. To base a test on the difference $\widehat{p}_1 - \widehat{p}_2$, we need its standard error. If the null hypothesis is true and $p_1 = p_2$, then it can be shown that the standard error of $\widehat{p}_1 - \widehat{p}_2$ is

$$\text{SE}(\widehat{p}_1 - \widehat{p}_2) = \sqrt{\widehat{p}_c(1 - \widehat{p}_c)(1/n_1 + 1/n_2)}$$

where $\widehat{p}_c$ is the pooled proportion from the two samples combined. For example, if $\widehat{p}_1 = 20/85$ and $\widehat{p}_2 = 34/115$, then $\widehat{p}_c = (20 + 34)/(85 + 115) = 54/200$.

Given this standard error, the rest is straightforward. Assuming that the sample sizes are reasonably large, the test statistic

$$z\text{-value} = \frac{\widehat{p}_1 - \widehat{p}_2}{\text{SE}(\widehat{p}_1 - \widehat{p}_2)}$$

has (approximately) a standard normal distribution. Therefore, the corresponding p-value for the test can be found with Excel's NORMSDIST function, as illustrated in the next example.

EXAMPLE 9.7

The ArmCo Company, a large manufacturer of automobile parts, has several plants in the United States. For years, ArmCo employees have complained that their suggestions for improvements in the manufacturing processes are ignored by upper management. In the spirit of employee empowerment, ArmCo management at the Midwest plant decided to initiate a number of policies to respond to employee suggestions. For example, a mailbox was located in a central location, and employees were encouraged to drop suggestions into this box. No such initiatives were taken at the other ArmCo plants. As expected, there was a great deal of employee enthusiasm at the Midwest plant shortly after the new policies were implemented, but the question was whether life would revert to normal and the enthusiasm would dampen with time.

To check this, 100 randomly selected employees at the Midwest plant and 300 employees from other plants were asked to fill out a questionnaire 6 months after the implementation of the new policies at the Midwest plant. Employees were instructed to respond to each item on the questionnaire by checking either a "yes" box or a "no" box. Two specific items on the questionnaire were:

■ Management at this plant is generally responsive to employee suggestions for improvements in the manufacturing processes.

■ Management at this plant is more responsive to employee suggestions now than it used to be.

The results of the questionnaire for these two items appear in rows 5 and 6 of Figure 9.26. (See the file EMPOWER1.XLS.) Does it appear that the policies at the Midwest plant are appreciated? Should ArmCo implement these policies in its other plants?

FIGURE 9.26   **Results for Employee Empowerment Example**

	A	B	C	D	E	F	G
1	**Employee empowerment results**						
2							
3	Item 1: Management responds				Item 2: Things have improved		
4		Midwest	Other			Midwest	Other
5	Yes	39	93		Yes	68	159
6	No	61	207		No	32	141
7	Totals	100	300		Totals	100	300
8							
9	Sample proportion yes	0.39	0.31			0.68	0.53
10	Pooled proportion yes	0.33				0.568	
11							
12	Difference between proportions	0.08		**Range names**		0.15	
13	Standard error of difference	0.054		Diff: B12		0.057	
14	Test statistic	1.473		PooledProp: B10		2.622	
15	p-value	0.070		SampProp1: B9		0.004	
16				SampProp2: C9			
17	Confidence interval for difference			SampSize1: B7			
18	Confidence level	95%		SampSize2: C7		95%	
19	Standard error of difference	0.056		StErr: B13		0.055	
20	z-multiple	1.960		TestStat: B14		1.960	
21	Lower confidence limit	-0.029				0.043	
22	Upper confidence limit	0.189				0.257	

Solution

For either questionnaire item we let p_1 be the proportion of "yes" responses we would obtain at the Midwest plant if the questionnaire were given to all of its employees. We define p_2 similarly for the other plants. Management certainly hopes to find a larger proportion of "yes" responses (to either item) at the Midwest plant than at the other plants, so the appropriate test is one-tailed, with the hypotheses set up as $H_0: p_1 - p_2 \leq 0$ versus $H_a: p_1 - p_2 > 0$. (We could also write these as $H_0: p_1 \leq p_2$ versus $H_a: p_1 > p_2$, but this has no effect on the test.)

The data from this type of questionnaire are usually given as *counts* of "yes" and "no" responses, as in Figure 9.26, but these easily translate into sample proportions. For the first questionnaire item, the sample proportions of "yes" responses are $\widehat{p}_1 = 39/100 = 0.39$ and $\widehat{p}_2 = 93/300 = 0.31$, for a difference of $\widehat{p}_1 - \widehat{p}_2 = 0.08$. The standard error of this difference, under the assumption that $p_1 = p_2$, uses the pooled proportion $\widehat{p}_c = (39 + 93)/(100 + 300) = 0.33$. This produces a standard error of 0.054, calculated in cell B13 with the formula

$$=\text{SQRT(PooledProp*(1-PooledProp)*(1/SampSize1+1/SampSize2))}$$

Then the test statistic is $0.08/0.054 = 1.473$, and the corresponding *p*-value for the test is the probability to the right of 1.473 in the standard normal distribution. Its value is 0.070, found in cell B15 with the formula

$$=\text{1-NORMSDIST(TestStat)}$$

A similar analysis for the second questionnaire item leads to a sample difference of $0.68 - 0.53 = 0.15$ and a *p*-value of 0.004.

These results should be fairly good news for management. There is moderate, but not overwhelming, support for the hypothesis that management at the Midwest plant is more responsive than at the other plants, at least as perceived by employees. There is convincing support for the hypothesis that things have improved more at the Midwest plant than at the other plants. Corresponding 95% confidence intervals for the differences between proportions appear in rows 21 and 22. Since they are almost completely positive, they reinforce the hypothesis-test findings. Moreover, they provide a range of plausible values for the differences between the population proportions.

The only real downside to these findings, from Midwest management's point of view, is the sample proportion $\widehat{p}_1$ for the first item. Only 39% of the sampled employees at that plant believe that management generally responds to their suggestions, even though 68% believe things are better than they used to be. A reasonable conclusion by ArmCo management is that they are on the right track at the Midwest plant, and the policies initiated there ought to be initiated at other plants, but more still needs to be done at *all* plants. ∎

P R O B L E M S

Level A

9 In the past, 60% of all undergraduate students enrolled at State University earned their degrees within 4 years of matriculation. A random sample of 36 students from the class that matriculated in the fall of 1994 was recently selected to test whether there has been a change in the proportion of students who graduate within 4 years. Administrators found that 15 of these 36 students graduated in the spring of 1998 (i.e., 4 academic years after matriculation).

   a Given the sample outcome, construct a 95% confidence interval for the relevant population proportion. Does this interval estimate suggest that there has been in a change in the proportion of students who graduate within 4 years? Why or why not?

b Given the sample outcome, construct a 99% confidence interval for the relevant population proportion. Does this interval estimate suggest that there has been in a change in the proportion of students who graduate within 4 years? Why or why not?

10 Continuing the previous problem, suppose now that State University administrators want to test the claim made by faculty that the proportion of students who graduate within 4 years at State University has fallen *below* the historical value of 60% this year. Use the given sample proportion to test this claim. Report a *p*-value and interpret it in the context of this statistical hypothesis test.

11 The director of admissions of a distinguished (i.e., top-20) MBA program is interested in studying the proportion of entering students in similar graduate business programs who have achieved a composite score on the Graduate Management Admissions Test (GMAT) in excess of 630. In particular, the admissions director believes that the proportion of students entering top-rated programs with such composite GMAT scores is now 50%. To test this hypothesis, he has collected a random sample of MBA candidates entering his program in the fall of 1998. He believes that these students' GMAT scores are indicative of the scores earned by their peers in his program and in competitors' programs. The GMAT scores for these 25 individuals are given in the file P9_11.XLS. Test the admission director's claim at the 5% significance level and report your findings. Does your conclusion change when the significance level is increased to 10%?

12 A market research consultant hired by the Pepsi-Cola Co. is interested in determining the proportion of consumers who favor Pepsi-Cola over Coke Classic in a particular urban location. A random sample of 250 consumers from the market under investigation is provided in the file P8_17.XLS.

a Construct a 99% confidence interval for the proportion of all consumers in this market who prefer Pepsi over Coke. Interpret this confidence interval for Pepsi's market researchers.

b Does the confidence interval in part **a** support the claim made by one of Pepsi-Cola's marketing managers that more than half of the consumers in this urban location favor Pepsi over Coke? Explain your answer.

c Comment on the sample size used by the market research consultant. Specifically, is the sample unnecessarily large? Why or why not?

13 The CEO of a medical supply company is committed to expanding the proportion of highly qualified women in the organization's staff of salespersons. He claims that the proportion of women in similar sales positions across the country in 1998 is less than 50%. Hoping to find support for his claim, he directs his assistant to collect a random sample of salespersons employed by his company, which is thought to be representative of sales staffs of competing organizations in the industry. These data are listed in the file P9_13.XLS. Test this manager's claim using the given sample data and report a *p*-value. Do you find statistical support for his hypothesis that the proportion of women in similar sales positions across the country is less than 50%?

14 Management of a software development firm would like to establish a wellness program during the lunch hour to enhance the physical and mental health of its employees. Before introducing the wellness program, management must first be convinced that a sufficiently large majority of its employees are not already exercising at lunchtime. Specifically, it plans to initiate the program only if less than 40% of its personnel take time to exercise prior to eating lunch. To make this decision, management has surveyed a random sample of 100 employees regarding their midday exercise activities. The results of the survey are given in the file P9_14.XLS.

a Using a 10% significance level, is there sufficient evidence for managers of this organization to initiate a corporate wellness program? Why or why not?

b Using a 1% significance level, is there sufficient evidence for managers of this organization to initiate a corporate wellness program? Why or why not?

15 The managing partner of a major consulting firm is trying to assess the effectiveness of expensive computer skills training given to all new entry-level professionals. In an effort to make such an assessment, she administers a computer skills test immediately before and after the training program to each of 40 randomly chosen employees. The pretraining and posttraining scores of these 40 individuals are recorded in the file P9_15.XLS.

a Using a 10% level of significance, do the given sample data support the claim that the organization's training program is increasing the new employee's working knowledge of computing?

b Using a 1% level of significance, do the given sample data support the claim that the organization's training program is increasing the new employee's working knowledge of computing?

16 A large buyer of household batteries wants to decide which of two equally priced brands to purchase. To do this, he takes a random sample of 100 batteries of each brand. The lifetimes, measured in hours, of the randomly chosen batteries are recorded in the file P9_16.XLS.

    a Using the given sample data, generate a 95% confidence interval for the difference between the mean lifetimes of brand 1 and brand 2 batteries. Based on this confidence interval, which brand should the buyer purchase?

    b Using the given sample data, generate a 99% confidence interval for the difference in the mean lifetimes of brand 1 and brand 2 batteries. Based on this confidence interval, which brand should the buyer purchase?

    c How can your analyses in parts **a** and **b** be related to hypothesis testing?

17 The managers of a chemical manufacturing plant are interested in determining whether recent safety training workshops have reduced the weekly number of reported safety violations at the facility. The management team has randomly selected weekly safety violation reports for each of 25 weeks prior to the safety training and 25 weeks after the safety workshops. These data are provided in the file P9_17.XLS. Given this evidence, is it possible to conclude that the safety workshops have been effective in reducing the number of safety violations reported per week? Report a p-value and interpret your findings for the management team.

18 A real estate agent has collected a random sample of 75 houses that were recently sold in a suburban community. She is particularly interested in comparing the appraised value and recent selling price of the houses in this particular market. The values of these two variables for each of the 75 randomly chosen houses are provided in the file P8_24.XLS. Using these sample data, test whether there exists a statistically significant mean difference between the appraised values and selling prices of the houses sold in this suburban community. Report a p-value. For which levels of significance is it appropriate to conclude that *no* difference exists between these two values?

19 The owner of two submarine sandwich shops located in Gainesville, Florida, would like to know how the mean daily sales of the first shop (located in the downtown area) compares to that of the second shop (located on the southwest side of town). In particular, he would like to know whether the mean daily sales levels of these two restaurants are essentially equal. He records the sales (in dollars) made at each location for 30 randomly chosen days. These sales levels are given in the file P9_19.XLS. Construct a 99% confidence level for the mean difference between the daily sales of restaurant 1 and restaurant 2. Use this confidence interval to answer the following questions:

    a Is it possible to conclude that a statistically significant mean difference exists at the 1% level of significance? Explain why or why not.

    b Is it possible to conclude that a statistically significant mean difference exists at the 5% level of significance? Explain why or why not.

    c Is it possible to conclude that a statistically significant mean difference exists at the 10% level of significance? Explain why or why not.

20 Suppose that an investor wants to compare the risks associated with two different stocks. One way to measure the risk of a given stock is to measure the variation in the stock's daily price changes. The investor obtains a random sample of 25 daily price changes for stock 1 and 25 daily price changes for stock 2. These data are provided in the file P9_20.XLS. Show how this investor can compare the risks associated with the two stocks by testing the null hypothesis that the variances of the stocks are equal. Use $\alpha = 0.10$ and interpret the results of the statistical test.

21 A manufacturing company is interested in determining whether a significant difference exists between the variance of the number of units produced per day by one machine operator and the similar variance for another machine operator. The file P9_21.XLS contains the number of units produced by operator 1 and operator 2, respectively, on each of 25 days. Note that these two sets of days are not necessarily the same, so you can assume that the two samples are *independent* of one another.

    a Do these sample data indicate a statistically significant difference at $\alpha = 0.10$? Explain your answer.

b If your conclusion in part **a** were incorrect, would you have committed a type I or type II error? Explain.

c At which values of α could you *not* reject the null hypothesis?

22 A large buyer of household batteries wants to decide which of two equally priced brands to purchase. To do this, he takes a random sample of 100 batteries of each brand. The lifetimes, measured in hours, of the batteries are recorded in the file P9_16.XLS. Before testing for the difference between the mean lifetimes of these two batteries, he must first determine whether the underlying population variances are equal.

a Perform a test for equal population variances. Report a p-value and interpret its meaning.

b Based on your conclusion in part **a**, which test statistic should be used in performing a test for the existence of a difference between population means?

23 Do undergraduate business students who major in finance earn, on average, higher annual starting salaries than their peers who major in marketing? Before addressing this question through a statistical hypothesis test, we should determine whether the variances of annual starting salaries of the two types of majors are equal. The file P9_23.XLS contains the starting salaries of 50 randomly selected finance majors and 50 randomly chosen marketing majors.

a Perform a test for equal population variances. Report a p-value and interpret its meaning.

b Based on your conclusion in part **a**, which test statistic should be used in performing a test for the existence of a difference between population means?

24 The CEO of a medical supply company is committed to expanding the proportion of highly qualified women in the organization's large staff of salespersons. Given the recent hiring practices of his human resources director, he claims that the company has increased the proportion of women in sales positions throughout the organization between 1993 and 1998. Hoping to find support for his claim, he directs his assistant to collect random samples of the salespersons employed by the company in 1993 and 1998. These data can be found in the file P9_13.XLS. Test the CEO's claim using the given sample data and report a p-value. Do you find statistical support for the efficacy of his committed strategy to hiring a greater proportion of female salespersons?

25 The director of admissions of a distinguished (i.e., top-20) MBA program is interested in studying the proportion of entering students in similar graduate business programs who have achieved a composite score on the Graduate Management Admissions Test (GMAT) in excess of 630. In particular, the admissions director believes that the proportion of students entering top-rated programs with such composite GMAT scores is higher in 1998 than it was in 1988. To test this hypothesis, he has collected random samples of MBA candidates entering his program in the fall of 1998 and in the fall of 1988. He believes that these students' GMAT scores are indicative of the scores earned by their peers in his program and in competitors' programs. The GMAT scores for the randomly selected students entering in each year are given in the file P9_11.XLS. Test the admission director's claim at the 5% significance level and report your findings. Does your conclusion change when the significance level is increased to 10%?

26 Managers of a software development firm have established a wellness program during the lunch hour to enhance the physical and mental health of their employees. Now, they would like to see whether the wellness program has increased the proportion of employees who exercise regularly during the lunch hour. To make this assessment, the managers surveyed a random sample of 100 employees about their noontime exercise habits *before* the wellness program was initiated. Later, *after* the program was initiated, another 100 employees were independently chosen and surveyed about their lunchtime exercise habits. The results of these two surveys are given in the file P9_14.XLS.

a Construct a 99% confidence interval for the difference in the proportions of employees who exercise regularly during their lunch hour before and after the implementation of the corporate wellness program.

b Does the confidence interval found in part **a** support the belief that the wellness program has increased the proportion of employees who exercise regularly during the lunch hour? If so, at which levels of significance is this claim supported?

c Would your results in parts **a** and **b** differ if the *same* 100 employees surveyed before the program were also surveyed after the program? Explain.

27 An Environmental Protection Agency official asserts that more than 80% of the plants in the northeast region of the United States meet air pollution standards. An antipollution advocate does not believe the EPA's claim. She takes a random sample of 64 plants in the northeast region and finds that 56 meet the federal government's pollution standards.

   a Does the sample information support the EPA's claim at the 5% level of significance?

   b For which values of the sample proportion (based on a sample size of 64) would the sample data support the EPA's claim? Assume that $\alpha = 0.05$.

   c Would the conclusion found in part **a** change if the sample proportion remained constant but the sample size increased to 124? Explain why or why not.

28 A television network decides to cancel one of its shows if it is convinced that less than 14% of the viewing public are watching this show.

   a If a random sample of 1500 households with televisions is selected, what sample proportion values will lead to this show's cancellation? Assume a 5% significance level.

   b What is the probability that this show will be canceled if 13.4% of all viewing households are watching it?

29 An economic researcher would like to know whether he can reject the null hypothesis, at the $\alpha = 0.10$ level, that no more than 20% of the households in Pennsylvania make more than $70,000 per year.

   a If 200 Pennsylvania households are chosen at random, how many of them would have to be earning more than $70,000 per year for the researcher to reject the null hypothesis?

   b Assuming that the true proportion of all Pennsylvania households with annual incomes of least $70,000 is 0.217, find the probability of *not* rejecting a *false* null hypothesis when the sample size is 200.

30 Senior partners of an accounting firm are concerned about recent complaints by some female managers that they are paid less than their male counterparts. In response to these charges, the partners direct their human resources director to record the salaries of female and male managers with equivalent education, work experience, and job performance. A random sample of these pairs of managers is provided in the file P9_30.XLS.

   a Do these data support the claim made by some female managers within this organization? Report and interpret a *p*-value.

   b Assuming a 5% significance level, which values of the sample mean difference between the female and male salaries would support the claim of discrimination against female managers?

31 Do undergraduate business students who major in finance earn, on average, higher annual starting salaries than their peers who major in marketing? Address this question through a statistical hypothesis test. The file P9_23.XLS contains the starting salaries of 50 randomly selected finance majors and 50 randomly selected marketing majors.

   a Is it appropriate to perform a paired-comparison *t*-test in this case? Explain why or why not.

   b Perform an appropriate hypothesis test with a 1% significance level. Summarize your findings.

   c How large would the difference between the mean starting salaries of finance and marketing majors have to be before you could conclude that finance majors earn more on average? Employ a 1% significance level in answering this question.

32 Consider a random sample of 100 households from a middle-class neighborhood that was the recent focus of an economic development study conducted by the local government. Specifically, for each of the 100 households, information was gathered on each of the following variables: family size, location of the household within the neighborhood, an indication of whether those surveyed owned or rented their home, gross annual income of the first household wage earner, gross annual income of the second household wage earner (if applicable), monthly home mortgage or rent payment, average monthly expenditure on utilities, and the total indebtedness (excluding the value of a home mortgage) of the household. The data are in the file P8_26.XLS.

Test for the existence of a significant difference between the mean indebtedness levels of the households in the first (i.e., SW) and second (i.e., NW) sectors of this community. Perform similar hypothesis tests for the differences between the mean indebtedness levels of households from all other pairs of locations (i.e., first and third, first and fourth, second and third, second and fourth, and third and fourth). Summarize your findings.

33 Elected officials in a small Florida town are preparing the annual budget for their community. They would like to determine whether their constituents living across town are typically paying the same amount in real estate taxes each year. Given that there are over 3000 homeowners in this small community, officials have decided to sample a representative subset of taxpayers and thoroughly study their tax payments. A randomly selected set of 170 homeowners is given in the file P9_33.XLS. Specifically, the elected officials would like to test for the existence of a statistical difference between the mean real estate tax bill paid by residents of the *first* neighborhood of this town and each of the remaining five neighborhoods (i.e., neighborhoods 2 through 6).

   a Before conducting any hypothesis tests on the difference between various pairs of mean real estate tax payments, perform a test for equal population variances for each pair of neighborhoods. For each pair, report a *p*-value and interpret its meaning.

   b Based on your conclusions in part **a**, which test statistic should be used in performing a test for the existence of a difference between population means in each pair?

   c Given your conclusions in part **b**, appropriately perform each of the tests for the existence of a difference between mean real estate tax payments in each pair of neighborhoods. For each pair, report a *p*-value and interpret its meaning.

34 Suppose that you sample two normal populations independently. The variances of these two populations are σ_1^2 and σ_2^2. You take random samples of sizes n_1 and n_2 and observe sample variances of s_1^2 and s_2^2.

   a If $n_1 = n_2 = 21$, how large must the fraction s_1/s_2 be before you can reject the null hypothesis that σ_1^2 is no greater than σ_2^2 at the 5% significance level?

   b Answer part **a** when $n_1 = n_2 = 41$.

   c If s_1 is 25% greater than s_2, approximately how large must n_1 and n_2 be if you are able to reject the null hypothesis in part **a** at the 5% significance level? Assume that n_1 and n_2 are equal.

35 Two teams of workers assemble automobile engines at a manufacturing plant in Michigan. Quality control personnel inspect a random sample of the teams' assemblies and judge each assembly to be acceptable or unacceptable. A random sample of 127 assemblies from team 1 shows 12 unacceptable assemblies. A similar random sample of 98 assemblies from team 2 shows 5 unacceptable assemblies.

   a Construct a 90% confidence interval for the difference between the proportions of unacceptable assemblies generated by the two teams.

   b Based on a review of the confidence interval found in part **a**, is there sufficient evidence to conclude, at the 10% significance level, that the two teams differ with respect to their proportions of unacceptable assemblies?

   c For which values of the difference between these two sample proportions could you conclude that a statistically significant difference exists? Assume that $\alpha = 0.10$.

36 A market research consultant hired by the Pepsi-Cola Co. is interested in determining whether there is a difference between the proportions of female and male consumers who favor Pepsi-Cola over Coke Classic in a particular urban location. A random sample of 250 consumers from the market under investigation is provided in the file P8_17.XLS.

   a After separating the 250 randomly selected consumers by *gender*, perform the statistical test and report a *p*-value. At which levels of α will the market research consultant conclude that there is essentially no difference between the proportions of female and male consumers who prefer Pepsi to Coke in this urban area?

   b Marketing managers at the Pepsi-Cola Co. have asked their market research consultant to explore further the potential differences in the proportions of women and men who prefer drinking Pepsi to Coke Classic. Specifically, Pepsi managers would like to know whether the potential difference between the proportions of female and male consumers who favor Pepsi varies by the *age* of the consumers. Using the same random sample of consumers as in part **a,** assess whether this difference varies across the four given age categories: *under 20, between 20 and 40, between 40 and 60,* and *over 60.* Employ a 10% significance level in performing each of the *six* required hypothesis tests. Summarize your conclusions in detail. Finally, what recommendations would you make to the marketing managers in light of your statistical findings?

37 The employee benefits manager of a small private university would like to determine whether differences exist in the proportions of various groups of full-time employees who prefer adopting the second (i.e., plan B) of three available health care plans in the forthcoming annual enrollment period. A reliable frame of the university's employees and their tentative health care preferences are given in the file P7_25.XLS.

    a First, select a simple random sample of 25 employees from *each* of three employee classifications: *administrative staff, support staff,* and *faculty.*

    b Use the three simple random samples obtained in part **a** to perform tests for differences in the proportions of employees within respective classifications who favor plan B in the coming year. For instance, the first such test should examine the potential difference between the proportion of administrative employees who favor plan B and the proportion of the support staff who prefer plan B.

    c Report a *p*-value for each of your hypothesis tests and interpret your results. How might the benefits manager use the information you have derived from these statistical tests?

38 Consider a random sample of 100 households from a middle-class neighborhood that was the recent focus of an economic development study conducted by the local government. Specifically, for each of the 100 randomly selected households, information was gathered on each of the following variables: family size, location of the household within the neighborhood, an indication of whether those surveyed owned or rented their home, gross annual income of the first household wage earner, gross annual income of the second household wage earner (if applicable), monthly home mortgage or rent payment, average monthly expenditure on utilities, and the total indebtedness (excluding the value of a home mortgage) of the household. The data are provided in the file P8_26.XLS.

    Researchers would like to use the available sample information to discern whether home ownership rates vary by household *location.* For example, is there a nonzero difference between the proportions of individuals who own their homes (as opposed to those who rent their homes) in households located in the first (i.e., SW) and second (i.e., NW) sectors of this community? Use the given sample to perform a test for the existence of a difference in home ownership rates in these two sectors as well as for those of other pairs of household locations. Assume that $\alpha = 0.05$. Interpret and summarize your results. (*Hint:* To be complete, you should construct and interpret a total of six hypothesis tests.)

39 For testing the difference between two proportions, we use $\sqrt{\hat{p}_c(1 - \hat{p}_c)(1/n_1 + 1/n_2)}$ as the approximate standard error of $\hat{p}_1 - \hat{p}_2$, where $\hat{p}_c$ is the pooled sample proportion. Explain why this is reasonable when the null-hypothesized value of $p_1 - p_2$ is zero. Why would this not be a good approximation when the null-hypothesized value of $p_1 - p_2$ is a nonzero number? What would you recommend using for the standard error of $\hat{p}_1 - \hat{p}_2$ in that case? ■

9.5   One-Way ANOVA

I n Sections 8.7.1 and 9.4.2 we discussed the two-sample procedure for analyzing the difference between two population means. A natural extension is to *more* than two population means. The resulting procedure is commonly called **one-way analysis of variance**, or **one-way ANOVA**. There are two typical situations where one-way ANOVA is used. The first is when there are several distinct populations. For example, consider recent graduates with BS degrees in one of three disciplines: Business, Engineering, and Computer Science. We might sample randomly from each of these populations to discover whether there are any significant differences between them with respect to mean starting salary.

A second situation where one-way ANOVA is used is in randomized experiments. In this case a *single* population is treated in one of several ways. For example, a pharmaceutical company might select a group of people who suffer from allergies and randomly assign each person to a different type of allergy medicine currently being developed. Then the question is whether any of the treatments differ from one another with respect to the mean amount of symptom relief.

The data analysis in these two situations is identical; only the interpretation of the results differs. For the sake of clarity, we will phrase this discussion in terms of the first situation, where we randomly sample from each of several populations. Let I be the number of populations, and denote the means of these populations by μ_1 through μ_I. The null hypothesis is that the I means are all equal, whereas the alternative is that they are not all equal. Note that this alternative admits many possibilities. With $I = 4$, for example, we could have $\mu_1 = \mu_2 = \mu_3 = 5$ and $\mu_4 = 10$, or we could have $\mu_1 = \mu_2 = 5$ and $\mu_3 = \mu_4 = 10$, or we could have $\mu_1 = 5, \mu_2 = 7, \mu_3 = 9$, and $\mu_4 = 10$. The alternative hypothesis simply specifies that *the means are not all equal*.

The one-way ANOVA procedure is usually run in two stages. In the first stage we test the null hypothesis of equal means. If the resulting *p*-value is not sufficiently small, then there is not enough evidence to reject the equal-means hypothesis, and the analysis stops. However, if the *p*-value is sufficiently small, we can conclude with some assurance that the means are not all equal. Then the second stage is to discover which means are significantly different from which other means. This latter analysis is usually accomplished via confidence intervals.

If one-way ANOVA is basically a test of differences between means, why is it called analysis of *variance*? The answer to this question is the key to the procedure. Consider the plot in Figure 9.27. Each point corresponds to a single observation, and each vertical scatter corresponds to the observations from a particular sample. The horizontal bars in the middle of each vertical scatter indicate the sample means. From this graph, would you conclude that the population means differ? Would your answer change if the data were instead as in Figure 9.28 (page 478)? We expect that it would.

The sample means in these two figures are the same, but the variances *within* each vertical scatter in Figure 9.27 are quite large relative to the variance *between* the sample means. In contrast, there is very little variance within each vertical scatter in Figure 9.28. In the first case the large "within" variance makes it difficult to infer whether there are really any differences between population means, whereas the small "within" variance in the second case makes it easy to infer differences between population means.

This is the essence of the ANOVA test. We compare variances *within* the individual samples to variance *between* the sample means. Only if the between variance is large relative

FIGURE 9.27 **Samples with Large Within Variation**

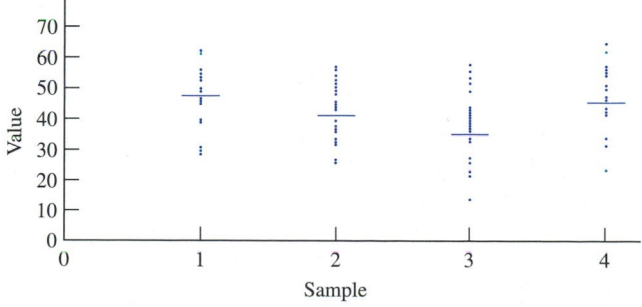

FIGURE 9.28 Samples with Small Within Variation

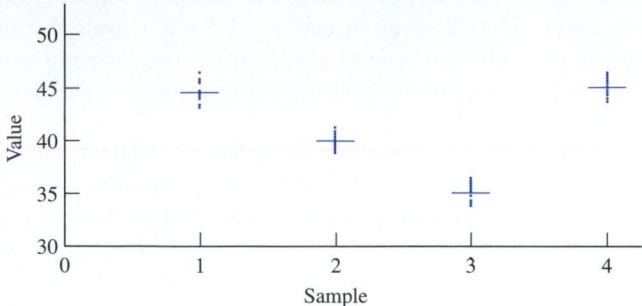

to the within variance can we conclude with any assurance that there are differences between population means—and reject the equal-means hypothesis.

The test itself is based on two assumptions: (1) the population variances are all equal to some common variance σ^2, and (2) the populations are normally distributed. These are analogous to the assumptions we made for the two-sample t test. Although these assumptions are never satisfied exactly in any application, we should keep them in mind and check for gross violations whenever possible. Fortunately, the test we present is fairly robust to violations of these assumptions, particularly when the sample sizes are large and roughly the same.

To run the test, let $\overline{Y}_i$, s_i^2, and n_i be the sample mean, sample variance, and sample size from sample i. Also, let n and $\overline{\overline{Y}}$ be the combined number of observations and the sample mean of all n observations. (We call $\overline{\overline{Y}}$ the **grand mean**.) Then a measure of the between variation is SSB (sum of squares between):

$$SSB = \sum_{i=1}^{I} n_i \left(\overline{Y}_i - \overline{\overline{Y}} \right)^2$$

Note that SSB is large if the individual sample means differ substantially from the grand mean $\overline{\overline{Y}}$, and this occurs only if they differ substantially from one another. A measure of the within variation is SSW (sum of squares within):

$$SSW = \sum_{i=1}^{I} (n_i - 1)s_i^2$$

This sum of squares is large if the individual sample variances are large. For example, SSW is much larger in Figure 9.27 than in Figure 9.28. However, SSB is the same in both figures.

Each of these sums of squares has an associated degrees of freedom, dfB and dfW:

$$dfB = I - 1$$

and

$$dfW = n - I$$

When we divide the sums of squares by their degrees of freedom, we obtain "mean squares," MSB and MSW:

$$MSB = \frac{SSB}{dfB}$$

and

$$MSW = \frac{SSW}{dfW}$$

Actually, it can be shown that MSW is a weighted average of the individual sample variances, where the sample variance s_i^2 receives weight $(n_i - 1)/(n - I)$. In this sense MSW is a pooled estimate of the common variance σ^2, just as in the two-sample procedure.

Finally, the ratio of these means squares is the test statistic we use:

$$F\text{-ratio} = \frac{MSB}{MSW}$$

Under the null hypothesis of equal population means, this test statistic has an F distribution with dfB and dfW degrees of freedom. If the null hypothesis is *not* true, then we would expect MSB to be large relative to MSW, as in Figure 9.28. Therefore, the p-value for the test is found by finding the probability to the *right* of the F-ratio in the F distribution with dfB and dfW degrees of freedom.

The elements of this test are usually presented in an **ANOVA table**, as we will see shortly. The "bottom line" in this table is the p-value. If it is sufficiently small, we can conclude that the population means are not all equal. Otherwise, we cannot reject the equal-means hypothesis.

If we do reject the equal-means hypothesis, then it is customary to examine confidence intervals for the differences between all pairs of population means. This can lead to quite a few confidence intervals. For example, if there are $I = 5$ samples, then there are 10 pairs of differences (the number of ways 2 means can be chosen from 5 means). As usual, the confidence interval for any difference $\mu_i - \mu_j$ is of the form

$$\overline{Y}_i - \overline{Y}_j \pm \text{multiplier} \times SE(\overline{Y}_i - \overline{Y}_j)$$

The appropriate standard error is

$$SE(\overline{Y}_i - \overline{Y}_j) = s_p\sqrt{1/n_i + 1/n_j}$$

where s_p is the pooled standard deviation, calculated as $\sqrt{MSW}$.

The appropriate multiplier for this confidence interval is

$$\text{multiplier} = \sqrt{(I - 1) \times F\text{-value}}$$

where F-value is the value that has probability 0.05 (for a 95% confidence level) to the right of it in the F distribution with dfB and dfW degrees of freedom. This multiple is larger than usual. Instead of its usual value of approximately 2, it is now typically from 2.5 to 3.5. The reason is that if we want to conclude with, say, 95% confidence that *each* of these confidence intervals includes the corresponding mean difference, we must make the confidence intervals relatively wide.

For any of these confidence intervals that does *not* include the value 0, we infer that the corresponding means are not equal. But if a confidence interval does include 0, we cannot conclude that the corresponding means are unequal.

We have presented the formulas for one-way ANOVA because we believe they lend some insight into the procedure. However, StatPro's one-way ANOVA procedure takes care of all the tedious calculations, as illustrated in the following example.

E X A M P L E   9 . 8

We discussed the ArmCo Company in Example 9.7. It initiated an employee empowerment program at its Midwest plant, and the reaction from employees was basically positive. Let's assume now that ArmCo has initiated this policy in all five of its plants—in the South,

Midwest, Northeast, Southwest, and West—and several months later it wants to see whether the policy is being perceived equally by employees across the plants. Random samples of employees at the five plants have been asked to rate the success of the empowerment policy on a 1 to 10 scale, 10 being the most favorable rating. The data appear in Figure 9.29.[7] (See the file EMPOWER2.XLS.) Is there any indication of mean differences across the plants? If so, which plants appear to differ from which others?

FIGURE 9.29 **Data for Empowerment Example**

	A	B	C	D	E
1	Empowerment results from several plants				
2					
3	South	Midwest	Northeast	Southwest	West
4	7	7	7	6	6
5	1	6	5	4	6
6	8	10	5	7	6
7	7	3	5	10	6
8	2	9	4	7	3
9	9	10	3	6	4
10	3	8	4	6	8
11	8	4	5	7	6
41	5	3	5	4	2
42	7	2	3	3	4
43	4	7	3	7	5
44		7	3	8	6
45		5	5	9	4
46		10	5	10	7
47		10		4	4
48		6		10	3
49		3		4	5
50		5		6	4
51		2			7
52		6			6
53		4			4
54		5			
55		2			
56		7			
57		8			
58		7			

Solution

First, note that the sample sizes are not equal. This could be because some employees opted not to cooperate or it could be due to other reasons. Fortunately, equal sample sizes are not necessary for the ANOVA test.

The output in Figure 9.30 consists of three basic parts: summary statistics, the ANOVA table, and confidence intervals. The summary statistics show that the Southwest has the largest mean rating, 6.745, and the Northeast has the smallest, 4.140, with the others in between. The sample standard deviations (or variances) vary somewhat across the plants, but not enough to invalidate the procedure. The side-by-side boxplots in Figure 9.31 illustrate these summary measures graphically. However, there is too much overlap between the boxplots to tell (graphically) whether the observed differences between plants are statistically significant.

---

[7]StatPro's one-way ANOVA procedure accepts the data in stacked or unstacked form. The data in this example are unstacked.

FIGURE 9.30   Analysis of Empowerment Data

	G	H	I	J	K	L	M
3	*Results of one-way ANOVA*						
4							
5	*Summary stats for samples*						
6			South	Midwest	Northeast	Southwest	West
7		Sample sizes	40	55	43	47	50
8		Sample means	5.600	5.400	4.140	6.745	4.980
9		Sample standard deviations	2.073	2.469	1.820	1.687	1.635
10		Sample variances	4.297	6.096	3.313	2.846	2.673
11		Weights for pooled variance	0.170	0.235	0.183	0.200	0.213
12							
13		Number of samples	5				
14		Total sample size	235				
15		Grand mean	5.383				
16		Pooled variance	3.904				
17		Pooled standard deviation	1.976				
18							
19	*OneWay ANOVA table*						
20		Source	SS	df	MS	F	p-value
21		Between variation	163.653	4	40.913	10.480	0.0000
22		Within variation	897.879	230	3.904		
23		Total variation	1061.532	234			
24							
25	*Simultaneous confidence intervals for mean differences*						
26		Confidence level	95.0%				
27							
28		Difference	Mean diff	Lower	Upper	Signif?	
29		South - Midwest	0.200	-1.075	1.475	No	
30		South - Northeast	1.460	0.113	2.808	Yes	
31		South - Southwest	-1.145	-2.465	0.175	No	
32		South - West	0.620	-0.682	1.922	No	
33		Midwest - Northeast	1.260	0.011	2.509	Yes	
34		Midwest - Southwest	-1.345	-2.563	-0.126	Yes	
35		Midwest - West	0.420	-0.779	1.619	No	
36		Northeast - Southwest	-2.605	-3.900	-1.310	Yes	
37		Northeast - West	-0.840	-2.117	0.436	No	
38		Southwest - West	1.765	0.518	3.011	Yes	

FIGURE 9.31   Boxplots for Empowerment Data

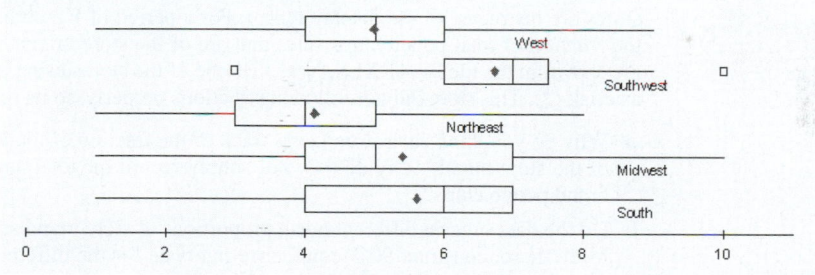

The ANOVA table in rows 19–22 shows the elements for the F test of equal means. All of it is based on the theory we developed above. The only part we didn't discuss is the Total variation in row 22. It is based on the total variation of all observations around the grand mean in cell I14, and is used mainly to aid in the calculations. (Note that SSB and SSW in cells I20 and I21 add up to the total sum of squares in cell I22. Similarly, the degrees of freedom add up in column J.) The F-ratio for the test is 10.480, in cell L20. Its corresponding p-value (to three decimal places) is 0.000. This leaves practically no doubt that the five population means are *not* all equal. Employees evidently do not perceive the empowerment policy equally across plants.

The 95% confidence intervals in rows 26–35 indicate which plants differ significantly from which others. For example, the mean for the Southwest plant is somewhere between 1.31 and 3.9 rating points above the mean for the Northeast plant. We see that the Southwest plant is rated significantly higher than the Northeast, West, and Midwest plants, and the South and Midwest plants are also rated significantly higher than the Northeast plant. Now it is up to ArmCo management to decide whether the magnitudes of these differences are *practically* significant, and, if so, what they can do to increase employee perceptions at the lower-rated plants. ■

PROBLEMS

Level A

40 An automobile manufacturer employs sales representatives who make calls on dealers. The manufacturer wishes to compare the effectiveness of four different call-frequency plans for the sales representatives. Thirty-two representatives are chosen at random from the sales force and randomly assigned to the four call plans (eight per plan). The representatives follow their plans for 6 months, and their sales for the 6-month study period are recorded. These data are given in the file P9_40.XLS.

a Do the sample data support the hypothesis that at least one of the call plans helps produce a higher average level of sales than some other call plan? Perform an appropriate statistical test and report a *p*-value.

b If the sample data indicate the existence of mean sales differences across the call plans, which plans appear to produce different average sales levels? Construct 95% confidence levels for the differences between all pairs of means to help answer this question.

41 Consider a large chain of supermarkets that sell their own brand of potato chips in addition to many other name brands. Management would like to know whether the type of display used for the store brand has any effect on sales. Because there are four types of displays being considered, management decides to choose 24 similar stores to serve as experimental units. A random six of these are instructed to use display type 1, another random six are instructed to use display type 2, a third random six are instructed to use display type 3, and the final six stores are instructed to use display type 4. For a period of 1 month, each store keeps track of the *fraction* of total potato chips sales that are of the store brand. The data for the 24 stores are shown in the file P9_41.XLS. Note that one of the stores using display 3 is marked with an asterisk (*). This store did not follow instructions properly, so its observation is disregarded.

a Why do you think each store keeps track of the fraction of total potato chips sales that are of the store brand? Why do they not simply record the total amount of sales of the store brand potato chips?

b Do the data suggest different mean proportions of store brand sales at the 10% significance level? If so, construct 90% confidence intervals for the differences between all pairs of mean proportions to identify which of the display types are associated with higher fractions of sales.

42 National Airlines recently introduced a daily early-morning nonstop flight between Houston and Chicago. The vice president of marketing for National Airlines decided to perform a statistical test to see whether National's average passenger load on this new flight is different from that of each of its two major competitors (which we will call competitor 1 and competitor 2). Ten early-morning flights were selected at random from each of the three airlines and the percent of *unfilled* seats on each flight was recorded. These data are stored in the file P9_42.XLS.

a Is there evidence that National's average passenger load on the new flight is different from that of its two competitors? Report a *p*-value and interpret the results of the statistical test.

b Select an appropriate significance level and construct confidence intervals for all pairs of differences between means. Which of these differences, if any, are statistically significant at the selected significance level?

43 Do graduates of undergraduate business programs with different majors tend to earn disparate average starting salaries? Consider the data given in the file P9_43.XLS.

   a Is there any reason to doubt the equal-variance assumption made in the one-way ANOVA model in this particular case? Support your response to this question.

   b Assuming that the variances of the four underlying populations are indeed equal, can you reject at the 10% significance level that the mean starting salary is the same for each of the given business majors? Explain why or why not.

   c Generate 90% confidence intervals for all pairs of differences between means. Which of these differences, if any, are statistically significant at $\alpha = 0.10$? ■

9.6 Tests for Normality

The final tests we discuss are tests for normality. As we have already seen, many statistical procedures are based on the assumption that population data are normally distributed. The tests in this section allow us to test this assumption. The null hypothesis is that the population is normally distributed, whereas the alternative is that the population distribution is not normal. Therefore, the burden of proof is on showing that the population distribution is *not* normal. Unless there is sufficient evidence to this effect, we will accept the normal assumption.

The first test we discuss is called a **chi-square goodness-of-fit** test. It is quite intuitive. We form a histogram of the sample data and compare this to the *expected* histogram we would observe if the data were normally distributed with the same mean and standard deviation as the sample. If the two histograms are sufficiently similar, we accept the null hypothesis of normality. Otherwise, we reject it.

The test is based on a numerical measure of the difference between the two histograms. Let C be the number of categories in the histogram, and let O_i be the observed number of observations in category i. Also, let E_i be the expected number of observations in category i if the population were normal with the same mean and standard deviation as the sample. Then we use the following goodness-of-fit measure as a test statistic:

$$\chi^2\text{-value} = \sum_{i=1}^{C}(O_i - E_i)^2/E_i$$

(Here, χ is the Greek letter chi.) If the null hypothesis of normality is true, this test statistic has (approximately) a chi-square distribution with $C - 3$ degrees of freedom. Because *large* values of the test statistic indicate a poor fit—the O_i's do not match up well with the E_i's—the *p*-value for the test is the probability to the right of the test statistic in the chi-square distribution with $C - 3$ degrees of freedom.

Although it is possible to perform this test manually, it is certainly preferable to rely on StatPro, as we demonstrate in the following example.

EXAMPLE 9.9

A company manufactures strips of metal that are supposed to have width 10 centimeters. For purposes of quality control, the manager plans to run some statistical tests on these strips. However, realizing that these statistical procedures assume normally distributed widths, he first tests this normality assumption on 90 randomly sampled strips. How should he proceed?

Solution

The sample data appear in Figure 9.32, where each width is measured to three decimal places. (See the file NORMTEST.XLS.) A number of summary measures also appear. These summary measures help the manager to select "reasonable" categories for a histogram of the data. After observing them, the manager chooses 10 categories for the histogram. The extreme categories are "less than or equal to 9.980" and "greater than 10.020," and the middle eight categories each have length 0.005.

FIGURE 9.32 **Data for Testing Normality**

	A	B	C	D	E	F	G
1	**Illustration of test for normality**						
2							
3	Part	Width			*Summary measures for selected variables*		
4	1	9.99				Width	
5	2	10.031			Count	90.000	
6	3	9.985			Mean	9.999	
7	4	9.983			Standard deviation	0.010	
8	5	10.004			Minimum	9.970	
9	6	10			Maximum	10.031	
10	7	9.992			First quartile	9.993	
11	8	9.996			Third quartile	10.006	
12	9	9.997			5th percentile	9.984	
13	10	9.993			95th percentile	10.014	
14	11	9.991					
89	86	9.977					
90	87	10.004					
91	88	10.007					
92	89	10.003					
93	90	9.996					

To run the test, we select the StatPro/Tests for Normality/Chi-square Test menu item, which leads to the same dialog box as in the Histogram procedure. After specifying the histogram categories in the usual way (upper limit of 9.98 for first category, 10 categories in all, typical length 0.005), we obtain the message in Figure 9.33, the histograms in Figure 9.34, and the numerical output in Figure 9.35. The histograms provide visual evidence of the goodness of fit. The solid bars represent the observed frequencies (the O_i's), and the hollow bars represent the expected frequencies for a normal distribution (the E_i's). The normal fit to the data appears to be quite good.

FIGURE 9.33 **StatPro Message for Chi-Square Test for Normality**

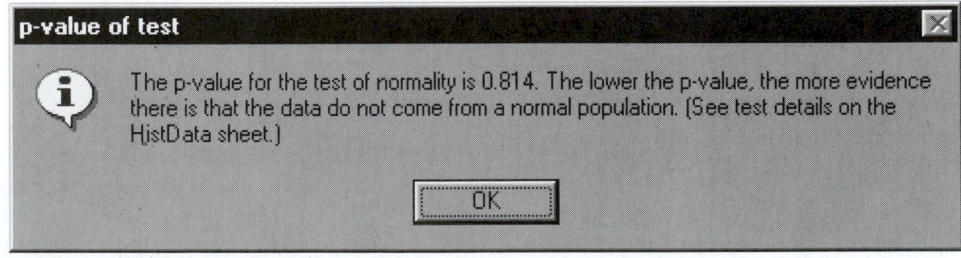

p-value of test

The p-value for the test of normality is 0.814. The lower the p-value, the more evidence there is that the data do not come from a normal population. (See test details on the HistData sheet.)

OK

FIGURE 9.34 **Observed and Normal Histograms**

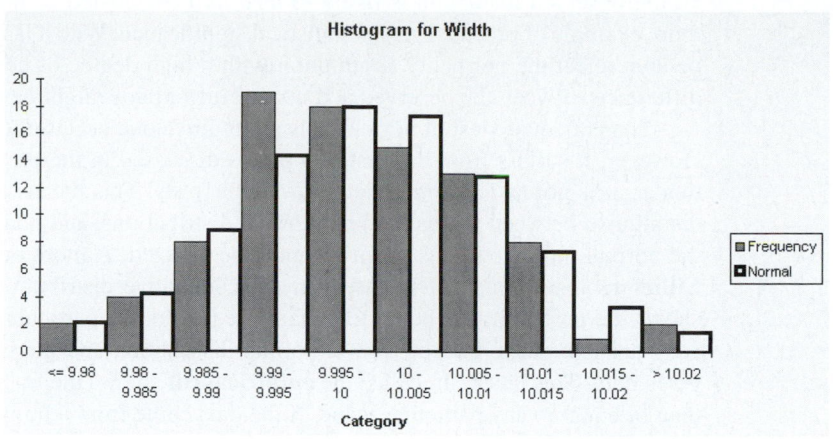

FIGURE 9.35 **Chi-square Test of Normality**

	A	B	C	D	E	F	G	H
1	Frequency table and normal test for Width							
2								
3	Upper limit	Category	Frequency	Normal	Dist measure		Test of normal fit	
4	9.98	<= 9.98	2	2.150	0.010		Chi-square statistic	3.693
5	9.985	9.98 - 9.985	4	4.277	0.018		p-value	0.814
6	9.99	9.985 - 9.99	8	8.936	0.098			
7	9.995	9.99 - 9.995	19	14.418	1.456			
8	10	9.995 - 10	18	17.964	0.000			
9	10.005	10 - 10.005	15	17.286	0.302			
10	10.01	10.005 - 10.01	13	12.846	0.002			
11	10.015	10.01 - 10.015	8	7.372	0.053			
12	10.02	10.015 - 10.02	1	3.267	1.573			
13		> 10.02	2	1.484	0.179			

The message in Figure 9.33 (based on the output in Figure 9.35) confirms this statistically. In Figure 9.35, each value in column D is an E_i, calculated as the total number of observations multiplied by the normal probability of being in the corresponding category. Column E contains the individual $(O_i - E_i)^2/E_i$ terms, and cell H4 contains their sum, the chi-square test statistic. The corresponding p-value in cell H5, 0.814, is calculated with the formula

=CHIDIST(TestStat,7)

This large p-value provides no evidence whatsoever of nonnormality. It implies that if we repeated this procedure on many random samples, each taken from a population known to be normal, we would obtain a fit at least this poor in about 81% of the samples. Stated differently, only about 19% of the fits would be *better* than the one we observed. Therefore, whatever statistical procedures the manager intends to use, he doesn't need to worry about the normality assumption. ■

We make three comments about this chi-square procedure. First, the test *does* depend on which (and how many) categories we use for the histogram. Reasonable choices are likely to lead to the same conclusion, but this is not guaranteed. Second, the test is not very effective unless the sample size is large, say, at least 80 or 100. Only then can we begin to see the true shape of the histogram and judge accurately whether it is normal. Finally, the test tends to be *too* sensitive if the sample size is really large. In this case any little "bump" on the observed histogram is likely to lead to a conclusion of nonnormality. This is one more example of practical versus statistical significance. With a large sample size we might be able reject the normality assumption with a high degree of certainty, but the practical difference between the observed and normal histograms might be unimportant.

The chi-square test of normality is an intuitive one because it is based on histograms. However, it suffers from the first two points discussed in the previous paragraph. In particular, it is not as *powerful* as other available tests. This means that it is often unable to distinguish between normal and nonnormal distributions, and hence it often fails to reject the normal null hypothesis when it should be rejected. A more powerful test is called the **Lilliefors test**.[8] This test is based on the cumulative distribution function (cdf), which shows the probability of being less than or equal to any particular value. Specifically, we compare two cdf's: the cdf from a normal distribution and the cdf corresponding to the given data. This latter cdf, called the **empirical cdf**, shows the fraction of observations less than or equal to any particular value. If the data come from a normal distribution, then the normal and empirical cdf's should be quite close. Therefore, the Lilliefors test compares the *maximum vertical distance* between the two functions and compares it to specially tabulated values. If this maximum vertical distance is sufficiently large, the normal null hypothesis can be rejected.

To run the Lilliefors test in StatPro, we select the StatPro/Tests of Normality/Lilliefors Test menu item and the variable to be tested. StatPro then shows a message and a corresponding graph of the normal and empirical cdf's. These outputs for the Width variable in Example 9.9 appear in Figures 9.36 and 9.37. The message indicates that the maximum vertical distance between the two curves is relatively small—not nearly large enough to reject the normal hypothesis. This conclusion agrees with the one based on the chi-square goodness-of-fit test, but the two tests do not agree on *all* data sets.

We conclude this section with a popular, but informal, test of normality. This is based on a plot called a **quantile-quantile** (or **Q-Q**) **plot**. Although the technical details for forming this plot are somewhat complex, it is basically a scatterplot of the standardized values from the data set versus the values we would expect if the data were perfectly normally distributed (with the same mean and standard deviation as in the data set). If the data are, in fact, normally distributed, then the points in this plot will tend to cluster around a 45° line. Any large deviations from a 45° line signal some type of nonnormality. Again, however, this is not a formal test of normality. A Q-Q plot is usually used only to obtain a general idea of whether the data are normally distributed and, if they are not, what type of nonnormality exists. For example, if points on the right of the plot are well *above* a 45° line, this is an indication that the largest observations in the data set are larger than we

FIGURE 9.36 Lilliefors Test Results from StatPro

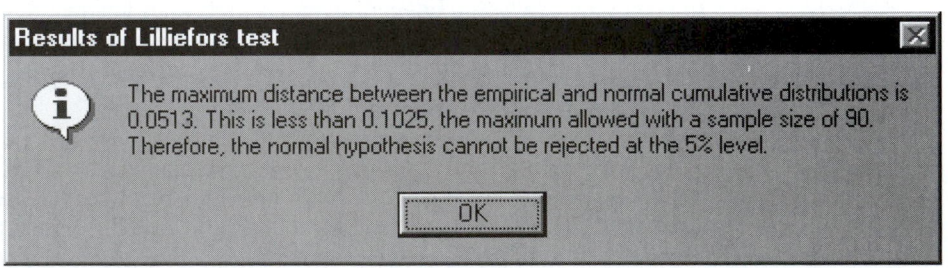

[8] This is actually a special case of the more general and widely known **Kolmogorov-Smirnoff** (or **K-S**) **test**.

FIGURE 9.37 **Normal and Empirical Cumulative Distribution Functions**

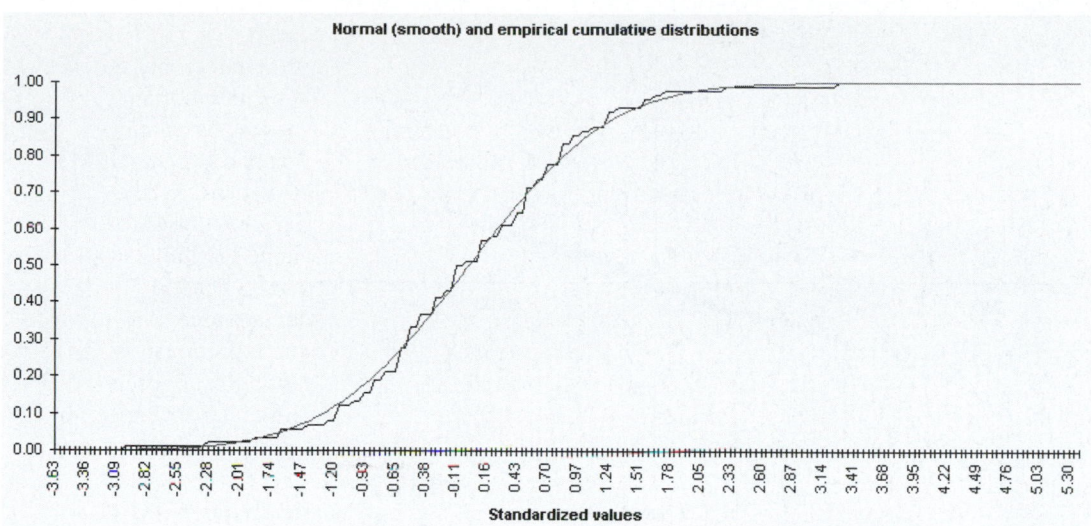

would expect from a normal distribution. Therefore, these points might be high-end outliers and/or a signal of positive skewness.

To obtain a Q-Q plot in StatPro, we use the StatPro/Tests of Normality/Q-Q Plot menu item and select the variable to be tested. The output for the Width data in Example 9.9 appears in Figures 9.38 and 9.39 (page 488). Although the points in this Q-Q plot do not all lie *exactly* on a 45° line, they are about as close to doing so as we can expect from real data. Therefore, there is no reason to question the normal hypothesis for these data—the same conclusion we reached with the chi-square and Lilliefors tests.

FIGURE 9.38 **StatPro Message from Q-Q Plot Procedure**

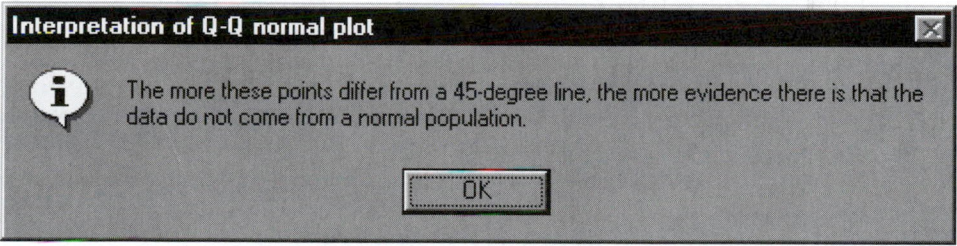

P R O B L E M S

Level A

44 A finance professor has just given a midterm examination in her corporate finance course. In particular, she is interested in determining whether the distribution of 100 exam scores is normally distributed. The data are in the file P2_5.XLS. Perform a chi-square goodness-of-fit test. Report and interpret the computed *p*-value. What can you conclude about normality?

FIGURE 9.39 Q-Q Plot for Width Data

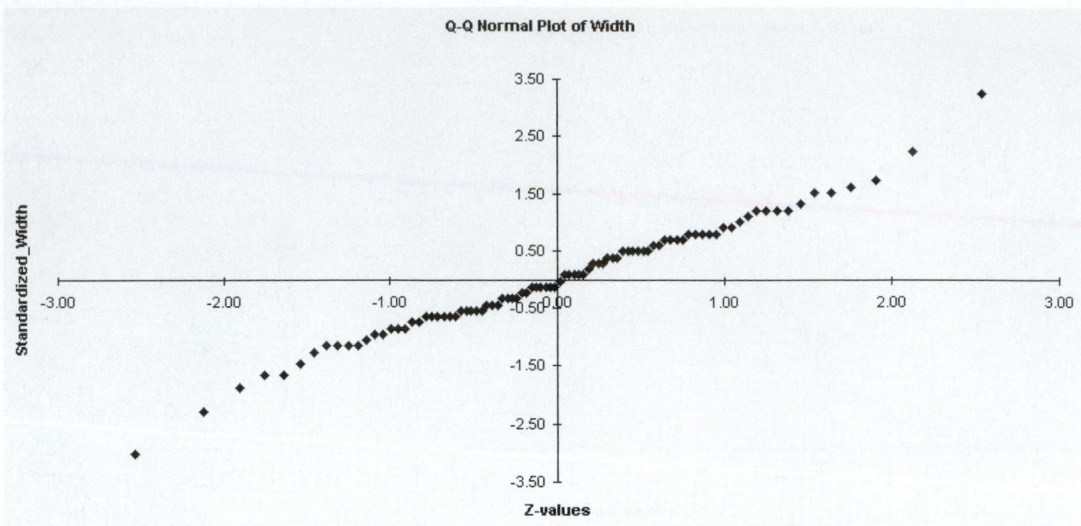

45 The annual base salaries for 100 students graduating from a reputable MBA program this year are of interest to those in the admissions office who are responsible for marketing the program to prospective students. The data are in the file P9_45.XLS. Are these salaries normally distributed? Perform a chi-square goodness-of-fit test. Report and interpret the computed p-value.

46 The manager of a local fast-food restaurant is interested in improving the service provided to customers who use the restaurant's drive-up window. As a first step in this process, the manager asks his assistant to record the time (in minutes) it takes to serve 100 different customers at the final window in the facility's drive-up system. The given 100 customer service times are all observed during the busiest hour of the day for this fast-food operation. The data are in the file P9_46.XLS. Prior to performing some statistical tests on these data, the manager's assistant needs to know whether the given customer service times are normally distributed. Perform a chi-square goodness-of-fit test. Report and interpret the computed p-value.

47 A manufacturer is interested in determining whether it can claim that the boxes of detergent it sells contain, on average, more than 500 grams of detergent. From past experience the manufacturer assumes that the amount of detergent in the boxes is normally distributed. The firm takes a random sample of 100 boxes and records the amount of detergent (in grams) in each box. Based on the data in the file P9_2.XLS, is it still reasonable for the manufacturer to assume that the amount of detergent in these boxes is normally distributed? Perform a chi-square goodness-of-fit test. Report and interpret the computed p-value.

48 An aircraft manufacturer needs to buy aluminum sheets with an average thickness of 0.05 inch. The manufacturer collects a random sample of 100 sheets from a potential supplier. The thickness of each sheet in this sample is measured (in inches) and recorded in the file P9_7.XLS. Are these measurements normally distributed? Using a 5% significance level, perform a chi-square goodness-of-fit test. Summarize your results.

49 A U.S. Navy recruiting center knows from past experience that the mean height of its recruits is 68 inches. The recruiting center wants to test the claim that the average height of this year's recruits is greater than 68 inches. To do this, recruiting personnel take a random sample of 64 recruits from the past year and record their heights (in inches). These data are provided in the file P9_4.XLS. Before conducting an appropriate statistical test, the recruiters would like to check whether the given distribution of heights is normally distributed.

a On the basis of the available information, do the recruiters find support for the normality assumption at the 10% significance level? Explain.

b On the basis of the available information, do the recruiters find support for the normality assumption at the 1% significance level? Explain.

50   The chi-square test for normality discussed in Section 9.6 is far from perfect. If the sample is too small, the test tends to accept the null hypothesis of normality for any population distribution even remotely bell shaped; that is, it is not **powerful** in detecting nonnormality. On the other hand, if the sample is very large, it will tend to reject the null hypothesis of normality for *any* data set.[9] Check this by using simulation. Simulate data from a normal distribution to illustrate that if the sample size is sufficiently large, there is a good chance that the null hypothesis will (wrongly) be rejected. Then simulate data from a nonnormal distribution (uniform or triangular, say) to illustrate that if the sample size is fairly small, there is a good chance that the null hypothesis will (wrongly) not be rejected. Summarize your findings in a short report. ■

9.7

Conclusion

The concepts and procedures we have discussed in this chapter occupy a cornerstone in both applied and theoretical statistics. Of particular importance is the interpretation of a *p*-value, especially since *p*-values are common outputs of all statistical software packages. A *p*-value summarizes the evidence in support of an alternative hypothesis, which is usually the hypothesis an analyst is trying to prove. Small *p*-values provide support for the alternative hypothesis, whereas large *p*-values provide little or no support for it.

Although hypothesis testing continues to be an important tool for analysts, it is important to note its limitations, particularly in business applications. First, given a choice between a confidence interval for some population parameter and a test of this parameter, we generally favor the confidence interval. For example, a confidence interval not only tells us whether a mean difference is 0, but it also gives us a plausible range for this difference. Second, many business *decision* problems cannot be handled adequately with hypothesis-testing procedures. Either they ignore important cost information or they treat the consequences of incorrect decisions (type I and type II errors) in an inappropriate way. Finally, the *statistical* significance at the core of hypothesis testing is sometimes quite different from the *practical* significance that is of most interest to business managers.

P R O B L E M S

Level A

51   The file P9_51.XLS contains the number of days 44 mothers spent in the hospital giving birth (in the year 1995). Before health insurance rules were changed (the change was effective January 1, 1995), the average number of days spent in a hospital by a new mother was 2 days. For a 0.05 level of significance, do the data in the file indicate (the research hypothesis) that women are now spending less time in the hospital after giving birth than they were prior to 1995? Explain your answer in terms of the *p*-value for the test.

52   Eighteen readers took a speed-reading course. The file P9_52.XLS contains the number of words that they could read before and after the course. Test the alternative hypothesis at the 5% significance level that reading speeds have increased, on average, as a result of the course. Explain your answer in terms of the *p*-value. Do you need to assume that reading speeds (before and after) are normally distributed? Exactly what assumption do you need?

53   Statistics show that a child 0–4 years of age has a 0.0002 probability of getting cancer in any given year. Assume that during each of the last 7 years there have been 100 children ages 0–4 whose parents work in the business school. Four of these children have gotten cancer. Use this

---

[9]Actually, all of the tests for normality suffer from this latter problem.

evidence to test whether the incidence of childhood cancer among children 0–4 whose parents work at the business school exceeds the national average. Write down your hypotheses and determine the appropriate p-value.

54 Blacks in a St. Louis suburb sued the city claiming they were discriminated against in school-teacher hiring. Of the city's population, 5.7% were black; of 405 teachers in the school system, 15 were black. Set up appropriate hypotheses and determine whether blacks are underrepresented. Does your answer depend on whether you use a one-tailed or two-tailed test? In discrimination cases, the Supreme Court always uses a two-tailed test with $\alpha = .05$. (Source: U.S. Supreme Court Case Hazlewood versus City of St. Louis)

55 In the past, monthly sales for HOOPS, a small software firm, have averaged $20,000 with standard deviation $4,000. During the last year sales averaged $22,000 per month. Does this indicate that monthly sales have changed (in a statistically significant sense)? Use $\alpha = .05$. Assume monthly sales are normally distributed.

56 Twenty people have rated a new beer on a taste scale of 0 to 100. Their ratings are in the file P9_56.XLS. Marketing has determined that the beer will be a success if the average taste rating exceeds 76. If we use $\alpha = 0.05$, is there sufficient evidence to conclude that the beer will be a success? Discuss your result in terms of a p-value. Assume ratings are normally distributed.

57 We have asked 22 people to rate a competitive beer on a taste scale of 0 to 100. Another 22 people rated our beer on a taste scale of 0 to 100. The file P9_57.XLS contains the results. Do these data provide sufficient evidence to conclude, at the $\alpha = 0.01$ level, that people believe our beer tastes better than the competition? Assume ratings are normally distributed.

58 Callaway is thinking about entering the golf ball market. The company will make a profit if its market share is more than 20%. A market survey indicates that 140 of 624 golf ball purchasers will buy a Callaway golf ball.

a Is this enough evidence to persuade Callaway to enter the golf ball market?

b How would you make the decision if you were Callaway management?

59 Sales of a new product will be profitable if the average sales per store exceeds 100 per week. The product was test marketed for 1 week at 10 stores, with the results listed in the file P9_59.XLS. Assume that sales at each store follow a normal distribution.

a Is this enough evidence to persuade the company to market the new product?

b How would you make the decision if you were deciding whether to market the new product?

60 We are interested in determining whether the position of Coca-Cola in a store affects sales. Specifically, does Coke sell better when it is placed in the front or middle of an aisle? The file P9_60.XLS contains sales of Coke at 10 stores when Coke was placed in the front of an aisle and at another 10 stores when Coke was placed in the back of an aisle. What are reasonable null and alternative hypotheses to test? Use the data to test them. What can you conclude?

61 Target wants to know whether red or blue coats sell better. The sales of red and blue coats last winter were measured at several different stores. The file P9_61.XLS contains the results. What are reasonable null and alternative hypotheses to test? Use the data to test them. What can you conclude?

62 Marsh Supermarket wants to know whether putting a color flyer in the local paper has a greater effect on sales than putting a black and white flyer in the paper. For the last 10 times a color flyer was put in the paper, Marsh compared sales (in thousands of dollars) to the last week (at the same store) for which a black and white flyer was put in the paper. The file P9_62.XLS contains the data. Formulate reasonable hypotheses and test them. What do you conclude?

63 In the past, the Algood Company has produced an average of 12,000 good parts per day. Since the compensation system was changed 15 days ago, the average production has been 12,100 good parts per day. The sample standard deviation of the number of good parts produced during the last 15 days is 400. Is this sufficient evidence to conclude, at the $\alpha = 0.10$ level, that the new compensation plan has improved productivity? Justify your answer with a p-value.

64 A hotel manager would like to know whether people who pay by different methods have different-sized bills, on average. He divides all customers into four categories: those who pay by check or cash, those who pay with VISA or MasterCard, those who pay with an American Express card, and those who use some other type of charge card. He then collects the data on daily bills listed in the file P9_64.XLS. (These bills contain the room charge, plus any other charges to the customer's account.) Use one-way ANOVA to help answer the manager's question, and write a short report to summarize your findings.

65 Although four similar-sized small-car models exhibit similar miles per gallon (mpg) sticker ratings, there is some skepticism as to whether their mean mpg values are really equal. To test this equal-means hypothesis, several cars of each model are driven for 10,000 miles under nearly identical driving conditions. The observed mpg values are listed in the file P9_65.XLS. Use one-way ANOVA to help decide whether the different models have equal mean mpg values, and write a short report to summarize your findings.

Level B

66 You are trying to determine whether male and female Central Bank employees having equal qualifications receive different salaries. The file P9_66.XLS contains the salaries (in thousands of dollars) for 9 male and 9 female employees. Assume salaries are normally distributed.

    a Assuming that each row of data represents paired observations, and using $\alpha = 0.05$, can you conclude that members of different genders are paid equally? Be sure to write down your hypotheses.

    b How would you collect data to ensure that the observations are actually paired?

67 You are trying to determine whether male and female Indiana University grads having equal qualifications receive different starting salaries for their first job. The file P9_67.XLS contains the starting salaries for 10 male and 10 female IU grads.

    a Assuming that each row of data represents paired observations, and using $\alpha = 0.05$, can you conclude that equally qualified people of different genders have the same starting salaries on average? Be sure to write down your null and alternative hypotheses.

    b How would you collect data to ensure that the observations are actually paired?

68 A recent study concluded that children born to mothers who take Prozac tend to have more birth defects than children born to mothers who do not take Prozac.

    a What do you think the null and alternative hypotheses were for this study?

    b If you were a spokesperson for Eli Lilly (the company that produces Prozac), how would you rebut the conclusions of this study?

69 Suppose you are the state superintendent of Tennessee public schools. You want to know whether decreasing the class size in grades 1–3 will improve student performance. Explain how you would set up a test to determine whether decreased class size will improve student performance. What hypotheses would you use in this experiment. (This was actually done and smaller class size did help, particularly with minority students.)

70 Do chief executive officers of large corporations in different industries typically earn disparate annual salaries? Consider the data in the file P2_13.XLS, which came from a recent survey of chief executive officers of the nation's 350 biggest businesses (*The Wall Street Journal*, April 9, 1998). In particular, we seek to discover whether significant differences exist between the mean levels of 1997 salaries earned by executives of *Technology* companies and those of each of the other seven company types. For instance, is the difference between the mean 1997 salaries of executives from *Technology* and *Basic Materials* companies significant?

    a Before conducting these hypothesis tests, perform a test for equal population variances for each pair of company types. For each pair, report a p-value and interpret it.

    b Based on your conclusions in part **a**, which test statistic should be used in performing a test for the existence of a difference between population means in each pair?

    c Given your conclusions in part **b**, perform a test for the existence of a difference in mean annual CEO salaries. For each pair of company types, report a p-value and interpret its meaning.

71 Is the overall cost of living higher or lower for urban areas in particular geographical regions of the United States? Consider the random sample of 80 urban areas provided in the file P9_71.XLS (Source: *ACCRA Cost of Living Index*). In particular, determine whether the mean composite (cost of living) value in urban areas of the northeastern states is higher than the mean composite value in urban areas of each of the following: (a) southeastern states, (b) central states, (c) southwestern states, and (d) northwestern states. Note that you will need to assign each of the urban areas in the given sample to one of these five geographical regions before you can proceed further.

a Before conducting any hypothesis tests on the difference between various pairs of mean composite values, perform a test for equal population variances in each pair of geographical regions. For each pair, report a p-value and interpret its meaning.

b Based on your conclusions in part **a**, which test statistic should be used in performing a test for a difference between population means in each pair?

c Given your conclusions in part **b**, perform a test for the difference between composite cost of living values in each pair of geographical regions. For each pair, report a p-value and interpret its meaning.

72 Consider a random sample of 100 households from a middle-class neighborhood that was the recent focus of an economic development study conducted by the local government. Specifically, for each of the 100 households in the sample, information was gathered on the gross annual income earned by the first wage earner of the household and on each of several other variables. The data are given in the file P8_26.XLS. Economic researchers would like to test for the existence of a significant difference between the mean annual income levels of the first household wage earners in the first (i.e., SW) and second (i.e., NW) sectors of this community. In fact, they intend to perform similar hypothesis tests for the differences between the mean annual income levels of the first household wage earners from all other pairs of locations (i.e., first and third, first and fourth, second and third, second and fourth, and third and fourth).

a Before conducting any hypothesis tests on the difference between various pairs of mean income levels, perform a test for equal population variances in each pair of locations. For each pair, report a p-value and interpret its meaning.

b Based on your conclusions in part **a**, which test statistic should be used in performing a test for the existence of a difference between population means?

c Given your conclusions in part **b**, perform a test for the existence of a difference in mean annual income levels in each pair of locations. For each pair, report a p-value and interpret its meaning.

73 A group of 25 husbands and wives were chosen randomly. Each person was asked to write the most he or she would be willing to pay for a new car (assuming they had decided to buy a new car). The results are shown in the file P9_73.TXT (an ASCII file). Can you accept the alternative hypothesis that the husbands are willing to spend more, on average, than the wives at the 5% significance level? What is the associated p-value?

74 A company is concerned with the high cholesterol levels of many of its employees. To help combat the problem, it opens an exercise facility and encourages its employees to use this facility. After a year, it chooses a random 100 employees who claim they use the facility regularly, and another 200 who claim they don't use it at all. The cholesterol levels of these 300 employees are checked, with the results shown in the file P9_74.XLS.

a Is this sample evidence "proof" that the exercise facility, when used, tends to lower the mean cholesterol level? Phrase this as a hypothesis-testing problem and do the appropriate analysis. Do you feel comfortable that your analysis answers the question definitively (one way or the other)? Why or why not?

b Repeat part **a**, but replace "mean level" with "percentage with level over 215." (The company believes that any level over 215 is dangerous.)

75 Suppose that you are trying to compare two populations on some variable (GMAT scores of men versus women, for example). Specifically, you are testing the null hypothesis that the means of the two populations are equal versus a two-tailed hypothesis. Are the following statements correct? Why or why not?

a A given difference (such as 5 points) between sample means from these populations will probably not be considered statistically significant if the sample sizes are small, but will probably be considered statistically significant if the sample sizes are large.

b Virtually any difference between the population means will lead to statistically significant sample results if the sample sizes are sufficiently large.

76 Continuing the previous problem, analyze part **b** in Excel as follows. Start with hypothetical population mean GMAT scores for men and women, along with population standard deviations. Enter these at the top of a spreadsheet. You can make the two means as close as you like, but not identical. In column A simulate a sample of men's GMAT scores with your mean and standard deviation. Do the same for women in column B. The sample sizes do not have to

be the same, but you can make them the same. Then run the test for the difference between two means. (The point of this problem is that if the population means are fairly close and you pick relatively small sample sizes, the sample mean differences probably won't be significant. If you find this, generate new samples of a larger sample size and redo the test. Now they might be significant. If not, try again with a still larger sample size. Eventually, you should get statistically significant differences.)

77 This problem concerns course scores (on a 0–100 scale) for a large undergraduate computer programming course. The class is composed of both underclassmen (freshmen and sophomores) and upperclassmen (juniors and seniors). Also, the students can be categorized according to their previous mathematical background from previous courses as "low" or "high" mathematical background. The data for these students are in the file P9_77.XLS. The variables are:

- Score: score on a 0–100 scale
- UpperCl: 1 for an upperclassman, 0 otherwise
- HighMath: 1 for a high mathematical background, 0 otherwise

For the following questions, assume that the students in this course represent a random sample from all college students who might take the course. This latter group is the "population."

a Find a 90% confidence interval for the population mean score for the course. Do the same for the mean of all upperclassmen. Do the same for the mean of all upperclassmen with a high mathematical background.

b The professor believes he has enough evidence to prove the research hypothesis that upperclassmen score at least 5 points better, on average, than lowerclassmen. Do you agree?

c If we consider a "good" grade to be one that is at least 80, is there enough evidence to reject the null hypothesis that the fraction of good grades is the same for students with low math backgrounds as those with high math backgrounds?

78 A cereal company wants to see which of two promotional strategies, supplying coupons in a local newspaper or including coupons in the cereal package itself, is more effective. (In the latter case, there is a sign on the package indicating the presence of the coupon inside.) The company randomly chooses 80 Kroger's stores around the country—all of approximately the same size and overall sales volume—and promotes its cereal one way at 40 of these sites, and the other way at the other 40 sites. (All are at different geographical locations, so local newspaper ads for one of the sites should not affect sales at any other site.) Unfortunately, as in many business "experiments," there is a factor beyond the company's control—namely, whether its main competitor at any particular site happens to be running a promotion of its own. The file P9_78.XLS has 80 observations on three variables:

- Sales: number of boxes sold during the first week of the company's promotion
- PromType:1 if coupons are in local paper, 0 if coupons are inside box
- CompProm:1 if main competitor is running a promotion, 0 otherwise

a Based on all 80 observations, find (1) the difference in sample mean sales between stores running the two different promotional types (and indicate which sample mean is larger), (2) the standard error of this difference, and (3) a 90% confidence interval for the population mean difference.

b Test whether the population mean difference is 0 (the null hypothesis) versus a two-tailed alternative. State whether you should accept or reject the null hypothesis, and why.

c Repeat part **b**, but now restrict the "population" to stores where the competitor is not running a promotion of its own.

d Based on data from all 80 observations, can you accept the (alternative) hypothesis, at the 5% level, that the mean company sales drops by at least 30 boxes when the competitor runs its own promotion (as opposed to not running its own promotion)?

e We often use the term "population" without really thinking what it means. If you talk about the population mean for the case, say, where coupons are put in boxes, explain in words exactly what this population mean refers to. ■

9.1 Regression Toward the Mean

In Chapters 11 and 12 we will study regression, a method for relating one variable to other explanatory variables. However, the term "regression" has sometimes been used in a slightly different way, meaning "regression toward the mean." The example often cited is of male heights. If a father is unusually tall, for example, his son will typically be taller than average but not as tall as the father. Similarly, if a father is unusually short, the son will typically be shorter than average but not as short as the father. We say that the son's height tends to regress toward the mean. This case will illustrate how regression toward the mean can occur.

Suppose a company administers an aptitude test to all of its job applicants. If an applicant scores below some value, he or she cannot be hired immediately but is allowed to retake a similar exam at a later time. In the interim the applicant can presumably study to prepare for the second exam. If we focus on the applicants who fail the exam the first time and then take it a second time, we would probably expect them to score better on the second exam. One plausible reason is that they are more familiar with the exam the second time. However, we will rule this out by assuming that the two exams are sufficiently different from one another. A second plausible reason is that the applicants have studied between exams, which has a beneficial effect. However, we will argue that even if studying has *no beneficial effect whatsoever*, these applicants will tend to do better the second time around. The reason is regression toward the mean. All of these applicants scored unusually low on the first exam, so they will tend to regress toward the mean on the second exam—that is, they will tend to score higher.

You can employ simulation to demonstrate this phenomenon, using the following model. Assume that the scores of *all* potential applicants are normally distributed with mean μ and standard deviation σ. Since we are assuming that any studying between exams has no beneficial effect, this distribution of scores is the *same* on the second exam as on the first. An applicant fails the first exam if his or her score is below some cutoff value L. Now, we would certainly expect scores on the two exams to be positively correlated, with some correlation ρ. That is, if everyone took both exams, then applicants who scored high on the first would tend to score high on the second, and those who scored low on the first would tend to score low on the second. (This isn't regression to the mean, but simply that some applicants are better than others.)

Given this model, you can proceed by simulating many pairs of scores, one pair for each applicant. The scores for each exam should be normally distributed with parameters μ and σ, but the trick is to make them correlated. You can use StatPro's BINORMAL_ function to do this. (Binormal is short for bivariate normal.) It takes a pair of means (both equal to μ), a pair of standard deviations (both equal to σ), and a correlation ρ as arguments, with the syntax =BINORMAL_(*means,stdevs,correlation*). To enter the formula, highlight two adjacent cells such as C6 and D6, type the formula, and press Ctrl-Shift-Enter. Then copy and paste to generate similar values for other applicants.

Once you have generated pairs of scores for many applicants, you should ignore all pairs except for those where the score on the first exam is less than L. (Sorting is suggested here, but "freeze" the random numbers first.) For these pairs, test whether the mean score on the second exam is *higher* than on the first, using a paired-samples test. If it is, you have demonstrated regression toward the mean. As you'll probably discover, however, the results will depend on the parameters you choose: μ, σ, ρ, and L. We encourage you to experiment with these. Assuming that you are able to demonstrate regression toward the mean, can you explain intuitively why it occurs?

9.2 Baseball Statistics

Baseball has long been the sport of statistics. Probably more statistics—both relevant and completely obscure—are kept on baseball games and players than for any other sport. During the early 1990s, the first author of this book was able to acquire an enormous set of baseball data.[10] It includes data on every at-bat for every player in every game for the 4-year period from 1987 to 1990. The majority of these data are on the CD-ROM that accompanies this book. (The bulk of the data are in eight large files with names such as 89AL.EXE—for the 1989 American League. See the BB_README.TXT file for detailed information about the files.) The files include data for approximately 500 player-years during this period. Each text file contains data for a particular player during an entire year, such as Barry Bonds during 1989, provided that the player had at least 500 at-bats during that year. Each record (row) of such a file lists the information pertaining to a single at-bat, such as whether the player got a hit, how many runners were on base, the earned-run-average (ERA) of the pitcher, and more.

The author analyzed these data to see whether batters tend to hit in "streaks," a phenomenon that has been debated for years among avid fans. [The results of this study are described in Albright (1993).] However, the data set is sufficiently rich to enable testing of any number of hypotheses. We challenge you to develop your own hypotheses and test them with these data.

9.3 The Wichita Anti-Drunk Driving Advertising Campaign[11]

Each year drinking and driving behavior are estimated to be responsible for approximately 24,000 traffic fatalities in the United States. Data show that a preponderance of this problem is due to the behavior of young males. Indeed, a disproportionate number of traffic fatalities are young people between 15 and 24 years of age. Market research among young people has suggested that this perverse behavior of driving automobiles while under the influence of alcoholic beverages might be reduced by a mass media communications/advertising program based on an understanding of the "consumer psychology" of young male drinking and driving. There is some precedent for this belief. Reduction in cigarette smoking over the last 25 years is often attributed in part to mass antismoking advertising campaigns. There is also precedent for being less optimistic, because past experimental campaigns against drunk driving have shown little success.

---

[10] The data were collected by volunteers of a group called Project Scoresheet. These volunteers attended each game and kept detailed records of virtually everything that occurred. Such detail is certainly not available in newspaper box scores—it is not even available on the Web!

[11] This case was contributed by Peter Kolesar from Columbia University.

Between March and August of 1986, an anti-drinking and driving advertising campaign was conducted in the city of Wichita, Kansas. In this federally sponsored experiment, several carefully constructed messages were aired on television and radio and also appeared in newspapers and on billboards. Unlike earlier and largely ineffective campaigns that depended on donated talent and media time, this test was sufficiently funded to create impressive anti-drinking and driving messages, and to place them so that the targeted audience would be reached. The messages were pretested before the program and the final version won an OMNI advertising award.

To evaluate the effectiveness of this anti-drinking and driving campaign, researchers collected before and after data (pre-program and post-program) of several types. In addition to data collection in Wichita, they also selected Omaha, Nebraska, as a "control" city. Omaha, another midwestern city on the Great Plains, was arguably similar to Wichita, but was not subjected to such an advertising campaign. The following tables contain some of the data gathered by researchers to evaluate the impact of the program.

Table 9.1 contains background demographics on the test and control cities. Table 9.2 contains data obtained from telephone surveys of 18-to-24-year-old males in both cities. The surveys were done using a random telephone dialing technique. They had an 88% response rate during the pre-program survey and a 91% response rate during the post-program survey. Respondents were asked whether they had driven under the influence or 4 or more alcoholic drinks, or 6 or more alcoholic drinks, at least once in the previous month. The pre-program data were collected in September 1985, and the post-program data were collected in September 1986.

Table 9.3 contains counts of fatal or incapacitating accidents involving young people gathered from the Kansas and Nebraska Traffic Safety Departments during the spring and summer months of 1985 (pre-program) and 1986 (during the program). The spring and summer months were defined to be the period from March to August. These data were taken by the research team as "indicators" of driving under the influence of alcohol. Researchers at first proposed to also gather data on the blood alcohol content of drivers

TABLE 9.1 Demographics for Wichita and Omaha

	Wichita	Omaha
Total population	411,313	483,053
Percent of age 15–24 years	19.2	19.5
Race:		
White	85	87
Black	8	9
Hispanic	4	2
Other	3	2
Percent high school graduates among those 18 years and older	75.4	79.9
Private car ownership	184,641	198,723

TABLE 9.2 Telephone Survey of 18-to-24-Year-old Males

	Wichita		Omaha	
	Pre-program	Post-program	Pre-program	Post-program
Respondents	205	221	203	157
Drove after 4 drinks	71	61	77	69
Drove after 6 drinks	42	37	45	38

TABLE 9.3 **Average Monthly Number of Fatal and Incapacitating Accidents, March to August**

TABLE 9.3 **Average Monthly Number of Fatal and Incapacitating Accidents, March to August**

Driver Group	Accident Type	Wichita 1985	Wichita 1986	Omaha 1985	Omaha 1986
18-to-24-Year-old Males	Total	68	55	41	40
	Single	13	13	13	14
	Night	36	35	25	26
15-to-24-Year-old Males and Females	Total	117	97	59	57
	Single	22	17	16	20
	Night	56	52	34	38

involved in fatal accidents. However, traffic safety experts pointed out that such data are often inconsistent and incomplete because police at the scene of a fatal accident have more pressing duties to perform than to gather such data. On the other hand, it is well established that alcohol is implicated in a major proportion of nighttime traffic fatalities, and for that reason, the data also focus on accidents at night among two classes of young people: the group of accidents involving 18-to-24-year-old males as a driver, and the group of accidents involving 15-to-24-year-old males and/or females as a driver.

The categories of accidents recorded were as follows:

■ Total: total count of all fatal and incapacitating accidents in the indicated driver group

■ Single vehicle: single vehicle fatal and incapacitating accidents in the indicated driver group

■ Nighttime: nighttime (8 P.M. to 8 A.M.) fatal and incapacitating accidents in the indicated driver group

It was estimated that if a similar 6-month advertising campaign were run nationally, it would cost about $25 million. The Commissioner of the U.S. National Highway Safety Commission had funded a substantial part of the study and needed to decide what, if anything, to do next.

10

Statistical Process Control

Successful Applications

Northern Telecom (Nortel) is a leading global provider of digital network hardware and software solutions for communications, information, entertainment, education, and commerce. As of 1996, it had annual worldwide revenues of $12.85 billion. Due to a 1995 U.S. Federal Communications Commission action, the auctioning of a section of frequency bandwidth reserved for advanced digital cellular communications, Nortel saw the opportunity to move into a new technology, personal communications services (PCS). The company decided to build a new manufacturing operation, Wireless Networks Raleigh (WNR) in Raleigh, North Carolina. The new plant was dedicated to manufacturing advanced cell-site base-station and antenna equipment, with many of the designs for the plant's products coming from Nortel operations in France and the United Kingdom. From the outset, senior managers recognized that state-of-the-art manufacturing practices were necessary for WNR. Among other things, this included computer-based data collection from the manufacturing processes, statistical process control on literally hundreds of product characteristics, and the ability to act on the information in a timely manner, both in North Carolina and in European sites.

A team of analysts created a decision support system to achieve these objectives. Their work is described in the article by Brinkley et al. (1998). A key component of the system is its statistical process control capability. The communications products developed at WNR contain circuit boards and other assembly items that must meet stringent quality specifications. To ensure that this happens, the system continually monitors hundreds of product characteristics and produces real-time control charts. Typical illustrations of these appear in Figures 10.1 and 10.2 on page 500. (Much of this chapter deals with the meaning and interpretation of such charts, so we urge you to take another look at them after you have studied this chapter.) The basic objectives of these charts are to show everyone involved—workers on the shop floor, design engineers, and senior managers—how the manufacturing process is currently operating and to suggest corrective actions in case the process is not behaving as desired. Such charts are in use in most manufacturing companies. However, an interesting aspect of the system developed by Nortel is that these charts (and the spreadsheet data on which they are based) are available instantly through the company's intranet—over the World Wide Web. For example, a design engineer in Paris can immediately see current data from Raleigh simply by logging onto the intranet.

This real-time capability cuts the time for data analysis and decision making tremendously, compared to the traditional methods of report generation and distribution.

The analysts developed and implemented this decision support system within a 12-month period at a cost of $500,000. The annual costs of supporting the system are approximately $800,000. Given that revenues in 1996 at WNR were already $320 million, this low system cost is very impressive. The company estimates that the direct benefits of the system, primarily from reduced work-in-process and reduced rework and scrap production, are over $1 million annually. However, there are other more qualitative benefits from the system. It has had a definite positive impact on customer satisfaction due to improved quality and reliability, and employee satisfaction has improved as a result of increased knowledge and empowerment.

FIGURE 10.1 $\overline{X}$ and R **Charts for Nortel System**

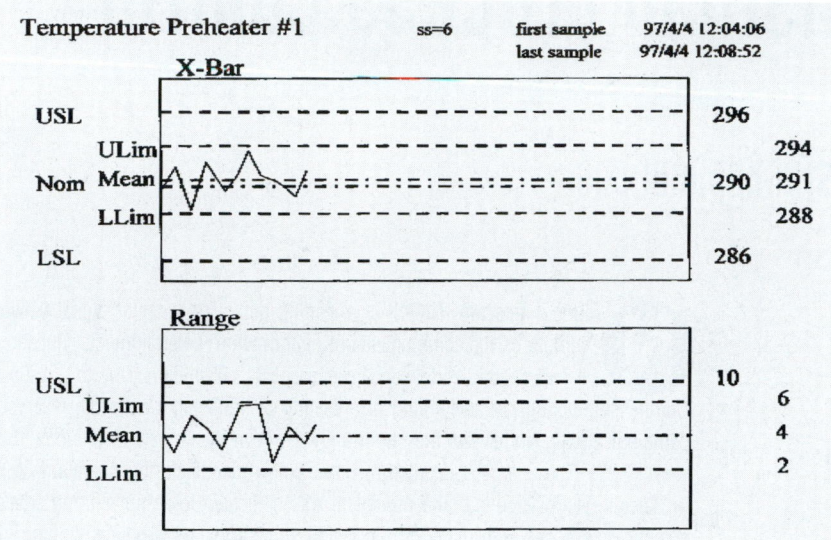

FIGURE 10.2 **Process Capability Chart for Nortel System**

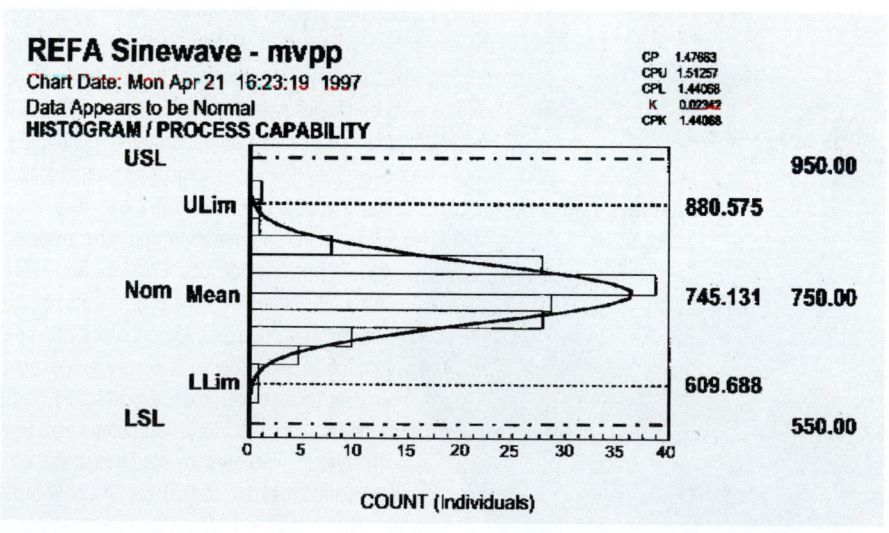

Introduction

O ne of the areas where statistics has had the largest impact in the business world is the area of quality. For many years quality was not emphasized, especially by U.S. companies. Gradually, spurred on by foreign competition, high levels of quality became a competitive advantage for the best companies, and today most companies are simply not competitive unless they have excellent quality. One of the best examples of this change is in the automobile industry. All we need to do is compare U.S. cars produced in the 1970s with those produced now to see the tremendous improvements in quality that have been achieved in the past decade. U.S. automobile manufacturers can now compete successfully with their Japanese and European counterparts, and much of this is due to the improvements in quality in U.S. manufacturing plants. Of course, this improvement in quality became *necessary* in the U.S. automobile industry. Without quality improvements, U.S. market shares would have continued to fall into the hands of foreign competitors.

The quality movement in the United States (and abroad) has taken on almost a religious fervor in recent years. It has spawned a number of acronyms, including TQM (total quality management), QC (quality control), SPC (statistical process control), QFD (quality function deployment), and others. Some of the best-known consultants and researchers in the area, including Joseph Juran, Genichi Taguchi, Philip Crosby, and W. Edwards Deming, have become business heroes and are commonly referred to as "quality gurus." Since its inception in 1987, there has been fierce competition for the Malcolm Baldrige National Quality Award, an award given to U.S. manufacturing and service companies on the basis of their superior quality initiatives and performance.

In the larger context, the quality movement comprises much more than just statistical or quantitative methods. It is also about leadership, worker empowerment, producer/supplier relationships, interest in the customer, and other broad business issues. However, a large part of the success of the quality movement is due to the increased use of quantitative methods, both in manufacturing and in service industries. Our focus in this chapter is on a set of quantitative tools generally referred to as **statistical process control** (or **SPC**).

There are various themes to SPC, but perhaps the two most important themes can be summarized as:

- Get it right the first time.
- Reduce variation.

In the past, quality was often synonymous with *inspection*. Completed parts or assemblies were routinely inspected for problems, and those that failed inspection were scrapped or sent back for rework. This emphasis on inspection is good in that it tries to keep faulty products from reaching the customer, but it is expensive. Time and resources used to fix mistakes could be used more profitably if there were no mistakes to fix. The quality gurus argued that it is much better to catch mistakes early in the production process, where they are less costly to fix, than to wait for final inspection. Besides, by focusing on the sources of problems early in the process, the *causes* of the problems become more apparent, and future problems can be prevented. Therefore, getting it right the first time is the focus of many quality program initiatives.

The second theme is to reduce variability. As Deming and others have preached, variability is the main culprit that hurts quality, and everything that is possible must be done to eliminate variability. However, to do so, we must be able to measure it and give workers a way to reduce it. This is exactly the objective of control charts, the statistical tool we will study throughout much of this chapter. Control charts enable an operator on the shop floor to see what a production process is currently doing. Then by following established guidelines, this operator and/or management can often root out the causes of variability and produce a better product—*before* it passes on to final inspection.

The quality movement and the statistical tools for quality improvement are usually discussed in the context of manufacturing. Indeed, much of the impetus for SPC came from manufacturing industries. However, the same ideas that have resulted in dramatic improvements in manufacturing apply to service industries. The banking industry, the hotel industry, and others also need to reduce variability and get it right the first time. Fortunately, these service industries can also benefit from control charts and other SPC tools. A bit more creativity is sometimes required to apply the tools appropriately, but it can be done.

10.2

Deming's 14 Points

W. Edwards Deming is probably more responsible than any other single individual for the recent emphasis on quality.[1] A statistician by trade, Deming took his theories and statistical tools to Japan shortly after World War II. At that time, of course, Japan was just starting to rebound from the devastation of the war. Deming taught the newly emerging Japanese industries the principles of quality management, for which they are now well known. He became a legend in Japan. In fact, the quality award Japan gives that is comparable to our Baldrige Award is called the Deming Prize.

However, Deming (and his teachings) remained largely unknown in the United States until the early 1980s. At that time, U.S. manufacturing industries were floundering with poor-quality products, and Deming—along with a few other quality gurus—began teaching them the statistical principles they would need to compete successfully. Today Deming's philosophy greatly influences decision making at many major U.S. companies, including Procter and Gamble, Xerox, Ford, and General Motors. In fact, the operation of the Saturn division of GM is based largely on Deming's philosophy.

Deming is perhaps best remembered for his famous 14 points, a list of precepts he taught in all of his seminars. We present and discuss these points here to give an overview of quality management. [They are adapted from Deming (1986).] As will be obvious, some of these 14 points are more quantitatively oriented than others. However, we reiterate that Deming was first and foremost a statistician who strongly believed in taking constant measurements and applying appropriate statistical techniques to reduce variation. He was no idle armchair philosopher!

1 **CONSTANCY OF PURPOSE. Create constancy of purpose toward improvement of product and service, allocating resources to provide for long-range needs rather than only short-term profitability, with a plan to become competitive, stay in business, and provide jobs.**

It is tempting for U.S. companies, whose attention has traditionally been on short-term financial measures, to adopt quality initiatives (with a lot of fanfare!) and then abandon them whenever they conflict with short-term objectives. This defeats the purpose of the quality initiatives. Besides, it leads employees to believe that this or that quality initiative is simply the "gimmick of the month." The only way to adopt Deming's teachings successfully is for management to "walk the talk" and show a constancy of purpose that the workers can appreciate.

---

[1]Deming died at the age of 93 in 1993.

2 THE NEW PHILOSOPHY. Adopt the new philosophy. We are in a new economic age, created in Japan. We can no longer live with commonly accepted levels of delays, mistakes, defective materials, and defective workmanship. Transformation of Western management style is necessary to halt the continued decline of industry.

The type of change Deming envisioned is not simply a few quick changes that can be adopted overnight. It is an entirely new philosophy, and most companies will have to completely rethink the way they do things. However, unless companies strive continually to move in this direction, they are doomed to lose out to their more enlightened competitors.

3 CEASE DEPENDENCE ON MASS INSPECTION. Eliminate the need for mass inspection as a way to achieve quality by building quality into the product in the first place. Require statistical evidence of built-in quality in both manufacturing and purchasing functions.

Companies should concentrate on *preventing* defects rather than detecting them. As we stated earlier, the traditional emphasis in American companies was on final inspection. Unfortunately, final inspection of a defective product does not always provide information on how to improve product quality. It is better to use control charts and other statistical tools to monitor product quality at each step of a process. Then quality problems can be corrected as they occur. Besides, 100% inspection is costly and delays deliveries, and it is not always accurate. To illustrate that 100% inspection is not always accurate, simply ask several people to count the number of "f"s on this page. (Most will miss the "f"s in "of.") So even if the inspectors know what they're looking for, they won't always find it.

4 END LOWEST-TENDER CONTRACTS. End the practice of awarding business solely on the basis of price tag.

It is sad but true that the lowest-price vendor may also have the lowest quality. Saving one cent on each "widget" placed in a car may later cost a company millions of dollars in repair costs and lawsuits due to accidents caused by the faulty part. Deming believed a company should use as few suppliers as possible. Ideally he believed a company should use a single supplier (called **single sourcing**). He argued that single sourcing leads to a trusting relationship that will increase the quality of goods produced. In accordance with Deming's teachings, the automobile companies have in recent years greatly reduced the number of suppliers they use. In this way they and their suppliers no longer play an adversary role but instead forge long-term relationships and work together to improve quality.

5 IMPROVE EVERY PROCESS. Improve constantly and forever the system of production and service, to improve quality and productivity, and thus constantly decrease costs.

Deming believed that unenlightened managers often respond only to crises—that is, they wait until things get so bad that they are impossible to ignore. It is much better to make improvements continually and thereby try to keep crises from occurring in the first place. The statistical tools we will discuss are intended to do this. By using them continually, companies are able to detect a problem almost immediately when it occurs, and they are generally able to learn more about their processes so that lasting improvements can be made.

6 INSTITUTE TRAINING. Institute modern methods of training for everybody's job, including management, to make better use of every employee.

Employees need to understand the entire process, not just their own jobs. Most Japanese companies, including Toyota, have adopted this philosophy. Deming believed that training is an investment for the long term in the company's most important assets, its employees. For example, in its early days, Motorola U (Motorola's employee training center) estimated a 3300% return on training at plants where managers supported the quality policy. Unfortunately, some companies fail to see the long-term value of worker training and scrap training programs as soon as financial resources become tight. Deming argued strongly that this is exactly the wrong strategy to take.

7 INSTITUTE LEADERSHIP OF PEOPLE. Adopt and institute leadership aimed at helping people to do a better job.

Supervisors should not focus on the negative. They should promote teamwork, not divisiveness, and they should stress quality, not quantity. One of Deming's most controversial views is his rejection of performance appraisals. He believed they undermine teamwork. His reasons are that (1) most variation is a part of the *system*, over which the workers have little or no control, so it makes little sense to reward or penalize workers for something they cannot control; (2) individual and departmental targets and objectives destroy cooperation between departments; and (3) reliance on pay as a motivator destroys pride in work and individual creativity. Deming saw the ideal leader as a coach and teacher, not a watchman. He believed that the primary objective of leadership should be to motivate people to work to their maximum level of performance. When they complain about "worker attitudes" as the cause of poor quality, they usually miss the real cause: the system itself. It is actually worse than this: When workers are placed under conditions that force them to do a poor job, they are likely to stop caring, in which case they will probably do an even worse job.

8 DRIVE OUT FEAR. Encourage effective two-way communication and other means to drive out fear throughout the organization so that everybody can work effectively and more productively for the company.

When all relationships between different levels of employees (workers versus supervisors, middle management versus upper management, and so on) are adversarial and based on fear, it is difficult to make improvements. Workers attempt to "hide" from their supervisors rather than cooperate with them, and each level of management is fed what the level below thinks it wants to hear. Fortunately, this style of management, once so prevalent in the United States, is now beginning to give way to one based on trust and cooperation.

9 BREAK DOWN BARRIERS. Break down barriers between departments and staff areas.

It is usually counterproductive to the company as a whole if the individual departments have little knowledge of one another's roles, and it is even worse if individual departments work only for their own good, not the good of the company. Fortunately, we are now seeing more cross-functional teams, often formed to tackle specific problems. Obviously, this brings different areas of expertise to the solution of problems, and it encourages cooperation.

10 ELIMINATE EXHORTATIONS. Eliminate the use of slogans, posters, and exhortations for the workforce, demanding zero defects and new levels of productivity, without providing methods.

Deming's point here is that it does little good to exhort workers to "do it right the first time" if the *system* prevents them from doing so. It actually discourages workers, since they are being exhorted to do something beyond their power to achieve. Management would be wiser to improve the system so that workers can do the jobs they are being asked to do.

11 ELIMINATE ARBITRARY NUMERICAL TARGETS. Eliminate work standards that prescribe quotas for the workforce and numerical goals for people in management.

Establishing arbitrary standards for workers can be counterproductive. On the one side, if the standard is set too low, workers will do just enough to meet the standard, when in fact they *could* accomplish more. On the other side, if the standard is set too high, workers will either become discouraged by the impossibility of meeting the standard or they will cut corners—and produce lower quality—in their attempt to turn out the numbers. A better approach is for management to provide helpful leadership and coaching so that workers can turn out better quality *and* achieve higher productivity. After all, which worker is more productive: a worker who produces 50 parts per hour, 10 of which require rework, or a worker who produces 45 parts per hour, all of which meet specifications?

12 PERMIT PRIDE OF WORKMANSHIP. Remove the barriers that rob hourly workers, and people in management, of their right to pride of workmanship.

This is similar to the previous point. Managers must provide the workers with the motivation and tools to perform their jobs as well as possible. Most workers don't want just to serve time at their jobs; they want to have pride in what they accomplish. Deming argued that when workers are placed in an environment where they can do their jobs properly, then productivity and quality will both improve, and the workers will be happier at what they do.

13 ENCOURAGE EDUCATION. Institute a vigorous program of education, and encourage self-improvement for everyone.

Whereas point 6 is concerned primarily with job training, this point is broader. It refers to self-improvement in any dimension. Deming's idea is that a better educated workforce is a more valuable one. It is better able to evolve with today's constantly changing technology, and it is more aware of broader business issues.

14 TOP MANAGEMENT COMMITMENT AND ACTION. Clearly define top management's permanent commitment to ever-improving quality and productivity, and their obligation to implement all of these principles.

This is essentially a summation of the other points. It says that if a company plans to initiate the quality improvements that are necessary to compete successfully in today's business world—as spelled out by the previous 13 points—then top management must lead the way. Otherwise, it won't happen.

Deming's 14 points are both a philosophy for becoming a quality leader and a prescription for how to do so. For the past several decades, Deming and his disciples have "spread the word" to numerous U.S. (and foreign) companies, and in many cases top management has taken the advice. We customers who now purchase high-quality cars, refrigerators, computers, and a host of other consumer items should thank Deming for his insights. They have resulted in lower prices, better and more useful features, and considerably longer times between repairs.

10.3

Basic Ideas Behind Control Charts

We now discuss control charts, one of the most important statistical tools available for reducing variability and improving quality. These types of charts were originally developed by Dr. Walter A. Shewhart of the Bell Telephone Laboratories in the 1920s, and they are still in widespread use today. They are generally easy to use, even for people not specifically trained in statistics, and they provide a wealth of information about a process.

To understand the reasoning behind control charts, we need to discuss two types of variability in a process. No process, whether it be in a manufacturing or a service company, ever produces outputs with *exactly* the same characteristics from item to item. There is always some variability. The question is whether the variability is an inherent part of the process or can be attributed to **assignable causes**. If the current variability in the output of a process is due entirely to the inherent nature of the process, then we say that its variability is due to **common causes** and that the process is **in statistical control**, or simply, **in control**. On the other hand, if some of the current variability of the process is due to specific assignable causes, such as a bad batch of raw materials, an improperly adjusted machine, a new operator unfamiliar with the process, or others, then we say that the process is **out of control**.

One of the main purposes of control charts is to monitor a process so that we can see when a process goes from an in-control condition to an out-of-control condition. When such a transition is discovered, then a person knowledgeable about the process (the operator of a machine, for example) can search for an assignable cause that led to the out-of-control condition and fix it, thereby bringing the process back into control.

It is important to realize that a process in control is not necessarily a good process. It could be making a lot of items "out of specs." There are two reasons we want to distinguish between in-control and out-of-control processes. First, an in-control process is at least *predictable*, regardless of whether it is any good. By measuring an in-control process, we can estimate the ability of the process to produce quality items. An out-of-control process, on the other hand, might not only be producing a lot of faulty items, but it is also *unpredictable*. It's difficult to change a process in some sensible way if we don't know exactly how good or bad it is.

The second reason is that the assignable causes that produce out-of-control behavior can often be corrected by the workers on the shop floor; that is, they generally do not require management intervention to correct. Once corrected, the process is brought back into control, and the charting can continue.

Unfortunately, there is little workers can do to improve an in-control process that has unacceptable variability. Control charts allow them to *measure* the amount of variability, but there is generally no way they can *reduce* the amount of variability without guidance from management. Essentially, workers are stuck with the current process, and (compare with Deming's point 10) no amount of encouragement or exhortation can enable them to produce a higher-quality product unless management makes a fundamental improvement in the process itself. Control charts can measure how well an in-control process is doing, but they can't improve a faulty process. That is the job of management.

Before looking at control charts in detail, we list the primary reasons they have become so popular.

1   **They improve productivity and lower costs.** Here we define productivity as the number of *good* items produced per hour. Control charts typically allow mistakes to be found (or prevented) early in the process—before they result in poor finished products. Therefore, instead of having workers spend a lot of time producing items that are eventually scrapped or require rework, control charts enable them to get it right the first time. Obviously, when workers spend their time producing good items, they are more productive and the costs of scrap and rework are minimized.

2   **They prevent unnecessary process adjustments.** Even an in-control process contains a certain amount of inherent common-cause variability. Without the guidance of control charts, a human operator is likely to respond to every observed up and down in the process. If the diameter of one part is too high, a downward adjustment of a machine might be made; if a subsequent diameter is too low, an upward adjustment might be made. However, if the process is actually in control and the observed ups and downs are really just "normal" amounts of variability, then such adjustments can actually make the process *worse*. Deming called this "tampering" and advised never to tamper with an in-control process. Control charts allow the operator to see when a process is

really in need of an adjustment—because it has gone out-of-control. As long as the process is in control, adjustments shouldn't be necessary.

3 **They provide diagnostic information about the process.** Control charts are similar to medical diagnostic tests. They not only signal when something is wrong, but they provide clues as to the cause of the problem. An experienced operator will monitor control charts for telltale signs of various problems. When these are spotted, then a search for assignable causes can be made, and in many cases problems can be fixed before they become major.

4 **They provide information about process capability.** Process capability is defined as the ability of a process to produce outputs that meet specifications. Obviously, managers want a high level of process capability. However, to achieve this, they need to know how well their *current* process is doing. Control charts help provide this information, at least when the process is in control. For example, a control chart might indicate that under current in-control conditions, approximately 6 out of every 1000 parts fail to meet specs. This is the process capability. Armed with this information, management can decide whether fundamental changes in the process are warranted.

10.4

Control Charts for Variables

There are two basic types of control charts: control charts for variables and control charts for attributes. Charts for variables are relevant when there is a measurable quantity, such as a diameter, a weight, or a thickness, that can be monitored. In this case the purpose of the chart is to see how this quantity varies through time. On the other hand, in many situations an item is judged to conform to specifications or not—it is either a good item or a bad one—in which case a control chart for *attributes* is appropriate. This type of chart tracks the proportion of conforming (or nonconforming) parts through time. An attributes chart is also appropriate for tracking the number of *defects* (such as paint blemishes, scratches, and so on) through time. We will discuss control charts for attributes in the next section.

In this section we will illustrate two of the most common types of variables control charts: the $\overline{X}$ chart and the R chart. Consider any product that has some measurable characteristic such as a diameter or a thickness. To produce $\overline{X}$ and R charts for this product, we typically proceed as follows. Every so often, say, every half hour, we randomly sample a small number of items and measure the characteristic. This "small number" is usually from 3 to 6, and the resulting sample of measurements is called a **subsample**. For the $\overline{X}$ chart we calculate the average of the measurements in the subsample, and for the R chart we calculate the range (maximum minus minimum) of the measurements in the subsample. Then we plot the sequence of averages ($\overline{X}$'s) and the sequence of ranges (R's) in time series plots.

The resulting time series plots are more informative when we add center lines and control limits. A center line indicates the average value that the $\overline{X}$'s (or R's) vary around. Control limits place upper and lower bounds on where the $\overline{X}$'s (or R's) should be for a process in control. The following example provides an illustration of these charts. We will follow it up with more details on how the charts are formed.

EXAMPLE 10.1

The file SODACANS.XLS contains data on the number of ounces of soda in cans labeled "12-ounce" cans. Every half hour, five cans of soda from a production process were measured for fill volume. This was done for 70 consecutive half-hour periods. Create and interpret the $\overline{X}$ and R charts.

Solution

Although $\overline{X}$ and R charts are quite easy to create by hand—this is the way they are usually created on the shop floor—the process is tedious and better suited for computer implementation. We have done so in StatPro and will explain the steps here. First, the SODACANS.XLS file is set up in the appropriate way for StatPro. There are five adjacent columns for the five observations taken each half hour. (These columns need not be adjacent, but it's natural for them to be.)

To use StatPro, place the cursor anywhere inside the data set and select the Stat-Pro/Quality Control/XBar, R Charts menu item. When prompted for variables, select the five adjacent observation variables, Obs1–Obs5. The next dialog box, shown in Figure 10.3, provides several options for building the charts. Fill it out as shown. We will plot data for only the first 30 half hours and base the control limits on these. Then provide a name (we used Wt1) for the sheets that StatPro will create.

FIGURE 10.3 **Dialog Box for $\overline{X}$, R Chart Options**

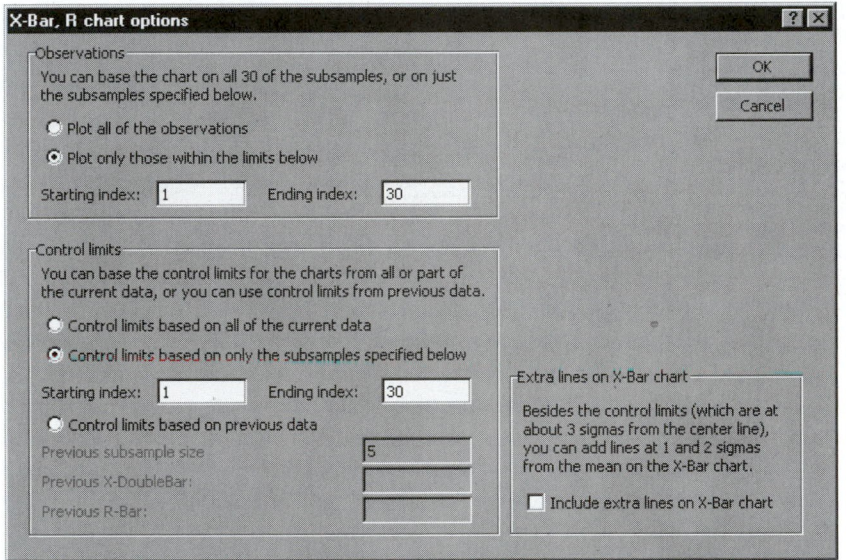

StatPro creates three new sheets. One (named Wt1Data) contains the data that the control charts are based on. The other two (named Wt1XBar and Wt1R) are chart sheets that contain the $\overline{X}$ and R charts. These appear in Figures 10.4 and 10.5. (We will soon discuss the buttons at the tops of these chart sheets.) On each chart we see that the points vary around a centerline and stay within upper and lower control limits (although one point on the $\overline{X}$ chart is very close to the upper limit). The behavior we see in these charts is typical *in-control* behavior. No points are outside of the control limits, and there is no obvious "nonrandom" behavior, such as an upward trend through time. Therefore, this process appears to be in control. If there are specifications on the soda cans—for example, the fill volume of a can should be between 11.88 and 12.20 ounces—then we could use the data (and the fact that the process is in control, that is, predictable) to estimate the percentage of *all* cans within specs.

FIGURE 10.4 $\overline{X}$ **Chart for Soda Can Fill Volumes**

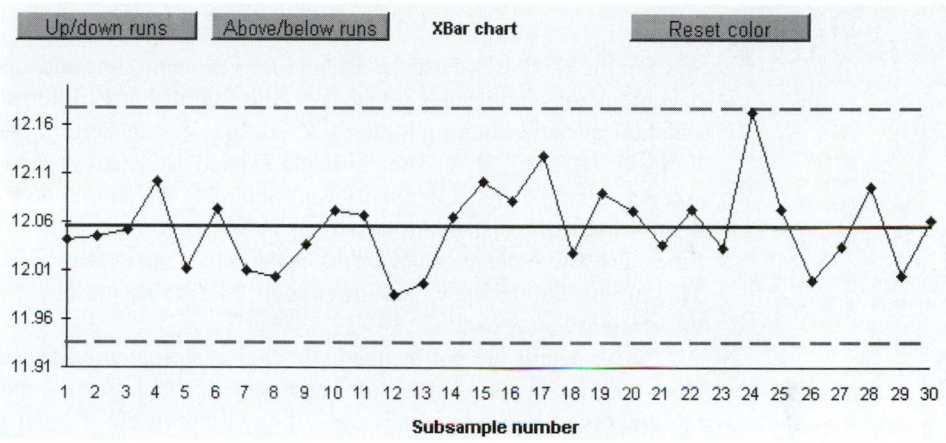

FIGURE 10.5 *R* **Chart for Soda Can Fill Volumes**

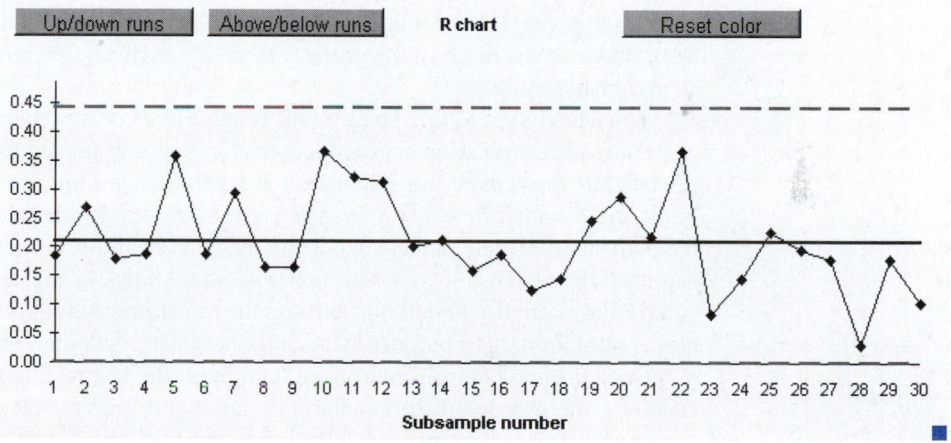

We now discuss in some detail how these charts are formed. The $\overline{X}$ chart is a plot of the subsample averages, that is, the individual $\overline{X}$'s. The centerline for this plot is the average of all $\overline{X}$'s, denoted $\overline{\overline{X}}$. The lower and upper control limits, denoted LCL and UCL, are approximately three standard deviations (of $\overline{X}$) on either side of the centerline, where the standard deviation of $\overline{X}$ is $\sigma/\sqrt{n}$ and n is the subsample size. However, it has been traditional to measure variability by *ranges* rather than standard deviations. (This is easier for nontechnical operators.) Fortunately, there is a simple relationship between them. If $\widehat{\sigma}$

is an estimate of the unknown standard deviation σ and $\overline{R}$ is the average of all R's (one from each subsample), then

$$\widehat{\sigma} = \overline{R}/d_2$$

where d_2 is a constant that depends only on the subsample size n.[2] The lower and upper control limits in the $\overline{X}$ chart are then given by

$$LCL = \overline{\overline{X}} - 3\widehat{\sigma}/\sqrt{n}$$

and

$$UCL = \overline{\overline{X}} + 3\widehat{\sigma}/\sqrt{n}$$

For the R chart, we use the average $\overline{R}$ as the centerline and again go out three standard deviations (of R) on either side to form the control limits. It turns out that the appropriate standard deviation is a multiple of $\overline{R}$, so that we can write the lower and upper control limits as $D_3\overline{R}$ and $D_4\overline{R}$. The constants D_3 and D_4 again depend only on the subsample size n and are tabulated in quality control books. We simply note that the "natural" lower control limit (three standard deviations below the centerline) can sometimes be negative. Since a negative range value doesn't make sense, we instead set $LCL = 0$ in these cases. This means that the upper and lower control limits are not always the same distance from the centerline in R charts.

These details are not as important as the interpretation and use of the charts. The R chart measures within-subsample variation over time. Each R measures the variability in the process *at a given point in time*. If any point in the R chart goes beyond the control limits, this is an indication that the variability has changed, and we can begin searching for a reason—an assignable cause.

We typically look at the R chart first. Because the control limits for the $\overline{X}$ chart depend on $\overline{R}$, they make little sense unless the R's are in control. Assuming, however, that the R chart indicates in-control behavior, we then shift our attention to the $\overline{X}$ chart. It shows subsample averages over time. Any point beyond the control limits suggests a shift, either up or down, in the mean of the process. If we see such a point, we can begin searching for an assignable cause.

The description to this point might suggest that control charting is a static, one-time procedure. However, it is actually a dynamic, ongoing procedure. Typically, a company periodically recalculates (or calculates for the first time, if this is a new process) the control limits for $\overline{X}$ and R by using a fresh set of subsamples. (At least 20 or 25 subsamples are recommended.) If any points are beyond the control limits, a search for assignable causes begins. If the search is successful, the problems are fixed. In any case, the points beyond the control limits are usually eliminated, and the remaining subsamples are used to reestimate new control limits. The purpose in this stage is to bring the process into control, if necessary.

Once the process is in control, we "continue" the control charts by plotting new points but using the just-established centerlines and control limits. We continue to do this until some type of out-of-control behavior is observed, at which time we search for assignable causes. As time proceeds, we learn more and more about the process. This learning not only enables us to keep the process from slipping out of control for extended periods of time, but it also enables us to make lasting improvements to the process. The following continuation of Example 10.1 illustrates how events might unfold.

---

[2] This and other constants below are tabulated in books on quality control. They have been incorported into StatPro automatically.

EXAMPLE 10.2

We now assume that the first 30 subsamples of soda can fill volumes, the ones used in Example 10.1, were used to determine centerlines and control limits for the $\overline{X}$ and R charts. When we plot the other 40 subsamples, using the *same* centerlines and control limits, what do we learn about the process?

Solution

As the dialog box in Figure 10.3 indicates, StatPro allows us to choose the subsamples to plot, as well as the subsamples to base the control limits on. Here we will plot all of the subsamples but base the control limits (and centerlines) only on subsamples 1–30. The dialog box should be filled out as shown in Figure 10.6. The resulting $\overline{X}$ and R charts appear in Figures 10.7 and 10.8 (page 512).

FIGURE 10.6   **Dialog Box for Continuation of Control Charts**

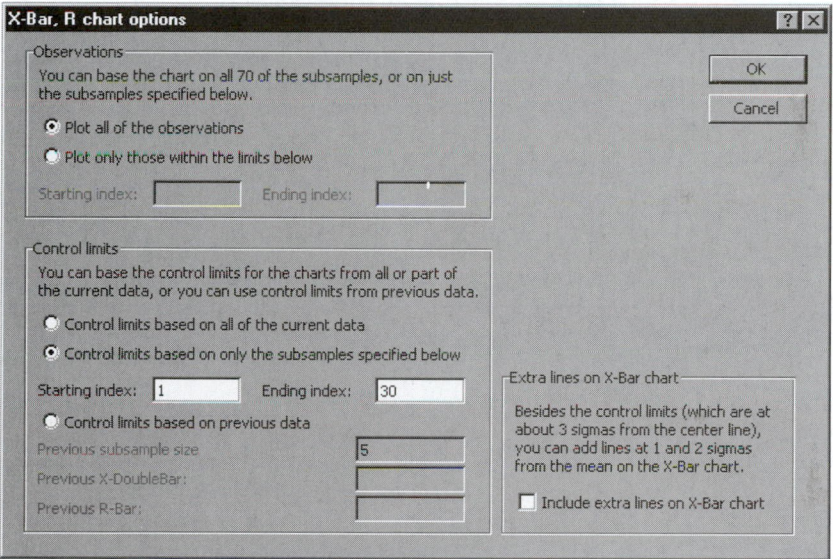

We first look at the R chart. It shows that the process stayed in control for at least 10 more half-hour periods beyond subsample 30. However, beginning shortly after subsample 40, the process variability appears to have increased (many points above the centerline), and finally two points, subsamples 49 and 53, jumped above the upper control limit. As if this weren't enough evidence of an upward shift in variability, we can also search for "runs" of at least eight points above or below the centerline by clicking on the "Above/below runs" button on the chart. (It is very unlikely to see a run this long in an in-control process.) If we click on this button, points 47–54 turn red, indicating a long run above the centerline.

Presumably, the operator of the process discovered the problem that was causing abnormally high variation and fixed it at around the time of subsample 55. After that point, the R chart goes back into control. However, at about this same time, the $\overline{X}$ chart suggests a downward shift in the process mean. Many points are below the centerline, and one finally crosses the lower control limit on subsample 63. Many machines have a mechanism for adjusting the mean to some target level, such as 12.05 ounces. In the present case it appears

FIGURE 10.7 $\overline{X}$ Chart for Continuation of Subsamples

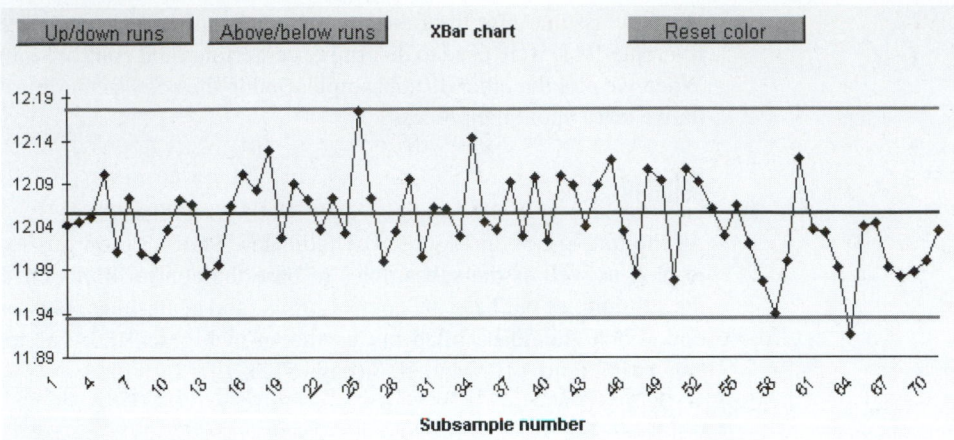

FIGURE 10.8 R Chart for Continuation of Subsamples

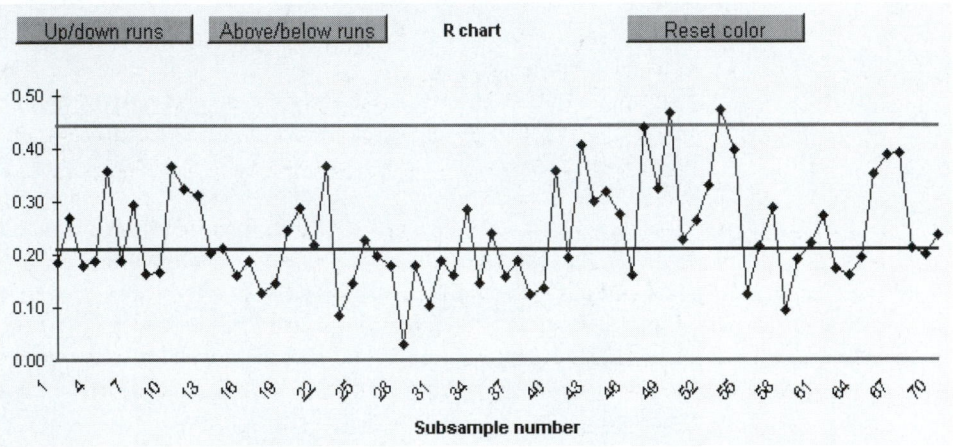

that this machine simply needs to be readjusted to bring its mean back up to the previous level. After this is done, both of the control charts should indicate an in-control process—at least until some other assignable causes force it back out of control again. ∎

This example illustrates how control charts allow an operator to monitor a process continuously and react quickly when problems are indicated. Without this continuous monitoring, out-of-control conditions could persist indefinitely, causing poor quality and higher costs.

10.4.1 Control Charts and Hypothesis Testing

It is enlightening to think of control charts in the context of hypothesis testing. We let the null and alternative hypotheses correspond to in-control and out-of-control conditions, respectively. As we monitor the process with control charts, there are two types of errors we can make. The first, a type I error, is when we react to an out-of-control indication when in fact the process is still in control. We call this a false alarm. For example, there is some chance that a process operating in control will produce a point beyond the control limits. In this case we might begin a search for assignable causes when there are none. We might also make an unnecessary adjustment to the process to bring it back into control (unnecessary because it is still *in* control).

We want to make the probability of a type I error fairly small. If it is too large, we react to too many false alarms and, in Deming's terminology, we tamper with the process. This could not only be costly, but it could actually cause an *increase* in the variability of the process. Therefore, we set the control limits fairly far apart—typically three standard deviations from the centerline—so that the chance of observing a point beyond them is very small.

To pursue this a bit further, assume that the $\overline{X}$'s are normally distributed. (Since each $\overline{X}$ is an average of several observations, the central limit theorem suggests that this normality assumption is reasonable.) Then we know that the probability of any $\overline{X}$ being more than three standard deviations from the mean is 0.0027. From this, we can calculate the mean number of subsamples, called the **average run length**, or ARL, until an in-control process produces a point beyond the control limits. It is simply[3]

$$ARL = 1/0.0027 \simeq 370$$

In other words, false alarms will be few and far between if the process remains in control.

Of course, the flip side is a type II error. This means that the process has gone out of control but the control charts do not indicate it. As usual, it is difficult to calculate the probability of a type II error because there are many types of out-of-control conditions that *could* occur. However, let's concentrate on one possible type of out-of-control condition, where the process variation remains constant but the mean shifts from μ to $\mu + k\sigma$, where k is some fixed constant. For example, if $k = 1$, then the process mean has shifted upward by one standard deviation. We would like to spot this shift immediately, but we won't spot it until an $\overline{X}$ falls above the upper control limit. How long, on average, will this take?

Assuming that the $\overline{X}$ chart has centerline μ, the upper control limit is $\mu + 3\sigma/\sqrt{n}$, and the mean of the process has shifted up to $\mu + \sigma$, we first calculate the probability that an $\overline{X}$ is above the upper control limit. Since $\overline{X}$ now has mean $\mu + \sigma$ and standard deviation $\sigma/\sqrt{n}$, the calculation is a typical normal probability calculation, where we subtract the mean and then divide by the standard deviation:

$$P(\overline{X} > \mu + 3\sigma/\sqrt{n}) = P\left(Z > \frac{(\mu + 3\sigma/\sqrt{n}) - (\mu + \sigma)}{\sigma/\sqrt{n}}\right) = P(Z > 3 - \sqrt{n})$$

Here, Z is normal with mean 0 and standard deviation 1. In the soda can example, $n = 5$, so this probability is

$$P(Z > 3 - \sqrt{5}) = P(Z > 0.764) = 0.222$$

Therefore, there is less than 1 chance in 4 that any particular $\overline{X}$ will be beyond the upper control limit. Another way of looking at it is to calculate the ARL, the expected number of subsamples until the out-of-control behavior is spotted:

$$ARL = 1/0.222 \simeq 4.5$$

For example, if subsamples are taken every half hour, it will take, on average, over 2 hours to realize that the process has gone out of control.

---

[3]An analogy is how long, on average, we would have to wait to roll double sixes with two dice. Since there are 36 possible outcomes for the two dice, the probability of double sixes on a single toss is 1/36. Therefore, the expected number of tosses until double sixes occurs is $1/(1/36) = 36$.

We would like to keep both type I and type II errors to a minimum. That is, we would like to minimize the number of false alarms, but at the same time we would like to spot out-of-control conditions quickly. One strategy is to sample more frequently. Instead of sampling every half hour, we could sample every 15 minutes. Another strategy is to increase the subsample size n from, say, 5 to 10. Both of these strategies are intended to decrease the ARL when the process goes out of control.

For example, if we use $n = 10$ instead of $n = 5$ in the above calculations, we obtain

$$P(Z > 3 - \sqrt{10}) = P(Z > -0.162) = 0.564$$

and

$$ARL = 1/0.564 \simeq 1.77$$

Now, assuming that we are still sampling every half hour, the average time to spot the out-of-control condition is less than an hour. Alternatively, if we keep $n = 5$ but sample every 15 minutes, then the previous ARL of 4.5 now translates to only slightly more than 1 hour.

10.4.2 Other Out-of-Control Indications

To this point, the only formal indication of an out-of-control process is a point beyond the control limits. There are a number of other possible indications of "nonrandom" behavior that we might want to react to. The usual ones that have been suggested include:

1   At least 8 upward (or downward) consecutive changes

2   At least 8 consecutive points above (or below) the centerline

3   At least 2 of 3 consecutive points beyond two standard deviations from the centerline (where both are on the *same* side of the centerline); usually applied only to $\overline{X}$ charts

4   At least 4 of 5 consecutive points beyond one standard deviation from the centerline (where all 4 are on the *same* side of the center line); usually applied only to $\overline{X}$ charts

For these last two conditions it is common to divide the region between the centerline and either control limit into three "zones" of width one standard deviation each, as indicated in Figure 10.9. Then condition 3 is called the **Zone A rule**, and condition 4 is called the **Zone B rule**. In either case the idea is that although points within zone A and zone B are within the control limits, it is unlikely that an in-control process would have this many nearby points in zone A or B.

StatPro places buttons on the charts to check for these four conditions. When any button is clicked, any offending points are colored red. To check conditions 3 and 4 on the $\overline{X}$ chart, the "Include extra lines on X-bar chart" box must be checked in the dialog box in Figure 10.6. If this is done for the soda can data in Example 10.2, you can check that none of conditions 1, 2, or 3 hold for the $\overline{X}$ chart, but condition 4 holds for two different sets of five consecutive points, as indicated in Figure 10.10. The fourth point in each five-point set in zone B is colored red. Since the five-point sets can overlap, there is actually just one red point on the chart, the point corresponding to subsample 69. (Subsamples 65–69 and 66–70 both satisfy condition 4, and subsample 69 is the fourth point in zone B of each of these five-point sequences.)

We do not want to overemphasize these (or any other) possible indications of out-of-control behavior. The more such conditions we check for, the more likely we will find false alarms. In a real situation an experienced operator is likely to give different emphasis to different out-of-control indications. For example, if he sees any of conditions 1–4, but no points beyond the control limits, he might start sampling more frequently—every 15

FIGURE 10.9 **Zones in an $\overline{X}$ Chart**

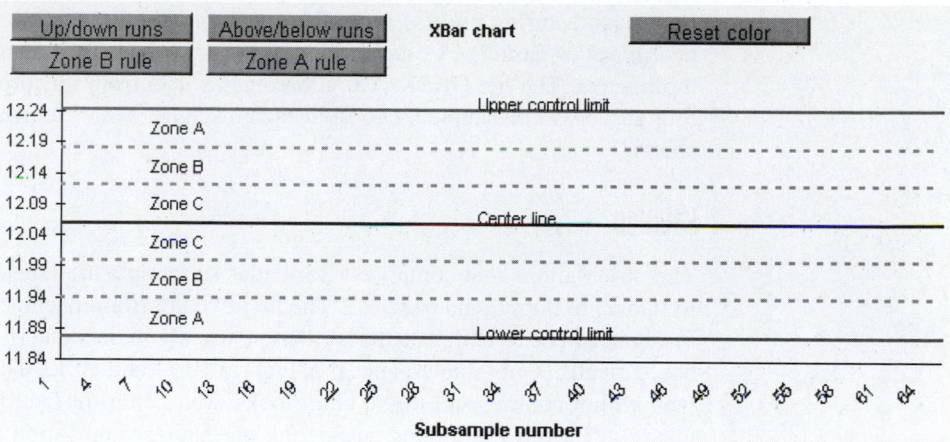

FIGURE 10.10 **Illustration of Zone B Rule**

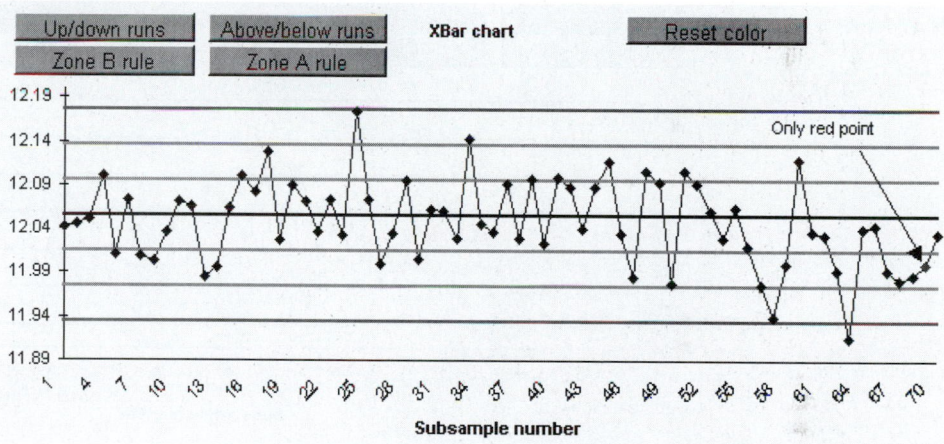

minutes instead of every half hour, say. If he then continues to see more instances of these conditions or see points beyond the control limits, he might start searching for assignable causes and possible fixes.

10.4.3 Rational Subsamples

The small number of observations taken periodically should be **rational subsamples**. This means that they should be taken in such a way that only common-cause variability can be attributed to the points in a particular subsample. There shouldn't be any assignable causes of variability that affect some of the points in the subsample and not others. Typically, rational subsamples are obtained by taking observations nearby in time. For example, every half hour we might examine five consecutive soda cans coming off the production line. However, the following example illustrates what can happen if we are not careful.

EXAMPLE 10.3

In a manufacturing process for gaskets, two parallel production machines produce identical types of gaskets. A crucial dimension of the gaskets is their thickness, measured in millimeters. The file GASKETS.XLS contains data from this process. Every 15 minutes, four gaskets were sampled, two from each machine. What can we learn from the $\overline{X}$ and R charts?

Solution

The observations that comprise a particular subsample are labeled (in the file) M1Obs1, M1Obs2, M2Obs1, and M2Obs2. The first two are from machine 1; the last two are from machine 2. The $\overline{X}$ and R charts for these data, where the centerline and control limits are based on all 50 subsamples, appear in Figures 10.11 and 10.12. The R chart looks perfectly well within control, and the $\overline{X}$ chart looks even better. In fact, it looks suspiciously *too* good, with almost no points outside the one standard deviation band, let alone the three

FIGURE 10.11 $\overline{X}$ **Chart for Gasket Data from Both Machines**

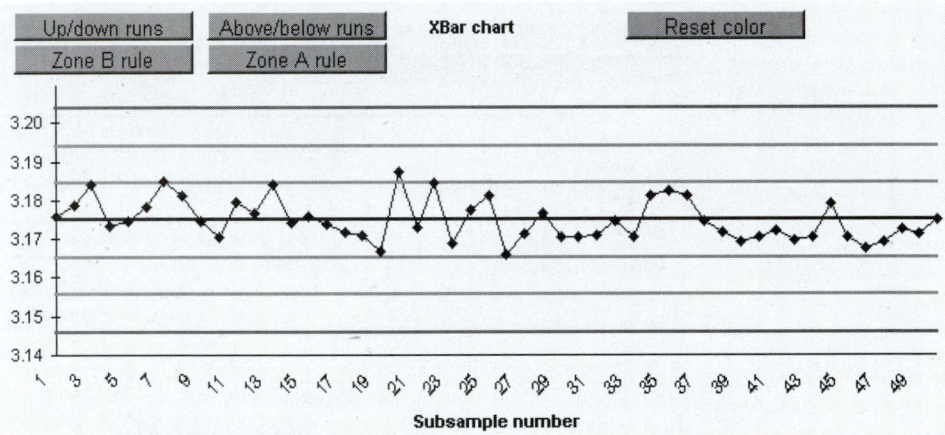

FIGURE 10.12 R **Chart for Gasket Data from Both Machines**

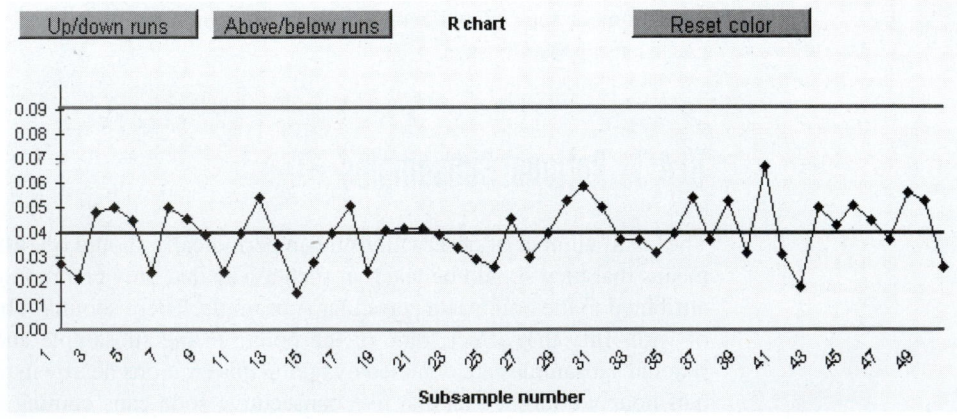

standard deviation band. The process appears to be in control, but is the small amount of variation in the $\overline{X}$ chart (relative to the control limits) telling us something?

A simple look at the data shows that the observations from machine 1 are consistently below those from machine 2. The variability in the data from each machine is roughly the same, but they are varying around *different means*. Think of what this does to the control charts. First, each R is probably a large value from machine 2 minus a small value from machine 1. So the R's are fairly large. This causes the control limits on the $\overline{X}$ chart to be fairly far apart. However, each $\overline{X}$ is an average of two typical machine 1 observations and two typical machine 2 observations. Such averages are not only fairly stable through time, but the highs tend to cancel out the lows. The result is the unusually low variability we see in Figure 10.11.

For the sake of illustration, we assume *four* observations were taken from each machine each half hour. (These are labeled M1Obs1–M1Obs4 and M2Obs1–M2Obs4 in the file.) Only the first two observations from each machine were used in the above control charts. A *rational* subsample philosophy would suggest separate control charts for each machine. It turns out (you can check this) that the control charts for machine 1, based on the subsamples of size 4, indicate perfect in-control behavior. However, the charts for machine 2, again based on subsamples of size 4, appear in Figures 10.13 and 10.14 (page 518). As we see from the R chart, the variability in machine 2 suddenly increased shortly after subsample 25. This causes one out-of-control point in the $\overline{X}$ chart and nearly another. Machine 2 should be checked for assignable causes!

FIGURE 10.13 $\overline{X}$ **Chart for Gaskets from Machine 2**

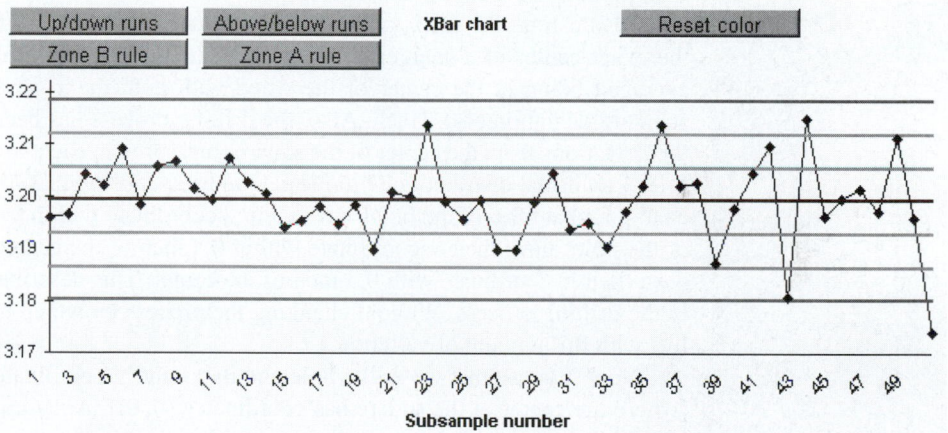

The problem here is that when we combine observations from the two machines into subsamples, the out-of-control behavior is masked by the mixing of highs and lows. We are unable to learn about each machine separately. Therefore, the lesson from this example is that observations within any particular subsample should come from a *single* process, not the mixture of two or more processes.

FIGURE 10.14   *R* Chart for Gaskets from Machine 2

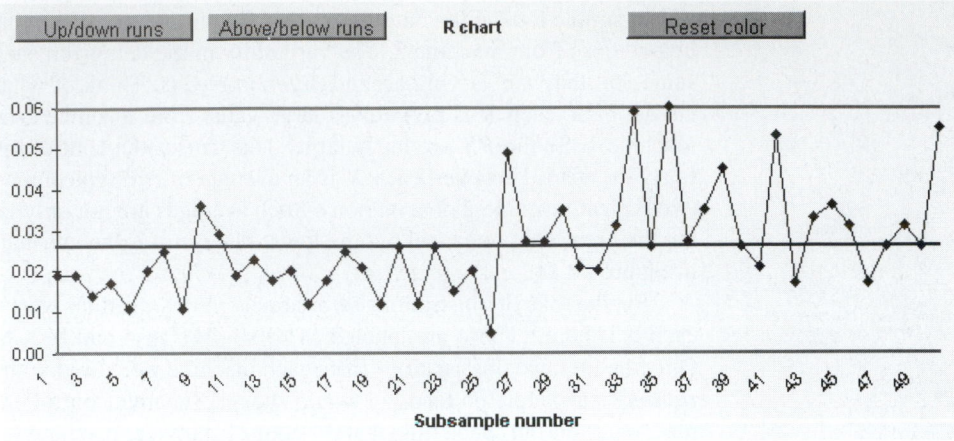

10.4.4   Deming's Funnel Experiment and Tampering

In the quest for reduced variability, it is tempting to make frequent small adjustments to a system. However, if the system is already in control, these adjustments can actually make a system *worse*. Deming called this "tampering" and often demonstrated it in his seminars with the following funnel experiment.

To illustrate the idea, suppose that we are in the business of drilling a tiny hole in the exact center of a square piece of wood. In the past, the holes we have drilled have averaged being in the center of the wood with both the x- and y-coordinates having a standard deviation of 0.1 inch. Also, the drilling process has been in control. Specifically, the deviations from the center of the square (measured in each of the x- and y-coordinates) follow a normal distribution with mean 0 and standard deviation 0.1 inch. This means, for example, that 68% of the holes have their x-coordinate within 0.1 inch of the center, 95% of the holes have their x-coordinate within 0.2 inch of the center, and 99.7% of the holes have their x-coordinate with 0.3 inch of the center. This describes the *inherent* variability in the drilling process. Without changing the process by which holes are drilled, we must live with this amount of variation.

Now suppose that we drill a hole and its x- and y-coordinates are $x = 0.1$ and $y = 0$ [where the center of the square has coordinates $(0, 0)$]. A natural reaction is to reduce (if possible) the x-setting of the drill by 0.1 inch to correct for the fact that the x-coordinate was too high. Then if the next hole has coordinates $x = -0.2$ and $y = 0.1$, we might try to increase the x-coordinate by 0.2 inch and decrease the y-coordinate by 0.1 inch. Deming's funnel experiment shows that this method of continually readjusting an in-control process— tampering—will actually *increase* the variability of the distance of the holes from the target. That is, tampering will generally make the process worse!

To illustrate the effects of tampering, Deming placed a funnel above a target on the floor and dropped small balls through the funnel in an attempt to hit the target. As he demonstrated, many balls did *not* hit the target. His goal, therefore, was to make the balls fall as close to the target as possible. Deming proposed four rules for adjusting the position of the funnel.

Rules for Funnel Experiment

1   Never move the funnel.

2   After each ball is dropped, move the funnel—*relative to its previous position*—to compensate for any error. To illustrate, suppose the funnel begins directly over the target, at coordinates $(0, 0)$. If the ball lands at $(0.5, 0.1)$ on the first drop, we compensate by repositioning the funnel at $(-0.5, -0.1)$. If the second drop has coordinates $(1, -2)$, we now reposition the funnel at $(-0.5 - 1, -0.1 - (-2)) = (-1.5, 1.9)$.

3   Move the funnel—*relative to its original position at* $(0, 0)$—to compensate for any error. If the ball lands at $(0.5, 0.1)$ on the first drop, we compensate by repositioning the funnel at $(-0.5, -1)$. If the second drop has coordinates $(1, -2)$, we now reposition the funnel at $(0 - 1, 0 - (-2)) = (-1, 2)$.

4   Always reposition the funnel directly over the last drop. Thus if the first ball lands at $(0.5, 1)$, we reposition the funnel to $(0.5, 1)$. If the second drop has coordinates $(1, 2)$, we reposition the funnel to $(1, 2)$. This rule might be followed, for example, by an automobile manufacturer's painting department. With each new batch of paint, they attempt to match the color of the previous batch, whether or not the previous color was "correct."

To see how these rules work, we run a simulation in Excel. We assume that the x-coordinate on each drop is normally distributed with a mean equal to the x-coordinate of the funnel position and a standard deviation of 1. A similar statement holds for the y-coordinate. Also, we assume that the x- and y-coordinates are selected independently of one another. These assumptions describe the inherent variability in the process of dropping the balls.

We now develop a spreadsheet to simulate the four rules. For each rule we simulate 50 consecutive drops of the ball and then use a data table to replicate the distance from the 50th drop to the target 100 times. A good rule should have a small average distance, and the standard deviation of the distances (across the replications) should also be small.

It helps to introduce some notation. Let $P_{x,t}$ and $P_{y,t}$ be the x- and y-coordinates of the position of the funnel just before drop t, where $P_{x,1}$ and $P_{y,1}$, the coordinates of the initial position, are both set to 0 for all of the rules. Also, let X_t and Y_t be the coordinates where drop t *actually* falls. Our assumptions imply that X_t and Y_t are normally distributed with means $P_{x,t}$ and $P_{y,t}$. The four rules determine the coordinates of the *next* funnel position, $P_{x,t+1}$ and $P_{y,t+1}$, as follows:

$$P_{x,t+1} = P_{x,t}, \qquad P_{y,t+1} = P_{y,t} \qquad \textbf{(Rule 1)}$$

$$P_{x,t+1} = P_{x,t} - X_t, \qquad P_{y,t+1} = P_{y,t} - Y_t \qquad \textbf{(Rule 2)}$$

$$P_{x,t+1} = 0 - X_t = -X_t, \qquad P_{y,t+1} = 0 - Y_t = -Y_t \qquad \textbf{(Rule 3)}$$

$$P_{x,t+1} = X_t, \qquad P_{y,t+1} = Y_t \qquad \textbf{(Rule 4)}$$

These equations allow us to simulate 50 consecutive drops for any of the four rules very easily in Excel. We illustrate this in Figure 10.15 (page 520) for rule 2. (See the file FUNNEL.XLS.) After entering zeros in cells B7 and C7, we enter the formula

$$=\text{NORMINV(RAND(),B7,1)}$$

in cell D7 and copy it to the range D7:E56 to generate normal random numbers with the appropriate means and standard deviation 1. Then we enter the formula

$$=\text{B7-D7}$$

in cell B8 and copy it to the range B8:C56. This implements the rule 2 positioning equations.

FIGURE 10.15   Simulation of Rule 2 for Funnel Experiment

	A	B	C	D	E
1	Deming's funnel experiment: Rule 2				
2					
3	Move funnel relative to its last position to compensate for error.				
4		Funnel positioned at:		Drop lands at:	
5	Drop	Xpos	Ypos	Xdrop	Ydrop
7	1	0	0	-0.13	0.57
8	2	0.13	-0.57	1.98	-3.43
9	3	-1.84	2.86	-1.18	1.62
10	4	-0.67	1.24	-1.24	0.12
11	5	0.58	1.12	1.16	1.41
12	6	-0.59	-0.28	1.44	0.07
13	7	-2.03	-0.35	-1.18	-0.80
14	8	-0.85	0.45	-1.30	1.59
54	48	2.68	-0.11	3.14	0.83
55	49	-0.46	-0.95	-1.74	1.20
56	50	1.28	-2.15	1.13	-1.81

After implementing each of the four rules for 50 drops, we use a data table, as shown in Figure 10.16, to replicate 100 times the distance from the 50th drop to the target for each rule. (Each distance is the square root of the sum of squares of the coordinates of the 50th drop.) The average, standard deviation, and maximum of the 100 distances appear in rows 5–7. Since we want these distances to be *small*, we see that rule 1 is performing best, with rule 2 following fairly close behind, and rules 3 and 4 performing terribly.

This behavior is reinforced by the histograms of the 100 replicated distances for each rule in Figures 10.17–10.20. (They are all shown on the same scale to facilitate comparisons.) As we see, most of the distances for rule 1 are within 2 units of the target and most of the distances for rule 2 are within 3 units of the target, but most of the distances for rules 3 and 4 are more than 9 units from the target. As Deming predicted, tampering with an in-control system never helps—and it can have very negative consequences.

FIGURE 10.16   Distances from Drop 50 to Target for Four Rules

	A	B	C	D	E	F
1	Data table for replicating distance from center of 50th drop					
2						
3	Summary measures for replications below					
4		Rule1	Rule2	Rule3	Rule4	
5	Average	1.28	1.87	9.11	9.58	
6	Stdev	0.65	0.88	4.98	4.99	
7	Maximum	3.60	4.36	24.96	25.91	
8						
9	Replication	Rule1	Rule2	Rule3	Rule4	
10	0	1.61	1.51	12.61	17.18	
11	1	1.08	3.11	9.73	16.56	
12	2	0.92	0.59	13.34	11.70	
13	3	0.38	1.84	6.91	1.88	
14	4	0.94	1.42	12.93	6.12	
15	5	0.92	3.63	3.01	13.16	
106	96	1.59	1.11	8.69	11.64	
107	97	0.23	0.98	16.46	1.33	
108	98	0.76	0.45	21.46	6.80	
109	99	2.49	2.90	13.93	2.42	
110	100	0.72	4.24	14.25	9.60	

FIGURE 1 0 . 1 7 **Histogram of Distances for Rule 1**

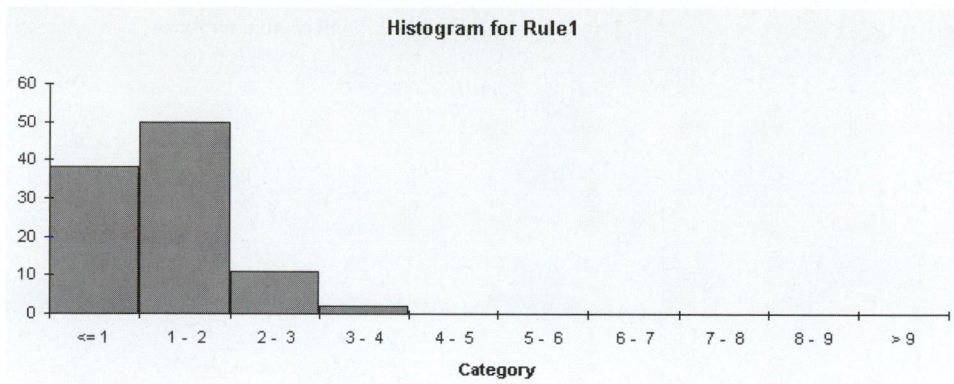

FIGURE 1 0 . 1 8 **Histogram of Distances for Rule 2**

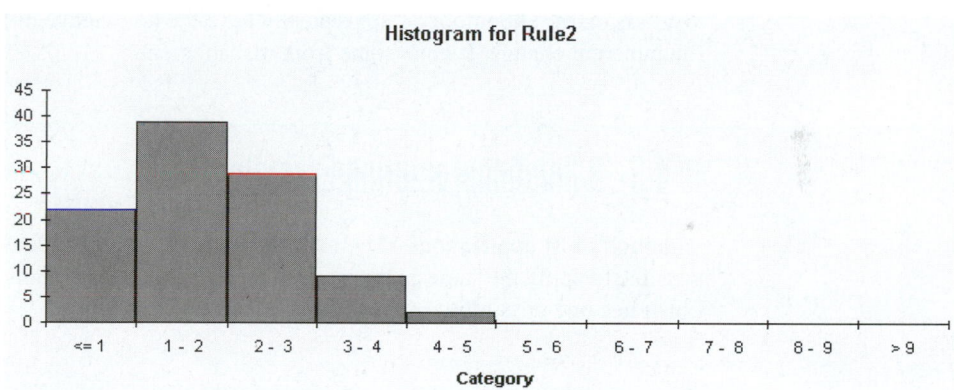

FIGURE 1 0 . 1 9 **Histogram of Distances for Rule 3**

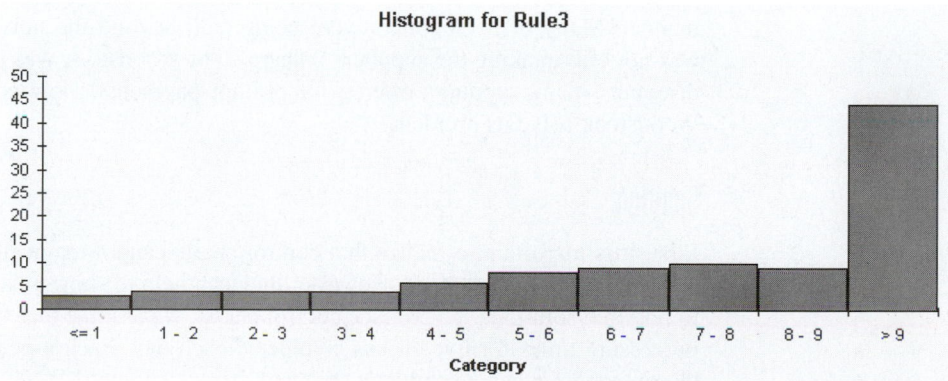

We conclude this discussion of the funnel experiment by noting that the system obtained by using rule 1, the leave-it-alone rule, is not necessarily a *good* system. It may indeed require improvement. The point, though, is that continual tampering with this system will not produce the required improvement; it will only tend to make things worse. The only way

FIGURE 10.20 Histogram of Distances for Rule 4

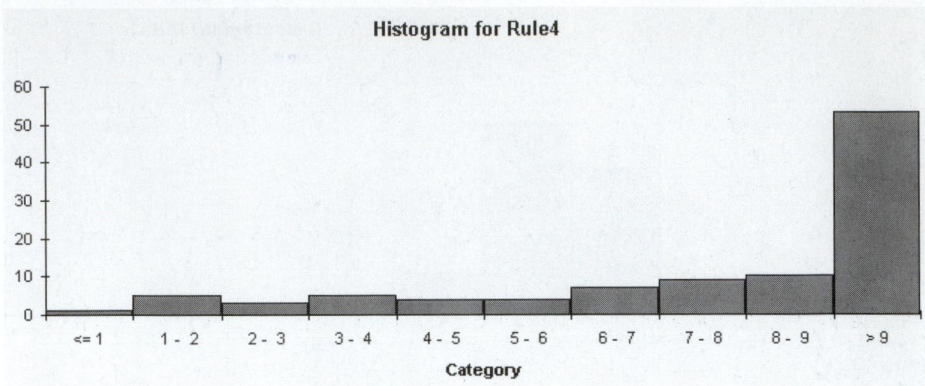

to make a lasting improvement to the system is for management to change it fundamentally. Workers on the shop floor do not typically have the knowledge or authority to make such a fundamental change. It must come from management.

10.4.5 A Nonmanufacturing Example

Although most applications of control charts are in the manufacturing area, it is certainly possible to apply the same analysis to nonmanufacturing problems. The following example illustrates one possibility.

EXAMPLE 10.4

The Woodstock Company, a company in the construction industry, had recently experienced considerable expansion of its business volume. Due in part to this expansion, the finance department of the company was having difficulty processing checks to suppliers in a timely manner. Many of its suppliers were being paid beyond the normal 30-day period. This was not only making the suppliers unhappy, but Woodstock was also failing to obtain the discounts many suppliers offered for prompt payments. How could control charts help Woodstock solve its problem?

Solution

First, it is important to realize that control charts cannot magically solve a problem such as the one Woodstock faced. However, they can help to show what is happening and point to possible solutions. To produce control charts, we assume that Woodstock measured the processing times for five checks completed each day. Each processing time is defined as the time from when a supplier's shipment is received until Woodstock sends the check to the supplier. The file CHECKS.XLS contains these processing times for 60 consecutive business days. Observations for the first 30 days were used to form control limits. The R chart (not shown here) for these 30 days is well within control, but the $\overline{X}$ chart, shown in Figure 10.21, indicates out-of-control points on days 7 and 10.

FIGURE 10.21 $\overline{X}$ **Chart for First 30 Days**

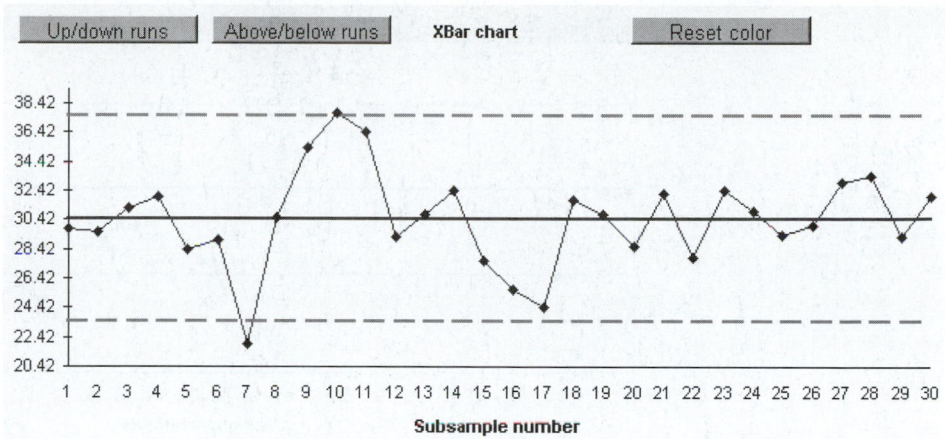

Upon closer examination, Woodstock learned that on day 7 the people in finance, trying to improve a process with high variability and large processing times, implemented a change in the check preparation process. However, this change backfired—it actually made things worse—and was eliminated after 5 days. This change is a clear example of an *assignable cause*. The points we observe in Figure 10.21 are actually the result of two separate processes, those without the change and those (points 7–11) with the change. To understand the original process, Woodstock needed to eliminate points 7–11 and form new charts. This was done, and the plots of days 1–6 and 12–30 (not shown here) showed statistical control.[4]

The process was now in statistical control, but this was no place to stop! Woodstock was alarmed at the high average processing times (about 30 days) and the high variability (average R's of nearly 12 days). Their management took a closer look at the check preparation process and discovered several unnecessary steps—duplicate paperwork and excessive "hand-offs" from one person to another. They took steps to streamline the process, and they continued to plot, using the control limits and centerlines from days 1–6 and 12–30. The $\overline{X}$ and R charts through day 60 (again, with days 7–11 eliminated) appear in Figures 10.22 and 10.23 (page 524).

These control charts both indicate out-of-control behavior, but of the kind Woodstock is happy to see. The R chart indicates a lower level of variability, and the $\overline{X}$ chart indicates a decreased average time to process checks. The R's are now averaging about 6.5 days, and the average check processing times are about 20 days. These improvements are a direct result of Woodstock's management interventions, but these interventions were prompted by observing control charts and trying to understand what was causing them.

Even after day 60, Woodstock should not rest on its laurels. First, it should recalculate control limits and centerlines, based on new data, say, from days 51–80. It could use these to check whether the improved process is in control with respect to the new limits. At least as importantly, it should continue to search for potential improvements in the process. If the average check preparation time could be reduced from 30 days to about 20 days, and the variability could be reduced as well, who's to say that further improvements are not possible?

[4]To do this in Excel, we copied the original data sheet to a new data sheet, deleted the rows corresponding to days 7–11, and formed control charts from the first 25 rows of this new data set.

FIGURE 10.22 $\overline{X}$ Chart for Days 1–60 (with Days 7–11 Eliminated)

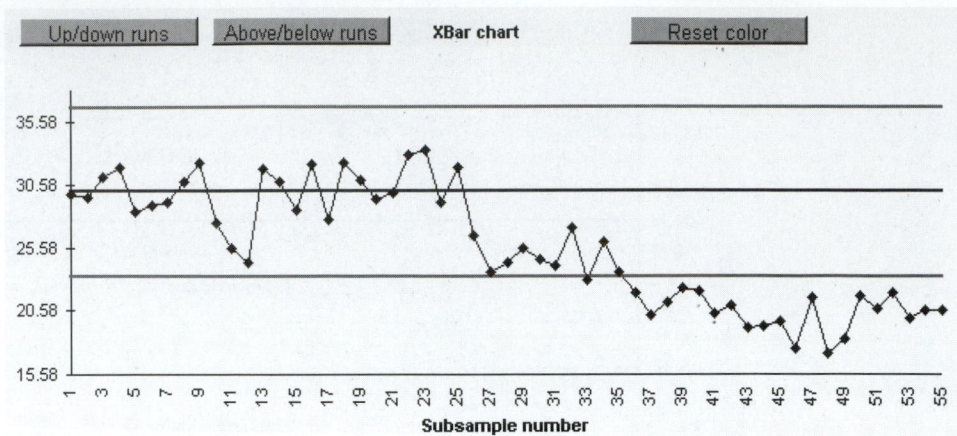

FIGURE 10.23 $\overline{X}$ Chart for Days 1–60 (with Days 7–11 Eliminated)

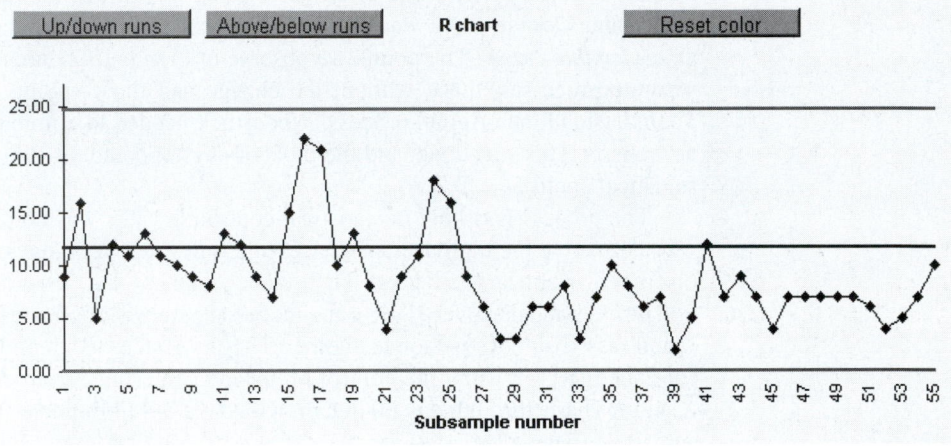

PROBLEMS

Level A

1   The file P10_1.XLS contains data on the amount of soda (in ounces) placed in aluminum cans by a particular filling process. Ideally, the filling process should place 12 ounces of soda in each can. Every hour, 4 cans of soda were randomly selected from the production process and measured for amount of fill. This was repeated for 25 consecutive hours. Generate and interpret $\overline{X}$ and R charts for the given data. Does this filling process appear to be in control?

2   The data in the file P10_2.XLS consist of 25 subsamples of 4 observations each on the diameters (measured in centimeters) of ball bearings produced by a manufacturing process. The target diameter of these ball bearings is 4 centimeters.

   a   Generate and interpret $\overline{X}$ and R charts for the given data. Based on these charts, does this manufacturing process appear to be in control?

   b   Are there any other indications that the given process may be out of control? If so, explain.

3 The data in the file P10_3.XLS consist of 25 subsamples of 6 observations each on the fill weights of cans of paint. The ideal fill weight of these paint cans is 20 pounds.

a Generate and interpret $\overline{X}$ and R charts for the given data. Does this filling process appear to be in control?

b Are there any other indications that the given process may be out of control? If so, explain.

4 Continuing the previous problem, operators have made an adjustment that they hope will improve the functioning of this process. The file P10_4.XLS contains 25 subsamples of 6 observations each on the fill weights of cans of paint, taken after the process was modified.

a Generate and interpret $\overline{X}$ and R charts for the given data. Which control limits do you believe are most appropriate? Explain. Does this filling process appear to be in control now?

b Are there any other indications that the given process may be out of control now? If so, explain.

c What advice would you give to the operators of this filling process based on your analysis of the latest sample information?

5 Producers of a particular brand of ready-to-eat breakfast cereal place, in theory, 15 ounces of cereal in each box of this product. In an effort to assess this stage of the manufacturing process, an operations manager gathers 25 subsamples of 4 observations each on the amount (measured in ounces) of cereal in selected boxes. These data are given in the file P10_5.XLS.

a Generate and interpret $\overline{X}$ and R charts for the given data. Does this process appear to be in control?

b Are there any other indications that the given process may be out of control? If so, explain.

c If your analysis reveals that a problem does exist with the process, what advice would you give to the manager of this operation?

6 The data in the file P10_6.XLS consist of 25 subsamples of 4 observations each on the lengths of particular bolts manufactured for use in large aircraft. The target length of these bolts is 37 centimeters.

a Generate and interpret $\overline{X}$ and R charts for the given data. Does this production process appear to be in control?

b Are there any other indications that the given process may be out of control? If so, explain.

7 Continuing the previous problem, managers have made an adjustment that they hope will improve the functioning of this process. The file P10_7.XLS contains 25 subsamples of 4 observations each on selected bolt lengths, taken after the production process was modified.

a Generate and interpret $\overline{X}$ and R charts for the given data. Which control limits do you believe are most appropriate? Explain. Does this production process appear to be in control now?

b Are there any other indications that the given process may be out of control now? If so, explain.

c What advice would you give to the operators of this production process based on your analysis of the latest sample information?

8 The operations manager of an airline check-in counter is interested in evaluating the service provided to the company's customers. In particular, she would like to make sure that customers are not waiting excessively long prior to being served at the check-in facility. Ideally, she would like to see that customers wait, on average, less than 7 minutes prior to being served at the check-in counter. The file P10_8.XLS contains the waiting times (in minutes) of 5 randomly selected passengers, observed during the same hour on each of 25 different days.

a Construct and interpret $\overline{X}$ and R charts for the given data. Based on these charts, does this service process appear to be in control?

b Are there any other indications that the given service process may be out of control? If so, explain.

c What specific advice would you give to the operations manager for improving customer service, at least in the short run?

9 Continuing the previous problem, the operations manager of this airline check-in counter has recently made some changes to the operation of the counter that she hopes will reduce customer waiting times. Again, she observes the waiting times of 5 randomly selected passengers during the same hour on each of another 25 days. These observations are given in the file P10_9.XLS. Characterize the impact of the operations manager's refinements on the performance of this service operation. Does this facility, with respect to customer waiting times, appear to be operating well now? Explain why or why not.

10 The file P10_10.XLS contains the breaking strengths (measured in pounds) of randomly selected pieces of a certain welded material. In particular, these data consist of 25 subsamples of 5 observed breaking strengths each. The target breaking strength of this welded material is 300 pounds.

    a Generate and interpret $\overline{X}$ and R charts for the given data. Does this production process appear to be in control?

    b Are there any other indications that the given process may be out of control? If so, explain.

    c If the process is out of control, which subsamples could be eliminated to achieve in-control behavior in the R chart? Why might it be legitimate to eliminate these subsamples?

11 The file P10_11.XLS contains data on the amount of liquid detergent (in ounces) placed in plastic containers by a particular filling process. Ideally, the filling process should place 100 ounces of detergent in each container. Every hour, 6 detergent containers were randomly selected from the production process and measured for amount of fill. This was repeated for 25 consecutive hours.

    a Generate and interpret $\overline{X}$ and R charts for the given data. Does this filling process appear to be in control?

    b Are there any other indications that the given process may be out of control? If so, explain.

    c Given your analysis of the sample information, what steps, if any, should be taken to adjust this filling process?

12 Management of a local bank is interested in assessing the process used in opening new checking accounts for bank customers. In particular, management would like to examine the time required to process a customer's request to open a new checking account. Currently, managers believe that it should typically take about 7 minutes to process such a request. The file P10_12.XLS contains the time required to process new checking account requests for each of 6 customers selected randomly on a given day. A different subsample of 6 customer requests was collected on each of 25 days. Generate and interpret $\overline{X}$ and R charts for the given data. Does this customer service process appear to be in control? Explain why or why not.

13 The manager of a supermarket would like to evaluate the effectiveness of a large freezer unit currently used to store excess supplies of various frozen food items in the supermarket's inventory. Specifically, the manager wants to determine whether the current freezer is maintaining the valuable store inventory at a roughly constant temperature of 7 degrees. To make this evaluation, he asks his assistant to take 6 temperature readings within the freezer at various points in the day for a total of 30 days. These measurements are given in P10_13.XLS.

    a Generate and interpret $\overline{X}$ and R charts for the given data. Do these data indicate the presence of one or more problems with the operation of this freezer? Explain.

    b How might you explain the trend in the R chart for subsamples 21 through 30?

    c What advice would you give to the supermarket manager regarding this freezer?

Level B

14 Consider a situation where a given process goes out of control but the relevant control charts do not indicate so. Assume that the process variation remains constant but the mean shifts from μ to $\mu + k\sigma$, where k is a fixed constant.

    a Provided that $k = 1.5$ and $n = 5$, what is the mean number of subsamples required for $\overline{X}$ to rise above the upper control limit?

    b Provided that $k = 1.5$ and $n = 9$, what is the mean number of subsamples required for $\overline{X}$ to rise above the upper control limit?

    c Provided that $k = 2.0$ and $n = 5$, what is the mean number of subsamples required for $\overline{X}$ to rise above the upper control limit?

15 Consider a situation where a given process goes out of control but the relevant control charts do not indicate so. Assume that the process variation remains constant but the mean shifts from μ to $\mu - k\sigma$, where k is a fixed constant.

    a Provided that $k = 1.0$ and $n = 4$, what is the mean number of subsamples required for $\overline{X}$ to fall below the lower control limit?

    b Provided that $k = 1.0$ and $n = 8$, what is the mean number of subsamples required for $\overline{X}$ to fall below the lower control limit?

    c Provided that $k = 0.5$ and $n = 4$, what is the mean number of subsamples required for $\overline{X}$ to fall below the lower control limit? ■

10.5   Control Charts for Attributes

Often there are no explicit measurements available. We may simply be able to check whether each item produced conforms to specifications or not. For example, a computer chip either works as it should or it doesn't. An item that fails to conform to specifications is called a **nonconforming** (or **defective**) item. When items can only be classified as conforming or nonconforming, then we typically chart the proportions that are conforming during consecutive periods of time. The resulting chart is called a **p chart**. It is one of several types of charts called **attributes** charts, where the term *attribute* indicates an "on/off" type of measurement: The item either has the attribute or it does not.

There are other types of attributes charts called **c charts** and **u charts**. These are used to chart the number (or rate) of defects in successive items, where a defect is any flaw in an item, such as a paint blemish on a car door, a defective weld in a pipeline, a broken rivet on an airplane wing, and so on. Clearly, different types of defects vary in their seriousness, and any combination of them could cause an item (a car door, for example) to be classified as nonconforming. We will not discuss c charts and u charts in this book, but they are very similar to the other control charts we discuss, and they can be formed easily with StatPro's Quality Control procedures.

10.5.1   The p Chart

We now discuss p charts in some detail. During consecutive periods of time, we sample a number of items from a process and label each of these as conforming or nonconforming. Specifically, suppose we sample n_i items during period i, and k_i of these fail to conform to specifications. The number n_i could either be *all* of the items produced during period i, or it could represent a sample of all items produced. Also, these sample sizes could be constant for all periods, or they could differ. In any case, we let $\widehat{p}_i$ be the proportion of nonconforming items in sample i:

$$\widehat{p}_i = k_i / n_i$$

A p chart is then a time series plot of the $\widehat{p}_i$'s.

The idea behind p charts is exactly the same as with $\overline{X}$ and R charts. We place a centerline and control limits on the chart in such a way that the $\widehat{p}_i$'s for an in-control process vary randomly around the centerline and almost never cross the control limits. The centerline is placed at the overall proportion of nonconforming items. This value, denoted by $\overline{p}$, is given by

$$\text{Centerline} = \overline{p} = \frac{\sum_i k_i}{\sum_i n_i} = \frac{\text{number of nonconforming items}}{\text{number of items produced}}$$

If the n_i's are constant across samples, then $\overline{p}$ is the average of the $\widehat{p}_i$'s.

To specify the control limits, we first examine the special case where the n_i's are constant and equal to a common value n. If we can assume that each item is nonconforming with some constant probability p, then we know from Chapter 5 that the number of nonconforming items in sample i is binomially distributed with mean np and standard deviation $\sqrt{np(1-p)}$. Equivalently, the sample proportion $\hat{p}$ has mean p and standard deviation $\sqrt{p(1-p)/n}$. Because p is typically unknown, we use the value $\bar{p}$ as an estimate of p to form the following control limits:

$$LCL = \bar{p} - 3\sqrt{\bar{p}(1-\bar{p})/n}$$

and

$$UCL = \bar{p} + 3\sqrt{\bar{p}(1-\bar{p})/n}$$

That is, we go out three standard deviations (of $\hat{p}$) on either side of the centerline value $\bar{p}$.

If the sample sizes are *not* equal, then each sample has its own control limits of the form

$$\bar{p} \pm 3\sqrt{\bar{p}(1-\bar{p})/n_i}$$

Now the denominator n_i varies from sample to sample instead of being constant. The effect is that the control limits vary through time and are not straight lines on the control chart. This is an annoying feature, so in practice the *average* of the n_i's is often used in place of the n_i's as a "common sample size" unless the n_i's differ greatly from one another. StatPro gives the user this option of using a common sample size even if the individual sample sizes are not equal.

The following example illustrates how a p chart can be constructed and interpreted. Although some of the details are different, the basic interpretation and use of p charts are exactly the same as with $\overline{X}$ and R charts. Specifically, they are monitored through time to provide a better understanding of a process and suggestions for possible improvement.

EXAMPLE 10.5

SoundTech is a company that manufactures electronic chips for sound systems in personal computers. Each chip is classified as conforming or nonconforming. The nonconforming chips cannot be used and are discarded. Each hour 75 chips are tested for conformance. These 75 chips represent a random sample of all chips that are produced in a given hour. The file CHIPS1.XLS lists the number of nonconforming chips (out of 75) for 25 consecutive hours. Is the process currently in control? Is it behaving well?

Solution

The mechanics of constructing a p chart with StatPro are very similar to those for $\overline{X}$ and R charts. The main difference is that the data can be set up in several ways. First, the data can either list the *numbers* of nonconforming items or the *fractions* of nonconforming items. (CHIPS1.XLS lists the former.) Second, a variable that lists the sample sizes, the n_i's, can either be present or absent. (There is such a variable in CHIPS1.XLS.) If the sample size variable is absent, then it is assumed that the sample sizes are constant, and you must enter this common value in a dialog box.

To create the p chart, we use StatPro's Quality Control/P Chart menu item. After the usual opening message, the dialog box in Figure 10.24 appears. For this example it should be filled out as shown. (Alternatively, the bottom option could be checked, in which case the value 75 should be entered manually in the box.) Next, the procedure prompts for the variable containing the numbers nonconforming and the sample size variable. (The

FIGURE 10.24   **Dialog Box for Specifying Variables for** *p* **Chart**

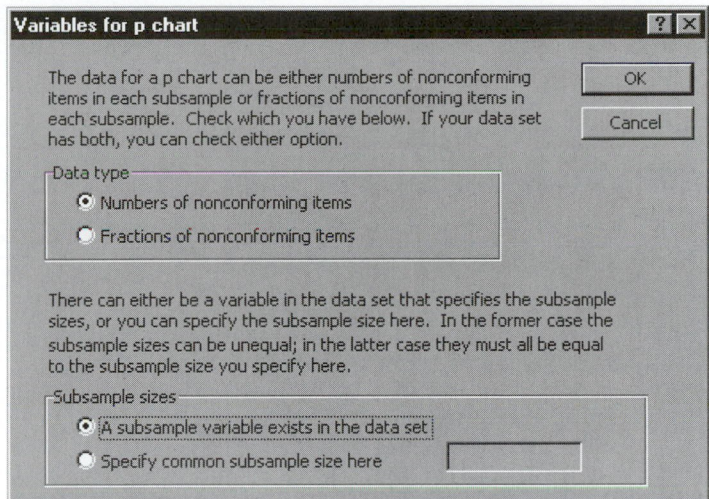

FIGURE 10.25   **Dialog Box for Other** *p* **Chart Options**

variables Nonconforming and SampSize should be selected for this example.) Next, the dialog box shown in Figure 10.25 appears. It is almost exactly the same as for $\overline{X}$ and R charts and should be filled in as shown. Finally, the procedure prompts for a sheet name. Two sheets are then created, one with the *p* chart and one with the data used to build it.

The *p* chart appears in Figure 10.26 (page 530). We see that the points, each of which indicates a proportion nonconforming, vary randomly around a centerline of $\overline{p} = 0.255$. The control limits are at 0.104 and 0.407, and no points are beyond the control limits. Therefore, the current process appears to be in control. But is it any good? We would argue that an average percent nonconforming of about 25% is *not* very good. As usual, an in-control process is *predictable* but not necessarily acceptable. SoundTech management should begin searching for improvements to its process. For example, they might select

FIGURE 10.26 *p* **Chart for Nonconforming Chips**

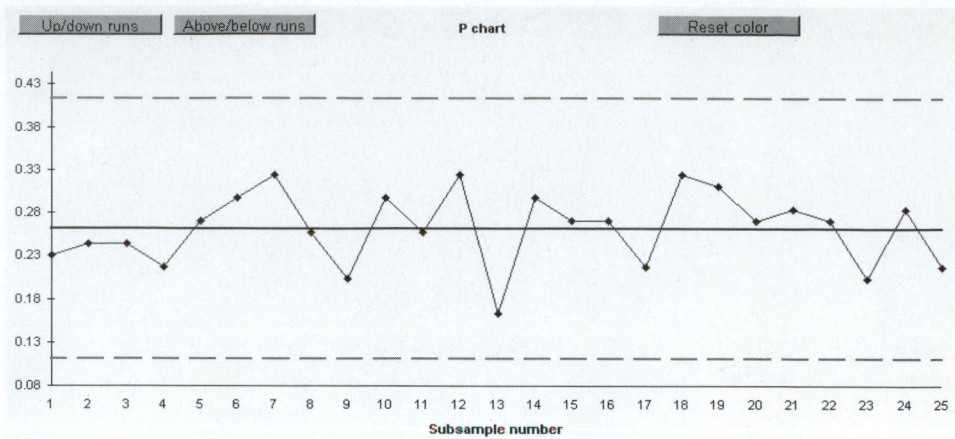

different suppliers of raw material, purchase new machinery, or institute better worker training. Then by charting future values, the company can see whether any improvements it employs have the desired effect.

For the sake of comparison, we illustrate a variation of this example where SoundTech samples a *different* number of chips each hour. For example, it might actually sample *all* chips produced, and production quantities might vary considerably from hour to hour. The file CHIPS2.XLS contains the data. The only difference is that the SampSize variable in this file is not constant. We have two options. We can fill out the dialog box in Figure 10.24 exactly as before, or we can check the bottom box and enter an "average" sample size. If we select the former option, the resulting *p* chart appears in Figure 10.27. As we see, the nonconstant sample sizes result in uneven control limits. Although we are still looking for points beyond the control limits, the bumpiness of these limits is somewhat distracting. Therefore, SoundTech might decide to base the chart on the average sample size (about 75). Fortunately, the practical difference between these two approaches is usually minor.

FIGURE 10.27 **A *p* Chart with Unequal Sample Sizes**

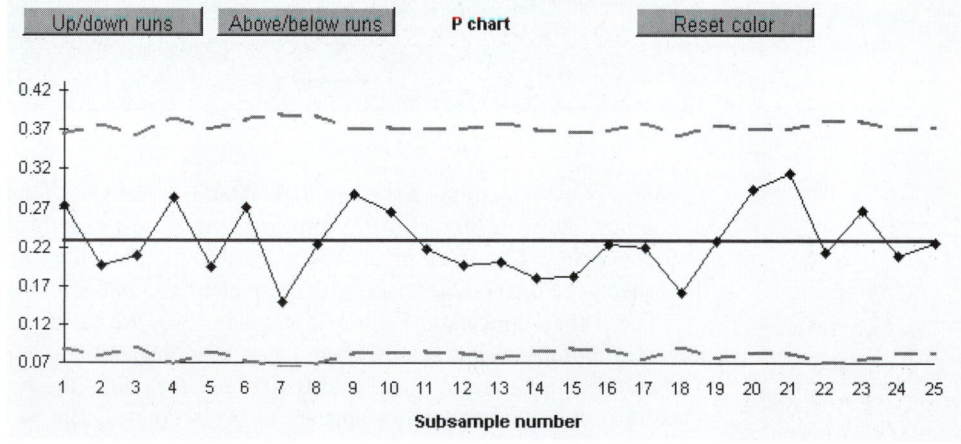

10.5.2 The Red Bead Experiment

Recall that several of Deming's 14 points concern the role of management in helping workers to do a better job. Deming believed that it is *not* management's role simply to exhort workers to do a better job. Management needs to change a system that prevents workers from performing up to standards. To illustrate this concept, Deming often used the following "red bead experiment." It illustrates clearly that in a system subject only to common-cause variation, some workers are bound to be the "best" on some days and "worst" on others, for no particular reasons (such as slacking off or working harder). It also illustrates how all workers can fail to live up to standards, through no fault of their own, if the system is not designed correctly.

The experiment is very simple. There is a large container of beads, 20% of which are red and 80% of which are white. Several people from the audience are asked to play the role of workers, while others from the audience are asked to help out as inspectors. Each of the workers gets a "paddle" with 50 holes, where each hole can hold a single bead. The rules of the game are that each worker must put his or her paddle into the container and pull out exactly 50 beads. Each such draw corresponds to one day's production quantity. That is, each worker "produces" exactly 50 beads per day. They are also told that red beads correspond to defectives. Each person's job is to produce no more than two defectives per day; their continued employment depends on it. The inspectors then count the number of red beads for each worker for each day's production and tally the results for all to see.

Let's say the workers' names are Jim, Tricia, Tom, and Lisa. Several things about the experiment are fairly obvious. First, the mechanics of the process make it impossible for workers to "fish" for all white beads. Therefore, every worker gets a random sample of 50 red and white beads on each draw from the container. Some days Jim will—totally by luck—get the most red beads, and other days he will get the fewest red beads. The same applies for the other workers. Certainly, there is no reason to reprimand Jim in the first case or reward him in the second. But Deming says that this is exactly what occurs in many job settings.

Second, the experiment is stacked against the workers. It is impossible for them, on most days, to draw two or fewer red beads. On average, each draw will result in 20%, or 10, red beads. For them to do their job as instructed, the *system* must change. For example, management could remove a lot of the red beads from the container. Even though all of this was obvious to the "workers" in Deming's experiments, it is interesting that many of them nevertheless tried their best to perform as instructed, and many were genuinely frustrated when they continued to draw too many red beads.

We can illustrate the red bead experiment with an Excel simulation, together with a *p* chart. The REDBEAD.XLS file contains the results. We first simulate the number of red beads for each worker on 30 successive days. (See Figure 10.28, page 532.) For each worker and each day, the number of red beads is a binomial random value based on 50 trials and probability 0.2 of "success" (a red bead) on each trial. To simulate such a value, we can use the BINOMIAL_ function built into StatPro.[5] That is, we enter the formula

$$=BINOMIAL\_(50,0.2)$$

in cell B6 and copy it to the range B6:E35.

We then sum the number of red beads per day in column F, and in columns G–J we record the "best" and "worst" workers each day. For example, the formulas in cells G6 and I6 are

$$=MIN(B6:E6)$$

---

[5]Alternatively, we could use Excel's built-in function CRITBINOM in the form =CRITBINOM(50,0.2,RAND()).

FIGURE 10.28 Simulation Results for Red Bead Experiment

	A	B	C	D	E	F	G	H	I	J
1	Red bead experiment									
2										
3	Simulation of 30 days									
4										
5	Day	Jim	Tricia	Tom	Lisa	Total	Best	Worst	Winner	Loser
6	1	10	8	11	10	39	8	11	Tricia	Tom
7	2	9	14	13	13	49	9	14	Jim	Tricia
8	3	13	11	6	8	38	6	13	Tom	Jim
9	4	6	20	11	17	54	6	20	Jim	Tricia
10	5	15	9	10	5	39	5	15	Lisa	Jim
11	6	13	6	11	9	39	6	13	Tricia	Jim
12	7	6	13	14	6	39	6	14	Jim	Tom
13	8	11	7	12	12	42	7	12	Tricia	Tom
14	9	9	10	9	13	41	9	13	Jim	Lisa
15	10	9	8	10	8	35	8	10	Tricia	Tom
16	11	10	4	5	11	30	4	11	Tricia	Lisa
17	12	6	9	11	12	38	6	12	Jim	Lisa
18	13	9	8	14	13	44	8	14	Tricia	Tom
19	14	8	14	13	8	43	8	14	Jim	Tricia
20	15	10	11	9	13	43	9	13	Tom	Lisa
21	16	5	16	14	11	46	5	16	Jim	Tricia
22	17	11	9	12	11	43	9	12	Tricia	Tom
23	18	12	6	15	2	35	2	15	Lisa	Tom
24	19	17	13	8	9	47	8	17	Tom	Jim
25	20	10	7	12	9	38	7	12	Tricia	Tom
26	21	6	10	11	10	37	6	11	Jim	Tom
27	22	8	8	13	10	39	8	13	Jim	Tom
28	23	10	8	9	8	35	8	10	Tricia	Jim
29	24	12	9	13	15	49	9	15	Tricia	Lisa
30	25	11	11	12	16	50	11	16	Jim	Lisa
31	26	10	9	11	9	39	9	11	Tricia	Tom
32	27	11	9	7	11	38	7	11	Tom	Jim
33	28	7	10	11	11	39	7	11	Jim	Tom
34	29	5	13	10	12	40	5	13	Jim	Tricia
35	30	14	10	12	8	44	8	14	Lisa	Jim
36										
37	Tally of winners and losers									
38		Wins	Losses							
39	Jim	12	7							
40	Tricia	11	5							
41	Tom	4	12							
42	Lisa	3	6							
43	Total	30	30							

and

$$=IF(G6=\$B6,"Jim",IF(G6=\$C6,"Tricia",IF(G6=\$D6,"Tom","Lisa")))$$

(Note that if there is a tie for best or worst, only one of the workers in the tie is listed.) Finally, we tally the winners and losers in the range B39:C42. The formula in B39 is

$$=COUNTIF(I\$6:I\$35,\$A39)$$

which is then copied to the range B39:C42.

Using the daily production quantities of red beads in column F, we can also create a *p* chart, as shown in Figure 10.29. It shows a process well in control. In particular, it shows how the daily proportion of red beads varies randomly around 0.2. Of course, this doesn't mean the workers are producing what management *wants* them to produce (no more than two red beads per day), but it certainly is not the workers' fault, and there is nothing they can do about it until the system changes.

If you look at this REDBEAD file, you'll see that all of the random numbers are "live," so that they change any time the spreadsheet recalculates. Therefore, you'll see

FIGURE 10.29 *p* **Chart for the Red Bead Experiment**

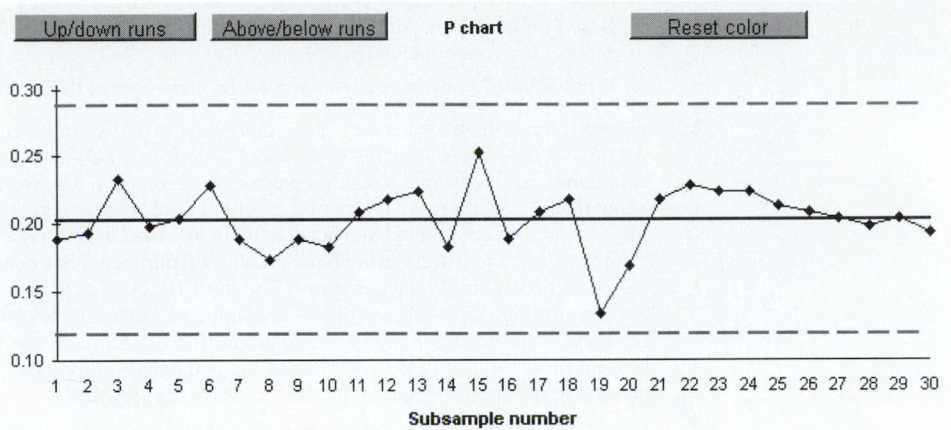

values different from those in Figures 10.28 and 10.29. However, they should all tell approximately the same story, as summarized below.

- Variation is inherent in any process.

- The system determines workers' performance; until it changes, workers are typically unable to improve their performance.

- Only management can change the system.

- Given an in-control process, some workers will *appear* to be best or worst on different days, but at least part of this is a matter of luck, not skill or working harder. When this is the case, rewards or reprimands are likely to do more harm than good.

PROBLEMS

Level A

16 Suppose that a manufacturer of electronic computer chips classifies each chip as either defective or nondefective. Each hour 100 electronic chips are randomly selected from a very large batch of chips and tested for possible defectiveness. The file P10_16.XLS lists the number of defective chips (out of the 100 sampled) found during each of 25 hours of production. Based on the given sample data, is this production process currently in control? Provide support for your conclusions.

17 Construct and interpret a *p* chart for the data provided in the file P10_17.XLS. These data consist of the number of defective units found in each of 25 samples with a common size of 200 units. Is this production process currently in control? Is it behaving "well"?

18 Continuing the previous problem, suppose that the given production process has been modified in an effort to reduce the variation in the proportion of defective items. An additional 25 samples that share a common size of 200 are gathered, and the number of defective items in each sample is recorded in the file P10_18.XLS. Have the refinements to this system achieved the desired result? Explain why or why not.

19 Construct and interpret a *p* chart for the data provided in the file P10_19.XLS. These data consist of the number of defective units found in each of 25 samples with a common size of 100 units. Is this production process currently in control? Is it behaving "well"?

20 Suppose that a manufacturer of a particular automotive part classifies each unit produced as either defective or nondefective. Each hour 200 parts are randomly selected from a very large batch of manufactured items and tested for possible defectiveness. The file P10_20.XLS lists the number of defective parts (out of the 200 sampled) found during each of 30 consecutive hours of production.

    a Based on the given sample data, is this production process currently in control? Provide support for your conclusions.

    b What advice, if any, would you give to the managers of this production process?

21 A new Internet-based bookstore ships thousands of books to its customers each week. The director of this firm's shipping department is concerned about a seemingly large number of complaints from customers regarding errors in shipments. The managers of the organization know that the future profitability of this virtual bookstore depends essentially on its ability to fill customer orders quickly and accurately. In an effort to investigate this problem further, the shipping director collects data on the number of shipments not conforming to corresponding customer orders for 25 days in a row. The file P10_21.XLS contains the number of reported nonconforming shipments out of the 75 shipments randomly selected on each of the 25 days. Do these data indicate a high average proportion of shipment errors? Is there an excessive amount of variability in the error rate of the company's shipments? If so, what can managers do both in the short run and long run to improve the situation?

22 Continuing the previous problem, the firm's shipping director has implemented a new quality control program within her department. She is interested in determining whether this program is reducing the mean error rate of the company's shipments. She also hopes that the quality control program will serve to reduce the variability in the proportion of book shipments not conforming to customer orders. To assess the efficacy of the new program, she obtains another set of sample data. The file P10_22.XLS contains the number of reported nonconforming shipments out of the 75 shipments randomly selected on each of 25 consecutive days *after* the implementation of the quality control program. Based on these data, does the program appear to be meeting the shipping director's goals? Explain why or why not.

23 Construct and interpret a *p* chart for the data provided in the file P10_23.XLS. These data consist of the proportion of defective heating control units found in each of 30 samples with a common size of 150 units. Is this production process currently in control? Is it behaving "well"?

24 Construct and interpret a *p* chart for the data provided in the file P10_24.XLS. These data consist of the proportion of defective lightbulbs found in each of 30 samples with a common size of 100 units. Is this production process currently in control? Is it behaving "well"?

25 Continuing the previous problem, the managers of this manufacturing process have implemented more stringent quality control procedures to reduce the variability of the lightbulbs' defective rate. The file P10_25.XLS contains the proportion of defective lightbulbs found in each of 30 samples (again, with a common size of 100 units) taken after the implementation of the new quality control procedures. Use these sample observations to assess the impact of the managers' corrective actions? Support your conclusions with a *p* chart.

26 Management of a new credit card company has recorded the number of nonconforming customer bills found in random samples of 150 bills obtained during the first 30 weeks of the firm's operation. These observations are provided in the file P10_26.XLS. Given this sample information, how would you evaluate the performance of this company with respect to the accuracy of produced customer bills? Support your assessment with a relevant control chart.

27 A mail-order clothing retailer is interested in improving the accuracy of its customer service agents who enter customer orders into the firm's computerized record system. To monitor the accuracy of the agents' data entry activities, a manager records the number of data entry errors detected in 150 randomly selected customer orders placed over the course of 1 month (i.e., 30 days). These data are stored in the file P10_27.XLS. Construct a *p* chart for the given sample data.

    a Based on the given sample data, is this data entry process currently in control? Provide support for your conclusion here.

    b What advice, if any, would you give to the managers of this process?

28 Construct and interpret a *p* chart for the data provided in the file P10_28.XLS. These data consist of the proportion of defective radar detectors found in each of 30 samples with a common size of 200 units. Is this production process currently in control? Is it behaving "well"? Comment on any discernible trend(s) in the *p* chart based on the given sample data.

29 Explain the difference in the actions a manager must take on a process when a point on a *p* chart exceeds the upper control limit versus when a point falls below the lower control limit.

30 Provided that $\overline{p} = 0.01$, determine a sample size large enough to avoid the construction of a p chart with a *negative* lower control limit. How does this required sample size change when $\overline{p}$ increases to 0.10?

31 To establish the subsample size n for a p chart, a probability of 0.95 is specified for finding at least one nonconforming item in any subsample of n items. If the process has an average nonconformance rate of 5%, what subsample size n should be used? If the process has an average nonconformance rate of 1%, what subsample size n should be used? (*Hint:* A binomial random variable X can be approximated by a Poisson random variable with parameter $\lambda = np$, where n is the subsample size and p is the underlying proportion of nonconforming items.)

32 For a fixed subsample size n, what values of $\overline{p}$ lead to a positive lower control limit on a p chart?

33 Use Excel to simulate Deming's red bead experiment, described in Section 10.5.2 of this text, with *six* workers instead of four. How do the results change when the number of workers is increased to six? What new conclusions, if any, emerge from your revision of this simulation? ■

10.6 Process Capability

Recall that one of the main goals of control charts is to bring a process into control so that it is predictable. In this section we assume that a process is in control, and we predict how capable it is of producing outputs that meet specifications. These specifications are typically set outside of a process from considerations of what an "acceptable" product is. For example, a team of engineers might determine that a machined rod can function properly only if its diameter is between 20.80 and 20.95 millimeters. Or a manager might decide that its check processing department is operating within acceptable limits only if check processing times are no more than 30 days. These examples illustrate what we *want* outputs to be. The question then is whether the current process is *capable* of meeting these specifications. When we analyze whether a process is able to meet set specifications, we call it a **process capability analysis**.

In a process capability analysis we are typically given lower and upper specification limits, denoted LSL and USL, and we want to calculate the proportion of outputs from a given process that fall within these limits.[6] Based on data generated from the process, we perform a probability calculation to see how capable the current process is of producing outputs within the specification limits. The following example illustrates a typical calculation.

EXAMPLE 10.6

A manufacturing process produces rods for a mechanical device. Engineers have determined that the diameters of the rods must be between 20.80 and 20.95 millimeters; rods with diameters outside these limits are unusable. As part of the standard control charting the company does, the data in the file RODS.XLS have been collected. Here diameters of six randomly selected rods were measured every half hour for several production shifts. How capable is this process of meeting engineering specifications?

---

[6] In some cases, such as in the check processing example, only one of the limits is relevant. In that example, $USL = 30$, but there is no lower limit of interest.

Solution

The Data sheet in the RODS.XLS file is set up exactly as we have seen in previous control chart examples. That is, there is a separate column for each observation in the subsamples of size 6. Therefore, we can—and should—examine $\overline{X}$ and R charts as a first step to see whether the current process is in control. If it *isn't* in control, then it lacks the predictability necessary to judge whether it is capable of meeting specifications. Fortunately, control charts show that the current process *is* in control. We show the $\overline{X}$ bar chart in Figure 10.30. Note that its centerline is 20.897 mm, and its lower and upper control limits are 20.867 mm and 20.928 mm. These values indicate how the process *is* operating. They might or might not bear any relationship to how we would *like* it to be operating.

FIGURE 10.30 $\overline{X}$ **Control Chart for Rod Diameters**

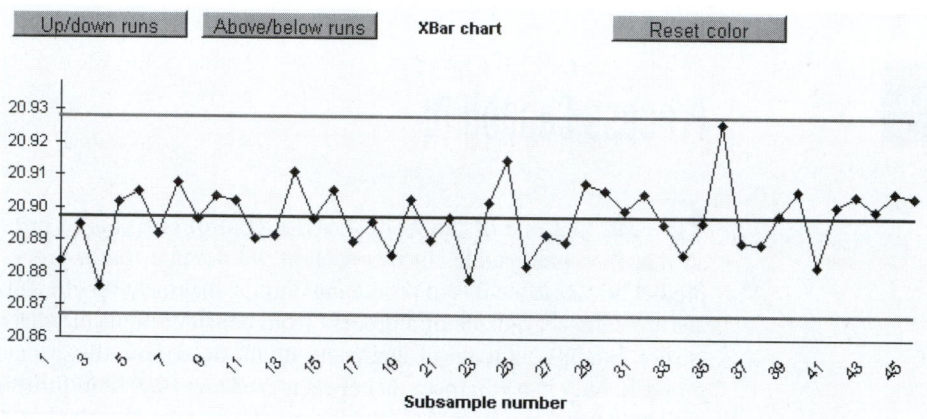

Now that we know the process is in control, hence predictable, we estimate the proportion of rods that fall within the specification limits $LSL = 20.80$ and $USL = 20.95$. One obvious way to do this is to count the number of *observed* rods with diameters within the limits. There are $45(6) = 270$ rods in the 45 subsamples, and a simple tally shows that none of the 270 diameters are less than the LSL, while four are greater than the USL. Therefore, the proportion within the limits is $266/270 = 0.985$.

However, this calculation uses only observed rods. What about other rods the process has been producing and will produce? To answer this question, we use a probability model. We assume the distribution of rod diameters is some standard distribution, typically the normal distribution, and then we do a probability calculation based on the estimated parameters of this distribution. We'll show this in a couple of steps.

First, is it reasonable to assume that rod diameters are normally distributed? We check this by creating a histogram of rod lengths. (To use StatPro to do this, we first need to obtain one long variable of 270 diameters. This can be done either manually by copying and pasting or with StatPro's Stack procedure.) The resulting histogram in Figure 10.31 indicates a reasonably bell-shaped distribution of diameters, so that a normal probability model can be used. The histogram also indicates that none of the diameters are near the LSL, and that only a few are above the USL.

Next, we use the normal probability model to calculate the probabilities of falling outside the specification limits. We assume a typical rod has a diameter that is normally distributed with mean and standard deviation equal to the *observed* mean and standard deviation from the sample. These are $\overline{X} = 10.897$ and $s = 0.025$. We then use the

FIGURE 10.31 **Histogram of Rod Diameters**

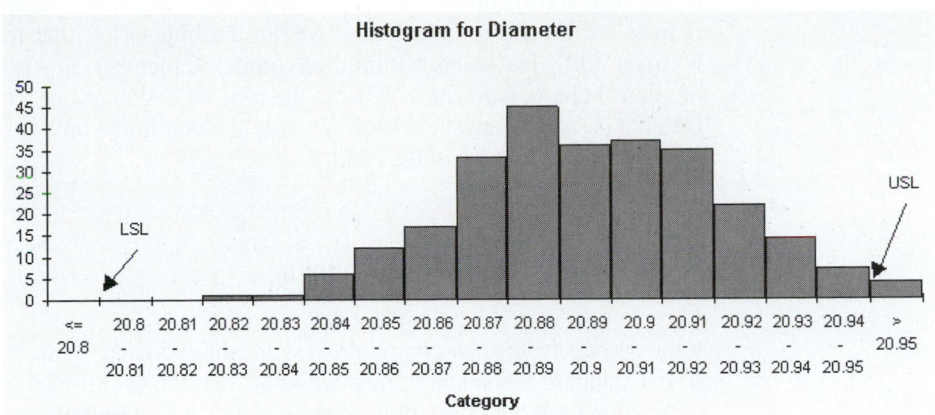

NORMDIST function to calculate the probability below the LSL and above the USL. (See Figure 10.32.) The formulas in cells N11 and N13 are

$$=NORMDIST(LSL,SampMean,SampStdev,1)$$

and

$$=1-NORMDIST(USL,SampMean,SampStdev,1)$$

We see that there is almost no probability of being below the LSL, but the probability of being above the USL is almost 0.02. Therefore, over 98% of rods should meet specifications if the process continues to operate as it is currently operating.

Although the probabilities of not meeting specifications are quite small, it is common to project the results to a *large* number of items. Specifically, the capability of a process is often quoted in parts per million (ppm). We have done this in cells N12 and N14 by multiplying each of the probabilities by 1,000,000. Surprisingly, the extremely small probability in cell N11 still implies that 60 ppm will fall below the LSL, and the probability in cell N13 implies that over 18,000 ppm will fall above the USL. Perhaps this process isn't as capable as we initially thought! Two other capability indices, denoted C_p and C_{pk}, are also listed in Figure 10.32. We will discuss them in the next subsection.

FIGURE 10.32 **Capability Analysis for Rod Diameters**

	L	M	N	O	P	Q
3		*Summary measures for selected variables*				
4			Diameter			
5		Mean	20.897			
6		Standard deviation	0.025	**Named ranges:**		
7				SampMean: N5		
8		**Normal probability calculations**		SampStdev: N6		
9		LSL	20.80	LSL: N9		
10		USL	20.95	USL: N10		
11		P(below LSL)	5.966E-05			
12		Per million	60			
13		P(above USL)	0.0181			
14		Per million	18093			
15						
16		**Capability indices**				
17		Cp	0.990			
18		Cpk	0.698			

Before continuing, we make one important point about control charts and specification limits. The specification limits, *LSL* and *USL*, should *not* be shown on a control chart. If lines are drawn at these limits, we get the impression that the purpose of the charts is to get all of the points within these limits. Remember, however, that the real purpose of control charts is to show us what the process *is* doing, not what we *want* it to do. As Deming preached, anyone who draws specification limits on a control chart doesn't really understand the purpose of the chart.

10.6.1 Process Capability Indexes

If the outputs from an in-control process are approximately normally distributed with mean μ and standard deviation σ, then we know that almost all of the items produced will be within three standard deviations of the mean, that is, within the interval $\mu \pm 3\sigma$. Note that this interval has length 6σ. On the other hand, we *want* the items to be within the interval from *LSL* to *USL*, an interval of length $USL - LSL$. One way to judge the capability of a process is to compare the lengths of these two intervals. Specifically, the capability index denoted by C_p is defined as

$$C_p = \frac{USL - LSL}{6\sigma} \tag{10.1}$$

To understand C_p, assume that the ideal output value, called the "target," is halfway between the *LSL* and the *USL*. Also, assume that the current mean μ of the process is equal to the target, and that the distance from the target to either specification limit is 3σ. Then $C_p = 1$, and we have the picture in Figure 10.33. In words, the current process is making just about what needs to be made, and the probability of falling outside the specification limits is only 0.0027 (the probability that a normally distributed random value is more than three standard deviations from the mean). Alternatively, the ppm beyond the specification limits is 2,700 [$= 0.0027(1,000,000)$].

Now consider changes from this "baseline" situation. There are essentially three ways we could make the process more or less capable: (1) we could change the specification limits, *LSL* and *USL*, (2) we could change the mean μ so that it is not equal to the target, and (3) we could increase or decrease the variability in the process, as measured by σ.

F I G U R E   1 0 . 3 3 **Distribution for a Process with $C_p = 1$**

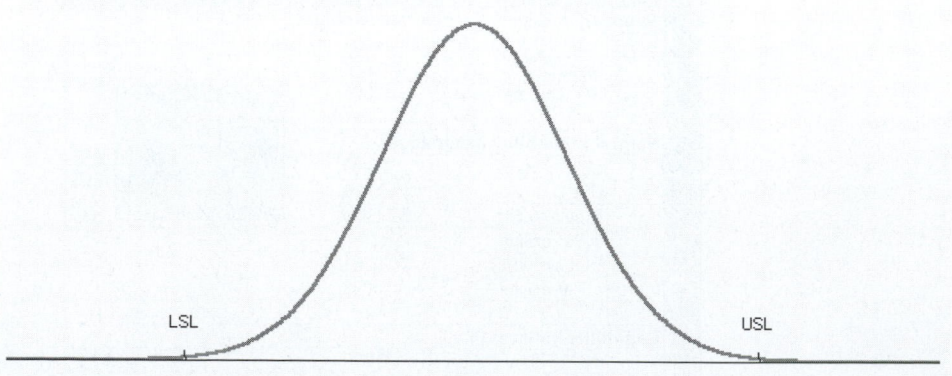

For the time being, we'll assume that LSL and USL are fixed because of engineering requirements and that μ continues to equal the target, so that only σ varies.

Figures 10.34 and 10.35 indicate two possible changes in σ. Figure 10.34 represents a *more* variable process, where the distance from the target to either specification limit is only 2σ. The specification limits haven't changed, but σ has increased. In this case $C_p = 4\sigma/6\sigma = .667$, and the probability of falling outside the specification limits is 0.045392 (45,392 ppm). On the other hand, Figure 10.35 represents a *less* variable process, where the distance from the target to either specification limit is now 4σ. Again, the specification limits haven't changed, but σ has decreased. In this case $C_p = 8\sigma/6\sigma = 1.333$, and the probability of falling outside the specification limits is 0.000064 (64 ppm). Clearly, the relationship of σ to the distance between the specification limits is crucial in determining the capability of the process, and we want C_p to be as large as possible. Most world-class manufacturers attempt to achieve a C_p of at least 1.333, and many even try to improve on this.

FIGURE 10.34 **Distribution for a Process with $C_p = 0.667$**

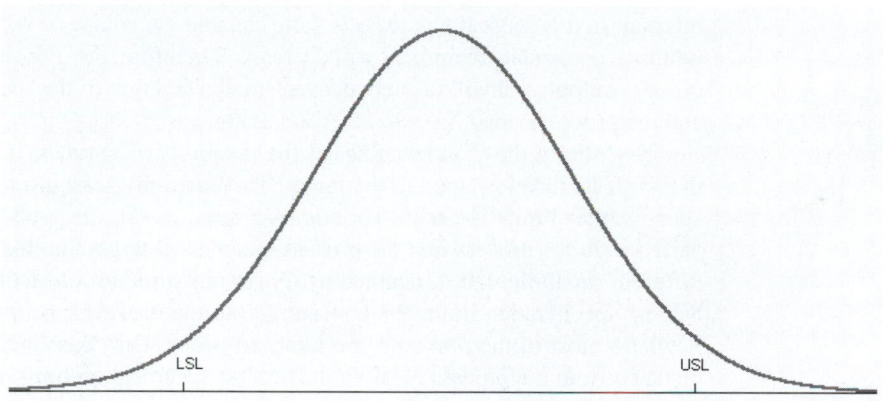

FIGURE 10.35 **Distribution for a Process with $C_p = 1.333$**

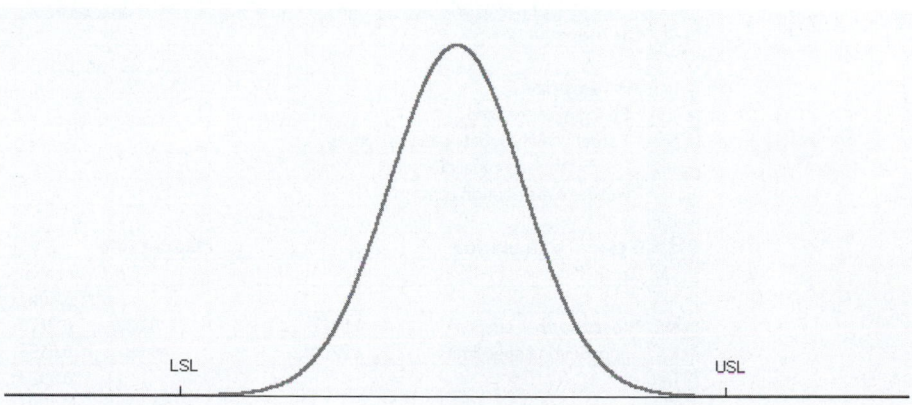

When the target is midway between the specification limits, the process mean is equal to the target, and the process is normally distributed, it can be shown that the probability of falling outside the specification limits is

$$P(\text{beyond specification limits}) = 2P(Z < -3C_p)$$

where Z is normal with mean 0 and standard deviation 1. We use this fact in Figure 10.36 to show the effect of C_p. (See the file CAPINDEX.XLS.) We treat C_p in cell B10 (range-named Cp) as an input. The formula in cell B12 is

$$=2*NORMSDIST(-3*Cp)$$

We then create the data table in columns D–F. Clearly, the ppm outside the specification limits decreases dramatically as C_p increases.

An equivalent way of thinking about C_p is by considering its reciprocal. For example, suppose that $C_p = 1.333$, so that its reciprocal is 3/4. Specifically, let's assume that $LSL = 92, USL = 108, \mu = 100$ (the target), and $\sigma = 2$. (Check that $C_p = 1.333$ for these parameters.) Then we know that the interval $\mu \pm 3\sigma$, which contains almost all of the items produced, is from 94 to 106, an interval of length 12. In contrast, the interval defined by the specification limits is from 92 to 108, an interval of length 16. Therefore, the $\pm 3\sigma$ interval within which the process outputs falls takes up only $12/16 = 3/4$ of the specification-limit interval. In this sense the process is quite capable. Of course, if we can decrease σ, then C_p will increase and its reciprocal will decrease. Therefore, the $\pm 3\sigma$ interval within which the process outputs fall will take up an even smaller fraction of the specification-limit interval, and the process capability will be even greater.

Essentially, the C_p index indicates the capability of a process if it is centered properly—that is, if its mean is equal to the target. Then the only reason for parts falling outside the specification limits is excess variation—a large σ—in the process. But what if there is variation in the process *and* the process mean is off target? In this case we need a slightly different capability index, denoted by C_{pk}, to measure how close the process mean is to the nearest specification limit. We concentrate on the *nearest* specification limit because this is where most of the problems are likely to occur. The "baseline" case is now where the distance from the process mean to the nearest specification limit is 3σ, for in this case the

FIGURE 10.36 **Effect of C_p on ppm Beyond Specification Limits**

	A	B	C	D	E	F
1	**Cp index**					
2						
3	**Assumptions:**					
4	Spec limits are fixed					
5	Target is midway between spec limits					
6	Process mean equals target					
7	Process distribution is normal					
8						
9	**Typical calculation**			**Data table**		
10	Cp	1			Cp P(beyond)	ppm
11					0.0027	2700
12	P(beyond spec limits)	0.0027		0.333	0.3178	317795
13	ppm beyond spec limits	2700		0.667	0.0454	45392
14				1	0.0027	2700
15				1.333	0.0001	64
16				1.667	0.0000	1
17				2	0.0000	0

process will be producing just about what we want it to produce. We define C_{pk} so that it is equal to 1 in this baseline case:

$$C_{pk} = \min\left\{ \frac{USL - \mu}{3\sigma}, \frac{\mu - LSL}{3\sigma} \right\} \qquad (10.2)$$

An illustration of C_{pk} similar to that for C_p in Figure 10.36 appears in Figure 10.37. (This is also in the CAPINDEX.XLS file.) Here we assume that the process is nearer to USL than to LSL. Then it can be shown that the probability of being beyond USL is $P(Z > 3C_{pk})$. Therefore, for any trial value of C_{pk} in cell B10 (range-named Cpk), we enter the formulas

$$=1\text{-NORMSDIST}(3*\text{Cpk})$$

and

$$1000000*\text{B12}$$

in cells B12 and B13. Using these, we form a data table in columns D–F to show how the process capability varies as C_{pk} varies. Of course, this shows only half of the story, the probability of being beyond specifications on the *high* side. But the probability of being beyond specifications on the *low* side is even smaller, since we assumed the process mean is closer to USL than to LSL.

To illustrate C_{pk} with data, we look again at Figure 10.32 from the example on rod diameters. Since $LSL = 20.80$ and $USL = 20.95$, the target is their midpoint, 20.875. However, the process mean, estimated by $\overline{X} = 20.897$, appears to be closer to the USL. Therefore, it is likely that most rods beyond the specification limits will be *above* the USL. We estimate σ for this process with the sample standard deviation, $s = 0.025$. Then the (estimated) C_{pk} is

$$C_{pk} = \frac{USL - \overline{X}}{3s} = \frac{20.95 - 20.897}{3(0.025)} = 0.698$$

FIGURE 10.37   **Effect of C_{pk} on ppm Beyond the Nearest Specification Limit**

	A	B	C	D	E	F
1	Cpk index					
2						
3	Assumptions:					
4	Spec limits are fixed					
5	Target is midway between spec limits					
6	Process mean doesn't equal the target (here we'll assume it's closer to USL than to LSL)					
7	Process distribution is normal					
8						
9	Typical calculation			Data table		
10	Cpk	1		Cpk	P(above USL)	ppm above USL
11					0.00135	1350
12	P(above USL)	0.00135		0.333	0.15890	158897
13	ppm above USL	1350		0.667	0.02270	22696
14				1	0.00135	1350
15				1.333	0.00003	32
16				1.667	0.00000	0
17				2	0.00000	0
18						
19						
20						
21				Because we're assuming the mean is closer		
22				to USL than to LSL, P(below LSL) and ppm		
23				below LSL are even smaller than these values.		

This is considerably below the baseline case where $C_{pk} = 1$, so that, as we see in Figure 10.32, the current process has a fairly large ppm beyond specifications—almost all on the high side.

If the C_{pk} is unacceptably small—and again, most world-class manufacturers try to achieve a value of at least 1.333—then there are two possibilities.[7] First, we could try to "center" the process by adjusting the process mean to the target. In this case C_p and C_{pk} coincide. If we could do this for the rod example, we could achieve a C_p value of 0.990, as shown in cell N17 in Figure 10.32. This would be much more acceptable than the current process. Alternatively, we could try to reduce the process variation, with or without a shift in the mean. By reducing σ, we automatically reduce C_{pk} (and C_p), regardless of whether the mean is on target.

Both C_p and C_{pk} are simply *indexes* of process capability. The larger they are, the more capable the process is. An equivalent descriptive measure is the "number of sigmas" of a process. A k-sigma process is one for which the distance from the process mean to the nearest specification limit is $k\sigma$. For example, a 3-sigma process is one where $C_{pk} = 1$, since this is exactly how C_{pk} is defined. (In case the process mean is on target, C_p also equals 1 for a 3-sigma process.) As we will discuss in more detail below, Motorola has become famous for its 6-sigma processes, where $C_{pk} = 2$. This is remarkable quality! It implies almost *no* items out of specifications per million items produced. This is because an item is out of specifications in a 6-sigma process only if it is beyond six standard deviations from the mean, an extremely unlikely event. Motorola and other world-class companies have achieved this by reducing variation to a bare minimum—and by continually searching for ways to reduce it even further.

We can summarize the ideas in this section as follows.

1 The C_p index is appropriate for processes where the mean is equal to the target value (midway between the specification limits). Processes with $C_p = 1$ produce about 2700 out-of-specification items per million, but this number decreases dramatically as C_p increases.

2 The C_{pk} index is appropriate for all processes, but it is especially useful when the mean is off target. (In case the mean is on target, C_p and C_{pk} are equivalent.) Processes with $C_{pk} = 1$ produce about 1350 out-of-specification items per million on the side nearest the target (and less on the other side), and again this number decreases dramatically as C_{pk} increases.

3 Both C_p and C_{pk} are only indices of process capability. However, they imply the probability of an item being beyond specifications (and the ppm beyond specifications), as illustrated in Figures 10.36 and 10.37.

4 A 3-sigma process has $C_{pk} = 1$, whereas a 6-sigma process has $C_{pk} = 2$. In general, the distance from the process mean to the nearest specification limit in a k-sigma process is $k\sigma$.

10.6.2 More on Motorola and 6-Sigma

We defined a k-sigma process as one where the distance from the target to either specification limit is $k\sigma$. Until the 1990s most companies were very content to achieve a 3-sigma process, that is, $C_p = 1$. Assuming that each part's measurement is normally distributed, they reasoned that 99.73% of all parts would be within specifications. Motorola questioned this wisdom on two counts:

---

[7]This assumes that changing the specification limits is *not* an option.

- Products are made of many parts. The probability that a product is acceptable is the probability that *all* parts making up the product are acceptable.

- When using control charts to monitor quality, shifts of 1.5 standard deviations or less in the process mean are difficult to detect. Therefore, when we are producing a product, there is a reasonable chance that the process mean will shift by as much as 1.5σ up or down without being detected (at least in the short run).

Given that the process mean might be as far as 1.5σ from the target and that a product is made up of *many* parts, a 3-sigma process might not be as good as we originally stated. Just how good is it?

Suppose a product is made up of m parts. We will calculate the probability that all m parts are within specifications when the process mean is 1.5σ above the target and the distance from the target to either specification limit is $k\sigma$.[8] That is, we are considering a k-sigma process with a process mean off center by an amount 1.5σ. Let X be the measurement for a typical part, and let p be the probability that X is within the specification limits, that is, $p = P(LSL < X < USL)$. If p_m is the probability that all m parts are within the specification limits, then assuming that all parts are identical and probabilistically independent, the multiplication rule for probability implies that $p_m = p^m$.

To calculate $p = P(LSL < X < USL)$, we need to standardize each term inside the probability by subtracting the process mean μ and dividing the difference by σ. Let T be the target. Then we have $LSL = T - k\sigma$ and $USL = T + k\sigma$ (since the process is a k-sigma process) and $\mu = T + 1.5\sigma$ (since the mean has shifted upward by an amount 1.5σ). Therefore, the standardized specification limits are

$$\frac{LSL - \mu}{\sigma} = \frac{(T - k\sigma) - (T + 1.5\sigma)}{\sigma} = -k - 1.5$$

and

$$\frac{USL - \mu}{\sigma} = \frac{(T + k\sigma) - (T + 1.5\sigma)}{\sigma} = k - 1.5$$

This implies that

$$p = P(-k - 1.5 < Z < k - 1.5) = P(Z < k - 1.5) - P(Z < -k - 1.5) \quad \textbf{(10.3)}$$

We can easily implement this in Excel, as shown in Figure 10.38. (See the file MULT-PART.XLS.) Equation (10.3) is implemented in cell B10 with the formula

$$=\text{NORMSDIST(A10-1 .5)-NORMSDIST(-A10-1 .5)}$$

and this probability is raised to the 10th, 100th, and 1000th powers in cells C10 to E10. All of this is then copied down for other values of k. As we see, a 3-sigma process (row 11) is not all that great. Almost 7% of its individual parts are out of specifications, about half of its 10-part products are out of specifications, and almost *all* of its 100-part and 1000-part products are out of specifications. In contrast, a 6-sigma process (row 14) is extremely capable, with only 0.34% of its 1000-part products out of specifications. No wonder Motorola's 5-year goal (as of 1992) was to achieve "6-sigma capability in everything we do."

By the way, if 1 minus the probability in cell B14 is multiplied by 1,000,000, the result is 3.4. (The *exact* value in cell B14 is 0.9999966; its format does not show it, however.) This value has become very well known in the quality world. It says that if a process is a 6-sigma process with the mean off target by an amount 1.5σ, then the process will produce only 3.4 ppm out of specifications. Again, this is remarkable quality!

The above analysis shows how we can calculate the capability of a process if we *know* it is a k-sigma process for any specific k. We conclude this section by asking a slightly

---

[8]The case where the process mean is 1.5σ *below* the target is completely analogous.

FIGURE 10.38 **Probability of Multipart Products Meeting Specifications**

	A	B	C	D	E
1	Process capability for multiple-part products				
2					
3	Assumptions:				
4	Each product has m identical, probabilistically independent parts				
5	The process is a k-sigma process				
6	The process mean is 1.5 stdevs above the target				
7					
8	Calculations				
9	k	p	p_{10}	p_{100}	p_{1000}
10	2	0.69123	0.02490	0.00000	0.00000
11	3	0.93319	0.50084	0.00099	0.00000
12	4	0.99379	0.93961	0.53638	0.00197
13	5	0.99977	0.99768	0.97700	0.79239
14	6	1.00000	0.99997	0.99966	0.99660

different question. If a company has produced many parts and has observed a certain fraction to be out of specifications, what is their estimated value of k? For example, suppose that after monitoring thousands of gaskets produced on its machines, a company has observed that 0.545% of them are out of specifications. Is this company's process a 3-sigma process, a 4-sigma process, or what?

To answer this question, we again assume a "worst-case" scenario where the mean is above the target by an amount 1.5σ. Then from equation (10.3), we know that the probability of being within specifications is

$$p = P(Z < k - 1.5) - P(Z < -k - 1.5)$$

if the process is a k-sigma process. However, we now know p from observed data, and we want to estimate k. This can be done with Excel's Goal Seek tool, as shown in Figure 10.39. (See the file KSIG.XLS.) First, we enter the observed fractions in and out of specifications in cells B7 and B8. Next, we enter *any* trial value of k in cell B10 and use it to calculate the probability of being within specifications in cell B12 with the formula

=NORMSDIST(B10–1 .5)-NORMSDIST(-B10–1 .5)

FIGURE 10.39 **Finding k for a k-sigma Process**

	A	B	C
1	Finding k for a k-sigma process		
2			
3	Assumption:		
4	Mean is 1.5 sigmas above target		
5			
6	Observed fractions		
7	Out of specs	0.00545	
8	Within specs	0.99455	
9			
10	Trial value of k	4.077	
11			
12	P(within specs)	0.99501	

Finally, we use the Tools/Goal Seek menu item and fill out the dialog box as in Figure 10.40. It immediately shows that this process is slightly better than a 4-sigma process.[9]

FIGURE 10.40   **Goal Seek Dialog Box Settings**

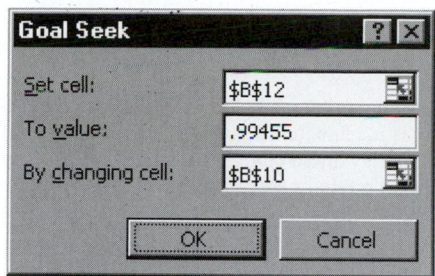

PROBLEMS

Level A

34 The file P10_1.XLS contains data on the amount of soda (in ounces) placed in aluminum cans by a particular filling process. The filling process should place between $LSL = 11.95$ ounces and $USL = 12.05$ ounces of soda in each can. Every hour, 4 cans of soda were randomly selected from the production process and measured for amount of fill. This was repeated for 25 consecutive hours.

   a Based on the given sample data, calculate the probabilities that this process will yield soda cans (i) falling below the lower specification limit and (ii) exceeding the upper specification limit.

   b Represent your results found in part **a** in parts per million (ppm).

   c Estimate C_p and C_{pk} in this case. If a difference exists between these two capability indexes, explain it.

35 The data in the file P10_7.XLS consist of 25 subsamples of 4 observations each on the lengths of particular bolts manufactured for use in large aircraft. The target length of these bolts is 37 centimeters. Furthermore, the bolt manufacturer has established $LSL = 36.95$ centimeters and $USL = 37.05$ centimeters.

   a Estimate C_p and the probability of meeting specifications. Evaluate C_p in this case. Is this a highly capable production process?

   b Estimate C_{pk} in this case. Does your estimate of C_{pk} differ from that of C_p computed in part **a**? If so, how do you explain this difference?

36 Management of a local bank is interested in assessing the process used in opening new checking accounts for bank customers. In particular, management would like to examine the time required to process a customer's request to open a new checking account. Currently, managers believe that it should take about 7 minutes to process such a request. Furthermore, they believe that the time required to process this type of request should be between $LSL = 5.5$ minutes and $USL = 8.5$ minutes. The file P10_12.XLS contains the time required to process new checking account requests for each of 6 customers selected randomly on a given day. A different subsample of 6 customer requests was collected on each of 25 days.

   a Estimate C_p and the probability of meeting specifications. Evaluate C_p in this case. Is this a highly capable production process?

---

[9]Note that Goal Seek's solution in cell B12 doesn't match the probability in cell B8 exactly, but it is close enough for all practical purposes.

b Estimate C_{pk} in this case. Does your estimate of C_{pk} differ from that of C_p computed in part **a**? If so, how do you explain this difference?

37 A computer printout shows that a certain process has a C_p of 1.50 and a C_{pk} of 0.80. Assuming that this process is in control, what do these two index values indicate about the capability of the process?

Level B

38 For a given process, can C_{pk} ever exceed C_p? Provide a mathematical and/or verbal argument to support your answer.

39 Suppose that a product is composed of 25 identical and probabilistically independent parts. Assume that this product is manufactured through the use of a k-sigma process with a process mean that is 1.25 standard deviations above the target mean. Assuming that $k = 3$, what proportion of these multipart products are *not* within specification limits? Answer this question again for the case where $k = 6$. Explain the difference between these two probabilities.

40 Suppose that a product is composed of m identical and probabilistically independent parts. Assume that this product is manufactured through the use of a 6-sigma process with a process mean that is 1.5 standard deviations below the target mean. Assuming that $m = 5$, what proportion of these multipart products are *not* within specification limits? Answer this question again for the cases where $m = 50$ and $m = 500$. Explain the differences among your three computed probabilities.

41 Suppose that after monitoring a large number of electronic computer chips, a manufacturer observes that 1% of them are out of specifications. Assume that the process mean exceeds the target mean by 1.25 standard deviations. Given this information, it is possible to conclude that this manufacturer is employing a k-sigma process. What is k approximately?

42 Suppose that after monitoring thousands of ball bearings, a manufacturer observes that 0.27% of them are out of specs. Assume that the process mean is 1.5 standard deviations below the target mean. Given this information, it is possible to conclude that this manufacturer is employing a k-sigma process. What is k approximately? ■

10.7

Conclusion

Ⓢome critics have claimed that the quality movement, with all of its acronyms, is a fad that will eventually lose favor in the business world. We do not believe this is true. In the past decade or two, many companies in the United States and abroad have embraced the teachings of Deming and others to gain a competitive advantage with superior quality. By now, quality has improved to such a level in many industries that superior quality no longer ensures a competitive advantage; it is a prerequisite for staying in business!

In this chapter we have discussed two quantitative tools from the quality movement: control charts and process capability analysis. It is clear from Deming's 14 points that there is much more to achieving quality than crunching numbers—for example, good management and worker training are crucial—but the use of proven statistical techniques is key to any program of continual improvement. The fanfare surrounding the quality movement may indeed die down in the future, but the careful monitoring of processes, together with the use of the statistical tools we have discussed, will still be required elements for companies that want to remain competitive.

PROBLEMS

Level A

43 To monitor product quality, Wintel inspects 30 chips each week and determines the fraction of defective chips. The resulting data are in the file P10_43.XLS. Construct $\overline{X}$ and R charts based on 12 weeks of data. Is week 5 out of control? Why or why not? Is week 6 out of control? Why or why not? What do these charts tell you about Wintel's production process?

44 Eleven samples of size 3 were taken in an effort to monitor the voltage held by a regulator. The data are in the file P10_44.XLS. A regulator meets specifications if it can hold between 40 and 60 volts.

    a Construct $\overline{X}$ and R charts for the data. Is the process in control?

    b Estimate C_p and the probability of meeting specifications.

45 You are the manager of a hospital emergency room. You are interested in analyzing the time patients wait to see a physician. For 25 samples of 5 patients each, the file P10_45.XLS contains the time each patient had to wait before seeing a physician. Construct and interpret $\overline{X}$ and R charts for this situation. Also answer the following questions:

    a We are 68% sure that a patient will wait between what two values (in minutes) to see a physician?

    b We are 95% sure that a patient will wait between what two values (in minutes) to see a physician?

    c We are 99.7% sure that a patient will wait between what two values (in minutes) to see a physician?

46 A mail-order company (Seas Beginning) processes 100 invoices per day. For each of several days, they have kept track of the number of invoices that contain errors. The data are in the file P10_46.XLS. Use these data to construct a p chart and then interpret the chart.

47 The file P10_47.XLS contains the measured diameters (in inches) reported by the production foreman of 500 rods produced by Rodco. A rod is considered acceptable if it is at least 1.0 inch in diameter. In the past the diameter of the rods produced by Rodco has followed a symmetric distribution.

    a Construct a histogram of these measurements.

    b Comment on any unusual aspects of the histogram.

    c Can you guess what might have caused the unusual aspect(s) of the histogram? (*Hint*: One of Deming's 14 points is to "Drive Out Fear.")

48 John makes 20 computers per day for Pathway computer. Production data appear in the file P10_48.XLS. Construct a control chart based on the number of defective computers produced during each of the last 30 days. Explain as fully as possible what you learn from this control chart.

49 For the data in the file P10_49.XLS, suppose $USL = 1.06$ inches and $LSL = 0.94$ inch.

    a Is the process in control? If it is out of control, describe any observed out-of-control pattern.

    b If possible, estimate C_p, C_{pk}, and the probability of meeting specifications.

50 For the data in the file P10_50.XLS, suppose that $LSL = 190$ and $USL = 210$.

    a Is the process in control? If it is out of control, describe any observed out-of-control pattern.

    b If possible, estimate C_p, C_{pk}, and the probability of meeting specifications.

51 For the data in the file P10_51.XLS, suppose that $LSL = 195$ and $USL = 205$.

    a Is the process in control? If it is out of control, describe any observed out-of-control pattern.

    b If possible, estimate C_p, C_{pk}, and the probability of meeting specifications.

52 Consider a k-sigma process.

    a If $k = 4$, determine the fraction of all parts that meet specifications and calculate C_p. Now suppose that a car consists of 1000 parts, each of which is governed by a 4-sigma process. What fraction of all cars will be perfect (meaning all 1000 parts meets specs)?

b Repeat part **a** for a 6-sigma process. Now can you see why companies like Motorola are not satisfied with anything less than a 6-sigma process?

53 A part is considered within specifications if its tensile strength is between 180 and 200. For 20 straight hours the tensile strength of 4 randomly chosen parts was measured. The data are in the file P10_53.XLS.

   a Is the process in control?

   b What is C_p?

   c What is the probability that the specifications will be met on a typical part?

54 Twelve samples of size 4 were taken in an effort to monitor the voltage held by a regulator. The data are in the file P10_54.XLS. A regulator meets specifications if it can hold between 18 and 56 volts. Estimate C_p and the probability of meeting specifications.

55 Suppose that the employees of D&D's each service 100 accounts per week. The file P10_55.XLS contains the number of accounts that each employee "messed up" during the week. Do these data indicate that Jake should receive a raise and Billy should be fired? Discuss.

Level B

56 Continuing the previous problem, the file P10_56.XLS contains 2 more weeks of data for D&D's.

   a By plotting each employee's weekly fraction of "mess ups," does it appear that Amanda is a problem? Discuss.

   b Now combine the 2 weeks of data for each employee and answer the question in part **a**.

57 A company has a 3-sigma process. What must the company do to change it to a 6-sigma process? Be as specific as possible.

58 For Ford to designate a supplier as Q-1 (its highest designation), Ford requires that the supplier have a C_p equal to 1.33. Currently your firm has $C_p = 1$. What must you do to increase your C_p to 1.33? Be as specific as possible.

59 How does continuous improvement manifest itself on a p chart? What about on $\overline{X}$ and R charts?

60 A screw manufacturer produces screws that are supposed to be 0.125 inch in diameter. A screw is deemed satisfactory if its diameter is between 0.124 inch and 0.126 inch. The company quality manager therefore uses an $\overline{X}$ chart with a centerline of 0.125 inch, a UCL of 0.126 inch, and an LCL of 0.124 inch. Why is this incorrect?

61 A sudden change in a particular production process has *lowered* the process mean by 1 standard deviation. It has been determined that the weight of the product being measured is approximately normally distributed. Furthermore, it is known that the recent change had virtually no effect on the variability of this process. What proportion of points is expected to fall outside the control limits on the $\overline{X}$ chart if the subsample size is 4? Compute this proportion again for the case where the subsample size is 9. Provide an explanation for the difference between these two proportions.

62 The SteelCo company manufactures steel rods. The specification limits on the lengths of these rods are from 95.6 inches to 95.7 inches. The process that produces these rods currently yields lengths that are normally distributed with mean 95.66 inches and standard deviation 0.025 inch.

   a What is the probability that a single rod will be within specification limits?

   b What is the probability that at least 90 of 100 rods will be within specification limits?

   c SteelCo's best customer currently buys 200 of these rods each day and pays the company $20 apiece. However, it gets a $40 refund for each rod that doesn't meet specifications. What is SteelCo's current expected profit per day? How small would its standard deviation need to be before it would net an expected $3900 per day?

63 Continuing the previous problem, suppose that SteelCo can pay money to reduce the standard deviation of the process. It costs e^{1000d} dollars to reduce the standard deviation from 0.025 to $0.025 - d$. (This reflects the fact that small reductions are fairly cheap, but large reductions are quite expensive.) If the company wants to make sure that at least 99% of all rods meet specifications, how much will it have to spend? (Remember that you evaluate e^x in Excel with the EXP function.)

64 In this problem we reconsider SteelCo from the previous two problems from a different point of view. Now we assume SteelCo doesn't know its process mean and standard deviation, so it uses sampling. The file P10_64.XLS lists 150 randomly sampled rod lengths.

   a Calculate a 95% confidence interval for the population mean length of all rods produced.

   b Continuing part **a**, find a 95% confidence interval for the population proportion that meet the specifications listed in at the top of the spreadsheet (the same as in the previous problem).

   c Using the sample standard deviation found in part **a** as a best guess for the population standard deviation, how large a sample size is required to achieve a 95% confidence interval for the mean of the form: "point estimate plus or minus 0.002"?

65 Simulation is useful to see how long it might take before an out-of-control condition is recognized by an $\overline{X}$ or R control chart. Proceed as follows:

   a Generate 30 subsamples of size $n = 5$ each, where each observation comes from a normal distribution with a given mean μ and standard deviation σ. (You can choose μ and σ.) Then "freeze" these values (with the Copy and PasteSpecial/Values commands), and form $\overline{X}$ and R control charts based on all 30 subsamples.

   b Below the subsamples in part **a**, generate 30 more subsamples of size $n = 5$ each, where each observation comes from a normal distribution with mean $\mu + k_1\sigma$ and standard deviation $k_2\sigma$. That is, the mean has shifted by an amount $k_1\sigma$, and the standard deviation has been multiplied by a factor k_2. The values k_1 and k_2 should be entered as input parameters that you can change easily. Initially, set $k_1 = 1.5$ and $k_2 = 1$, although you can try other values in a follow-up sensitivity analysis. Do *not* freeze the observations in these 30 new subsamples. Create new $\overline{X}$ and R control charts that plot all 60 subsamples but have the *same* control limits from part **a**. By pressing the F9 key and/or changing the values in the k_1 and k_2 input cells, you change the behavior of the control charts.

   c Write up your results. In particular, indicate how long it takes for the control charts to realize that the process is out of control with respect to the *original* control limits, and how this depends on k_1 and k_2.

66 Are all "capable" processes the same? Consider the data in the file P10_66.XLS. The data in the sheets Process1 and Process2 come from two processes that produce the same type of part. These parts should be within the specification limits 10.45 inches to 10.55 inches, with a target of 10.50 inches. Are both processes capable of staying within the specification limits? If you were a manufacturer and had to select one of these processes as a supplier of parts, which would you choose? Why?

67 Continuing the previous problem, one of the leading quality gurus, Genichi Taguchi of Japan, suggested the idea of a **quadratic loss function** when judging quality. Rather than saying that a part is "good" when its measurement falls within specification limits and is "bad" otherwise, the quadratic loss function estimates the part's quality as $(x - T)^2$, where x is the part's measurement and T is the target measurement.

   a Using this loss function, estimate the average quality of parts from process 1, given the data in the file P10_66.XLS and a target of 10.50 inches. Do the same for process 2. Which process appears to be better?

   b Explain intuitively why a quadratic loss function might be preferable to a simple 0–1 function (where a part either meets specifications or it doesn't) when assessing quality.

68 A manufacturer supplies a certain type of assembly to customers. The manufacturer recognizes the advantages of control charts and uses them consistently. In the past month, its $\overline{X}$ and R charts for the assembly indicated a process well within control. For these charts, 100 subsamples of size $n = 5$ each were used. In addition, the manufacturer compared the 100 $\overline{X}$'s to the specification limits set by one of its customers. Only 2 out of these 100 averages were outside the specification limits. This was good news because the customer was willing to accept orders with no more than 5% out of specifications. However, the manufacturer was shocked when the customer rejected an order for 1000 assemblies. The customer claimed that it inspected 50 of the 1000 assemblies, and 10% (i.e., 5) of them were out of specifications. What is going on here? Is it likely that the customer could see so many bad assemblies, given what the manufacturer observed in its process? Perform appropriate calculations, and write up your results in a short report. Make whatever assumptions you deem relevant.

69 A type of assembly is produced by gluing 5 identical wafers together in a sandwich-like arrangement. The critical dimension of this assembly is its width, the sum of the widths of the 5 wafers. The specifications for the assembly width are from 4.95 inches to 5.05 inches, with a target of 5.00 inches. The manufacturer wants at least 99.5% of the assemblies to meet specifications. Based on a lot of evidence, the individual wafer widths are normally distributed with mean 5.00 inches and some standard deviation σ.

a One engineer, Bob Smith, argues that the company should try to achieve a value of σ (through appropriate changes in the process) such that 99.5% of all *individual* wafer widths are between 0.99 inch and 1.01 inches. What value of σ is necessary to achieve this?

b A second engineer, Ed Jones, argues that Smith is solving the wrong problem. Instead, he says, the company should try to achieve a value of σ such that the *sum* of 5 normally distributed random values has only a 0.5% chance of falling outside the interval from 4.95 inches to 5.05 inches. What value of σ is necessary to achieve this?

c Which of the engineers is solving the "correct" problem? If the company follows the advice of the wrong engineer, will it err on the high side (too many assemblies out of specifications) or the low side? Is there any disadvantage to erring on the low side? ■

Charlie Hobbs, production manager of the 120-employee Rock Isle Plant of the Plastron Division of Intergalactica Chemicals Ltd., stared at the tables of reject data his people had gathered over the last 3 months. Hobbs wanted to use these data to help justify the purchase of a new lamination press. Past proposals for a new press had been rejected by Intergalactica Corporate Finance. But now that Intergalactica had embarked on a new Total Quality Management program, perhaps some fancy quality statistics would dazzle the people at headquarters.

The Plastron Division with $32 million in sales and $8 million in net revenues is the smallest and most profitable of Intergalactica Chemicals Ltd.'s 14 business units. Plastron manufactures a variety of laminated resin impregnated paper products. Its lead product is a laminate board, trademarked under the name "Plastfoam," that has a wide variety of applications in commercial art and photography. The product is a very high-quality hard-surfaced, rigid but lightweight, multi-layered polystyrene foam core board that is used for direct photographic and lithographic printing as well as for mounting of displays, photographs, and the like. Plastfoam facing is made by first saturating a special heavy absorbent paper in a proprietary blend of plastic resins, and then drying the paper to form a rigid yet somewhat rough-surfaced material. Next, these rough-faced resin impregnated sheets are pressed under heat (calendered) to form a very smooth and rather hard material similar to the well-known "Formica" surface that is frequently used as countertops. Then, two of these smooth faces are glued to the top and bottom of a polystyrene foam core to form a "sandwich." The final step in the production process is edge trimming and packaging. The resulting Plastfoam product is considered the "Cadillac" of the industry and commands a premium price that makes it Plastron's most profitable product line by far. As noted earlier, the Plastron Division also manufactures a variety of resin impregnated paper base materials that are used as facings in some economy brands of furniture. These products share some of the same production facilities and personnel with the Plastfoam product. Production scheduling and product changeovers are serious issues in the plant.

Key purchased input materials include the specialty absorbent paper that gets impregnated, several types of resins that Plastron blends to create its unique recipe for the saturation process, the large styrofoam blocks that are cut to size in-house, glues, and dyes. A rough schematic of the main production processes is shown in Figures 10.41 and

FIGURE 10.41   **Plastron Product**

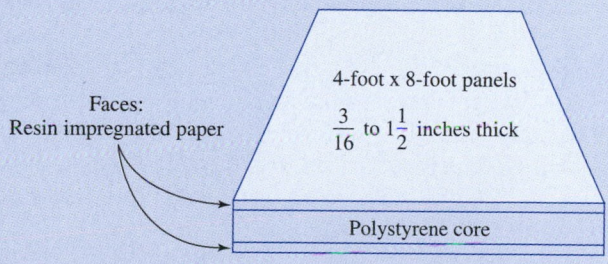

Faces:
Resin impregnated paper

4-foot x 8-foot panels
$\frac{3}{16}$ to $1\frac{1}{2}$ inches thick

Polystyrene core

[10]These cases were contributed by Professor Peter Kolesar at Columbia University.

FIGURE 10.42 **Plastron Production Process**

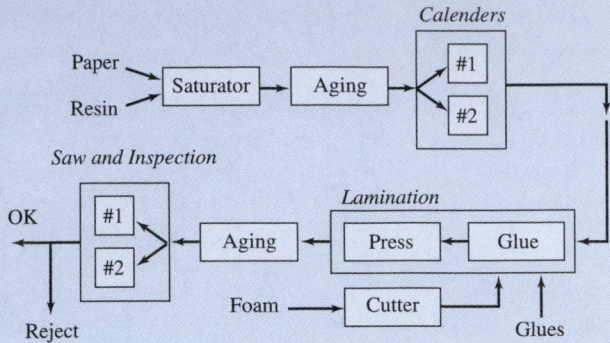

10.42. The physical production facilities employed include: two resin mixing tanks, the paper saturator—similar in appearance to a paper machine and 150 feet long, two converted multi-opening retrofitted plywood presses used for calendering, two hot wire styrofoam cutters, a hot glue applicator and hot glue press, two edge trimmers, and inspection/packing stands.

The production line uses technology that was adapted by Plastron from other purposes, and it has been in place essentially unchanged for about 14 years. The typical flow time of product through the system is 19 days. Of this time, about 5 days are designed for "curing" the product between saturation and calendering and 1 day for setting the glue after the glue press. Over the last 6 months, actual flow times from saturation to packing have varied from a minimum of 11 days to a maximum of 31 days.

Intergalactica Chemicals Ltd., the parent of the Plastron Division, is a global enterprise with 14 very diverse chemical process business units. Overall, Intergalactica has $14 billion in sales and 73,000 employees on three continents. The corporation recently embarked on a corporation-wide quality improvement program called the Intergalactica Quality Process. Twelve weeks ago, just before he began the collection of detailed end-of-the-line reject data, Charlie Hobbs had completed an intensive statistically focused 1-week quality improvement training session at the new "Intergalactica Corporate Quality College."

At Quality College, Hobbs was exposed to the basic principles and tools of statistical process control. The course aim was to enable the participants to help move the company toward its 5-year corporate goals of "total process control and process capability." It emphasized the concept that measurement and data are the keys to quality and productivity improvement. On returning to the Rock Isle Plant, Hobbs realized that the available historical data on product quality at Plastron were quite limited—they kept only overall monthly reject rates by product. Therefore, as his first step, Hobbs instituted a systematic recording of detailed counts of panels rejected at the end of the production process—by cause of rejection.

Just before packing, each (4 ft by 8 ft) finished Plastfoam panel is inspected. There, under special lighting, the panels are rotated by two workers and each side is examined visually for defects. Thus, all output is subjected to 100% visual inspection before shipment. Although the Plastfoam product line is quite profitable and, as mentioned earlier, is thought of as the "Cadillac" of the industry, historical reject rates have been very high—in some months as bad as 20%.

So, Charlie Hobbs had 3 months of defect data available (see the file PLASTRON.XLS), and he had to decide what to do next. His data confirmed that delaminations had been the most frequent or second most frequent cause of rejects in each of the last 3 months.

(Delamination means that the Plastfoam sandwich had partially separated.) Hobbs had expected that delaminations would be near the top of the charts. Indeed, that was why he wanted a new lamination press. Now, he wanted to do more with the numbers. One of the articles Hobbs had read at Intergalactica Quality College quoted W. Edwards Deming, the dean of American quality experts, as saying that " 85% of the problems are with the system!" Hobbs read that as "85% of the delaminations are due to the lamination press."

What kind of case could Hobbs make with these data for a new press?

CASE STUDY **10.2   Paper Production for Fornax at the Pluto Mill**

Ed Michaels, the recently appointed director of quality assurance at Great Western Papelco's Pluto Mill, did not much like what he had just heard at the mill's morning meeting. This meeting, a long-standing Pluto Mill tradition, was attended by the mill manager, his direct reports, and most of their direct reports—typically 17 persons. It was held each day at the start of the first shift. The nominal purpose of the morning meeting was general communication and planning, but, in fact, most of the discussion usually focused on things that had gone wrong during the previous day, firefighting efforts under way, and the like. The wrap-up of the morning meeting was a report on the previous day's production and shipment figures. An enormous chart plotting daily tons shipped dominated the conference room wall, and before the meeting started, the production manager was obliged to have yesterday's figures posted. The mill manager was obliged to telephone these figures personally to Salt Lake City headquarters as soon as the meeting ended—usually to the White Paper Group vice president himself.

This morning there had been a special topic—the upcoming run of Fornax reproduction paper, the first to happen at the Pluto Mill in more than 6 weeks. The schedule called for 2400 tons of paper with production to start on Monday morning, if the paper makers could get the paper machine tuned up in time. The group vice president of White Papers, George Philliston, was leaning heavily on the Pluto mill manager, Rich Johnson, not to repeat the disastrous customer rejection that had occurred on the last run of Fornax paper. At the morning meeting, Ed and the Pluto Mill quality improvement lead team had been charged to help "do it right this time," and he was worried.

This was a crucial time for Great Western and the Pluto Mill. The Great Western Papelco Company, a large, fully integrated forest products company, was just 8 months into a massive, company-wide total quality management effort that had been named "Quality Is Everything." To kick off this effort, all mill management had been through a $2\frac{1}{2}$-day quality awareness training, new quality posters were on the walls of the company conference rooms, and Ed Michaels had been the first person appointed to hold the new position of mill director of quality assurance. In this job, Ed reported directly to Rich Johnson, the mill manager. Ed had, of course, gone through the $2\frac{1}{2}$ day course and, in addition, had just returned from a 1-week training course on statistical methods for quality improvement, run by nearby Erehwon University.

Many new and very technical ideas had been covered in those $4\frac{1}{2}$ days at Erehwon. Ed came back to Pluto with a binder of notes that was fully 3 inches thick, a new calculator, and a diskette with statistical process control (SPC) software. Pareto charts, control charts, C_p ratios, Ishikawa diagrams, and standard deviations filled his mind. In 3 months Ed would be going back for a second week of training that promised to include regression analysis, experimental design, and hypothesis testing. (It had been 17 years since his last math course in college.) Some of Ed's colleagues in the mill, and indeed Rich Johnson, the mill manager, expected this new methodology of SPC to be the silver bullet that would magically solve Pluto's serious quality problems. Ed wryly noted that Rich, a crafty old-timer, had scheduled himself to be out of town during the original quality awareness training. "Ed, I'm counting on you to lead this quality effort," were his parting words.

Indeed, there were many serious quality problems. A task force consisting of outside consultants had, at the outset of the Quality Is Everything program, estimated that quality nonconformance costs at the Pluto Mill were an incredible 19% of revenues. Fully 70% of all plant overtime had been traced to specific quality problems, many shipments of even commodity-grade product had nonconformances on one or more specifications, Monday morning absenteeism was 11%, and the list goes on.

Members of the senior management team of Great Western Papelco were already talking enthusiastically about the positive impact on corporate profits if even half of these quality-related costs could be reduced through SPC. But Ed Michaels, no newcomer himself to Great Western Papelco or to the Pluto Mill, had seen a series of quality programs introduced over the years with great fanfare, but little follow-up or long-term effect. There had been a Zero Defects program in the late 1960's, then a Quality Circle initiative in 1978, and the latest program had been an Overhead Value Analysis in 1982. Though each program had brought initial benefits, none had delivered on its long-term promises and, in fact, had left most employees cynical or worse. "At least half the mill probably thinks Quality Is Everything will be another fiasco," mused Ed, "and this time I'm the point man." Ed knew that senior management had discussed the shortcomings of the past programs and was stating forcefully that Quality Is Everything would be different, but he wondered how real their commitment would be as the paper market continued to soften, and both prices and sales volumes dropped.

The Pluto Mill, one of seven paper mills in the White Paper Group of Great Western Papelco, manufactures a variety of white papers for high-speed printing and reprographic applications. The Pluto Mill, indeed Great Western itself, has a very fragile relationship with the Fornax Corporation, a major producer of reprographic equipment. Pluto produces $8\frac{1}{2}$ x 11 inch paper for the Fornax Corporation, which is sold under the Fornax Company label, and is used in the Fornax Fourth-Generation Super-Duper Hi-Speed Laser-Phasor Publishing System. Recently, Pluto made a large run of "Fornax" paper that, according to the tests done at the paper mill, met Fornax quality specifications. Nevertheless, the shipment was rejected by the customer when it was inspected upon receipt at the Fornax warehouse. The rejection was based on physical testing done according to a military standard statistical sampling plan. The tests were done at Fornax's own lab by the Fornax Quality Assurance Department.

This situation caused a crisis at the Pluto Mill, as the return of the entire Fornax shipment cost Great Western Papelco well over $100,000. (What do you do with over 800,000 reams of paper in Fornax wrapping and labels?) Of course, Fornax itself lost $25,000 and more than a little customer goodwill when the shipment was rejected. This loss was particularly acute as Fornax's just-in-time inventory system depends on timely and high-quality shipments. Unable to meet its own customers' needs, Fornax had to special-order paper from one of its other suppliers. To make matters worse, this recent rejection was just one in a long series of similar incidents between Great Western Papelco and Fornax.

Great Western Papelco has ten paper machines in its system that are nominally capable of producing Fornax paper, but only one, machine C at Pluto, has been "qualified" to supply Fornax, and though qualified, it frequently has trouble meeting the specifications. The operators at the Pluto Mill often take more than a day to change over to Fornax production from the company's own "Great Western High-Speed Reproduction Paper," whose quality specifications, essentially those of the industry at large, are looser than those of the Fornax brand. A paper machine operates continuously so that during these changeovers, a great deal of off-quality paper is made as the operators literally fight the paper machine to bring all 24 key quality characteristics within the customer's specifications. It is true that, while some changeovers have gone remarkably smoothly, on one occasion last year it actually took over 4 days to begin the Fornax run! In contrast, the quality of several other Fornax paper suppliers is apparently high enough that many of their paper machines are qualified, and their quality history is so high that their product is only "skip-lot" inspected. Under such skip-lot plans, Fornax does much less testing, essentially showing confidence in the suppliers' abilities to consistently meet the Fornax needs and specifications.

At the Pluto Mill, "Fornax" paper is produced continuously on paper machine C, at a rate of about 20 tons per hour. The linear speed of the machine is about 20 miles per hour. As the paper comes off the dry end of the machine, it is rolled onto huge reels, each of which is about 20 tons in weight, 20 miles long, and 20 feet wide.[11] Thus, it takes about 1 hour to produce such a reel of paper. After production, reels are rewound and cut, across the paper machine direction, into 10-mile-long "sets" (still 20 feet wide) and then rewound again and slit four times, again along the paper machine direction, into 5-foot-wide rolls from which the paper is finally cut into $8\frac{1}{2}$ x 11 inch sheets. This last operation is done on a machine called the "WilSheeter," which handles 6 rolls at a time. At the back end of the sheeter, the paper is packaged into 500-sheet reams, labeled, and then packed for Fornax in 20-ream cartons. The run in question consisted of 132 reels, or 2640 tons of paper.

Many of the more than 20 quality characteristics measured on each reel of paper are of concern to Fornax and have caused the Pluto Mill problems in the past. The key issues lately, however, appear to have been moisture content, smoothness, and curl. Moisture content was the chief complaint on the last Fornax run. It affects both the printability of the paper and the speed and ease with which it goes through the complex Fornax machines. These state-of-the-art reproduction devices take ream paper in at one end and produce completely bound reports at the other. Their high speed, high quality, and versatility are important competitive edges in Fornax Company's own struggles to regain share in the market it once dominated. The high quality and low cost of the duplication machines offered by several competitors had nearly knocked Fornax out of the market.

Part of the Fornax corporate strategy to regain market share is an intensive total quality management effort incorporating a thorough vendor qualification program. Fornax engineers have often visited the Pluto Mill, sometimes during Fornax runs, and it was they who had first introduced some key statistical and quality improvement ideas to Pluto personnel. Although Fornax has provided help and encouragement to Pluto for some time, it appears that their patience is running very thin. Fornax procurement personnel rather bluntly reminded Great Western Papelco's vice president, George Philliston, of their intention to reduce the number of suppliers by half over a 3-year period. By the way, as Great Western well knows, Fornax is able to market reproduction paper wrapped under its own Fornax brand name at a premium price that is well above that of Great Western's own products. Sales of this product make a handsome contribution to Fornax's profitability. Ironically, due to Pluto's difficulty in changing over to Fornax product and its frequent necessity to cull out "off-spec" paper made during the run, it was suspected by some in the mill that they actually lost money on many Fornax runs. On the other hand, it was a help to Great Western sales people to tell other customers for commodity grades that machine C was Fornax qualified. If only they really knew how tenuous that qualification was!

Fornax insists on 90% compliance to its $4.0 \pm 0.5\%$ moisture specifications (3.5% to 4.5% moisture). The Pluto Mill paper makers claim that achieving compliance to moisture specifications on their own is not too difficult. The problem, they claim, is that moisture is frequently adjusted to bring other characteristics into compliance. Smoothness has been

[11]The size of this machine alone was seen by the paper makers as a potential problem. No other paper machine close to this size was qualified to run Fornax paper.

another long-standing concern, and the paper makers say that adjustments in moisture, caliper, and basis weight are continually being made to get smoothness within specifications. ("Caliper" is a measure of paper thickness in thousandths of an inch, while "basis weight," recorded in pounds per 500 sheets, is essentially a measure of density.) These quality characteristics are dependent on many factors that are under the nominal control of the paper makers, including the machine speed, a variety of temperatures, pressures and nip clearances, and the distribution and quality of the pulp as it is laid down on the moving wire web at the head of the paper machine. While there are, therefore, many parameters under their influence, selecting an optimal control strategy has proven to be far from easy.

The effects of many parameters often go in opposite directions. For example, increasing machine speed decreases basis weight while simultaneously increasing moisture. Increasing steam flow after the size press increases both caliper and smoothness, but it decreases moisture. In addition, the physical characteristics of the incoming pulp are crucial and can vary considerably from batch to batch. Paper makers around Great Western frequently say, "Making paper is one-third art, one-third science, and one-third luck with a pinch of black magic. The day nature produces cylindrical, knot-free identical trees is the day paper making becomes pure science!"

As part of the organizational architecture of Great Western's Quality Is Everything company-wide total quality program, each paper mill has formed a quality improvement lead team. In his role as director of quality assurance, Ed Michaels is the Pluto Mill's lead team leader/facilitator. However, he and his team have, as yet, had very little hands-on experience using the tools of statistical problem solving. No specific quality improvement tasks had yet been selected for attack when mill manager Rich Johnson charged Ed and his team with taking on the Fornax problem. Ed is uncomfortable with starting on such a high-impact, high-visibility problem that has defied the efforts of so many others at the mill for so long, but he has little choice. The Pluto Mill culture is such that when Rich Johnson says "jump" the only question is "how high?"

The Pluto quality improvement lead team will meet in the morning to consider the Fornax moisture problem in light of the warnings from the Great Western sales department: Fornax management is so unhappy with recent quality that Great Western is in danger of losing the valuable Fornax account if another lot is rejected. Indeed, it is widely rumored that Fornax continues to give business to Pluto largely to keep them as a back-up against the possibility of supply disruption due to the volatile labor relations in the paper industry. With a large Fornax run scheduled for next week, group vice president Philliston wants to know what actions the Mill is planning to take so that this run meets Fornax specifications.

1   Taking advantage of the statistics training that he just went through, Ed Michaels wants to see what he can learn from the Pluto RRDB (Really Reel Data Base) about past and potential quality problems. Since the last run was rejected because of low moisture, Ed is focusing attention on the data in the file PLUTO.XLS, which gives the moisture measurements from the RRDB for the 132 reels from the rejected run. The moisture measurements contained in this data set are the result of physical tests conducted on a single, 12-inch square sample cut off the end of each reel—at its center "across the reel." It takes approximately half an hour to get the sample to the lab, conduct the moisture test, and report the results back to the machine operator. (Moisture is measured by weighing the sample sheet, baking it for 8 minutes at 100°C and then weighing it again. The weight loss is presumed to be due to evaporation of water.

Your assignment is to perform such statistical analysis on this data set that might be useful to Ed and his team in understanding and resolving their problem. The following issues are among those that Ed thinks might be relevant to an understanding of Great Western's problem:

a   Great Western's management has traditionally dealt with quality issues in terms of averages such as moisture averaged over a reel, averaged over a run, or averaged over a month. How well does the average reel moisture over the run conform to the Fornax specifications of 3.5% to 4.5%? How well do the individual reel moistures conform to the Fornax specifications? What should the specification apply to anyway—averages, individuals, samples, or the whole run? What would senior management at Great Western think? At Fornax?

b   Pluto Mill management has reminded the Great Western sales department that traditional industry standards on this grade of paper are $4.0 \pm 1.0\%$. How well do the individual reel moistures conform to these weaker standards? The Pluto Mill manager has complained, "Isn't the problem the inconsistency between Fornax and the rest of the industry?"

c   The next Fornax run is scheduled to be 120 reels. How many of those reels can Ed expect to meet Fornax specifications? How far off could he be in this prediction? Could he give the Great Western sales department a range on the number of "off-spec" reels that might be produced? If the mill were to run an extra number of reels and cull out the off-spec paper, how many reels would they have to run to be certain of getting 120 good ones?

d   Dr. D. Vader of the Fornax quality assurance department devised the sampling inspection plan that was used by Fornax when it rejected the recent run. Vader's starting point was the frequently used MIL-STD 105D plan (which he modified because Pluto ships in FIFO order and Fornax and Pluto are collaborating on a "just in time" inventory program). Thus, the testing at Fornax is done up front and just in time to decide whether the rest of the shipment should be unloaded from the rail cars. In Vader's plan, one carton of paper is selected at random from each of the first 14 reels of paper received from Pluto. Then, 5 reams are selected at random from each carton, and 5 sheets are selected at random from each ream. On the basis of these data (only $14 \times 5 \times 5 = 350$ sheets of paper out of the more than 429 million sheets in the run), Fornax rejected the entire shipment! Mill management is asking Ed how such data could have led to the lot rejection. "Didn't our own tests, made before shipment, show that we met specs?" The Fornax Company has not given Great Western any specifics on their data. All that Ed knows is that, according to Vader, 58 of the 350 sampled sheets were below and 1 sheet was above the moisture specs. Aren't these data, Ed mused, inconsistent with the numbers in the RRDB table? What insight can Ed get from his own RRDB records? Is such a small sample enough to assure that Fornax is getting 90% compliance on such a large production run? Are the results—as political pollsters put it—within an allowable margin of error? Might Fornax have made an error in testing? What could explain the differences?

2   As mentioned above, the next run will be starting on Monday morning—if the paper makers can manage the changeover in a timely fashion. Besides working harder and putting forth "best efforts," what can the Pluto Mill do to assure that there will not be a repetition of last month's disastrous product rejection? Ed Michaels would like to put his statistical training to work to do some root-cause problem solving, but how?

3   Great Western sales and marketing are chagrined at the potential loss of Fornax as a customer. Indeed, they expect that quality standards will be even stricter in the future, and if Great Western is ever to hold on in this product line, or penetrate new markets, real quality improvement will be necessary. It is clear to senior management that the company's quality status has slipped and that Great Western is far from being the quality leader it once was in the industry. Perhaps the Fornax problem is a blessing in disguise. The Pluto Mill, together with corporate engineering, has developed a proposal to spend $23 million to upgrade the wet end of the paper machine in an attempt to cure a variety of performance problems, most particularly

"curl." Curl also affects how easily paper runs through a duplicator without jamming. It has been a frequent problem with Fornax. Bigabeta, Inc., a leading supplier of paper machine equipment, assures Great Western that the proposed upgrade to machine C will, among other things, ease the Fornax moisture and smoothness problems. Unfortunately, the recent history of such capital projects at Great Western has been disappointing, to say the least. Over the last 10 years, fully 60% of funded projects have failed to live up to their projected impacts. The Great Western board of directors is uneasy about the efficacy of their capital funding process. Something appears to be broken in how these projects are approved or implemented, but what is it?

a What light do the data in the file PLUTO.XLS cast on the worthiness of this capital proposal for the moisture problem? Of course, in reality a variety of financial and marketing analyses would be necessary, but in the spirit of the case, focus on the process performance itself.

b In addition to the types of financial information that usually accompany such capital requests, what other data would you request in evaluating this proposal?

c Ed himself is no longer as confident as he once was that technology itself will be a cure to the problems on machine C. He wonders, "Is this paper machine potentially capable of meeting the Fornax specifications? Is the problem in the paper machine, or in how the paper machine is operated? Could the problem be (as claimed by the machine operators) in the pulping process upstream? And how does all this relate to the smoothness, abrasion, and curl problems they have had on Fornax paper over the past several months?"

4 From the Fornax view, what do you think about the Fornax specifications and testing? Do you have any suggestions for improvement?

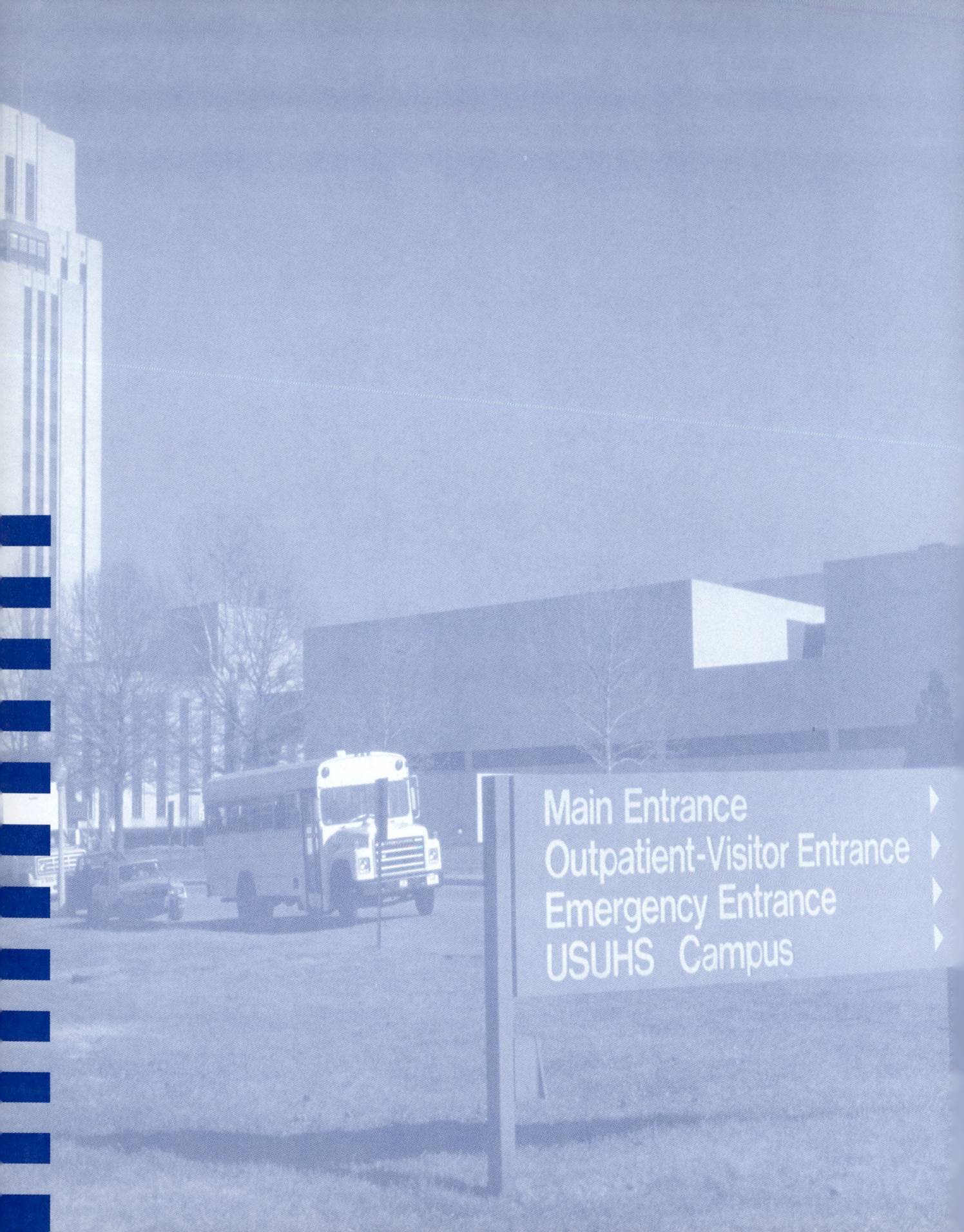

Main Entrance ▶
Outpatient-Visitor Entrance ▶
Emergency Entrance ▶
USUHS Campus ▶

11

Regression Analysis: Estimating Relationships

Successful Applications

Regression analysis is an extremely flexible tool that can aid decision making in many areas. Kimes and Fitzsimmons (1990) describe how it has been used by La Quinta Motor Inns, a moderately priced hotel chain oriented toward serving the business traveler, to help make site location decisions. Location is one of the most important decisions for a lodging firm. All hotel chains search for ideal locations and often compete against each other for the same sites. A hotel chain that can select good sites more accurately and quickly than its competition has a distinct competitive advantage.

Kimes and Fitzsimmons, academics hired by La Quinta to model their site location decision process, used regression analysis. They collected data on 57 mature inns belonging to La Quinta during a 3-year business cycle. The data included profitability for each inn (defined as operating margin percentage—profit plus depreciation and interest expenses, divided by the total revenue), as well as a number of potential explanatory variables that could be used to predict profitability. These explanatory variables fell into five categories: competitive characteristics (such as number of hotel rooms in the vicinity and average room rates); demand generators (such as hospitals and office buildings within a 4-mile radius that might attract customers to the area); demographic characteristics (such as local population, unemployment rate, and median family income); market awareness (such as years inn has been open and state population per inn); and physical considerations (such as accessibility, distance to downtown, and sign visibility).

The analysts then determined which of these potential explanatory variables were most highly correlated (positively or negatively) with profitability and entered these variables into a regression equation for profitability. The estimated regression equation was

$$\text{Predicted Profitability} = 39.05 - 5.41\text{StatePop} + 5.81\text{Price}$$

$$-3.09\sqrt{\text{MedIncome}} + 1.75\text{ColStudents}$$

where StatePop is the state population (1000's) per inn, Price is the room rate for the inn, MedIncome is the median income ($1000's) of the area, ColStudents is the number of college students (1000's) within 4 miles, and all variables in this equation are standardized to have mean 0 and standard deviation 1. This equation predicts that profitability will increase when room rate and the number of college students *increase* and when state population and median income *decrease*. The R^2 value (to be discussed in this chapter) was a respectable 0.51, indicating a reasonable predictive ability. Using good statistical practice, the analysts validated this equation by feeding it explanatory variable data on a set of *different* inns, attempting to predict profitability for these new inns. The validation was a success—the regression equation predicted profitability fairly accurately for this new set of inns.

La Quinta management, however, was not as interested in predicting the exact profitability of inns as in predicting which would be profitable and which would be unprofitable. A cutoff value of 35% for operating margin was used to divide the profitable inns from the unprofitable inns. (Approximately 60% of the inns in the original sample were profitable by this definition.) The analysts were still able to use the regression equation they had developed. For any prospective site, they used the regression equation to predict profitability, and if the predicted value was sufficiently high, they predicted that this site would be profitable. They selected a decision rule—that is, how high was "sufficiently high"—from considerations of the two potential types of errors. One type of error, a false positive, was predicting that a site would be profitable when in fact it was headed for unprofitability. The opposite type of error, a false negative, was predicting that a site would be unprofitable (and rejecting the site) when in fact it would have been profitable. La Quinta management was more concerned about false positives, so it was willing to be conservative in its decision rule and miss a few potential opportunities for profitable sites.

Since the time of the study, La Quinta has implemented the regression model in spreadsheet form. For each potential site, it collects data on the relevant explanatory variables, uses the regression equation to predict the site's profitability, and applies the decision rule on whether to build or not build. Of course, the model's recommendation is only that—a recommendation. Top management has the ultimate say on whether any site is used or not. As Sam Barshop, then chairman of the board and president of La Quinta Motor Inns stated, "We currently use the model to help us in our site-screening process and have found that it has raised the 'red flag' on several sites we had under consideration. We plan to continue using and updating the model in the future in our attempt to make La Quinta a leader in the business hotel market." ■

11.1 Introduction

Ⓡegression analysis is the study of relationships between variables. It is one of the most useful tools for a business analyst because it applies to so many situations. Some potential uses of regression analysis in business include the following:

- How do wages of employees depend on years of experience, years of education, and gender?

- How does the current price of a stock depend on its own past values, as well as the current and past values of a market index?

- How does a company's current sales level depend on its current and past advertising levels, the advertising levels of its competitors, the company's own past sales levels, and the general level of the market?

- How does the unit cost of producing an item depend on the total quantity of items that have been produced?

- How does the selling price of a house depend on such factors as the appraised value of the house, the square footage of the house, the number of bedrooms in the house, and perhaps others?

Each of these questions asks how a single variable, such as selling price or employee wages, depends on other relevant variables. If we can estimate this relationship, then we can not only better understand how the world operates, but we can also do a better job of predicting the variable in question. For example, we can not only understand how a company's sales are affected by its advertising, but we can also use the company's records of current and past advertising levels to predict future sales.

The branch of statistics that studies such relationships is called **regression analysis**, and is the subject of this chapter and the next. Regression analysis is one of the most pervasive of all statistical methods in the business world. This is because of its generality and applicability. Even when we restrict the analysis to a special case of regression analysis called **linear regression**, as we will do here, the number of potential applications is virtually unlimited.

There are several ways to categorize regression analysis. One categorization is based on the overall purpose of the analysis. As suggested above, there are two potential objectives of regression analysis: to understand how the world operates and to make predictions. Either of these objectives might be paramount in any particular application. If the variable in question is employee wages and we are using variables such as years of experience, years of education, and gender to explain wage levels, then the purpose of the analysis is probably to understand how the world operates—that is, to explain how the variables combine in any given company to determine wages. More specifically, the purpose of the analysis might be to discover whether there is any gender discrimination in wages, after allowing for differences in work experience and education level.

On the other hand, the primary objective of the analysis might be prediction. A good example of this is when the variable in question is company sales, and variables such as advertising and past sales levels are used as explanatory variables. In this case it is certainly important for the company to know how the relevant variables impact its sales. But the company's primary objective is probably to predict *future* sales levels, given current and past values of the explanatory variables. The company might also use a regression model for a what-if analysis, where it predicts future sales for many conceivable patterns of advertising and then selects its advertising level on the basis of these predictions.

Fortunately, the same regression analysis enables us to solve both problems simultaneously. That is, it indicates how the world operates and it enables us to make predictions. So although the objectives of regression studies might differ, the same basic analysis always applies.

A second categorization of regression analysis is based on the type of data being analyzed. There are two basic types: cross-sectional data and time series data. Cross-sectional data are usually data gathered from approximately the same period of time from a cross section of a population. The housing and wage examples mentioned earlier are typical cross-sectional studies. The first concerns a sample of houses, presumably sold during a short period of time, such as houses sold in Florida during the first couple of months of 1998. The second concerns a sample of employees observed at a particular point in time, such as a sample of automobile workers observed at the beginning of 1997.

In contrast, time series studies involve one or more variables that are observed at several, usually equally-spaced, points in time. The stock price example mentioned earlier fits this description. We observe the price of a particular stock and possibly the price of a market index at the beginning of every week, say, and then try to explain the movement of the stock's price through time.

Regression analysis can be applied equally well to cross-sectional and time series data. In either case we might be attempting to understand how the world operates or make predictions. However, there are technical reasons for treating time series analysis somewhat differently. The primary reason is that time series variables are usually related to their own past values. This property of many time series variables is called **autocorrelation**, and it adds complications to the analysis that we will discuss briefly.

A third categorization of regression analysis involves the number of explanatory variables in the analysis. First, we need to introduce some terms. In every regression study there is a single variable that we are trying to explain or predict. This is called the **response** variable or the **dependent** variable. To help explain or predict the response variable, we use one or more **explanatory** variables. These explanatory variables are also called **predictor** variables or **independent** variables. If there is a single explanatory variable, the analysis is called **simple regression**. If there are several explanatory variables, it is called **multiple regression**.[1]

There are important differences between simple and multiple regression. The primary difference, as the name implies, is that simple regression is simpler. The calculations are simpler, the interpretation of output is somewhat simpler, and fewer complications can occur. We will begin with simple regression examples to introduce the ideas of regression. But we will soon see that simple regression is no more than a special case of multiple regression, and there is little need to single it out for separate discussion—especially when computer software is available to perform the calculations in either case.

A fourth and final categorization of regression analysis concerns linear versus nonlinear models. As mentioned earlier, the only type of regression analysis we will study is *linear* regression. Generally, this means that the relationships between variables are *straight-line* relationships, whereas the term *nonlinear* implies curved relationships. By focusing on linear regression, it might appear that we are ignoring the many real-world relationships that are clearly nonlinear. Fortunately, linear regression can often be used to estimate nonlinear relationships. As we will see, the term *linear regression* is more general than it appears. Admittedly, many of the relationships we will study can be explained adequately by straight lines. But it is also true that many nonlinear relationships can be "linearized" by suitable mathematical transformations. Therefore, the only relationships we are ignoring in this book are those—and there are some—that cannot be transformed to linear. Such relationships can be studied, but only by advanced methods beyond the level of this book.

In this chapter we will focus on line-fitting and curve-fitting, that is, on estimating equations that describe relationships between variables. We will also discuss the interpretation of these equations, and we will provide a couple of numerical measures that indicate the goodness of fit of the equations we estimate. In the next chapter we will extend the analysis to statistical inference of regression output. As we will see, this chapter focuses only on a small part of the available regression output, but it is an extremely important part and one we should thoroughly understand before proceeding to the more complex issues in the next chapter.

11.2

Scatterplots: Graphing Relationships

A good way to begin any regression analysis is to draw one or more scatterplots. As we learned in Chapter 2, a scatterplot is a graphical plot of two variables, an X and a Y. Consider a data set with n observations, where for each observation there are at least two variables. We choose two of these variables and label them X and Y. Then for each of the observations, we plot the X and Y values as a point on a two-dimensional graph. The

---

[1]The traditional terms used in regression are *dependent* and *independent* variables. However, because these terms can cause confusion with probabilistic independence, a totally different concept, there has been an increasing use of the terms *response* and *explanatory* variables. We will use the latter terms in this book.

scatterplot is the resulting scatter of points. If there is any relationship between the two variables, it is usually apparent from the scatterplot.

The following example, which we will carry throughout this chapter, illustrates the usefulness of scatterplots. It is a typical example of cross-sectional data.

EXAMPLE 11.1

Pharmex is a chain of drugstores that operate around the country. To see how effective its advertising and other promotional activities are, the company has collected data from 50 randomly selected metropolitan regions. In each region it has compared its own promotional expenditures and sales to those of the leading competitor in the region over the past year. There are two variables:

■ Promote: Pharmex's promotional expenditures as a percentage of those of the leading competitor

■ Sales: Pharmex's sales as a percentage of those of the leading competitor

Note that each of these variables is an "index," not a dollar amount. For example, if Promote equals 95 for some region, this tells us only that Pharmex's promotional expenditures in that region are 95% as large as those for the leading competitor in that region. The company expects that there is a positive relationship between these two variables, so that regions with relatively more expenditures have relatively more sales. However, it is not clear what the nature of this relationship is. The data are listed in the file PHARMEX.XLS. (See Figure 11.1 for a partial listing of the data.) What type of relationship, if any, is apparent in a scatterplot?

FIGURE 11.1 **Data for Drugstore Example**

	A	B	C	D	E	F
1	Data on drugstore promotional expenditures and sales					
2						
3	Note: each value is a percentage of what the leading competitor did					
4						
5	Region	Promote	Sales			
6	1	77	85			
7	2	110	103			
8	3	110	102			
9	4	93	109			
10	5	90	85			
11	6	95	103			
12	7	100	110			
13	8	85	86			
14	9	96	92			
15	10	83	87			
53	48	100	98			
54	49	95	108			
55	50	96	87			

Solution

First, recall from Chapter 2 that there are two ways to create a scatterplot in Excel. We can use Excel's Chart Wizard to create an X-Y chart, or we can use StatPro's Scatterplot procedure. The advantage of the latter is that the X variable (the one on the horizontal axis)

doesn't need to be to the left of the *Y* variable in the data set, so we generally favor its use in regression applications.

Which variable should be on the horizontal axis? In regression we always put the explanatory variable on the horizontal axis and the response variable on the vertical axis. In this example the store believes large promotional expenditures tend to "cause" larger values of sales, so we put Sales on the vertical axis and Promote on the horizontal axis. The resulting scatterplot appears in Figure 11.2.[2]

F I G U R E   1 1 . 2   Scatterplot of Sales versus Promote

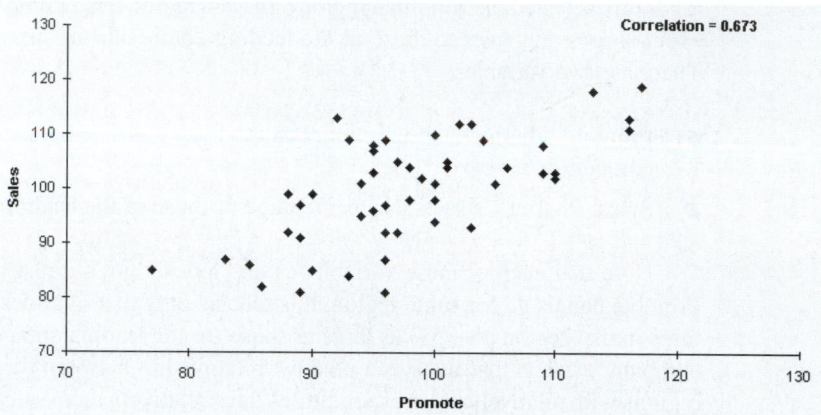

This scatterplot indicates that there is indeed a positive relationship between Promote and Sales—the points tend to rise from bottom left to top right—but the relationship is not perfect. If it were perfect, a given value of Promote would prescribe the value of Sales exactly. Clearly, this is not the case. For example, there are five regions with promotional values of 96 but different sales values. So the scatterplot indicates that while the variable Promote might be helpful for predicting the Sales value, it won't yield perfect predictions.

Note the correlation of 0.673 shown at the top of Figure 11.2. The StatPro add-in inserts this value automatically to indicate the strength of the linear relationship between the two variables. For now, just note that it is positive and its magnitude is moderately large. We will say more about correlations in the next section.

Finally, we say something about causation. There is a tendency for an analyst (such as a drugstore manager) to say that larger promotional expenses *cause* larger sales values. However, unless the data are obtained in a carefully controlled experiment—which is certainly not the case here—we can never make definitive statements about causation in regression analysis. The reason is that we can almost never rule out the possibility that some other variable is causing the variation in *both* of the observed variables. While this might be unlikely in this drugstore example, it is still a possibility. ■

The following example uses time series data to illustrate several other features of scatterplots. We will also follow this example throughout the chapter.

---

[2] The scatterplots you obtain with StatPro might not look exactly like those we show here. We have used some of Excel's many chart-editing features to modify the graphs slightly. For example, we often change the scale and the number formatting on the axes.

EXAMPLE 11.2

The Bendrix Company manufactures various types of parts for automobiles. The manager of the factory wants to get a better understanding of overhead costs. These overhead costs include supervision, indirect labor, supplies, payroll taxes, overtime premiums, depreciation, and a number of miscellaneous items such as insurance, utilities, and janitorial and maintenance expenses. Some of these overhead costs are "fixed" in the sense that they do not vary appreciably with the volume of work being done, whereas others are "variable" and do vary directly with the volume of work. The fixed overhead costs tend to come from the supervision, depreciation, and miscellaneous categories, whereas the variable overhead costs tend to come from the indirect labor, supplies, payroll taxes, and overtime premiums categories. However, it is not easy to draw a clear line between the fixed and variable overhead components.

The Bendrix manager has tracked total overhead costs over the past 36 months. To help "explain" these, he has also collected data on two variables that are related to the amount of work done at the factory. These variables are:

■ MachHrs: number of machine hours used during the month

■ ProdRuns: the number of separate production runs during the month

The first of these is a direct measure of the amount of work being done. To understand the second, we note that Bendrix manufactures parts in fairly large batches. Each batch corresponds to a production run. Once a production run is completed, the factory must "set up" for the next production run. During this setup there is typically some downtime while the machinery is reconfigured for the part type scheduled for production in the next batch. Therefore, the manager believes both of these variables might be responsible (in different ways) for variations in overhead costs. Do scatterplots support this belief?

Solution

The data appear in Figure 11.3 on page 568. (See the BENDRIX1.XLS file.) Each observation (row) corresponds to a single month. We want to investigate any possible relationship between the Overhead variable and the MachHrs and ProdRuns variables, but because these are time series variables, we should also be on the lookout for any relationships between these variables and the Month variable. That is, we should investigate any time series behavior in these variables.

This data set illustrates, even with a modest number of variables, how the number of potentially useful scatterplots can grow quickly. At the very least, we should examine the scatterplot between each potential explanatory variable (MachHrs and ProdRuns) and the response variable (Overhead). These appear in Figures 11.4 and 11.5. We see that Overhead tends to increase as either MachHrs increases or ProdRuns increases. However, both relationships are far from perfect.

To check for possible time series patterns, we can also create a time series plot for any of the variables. (Actually, this is equivalent to a scatterplot of the variable versus Month, with the points joined by lines.) One of these, the time series plot for Overhead, appears in Figure 11.6 (page 569). It shows a fairly random pattern through time, with no apparent upward trend or other obvious time series pattern. You can check that time series plots of the MachHrs and ProdRuns variables also indicate no obvious time series patterns.

FIGURE 11.3   Data for Bendrix Overhead Example

	A	B	C	D
1	Monthly data on manufacturing overhead costs			
2				
3	Month	MachHrs	ProdRuns	Overhead
4	1	1539	31	99798
5	2	1284	29	87804
6	3	1490	27	93681
7	4	1355	22	82262
8	5	1500	35	106968
9	6	1777	30	107925
10	7	1716	41	117287
11	8	1045	29	76868
12	9	1364	47	106001
13	10	1516	21	88738
37	34	1723	35	107828
38	35	1413	30	88032
39	36	1390	54	117943

FIGURE 11.4   Scatterplot of Overhead versus Machine Hours

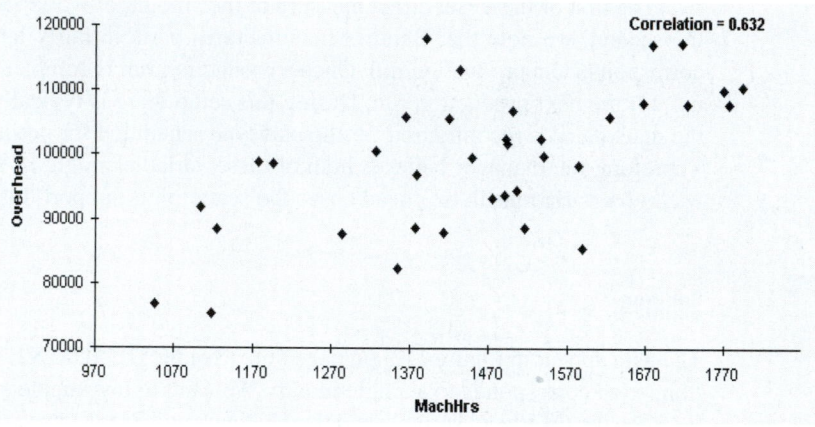

FIGURE 11.5   Scatterplot of Overhead versus Production Runs

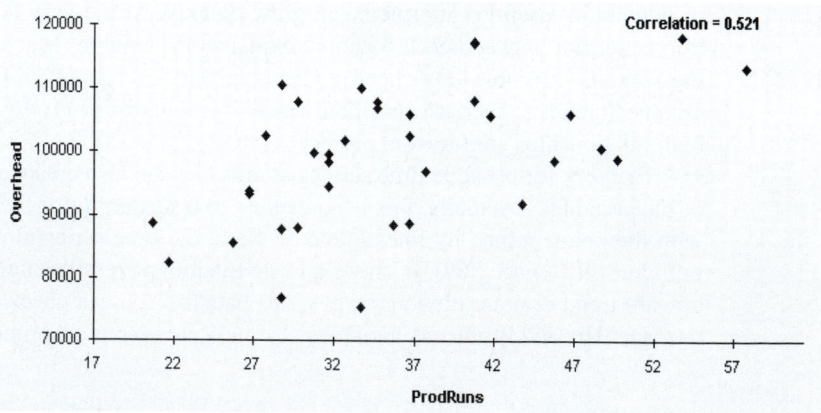

FIGURE 11.6 **Time Series Plot of Overhead versus Month**

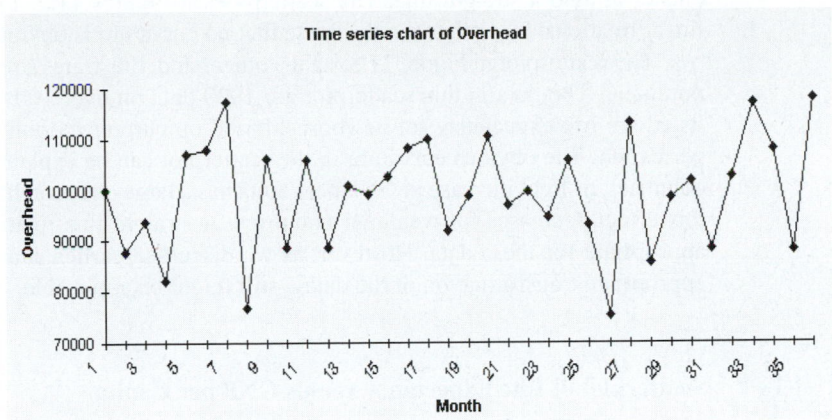

Finally, when there are multiple explanatory variables, we can check for relationships among them. The scatterplot of MachHrs versus ProdRuns appears in Figure 11.7. (Either variable could be chosen for the vertical axis.) This "cloud" of points indicates no relationship worth pursuing.

FIGURE 11.7 **Scatterplot of Machine Hours versus Production Runs**

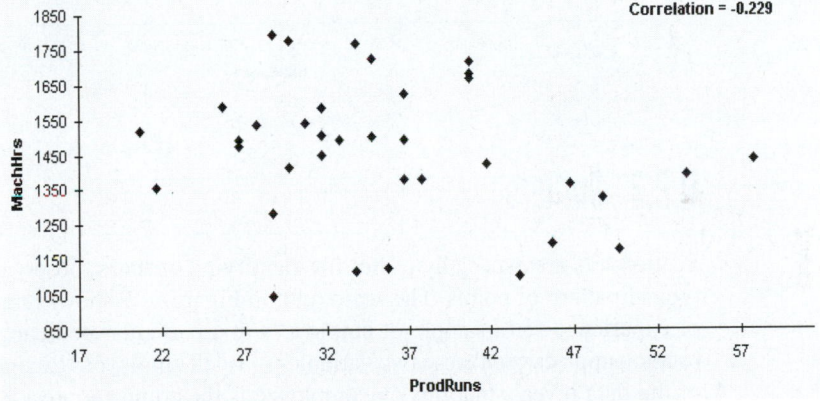

In summary, the Bendrix manager should continue to explore the positive relationship between Overhead and each of the MachHrs and ProdRuns variables. However, none of the variables appears to have any time series behavior, and the two potential explanatory variables do not appear to be related to each other. ∎

11.2.1 Linear Versus Nonlinear Relationships

Scatterplots are extremely useful for detecting behavior that might not be obvious otherwise. We illustrate some of these in the next few subsections. First, the typical relationship we hope to see is a straight-line, or *linear*, relationship. This doesn't mean that all points lie on a straight line—this is too much to expect in business data—but that the points tend to cluster around a straight line. The scatterplots in Figures 11.2, 11.4, and 11.5 all exhibit linear relationships, at least in the sense that no curvature is obvious.

The scatterplot in Figure 11.8, on the other hand, illustrates a relationship that is clearly nonlinear. The data in this scatterplot are 1990 data on over 100 countries. The variables listed are life expectancy (of newborns, based on current mortality conditions) and GNP per capita. The obvious curvature in the scatterplot can be explained as follows. For poor countries, a slight increase in GNP per capita has a large effect on life expectancy. However, this effect decreases for wealthier countries. A straight-line relationship is definitely not appropriate for these data. However, as we discussed earlier, *linear* regression—after an appropriate transformation of the data—still might be applicable.

FIGURE 11.8 **Scatterplot of Life Expectancy versus GNP per Capita**

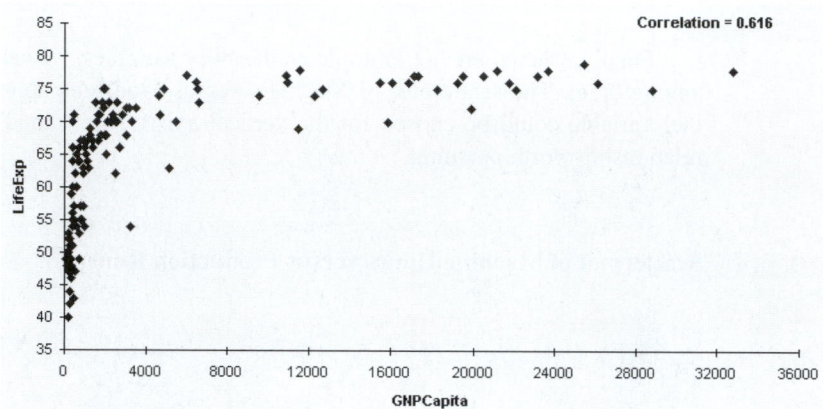

11.2.2 Outliers

Scatterplots are especially useful for identifying **outliers**, observations that lie outside the typical pattern of points. The scatterplot in Figure 11.9 shows annual salaries versus years of experience for a sample of employees at a particular company. There is a clear linear relationship between these two variables—for all employees except for one. Closer scrutiny of the data reveals that this one employee is the company president, whose salary is well above that of all the other employees!

Although scatterplots are good for detecting outliers, they do not necessarily indicate what we ought to do about any outliers we find. This depends entirely on the particular situation. If we are attempting to investigate the salary structure for "typical" employees at a company, then we probably should not include the company president. First, the president's salary is not determined in the same way as the salaries for typical employees. Second, if we do include the president in the analysis, it can greatly distort the results for the mass of typical employees. In other situations, however, it might *not* be appropriate to eliminate outliers just to make the analysis come out more nicely.

It is difficult to generalize about the treatment of outliers, but the following points are worth noting.

■   If an outlier is clearly not a member of the population of interest, then it is probably best to delete it from the analysis. This is the case for the company president in Figure 11.9.

FIGURE 11.9 **Scatterplot of Salary versus Years of Experience**

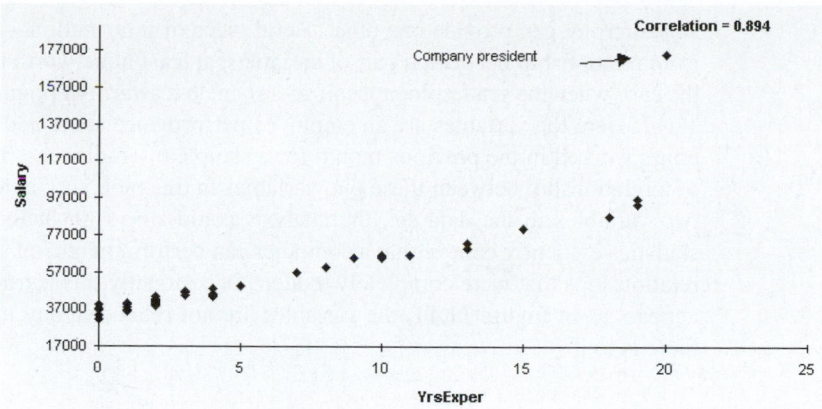

- If it isn't clear whether outliers are members of the relevant population, we should run the regression analysis with them and without them. If the results are practically the same in both cases, then it is probably best to report the results with the outliers included. Otherwise, we should report both sets of results with a verbal explanation of the outliers.

11.2.3   Unequal Variance

Occasionally, there is a clear relationship between two variables, but the variance of the response variable depends on the value of the explanatory variable. We saw a good example of this in the catalog data in Chapter 3. (See Example 3.11.) Figure 11.10 reproduces one of the scatterplots from the data in that example. It shows AmountSpent versus Salary for the customers in the data set. There is a clear linear relationship, but the variability of AmountSpent increases as Salary increases. This is evident from the "fan" shape. As we will see in the next chapter, this unequal variance violates one of the assumptions of linear regression analysis, and there are special techniques to deal with it.

FIGURE 11.10   **Unequal Variance of Response Variable in a Scatterplot**

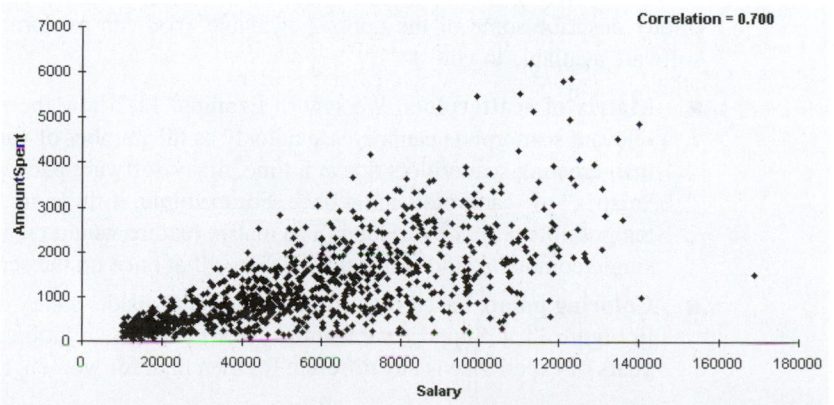

11.2.4 No Relationship

A scatterplot can provide one other useful piece of information—it can indicate that there is *no* relationship between a pair of variables, at least none worth pursuing. This is usually the case when the scatterplot appears as a shapeless swarm of points, as illustrated in Figure 11.11. Here the variables are an employee performance score and the number of overtime hours worked in the previous month for a sample of employees. There is virtually no hint of a relationship between these two variables in this plot, and, at least if these are the only two variables in the data set, the analysis could stop right here. Many people who use statistics evidently believe that a computer can perform magic on a set of numbers and find relationships that were completely hidden. Occasionally this is true, but when a scatterplot appears as in Figure 11.11, the variables are not related in any useful way, and that's all there is to it.

FIGURE 11.11 **An Example of No Relationship**

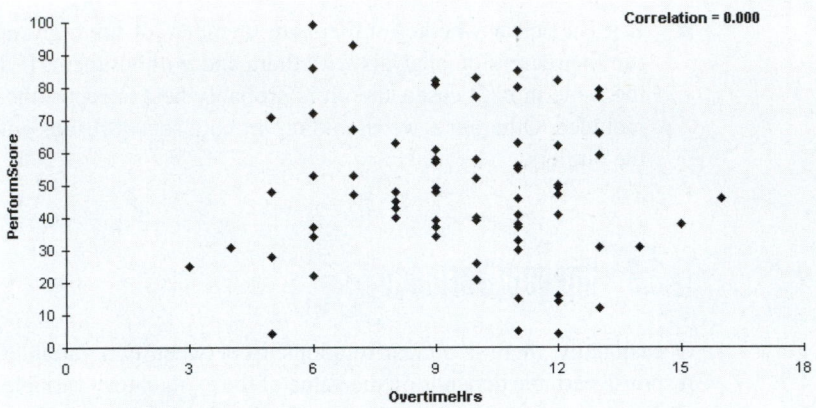

11.2.5 Other Scatterplot Features

Scatterplots are a useful way to begin nearly any regression analysis. In Excel they are fairly easy to construct, especially with an add-in such as StatPro. However, spreadsheet packages do have their limitations relative to special-purpose statistical software packages such as SPSS, Minitab, SAS, StatGraphics, and many others. The options for exploring data with scatterplots in these packages are very powerful and quite easy to use. We will briefly describe some of the options available. You can explore these depending on the software available to you.

- **Matrix of scatterplots.** We saw in Example 11.2 how the number of potentially relevant scatterplots can increase quickly as the number of variables increases. Rather than creating scatterplots one at a time, many software packages allow us to create a "matrix" of scatterplots all at once. For example, if there are five variables, there are ten possible *pairs* of variables. The matrix feature would create all ten of these with a single command, and we could see them all at once on the screen.

- **Coloring points based on a third variable.** Consider salary data such as those shown in Figure 11.9. Suppose we want to see whether the relationship between salary and years of experience is any different for men than for women. Some statistical software allows us to create a scatterplot of salary versus years of experience for all employees, but with the points for men colored (or shaped) differently than the points for women.

- **Brushing points based on a third variable.** The previous option is based on coloring points according to a variable with only two categories (for example, men and women). A similar idea is to color points based on a *continuous* third variable. For example, suppose we want to see how an employee's current performance score (given by a supervisor) affects the relationship between salary and years of experience. Some statistical software allows us to color the points in the scatterplot differently depending on a cutoff value for the performance score. For example, we might color all points blue for employees with performance scores less than 50 and color all other points red. In addition, it is usually easy to change the cutoff value and have the software recolor the points automatically.

- **Three-dimensional plots.** A final possibility is to show a "3-D" scatterplot of three variables simultaneously. Although these 3-D plots are often difficult to visualize on a two-dimensional computer screen, many software packages allow us to "rotate" the plot through various angles. A relationship that is not at all obvious from one angle might be apparent from another angle.

We are not claiming that a clever user could not accomplish these features with Excel—either with Excel's built-in capabilities or with its Visual Basic for Applications programming language. This is quite possible. The point, however, is that many special-purpose statistical software packages have this functionality built into them and are quite easy to use.

Correlations: Indicators of Linear Relationships

Scatterplots provide graphical indications of relationships, whether they be linear, non-linear, or essentially nonexistent. Correlations are numerical summary measures that indicate the strength of relationships between pairs of variables.[3] A correlation between a pair of variables is a single number that summarizes the information in a scatterplot. A correlation can be very useful, but it has an important limitation: it can only measure the strength of a *linear* relationship. If there is a nonlinear relationship, as suggested by a scatterplot, the correlation can be completely misleading. With this important limitation in mind, let's look a bit more closely at correlations.

The usual notation for a correlation between two variables X and Y is r_{XY}. The subscripts can be omitted if the variables are clear from the context of the problem. The formula for r_{XY} is given below. Note that it is a sum of products in the numerator, divided by the product $s_X s_Y$ of the sample standard deviations of X and Y. This requires a considerable amount of computation, so that correlations are almost always computed by software packages.

$$r_{XY} = \frac{\sum(X_i - \overline{X})(Y_i - \overline{Y})/(n-1)}{s_X s_Y} \qquad \textbf{(11.1)}$$

The numerator of equation (11.1) is also a measure of association between two variables X and Y. It is called the **covariance** between X and Y. Like a correlation, a covariance is a

---

[3]This section includes some material from Section 3.7, but it is repeated here for convenience.

single number that measures the strength of the linear relationship between two variables. By looking at the sign of the covariance or correlation—plus or minus—we can tell whether the two variables are positively or negatively related. The drawback to a covariance, however, is that its magnitude depends on the units in which the variables are measured.

To illustrate, the covariance between Overhead and MachHrs in the Bendrix manufacturing data set is 1,333,138. (It can be found with Excel's COVAR function or with StatPro.) However, if we divide each overhead value by 1000, so that overhead costs are expressed in thousands of dollars, and we divide each value of MachHrs by 100, so that machine hours are expressed in hundreds of hours, the covariance decreases by a factor of 100,000 to 13.33138. This is in spite of the fact that the basic relationship between these variables has not changed and the revised scatterplot has exactly the same shape. For this reason it is often difficult to interpret the magnitude of a covariance, and we concentrate instead on correlations.

Unlike covariances, correlations have the attractive property that they are completely unaffected by the units in which the variables are measured. The rescaling described in the previous paragraph has absolutely no effect on the correlation between Overhead and MachHrs. It is 0.632 in either case. Moreover, all correlations are between −1 and +1, inclusive. The sign of a correlation, plus or minus, determines whether the linear relationship between two variables is positive or negative. In this respect, a correlation is just like a covariance. However, the strength of the linear relationship between the variables is measured by the absolute value, or magnitude, of the correlation. The closer this magnitude is to 1, the stronger the linear relationship.

A correlation equal to zero or near zero indicates practically no linear relationship. A correlation with magnitude close to 1, on the other hand, indicates a strong linear relationship. At the extreme, a correlation equal to −1 or +1 occurs only when the linear relationship is perfect—that is, when all points in the scatterplot lie on a single straight line. Although such extremes practically never occur in business applications, "large" correlations, say, greater than 0.9 in magnitude, are not at all uncommon.

Looking back at the scatterplots for the Pharmex drugstore data in Figure 11.2, we see that the correlation between Sales and Promote is positive—as we would guess from the upward-sloping scatter of points—and that it is equal to 0.673. This is a moderately large correlation. It indicates what we see in the scatterplot, namely, that the points vary considerably around any particular straight line.

Similarly, the scatterplots for the Bendrix manufacturing data in Figures 11.4 and 11.5 indicate moderately large positive correlations, 0.632 and 0.521, between Overhead and MachHrs and between Overhead and ProdRuns. However, the correlation indicated in Figure 11.7 between MachHrs and ProdRuns, −0.229, is quite small and indicates almost no relationship between these two variables.

We must be a bit more careful when interpreting the correlations in Figures 11.8 and 11.9. The scatterplot between life expectancy and GNP per capita in Figure 11.8 is obviously nonlinear, and correlations are relevant descriptors only for *linear* relationships. If anything, the correlation of 0.616 in this example tends to underestimate the true strength of the relationship—the nonlinear one—between life expectancy and GNP per capita. In contrast, the correlation between salary and years of experience in Figure 11.9 is large, 0.894, but it is not nearly as large as it would be if the outlier were omitted. (It is then 0.992.) This example illustrates the considerable effect a single outlier can have on a correlation.

An obvious question is whether a given correlation is "large." This is a difficult question to answer directly. Clearly, a correlation such as 0.992 is quite large—the points tend to cluster very closely around a straight line. Similarly, a correlation of 0.034 is quite small—the points tend to be a shapeless swarm. But there is a continuum of in-between values, as exhibited in Figures 11.2, 11.4, and 11.5. We will give a more definite answer to this question when we examine the *square* of the correlation later in this chapter.

As for calculating correlations, there are two possibilities in Excel. To calculate a *single* correlation r_{XY} between variables X and Y, we can use Excel's CORREL function in the form

$$=\text{CORREL}(X\text{-range}, Y\text{-range})$$

Alternatively, we can use StatPro to obtain a whole table of correlations between a set of variables.

Finally, we reiterate the important limitation of correlations (and covariances), namely, that they apply only to *linear* relationships. If a correlation is close to zero, we cannot automatically conclude that there is no relationship between the two variables. We should look at a scatterplot first. The chances are that the points are a shapeless swarm and that no relationship exists. But it is also possible that the points cluster around some curve. In this case the correlation is misleading, and the nonlinear shape should be analyzed further.

Simple Linear Regression

Scatterplots and correlations are very useful for indicating linear relationships and the strengths of these relationships. But they do not actually *quantify* the relationships. For example, we know from the Pharmex drugstore data that sales are related to promotional expenditures. But from the knowledge presented so far, we do not know exactly what this relationship is. If the expenditure index for a given region is 95, what would we predict this region's sales index to be? Or if one region's expenditure index is 5 points higher than another region's, we would expect the former to have a larger sales index, but how much larger? To answer these questions, we need to quantify the relationship between the response variable Sales and the explanatory variable Promote.

In this section we answer these types of questions for simple linear regression, where there is a *single* explanatory variable. We do so by fitting a straight line through the scatterplot of the response variable Y versus the explanatory variable X and then basing the answers to the questions on the fitted straight line. But which straight line? We address this issue next.

11.4.1 Least Squares Estimation

The scatterplot between Sales and Promote, repeated in Figure 11.12 (page 576), hints at a linear relationship between these two variables. It would not be difficult to draw a straight line through these points to produce a reasonably good fit. In fact, a possible linear fit is indicated in the graph. But we will proceed more systematically than simply drawing lines freehand. Specifically, we will choose the line that makes the vertical distances from the points to the line as small as possible, as explained below.

Consider the magnified graph in Figure 11.13. Here we show several points in the scatterplot, along with a line drawn through them. Note that the vertical distance from the horizontal axis to any point, which is just the value of Sales for that point, can be decomposed into two parts: the vertical distance from the horizontal axis to the line, and the vertical distance from the line to the point. The first of these is called the **fitted value**, and the second is called the **residual**. The idea is very simple. By using a straight line to reflect the relationship between Sales and Promote, we expect a given Sales to be at the

FIGURE 11.12 **Scatterplot with Possible Linear Fit Superimposed**

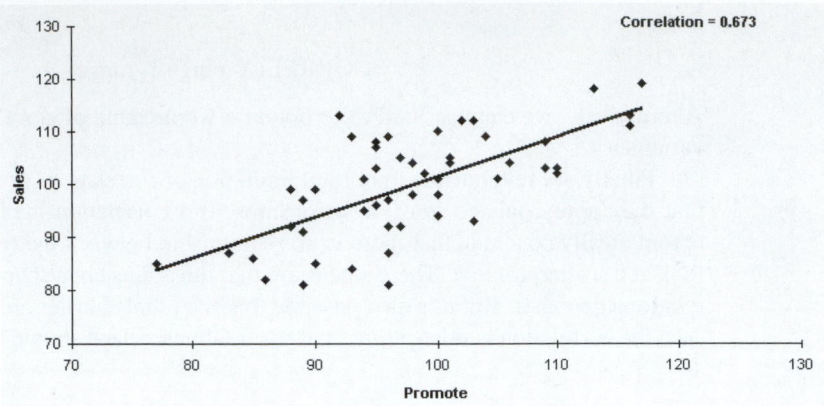

FIGURE 11.13 **Fitted Values and Residuals**

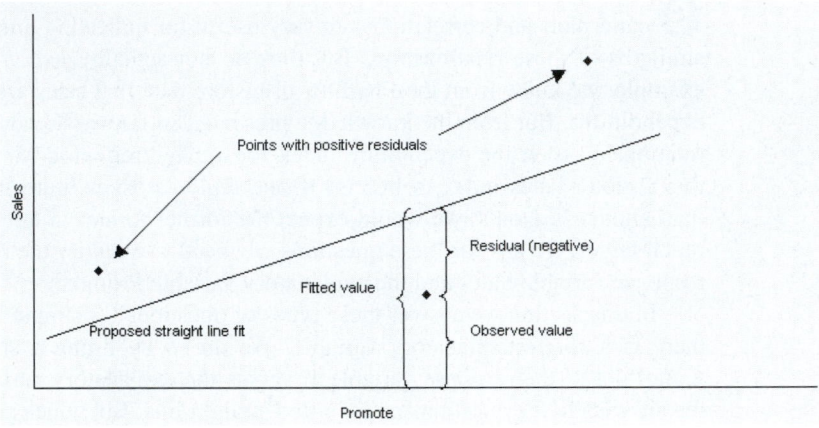

height of the line above any particular value of Promote. That is, we expect Sales to equal the fitted value.

But the relationship is not perfect. Not all (perhaps not any) of the points lie exactly on the line. The differences are the residuals. They show how much the observed values differ from the fitted values. If a particular residual is positive, the corresponding point is above the line; if it is negative, the point is below the line. The only time a residual is zero is when the point lies directly on the line. The relationship between observed values, fitted values, and residuals is very general and is stated below.

$$\text{Observed value} = \text{Fitted value} + \text{Residual}$$

We can now explain how to choose the "best-fitting" line through the points in the scatterplot. We choose the one with the *smallest sum of squared residuals*. The resulting line is called the **least squares** line. Why do we use the sum of *squared* residuals? Why not minimize some other measure of the residuals? First, we do not simply minimize the sum of the residuals because the positive residuals would cancel the negative residuals. In fact, the least squares line has the property that the sum of the residuals is always exactly zero. To adjust for this, we could minimize the sum of the *absolute values* of the residuals, and this is a perfectly reasonable procedure. However, for technical reasons it is not the procedure usually chosen. We settle on the sum of squared residuals because this method is deeply rooted in statistical tradition, and it works well.

The minimization problem itself is a calculus problem that we will not discuss here. Virtually all statistical software packages perform this minimization automatically, so we need not be concerned with the technical details. However, we will provide the formulas for the least squares line.

Recall from basic algebra that the equation for any straight line can be written as

$$Y = a + bX$$

Here, a is the Y-intercept of the line, the value of Y when $X = 0$, and b is the slope of the line, the change in Y when X increases by one unit. Therefore, to specify the least squares line, all we need to specify is the slope and intercept. These are given by

$$b = \frac{\sum(X_i - \overline{X})(Y_i - \overline{Y})}{\sum(X_i - \overline{X})^2} = r_{XY}\frac{s_X}{s_Y}$$

and

$$a = \overline{Y} - b\overline{X}$$

We have presented these formulas primarily for conceptual purposes, not for hand calculations—the computer can take care of the calculations. From the right-hand formula for b, we see that it is closely related to the correlation between X and Y. Specifically, if we keep the standard deviations, s_X and s_Y, of X and Y constant, then the slope b of the least squares line varies directly with the correlation between the two variables. A relationship with a large correlation (negative or positive) has a steep slope, and a relationship with a small correlation has a shallow slope. At the extreme, a nonrelationship with a correlation of 0 has a slope of 0; that is, it results in a horizontal line. The effect of the formula for a is not quite as interesting. It simply forces the least squares line to go through the point of sample means, $(\overline{X}, \overline{Y})$.

It is easy to obtain the least squares line in Excel, either by using Excel's built-in Analysis ToolPak or StatPro's Simple Regression procedure. We illustrate the latter in the following continuations of Examples 11.1 and 11.2.

EXAMPLE 11.1 [CONTINUED]

Find the least squares line for the Pharmex drugstore data, using Sales as the response variable and Promote as the explanatory variable.

Solution

We use the StatPro/Regression Analysis/Simple menu item. After specifying that Sales is the response (dependent) variable and that Promote is the explanatory (independent) variable, we see the dialog box in Figure 11.14 (page 578). This gives us the option of creating several scatterplots involving the fitted values and residuals. We suggest checking the first and third options, as shown.

The regression output includes three parts. The first two are a list of fitted values and residuals, placed in columns next to the data set, and any scatterplots selected from the dialog box in Figure 11.14. We will look at these shortly. The third part of the output is the most important. It is shown in Figure 11.15.

FIGURE 11.14 **Dialog Box for Scatterplot Options in Simple Regression Procedure**

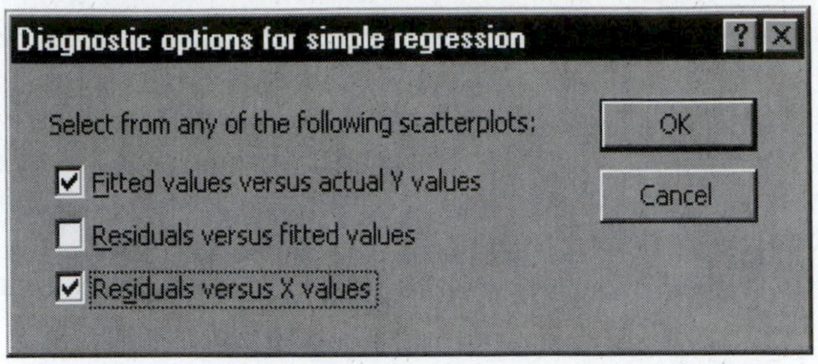

FIGURE 11.15 **Regression Output for Drugstore Example**

	A	B	C	D	E	F	G
1	***Results of simple regression for Sales***						
2							
3	*Summary measures*						
4		Multiple R	0.6730				
5		R-Square	0.4529				
6		Adj R-Square	0.4415				
7		StErr of Est	7.3947				
8							
9	*ANOVA Table*						
10		Source	df	SS	MS	F	p-value
11		Explained	1	2172.8804	2172.8804	39.7366	0.0000
12		Unexplained	48	2624.7396	54.6821		
13							
14	*Regression coefficients*						
15			Coefficient	Std Err	t-value	p-value	
16		Constant	25.1264	11.8826	2.1146	0.0397	
17		Promote	0.7623	0.1209	6.3037	0.0000	

We will eventually learn what all of the output in Figure 11.15 means, but for now, we will concentrate on only a small part of it. Specifically, we find the intercept and slope of the least squares line under the Coefficient label in cells C16 and C17. They imply that the equation for the least squares line is[4]

$$\text{Predicted Sales} = 25.1264 + 0.7623\text{Promote}$$

Excel Tip *The Simple Regression procedure in StatPro uses Excel formulas to calculate all of the regression output. It takes advantage of several built-in statistical functions available in Excel. Take a look at cells C4, C5, C7, C16, and C17 of the Regress sheet in the PHARMEX.XLS file. You'll see how Excel's statistical functions CORREL, RSQ, STEYX, INTERCEPT, and SLOPE are used. Also, look at the Fitted Values and Residuals columns to see how the TREND function is used. For now, note specifically that the slope and intercept of the least squares line can be calculated directly with the formulas*

$$=SLOPE(Y\text{-}range, X\text{-}range)$$

and

$$=INTERCEPT(Y\text{-}range, X\text{-}range)$$

[4]We will always report the left side of the estimated regression equation as the *predicted* value of the response variable. It is not the *actual* value of the response variable because the observations do not all lie on the estimated regression line.

*These formulas (with the appropriate X and Y ranges) can be entered anywhere in a spreadsheet to obtain the slope and intercept for a **simple** regression equation—no add-ins are necessary.*

We can interpret this equation as follows. The slope, 0.7623, indicates that the sales index tends to increase by about 0.76 for each unit increase in the promotional expenses index. Alternatively, if we compare two regions, where region 2 spends one unit higher than region 1, we predict the sales index for region 2 to be 0.76 larger than the sales index for region 1. The interpretation of the intercept is less important. It is literally the predicted sales index for a region that does no promotions. However, no region in the sample has anywhere near a zero promotional value. Therefore, in a situation like this, where the range of observed explanatory variable values does not include 0, it is best to think of the intercept term as an "anchor" for the least squares line that allows us to predict Y values for the range of *observed X* values.

A useful graph in almost any regression analysis is a scatterplot of residuals (on the vertical axis) versus fitted values. This scatterplot for the Pharmex data appears in Figure 11.16. We typically examine such a scatterplot for any striking patterns. A "good" fit not only has small residuals, but it has residuals scattered *randomly* around 0 with no apparent pattern. This appears to be the case for the Pharmex data.

FIGURE 11.16 **Scatterplot of Residuals versus Fitted Values in Pharmex Example**

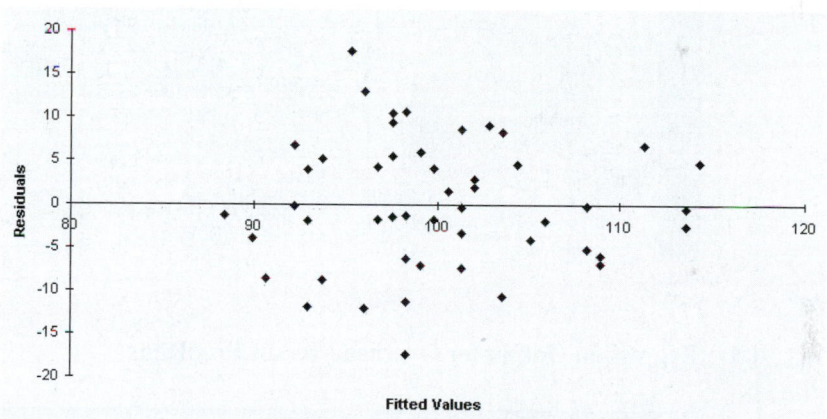

EXAMPLE 11.2 [CONTINUED]

The Bendrix manufacturing data set has two potential explanatory variables, MachHrs and ProdRuns. Eventually, we will estimate a regression equation with *both* of these variables included. However, if we include only one at a time, what do they tell us about overhead costs?

Solution

The regression output for Overhead with MachHrs as the single explanatory variable appears in Figure 11.17 (page 580). The output when ProdRuns is the only explanatory variable appears in Figure 11.18. The two least squares lines are therefore

$$\text{Predicted Overhead} = 48,621 + 34.7\text{MachHrs} \tag{11.2}$$

and

$$\text{Predicted Overhead} = 75{,}606 + 655.1\text{ProdRuns} \qquad \textbf{(11.3)}$$

Clearly, these two equations are quite different, although each effectively breaks Overhead into a fixed component and a variable component. Equation (11.2) implies that the fixed component of overhead is about \$48,621. Bendrix can expect to incur this amount even if zero machine hours are used. The variable component is the 34.7MachHrs term. It implies that the expected overhead increases by about \$35 for each extra machine hour. Equation (11.3), on the other hand, breaks overhead down into a fixed component of \$75,606 and a variable component of about \$655 per each production run.

The difference between these two equations can be attributed to the fact that neither tells the whole story. If the manager's goal is to split overhead into a fixed component and

FIGURE 11.17 **Regression Output for Overhead versus MachHrs**

	A	B	C	D	E	F	G
1	Results of simple regression for Overhead						
2							
3	Summary measures						
4		Multiple R	0.6319				
5		R-Square	0.3993				
6		Adj R-Square	0.3816				
7		StErr of Est	8584.7394				
8							
9	ANOVA Table						
10		Source	df	SS	MS	F	p-value
11		Explained	1	1665463368.3416	1665463368.3416	22.5986	0.0000
12		Unexplained	34	2505723491.6584	73697749.7547		
13							
14	Regression coefficients						
15			Coefficient	Std Err	t-value	p-value	
16		Constant	48621.3546	10725.3327	4.5333	0.0001	
17		MachHrs	34.7022	7.2999	4.7538	0.0000	

FIGURE 11.18 **Regression Output for Overhead versus ProdRuns**

	A	B	C	D	E	F	G
1	Results of simple regression for Overhead						
2							
3	Summary measures						
4		Multiple R	0.5205				
5		R-Square	0.2710				
6		Adj R-Square	0.2495				
7		StErr of Est	9457.2395				
8							
9	ANOVA Table						
10		Source	df	SS	MS	F	p-value
11		Explained	1	1130247999.2618	1130247999.2618	12.6370	0.0011
12		Unexplained	34	3040938860.7382	89439378.2570		
13							
14	Regression coefficients						
15			Coefficient	Std Err	t-value	p-value	
16		Constant	75605.5157	6808.6106	11.1044	0.0000	
17		ProdRuns	655.0707	184.2747	3.5549	0.0011	

a variable component, then the variable component should include *both* of the measures of work activity (and maybe even others) to give a more complete explanation of overhead. We will see how to do this when we reanalyze this example with multiple regression. ∎

11.4.2 Standard Error of Estimate

In a typical simple regression model, the expression $a + bX$ is the fitted value of Y. Graphically, it is the height of the estimated line above the value X. We often denote it by $\widehat{Y}$ (pronounced Y-hat)[5]:

$$\widehat{Y} = a + bX \tag{11.4}$$

Then a typical residual, denoted by e, is the difference between the observed value Y and the fitted value $\widehat{Y}$:

$$e = Y - \widehat{Y} \tag{11.5}$$

We show some of the fitted values and associated residuals for the Pharmex drugstore example in Figure 11.19. Although the fitted values in column D were calculated automatically by StatPro, there are two ways we can calculate them "manually." First, we can use Excel's TREND function. To do so, highlight the range where the fitted values will go (D6:D55), type the formula

$$=\text{TREND}(Y\text{-range}, X\text{-range})$$

(where the appropriate Y and X ranges are used), and press Ctrl-Shift-Enter. Alternatively, we can calculate the fitted value corresponding to each X value directly from equation (11.4), using the estimated values of a and b in the regression output. In either case we can then calculate the residuals from equation (11.5).

FIGURE 11.19   **Fitted Values and Residuals for Pharmex Example**

	A	B	C	D	E	F
1	Data on drugstore promotional expenditures and sales					
2						
3	Note: each value is a percentage of what the leading competitor did					
4						
5	Region	Promote	Sales	Fitted Values	Residuals	
6	1	77	85	83.8232	1.1768	
7	2	110	103	108.9790	-5.9790	
8	3	110	102	108.9790	-6.9790	
9	4	93	109	96.0200	12.9800	
10	5	90	85	93.7331	-8.7331	
11	6	95	103	97.5446	5.4554	
12	7	100	110	101.3561	8.6439	
13	8	85	86	89.9216	-3.9216	
14	9	96	92	98.3069	-6.3069	
15	10	83	87	88.3970	-1.3970	
53	48	100	98	101.3561	-3.3561	
54	49	95	108	97.5446	10.4554	
55	50	96	87	98.3069	-11.3069	

[5] We could write Predicted Y instead of $\widehat{Y}$, but the latter notation is more common in the statistics literature.

The magnitudes of the residuals provide a good indication of how useful the regression line is for predicting Y values from X values. However, because there are numerous residuals, it is useful to summarize them with a single numerical measure. This measure, called the **standard error of estimate** and denoted s_e, is essentially the standard deviation of the residuals. It is given by

$$s_e = \sqrt{\frac{\sum e_i^2}{n-2}}$$

(11.6)

Actually, because the average of the residuals from a least squares fit is always 0, this is identical to the standard deviation of the residuals except that we use the denominator $n-2$ rather than the usual $n-1$. As we'll see in more generality later on, the rule is to subtract the number of parameters being estimated from the sample size n to obtain the denominator. Here there are two parameters being estimated: the intercept a and the slope b.

The usual rules of thumb for standard deviations can be applied to the standard error of estimate. For example, we expect about 2/3 of the residuals to be within one standard error of their mean (which is 0). Stated another way, we expect about 2/3 of the observed Y values to be within one standard error of the corresponding fitted $\widehat{Y}$ values. Similarly, we expect about 95% of the observed Y values to be within two standard errors of the corresponding fitted $\widehat{Y}$ values.[6]

The standard error of estimate s_e is included in all regression outputs. Alternatively, it can be calculated directly with Excel's STEYX function in the form

=STEYX(Y-range,X-range)

The standard error for the Pharmex data appears in cell C7 of Figure 11.15. Its value, approximately 7.39, indicates the typical error we are likely to make when we use the fitted value (based on the regression line) to predict sales from promotional expenses. More specifically, if we use the regression equation to predict sales for many regions, based on the promotional expenses in each region, then about 2/3 of the predictions will be within 7.39 of the actual sales values, and about 95% of the predictions will be within two standard errors, or 14.78, of the actual sales values.

Is this level of accuracy good? One measure of comparison is the standard deviation of the sales variable, namely, 9.90. (This is obtained by the usual STDEV function applied to the observed sales values.) It can be interpreted as the standard deviation of the residuals around a *horizontal* line positioned at the mean value of Sales. This would be the relevant regression line if there were no explanatory variables—that is, if we ignored Promote. In other words, it is a measure of the prediction error we would make if we used the sample mean of Sales as the prediction for *every* region and ignored Promote. The fact that the standard error of estimate, 7.39, is not much less than 9.90 means that the Promote variable adds a relatively small amount to prediction accuracy. We can do nearly as well without it as with it. We would certainly prefer a standard error of estimate *well* below 9.90.

We can often use the standard error of estimate to judge which of several potential regression equations is the most useful. In the Bendrix manufacturing example we estimated two regression lines, one using MachHrs and one using ProdRuns. From Figures 11.17 and 11.18, their standard errors are approximately \$8585 and \$9457. These imply that MachHrs is a slightly better predictor of overhead. The predictions based on MachHrs will tend to be slightly more accurate than those based on ProdRuns. Of course, we might guess that predictions based on *both* predictors will yield even more accurate predictions, and this is definitely the case, as we will see when we discuss multiple regression.

---

[6] This requires that the residuals be at least approximately normally distributed, a requirement we will discuss more fully in the next chapter.

11.4.3 R-Square: The Coefficient of Determination

We now discuss another important measure of the goodness of fit of the least squares line. This is called the **coefficient of determination**, or simply R^2. Along with the standard error of estimate s_e, it is the most frequently quoted measure in applied regression analysis. Its value is always between 0 and 1, and it can be interpreted as the *fraction of variation of the response variable explained by the regression line*. (It is often expressed as a percentage, so that we talk about the *percentage* of variation explained by the regression line.)

To see more precisely what this means, we look into the derivation of R^2. In the previous section we suggested that one way to measure the regression equation's ability to predict is to compare the standard error of estimate, s_e, to the standard deviation of the response variable, s_Y. The idea is that s_e is (essentially) the standard deviation of the residuals, whereas s_Y is the standard deviation of the residuals that we would obtain from a horizontal regression line at height $\overline{Y}$, the response variable's mean. Therefore, if s_e is small compared to s_Y (that is, if s_e/s_Y is small), then the regression line has evidently done a good job in explaining the variation of the response variable.

The R^2 measure is based on this idea. Its formula is

$$R^2 = 1 - \frac{\sum e_i^2}{\sum (Y_i - \overline{Y})^2} \tag{11.7}$$

(This value is obtained automatically with StatPro's regression procedure, or it can be calculated with Excel's RSQ function.) Equation (11.7) indicates that when the residuals are small, then R^2 will be close to 1, but when they are large, R^2 will be close to 0.

We see from cell C5 of Figure 11.15 that the R^2 measure for the Pharmex drugstore data is 0.453. In words, the single explanatory variable Promote is able to explain only 45.3% of the variation in the Sales variable. This is not particularly good—the same conclusion we made when we based goodness of fit on s_e. There is still 54.7% of the variation left unexplained. Of course, we would like R^2 to be as close to 1 as possible. Usually, the only way to increase it is to use better and/or more explanatory variables.

Analysts often compare equations on the basis of their R^2 values. We see from Figures 11.17 and 11.18 that the R^2 values using MachHrs and ProdRuns as single explanatory variables for the Bendrix overhead data are 39.9% and 27.1%. These provide one more piece of evidence that MachHrs is a slightly better predictor of Overhead than ProdRuns. Of course, they also suggest that the percentage of variation of Overhead explained could be increased by including *both* variables in a single equation. This is true, as we will see shortly.

There is a good reason for the notation R^2. It turns out that R^2 is the square of the correlation between the observed Y values and the fitted $\widehat{Y}$ values. This correlation appears in all regression outputs. For the Pharmex data it is 0.673, as seen in cell C4 of Figure 11.15. Aside from rounding error, the square of 0.673 is 0.453, the R^2 value right below it. In the case of simple linear regression, when there is only a single explanatory variable in the equation, the correlation between the Y variable and the fitted $\widehat{Y}$ values is the same as the absolute value of the correlation between the Y variable and the explanatory X variable. For the Pharmex data we already saw that the correlation between Sales and Promote is indeed 0.673.

This interpretation of R^2 as the square of a correlation helps to decide the issue of when a correlation is "large." For example, if the correlation between two variables Y and X is ± 0.8, we know that the regression of Y on X will produce an R^2 of 0.64; that is, the regression with X as the only explanatory variable will explain 64% of the variation in Y. If the correlation drops to ± 0.7, this percentage drops to 49%; if the correlation increases to ± 0.9, the percentage increases to 81%. The point is that before a single variable X can explain a large percentage of the variation in some other variable Y, the two variables must be highly correlated—in *either* a positive or negative direction.

PROBLEMS

Level A

1 Explore the relationship between the selling prices (Y) and the appraised values (X) of the 150 homes in the file P2_7.XLS by estimating a simple linear regression model. Also, compute the standard error of estimate s_e and the coefficient of determination R^2 for the estimated least squares line. Interpret these measures and the least squares line for these data.

   a Is there evidence of a *linear* relationship between the selling price and appraised value? If so, characterize the relationship (i.e., indicate whether the relationship is a positive or negative one, a strong or weak one, etc.).

   b For which of the two remaining variables, the size of the home and the number of bedrooms in the home, is the relationship with the home's selling price *stronger*? Justify your choice with additional simple linear regression models.

2 What is the relationship between the number of short-term general hospitals (Y) and the number of general or family physicians (X) in U.S. metropolitan areas? Explore this question by estimating a simple linear regression model using the data in the file P2_17.XLS. Interpret your estimated regression model as well as the coefficient of determination R^2.

3 Motorco produces electric motors for use in home appliances. One of the company's production managers is interested in examining the relationship between the dollars spent per month in inspecting finished motor products (X) and the number of motors produced during that month that were returned by dissatisfied customers (Y). He has collected the data in the file P2_18.XLS to explore this relationship for the past 36 months. Generate a simple linear regression model using the given data and interpret it for this production manager. Also, compute and interpret s_e and R^2 for these data.

4 The owner of the Original Italian Pizza restaurant chain would like to understand which variable most strongly influences the sales of his specialty, deep-dish pizza. He has gathered data on the monthly sales of deep-dish pizzas at his restaurants and observations on other potentially relevant variables for each of his 15 outlets in central Pennsylvania. These data are provided in the file P11_4.XLS. Estimate a simple linear regression model between the quantity sold (Y) and each of the following candidates for the best explanatory variable: average price of deep-dish pizzas, monthly advertising expenditures, and disposable income per household in the areas surrounding the outlets. Which variable is *most* strongly associated with the number of pizzas sold? Be sure to explain your choice.

5 The human resources manager of DataCom, Inc. wants to examine the relationship between annual salaries (Y) and the number of years employees have worked at DataCom (X). These data have been collected for a sample of employees and are given in the file P11_5.XLS.

   a Estimate the relationship between Y and X. Interpret the least squares line.

   b How well does the estimated simple linear regression model fit the given data? Document your answer.

6 Consider the relationship between the size of the population (X) and the average household income level for residents of U.S. towns (Y). What do you expect the relationship between these two variables to be? Using the data in the file P2_24.XLS, produce and interpret a simple linear regression model involving these two variables. How well does the estimated model fit the given data?

7 Examine the relationship between the average utility bills for homes of a particular size (Y) and the average monthly temperature (X). The data in the file P11_7.XLS include the average monthly bill and temperature for each month of the past year.

   a Use the given data to estimate a simple linear regression model. Interpret the least squares line.

   b How well does the estimated regression model fit the given data? How might we do a better job of explaining the variation of the average utility bills for homes of a certain size?

8 The U.S. Bureau of Labor Statistics provides data on the year-to-year percentage changes in the wages and salaries of workers in private industries, including both "white-collar" and "blue-collar" occupations. Here we consider these data for the years 1980–1996 in the file P2_56.XLS. Is there evidence of a strong relationship between the yearly changes in the wages

and salaries of white-collar and blue-collar workers in the United States over the given time period? Answer this question by estimating and interpreting a simple linear regression model.

9   Management of a home appliance store in Charlotte would like to understand the growth pattern of the monthly sales of VCR units over the past 2 years. The managers have recorded the relevant data in an Excel spreadsheet, which can be found in the file P11_9.XLS. Have the sales of VCR units been growing linearly over the past 24 months? Using simple linear regression, explain why or why not.

10 Do the sales prices of houses in a given community vary systematically with their sizes (as measured in square feet)? Attempt to answer this question by estimating a simple regression model where the sales price of the house is the response variable and the size of the house is the explanatory variable. Use the sample data given in the file P11_10.XLS. Interpret your estimated model and the associated coefficient of determination R^2.

11 The file P11_11.XLS contains observations of the American minimum wage during each of the years from 1950 through 1994. Has the minimum wage been growing at roughly a *constant* rate over this period? Use simple linear regression analysis to address this question. Explain the results you obtain.

12 Based on the data in the file P2_25.XLS from the U.S. Department of Agriculture, explore the relationship between the number of farms (X) and the average size of a farm (Y) in the United States between 1950 and 1997. Specifically, generate a simple linear regression model and interpret it.

13 Estimate the relationship between monthly electrical power usage (Y) and home size (X) using the data in the file P11_13.XLS. Interpret your computer-generated results. How well does a simple linear regression model explain the variation in monthly electrical power usage?

14 The *ACCRA Cost of Living Index* provides a useful and reasonably accurate measure of cost of living differences among a large number of urban areas. Items on which the index is based have been carefully chosen to reflect the different categories of consumer expenditures. The data are in the file P2_19.XLS. Use the given data to estimate simple linear regression models to explore the relationship between the composite index (i.e., response variable) and each of the various expenditure components (i.e., explanatory variable).

    a Which expenditure component has the *strongest* linear relationship with the composite index?

    b Which expenditure component has the *weakest* linear relationship with the composite index?

15 The management of Beta Technologies, Inc., is trying to determine the variable that best explains the variation of employee salaries using a sample of 52 full-time employees in the file P2_1.XLS. Estimate simple linear regression models to identify which of the following has the *strongest* linear relationship with annual salary: the employee's gender, age, number of years of relevant work experience prior to employment at Beta, number of years of employment at Beta, or number of years of post-secondary education. Provide support for your conclusion. ∎

Multiple Regression

In general, there are two possible approaches to obtaining improved fits. The first is to examine a scatterplot of residuals for nonlinear patterns and then make appropriate modifications to the regression equation. We will discuss this approach later in this chapter. The second approach is much more straightforward—we simply add more explanatory variables to the regression equation. In the Bendrix manufacturing example we deliberately included only a single explanatory variable in the equation at a time so that we could keep the equations simple. But because scatterplots indicate that both explanatory variables are also related to Overhead, we ought to try including both in the regression equation. With any luck, the linear fit should improve.

When several explanatory variables are included in the equation, we move into the realm of multiple regression, so there are a few new ideas. First, assuming there are only two explanatory variables, the line we are fitting to the data is really a *plane* in three-dimensional space. There is one dimension for the response variable and one for each explanatory variable. Although we can imagine a flat plane passing through a swarm of points, it is difficult to graph this on a two-dimensional screen. If there are more than two explanatory variables, then we can only imagine the regression plane; drawing in four dimensions (or higher dimensions) is impossible. Nevertheless, it is still possible to find the least squares regression equation numerically. It is still the equation that minimizes the sum of squared residuals, and it is calculated by most statistical packages, including StatPro.

11.5.1 Interpretation of Regression Coefficients

If Y is the response variable and X_1 through X_k are the explanatory variables, then a typical multiple regression equation has the form

$$Y = a + b_1X_1 + b_2X_2 + \cdots + b_kX_k \tag{11.8}$$

Here, a is again the Y-intercept, and b_1 through b_k are the slopes. Collectively, we refer to a and the b's in equation (11.8) as the **regression coefficients**. The intercept a is the expected value of Y when all of the X's equal 0. Of course, this makes sense only if it is practical for all of the X's to equal 0. Each slope coefficient is the expected change in Y when this particular X increases by one unit and the other X's in the equation remain constant. For example, b_1 is the expected change in Y when X_1 increases by one unit and the other X's in the equation, X_2 through X_k, remain constant.

This extra proviso, "when the other X's in the equation remain constant," is very important for the interpretation of the regression coefficients. In particular, it means that the estimates of the b's depend on which other X's are included in the regression equation. We illustrate these ideas in the following continuation of the Bendrix manufacturing example.

E X A M P L E   1 1 . 2   [C O N T I N U E D]

Estimate and interpret the equation for Overhead when both explanatory variables, MachHrs and ProdRuns, are included in the regression equation.

Solution

Unlike the situation with simple regression, we do not even attempt to provide formulas for the regression coefficients in multiple regression. These require matrix algebra and are best left for a more technical course. Instead, we rely on computer software such as the StatPro add-in. To obtain the output, we use the StatPro/Regression Analysis/Multiple menu item, select Overhead as the response (dependent) variable, and select MachHrs and ProdRuns as the explanatory (independent) variables. The dialog box shown in Figure 11.20 then gives us options of which scatterplots to obtain and whether we want columns of fitted values and residuals placed next to the data set. We filled it in as shown in the figure, selecting scatterplots of the fitted values versus the observed values and residuals versus fitted values, and requesting columns of fitted values and residuals.

The main regression output appears in Figure 11.21. The coefficients in the range C16:C18 indicate that the estimated regression equation is

$$\text{Predicted Overhead} = 3997 + 43.54\text{MachHrs} + 883.62\text{ProdRuns} \tag{11.9}$$

FIGURE 11.20 **Dialog Box of Options with Multiple Regression Procedure**

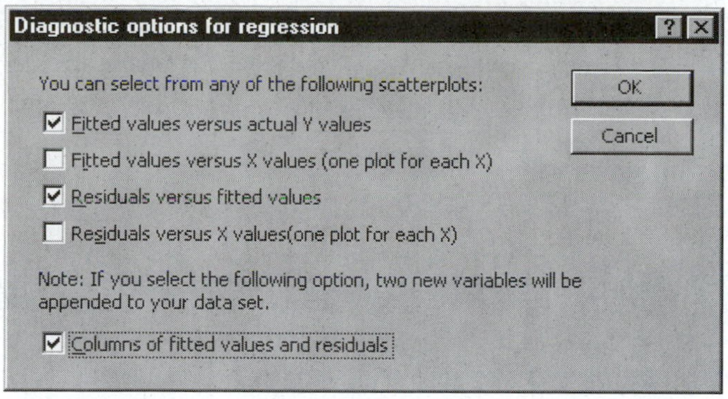

FIGURE 11.21 **Multiple Regression Output for Bendrix Example**

	A	B	C	D	E	F	G
1	Results of multiple regression for Overhead						
2							
3	Summary measures						
4		Multiple R	0.9308				
5		R-Square	0.8664				
6		Adj R-Square	0.8583				
7		StErr of Est	4108.9932				
8							
9	ANOVA Table						
10		Source	df	SS	MS	F	p-value
11		Explained	2	3614020652.0000	1807010326.0000	107.0261	0.0000
12		Unexplained	33	557166208.0000	16883824.4848		
13							
14	Regression coefficients						
15			Coefficient	Std Err	t-value	p-value	
16		Constant	3996.6782	6603.6509	0.6052	0.5492	
17		MachHrs	43.5364	3.5895	12.1289	0.0000	
18		ProdRuns	883.6179	82.2514	10.7429	0.0000	

The interpretation of equation (11.9) is that if the number of production runs is held constant, then the overhead cost is expected to increase by $43.54 for each extra machine hour, and if the number of machine hours is held constant, the overhead cost is expected to increase by $883.62 for each extra production run. The Bendrix manager can interpret the intercept, $3997, as the fixed component of overhead. The slope terms involving MachHrs and ProdRuns are the variable components of overhead.

It is interesting to compare equation (11.9) with the separate equations for Overhead involving only a single variable each. From the previous section these are

$$\text{Predicted Overhead} = 48{,}621 + 34.7 \text{MachHrs}$$

and

$$\text{Predicted Overhead} = 75{,}606 + 655.1 \text{ProdRuns}$$

Note that the coefficient of MachHrs has increased from 34.7 to 43.5 and the coefficient of ProdRuns has increased from 655.1 to 883.6. Also, the intercept is now lower than either intercept in the single-variable equations. In general, it is difficult to guess the changes that will occur when we introduce more explanatory variables into the equation, but it is likely that changes will occur.

The reasoning is that when MachHrs is the only variable in the equation, we are obviously *not* holding ProdRuns constant—we are ignoring it—so in effect the coefficient 34.7 of MachHrs indicates the effect of MachHrs *and* the omitted ProdRuns on Overhead. But when we include both variables, then the coefficient 43.5 of MachHrs indicates the effect of MachHrs only, holding ProdRuns constant. Because the coefficients of MachHrs in the two equations have different *meanings*, it is not surprising that we obtain different numerical estimates of them. ■

11.5.2 Interpretation of Standard Error of Estimate and R-Square

The multiple regression output in Figure 11.21 is very similar to simple regression output.[7] In particular, cells C5 and C7 again show R^2 and the standard error of estimate s_e. Also, the square root of R^2 appears in cell C4. We interpret these quantities almost exactly as in simple regression. The standard error of estimate is essentially the standard deviation of residuals, but it is now given by the formula

$$s_e = \sqrt{\frac{\sum e_i^2}{n-3}}$$

That is, the denominator is now $n-3$. In general, we subtract the number of regression coefficients from the sample size to obtain this denominator.

However, we interpret s_e exactly as before. It is a measure of the prediction error we are likely to make when we use the multiple regression equation to predict the response variable. In this example about 2/3 of the predictions should be within one standard error, or $4109, of the actual overhead cost. By comparing this with the standard errors from the single-variable equations for Overhead, $8585 and $9457, we see that the multiple regression equation is likely to provide predictions that are more than twice as accurate as the single-variable equations—quite an improvement!

The R^2 value is again the percentage of variation of the response variable explained by the combined set of explanatory variables. In fact, it even has the same formula as before [see equation (11.7)]. For the Bendrix data we see that MachHrs and ProdRuns combine to explain 86.6% of the variation in Overhead. This is a big improvement over the single-variable equations that were able to explain only 39.9% and 27.1% of the variation in Overhead. Remarkably, the combination of the two explanatory variables explains a larger percentage than the *sum* of their individual effects. This is not common, but as this example shows, it is possible.[8]

The square root of R^2 shown in cell C4 is again the correlation between the fitted values and the observed values of the response variable. For the Bendrix data the correlation between them is 0.931, quite high. A graphical indication of this high correlation can be seen in one of the scatterplots we requested, the plot of fitted versus observed values of Overhead. This scatterplot appears in Figure 11.22. If the regression equation gave *perfect* predictions, then all of the points in this plot would lie on a 45-degree line—each fitted value would *equal* the corresponding observed value. Although a perfect fit virtually never occurs, the closer the points are to a 45-degree line, the better the fit is, as indicated by R^2 or its square root.

---

[7] One difference, however, is that the StatPro multiple regression output is not linked to the data by formulas. If the data change, you must rerun the Multiple Regression procedure to update the output.

[8] It is so uncommon, in fact, that none of the authors realized that it could occur. However, we checked our figures—there are no errors in the calculations!

FIGURE 11.22 **Scatterplot of Fitted Values versus Observed Values of Overhead**

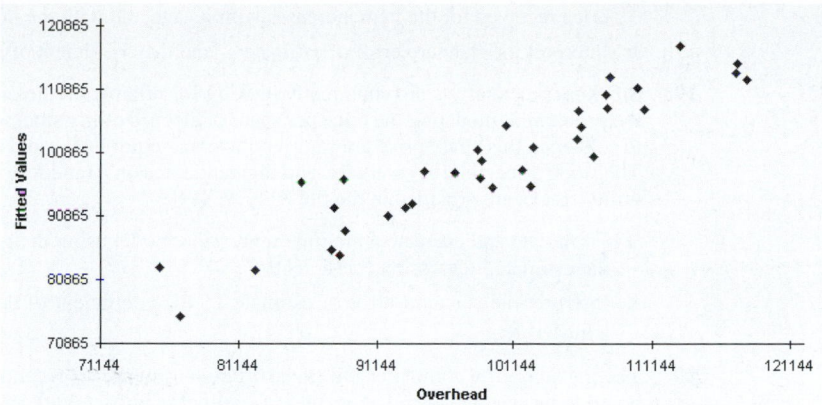

Although the R^2 value is one of the most frequently quoted values from a regression analysis, it does have one serious drawback—it can only *increase* when extra explanatory variables are added to an equation. This can lead to "fishing expeditions," where we keep adding variables to an equation, some of which have no conceptual relationship to the response variable, just to inflate the R^2 value. To "penalize" the addition of extra variables that do not really belong, an **adjusted** R^2 value is typically listed in regression outputs. This adjusted value appears in cell C6 of Figure 11.21. Although it has no direct interpretation as "percentage of variation explained," it *can* decrease when extra explanatory variables that do not really belong are added to an equation. Therefore, it is a useful index that we can monitor. If we add variables and the adjusted R^2 *decreases*, then the extra variables are essentially not pulling their weight and should probably be omitted. We will have much more to say about the issue of which variables to include in the next chapter.

PROBLEMS

Level A

16   A trucking company wants to predict the yearly maintenance expense (Y) for a truck using the number of miles driven during the year (X_1) and the age of the truck (X_2, in years) at the beginning of the year. The company has gathered the data given in the file P11_16.XLS. Note that each observation corresponds to a particular truck.

 a   Formulate and estimate a multiple regression model using the given data. Interpret each of the estimated regression coefficients.

 b   Compute and interpret the standard error of estimate s_e and the coefficient of determination R^2 for these data.

17   DataPro is a small but rapidly growing firm that provides electronic data-processing services to commercial firms, hospitals, and other organizations. For each of the past 12 months, DataPro has tracked the number of contracts sold, the average contract price, advertising expenditures, and personal selling expenditures. These data are provided in P11_17.XLS. Assuming that the number of contracts sold is the response variable, estimate a multiple regression model with three explanatory variables. Interpret each of the estimated regression coefficients and the coefficient of determination R^2.

18   An antique collector believes that the price received for a particular item increases with its age and with the number of bidders. The file P11_18.XLS contains data on these three variables for 32 recently auctioned comparable items.

a Formulate and estimate a multiple regression model using the given data. Interpret each of the estimated regression coefficients. Is the antique collector correct in believing that the price received for the item increases with its age and with the number of bidders?

b Interpret the standard error of estimate s_e and the coefficient of determination R^2.

19 Stock market analysts are continually looking for reliable predictors of stock prices. Consider the problem of modeling the price per share of electric utility stocks (Y). Two variables thought to influence this stock price are return on average equity (X_1) and annual dividend rate (X_2). The stock price, returns on equity, and dividend rates on a randomly selected day for 16 electric utility stocks are provided in the file P11_19.XLS.

a Formulate and estimate a multiple regression model using the given data. Interpret each of the estimated regression coefficients.

b Interpret the standard error of estimate s_e, the coefficient of determination R^2, and the adjusted R^2.

20 The manager of a commuter rail transportation system was recently asked by her governing board to determine which factors have a significant impact on the demand for rides in the large city served by the transportation network. The system manager has collected data on variables thought to be possibly related to the number of weekly riders on the city's rail system. The file P11_20.XLS contain these data.

a What are the expected signs of the coefficients of the explanatory variables in this multiple regression model? Provide reasoning for each of your stated expectations. (Answer this *before* using regression.)

b Formulate and estimate a multiple regression model using the given data. Interpret each of the estimated regression coefficients. Are the signs of the estimated coefficients consistent with your expectations as stated in part **a**?

c What proportion of the total variation in the number of weekly riders is *not* explained by this estimated multiple regression model?

21 Consider the enrollment data for *Business Week*'s top 50 U.S. graduate business programs in the file P2_3.XLS. Use these data to estimate a multiple regression model to assess whether there is a systematic relationship between the total number of full-time students and the following explanatory variables: (i) the proportion of female students, (ii) the proportion of minority students, and (iii) the proportion of international students enrolled at these distinguished business schools.

a Interpret the coefficients of your estimated regression model. Do any of these results surprise you? Explain.

b How well does your estimated regression model fit the given data?

22 David Savageau and Geoffrey Loftus, the authors of *Places Rated Almanac* (published in 1997 by Macmillan) have ranked 325 metropolitan areas in the United States with consideration of the following aspects of life in each area: cost of living, transportation, jobs, education, climate, crime, arts, health, and recreation. The data are in the file P2_55.XLS.

a Use multiple regression analysis to explore the relationship between the metropolitan area's overall score and the set of potential explanatory variables.

b Interpret each of the estimated coefficients in the regression model. Are the signs of the estimated coefficients consistent with your expectations? If not, can you explain any discrepancies between your findings and expectations?

c Does the given set of explanatory variables do a good job of explaining changes in the overall score? Explain why or why not.

Level B

23 The owner of a restaurant in Bloomington, Indiana, has recorded sales data for the past 19 years. He has also recorded data on potentially relevant variables. The entire data set appears in the file P11_23.XLS.

a Estimate a simple linear regression model involving annual sales (the explanatory variable) and the size of the population residing within 10 miles of the restaurant (the explanatory variable). Interpret R^2.

b Add another explanatory variable—annual advertising expenditures—to the regression model in part **a**. Estimate and interpret this expanded model. How does the R^2 value for this multiple regression model compare to that of the simple regression model estimated in part **a**? Explain any difference between the two R^2 values. Compute and interpret the *adjusted* R^2 value for the revised model.

c Add one more explanatory variable to the multiple regression model estimated in part **b**. In particular, estimate and interpret the coefficients of a multiple regression model that includes the *previous* year's advertising expenditure. How does the inclusion of this third explanatory variable affect the R^2 and adjusted R^2 values, in comparison to the corresponding values for the model of part **b**? Explain any changes in these values.

24 A regional express delivery service company recently conducted a study to investigate the relationship between the cost of shipping a package (Y), the package weight (X_1), and the distance shipped (X_2). Twenty packages were randomly selected from among the large number received for shipment, and a detailed analysis of the shipping cost was conducted for each package. These sample observations are given in the file P11_24.XLS.

a Estimate a simple linear regression model involving shipping cost and package weight. Interpret the slope coefficient of the least squares line as well as the computed value of R^2.

b Add another explanatory variable—distance shipped—to the regression model in part **a**. Estimate and interpret this expanded model. How does the R^2 value for this multiple regression model compare to that of the simple regression model estimated in part **a**? Explain any difference between the two R^2 values. Compute and interpret the *adjusted* R^2 value for the revised model.

25 Using the sample data given in the file P11_10.XLS, formulate a multiple regression model to predict the sales price of houses in a given community.

a Add one explanatory variable at a time and estimate each partial regression equation. Report and explain changes in the standard error of estimate s_e, the coefficient of determination R^2, and the adjusted R^2 as each explanatory variable is added to the model.

b Interpret each of the estimated regression coefficients in the full model.

c What proportion of the total variation in the sales price is explained by the multiple regression model that includes all four explanatory variables? ■

Modeling Possibilities

Once we move from simple to multiple regression, the floodgates open. All types of explanatory variables are potential candidates for inclusion in the regression equation. In this section we will examine several new types of explanatory variables. These include "dummy" variables, interaction terms, and nonlinear transformations. The techniques in this section provide us with many alternative approaches to modeling the relationship between a response variable and potential explanatory variables. In many applications these techniques produce much better fits than we could obtain without them.

As the title of this section suggests, these techniques are modeling *possibilities*. They provide a wide variety of explanatory variables to choose from. However, this does not mean that it is wise to include all or even many of these new types of explanatory variables in any particular regression equation. The chances are that only a few, if any, will significantly improve the linear fit. Knowing which explanatory variables to include requires a great deal of practical experience with regression, as well as a thorough understanding of the particular problem to be solved. The material in this section should *not* be an excuse for a mindless fishing expedition.

11.6.1 Dummy Variables

Some potential explanatory variables are categorical and cannot be measured on a quantitative scale. However, these categorical variables are often related to the response variable, so we need a way to include them in a regression equation. The trick is to use **dummy** variables, also called **indicator** or **0–1** variables. Dummy variables are variables that indicate the category a given observation is in. If a dummy variable for a given category equals 1, the observation is in that category; if it equals 0, the observation is not in that category.

There are basically two situations. The first and perhaps most common situation is when a categorical variable has only two categories. A good example of this is a "gender" variable that has the two categories "male" and "female." In this case we need only a *single* dummy variable, and we have the choice of assigning the 1's to either category. If we label the dummy variable Gender, then we can code Gender as 1 for males and 0 for females, or we can code Gender as 1 for females and 0 for males. We just need to be consistent and specify explicitly which coding scheme we are using.

The other situation is when there are more than two categories. A good example of this is when we have quarterly time series data and we want to treat the quarter of the year as a categorical variable with four categories, 1–4. Then we can create four dummy variables, Q1–Q4. For example, Q2 equals 1 for all second-quarter observations and equals 0 for all other observations. Although we can create four dummy variables, we will see that only three of them—*any* three—should be used in a regression equation.

The following example illustrates how we form, use, and interpret dummy variables in regression analysis.

EXAMPLE 11.3

The Fifth National Bank of Springfield is facing a gender discrimination suit.[9] The charge is that its female employees receive substantially smaller salaries than its male employees. The bank's employee database is listed in the file BANK.XLS. For each of its 208 employees, the data set includes the following variables:

- EducLev: education level, a categorical variable with categories 1 (finished high school), 2 (finished some college courses), 3 (obtained a bachelor's degree), 4 (took some graduate courses), 5 (obtained a graduate degree)

- JobGrade: a categorical variable indicating the current job level, the possible levels being 1–6 (6 is highest)

- YrHired: year employee was hired

- YrBorn: year employee was born

- Gender: a categorical variable with values "Female" and "Male"

- YrsPrior: number of years of work experience at another bank prior to working at Fifth National

- PCJob: a dummy variable with value 1 if the employee's current job is computer-related and value 0 otherwise

- Salary: current annual salary in thousands of dollars

Figure 11.23 lists a few of the observations. Do these data provide evidence that females are discriminated against in terms of salary?

---

[9]This example and the accompanying data set are based on a real case. Only the bank's name has been changed.

FIGURE 11.23 **Selected Data for Bank Example**

	A	B	C	D	E	F	G	H	I
1	Bank salary data								
2									
3	Employee	EducLev	JobGrade	YrHired	YrBorn	Gender	YrsPrior	PCJob	Salary
4	1	3	1	92	69	Male	1	No	32
5	2	1	1	81	57	Female	1	No	39.1
6	3	1	1	83	60	Female	0	No	33.2
7	4	2	1	87	55	Female	7	No	30.6
8	5	3	1	92	67	Male	0	No	29
9	6	3	1	92	71	Female	0	No	30.5
10	7	3	1	91	68	Female	0	No	30
11	8	3	1	87	62	Male	2	No	27
12	9	1	1	91	33	Female	0	No	34
13	10	3	1	86	64	Female	0	No	29.5
209	206	5	6	63	33	Male	0	No	88
210	207	5	6	60	36	Male	0	No	94
211	208	5	6	62	33	Female	0	No	30

Solution

A naive approach to this problem compares the average female salary to the average male salary. This can be done with a pivot table, as in Chapter 2, or with a more formal hypothesis test, as in Chapter 9. Using these methods, we find that the average of all salaries is $39,922, the female average is $37,210, the male average is $45,505, and the difference between the male and female averages is statistically significant at any reasonable level of significance. The females are definitely earning less, but perhaps there is a reason for this. They might have lower education levels, they might have been hired more recently, they might be working at lower job grades, and so on. The question is whether the difference between female and male salaries is still evident after taking these other attributes into account. This is a perfect task for regression.

We first need to create dummy variables for the various categorical variables. We can do this manually with IF functions or we can use StatPro's Dummy Variable procedure. To do it manually, we can create a dummy variable Female based on Gender in column J by entering the formula

$$=IF(F4=\text{"Female"},1,0)$$

in cell J4 and copying it down. Note that we are coding the females as 1's and the males as 0's. (The quotes are necessary when a nonnumerical value is used in an IF function.)

StatPro's Dummy Variable procedure is somewhat easier, especially when there are multiple categories. For example, to create five dummies, Ed_1–Ed_5, for each of the education levels, we can use the StatPro/Data Utilities/Create Dummy Variables menu item, select the "Create several dummies from a categorical variable" option, select the EducLev variable to base the dummies on, and (after the dummies have been created) change their default names to Ed_1–Ed_5. This procedure simply enters IF functions in the dummy cells, exactly as we would do manually. We can follow the same procedure to create six dummies, Job_1–Job_6, for the job grade categories.

Sometimes we might want to collapse several categories. For example, we might want to collapse the five education categories into three categories: 1, (2,3), and (4,5). The new second category includes employees who have taken undergraduate courses or have completed a bachelor's degree, and the new third category includes employees who have taken graduate courses or have completed a graduate degree. It is easy to do this. We simply add the Ed_2 and Ed_3 columns to get the dummy for the new second category, and similarly add the Ed_4 and Ed_5 columns for the new third category.

Once the dummies have been created, we can run a regression analysis with Salary as the response variable, using any combination of numerical and dummy explanatory variables. However, there are two rules we must follow:

- We shouldn't use any of the *original* categorical variables, such as EducLev, that the dummies are based on.
- We should use *one less dummy* than the number of categories for any categorical variable.

This second rule is a technical one. If we violate it, the statistical software will give us an error message. For example, if we want to use education level as an explanatory variable, we should enter only five of the six dummies Ed_1–Ed_6. *Any* five of these can be used. The omitted dummy then corresponds to the **reference** category. As we will see, the interpretation of the dummy variable coefficients are all relevant to this reference category. When there are only two categories, as with the gender variable, we typically name the variable with the category, such as Female, that corresponds to the 1's. If we create the dummy variables manually, we probably do not even bother to create a Male dummy. In this case "Male" automatically becomes the reference category.

To get used to dummy variables in regression, we will proceed in several stages in this example. We first estimate a regression equation with only one explanatory variable, Female. The output appears in Figure 11.24. The resulting equation is

$$\text{Predicted Salary} = 45.505 - 8.296\text{Female} \qquad \textbf{(11.10)}$$

To interpret this equation, recall that Female has only two possible values, 0 and 1. If we substitute Female=1 into equation (11.10), we obtain

$$\text{Predicted Salary} = 45.505 - 8.296(1) = 37.209$$

Since Female=1 corresponds to females, this equation simply indicates the average female salary. Similarly, if we substitute Female=0 into equation (11.10), we obtain

$$\text{Predicted Salary} = 45.505 - 8.296(0) = 45.505$$

Since Female=0 corresponds to males, this equation indicates the average male salary. Therefore, the interpretation of the -8.296 coefficient of the Female dummy variable is straightforward. It is the average female salary relative to the reference (male) category—females get paid $8296 less on average than males.

Obviously, equation (11.10) tells only part of the story. It ignores all information except for gender. We expand this equation by adding the experience variables YrsPrior and YrsExper, where YrsExper is years of experience with Fifth National and is calculated in a new column as 95 minus YrHired. (Remember that the data are from 1995.) The output with the Female dummy variable and these two experience variables appears in Figure 11.25. The corresponding regression equation is

$$\text{Predicted Salary} = 35.492 + 0.988\text{YrsExper} + 0.131\text{YrsPrior} - 8.080\text{Female} \quad \textbf{(11.11)}$$

It is again useful to write equation (11.11) in two forms: one for females (substituting Female=1) and one for males (substituting Female=0). After doing the arithmetic, they become

$$\text{Predicted Salary} = 27.412 + 0.988\text{YrsExper} + 0.131\text{YrsPrior}$$

and

$$\text{Predicted Salary} = 35.492 + 0.988\text{YrsExper} + 0.131\text{YrsPrior}$$

Except for the intercept term, these equations are identical. We can now interpret the coefficient -8.080 of the Female dummy variable as the average salary disadvantage for

FIGURE 11.24 **Output for Bank Example with a Single Explanatory Variable**

	A	B	C	D	E	F	G
1	*Results of multiple regression for Salary*						
2							
3	*Summary measures*						
4		Multiple R	0.3465				
5		R-Square	0.1201				
6		Adj R-Squar	0.1158				
7		StErr of Est	10.5843				
8							
9	*ANOVA Table*						
10		Source	df	SS	MS	F	p-value
11		Explained	1	3149.6346	3149.6346	28.1151	0.0000
12		Unexplained	206	23077.4727	112.0266		
13							
14	*Regression coefficients*						
15			Coefficient	Std Err	t-value	p-value	
16		Constant	45.5054	1.2835	35.4534	0.0000	
17		Female	-8.2955	1.5645	-5.3024	0.0000	

FIGURE 11.25 **Regression Output with Two Numerical Explanatory Variables Included**

	A	B	C	D	E	F	G
1	*Results of multiple regression for Salary*						
2							
3	*Summary measures*						
4		Multiple R	0.7016				
5		R-Square	0.4923				
6		Adj R-Squar	0.4848				
7		StErr of Est	8.0794				
8							
9	*ANOVA Table*						
10		Source	df	SS	MS	F	p-value
11		Explained	3	12910.6678	4303.5559	65.9279	0.0000
12		Unexplained	204	13316.4395	65.2767		
13							
14	*Regression coefficients*						
15			Coefficient	Std Err	t-value	p-value	
16		Constant	35.4917	1.3410	26.4661	0.0000	
17		YrsPrior	0.1313	0.1809	0.7259	0.4687	
18		Female	-8.0802	1.1982	-6.7438	0.0000	
19		YrsExper	0.9880	0.0809	12.2083	0.0000	

females relative to males *after controlling for job experience*. Gender discrimination still appears to be a very plausible conclusion. However, note that the R^2 value is only 49.2%. Perhaps there is still more of the story to tell.

We next add job grade to the equation by including five of the six job grade dummies. Although *any* five could be used, we use Job_2–Job_6, so that the lowest level becomes the reference category. The resulting output appears in Figure 11.26. The estimated regression equation is now

$$\text{Predicted Salary} = 30.230 + 0.408\text{YrsExper} + 0.149\text{YrsPrior} - 1.962\text{Female}$$
$$+2.575\text{Job\_2} + 6.295\text{Job\_3} + 10.475\text{Job\_4}$$
$$+16.011\text{Job\_5} + 27.647\text{Job\_6} \hspace{2cm} \textbf{(11.12)}$$

FIGURE 11.26 **Regression Output with Job Grade Dummies Included**

	A	B	C	D	E	F	G
1	*Results of multiple regression for Salary*						
2							
3	*Summary measures*						
4		Multiple R	0.8616				
5		R-Square	0.7423				
6		Adj R-Squar	0.7320				
7		StErr of Est	5.8275				
8							
9	*ANOVA Table*						
10		Source	df	SS	MS	F	p-value
11		Explained	8	19469.1336	2433.6417	71.6627	0.0000
12		Unexplained	199	6757.9736	33.9597		
13							
14	*Regression coefficients*						
15			Coefficient	Std Err	t-value	p-value	
16		Constant	30.2296	1.1730	25.7705	0.0000	
17		YrsPrior	0.1489	0.1320	1.1286	0.2604	
18		Female	-1.9622	1.0051	-1.9523	0.0523	
19		Job_2	2.5753	1.1821	2.1786	0.0305	
20		Job_3	6.2947	1.1703	5.3786	0.0000	
21		Job_4	10.4745	1.3676	7.6588	0.0000	
22		Job_5	16.0114	1.5593	10.2681	0.0000	
23		Job_6	27.6472	2.4176	11.4357	0.0000	
24		YrsExper	0.4084	0.0778	5.2522	0.0000	

Now there are two categorical variables involved, gender and job grade. However, we can still write a separate equation *for any combination* of categories by setting the dummies to the appropriate values. For example, the equation for females at the fifth job grade is found by setting Female=1 and Job_5=1, and setting the other job dummies equal to 0. After terms are combined, this equation is

$$\text{Predicted Salary} = 44.279 + 0.408\text{YrsExper} + 0.150\text{YrsPrior}$$

The intercept 44.279 is the intercept from equation (11.12), 30.230, plus the coefficients of Female and Job_5.

We can interpret equation (11.12) as follows. For either gender and any job grade, the expected increase in salary for one extra year of experience with Fifth National is $408; the expected increase in salary for one extra year of prior experience with another bank is $149. The coefficients of the job dummies indicate the average increase in salary an employee can expect relative to the reference (lowest) job grade. For example, an employee in job grade 4 can expect to earn $10,475 more than an employee in job grade 1, given that they have the same experience levels and are of the same gender. Finally, the key coefficient, the negative $1962 for females, indicates the average salary disadvantage for females relative to males, given that they have the same experience levels *and* are in the same job grade. Note that the R^2 value is now 74.2%, quite a bit larger than the R^2 value from equation (11.11). We appear to be getting closer to the "truth."

Although the "penalty" for females in equation (11.12) is still substantial, it is less than a fourth of the penalty we saw in equations (11.10) and (11.11). It appears that females might be getting paid less on average partly because they are in the lower job categories. We can check whether females are disproportionately in the lower job categories with a pivot table. We use Excel's pivot table tool, putting JobGrade in the row area, Gender in the column area and the count of *any* variable in the data area. If we express counts as percentages of the columns, we obtain the pivot table in Figure 11.27.

FIGURE 11.27   **Pivot Table of Job Grade Counts for Bank Data**

	A	B	C	D
1	Count	Gender		
2	JobGrade	Female	Male	Grand Total
3	1	34.29%	17.65%	28.85%
4	2	20.71%	19.12%	20.19%
5	3	25.71%	10.29%	20.67%
6	4	12.14%	16.18%	13.46%
7	5	6.43%	17.65%	10.10%
8	6	0.71%	19.12%	6.73%
9	Grand Total	100.00%	100.00%	100.00%

Clearly, females tend to be concentrated at the lower job grades. For example, 28.85% of all employees are at the lowest job grade, but 34.29% of all females are at this grade and only 17.65% of males are at this grade. The opposite is true at the higher job grades. This certainly helps to explain why females get lower salaries on average, but it doesn't explain why females are at the lower job grades in the first place. We won't be able to provide a thorough analysis of this issue, but we will add one more piece to the puzzle—for now—by adding education level (using the dummies Ed_2–Ed_5), age (calculated as 95 minus YrBorn), and PCJob to equation (11.12). The resulting output appears in Figure 11.28. We do not list the full equation here, but the coefficients can be seen from the output. This equation doesn't appear to add much to equation (11.12). The R^2 value has increased only slightly to 76.5%, and the adjusted R^2 value has barely increased at all. The penalty for being a female, $2555, is now slightly greater than its previous value of $1962.

At face value we can interpret the coefficients of the education dummies in this expanded equation as the benefit (or loss, if negative) of extra education relative to a high school diploma, the reference category. For example, the benefit of a bachelor's degree over a high school diploma is $528, given that all the other variables in the equation are held constant. However, for reasons we will discuss in the next chapter, the coefficients of the education dummies Ed_2–Ed_4 are not very stable estimates, and we shouldn't put too much faith in them. The coefficient of PCJob implies that an employee with a computer-related job can expect an extra $4923 in salary relative to an employee without a computer-related job, provided that the other variables in the equation are the same for both employees. The Age coefficient is quite small and indicates that age has little effect—in addition to the effects of the other variables—on salary.

The main conclusion we can draw from the output in Figure 11.28 (page 598) is that there is still a plausible case to be made for discrimination against females, even after including information on all of the variables in the database in the regression equation. We'll conclude this example for now, but there is still more we will say about it in the next two sections.

FIGURE 11.28 Regression Output with Other Variables Added

	A	B	C	D	E	F	G
1	*Results of multiple regression for Salary*						
2							
3	*Summary measures*						
4		Multiple R	0.8748				
5		R-Square	0.7652				
6		Adj R-Squar	0.7482				
7		StErr of Est	5.6481				
8							
9	*ANOVA Table*						
10		Source	df	SS	MS	F	p-value
11		Explained	14	20070.2508	1433.5893	44.9390	0.0000
12		Unexplained	193	6156.8564	31.9008		
13							
14	*Regression coefficients*						
15			Coefficient	Std Err	t-value	p-value	
16		Constant	29.6899	2.4900	11.9236	0.0000	
17		YrsPrior	0.1677	0.1404	1.1943	0.2338	
18		PCJob	4.9228	1.4738	3.3402	0.0010	
19		Female	-2.5545	1.0120	-2.5242	0.0124	
20		Ed_2	-0.4856	1.3987	-0.3472	0.7289	
21		Ed_3	0.5279	1.3575	0.3889	0.6978	
22		Ed_4	0.2852	2.4047	0.1186	0.9057	
23		Ed_5	2.6908	1.6209	1.6601	0.0985	
24		Job_2	1.5645	1.1858	1.3194	0.1886	
25		Job_3	5.2194	1.2624	4.1345	0.0001	
26		Job_4	8.5948	1.4960	5.7451	0.0000	
27		Job_5	13.6594	1.8743	7.2879	0.0000	
28		Job_6	23.8324	2.7999	8.5119	0.0000	
29		YrsExper	0.5156	0.0980	5.2621	0.0000	
30		Age	-0.0090	0.0577	-0.1553	0.8767	

11.6.2 Interaction Terms

Suppose that we regress a variable Y on a numerical variable X and a dummy variable D. If the estimated equation is of the form

$$\widehat{Y} = a + b_1 X + b_2 D \tag{11.13}$$

then, as in previous section, we can break this equation down into two separate equations:

$$\widehat{Y} = (a + b_2) + b_1 X$$

and

$$\widehat{Y} = a + b_1 X$$

The first corresponds to $D = 1$, and the second corresponds to $D = 0$. The only difference between these two equations is the intercept term; the slope for each is b_1. Geometrically, they correspond to two *parallel* lines that are a distance b_2 apart. For example, if D corresponds to gender, then there is a female line and a parallel male line. The effect of X on Y is the same for females and males. When X increases by one unit, we predict Y to change by b_1 units for males or females.

In effect, when we include *only* a dummy variable in a regression equation, as in equation (11.13), we are allowing the intercepts of the two lines to differ (by an amount b_2), but we are *forcing* the lines to be parallel. Sometimes we want to allow them to have different slopes, in addition to possibly different intercepts. We can do this with an **interaction** variable. Algebraically, an interaction variable is the *product* of two variables. Its effect is to allow the effect of one of the variables on Y to depend on the value of the other variable.

Suppose we create the interaction variable XD (the product of X and D) and then estimate the equation

$$\widehat{Y} = a + b_1 X + b_2 D + b_3 XD$$

As usual, we rewrite this equation as two separate equations, depending on whether $D = 0$ or $D = 1$. If $D = 1$, we combine terms to write

$$\widehat{Y} = (a + b_2) + (b_1 + b_3)X$$

If $D = 0$, the dummy and interaction terms drop out and we obtain

$$\widehat{Y} = a + b_1 X$$

The notation is not important. The important part is that the interaction term, $b_3 XD$, allows the slope of the regression line to differ between the two categories.

The following continuation of the bank discrimination example illustrates one possible use of interaction variables.

EXAMPLE 11.3 [CONTINUED]

Earlier we estimated an equation for Salary using the numerical explanatory variables YrsExper and YrsPrior and the dummy variable Female. If we drop the YrsPrior variable from this equation (for simplicity) and rerun the regression, we obtain the equation

$$\text{Predicted Salary} = 35.824 + 0.981\,\text{YrsExper} - 8.012\,\text{Female} \qquad \textbf{(11.14)}$$

The R^2 value for this equation is 49.1%. If we decide to include an interaction variable between YrsExper and Female in this equation, what is its effect?

Solution

We first need to form an interaction variable that is the product of YrsExper and Female. This can be done in two ways in Excel. We can do it manually by introducing a new variable that contains the product of the two variables involved, or we can use the StatPro/Data Utilities/Create Interaction Variable(s) menu item. For the latter, we select Female and YrsExper as the variables to be used to create an interaction variable, and we do not check either of the boxes in the next dialog box—we do *not* want either to be treated as a categorical variable.[10]

Once the interaction variable has been created, we include it in the regression equation in addition to the other variables in equation (11.14). The multiple regression output appears in Figure 11.29 (page 600). The estimated regression equation is

$$\text{Predicted Salary} = 30.430 + 1.528\,\text{YrsExper} + 4.098\,\text{Female}$$

$$-1.248\,\text{YrsExper\_Female}$$

(where YrsExper_Female is StatPro's default name for the interaction variable). As in the

---

[10]See the online help in StatPro for this data utility. It explains the options for creating interaction variables.

FIGURE 11.29 **Regression Output with an Interaction Variable**

	A	B	C	D	E	F	G
1	*Results of multiple regression for Salary*						
2							
3	*Summary measures*						
4		Multiple R	0.7991				
5		R-Square	0.6386				
6		Adj R-Square	0.6333				
7		StErr of Est	6.8163				
8							
9	*ANOVA Table*						
10		Source	df	SS	MS	F	p-value
11		Explained	3	16748.8748	5582.9583	120.1620	0.0000
12		Unexplained	204	9478.2324	46.4619		
13							
14	*Regression coefficients*						
15			Coefficient	Std Err	t-value	p-value	
16		Constant	30.4300	1.2166	25.0129	0.0000	
17		Female	4.0983	1.6658	2.4602	0.0147	
18		YrsExper	1.5278	0.0905	16.8887	0.0000	
19		Female_YrsExp	-1.2478	0.1367	-9.1296	0.0000	

general discussion, it is useful to write this as two separate equations, one for females and one for males. The female equation (Female=1) is

$$\text{Predicted Salary} = (30.430 + 4.098) + (1.528 - 1.248)\text{YrsExper}$$

$$= 34.528 + 0.280\text{YrsExper}$$

and the male equation (Female=0) is

$$\text{Predicted Salary} = 30.430 + 1.528\text{YrsExper}$$

Graphically, these equations appear as in Figure 11.30. The *Y*-intercept for the female line is slightly higher—females with no experience with Fifth National tend to start out slightly higher than males—but the slope of the female line is much lower. That is, males tend to move up the salary ladder much more quickly than females. Again, this provides another argument, although a somewhat different one, for gender discrimination against

FIGURE 11.30 **Nonparallel Female and Male Salary Lines**

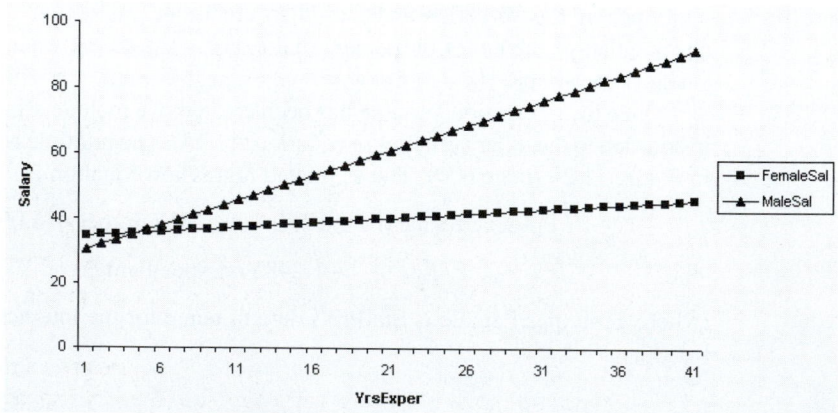

females. By the way, note that the R^2 value with the interaction variable has increased from 49.1% to 63.9%. The interaction variable has definitely added to the explanatory power of the equation. ■

This example illustrates just one possible use of interaction variables. The product of any two variables, a numerical and a dummy variable, two dummy variables, or even two numerical variables, can be used. The trick is to interpret the results correctly, and the easiest way to do this is the way we've been doing it—by writing several separate equations and seeing how they differ. To illustrate one further possibility (among many), suppose we include the variables YrsExper, Female, and HighJob in the equation for Salary, along with interactions between Female and YrsExper and between Female and HighJob. Here, HighJob is a new dummy variable that is 1 for job grades 4–6 and is 0 for job grades 1–3. (It can be calculated as the sum of the dummies Job_4–Job_6.) The resulting equation is

$$\text{Predicted Salary} = 28.168 + 1.261\text{YrsExper} + 9.242\text{HighJob} + 6.601\text{Female}$$

$$-1.224\text{Female\_YrsExper} + 1.564\text{Female\_HighJob} \qquad \textbf{(11.15)}$$

and the R^2 value is now a hefty 76.6%.

The interpretation of equation (11.15) is quite a challenge because it is really composed of four separate equations, one for each combination of Female and HighJob. For females in the high job category, the equation becomes

$$\text{Predicted Salary} = (28.168 + 9.242 + 6.601 + 1.564) + (1.261 - 1.224)\text{YrsExper}$$

$$= 45.575 + 0.037\text{YrsExper}$$

and for females in the low job category it is

$$\text{Predicted Salary} = (28.168 + 6.601) + (1.261 - 1.224)\text{YrsExper}$$

$$= 34.769 + 0.037\text{YrsExper}$$

Similarly, for males in the high job category, the equation becomes

$$\text{Predicted Salary} = (28.168 + 9.242) + 1.261\text{YrsExper}$$

$$= 37.410 + 1.261\text{YrsExper}$$

and for males in the low job category it is

$$\text{Predicted Salary} = 28.168 + 1.261\text{YrsExper}$$

Putting this into words, we can interpret the various coefficients as follows:

- The intercept 28.168 is the average *starting* salary (that is, with no experience at Fifth National) for males in the low job category.
- The coefficient 1.261 of YrsExper is the expected increase in salary per extra year of experience for males (in either job category).
- The coefficient 9.242 of HighJob is the expected salary "premium" for males starting in the high job category instead of the low job category.
- The coefficient 6.601 of Female is the expected starting salary premium for females relative to males, given that they start in the low job category.
- The coefficient −1.224 of Female_YrsExper is the penalty per extra year of experience for females relative to males—that is, male salaries increase this much more than female salaries each year.
- The coefficient 1.564 of Female_HighJob is the extra premium (in addition to the male premium) for females starting in the high job category instead of the low job category.

As we see, there are pros and cons to adding interaction variables. On the plus side, they allow for more complex and interesting models, and they can provide significantly better fits. On the minus side, they can become extremely difficult to interpret correctly. Therefore, we recommend that they be added only when there is good economic and statistical justification for doing so.

11.6.3 Nonlinear Transformations

The general linear regression equation has the form

$$\widehat{Y} = a + b_1 X_1 + b_2 X_2 + \cdots + b_k X_k$$

It is *linear* in the sense that the right-hand side of the equation is a constant plus a sum of products of constants and variables. However, there is no requirement that the response variable Y or the explanatory variables X_1 through X_k be *original* variables in the data set. Most often they are, but they are also allowed to be transformations of original variables. We already saw one example of this in the previous section with interaction variables. They are not original variables but are instead products of original (or even transformed) variables. We enter them in the same way as original variables; only the interpretation differs. In this section we will look at several nonlinear transformations of variables. These are often used because of curvature detected in scatterplots. They can also arise because of economic considerations. That is, economic theory often leads us to particular nonlinear transformations.

There are actually two cases we should distinguish. We can transform the response variable Y or we can transform any of the explanatory variables, the X's. We can also do both. In either case there are a few nonlinear transformations that are typically used. These include the natural logarithm, the square root, the reciprocal, and the square. The point of any of these is usually to "straighten out" the points in a scatterplot. If several different transformations straighten out the data equally well, then we prefer the one that is easiest to interpret.

We begin with a small example where only the X variable needs to be transformed.

E X A M P L E   1 1 . 4

The Public Service Electric Company produces different quantities of electricity each month, depending on the demand. The file POWER.XLS lists the number of units of electricity produced (Units) and the total cost of producing these (Cost) for a 36-month period. The data appear in Figure 11.31. How can regression be used to analyze the relationship between Cost and Units?

Solution

A good place to start is with a scatterplot of Cost versus Units. This appears in Figure 11.32. It indicates a definite positive relationship and one that is nearly linear. However, there is also some evidence of curvature in the plot. The points increase slightly less rapidly as Units increases from left to right. In economic terms, there may be economies of scale, where the marginal cost of electricity decreases as more units of electricity are produced.

Nevertheless, we first use regression to estimate a *linear* relationship between Cost and Units. The resulting regression equation is

$$\text{Predicted Cost} = 23{,}651 + 30.53\text{Units}$$

The corresponding R^2 and s_e are 73.6% and $2734. We also requested a scatterplot of

FIGURE 11.31   Data for Electric Power Example

	A	B	C	D
1	Data on cost versus production level			
2				
3	Month	Cost	Units	
4	1	45623	601	
5	2	46507	738	
6	3	43343	686	
7	4	46495	736	
8	5	47317	756	
9	6	41172	498	
10	7	43974	828	
11	8	44290	671	
12	9	29297	305	
13	10	47244	637	
37	34	46295	667	
38	35	45218	705	
39	36	45357	637	

FIGURE 11.32   Scatterplot of Cost Versus Units for Electricity Example

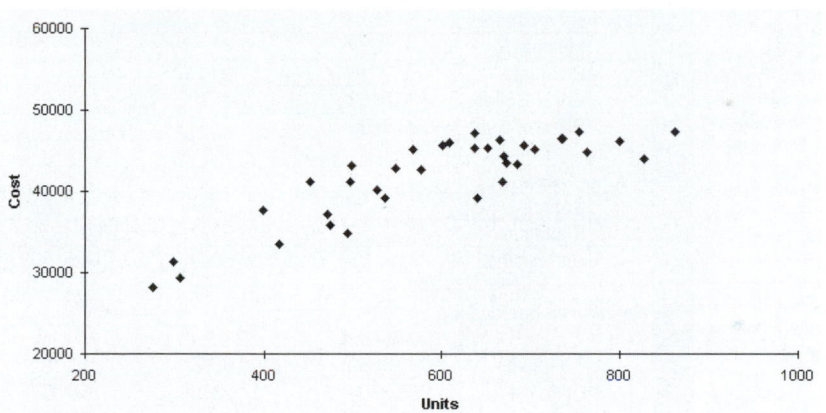

the residuals versus the fitted values, always a good idea when nonlinearity is suspected. This plot is shown in Figure 11.33 (page 604). The sign of nonlinearity in this plot is that the residuals to the far left and the far right are all negative, whereas the majority of the residuals in the middle are positive. Admittedly, the pattern is far from perfect—there are quite a few negative residuals in the middle—but the plot does hint at nonlinear behavior.

This negative–positive–negative behavior of residuals suggests a *parabola*—that is, a quadratic relationship with the *square* of Units included in the equation. We first create a new variable Sqr_Units in the data set. This can be done manually (with the formula =C4^2 in cell D4, copied down) or with the StatPro/Data Utilities/Transform Variables menu item. This latter method is easier to use and allows us to transform several variables simultaneously. Then we use multiple regression to estimate the equation for Cost with *both* explanatory variables, Units and Sqr_Units, included. The resulting equation, as shown in Figure 11.34, is

$$\text{Predicted Cost} = 5793 + 98.35\text{Units} - 0.0600\text{Sqr\_Units} \qquad \textbf{(11.16)}$$

Note that R^2 has increased to 82.2% and s_e has decreased to \$2281.

FIGURE 11.33 **Residuals from a Straight-Line Fit**

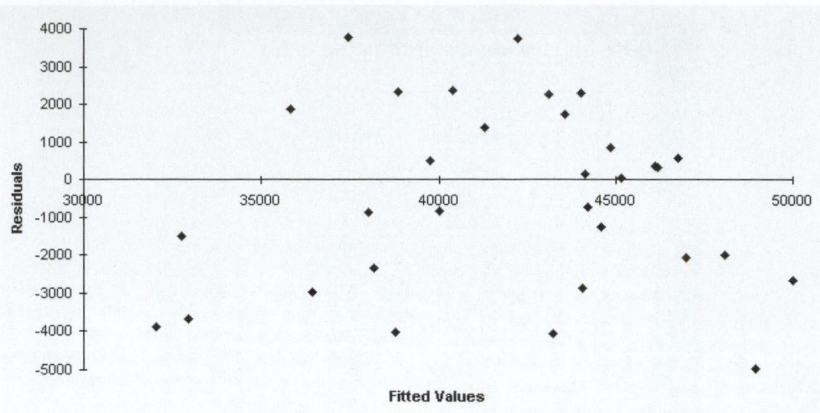

FIGURE 11.34 **Regression Output with Squared Term Included**

	A	B	C	D	E	F	G
1	*Results of multiple regression for Cost*						
2							
3	*Summary measures*						
4		Multiple R	0.9064				
5		R-Square	0.8216				
6		Adj R-Square	0.8108				
7		StErr of Est	2280.7998				
8							
9	*ANOVA Table*						
10		Source	df	SS	MS	F	p-value
11		Explained	2	790511520.9722	395255760.4861	75.9808	0.0000
12		Unexplained	33	171667568.0000	5202047.5152		
13							
14	*Regression coefficients*						
15			Coefficient	Std Err	t-value	p-value	
16		Constant	5792.7983	4763.0586	1.2162	0.2325	
17		Units	98.3504	17.2369	5.7058	0.0000	
18		Sqr_Units	-0.0600	0.0151	-3.9806	0.0004	

One way to see how this regression equation fits the scatterplot of Cost versus Units (in Figure 11.32) is to use Excel's trendline option. To do so, activate the scatterplot, click on any point, use the Chart/Add Trendline menu item, click on the Type tab, and select the Polynomial type or order 2, that is, a quadratic. (This is for Excel 97. For Excel 5 and 95, use the Insert/Trendline menu item instead.) A graph of equation (11.16) is superimposed on the scatterplot, as shown in Figure 11.35. It shows a reasonably good fit, plus an obvious curvature.

The main downside to a quadratic regression equation, as in equation (11.16), is that there is no easy interpretation of the coefficients of Units and Sqr_Units. For example, we can't conclude from the 98.35 coefficient of Units that Cost increases by 98.35 dollars when Units increases by 1. The reason is that when Units increases by 1, Sqr_Units doesn't stay constant; it *also* increases. All we can say is that the terms in equation (11.16) combine to explain the nonlinear relationship between units produced and total cost.

A final note about this equation concerns the coefficient of Sqr_Units, −0.0600. First, the fact that it is negative makes the parabola bend "downward." This produces the de-

FIGURE 11.35   Quadratic Fit in Electricity Example

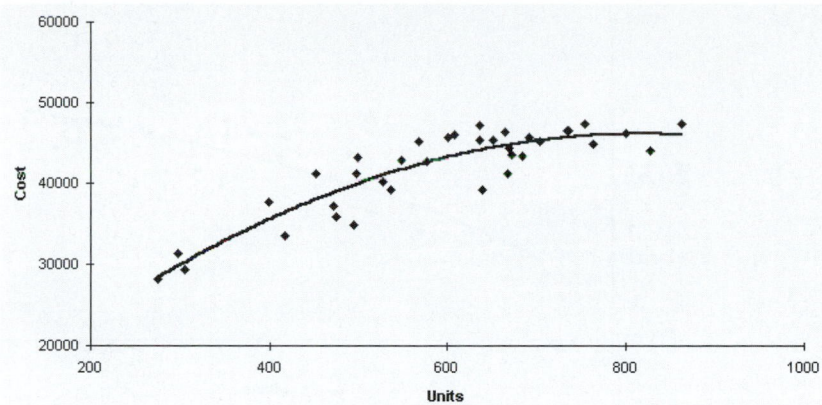

creasing marginal cost behavior, where every extra unit of electricity incurs a smaller cost. Actually, the curve described by equation (11.16) eventually goes downhill for large values of Units, but this part of the curve is irrelevant because the company evidently never produces such large quantities. Second, we shouldn't be fooled by the small magnitude of this coefficient. Remember that it is the coefficient of Units *squared*, which is a large quantity. Therefore, the effect of the product -0.0600Sqr_Units is sizable.

There is at least one other possibility we might examine. Rather that a quadratic fit, we could try a logarithmic fit. In this case we create a new variable, Log_Units, the natural logarithm of Units, and then regress Cost against the *single* variable Log_Units. To create the new variable, we can either proceed manually with Excel's LN function or we can use StatPro/Data Utilities/Transform Variables menu item. Also, we can superimpose a logarithmic curve on the scatterplot of Cost versus Units by using Excel's trendline feature with the logarithmic option. This curve appears in Figure 11.36 (page 606). To the naked eye, it appears to be similar, and about as good a fit, as the quadratic curve in Figure 11.35.

The resulting regression equation is

$$\text{Predicted Cost} = -63{,}993 + 16{,}654\text{Log\_Units} \qquad \textbf{(11.17)}$$

and the R^2 and s_e values are 79.8% and 2393. These latter values indicate that the logarithmic fit is not quite as good as the quadratic fit. However, the advantage of the logarithmic equation is that it is easier to interpret. In fact, one reason logarithmic transformations of variables are used as widely as they are in regression analysis is that they are fairly easy to interpret.

In the present case, where the log of an *explanatory* variable is used, we can interpret its coefficient as follows. Suppose that Units increases by 1%, for example, from 600 to 606. Then equation (11.17) implies that the expected Cost will increase by approximately $0.01(16{,}654) = 166.54$ dollars. In words, every 1% increase in Units is accompanied by an expected \$166.54 increase in Cost.[11] Note that for larger values of Units, a 1% increase represents a larger absolute increase (from 700 to 707 instead of from 600 to 606, say). But each such 1% increase entails the *same* increase in Cost. This is another way of describing the decreasing marginal cost property.

---

[11]In general, if b is the coefficient of the log of X, then the expected change in Y when X increases by 1% is approximately 0.01 times b.

FIGURE 11.36 Logarithmic Fit to Electricity Data

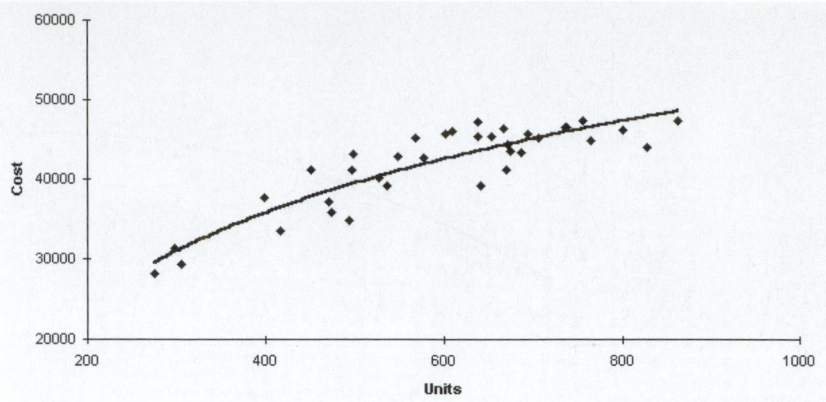

The electricity example has shown two possible nonlinear transformations of the *explanatory* variable (or variables) that we can use. All we need to do is create the transformed X's and run the regression. The interpretation of statistics such as R^2 and s_e is exactly the same as before; only the interpretation of the coefficients of the transformed X's changes. It is also possible to transform the response variable Y. Now, however, we must be careful when interpreting summary statistics such as R^2 and s_e, as we explain in the following examples.

Each of these examples transforms the response variable Y by taking its natural logarithm and then using the log of Y as the new response variable. This approach is taken in a wide variety of business applications. Essentially, it is often a good option when the distribution of Y is skewed to the right, with a few very large values and many small to medium values. The effect of the logarithm transformation is to spread the small values out and squeeze the large values together, making the distribution more symmetric. This is illustrated in Figures 11.37 and 11.38 for a hypothetical distribution of household incomes. The histogram of incomes in Figure 11.37 is clearly skewed to the right. However, the histogram of the natural log of income in Figure 11.38 is much more nearly symmetric—and, for technical reasons, more suitable for use as a response variable in regression.

FIGURE 11.37 Skewed Distribution of Income

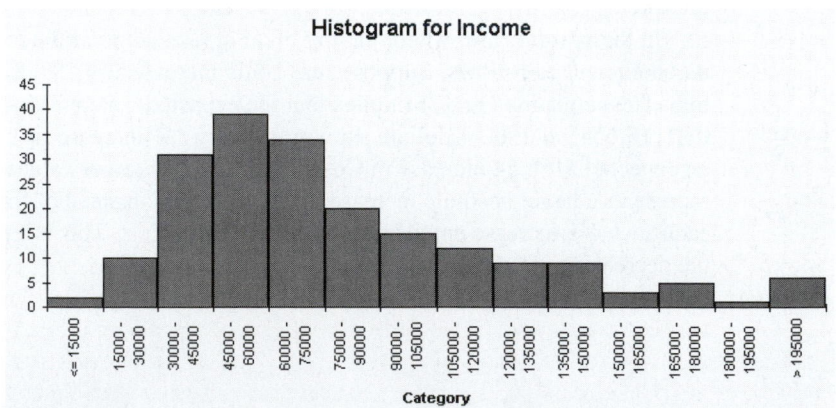

FIGURE 11.38   **Symmetric Distribution of Log_Income**

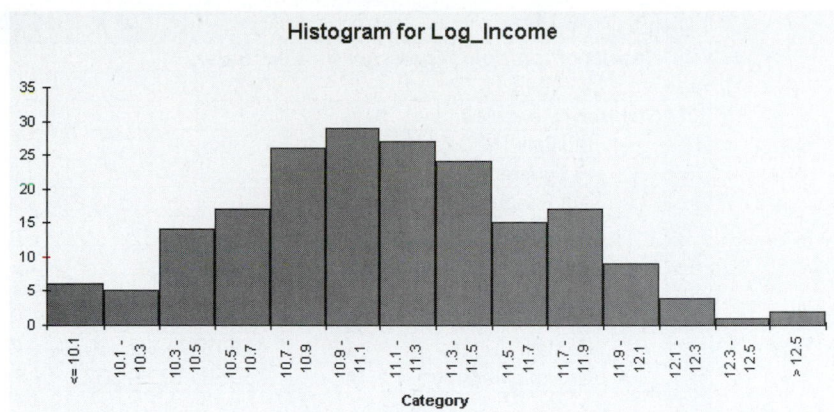

EXAMPLE 11.3 [CONTINUED]

Returning to the bank discrimination example, a glance at the distribution of salaries of the 208 employees shows some skewness to the right—a few employees make substantially more than the majority of employees. Therefore, it might make sense to use the natural logarithm of Salary instead of Salary as the response variable. If we do this, how do we interpret the results?

Solution

All of the analyses we did earlier with this data set could be repeated except with Log_Salary as the response variable. For the sake of discussion, we look only at the regression equation with Female and YrsExper as explanatory variables. After we create the Log_Salary variable and run the regression, we obtain the output in Figure 11.39 (page 608). The estimated regression equation is

$$\text{Predicted Log\_Salary} = 3.5829 + 0.0188\text{YrsExper} - 0.1616\text{Female} \qquad \textbf{(11.18)}$$

The R^2 and s_e values are 42.4% and 0.1794. For comparison, when this same equation was estimated with Salary as the response variable, R^2 and s_e were 49.1% and 8.070.

We first interpret R^2 and s_e. Neither is directly comparable to the R^2 or s_e value with Salary as the response variable. Recall that R^2 in general is the percentage of the response variable explained by the regression equation. The problem here is that the two R^2 values are percentages explained of *different* response variables, Log_Salary and Salary. The fact that one is smaller than the other (42.4% versus 49.1%) does not necessarily mean that it corresponds to a "worse" fit. They simply aren't comparable.

The situation is even worse with s_e. Each s_e is a measure of a typical residual, but the residuals in the Log_Salary equation are in log dollars, whereas the residuals in the Salary equation are in dollars. These units are completely different. For example, the log of $1000 is only 6.91. Therefore, it is no surprise that s_e for the Log_Salary is *much* smaller than s_e for the Salary equation. If we want comparable standard error measures for the two equations, we should take antilogs of fitted values from the Log_Salary equation to convert them back to dollars, subtract these from the original Salary values, and take the standard deviation of these "residuals." (The EXP function in Excel can be used to take antilogs.) You can check

FIGURE 11.39   **Regression Output with Log_Salary as Response Variable**

	A	B	C	D	E	F	G
1	*Results of multiple regression for Log_Salary*						
2							
3	*Summary measures*						
4		Multiple R	0.6514				
5		R-Square	0.4243				
6		Adj R-Square	0.4187				
7		StErr of Est	0.1794				
8							
9	*ANOVA Table*						
10		Source	df	SS	MS	F	p-value
11		Explained	2	4.8613	2.4307	75.5556	0.0000
12		Unexplained	205	6.5950	0.0322		
13							
14	*Regression coefficients*						
15			Coefficient	Std Err	t-value	p-value	
16		Constant	3.5829	0.0280	128.0326	0.0000	
17		Female	-0.1616	0.0265	-6.0936	0.0000	
18		YrsExper	0.0188	0.0018	10.5556	0.0000	

that the resulting standard deviation is 7.774.[12] This is somewhat smaller than s_e from the Salary equation, an indication of a slightly *better* fit.

Finally, we interpret equation (11.18) itself. Fortunately, this is fairly easy. When the response variable is Log_Y and a term on the right-hand side of the equation is of the form bX, then whenever X increases by one unit, $\widehat{Y}$ changes by a constant *percentage*, and this percentage is approximately equal to b (written as a percentage). For example, if $b = 0.035$, then when X increases by one unit, $\widehat{Y}$ increases by approximately 3.5%. Applied to equation (11.18), this means that for each extra year of experience with Fifth National, an employee's salary can be expected to increase by about 1.88%. To interpret the Female coefficient, note that the only possible increase in Female is 1 unit (from 0 for male to 1 for female). When this occurs, the expected percentage *decrease* in salary is approximately 16.16%. In other words, equation (11.18) implies that females can expect to make about 16% less than men for comparable years of experience. ■

We are not necessarily claiming that the bank data are fit better with Log_Salary as the response variable than with Salary—it appears to be a virtual toss-up. However, the lessons from this example are important in general. They are as follows.

1   The R^2 values with Y and Log_Y as response variables are not directly comparable. They are percentages explained of *different* variables.

2   The s_e values with Y and Log_Y as response variables are usually of totally different magnitudes. To make the s_e from the log equation comparable, we need to go through the procedure described in the example, so that the residuals are in *original* units.

3   To interpret any term of the form bX in the log equation, we first express b as a percentage. For example $b = 0.035$ becomes 3.5%. Then when X increases by one unit, the expected *percentage* change in Y is approximately this percentage b.

---

[12] To make the two "standard deviations" comparable, we use the denominator $n - 3$ in each.

The log transformation of a response variable Y is used frequently. This is partly because it induces nice statistical properties (such as making the distribution of Y more symmetric). But an important advantage of this transformation is its ease of interpretation in terms of percentage changes.

Constant Elasticity Relationships A particular type of nonlinear relationship that has firm grounding in economic theory is called a **constant elasticity** relationship. It is also called a **multiplicative** relationship. It has the form

$$Y = aX_1^{b_1} X_2^{b_2} \cdots X_k^{b_k} \qquad (11.19)$$

One property of this type of relationship is that the effect of a change on any explanatory variable X_i on Y depends on the levels of the other X's in the equation. This is not true for the *additive* relationships

$$Y = a + b_1 X_1 + b_2 X_2 + \cdots + b_k X_k$$

that we have been discussing. For additive relationships, when any X_i increases by one unit, Y changes by b_i units, regardless of the levels of the other X's.

The term "constant elasticity" comes from economics. Economists define the elasticity of Y with respect to X as the percentage change in Y that accompanies a 1% increase in X. Often this is in reference to a demand–price relationship. Then the "price elasticity" is the percentage decrease in demand when price increases by 1%. Usually, the elasticity depends on the current value of X. For example, the price elasticity when the price is \$35 might be different than when the price is \$50. However, when the relationship is of the form

$$Y = aX^b$$

then the elasticity is *constant*, the same for any value of X. Moreover, it is approximately equal to the exponent b. For example, if $Y = 2X^{-1.5}$, then the constant elasticity is approximately -1.5, so that when X increases by 1%, Y decreases by approximately 1.5%.

The constant elasticity property carries over to the multiple-X relationship in equation (11.19). Then each exponent is the approximate elasticity for its X. For example, if $Y = 2X_1^{-1.5} X_2^{0.7}$, then we can make the following statements:

- When X_1 increases by 1%, Y decreases by approximately 1.5%, regardless of the current values of X_1 and X_2.

- When X_2 increases by 1%, Y increases by approximately 0.7%, regardless of the current values of X_1 and X_2.

We can use linear regression to estimate the nonlinear relationship in equation (11.19) by taking natural logarithms of *all* variables. Here we exploit two properties of logarithms: (1) the log of a product is the sum of the logs, and (2) the log of X^b is b times the log of X. Therefore, taking logs of both sides of equation (11.19) gives

$$\text{Log\_}Y = \text{Log\_}a + b_1 \text{Log\_}X_1 + \cdots + b_k \text{Log\_}X_k$$

This equation is *linear* in the log variables Log_Y and Log_X_1 through Log_X_k, so it can be estimated in the usual way with multiple regression. We can then interpret the coefficients of the explanatory variables directly as elasticities. The following example illustrates the method.

EXAMPLE 11.5

The file CARDEMAND.XLS contains annual data (1970–1987) on domestic auto sales in the United States. The data are listed in Figure 11.40. The variables are defined as

- Quantity: annual domestic auto sales (in number of units)
- Price: real price index of new cars
- Income: real disposable income
- Interest: prime rate of interest

FIGURE 11.40 **Data for Automobile Demand Example**

	A	B	C	D	E
1	Car demand data				
2					
3	Year	Quantity	Price	Income	Interest
4	1970	7,115,270	107.6	1668.1	7.91%
5	1971	8,676,410	112	1728.4	5.72%
6	1972	9,321,310	111	1797.4	5.25%
7	1973	9,618,510	111.1	1916.3	8.03%
8	1974	7,448,340	117.5	1896.6	10.81%
9	1975	7,049,840	127.6	1931.7	7.86%
10	1976	8,606,860	135.7	2001	6.84%
11	1977	9,104,930	142.9	2066.6	6.83%
12	1978	9,304,250	153.8	2167.4	9.06%
13	1979	8,316,020	166	2212.6	12.67%
14	1980	6,578,360	179.3	2214.3	15.27%
15	1981	6,206,690	190.2	2248.6	18.87%
16	1982	5,756,610	197.6	2261.5	14.86%
17	1983	6,795,230	202.6	2331.9	10.79%
18	1984	7,951,790	208.5	2469.8	12.04%
19	1985	8,204,690	215.2	2542.2	9.93%
20	1986	8,222,480	224.4	2645.1	8.33%
21	1987	7,080,890	232.5	2676.1	8.22%

Estimate and interpret a multiplicative (constant elasticity) relationship between Quantity and Price, Income, and Interest.

Solution

We first take natural logs of all four variables. (This can be done in one step with the StatPro/Data Utilities/Transform Variables menu item or we can use Excel's LN function.) We then use multiple regression, with Log_Quantity as the response variable and Log_Price, Log_Income, and Log_Interest as the explanatory variables. The resulting output is shown in Figure 11.41. The corresponding equation for Log_Quantity is

$$\text{Predicted Log\_Quantity} = 4.675 - 1.185\text{Log\_Price} + 2.183\text{Log\_Income}$$

$$-0.191\text{Log\_Interest}$$

If we like, we can convert this back to original variables, that is, back to multiplicative form, by taking antilogs. The result is

$$\text{Predicted Quantity} = 107.198\text{Price}^{-1.185}\text{Income}^{2.183}\text{Interest}^{-0.191}$$

where the constant 107.198 is the antilog of 4.675 (and is calculated in Excel with the EXP function).

In either form the equation implies that the elasticities are approximately equal to -1.185, 2.183, and -0.191. When Price increases by 1%, Quantity tends to decrease by about 1.185%; when Income increases by 1%, Quantity tends to increase by about 2.183%; and when Interest increases by 1%, Quantity tends to decrease by about 0.191%.

Does this multiplicative equation provide a better fit to the automobile data than an additive relationship? Without doing considerably more work, it is difficult to answer this

FIGURE 11.41 **Regression Output for Multiplicative Relationship**

	A	B	C	D	E	F	G
1	*Results of multiple regression for Log_Quantity*						
2							
3	*Summary measures*						
4		Multiple R	0.8445				
5		R-Square	0.7132				
6		Adj R-Square	0.6517				
7		StErr of Est	0.0887				
8							
9	*ANOVA Table*						
10		Source	df	SS	MS	F	p-value
11		Explained	3	0.2738	0.0913	11.6043	0.0004
12		Unexplained	14	0.1101	0.0079		
13							
14	*Regression coefficients*						
15			Coefficient	Std Err	t-value	p-value	
16		Constant	4.6747	3.2631	1.4326	0.1739	
17		Log_Price	-1.1845	0.3619	-3.2732	0.0056	
18		Log_Income	2.1828	0.6584	3.3151	0.0051	
19		Log_Interest	-0.1906	0.0811	-2.3501	0.0340	

question with any certainty. As we discussed in the previous example, it is *not* sufficient to compare R^2 and s_e values for the two fits. Again, the reason is that one has Log_Quantity as the response variable, while the other has Quantity, so the R^2 and s_e measures aren't comparable. We will simply state that the multiplicative relationship provides a reasonably good fit (for example, a scatterplot of its fitted values versus residuals shows no unusual patterns), and it makes sense economically. ■

One final example of a multiplicative relationship is the **learning curve** model. A learning curve relates the unit production time (or cost) to the cumulative volume of output since that production process first began. Empirical studies indicate that production times tend to decrease by a relatively constant *percentage* every time cumulative output doubles. To model this phenomenon, let Y be the time required to produce a unit of output, and let X be the cumulative amount of output that has been produced. If we assume that the relationship between Y and X is of the form

$$Y = aX^b$$

then it can be shown that whenever X doubles, Y decreases to a *constant* percentage of its previous value. This constant is often called the **learning rate**. For example, if the learning rate is 80%, then each doubling of cumulative production yields a 20% reduction in unit production time. It can be shown that the learning rate satisfies the equation

$$b = \ln(\text{learning rate}) / \ln(2) \tag{11.20}$$

(where "ln" refers to the natural logarithm). So once we estimate b, we can use equation (11.20) to estimate the learning rate.

The following example illustrates a typical application of the learning curve model.

EXAMPLE 11.6

The Presario Company produces a variety of small industrial products. It has just finished producing 22 batches of a new product (new to Presario) for a customer. The file LEARN-ING.XLS contains the times (in hours) to produce each batch. These data are listed in Figure 11.42. Clearly, the times have tended to decrease as Presario has gained more experience in making the product. Does the multiplicative learning model apply to these data, and what does it imply about the learning rate?

FIGURE 11.42   **Data for Learning Curve Example**

	A	B
1	**Learning curve effect**	
2		
3	Batch	Time
4	1	125.00
5	2	110.87
6	3	105.35
7	4	103.34
8	5	98.98
9	6	99.90
10	7	91.49
11	8	93.10
12	9	92.23
13	10	86.19
14	11	82.09
15	12	82.32
16	13	87.67
17	14	81.72
18	15	83.72
19	16	81.53
20	17	80.46
21	18	76.53
22	19	82.06
23	20	82.81
24	21	76.52
25	22	78.45

Solution

One way to check whether the multiplicative learning model is reasonable is to create the log variables Log_Time and Log_Batch in the usual way and then see whether a scatterplot of Log_Time versus Log_Batch is approximately *linear*. The multiplicative model implies that it should be. Such a scatterplot appears in Figure 11.43, along with a superimposed linear trend line. The fit appears to be quite good.

To estimate the relationship, we regress Log_Time on Log_Batch. The resulting equation is

$$\text{Predicted Log\_Time} = 4.834 - 0.155 \text{Log\_Batch} \qquad \textbf{(11.21)}$$

There are a couple of ways of interpreting this equation. First, because it is based on a multiplicative relationship, we can interpret the coefficient −0.155 as an elasticity. That is, when Batch increases by 1%, Time tends to decrease by approximately 0.155%.

FIGURE 11.43 **Scatterplot of Log Variables with Linear Trend Superimposed**

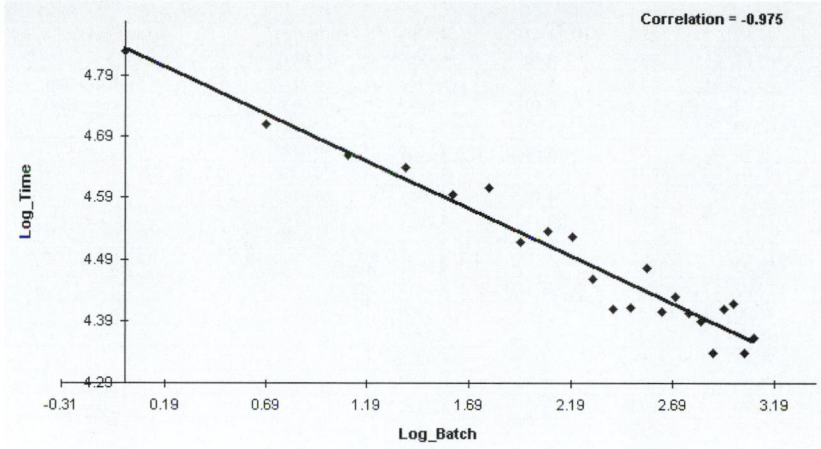

Although this interpretation is correct, it is not as useful as the "doubling" interpretation we discussed above. We know from equation (11.20) that the estimated learning rate satisfies

$$-0.155 = \ln(\text{learning rate}) / \ln(2)$$

Solving for the learning rate (multiply through by $\ln(2)$ and then take antilogs), we find that it is 0.898, or approximately 90%. In words, whenever cumulative production doubles, the time to produce a batch decreases by about 10%.

Presario could use this regression equation to predict future production times. For example, suppose the customer places an order for 15 more batches of the same product. Note that Presario is already partway up the learning curve, that is, these batches are numbers 23–37, and the company already has experience producing the product. We can use equation (11.21) to predict the log of production time for each batch, then take their antilogs and sum them to obtain the total production time. The calculations are shown in rows 26–41 of Figure 11.44 (page 614). We enter the batch numbers and calculate their logs in columns A and C. Then we substitute the values of Log_Batch in column C into equation (11.21) to obtain the predicted values of Log_Time in column E. Finally, we use Excel's EXP function to calculate the antilogs of these predictions in column B, and we calculate their sum in cell B41. The total predicted time to finish the order is about 1115 hours. ∎

PROBLEMS

Level A

26   In a study of housing demand, a county assessor is interested in developing a regression model to estimate the selling price of residential properties within her jurisdiction. She randomly selects 15 houses and records the selling price in addition to the following values: the size of the house (in hundreds of square feet), the total number of rooms in the house, the age of the house, and an indication of whether the house has an attached garage. These data are stored in the file P11_26.XLS.

   a   Estimate and thoroughly interpret a multiple regression model that includes the four potential explanatory variables.

   b   Evaluate the estimated regression model's goodness of fit.

   c   Use the estimated model to predict the sales price of a 3000-square-foot, 20-year-old home that has 7 rooms but no attached garage.

FIGURE 11.44 Using the Learning Curve Model for Predictions

	A	B	C	D	E	F	G	H	I	J
16	13	87.67	2.56	4.47	4.4364	0.0371		Regression coefficients		
17	14	81.72	2.64	4.40	4.4250	-0.0217				Coefficient
18	15	83.72	2.71	4.43	4.4143	0.0132			Constant	4.8340
19	16	81.53	2.77	4.40	4.4043	-0.0033			Log_Batch	-0.1550
20	17	80.46	2.83	4.39	4.3949	-0.0071				
21	18	76.53	2.89	4.34	4.3860	-0.0483				
22	19	82.06	2.94	4.41	4.3776	0.0298				
23	20	82.81	3.00	4.42	4.3697	0.0469				
24	21	76.52	3.04	4.34	4.3621	-0.0246				
25	22	78.45	3.09	4.36	4.3549	0.0076				
26	23	77.32	3.1355		4.3480					
27	24	76.82	3.1781		4.3414					
28	25	76.33	3.2189		4.3351					
29	26	75.87	3.2581		4.3290					
30	27	75.43	3.2958		4.3232					
31	28	75.00	3.3322		4.3175					
32	29	74.60	3.3673		4.3121					
33	30	74.20	3.4012		4.3068	Predictions				
34	31	73.83	3.4340		4.3017					
35	32	73.47	3.4657		4.2968					
36	33	73.12	3.4965		4.2921					
37	34	72.78	3.5264		4.2874					
38	35	72.45	3.5553		4.2829					
39	36	72.14	3.5835		4.2786					
40	37	71.83	3.6109		4.2743					
41		1115.18		Predicted total time						
42				for next 15 batches						
43										

27 A manager of boiler drums wants to use regression analysis to predict the number of worker-hours needed to erect the drums in future projects. Consequently, data for 36 randomly selected boilers were collected. In addition to worker-hours (Y), the variables measured include boiler capacity, boiler design pressure, boiler type, and drum type. All of these measurements can be found in the file P11_27.XLS.

   a Formulate an appropriate multiple regression model to predict the number of worker-hours needed to erect boiler drums.

   b Estimate the formulated model using the given sample data, and interpret the estimated regression coefficients.

   c According to the estimated regression model, what is the difference between the mean number of worker-hours required for erecting industrial and utility field boilers?

   d According to the estimated regression model, what is the difference between the mean number of worker-hours required for erecting boilers with steam drums and those with mud drums?

   e Given the estimated regression model, predict the number of worker-hours needed to erect a utility-field, steam-drum boiler with a capacity of 550,000 pounds per hour and a design pressure of 1400 pounds per square inch.

   f Given the estimated regression model, predict the number of worker-hours needed to erect an industrial-field, mud-drum boiler with a capacity of 100,000 pounds per hour and a design pressure of 1000 pounds per square inch.

28 Suppose that a regional express delivery service company wants to estimate the cost of shipping a package (Y) as a function of cargo type, where cargo type includes the following possibilities: fragile, semifragile, and durable. Costs for 15 randomly chosen packages of approximately the same weight and same distance shipped, but of different cargo types, are provided in the file P11_28.XLS.

   a Formulate an appropriate multiple regression model to predict the cost of shipping a given package.

b Estimate the formulated model using the given sample data, and interpret the estimated regression coefficients.

c According to the estimated regression model, which cargo type is the *most* costly to ship? Which cargo type is the *least* costly to ship?

d How well does the estimated model fit the given sample data? How can the model's goodness of fit be improved?

e Given the estimated regression model, predict the cost of shipping a package with semifragile cargo.

29 The file P11_11.XLS contains observations of the American minimum wage during each of the years from 1950 through 1994. Has the minimum wage been growing at roughly a *constant* rate over this period?

a Generate a scatterplot diagram for these data. Comment on the observed behavior of the minimum wage over time.

b Formulate and estimate an appropriate regression model to explain the variation of the American minimum age over the given time period. Interpret the estimated regression coefficients.

c Analyze the estimated model's residuals. Is your estimated regression model adequate? If not, return to part **b** and revise your model. Continue to revise the model until your results are satisfactory.

30 Formulate a regression model that adequately estimates the relationship between monthly electrical power usage (Y) and home size (X) using the data in the file P11_13.XLS. Interpret your computer-generated results. How well does your model explain the variation in monthly electrical power usage?

31 An insurance company wants to determine how its annual operating costs depend on the number of home insurance (X_1) and automobile insurance (X_2) policies that have been written. The file P11_31.XLS contains relevant information for 10 branches of the insurance company. The company believes that a multiplicative model might be appropriate because operating costs typically increase by a constant percentage as the number of either type of policy increases by a given percentage. Use the given data to estimate a multiplicative model for this insurance company. Interpret your computer-generated results. Does a multiplicative model provide a good fit with these data?

32 Suppose that an operations manager is trying to determine the number of labor hours required to produce the *i*th unit of a certain product. Consider the data provided in the file P11_32.XLS. For example, the second unit produced required 517 labor hours, and the 600th unit required 34 labor hours.

a Use the given data to estimate a relationship between the total number of units produced and the labor hours required to produce the last unit in the total set. Interpret your findings.

b Use your estimated relationship to predict the number of labor hours that will be needed to produce the 800th unit.

Level B

33 The human resources manager of DataCom, Inc. wants to predict the annual salaries of given employees using the following explanatory variables: the number of years of prior relevant work experience, the number of years of employment at DataCom, the number of years of education beyond high school, the employee's gender, the employee's department, and the number of individuals supervised by the given employee. These data have been collected for a sample of employees and are given in the file P11_5.XLS.

a Formulate an appropriate multiple regression model to predict the annual salary of a given DataCom employee.

b Estimate the formulated model using the given sample data, and interpret the estimated regression coefficients.

c According to the estimated regression model, is there a difference between the mean salaries earned by male and female employees at DataCom? If so, how large is the difference?

d According to the estimated regression model, is there a difference between the mean salaries earned by employees in the sales department and those in the advertising department at DataCom? If so, how large is the difference?

e According to the estimated regression model, in which department are DataCom employees paid the *highest* mean salary? In which department are DataCom employees paid the *lowest* mean salary?

f Given the estimated regression model, predict the annual salary of a female employee who served in a similar department at another company for 10 years prior to coming to work at DataCom. This woman, a graduate of a 4-year collegiate business program, has been supervising 12 subordinates in the purchasing department since joining the organization 5 years ago.

34 Does the rate of violent crime acts vary across different regions of the United States?

a Using the data in the file P11_34.XLS, develop and estimate an appropriate regression model to explain the variation in acts of violent crime across the four established regions of the United States. Thoroughly interpret the estimated model. Rank the four regions from highest to lowest according to their mean violent crime rate.

b How would you modify the regression model in part **a** to account for possible differences in the violent crime rate across the various subdivisions of the given regions? Estimate your revised model and interpret your findings. Rank the nine subdivisions from highest to lowest according to their mean violent crime rate.

35 Suppose that you are interested in predicting the price of a laptop computer based on its various features. The file P11_35.XLS contains observations on the sales price and a number of potentially relevant variables for a randomly chosen sample of laptop computers.

a Formulate a multiple regression model that includes all potential explanatory variables and estimate it with the given sample data.

b Interpret the estimated regression equation. Be sure to indicate the impact of each attribute on the computer's sales price. For example, what impact does the monitor type have on the average sales price of a laptop computer?

c How well does the estimated regression model fit the data given in the file P11_35.XLS?

d Use the estimated regression equation to predict the price of a laptop computer with the following features: a 60-megahertz processor, a battery that holds its charge for 240 minutes, 32-megabytes of RAM, a DX chip, a color monitor, a mouse pointing device, and a 24-hour, toll-free customer service hotline.

36 Continuing Problem 18, suppose that the antique collector believes that the *rate of increase* of the auction price with the age of the item will be driven upward by a large number of bidders. How would you revise the multiple regression model developed previously to model this feature of the problem?

a Estimate your revised model using the data in the file P11_18.XLS.

b Interpret each of the estimated coefficients in your revised model.

c Does this revised model fit the given data better than the original multiple regression model? Explain why or why not.

37 Continuing Problem 19, revise the multiple regression model developed previously to include an interaction term between the return on average equity (X_1) and annual dividend rate (X_2).

a Estimate your revised model using the data provided in the file P11_19.XLS.

b Interpret each of the estimated coefficients in your revised model. In particular, how do you interpret the coefficient for the interaction term in the revised model?

c Does this revised model fit the given data better than does the original multiple regression model? Explain why or why not.

38 Continuing Problem 24, suppose that one of the managers of this regional express delivery service company is trying to decide whether to add an interaction term involving the package weight (X_1) and the distance shipped (X_2) in the multiple regression model developed previously.

a Why would the manager want to add such a term to the regression equation?

b Estimate the revised model using the data given given in the file P11_24.XLS.

c Interpret each of the estimated coefficients in your revised model. In particular, how do you interpret the coefficient for the interaction term in the revised model?

d Does this revised model fit the given data better than the original multiple regression model? Explain why or why not. ■

Validation of the Fit

The fit from a regression analysis is often overly optimistic. When we use the least squares procedure on a given set of data, we exploit all of the idiosyncrasies of the particular data to obtain the best possible fit. There is no guarantee that the fit will be as good when the estimated regression equation is applied to *new* data. In fact, it usually isn't. This is particularly important when our goal is to use the regression equation to predict new values of the response variable. The usual situation is that we use a given data set to estimate a regression equation. Then we gather new data on the *explanatory* variables and use these, along with the already-estimated regression equation, to predict the new (but unknown) values of the response variable.

One way to see whether this procedure will be successful is to split the original data set into two subsets—one subset for estimation and one subset for validation. We estimate the regression equation from the first subset. Then we substitute the values of explanatory variables from the second subset into this equation to obtain predicted values for the response variable. Finally, we compare these predicted values with the known values of the response variable in the second subset. If the agreement is good, there is reason to believe that the regression equation will predict well for new data.

This validation procedure is fairly simple to perform in Excel. We illustrate it for the Bendrix manufacturing data in Example 11.2. There we used 36 monthly observations to regress Overhead on MachHrs and ProdRuns. For convenience, we repeat the regression output in Figure 11.45. In particular, it shows an R^2 value of 86.6% and an s_e value of $4109.

FIGURE 11.45 **Multiple Regression Output for Bendrix Example**

	A	B	C	D	E	F	G
1	*Results of multiple regression for Overhead*						
2							
3	*Summary measures*						
4		Multiple R	0.9308				
5		R-Square	0.8664				
6		Adj R-Square	0.8583				
7		StErr of Est	4108.9932				
8							
9	*ANOVA Table*						
10		Source	df	SS	MS	F	p-value
11		Explained	2	3614020652.0000	1807010326.0000	107.0261	0.0000
12		Unexplained	33	557166208.0000	16883824.4848		
13							
14	*Regression coefficients*						
15			Coefficient	Std Err	t-value	p-value	
16		Constant	3996.6782	6603.6509	0.6052	0.5492	
17		MachHrs	43.5364	3.5895	12.1289	0.0000	
18		ProdRuns	883.6179	82.2514	10.7429	0.0000	

Now suppose that this data set is from one of Bendrix's two plants. The company would like to predict overhead costs for the other plant by using data on machine hours and production runs at the other plant. The first step is to see how well the regression from Figure 11.45 fits data from the other plant. We perform this validation on the 36 months of data shown in Figure 11.46. The validation results also appear in this figure.

FIGURE 11.46 **Validation of Bendrix Regression Results**

	A	B	C	D	E	F
1	Validation data					
2						
3	Coefficients from regression equation (based on original data)					
4		Constant	MachHrs	ProdRuns		
5		3996.6782	43.5364	883.6179		
6						
7	Comparison of summary measures					
8		Original	Validation			
9	R-Square	0.8664	0.7733			
10	StErr of Est	4108.99	5251.53			
11						
12	Month	MachHrs	ProdRuns	Overhead	Fitted	Residual
13	1	1374	24	92414	85023	7391
14	2	1510	35	92433	100663	-8230
15	3	1213	21	81907	75362	6545
16	4	1629	27	93451	98775	-5324
17	5	1858	28	112203	109629	2574
18	6	1763	40	112673	116096	-3423
19	7	1449	44	104091	105960	-1869
20	8	1422	46	104354	106552	-2198
45	33	1534	38	104946	104359	587
46	34	1529	29	94325	96189	-1864
47	35	1389	47	98474	105999	-7525
48	36	1350	34	90857	92814	-1957

To obtain the results in this figure, we proceed as follows:

1. **Copy old results.** Copy the results from the original regression to the ranges B5:D5 and B9:B10.

2. **Calculate fitted values and residuals.** The fitted values are now the predicted values of overhead for the other plant, based on the original regression equation. We find these by substituting the new values of MachHrs and ProdRuns into the original equation. To do so, enter the formula

    =$B$5+SUMPRODUCT($C$5:$D$5,B13:C13)

    in cell E13 and copy it down. Then calculate the residuals (prediction errors for the other plant) by entering the formula

    =D13-E13

    in cell F13 and copying it down.

3. **Calculate summary measures.** We see how well the original equation fits the new data by calculating R^2 and s_e values. Recall that R^2 in general is the square of the correlation between observed and fitted values. Therefore, enter the formula

    =CORREL(E13:E48,D13:D48)^2

in cell C9. The s_e value is essentially the standard deviation of the residuals, but it uses the denominator $n - 3$ (when there are two explanatory variables) rather than $n - 1$. Therefore, enter the formula

$$=SQRT(35/33)*STDEV(F13:F48)$$

in cell C10.

The results in Figure 11.46 are typical. The validation results are usually not as good as the original results. The value of R^2 has decreased from 86.6% to 77.3%, and the value of s_e has increased from $4109 to $5252. Nevertheless, Bendrix may conclude that the original regression equation is adequate for making future predictions at either plant.

11.8 Conclusion

The material in this chapter has illustrated how to fit an equation to a set of points and how to interpret the resulting equation. We have also discussed two measures, R^2 and s_e, that indicate the goodness of fit of the regression equation. Although the general technique is called *linear* regression, we have seen how it can be used to estimate nonlinear relationships through suitable transformations of variables. We are not finished with our study of regression, however. In the next chapter we will make some statistical assumptions about the regression model and then discuss the types of inferences that can be made from regression output. In particular, we will discuss the accuracy of the estimated regression coefficients, the accuracy of predictions made from the regression equation, and the general topic of which explanatory variables "belong" in the regression equation.

PROBLEMS

Level A

39 Many companies manufacture products that are at least partially produced using chemicals (for example, paint, gasoline, and steel). In many cases, the quality of the finished product is a function of the temperature and pressure at which the chemical reactions take place. Suppose that a particular manufacturer wants to model the quality (Y) of a product as a function of the temperature (X_1) and the pressure (X_2) at which it is produced. The file P11_39.XLS contains data obtained from a carefully designed experiment involving these variables. Note that the assigned quality score can range from a maximum of 100 to a minimum of 0 for each manufactured product.

    a Formulate a multiple regression model that includes the two given explanatory variables. Estimate the model using the given sample data. Does the estimated model fit the data well?

    b Interpret each of the estimated coefficients in the multiple regression model.

    c Consider adding a term to model a possible interaction between the two explanatory models. Reformulate the model and estimate it again using the given data. Does the inclusion of the interaction term improve the model's goodness of fit?

    d Interpret each of the estimated coefficients in the revised model. In particular, how do you interpret the coefficient for the interaction term in the revised model?

40 Suppose that a power company located in southern Alabama wants to predict the peak power load (i.e., the maximum amount of power that must be generated each day to meet demand) as a function of the daily high temperature (X). A random sample of 25 summer days is chosen, and the peak power load and the high temperature are recorded on each day. The file P11_40.XLS contains these observations.

a Generate a scatterplot diagram for these data. Comment on the observed relationship between the response variable and explanatory variable.

b Formulate and estimate an appropriate regression model to predict the peak power load for this power company. Interpret the estimated regression coefficients.

c Analyze the estimated model's residuals. Is your estimated regression model adequate? If not, return to part **b** and revise your model. Continue to revise the model until your results are satisfactory.

d Use the final version of your model to predict the peak power load on a summer day with a high temperature of 100 degrees.

41 Management of a home appliance store in Charlotte would like to understand the growth pattern of the monthly sales of VCR units over the past 2 years. Managers have recorded the relevant data in an Excel spreadsheet, which can be found in the file P11_9.XLS. Have the sales of VCR units been growing *linearly* over the past 24 months?

a Generate a scatterplot diagram for these data. Comment on the observed behavior of monthly VCR sales at this store over time.

b Formulate and estimate an appropriate regression model to explain the variation of monthly VCR sales over the given time period. Interpret the estimated regression coefficients.

c Analyze the estimated model's residuals. Is your estimated regression model adequate? If not, return to part **b** and revise your model. Continue to revise the model until your results are satisfactory.

42 Chipco, a small computer chip manufacturer, wants to be able to forecast monthly operating costs as a function of the number of units produced during a month. They have collected the 16 months of data in the file P11_42.XLS.

a Determine an equation that can be used to predict monthly production costs from units produced. Are there any outliers?

b How could the regression line obtained in part **a** be used to determine whether the company was efficient or inefficient during any particular month?

43 The file P11_43.XLS contains data on the following variables for several underdeveloped countries:

- Infant mortality rate
- Per capita GNP
- Percentage of people completing primary school
- Percentage of adults who can read (adult literacy)

Use these data to determine which of the given variables (by itself) best predicts infant mortality. Can you give an explanation for your answer?

44 The file P11_44.XLS contains data that relate the unit cost of producing a fuel pressure regulator to the cumulative number of fuel pressure regulators produced at the Ford plant in Bedford. For example, the 4000th unit cost $13.70 to produce.

a Fit a learning curve to these data.

b We would predict that doubling cumulative production reduces the cost of producing a regulator by what amount?

45 The "beta" of a stock is found by running a regression with the explanatory variable being the monthly return on a market index and the response variable being the monthly return on the stock. The beta of the stock is then the slope of this regression.

a Explain why most stocks have a positive beta.

b Explain why a stock with a beta with absolute value greater than 1 is more volatile than the market and a stock with a beta less than 1 (in absolute value) is less volatile than the market.

c Use the data in the file P11_45.XLS to estimate the beta for Ford Motor Company.

d What percentage of the variation in Ford's return is explained by market variation? What percentage is unexplained by market variation?

e Verify that the beta for Ford is given by

$$\frac{\text{Covariance between Ford and Market}}{\text{Variance of Market}}$$

Also, verify that the correlation between Ford return and Market return is the square root of R^2.

46 The file P11_46.XLS contains monthly returns on Anheiser-Busch (AB) and a market index for the period 1988–1993. Use these data to answer the following questions:

a What percentage of the variation in the return in AB is explained by variation in the market? What percentage is unexplained by variation in the market?

b Predict the change in AB during a month in which the market goes up by 2%.

c Use Excel's CORREL functions to determine the correlation between the return on AB and the market. Verify that this correlation between AB and the market is equal to the square root of R^2 from the regression output.

d Estimate the beta (refer to Problem 45) for AB by using regression. Then verify that it can also be found (using Excel's COVAR and VAR functions) from

$$\frac{\text{Covariance between AB and Market}}{\text{Variance of Market}}$$

47 Investors are interested in knowing whether estimates of stock betas based on past history are good predictors of future betas. How could you use a data set that gives monthly returns on several stocks over a 5-year period to see whether this is true?

48 The file P11_48.XLS contains monthly sales (in thousands) and price of a popular candy bar.

a Describe the type of relationship between price and sales (linear, nonlinear, strong, weak).

b What percentage of variation in monthly sales is explained by variation in price? What percentage is unexplained?

c If the price of the candy bar is 55 cents, predict monthly candy bar sales.

d Use the regression output to determine the correlation between price and candy bar sales.

e Are there any outliers?

49 The file P11_49.XLS contains the amount of money spent advertising a product (in thousands of dollars) and the number of units sold (in millions) for 8 months.

a Assume that the only factor influencing monthly sales is advertising. Fit the following three curves to these data: linear ($Y = a + bX$), exponential ($Y = ab^X$), and power ($Y = aX^b$). Which equation best fits the data?

b Interpret the best-fitting equation.

c Using the best-fitting equation, predict sales during a month in which $60,000 is spent on advertising.

50 Callaway Golf is trying to determine how the price of a set of clubs affects the demand for clubs. The file P11_50.XLS contains the price of a set of clubs (in dollars) and the monthly sales (in millions of sets sold).

a Assume the only factor influencing monthly sales is price. Fit the following three curves to these data: linear ($Y = a + bX$), exponential ($Y = ab^X$), and power ($Y = aX^b$). Which equation best fits the data?

b Interpret your best-fitting equation.

c Using the best-fitting equation, predict sales during a month in which the price is $470.

51 The number of cars per 1000 people is known for virtually every country in the world. For many countries, however, per capita income is not known. Can you think of a way to estimate per capita income for countries where it is unknown?

52 The file P11_52.XLS contains the cost (in 1990 dollars) of making a 3-minute phone call from London to New York. Use regression to estimate how (or whether) the cost of a London to New York call has declined over time. Based on these data, predict the cost of a 3-minute phone call in the year 2000. (Source: *The Economist*, September 28, 1996)

53 The file P11_53.XLS contains the databit power per chip for computers. Use regression to estimate how databit power per chip has changed over time. (This result is called Moore's law.) Also predict the databit power per chip in the year 2000. Do you think Moore's law can continue indefinitely? (Source: *One World Ready or Not,* by William Greider, 1996)

54   The file P11_54.XLS contains the cost of building (in hundreds of millions of dollars) a plant to produce RAM chips for PCs. Use regression to estimate how (or whether) the cost of building a RAM plant has increased over time. Predict the cost of building a RAM plant in the year 2000. (Source: *One World Ready or Not,* by William Greider, 1996)

55   The file P11_55.XLS contains the unit cost of producing a unit of computer memory, as a function of the number of units of computer memory that have been produced to date. Use regression to analyze how (or whether) the price of a bit of memory has changed as more memory has been produced (Source: *Every Investor's Guide to High-Tech Stocks*, by Michael Murphy, 1998)

56   The Baker Company wants to develop a budget to predict how overhead costs vary with activity levels. Management is trying to decide whether direct labor hours (DLH) or units produced is the better measure of activity for the firm. Monthly data for the preceding 24 months appear in the file P11_56.XLS. Use regression analysis to determine which measure, DLH or Units (or both), should be used for the budget. How would the regression equation be used to obtain the budget for the firm's overhead costs?

57   The auditor of Kiely Manufacturing is concerned about the number and magnitude of year-end adjustments that are made annually when the financial statements of Kiely Manufacturing are prepared. Specifically, the auditor suspects that the management of Kiely Manufacturing is using discretionary write-offs to manipulate the reported net income. To check this, the auditor has collected data from 25 firms that are similar to Kiely Manufacturing in terms of manufacturing facilities and product lines. The cumulative reported third quarter income and the final net income reported are listed in the file P11_57.XLS for each of these 25 firms. If Kiely Manufacturing reported a cumulative third quarter income of $2,500,000 and a preliminary net income of $4,900,000, should the auditor conclude that the relationship between cumulative third quarter income and the annual income for Kiely Manufacturing differs from that of the 25 firms in this sample? Explain why or why not.

Level B

58   An economic development researcher wants to understand the relationship between the size of the monthly home mortgage or rent payment for households in a particular middle-class neighborhood and the following set of household variables: family size, approximate location of the household within the neighborhood, an indication of whether those surveyed own or rent their home, gross annual income of the first household wage earner, gross annual income of the second household wage earner (if applicable), average monthly expenditure on utilities, and the total indebtedness (excluding the value of a home mortgage) of the household. Observations on each of these variables for a large sample of households are recorded in the file P2_54.XLS.

a   Beginning with *family size*, iteratively add one explanatory variable and estimate the resulting regression equation to explain the variation in the monthly home mortgage or rent payment. If adding any explanatory variable causes the *adjusted R^2* measure to fall, do not include that variable in subsequent versions of the regression model. Otherwise, include the variable and consider adding the next variable in the set. Which variables are included in the final version of your regression model?

b   Interpret the final estimated regression equation you obtained through the process outlined in part **a**. Also, report and interpret the standard error of estimate s_e, the coefficient of determination R^2, and the adjusted R^2 for the final estimated model.

59   (Based on an actual court case in Philadelphia) In the 1994 congressional election, the Republican candidate outpolled the Democratic candidate by 400 votes (excluding absentee ballots). The Democratic candidate outpolled the Republican candidate by 500 absentee votes. The Republican candidate sued (and won), claiming that vote fraud must have played a role in the absentee ballot count. The Republican's lawyer ran a regression to predict (based on past elections) how the absentee ballot margin could be predicted from the votes tabulated on voting machines. Selected results are given in the file P11_59.XLS. Show how this regression could be used by the Republican to prove his claim of vote fraud. (*Hint*: Is the 1994 result an outlier?)

60   The file P11_60.XLS contains data on the price of new and used Taurus sedans. All prices for used cars are from 1995. For example, a new Taurus bought in 1985 cost $11,790 and the

wholesale used price of that car in 1995 was $1700. A new Taurus bought in 1994 cost $18,680 and it could be sold used in 1995 for $12,600.

a You want to predict the resale value (as a percentage of the original price of the vehicle) as a function of the vehicle's age. Find an equation to do this. (You should try at least two different equations and choose the one with the best fit.)

b Suppose all police cars are Ford Tauruses. If you were the business manager for the New York Police Department, what use would you make of your findings from part **a**?

61 (The data for this problem are fictitious, but they are not far off.) For each of the top 25 business schools, the file P11_61.XLS contains the average salary of a professor. Thus, for Indiana University (number 15 in the rankings), the average salary is $46,000. Use this information and regression to show that IU is doing a great job with its available resources.

62 Suppose the correlation between the average height of parents and the height of their firstborn male child is 0.5. You are also told that:

- The average height of all parents is 66 inches.

- The standard deviation of the average height of parents is 4 inches.

- The average height of all male children is 70 inches.

- The standard deviation of the height of all male children is 4 inches.

If a mother and father are 73 and 80 inches tall, respectively, how tall do you predict their son to be? Explain why this is called "regression toward the mean."

63 Do increased taxes increase or decrease economic growth? Table 11.1 gives tax revenues as a percentage of Gross Domestic Product (GDP) and the average annual percentage growth in GDP per capita for nine countries during the years 1970–1994. Do these data support or contradict the dictum of supply-side economics? (Source: *The Economist*, August 24, 1996)

TABLE 11.1 **Economic Data from Nine Countries**

Country	Tax revenues as % of GDP	Average annual growth in GDP per capita
Japan	26%	3.1%
U.S.	27%	1.6%
Italy	33%	2.5%
Canada	34%	2.0%
Switzerland	30%	1.0%
Britain	36%	1.9%
Germany	38%	2.2%
France	42%	1.9%
Sweden	49%	1.1%

64 For each of the four data sets in the file P11_64.XLS, calculate the least squares line. For which of these data sets would you feel comfortable in using the least squares line to predict Y? (Source: Frederic Anscombe, *The American Statistician*)

65 Suppose we run a regression on a data set of X's and Y's and obtain a least squares line of $Y = 12 - 3X$.

a If we double each value of X, what is the new least squares line?

b If we triple each value of Y, what is the new least squares line?

c If we add 6 to each value of X, what is the new least squares line?

d If we subtract 4 from each value of Y, what is the new least squares line?

66 The file P11_66.XLS contains monthly cost accounting data on overhead costs, machine hours, and direct material costs. This problem will help you explore the meaning of R^2 and the relationship between R^2 and correlations.

a Create a table of correlations between the individual variables.

b If you ignored the two explanatory variables MachHrs and DirMatCost and predicted each OHCost as the *mean* of all OHCosts, then a typical "error" would be OHCost minus the mean of all OHCosts. Find the sum of squared errors using this form of prediction, where the sum is over all observations.

c Now run three regressions: (1) OHCost versus MachHrs, (2) OHCost versus DirMatCost, and (3) OHCost versus both MachHrs and DirMatCost. (The first two are simple regressions, the third is a multiple regression.) For each, find the sum of squared residuals, and divide this by the sum of squared errors from part **b**. What is the relationship between this ratio and the associated R^2 for that equation? (Now do you see why R^2 is referred to as the percentage of variation explained?)

d For the first two regressions in part **c**, what is the relationship between R^2 and the corresponding correlation between the response and explanatory variable? For the third regression it turns out that the R^2 can be expressed as a complicated function of all three correlations in part **a**, that is, not just the correlations between the response variable and each explanatory variable, but also the correlation between the explanatory variables. Note that this R^2 is not just the sum of the R^2 values from the first two regressions in part **c**. Why do you think this is true, intuitively? However, R^2 for the multiple regression is still the square of a correlation—namely, the correlation between the observed and predicted values of OHCost. Verify that this is the case for these data.

67 The file P11_67.XLS contains hypothetical starting salaries (in $1000's) for MBA students directly after graduation. The file also lists their years of experience prior to the MBA program and their class standing in the MBA program (on a 0–100 scale).

a Estimate the regression equation with Salary as the response variable and Exper and Class as the explanatory variables. What does this equation imply? What does the standard error of estimate s_e tell you? What about R^2?

b Repeat part **a**, but now include the interaction term Exper*Class (the product) in the equation as well as Exper and Class individually. Answer the same questions as in part **a**. What evidence is there that this extra variable (the interaction variable) is worth including? How do you interpret this regression equation?

68 In a study published in 1985 in *Business Horizons*, Platt and McCarthy employed multiple regression analysis to explain variations in compensations among the CEOs of large companies. Their primary objective was to discover whether levels of compensations are affected more by short-run considerations—"I'll earn more now if my company does well in the short run"—or long-run considerations—"My best method for obtaining high compensation is to stay with my company for a long time." The study used as its response variable the total compensation for each of the 100 highest paid CEOs in 1981. This variable was defined as the sum of salary, bonuses, and other benefits (measured in $1000's).

The following potential explanatory variables were considered. To capture short-run effects, the average of the company's previous 5 years' percentage changes in earnings per share (EPS) and the projected percentage change in next year's EPS were used. To capture the long-run effect, age and years as CEO, two admittedly correlated variables, were used. Dummy variables for the CEO's background (finance, marketing, and so on) were also considered. Finally, the researchers considered several nonlinear and interaction terms based on these variables. The best-fitting equation was the following:

$$\text{TotComp} = -3493 + 898.7(\text{Years as CEO}) + 9.28(\text{Years as CEO})^2$$

$$-17.19(\text{Years as CEO})(\text{Age}) + 88.27\text{Age} + 867.4\text{Finance}$$

(The last variable represents a dummy variable, equal to 1 if the CEO had a finance background, 0 otherwise.) The corresponding R^2 was 19.4%.

a Explain what this equation implies about CEO compensations.

b The researchers drew the following conclusions. First, it appears that CEOs should indeed concentrate on long-run considerations—namely, those that keep them on their jobs the longest. Second, the absence of the short-run company-related variables from the equations helps to confirm the conjecture that CEOs who concentrate on earning the quick buck for their companies may not be acting in their best self-interest. Finally, the positive coefficient of the dummy variable may imply that financial people possess skills that are vitally important, and firms therefore outbid one another for the best financial talent. Based on the data given, do you agree with these conclusions?

c Consider a CEO (other than those in the study) who has been in his position for 10 years and has a financial background. Predict his total yearly compensation (in $1000's) if he is

50 years old; if he is 55 years old. Explain why the difference between these two predictions is not 5(88.27), where 88.27 is the coefficient of the Age variable.

69 The Wilhoit Company has observed that there is a linear relationship between indirect labor expense (ILE) and direct labor hours (DLH). Data for direct labor hours and indirect labor expense for 18 months are given in the file P11_69.XLS. At the start of month 7, all cost categories in the Wilhoit Company increased by 10%, and they stayed at this level for months 7–12. Then at the start of month 13, another 10% across-the-board increase in all costs occurred, and the company operated at this price level for months 13–18.

  a Plot the data. Verify that the relationship between ILE and DLH is approximately linear within each 6-month period. Use regression (three times) to estimate the slope and intercept during months 1–6; during months 7–12; during months 13–18.

  b Use regression to fit a straight line to all 18 data points simultaneously. What values of the slope and intercept do you obtain?

  c Perform a price level adjustment to the data and re-estimate the slope and intercept using all 18 data points. Assuming no cost increases for month 19, what is your prediction for indirect labor expense if there are 35,000 direct labor-hours in month 19?

  d Interpret your results. What causes the difference in the linear relationship estimated in parts **b** and **c**?

70 The Bohring Company manufactures a sophisticated radar unit that is used in a fighter aircraft built by Seaways Aircraft. The first 50 units of the radar unit have been completed, and Bohring is preparing to submit a proposal to Seaways Aircraft to manufacture the next 50 units. Bohring wants to submit a competitive bid, but at the same time, it wants to ensure that all the costs of manufacturing the radar unit are fully covered. As part of this process, Bohring is attempting to develop a standard for the number of labor hours required to manufacture each radar unit. Developing a labor standard has been a continuing problem in the past. The file P11_70.XLS lists the number of labor hours required for each of the first 50 units of production. Bohring accountants want to see whether regression analysis, together with the concept of learning curves, can help solve the company's problem. ■

11.1   Quantity Discounts at the FirmChair Company

The FirmChair Company manufactures customized wood furniture and sells the furniture in large quantities to major furniture retailers. Jim Bolling has recently been assigned to analyze the company's pricing policy. He has been told that quantity discounts were usually given. For example, for one type of chair, the pricing changed at quantities of 200 and 400—that is, these were the quantity "breaks," where the marginal cost of the next chair changed. For this type of chair, the file FIRMCHAIR.XLS contains the quantity and total price to the customer for 81 orders. Use regression to help Jim discover the pricing structure that FirmChair evidently used. (*Note*: A linear regression of TotPrice versus Quantity will give you a "decent" fit, but you can do much better by introducing appropriate variables into the regression.)

11.2   Housing Price Structure in MidCity

Sales of single-family houses have been brisk in MidCity this year. This has especially been true in older, more established neighborhoods, where housing is relatively inexpensive compared to the new homes being built in the newer neighborhoods. Nevertheless, there are also many families who are willing to pay a higher price for the prestige of living in one of the newer neighborhoods. The file MIDCITY.XLS contains data on 128 recent sales in MidCity. For each sale, the file shows the neighborhood (1, 2, or 3) in which the house is located, the number of offers made on the house, the square footage, whether the house is made primarily of brick, the number of bathrooms, the number of bedrooms, and the selling price. Neighborhoods 1 and 2 are more traditional neighborhoods, whereas neighborhood 3 is a newer, more prestigious, neighborhood.

Use regression to estimate and interpret the pricing structure of houses in MidCity. Here are some considerations.

1   Is there a "premium" for a brick house, everything else being equal?

2   Is there a premium for a house in neighborhood 3, everything else being equal?

3   Is there an *extra* premium for a brick house in neighborhood 3, in addition to the usual premium for a brick house?

4   For purposes of estimation and prediction, could neighborhoods 1 and 2 be collapsed into a single "older" neighborhood?

11.3 **Demand for French Bread at Howie's**

Howie's Bakery is one of the most popular bakeries in town, and the favorite at Howie's is French bread. Each day of the week, Howie's bakes a number of loaves of French bread, more or less according to a daily schedule. To maintain its fine reputation, Howie's gives away to charity any loaves not sold on the day they are baked. Although this occurs frequently, it is also common for Howie's to run out of French bread on any given day—more demand than supply. In this case, no extra loaves are baked that day; the customers have to go elsewhere (or come back to Howie's the next day) for their French bread. Although French bread at Howie's is always popular, Howie's stimulates demand by running occasional 10% off sales.

Howie's has collected data for 20 consecutive weeks, 140 days in all. These data are listed in the file HOWIES.XLS. The variables are Day (Monday–Sunday), Supply (number of loaves baked that day), OnSale (whether French bread is on sale that day), and Demand (loaves actually sold that day). Howie's would like you to see whether regression can be used successfully to estimate Demand from the other data in the file. Howie reasons that if these other variables can be used to predict Demand, then he might be able to determine his daily supply (number of loaves to bake) in a more cost-effective way.

How successful is regression with these data? Is Howie correct that regression can help him determine his daily supply? Is any information "missing" that would be useful? How would you obtain it? How would you use it? Is this extra information *really* necessary?

11.4 **Investing for Retirement**

Financial advisors offer many types of advice to customers, but they generally agree that one of the best things people can do is invest as much as possible in tax-deferred retirement plans. Not only are the earnings from these investments exempt from income tax (until retirement), but the investment itself is tax-exempt. This means that if a person invests, say, $10,000 income of his $100,000 income a tax-deferred retirement plan, he pays income tax that year on only $90,000 of his income. This is probably the best method available to most people for avoiding tax payments. However, which group takes advantage of this attractive investment opportunity: everyone, people with low salaries, people with high salaries, or who?

The file RETIREPLAN.XLS lets you investigate this question. It contains data on 194 couples: number of dependent children, combined annual salary of husband and wife, current mortgage on home, average amount of other (nonmortgage) debt, and percentage of combined income invested in tax-deferred retirement plans (assumed to be limited to 15%, which is realistic). Using correlations, scatterplots, and regression analysis, what can you conclude about the tendency to invest in tax-deferred retirement plans in this group of people?

12

Regression Analysis: Statistical Inference

Successful Applications

Do fast-food chains price discriminate on the basis of race and income characteristics of an area? One researcher, Kathryn Graddy, has provided evidence that they do (Graddy, 1997). She gathered data from over 300 fast-food restaurants, including Burger King, Wendy's, KFC, and Roy Rogers, in New Jersey and eastern Pennsylvania locations. Using regression, she estimated that after taking income, cost, and other differences between restaurants into account, meal prices increase approximately 5% for each 50% increase in the black population. More simply, when all else is equal, prices tend to be slightly higher in areas with larger percentages of blacks.

Graddy's principal research question was whether prices charged for fast-food meals tend to be affected by the race characteristics of an area. However, she had to be very careful to account for other factors that might affect prices. This is a strength of regression. It allows a researcher to *control* for other factors that might also affect a response variable—in this case, price. Graddy used economic theory to suggest several types of explanatory variables that she should include in her regression equation. Then she operationalized these as well as possible, based on the data she was able to obtain. The three types of explanatory variables she believed were necessary were cost variables, competition variables, and race and income variables.

Obviously, cost variables influence price. The costs can include occupancy expenses; payroll expenses; and publicity, food, and packaging expenses. The cost variables she used were (1) the log of the average starting wage in each store; (2) the number of full-time-equivalent employees at each store; (3) an index of crime in the area (which could affect maintenance and insurance costs); (4) the log of the median value of owner-occupied housing units (as a proxy for real-estate expenses) in the area; and (5) a state dummy variable (New Jersey versus Pennsylvania) to control for possible cost differences for operating in different states. Competitive facators can also affect price. Graddy used several variables to capture differences in competitive characteristics. Specifically, she chose (1) a dummy variable for whether a store is company owned or franchised; (2) the proportion of the population without a car (because people without cars have difficulty dining outside of their neighborhood); and (3) a dummy variable to indicate whether there are more than three stores in the area or three or fewer. Finally, for the race and income variables, she included (1) the log of the median family income in the area; (2) the proportion of the population that is black; and (3) the proportion of the population below the poverty level for each zip code area in which a store is located.

Graddy's article is not easy reading. When performing a study as this, particularly in the sensitive area of race discrimination, a researcher needs to document her methodology very carefully to convince readers that her principal findings are not the result of improper statistical analysis. On the surface, her results appear to indicate that there is racial discrimination, in the form of higher prices, at these fast-food restaurants. However, could this result be due to the particular explanatory variables, or the forms of these variables, that were entered in the regression equation? Could the results be due to variables omitted from the equation? And even if the results are statistically correct, can we conclude that there is some type of *deliberate* racial discrimination at these restaurants?

Graddy does her best to address these questions, although no *statistical* analysis can ever answer the last question with complete assurance. She runs a number of variations of the original regression equation, using different subsets of explanatory variables, and finds that the same essential price discrimination continues to appear. She also discusses possible reasons for the price discrimination findings *besides* deliberate racial discrimination. For example, it might be that differences in prices arise because the crime index she used does not adequately reflect differences in insurance costs or the perceived risk of operating in different areas. Or it is possible that franchise owners who operate stores in areas with a high proportion of black customers own fewer restaurants, which could result in fewer economies of scale at the management level. There are many alternative economic explanations of the results. As Graddy concludes, "Explanations based on price discrimination, either due to differences in elasticities, differences in competition, or a taste for discrimination, cannot be excluded, however. More research into the incidence, cause, and effects of price differences that are correlated with race would appear to be warranted." ■

Introduction

In the previous chapter we learned how to fit a regression equation to a set of points by using the least squares method. The purpose of this regression equation is to provide a good fit to the points in the sample so that we can understand the relationship between a response variable and one or more explanatory variables. The entire emphasis of the discussion in the previous chapter was on the observations in the sample. In this chapter we take a slightly different point of view. Now we assume that the observations in the sample are taken from some larger population. For example, the sample of 50 regions from the Pharmex drugstore example could represent a sample of all the regions where Pharmex does business. If that is the case, then we might be interested in the relationship between variables in the entire population, not just in the sample.

There are two basic problems we will discuss in this chapter. The first has to do with the population regression equation. We want to infer its characteristics—that is, its intercept and slope term(s)—from the corresponding terms estimated by least squares. We also want to know which explanatory variables "belong" in the equation. We have seen that there are typically a large number of *potential* explanatory variables, and it is often not clear which of these do the best job of explaining variation in the response variable. In addition, we would like to infer whether there is any population regression equation worth pursuing. It might be that the potential explanatory variables provide very little explanation of the response variable, based on the sample data.

The second problem we will discuss in this chapter is prediction. We touched on the prediction problem in the previous chapter, but there it was primarily in the context of predicting the response variable for part of the sample held out for validation purposes. In reality, we had the values of the response variable for that part of the sample, so prediction was not really necessary. Now we will go beyond the sample and predict values of the response variable for *new* observations. There is no way to check the accuracy of these predictions, at least not right away, because the true values of the response variable are not yet known. However, we will provide prediction intervals to measure the accuracy of the predictions.

12.2

The Statistical Model

To perform statistical inference in a regression context, we must first make several assumptions about the population. Throughout the analysis these assumptions remain exactly that—they are only assumptions, not facts. These assumptions represent an idealization of reality, and as such, they are never likely to be entirely satisfied for the population in any real study. From a practical point of view, all we can ask is that they represent a close approximation to reality. If this is the case, then the analysis in this chapter is valid. But if the assumptions are grossly violated, we should be very suspicious of the statistical inferences that are based on these assumptions. Although we can never be entirely certain of the validity of the assumptions, there are ways to check for gross violations, and we will discuss some of these.

Regression Assumptions

1   There is a population regression line. It joins the means of the response variable for all values of the explanatory variables. For any fixed values of the explanatory variables, the mean of the errors is 0.

2   For any values of the explanatory variables, the standard deviation of the response variable is a constant, the same for all such values.

3   For any values of the explanatory variables, the response variable is normally distributed.

4   The errors are probabilistically independent.

Since these assumptions are so crucial to the regression analysis that follows, it is important to understand exactly what they mean. Assumption 1 is probably the most important. It implies that for some set of explanatory variables, there is an exact linear relationship in the population between the *means* of the response variable and the values of the explanatory variables.

To explain assumption 1 in more detail, we introduce some notation. Let Y be the response variable, and assume that there are k explanatory variables, X_1 through X_k. Let $\mu_{Y|X_1,\ldots,X_k}$ be the mean of all Y's for *fixed* values of the X's. Then assumption 1 implies that there is an exact linear relationship between the mean $\mu_{Y|X_1,\ldots,X_k}$ and the X's. Specifically, it implies that there are coefficients α and β_1 through β_k such that the following equation holds for all values of the X's:

$$\mu_{Y|X_1,\ldots,X_k} = \alpha + \beta_1 X_1 + \cdots + \beta_k X_k \tag{12.1}$$

In the terminology of the previous chapter, α is the intercept term, and β_1 through β_k are the slope terms. We use Greek letters for these coefficients to denote that they are *unobservable* population parameters. Assumption 1 implies the existence of a population regression equation and the corresponding α and β's. However, it tells us nothing about the values of these parameters. We still need to estimate them from sample data, and we will continue to use the least squares method to do so.

Equation (12.1) says that the *means* of the Y's lie on the population regression line. However, we know from a scatterplot that most *individual* Y's do not lie on this line. The vertical distance from any point to the line is called an **error term**.[1] The error for any point, labeled ε, is the difference between Y and $\mu_{Y|X_1,\ldots,X_k}$, that is,

$$Y = \mu_{Y|X_1,\ldots,X_k} + \varepsilon$$

By substituting the assumed linear form for $\mu_{Y|X_1,\ldots,X_k}$, we obtain

$$Y = \alpha + \beta_1 X_1 + \cdots + \beta_k X_k + \varepsilon \tag{12.2}$$

This equation states that each value of Y is equal to a fitted part plus an error term. The fitted part is the linear expression $\alpha + \beta_1 X_1 + \cdots + \beta_k X_k$. The error term ε is sometimes positive, in which case the point is above the regression line, and sometimes negative, in which case the point is below the regression line. The last part of assumption 1 states that these errors average to 0 in the population, so that the positive errors cancel the negative errors.

Assumption 2 concerns variation around the population regression line. Specifically, it states that the variation of the Y's about the regression line is the *same*, regardless of the values of the X's. A technical term for this property is **homoscedasticity**. We prefer a simpler term: **constant error variance**. In the Pharmex example (Example 11.1), constant error variance implies that the variation in Sales values is the same regardless of the value of Promote. As another example, consider the Bendrix manufacturing example (Example 11.2). There we related overhead costs (Overhead) to the number of machine hours (MachHrs) and the number of production runs (ProdRuns). Constant error variance implies that overhead costs vary just as much for small values of MachHrs and ProdRuns as for large values—or any values in between.

There are many applications in which assumption 2 is questionable. The variation in Y often increases as X increases—a violation of assumption 2. We saw an example of this in Figure 11.10 (repeated here in Figure 12.1), which is based on the HyTex mail-order data in Example 3.11 from Chapter 3. This scatterplot shows AmountSpent versus Salary for a sample of HyTex's customers. Clearly, the variation in AmountSpent increases as Salary increases, which makes intuitive sense. Customers with small salaries have little disposable income, so they all tend to spend small amounts for mail-order items. Customers with large salaries have more disposable income. Some of them spend a lot of it on mail-order items and some spend only a little of it—hence a larger variation. Scatterplots with this "fan" shape are not at all uncommon in real studies, and they exhibit a clear violation of assumption 2. We say that the data in this graph exhibit **heteroscedasticity**, or more simply, **nonconstant error variance**.

The easiest way to detect nonconstant error variance is through a visual inspection of a scatterplot. We draw a scatterplot of the response variable versus an explanatory variable X and see whether the points vary more for some values of X than for others. We can also examine the residuals with a residual plot, where residual values are on the vertical axis and some other variable (Y or one of the X's) is on the horizontal axis. If the residual plot

---

[1] An error term ε is close to, but not the same as, a residual e. An error term is the vertical distance from a point to the (unobservable) population regression line. A residual is the vertical distance from a point to the estimated regression line. Residuals can be calculated from observed data; error terms cannot.

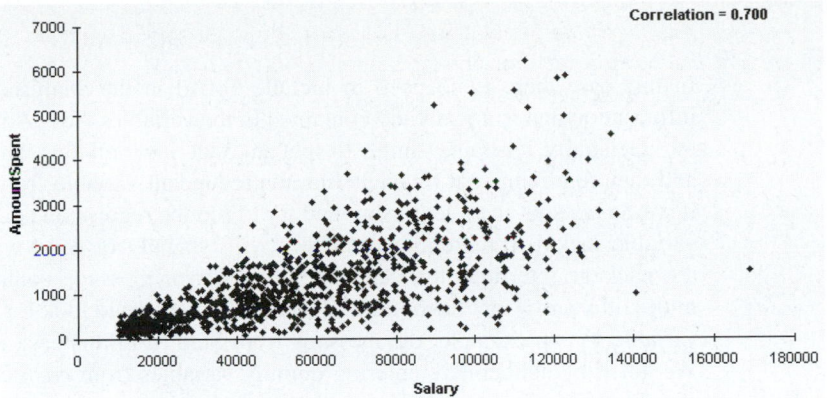

exhibits a fan shape or other evidence of nonconstant error variance, this also indicates a violation of assumption 2.

Assumption 3 states that the errors are normally distributed. We can check this by forming a histogram or a Q–Q plot of the residuals. If assumption 3 holds, then the histogram should be approximately symmetric and bell-shaped, and the points in the Q–Q plot should be close to a 45° line. But if there is an obvious skewness, too many residuals more than, say, two standard deviations from the mean, or some other nonnormal property, then this indicates a violation of assumption 3.

Finally, assumption 4 requires probabilistic independence of the errors. Intuitively, this assumption means that information on some of the errors provides no information on other errors. For example, if we are told that the overhead costs for months 1–4 are all above the regression line (positive residuals), we cannot infer anything about the residual for month 5 if assumption 4 holds.

For cross-sectional data there is generally little reason to doubt the validity of assumption 4 unless the observations are ordered in some particular way. For cross-sectional data we generally take assumption 4 for granted. However, for time series data, assumption 4 is often violated. This is because of a property called **autocorrelation**. For now, we simply mention that one output given automatically in most regression packages is the **Durbin-Watson statistic**. The Durbin-Watson statistic is one measure of autocorrelation and thus it measures the extent to which assumption 4 is violated. We can usually ignore it in cross-sectional studies, but it is important for time series data. We briefly discuss this Durbin-Watson statistic toward the end of this and the next chapter.

One other assumption is important for numerical calculations. We must assume that no explanatory variable is an *exact* linear combination of any other explanatory variables. Another way of stating this is that there is no exact linear relationship between any set of explanatory variables. This would occur, for example, if one variable were an exact multiple of another, or if one variable were equal to the sum of several other variables. More generally, it occurs if one of the explanatory variables can be written as a weighted sum of several of the others.

If such a relationship holds, it means that there is *redundancy* in the data. One of the X's could be eliminated without any loss of information. A simple example is the following. Suppose that MachHrs1 is machine hours measured in hours, and MachHrs2 is machine hours measured in *hundreds* of hours. Then it is clear that these two variables contain exactly the same information, and either of them could be eliminated.

Another example is the following. Suppose that Ad1, Ad2, and Ad3 are the amounts spent on radio ads, television ads, and newspaper ads. Also, suppose that TotAd is the amount spent on radio, television, and newspaper ads combined. Then there is an exact linear relationship among these variables:

$$\text{TotAd} = \text{Ad1} + \text{Ad2} + \text{Ad3}$$

In this case there is no need to include TotAd in the analysis because it contains no information that is not already contained in the variables Ad1, Ad2, and Ad3.

Generally, it is fairly simple to spot an exact linear relationship such as the ones above, and then to eliminate it by excluding the redundant variable from the analysis. However, if we do *not* spot the relationship and try to run the regression analysis with the redundant variable included, regression packages will typically respond with an error message. If the package interrupts the analysis with an error message containing the words "exact multicollinearity" or "linear dependence," then we should look for a redundant explanatory variable. As an example, the message from StatPro in this case is shown in Figure 12.2. We got it by deliberately entering dummy variables from *each* category of a categorical variable—something we have warned *not* to do.

FIGURE 12.2 **Error Message from StatPro Indicating Exact Multicollinearity**

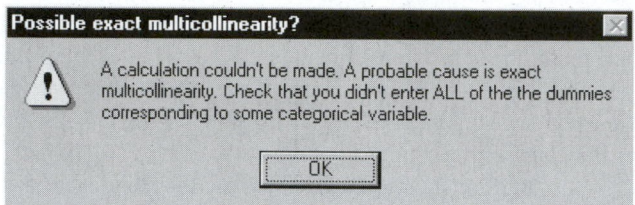

Although this problem can be a nuisance, it is usually caused by an oversight and can be fixed easily by eliminating a redundant variable. A more common and serious problem is **multicollinearity**, where explanatory variables are highly, but not exactly, correlated. A typical example is an employee's years of experience and age. Although these two variables are not equal for all employees, they are likely to be very highly correlated. If they are both included as explanatory variables in a regression analysis, the computer will not issue any error messages, but the estimates it produces might be unreliable. We will discuss multicollinearity in more detail later in this chapter.

12.3

Inferences About the Regression Coefficients

In this section we show how to make inferences about the population regression coefficients from sample data. We begin by making the assumptions discussed in Section 12.2. In particular, the first assumption states that there is a population regression line. Equation (12.2) for this line is repeated below:

$$Y = \alpha + \beta_1 X_1 + \cdots + \beta_k X_k + \varepsilon$$

We refer to α and the β's collectively as the **regression coefficients**. Again, Greek letters are used to indicate that these quantities are unknown and unobservable. Actually, there is one other unknown constant in the model, the variance of the error terms. Regression assumption 2 states that these errors have a constant variance, the same for all values of the X's. We label this constant variance σ^2. Equivalently, the common standard deviation of the errors is σ.

This is how it looks in theory. There is a fixed set of explanatory variables, and given these variables, the problem is to estimate α, the β's, and σ. In practice, however, it is not this straightforward. In real regression applications the choice of relevant explanatory variables is almost never obvious. There are at least two guiding principles—relevance and data availability. We certainly want variables that are related to the response variable. The best situation is when there is an established economic or physical theory to guide us. For example, economic theory suggests that the demand for a product (response variable) is related to its price (possible explanatory variable). But there are not enough established theories to cover every situation. We often have to use the available data, plus some trial and error, to determine a *useful* set of explanatory variables. In this sense, it is usually pointless to search for one single "true" population regression equation. Instead, we typically estimate several competing models, each with a different set of explanatory variables, and ultimately select one of them as being the most useful.

Deciding which explanatory variables to include in a regression equation is probably the most difficult part of any applied regression analysis. Available data sets frequently offer an overabundance of potential explanatory variables. In addition, it is possible and often useful to create new variables from original variables, such as their logarithms. So where do we stop? Is it best to include every conceivable explanatory variable that might be related to the response variable? One overriding principle is **parsimony**—explaining the most with the least. For example, if we can explain a response variable just as well (or nearly as well) with two explanatory variables as with ten explanatory variables, then the principle of parsimony says to use only two. Models with fewer explanatory variables are generally easier to interpret, so we prefer them whenever possible.

Before we can determine which equation has the "best" set of explanatory variables, however, we must be able to estimate the unknown parameters for a given equation. That is, for a given set of explanatory variables X_1 through X_k, we must be able to estimate α, the β's, and σ. We learned how to find point estimates of these parameters in the previous chapter. The estimates of α and the β's are the least squares estimates of the intercept and slope terms. For example, we used the 36 months of overhead data in the Bendrix example to estimate the equation

$$\text{Predicted Overhead} = 3997 + 43.54\text{MachHrs} + 883.62\text{ProdRuns}$$

This implies that the least squares estimates of α, β_1, and β_2 are 3997, 43.54, and 883.62. Furthermore, because the residuals are really estimates of the error terms, the standard error of estimate s_e is an estimate of σ. For the same overhead equation this estimate is $s_e = \$4109$.

However, we know from Chapters 8 and 9 that there is more to statistical estimation than finding point estimates of population parameters. Each potential sample from the population would typically lead to *different* point estimates. For example, if Bendrix estimated the equation for overhead from a different 36-month period, the results would almost certainly be different. Therefore, the question is how these point estimates vary from sample to sample.

12.3.1 Sampling Distribution of the Regression Coefficients

The key idea is again sampling distributions. Recall that the sampling distribution of any statistic derived from sample data is the distribution of this statistic over all possible samples. This idea can be applied to the least squares estimate of a regression coefficient. For example, the sampling distribution of b_1, the least squares estimate of β_1, is the distribution of b_1's we would see if we observed many samples and ran a least squares regression on each of them.

Fortunately, mathematicians have used theoretical arguments to find the required sampling distributions. We state the main result as follows. Let β_i be any of the β's, and let b_i be the least squares estimate of β_i. Then if the regression assumptions hold, the standardized value $(b_i - \beta_i)/s_i$ has a t distribution with $n - k - 1$ degrees of freedom. Here, k is the number of explanatory variables included in the equation, and s_i is the estimated standard deviation of the sampling distribution of b_i.

This important result can be interpreted as follows. First, the estimate b_i is *unbiased* in the sense that its mean is β_i, the true but unknown value of the slope. If we calculated b_i's from repeated samples, some would underestimate β_i and others would overestimate β_i, but on average they would be on target.

Second, the estimated standard deviation of b_i is labeled s_i. It is usually called the **standard error of b_i**. This standard error is related to the standard error of estimate s_e, but it is not the same. Generally, the formula for s_i is quite complicated, and it is not shown here, but its value is printed in all standard regression outputs. It measures how much the b_i's would vary from sample to sample. A small value of s_i is preferred—it means that b_i is a more accurate estimate of the true coefficient β_i.

Finally, the shape of the distribution of b_i is symmetric and bell-shaped. The relevant distribution is the t distribution with $n - k - 1$ degrees of freedom.

We have stated this result for a typical coefficient of one of the X's. These are usually the coefficients of most interest. However, exactly the same result holds for the intercept term α. Now we will see how to use this result.

EXAMPLE 12.1

This example is a continuation of the Bendrix manufacturing example from the previous chapter. As before, the response variable is Overhead and the explanatory variables are MachHrs and ProdRuns. What inferences can we make about the regression coefficients?

Solution

When we use StatPro's Multiple Regression procedure, we obtain the output shown in Figure 12.3. (See the file BENDRIX.XLS.) This output is practically identical to regression

FIGURE 12.3   **Regression Output for Bendrix Example**

	A	B	C	D	E	F	G
1	Results of multiple regression for Overhead						
2							
3	Summary measures						
4		Multiple R	0.9308				
5		R-Square	0.8664				
6		Adj R-Square	0.8583				
7		StErr of Est	4108.9932				
8							
9	ANOVA Table						
10		Source	df	SS	MS	F	p-value
11		Explained	2	3614020652.0000	1807010326.0000	107.0261	0.0000
12		Unexplained	33	557166208.0000	16883824.4848		
13							
14	Regression coefficients						
15			Coefficient	Std Err	t-value	p-value	
16		Constant	3996.6782	6603.6509	0.6052	0.5492	
17		MachHrs	43.5364	3.5895	12.1289	0.0000	
18		ProdRuns	883.6179	82.2514	10.7429	0.0000	

outputs from all other statistical software packages. We have already seen that the estimates of the regression coefficients appear under the label Coefficient in the range C16:C18. These values estimate the true, but unobservable, population coefficients. The next column, labeled Std Err, shows the s_i's. Specifically, 3.590 is the standard error of the coefficient of MachHrs, and 82.251 is the standard error of the coefficient of ProdRuns.

The b_i's represent point estimates of the β_i's, based on this particular sample. The s_i's indicate the accuracy of these point estimates. For example, the point estimate of β_1, the effect on Overhead of a one-unit increase in MachHrs, is 43.536. We are about 95% confident that the true β_1 is within two standard errors of this point estimate, that is, from 36.357 to 50.715. Similar statements can be made for the coefficient of ProdRuns and the intercept (Constant) term. ■

12.3.2 Confidence Intervals for the Regression Coefficients

As with any population parameters, we can use the sample data to obtain confidence intervals for the regression coefficients. For example, the preceding paragraph implies that an approximate 95% confidence interval for the coefficient of MachHrs extends from 36.357 to 50.715. More precisely, a confidence interval for any β_i is of the form

$$b_i \pm t\text{-multiple} \times s_i$$

where the t-multiple depends on the confidence level and the degrees of freedom (here $n - k - 1$). For example, the relevant t-multiple for the Bendrix data, assuming we want a 95% confidence interval, is the value that cuts off probability 0.025 of the t distribution with $36 - 2 - 1 = 33$ degrees of freedom. [It is 2.035 and can be found in Excel with the function TINV(0.05,33).] Using this multiple gives a 95% confidence interval from 36.234 to 50.839, as shown in Figure 12.4.

Many computer packages routinely provide 95% confidence intervals for the β_i's, so that no calculation is necessary. The StatPro add-in does not provide these confidence intervals automatically, but they are easy to obtain with Excel's TINV function, as shown in Figure 12.4 for the Bendrix data. Once we obtain the regression output through row 18 with StatPro, we can calculate lower confidence limits by entering the formula

=C16-TINV(1-$C$21,33)*D16

in cell C23 and copying down. The upper confidence limits in column D are the same except with a plus sign before TINV.

FIGURE 12.4 **Confidence Intervals for Regression Coefficients**

	A	B	C	D	E	F
14	Regression coefficients					
15			Coefficient	Std Err	t-value	p-value
16		Constant	3996.6782	6603.6509	0.6052	0.5492
17		MachHrs	43.5364	3.5895	12.1289	0.0000
18		ProdRuns	883.6179	82.2514	10.7429	0.0000
19						
20	Confidence intervals for regression coefficients					
21		Confidence level	95%			
22			Lower limit	Upper limit		
23		Constant	-9438.561	17431.918		
24		MachHrs	36.234	50.839		
25		ProdRuns	716.276	1050.960		

12.3.3 Hypothesis Tests for the Regression Coefficients

There is another important piece of information in regression outputs: the t-values for the individual regression coefficients. These are shown in the "t-value" column of the regression output in Figure 12.4. The formula for a t-value is simple. It is the ratio of the estimated coefficient to its standard error:

$$t\text{-value} = b_i/s_i$$

Therefore, it indicates how many standard errors the regression coefficient is from 0. For example, the t-value for MachHrs is about 12.13, so we know that the regression coefficient of MachHrs, 43.536, is over 12 standard errors to the right of 0. Similarly, the coefficient of ProdRuns is more than 10 of its standard errors to the right of 0.

A t-value can be used in an important hypothesis test for the corresponding regression coefficient. To motivate this test, suppose that we want to decide whether a particular explanatory variable belongs in the regression equation. A sensible criterion for making this decision is to check whether the corresponding regression coefficient is 0. If a variable's coefficient is 0, there is no point in including this variable in the equation; the 0 coefficient will cancel its effect on the response variable.

Therefore, it is reasonable to test whether a variable's coefficient is 0. This is usually tested versus a *two-tailed* alternative. The null and alternative hypotheses are of the form $H_0: \beta_i = 0$ versus $H_a: \beta_i \neq 0$. If we can reject the null hypothesis and conclude that this coefficient is *not* 0, then we have an argument for including the variable in the regression equation. Conversely, if we cannot reject the null hypothesis, we might decide to eliminate this variable from the equation.

The t-value for a variable allows us to run this test easily. We simply compare the t-value in the regression output with a tabulated t-value and reject the null hypothesis only if the t-value from the computer output is greater in magnitude than the tabulated t-value. If the test is run at the 5% significance level, for example, then the appropriate tabulated t-value can be found in Excel with TINV($0.05, n - k - 1$), the same t-value used above for confidence intervals.

Most computer packages, including StatPro, make this test even easier to run by reporting the corresponding p-value for the test. This eliminates the need for finding the tabulated t-value (or using the TINV function). The p-value is interpreted exactly as in Chapter 9. It is the probability (in both tails) of the relevant t distribution beyond the listed t-value. For example, referring again to Figure 12.4, the t-value for MachHrs is 12.13, and the associated p-value (rounded to four decimal places) is 0.0000. This means that there is virtually no probability beyond the observed t-value. In words, we are still not exactly sure of the true coefficient of MachHrs, but we are sure it is not 0. The same can be said for the coefficient of ProdRuns.

We will soon say even more about these t-values and how they can help to decide which variables to include or exclude in a regression equation. But we first make the following points about hypothesis tests for regression coefficients.

1   A t-value is usually reported for the intercept (constant) term in the equation, as well as for the other coefficients. However, this information is often of little relevance. The reason is that there is often no practical reason for testing whether the intercept is 0. There are rare situations where an intercept equal to 0 has a meaningful interpretation, and in such situations the hypothesis test is relevant.

2   The test of $\beta_i = 0$ versus a two-tailed alternative at the 5% level, say, can also be run by calculating a 95% confidence interval for β_i and rejecting the null hypothesis if 0 is not within the confidence interval. That is, if a 95% confidence interval for β_i extends from a negative number to a positive number, we cannot reject the null hypothesis that $\beta_i = 0$.

3 The above test, a two-tailed test of whether a particular β_i is 0, is only one of many hypothesis tests that can be run. For example, consider a sample of houses that have been sold recently. We would like to regress the selling prices of the houses on their appraised values, as obtained by a professional appraiser. Now, it is pretty clear, even before the data are observed, that selling prices will be *positively* related to appraised values. Therefore, there isn't much point in testing whether the coefficient of AppraisedValue is 0.

A more interesting test in this example is whether the coefficient of AppraisedValue is less than or greater than 1. If it is less than 1, say, then every extra dollar of appraised value contributes *less than* an extra dollar to the selling price. Therefore, we might run the one-tailed test of $H_0: \beta \geq 1$ versus $H_a: \beta < 1$. (We could also run a two-tailed test. It just depends on what we're trying to prove.) In this case we would base the test on the test statistic

$$t\text{-value} = \frac{b_1 - 1}{s_1}$$

where b_1 and s_1 are the coefficient and standard error of AppraisedValue in the regression output. Its p-value could be calculated in Excel with the function TDIST(ABS(t-value),$n - 2$,1). This t-value and the corresponding p-value are *not* reported in computer outputs, but they are easy to obtain.

The point here is that most computer outputs provide the ingredients for a very natural test—whether a given regression coefficient is 0. Virtually no work is needed to perform this test because the t-value and p-value are given in the regression output. But other hypothesis tests on the coefficients are sometimes relevant, and they can be performed easily with Excel formulas.

PROBLEMS

Level A

1 Explore the relationship between the selling prices (Y) and the appraised values (X) of the 150 homes in the file P2_7.XLS by estimating a simple linear regression model. Construct a 95% confidence interval for the model's slope (i.e., β_1) parameter. What does this confidence interval tell you about the relationship between Y and X for these data?

2 The owner of the Original Italian Pizza restaurant chain would like to predict the sales of his specialty, deep-dish pizza. He has gathered data on the monthly sales of deep-dish pizzas at his restaurants and observations on other potentially relevant variables for each of his 15 outlets in central Pennsylvania. These data are provided in the file P11_4.XLS.

    a Estimate a multiple regression model between the quantity sold (Y) and the following explanatory variables: average price of deep-dish pizzas, monthly advertising expenditures, and disposable income per household in the areas surrounding the outlets.

    b Is there evidence of any violations of the key assumptions of regression analysis in this case?

    c Which of the variables in this model have regression coefficients that are statistically different from 0 at the 5% significance level?

    d Given your findings in part **c**, which variables, if any, would you choose to remove from the model estimated in part **a**? Explain your decision.

3 The *ACCRA Cost of Living Index* provides a useful and reasonably accurate measure of cost of living differences among a large number of urban areas. Items on which the index is based have been carefully chosen to reflect the different categories of consumer expenditures. The data are in the file P2_19.XLS.

    a Use multiple regression to explore the relationship between the composite index (response variable) and the various expenditure components (explanatory variables).

    b Is there evidence of any violations of the key assumptions of regression analysis?

c Which of the variables in this model have regression coefficients that are statistically different from 0 at the 5% significance level?

d Given your findings in part **c**, which variables, if any, would you choose to remove from the model estimated in part **a**? Explain your decision.

4 A trucking company wants to predict the yearly maintenance expense (Y) for a truck using the number of miles driven during the year (X_1) and the age of the truck (X_2, in years) at the beginning of the year. The company has gathered the information given in the file P11_16.XLS. Note that each observation corresponds to a particular truck.

a Formulate and estimate a multiple regression model using the given data.

b Does autocorrelation, multicollinearity, or heteroscedasticity appear to be a problem?

c Construct 95% confidence intervals for the regression coefficients of X_1 and X_2. Based on these interval estimates, which variables, if any, would you choose to remove from the model estimated in part **a**? Explain your decision.

5 Based on the data in the file P2_25.XLS from the U.S. Department of Agriculture, explore the relationship between the number of farms (X) and the average size of a farm (Y) in the United States between 1950 and 1997.

a Use the given data to estimate a simple linear regression model.

b Test whether there is sufficient evidence to conclude that the slope parameter (i.e., β_1) is *less than* 0. Use a 5% significance level.

c Based on your finding in part **b**, is it possible to conclude that a linear relationship exists between the number of farms and the average farm size between 1950 and 1997? Explain.

Level B

6 Consider the relationship between the size of the population (X) and the average household income level (Y) for residents of U.S. towns.

a Using the data in the file P2_24.XLS, estimate a regression model involving these two variables.

b Does autocorrelation, multicollinearity, or heteroscedasticity appear to be a problem?

c Test whether there is sufficient evidence to conclude that the slope parameter (i.e., β_1) is *greater than* 0.0035. Use a 5% significance level.

d Based on your finding in part **c**, is it possible to conclude that a linear relationship exists between the size of the population and the average household income level for residents of U.S. towns? Explain. ■

Multicollinearity

Recall that the coefficient of any variable in a regression equation indicates the effect of this variable on the response variable, provided that the other variables in the equation remain constant. Another way of stating this is that the coefficient represents the effect of this variable on the response variable *in addition to* the effects of the other variables in the equation. For example, if MachHrs and ProdRuns are included in the equation for Overhead, then the coefficient of MachHrs indicates the *extra* amount MachHrs explains about variation in Overhead, in addition to the amount already explained by ProdRuns. Similarly, the coefficient of ProdRuns indicates the extra amount ProdRuns explains about variation in Overhead, in addition to the amount already explained by MachHrs. Therefore, the relationship between an explanatory variable X and the response variable Y is not always accurately reflected in the coefficient of X; it depends on which *other* X's are included or not included in the equation.

This is especially true when there is a linear relationship between two or more *explanatory* variables, in which case we have **multicollinearity**. By definition, multicollinearity is the presence of a fairly strong linear relationship between two or more explanatory variables, and it can make estimation difficult. Consider the following example. It is a rather trivial example, but it is useful for illustrating the potential effects of multicollinearity.

EXAMPLE 12.2

We want to explain a person's height by means of foot length. The response variable is Height, and the explanatory variables are Right and Left, the length of the right foot and the left foot, respectively. What can occur when we regress Height on *both* Right and Left?

Solution

Admittedly, there is no need to include both Right and Left in an equation for Height—either one of them would do—but we include them both to make a point. Now, it is likely that there is a large correlation between height and foot size, so we would expect this regression equation to do a good job. For example, the R^2 value will probably be large. But what about the coefficients of Right and Left? Here there is a problem. The coefficient of Right indicates the right foot's effect on Height in addition to the effect of the left foot. This additional effect is probably minimal. That is, after the effect of Left on Height has already been taken into account, the extra information provided by Right is probably minimal. But it goes the other way also. The extra effect of Left, in addition to that provided by Right, is probably minimal.

To show what can happen numerically, we generated a hypothetical data set of heights and left and right foot lengths. (See the file HEIGHT.XLS.) We did this so that, except for random error, height is approximately 32 plus 3.2 times foot length (all expressed in inches). As shown in Figure 12.5, the correlation between Height and either Right or Left in our data set is quite large, and the correlation between Right and Left is very close to 1.

FIGURE 12.5 **Correlations in Height versus Foot Length Example**

	E	F	G	H	I
3	*Table of correlations*				
4			Height	Right	Left
5		Height	1.000		
6		Right	0.903	1.000	
7		Left	0.900	0.999	1.000

The regression output when both Right and Left are entered in the equation for Height appears in Figure 12.6 (page 642). This tells a somewhat confusing story. The multiple R and the corresponding R^2 are about what we would expect, given the correlations between Height and either Right or Left in Figure 12.5. In particular, the multiple R is close to the correlation between Height and either Right or Left. Also, the s_e value is quite good. It implies that predictions of height from this regression equation will typically be off by only about 2 inches.

However, the coefficients of Right and Left are not at all what we might expect, given that we generated heights as approximately 32 plus 3.2 times foot length. In fact, the coefficient of Left is the wrong sign—it is *negative*! Besides this "wrong" sign, the tip-off that there is a problem is that the t-value of Left is quite small and the corresponding

FIGURE 12.6

Regression Output for Height versus Foot Length Example

	A	B	C	D	E	F	G
1	*Results of multiple regression for Height*						
2							
3	*Summary measures*						
4		Multiple R	0.9042				
5		R-Square	0.8176				
6		Adj R-Square	0.8140				
7		StErr of Est	2.0041				
8							
9	*ANOVA Table*						
10		Source	df	SS	MS	F	p-value
11		Explained	2	1836.3845	918.1923	228.6003	0.0000
12		Unexplained	102	409.6916	4.0166		
13							
14	*Regression coefficients*						
15			Coefficient	Std Err	t-value	p-value	
16		Constant	31.7603	1.9595	16.2087	0.0000	
17		Right	6.8229	3.4285	1.9901	0.0493	
18		Left	-3.6448	3.4411	-1.0592	0.2920	

p-value is quite large. Judging by this, we might conclude that Height and Left are either not related or are related negatively. But we know from Figure 12.5 that both of these conclusions are false. In contrast, the coefficient of Right has the "correct" sign, and its *t*-value and associated *p*-value do imply statistical significance, at least at the 5% level. However, this happened mostly by chance. Slight changes in the data could change the results completely—the coefficient of Right could become negative and insignificant, or both coefficients could become insignificant.

The problem is that although both Right and Left are clearly related to Height, it is impossible for the least squares method to distinguish their *separate* effects. Note that the regression equation does estimate the combined effect fairly well—the sum of the coefficients of Right and Left is $6.823 + (-3.645) = 3.178$. This is close to the coefficient 3.2 we used to generate the data. Also, the estimated intercept 31.760 is close to the intercept 32 we used to generate the data. Therefore, the estimated equation will work well for predicting heights. It just does not have reliable estimates of the individual coefficients of Right and Left.

To see what happens when either Right or Left is excluded from the regression equation, we show the results of *simple* regression. When Right is the only variable in the equation, it becomes

$$\text{Predicted Height} = 31.546 + 3.195\text{Right}$$

The R^2 and s_e values are 81.6% and 2.005, and the *t*-value and *p*-value for the coefficient of Right are now 21.34 and 0.0000—very significant. Similarly, when Left is the only variable in the equation, it becomes

$$\text{Predicted Height} = 31.526 + 3.197\text{Left}$$

The R^2 and s_e values are 81.1% and 2.033, and the *t*-value and *p*-value for the coefficient of Left are 20.99 and 0.0000—again very significant. Clearly, both of these equations tell almost identical stories, and they are much easier to interpret than the equation with both Right and Left included. ∎

This example illustrates an extreme form of multicollinearity, where two explanatory variables are very highly correlated. In general, there are various degrees of multicollinearity. In each of them, there is a linear relationship between two or more explanatory variables, and this relationship makes it difficult to estimate the individual effect of the X's on the response variable. The symptoms of multicollinearity can be "wrong" signs of the coefficients, smaller-than-expected t-values, and larger-than-expected (insignificant) p-values. In other words, variables that are really related to the response variable can look like they aren't related, based on their p-values. The reason is that their effects on Y are already explained by other X's in the equation.

Sometimes multicollinearity is easy to spot and treat. For example, it would be silly to include both Right and Left foot length in the equation for Height. They are obviously very highly correlated and only one is needed in the equation for Height. We should exclude one of them—either one—and reestimate the equation. However, multicollinearity is not usually this easy to treat or even diagnose.

Suppose, for example, that we want to use regression to explain variations in salary. Three potentially useful explanatory variables are age, years of experience in the company, and years of experience in the industry. It is very likely that each of these is positively related to salary, and it is also very likely that they are very closely related to each other. However, it isn't clear which, if any, we should exclude from the regression equation. If we include all three, we are likely to find that at least one of them is insignificant (high p-value), in which case we might consider excluding it from the equation. If we do so, the s_e and R^2 values will probably not change very much—the equation will provide equally good predicted values—but the coefficients of the variables that remain in the equation could change considerably.

PROBLEMS

Level A

7   Using the data given in P11_10.XLS, estimate a multiple regression equation to predict the sales price of houses in a given community. Employ all available explanatory variables. Is there evidence of multicollinearity in this model? Explain why or why not.

8   Consider the enrollment data for *Business Week*'s top 50 U.S. graduate business programs in the file P2_3.XLS. Use these data to estimate a multiple regression model to assess whether there is a systematic relationship between the total number of full-time students and the following explanatory variables: (i) the proportion of female students, (ii) the proportion of minority students, and (iii) the proportion of international students enrolled at these distinguished business schools.

   a   Determine whether each of the regression coefficients for the explanatory variables in this model is statistically different from 0 at the 5% significance level. Summarize your findings.

   b   Is there evidence of multicollinearity in this model? Explain why or why not.

9   The manager of a commuter rail transportation system was recently asked by her governing board to determine the factors that have a significant impact on the demand for rides in the large city served by the transportation network. The system manager has collected data on variables that might be related to the number of weekly riders on the city's rail system. The file P11_20.XLS contains these data.

   a   Estimate a multiple regression model using all of the available explanatory variables. Perform a test of significance for each of the model's regression coefficients. Are the signs of the estimated coefficients consistent with your expectations?

   b   Is there evidence of multicollinearity in this model? Explain why or why not. If multicollinearity appears to be present, explain what you would do to eliminate this problem.

10 The human resources manager of DataCom, Inc., wants to examine the relationship between annual salaries (Y) and the number of years employees have worked at DataCom (X). These data have been collected for a sample of employees and are given in the file P11_5.XLS.

    a Estimate the relationship between Y and X using simple linear regression analysis. Is there evidence to support the hypothesis that the coefficient for the number of years employed is statistically different from 0 at the $\alpha = 0.05$ level?

    b Next, formulate a multiple regression model to explain annual salaries of DataCom employees with X and X^2 as explanatory variables. Estimate this model using the given data. Perform relevant hypothesis tests to determine the significance of the regression coefficients of these two variables. Let $\alpha = 0.05$. Summarize your findings.

    c How do you explain your findings in part **b** in light of the results found in part **a**?

11 The owner of a restaurant in Bloomington, Indiana, has recorded sales data for the past 19 years. He has also recorded data on potentially relevant variables. The data appear in the file P11_23.XLS.

    a Estimate a multiple regression equation that includes annual sales as the response variable and the following explanatory variables: year, size of the population residing within 10 miles of the restaurant, annual advertising expenditures, and advertising expenditures in the *previous* year.

    b Which of the explanatory variables have significant effects on sales at the 10% significance level? Do any of these results surprise you? Explain why or why not.

    c Exclude all insignificant explanatory variables from the full model and estimate the reduced model. Comment on the significance of each remaining explanatory variable. Again, use a 10% significance level.

    d Based on your analysis of this problem, does multicollinearity appear to be present in the original or reduced versions of the model? Provide the reasoning behind your response. ■

12.5

Include/Exclude Decisions

I n this section we make further use of the t-values of regression coefficients. In particular, we will see how they can be used to make include/exclude decisions for explanatory variables in a regression equation. From Section 12.3 we know that a t-value can be used to test whether a population regression coefficient is 0. But does this mean that we should automatically include a variable if its t-value is significant and automatically exclude it if its t-value is not significant? The decision is not always this simple.

The bottom line is that we are always trying to get the best fit possible, and because of the principle of parsimony, we want to use the fewest number of variables. This presents a trade-off, where there are often no easy answers. On the one hand, more variables certainly increase R^2 and they usually reduce the standard error of estimate s_e. On the other hand, fewer variables are better for parsimony. Therefore, we present several guidelines. These guidelines are not hard and fast rules, and they are sometimes contradictory. In real applications there are often several equations that are equally good for all practical purposes, and it is rather pointless to search for a single "true" equation.

Guidelines for Including/Excluding Variables in a Regression Equation

1 Look at a variable's t-value and its associated p-value. If the p-value is above some accepted significance level, such as 0.05, then this variable is a candidate for exclusion.

2 Check whether a variable's t-value is less than 1 or greater than 1 in magnitude. If it is less than 1, then s_e will decrease (and adjusted R^2 will increase) if this variable is excluded from the equation. If it is greater than 1, the opposite will occur. These are mathematical facts. Because of them, some statisticians advocate excluding variables with t-values less than 1, and including variables with t-values greater than 1.

3 Look at t-values and p-values, rather than correlations, when making include/exclude decisions. An explanatory variable can have a fairly high correlation with the response variable, but because of *other* variables included in the equation, it might not be needed. This would be reflected in a low t-value and a high p-value, and this variable could possibly be excluded for reasons of parsimony. This often occurs in the presence of multicollinearity.

4 When there is a group of variables that are in some sense logically related, it is sometimes a good idea to include all of them or exclude all of them. In this case, their individual t-values should not be used. Instead, the "partial F test" discussed in Section 12.8 should be used.

5 Use economic and/or physical theory to decide whether to include or exclude variables, and put less reliance on t-values and/or p-values. The idea is that some variables might really *belong* in an equation because of their theoretical relationship with the response variable, and their low t-values, possibly the result of an unlucky sample, should not disqualify them from being in the equation. Similarly, a variable that has no economic or physical relationship with the response variable might have gotten a significant t-value just by chance. This does not necessarily mean that it should be included in the equation. We should not use a computer package blindly to hunt for "good" explanatory variables. We should have some idea, before running the package, which variables belong and which do not.

Again, these guidelines can give contradictory signals. Specifically, guideline 2 bases the include/exclude decision on whether the magnitude of the t-value is greater or less than 1. However, analysts who base the decision on statistical significance at the usual 5% level, as in guideline 1, typically exclude a variable from the equation unless its t-value is at least 2 (approximately). This latter approach is more stringent—fewer variables will be retained—but it is probably the more popular approach. However, either approach is likely to result in "similar" equations for all practical purposes.

We illustrate how these guidelines can be used in the following example. It uses a slightly modified version of the data set on HyTex's mail-order customers from Chapter 3.

EXAMPLE 12.3

The file CATALOGS1.XLS contains data on 1000 customers who purchased mail-order products from the HyTex Company in 1998. Recall from Example 3.11 in Chapter 3 that HyTex is a direct marketer of stereo equipment, personal computers, and other electronic products. HyTex advertises entirely by mailing catalogs to its customers, and all of its orders are taken over the telephone. The company spends a great deal of money on its catalog mailings, and it wants to be sure that this is paying off in sales. For each customer there are data on the following variables:

- Age: age of the customer as of the end of 1998
- Gender: coded as 1 for males, 0 for females
- Own_Home: coded as 1 if customer owns a home, 0 otherwise
- Married: coded as 1 if customer is currently married, 0 otherwise

- Close: coded as 1 if customer lives reasonably close to a shopping area that sells similar merchandise, 0 otherwise
- Salary: combined annual salary of customer and spouse (if any)
- Children: number of children living with customer
- Customer97: coded as 1 if customer purchased from HyTex during 1997, 0 otherwise
- Spent97: total amount of purchases made from HyTex during 1997
- Catalogs: number of catalogs sent to the customer in 1998
- Spent98: total amount of purchases made from HyTex during 1998

Estimate and interpret a regression equation for Spent98 based on all of these variables.

Solution

First, if you compare this data set to the data set in Chapter 3, you'll see that we made the following modifications to simplify the regression analysis.

- Age is now a continuous variable, not a categorical variable with three categories.
- The dummy variables Gender, Married, Own_Home, and Close are now coded as 1 and 0, not as 1 and 2. This allows us to interpret their coefficients as we discussed in the previous chapter.
- Before, we had a History variable with four categories, depending on how much, if any, the customer purchased from HyTex in the previous year. Now we use the dummy variable Customer97 to indicate whether the customer purchased anything from HyTex in the previous year. We also use the continuous variable Spent97 for the amount purchased the previous year. Of course, if Customer97 equals 0, so does Spent97.

With this much data, 1000 observations, we can certainly afford to set aside part of the data set for validation, as discussed in Section 11.7. Although any split can be used, we decided to base the regression on the first 250 observations and use the other 750 for validation.

We begin by entering all of the potential explanatory variables. Our goal is then to exclude variables that aren't necessary, based on their t-values and p-values. The multiple regression output with all explanatory variables appears in Figure 12.7. It indicates a fairly good fit. The R^2 value is 79.1% and s_e is about \$424. When we consider that the actual amounts spent in 1998 vary from a low of under \$50 to a high of over \$5500, with a median of about \$950, a typical prediction error of around \$424 is decent but not great.

From the p-value column, we see that there are three variables, Age, Own_Home, and Married, that have p-values well above 0.05. These are the obvious candidates for exclusion from the equation. We could rerun the equation with all three of these variables excluded, but it is better to proceed one step at a time. It is possible that when one of these variables is excluded, another one of them will become significant (the Right–Left foot phenomenon).

Actually, this did not happen. We first excluded the variable with the largest p-value, Age, and reran the regression. At this point, Own_Home and Married still had large p-values, and all other variables had small p-values. Next, we excluded Married, the variable with the largest remaining p-value, and reran the regression. Now, only Own_Home had a large p-value, so we ran one more regression with this variable excluded. The resulting output appears in Figure 12.8. As we see, the R^2 and s_e values of 79.0% and \$423 are practically as good as they were with all variables included, and all of the t-values are now large (well above 2 in absolute value) and the p-values are all small (well below 0.05).

FIGURE 12.7 Regression Output with All Explanatory Variables Included

	A	B	C	D	E	F	G
1	*Results of multiple regression for Spent98*						
2							
3	*Summary measures*						
4		Multiple R	0.8893				
5		R-Square	0.7908				
6		Adj R-Square	0.7820				
7		StErr of Est	423.8584				
8							
9	*ANOVA Table*						
10		Source	df	SS	MS	F	p-value
11		Explained	10	162299316.1832	16229931.6183	90.3390	0.0000
12		Unexplained	239	42937764.0000	179655.9163		
13							
14	*Regression coefficients*						
15			Coefficient	Std Err	t-value	p-value	
16		Constant	257.3477	132.9876	1.9351	0.0542	
17		Age	0.1884	1.7626	0.1069	0.9150	
18		Gender	-124.0805	55.7627	-2.2252	0.0270	
19		Own_Home	62.2752	60.7581	1.0250	0.3064	
20		Married	49.8426	70.1742	0.7103	0.4782	
21		Close	-282.7266	71.7762	-3.9390	0.0001	
22		Salary	0.0143	0.0017	8.4930	0.0000	
23		Children	-155.2858	31.5902	-4.9156	0.0000	
24		Customer97	-729.7213	92.3670	-7.9002	0.0000	
25		Spent97	0.4725	0.0782	6.0447	0.0000	
26		Catalogs	42.5806	4.3503	9.7880	0.0000	

FIGURE 12.8 Regression Output with Insignificant Variables Excluded

	A	B	C	D	E	F	G
1	*Results of multiple regression for Spent98*						
2							
3	*Summary measures*						
4		Multiple R	0.8885				
5		R-Square	0.7895				
6		Adj R-Square	0.7834				
7		StErr of Est	422.5169				
8							
9	*ANOVA Table*						
10		Source	df	SS	MS	F	p-value
11		Explained	7	162035108.1832	23147872.5976	129.6650	0.0000
12		Unexplained	242	43201972.0000	178520.5455		
13							
14	*Regression coefficients*						
15			Coefficient	Std Err	t-value	p-value	
16		Constant	269.8643	108.5596	2.4859	0.0136	
17		Gender	-130.3226	55.2112	-2.3604	0.0190	
18		Close	-287.5537	70.8671	-4.0576	0.0001	
19		Salary	0.0154	0.0014	11.1924	0.0000	
20		Children	-158.4511	31.3378	-5.0562	0.0000	
21		Customer97	-724.0651	91.5870	-7.9058	0.0000	
22		Spent97	0.4699	0.0777	6.0452	0.0000	
23		Catalogs	42.6638	4.3204	9.8751	0.0000	

We can interpret this final regression equation as follows:

- The coefficient of Gender implies that an average male customer spent about $130 less than an average female customer, all other variables being equal. Similarly, an average customer living close to stores with this type of merchandise spent about $288 less than an average customer living far from such stores.

- The coefficient of Salary implies that, on average, about 1.5 cents of every extra salary dollar was spent on HyTex merchandise.

- The coefficient of Children implies that about $158 *less* was spent for every extra child living at home.

- The Customer97 and Spent97 terms are somewhat more difficult to interpret. First, both of these terms are 0 for customers who didn't purchase from HyTex in 1997. For those who did, the terms become $-724 + 0.47$Spent97. The coefficient 0.47 implies that each extra dollar spent in 1997 can be expected to contribute an extra 47 cents in 1998. The -724 literally means that if we compare a customer who didn't purchase from HyTex in 1997 to another customer who purchased only a tiny amount, the latter would be expected to spend about $724 less than the former in 1998. However, there were none of the latter customers in the data set. A look at the data shows that of all customers who purchased from HyTex in 1997, almost all spent at least $100 and most spent considerably more. In fact, the median amount spent by these customers in 1997 was about $900 (the median of all positive values for the Spent97 variable). If we substitute this median value into the expression $-724 + 0.47$Spent97, we obtain -301. Therefore, this "median" spender from 1997 can be expected to spend about $301 less in 1998 than the 1997 nonspender.

- The coefficient of Catalogs implies that each extra catalog can be expected to generate about $43 in extra spending.

We conclude this example with a couple of cautionary notes. First, when we validate this final regression equation on the other 750 customers, using the procedure from Section 11.7, we find R^2 and s_e values of 75.7% and $485. Actually, these aren't bad. They show only a little deterioration from the values based on the original 250 customers. Second, we haven't tried all possibilities yet. We haven't tried nonlinear or interaction variables, nor have we looked at different coding schemes (such as treating Catalogs as a categorical variable and using dummy variables to represent it); we haven't checked for nonconstant error variance (remember that Figure 12.1 is based on this data set) or looked at the potential effects of outliers. ■

PROBLEMS

Level A

12 David Savageau and Geoffrey Loftus, the authors of *Places Rated Almanac* (published in 1997 by Macmillan) have ranked 325 metropolitan areas in the United States with consideration of the following aspects of life in each area: cost of living, transportation, jobs, education, climate, crime, arts, health, and recreation. The data are in the file P2_55.XLS. Use multiple regression analysis to explore the relationship between the metropolitan area's overall score and the set of aforementioned numerical factors. Which explanatory variables should be included in a final version of this regression model? Justify your choices.

13 A manager of boiler drums wants to use regression analysis to predict the number of worker-hours needed to erect the drums in future projects. Consequently, data for 36 randomly selected boilers were collected. In addition to worker-hours (Y), the variables measured include boiler capacity, boiler design pressure, boiler type, and drum type. All of these measurements are listed in the file P11_27.XLS. Estimate an appropriate multiple regression model to predict the number of worker-hours needed to erect given boiler drums using all available explanatory variables. Which explanatory variables should be included in a final version of this regression model? Justify your choices.

14 An economic development researcher wants to understand the relationship between the size of the monthly home mortgage or rent payment for households in a particular middle-class neighborhood and the following set of household variables: family size, approximate location of the household within the neighborhood, an indication of whether those surveyed own or rent their home, gross annual income of the first household wage earner, gross annual income of the second household wage earner (if applicable), average monthly expenditure on utilities, and the total indebtedness (excluding the value of a home mortgage) of the household. Observations on each of these variables for a large sample of households are recorded in the file P2_54.XLS.

   a In an effort to explain the variation in the size of the monthly home mortgage or rent payment, estimate a multiple regression model that includes all of the aforementioned household explanatory variables.

   b Using your regression output, determine which of the explanatory variables should be *excluded* from the regression equation. Explain why you decide to remove each such variable.

15 Managers at Beta Technologies, Inc., have collected current annual salary figures and potentially related data for a random sample of 52 of the company's full-time employees. The data are in the file P2_1.XLS. These data include each selected employee's gender, age, number of years of relevant work experience prior to employment at Beta, the number of years of employment at Beta, and the number of years of post-secondary education.

   a Estimate a multiple regression model to explain the variation in employee salaries at Beta Technologies using all of the potential explanatory variables.

   b Using your regression output, determine which of the explanatory variables should be *excluded* from the regression equation. Provide reasoning for your decision to remove each such variable.

16 Stock market analysts are continually looking for reliable predictors of stock prices. Consider the problem of modeling the price per share of electric utility stocks (Y). Two variables thought to influence such a stock price are return on average equity (X_1) and annual dividend rate (X_2). The stock price, returns on equity, and dividend rates on a randomly selected day for 16 electric utility stocks are provided in the file P11_19.XLS.

   a Estimate a multiple regression model using the given data. Include linear terms as well as an interaction term involving the return on average equity (X_1) and annual dividend rate (X_2).

   b Which of the three explanatory variables (X_1, X_2, and X_1X_2) should be included in a final version of this regression model? Explain. Does your conclusion make sense in light of your knowledge of corporate finance? ■

12.6 Stepwise Regression

Multiple regression represents an improvement over simple regression because it allows any number of explanatory variables to be included in the analysis. Sometimes, however, the large number of potential explanatory variables makes it difficult to know which variables to include. Many statistical packages provide some assistance by including automatic equation-building options. These options estimate a series of regression equations by successively adding (or deleting) variables according to prescribed rules. Generically, the methods are referred to as **stepwise regression**.

Before discussing how stepwise procedures work, consider a naive approach to the problem. We have already looked at correlation tables for indications of linear relationships. Why not simply include all explanatory variables that have large correlations with the response variable? There are two reasons for not doing this. First, although a variable is highly correlated with the response variable, it might also be highly correlated with other explanatory variables. Therefore, this variable might not be needed in the equation once the other explanatory variables have been included.

Second, even if a variable's correlation with the response variable is small, its contribution when it is included with a number of other explanatory variables can be greater than anticipated. Essentially, this variable can have something unique to say about the response variable that none of the other variables provides, and this fact might not be apparent from the correlation table.

For these reasons it is sometimes useful to let the computer discover the best combination of variables by means of a stepwise procedure. There are a number of procedures for building equations in a stepwise manner, but there is a basic idea common to all of them. Suppose that we have an existing regression equation and we want to add another variable to this equation from a set of variables not yet included. At this point, the variables already in the equation have explained a certain percentage of the variation of the response variable. The residuals represent the part still unexplained. Therefore, in choosing the next variable to enter the equation, we pick the one that is most highly correlated with the current residuals. If none of the remaining variables is highly correlated with the residuals, we might decide to quit. This is the essence of stepwise regression. However, besides adding variables to the equation, a stepwise procedure might delete a variable. This is sometimes reasonable because a variable entered early in the procedure might no longer be needed, given the presence of other variables that have entered since.

Many statistical packages have three types of equation-building procedures: **forward**, **backward**, and **stepwise**. A forward procedure begins with no explanatory variables in the equation and successively adds one at a time until no remaining variables make a significant contribution. A backward procedure begins with all potential explanatory variables in the equation and deletes them one at a time until further deletion would do more harm than good. Finally, a true stepwise procedure is much like a forward procedure, except that it also considers possible deletions along the way. All of these procedures have the same basic objective—namely, to find an equation with a small s_e and a large R^2 (or adjusted R^2). There is no guarantee that they will all produce exactly the same final equation, but in most cases their final results are very similar. The important thing to realize is that the equations estimated along the way, including the final equation, are estimated exactly as before—by least squares. Therefore, none of these procedures produces any new results. They merely take the burden off the user of having to decide ahead of time which variables to include in the equation.

The StatPro add-in implements each of the forward, backward, and stepwise procedures. To use them, we select the response variable and a set of *potential* explanatory variables. Then we specify the criterion for adding and/or deleting variables from the equation. This can be done in two ways, with an F-value or a p-value. We suggest using p-values because they are easier to understand, but either method is easy to use. In the p-value method, we select a p-value such as 0.05. If the regression coefficient for a potential entering variable would have a p-value less than 0.05 (if it were entered), then it is a candidate for entering (if the forward or stepwise procedure is used). The procedure selects the variable with the *smallest* p-value as the next entering variable. Similarly, if any currently included variable has a p-value greater than 0.05, then (with the stepwise and backward procedures) it is a candidate for leaving the equation. The methods stop when there are no candidates (according to their p-values) for entering or leaving the current equation.

The following continuation of the HyTex mail-order example illustrates these stepwise procedures.

EXAMPLE 12.3 [CONTINUED]

The analysis of the HyTex mail-order data (for the first 250 customers in the data set) resulted in a regression equation that included all potential explanatory variables except for Age, Own_Home, and Married. We excluded these because their t-values were large and their p-values were small (less than 0.05). Do forward, backward, and stepwise procedures produce the same regression equation for the amount spent in 1998?

Solution

Each of these options is found under the StatPro/Regression Analysis menu item. In each, we specify Spent98 as the response variable and select all of the other variables (besides Customer) as potential explanatory variables. We then see a dialog box as in Figure 12.9 where we choose p-values or F-values as the appropriate criterion. (We chose p-values.) Next we see a dialog box as in Figure 12.10 where we choose the particular p-value or F-value for entering or leaving. (This particular dialog box is for the stepwise procedure, so we must choose a p-value for entering *and* for leaving. The latter cannot be less than the former, but they can be equal, as we show here. Note that the *default* p-value for leaving is 0.10; we selected 0.05 instead.)

FIGURE 12.9   **Dialog Box for Choosing Criterion in Stepwise Procedure**

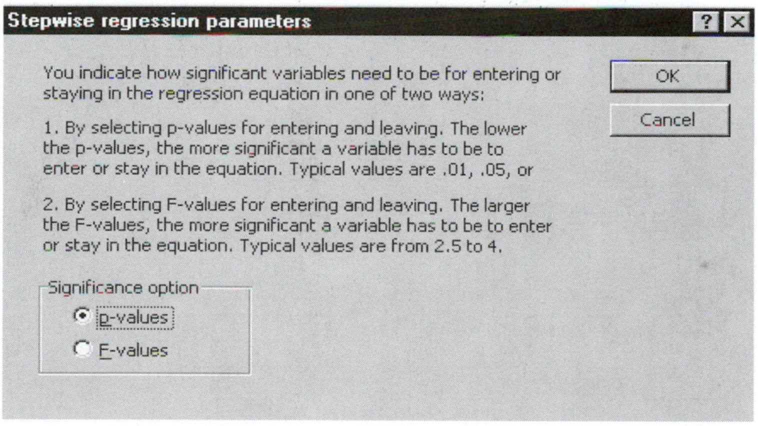

FIGURE 12.10   **Dialog Box for Choosing p-values for Entering and Leaving**

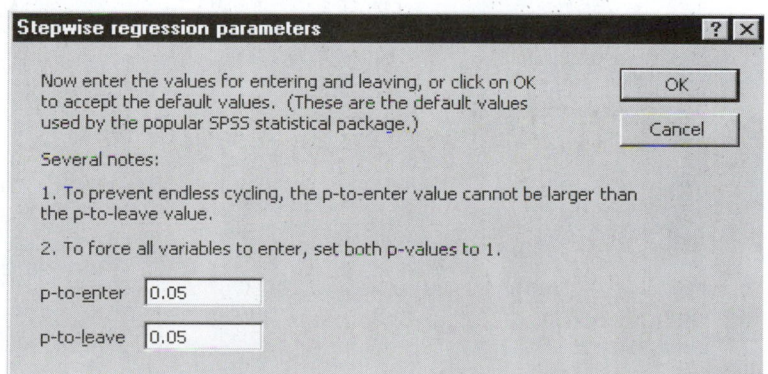

It turns out that each procedure produces a *final* equation that is exactly the same as we obtained earlier, with all variables except Age, Own_Home, and Married included. This often happens, but not always. The stepwise and forward procedures add the variables in the order Salary, Catalogs, Children, Close, Customer97, Spent97, and Gender. The backward procedure, which starts with *all* variables in the equation, eliminates variables in the order Age, Married, and Own_Home.

A sample of the stepwise output appears in Figure 12.11. For each step of the procedure, we see which variable enters or leaves the equation. We also see the usual regression output for all the variables in the equation at that step, along with percentage changes in the key summary measures from the previous step to the current step. Again, however, the final equation's output is *exactly* the same as if we used multiple regression with these particular variables.

FIGURE 12.11 **Regression Output from Stepwise Procedure**

	A	B	C	D	E	F	G
1	*Results of stepwise regression for Spent98*						
2							
3	*Step 1 - Entering variable: Salary*						
4							
5	*Summary measures*						
6		Multiple R	0.6624				
7		R-Square	0.4387				
8		Adj R-Square	0.4365				
9		StErr of Est	681.5285				
10							
11	*ANOVA Table*						
12		Source	df	SS	MS	F	p-value
13		Explained	1	90045768.1832	90045768.1832	193.8631	0.0000
14		Unexplained	248	115191312.0000	464481.0968		
15							
16	*Regression coefficients*						
17			Coefficient	Std Err	t-value	p-value	
18		Constant	57.1089	91.6991	0.6228	0.5340	
19		Salary	0.0203	0.0015	13.9235	0.0000	
39							
126	*Step 7 - Entering variable: Gender*						
127							
128	*Summary measures*			Change	% Change		
129		Multiple R	0.8885	0.0027	%0.3		
130		R-Square	0.7895	0.0048	%0.6		
131		Adj R-Square	0.7834	0.0041	%0.5		
132		StErr of Est	422.5169	-3.9560	-%0.9		
133							
134	*ANOVA Table*						
135		Source	df	SS	MS	F	p-value
136		Explained	7	162035108.1832	23147872.5976	129.6650	0.0000
137		Unexplained	242	43201972.0000	178520.5455		
138							
139	*Regression coefficients*						
140			Coefficient	Std Err	t-value	p-value	
141		Constant	269.8643	108.5596	2.4859	0.0136	
142		Salary	0.0154	0.0014	11.1924	0.0000	
143		Catalogs	42.6638	4.3204	9.8751	0.0000	
144		Children	-158.4511	31.3378	-5.0562	0.0000	
145		Close	-287.5537	70.8671	-4.0576	0.0001	
146		Customer97	-724.0651	91.5870	-7.9058	0.0000	
147		Spent97	0.4699	0.0777	6.0452	0.0000	
148		Gender	-130.3226	55.2112	-2.3604	0.0190	

Stepwise regression or any of its variations can be very useful for narrowing down the set of all possible explanatory variables to a set that is useful for explaining a response variable. However, these procedures should not be used as a substitute for thoughtful analysis. With the availability of such procedures in statistical software packages, there is sometimes a tendency to turn the analysis over to the computer and accept its output. A good analyst does not just collect as much data as possible, throw it into a computer package, and blindly report the results. There should always be some rationale, whether it be based on economic theory, business experience, or common sense, for the variables that we use to explain a given response variable. A thoughtless use of stepwise regression can sometimes capitalize on chance to obtain an equation with a reasonably large R^2 but no useful or practical interpretation.

PROBLEMS

Level A

17 Suppose that you are interested in predicting the price of a laptop computer based on its various features. The file P11_35.XLS contains observations on the sales price and a number of potentially relevant variables for a randomly chosen sample of laptop computers. Employ stepwise regression to decide which explanatory variables to include in a regression equation. Use the p-value method with a cutoff value of 0.05. Summarize your findings.

18 Does the rate of violent crime acts vary across different regions of the United States? Using the data in P11_34.XLS and a stepwise regression procedure, develop an appropriate regression model to explain the variation in acts of violent crime across the United States. Use the p-value method with a cutoff value of 0.05. Summarize your results.

19 In a study of housing demand, a county assessor is interested in developing a regression model to estimate the selling price of residential properties within her jurisdiction. She randomly selects 15 houses and records the selling price in addition to the following values: the size of the house (in hundreds of square feet), the total number of rooms in the house, the age of the house, and an indication of whether the house has an attached garage. These data are stored in the file P11_26.XLS.

a Use stepwise regression to decide which explanatory variables should be included in the assessor's statistical model. Use the p-value method with a cutoff value of 0.05. Summarize your findings.

b How do your results in part **a** change when the critical p-value for evaluating a potential entering variable is increased to 0.10? Explain any differences between the regression equation obtained here and the one found in part **a**.

20 Continuing Problem 2, employ stepwise regression to evaluate your conclusions regarding the specification of a regression model to predict the sales of deep-dish pizza by the Original Italian Pizza restaurant chain. Sample observations on all potentially relevant variables are provided in P11_4.XLS. Use the p-value method with a cutoff value of 0.05. Compare your conclusions in Problem 2 with those derived from a stepwise regression procedure in completing this problem.

21 Continuing Problem 3, employ stepwise regression to evaluate your conclusions regarding the specification of a regression model to explain the variation in values of the ACCRA Cost of Living Index. Data on potentially relevant expenditure components (i.e., explanatory variables) are provided in the file P2_19.XLS. Use the p-value method with a cutoff value of 0.05. Compare your conclusions in Problem 3 with those derived from a stepwise regression procedure in completing this problem.

Level B

22 What factors are truly useful in predicting a chief executive officer's annual base salary? Explore this question by employing a stepwise regression procedure on potentially relevant variables for which survey data have been collected and recorded in the file P2_13.XLS. Assess only those variables that make economic sense in predicting CEO base salaries. Also, consider incorporating a set of categorical variables to account for any potential variation in the base salaries that is explained by the CEO's company type. Use the p-value method with a cutoff value of 0.10. Summarize your findings. ■

A Test for the Overall Fit: The ANOVA Table

The t-values for the regression coefficients allow us to see which of the potential explanatory variables are useful in explaining the response variable. But it is conceivable that *none* of these variables does a very good job. That is, it is conceivable that the entire group of explanatory variables explains only an insignificant portion of the variability of the response variable. Although this is the exception rather than the rule in most real applications, it can certainly happen. An indication of this is that we obtain a very small R^2 value. Because R^2 is the square of the correlation between the observed values of the response variable and the fitted values from the regression equation, another indication of a lack of fit is that this correlation (the "multiple R") is small. In this section we state a formal procedure for testing the overall fit, or explanatory power, of a regression equation.

Suppose that the response variable is Y and the explanatory variables are X_1 through X_k. Then the proposed population regression equation is

$$Y = \alpha + \beta_1 X_1 + \cdots + \beta_k X_k + \varepsilon$$

To say that this equation has absolutely no explanatory power means that the same value of Y will be predicted regardless of the values of the X's. In this case it makes no difference which values of the X's we use because they all lead to the same predicted value of Y. But the only way this can occur is if all of the β's are 0. So the formal hypothesis we test in this section is $H_0: \beta_1 = \cdots = \beta_k = 0$ versus the alternative that at least one of the β's is not 0. In words, the null hypothesis is that this set of explanatory variables has no power to explain the variation in the response variable Y. If we can reject the null hypothesis, as we can in the majority of applications, this means that the explanatory variables *as a group* provide at least some explanatory power.

At first glance it might appear that we can test this null hypothesis by looking at the individual t-values. If they are all small (statistically insignificant), then we can accept the null hypothesis of no fit; otherwise, we can reject it. However, Example 12.2 of Height versus Left and Right (foot size) indicates why this procedure might not work. In this example, the variables Left and Right definitely provide some explanatory power for predicting Height, but the extremely high correlation between Left and Right can possibly lead to small t-values for *both* variables. The point is that a group of small t-values is not an automatic guarantee of an equation's lack of explanatory power.

The alternative is to use an F test. This is sometimes referred to as the ANOVA (analysis of variance) test because the elements for calculating the required F-value are shown in an ANOVA table.[2] In general, an ANOVA table analyzes different sources of variation. In the case of regression, the variation in question is the variation of the response variable Y. The "total variation" of this variable is the sum of squared deviations about the mean and is labeled SST (sum of squares total)

$$SST = \sum (Y_i - \overline{Y})^2$$

The ANOVA table splits this total variation into two parts, the part *explained* by the regression equation, and the part left *unexplained*. The unexplained part is the sum of squared residuals, usually labeled SSE (sum of squared errors):

$$SSE = \sum e_i^2 = \sum (Y_i - \widehat{Y}_i)^2$$

---

[2] This ANOVA table is similar to the ANOVA table we discussed in the optional Section 9.5. However, we repeat the necessary material here for those who didn't cover Section 9.5.

The explained part is then the difference between the total and unexplained variation. It is usually labeled SSR (sum of squares due to regression):

$$SSR = SST - SSE$$

The F test is a formal procedure for testing whether the explained variation is "large" compared to the unexplained variation. Specifically, each of these sources of variation has an associated degrees of freedom (df). For the explained variation, df= k, the number of explanatory variables. For the unexplained variation, df= $n - k - 1$, the sample size minus the total number of coefficients (including the intercept term). When we divide the explained or unexplained variation by its degrees of freedom, the result is called a mean square, or MS. The two mean squares we need are MSR and MSE, given by

$$MSR = \frac{SSR}{k}$$

and

$$MSE = \frac{SSE}{n - k - 1}$$

Note that MSE is the square of the standard error of estimate, that is,

$$MSE = s_e^2$$

Finally, the ratio of these mean squares is the required F-ratio for the test:

$$F\text{-ratio} = \frac{MSR}{MSE}$$

When the null hypothesis of no explanatory power is true, this F-ratio has an F distribution with k and $n - k - 1$ degrees of freedom. If the F-ratio is small, then the explained variation is small relative to the unexplained variation, and there is evidence that the regression equation provides little explanatory power. But if the F-ratio is large, then the explained variation is large relative to the unexplained variation, and we can conclude that the equation does have some explanatory power.

As usual, the F-ratio has an associated p-value that allows us to run the test easily. In this case the p-value is the probability to the *right* of the observed F-ratio in the appropriate F distribution. This p-value is reported in most regression outputs, along with the rest of the elements that lead up to it. If it is sufficiently small, less than 0.05, say, then we can conclude that the explanatory variables as a whole have at least some explanatory power.

Although this test is run routinely in most applications, there is often little doubt that the equation has some explanatory power; the only questions are how much, and which explanatory variables provide the best combination. In such cases the F-ratio from the ANOVA table is typically "off the charts" and the corresponding p-value is practically 0. On the other hand, F-ratios, particularly large ones, should not necessarily be used to choose between equations with different explanatory variables included.

For example, suppose that one equation with three explanatory variables has an F-ratio of 54 with an extremely small p-value—obviously very significant. Also, suppose that another equation that includes these three variables plus a few more has an F-ratio of 37 and also has a very small p-value. (When we say small, we mean *small*. These p-values are probably listed, to four decimal places, as 0.0000.) Is the first equation better because its F-ratio is higher? Not necessarily. The two F-ratios imply only that both of these equations have a good deal of explanatory power. It is better to look at their s_e values (or adjusted R^2 values) and their t-values to choose between them.

None of the examples we have examined in this chapter or the previous chapter are even close to having *no* explanatory power. Therefore, their ANOVA tables are of little interest. Nevertheless, to illustrate the method, we reexamine the Bendrix manufacturing data from Example 12.1.

EXAMPLE 12.1 [CONTINUED]

Does the ANOVA table for the Bendrix manufacturing data indicate that the combination MachHrs and ProdRuns has at least some ability to explain variation in Overhead?

Solution

The ANOVA table is automatically given in any StatPro regression output. The output for this example was given earlier in Figure 12.3 and is repeated here in Figure 12.12. The ANOVA table appears in rows 9–12. (Some packages also list a "Total" row at the bottom of the table to show SST and its degrees of freedom. However, these aren't really necessary.) We see the degrees of freedom in column B, the sums of squares in column C, the mean squares in column D, the F-ratio in cell E11, and its associated p-value in cell F11. As predicted, this F-ratio is "off the charts," and the p-value is practically 0.

FIGURE 12.12 **Regression Output for Bendrix Example**

	A	B	C	D	E	F	G
1	Results of multiple regression for Overhead						
2							
3	Summary measures						
4		Multiple R	0.9308				
5		R-Square	0.8664				
6		Adj R-Square	0.8583				
7		StErr of Est	4108.9932				
8							
9	ANOVA Table						
10		Source	df	SS	MS	F	p-value
11		Explained	2	3614020652.0000	1807010326.0000	107.0261	0.0000
12		Unexplained	33	557166208.0000	16883824.4848		
13							
14	Regression coefficients						
15			Coefficient	Std Err	t-value	p-value	
16		Constant	3996.6782	6603.6509	0.6052	0.5492	
17		MachHrs	43.5364	3.5895	12.1289	0.0000	
18		ProdRuns	883.6179	82.2514	10.7429	0.0000	

This information wouldn't be much comfort for the Bendrix manager who is trying to understand the causes of variation in overhead costs. This manager already *knows* that machine hours and production runs are related positively to overhead costs—everyone in the company knows that! What he really wants is a set of explanatory variables that yields a high R^2 and a low s_e. The low p-value in the ANOVA tables does not guarantee these. All it guarantees is that MachHrs and ProdRuns are of "some help" in explaining variations in Overhead. ■

As this example indicates, the ANOVA table can be used as a screening device. If the explanatory variables do not explain a significant percentage of the variation in the response variable, then we can either discontinue the analysis or search for an entirely new set of explanatory variables. But even if the F-ratio in the ANOVA table is extremely significant, there is no guarantee that the regression equation provides a good enough fit for practical uses. This depends on other measures such as s_e and R^2.

PROBLEMS

Level A

23 An antique collector believes that the price received for a particular item increases with its age and the number of bidders. The file P11_18.XLS contains data on these three variables for 32 recently auctioned comparable items.

    a Estimate an appropriate multiple regression model using the given data.

    b Interpret the computer-generated ANOVA table for this model. In particular, does this set of explanatory variables provide at least some power in explaining the variation in price? Report a p-value for this hypothesis test.

24 Consider the enrollment data for *Business Week*'s top 50 U.S. graduate business programs in the file P2_3.XLS. Use these data to estimate a multiple regression model to assess whether there is a systematic relationship between the total number of full-time students and the following explanatory variables: (i) the proportion of female students, (ii) the proportion of minority students, and (iii) the proportion of international students enrolled at these distinguished business schools. Next, interpret the ANOVA table for this model. In particular, does this set of explanatory variables provide at least some power in explaining the variation in total full-time enrollment at the top graduate business programs? Report a p-value for this hypothesis test.

25 The U.S. Bureau of Labor Statistics provides data on the year-to-year percentage changes in the wages and salaries of workers in private industries, including both "white-collar" and "blue-collar" occupations. Here we consider these data for the years 1980–1996 in the file P2_56.XLS. Is there evidence of a linear relationship between the yearly changes in the wages and salaries of "white-collar" (Y) and "blue-collar" (X) workers in the United States over the given time period? Begin to answer this question by estimating a simple linear regression model.

    a Construct a 95% confidence interval for the model's slope (i.e., β_1) parameter. Interpret this interval estimate to answer the question posed above.

    b Interpret the ANOVA table for this model. In particular, does the explanatory variable included in this simple regression model provide at least some power in explaining the variation in the response variable? Report a p-value for this hypothesis test.

    c What is the relationship between the computed t-ratio for the estimated coefficient of the explanatory variable and the computed F-ratio found in the ANOVA section of the output? Do these two test statistic values provide the same indication regarding a possible relationship between yearly changes in the wages and salaries of white-collar and blue-collar workers? Explain why or why not.

26 Suppose that a regional express delivery service company wants to estimate the cost of shipping a package (Y) as a function of cargo type, where cargo type includes the following possibilities: fragile, semifragile, and durable. Costs for 15 randomly chosen packages of approximately the same weight and same distance shipped, but of different cargo types, are provided in the file P11_28.XLS.

    a Estimate an appropriate multiple regression model to predict the cost of shipping a given package.

    b Interpret the computer-generated ANOVA table for this model. In particular, do the explanatory variables included in your model formulated in part **a** provide at least some power in explaining the variation in the cost of shipping a package? Report a p-value for this hypothesis test.

27 A simple linear regression with 11 observations yielded the ANOVA table in Table 12.1.

TABLE 12.1 **ANOVA Table**

	Degrees of Freedom	Sum of Squares
Regression		1000
Error		
Total		2500

a Complete this ANOVA table.

b Using $\alpha = 0.05$, test the hypothesis of no linear regression.

Level B

28 Suppose you find the ANOVA table shown in Table 12.2 for a simple linear regression.

TABLE 12.2 **ANOVA Table**

	Sum of Squares	Degrees of Freedom
SSR	20	
SSE		4
SST	100	

a Find the correlation between X and Y. Assume the slope of the least squares line is negative.

b Find the p-value for the test of the hypothesis of no linear regression. ∎

12.8

The Partial F Test

There are many situations where a set of explanatory variables form a logical group. It is then common to include all of the variables in the equation or exclude all of them. An example of this is when one of the explanatory variables is categorical with more than two categories. In this case we model it by including dummy variables—one less than the number of categories. If we decide that the categorical variable is worth including, we might want to keep all of the dummies. Otherwise, we might exclude all of them. We will look at an example of this type below.

For now, consider the following general situation. We have already estimated an equation that includes the variables X_1 through X_j, and we are proposing to estimate a larger equation that includes X_{j+1} through X_k in addition to the variables X_1 through X_j. That is, the larger equation includes all of the variables from the smaller equation, but it also includes $k - j$ extra variables. These extra variables are the ones that form a group. We assume that it makes logical sense to include all of them or none of them.

In this section we describe a test to determine whether the extra variables provide enough *extra* explanatory power as a group to warrant their inclusion in the equation. The test is called the partial F test. The original equation is called the **reduced** equation, and the larger equation is called the **complete** equation. In simple terms, the partial F test tests whether the complete equation is significantly better than the reduced equation.

The test itself is intuitive. We use the output from the ANOVA tables of the reduced and complete equations to form an F-ratio. This ratio measures how much the sum of squared residuals, SSE, *decreases* by including the extra variables in the equation. It *must* decrease by some amount because the sum of squared residuals cannot increase when extra variables are added to an equation. But if it is does not decrease sufficiently, then the extra variables might not explain enough to warrant their inclusion in the equation, and we should probably exclude them. The F-ratio measures this. If it is sufficiently large, then we can conclude that the extra variables are worth including; otherwise, we can safely exclude them.

To state the test formally, we first state the relevant hypotheses. Let β_{j+1} through β_k be the coefficients of the extra variables in the complete equation. Then the null hypothesis is that these extra variables have no effect on the response variable; that is,

$H_0: \beta_{j+1} = \cdots = \beta_k = 0$. The alternative is that at least one of the extra variables has an effect on the response variable, so that at least one of these β's is not 0.

To run the test, we estimate both the reduced and complete equations and look at the associated ANOVA tables. Let SSE_R and SSE_C be the sums of squared errors from the reduced and complete equations, respectively. Also, let MSE_C be the mean square error for the complete equation. All of these quantities appear in the ANOVA tables. Next, we form the following F-ratio:

$$F\text{-ratio} = \frac{(SSE_R - SSE_C)/(k - j)}{MSE_C} \qquad (12.3)$$

Note that the numerator includes the reduction in sum of squared errors discussed above. If the null hypothesis is true, then this F-ratio has an F distribution with $k - j$ and $n - k - 1$ degrees of freedom. If it is sufficiently large, we reject H_0. As usual, the best way to run the test is to find the p-value corresponding to this F-ratio. This is the probability beyond the calculated F-ratio in the F distribution with $k - j$ and $n - k - 1$ degrees of freedom. In words, we reject the hypothesis that the extra variables have no explanatory power if this p-value is sufficiently small, less than 0.05, say.

This F-ratio and corresponding p-value are *not* part of the StatPro regression output. However, they are fairly easy to obtain. We run two regressions, one for the reduced equation and one for the complete equation, and use the appropriate values from their ANOVA tables to calculate the F-ratio in equation (12.3). Then we use Excel's FDIST function in the form FDIST(F-ratio, $k - j$, $n - k - 1$) to calculate the corresponding p-value. The procedure is illustrated in the following example. It uses the bank discrimination data from Example 11.3 of the previous chapter.

E X A M P L E   1 2 . 4

Recall from Example 11.3 that Fifth National Bank has 208 employees. The data for these employees are stored in the file BANK.XLS. In the previous chapter we ran several regressions for Salary to see whether there is convincing evidence of salary discrimination against females. We will continue this analysis here. First, we'll regress Salary versus the Female dummy, YrsExper, and the interaction between Female and YrsExper, labeled Fem_YrsExper. This will be the reduced equation. Then we'll see whether the JobGrade dummies Job_2 to Job_6 add anything significant to the reduced equation. If so, we will then see whether the interactions between the Female dummy and the JobGrade dummies, labeled Fem_Job2 to Fem_Job6, add anything significant to what we already have. If so, we'll finally see whether the education dummies Ed_2 to Ed_5 add anything significant to what we already have.

Solution

First, note that we created all of the dummies and interaction variables with StatPro's Data Utilities procedures. These could be entered directly with Excel functions (see the formulas in the AnalysisData sheet of the BANK.XLS file for details), but StatPro makes the process much quicker and easier. Also, note that we have used three sets of dummies, for gender, job grade, and education level. When we use these in a regression equation, the dummy for one category of each should always be excluded; it is the reference category. The reference categories we have used are "male," job grade 1, and education level 1.

The output for the "smallest" equation, using Female, YrsExper, and Fem_YrsExper as explanatory variables, appears in Figure 12.13 (page 660). (We put this output in a sheet called Reduced.) We're off to a good start. These three variables already explain 63.9% of the variation in Salary.

FIGURE 12.13 Reduced Equation for Bank Example

	A	B	C	D	E	F	G
1	*Results of multiple regression for Salary*						
2							
3	*Summary measures*						
4		Multiple R	0.7991				
5		R-Square	0.6386				
6		Adj R-Square	0.6333				
7		StErr of Est	6.8163				
8							
9	*ANOVA Table*						
10		Source	df	SS	MS	F	p-value
11		Explained	3	16748.8748	5582.9583	120.1620	0.0000
12		Unexplained	204	9478.2324	46.4619		
13							
14	*Regression coefficients*						
15			Coefficient	Std Err	t-value	p-value	
16		Constant	30.4300	1.2166	25.0129	0.0000	
17		Female	4.0983	1.6658	2.4602	0.0147	
18		YrsExper	1.5278	0.0905	16.8887	0.0000	
19		Fem_YrsExper	-1.2478	0.1367	-9.1296	0.0000	

FIGURE 12.14 Equation with Job Dummies Added

	A	B	C	D	E	F	G
1	*Results of multiple regression for Salary*						
2							
3	*Summary measures*						
4		Multiple R	0.9005				
5		R-Square	0.8109				
6		Adj R-Square	0.8033				
7		StErr of Est	4.9916				
8							
9	*ANOVA Table*						
10		Source	df	SS	MS	F	p-value
11		Explained	8	21268.7391	2658.5924	106.7004	0.0000
12		Unexplained	199	4958.3682	24.9164		
13							
14	*Regression coefficients*						
15			Coefficient	Std Err	t-value	p-value	
16		Constant	26.1042	1.1054	23.6143	0.0000	
17		Female	6.0633	1.2663	4.7881	0.0000	
18		Job_2	2.5965	1.0101	2.5705	0.0109	
19		Job_3	6.2214	0.9982	6.2328	0.0000	
20		Job_4	11.0720	1.1726	9.4423	0.0000	
21		Job_5	14.9466	1.3402	11.1521	0.0000	
22		Job_6	17.0974	2.3907	7.1517	0.0000	
23		YrsExper	1.0709	0.1020	10.4975	0.0000	
24		Fem_YrsExper	-1.0211	0.1187	-8.6001	0.0000	
25							
26	Partial F test for including Job dummies						
27		df numerator	5				
28		df denominator	199				
29		F ratio	36.2802				
30		p-value	0.0000				

The output for the next equation, which adds the explanatory variables Job_2 to Job_6, appears in Figure 12.14. (We put this output in a sheet called Complete.) This equation appears to be much better. For example, R^2 has increased to 81.1%. We check whether it is *significantly* better with the partial F test in rows 26–30. (This part of the output is not given by StatPro; we have to enter it manually.) The degrees of freedom in cell C27 is 5, the number of *extra* variables. The degrees of freedom in cell C28 is the same as the value in cell C12, the degrees of freedom for SSE. Then we calculate the F-ratio in cell C29 with the formula

$$=((\text{Reduced!D12-D12})/\text{C27})/\text{E12}$$

where Reduced!D12 refers to SSE for the reduced equation from the Reduced sheet. Finally, we calculate the corresponding p-value in cell C30 with the formula

$$=\text{FDIST(C29,C27,C28)}$$

It is practically 0, so there is no doubt that the job grade dummies add significantly to the explanatory power of the equation.

Do the interactions between the Female dummy and the job dummies add anything more? We again use the partial F test, but now the previous *complete* equation becomes the new *reduced* equation, and the equation that includes the new interaction terms becomes the new complete equation. The output for this new complete equation appears in Figure 12.15 (page 662). (We put this output in a sheet called MoreComplete.) We perform the partial F test in rows 31–35 exactly as before. For example, the formula for the F-ratio in cell C34 is

$$=((\text{Complete!D12-D12})/\text{C32})/\text{E12}$$

Note how the SSE_R term in equation (12.3) now comes from the Complete sheet since this sheet contains the current *reduced* equation. As we see, the terms "reduced" and "complete" are relative. What is complete in one stage becomes reduced in the next stage. In any case, the p-value in cell C35 is again extremely small, so there is no doubt that the interaction terms add significantly to what we already had (even though R^2 has increased from 81.1% to only 84.0%).

Finally, we add the education dummies. The resulting output is shown in Figure 12.16 (page 663). (We put this output in a sheet called EvenMoreComplete.) Again, we see how the terms reduced and complete are relative. This output now corresponds to the complete equation, and the previous output corresponds to the reduced equation. The formula in cell C38 for the F-ratio is now

$$=((\text{MoreComplete!D12-D12})/\text{C36})/\text{E12}$$

Its SSE_R value comes from the MoreComplete sheet. Note that the increase in R^2 is from 84.0% to only 84.7%. Also, the p-value is not extremely small. According to the partial F test, it is not quite enough to qualify for statistical significance at the 5% level. Based on this evidence, there is not much to gain from including the education dummies in the equation, so we would probably elect to exclude them.

Before leaving this example, we make several comments. First, the partial test is *the* formal test of significance for an extra set of variables. Many users look only at the R^2 and/or s_e values to check whether extra variables are doing a "good job." For example, they might cite that R^2 went from 81.1% to 84.0% or that s_e went from 4.992 to 4.656 as evidence that extra variables provide a "significantly" better fit. Although these are important indicators, they are not the basis for a formal hypothesis test.

Second, if the partial F test shows that a block of variables is significant, it does not imply that each variable in this block is significant. Some of these variables can have low t-values. Consider Figure 12.15, for example. We are able to conclude that the Female/Job interactions as a whole are significant. But three of these interactions, Fem_Job2 to Fem_Job4 are clearly not significant, and Fem_Job5 is borderline. In fact, Fem_Job6

FIGURE 12.15   Regression Output with Interaction Terms Added

	A	B	C	D	E	F	G
1	*Results of multiple regression for Salary*						
2							
3	*Summary measures*						
4		Multiple R	0.9163				
5		R-Square	0.8396				
6		Adj R-Square	0.8289				
7		StErr of Est	4.6564				
8							
9	*ANOVA Table*						
10		Source	df	SS	MS	F	p-value
11		Explained	13	22020.7615	1693.9047	78.1242	0.0000
12		Unexplained	194	4206.3457	21.6822		
13							
14	*Regression coefficients*						
15			Coefficient	Std Err	t-value	p-value	
16		Constant	26.5155	1.4324	18.5112	0.0000	
17		Female	4.7245	1.7354	2.7225	0.0071	
18		Job_2	3.3410	1.8642	1.7922	0.0747	
19		Job_3	7.8720	2.2149	3.5540	0.0005	
20		Job_4	10.6919	1.9567	5.4643	0.0000	
21		Job_5	13.1464	1.9931	6.5958	0.0000	
22		Job_6	20.9794	2.7676	7.5803	0.0000	
23		YrsExper	0.9608	0.1042	9.2214	0.0000	
24		Fem_YrsExper	-0.8060	0.1303	-6.1845	0.0000	
25		Fem_Job2	-0.9434	2.1640	-0.4359	0.6634	
26		Fem_Job3	-1.9350	2.4414	-0.7926	0.4290	
27		Fem_Job4	0.4338	2.3750	0.1827	0.8553	
28		Fem_Job5	4.8734	2.6232	1.8578	0.0647	
29		Fem_Job6	-27.3274	5.7700	-4.7361	0.0000	
30							
31	*Partial F test for including job interactions with Female*						
32		df numerator	5				
33		df denominator	194				
34		F ratio	6.9368				
35		p-value	0.0000				

is the only one that is clearly significant. Some analysts favor excluding the *individual* variables that aren't significant, whereas others favor keeping the whole block or excluding the whole block. We lean toward the latter but recognize that either approach is valid—and the results are nearly the same either way.

Third, producing all of these outputs and doing the partial F tests is a lot of work. Therefore, we included a "Block" option in StatPro to make life easier. To run the analysis in this example in one step, we use the StatPro/Regression Analysis/Block menu item. After selecting Salary as the response variable, we see the dialog box in Figure 12.17 and fill it out as shown. We want four blocks of explanatory variables, and we want a given block to enter only if it passes the partial F test at the 5% level. In later dialog boxes, we then specify the explanatory variables in each block. Block 1 has Female, YrsExper, and Fem_YrsExper, block 2 has the job grade dummies, and so on.

Once we have specified all of this, the regression calculations are done in stages. At each stage, the partial F test checks whether a block is significant. If so, the variables in this block enter and we progress to the next stage. If not, the process ends; neither this block nor any later blocks are entered.

FIGURE 12.16 **Regression Output with Education Dummies Added**

	A	B	C	D	E	F	G
1	*Results of multiple regression for Salary*						
2							
3	*Summary measures*						
4		Multiple R	0.9205				
5		R-Square	0.8473				
6		Adj R-Square	0.8336				
7		StErr of Est	4.5914				
8							
9	*ANOVA Table*						
10		Source	df	SS	MS	F	p-value
11		Explained	17	22221.6888	1307.1582	62.0060	0.0000
12		Unexplained	190	4005.4185	21.0811		
13							
14	*Regression coefficients*						
15			Coefficient	Std Err	t-value	p-value	
16		Constant	26.0205	1.6784	15.5027	0.0000	
17		Female	4.3738	1.7247	2.5360	0.0120	
18		Ed_2	-0.6648	1.1204	-0.5933	0.5537	
19		Ed_3	0.6124	1.0823	0.5658	0.5722	
20		Ed_4	0.0491	1.9616	0.0250	0.9800	
21		Ed_5	2.8082	1.3035	2.1543	0.0325	
22		Job_2	2.6973	1.8757	1.4380	0.1521	
23		Job_3	6.8626	2.2492	3.0511	0.0026	
24		Job_4	8.7459	2.0547	4.2565	0.0000	
25		Job_5	10.5796	2.1800	4.8530	0.0000	
26		Job_6	18.2024	2.9402	6.1908	0.0000	
27		YrsExper	1.0024	0.1045	9.5878	0.0000	
28		Fem_YrsExper	-0.7608	0.1299	-5.8584	0.0000	
29		Fem_Job2	-0.7138	2.1484	-0.3323	0.7401	
30		Fem_Job3	-1.7529	2.4305	-0.7212	0.4717	
31		Fem_Job4	1.0232	2.3839	0.4292	0.6683	
32		Fem_Job5	5.2410	2.6231	1.9980	0.0471	
33		Fem_Job6	-29.3752	5.7539	-5.1053	0.0000	
34							
35	Partial F test for including education dummies						
36		df numerator	4				
37		df denominator	190				
38		F ratio	2.3828				
39		p-value	0.0530				

FIGURE 12.17 **Dialog Box for StatPro's Block Regression Option**

Block regression options

Enter the number of blocks of explanatory variables and the p-value used to test whether any block can enter.

Note: To force all blocks to enter, enter a p-value of 1.

Number of blocks: 4

p-value for each block: 0.05

OK   Cancel

FIGURE 12.18 First Part of Block Regression Output

	A	B	C	D	E	F	G
1	**Results of block regression for Salary**						
2							
3	**Block 1 enters (corresponding variables shown in bold)**						
4							
5	*Summary measures*						
6		Multiple R	0.7991				
7		R-Square	0.6386				
8		Adj R-Square	0.6333				
9		StErr of Est	6.8163				
10							
11	*ANOVA Table*						
12		Source	df	SS	MS	F	p-value
13		Explained	3	16748.8748	5582.9583	120.1620	0.0000
14		Unexplained	204	9478.2324	46.4619		
15							
16	*Regression coefficients*						
17			Coefficient	Std Err	t-value	p-value	
18		Constant	30.4300	1.2166	25.0129	0.0000	
19		**Female**	4.0983	1.6658	2.4602	0.0147	
20		**YrsExper**	1.5278	0.0905	16.8887	0.0000	
21		**Fem_YrsExper**	-1.2478	0.1367	-9.1296	0.0000	
22							
23	**Block 2 enters (corresponding variables shown in bold)**						
24							
25	*Summary measures*			Change	% Change		
26		Multiple R	0.9005	0.1014	%12.7		
27		R-Square	0.8109	0.1723	%27.0		
28		Adj R-Square	0.8033	0.1700	%26.9		
29		StErr of Est	4.9916	-1.8247	-%26.8		
30							
31	*ANOVA Table*						
32		Source	df	SS	MS	F	p-value
33		Explained	8	21268.7391	2658.5924	106.7004	0.0000
34		Unexplained	199	4958.3682	24.9164		
35							
36	*Regression coefficients*						
37			Coefficient	Std Err	t-value	p-value	
38		Constant	26.1042	1.1054	23.6143	0.0000	
39		Female	6.0633	1.2663	4.7881	0.0000	
40		YrsExper	1.0709	0.1020	10.4975	0.0000	
41		Fem_YrsExper	-1.0211	0.1187	-8.6001	0.0000	
42		**Job_2**	2.5965	1.0101	2.5705	0.0109	
43		**Job_3**	6.2214	0.9982	6.2328	0.0000	
44		**Job_4**	11.0720	1.1726	9.4423	0.0000	
45		**Job_5**	14.9466	1.3402	11.1521	0.0000	
46		**Job_6**	17.0974	2.3907	7.1517	0.0000	

The output from this procedure appears in Figures 12.18 and 12.19. (It wouldn't all fit in a single figure.) This output is basically a repetition of Figures 12.13, 12.14, and 12.15. However, note in rows 26–29 and 51–54 the percentage changes in the key summary statistics from one block to the next. Also, note that the output with the final block, the education dummies, does not appear at all. This block did not pass the partial F test at the 5% level, so it does not appear in the output.

FIGURE 12.19   Second Part of Block Regression Output

	A	B	C	D	E	F	G
48	**Block 3 enters (corresponding variables shown in bold)**						
49							
50	*Summary measures*			Change	% Change		
51		Multiple R	0.9163	0.0158	%1.8		
52		R-Square	0.8396	0.0287	%3.5		
53		Adj R-Square	0.8289	0.0255	%3.2		
54		StErr of Est	4.6564	-0.3352	-%6.7		
55							
56	*ANOVA Table*						
57		Source	df	SS	MS	F	p-value
58		Explained	13	22020.7615	1693.9047	78.1242	0.0000
59		Unexplained	194	4206.3457	21.6822		
60							
61	*Regression coefficients*						
62			Coefficient	Std Err	t-value	p-value	
63		Constant	26.5155	1.4324	18.5112	0.0000	
64		Female	4.7245	1.7354	2.7225	0.0071	
65		YrsExper	0.9608	0.1042	9.2214	0.0000	
66		Fem_YrsExper	-0.8060	0.1303	-6.1845	0.0000	
67		Job_2	3.3410	1.8642	1.7922	0.0747	
68		Job_3	7.8720	2.2149	3.5540	0.0005	
69		Job_4	10.6919	1.9567	5.4643	0.0000	
70		Job_5	13.1464	1.9931	6.5958	0.0000	
71		Job_6	20.9794	2.7676	7.5803	0.0000	
72		**Fem_Job2**	-0.9434	2.1640	-0.4359	0.6634	
73		**Fem_Job3**	-1.9350	2.4414	-0.7926	0.4290	
74		**Fem_Job4**	0.4338	2.3750	0.1827	0.8553	
75		**Fem_Job5**	4.8734	2.6232	1.8578	0.0647	
76		**Fem_Job6**	-27.3274	5.7700	-4.7361	0.0000	

Finally, we have concentrated on the partial F test and statistical significance in this example. We don't want you to lose sight, however, of the bigger picture. Once we have decided on a "final" regression equation, say, the one in Figure 12.15, we need to analyze its implications for the problem at hand. In this case the bank is interested in possible salary discrimination against females, so we should interpret this final equation in these terms. We will not go through this exercise again here—we did similar interpretations in the previous chapter. Our point is simply that you shouldn't get so caught in the details of statistical significance that you lose sight of the original purpose of the analysis! ■

PROBLEMS

Level A

29 A regional express delivery service company recently conducted a study to investigate the relationship between the cost of shipping a package (Y), the package weight (X_1), and the distance shipped (X_2). Twenty packages were randomly selected from among the large number received for shipment and a detailed analysis of the shipping cost was conducted for each package. These sample observations are given in the file P11_24.XLS.

    a Estimate a multiple regression model involving the two given explanatory variables. Using the ANOVA table, perform and interpret the result of an F test. Use a 5% significance level in making the statistical decision in this case.

b Is it worthwhile to add the terms X_1^2 and X_2^2 to the regression equation of part **a**? Base your decision here on a partial F test. Once again, employ a 5% significance level in performing this test.

c Is it worthwhile to add the term $X_1 X_2$ to the most appropriate reduced equation as determined in part **b**? Again, perform a partial F test with a 5% significance level.

d Based on the previous findings, what regression equation should this company use in predicting the cost of shipping a package? Defend your recommendation.

30 Suppose you are interested in predicting the price of a laptop computer based on its features. The file P11_35.XLS contains observations on the sales price and a number of potentially relevant variables for a randomly chosen sample of laptop computers.

a Estimate a multiple regression model that predicts the price of a laptop computer using the following quantitative variables: the speed of the computer's CPU, the length of time the computer's battery maintains its charge, and the size of the computer's RAM. Assess this set of explanatory variables with an F test, and report a p-value.

b Do explanatory variables that model the computer's chip type and monitor type contribute significantly to the prediction of the laptop's sales price? Let the equation estimated in part **a** serve as the reduced equation in a partial F test. Employ a 5% significance level in conducting the appropriate hypothesis test in this case.

c Do explanatory variables that model the computer's pointing device and the availability of a help line for buyers contribute significantly to the prediction of the laptop's sales price? Let the most appropriate equation found from the analysis in part **b** serve as the reduced equation in a partial F test. Again, employ a 5% significance level in conducting the appropriate hypothesis test in this case.

31 Many companies manufacture products that are at least partially produced using chemicals (for example, paint, gasoline, and steel). In many cases, the quality of the finished product is a function of the temperature and pressure at which the chemical reactions take place. Suppose that a particular manufacturer wants to model the quality (Y) of a product as a function of the temperature (X_1) and the pressure (X_2) at which it is produced. The file P11_39.XLS contains data obtained from a designed experiment involving these variables. Note that the assigned quality score can range from a minimum of 0 to a maximum of 100 for each manufactured product.

a Estimate a multiple regression model that includes the two given explanatory variables. Assess this set of explanatory variables with an F test, and report a p-value.

b Conduct a partial F test to decide whether it is worthwhile to add second-order terms (i.e., X_1^2, X_2^2, and $X_1 X_2$) to the multiple regression equation estimated in part **a**. Employ a 5% significance level in conducting this hypothesis test.

c Which regression equation is the most appropriate one for modeling the quality of the given product? Bear in mind that a good statistical model is usually parsimonious.

Level B

32 Continuing Problem 23, we'll refer to the original multiple regression model (i.e., the one that includes the age of the auctioned item and the number of bidders as explanatory variables) as the *reduced* equation. Suppose now that the antique collector believes that the *rate of increase* of the auction price with the age of the item will be driven upward by a large number of bidders.

a Revise the multiple regression model developed previously to model this additional feature of the problem. Estimate this larger regression equation, which we call the *complete* equation, using the sample data in the file P11_18.XLS.

b Perform a partial F test to check whether the complete equation is significantly better than the reduced equation. Use a 5% level of significance.

33 An economic development researcher wants to understand the relationship between the size of the monthly home mortgage or rent payment for households in a particular middle-class neighborhood and the following set of household variables: family size, approximate location of the household within the neighborhood, an indication of whether those surveyed owned or rented their home, gross annual income of the first household wage earner, gross annual income of the second household wage earner (if applicable), average monthly expenditure on utilities, and the total indebtedness (excluding the value of a home mortgage) of the household.

Observations on these variables for a large sample of households are recorded in the file P2_54.XLS.

a To explain the variation in the size of the monthly home mortgage or rent payment, formulate a multiple regression model that includes all of the *quantitative* household variables in the aforementioned set. Estimate this model using the given sample data. Perform an *F* test of the model's overall significance, and report a *p*-value.

b Determine whether the set of *qualitative* (i.e., categorical) variables that models the location of the household within the neighborhood adds significantly to explaining the variation in the size of the monthly home mortgage or rent payment. Use a 5% significance level in conducting this hypothesis test.

c Determine whether it is worthwhile to add a variable that models whether the home is owned or rented to the most appropriate regression equation from part **b**. Again, use a 5% significance level in conducting this hypothesis test. ■

Outliers

In all of the regression examples we have analyzed to this point, we have ignored the possibility of outliers. Unfortunately, in many real applications we cannot afford to ignore outliers. They are often present, and they can often have a substantial effect on the results. In this section we will briefly discuss outliers in the context of regression—how to detect them and what to do about them.

We tend to think of an outlier as an observation that has an extreme value for at least one variable. For example, if salaries in a data set are mostly in the $40,000–$80,000 range, but one salary is $350,000, then this observation is a clear outlier with respect to salary. However, in a regression context outliers are not always this obvious. In fact, an observation can be considered an outlier for several reasons, and some types of outliers can be difficult to detect. An observation can be an outlier for one or more of the following reasons.

1 It has an extreme value for one or more variables.

2 Its value of the response variable is much larger or smaller than predicted by the regression line, and its residual is abnormally large in magnitude. An example appears in Figure 12.20 (page 668). The line in this scatterplot fits most of the points, but it misses badly on the one obvious outlier. This outlier has a large positive residual, but its *Y* value is not abnormally large. Its *Y* value is only large relative to points with the same *X* value that it has.

3 Its residual is not only large in magnitude, but this point "tilts" the regression line toward it. An example appears in Figure 12.21. The two lines shown are the regression lines with the outlier and without it. If we keep the outlier, it makes a big difference on the slope and intercept of the regression line. This type of outlier is called an **influential** point—for the obvious reason.

4 Its values of individual explanatory variables are not extreme, but they fall outside the general pattern of the other observations. An example appears in Figure 12.22 (page 669). Here, we assume that the two variables shown, YrsExper (years of experience) and Rating (an employee's performance rating) are both explanatory variables for some other response variable (Salary) that isn't shown in the plot. The obvious outlier does not have an abnormal value of either YrsExper or Rating, but it falls well outside the pattern of most employees.

Once we've identified outliers, there is still the thorny problem of what to do with them. In most cases the regression output will look "nicer" if we delete outliers, but this

FIGURE 12.20 Outlier with a Large Residual

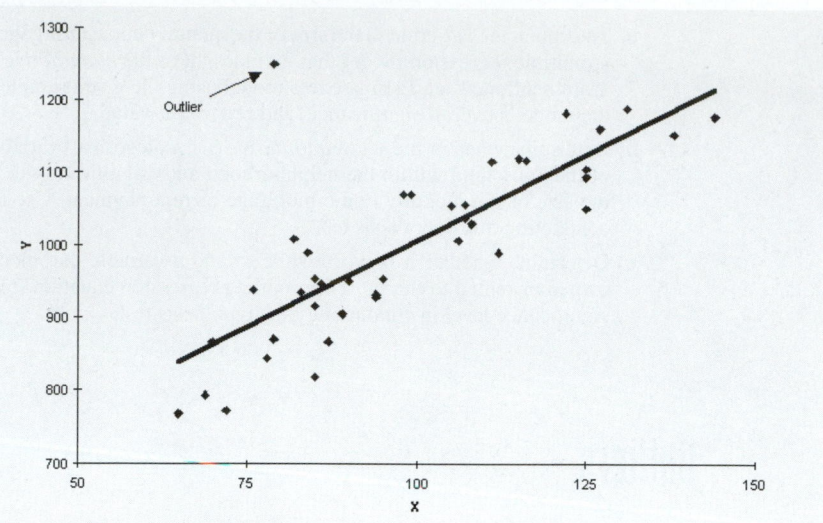

FIGURE 12.21 Outlier That Tilts the Regression Line

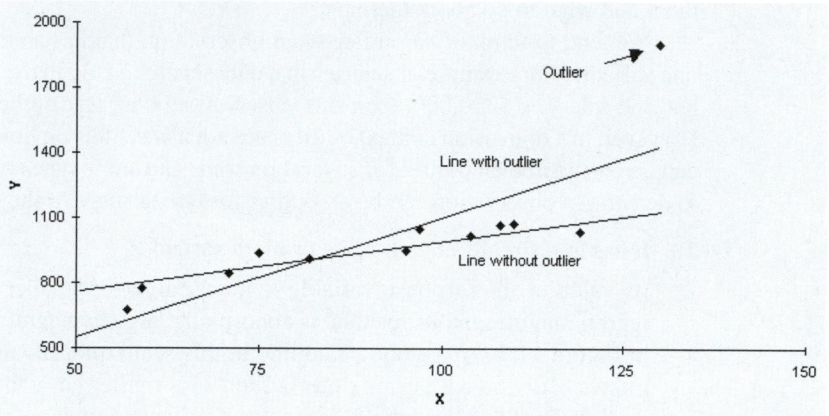

is not necessarily appropriate. If we can argue that the outlier isn't really a member of the relevant population, then it is appropriate and probably best to delete it. But if no such argument can be made, then it is not really appropriate to delete the outlier just to make the analysis come out better. Perhaps the best advice in this case is the advice we gave in the previous chapter. Run the analysis with the outliers and without them. If the key outputs do not change much, then it does not really matter whether the outliers are included or not. If the key outputs do change substantially, then report the results both with and without the outliers, along with a verbal explanation.

We illustrate this procedure in the following continuation of the bank discrimination example.

FIGURE 12.22 **Outlier Outside Pattern of Explanatory Variables**

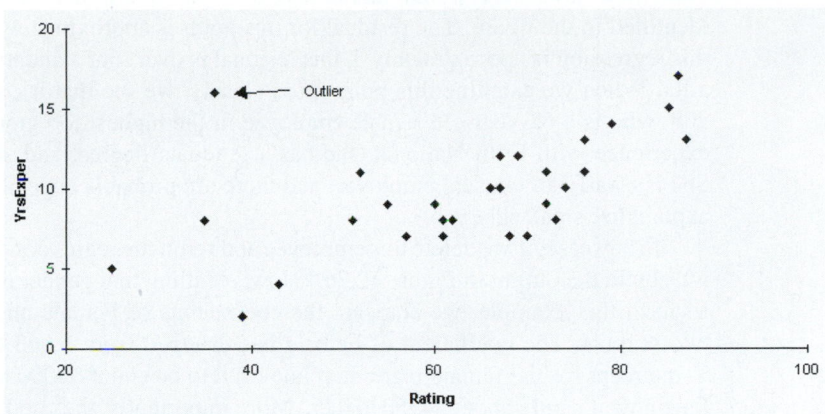

EXAMPLE 12.4 [CONTINUED]

Of the 208 employees at Fifth National Bank, are there any obvious outliers? In what sense are they outliers? Does it matter to the regression results, particularly those concerning gender discrimination, whether the outliers are removed?

Solution

There are several places we could look for outliers. An obvious place is the Salary variable. The boxplot in Figure 12.23 shows that there are several employees making substantially more in salary than most of the employees. (See the file BANK.XLS.) We could consider these outliers and remove them, arguing perhaps that these are senior managers who shouldn't be included in the discrimination analysis. We leave it to you to check whether the regression results are any different with these high-salary employees than without them.

Another place to look is at a scatterplot of the residuals versus the fitted values. This type of plot (offered as an option by StatPro) shows points with abnormally large residuals. For example, we ran the regression with Female, YrsExper, Fem_YrsExper, and the five job

FIGURE 12.23 **Boxplot of Salaries for Bank Data**

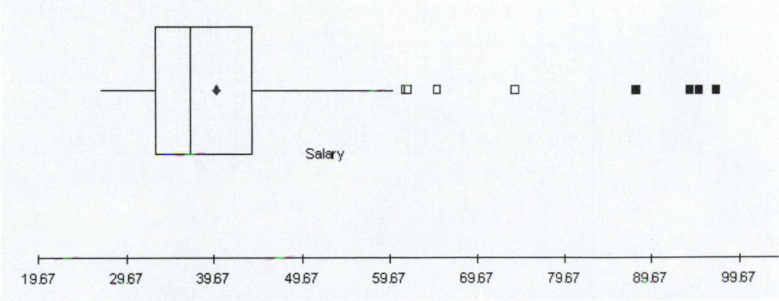

grade dummies, and we obtained the output and scatterplot in Figures 12.24 and 12.25. This scatterplot has several points that could be considered outliers, but we focus on the point identified in the figure. The residual for this point is approximately −21. Given that s_e for this regression is approximately 5, this residual is over four standard errors below 0—quite a lot. When we examine this point more closely, we see that it corresponds to employee 208, who is a 62-year-old female employee in the highest job grade. She has 33 years of experience with Fifth National, she has a graduate degree, and she earns only $30,000. She is clearly an unusual employee, and there are probably special circumstances that can explain her small salary.

In any case, if we delete this employee and rerun the regression with the same variables, we obtain the output in Figure 12.26.[3] Now, recalling that gender discrimination is the key issue in this example, we compare the coefficients of Female and Fem_YrsExper in the two outputs. The coefficient of Female has dropped from 6.063 to 4.353. In words, the Y-intercept for the female regression line used to be about $6000 higher than for the male line; now it's only about $4350 higher. More importantly, the coefficient of Fem_YrsExper

	A	B	C	D	E	F	G
1	Results of multiple regression for Salary						
2							
3	Summary measures						
4		Multiple R	0.9005				
5		R-Square	0.8109				
6		Adj R-Square	0.8033				
7		StErr of Est	4.9916				
8							
9	ANOVA Table						
10		Source	df	SS	MS	F	p-value
11		Explained	8	21268.7391	2658.5924	106.7004	0.0000
12		Unexplained	199	4958.3682	24.9164		
13							
14	Regression coefficients						
15			Coefficient	Std Err	t-value	p-value	
16		Constant	26.1042	1.1054	23.6143	0.0000	
17		Female	6.0633	1.2663	4.7881	0.0000	
18		Job_2	2.5965	1.0101	2.5705	0.0109	
19		Job_3	6.2214	0.9982	6.2328	0.0000	
20		Job_4	11.0720	1.1726	9.4423	0.0000	
21		Job_5	14.9466	1.3402	11.1521	0.0000	
22		Job_6	17.0974	2.3907	7.1517	0.0000	
23		YrsExper	1.0709	0.1020	10.4975	0.0000	
24		Fem_YrsExper	-1.0211	0.1187	-8.6001	0.0000	

[3]As it turns out, this employee is the last observation in the data set. An easy way to run the regression (with StatPro) without this employee is to insert a blank row above her row and then position the cursor anywhere above this blank row.

670 *Chapter 12 Regression Analysis: Statistical Inference*

FIGURE 12.25
Scatterplot of Residuals versus Fitted Values with Outlier Identified

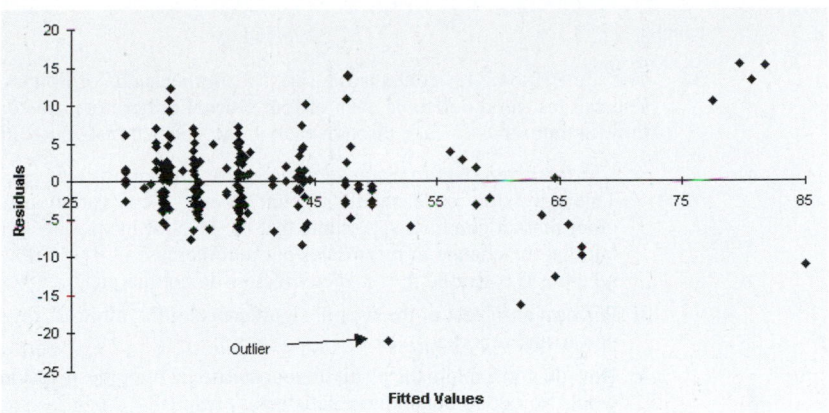

FIGURE 12.26
Regression Output with Outlier Excluded

	A	B	C	D	E	F	G
1	*Results of multiple regression for Salary*						
2							
3	*Summary measures*						
4		Multiple R	0.9130				
5		R-Square	0.8336				
6		Adj R-Square	0.8269				
7		StErr of Est	4.6857				
8							
9	*ANOVA Table*						
10		Source	df	SS	MS	F	p-value
11		Explained	8	21780.9962	2722.6245	124.0064	0.0000
12		Unexplained	198	4347.1909	21.9555		
13							
14	*Regression coefficients*						
15			Coefficient	Std Err	t-value	p-value	
16		Constant	26.7103	1.0440	25.5840	0.0000	
17		Female	4.3531	1.2321	3.5331	0.0005	
18		Job_2	2.7179	0.9485	2.8655	0.0046	
19		Job_3	6.2572	0.9370	6.6777	0.0000	
20		Job_4	10.9838	1.1008	9.9777	0.0000	
21		Job_5	15.4645	1.2619	12.2547	0.0000	
22		Job_6	22.3234	2.4530	9.1004	0.0000	
23		YrsExper	0.8977	0.1012	8.8675	0.0000	
24		Fem_YrsExper	-0.7206	0.1252	-5.7578	0.0000	

has changed from -1.021 to -0.721. This coefficient indicates how much less steep the female line for Salary versus YrsExper is than the male line. So a change from -1.021 to -0.721 indicates *less* discrimination against females now than before. In other words, this unusual female employee accounts for a good bit of the discrimination argument—although a strong argument still exists even without her. ∎

PROBLEMS

Level A

34 The file P12_34.XLS contains the sales, Y, in thousands of dollars per week, for randomly selected fast-food outlets in each of four cities. Furthermore, this data set includes the traffic flow, in thousands of cars, through each of the selected fast-food outlets.

   a Use the given data to estimate a model for predicting sales as a function of traffic flow. This regression model should account for city-to-city variations that might be due to size or other market conditions. Assume that the level of mean sales will differ from city to city, but that the change in mean sales per unit increase in traffic flow will remain the same for all cities (i.e., traffic flow and city factors do not interact).

   b Perform an F test of the overall significance of the multiple regression model estimated in part **a**, and report a p-value.

   c How do you explain the result of your statistical hypothesis test in part **b**? What, if anything, would you do to obtain more satisfactory results?

35 A manufacturing firm wants to determine whether a relationship exists between the number of work-hours an employee misses per year (Y) and the employee's annual wages (X). The data provided in the file P12_35.XLS are based on a random sample of 15 employees from this organization.

   a Estimate a simple linear regression model using the sample data. How well does the estimated model fit the sample data?

   b Perform an F test for the existence of a linear relationship between Y and X. Use a 5% level of significance.

   c How do you explain the results you have found in parts **a** and **b**?

   d Suppose you learn that the 10th worker in the sample has been fired for missing an excessive number of work-hours during the past year. In light of this information, how would you proceed to estimate the relationship between the number of work-hours an employee misses per year and the employee's annual wages, using the available information? If you decide to revise your estimate of this regression equation, repeat parts **a** and **b**.

Level B

36 Statistician Frank J. Anscombe created a data set to illustrate the importance of doing more than just examining the standard computer-generated regression output. These data are provided in the file P12_36.XLS.

   a Regress Y_1 on X. How well does the estimated model fit the data? Is there evidence of a linear relationship between Y_1 and X at the 5% significance level?

   b Regress Y_2 on X. How well does the estimated model fit the data? Is there evidence of a linear relationship between Y_2 and X at the 5% significance level?

   c Regress Y_3 on X. How well does the estimated model fit the data? Is there evidence of a linear relationship between Y_3 and X at the 5% significance level?

   d Regress Y_4 on X_4. How well does the estimated model fit the data? Is there evidence of a linear relationship between Y_4 and X_4 at the 5% significance level?

   e Compare these four simple linear regression models (i) in terms of goodness of fit and (ii) in terms of overall statistical significance.

   f How do you explain the above findings, considering that each of the regression equations is based on a *different* set of variables?

   g What role, if any, do outliers have upon each of these estimated regression models? ■

Violations of Regression Assumptions

M uch of the theoretical research in the area of regression has dealt with violations of the regression assumptions in Section 12.2. There are three issues: how to detect violations of the assumptions, what goes wrong if we ignore violations, and what to do about them if they are detected. Detection is usually relatively easy. We can look at scatterplots, histograms, and time series plots for visual signs of violations, and there are a number of numerical measures (many not covered here) that have been developed for diagnostic purposes. The second issue, what goes wrong if we ignore violations, depends on the type of violation and its severity. The third issue is the most difficult. There are some relatively easy fixes and some that are well beyond the level of this book. In this section we will briefly discuss some of the most common violations and a few possible remedies for them.

12.10.1 Nonconstant Error Variance

The second regression assumption states that the variance of the errors should be *constant* for all values of the explanatory variables. This is a lot to ask, and it is almost always violated to some extent. Fortunately, mild violations do not have much effect on the validity of the output, so we may usually ignore them.

However, one particular form of nonconstant error variance occurs fairly often and should be dealt with. This is the "fan shape" we saw in the scatterplot of Amount_Spent versus Salary in Figure 12.1. As salaries increase, the variability of amounts spent also increases. Although this fan shape appears in the scatterplot of the response variable Amount_Spent versus the explanatory variable Salary, it also appears in the scatterplot of residuals versus fitted values when we regress Amount_Spent versus Salary. If we ignore this nonconstant error variance, then the standard error of the regression coefficient of Salary is inaccurate, so that a confidence interval for this coefficient or a hypothesis test concerning it can be misleading.

There are at least two ways to deal with this fan-shape phenomenon. The first is to use a different estimation method than least squares. It is called **weighted least squares**, and it is an option available in many statistical software packages. However, it is fairly advanced and it is not available with Excel (or StatPro), so we won't discuss it here.

The second method is simpler. When we see a fan shape, where the variability increases from left to right in a scatterplot, we can try a logarithmic transformation of the response variable. The reason this often works is that the logarithmic transformation squeezes the large values closer together and pulls the small values farther apart. The scatterplot of the log of Amount_Spent versus Salary appears in Figure 12.27 (page 674). (This is the same mail-order data set used in Example 3.11 in Chapter 3. See the file CATALOGS.XLS from that chapter.) Clearly, the fan shape evident in Figure 12.1 is gone.

This logarithmic transformation is not a magical cure for all instances of nonconstant error variance. For example, it appears to have introduced some curvature into the plot in Figure 12.27. However, as we discussed in the previous chapter, whenever the distribution of the response variable is heavily skewed to the right, as it often is, the logarithmic transformation is worth exploring.

FIGURE 12.27 Scatterplot without Fan Shape

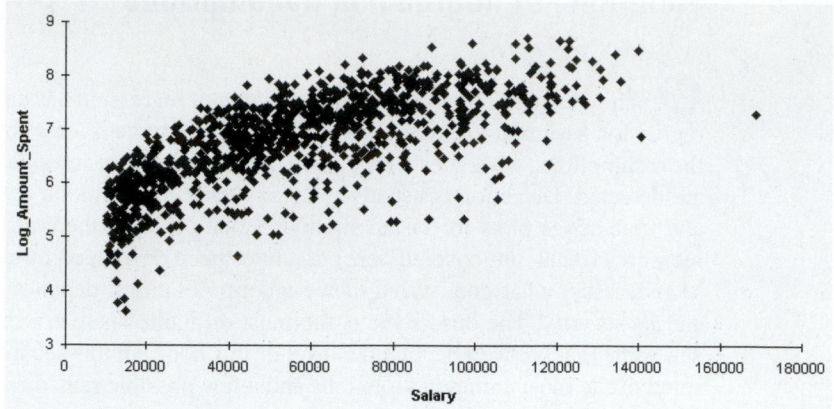

12.10.2 Nonnormality of Residuals

The third regression assumption states that the error terms are normally distributed. We can check this assumption fairly easily by forming a histogram of the residuals. We can even perform a formal test of normality of the residuals by using the procedures discussed in Section 9.6 of Chapter 9. However, unless the distribution of the residuals is severely nonnormal, the inferences we make from the regression output are still approximately valid. In addition, a form of nonnormality often encountered is skewness to the right, and this can often be remedied by the same logarithmic transformation of the response variable that remedies nonconstant error variance.

12.10.3 Autocorrelated Residuals

The fourth regression assumption states that the error terms are probabilistically independent. This assumption is usually valid for cross-sectional data, but it is often violated for time series data. The problem with time series data is that the residuals are often correlated with nearby residuals, a property called **autocorrelation**. The most frequent type of autocorrelation is positive autocorrelation. For example, if residuals separated by 1 month are autocorrelated—this is called **lag 1 autocorrelation**—in a positive direction, then an overprediction in January, say, will likely lead to an overprediction in February, and an underprediction in January will likely lead to an underprediction in February. If this autocorrelation is large, then serious prediction errors can occur if it isn't dealt with appropriately.

A numerical measure has been developed to check for lag 1 autocorrelation. It is called the **Durbin–Watson statistic** (after the two statisticians who developed it), and it is quoted automatically in the regression output of many statistical software packages. The Durbin–Watson (DW) statistic is scaled to be between 0 and 4. Values close to 2 indicate very little lag 1 autocorrelation, values below 2 indicate positive autocorrelation, and values above 2 indicate negative autocorrelation.

Since *positive* autocorrelation is the usual culprit, the question becomes how much below 2 the DW statistic must be before we should react. There is a formal hypothesis test for answering this question, and a set of tables appears in many statistics texts. Without going into the details, we will simply state that when the number of time series observations, n, is about 30 and the number of explanatory variables is fairly small, say, 1 to 5, then any DW statistic less than 1.2 should get our attention. If n increases to around 100, then we shouldn't be concerned unless the DW statistic is below 1.5.

If e_i is the ith residual, then the formula for the DW statistic is

$$DW = \frac{\sum_{i=2}^{n}(e_i - e_{i-1})^2}{\sum_{i=1}^{n} e_i^2}$$

This is obviously not very attractive for hand calculation, so we have included the DW function in the StatPro add-in. To use it, run any regression and check the option to supply columns of fitted values and residuals. (This option is automatic with the Simple Regression procedure.) Then enter the formula

$$=DW(ResidRange)$$

in any cell, substituting the actual range of residuals for "ResidRange."

The following continuation of Example 12.1 with the Bendrix manufacturing data—the only time series data set we've analyzed with regression—checks for possible lag 1 autocorrelation.

EXAMPLE 12.1 [CONTINUED]

Is there any evidence of lag 1 autocorrelation in the Bendrix data when Overhead is regressed on MachHrs and ProdRuns?

Solution

We run the usual multiple regression and check that we want columns of fitted values and residuals appended to the data set. The results (with some rows hidden) appear in Figure 12.28. (See the file BENDRIX.XLS.) The residuals are listed in column F. Each represents how much the regression overpredicts (if negative) or underpredicts (if positive) the overhead cost for that month. We can check for lag 1 autocorrelation in two ways, with the DW statistic and by examining the time series graph of the residuals in Figure 12.29.

FIGURE 12.28 **Regression Output with Residuals and DW Statistic**

	A	B	C	D	E	F	G	H
1	Monthly data on manufacturing overhead costs							
2								
3	Month	MachHrs	ProdRuns	Overhead	Fitted Values	Residuals		Durbin-Watson
4	1	1539	31	99798	98391.351	1406.649		1.3131
5	2	1284	29	87804	85522.333	2281.667		
6	3	1490	27	93681	92723.595	957.405		
7	4	1355	22	82262	82428.092	-166.092		
8	5	1500	35	106968	100227.903	6740.097		
9	6	1777	30	107925	107869.395	55.605		
10	7	1716	41	117287	114933.472	2353.528		
11	8	1045	29	76868	75117.134	1750.866		
12	9	1364	47	106001	104910.368	1090.632		
13	10	1516	21	88738	88553.834	184.166		
37	34	1723	35	107828	109936.520	-2108.520		
38	35	1413	30	88032	92022.147	-3990.147		
39	36	1390	54	117943	112227.640	5715.360		

FIGURE 12.29 **Time Series Graph of Residuals**

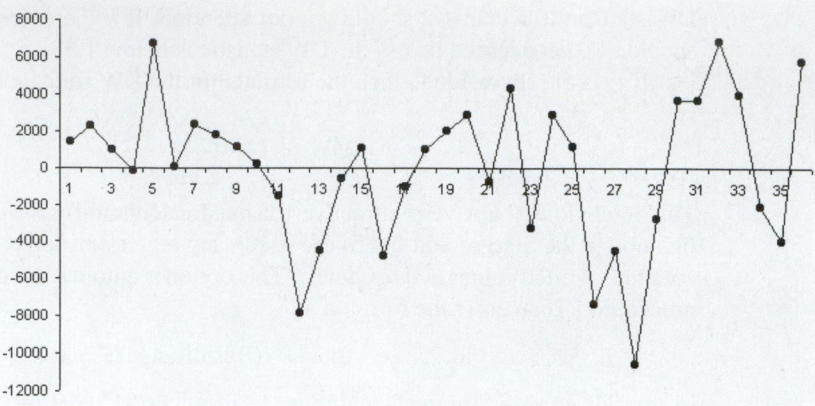

We calculate the DW statistic in cell H4 of Figure 12.28 with the formula

$$=DW(F4:F39)$$

(Remember that DW is *not* a built-in Excel function. It is available only if StatPro is loaded.) Based on our guidelines for DW values, 1.3131 suggests positive autocorrelation—it is less than 2—but not enough to cause concern.[4] This general conclusion is supported by the time series graph. Serious autocorrelation of lag 1 would tend to show long runs of residuals alternating above and below the horizontal axis—positives would tend to follow positives, and negatives would tend to follow negatives. There is some indication of this behavior in the graph but not an excessive amount. ■

What should we do if the DW statistic signals significant autocorrelation? Unfortunately, the answer to this question would take us much deeper into time series analysis than we can go in this book. Suffice it to say that time series analysis in the context of regression can become very complex, and there are no easy fixes for the autocorrelation that often occurs.

PROBLEMS

Level A

37 Motorco produces electric motors for use in home appliances. One of the company's production managers is interested in examining the relationship between the dollars spent per month in inspecting finished motor products (X) and the number of motors produced during that month that were returned by dissatisfied customers (Y). He has collected the data in the file P2_18.XLS to explore this relationship for the past 36 months.

a Generate a simple linear regression model using the given data and interpret it for this production manager.

b Conduct an appropriate hypothesis test for the existence of a linear relationship between Y and X in this case, and report a p-value.

c Examine the residuals of the estimated regression equation. Do you see evidence of any violations of the assumptions regarding the errors of the regression model?

---

[4] A more formal test, using Durbin–Watson tables, supports this conclusion.

d Conduct a Durbin–Watson test on the model's residuals. Interpret the result of this test for the production manager.

e In light of your result in part **d**, do you recommend modifying the original regression model? If so, how would you revise it?

38 Examine the relationship between the average utility bills for homes of a particular size (Y) and the average monthly temperature (X). The data in the file P11_7.XLS include the average monthly bill and temperature for each month of the past year.

a Use the given data to estimate a simple linear regression model. How well does the estimated regression model fit the given data?

b Conduct an appropriate hypothesis test for the existence of a linear relationship between Y and X, and report a p-value.

c Examine the residuals of the estimated regression equation. Do you see evidence of any violations of the assumptions regarding the errors of the regression model?

d Conduct a Durbin–Watson test on the model's residuals. Interpret the result of this test.

e In light of your result in part **d**, do you recommend modifying the original regression model? If so, how would you revise it?

39 The manager of a commuter rail transportation system was recently asked by her governing board to predict the demand for rides in the large city served by the transportation network. The system manager has collected data on variables thought to be related to the number of weekly riders on the city's rail system. The file P11_20.XLS contains these data.

a Estimate a multiple regression model using all of the available explanatory variables.

b Conduct and interpret the result of an F test on the given model. Employ a 5% level of significance in conducting this statistical hypothesis test.

c Is there evidence of autocorrelated residuals in this model? Explain why or why not. ■

Prediction

Once we have estimated a regression equation from a set of data, we might want to use this equation to predict the value of the response variable for *new* observations. As an example, suppose that a retail chain is considering opening a new store in one of several proposed locations. It naturally wants to choose the location that will result in the largest revenues. The problem is that the revenues for the new locations are not yet known. They can be observed only after stores are opened in these locations, and the chain cannot afford to open more than one store at the current time. An alternative is to use regression analysis. Using data from *existing* stores, the chain can run a regression of the response variable revenue on several explanatory variables such as population density, level of wealth in the vicinity, number of competitors nearby, ease of access given the existing roads, and so on.

Assuming that the regression equation has a reasonably large R^2 and, even more important, a reasonably small s_e, the chain can then use this equation to predict revenues for the proposed locations. Specifically, it will gather values of the explanatory variables for each of the proposed locations, substitute these into the regression equation, and look at the predicted revenue for each proposed location. All else being equal, it will probably choose the location with the highest predicted revenue.

As another example, suppose that we are trying to explain the starting salaries for undergraduate college students. We want to predict the *mean* salary of all graduates with certain characteristics, such as all male marketing majors from state-supported universities. To do this, we first gather salary data from a sample of graduates from various universities. Included in this data set are relevant explanatory variables for each graduate in the sample, such as the type of university, the student's major, GPA, years of work experience, and so on. We then use these data to estimate a regression equation for starting salary and substitute the relevant values of the explanatory variables into the regression equation to obtain the required prediction.

The above two examples illustrate two types of prediction problems in regression. The first problem, illustrated by the retail chain example, is probably the more common of the two. Here we are trying to predict the value of the response variable for one or more *individual* members of the population. In this specific example we are trying to predict the future revenue for several potential locations of the new store. In the second problem, illustrated by the salary example, we are trying to predict the *mean* of the response variable for all members of the population with certain values of the explanatory variables. In the first problem we are predicting an individual value; in the second problem we are predicting a mean.

The second problem is inherently easier than the first in the sense that the resulting prediction is more accurate. The reason should be intuitive. Recall that the mean of the response variable for any fixed values of the explanatory variables lies on the population regression line. Therefore, if we can accurately estimate this line—that is, if we can accurately estimate the regression coefficients—we can accurately predict the required mean. In contrast, most individual points do *not* lie on the population regression line. Therefore, even if our estimate of the population regression line is perfectly accurate, we still cannot predict exactly where an individual point will fall.

Stated another way, when we predict a mean, there is a single source of error—the possibly inaccurate estimates of the regression coefficients. But when we predict an individual value, there are two sources of error—the inaccurate estimates of the regression coefficients and the inherent variation of individual points around the regression line. Actually, this second source of error often dominates the first.

We illustrate these comments in Figure 12.30. For the sake of illustration, the response variable is salary and the single explanatory variable is years of experience with the company. Let's suppose that we want to predict either the salary for a particular employee with 10 years of experience or the mean salary of all employees with 10 years of experience. The two lines in this graph represent the population regression line (which in reality is unobservable) and the estimated regression line. For each prediction problem the point prediction—the best guess—is the value above 10 on the estimated regression line. The error in predicting the mean occurs because the two lines in the graph are not the same, that is, the estimated line is not quite correct. The error in predicting the individual value (the point shown in the graph) occurs because the two lines are not the same and also because this point does not lie on the population regression line.

FIGURE 12.30   **Prediction Errors for an Individual and a Mean**

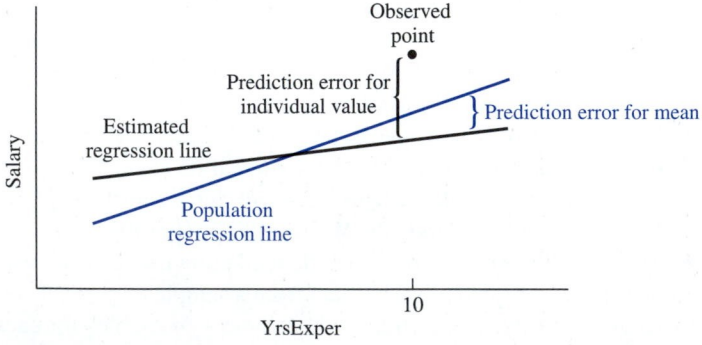

One general aspect of prediction becomes apparent by looking at this graph. If we let X's denote the explanatory variables, predictions for values of the X's close to their means are likely to be more accurate than predictions for X's far from their means. In the graph, the mean years of experience is about 7. (This is approximately where the two lines cross.) Because the slopes of the two lines are different, they get farther apart as YrsExper gets farther away from 7 (on either side). As a result, predictions tend to become less accurate.

This phenomenon shows up as higher standard errors of prediction as the X's get farther away from their means. However, for extreme values of the X's, there is another problem. Suppose, for example, that all values of YrsExper in the data set are between 1 and 15, and we attempt to predict the salary for an employee with 25 years of experience. This is called **extrapolation**; we are attempting to predict beyond the limits of the sample.

The problem here is that there is no guarantee, and sometimes no reason to believe, that the relationship within the range of the sample is valid outside of this range. It is perfectly possible that the effect of years of experience on salary is considerably different in the 25-year range than in the range of the sample. If it is, then extrapolation is bound to yield inaccurate predictions. In general, we should try to avoid extrapolation whenever possible. If we really want to predict the salaries of employees with 25-plus years of experience, then we should include some employees of this type in the original sample.

We now discuss how to make predictions and how to estimate their accuracy, both for individual values and for means. To keep it simple, we first assume that there is a single explanatory variable X. We choose a fixed "trial" value of X, labeled X_0, and predict the value of a single Y or the mean of all Y's when $X = X_0$. For both prediction problems the point prediction, or best guess, is found by substituting into the right-hand side of the estimated regression equation. Graphically, this is the height of the estimated regression line above X_0.

To measure the accuracy of these point predictions, we calculate a standard error for each prediction. These standard errors can be interpreted in the usual way. For example, we are about 68% certain that the actual values will be within one standard error of the point predictions, and we are about 95% certain that the actual values will be within two standard errors of the point predictions. For the individual prediction problem, the standard error is labeled s_{ind} and is given by

$$s_{\text{ind}} = s_e \sqrt{1 + \frac{1}{n} + \frac{(X_0 - \overline{X})^2}{\sum_{i=1}^{n}(X_i - \overline{X})^2}} \simeq s_e \qquad (12.4)$$

As indicated by the approximate equality on the right, when the sample size n is large and X_0 is fairly close to $\overline{X}$, the last two terms inside the square root are relatively small, and this standard error of prediction can be approximated by s_e, the standard error of estimate.

For the prediction of the mean, the standard error is labeled s_{mean} and is given by

$$s_{\text{mean}} = s_e \sqrt{\frac{1}{n} + \frac{(X_0 - \overline{X})^2}{\sum_{i=1}^{n}(X_i - \overline{X})^2}} \simeq s_e / \sqrt{n} \qquad (12.5)$$

Here, if X_0 is fairly close to $\overline{X}$, then the last term inside the square root is relatively small, and this standard error of prediction is approximately $s_e / \sqrt{n}$.

These standard errors can be used to calculate a 95% prediction interval for an individual value and a 95% confidence interval for a mean value. Exactly as in Chapter 8, we go out a t-multiple of the relevant standard error on either side of the point prediction. The t-multiple is the value that cuts off 0.025 probability in the right-hand tail of a t distribution with $n - 2$ degrees of freedom.

The term *prediction* interval (rather than confidence interval) is used for an individual value because an individual value of Y is not a population *parameter*. However, the interpretation is basically the same. If we calculate a 95% prediction interval for many members of the population, we expect their actual Y values to fall within the corresponding prediction intervals about 95% of the time.

To see how all of this can be implemented in Excel, we revisit the Pharmex drugstore data set, where a sales index is regressed on a promotional expenditures index for a sample of 50 regions.

EXAMPLE 12.5

Besides the 50 regions in the data set, Pharmex does business in five other regions, which have promotional expenses indexes of 114, 98, 84, 122, and 101. Find the predicted Sales and a 95% prediction interval for each of these regions. Also, find the *mean* Sales for all regions with each of these values of Promote, along with 95% confidence intervals for these means.

Solution

This example cannot be solved with StatPro, but it is relatively easy with Excel's built-in functions.[5] We illustrate the procedure in Figure 12.31. (See the file PHARMEX.XLS.) The original data appear in columns B and C. We use the range names SalesOld and PromoteOld for the data in these columns. The new regions appear to the right in rows 9–13. Their given values of Promote are in the range G9:G13, which we name PromoteNew. To obtain the predicted sales for these regions, we use Excel's TREND function by highlighting the range H9:H13, typing the formula

$$=TREND(SalesOld,PromoteOld,PromoteNew)$$

and pressing Ctrl-Shift-Enter. This substitutes the new values of the explanatory variable (in the third argument) into the regression equation based on the data from the first two arguments. We can then use these same predictions in rows 19–23 for the mean sales values. For example, we predict the same Sales value of 112.03 for a single region with Promote equal to 114 or the mean of all regions with this value of Promote.

According to equation (12.4), the *approximate* standard error of prediction for any individual value is s_e, calculated in cell H6 with the formula

$$=STEYX(SalesOld,PromoteOld)$$

The more exact standard error of prediction depends on the value of Promote. To calculate it from equation (12.4), we enter the formula

$$=\$H\$6*SQRT(1+1/50+(G9-AVERAGE(PromoteOld))\hat{}2/(48*STDEV(PromoteOld))\hat{}2)$$

in cell I9 and copy it down through cell I13. We then calculate the lower and upper limits of 95% prediction intervals in columns J and K. These use the t-multiple in cell I3, obtained with the formula

$$=TINV(0.05,73)$$

The formulas in cells J9 and K9 are then

$$=H9-\$I\$3*I9$$

and

$$=H9+\$I\$3*I9$$

which we copy down to row 13.

---

[5] We intend to incorporate this capability into StatPro.

FIGURE 12.31 Prediction in Simple Regression

	A	B	C	D	E	F	G	H	I	J	K
1	Pharmez drugstore data										
2											
3	Original data (used to estimate regression)					t-multiple for prediction intervals			1.993		
4											
5	Region	Promote	Sales			Predictions for individual customers					
6	1	77	85			Approximate std err		7.395			
7	2	110	103								
8	3	110	102			Region	Promote	Pred Sales	Std Err	Lower limit	Upper limit
9	4	93	109			51	114	112.03	7.474	97.13	126.92
10	5	90	85			52	98	99.83	7.468	84.95	114.72
11	6	95	103			53	84	89.16	7.472	74.27	104.05
12	7	100	110			54	122	118.13	7.480	103.22	133.04
13	8	85	86			55	101	102.12	7.469	87.23	117.00
14	9	96	92								
15	10	83	87			Prediction of means					
16	11	88	99			Approximate std err		1.046			
17	12	94	101								
18	13	104	109				Promote	Pred Mean	Std Err	Lower limit	Upper limit
19	14	89	81				114	112.03	1.084	109.87	114.19
20	15	95	107				98	99.83	1.046	97.75	101.92
21	16	94	95				84	89.16	1.074	87.02	91.30
22	17	96	109				122	118.13	1.129	115.88	120.38
23	18	92	113				101	102.12	1.047	100.03	104.21
24	19	93	84								
52	47	98	104								
53	48	100	98								
54	49	95	108								
55	50	96	87								

The calculations for the mean predictions in rows 19–23 are almost identical. The only difference is that the approximate standard error [from equation (12.5)] is $s_e/\sqrt{75}$, calculated in cell H16. The more exact standard errors in column I are then calculated from equation (12.5) by entering the formula

=$H$6*SQRT(1/50+(G9-AVERAGE(PromoteOld))^2/(48*STDEV(PromoteOld))^2)

in cell I19 and copying down.

We have gone through these rather tedious calculations to make several points. First, the approximate standard errors in equations (12.4) and (12.5), s_e and $s_e/\sqrt{n}$, are usually quite accurate. (Compare these with the values in column I.) This is fortunate because the exact standard errors are difficult to calculate and are not always given in statistical software packages. This is particularly the case in *multiple* regression, which we will discuss shortly. Second, a simple rule of thumb for calculating individual 95% prediction intervals is to go out an amount $2s_e$ on either side of the predicted values. Again, this is not exactly correct, but as the calculations in this example indicate, it works quite well.[6]

Finally, we see from the wide prediction intervals how much uncertainty remains. For example, the prediction interval for a region with Promote equal to 114 extends from 97.13 to 126.92. This implies that the point prediction for this region, 112.03, contains a considerable amount of uncertainty. The reason is the relatively large standard error of estimate, s_e. If we could halve the value of s_e, the length of the prediction interval would be only half as large. Contrary to what you might expect, this is not a sample size problem. That is, a larger sample size would almost surely *not* produce a smaller value of s_e. The whole problem is that Promote is not highly correlated with Sales. The only way to decrease s_e and

---

[6]These approximate standard errors are least accurate when the values of the explanatory variables used in the prediction are far from their mean values in the original data set. In this case, the *exact* standard errors of prediction can be considerably larger.

get more accurate predictions is to find other explanatory variables that are more closely related to Sales. ■

The situation is only slightly different for multiple regression. Again, to find a point prediction in either prediction problem, we substitute the trial values of the X's into the right-hand side of the estimated regression equation. The formulas for the standard errors of prediction, however, are considerably more complex and are not given here. Some (but not all) statistical packages provide these standard errors. Fortunately, we can again approximate the standard error of an individual value by s_e and the standard error of a mean by $s_e/\sqrt{n}$. We illustrate this in the following continuation of the bank discrimination example.

EXAMPLE 12.4 [CONTINUED]

Consider the following three male employees at Fifth National:

■ Employee 5 makes $29,000, is in job grade 1, and has 3 years of experience at the bank.

■ Employee 156 makes $45,000, is in job grade 4, and has 6 years of experience at the bank.

■ Employee 198 makes $60,000, is in job grade 6, and has 12 years of experience at the bank.

Using the regression equation for Salary that includes the explanatory variables Female, YrsExper, Fem_YrsExper, and the job grade dummies Job_2 to Job_6, check that the predicted salaries for these three employees are close to their actual salaries. Then predict the salaries these employees would obtain if they were females. How large are the discrepancies? (When estimating the equation, exclude the last employee, employee 208, whom we diagnosed as an outlier in Section 12.9.)

Solution

The analysis appears in Figure 12.32. The top part includes the variables we need for this analysis. Note how employee 208 has been separated from the rest of the data, so that she is not included in the regression analysis. The usual regression output is not shown, but the standard error of estimate and estimated coefficients have been copied to cell B216 and the range B218:J218.

The values for male employees 5, 156, and 198 have been copied to the range B222:B224. We can then substitute their values into the regression equation to obtain their predicted salaries in column A. The formula in cell A222, for example, is

=$B$218+SUMPRODUCT($C$218:$J$218,C222:J222)

Clearly, the predictions are quite good for these three employees. The worst prediction is off by less than $2000.

To see what would happen if these employees were females, we need to adjust the values of the explanatory variables Female and Fem_YrsExper. For each employee in rows 227–229, the value of Female becomes 1, and the value of Fem_YrsExper becomes the same as the value of YrsExper (because it is equal to the product of Female and YrsExper, and Female equals 1). Copying the formula in A222 down to these rows gives the predicted salaries for the females.

FIGURE 12.32 Predictions for Selected Bank Employees

	A	B	C	D	E	F	G	H	I	J
1	Bank salary data with extra variables added									
2										
3	Employee	Salary	Female	Job_2	Job_3	Job_4	Job_5	Job_6	YrsExper	Fem_YrsExper
4	1	32	0	0	0	0	0	0	3	0
5	2	39.1	1	0	0	0	0	0	14	14
6	3	33.2	1	0	0	0	0	0	12	12
7	4	30.6	1	0	0	0	0	0	8	8
8	5	29	0	0	0	0	0	0	3	0
9	6	30.5	1	0	0	0	0	0	3	3
10	7	30	1	0	0	0	0	0	4	4
11	8	27	0	0	0	0	0	0	8	0
209	206	88	0	0	0	0	0	1	32	0
210	207	94	0	0	0	0	0	1	35	0
211										
212	Outlier omitted from analysis									
213	208	30	1	0	0	0	0	1	33	33
214										
215	Predictions for new customers									
216	Std Err	4.686								
217	Coefficients	Constant	Female	Job_2	Job_3	Job_4	Job_5	Job_6	YrsExper	Fem_YrsExper
218		26.7103	4.3531	2.7179	6.2572	10.9838	15.4645	22.3234	0.8977	-0.7206
219										
220	Males									
221	Predicted	Actual	Values of explanatory variables							
222	29.4033	29	0	0	0	0	0	0	3	0
223	43.0801	45	0	0	0	1	0	0	6	0
224	59.8058	60	0	0	0	0	0	1	12	0
225	Females									
226	Predicted	# of sterrs	Values of explanatory variables							
227	31.5946	0.554	1	0	0	0	0	0	3	3
228	43.1096	-0.403	1	0	0	1	0	0	6	6
229	55.5116	-0.958	1	0	0	0	0	1	12	12

One way to compare the females to the males is to enter the formula

=(A227-B222)/$B$216

in cell B227 and copy it down. This is the number of standard errors the predicted female salary is above (if positive) or below (if negative) the actual male salary. As we discussed earlier with this data set, females with only a few years of experience actually tend to make *more* than males. But the opposite occurs for employees with many years of experience. For example, male employee 198 is earning just about what the regression equation predicts he should earn. But if he were female, we would predict a salary about $4500 below the male, almost a full standard error lower. ■

Technical Note about Standard Error of Prediction Neither Excel nor the StatPro add-in provides the exact standard error of prediction for an individual prediction in multiple regression. However, there is a simple (though tedious) way to obtain this standard error for any given values of the explanatory variables. For the sake of discussion, assume there are three explanatory variables, X_1, X_2, and X_3, and we want to predict Y when the values of these X's are 25, 72, and 5. The trick is to create three new variables (in new columns) that are "shifted" versions of the X's, shifted by the amounts 25, 72, and 5. For example, the first shifted variable is $X_1 - 25$. If we regress Y on the *shifted* X's, then the predicted value of Y is the estimated intercept term (in the "Constant" row of the regression output). Let s_{int} be the standard error of this intercept term, which is also listed in the regression output. Then the standard error of prediction is $\sqrt{s_e^2 + s_{int}^2}$. We tried this method for the female employee in row 227 of Figure 12.32. It gave a standard error of prediction of $4752, slightly larger than the approximate value of $s_e = \$4686$ but probably close enough for all practical purposes.

PROBLEMS

Level A

40 The human resources manager of DataCom, Inc., wants to predict the annual salaries of given employees using the following explanatory variables: (1) the number of years of prior relevant work experience, (2) the number of years of employment at DataCom, (3) the number of years of education beyond high school, (4) the employee's gender, (5) the employee's department, and (6) the number of individuals supervised by the given employee. These data have been collected for a sample of employees and are given in the file P11_5.XLS.

   a Estimate an appropriate multiple regression model to predict the annual salary of a given DataCom employee.

   b Conduct and interpret the result of an F test on the given model. Employ a 5% level of significance in conducting this statistical hypothesis test.

   c Given the estimated regression model, predict the annual salary of a male employee who served in a similar department at another company for 5 years prior to coming to work at DataCom. This man, a graduate of a 4-year collegiate business program, has been supervising 6 subordinates in the sales department since joining the organization 7 years ago.

   d Find a 95% prediction interval for the salary earned by a DataCom employee as characterized in part c.

   e Find a 95% confidence interval for the mean salary earned by all DataCom employees sharing the characteristics provided in part c.

   f How do you explain the difference between the widths of the intervals in parts d and e?

41 Suppose you are interested in predicting the price of a laptop computer based on its various features. The file P11_35.XLS contains observations on the sales price and on a number of potentially relevant variables for a randomly chosen sample of laptop computers.

   a Estimate a multiple regression model that includes all available explanatory variables.

   b Conduct and interpret the result of an F test on the given model. Employ a 5% level of significance in conducting this statistical hypothesis test.

   c Use the estimated regression equation to predict the price of a laptop computer with the following features: a 50-megahertz processor, a battery that holds its charge for 180 minutes, 20 megabytes of RAM, a DX chip, a color monitor, a trackball pointing device, and a 24-hour, toll-free customer service hotline.

   d Find a 99% prediction interval for the price of a laptop computer as characterized in part c.

   e Find a 99% confidence interval for the average price of all laptop computers sharing the characteristics provided in part c.

   f How do you explain the difference between the widths of the intervals in parts d and e?

42 Suppose that a power company located in southern Alabama wants to predict the peak power load (i.e., Y, the maximum amount of power that must be generated each day to meet demand) as a function of the daily high temperature (X). A random sample of 25 summer days is chosen, and the peak power load and the high temperature are recorded on each day. The file P11_40.XLS contain these observations.

   a Use the given data to estimate a simple linear regression model. How well does the estimated regression model fit the given data?

   b Conduct an appropriate hypothesis test for the existence of a linear relationship between Y and X, and report a p-value.

   c Examine the residuals of the estimated regression equation. Do you see evidence of any violations of the assumptions regarding the errors of the regression model?

d Conduct a Durbin–Watson test on the model's residuals. Interpret the result of this test.

e Given your result in part **d**, do you recommend modifying the original regression model in this case? If so, how would you revise it?

f Use the final version of your regression model to predict the peak power load on a summer day with a high temperature of 90 degrees.

g Find a 95% prediction interval for the peak power load on a summer day with a high temperature of 90 degrees.

h Find a 99% confidence interval for the average peak power load on all summer days with a high temperature of 90 degrees. ■

12.12   Conclusion

In these two chapters on regression, we have seen how useful regression analysis can be for a variety of business applications and how statistical software such as the StatPro add-in in Excel enables us to obtain relevant output—both graphical and numerical—with very little effort. However, we have also seen that there are many concepts that need to be understood well before regression analysis can be used appropriately. Given the user-friendly software currently available, it is all too easy to generate enormous amounts of regression output and then misinterpret or misuse much of it.

At the very least, you should (1) be able to interpret the standard regression output, including statistics on the regression coefficients, summary measures such as R^2 and s_e, and the ANOVA table, (2) know what to look for in the many scatterplots available, (3) know how to use dummy variables, interaction terms, and nonlinear transformations to improve a fit, and (4) be able to spot clear violations of the regression assumptions. However, we haven't covered everything. Indeed, many entire books are devoted exclusively to regression analysis. Therefore, you should recognize when you *don't* know enough to handle a regression problem such as nonconstant error variance or autocorrelation appropriately. In this case you should consult a statistical expert.

PROBLEMS

Level A

43 For 12 straight weeks you have observed the sales (in number of cases) of canned tomatoes at Mr. D's. Each week you kept track of the following:

■ Was a promotional notice placed in all shopping carts for canned tomatoes?

■ Was a coupon given for canned tomatoes?

■ Was a price reduction (none, 1, or 2 cents off) given?

The file P12_43.XLS contains these data.

a Use multiple regression to determine how the above factors influence sales.

b Discuss whether your final equation has any problems with autocorrelation, heteroscedasticity, or multicollinearity.

c Predict sales of canned tomatoes during a week in which Mr. D's uses a shopping cart notice, a coupon, and a 1-cent price reduction.

44 The file P12_44.XLS contains data on pork sales. Price is in dollars per hundred pounds, quantity sold is in billions of pounds, per capita income is in dollars, U.S. population is in millions, and GNP is in billions of dollars.

a Use the data to develop a regression equation that could be used to predict the quantity of pork sold during future periods. Does heteroscedasticity, autocorrelation, or multicollinearity appear to be a problem?

b Suppose that during each of the next two quarters, price is 45, U.S. population is 240, GNP is 2620, and per capita income is 10,000. (These are in the units described above.) Predict the quantity of pork sold during each of the next two quarters.

45 The file P12_45.XLS contains monthly sales (in thousands of dollars) for a photography studio and the price charged per portrait during each month. Suppose we try to predict the current month's sales from last month's sales and the current month's price.

a If the price of a portrait during month 21 is $10, predict month 21 sales.

b Does autocorrelation, multicollinearity, or heteroscedasticity appear to be a problem?

46 The file P12_46.XLS contains data on a motel chain's revenue and advertising.

a Use the data and multiple regression to make predictions for the motel chain's revenues during the next four quarters. Assume that advertising during each of the next four quarters is $50,000.

b Does autocorrelation appear to be a problem?

47 The file P12_47.XLS contains the quarterly revenues (in millions of dollars) of Washington Gas and Light for the years 1992–1997. We want to use these data to build a multiple regression model that can be used to forecast future revenues.

a Which variables should be included in the regression? Explain your rationale for including or excluding variables.

b Interpret the coefficients of your final equation.

c Make a forecast for revenues during the first quarter of 1987. Also, estimate the probability that 1987 Quarter 1 revenues will be at least $150 million dollars. (*Hint*: Use the standard error of prediction and the fact that the errors are approximately normally distributed.)

48 The file P12_48.XLS contains the following data for several underdeveloped countries:

- Infant mortality rate
- Adult literacy rate
- Percentage of students finishing primary school
- Per capita GNP

a Use these data to develop an equation that can be used to predict the infant mortality rate. Justify your equation.

b Are there any outliers? If so, what happens if you omit them? *Should* they be omitted?

c Interpret the coefficients in your equation.

d Does heteroscedasticity or multicollinearity appear to be a problem?

e Why is autocorrelation not important in this problem?

f Within what amount should 95% of our predictions for the infant mortality rate be accurate?

g For a country with a $2000 GNP, 90% adult literacy, and 80% finishing primary school, the regression implies that there is a 1% chance of infant mortality exceeding what value? (*Hint*: Use the standard error of prediction and the fact that the errors are approximately normally distributed.)

49 The file P12_49.XLS contains the following information for the years 1962–1987:

- Millions of gallons of gasoline consumed
- Service station price of gasoline in cents (ignoring taxes)
- Retail price of gasoline (in cents including taxes)
- CPI (Consumer Price Index, with 1967 as base year)
- CPI for public transportation
- Registered cars (thousands)
- Miles per gallon (average for cars)
- Disposable income (in 1982 dollars)

Our goal is to use these data to determine which factors influence demand for gasoline.

    a Run a regression with all potential explanatory variables used to predict gasoline demand. Are you disappointed in the *t*-values for several variables? Explain.

    b Calculate a correlation matrix for the potential explanatory variables. With this in mind, why it is reasonable to delete service station price, CPI for public transportation, and number of registered vehicles as explanatory variables?

    c Now run the regression with the remaining explanatory variables. Are all the variables significant at the 0.05 level?

    d Are there any outliers? If so, what happens if you omit them? *Should* they be omitted?

    e Does autocorrelation or heteroscedasticity appear to be present?

    f Interpret the coefficient of each variable in your final equation.

50 Recall the movie star data from Chapter 2 (in the file ACTORS.XLS).

    a Determine an equation to predict salary on the basis of gender, domestic gross, and foreign gross. Make sure all variables in your equation are significant at the 0.15 level.

    b Interpret the coefficients in your equation.

    c Does your equation exhibit any autocorrelation, heteroscedasticity, or multicollinearity?

    d Identify and interpret any outliers.

51 You are trying to determine how the marketing mix influences the sale of Cornpone cereal. The file P12_51.XLS contains the following information for 17 consecutive weeks. (*Note:* Weekly sales are in millions of boxes.)

    ■ Was price cut during the week?

    ■ Was there a prize in the package?

    ■ Was there a coupon in the package?

    a Use these data to determine an equation that can be used to predict weekly Cornpone sales. (Ignore any possible effect of trend.) Make sure all variables in your equation are significant at the 0.15 level.

    b Interpret the coefficients in your equation.

    c Are there any outliers?

    d Is either multicollinearity or autocorrelation a problem?

    e During a week in which there is a price cut and both a prize and a coupon are in the package, what is the probability that sales will be less than 50 million boxes? You may assume that heteroscedasticity and autocorrelation are not problems. (*Hint:* Use the standard error of prediction and the fact that the errors are approximately normally distributed.)

52 The belief that larger majorities for a president in a presidential election help the president's party increase its representation in the House and Senate is called the "coat-tail" effect. The file P12_52.XLS gives the percent by which each president since 1948 won the election and the number of seats in the House and Senate gained (or lost) during each election. Are these data consistent with the idea of presidential coat-tails? (Source: *Wall Street Journal,* September 10, 1996)

53 The file P12_53.XLS lists the U.S. unemployment rate, the percentage growth in the U.S. economy (in real terms), and the percentage growth in prices for years 1960–1996. Determine how changes in unemployment, economic growth, and price changes are related. (Source: *1998 Wall Street Journal Almanac*)

54 The file P12_54 contains the golf handicap and an index of their company's stock performance over the last three years for 50 CEOs. A higher index indicates a better stock performance, whereas a lower handicap indicates better golfing ability. For example, Jerry Choate, the CEO of Allstate, has a 10.1 golf handicap, and his company's stock performance index is 83. (The maximum possible stock performance index is 100.) The May 31, 1998, *New York Times* reported that these data indicate that better golfers make better CEOs. What do you think?

55 When potential workers apply for a job that requires extensive manual assembly of small intricate parts, they are initially given three different tests to measure their manual dexterity. The ones who are hired are then periodically given a performance rating on a 0–100 scale that combines their speed and accuracy in performing the required assembly operations. The file P12_55.XLS lists the test scores and performance ratings for a randomly selected group of employees. It also lists their seniority (months with the company) at the time of the performance rating.

a Look at a matrix of correlations. Can you say with certainty (based only on these correlations) that the R^2 value for the regression will be at least 35%? Why or why not?

b Is there any evidence (from the correlation matrix) that multicollinearity will be a problem? Why or why not?

c Run the regression of JobPerf versus all four independent variables. List the equation, the value of R^2, and the value of s_e. Do all of the coefficients have the signs you would expect? Briefly explain.

d Referring to the equation in part **c**, if a worker (outside of the 80 in the sample) has 15 months of seniority and test scores of 57, 71, and 63, give a prediction and an approximate 95% prediction interval for this worker's JobPerf score.

e One of the t-values for the coefficients in part **c** is less than 1. Explain briefly why this occurred. Does it mean that this variable is not related to JobPerf?

f Arguably, the three test measures provide overlapping (or redundant) information. For the sake of parsimony (explaining "the most with the least"), it might be sensible to regress JobPerf versus only two explanatory variables, Sen and AvgTest, where AvgTest is the average of the three test scores—that is, AvgTest = (Test1 + Test2 + Test3)/3. Run this regression and report the same measures as in part **c**: the equation itself, R^2, and s_e. Would you argue that this equation is "just as good as" the equation in part **c**? Explain briefly.

56 Nicklaus Electronics manufactures electronic components used in the computer and space industries. The annual rate of return on the market portfolio and the annual rate of return on Nicklaus Electronics stock for the last 36 months are shown in the file P12_56.XLS. The company wants to calculate the "systematic risk" of its common stock. (It is systematic in the sense that it represents the part of the risk that Nicklaus shares with the market as a whole.) The rate of return Y_t in period t on a security is hypothesized to be related to the rate of return m_t on a market portfolio by the equation

$$Y_t = a + bm_t + e_t$$

Here, a is the risk-free rate of return, b is the security's systematic risk, and e_t is an error term. Using the data available, estimate the systematic risk of the common stock of Nicklaus Electronics. Would you say that Nicklaus stock is a "risky" investment? Why or why not?

57 The auditor of Kaefer Manufacturing uses regression analysis during the analytical review stage of the firm's annual audit. The regression analysis attempts to uncover relationships that exist between various account balances. Any such relationship is subsequently used as a preliminary test of the reasonableness of the reported account balances. The auditor wants to determine whether a relationship exists between the balance of accounts receivable at the end of the month and that month's sales. The file P12_57.XLS contains data on these two accounts for the last 36 months. It also shows the sales levels two months prior to month 1.

a Is there any statistical evidence to suggest a relationship between the monthly sales level and accounts receivable?

b Referring to part **a**, would the relationship be described any better by including this month's sales and the previous month's sales (called lagged sales) in the equation for accounts receivable? What about adding the sales from more than a month ago to the equation? For this problem, why might it make accounting sense to include lagged sales variables in the equation? How do you interpret their coefficients?

c During month 37, which is a fiscal year-end month, the sales were $1,800,000. The reported accounts receivable balance was $3,000,000. Does this reported amount seem consistent with past experience? Explain.

58 A company gives prospective managers four separate tests for judging their potential. For a sample of 30 managers, the test scores and the subsequent job effectiveness ratings (JobEff) given 1 year later are listed in the file P12_58.XLS.

a Look at scattergrams and the table of correlations for these five variables. Does it appear that a multiple regression equation for JobEff, with the test scores as explanatory variables, will be successful? Can you foresee any problems in obtaining accurate estimates of the individual regression coefficients?

b Estimate the regression equation that includes all four test scores, and find 95% confidence intervals for the coefficients of the explanatory variables. How can you explain the negative coefficient of Test3, given that the correlation between JobEff and Test3 is positive?

c Can you reject the null hypothesis that these test scores, as a whole, have no predictive ability for job effectiveness at the 1% level? Why or why not?

d If a new prospective manager has test scores of 83, 74, 65, and 77, what do you predict his job effectiveness rating will be in 1 year? What is the approximate standard error of this prediction?

Level B

59 Confederate Express is attempting to determine how its monthly shipping costs depend on the number of units shipped during a month. The file P12_59.XLS contains the number of units shipped and total shipping costs for the last 15 months.

a Use regression to determine a relationship between units shipped and monthly shipping costs.

b Plot the errors for the predictions in order of time sequence. Is there any unusual pattern?

c We have been told that there was a trucking strike during months 11–15, and we believe that this might have influenced shipping costs. How could the answer to part **a** be modified to account for the effects of the strike? After accounting for the effects of the strike, does the unusual pattern in part **b** disappear?

60 You are trying to determine the effects of three packaging displays (A, B, and C) on sales of toothpaste. The file P12_60.XLS contains the number of cases of toothpaste sold for 9 consecutive weeks. The type of store (GR = grocery, DI = discount, and DE = department store) and the store location (U = urban, S = suburban, and R = rural) are also listed.

a Run a multiple regression to determine how the type of store, display, and store location influence sales. Which potential explanatory variables should be included in the equation? Explain your rationale for including or excluding variables.

b What type of store, store location, and display appears to maximize sales?

c For the type of store in your part **b** answer, estimate the probability that 80 or more cases of toothpaste will be sold during a week. (*Hint*: Use the standard error of prediction and the fact that the errors are approximately normally distributed.)

d Does multicollinearity or autocorrelation seem to be a problem?

61 You want to determine the variables that influence bus usage in major American cities. For 24 cities, the following data are listed in the file P12_61.XLS:

■ Bus travel (annual, in thousands of hours)
■ Income (average per capita income)
■ Population (in thousands)
■ Land area (in square miles)

a Use these data to fit the equation

$$BusTravel = \beta_0 Income^{\beta_1} Population^{\beta_2} LandArea^{\beta_3}$$

b Are all variables significant at the 0.05 level?

c Interpret the values of β_1, β_2, and β_3.

62 The file P12_62.XLS contains the following information for the years 1970–1987:

■ Domestic auto sales (in thousands)
■ Real price index for new car prices (where $1967 = 100$ is the base index)
■ Real disposable income (in 1982 dollars)
■ Interest rate

a Fit a multiplicative model that can be used to predict domestic auto sales. Make sure all variables are significant at the 0.10 level.

b Are there any outliers? If so, what happens if you omit them? *Should* they be omitted?

c Interpret the coefficients of your final equation.

d During a year in which the real price index is 250, the interest rate is 12%, and real disposable income per person is $3500, there is a 5% chance that car sales will be less than or equal to what value? (*Hint*: Use the standard error of prediction and the fact that the errors are approximately normally distributed.)

63 Mattel has assigned you to analyze the factors influencing Barbie sales. The number of Barbie dolls sold (in millions) during the last 23 years is given in the file P12_63.XLS. Year 23 is last year, year 22 is the year before that, and so on. The following factors are thought to influence Barbie sales:

- Was there a recession?
- Were Barbies on sale at Christmas?
- Was there an upward trend over time?

a Determine an equation that can be used to predict annual Barbie sales. Make sure that all variables in your equation are significant at the 0.15 level.

b Interpret the coefficients in your equation.

c Are there any outliers?

d Is heteroscedasicity or autocorrelation a problem?

e During the current year (year 24), a recession is predicted and Barbies will be put on sale at Christmas. There is a 1% chance that sales of Barbies will exceed what value? You may assume here that heteroscedasticity and autocorrelation are not a problem. (*Hint*: Use the standard error of prediction and the fact that the errors are approximately normally distributed.)

64 The capital asset pricing model (CAPM) is a cornerstone of finance. To apply the CAPM, we assume that each stock has a risk measure (called the beta of the stock) associated with it. Then the CAPM asserts that

- The expected return on $1 invested in a stock is a linear function of the stock's beta.
- $1 invested in a stock with a 0 beta will earn an annual return equal to the risk-free interest rate (r_f) on 90-day treasury bills.
- $1 invested in a stock with a beta of 1 will yield an annual return equal to the annual return (r_m) on the market portfolio.

a Formulate a population regression model incorporating the above features of the CAPM. The explanatory variable is the stock's beta and the response variable is the annual return on $1 invested in the stock.

b Given the data in Table 12.3, test the adequacy of the model developed in part **a**. Assume $r_f = 0.09$ and $r_m = 0.18$.

TABLE 12.3 **Stock Returns and Betas**

Company	Beta	Annual Return
AT&T	0.56	0.14
IBM	1.07	0.19
GM	0.76	0.16
Polaroid	2.17	0.28
Chrysler	1.04	0.18

65 How does inflation in a country affect changes in exchange rates? The file P12_65.XLS contains the following information for 11 countries.

- Ratio of percentage increase in prices in local country to percentage increase in U.S. prices from 1973 to 1995.
- Ratio of 1995 units of local currency per dollar to 1973 units of local currency per dollar.

  Use these data to explain how inflation affects exchange rates. Do you have an explanation for these results? (Source: *The Economist*, January 20, 1996)

66 The file P12_66.XLS shows the "yield curve" (at monthly intervals) for the years 1985–1992. For example, in January 1985 the annual rate on a 3-month T-bill was 7.76% and the annual rate on a 30-year government bond was 11.45%. Use regression to determine which interest rates tend to move together most closely. (Source: International Investment and Exchange Database Developed by Craig Holden, Indiana University School of Business)

67 The Keynesian school of macroeconomics believes that increased government spending leads to increased growth. The file P12_67.XLS contains the following data for years 1992–1995:

■ Government spending as percentage of GDP (gross domestic product)

■ Percentage annual growth in annual GDP

Are these data consistent with the Keynesian school of economics? (Source: *Wall Street Journal*)

68 The June 1997 issue of *Management Accounting* gave the following rule for predicting your current salary if you are a managerial accountant. Take $31,865. Next, add $20,811 if you are top management, add $3604 if you are senior management, or subtract $11,419 if you are entry management. Then add $1105 for every year you have been a managerial accountant. Add $7600 if you have a master's degree or subtract $12,467 if you have no college degree. Add $11,257 if you have a professional certification. Finally, add $8667 if you are male.

a How do you think the journal derived this "method" of estimating an accountant's current salary? Be specific.

b How could a managerial accountant use this information to determine whether he or she is significantly underpaid?

69 Suppose you are trying to use regression to predict the current salary of a major league baseball player. What variables might you use?

70 The file P12_70.XLS contains sample data on annual sales for Prozac, a drug produced by Ely Lilly. For each year, the file lists the price per day of therapy (DOT) charged for Prozac and total Prozac sales (in millions of DOT) for the year. Assuming that price is the only factor influencing Prozac sales, determine the number of DOT of Prozac that Lilly should produce for the year to ensure that there is only a 1% chance that Lilly runs out of Prozac. Assume the current price of Prozac is $1.75. (*Hint*: Use the standard error of prediction and the fact that the errors are approximately normally distributed.)

71 A business school committee was charged with studying admissions criteria to the school. Until that time, only juniors were admitted. Part of the committee's task was to see whether freshman courses would be equally good predictors of success as freshman and sophomore courses combined. Here, we'll take "success" to mean doing well in A-core (a combination of the junior level finance, marketing, and production courses, F301, M301, and P301). The file P12_71.XLS contains data on 250 students who had just completed A-core. For each student, the file lists their grades in the following courses:

■ M118 (freshman)—finite math

■ M119 (freshman)—calculus

■ K201 (freshman)—computers

■ W131 (freshman)—writing

■ E201, E202 (sophomore)—micro- and macroeconomics

■ L201 (sophomore)—business law

■ A201, A202 (sophomore)—accounting

■ E270 (sophomore)—statistics

■ A-core (junior)—finance, marketing, and production

Except for A-core, each value is a grade point for a specific course (such as 3.7 for an A−). For A-core, each value is the average grade point for the three courses comprising A-core.

a The A-core grade point will be the eventual response variable in a regression analysis. Look at the correlations between all variables. Is multicollinearity likely to be a problem? Why or why not?

b Run a multiple regression using all of the potential explanatory variables. Now, eliminate the variables as follows. (This is a reasonable variation of the procedures discussed in the chapter.) Look at 95% confidence intervals for their coefficients (as usual, not counting the intercept term). Any variable whose confidence interval contains the value 0 is a candidate for exclusion. For all such candidates, eliminate the variable with the t-value lowest in magnitude. Then rerun the regression, and use the same procedure to possibly exclude another variable. Keep doing this until 95% confidence intervals of the coefficients of all remaining variables do *not* include 0. Report this final equation, its R^2 value, and its standard error of estimate s_e.

c Give a quick summary of the properties of the equation in part **b**. Specifically, (i) do the variables have the "correct" signs, (ii) which courses tend to be the best predictors, (iii) are the predictions from this equation likely to be much good, and (iv) are there any obvious violations of the regression assumptions?

d Redo part **b**, but now use as your potential explanatory variables only courses taken in the freshman year. As in part **b**, report the final equation, its R^2, and its standard error of estimate s_e.

e Briefly, do you think there is enough predictive power in the freshman courses, relative to the freshman and sophomore courses combined, to change to a sophomore admit policy? (Answer only on the basis of the regression results; don't get into other merits of the argument.)

72 The file P12_72.XLS has data on several countries. The variables are listed below.

- ■ Country: name of country
- ■ GNPCapita: GNP per capita
- ■ PopGrowth: average annual percentage change in population, 1980–1990
- ■ Calorie: daily per capita calorie content of food used for domestic consumption
- ■ LifeExp: average life expectancy of newborn given current mortality conditions
- ■ Fertility: births per woman given current fertility rates

With data such as these, cause and effect are difficult to determine. For example, does low LifeExp cause GNPCapita to be low, or vice versa? Therefore, the purpose of this problem is to experiment with the following sets of response and explanatory variables. In each case, look at scatterplots (and use economic reasoning) to find and estimate the best form of the equation, using only linear and logarithmic variables. Then interpret precisely what each equation is saying.

a Response: LifeExp; Explanatories: Calorie, Fertility
b Response: LifeExp; Explanatories: GNPCapita, PopGrowth
c Response: GNPCapita; Explanatories: PopGrowth, Calorie, Fertility

73 Suppose that an economist has been able to gather data on the relationship between demand and price for a particular product. After analyzing scatterplots and using economic theory, the economist decides to estimate an equation of the form $Q = aP^b$, where Q is quantity demanded and P is price. An appropriate regression analysis is then performed, and the estimated parameters turn out to be $a = 1000$ and $b = -1.3$. Now consider two scenarios: (1) the price increases from $10 to $12.50; (2) the price increases from $20 to $25.

a Do you expect the percentage decrease in demand to be the same in scenario (1) as in scenario (2)? Why or why not?

b What is the expected percentage decrease in demand in scenario (1); in scenario (2)? Be as exact as possible. (*Hint*: Remember from economics that an elasticity shows directly what happens for a "small" percentage change in price. These changes aren't that small, so you'll have to do some calculating.)

74 A human resources analyst believes that in a particular industry, the wage rate ($/hr) is related to seniority by an equation of the form $W = ae^{bS}$, where W equals wage rate and S equals seniority (in years). However, the analyst suspects that both parameters, a and b, might depend on whether the workers belong to a union or not. Therefore, the analyst gathers data on a number of workers, both union and nonunion, and estimates the following equation with regression:

$$\ln(W) = 2.14 + 0.027S + 0.12U + 0.006SU$$

Here $\ln(W)$ is the natural log of W, U is 1 for union workers and 0 for nonunion workers, and SU is the product of S and U.

a According to this model, what is the predicted wage rate for a nonunion worker with 0 years of seniority? What is it for a union worker with 0 years of seniority?

b Explain exactly what this equation implies about the predicted effect of seniority on wage rate for a nonunion worker; for a union worker.

75 A company has recorded its overhead costs, machine hours, and labor hours for the past 60 months. The data are in the file P12_75.XLS. The company decides to use regression to explain its overhead hours linearly as a function of machine hours and labor hours. However, recognizing good statistical practice, it decides to estimate a regression equation for the first 36 months, then validate this regression with the data from the last 24 months. That is, it will substitute the values of machine and labor hours from the last 24 months into the regression equation that is based on the first 36 months and see how well it does.

a Run the regression for the first 36 months. Explain briefly why the coefficient of labor hours is not significant.

b For this part, use the regression equation from part **a** with both variables still in the equation (even though one was insignificant). Fill in the fitted and residual columns for months 37–60. Then do relevant calculations to see whether the R^2 (or multiple R) and the standard error of estimate s_e are as good for these 24 months as they are for the first 36 months. Explain your results briefly. (*Hint*: Remember the meaning of the multiple R and the standard error of estimate.)

76 Pernavik Dairy produces and sells a wide range of dairy products. Because most of the dairy's costs and prices are set by a government regulatory board, most of the competition between the dairy and its competitors takes place through advertising. The controller of Pernavik has developed the sales and advertising levels for the last 52 weeks. These appear in the file P12_76.XLS. Note that the advertising levels for the three weeks prior to week 1 are also listed. The controller wonders whether Pernavik is spending too much money on advertising. He argues that the company's contribution-margin ratio is about 10%. That is, 10% of each sales dollar goes toward covering fixed costs. This means that each advertising dollar has to generate at least $10 of sales or the advertising is not cost-effective. Use regression to determine whether advertising dollars are generating this type of sales response. (*Hint*: It is very possible that the sales value in any week is affected not only by advertising this week, but also by advertising levels in the past one, two, or three weeks. These are called "lagged" values of advertising. Try regression models with lagged values of advertising included, and see whether you get better results.)

77 The Pierce Company manufactures drill bits. The production of the drill bits occurs in lots of 1000 units. Due to the intense competition in the industry and the correspondingly low prices, Pierce has undertaken a study of the manufacturing costs of each of the products it manufactures. One part of this study concerns the overhead costs associated with producing the drill bits. Senior production personnel have determined that the number of lots produced, the direct labor hours used, and the number of production runs per month might help to explain the behavior of overhead costs. The file P12_77.XLS contains the data on these variables for the past 36 months.

a See how well you can predict overhead costs on the basis of these variables with a linear regression equation. Why might you be disappointed with the results?

b A production supervisor believes that labor hours and the number of production run setups affect overhead because Pierce uses a lot of supplies when it is working on the machines and because the machine setup time for each run is charged to overhead. As he says, "When the rate of production increases, we use overtime until we can train the additional people that we require for the machines. When the rate of production falls, we incur idle time until the surplus workers are transferred to other parts of the plant. So it would seem to me that there will be an additional overhead cost whenever the level of production changes. I would also say that because of the nature of this rescheduling process, the bigger the change in production, the greater the effect of the change in production on the increase in overhead." How might you use this information to find a better regression equation than in part **a**? (*Hint*: Develop a new explanatory variable, and use the fact that the number of lots produced in the month preceding month 1 was 5964.)

78 Danielson Electronics manufactures color television sets for sale in a highly competitive marketplace. Recently Ron Thomas, the marketing manager of Danielson Electronics, has been complaining that the company is losing market share because of a poor-quality image, and he has asked that the company's major product, the 25-inch console model, be redesigned to incorporate a higher quality level. The company general manager, Steve Hatting, is considering the request to improve the product quality but is not convinced that consumers will be willing to pay the additional expense for improved quality.

As the company controller, you are in charge of determining the cost effectiveness of improving the quality of the television sets. With the help of the marketing staff, you have obtained a summary of the average retail price of the company's television set and the prices of 29 competitive sets. In addition, you have obtained from *The Shoppers' Guide*, a magazine that evaluates and reports on various consumer products, a quality rating of the television sets produced by Danielson Electronics and its competitors. The file P12_78.XLS summarizes these data. According to *The Shoppers' Guide*, the quality rating, which varies from 0 to 10 (10 being the highest level of quality), considers such factors as the quality of the picture, the frequency of repair, and the cost of repairs. Discussions with the product design group suggest that the cost of manufacturing this type of television set is $125 + Q^2$, where Q is the quality rating.

a Regress AvgPrice versus QualityRating. Does the regression equation imply that customers are willing to pay a premium for quality? Explain.

b Given the results from part **a**, is there a preferred level of quality for this product? Assume that the quality level will affect only the price charged and not the level of sales of the product.

c How might you answer part **b** if the level of sales is also affected by the quality level (or alternatively, if the level of sales is affected by price)?

79 The file P12_79.XLS contains 1987 data on gasoline consumption and several economic variables. The variables are: gasoline consumption for passenger cars (GasUsed), service station price excluding taxes (SSPrice), retail price of gasoline including state and federal taxes (RPrice), Consumer Price Index for all items (CPI), Consumer Price Index for public transportation (CPIT), number of registered passenger cars (Cars), average miles traveled per gallon (MPG), and real per capita disposable income (DispInc). (Sources: *Basic Petroleum Data Book*, published by the American Petroleum Institute, 1989, and *Economic Report of the President*, 1988)

a Regress GasUsed linearly versus CPIT, Cars, MPG, DispInc, and DefRPrice, where DefRPrice is the deflated retail price of gasoline (RPrice divided by CPI). What signs would you expect the coefficients to have? Do they have these signs? Which of the coefficients are statistically significant at the 0.05 level?

b The government made the claim that for every 1 cent of tax on gasoline, there would be a $1 billion increase in tax revenue. Use the estimated equation in part **a** to support or refute the government's claim.

80 On October 30, 1995, the citizens of Quebec went to the polls to decide the future of their province. They were asked to vote "Yes" or "No" to whether Quebec, a predominantly French-speaking province, should secede from Canada and become a sovereign country. The "No" side was declared the winner, but only by a thin margin. Immediately following the vote, however, allegations began to surface that the result was closer than it should have been. (Source: Cawley and Sommers (1996)). In particular, the ruling separatist Parti Quebecois, whose job was to decide which ballots were rejected, was accused by the "No" voters of systematic electoral fraud by voiding thousands of "No" votes in the predominantly allophone and anglophone electoral divisions of Montreal. (An allophone refers to someone whose first language is neither English nor French. An anglophone refers to someone whose first language is English.)

Cawley and Sommers examined whether electoral fraud had been committed by running a regression, using data from the 125 electoral divisions in the October 1995 referendum. The response variable was REJECT, the percentage of rejected ballots in the electoral division. The explanatory variables were:

■ ALLOPHONE: percentage of allophones in the electoral division

■ ANGLOPHONE: percentage of anglophones in the electoral division

■ REJECT94: percentage of rejected votes from that electoral division during a similar referendum in 1994

■ LAVAL: dummy variable equal to 1 for electoral divisions in the Laval region, 0 otherwise

■ LAV_ALL: interaction (i.e., product) of LAVAL and ALLOPHONE

The estimated regression equation (with t-values in parentheses) is

$$\text{Prediced REJECT} = \underset{(5.68)}{1.112} + \underset{(4.34)}{0.020}\,\text{ALLOPHONE} + \underset{(0.12)}{0.001}\,\text{ANGLOPHONE}$$

$$+ \underset{(2.64)}{0.223}\,\text{REJECT94} - \underset{(-8.61)}{3.773}\,\text{LAVAL} + \underset{(15.62)}{0.387}\,\text{LAV\_ALL}$$

The R^2 value was 0.759. Based on this analysis, Cawley and Sommers state that, "The evidence presented here suggests that there were voting irregularities in the October 1995 Quebec referendum, especially in Laval." Discuss how they came to this conclusion.

81 Suppose we are trying to explain variations in salaries for technicians in a particular field of work. The file P12_81.XLS contains annual salaries for 200 technicians. It also shows how many years of experience each technician has, as well as his or her education level. There are four education levels, as explained in the comment in cell D3. Three suggestions are put forth for the relationship between Salary and these two explanatory variables:

- We should regress Salary linearly versus the two given variables, YrsExper and EducLev.

- All that really matters in terms of education is whether the person got a college degree or not. Therefore, we should regress Salary linearly versus YrsExper and a dummy variable indicating whether he or she got a college degree.

- Each level of education might result in different jumps in salary. Therefore, we should regress Salary linearly versus YrsExper and dummy variables for the different education levels.

a Run the indicated regressions for each of these three suggestions. Then (i) explain what each equation is saying and how the three are different (focus here on the coefficients), (ii) which you prefer, and (iii) whether (or how) the regression results in your preferred equation contradict the average salary results shown in the PivTab sheet of the file.

b Consider the four workers shown on the Predict sheet of the file. (These are four new workers, not among the original 200.) Using your preferred equation, calculate a predicted salary and an approximate 95% prediction interval for each of these four workers.

c It turns out (you don't have to check this) that the interaction between years of experience and education level is *not* significant for this data set. In general, however, argue why we might expect an interaction between them for salary data of technical workers. What form of interaction would you suspect? (There is not necessarily one right answer, but argue convincingly one way or the other, that is, for a positive or a negative interaction.) ■

The Artsy Corporation has been sued in the U.S. Federal Court on charges of sex discrimination in employment under Title VII of the Civil Rights Act of 1964.[8] The litigation at contention here is a "class-action" lawsuit brought on behalf of all females who were employed by the company, or who had applied for work with the company, between 1979 and 1987. Artsy operates in several states, runs four quite distinct businesses, and has many different types of employees. The allegations of the plaintiffs deal with issues of hiring, pay, promotions, and other "conditions of employment."

In such large class-action employment discrimination lawsuits, it has become common for statistical evidence to play a central role in the determination of guilt or damages. In an interesting twist on typical legal procedures, a precedent has developed in these cases that plaintiffs may make a "prima-facie" case purely in terms of circumstantial statistical evidence. If that statistical evidence is reasonably strong, the burden of proof shifts to the defendants to rebut the plaintffs' statistics with other data, other analyses of the same data, or nonstatistical testimony. In practice, statistical arguments often dominate the proceedings of such Equal Employment Opportunity (EEO) cases. Indeed, in this case the statistical data used as evidence filled numerous computer tapes, and the supporting statistical analysis comprised thousands of pages of printouts and reports. We will work here with a typical subset that pertains to one contested issue at one of the company's locations.

The data in the file ARTSY.XLS relate to the pay of 256 employees on the hourly payroll at one of the company's production facilities. The data include: an identification number (ID) that would permit us to identify the person by name or social security number, the person's gender (Gender), where 0 denotes female and 1 denotes male, the person's job grade in 1986 (Grade), the length of time (in years) the person had been in that job grade as of December 31, 1986 (TInGrade), and the person's weekly pay rate as of December 31, 1986 (Rate). These data permit a statistical examination of one of the issues in the case— fair pay for female employees. We deal with one of three pay classes of employees—those on the biweekly payroll, and at one of the company's locations at Pocahantus, Maine.

The plaintiffs' attorneys have proposed settling the pay issues in the case for this group of female employees for a "back pay" lump payment to female employees of 25% of their pay during the period 1979 to 1987. It is our task to examine the data statistically for evidence in favor of, or against, the charges. We are to advise the lawyers for the company on how to proceed. Consider the following issues as they have been laid out to us by the attorneys representing the firm:

1   Overall, how different is pay by gender? Are the differences in pay statistically significant? Does a statistical significance test have meaning in a case like this? If so, how should it be performed? Lay out as succinctly as possible the arguments that you anticipate the plaintiffs will make with this data set.

2   The company wishes to argue that a legitimate explanation of the pay rate differences may be the difference in job grades. (In this analysis, we will tacitly assume that each person's job grade is, in fact, appropriate for him or her, even though the plaintiffs' attorneys have charged that females have been unfairly kept in the lower grades. Other statistical data, not available here, are used in that analysis.) The

---

[7]This case was contributed by Peter Kolesar from Columbia University.

[8]Artsy is an actual corporation, and the data given in this case are real, but the name has been changed to protect the firm's true identity.

lawyers ask, "Is there a relatively easy way to understand, analyze, and display the pay differences by job grade? Is it easy enough that it could be presented to an average jury without confusing them?" Again, use the data to anticipate the possible arguments of the plaintiffs. To what extent does job grade appear to explain the pay rate differences between the genders? Propose and carry out appropriate hypothesis tests or confidence intervals to check whether the difference in pay between genders is statistically significant within each of the grades.

3. In the actual case, the previous analysis suggested to the attorneys that differences in pay rates are due, at least in part, to differences in job grades. They had heard that in another EEO case, the dependence of pay rate on job grade had been investigated with regression analysis. Perform a simple linear regression of pay rate on job grade for them. Interpret the results fully. Is the regression significant? How much of the variability in pay does job grade account for? Carry out a full check of the quality of your regression. What light does this shed on the pay fairness issue? Does it help or hurt the company? Is it fair to the female employees?

4. It is argued that seniority within a job grade should be taken into account because the company's written pay policy explicitly calls for the consideration of this factor. How different are times in grade by gender? Are they enough to matter?

5. The Artsy legal team wants an analysis of the simultaneous influence of grade and time in grade on pay. Perform a multiple regression of pay rate versus grade and time in grade. Is the regression significant? How much of the variability in pay rates is explained by this model? Will this analysis help your clients? Could the plaintiffs effectively attack it? Consider residuals in your analysis of these issues.

6. Organize your analyses and conclusions in a brief report summarizing your findings for your client, the Artsy Corporation. Be complete but succinct. Be sure to advise them on the settlement issue. Be as forceful as you can be in arguing "the Artsy Case" without misusing the data or statistical theory. Apprise your client of the risks they face by developing the forceful and legitimate counterargument the female plaintiffs could make.

CASE STUDY   12.2   Heating Oil at Dupree Fuels Company[9]

Dupree Fuels Company is facing a difficult problem. Dupree sells heating oil to residential customers. Given the amount of competition in the industry, both from other home heating oil suppliers and from electric and natural gas utilities, the price of the oil supplied and the level of service are critical in determining a company's success. Unlike electric and natural gas customers, oil customers are exposed to the risk of running out of fuel. Home heating oil suppliers therefore have to guarantee that the customer's oil tank will not be allowed to run dry. In fact, Dupree's service pledge is, "50 free gallons on us if we let you run dry." Beyond the cost of the oil, however, Dupree is concerned about the perceived reliability of his service if a customer is allowed to run out of oil.

[9]Case Studies 12.2–12.4 are based on problems from *Advanced Management Accounting*, 2nd edition, by Robert S. Kaplan and Anthony A. Atkinson, Prentice Hall, 1989. We thank them for allowing us to adopt their problems.

To estimate customer oil use, the home heating oil industry uses the concept of "degree days." A degree day is equal to the difference between the average daily temperature and 68 degrees Fahrenheit. So if the average temperature on a given day is 50, the degree days for that day will be 18. (If the degree day calculation results in a negative number, the degree days number is recorded as 0.) By keeping track of the number of degree days since the customer's last oil fill, by knowing the size of the customer's oil tank, and by estimating the customer's oil consumption as a function of the number of degree days, the oil supplier can estimate when the customer is getting low on fuel and then resupply the customer.

Dupree has used this scheme in the past but is disappointed with the results and the computational burdens it places on the company. First, the system requires that a consumption-per-degree-day figure be estimated for each customer to reflect that customer's consumption habits, size of home, quality of home insulation, and family size. Because Dupree has over 1500 customers, the computational burden of keeping track of all of these customers is enormous. Second, the system is crude and unreliable. The consumption per degree day for each customer is computed by dividing the oil consumption during the preceding year by the degree days during the preceding year. Customers have tended to use less fuel than estimated during the colder months and more fuel than estimated during the warmer months. This means that Dupree is making more deliveries than necessary during the colder months and customers are running out of oil during the warmer months.

Dupree wants to develop a consumption estimation model that is practical and more reliable. The following data are available in the file DUPREE.XLS:

- The number of degree days since the last oil fill and the consumption amounts for 67 customers.

- The number of people residing in the homes of each of the 67 customers. Dupree thinks that this might be important in predicting the oil consumption of customers using oil-fired hot water heaters because it provides an estimate of the hot-water requirements of each customer. Each of the customers in this sample uses an oil-fired hot water heater.

- An assessment, provided by Dupree sales staff, of the home type of each of these 67 customers. The home type classification, which is a number between 1 and 5, is a composite index of the home size, age, exposure to wind, level of insulation, and furnace type. A low index implies a lower oil consumption per degree day, and a high index implies a higher consumption of oil per degree day. Dupree thinks that the use of such an index will allow them to estimate a consumption model based on a sample data set and then to apply the same model to predict the oil demand of each of his customers.

Use regression to see whether a statistically reliable oil consumption model can be estimated from the data.

12.3 Developing a Flexible Budget at the Gunderson Plant

The Gunderson Plant manufactures the industrial product line of FGT Industries. Plant management wants to be able to get a good, yet quick, estimate of the manufacturing overhead costs that can be expected each month. The easiest and simplest method to accomplish this task is to develop a flexible budget formula for the manufacturing overhead costs. The plant's accounting staff has suggested that simple linear regression be used to determine the behavior pattern of the overhead costs. The regression data can provide the basis for the flexible budget formula. Sufficient evidence is available to conclude that manufacturing overhead costs vary with direct labor hours. The actual direct labor hours and the corresponding manufacturing overhead costs for each month of the last 3 years have been used in the linear regression analysis.

The 3-year period contained various occurrences not uncommon to many businesses. During the first year, production was severely curtailed during 2 months due to wildcat strikes. In the second year, production was reduced in 1 month because of material shortages, and increased significantly (scheduled overtime) during 2 months to meet the units required for a one-time sales order. At the end of the second year, employee benefits were raised significantly as the result of a labor agreement. Production during the third year was not affected by any special circumstances. Various members of Gunderson's accounting staff raised some issues regarding the historical data collected for the regression analysis. These issues were as follows.

■ Some members of the accounting staff believed that the use of data from all 36 months would provide a more accurate portrayal of the cost behavior. While they recognized that any of the monthly data could include efficiencies and inefficiencies, they believed these efficiencies and inefficiencies would tend to balance out over a longer period of time.

■ Other members of the accounting staff suggested that only those months that were considered normal should be used so that the regression would not be distorted.

■ Still other members felt that only the most recent 12 months should be used because they were the most current.

■ Some members questioned whether historical data should be used at all to form the basis for a flexible budget formula.

The accounting department ran two regression analyses of the data—one using the data from all 36 months and the other using only the data from the last 12 months. The information derived from the two linear regressions is shown below (t-values shown in parentheses). The 36-month regression is

$$OH_t = 123,810 + \underset{(1.64)}{1.60}\, DLH_t, \quad R^2 = 0.32$$

The 12-month regression is

$$OH_t = 109,020 + \underset{(3.01)}{3.00}\, DLH_t, \quad R^2 = 0.48$$

Questions

1 Which of the two results (12 months versus 36 months) would you use as a basis for the flexible budget formula?

2   How would the four specific issues raised by the members of Gunderson's accounting staff influence your willingness to use the results of the statistical analyses as the basis for the flexible budget formula? Explain your answer.

12.4   Forecasting Overhead at Wagner Printers

Wagner Printers performs all types of printing including custom work, such as advertising displays, and standard work, such as business cards. Market prices exist for standard work, and Wagner Printers must match or better these prices to get the business. The key issue is whether the existing market price covers the cost associated with doing the work. On the other hand, most of the custom work must be priced individually. Because all custom work is done on a job-order basis, Wagner routinely keeps track of all the direct labor and direct materials costs associated with each job. However, the overhead for each job must be estimated. The overhead is applied to each job using a predetermined (normalized) rate based on estimated overhead and labor hours. Once the cost of the prospective job is determined, the sales manager develops a bid that reflects both the existing market conditions and the estimated price of completing the job.

In the past, the normalized rate for overhead has been computed by using the historical average of overhead per direct labor hour. Wagner has become increasingly concerned about this practice for two reasons. First, it hasn't produced accurate forecasts of overhead in the past. Second, technology has changed the printing process, so that the labor content of jobs has been decreasing, and the normalized rate of overhead per direct labor hour has steadily been increasing. The file WAGNER.XLS shows the overhead data that Wagner has collected for its shop for the past 52 weeks. The average weekly overhead for the last 52 weeks is $54,208, and the average weekly number of labor hours worked is 716. Therefore, the normalized rate for overhead that will be used in the upcoming week is about $76 (= 54,208/716) per direct labor hour.

Questions

1   Determine whether you can develop a more accurate estimate of overhead costs.

2   Wagner is now preparing a bid for an important order that may involve a considerable amount of repeat business. The estimated requirements for this project are 15 labor hours, 8 machine hours, $150 direct labor cost, and $750 direct material cost. Using the existing approach to cost estimation, Wagner has estimated the cost for this job as $2040 (= 150 + 750 + (76 × 15)). Given the existing data, what cost would you estimate for this job?

13

Time Series Analysis and Forecasting

Successful Applications

How much quantitative analysis occurs at fast-food restaurants? At Taco Bell, a lot! This is described in an article by Huerter and Swart (1998). This article explains the approach to labor management that has occurred at Taco Bell restaurants over the past decade. Labor is a large component of costs at Taco Bell. Approximately 30% of every sales dollar goes to labor. However, the unique characteristics of fast-food restaurants make it difficult to plan labor utilization efficiently. In particular, the Taco Bell product—food—cannot be inventoried; it must be made fresh at the time the customer orders it. Because of shifting demand throughout any given day, where the lunch period accounts for approximately 52% of a day's sales and as much as 25% of a day's sales can occur during the busiest hour, labor requirements vary greatly throughout the day. If too many workers are on hand during slack times, they are paid for doing practically nothing. Worse than that, however, are the lost sales (and unhappy customers) that occur if too few workers are on hand during peak times. Prior to 1988, Taco Bell made very little effort to manage the labor problem in an efficient, centralized manner. It simply allocated about 30% of each store's sales to the store managers and let them allocate it as best they could—not always with good results.

In 1988 Taco Bell initiated its "value meal" deals, where certain meals were priced as low as 59 cents. This increased demand to the point where management could no longer ignore the labor allocation problem. Therefore, in-store computers were installed, data from all stores were collected, and a team of analysts was assigned the task of developing a cost-efficient labor allocation system. This system, which has now been fully integrated into all Taco Bell stores since 1993, is composed of three subsystems: (1) a forecasting subsystem that, for each store, forecasts the arrival rate of customers by 15-minute interval by day of week; (2) a simulation subsystem that, for each store, simulates the congestion and number of lost customers that will occur for any customer arrival rate, given a specific number (and deployment) of workers; and (3) an optimization subsystem that, for each store, indicates the minimum cost allocation of workers, subject to various constraints, such as a minimum service level and a minimum shift length for workers.[1] Although all three of these subsystems are important, the forecasting subsystem is where it all

[1] We will analyze a similar labor allocation problem at the beginning of Chapter 15.

starts. Each store must have a reasonably accurate forecast of future customer arrival rates, broken down by small time intervals (such as 11:15 A.M. to 11:30 A.M. on Friday), before labor requirements can be predicted and labor allocations can be made in an intelligent manner. Like many real-world forecasting systems, Taco Bell's has two important characteristics: (1) it requires extensive data, which have been made available by the in-store computer systems, and (2) the eventual forecasting method used is mathematically a fairly simple one, namely, 6-week moving averages, which we will study in this chapter.

Simple or not, the forecasts, as well as the other system components, have enabled Taco Bell to cut costs and increase profits considerably. In its first four years, 1993–1996, the labor management system is estimated to have saved Taco Bell approximately $40.34 million in labor costs. Because the number of Taco Bell stores is constantly increasing, the annual company-wide savings from the system will certainly grow in the future. In addition, the focus on quantitative analysis has produced other side benefits for Taco Bell. Its service is now better and more consistent across stores, with many fewer customers leaving because of slow service. Also, the quantitative models developed have enabled Taco Bell to evaluate the effectiveness of various potential productivity enhancements, including self-service drink islands, customer-activated touch screens for ordering, and smaller kitchen areas. So the next time you order food from Taco Bell, you can be assured that there is definitely a method to the madness! ■

Introduction

M any decision-making applications depend on a forecast of some quantity. Here are several examples.

■ When a service organization, such as a fast-food restaurant, plans its staffing over some time period, it must forecast the customer demand as a function of time. This might be done at a very detailed level, such as the demand in successive half-hour periods, or at a more aggregate level, such as the demand in successive weeks.

■ When a company plans its ordering or production schedule for a product it sells to the public, it must forecast the customer demand for this product so that it can stock appropriate quantities—neither too much nor too little.

■ When an organization plans to invest in stocks, bonds, or other financial instruments, it typically attempts to forecast movements in stock prices and interest rates.

■ When government representatives plan policy, they attempt to forecast movements in macroeconomic variables such as inflation, interest rates, and unemployment.

Unfortunately, forecasting is a very difficult task, both in the short run and in the long run. Typically, we base forecasts on observations made in the past. We investigate past behavior, search for patterns or relationships, and then we make forecasts. There are two problems with this approach. The first is that it is not always easy to uncover historical patterns or relationships. In particular, it is often difficult to separate the noise, or random behavior, from the underlying patterns. Some forecasts can even overdo it, by attributing importance to patterns that are in fact random variations and are unlikely to repeat themselves.

The second problem is that there are no guarantees that past patterns will continue in the future. The OPEC countries could raise their oil prices again, a company's competitor could introduce a new product into the market, the bottom could fall out of the stock market, and so on. Each of these shocks to the system being studied could drastically alter the future in a highly unpredictable way. This partly explains why forecasts are almost always wrong. Unless they have inside information to the contrary, forecasters must assume that history will repeat itself. But we all know that history does *not* always repeat itself. Therefore, there are many famous forecasts that turned out to be way off the mark, even though the forecasters made reasonable assumptions and used standard forecasting techniques. Nevertheless, forecasts are required constantly, so fear of failure is no excuse for not giving it our best effort.

13.2 Forecasting Methods: An Overview

There are many forecasting methods available, and all practitioners have their favorites. To say the least, there is little agreement among practitioners or theoreticians as to the best forecasting method. The methods can generally be divided into three groups: (1) **judgmental** methods, (2) **extrapolation** (or **time series**) methods, and (3) **econometric** (or **causal**) methods. The first of these is basically nonquantitative and will not be discussed here; the last two are quantitative. In this section we will describe extrapolation and econometric methods in some generality. In the rest of the chapter, we will go into more detail, particularly about the extrapolation methods.

13.2.1 Extrapolation Methods

Extrapolation methods are quantitative methods that use past data of a time series variable—and nothing else, except possibly time itself—to forecast future values of the variable. The idea is that we can use past movements of a variable, such as company sales or U.S. exports to Japan, to forecast its future values. There are many extrapolation methods available, including trend-based regression, exponential smoothing, moving averages, and autoregression models. Some of these methods are relatively simple, both conceptually and in terms of the calculations required, whereas others are quite complex.

All of these extrapolation methods search for *patterns* in the historical series and then extrapolate these patterns into the future. Some try to track long-term upward or downward trends and then project these. Some try to track the seasonal patterns (sales up in November and December, down in other months, for example) and then project these. Basically, the more complex the method, the more closely it tries to track historical patterns. Researchers have long believed that it is an asset of a method to be able to track the ups and downs—the zigzags on a graph—of a time series. This has led to voluminous research and increasingly complex methods. But is complexity always better?

Surprisingly, empirical evidence shows that it is sometimes worse. This is documented in the quarter-century review article by Armstrong (1986) and the article by Schnarrs and Bavuso (1986). They document a number of empirical studies on literally thousands of time series forecasts where complex methods fared no better, and often worse, than simple methods. In fact, the Schnarrs/Bavuso article presents evidence that a naive forecast from a "random walk" model often outperforms all of the more sophisticated extrapolation methods.[2]

---

[2] With this naive model we forecast that next period's value will be the same as this period's value. So if today's closing stock price is 51.375, we forecast that tomorrow's closing stock price will be 51.375. We will discuss random walks in more detail in Section 13.3.

The evidence in favor of simpler models is not accepted by everyone, particularly not those who have spent years investigating complex models, and complex models continue to be studied and used. However, there is a very plausible reason why simple models might provide better forecasts. The whole idea behind extrapolation methods is to extrapolate historical patterns into the future. But it is often difficult to determine which patterns are real and which represent noise, that is, random ups and downs that are not likely to repeat themselves. Also, if something important changes (a competitor introduces a new product or interest rates increase, for example), it is always possible that the historical patterns will change. A potential problem with complex methods is that they often track the historical series *too* closely. That is, they often track patterns that are really noise. Simpler methods, on the other hand, track only the most basic underlying patterns and therefore can be more flexible and accurate in forecasting the future.

13.2.2 Econometric Models

Econometric models, also called **causal** models, use regression to forecast a time series variable by means of other explanatory time series variables. For example, a company might use a causal model to regress future sales on its advertising level, the population income level, the interest rate, and possibly others. Because we have already discussed regression models in some depth, we will not devote much time to econometric models in this chapter; the mechanics are largely the same as in any regression analysis. However, based on the empirical evidence presented in Armstrong (1985, 1986), here are a few possibly surprising findings.

- It is not necessary to include a lot of explanatory variables in the analysis. It is better to choose a small number of variables that, based on prior evidence, are believed to affect the response variable.

- It is important to select the proper *conceptual* explanatory variables. For example, in forecasting sales, appropriate conceptual variables might be market size, ability to buy, consumer needs, and price. However, the *operational* measures of these conceptual variables are relatively unimportant for forecast accuracy. For example, different measures of buying power might lead to comparable sales forecasts.

- Stepwise regression procedures allow the model builder to search through many possible explanatory variables to find the best model. This sounds good, and it is attractive given the access to powerful statistical software packages. However, it can lead to poor forecasts because it substitutes computer technology for sound judgment and prior theory. The moral is that we shouldn't throw everything but the kitchen sink into the regression package and hope for the best. Some judgment regarding the variables to include may lead to better forecasts.

- High-precision data on the explanatory variables are not essential. Armstrong (1986) quotes studies where models requiring forecasts of the explanatory variables did better than those where no such forecasts were required. This is contrary to intuition. We might expect that the forecasting error in the explanatory variables would lead to extra forecasting error in the response variable. This is apparently not always the case. However, the same does not hold for the response variable. It is important to have high-quality data on this variable.

- It might be a good idea to break the causal relationship into a causal chain of relationships and then estimate each part of the chain by a separate regression equation. For example, in a study of product sales, the first stage of the chain might regress price on such variables as wage rates, taxes, and warranty costs. These price predictions could then be entered into a model that predicts product sales per capita as a function of personal consumption expenditures per capita and product price. The third stage could then predict the market size as a function of total population, literacy, age, and employment. Finally, the fourth stage could regress total product sales on the predicted values of product sales per capita and market size.

- The divide-and-conquer strategy outlined in the previous point is simpler than the complex simultaneous equation approach taught in many upper-level econometrics courses. The idea behind simultaneous equations is that there are several response (or endogenous) variables that cause changes in one another (Y_1 causes a change in Y_2, which in turn causes a change in Y_1, and so on). Therefore, the regression model consists of several equations, each of which has its own response variable. According to Armstrong, despite great expenditures of time and money by the best and brightest econometricians, simultaneous equations have not been found to be of value in forecasting.

- The functional form of the relationship may not be terribly important. In particular, complex nonlinear relationships do not appear to improve forecast accuracy. However, in addition to the basic linear additive model, the constant-elasticity multiplicative model

$$Y = aX_1^{b_1} X_2^{b_2} \cdots X_k^{b_k}$$

which can be transformed to a linear additive model by taking logarithms, has strong theoretical support and has done well in applications.

- A great deal of research has gone into the autocorrelation structure of econometric models. This is difficult analysis for most practitioners. Fortunately, empirical studies show that it produces only marginal gains in forecast accuracy.

- Econometric models appear to be most useful, relative to other forecasting methods, when *large* changes in the explanatory variables are expected. But in this case it is important to be able to forecast the direction of change in the explanatory variables accurately.

Armstrong summarizes his empirical findings on econometric models succinctly: "There are two important rules in the use of econometric methods, (1) keep it simple and (2) don't make mistakes. If you obey rule 1, rule 2 becomes easier to follow." He acknowledges that rule 1 runs contrary to the thinking of many academic researchers, even practitioners. But the empirical evidence simply does not support the claim that complexity and forecast accuracy are inevitably related.

13.2.3 Combining Forecasts

There is one other general forecasting method that is worth mentioning. In fact, it has attracted a lot of attention in recent years, and many researchers believe that it has great potential for increasing forecast accuracy. The method is simple—combine two or more forecasts to obtain the final forecast. The reasoning behind this method is also simple—the forecast errors from different forecasting methods may cancel one another. The forecasts that are combined can be of the same general type—extrapolation forecasts, for example—or they can be of different types, such as judgmental and extrapolation. The *number* of forecasts to combine and the *weights* to use in combining them have been the subject of several research studies.

Although the findings are not entirely consistent, it appears that the marginal benefit from each individual forecast after the first two or three is minor. Also, there is not much evidence to suggest that the simplest weighting scheme—weight each forecast equally, that is, average them—is any less accurate than more complex weighting schemes.

13.2.4 General Notation and Formulas

First, we introduce a bit of notation and discuss some aspects common to most forecasting methods. In general, we let Y denote the variable we want to forecast. Then Y_t denotes the observed value of Y at time t. Typically, the first observation (the most distant one) corresponds to period $t = 1$, and the last observation (the most recent one) corresponds to period $t = T$, so that T denotes the number of historical observations of Y. The periods themselves might be weeks, months, quarters, years, or any other convenient unit of time.

Suppose we have just observed Y_{t-k} and want to make a "k-period-ahead" forecast; that is, we want to use the information through time $t - k$ to forecast Y_t. Then we denote the resulting forecast by $F_{t-k,t}$. The first subscript denotes the period in which the forecast is made, and the second subscript denotes the period being forecasted. As an example, if the data are monthly and September 1999 corresponds to $t = 67$, then a forecast of Y_{69}, the value in November 1999, would be labeled $F_{67,69}$. The **forecast error** is the difference between the actual value and the forecast. It is denoted by E with appropriate subscripts. Specifically, the forecast error associated with $F_{t-k,t}$ is $E_{t-k,t}$:

$$E_{t-k,t} = Y_t - F_{t-k,t}$$

This double-subscript notation is necessary to specify when the forecast is being made and which period is being forecasted. However, the former is generally clear from context. Therefore, to simplify the notation, we will usually drop the first subscript and write F_t and E_t to denote the forecast of Y_t and the error in this forecast.

There are actually two steps in any forecasting procedure. The first step is to build a model that fits the historical data well. The second step is to use this model to forecast the future. Most of the work goes into the first step. For any trial model we see how well it "tracks" the known values of the time series. Specifically, we calculate the one-period-ahead forecasts F_t (or more precisely, $F_{t-1,t}$) from the model and compare these to the known values, Y_t, for each t in the historical time period. We attempt to find a model that produces small forecast errors, E_t. We expect that if the model forecasts the *historical* data well, it will also forecast *future* data well.

Forecasting software packages typically report several summary measures of the forecast errors. The most important of these are MAE (mean absolute error), RMSE (root mean square error), and MAPE (mean absolute percentage error). These are defined below. Fortunately, models that make any one of these measures small tend to make the others small, so that we can choose whichever measure we want to minimize. In the following formulas, N denotes the number of terms in each sum. This value is typically slightly less than T, the number of historical observations, because it is not usually possible to provide a forecast for each historical period.

$$\text{MAE} = \left(\sum_{t=1}^{N} |E_t| \right) / N \tag{13.1}$$

$$\text{RMSE} = \sqrt{\left(\sum_{t=1}^{N} E_t^2 \right) / N} \tag{13.2}$$

$$\text{MAPE} = 100\% \times \left(\sum_{t=1}^{N} |E_t / Y_t| \right) / N \tag{13.3}$$

RMSE is similar to a standard deviation in that the errors are squared; because of the square root, its units are the same as those of the forecasted variable. The MAE is similar to the RMSE, except that absolute values of errors are used instead of squared errors. The MAPE is probably the most easily understood measure because it does not depend on the units of the forecasted variable; it is always stated as a percentage. For example, the statement that the forecasts are off on average by 2% has an obvious meaning.

Forecasting software packages are sometimes able to choose the best model from a given class (such as the best exponential smoothing model) by minimizing MAE, RMSE, or MAPE. However, because the details of the package are not always given, we might not be absolutely sure which of these measures is being minimized. Fortunately, this is probably not too important. For example, a model with a small RMSE typically has a small MAPE and MAE. In any case, small values of these measures only guarantee that the model forecasts the *historical* observations well. There is still no guarantee that the model will forecast *future* values accurately.

We will now examine a number of useful forecasting models. You should be aware that more than one of these models can be appropriate for any particular time series data. For example, a random walk model and an autoregression model might be equally effective for forecasting stock price data. (Remember also that we can combine forecasts from more than one model to obtain a possibly better forecast.) We will try to give some insights into choosing the best type of model for various types of time series data. But ultimately the choice depends on the experience of the user.

13.3   Random Series

The simplest time series model is the **random** model. In a random model the observations vary around a constant mean, have a constant variance, and are probabilistically independent of one another. Intuitively, a random time series has no time series pattern whatsoever. The observations do not tend to trend upward or downward, the variance does not increase through time, and the observations in one period do not tend to be larger than those in any other periods.

It is probably easier to understand the random model by seeing time series that are *not* random. The time series plots in Figures 13.1–13.5 (pages 710–711) illustrate some common nonrandom patterns. In Figure 13.1, there is an upward trend. In Figure 13.2, the variance is increasing through time (larger zigzags to the right). Figure 13.3 exhibits seasonality, where observations in certain months are consistently larger than those in other months. There is a "meandering" pattern in Figure 13.4, where large observations tend to be followed by other large observations, and small observations tend to be followed by other small observations. Finally, the opposite behavior of Figure 13.4 is illustrated in Figure 13.5. Here, there are too *many* zigzags—large observations tend to follow small observations, and small observations tend to follow large observations.

A random model can be written as

$$Y_t = \mu + \varepsilon_t \tag{13.4}$$

Here, μ is a constant, the average of the Y_t's, and ε_t is the residual (or error) term. We assume that the residuals have mean 0, variance σ^2, and are probabilistically independent of one another. In words, the observations vary around the mean μ and have variance σ^2. If the residuals are normally distributed (which is *not* an assumption of the random model), then about 2/3 of the observations will be within the interval $\mu \pm \sigma$, and about 95% of the observations will be within the interval $\mu \pm 2\sigma$.

FIGURE 13.1 **A Series with Trend**

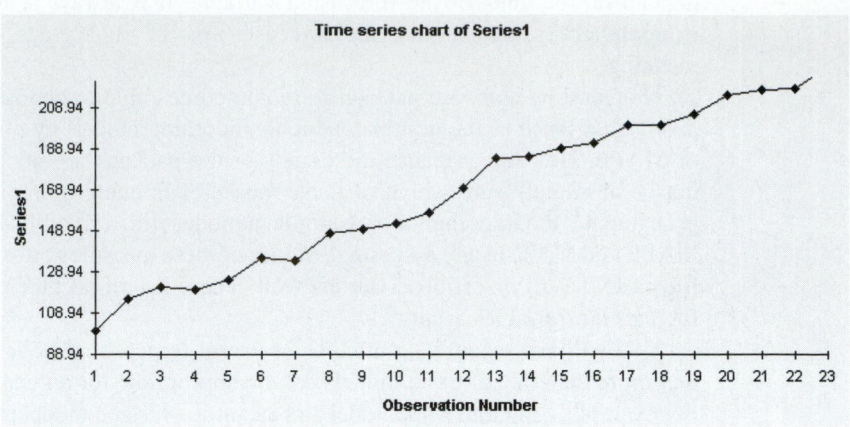

FIGURE 13.2 **A Series with Increasing Variance Through Time**

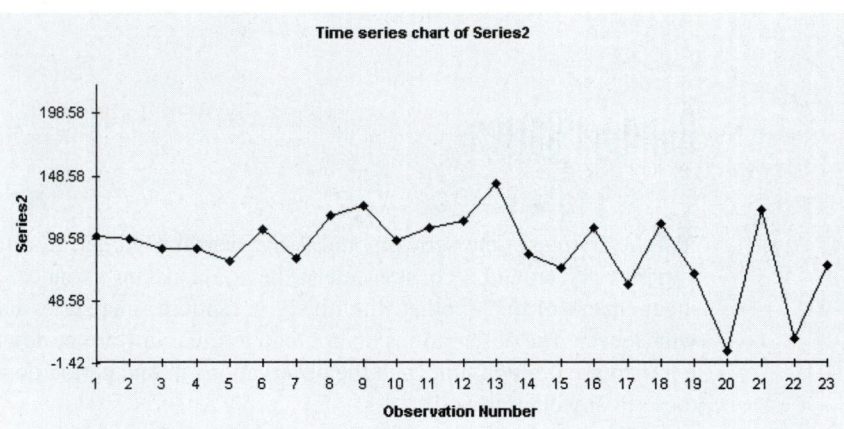

FIGURE 13.3 **A Series with Seasonality**

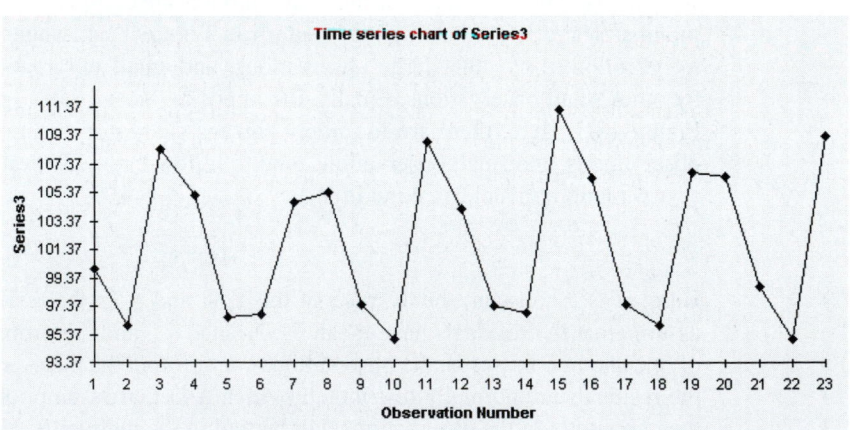

FIGURE 13.4 **A Series That Meanders**

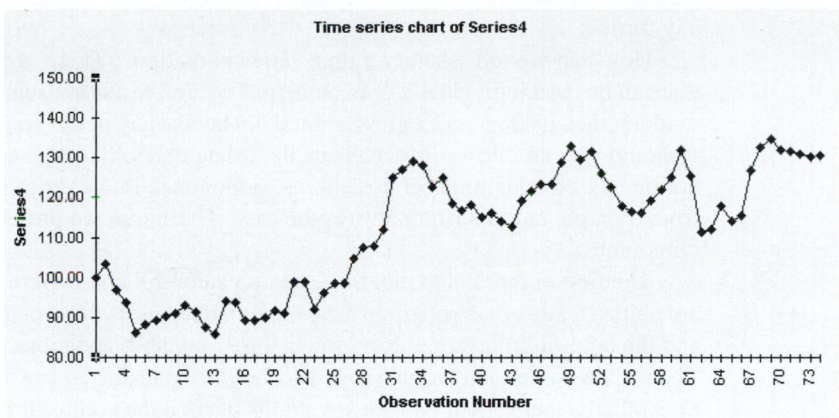

FIGURE 13.5 **A Series That Zigzags Frequently**

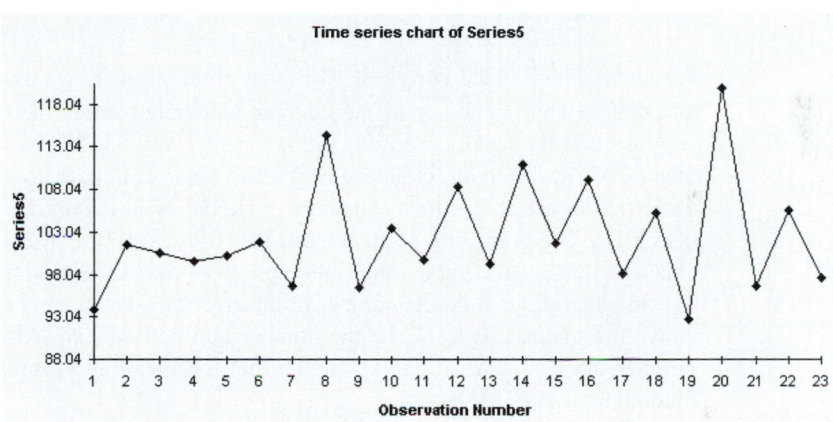

There are two situations where random time series occur. The first is when the *original* time series is random. For example, when studying the time pattern of diameters of individual parts from a manufacturing process, we might discover that the successive diameters behave like a random time series. In this case we can essentially ignore the fact that the observations are being collected through time, and treat them as a random sample from a distribution with mean μ and standard deviation σ. In forecasting terms, this means that the best forecast of any future observation is simply μ, and a corresponding 95% forecast interval is approximately $\mu \pm 2\sigma$. That is, we can expect 95% of future observations to be within this interval. If we don't know μ or σ, we can instead use the sample mean $\overline{Y}$ and the sample standard deviation s from the historical data.

The second situation where a random series occurs is more common. This is when we fit a model to a time series to obtain an equation of the form

$$Y_t = \text{fitted part} + \text{residual} \tag{13.5}$$

Although the fitted part varies from model to model, its essential feature is that it describes any underlying time series pattern in the original data. The residual is then whatever is left, and we hope that the series of residuals is random with mean $\mu = 0$. The fitted part is used to make forecasts, and the residuals, often called noise, are forecasted to be zero. Indeed, the primary goal in this chapter is to model Y_t as a fitted part plus noise, where the fitted part includes any forecastable pattern in the series, and the noise is impossible to model any further.

How can we tell whether a time series is random? There are several possible checks that can be used individually or in tandem. The simplest is a visual check. If a time series is random, then its time series graph should *not* be like any of the graphs in Figures 13.1–13.5. It should vary around a constant mean, its variance should remain constant, and there should not be any obvious time series patterns. Sometimes it is easy to spot a nonrandom series from a graph, but this is not always the case. Therefore, we present three other checks for randomness.

The first of these is to plot the series on a control chart. Here, *individual* observations are plotted (rather than subgroup means), the centerline is the average of the observations, $\overline{Y}$, and the control limits are plus or minus three standard deviations ($3s$) from the centerline. Then if the series is random, it should be "in control," as we discussed in Chapter 10. Specifically, there should not be any points beyond the control limits, and there should not be any patterns of the type we discussed for quality control charts.

13.3.1 The Runs Test

A second check is the **runs test**. For each observation Y_t we associate a 1 if $Y_t \geq \overline{Y}$ and a 0 if $Y_t < \overline{Y}$.[3] The Y_t series then has an associated series of 0's and 1's. For example, suppose that the successive observations are 87, 69, 53, 57, 94, 81, 44, 68, and 77, with mean $\overline{Y} = 70$. Then the sequence of 0's and 1's is 1, 0, 0, 0, 1, 1, 0, 0, 1; four of the nine observations are above the mean and five are below it. A **run** is a consecutive sequence of 0's or 1's. The preceding sequence has five runs: 1; 0 0 0; 1 1; 0 0; and 1. The runs test checks whether this is about the right number of runs for a random series.

In general, let T be the number of observations, let T_A be the number of observations above the mean, and let T_B be the number below the mean. Also, let R be the observed number of runs. Then it can be shown that the mean and standard deviation of R for a random series are

$$E(R) = \frac{T + 2T_A T_B}{T} \tag{13.6}$$

and

$$\text{Stdev}(R) = \sqrt{\frac{2T_A T_B (2T_A T_B - T)}{T^2 (T - 1)}} \tag{13.7}$$

Also, when T is reasonably large ($T > 20$ is suggested), the distribution of R is approximately normal. Therefore, if we define Z by

$$Z = \frac{R - E(R)}{\text{Stdev}(R)} \tag{13.8}$$

then Z is approximately normally distributed with mean 0 and standard deviation 1.

We can base a statistical test on the value of Z. Specifically, if the absolute value of Z is greater than 1.96, then we can reject the null hypothesis of randomness at the 5% significance level.

Note that if Z is large and positive, then there are *more* runs than expected. This means there is too much zigzagging in the time series graph. On the other hand, if the magnitude

---

[3]The runs test can also be based on the sample median of the Y's instead of the sample mean.

of Z is large but Z is negative, then there are *fewer* runs than expected. This situation is more common. Here the observations tend to stay above the mean (or below the mean) for longer stretches than we would expect in a random series.

In the small example above, $T = 9$, $T_A = 4$, $T_B = 5$, and $R = 5$. Under a randomness hypothesis, the mean and standard deviation of the number of runs, from equations (13.6) and (13.7), are

$$E(R) = \frac{9 + 2(4)(5)}{9} = 5.44$$

and

$$\text{Stdev}(R) = \sqrt{\frac{2(4)(5)[2(4)(5) - 9]}{9^2(9 - 1)}} = 1.38$$

The corresponding Z-value is

$$Z = \frac{5 - 5.44}{1.38} = -0.32$$

This value of Z is certainly not extreme, so there is little evidence of nonrandomness; the observed number of runs is very close to the expected number under a hypothesis of randomness.

We can also perform the runs test easily within Excel, as illustrated in the following example.

EXAMPLE 13.1

Monthly sales for a chain of stereo retailers are listed in the file STEREO.XLS. They cover the period from the beginning of 1995 to the end of 1998, during which there was no upward or downward trend in sales and no clear seasonal peaks or valleys. This behavior is apparent in the time series chart of sales shown in Figure 13.6. It is possible that this series is random. Does a runs test support this conjecture?

FIGURE 13.6 **Time Series Plot of Stereo Sales**

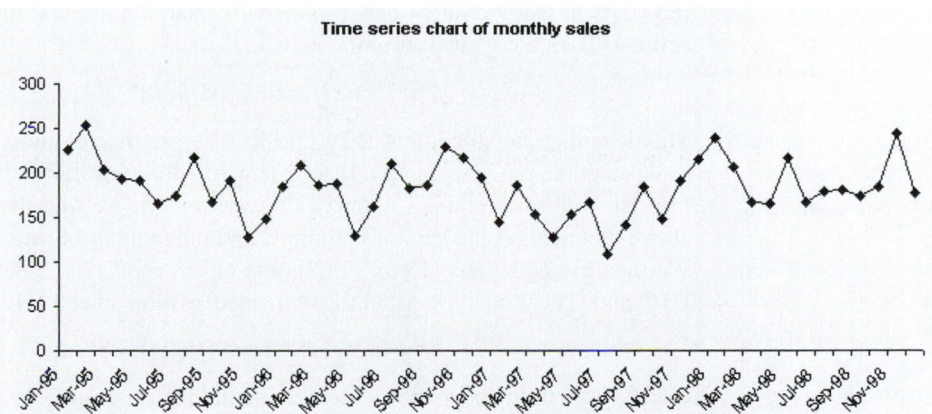

Solution

We use the StatPro Runs Test procedure, found under the StatPro/Statistical Inference/Runs Test menu item. We must specify the time series variable (Sales) and the cutoff value for the test, which can be the mean, the median, or even a user-specified value. In this case we select the mean to obtain the output shown in Figure 13.7. Note that StatPro adds two new variables, Sales_High and Sales_NewRun, as well as the elements for the test. The values in the Sales_High are 1 or 0, depending on whether the corresponding sales values are above or below the mean. For example, the formula in cell C4 is[4]

$$=IF(B4>=AVERAGE(Sales),1,0)$$

which is then copied down column C.

FIGURE 13.7 Runs Test for Randomness

	A	B	C	D	E	F	G	H
1	Runs test for randomness of sales							
2								
3	Month	Sales	Sales_High	Sales_NewRun			Runs Test Results	
4	Jan-95	226	1	1			Number of obs	48
5	Feb-95	254	1	0			Number above cutoff	26
6	Mar-95	204	1	0			Number below cutoff	22
7	Apr-95	193	1	0			Number of runs	20
8	May-95	191	1	0				
9	Jun-95	166	0	1			E(R)	24.833
10	Jul-95	175	0	0			Stdev(R)	3.403
11	Aug-95	217	1	1			Z-value	-1.420
12	Sep-95	167	0	1			p-value (2-tailed)	0.155
13	Oct-95	192	1	1				
14	Nov-95	127	0	1				
15	Dec-95	148	0	0				
48	Sep-98	175	0	0				
49	Oct-98	185	1	1				
50	Nov-98	245	1	0				
51	Dec-98	177	0	1				

The values in the Sales_NewRun column are also 1 or 0, depending on whether a *new* run starts in that month. A new run certainly starts in the first month, so a 1 is entered in cell D4. Then the typical formula, in cell D5, is

$$=IF(C5=C4,0,1)$$

This is copied down column D. It checks whether the column C value this month is the same as in the previous month. If so, a new run does not start; otherwise, it does.

The rest of the output is fairly straightforward. We find the number of observations above the mean as the sum of column C and the number of runs as the sum of column D. We then use equations (13.6), (13.7), and (13.8) for $E(R)$, Stdev(R), and Z in cells H9, H10, and H11. Finally, we find the two-sided p-value in cell H12 with the formula

$$=2*(1-NORMSDIST(ABS(Z)))$$

It is the probability beyond Z under the standard normal curve. We use the factor 2 to obtain the probability in *both* tails.

---

[4]Actually, the formulas are slightly more complicated than shown here because they check for missing data.

The output shows that there is some evidence of not enough runs. The expected number of runs under randomness is 24.833, and there are only 20 runs for this series. However, the evidence is certainly not overwhelming—the p-value is only 0.155. If we ran this test as a one-tailed test, checking only for too *few* runs, then the appropriate p-value would be 0.078, half of the value shown in cell H12. The conclusion in either case is that sales do not tend to "zigzag" as much as a random series—highs tend to follow highs and lows tend to follow lows—but the evidence in favor of nonrandomness is not overwhelming. ■

13.3.2 Autocorrelation

Recall that the successive observations in a random series are probabilistically independent of one another. Many time series violate this property and are instead **autocorrelated**. The "auto" means that successive observations are correlated with one other. For example, in the most common form of autocorrelation, *positive* autocorrelation, large observations tend to follow large observations, and small observations tend to follow small observations. In this case the runs test is likely to pick it up, because there will be fewer runs than expected and the corresponding Z-value for the runs test will be significantly negative. Another way to check for the same nonrandomness property is to calculate the autocorrelations of the time series.

To understand autocorrelations it is first necessary to understand what it means to **lag** a time series. This concept is easy to understand in spreadsheets. We'll again use the monthly stereo sales data for 1995–1998 in the STEREO.XLS file. To lag by 1 month, we simply "push down" the series by one row. See column C of Figure 13.8. Note that there is a blank cell at the top of the lagged series (in cell C4). We can continue to push the series down one row at a time to obtain other lags. For example, the lag 3 version of the series appears in the range E7:E54. Now there are three missing observations at the top. Note that in December 1995, say, the first, second, and third lags correspond to the observations in November 1995, October 1995, and September 1995, respectively. That is, lags are simply previous observations, removed by a certain number of periods from the present time. In general, the lag k observation corresponding to period t is Y_{t-k}. These lagged columns can be obtained by copying and pasting the original series or by using the StatPro/Data Utilities/Lag Series menu item.

FIGURE 13.8 Lags and Autocorrelations for Stereo Sales

	A	B	C	D	E	F	G	H	I	J
1	Illustration of lagging and autocorrelation									
2										
3	Month	Sales	Sales_Lag1	Sales_Lag2	Sales_Lag3			*Autocorrelations*		
4	Jan-95	226	·	·	·				Lag	Autocorr	StErr
5	Feb-95	254	226	·	·			1	**0.3492**	0.1443
6	Mar-95	204	254	226	·			2	0.0772	0.1443
7	Apr-95	193	204	254	226			3	0.0814	0.1443
8	May-95	191	193	204	254			4	-0.0095	0.1443
9	Jun-95	166	191	193	204			5	-0.1353	0.1443
10	Jul-95	175	166	191	193			6	0.0206	0.1443
11	Aug-95	217	175	166	191					
12	Sep-95	167	217	175	166					
48	Sep-98	175	181	179	168					
49	Oct-98	185	175	181	179					
50	Nov-98	245	185	175	181					
51	Dec-98	177	245	185	175					

Then the autocorrelation of lag k, for any integer k, is essentially the correlation between the original series and the lag k version of the series. For example, in Figure 13.8 the lag 1 autocorrelation is the correlation between the observations in columns B and C. Similarly, the lag 2 autocorrelation is the correlation between the observations in columns B and D.[5]

We have shown the lagged versions of Sales in Figure 13.8, and we have explained autocorrelations in terms of these lagged variables, to help motivate the concept of autocorrelation. However, we can use StatPro's Autocorrelation procedure directly, *without* forming the lagged variables, to calculate autocorrelations. This is illustrated in the following continuation of Example 13.1.

EXAMPLE 13.2

The runs test on the stereo sales data suggests that the pattern of sales is not completely random. Large values tend to follow large values, and small values tend to follow small values. Do autocorrelations support this conclusion?

Solution

We use StatPro's Autocorrelation procedure, found under the StatPro/Summary Stats/Autocorrelations menu item. It requires us to specify the time series variable (Sales), the number of lags we want (we chose 6), and whether we want a chart of the autocorrelations. This chart is called a **correlogram**. The resulting autocorrelations and correlogram appear in Figures 13.8 and 13.9. A typical autocorrelation of lag k indicates the relationship between observations k periods apart. For example, the autocorrelation of lag 3, 0.0814, indicates that there is very little relationship between observations separated by 3 months.

How large is a "large" autocorrelation? Under the assumption of randomness, it can be shown that the standard error of any autocorrelation is approximately $1/\sqrt{T}$, in this case $1/\sqrt{48} = 0.1443$. (Recall that T denotes the number of observations in the series.) If the

FIGURE 13.9   **Correlogram for Stereo Sales**

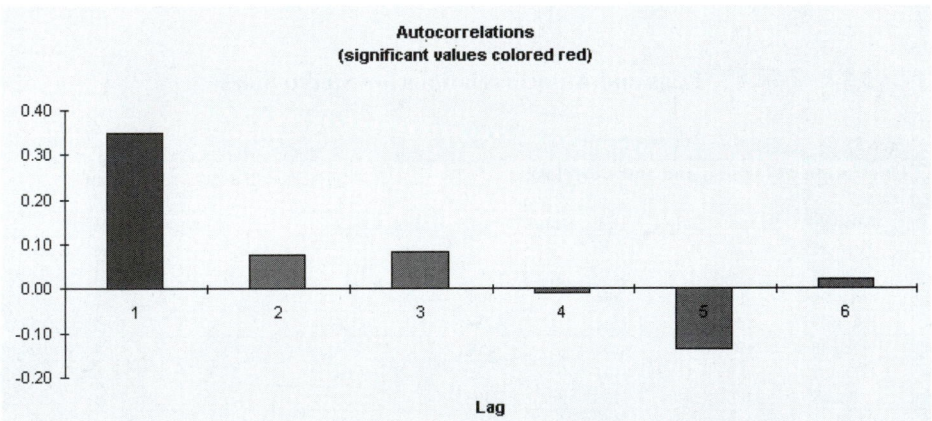

---

[5] We'll ignore the exact details of the calculations here. Just be aware that the formula for autocorrelations that is usually used differs slightly from the correlation formula in Chapter 3. However, the difference is very slight and of little practical importance.

series is truly random, then only an occasional autocorrelation should be larger than two standard errors in magnitude. Therefore, any autocorrelation that *is* larger than two standard errors in magnitude is worth our attention. These significantly nonzero autocorrelations are boldfaced in the numerical output and shown in red in the chart. The only "large" autocorrelation for the sales data is the first, or lag 1, autocorrelation of 0.3492. The fact that it is *positive* indicates once again that there is some tendency for large sales values to follow large sales values and for small to follow small. The autocorrelations for other lags are less than two standard errors in magnitude and can be considered "noise." ■

Typically, we can ask for autocorrelations up to as many lags as we like. However, there are several practical considerations to keep in mind. First, it is common practice to ask for no more lags than 25% of the number of observations. For example, if there are 48 observations, we should ask for no more than 12 autocorrelations (lags 1–12).

Second, the first few lags are typically the most important. Intuitively, if there is any relationship between successive observations, it is likely to be between nearby observations. The June 1996 observation is more likely to be related to the May 1996 observation than to the October 1995 observation. It sometimes happens that there is a fairly large spike in the correlogram at some large lag, such as lag 9. However, this can often be ignored as a random "blip" unless there is some obvious reason for its occurrence. A similarly large autocorrelation at lag 1 or 2 should usually be taken more seriously. The one exception to this is a *seasonal* lag. For example, for monthly data an autocorrelation at lag 12 corresponds to a relationship between observations a year apart, such as May 1996 and May 1995. If this autocorrelation is significantly large, it probably should not be ignored.

We conclude this section with an example of a time series that passes all of the checks for randomness.

EXAMPLE 13.3

The dollar demand for a certain class of parts at a local retail store has been recorded for 82 consecutive days. (See the file DEMAND.XLS.) A time series plot of these demands appears in Figure 13.10. The store manager wants to forecast future demands. In particular, he wants to know whether there is any significant time pattern to the historical demands or whether the series is essentially random.

FIGURE 13.10   **Time Series Plot of Demand for Parts**

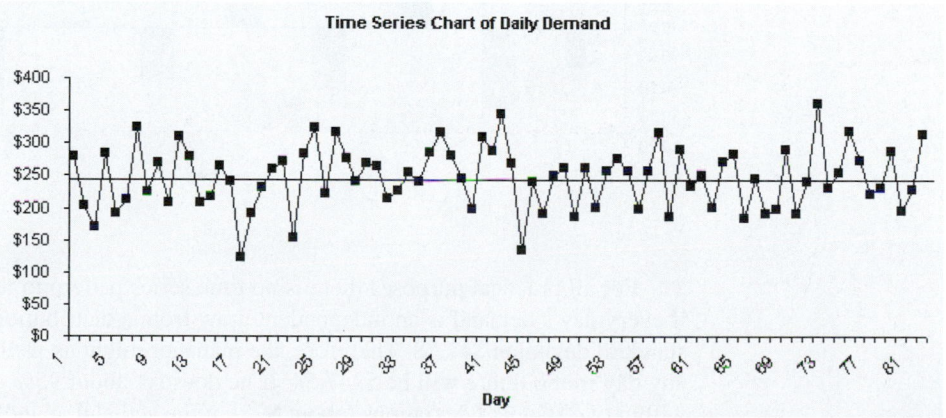

Solution

A visual inspection of the time series graph in Figure 13.10 shows that demands vary randomly around the sample mean of $247.54 (shown as the horizontal centerline). The variance appears to be constant through time, and there are no obvious time series patterns. To check formally whether this apparent randomness holds, we perform the runs test (runs above and below the mean) and calculate the first 10 autocorrelations. The numerical output appears in Figure 13.11, and the associated correlogram appears in Figure 13.12. The p-value for the runs test is relatively large, 0.118—although there are somewhat *more* runs than expected—and none of the autocorrelations is significantly large. These findings are consistent with randomness.

FIGURE 13.11 **Autocorrelations and Runs Test for Demand Data**

	J	K	L	M	N	O	P	Q
1								
2								
3	*Autocorrelations*					*Runs Test Results*		
4		Lag	Autocorr	StErr			Number of obs	82
5		1	-0.0653	0.1104			Number above cutoff	42
6		2	-0.1345	0.1104			Number below cutoff	40
7		3	0.1933	0.1104			Number of runs	49
8		4	-0.1024	0.1104				
9		5	0.0388	0.1104			E(R)	41.976
10		6	-0.0862	0.1104			Stdev(R)	4.497
11		7	0.0107	0.1104			Z-value	1.562
12		8	-0.1492	0.1104			p-value (2-tailed)	0.118
13		9	-0.1151	0.1104				
14		10	-0.0506	0.1104				

FIGURE 13.12 **Correlogram for Demand Data**

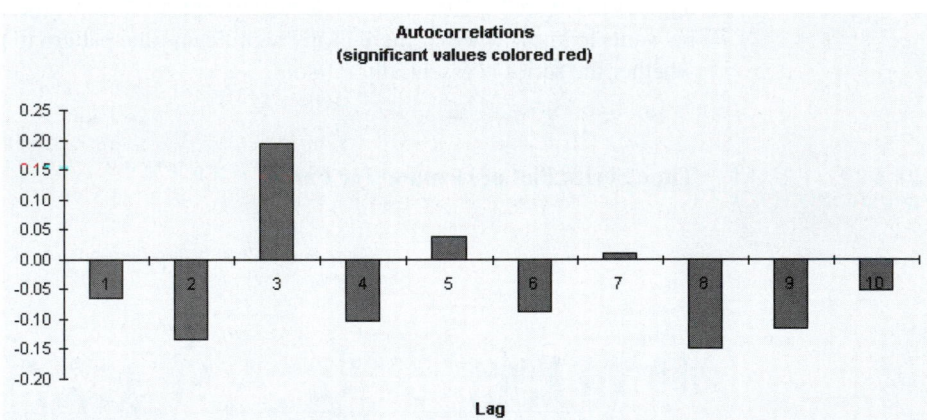

For all practical purposes there is no time series pattern to these demand data. It is as if every day's demand is an independent draw from a distribution with mean $247.54 and standard deviation $47.78. Therefore, the manager might as well forecast that demand for any day in the future will be $247.54. If he does so, about 95% of his forecasts should be within two standard deviations (about $95) of the actual demands. ∎

PROBLEMS

Level A

1 The file P13_1.XLS contains the number of airline tickets sold by the CareFree Travel Agency each month from January 1995 to December 1998. Is this time series *random*? Perform a runs test and compute a few autocorrelations to support your answer.

2 The file P13_2.XLS contains the weekly sales at a local bookstore for each of the past 25 weeks. Is this time series *random*? Perform a runs test and compute a few autocorrelations to support your answer.

3 The number of employees on the payroll at a food processing plant is recorded at the start of each month from January 1996 to December 1998. These data are provided in the file P13_3.XLS. Perform a runs test and compute a few autocorrelations to determine whether this time series is random.

4 The quarterly numbers of applications for home mortgage loans at a branch office of Northern Central Bank from the first quarter of 1993 to the fourth quarter of 1998 are recorded in the file P13_4.XLS. Perform a runs test and compute a few autocorrelations to determine whether this time series is random.

5 The number of reported accidents at a manufacturing plant located in Flint, Michigan, was recorded at the start of each month from January 1996 to December 1998. These data are provided in the file P13_5.XLS. Is this time series *random*? Perform a runs test and compute a few autocorrelations to support your answer.

6 The file P13_6.XLS contains the weekly sales at the local outlet of WestCoast Video Rentals for each of the past 36 weeks. Perform a runs test and compute a few autocorrelations to determine whether this time series is random.

Level B

7 Determine whether the RAND() function in Excel actually generates a random stream of numbers. Generate at least 100 random numbers to perform this test. Summarize your findings.

8 Use a runs test and calculate autorrelations to decide whether the random series explained in each part below are random. For each part, generate at least 100 random numbers in the series.

a A series of independent normally distributed values, each with mean 70 and standard deviation 5.

b A series where the first value is normally distributed with mean 70 and standard deviation 5, and each succeeding value is normally distributed with mean equal to the *previous* value and standard deviation 5. (For example, if the fourth value is 67.32, then the fifth value will be normally distributed with mean 67.32.)

c A series where the first value, Y_1, is normally distributed with mean 70 and standard deviation 5, and each succeeding value, Y_t, is normally distributed with mean $(1 + a_t)Y_{t-1}$ and standard deviation $5(1 + a_t)$, where the a_t's are independent, normally distributed values with mean 0 and standard deviation 0.2. (For example, if $Y_{t-1} = 67.32$ and $a_t = -0.2$, then Y_t will be normally distributed with mean $0.8(67.32) = 53.856$ and standard deviation $0.8(5) = 4$.) ∎

13.4

The Random Walk Model

Random series are sometimes building blocks for other time series models. The model we now discuss, the **random walk** model, is an example of this. In a random walk model the series itself is not random. However, its *differences*—that is, the changes from one period to the next—are random. This type of behavior is typical of stock price data (as well as various other time series data). For example, the graph in Figure 13.13 (page 720) shows monthly Dow Jones averages from January 1988 through March 1992. (See the file DOW.XLS.)

FIGURE 13.13   Time Series Plot of Dow Jones Index

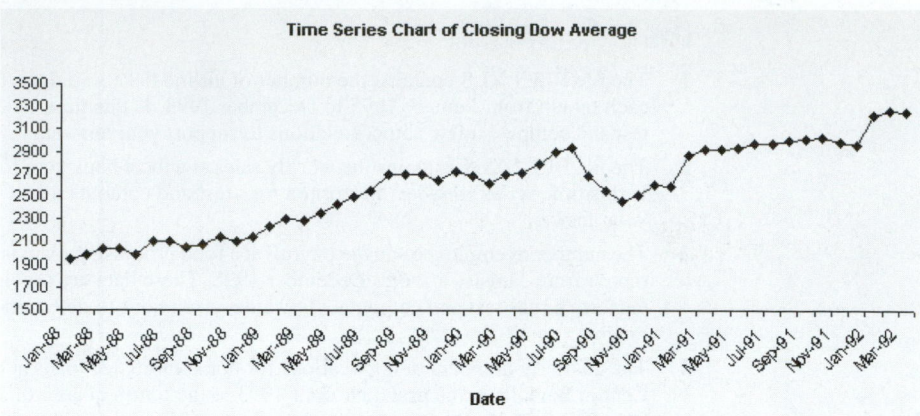

This series is not random, as can be seen from its gradual upward trend. (Although the runs test and autocorrelations are not shown for the series itself, they confirm that the series is not random. There are significantly *fewer* runs than expected, and the autocorrelations are significantly *positive* for many lags.)

If we were standing in March 1992 and were asked to forecast the Dow Jones average for the next few months, it is intuitive that we would not use the average of the historical values as our forecast. This forecast would probably be too low because the series has an upward trend. Instead, we would base our forecast on the most recent observation. This is exactly what the random walk model does.

An equation for the random walk model is

$$Y_t = Y_{t-1} + \mu + \varepsilon_t \tag{13.9}$$

where μ is a constant and ε_t is a random series (noise) with mean 0 and some standard deviation σ. If we let $DY_t = Y_t - Y_{t-1}$, the change in the series from time t to time $t-1$ (where D stands for difference), then we can write the random walk model as

$$DY_t = \mu + \varepsilon_t \tag{13.10}$$

This implies that the differences form a random series with mean μ and standard deviation σ. An estimate of μ is the average of the differences, labeled $\overline{Y}_D$, and an estimate of σ is the sample standard deviation of the differences, labeled s_D.

In words, a series that behaves according to this random walk model has random differences, and the series tends to trend upward (if $\mu > 0$) or downward (if $\mu < 0$) by an amount μ each period. If we are standing in period t and want to make a forecast F_{t+1} of Y_{t+1}, then a reasonable forecast is

$$F_{t+1} = Y_t + \overline{Y}_D \tag{13.11}$$

That is, we add the estimated trend to the current observation to forecast the next observation. We illustrate this method in the following example of the Dow Jones data.

EXAMPLE 13.4

Given the monthly Dow Jones data in the file DOW.XLS, check that it satisfies the assumptions of a random walk, and use the random walk model to forecast the value for April 1992.

Solution

We've already seen that the Dow Jones series itself is not random, due to the upward trend, so we form the differences in column C of Figure 13.14. The formula in cell C7 is

$$=B7-B6$$

which we copy down column C. (Notice that the difference series necessarily has a missing value in cell C6.) A graph of these differences is shown in Figure 13.15 (page 722). It appears to be a much more random series, varying around the mean difference 26.00 (in cell C58). The runs test appears in column H. It shows that there is absolutely no evidence of nonrandom differences; the observed number of runs is almost identical to the expected number. Similarly, the autocorrelations (not shown here) are all small except for a random "blip" at lag 11. Because there is probably no reason to believe that values 11 months apart really *are* related, we would tend to ignore this autocorrelation.

Assuming the random walk model is adequate, the forecast of April 1992 made in March 1992 is the observed March value, 3247.42, plus the mean difference, 26.00, or 3273.42. A measure of the forecast accuracy is provided by the standard deviation, $s_D = 84.65$, of the differences in cell C59. We can be 95% certain that our forecast is off by no more than $2s_D$, or about 170.

If we want to forecast farther into the future, say, 3 months ahead, based on data through March 1992, we would add the most recent value, 3247.42, to three times the mean difference, 26.00. That is, we just project the trend that far into the future. The corresponding standard deviation turns out to be $\sqrt{3}s_D$. However, we caution about forecasting too far into

FIGURE 13.14 Differences for Dow Jones Data

	A	B	C	D	E	F	G	H
1	Monthly Dow Jones average closing index, Jan 88 to Mar 92							
2								
3	A random walk?							
4								
5	Date	Dow	Diff	Diff_High	Diff_NewRun		Runs test values	
6	Jan-88	1947.35						
7	Feb-88	1980.65	33.3	1	1		T	50
8	Mar-88	2044.31	63.66	1	0		T_A	26
9	Apr-88	2036.13	-8.18	0	1		T_b	24
10	May-88	1988.91	-47.22	0	0		R	26
11	Jun-88	2104.94	116.03	1	1			
12	Jul-88	2104.22	-0.72	0	1		E(R)	25.96
13	Aug-88	2051.29	-52.93	0	0		StDev(R)	3.49
14	Sep-88	2080.06	28.77	1	1		Z	0.01
15	Oct-88	2144.31	64.25	1	0		p-value	0.99
16	Nov-88	2099.04	-45.27	0	1			
17	Dec-88	2148.58	49.54	1	1			
56	Mar-92	3247.42	-9.85	0	1			
57								
58	Means	2585.64	26.00					
59	StDevs	373.80	84.65					

FIGURE 13.15 Time Series Plot of Dow Differences

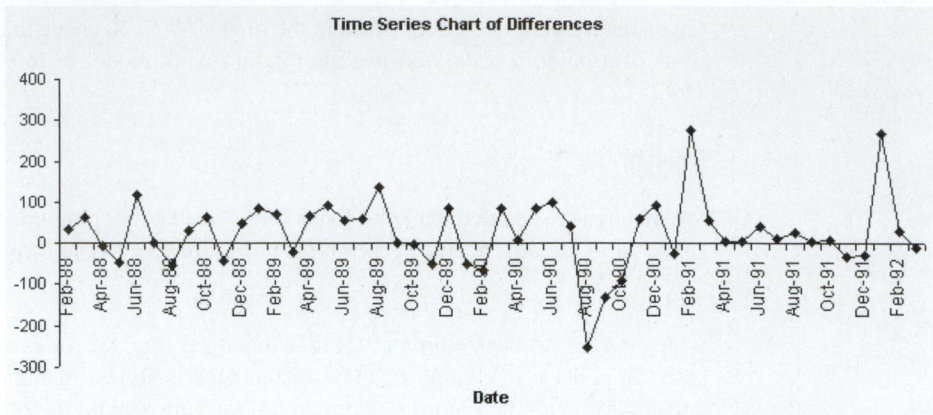

the future, especially for such a volatile series such as the Dow. In fact, the whole nature of the *future* series can change. For example, we all know that the Dow went through the roof shortly after the period in this example. It is unlikely that *any* automatic forecasting model could have predicted the dramatic upward trend in the Dow we saw through the mid to late 1990s. ■

PROBLEMS

Level A

9 The file P13_9.XLS contains the daily closing prices of American Express stock from July 21, 1997 through July 20, 1998.

  a Use the random walk model to forecast the closing price of this stock on July 21, 1998.

  b We can be about 95% certain that the forecast made in part **a** is off by no more than how many dollars?

10 The closing value of the AMEX Airline Index for each trading day from July 21, 1997 through July 21, 1998 is given in the file P13_10.XLS.

  a Use the random walk model to forecast the closing price of this stock on July 22, 1998.

  b We can be about 68% certain that the forecast made in part **a** is off by no more than how many dollars?

11 The file P13_11.XLS contains the daily closing prices of Chevron stock from July 21, 1997 through July 20, 1998.

  a Use the random walk model to forecast the closing price of this stock on July 21, 1998.

  b We can be about 99.7% certain that the forecast made in part **a** is off by no more than how many dollars?

12 The closing value of the Dow Jones Industrial Index for each trading day from March 31, 1998 through July 21, 1998 is provided in the file P13_12.XLS.

  a Use the random walk model to forecast the closing price of this stock on July 22, 1998.

  b Use the random walk model to forecast the closing price of this stock on July 29, 1998.

  c Would it be wise to use the random walk model to forecast the closing price of this stock for a trading day approximately *one month* after July 21, 1998? Explain why or why not.

13   Continuing the previous problem, consider the differences between consecutive closing values of the Dow Jones Industrial Index for the given set of trading days. Do these differences form a random series? Demonstrate why or why not.

14   The closing price of a share of J.P. Morgan's stock for each trading day from July 21, 1997 through July 21, 1998 is recorded in the file P13_14.XLS.

   a   Use the random walk model to forecast the closing price of this stock on July 24, 1998.

   b   We can be about 68% certain that the forecast made in part **a** is off by no more than how many dollars?

15   The purpose of this problem is to get you used to the concept of autocorrelation in a time series. You could do it with any time series, but here you should use the series of Wal-Mart daily stock prices from the beginning of 1992 through the end of July 1992. The data are in the file P13_15.XLS.

   a   First, do it the "easy" way. Use the Autocorrelations procedure in StatPro to get a list of autocorrelations and a corresponding correlogram. You can choose the number of lags.

   b   Now do it the "hard" way. Create columns of lagged versions of the Close variable—3 or 4 lags will suffice. Next, look at scatterplots of Close versus its first few lags. If the autocorrelations are large, you should see fairly tight scatters—that's what autocorrelation is all about. Also, generate a correlation matrix to see the correlations between Close and its first few lags. These should be approximately the same as the autocorrelations from part **a**. (Autocorrelations are calculated slightly differently than regular correlations, which accounts for any slight discrepancies you might notice, but these discrepancies should be minor.)

   c   Create the first differences of Close in a new column. (You can do this manually with formulas, or you can use StatPro's Differences procedure under Utilities.) Now repeat parts **a** and **b** with the differences instead of the original closing prices—that is, examine the autocorrelations of the differences. They should be small, and the scattergrams of the differences versus lags of the differences should be "swarms." This illustrates what happens when the differences of a time series variable have "insignificant" autocorrelations.

   d   Write a short report of your findings.

Level B

16   Consider a random walk model with the following equation: $Y_t = Y_{t-1} + 500 + \varepsilon_t$, where ε_t is a normally distributed random series with mean 0 and standard deviation 10.

   a   Use Excel to generate a time series that behaves according to this random walk model.

   b   Use the time series you constructed in part **a** to forecast the next observation.

17   The file P13_17.XLS contains the daily closing prices of Procter & Gamble stock from July 21, 1997 to July 20, 1998. Use only the data from the beginning of the period (through June 19, 1998) to estimate the trend component of the random walk model (i.e., assume that it is currently June 19, 1998 and you want to forecast the time series from this point onward). Next, use the estimated random walk model to forecast the behavior of the time series from June 22 to July 20 of 1998. Comment on the accuracy of the generated forecasts over this period. How could you improve the forecasts as you progress through these next 20 trading days?   ■

13.5

Autoregression Models

A regression-based extrapolation method is to regress the current value of the time series on past (lagged) values. This is called **autoregression**, where the "auto" means that the explanatory variables in the equation are lagged values of the response variable, so that we are regressing the response variable on lagged versions of itself. This procedure is fairly straightforward on a spreadsheet. We first create lags of the response variable and then use a regression procedure to regress the original column on the lagged columns. Some trial and error is generally required to see how many lags are useful in the regression equation. The following example illustrates the procedure.

EXAMPLE 13.5

A retailer has recorded its weekly sales of hammers (units purchased) for the past 42 weeks. (See the file HAMMERS.XLS.) A graph of this time series appears in Figure 13.16. It reveals a "meandering" behavior. The values begin high and stay high awhile, then get lower and stay lower awhile, then get higher again. (This behavior could be caused by any number of things, including the weather, increases and decreases in building projects, and possibly others.) How useful is autoregression for modeling these data and how would it be used for forecasting?

FIGURE 13.16 **Time Series Plot of Sales of Hammers**

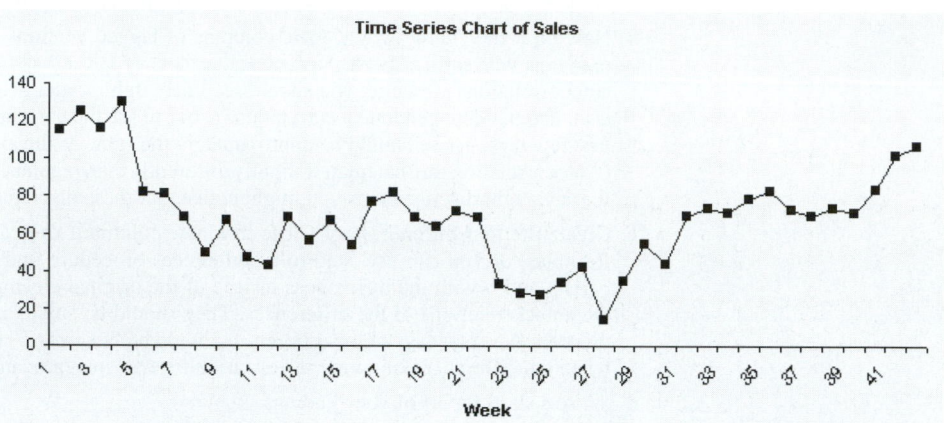

Solution

A good place to start is with the autocorrelations of the series. These indicate whether the Sales variable is linearly related to any of its lags. The first six autocorrelations are shown in Figure 13.17. The first three of them are significantly positive, and then they decrease. Based on this information, we create three lags of Sales and run a regression of Sales versus these three lags.[6] The output from this regression appears in Figure 13.18. We see that R^2 is fairly high, about 57%, and that s_e is about 15.7. However, the p-values for lags 2 and 3 are both quite large. It appears that once the first lag is included in the regression equation, the other two are not really needed.

Therefore, we reran the regression with only the first lag included. (Actually, we first omitted only the third lag. But the resulting output showed that the second lag was still insignificant.) The regression output with only the first lag included appears in Figure 13.19 (page 726). In addition, a graph of the response and fitted variables, that is, the original Sales variable and its forecasts, appears in Figure 13.20. (This latter graph was formed from the Week, Sales, and Fitted columns.) The estimated regression equation is

$$\text{Forecasted Sales}_t = 13.763 + 0.793\text{Sales}_{t-1}$$

The associated R^2 and s_e values are approximately 65% and 15.4. The R^2 value is a measure of the reasonably good fit we see in Figure 13.20, whereas s_e is a measure of the likely

---

[6] If you use StatPro's Multiple Regression procedure, make sure to check the box dealing with missing values. There *are* missing values of the lagged variables in the first few rows.

FIGURE 13.17 Correlogram for Hammer Sales Data

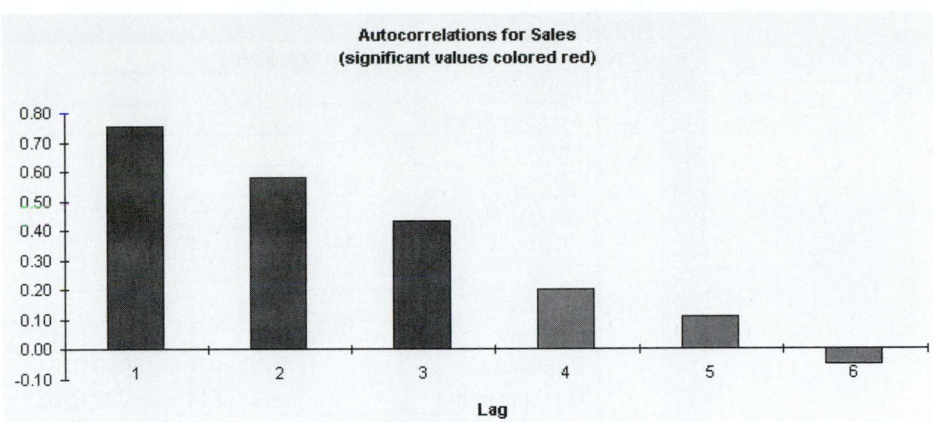

FIGURE 13.18 Autoregression Output with Three Lagged Variables

	A	B	C	D	E	F	G
1	*Results of multiple regression for Sales*						
2							
3	*Summary measures*						
4		Multiple R	0.7573				
5		R-Square	0.5736				
6		Adj R-Square	0.5370				
7		StErr of Est	15.7202				
8							
9	*ANOVA Table*						
10		Source	df	SS	MS	F	p-value
11		Explained	3	11634.2001	3878.0667	15.6927	0.0000
12		Unexplained	35	8649.3896	247.1254		
13							
14	*Regression coefficients*						
15			Coefficient	Std Err	t-value	p-value	
16		Constant	15.4986	7.8820	1.9663	0.0572	
17		Sales_Lag1	0.6398	0.1712	3.7364	0.0007	
18		Sales_Lag2	0.1523	0.1987	0.7665	0.4485	
19		Sales_Lag3	-0.0354	0.1641	-0.2159	0.8303	

forecast error for short-term forecasts. It implies that a short-term forecast could easily be off by as much as two standard errors, or about 31 hammers.

To use the regression equation for forecasting *future* sales values, we substitute known or forecasted sales values in the right-hand side of the equation. Specifically, the forecast for week 43, the first week after the data period, is

$$\text{Forecasted Sales}_{43} = 13.763 + 0.793\text{Sales}_{42} = 13.763 + 0.793(107) \simeq 98.6$$

Here we use the *known* value of sales in week 42. However, the forecast for week 44 requires the *forecasted* value of sales in week 43:

$$\text{Forecasted Sales}_{44} = 13.763 + 0.793\text{Forecasted Sales}_{43}$$

$$= 13.763 + 0.793(98.6) \simeq 92.0$$

FIGURE 13.19 **Autoregression Output with a Single Lagged Variable**

	A	B	C	D	E	F	G
1	*Results of multiple regression for Sales*						
2							
3	*Summary measures*						
4		Multiple R	0.8036				
5		R-Square	0.6458				
6		Adj R-Square	0.6367				
7		StErr of Est	15.4476				
8							
9	*ANOVA Table*						
10		Source	df	SS	MS	F	p-value
11		Explained	1	16969.9761	16969.9761	71.1146	0.0000
12		Unexplained	39	9306.5117	238.6285		
13							
14	*Regression coefficients*						
15			Coefficient	Std Err	t-value	p-value	
16		Constant	13.7634	6.7906	2.0268	0.0496	
17		Sales_Lag1	0.7932	0.0941	8.4329	0.0000	

FIGURE 13.20 **Forecasts from Autoregression**

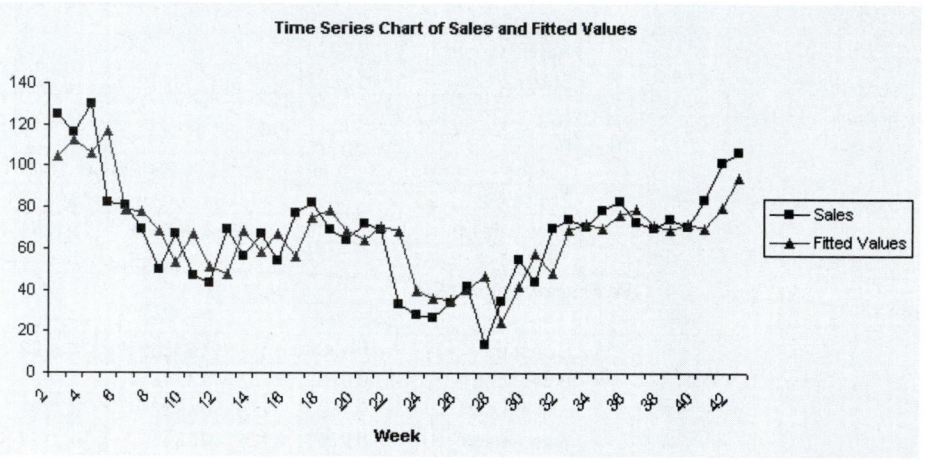

Perhaps these two forecasts of future sales values are on the mark, and perhaps they are not. The only way we'll know for certain is by observing future sales values. However, it is interesting that in spite of the *upward* movement in the series in the last 3 weeks, the forecasts for weeks 43 and 44 are for *downward* movements. This is a combination of two properties of the regression equation. First, the coefficient of $Sales_{t-1}$, 0.793, is positive. Therefore, the equation forecasts that large sales will be followed by large sales, that is, positive autocorrelation. Second, however, this coefficient is less than 1, and this provides a dampening effect. The equation forecasts that a large will follow a large, but not *that* large. ∎

Sometimes an autoregression model is virtually equivalent to another forecasting model. As an example, consider the Dow Jones data that were modeled as a random walk. If we regress the Dow versus its first lag (see the file DOW.XLS), we obtain the following autoregression equation:

$$\text{Forecasted Dow}_t = 88.94 + 0.976\text{Dow}_{t-1}$$

The coefficient of the lag term, 0.976, is nearly equal to 1. If this coefficient were 1, then we could write the equation as

$$\text{Forecasted Dow}_t - \text{Dow}_{t-1} = \text{constant}$$

(The constant on the right would not necessarily equal 88.94.) But this is just the random walk model. Therefore, we see that a random walk model is a special case of an autoregression model. However, autoregression models are much more general.

PROBLEMS

Level A

18 Consider the Consumer Price Index, which provides the annual percentage change in consumer prices, for the period from 1914 through 1996. The data are in the file P2_26.XLS.

a Compute the first six autocorrelations of this time series.

b Use the results of part **a** to specify one or more "promising" autoregression models. Estimate each model with the available data. Which model provides the best fit to the given data?

c Use the best autoregression model from part **b** to produce a forecast of the CPI in 1997. Also, provide a measure of the likely forecast error.

19 The Consumer Confidence Index attempts to measure people's feelings about general business conditions, employment opportunities, and their own income prospects. The file P2_28.XLS contains the annual average values of the CCI for the period 1967–1996.

a Compute the first six autocorrelations of this time series.

b Use the results of part **a** to specify one or more "promising" autoregression models. Estimate each model with the available data. Which model provides the best fit to the given data?

c Use the best autoregression model from part **b** to produce a forecast of the CCI in 1997. Also, provide a measure of the likely forecast error.

20 Consider the proportion of Americans under the age of 18 living below the poverty level for each of the years 1959–1996. The data are in the file P2_29.XLS.

a Compute the first six autocorrelations of this time series.

b Use the results of part **a** to specify one or more "promising" autoregression models. Estimate each model with the available data. Which model provides the best fit to the given data?

c Use the best autoregression model from part **b** to produce a forecast of the proportion of American children living below the poverty level in 1997. Also, provide a measure of the likely forecast error.

21 Examine the trend in the annual average values of the discount rate for the period 1977–1996. The data are in the file P2_30.XLS.

a Specify one or more "promising" autoregression models based on autocorrelations of this time series. Estimate each model with the available data. Which model provides the best fit to given data?

b Use the best autoregression model from part **a** to produce forecasts of the discount rate in 1997 and 1998.

22 The file P2_34.XLS contains the annual cigar consumption *per capita* in the United States for selected years between 1920 and 1996.

a Specify one or more "promising" autoregression models based on autocorrelations of this time series. Estimate each model with the available data. Which model provides the best fit to the given data?

b Use the best autoregression model from part **a** to produce forecasts of the cigar consumption per capita in 1997, 1998, and 1999.

23 Consider the average annual interest rates on 30-year fixed mortgages in the United States during the period 1972–1996. The data are recorded in the file P2_35.XLS.

a Specify one or more "promising" autoregression models based on autocorrelations of this time series. Estimate each model with the available data. Which model provides the best fit to the given data?

b Use the best autoregression model from part **a** to produce forecasts of the average annual interest rates on 30-year fixed mortgages in 1997, 1998, and 1999.

24 The file P13_24.XLS lists the monthly unemployment rates for the last 10 years. A common way to forecast time series is by using regression with lagged variables.

a Predict future monthly unemployment rates using some combination of the unemployment rates for the last 4 months. For example, you might use last month's unemployment rate and the unemployment rate from 3 months ago as explanatory variables. Make sure all variables that you finally decide to keep in your equation are significant at the 0.15 level.

b Do the residuals in your equation exhibit any autocorrelation?

c Predict the November 1997 unemployment rate.

d There is a 5% chance that the November 1997 unemployment rate will be less than what value?

e What is the probability the November 1997 unemployment rate will be less than 5%?

Level B

25 The unit sales of a new drug for the first 25 months after its introduction to the marketplace are recorded in the file P13_15.XLS. Specify one or more "promising" autoregression models based on autocorrelations of this time series. Estimate each model with the available data. Which model provides the best fit to the given data? Use the best autoregression model you found to forecast the sales of this new drug in the 26th month. (*Hint:* Recall what we learned in Section 6 of Chapter 11 about modeling these data.)

26 The file P13_2.XLS contains the weekly sales at a local bookstore for each of the past 25 weeks.

a Specify one or more "promising" autoregression models based on autocorrelations of this time series. Estimate each model with the available data. Which model provides the best fit to the given data?

b What general result emerges from your analysis in part **a**? In other words, what is the most appropriate autoregression model for any given *random* time series?

c Use the best autoregression model from part **a** to produce forecasts of the weekly sales at this bookstore for the next 3 weeks.

27 The file P13_17.XLS contains the daily closing prices of Procter & Gamble stock from July 21, 1997 to July 20, 1998.

a Use only the data from the beginning of the period (through June 19, 1998) to estimate an appropriate autoregression model (i.e., assume that it is currently June 19, 1998 and you want to forecast the time series from this point onward).

b Next, use the estimated autoregression model to forecast the behavior of the time series from June 22 to July 20 of 1998. Comment on the accuracy of the generated forecasts over this period.

c How well does the autoregression model perform in comparison to the random walk model with respect to the accuracy of these forecasts? Explain any significant differences between the forecasting abilities of the two models. ■

Regression-Based Trend Models

Many time series follow a long-term trend except for random variation. This trend can be upward or downward. A straightforward way to model this trend is to estimate a regression equation for Y_t, using time t as the *single* explanatory variable. In this section we will discuss the two most frequently used trend models, **linear** trend and **exponential** trend.

13.6.1 Linear Trend

A linear trend means that the time series variable changes by a constant *amount* each time period. The relevant equation is

$$Y_t = a + bt + \varepsilon_t \qquad \text{(13.12)}$$

where, as in previous regression equations, a is the intercept, b is the slope, and ε_t is an error term. The interpretation of b is that it represents the expected change in the series from one period to the next. If b is positive, the trend is upward; if b is negative, the trend is downward. The intercept term a is less important. It literally represents the expected value of the series at time $t = 0$. If time t is coded so that the first observation corresponds to $t = 1$, then a is where we expect the series to have been one period before we started observing. However, it is possible that time is coded in another way. For example, we might have annual data that start in 1985. Then the first value of t might be entered as 1985, which means that the intercept a corresponds to a period 1985 years earlier! Clearly, we would not take its value literally in this case.

As always, the graph of the time series is a good place to start. It indicates whether a linear trend model is likely to provide a good fit. Generally, the graph should rise or fall at approximately a constant rate through time, without too much random variation. But even if there is a lot of random variation—a lot of zigzags—fitting a linear trend to the data might still be a good starting point. Then the *residuals* from this trendline, which should have no remaining trend, could possibly be modeled by some other method in this chapter.

EXAMPLE 13.6

The file REEBOK.XLS includes quarterly sales data for Reebok from first quarter 1986 through second quarter 1996. The time series plot of these data is shown in Figure 13.21 (page 730). Sales increase from $174.52 million in the first quarter to $817.57 million in the final quarter. How well does a linear trend fit these data? Are the residuals from this fit random?

Solution

The plot in Figure 13.21 indicates an obvious upward trend with little or no curvature. Therefore, a linear trend is certainly plausible. We use regression to estimate the linear fit, where Sales is the response variable and Time is the single explanatory variable. Note in the file that we have two columns that indicate time. The Time variable is coded 1–42 and is used as the explanatory variable in the regression. The Quarter variable simply labels the quarters (Q1-86 to Q2-96) and is used only to label the horizontal axis in Figure 13.21; it is

FIGURE 13.21   Time Series Plot of Reebok Sales

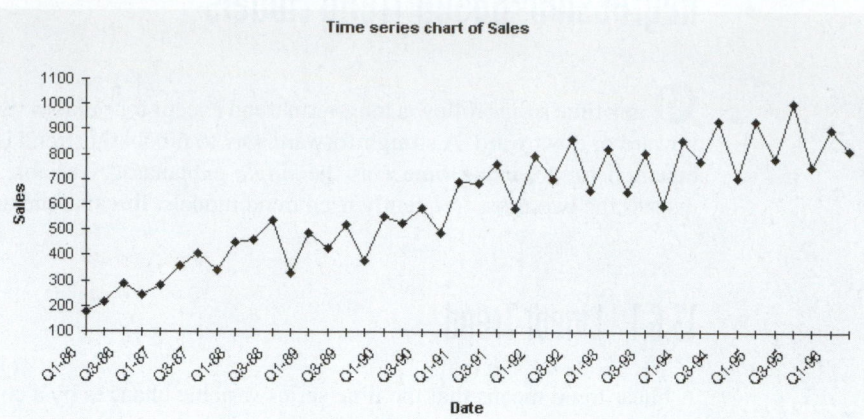

not used for any numerical calculations. The regression output in Figure 13.22 shows that the estimated equation is

$$\text{Forecasted Sales} = 244.82 + 16.53\text{Time}$$

with R^2 and s_e values of 83.8% and $90.38 million. The linear trendline, superimposed on the sales data in Figure 13.23, appears to be a decent fit. It implies that sales are increasing by about $16.53 million per quarter during this time period.

The fit is far from perfect, however. First, the s_e value, $90.38 million, is an indication of the typical forecast error. This is substantial, approximately equal to 11% of the final quarter's sales. Furthermore, there is some regularity to the forecast errors, shown in Figure 13.24. They zigzag more than a random series. There is possibly some seasonal pattern in the sales data, which we might be able to pick up with a more sophisticated forecasting method. However, the basic linear trend is sufficient as a first approximation to the behavior of sales.

FIGURE 13.22   Regression Output for Linear Trend

	A	B	C	D	E	F	G
1	*Results of multiple regression for Sales*						
2							
3	*Summary measures*						
4		Multiple R	0.9152				
5		R-Square	0.8377				
6		Adj R-Square	0.8336				
7		StErr of Est	90.3844				
8							
9	*ANOVA Table*						
10		Source	df	SS	MS	F	p-value
11		Explained	1	1686121.5556	1686121.5556	206.3964	0.0000
12		Unexplained	40	326773.3750	8169.3344		
13							
14	*Regression coefficients*						
15			Coefficient	Std Err	t-value	p-value	
16		Constant	244.8154	28.3989	8.6206	0.0000	
17		Time	16.5304	1.1506	14.3665	0.0000	

FIGURE 13.23 **Time Series Plot with Linear Trend Superimposed**

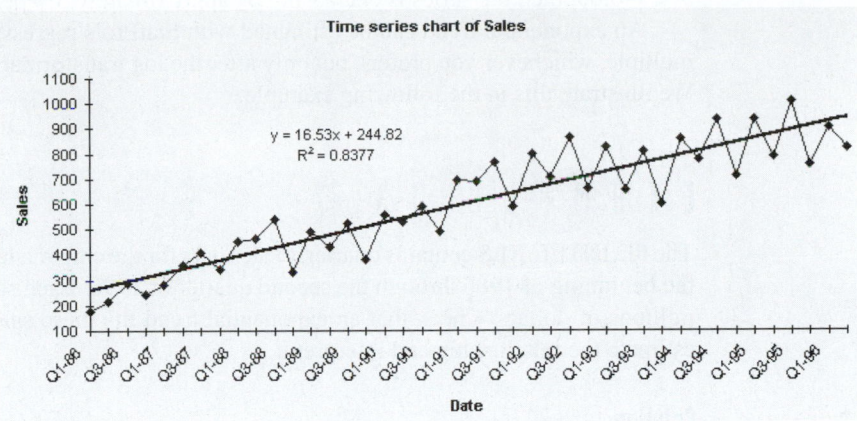

FIGURE 13.24 **Time Series Plot of Forecast Errors**

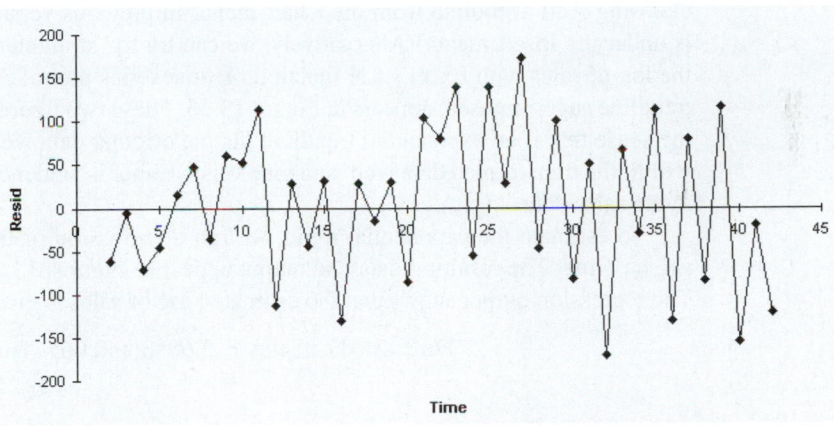

13.6.2 Exponential Trend

In contrast to a linear trend, an exponential trend is appropriate when the time series changes by a constant *percentage* (as opposed to a constant dollar amount) each period. Then the appropriate regression equation is

$$Y_t = ce^{bt}u_t \qquad (13.13)$$

where c and b are constants, and u_t represents a *multiplicative* error term. By taking logarithms of both sides, and letting $a = \ln(c)$ and $\varepsilon_t = \ln(u_t)$, we obtain a linear equation that can be estimated by the usual linear regression method. However, note that the response variable is now the logarithm of Y_t:

$$\ln(Y_t) = a + bt + \varepsilon_t \qquad (13.14)$$

Because the computer does the calculations, our main responsibility is to interpret the final result. This is not too difficult. It can be shown that the coefficient b (expressed as a percentage) is approximately the percentage change per period. For example, if $b = 0.05$, then the series is increasing by approximately 5% per period.[7] On the other hand, if $b = -0.05$, then the series is decreasing by approximately 5% per period.

An exponential trend can be estimated with StatPro's regression procedure (simple or multiple, whichever you prefer), but only after the log transformation has been made on Y_t. We illustrate this in the following example.

EXAMPLE 13.7

The file INTEL.XLS contains quarterly sales data for the chip manufacturing firm Intel from the beginning of 1986 through the second quarter of 1996. Each sales value is expressed in millions of dollars. Check that an exponential trend fits these sales data fairly well. Then estimate the relationship and interpret it.

Solution

The time series plot of sales in Figure 13.25 shows that sales are clearly increasing at an *increasing* rate, which a linear trend would not capture. The smooth curve in this figure is an exponential trendline, which appears to be an adequate fit. (In Excel 97, we get it by choosing Add Trendline from the Chart menu. In previous versions of Excel, this option is under the Insert menu.) Alternatively, we can try to "straighten out" the data by taking the log of sales with Excel's LN function. A time series plot of the log data, with a *linear* trendline superimposed, appears in Figure 13.26. These two figures go together logically in the sense that if an exponential trendline fits the original data well, then a linear trendline will fit the transformed data well, and vice versa. Either is evidence of an exponential trend in the sales data.

To estimate the exponential trend, we run a regression of the log of sales, LnSales, versus Time. The resulting data and output appear in Figures 13.27 and 13.28 (page 734). The regression output shows that the estimated log of sales is given by

$$\text{Forecasted LnSales} = 5.6883 + 0.0657\text{Time}$$

FIGURE 13.25   **Time Series Plot of Sales with Exponential Trend Superimposed**

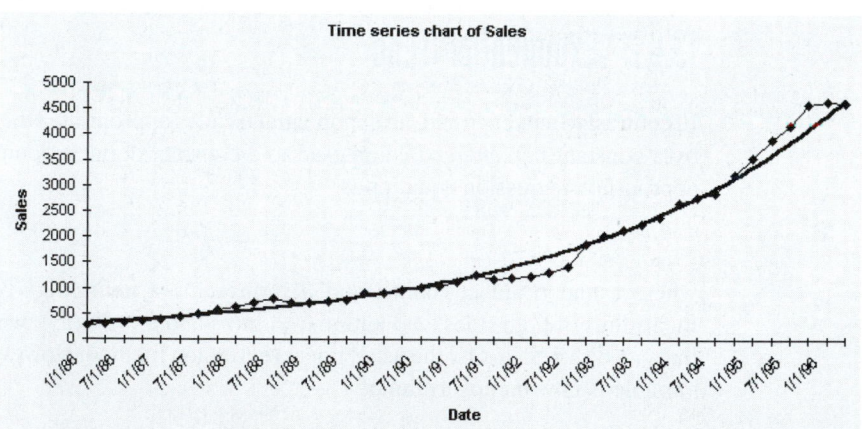

---

[7]A more accurate estimate of this percentage change is $e^b - 1$. For example, when $b = 0.05$, this is $e^b - 1 = 5.13\%$.

FIGURE 13.26   Time Series Plot of Log Sales with Linear Trend Superimposed

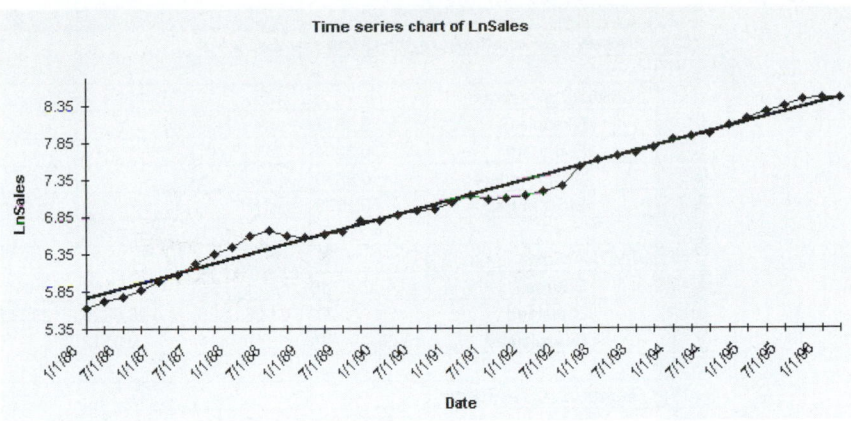

Alternatively, by taking antilogs we obtain an estimated equation for Sales:

$$\text{Forecasted Sales} = 295.377e^{0.0657\text{Time}}$$

(Note that the antilog of the constant 5.6883 appears in cell J25. We can calculate it with Excel's EXP function.) Looking at the coefficient of Time, we can say that Intel's sales are increasing by approximately 6.6% per quarter during this period. This translates to an annual percentage increase of about 29%! Perhaps the slight tailing off that we see at the right of Figure 13.25 indicates that Intel can't keep up this fantastic rate forever.

It is important to view the R^2 and s_e values (in cells J7 and J9) with caution. Each is based on log units, not original units. To produce similar measures in original units, we need to forecast sales in column E. This is actually a two-step process. (From here on, we have to create the output—StatPro does not provide it automatically.) We first forecast the log of sales, and then we take the antilog with Excel's EXP function. Specifically, the formula in cell E4 is

=EXP($J$18+$J$19*A4)

FIGURE 13.27   Data Setup for Regression of Exponential Trend

	A	B	C	D	E	F
1	Quarterly data on Intel sales ($ millions)					
2						
3	Time	Date	Sales	LnSales	FittedSales	ResidSales
4	1	1/1/86	280.05	5.6350	315.45	-35.39
5	2	4/1/86	305.18	5.7209	336.88	-31.70
6	3	7/1/86	324.14	5.7812	359.77	-35.63
7	4	10/1/86	355.64	5.8739	384.21	-28.57
8	5	1/1/87	394.53	5.9777	410.31	-15.78
9	6	4/1/87	438.96	6.0844	438.19	0.76
10	7	7/1/87	501.13	6.2169	467.96	33.16
11	8	10/1/87	572.49	6.3500	499.76	72.73
12	9	1/1/88	635.81	6.4549	533.71	102.09
13	10	4/1/88	726.68	6.5885	569.97	156.71
14	11	7/1/88	784.94	6.6656	608.70	176.24
43	40	10/1/95	4580.00	8.4295	4095.37	484.63
44	41	1/1/96	4644.00	8.4433	4373.62	270.38
45	42	4/1/96	4621.00	8.4384	4670.78	-49.78

FIGURE 13.28   Regression Ouput for Exponential Trend

	H	I	J	K	L	M	N
3	*Results of multiple regression for LnSales*						
4							
5	*Summary measures*						
6		Multiple R	0.9917				
7		R-Square	0.9834				
8		Adj R-Square	0.9830				
9		StErr of Est	0.1060				
10							
11	*ANOVA Table*						
12		Source	df	SS	MS	F	p-value
13		Explained	1	26.6625	26.6625	2373.2787	0.0000
14		Unexplained	40	0.4494	0.0112		
15							
16	*Regression coefficients*						
17			Coefficient	Std Err	t-value	p-value	
18		Constant	5.6883	0.0333	170.8029	0.0000	
19		Time	0.0657	0.0013	48.7163	0.0000	
20							
21	**Summary measures in original units**						
22		R-Square	0.988				
23		StErr of Est	159.698				
24							
25		Antilog of const	295.377				

The residuals in column F are then actual sales in column C minus fitted sales in column E. Once we have these, we can find the appropriate R^2 and s_e values in cells J22 and J23. As usual, R^2 is the square of the correlation between actual and fitted sales values, so the formula in cell J22 is

$$=\text{CORREL(Sales,FittedSales)}^2$$

Then s_e is the square root of the sum of squared residuals divided by $n - 2$. We can calculate this in cell J23 by using Excel's SUMSQ (sum of squares) function:

$$=\text{SQRT(SUMSQ(ResidSales)/40)}$$

The R^2 value of 0.988 indicates that there is a very high correlation between the actual and fitted sales values. In other words, the exponential fit is a very good one. However, the s_e value of 159.698 (in millions of dollars) indicates that forecasts based on this exponential fit could still be fairly far off.   ■

Whenever we observe a time series that is increasing at an increasing rate (or decreasing at a decreasing rate), an exponential trend model is worth trying. The key to the analysis is to regress the *logarithm* of the time series variable versus time. The coefficient of time, written as a percentage, is then the percentage increase (if positive) or decrease (if negative) per period. However, as we saw in the example, the typical regression measures, R^2 and s_e, should be recalculated in original units. If they are quoted exactly as they appear in a regression output, they (especially s_e) can be very misleading.

PROBLEMS

Level A

28 The file P13_1.XLS contains the number of airline tickets sold by the CareFree Travel Agency each month from January 1995 to December 1998.

    a Does a linear trend appear to fit these data well? If so, estimate and interpret the linear-trend model for this time series. Also, interpret the R^2 and s_e values.

    b Provide an indication of the typical forecast error generated by the estimated model in part **a**.

    c Is there evidence of some seasonal pattern in these sales data? If so, characterize the seasonal pattern.

29 The file P13_29.XLS contains the daily closing prices of Wal-Mart stock from July 21, 1997 to July 20, 1998. Does an exponential trend fit these data well? If so, estimate and interpret the exponential-trend model for this time series. Also, interpret the R^2 and s_e values.

30 This file P13_30.XLS contains annual data on the amount of life insurance in force in the United States from 1945 to 1981. Fit an exponential growth curve to these data. Write a short report to summarize your findings.

31 The file P13_31.XLS contains 5 years of monthly data on sales (number of units sold) for a particular company. The data set begins in January 1995. The company suspects that except for random noise, its sales are growing by a constant *percentage* each month and that they will continue to do so for at least the near future.

    a Explain briefly whether the plot of the series visually supports the company's suspicion.

    b Fit the appropriate regression model to the data. Report the resulting equation and state explicitly what it says about the percentage growth per month.

    c What are the RMSE and MAPE for the forecast model in part **b**? In words, what do they measure? Considering their magnitudes, does the model seem to be doing a good job?

    d In words, how does the model make forecasts for future months? Specifically, if you had the forecast value for December 1999 (the last month in the data set), what simple arithmetic could you use to obtain forecasts for the next few months?

32 The file P13_32.XLS contains quarterly data on GDP from 1966-I to 1991-IV. (The data are expressed in billions of current dollars, they are seasonally adjusted, and they represent annualized rates.)

    a Look at a time series plot of GDP. Does it suggest a linear relationship; an exponential relationship?

    b Use regression to estimate an exponential relationship between GDP and Time. Interpret the associated "constant" term and the "slope" term. Would you say that the fit is good?

Level B

33 The file P13_33.XLS contains monthly time series data on corporate bond yields from January 1975 to March 1992. These are averages of daily figures, and each is expressed as an annual rate. The variables are:

    ■   Yield: average yield on corporate bonds

    ■   YieldAAA: average yield on AAA bonds

    ■   YieldAA: average yield on AA bonds

    ■   YieldA: average yield on A bonds

    ■   YieldBAA: average yield on BAA bonds

    If you examine the Yield variable, you will notice that the autocorrelations of the series are not only large for many lags, but that the lag 1 autocorrelation of the *differences* is significant. This is very common. It means that the series is not a random walk and that it is probably possible to provide a better forecast than the "naive" forecast from the random walk model. Here is the idea. The large lag 1 autocorrelation of the differences means that the differences are related to the first lag of the differences. This relationship can be estimated by creating the difference variable and a lag of it, then regressing the former on the latter, and finally using this information to forecast the original Yield variable.

a Verify that the autocorrelations are as described above, and form the difference variable and the first lag of it. Call these DYield and L1DYield (where D is for difference, L1 is for first lag).

b Run a regression with DYield as the response variable and L1DYield as the single explanatory variable. In terms of the original variable Yield, this equation can be written as

$$\text{Yield}_t - \text{Yield}_{t-1} = a + b(\text{Yield}_{t-1} - \text{Yield}_{t-2})$$

Solving for Yield_t, this is equivalent to the following equation that can be used for forecasting:

$$\text{Yield}_t = a + (1 + b)\text{Yield}_{t-1} - b\text{Yield}_{t-2}$$

Try it—that is, try forecasting April 1992 from the known February and March 1992 values. How might you forecast the May 1992 and June 1992 values? (*Hint*: If you do not have an *observed* value to use in the right side of the equation, use a forecasted value.)

c The autocorrelation structure led us to the equation in part **b**. That is, the autocorrelations of the original series took a long time to die down, so we looked at the autocorrelations of the differences, and the large spike at lag 1 led to regressing L1DYield on DYield. In turn, this led ultimately to an equation for Yield_t in terms of its first two lags. Now see what you would have obtained if you had tried regressing Yield_t on its first two lags in the first place—that is, if you had used regression to estimate the equation

$$\text{Yield}_t = a + b_1\text{Yield}_{t-1} + b_2\text{Yield}_{t-2}$$

When you use multiple regression to estimate this equation, do you get the same equation as in part **b?**

34 The unit sales of a new drug for the first 25 months after its introduction to the marketplace are recorded in the file P13_25.XLS.

a Estimate a linear trend equation using the given data. How well does the linear trend fit these data? Are the residuals from this linear trend model *random*?

b If the residuals from this linear trend model are *not* random, propose another regression-based trend model that more adequately explains the long-term trend in this time series. Estimate the alternative model(s) using the given data. Check the residuals from the model(s) for randomness. Summarize your findings.

c Given the best estimated model of the trend in this time series, interpret R^2 and s_e. ∎

13.7 Moving Averages

Perhaps the simplest and one of the most frequently used extrapolation methods is the method of **moving averages**. To implement the moving averages method, we first choose a **span**, the number of terms in each moving average. Let's say the data are monthly and we choose a span of 6 months. Then the forecast of next month's value is the average of the most recent 6 months' values. For example, we average January–June to forecast July, we average February–July to forecast August, and so on. This procedure is the reason for the term *moving* averages.

The role of the span is important. If the span is large—say, 12 months—then many observations go into each average, and extreme values have relatively little effect on the forecasts. The resulting series of forecasts will be much smoother than the original series. (For this reason, the moving average method is called a **smoothing** method.) In contrast, if the span is small—say, 3 months—then extreme observations have a larger effect on the forecasts, and the forecast series will be much less smooth. In the extreme, if the span is 1, there is no smoothing effect at all. The method simply forecasts next month's value to be the same as the current month's value. (This is often called the **naive** forecasting model. It is a special case of the random walk model we discussed earlier, with the mean difference equal to zero.)

What span should we use? This requires some judgment. If we believe the ups and downs in the series are random noise, then we don't want future forecasts to react too quickly to these ups and downs, and we should use a relatively large span. But if we want to track every little zigzag—under the belief that each up or down is predictable—then we should use a smaller span. We shouldn't be fooled, however, by a plot of the (smoothed) forecast series superimposed on the original series. This graph will almost always look better when a small span is used, because the forecast series will appear to track the original series better. Does this mean it will always provide better future forecasts? Not necessarily. There is little point in tracking random ups and downs closely if they represent unpredictable noise.

The following example, a continuation of Example 13.4, illustrates the use of moving averages on the Dow Jones index.

EXAMPLE 13.8

We again look at the Dow Jones monthly data from January 1988 through March 1992. (See the file DOW.XLS.) How well do moving averages track this series when the span is 3 months; when the span is 12 months? What about future forecasts, that is, beyond March 1992?

Solution

Although the moving averages method is quite easy to implement in Excel—we just form an average of the appropriate span and copy it down—it can be tedious. Therefore, we call on the Forecasting procedure of StatPro. Actually, this procedure is fairly general in that it allows us to forecast with several methods, either with or without taking seasonality into account. Since this is our first exposure to this procedure, we'll go through it in some detail in this example. In later examples, we'll mention some of its other capabilities.

To use the StatPro Forecasting procedure, the cursor needs to be in a data set with time series data. The data set can contain a "date" variable (for labeling charts), but this is not required. We use the StatPro/Forecasting menu item and eventually choose Dow as the variable to analyze. We then see several dialog boxes, the first of which appears in Figure 13.29 (page 738). Here we specify the timing. Are the data annual, quarterly, and so on, and (if relevant) what year and period do they begin? We can also elect to "hold out" a subset of the data for validation purposes, and we can specify how many periods to forecast into the future. (If we hold out several periods at the end of the data set for validation, then any model that is built is estimated only for the non-hold-out observations, and summary measures are reported for the non-hold-out and hold-out subsets separately.) Figure 13.29 shows that the Dow data are monthly, they begin in the first month of 1988, we do not hold out any data for validation, and we want to forecast 12 months into the future.

In the next dialog box, shown in Figure 13.30, we specify which forecasting method to use and any parameters of that method. Here we are using the moving averages method with a span of 3 (or 12). Also, we indicate in this dialog box that the data are *not* seasonal. We next see a dialog box that allows us to request various time series plots, and finally we get the usual choice of whether to report the output on the current worksheet or a new worksheet.

The output consists of several parts, as shown in Figures 13.31–13.34 (pages 739–740). First, the forecasts and forecast errors are shown for the historical period of the data. Actually, with moving averages we lose some forecasts at the beginning of the period. For

FIGURE 13.29   Timing Dialog Box for StatPro Forecasting Procedure

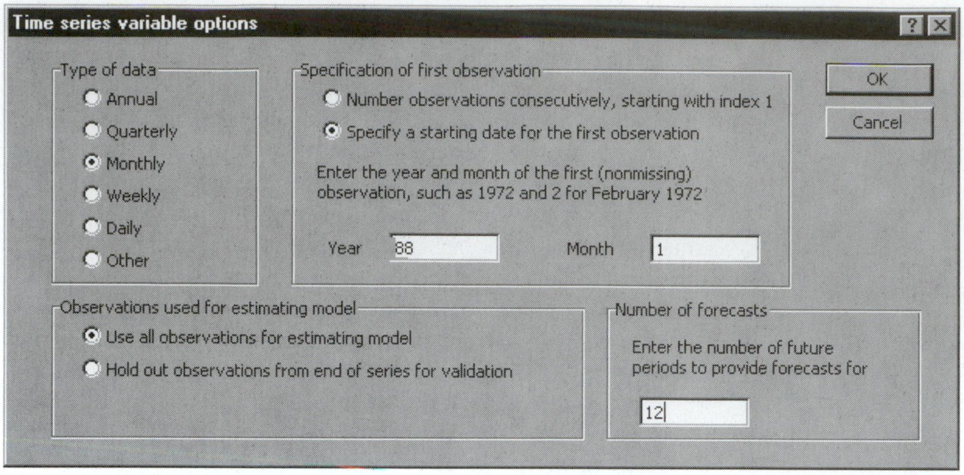

FIGURE 13.30   Method Dialog Box for StatPro Forecasting Procedure

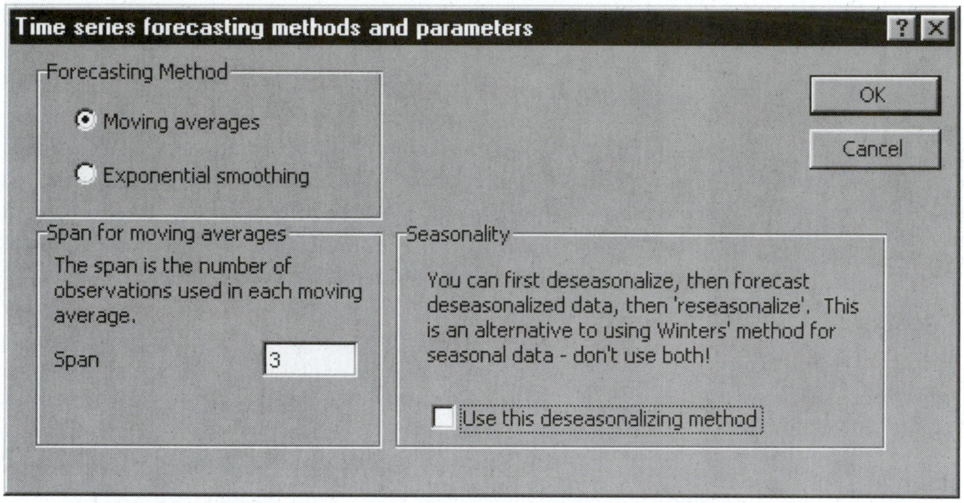

example, we lose three when the span is 3 because we don't have enough *previous* data to calculate these early averages. If we ask for *future* forecasts, they are shown in red at the bottom of the data series. Of course, there are no accompanying forecast errors because we don't yet have observations for these future periods. To the left of all this, we see the summary measures MAE, RMSE, and MAPE of the forecast errors. Finally, if we ask for any time series plots, these appear on separate sheets.

The essence of the forecasting method is very simple and is captured in column F of Figure 13.31 (for a span of 3). It uses the formula

$$=\text{AVERAGE}(\$E2:\$E4)$$

in cell F5, which is then copied down. The forecast errors are then just the differences between columns E and F. For the future periods, the forecast formulas use observations when they are available. If they are not available, previous forecasts are used. For example, the value in cell F54, the forecast for May 1992, is the average of the *observed* values in

FIGURE 13.31 Moving Averages Output with Span 3

	A	B	C	D	E	F	G
1	*Forecasting results for Dow*			Date	Observation	Forecast	Error
2				Jan-88	1947.350		
3	**Moving averages**			Feb-88	1980.650		
4				Mar-88	2044.310		
5	Span	3		Apr-88	2036.130	1990.770	45.360
6				May-88	1988.910	2020.363	-31.453
7	**Estimation period**			Jun-88	2104.940	2023.117	81.823
8				Jul-88	2104.220	2043.327	60.893
9	MAE	94.9825		Aug-88	2051.290	2066.023	-14.733
10	RMSE	121.8219		Sep-88	2080.060	2086.817	-6.757
11	MAPE	3.57%		Oct-88	2144.310	2078.523	65.787
12				Nov-88	2099.040	2091.887	7.153
13				Dec-88	2148.580	2107.803	40.777
49				Dec-91	2958.640	3005.403	-46.763
50				Jan-92	3227.060	2988.167	238.893
51				Feb-92	3257.270	3057.273	199.997
52				Mar-92	3247.420	3147.657	99.763
53				Apr-92		3243.917	
54				May-92		3249.536	
55				Jun-92		3246.957	
56				Jul-92		3246.803	
57				Aug-92		3247.765	
58				Sep-92		3247.175	
59				Oct-92		3247.248	
60				Nov-92		3247.396	
61				Dec-92		3247.273	
62				Jan-93		3247.306	
63				Feb-93		3247.325	
64				Mar-93		3247.301	

FIGURE 13.32 Moving Averages Output with Span 12

	A	B	C	D	E	F	G
1	*Forecasting results for Dow*			Date	Observation	Forecast	Error
2				Jan-88	1947.350		
3	**Moving averages**			Feb-88	1980.650		
4				Mar-88	2044.310		
5	Span	12		Apr-88	2036.130		
6				May-88	1988.910		
7	**Estimation period**			Jun-88	2104.940		
8				Jul-88	2104.220		
9	MAE	210.5725		Aug-88	2051.290		
10	RMSE	226.5329		Sep-88	2080.060		
11	MAPE	7.71%		Oct-88	2144.310		
12				Nov-88	2099.040		
13				Dec-88	2148.580		
49				Dec-91	2958.640	2900.355	58.285
50				Jan-92	3227.060	2929.332	297.728
51				Feb-92	3257.270	2982.620	274.650
52				Mar-92	3247.420	3015.473	231.948
53				Apr-92		3042.748	
54				May-92		3052.516	
55				Jun-92		3062.857	
56				Jul-92		3070.750	
57				Aug-92		3078.463	
58				Sep-92		3084.495	
59				Oct-92		3090.673	
60				Nov-92		3096.584	
61				Dec-92		3105.790	
62				Jan-93		3118.052	
63				Feb-93		3108.968	
64				Mar-93		3096.610	

February and March and the *forecasted* value in April. Finally, the summary formulas in the range B9:B11 implement equations (13.1), (13.2), and (13.3).[8]

The plots in Figures 13.33 and 13.34 show the behavior of the forecasts. The forecasts with span 3 appear to track the data better, whereas the forecast series with span 12 is considerably smoother—it reacts less to the ups and downs of the series. The summary measures MAE, RMSE, and MAPE confirm that moving averages with span 3 forecast the *known* observations better. For example, the forecasts are off by about 3.6% with span 3, versus 7.7% with span 12. Nevertheless, there is no guarantee that a span of 3 is better for forecasting *future* observations.

FIGURE 13.33   **Moving Averages Forecasts with Span 3**

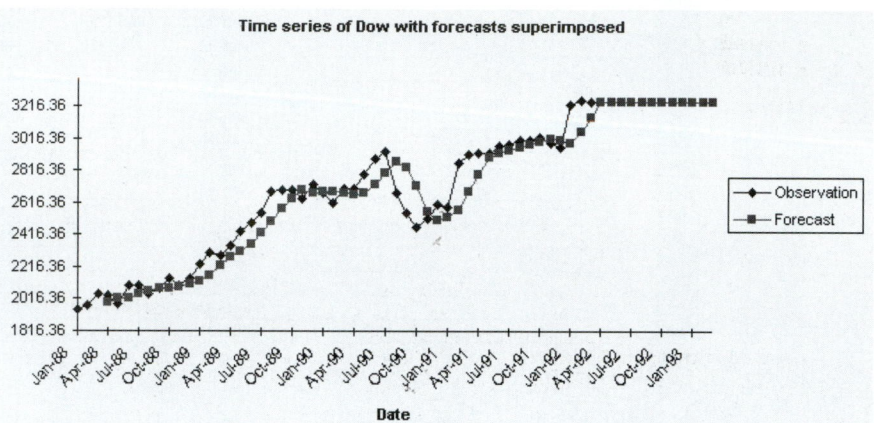

FIGURE 13.34   **Moving Averages Forecasts with Span 12**

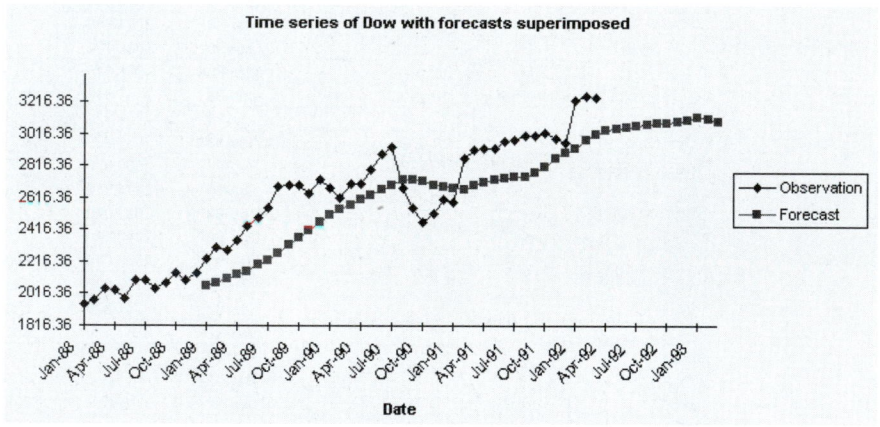

The moving average method we have presented is the simplest of a group of moving average methods used by professional forecasters. We *smoothed* exactly once; that is, we

---

[8] If you want to learn some interesting features of Excel, take a close look at the formulas in these three cells. The formulas with curly brackets around them are *array* formulas. To enter them, type the formula without the curly brackets and then press Ctrl-Shift-Enter.

took moving averages of several observations at a time and used these as forecasts. More complex methods smooth more than once, basically to get rid of random noise. They take moving averages, then moving averages of these moving averages, and so on for several stages. This can become quite complex, but the objective is quite simple—to smooth the data so that we can see underlying patterns.

PROBLEMS

Level A

35 The file P13_9.XLS contains the daily closing prices of American Express stock from July 21, 1997 to July 20, 1998.

a Using a span of 3 days, forecast the price of this stock on July 21, 1998 with the moving average method. How well does this method with span 3 forecast the known observations in this data set?

b Repeat part **a** with a span of 10.

c Which of these two spans appears to be more appropriate? Explain your choice.

36 The closing value of the AMEX Airline Index for each trading day from July 21, 1997 to July 21, 1998 is given in the file P13_10.XLS.

a How well does the moving average method track this series when the span is 4 days; when the span is 12 days?

b Using the more appropriate span, forecast the closing value of this index on July 22, 1998 with the moving average method.

37 The closing value of the Dow Jones Industrial Index for each trading day from March 31, 1998 to July 21, 1998 is provided in the file P13_12.XLS.

a Using a span of 2 days, forecast the price of this stock on July 22, 1998 with the moving average method. How well does the moving average method with span 2 forecast the known observations in this data set?

b Repeat part **a** with a span of 5 days; with a span of 15 days.

c Which of these three spans appears to be most appropriate? Explain your choice.

38 The file P13_29.XLS contains the daily closing prices of Wal-Mart stock from July 21, 1997 to July 20, 1998. Use the moving average method with a carefully chosen span to forecast this time series for July 21 through July 24 of 1998. Defend your choice of the span used.

39 The Consumer Confidence Index attempts to measure people's feelings about general business conditions, employment opportunities, and their own income prospects. The file P2_28.XLS contains the annual average values of the CCI for the period 1967–1996. Use the moving average method with a carefully chosen span to forecast this time series in 1997 and 1998. Defend your choice of the span used here.

Level B

40 Consider the file P2_37.XLS, which contains total monthly U.S. retail sales data for the years 1993–1996. While retaining the final 6 months of observations for validation purposes, use the method of moving averages with a carefully chosen span to forecast U.S. retail sales in 1997. Comment on the performance of your model. What makes this time series more challenging to forecast?

41 Consider a random walk model with the following equation: $Y_t = Y_{t-1} + \varepsilon_t$, where ε_t is a random series with mean 0 and standard deviation 1. Specify a moving average model that is equivalent to this random walk model. In particular, what is the appropriate size of the span in the equivalent moving average model? Describe the smoothing effect of this span choice. ■

Exponential Smoothing

There are two possible criticisms of the moving averages method. First, it puts equal weight on each value in a typical moving average when making a forecast. Many people would argue that if next month's forecast is to be based on the previous 12 months' observations, then more weight ought to be placed on the more recent observations. The second criticism is that the moving averages method requires a lot of data storage. This is particularly true for companies that routinely make forecasts of hundreds or even thousands of items. If 12-month moving averages are used for 1000 items, then 12,000 values are needed for next month's forecasts. This may or may not be a concern considering today's relatively inexpensive computer storage capabilities.

Exponential smoothing is a method that addresses both of these criticisms. It bases its forecasts on a weighted average of past observations, with more weight put on the more recent observations, and it requires very little data storage. In addition, it is not difficult for most business people to understand, at least conceptually. Therefore, this method finds widespread use in the business world, particularly when frequent and automatic forecasts of many items are required.

There are many versions of exponential smoothing. The simplest is called, surprisingly enough, **simple** exponential smoothing. It is relevant when there is no pronounced trend or seasonality in the series. If there is a trend but no seasonality, then **Holt's** method is applicable. If, in addition, there is seasonality, then **Winters'** method can be used. This does not exhaust the list of exponential smoothing models—researchers have invented many other variations—but these three models will suffice for us.

13.8.1 Simple Exponential Smoothing

We now examine simple exponential smoothing in some detail. We first introduce two new terms. Every exponential model has at least one **smoothing constant**, which is always between 0 and 1. Simple exponential smoothing has a single smoothing constant denoted by α. (Its role will be discussed shortly.) The second new term is L_t, called the **level** of the series at time t. This value is not observable but can only be estimated. Essentially, it is where we think the series would be at time t if there were no random noise. Then the simple exponential smoothing method is defined by the following two equations, where F_{t+k} is the forecast of Y_{t+k} made at time t:

$$L_t = \alpha Y_t + (1 - \alpha)L_{t-1} \tag{13.15}$$

$$F_{t+k} = L_t \tag{13.16}$$

Even though you usually won't have to substitute into these equations manually, you should understand what they say. Equation (13.15) shows how to update the estimate of the level. It is a weighted average of the current observation, Y_t, and the previous level, L_{t-1}, with respective weights α and $1 - \alpha$. Equation (13.16) shows how forecasts are made. It says that the k-period-ahead forecast, F_{t+k}, made of Y_{t+k} in period t is the most recently estimated level, L_t. This is the *same* for any value of $k \geq 1$. The idea is that in simple exponential smoothing, we believe that the series is not really going anywhere. So as soon as we estimate where the series ought to be in period t (if it weren't for random noise), we forecast that this is where it will also be in any future period.

The smoothing constant α is analogous to the span in moving averages. There are two ways to see this. The first way is to rewrite equation (13.15), using the fact that the forecast error, E_t, made in forecasting Y_t at time $t-1$ is $Y_t - F_t = Y_t - L_{t-1}$. A bit of algebra then gives

$$L_t = L_{t-1} + \alpha E_t \tag{13.17}$$

This says that the next estimate of the level is adjusted from the previous estimate by adding a multiple of the most recent forecast error. This makes sense. If our previous forecast was too high, then E_t is negative, and we adjust the estimate of the level downward. The opposite is true if our previous forecast was too low. However, equation (13.17) says that we do not adjust by the entire magnitude of E_t, but only by a fraction of it. If α is small, say $\alpha = 0.1$, then the adjustment is minor; if α is close to 1, the adjustment is large. So if we want to react quickly to movements in the series, we choose a large α; otherwise, we choose a small α.

Another way to see the effect of α is to substitute recursively into the equation for L_t. If you are willing to go through some algebra, you can verify that L_t satisfies

$$L_t = \alpha Y_t + \alpha(1-\alpha)Y_{t-1} + \alpha(1-\alpha)^2 Y_{t-2} + \alpha(1-\alpha)^3 Y_{t-3} + \cdots \tag{13.18}$$

where this sum extends back to the first observation at time $t = 1$. Equation (13.18) shows how the exponentially smoothed forecast is a weighted average of previous observations. Furthermore, because $1 - \alpha$ is less than 1, the weights on the Y's decrease from time t backward. Therefore, if α is close to 0, then $1 - \alpha$ is close to 1 and the weights decrease very slowly. In other words, observations from the distant past continue to have a large influence on the next forecast. This means that the graph of the forecasts will be relatively smooth, just as with a large span in the moving averages method. But when α is close to 1, the weights decrease rapidly, and only very recent observations have much influence on the next forecast. In this case forecasts react quickly to sudden changes in the series.

What value of α should we use? There is no universally accepted answer to this question. Some practitioners recommend always using a value around 0.1 or 0.2. Others recommend experimenting with different values of α until a measure such as RMSE or MAPE is minimized. Some packages even have an optimization feature to find this optimal value of α. (This is the case with StatPro.) But just as we discussed in the moving averages section, the value of α that tracks the historical series most closely does not necessarily guarantee the most accurate *future* forecasts.

EXAMPLE 13.9

The file EXXON.XLS contains data on quarterly sales (in millions of dollars) for the period from 1986 through the second quarter of 1996. A time series chart of these sales in Figure 13.35 (page 744) shows that there is some evidence of an upward trend in the early years, but that there is no obvious trend during the 1990s. Does a simple exponential smoothing model track these data well? How do the forecasts depend on the smoothing constant α?

Solution

We will use StatPro to implement the simple exponential smoothing model, specifically equations (13.15) and (13.16). We do this again with the StatPro/Forecasting menu item. We first specify that the data are quarterly, beginning in quarter 1 of 1986, we do not hold out any of the data for validation, and we ask for 8 quarters of future forecasts. We then fill out the next dialog box as shown in Figure 13.36. That is, we select the exponential smoothing option in the upper left, select the Simple option, choose a smoothing constant (0.2 was chosen here, but any other value could be chosen) and elect not to optimize, and

FIGURE 13.35   Time Series Plot of Exxon Sales

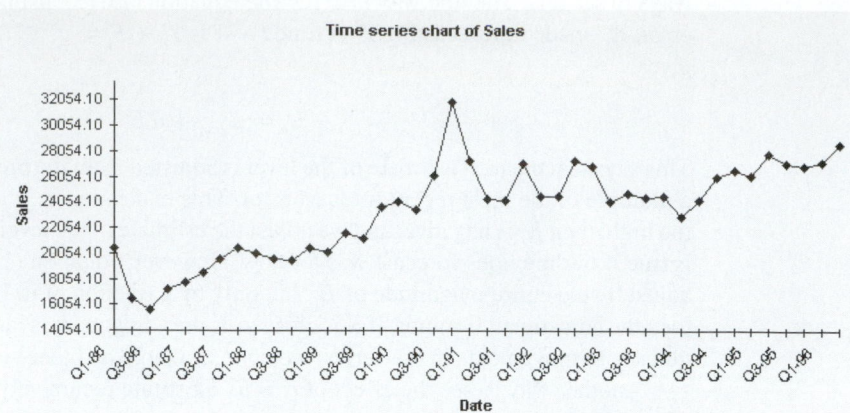

FIGURE 13.36   Method Dialog Box for StatPro Forecasting Procedure

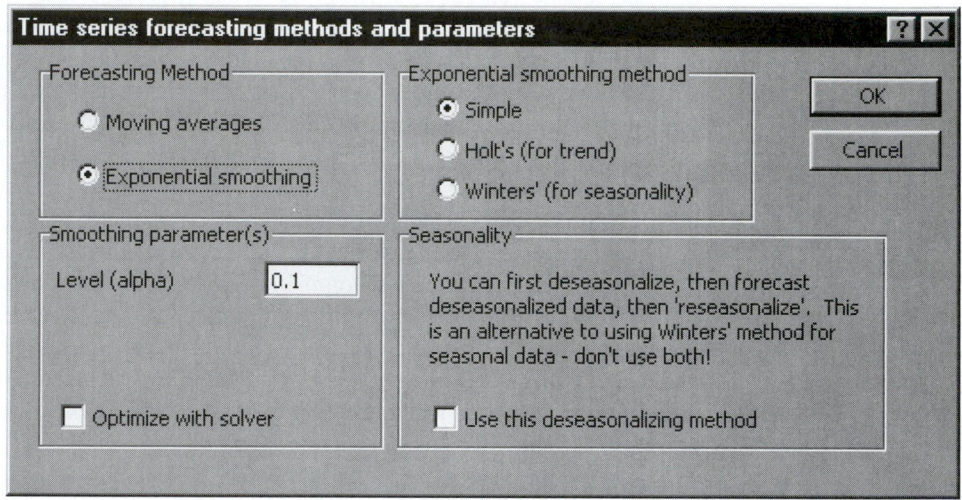

specify that the data are not seasonal. On the next dialog sheet we ask for time series charts of the series with the forecasts superimposed and the series of forecast errors.

The results appear in Figures 13.37, 13.38, and 13.39. The heart of the method takes place in columns F, G, and H of Figure 13.37. Column F calculates the smoothed levels (L_t) from equation (13.15), column G calculates the forecasts (F_t) from equation (13.16), and column H calculates the forecast errors (E_t) as the observed values minus the forecasts. For example, the formulas in row 6 are

$$=Alpha*E6+(1-Alpha)*F5$$

$$=F5$$

and

$$=E6-G6$$

FIGURE 13.37 Simple Exponential Smoothing Output

	A	B	C	D	E	F	G	H
1	*Forecasting results for Sales*			Date	Observation	SmLevel	Forecast	Error
2				Q1-86	20468.003	20468.003		
3	**Simple exponential smoothing**			Q2-86	16529.003	19680.203	20468.003	-3939.000
4				Q3-86	15673.003	18878.763	19680.203	-4007.200
5	Smoothing constant(s)			Q4-86	17218.003	18546.611	18878.763	-1660.760
6	Level	0.200		Q1-87	17781.003	18393.489	18546.611	-765.608
7				Q2-87	18588.003	18432.392	18393.489	194.514
8	**Estimation period**			Q3-87	19600.003	18665.914	18432.392	1167.611
9				Q4-87	20447.003	19022.132	18665.914	1781.089
10	MAE	1730.2410		Q1-88	20045.003	19226.706	19022.132	1022.871
11	RMSE	2324.5773		Q2-88	19614.003	19304.166	19226.706	387.297
12	MAPE	7.37%		Q3-88	19465.003	19336.333	19304.166	160.837
13				Q4-88	20433.667	19555.667	19336.333	1096.670
43				Q2-96	28561.000	26855.615	26429.269	2131.731
44				Q3-96			26855.615	
45				Q4-96			26855.615	
46				Q1-97			26855.615	
47				Q2-97			26855.615	
48				Q3-97			26855.615	
49				Q4-97			26855.615	
50				Q1-98			26855.615	
51				Q2-98			26855.615	

FIGURE 13.38 Plot of Forecasts from Simple Exponential Smoothing

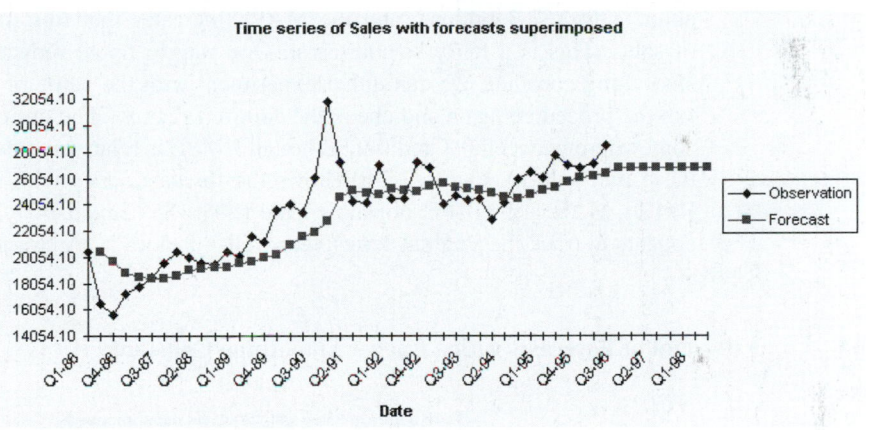

FIGURE 13.39 Plot of Forecast Errors from Simple Exponential Smoothing

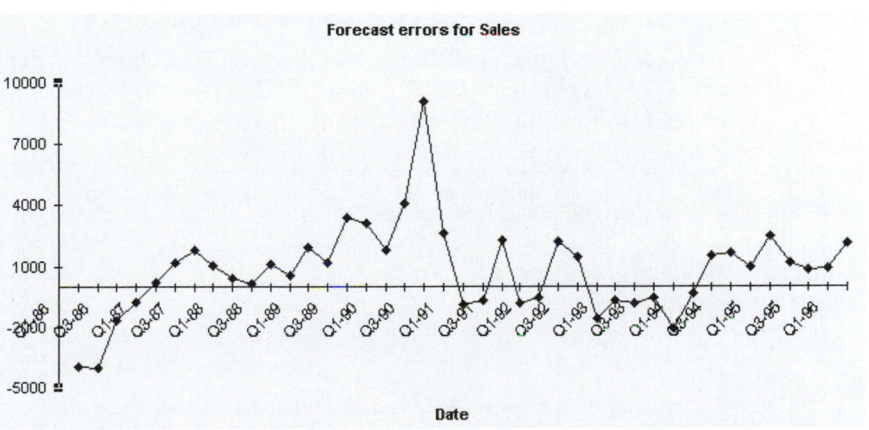

One exception to this scheme is in row 2. Every exponential smoothing method requires *initial* values, in this case the initial smoothed level in cell F2. There is no way to calculate this value, L_1, from equation (13.15) because the *previous* value, L_0, is unknown. Different implementations of exponential smoothing initialize in different ways. We have simply set L_1 equal to Y_1 (in cell E2). The effect of initializing in different ways is usually minimal because any effect of early data is usually washed out as we forecast into the future. In the present example, data from 1986 have little effect on forecasts of 1996 and beyond.

Note that the 8 future forecasts (rows 44 down) are all equal to the last calculated smoothed level, the one for second quarter of 1996 in cell F43. The fact that these remain constant is a consequence of the assumption behind *simple* exponential smoothing, namely, that the series is not really going anywhere. Therefore, the last smoothed level is the best indication of future values of the series we have.

Figure 13.38 shows the forecast series superimposed on the original series. We see the obvious smoothing effect of a relatively small α level. The forecasts don't track the series very well, but if the various zigzags in the original series are really random noise, then perhaps we don't want the forecasts to track these random ups and downs too closely. Perhaps we instead prefer a forecast series that emphasizes the basic underlying pattern. Figure 13.39 shows the time series of forecast errors. Although these errors are sometimes quite large, they do appear to be fairly random.

We see several summary measures of the forecast errors from Figure 13.37. The RMSE and MAE indicate that the forecasts from this model are typically off by a magnitude of about 2300 ($2.3 billion), and the MAPE indicates that this magnitude is about 7.4% of sales. This is a fairly sizable error. One way to try to reduce it is to use a different smoothing constant. We can either experiment with the value of α in cell B6, or we can run the procedure again and check the "optimize" box.[9] The optimal α for this example is somewhere between 0.8 and 0.9 (although RMSE is relatively constant for any α between these two values). Figure 13.40 shows the forecast series with $\alpha = 0.85$. (Its values of RMSE, MAE, and MAPE, not shown, are 1885, 1355, and 5.74%.) The forecast series now appears to track the original series very well—or does it? A closer look shows that we are

FIGURE 13.40 **Plot of Forecasts with a Larger Smoothing Constant**

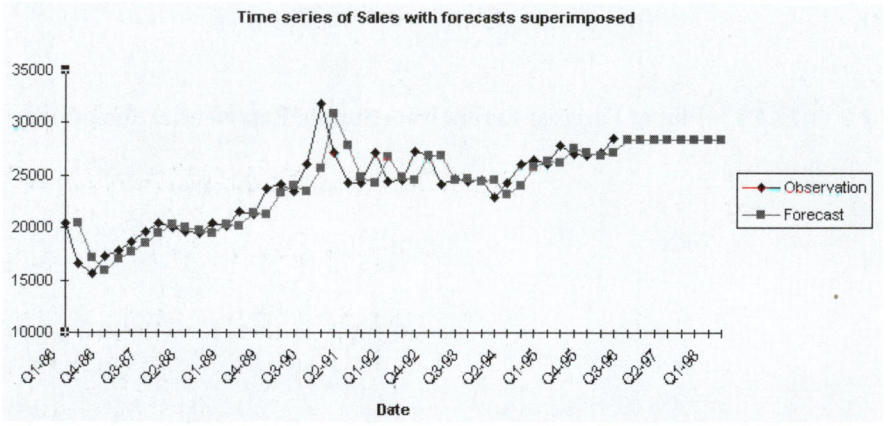

[9]This runs Excel's Solver to find the value of α that minimizes RMSE, subject to $0 \leq \alpha \leq 1$. Sometimes, as in the current example, the Solver will not converge to any solution if we start at the default value $\alpha = 0.1$. In this case it is best to try a different initial value of α.

essentially forecasting each quarter's sales value by the *previous* sales value. Therefore, any time the series changes much from one quarter to the next, the forecast will be way off. There is no doubt that $\alpha = 0.85$ gives lower summary measures for the forecast errors, but it is possibly reacting too quickly to random noise and might not really be showing us the basic underlying pattern of sales that we see with $\alpha = 0.2$. ■

13.8.2 Holt's Model for Trend

The simple exponential smoothing model generally works well if there is no obvious trend in the series. But if there is a trend, then this method consistently lags behind it. For example, if the series is constantly increasing, simple exponential smoothing forecasts will be consistently low. Holt's method rectifies this by dealing with trend explicitly. In addition to the level of the series, L_t, Holt's method includes a trend term, T_t, and a corresponding smoothing constant β. The interpretation of L_t is exactly as before. The interpretation of T_t is that it represents an estimate of the change in the series from one period to the next. The equations for Holt's model are as follows.

$$L_t = \alpha Y_t + (1 - \alpha)(L_{t-1} + T_{t-1}) \qquad \textbf{(13.19)}$$

$$T_t = \beta(L_t - L_{t-1}) + (1 - \beta)T_{t-1} \qquad \textbf{(13.20)}$$

$$F_{t+k} = L_t + kT_t \qquad \textbf{(13.21)}$$

These equations are not as bad as they look. (And don't forget that the computer typically does all of the calculations for you.) Equation (13.19) says that the updated level is a weighted average of the current observation and the previous level plus the estimated change. Equation (13.20) says that the updated trend term is a weighted average of the difference between two consecutive levels and the previous trend term. Finally, equation (13.21) says that the k-period-ahead forecast made in period t is the estimated level plus k times the estimated change per period.

Everything we said about α for simple exponential smoothing applies to both α and β in Holt's model. The new smoothing constant β controls how quickly the method reacts to perceived changes in the trend. If β is small, the method reacts slowly. If it is large, the method reacts more quickly. Of course, there are now two smoothing constants to select. Some practitioners suggest using a small value of α (0.1 to 0.2, say) and setting β equal to α. Others suggest using an optimization option (available in StatPro) to select the "best" smoothing constants. We illustrate the possibilities in the following example.

EXAMPLE 13.10

We return to the Dow Jones data from Examples 13.4 and 13.8. (See the file DOW.XLS.) Again, these are average monthly closing prices from January 1988 through March 1992. Recall that there is a definite upward trend in this series. In this example we investigate whether simple exponential smoothing can capture the upward trend. Then we see whether Holt's exponential smoothing method can make an improvement.

Solution

The graph in Figure 13.41 (page 748) shows how a simple exponential smoothing model handles this trend, using $\alpha = 0.2$. Its summary error measures are not bad (MAPE is 5.38%,

FIGURE 13.41 **Plot of Forecasts from Simple Exponential Smoothing**

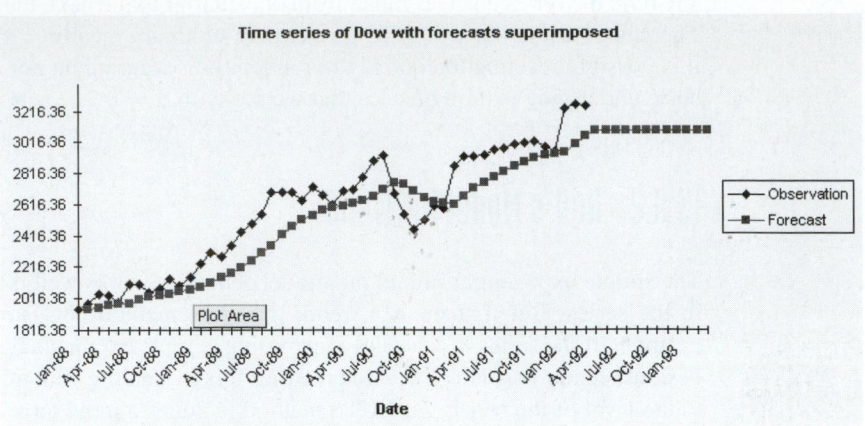

FIGURE 13.42 **Plot of Forecasts from Holt's Method**

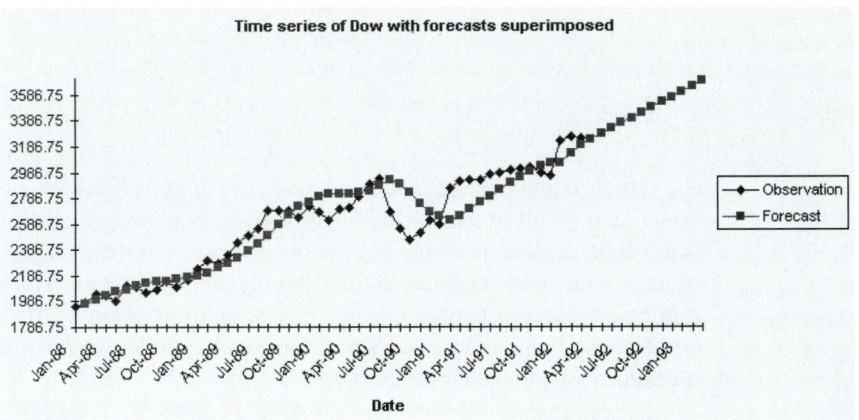

for example), but the forecast series is obviously lagging behind the original series. Also, the forecasts for the next 12 months are constant, because no trend is built into the model. In contrast, the graph in Figure 13.42 shows forecasts from Holt's model with $\alpha = \beta = 0.2$. The forecasts are still far from perfect (MAPE is now 4.01%), but at least the upward trend has been captured. This model appears likely to make better future forecasts than the simple exponential smoothing model.

To produce the output from Holt's method with StatPro (part of which is shown in Figure 13.43), we proceed exactly as with the simple exponential smoothing procedure. The only difference is that we now get to choose two smoothing parameters. The output in Figure 13.43 is also very similar to simple exponential smoothing output, except that there is now an extra column (column G) for the estimated trend. You can check that the formulas in columns F, G, and H implement equations (13.19), (13.20), and (13.21) for Holt's method. As before, there is an initialization problem in row 2. These require values of L_1 and T_1 to get the method started. Different implementations of Holt's method obtain these initial values in slightly different ways, but the effect is fairly minimal in most cases. (You can check cells F2 and G2 to see how StatPro does it.)

Before leaving this example, we mention that the smoothing constants used above are *not* optimal. In fact, if we use StatPro's optimize option to find the best α (for simple

FIGURE 13.43   Output from Holt's Method

	A	B	C	D	E	F	G	H	I
1	*Forecasting results for Dow*			Date	Observation	SmLevel	SmTrend	Forecast	Error
2				Jan-88	1947.350	1947.350	25.492		
3	**Holt's exponential smoothing**			Feb-88	1980.650	1974.403	25.804	1972.842	7.808
4				Mar-88	2044.310	2009.028	27.568	2000.207	44.103
5	Smoothing constant(s)			Apr-88	2036.130	2036.503	27.549	2036.596	-0.466
6	Level	0.200		May-88	1988.910	2049.024	24.544	2064.052	-75.142
7	Trend	0.200		Jun-88	2104.940	2079.842	25.799	2073.567	31.373
8				Jul-88	2104.220	2105.356	25.742	2105.640	-1.420
9	**Estimation period**			Aug-88	2051.290	2115.137	22.549	2131.098	-79.808
10				Sep-88	2080.060	2126.161	20.244	2137.686	-57.626
11	MAE	106.3884		Oct-88	2144.310	2145.986	20.161	2146.405	-2.095
12	RMSE	136.9544		Nov-88	2099.040	2152.725	17.476	2166.147	-67.107
13	MAPE	4.01%		Dec-88	2148.580	2165.877	16.611	2170.202	-21.622
14				Jan-89	2234.680	2192.927	18.699	2182.489	52.191
49				Dec-91	2958.640	3035.074	26.527	3054.182	-95.542
50				Jan-92	3227.060	3094.693	33.146	3061.601	165.459
51				Feb-92	3257.270	3153.725	38.323	3127.839	129.431
52				Mar-92	3247.420	3203.122	40.530	3192.048	55.372
53				Apr-92				3243.660	
54				May-92				3284.198	
55				Jun-92				3324.736	
56				Jul-92				3365.274	
57				Aug-92				3405.811	
58				Sep-92				3446.349	
59				Oct-92				3486.887	
60				Nov-92				3527.425	
61				Dec-92				3567.963	
62				Jan-93				3608.500	
63				Feb-93				3649.038	
64				Mar-93				3689.576	

exponential smoothing) or the best α and β (for Holt's method), we find that the best α in both cases is 1.0 and the best β is 0.0. This is certainly not always the case for all time series data, but it occurs for these Dow data. According to these parameters, the best forecast of next month's value is this month's value plus a constant trend. In other words, the optimal exponential smoothing model is again a random walk model! ■

13.8.3 Winters' Model for Seasonality

So far we have said practically nothing about seasonality. Seasonality is defined as the consistent month-to-month (or quarter-to-quarter) differences that occur each year. For example, there is seasonality in beer sales—high in the summer months, lower in other months. Toy sales are also seasonal, with a huge peak in the months preceding Christmas. In fact, if you start thinking about time series variables that you are familiar with, the majority of them probably have some degree of seasonality.

How do we know whether there is seasonality in a time series? The easiest way is to check whether a plot of the time series has a *regular* pattern of ups and/or downs in particular months or quarters. Although random noise can sometimes obscure such a pattern, the seasonal pattern is usually fairly obvious. (Some time series software packages have special types of graphs for spotting seasonality, but we won't discuss these here.)

There are basically two extrapolation methods for dealing with seasonality. We can either use a model that takes seasonality into account explicitly and forecasts it, or we can first **deseasonalize** the data, then forecast the deseasonalized data, and finally adjust the forecasts for seasonality. The exponential smoothing model we discuss here, Winters' model, is of the first type. It attacks seasonality directly. In the next section we will see how to deseasonalize data so that the second approach can be used.

Seasonal models are usually classified as **additive** or **multiplicative**. Suppose that we have monthly data, and that the average of the 12 monthly values for a typical year is 150. An additive model finds seasonal indexes, one for each month, that we *add* to the monthly average, 150, to get a particular month's value. For example, if the index for March is 22, then we expect a typical March value to be $150 + 22 = 172$. If the seasonal index for September is -12, then we expect a typical September value to be $150 - 12 = 138$. A multiplicative model also finds seasonal indexes, but we *multiply* the monthly average by these indexes to get a particular month's value. Now if the index for March is 1.3, we expect a typical March value to be $150(1.3) = 195$. If the index for September is 0.9, then we expect a typical September value to be $150(0.9) = 135$.

Either an additive or a multiplicative model can be used to forecast seasonal data. However, because multiplicative models are somewhat easier to interpret (and have worked well in applications), we will focus on them. Note that the seasonal index in a multiplicative model can be interpreted as a percentage. Using the figures in the previous paragraph as an example, March tends to be 30% above the monthly average, whereas September tends to be 10% below it. Also, the seasonal indexes in a multiplicative model should sum to the number of seasons (12 for monthly data, 4 for quarterly data). Computer packages typically ensure that this happens.

We now turn to Winters' exponential smoothing model. It is very similar to Holt's model—it again has level and trend terms and corresponding smoothing constants α and β—but it also has seasonal indexes and a corresponding smoothing constant γ (gamma). This new smoothing constant γ controls how quickly the method reacts to perceived changes in the pattern of seasonality. If γ is small, the method reacts slowly. If it is large, the method reacts more quickly. As with Holt's model, there are equations for updating the level and trend terms, and there is one extra equation for updating the seasonal indexes. For completeness, we list these equations below, but they are clearly too complex for hand calculation and are best left to the computer. In equation (13.24), S_t refers to the multiplicative seasonal index for period t. In equations (13.22), (13.24), and (13.25), M refers to the number of seasons ($M = 4$ for quarterly data, $M = 12$ for monthly data).

$$L_t = \alpha \frac{Y_t}{S_{t-M}} + (1 - \alpha)(L_{t-1} + T_{t-1}) \qquad \textbf{(13.22)}$$

$$T_t = \beta(L_t - L_{t-1}) + (1 - \beta)T_{t-1} \qquad \textbf{(13.23)}$$

$$S_t = \gamma \frac{Y_t}{L_t} + (1 - \gamma)S_{t-M} \qquad \textbf{(13.24)}$$

$$F_{t+k} = (L_t + kT_t)S_{t+k-M} \qquad \textbf{(13.25)}$$

To see how the forecasting in equation (13.25) works, suppose we have observed data through June and want a forecast for the coming September, that is, a 3-month-ahead forecast. (In this case t refers to June and $t + k = t + 3$ refers to September.) Then we first add 3 times the current trend term to the current level. This gives a forecast for September that would be appropriate if there were no seasonality. Next, we multiply this forecast by the most recent estimate of September's seasonal index (the one from the previous September) to get the forecast for September. Of course, the computer does all of the arithmetic, but this is basically what it is doing. We illustrate the method in the following example.

EXAMPLE 13.11

The data in the COCACOLA.XLS file represent quarterly sales (in millions of dollars) for Coca Cola from quarter 1 of 1986 through quarter 2 of 1996. As we might expect, there has been an upward trend in sales during this period, and there is also a fairly regular seasonal pattern, as shown in Figure 13.44. Sales in the warmer quarters, 2 and 3, are consistently higher than in the colder quarters, 1 and 4. How well can Winters' method track this upward trend and seasonal pattern?

FIGURE 13.44 **Time Series Plot of Coca Cola Sales**

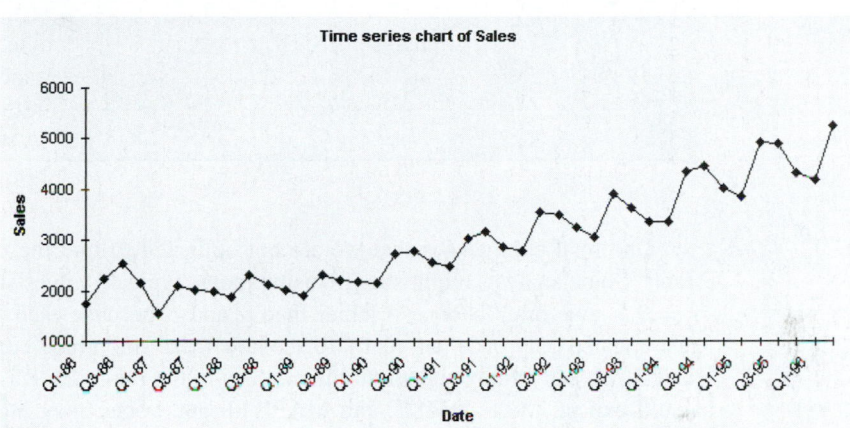

Solution

To use Winters' method with StatPro, we proceed exactly as with any of the other exponential smoothing methods. In particular, we fill out the second main dialog box as shown in Figure 13.45 (page 752). Note that the "Use this deseasonalizing method" option at the bottom right has been disabled. It wouldn't make much sense to deseasonalize *and* use Winters' method; we use one or the other. Also, we have elected to optimize the smoothing constants, but this is optional.

Parts of the output are shown in Figure 13.46. The following points are worth noting. (1) The optimal smoothing constants (those that minimize RMSE) are $\alpha = 1.0$, $\beta = 0.0$, and $\gamma = 0.244$. Intuitively, these mean that we react right away to changes in level, we never react to changes in trend, and we react fairly slowly to changes in the seasonal pattern. (2) If we ignore seasonality, the series is trending upward at a rate of 67.107 per quarter (see column G). This is our initial estimate of trend and, because $\beta = 0$, it never changes. (3) The seasonal pattern stays constant throughout this 10-year period. The seasonal indexes, shown in column H, are 0.879, 1.096, 1.064, and 0.961. For example, quarter 1 is about 12% below the yearly average, and quarter 2 is almost 10% above the yearly average. (4) The forecast series tracks the actual series quite well. For example, MAPE is 3.95%, meaning that on average our forecasts are only about 4% in error.

The plot of the forecasts superimposed on the original series, shown in Figure 13.47 (page 753), indicates that Winters' method clearly picks up the seasonal pattern and the upward trend and projects both of these into the future. (We asked for forecasts of 8 future quarters.) In later examples, we will investigate whether other seasonal forecasting methods can do this well.

FIGURE 13.45 Method Dialog Box from StatPro Forecasting Procedure

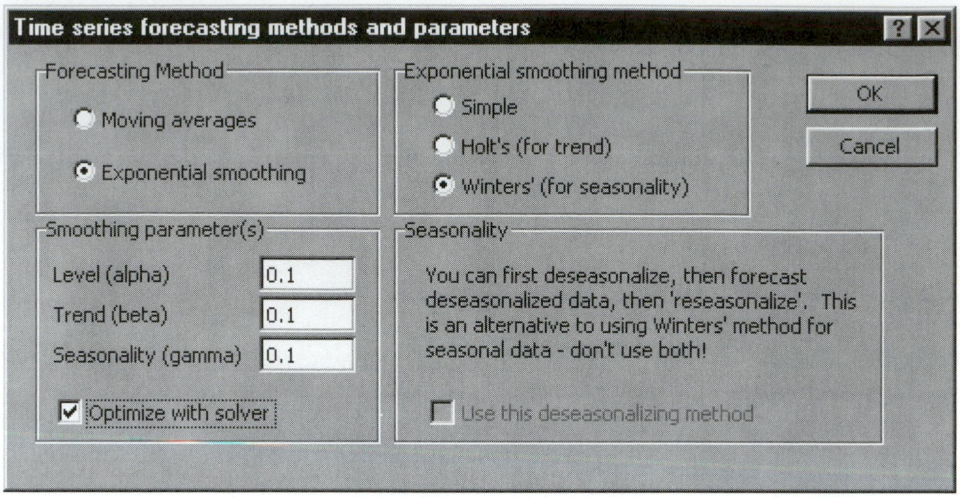

Time series forecasting methods and parameters

Forecasting Method
- ○ Moving averages
- ● Exponential smoothing

Exponential smoothing method
- ○ Simple
- ○ Holt's (for trend)
- ● Winters' (for seasonality)

OK
Cancel

Smoothing parameter(s)

Level (alpha)	0.1
Trend (beta)	0.1
Seasonality (gamma)	0.1

☑ Optimize with solver

Seasonality

You can first deseasonalize, then forecast deseasonalized data, then 'reseasonalize'. This is an alternative to using Winters' method for seasonal data - don't use both!

☐ Use this deseasonalizing method

One final comment is that we are not obligated to find the *optimal* smoothing constants. Some analysts might suggest using more "typical" values such as $\alpha = \beta = 0.2$ and $\gamma = 0.5$. (We often choose γ larger than α and β because each season's seasonal index gets updated only once per year.) To see how these smoothing constants would affect the results, we can simply substitute their values in the range B6:B8 of Figure 13.46. As we would expect, MAE, RMSE, and MAPE all get worse (they increase to 141, 191, and 5.48%, respectively), but a plot of the forecasts superimposed on the original sales data still indicates a very good fit.

FIGURE 13.46 Output from Winters' Method

	A	B	C	D	E	F	G	H	I	J
1	*Forecasting results for Sales*			Date	Observation	SmLevel	SmTrend	SmSeason	Forecast	Error
2				Q1-1986	1734.827	1973.930	67.107	0.879		
3	**Winters' exponential smoothing**			Q2-1986	2244.961	2048.133	67.107	1.096	2237.183	7.778
4				Q3-1986	2533.805	2380.639	67.107	1.064	2251.331	282.474
5	Smoothing constant(s)			Q4-1986	2154.963	2243.139	67.107	0.961	2351.527	-196.564
6	Level	1.000		Q1-1987	1547.819	1761.147	67.107	0.879	2030.406	-482.587
7	Trend	0.000		Q2-1987	2104.412	1919.907	67.107	1.096	2003.952	100.460
8	Seasonality	0.244		Q3-1987	2014.363	1892.597	67.107	1.064	2114.855	-100.492
9				Q4-1987	1991.747	2073.245	67.107	0.961	1882.670	109.077
10	**Estimation period**			Q1-1988	1869.050	2126.652	67.107	0.879	1881.091	-12.041
11				Q2-1988	2313.632	2110.784	67.107	1.096	2404.582	-90.950
12	MAE	101.2270		Q3-1988	2128.320	1999.666	67.107	1.064	2318.012	-189.692
13	RMSE	136.0574		Q4-1988	2026.829	2109.762	67.107	0.961	1985.529	41.300
14	MAPE	3.95%		Q1-1989	1910.604	2173.933	67.107	0.879	1913.185	-2.581
15				Q2-1989	2331.165	2126.779	67.107	1.096	2456.407	-125.242
40				Q3-1995	4895.000	4599.103	67.107	1.064	4864.389	30.611
41				Q4-1995	4333.000	4510.297	67.107	0.961	4482.784	-149.784
42				Q1-1996	4194.000	4772.039	67.107	0.879	4022.942	171.058
43				Q2-1996	5253.000	4792.442	67.107	1.096	5304.193	-51.193
44				Q3-1996					5172.203	
45				Q4-1996					4732.993	
46				Q1-1997					4388.867	
47				Q2-1997					5547.226	
48				Q3-1997					5457.903	
49				Q4-1997					4990.870	
50				Q1-1998					4624.782	
51				Q2-1998					5841.452	

FIGURE 13.47 **Plot of Forecasts from Winters' Method**

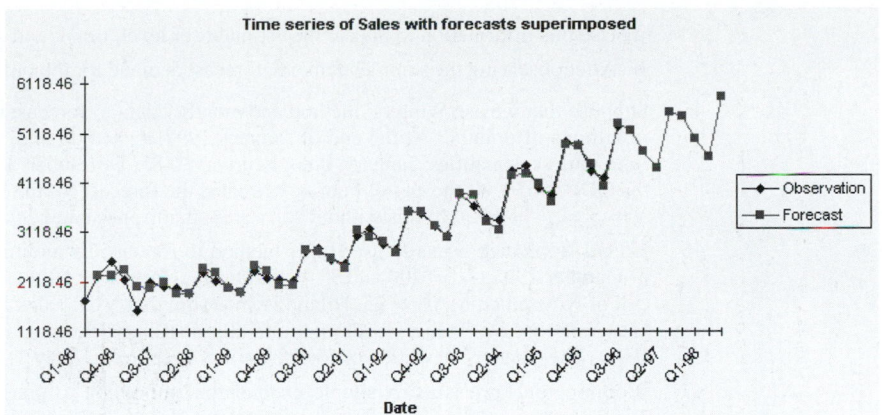

The three exponential smoothing methods we have examined are not the only ones available. For example, there are linear and quadratic models available in some software packages. These are somewhat similar to Holt's model except that they use only a single smoothing constant. There are also adaptive exponential smoothing models, where the smoothing constants themselves are allowed to change through time. Although these more complex models have been studied thoroughly in the academic literature and are used by some practitioners, they typically offer only marginal gains in forecast accuracy over the models examined here.

PROBLEMS

Level A

42 Hicks' Drugs is using simple exponential smoothing to predict monthly electric shaver sales. At the end of October 1997, Hicks' forecast for December 1997 sales was 40. In November, 50 shavers were sold, and during December, 45 shavers were sold. At the end of December 1997, what is Hicks' forecast for the total number of shavers that will be sold during March and April of 1998? Use $\alpha = 0.50$.

43 Suppose that simple exponential smoothing (with $\alpha = 0.2$) is used to forecast monthly beer sales at Gordon's liquor store. After April's demand is observed, the forecasted demand for May is 4000 cans of beer. Do the following without software—that is, use hand calculation.

a At the beginning of May, what is the forecast of July's beer sales?

b Suppose that actual demands during May and June are as follows: May, 4500 cans of beer; June, 3500 cans of beer. After observing June's demand, what is the forecast for July's demand?

c Based on the data from part **b**, the demands during May and June average to $(4500 + 3500)/2 = 4000$ cans per month. This is the same as the forecast for monthly sales before we observed the May and June data. Yet after we observe the May and June demands for beer, our forecast for July demand has decreased from what it was at the end of April. Why?

44 Continuing the previous problem, suppose that we are forecasting quarterly sales for soda at Gordon's liquor store using Winters' method. We are given the following information:

Seasonal factors: fall = 0.8, spring = 1.2, winter = 0.7, summer = 1.3

Current level estimate = 400 cases per quarter

Current trend estimate = 40 cases per quarter

$$\alpha = 0.2, \quad \beta = 0.3, \quad \gamma = 0.5$$

Also, 650 cases were sold during the summer quarter. Do the following without software—that is, use hand calculation.

a Use this information to update the estimates of level, trend, and seasonality.

b After observing the summer demand, forecast demand for the fall quarter and winter quarter.

45 Suppose that we use Winters' method and monthly data to forecast the GDP. (All numbers are in billions of dollars.) At the end of January 1997, $L_t = 600$ and $T_t = 5$. We are given the following seasonalities: January, 0.80; February, 0.85; December, 1.2. During February 1997, the GDP is 630. At the end of February, what is the forecast for the December 1997 GDP? Use $\alpha = \beta = \gamma = 0.5$. (Do this without software—that is, use hand calculation.)

46 Hiland Appliance wants to use Holt's method to forecast its monthly VCR sales. At the end of October 1997, $L_t = 200$ and $T_t = 10$. During November 1997, 230 VCRs are sold. At the end of November, MAE = 25. Hiland is 95% sure that VCR sales for December 1997 will be between what two values, assuming normally distributed forecast errors? Use $\alpha = \beta = 0.5$. (*Hint*: The standard deviation of forecast errors is approximately 1.25 times MAE.)

47 Bloomington Ford is using simple exponential smoothing to predict monthly auto sales. The company believes that sales do not exhibit trend or seasonality, so simple exponential smoothing has yielded satisfactory forecasts in the past. Each March, however, Bloomington Ford has observed that sales tend to exceed the simple exponential smoothing forecast (made in February) by 200. Suppose that at the end of February 1997, $L_t = 600$. During March 1997, 900 cars are sold.

a Using $\alpha = 0.3$, determine (at the end of March 1997) a forecast for April 1997 car sales.

b Assume that at the end of March, MAE = 60. Bloomington Ford can be 95% sure that April sales will be between what two values, assuming normally distributed forecast errors? (*Hint*: The standard deviation of forecast errors is approximately 1.25 times MAE.)

48 The University Credit Union is open Monday through Saturday. Winters' method is being used (with $\alpha = \beta = \gamma = 0.5$) to predict the number of customers entering the bank each day. After incorporating the arrivals of 16 October 1996, $L_t = 200$, $T_t = 1$, and the "seasonalities" are as follows: Monday, 0.90; Tuesday, 0.70; Wednesday, 0.80; Thursday, 1.1; Friday, 1.2; Saturday, 1.3. For example, the number of customers entering the bank on a typical Monday is 90% of the number of customers entering the bank on an average day. On Tuesday, 17 October 1996, 182 customers enter the bank. At the close of business on 17 October 1996, forecast the number of customers who will enter the bank on 25 October 1996.

49 TOD Chevy is using Holt's method to forecast weekly car sales. Currently, the level is estimated to be 50 cars per week, and the trend is estimated to be 6 cars per week. During the current week, 30 cars are sold. After observing the current week's sales, forecast the number of cars 3 weeks from now. Use $\alpha = \beta = 0.3$.

50 Last National Bank is using Winters' method (with $\alpha = 0.2$, $\beta = 0.1$, and $\gamma = 0.5$) to forecast the number of customers served each day. The bank is open Monday through Friday. At present, the following "seasonalities" have been estimated: Monday, 0.80; Tuesday, 0.90; Wednesday, 0.95; Thursday, 1.10; Friday, 1.25. A seasonality of 0.80 for Monday means that on a Monday, the number of customers served by the bank tends to be 80% of the average daily value. Currently, the level is estimated to be 20 customers, and the trend is estimated to equal 1 customer. After observing that 30 customers are served by the bank on Monday, forecast the number of customers who will be served by the bank on Wednesday.

51 We have been assigned to forecast the number of aircraft engines ordered each month by Commins Engine Company. At the end of February, the forecast is that 100 engines will be ordered during April. Then during March, 120 engines are actually ordered.

a Using $\alpha = 0.3$, determine a forecast (at the end of March) for the number of orders placed during April; during May. Use simple exponential smoothing.

b Suppose MAE = 16 at the end of March. At the end of March, Commins can be 68% sure that April orders will be between what two values, assuming normally distributed forecast errors? (*Hint*: The standard deviation of forecast errors is approximately 1.25 times MAE.)

52 Suppose that Winters' method is used to forecast quarterly U.S. retail sales (in billions of dollars). At the end of the first quarter of 1997, $L_t = 300$, $T_t = 30$, and the seasonal indexes are as follows: quarter 1, 0.90; quarter 2, 0.95; quarter 3, 0.95; quarter 4, 1.20. During the second quarter of 1997, retail sales are $360 billion. Assume $\alpha = 0.2$, $\beta = 0.4$, and $\gamma = 0.5$.

a At the end of the second quarter of 1997, develop a forecast for retail sales during the fourth quarter of 1997.

b At the end of the second quarter of 1997, develop a forecast for the second quarter of 1998.

53 Simple exponential smoothing with $\alpha = 0.3$ is being used to forecast sales of radios at Lowland Appliance. Forecasts are made on a monthly basis. After August radio sales are observed, the forecast for September is 100 radios.

a During September, 120 radios are sold. After observing September sales, what do we forecast for October radio sales? For November radio sales?

b It turns out that June sales were recorded as 10 radios. Actually, however, 100 radios were sold in June. After correcting for this error, develop a forecast for October radio sales.

Level B

54 Holt's method assumes an additive trend. For example, a trend of 5 means that the level will increase by 5 units per period. Suppose there is actually a **multiplicative trend**. For example, if the current estimate of the level is 50 and the current estimate of the trend is 1.2, we would predict demand to increase by 20% per period. So we would forecast the next period's demand to be 50(1.2) and forecast the demand 2 periods in the future to be $50(1.2)^2$. If we want to use a multiplicative trend in Holt's method, we should use the following equations:

$$L_t = \alpha y_t + (1 - \alpha)(I)$$
$$T_t = \beta(II) + (1 - \beta)T_{t-1}$$

a Determine (I) and (II).

b Suppose we are working with monthly data and month 12 is December, month 13 is January, and so on. Also suppose that $L_{12} = 100$ and $T_{12} = 1.2$. Suppose $Y_{13} = 200$. At the end of month 13, what is the prediction for Y_{15}? Assume $\alpha = \beta = 0.5$ and a multiplicative trend.

55 In our discussion of Winters' method, a monthly seasonality of 0.80 for January, say, means that during January, air conditioner sales are expected to be 80% of the sales during an average month. An alternative approach to modeling seasonality, called an **additive model**, is to let the seasonality factor for each month represent how far above average AC sales will be during the current month. For instance, if $S_{Jan} = -50$, then AC sales during January are expected to be 50 less than AC sales during an average month. (This is 50 ACs, not 50%.) If $S_{July} = 90$, then AC sales during July are expected to be 90 more than AC sales during an average month. Let

S_t = Seasonality for month t after observing month t demand

L_t = Estimate of level after observing month t demand

T_t = Estimate of trend after observing month t demand

Then the Winters' method equations given in the text should be modified as follows:

$$L_t = \alpha(I) + (1 - \alpha)(L_{t-1} + T_{t-1})$$
$$T_t = \beta(L_t - L_{t-1}) + (1 - \beta)T_{t-1}$$
$$s_t = \gamma(II) + (1 - \gamma)s_{t-12}$$

a Determine (I) and (II).

b Suppose that month 13 is January, $L_{12} = 30$, $T_{12} = -3$, $S_1 = -50$, and $S_2 = -20$. Let $\alpha = \gamma = \beta = 0.5$. Suppose 12 ACs are sold during month 13. At the end of month 13, what is the prediction for AC sales during month 14 using an additive model?

56 Winters' method assumes a multiplicative seasonality but an additive trend. For example, a trend of 5 means that the level will increase by 5 units per period. Suppose that there is actually a *multiplicative* trend. Then (ignoring seasonality) if the current estimate of the level is 50 and the current estimate of the trend is 1.2, we would predict demand to increase by 20% per period. So we would forecast the next period's demand to be 50(1.2) and forecast the demand 2 periods in the future to be $50(1.2)^2$. If we want to use a multiplicative trend in Winters' method, we should use the following equations (assuming a period is a month):

$$L_t = \alpha \left(\frac{Y_t}{S_{t-12}} \right) + (1 - \alpha)(I)$$

$$T_t = \beta(II) + (1 - \beta)T_{t-1}$$

$$S_t = \gamma \left(\frac{Y_t}{L_t} \right) + (1 - \gamma)S_{t-12}$$

a Determine (I) and (II).

b Suppose that we are working with monthly data and month 12 is December, month 13 is January, and so on. Also suppose that $L_{12} = 100$, $T_{12} = 1.2$, $S_1 = 0.90$, $S_2 = 0.70$, and $S_3 = 0.95$. Also, suppose $Y_{13} = 200$. At the end of month 13, what is the prediction for Y_{15} using $\alpha = \beta = \gamma = 0.5$ and a multiplicative trend?

57 A version of simple exponential smoothing can be used to predict the outcome of sporting events. To illustrate, consider pro football. We first assume that all games are played on a neutral field. Before each day of play, we assume that each team has a rating. For example, if the rating for the Bears is +10 and the rating for the Bengals is +6, we predict the Bears to beat the Bengals by $10 - 6 = 4$ points. Suppose that the Bears play the Bengals and win by 20 points. For this game, we "underpredicted" the Bears' performance by $20 - 4 = 16$ points. Assuming that the best α for pro football is $\alpha = 0.10$, we would increase the Bears' rating by $16(0.1) = 1.6$ and decrease the Bengals' rating by 1.6 points. In a rematch, the Bears would then be favored by $(10 + 1.6) - (6 - 1.6) = 7.2$ points.

a How does this approach relate to the equation $L_t = L_{t-1} + \alpha e_t$?

b Suppose that the home field advantage in pro football is 3 points; that is, home teams tend to outscore visiting teams by an average of 3 points a game. How could the home field advantage be incorporated into this system?

c How might we determine the *best* α for pro football?

d How might we determine ratings for each team at the beginning of the season?

e Suppose we apply this method to predict pro football (16-game schedule), college football (11-game schedule), college basketball (30-game schedule), and pro basketball (82-game schedule). Which sport do you think would have the smallest optimal α; the largest optimal α? Why?

f Why might this approach yield poor forecasts for major league baseball? ∎

Deseasonalizing: The Ratio-to-Moving-Averages Method

You have all probably seen references to time series data that have been *deseasonalized*. In this section we will discuss why this is done and how it is done. We will also see how it can be used to forecast seasonal time series.[10] First, data are often published in deseasonalized form so that readers can spot trends more easily. For example, if we see a time series of sales that has not been deseasonalized, and it shows a large increase from November to December, we might not be sure whether this represents a real increase in sales or a seasonal phenomenon (Christmas sales). However, if this increase is really just a seasonal effect, then the deseasonalized version of the series will show no such increase in sales.

Government economists and statisticians have a variety of sophisticated methods for deseasonalizing time series data, but they are all variations of the **ratio-to-moving-averages** method described here. This method is applicable when we believe that seasonality is

---

[10]This method is an alternative to Winters' method for dealing with seasonality. The two methods usually, but not always, give similar forecasts.

multiplicative, as described in the previous section. Our job is to find the seasonal indexes, which can then be used to deseasonalize the data. For example, if we estimate the index for June to be 1.3, this means that June's values are typically about 30% larger than the average for all months. Therefore, to deseasonalize a June value, we divide it by 1.3 (to make it smaller). Similarly, if February's index is 0.85, then February's values are 15% below the average for all months. So to deseasonalize a February value, we again divide it by 0.85 (to make it larger).

To find the seasonal index for June 91 (or any other month) in the first place, we essentially divide June's observation by the average of the 12 observations surrounding June. (This is the reason for the term "ratio" in the name of the method.) There is one minor problem with this approach. June 91 isn't exactly in the middle of any 12-month sequence. If we use the 12 months from January 91 to December 91, June 91 is in the *first* half of the sequence; if we use the 12 months from December 90 to November 91, June 91 is in the *last* half of the sequence. Therefore, it is best to compromise by averaging the January-to-December and December-to-November averages. This is called a **centered** average. Then the seasonal index for June is June's observation divided by this centered average. The following equation shows more specifically how it works.

$$\text{Jun91 index} = \frac{\text{Jun91}}{\left(\frac{\text{Dec90}+\cdots+\text{Nov91}}{12} + \frac{\text{Jan91}+\cdots+\text{Dec91}}{12}\right)/2}$$

The only remaining question is how to combine all of the indexes for any specific month such as June. After all, if we have data for several years, the above procedure produces several June indexes, one for each year. The usual way to combine them is simply to average them. This single average index for June is then used to deseasonalize *all* of the June observations.

Once the seasonal indexes are obtained, we divide each observation by its seasonal index to deseasonalize the data. The deseasonalized data can then be forecasted by any of the methods we have described (other than Winters' method, which wouldn't make much sense). For example, we could use Holt's method or the moving average method to forecast the deseasonalized data. Finally, we "reseasonalize" the forecasts by *multiplying* them by the seasonal indexes.

As this description suggests, the method is not meant for hand calculations! However, it is straightforward to implement in StatPro, as we illustrate in the following example.

EXAMPLE 13.12

We return to the Coca Cola sales data from Example 13.11. (See the file COCACOLA.XLS.) Is it possible to obtain the same forecast accuracy with the ratio-to-moving-averages method as we obtained with Winters' method?

Solution

The answer to this question depends on which forecasting method we use to forecast the *deseasonalized* data. The ratio-to-moving-averages method only provides a means for deseasonalizing the data and providing seasonal indexes. Beyond this, any method can be used to forecast the deseasonalized data, and some methods obviously work better than others. For this example, we compared two possibilities: the moving averages method with a span of 4 quarters, and Holt's exponential smoothing method optimized. However, we show the results only for the latter. Because the deseasonalized series still has a clear upward trend, we would expect Holt's method to do well, and we would expect the moving averages forecasts to lag behind the trend. This is exactly what occurred. For example, the values of MAPE for the two methods are 6.97% (moving averages) and 3.78% (Holt's).

To implement this latter method in StatPro, we proceed exactly as before, but this time we check the "Use this deseasonalizing method" box in the dialog box in Figure 13.45. (Now Holt's option will be checked, so the deseasonalizing option will be enabled.) By checking the deseasonalizing option, we then get a larger selection of optional charts. We can see charts of the deseasonalized data and/or the original "reseasonalized" data.

FIGURE 13.48 **Summary Measures for Forecast Errors**

	A	B	C
1	*Forecasting results for Sales*		
2			
3	**Holt's exponential smoothing**		
4			
5	Smoothing constant(s)		
6	Level	0.898	
7	Trend	0.000	
8			
9	**Estimation period**		
10		Deseas	Actual
11	MAE	98.7705	97.1839
12	RMSE	141.5835	135.3411
13	MAPE	3.78%	3.78%

Selected outputs are shown in Figures 13.48–13.51. Figures 13.48 and 13.49 show the numerical output. In particular, Figure 13.49 shows the seasonal indexes from the ratio-to-moving averages method in column G. These are virtually identical to the seasonal indexes we found using Winters' method, although the methods are mathematically different. Column H contains the deseasonalized sales (column F divided by column G), columns I–L implement Holt's method on the deseasonalized data, and columns M and N are the "reseasonalized" forecasts and errors.

The deseasonalized data, with forecasts superimposed, appear in Figure 13.50. Here we see only the smooth upward trend with no seasonality, which Holt's method is able

FIGURE 13.49 **Ratio-to-Moving-Averages Output**

	E	F	G	H	I	J	K	L	M	N
1	Date	Observation	SeasIndex	DeseasObs	SmLevel	SmTrend	DeseasFCast	DeseasError	Forecast	Error
2	Q1-86	1734.827	0.879	1973.930	1973.930	67.107				
3	Q2-86	2244.961	1.096	2048.133	2047.409	67.107	2041.037	7.095	2237.184	7.777
4	Q3-86	2533.805	1.064	2380.639	2353.512	67.107	2114.517	266.122	2250.561	283.244
5	Q4-86	2154.963	0.961	2243.139	2261.231	67.107	2420.620	-177.480	2325.467	-170.504
6	Q1-87	1547.819	0.879	1761.148	1818.963	67.107	2328.338	-567.190	2046.305	-498.486
7	Q2-87	2104.412	1.096	1919.906	1916.457	67.107	1886.070	33.836	2067.324	37.088
8	Q3-87	2014.363	1.064	1892.597	1901.869	67.107	1983.565	-90.968	2111.184	-96.821
9	Q4-87	1991.747	0.961	2073.245	2062.617	67.107	1968.977	104.268	1891.577	100.170
10	Q1-88	1869.050	0.879	2126.652	2126.965	67.107	2129.724	-3.072	1871.750	-2.700
11	Q2-88	2313.632	1.096	2110.783	2119.273	67.107	2194.073	-83.290	2404.926	-91.294
12	Q3-88	2128.320	1.064	1999.665	2018.698	67.107	2186.380	-186.715	2327.048	-198.728
13	Q4-88	2026.829	0.961	2109.762	2107.320	67.107	2085.805	23.958	2003.813	23.016
41	Q4-95	4333.000	0.961	4510.297	4525.823	67.107	4662.610	-152.313	4479.326	-146.326
42	Q1-96	4194.000	0.879	4772.039	4753.782	67.107	4592.930	179.109	4036.587	157.413
43	Q2-96	5253.000	1.096	4792.440	4795.340	67.107	4820.889	-28.450	5284.184	-31.184
44	Q3-96		1.064				4862.447		5175.288	
45	Q4-96		0.961				4929.555		4735.777	
46	Q1-97		0.879				4996.662		4391.414	
47	Q2-97		1.096				5063.769		5550.405	
48	Q3-97		1.064				5130.877		5460.988	
49	Q4-97		0.961				5197.984		4993.654	
50	Q1-98		0.879				5265.091		4627.329	
51	Q2-98		1.096				5332.199		5844.631	

to track very well. Then Figure 13.51 shows the results of reseasonalizing. Again, the forecasts track the actual sales data very well. In fact, we see that the summary measures of forecast errors (in Figure 13.48, range C11:C13) are quite comparable to those from Winters' method. The reason is that both arrive at virtually the same seasonal pattern.

FIGURE 13.50 **Forecast Plot of Deseasonalized Series**

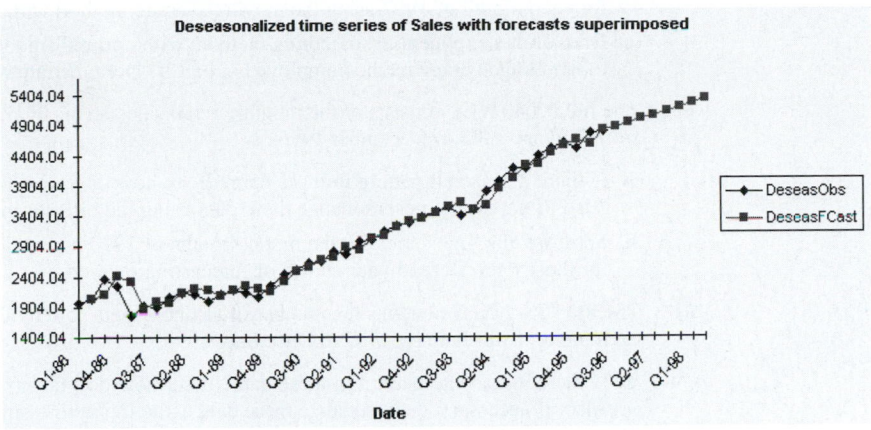

FIGURE 13.51 **Forecast Plot of Reseasonalized (Original) Series**

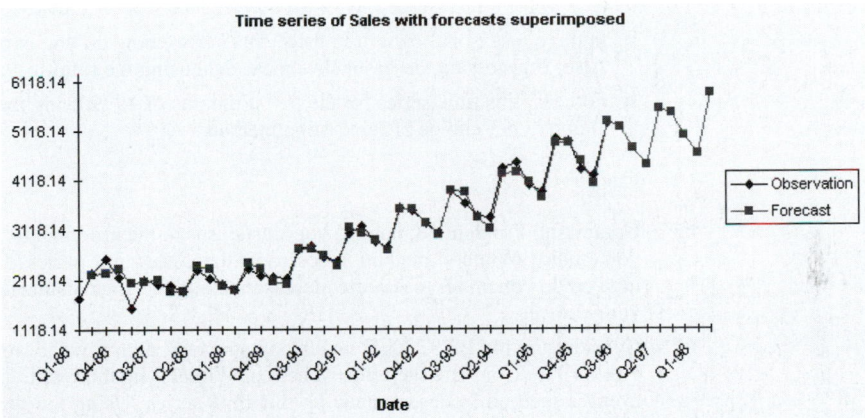

PROBLEMS

Level A

58 The file P2_38.XLS contains monthly retail sales of U.S. liquor stores from January 1993 to December 1996.

a Is seasonality present in these data? If so, characterize the seasonality pattern and then deseasonalize this time series using the ratio-to-moving-average method.

b If you decided to deseasonalize this time series in part **a**, forecast the deseasonalized data for each month of 1997 using the moving average method with an appropriate span.

c Does Holt's exponential smoothing method, with optimal smoothing constants, outperform the moving average method employed in part **b**? Demonstrate why or why not.

59 The file P2_39.XLS contains monthly time series data for total U.S. retail sales of building materials (which includes retail sales of building materials, hardware and garden supply stores, and mobile home dealers).

a Is seasonality present in these data? If so, characterize the seasonality pattern and then deseasonalize this time series using the ratio-to-moving-average method.

b If you decided to deseasonalize this time series in part **a**, forecast the deseasonalized data for each month of 1997 using the moving average method with an appropriate span.

c Does Holt's exponential smoothing method, with optimal smoothing constants, outperform the moving average method employed in part **b**? Demonstrate why or why not.

60 The file P2_40.XLS consists of the monthly retail sales levels of U.S. gasoline service stations from January 1993 to December 1996.

a Is there a seasonal pattern in these data? If so, how do you explain this seasonal pattern? Also, if necessary, deseasonalize these data using the ratio-to-moving-average method.

b Forecast this time series for the first 4 months of 1997 using the most appropriate method for these data. Defend your choice of forecasting method.

61 The file P13_1.XLS contains the number of airline tickets sold by the CareFree Travel Agency each month from January 1995 to December 1998.

a Is there a seasonal pattern in these data? If so, how do you explain this seasonal pattern? Also, if necessary, deseasonalize these data using the ratio-to-moving-average method.

b Forecast this time series for the first 4 months of 1999 using the most appropriate method for these data. Defend your choice of forecasting method.

62 The number of employees on the payroll at a food processing plant is recorded at the start of each month from January 1996 to December 1998. These data are provided in the file P13_3.XLS.

a Is there a seasonal pattern in these data? If so, how do you explain this seasonal pattern? Also, if necessary, deseasonalize these data using the ratio-to-moving-average method.

b Forecast this time series for the first 4 months of 1999 using the most appropriate method. Defend your choice of forecasting method.

Level B

63 Continuing Problem 58, how do your responses to the aforementioned questions change when you employ Winters' method in deseasonalizing this time series? Explain. Which forecasting method do you prefer to use after deseasonalizing the given data with Winters' method? Defend your choice.

64 Consider the file P2_37.XLS, which contains total monthly U.S. retail sales data for the years 1993–1996. Compare the effectiveness of Winters' method with that of the ratio-to-moving-average method in deseasonalizing this time series. Using the deseasonalized time series generated by each of these two methods, forecast U.S. retail sales with the most appropriate method. Defend your choice of forecasting method. ■

13.10

Estimating Seasonality with Regression

E arlier we saw two methods for dealing with seasonality: Winters' exponential smoothing model and the ratio-to-moving-averages method for deseasonalizing time series data. We now examine a regression approach that uses dummy variables for the seasons. As an example, suppose that the data are quarterly data with a possible linear trend. Then we might introduce dummy variables Q_1, Q_2, and Q_3 for the first three quarters (using quarter 4 as the reference quarter) and estimate the equation

$$\widehat{Y}_t = a + bt + b_1 Q_1 + b_2 Q_2 + b_3 Q_3$$

Then the coefficients of the dummy variables, b_1, b_2 and b_3, indicate how much each quarter differs from the reference quarter, quarter 4.

For example, if the estimated equation is

$$\widehat{Y}_t = 130 + 25t + 15Q_1 + 5Q_2 - 20Q_3$$

then the average increase from one quarter to the next is 25 (the coefficient of t). This is the trend effect. However, quarter 1 averages 15 units higher than quarter 4, quarter 2 averages 5 units higher than quarter 4, and quarter 3 averages 20 units lower than quarter 4. These coefficients indicate the effect of seasonality.

As discussed in Chapter 12, it is also possible to estimate a *multiplicative* model using dummy variables for seasonality (and possibly time for trend). Then we would estimate

$$\widehat{Y}_t = a e^{bt} e^{b_1 Q_1} e^{b_2 Q_2} e^{b_3 Q_3}$$

or, after taking logs,

$$\ln \widehat{Y}_t = \ln a + bt + b_1 Q_1 + b_2 Q_2 + b_3 Q_3$$

One advantage of this approach is that it provides a model with *multiplicative* seasonal factors. It is also fairly easy to interpret the regression output, as illustrated in the following continuation of the Coca Cola example.

E X A M P L E 1 3 . 1 3

Returning to the Coca Cola sales data (see the file COCACOLA.XLS), does a regression approach provide forecasts that are as accurate as those provided by the other seasonal methods in this chapter?

Solution

We illustrate the multiplicative approach, although an additive approach is also possible. Figure 13.52 (page 762) illustrates the data setup. Besides the Sales and Time variables, we need dummy variables for three of the four quarters (these were created manually), and a Log_Sales variable. The other output in this figure will be discussed below. We then use multiple regression, with Log_Sales as the response variable, and Time, Q1, Q2, and Q3 as the explanatory variables.

The regression output appears in Figure 13.53. Of particular interest are the coefficients of the explanatory variables. Recall that for a log response variable, these coefficients can be interpreted as *percentage* changes in the original sales variable. Specifically, the coefficient of Time means that deseasonalized sales increase by about 2.4% per quarter. Also, the coefficients of Q1, Q2, and Q3 mean that sales in quarters 1, 2, and 3 are, respectively, about 8% below, 13.7% above, and 10.4% above sales in the reference quarter, quarter 4. This pattern is quite comparable to the pattern of seasonal indexes we saw in Examples 13.11 and 13.12 for these data.

To compare the forecast accuracy of this method with earlier examples, we must go through several steps manually. The multiple regression procedure in StatPro provides (as an option) the fitted values and residuals for the log of sales, as shown in columns H and I of Figure 13.54 (page 763). Then we need to take antilogs in column J to obtain forecasts of the original sales data, and subtract these from the sales data to obtain forecast errors in

FIGURE 13.52 Data Setup for Multiplicative Model with Dummies

	A	B	C	D	E	F	G
1	Coca Cola quarterly sales						
2							
3	Quarter	Sales	Time	Q1	Q2	Q3	Log_Sales
4	Q1-86	1734.83	1	1	0	0	7.45866298
5	Q2-86	2244.96	2	0	1	0	7.71644343
6	Q3-86	2533.80	3	0	0	1	7.8374774
7	Q4-86	2154.96	4	0	0	0	7.67552883
8	Q1-87	1547.82	5	1	0	0	7.34460212
9	Q2-87	2104.41	6	0	1	0	7.65179137
10	Q3-87	2014.36	7	0	0	1	7.60805829
11	Q4-87	1991.75	8	0	0	0	7.59676742
42	Q3-95	4895.00	39	0	0	1	8.49596955
43	Q4-95	4333.00	40	0	0	0	8.37401542
44	Q1-96	4194.00	41	1	0	0	8.34141021
45	Q2-96	5253.00	42	0	1	0	8.56655462

FIGURE 13.53 Regression Output for Multiplicative Model

	A	B	C	D	E	F	G
1	Results of multiple regression for Log_Sales						
2							
3	Summary measures						
4		Multiple R	0.9697				
5		R-Square	0.9404				
6		Adj R-Square	0.9340				
7		StErr of Est	0.0823				
8							
9	ANOVA Table						
10		Source	df	SS	MS	F	p-value
11		Explained	4	3.9538	0.9884	145.9732	0.0000
12		Unexplained	37	0.2505	0.0068		
13							
14	Regression coefficients						
15			Coefficient	Std Err	t-value	p-value	
16		Constant	7.3946	0.0348	212.6519	0.0000	
17		Time	0.0242	0.0010	23.0503	0.0000	
18		Q1	-0.0795	0.0360	-2.2110	0.0333	
19		Q2	0.1368	0.0360	3.8056	0.0005	
20		Q3	0.1042	0.0368	2.8315	0.0075	

column K. Using these errors in column K, we can then use the formulas that were used in StatPro's forecasting procedure to obtain the summary measures MAE, RMSE, and MAPE. As we see, the forecasts are not quite as accurate as before (for example, MAPE is 5.36% as compared to earlier MAPEs of about 3.8%), but a plot of the forecasts superimposed on the original data, shown in Figure 13.55, shows that the method again tracks the data very well.

FIGURE 13.54 Forecast Errors and Summary Measures

	A	B	H	I	J	K	L	M	N
1	Coca Cola quarterly sales								
2									
3	Quarter	Sales	Fitted logs	Resids logs	FCasts	FCast Errors		Summary stats	
4	Q1-86	1734.83	7.339	0.119	1539.52	195.31			
5	Q2-86	2244.96	7.580	0.137	1958.13	286.83		MAE	286.83
6	Q3-86	2533.80	7.571	0.266	1941.72	592.09		RMSE	186.07
7	Q4-86	2154.96	7.491	0.184	1792.30	362.67		MAPE	5.36%
8	Q1-87	1547.82	7.436	-0.091	1695.77	-147.95			
9	Q2-87	2104.41	7.676	-0.025	2156.87	-52.46			
10	Q3-87	2014.36	7.668	-0.060	2138.79	-124.43			
11	Q4-87	1991.75	7.588	0.009	1974.21	17.54			
42	Q3-95	4895.00	8.441	0.055	4634.78	260.22			
43	Q4-95	4333.00	8.361	0.013	4278.12	54.88			
44	Q1-96	4194.00	8.306	0.036	4047.72	146.28			
45	Q2-96	5253.00	8.546	0.020	5148.35	104.65			

FIGURE 13.55 Plot of Forecasts for Multiplicative Model

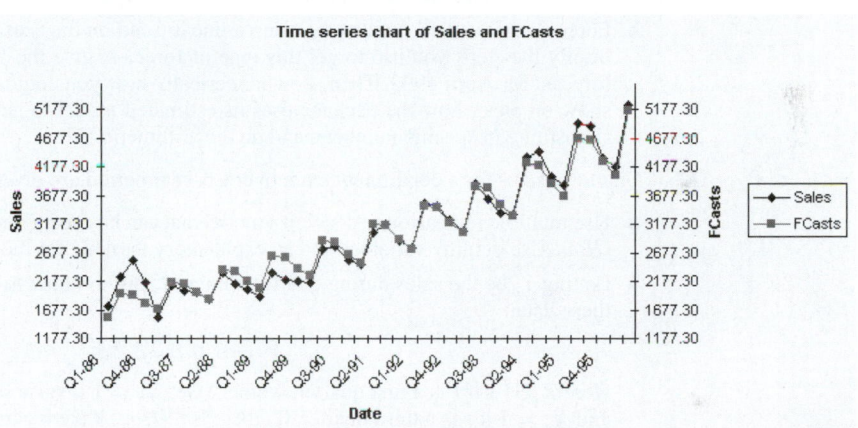

This method of detecting seasonality by using dummy variables in a regression equation is always an option. The other variables included in the regression equation could be time t, lagged versions of Y_t, and/or current or lagged versions of other independent variables. These variables would capture any time series behavior other than seasonality. Just remember that there is always one less dummy variable than the number of seasons. If the data are quarterly, then three dummies are needed; if the data are monthly, then eleven dummies are needed. If the coefficients of any of these dummies turn out to be statistically insignificant, they can be omitted from the equation. Then the omitted terms are in effect combined with the reference season. For example, if the Q_1 term above were omitted, then quarters 1 and 4 would essentially be combined and treated as the reference season, and the other two seasons would be compared to them through their dummy variable coefficients.

PROBLEMS

Level A

65 Suppose that a time series consisting of 6 years (1993–1998) of quarterly data exhibits definite seasonality. In fact, assume that the seasonal indexes turn out to be 0.75, 1.45, 1.25, and 0.55.

a If the last four observations of the series (the four quarters of 1998) are 2502, 4872, 4269, and 1924, calculate the deseasonalized values for the four quarters of 1998.

b Suppose that a plot of the deseasonalized series shows an upward linear trend, except for some random noise. Therefore, a linear regression of this series versus time is estimated, and it produces the equation

$$\text{Predicted deseasonalized value} = 2250 + 51\text{Quarter}$$

Here the time variable "Quarter" is coded so that Quarter = 1 corresponds to first quarter 1993, Quarter = 24 corresponds to fourth quarter 1994, and the others fall in between. Forecast the actual (not deseasonalized) values for the four quarters of 1999.

66 The file P13_66.XLS contains monthly data on federal receipts of taxes from January 1985 to March 1992. There are two variables: IndTax (taxes from individuals) and CorpTax (corporate taxes). For this problem, work only with IndTax.

a What evidence is there that seasonality is important in this series? Find seasonal indexes (by any method you like) and state briefly what they mean.

b Forecast the next 12 months by using a linear trend on the seasonally adjusted data. State briefly the steps you use to get this type of forecast, give the final RMSE, MAPE, and forecast for April 1992. Then show numerically how you could replicate this forecast, i.e., show on paper how the package uses its estimated model to get the April 1992 forecast. (Substitute in specific numbers, and do the arithmetic.)

67 Quarterly sales for a department store over a 6-year period are given in the file P13_67.XLS.

a Use multiple regression to develop a model that can be used to predict future quarterly sales. (*Hint*: Use dummy variables and an explanatory variable for the quarter number, 1–24.)

b Letting Y_t be the sales during quarter number t, discuss how to fit the following model to these data.

$$Y_t = \beta_0 \beta_1^t \beta_2^{X_1} \beta_3^{X_2} \beta_4^{X_3}$$

Here $X_1 = 1$ if t is a first quarter, 0 otherwise; $X_2 = 1$ if t is a second quarter, 0 otherwise; and $X_3 = 1$ if t is a third quarter, 0 otherwise. (*Hint*: Take logarithms of both sides.)

c Interpret the answer to part **b**.

d Which model appears to yield better predictions for sales, the one in part **a** or the one in part **b**?

68 Confederate Express Service is attempting to determine how its shipping costs for a month depend on the number of units shipped during a month. The number of units shipped and total shipping cost for the last 15 months are given in the file P13_68.XLS.

a Determine a relationship between units shipped and monthly shipping cost.

b Plot the errors for the predictions in order of time sequence. Is there any unusual pattern?

c We have been told that there was a trucking strike during months 11–15, and we believe that this might have influenced shipping costs. How could the answer to part **a** be modified to account for the effect of the strike? After accounting for this effect, does the unusual pattern in part **b** disappear?

Level B

69 Consider the file P2_37.XLS, which contains total monthly U.S. retail sales data for the years 1993–1996. Does a regression approach for estimating seasonality provide forecasts that are as accurate as those provided by (i) Winters' method and (ii) the ratio-to-moving-average method? Compare the summary measures of forecast errors associated with each method for deseasonalizing the given time series. Summarize your findings after performing these comparisons.

70 The file P2_39.XLS contains monthly time series data for total U.S. retail sales of building materials (which includes retail sales of building materials, hardware and garden supply stores, and mobile home dealers). Does a regression approach for estimating seasonality provide forecasts that are as accurate as those provided by (i) Winters' method and (ii) the ratio-to-moving-average method? Compare the summary measures of forecast errors associated with each method for deseasonalizing the given time series. Summarize your findings after performing these comparisons. ∎

Econometric Models

Most of the models in this chapter use only previous values of a time series variable Y to forecast future values of Y. A natural extension is to use one or more *other* time series variables, via a regression equation, to forecast Y. For example, if a company wants to forecast its monthly sales, it might use its own past advertising levels and/or macroeconomic variables such as GDP and the prime interest rate to forecast future sales. We will not study this approach in any detail because it can become quite complex mathematically. However, there are a few points worth making.

Let X be a potential explanatory variable, such as the company's advertising level or GDP. Then either X_t or any of its lags could be used as explanatory variables in a regression equation for Y_t. If X_t itself is included, it is called a **coincident** indicator of Y_t. If only its lags are included, it is called a **leading** indicator of Y_t. As an example, suppose that Y_t represents a company's sales during month t and X_t represents its advertising level during month t. It is certainly plausible that current sales are determined more by past months' advertising levels than by the current month's level. In this case advertising is a leading indicator of sales, and the advertising terms that should be included in the equation are X_{t-1}, X_{t-2}, and so on. The number of lags that should be included is difficult to specify ahead of time. In practice, we might begin by including a fairly large number of lags and then discard those with insignificant coefficients in the regression output.

If we decide to use a coincident indicator, the problem is a practical one—namely, that the value of X_t is probably not known at the time we are forecasting Y_t. Hence, it must *also* be forecasted. For example, if we believe that GDP is a coincident indicator of a company's sales, then we must first forecast GDP before we can use it to forecast sales. This may be a more difficult problem than forecasting sales itself! So from a practical point of view, we would like the variables on the right-hand side of the regression equation—the explanatory variables—to be *known* at the time the forecast is being made.

Once we have decided which variables to use as explanatory variables, the analysis itself is carried out exactly as with any other regression analysis, and the diagnostic tools are largely the same as with regression of cross-sectional data. However, there are several things to be aware of. First, because the explanatory variables are often lagged variables, either of the dependent variable or of some other explanatory variables, we will have to create these lagged variables to use them in the regression equation. (This can be done easily with StatPro's Lagged Variables procedure.)

Second, a problem we discussed only briefly in Chapters 11 and 12 is autocorrelation of the residuals. Recall that in the least squares estimation procedure, the residuals automatically average to zero. However, autocorrelation of the residuals means that errors in one period are not independent of errors in previous periods. The most common type of residual autocorrelation, *positive* autocorrelation, implies that if the forecast is on the high side in one period, it is likely to be on the high side the next period. Or if the forecast is on the low side in one period, it is likely to be on the low side the next period. We can detect residual autocorrelation by capturing the residuals and then looking at their autocorrelations to see if any are statistically significant.

Many regression outputs also include the **Durbin–Watson** statistic to check for lag 1 autocorrelation, as we discussed in Section 12.10. Recall that the value of this statistic is always between 0 and 4. If the Durbin–Watson statistic is near 2, then autocorrelation is not a problem. However, if it is significantly less than 2 (as measured by special tables), then there is significant positive autocorrelation, whereas if it is significantly greater than 2, there is significant negative autocorrelation. Actually, the Durbin–Watson statistic tests only for autocorrelation of lag 1, not for any higher lags. Therefore, a graph of the autocorrelations (a correlogram) provides more complete information than is contained in the Durbin–Watson statistic alone.

StatPro does not automatically report the Durbin–Watson statistic. However, it does provide a function, DW, for calculating this statistic. Assuming that StatPro has been added in, DW works like any other Excel function (such as the SUM function). It takes a single argument, a range. This range is typically the range containing the residuals from a regression run. For example, if the residuals are contained in the range F5:F30, we can obtain the Durbin–Watson statistic by entering the formula

$$=DW(F5:F30)$$

in any blank cell.

If a regression model does contain significant residual autocorrelation, this is generally a sign that the model is not as good as it could be. Perhaps we have not included the best set of explanatory variables or perhaps we have not used the best form of the response variable. This is a very complex topic, and we cannot do it justice here. Suffice it to say that a primary objective of any forecasting model, including econometric models, is to end up with uncorrelated residuals. This is easy to say, but it is often difficult to obtain, and we admit that the work necessary to eliminate residual autocorrelation is not always worth the extra effort in terms of more accurate forecasts.

An important final point is that two time series, Y_t and X_t, may be highly correlated, and hence produce a promising regression output, even though they are not really related at all. Suppose, for example, that both series are dominated by upward trends through time but are in no way related. Because they are both trending upward, it is very possible that they will have a large positive correlation, which means that the regression of Y_t on X_t has a large R^2 value. This is called a **spurious correlation** because it suggests a relationship that does not really exist. In such a case it is sometimes better to use an extrapolation model to model Y_t and then regress the *residuals* of Y_t on X_t. Intuitively, we first see how much of the behavior of the Y_t series can be explained by its own past values. Then we regress whatever remains on the X_t series.

We will not pursue this strategy here, but it does suggest how complex a rigorous econometric analysis can be. It is not just a matter of loading Y's and X's into a computer package and running the "obvious" regression. The output could look good, but it could also be very misleading!

13.12

Conclusion

W e have covered a lot of ground in this chapter. Because forecasting is such an important activity in business, it has received a tremendous amount of attention by both academicians and practitioners. All of the methods discussed in this chapter—and more—are actually used, often on a day-to-day basis. There is really no point in arguing which of these methods is best. All of them have their strengths and weaknesses. The most important point is that when they are applied properly, they have all been found to be useful in real business applications.

PROBLEMS

Level A

71   The file P13_71.XLS contains quarterly revenues of Toys 'R Us for the years 1992–1995. Discuss the seasonal and trend components of the growth of Toys 'R Us revenues. Also, use any reasonable forecasting method to forecast quarterly revenues for 1996. Explain your choice of forecasting method.

72   The file P13_72.XLS contains 1991–1997 quarterly revenues and earnings per share (EPS) for the following companies: Mattel, McDonald's, Eli Lilly, General Motors, Microsoft, AT&T, Nike, GE, Coca-Cola, and Ford. (Source: Standard and Poor's 500 Guide: 1998)

   a For each company, use a regression model with trend and seasonal components to forecast revenues and EPS.

   b For each company, use Winters' method to forecast revenues and EPS.

   c For each company, which method appears to be more accurate?

73   The file P13_73.XLS contains the sales in (millions of dollars) for Sun Microsystems for the years 1987–1993.

   a Use these data to predict the company's 1994 and 1995 sales. You need consider only a linear and exponential trend, but you should justify the equation you choose.

   b In words, how do your predictions of sales increase from year to year?

   c Are there any outliers?

74   The file P13_74.XLS contains the sales in (millions of dollars) for Procter & Gamble for the years 1984–1993.

   a Use these data to predict 1994 and 1995 Procter & Gamble sales. You need consider only a linear and exponential trend, but you should justify the equation you choose.

   b Use your answer from part **a** to explain how your predictions of Procter & Gamble sales increase from year to year.

   c Are there any outliers?

   d We can be approximately 95% sure that 1995 Procter & Gamble sales will be between what two values?

75   The file P13_75.XLS lists the 1984–1995 sales of Nike. Forecast 1996 and 1997 sales with a linear or exponential trend. Are there any outliers in your predictions for 1984–1995?

76   The file P13_76.XLS contains data on pork sales. Price is in dollars per hundred pounds sold, quantity sold is in billions of pounds, per capita income is in dollars, U.S. population is in millions, and GNP is in billions of dollars.

   a Use these data to develop a regression equation that could be used to predict the quantity of pork sold during future periods. Is autocorrelation, heteroscedasticity, or multicollinearity a problem?

   b Suppose that during each of the next two quarters, price is $45, U.S. population is 240, GNP is 2620, and per capita income is $10,000. (All of these are expressed in the units described above.) Predict the quantity of pork sold during each of the next 2 quarters.

   c We expect our prediction of pork sales to be accurate within what value 68% of the time?

   d Use Winters' method to develop a forecast of pork sales during the next 2 quarters.

77   The file P13_77.XLS contains data on a motel chain's revenue and advertising.

   a Use these data and multiple regression to make predictions of the motel chain's revenues during the next 4 quarters. Assume that advertising during each of the next 4 quarters is $50,000. (*Hint*: Try using advertising, lagged by 1 quarter, as an explanatory variable.)

b Use simple exponential smoothing to make predictions for the motel chain's revenues during the next 4 quarters.

c Use Holt's method to make forecasts for the motel chain's revenues during the next 4 quarters.

d Use Winters' method to determine predictions for the motel chain's revenues during the next 4 quarters.

e Which of these forecasting methods would you expect to be the most reliable for these data?

78 The file P13_78.XLS contains data on monthly U.S. housing sales (in thousands of houses) for 1967–1972.

a Using Winters' method, find values of α, β, and γ that yield an RMSE as small as possible.

b Although we have not discussed autocorrelation for smoothing methods, good forecasts derived from smoothing methods should exhibit no autocorrelation. Do the forecast errors for this problem exhibit autocorrelation?

c It has been stated that if only trend and seasonality are important factors, then α should be at most 0.5. Explain why this problem produced $\alpha > 0.5$.

d At the end of December 1972, what is the forecast of housing sales during the first 3 months of 1973?

79 Let Y_t be the sales during month t (in thousands of dollars) for a photography studio, and let P_t be the price charged for portraits during month t. The data are in the file P13_79.XLS. Use regression to fit the following model to these data:

$$Y_t = \beta_0 + \beta_1 Y_{t-1} + \beta_2 P_t + \varepsilon_t$$

This equation indicates that last month's sales and the current month's price are explanatory variables. The last term, ε_t, is an error term.

a If the price of a portrait during month 21 is $10, what would we predict for sales in month 21?

b Does there appear to be a problem with autocorrelation, heteroscedasticity, or multi-collinearity?

80 The file P13_80.XLS gives quarterly auto sales, GNP, interest rates and unemployment rates.

a With all but the most recent 2 years of data, use regression to forecast auto sales. Carefully interpret the coefficients in your final equation.

b Use all but the most recent 2 years of data to develop an exponential smoothing model to forecast future auto sales.

c To *validate* your model, determine which model does the best job of forecasting for the most recent 2 years of data. It is usually recommended to hold back some of your data to validate any forecast model. This helps avoid "overfitting."

Level B

81 The file P13_81.XLS gives monthly exchange rates (dollars per unit of local currency) for 25 countries. Technical analysts believe that by charting past changes in exchange rates, it is possible to predict future changes of exchange rates. After analyzing the autocorrelations for these data, do you believe that technical analysis has potential?

82 The file P13_82.XLS contains 5 years of monthly data, starting in January 1995, for a particular company. The first variable is Time (1–60). The second variable, Sales1, has data on sales of a product. Note that Sales1 increases linearly throughout the period, with only a minor amount of "noise." (The third variable, Sales2, will be discussed and used in the next problem.) For this problem use the Sales1 variable to see how the following forecasting methods are able to track a linear trend.

a Forecast this series with the moving average method with various spans such as 3, 6, and 12. What can you conclude?

b Forecast this series with simple exponential smoothing with various smoothing constants such as 0.1, 0.3, 0.5, and 0.7. What can you conclude?

c Now repeat part **b** with Holt's exponential smoothing method, again for various smoothing constants. Can you do significantly better than in parts **a** and **b**?

d What can you conclude from your findings in parts **a**, **b**, and **c** about forecasting this type of series?

83 The Sales2 variable in the file from Problem 82 was created from the Sales1 variable by multiplying by monthly seasonal factors. Basically, the summer months are high and the winter months are low. This might represent the sales of a product that has a linear trend and seasonality.

a Repeat parts **a**, **b**, and **c** from the previous problem to see how well these forecasting methods can deal with trend *and* seasonality.

b Now use Winters' method, with various values of the three smoothing constants, to forecast the series. Can you do much better? Which smoothing constants work well?

c Use the ratio-to-moving-average method, where you first do the seasonal decomposition and then forecast (by any appropriate method) the deseasonalized series. Does this do as well as, or better than, Winters' method?

d What can you conclude from your findings in parts **a**, **b**, and **c** about forecasting this type of series?

84 The file P13_84.XLS contains monthly time series data on federal expenditures in various categories. The time period extends from January 1982 to March 1992. All values are in billions of current dollars. The variables are:

■ Defense: expenditures on national defense

■ Science: expenditures on science, space, and technology

■ Energy: expenditures on energy

■ Environ: expenditures on natural resources and environment

■ Trans: expenditures on transportation

Analyze the Science variable by (i) simple exponential smoothing, (ii) Holt's method, (iii) simple exponential smoothing on the trend-adjusted data (the residuals from regressing linearly versus time), and (iv) moving averages on the adjusted or unadjusted data. Experiment with the smoothing constants [or span in (iv)], or use the optimize feature. Do any of these methods produce significantly better fits than the others as measured by RMSE or MAPE?

85 The data in the file P13_85.XLS represent annual changes in the average surface air temperature of the earth from 1880 to 1985. (The source doesn't say exactly how this was measured.) A look at the time series shows a gradual upward trend, starting with negative values and ending with (mostly) positive values. This might be used to support the theory of global warming.

a Is this series a random walk? Explain.

b Regardless of your answer in part **a**, use a random walk model to forecast the 1986 value of the series. What is your forecast, and what is an approximate 95% forecast interval?

c Forecast the series in three ways: (i) simple exponential smoothing ($\alpha = 0.35$), (ii) Holt's method ($\alpha = 0.5$, $\beta = 0.1$), and (iii) simple exponential smoothing ($\alpha = 0.3$) on trend-adjusted data, that is, the residuals from regressing linearly versus time. (These smoothing constants are close to "optimal.") For each of these, list the MAPE, the RMSE, and the forecast for 1986. Also, comment on any "problems" with forecast errors from any of these three approaches. Finally, compare the "qualitative" features of the three forecasts (for example, how do their short-run or longer-run forecasts differ?). Is any one of the methods clearly superior to the others?

d Does your analysis predict convincingly that global warming would occur during the years 1986–1995? Explain. ■

The Indiana University Credit Union Eastland Plaza Branch was having trouble getting the correct staffing levels to match customer arrival patterns. On some days, the number of tellers was too high relative to the customer traffic, so that tellers were often idle. On other days, the opposite occurred. Long customer waiting lines formed because the relatively few tellers could not keep up with the number of customers. The credit union manager, James Chilton, knew that there was a problem, but he had little of the quantitative training he believed would be necessary to find a better staffing solution. James figured that the problem could be broken down into three parts. First, he needed a reliable forecast of each day's number of customer arrivals. Second, he needed to translate these forecasts into staffing levels that would make an adequate trade-off between teller idleness and customer waiting. Third, he needed to translate these staffing levels into individual teller work assignments—who should come to work when.

The last two parts of the problem require analysis tools (queueing and scheduling) that we have not covered. However, you can help James with the first part—forecasting. The file CREDITUNION.XLS lists the number of customers entering this credit union branch each day of the past year. It also lists other information: the day of the week, whether the day was a staff or faculty payday, and whether the day was the day before or after a holiday. Use this data set to develop one or more forecasting models that James could use to help solve his problem. Based on your model(s), make any recommendations about staffing that appear reasonable.

Amanta Appliances sells two styles of refrigerators at over 50 locations in the Midwest. The first style is a relatively expensive model, whereas the second is a standard, less expensive model. Although weekly demand for these two products is fairly stable from week to week, there is enough variation to concern management at Amanta. There have been relatively unsophisticated attempts to forecast weekly demand, but they haven't been very successful. Sometimes demand (and the corresponding sales) are lower than forecasted, so that inventory costs are high. Other times the forecasts are too low. When this happens and on-hand inventory is not sufficient to meet customer demand, Amanta requires expedited shipments to keep customers happy—and this nearly wipes out Amanta's profit margin on the expedited units.[11] Profits at Amanta would almost certainly increase if demand could be forecasted more accurately.

Data on weekly sales of both products appear in the file AMANTA.XLS. A time series chart of the two sales variables indicates what Amanta management expected—namely, there is no evidence of any upward or downward trends or of any seasonality. In fact, it might appear that each series is an unpredictable sequence of random ups and downs.

---

[11]Because Amanta uses expediting when necessary, its sales each week are equal to its customer demands. Therefore, we use the terms *demand* and *sales* interchangeably.

But is this really true? Is it possible to forecast either series, with some degree of accuracy, with an extrapolation method (where only past values of *that* series are used to forecast current and future values)? What method appears to be best? How accurate is it? Also, is it possible, when trying to forecast sales of one product, to somehow incorporate current or past sales of the *other* product in the forecast model? After all, these products might be "substitute" products, where high sales of one go with low sales of the other, or they might be complementary products, where sales of the two products tend to move in the *same* direction.

14

Introduction to Optimization Modeling

Successful Applications

As we will see in this chapter, linear programming (LP) can be used for product mix decisions and inventory planning. This was the case at Libbey-Owens-Ford (LOF), a large plate glass company with 9000 employees and annual sales of $900 million. In the article "Integrated Production, Distribution, and Inventory Planning at Libbey-Owens-Ford," Martin et al. (1993) describe the process of building and implementing a large-scale LP model of the plate glass production and distribution process at LOF. The model (named FLAGPOL for *FLA*t *G*lass *P*roducts *O*ptimization Mode*L*) deals with four manufacturing plants, over 200 separate glass products, and over 40 demand centers in a 12-month planning horizon. The development of the model took over 2 years to complete, but since then it has resulted in annual savings of over $2 million.

The production of plate glass is an extremely complex manufacturing process. The glass is produced in large batches, each batch producing a certain color or tint of glass. The batches are large because the time required to change from one tint to another is very long (on the order of 2 to 4 days). Therefore, production occurs in cycles of approximately 10 months, and a particular tint is produced only once during a cycle. Given these long cycles, inventory planning is crucial. The production quantity of a particular tint in a cycle must be large enough to cover orders, both planned and forecasted, for a long period of time. Another complication is the cutting process. The glass is produced in long "ribbons" that can be cut to various dimensions. If the cuts are made during the production processing, yields tend to be higher than if they are made off-line, after processing. However, off-line cuts are sometimes necessary when orders arrive for nonstandard dimensions of glass.

The management at LOF decided that the complexity of the entire process necessitated a formal model. Therefore, the company appointed a task force to develop an LP model of the process. Since the task force included staff members from finance, marketing, MIS, materials management, transportation, production planning, and representatives from the plants, the scope of the resulting model became very broad. The first step was to develop the database that would support the model. This was a major undertaking because data were required on market demand and sales prices, freight rates, production rates and yields, manufacturing costs, inventory levels, and interplant rail schedules. Once these data were available, the FLAGPOL model was then built, tested, and finally implemented. The implementation process itself took about 9 months. During this time, several changes to the original model were required. For example, the company realized that differences in the cost accounting systems of the various plants needed to be addressed. Also, the model's reports were redesigned to make them more useful and comprehensible to the eventual users.

Now that FLAGPOL is fully implemented, it is run 10 to 20 times each month for short-run tactical plans, as well as for longer-range strategical decisions. At the tactical level, the model recommends how much of each product to produce at each plant each month, how much of each product to ship between plants each month, how much of each product to cut off-line at each plant each month, and how much inventory to hold of each product at each plant each month. At the strategic level, FLAGPOL has been used to address such issues as (1) planning the transition from a two-plant operation to a four-plant operation, (2) introducing new products or eliminating existing products from plants, (3) developing schedules for major construction and plant maintenance, and (4) analyzing possible locations and sizing for new facilities. Management at LOF now considers FLAGPOL an integral part of the company's planning process. It helps the company to reduce costs, increase profits, and enhance overall customer service. ■

14.1 Introduction

I n this chapter we introduce spreadsheet optimization, one of the most powerful and flexible methods of quantitative analysis. The specific type of optimization we will discuss is **linear programming** (LP). LP is used in all types of organizations, often on a daily basis, and it is used to solve an extremely wide variety of problems. These include problems in human resource scheduling, inventory management, selection of advertising media, bond trading, management of cash flows, operation of an electrical utility's hydroelectric system, routing of delivery vehicles, blending in oil refineries, hospital staffing, and many others. The goal of this chapter is to introduce the basic elements of LP: the types of problems it can solve, how LP problems can be modeled in Excel, and how Excel's powerful add-in, Solver, can be used to find optimal solutions. Then in the next chapter we will examine a variety of LP applications, and we will also look at applications of integer and nonlinear programming, two important extensions of LP.

14.2 A Brief History of Linear Programming

A brief history of LP is enlightening. Mathematically, every LP problem involves optimizing a linear function subject to several linear constraints, expressed as linear inequalities or equalities. For example, the objective might be profit, and the constraints might be upper limits on resource availabilities. Until World War II, mathematicians knew a great deal, at least theoretically, about systems of linear equations and inequalities. They realized that a huge number of arithmetic operations are necessary to solve such systems, and without computing power, humans are not able to perform the required calculations in a reasonable amount of time. Therefore, no one seriously considered their potential usefulness.

During World War II, however, two things fortuitously came together. First, complex military logistics problems arose that could be modeled as LP problems (although the name "linear programming" did not yet exist). Second, computers were just being developed. All that was needed was a method for solving this new class of problem—a method that could take advantage of computer power. Fortunately, a young mathematician, George Dantzig, developed a method he called the **simplex method**. It involved a systematic, arithmetic-intensive search through the set of all possible solutions for the solution that optimized a given objective. It appeared to work efficiently on the problems he tried, and it was not too difficult to program on a computer.

The surprising thing is that Dantzig's method, with relatively minor modifications, is still the most important solution method for LP problems. For reasons that are not entirely understood even by mathematicians, it works quickly on problems that are orders of magnitude larger than any problems Dantzig could have imagined in the early days, and all large companies now own (or have access to) a commercial version of the simplex computer code. Recently, an entirely different type of solution method developed by Narendra Karmarkar at Bell Labs has emerged as a competitor to the simplex method, particularly for extremely large problems, but the simplex method is still comfortably in first place.

14.3

Introduction to LP Modeling

We will not learn the simplex method. Instead, we will learn how to formulate problems as LP models. Once a problem is properly formulated, we will see that it is fairly easy to solve it on a computer and interpret the resulting solution. Actually, there are two ways to formulate an LP problem, the traditional algebraic way and the more recent spreadsheet way. We will illustrate both methods in this chapter, just for comparison. However, in the next chapter we will focus exclusively on spreadsheet formulations.

The first problem we will examine is often considered the prototype LP problem. The basic problem is to select the optimal mix of products to produce to maximize profit. We will refer to it as the **product mix** problem.

EXAMPLE 14.1

The Monet Company produces four types of picture frames, which we label 1, 2, 3, and 4. The four types of frames differ with respect to size, shape, and materials used. Each type requires a certain amount of skilled labor, metal, and glass, as shown in Table 14.1. This table also lists the unit selling price Monet charges for each type of frame. During the coming week Monet can purchase up to 4000 hours of skilled labor, 6000 ounces of metal, and 10,000 ounces of glass. The unit costs are $8.00 per labor hour, $0.50 per ounce of metal, and $0.75 per ounce of glass. Also, market constraints are such that it is impossible to sell more than 1000 type 1 frames, 2000 type 2 frames, 500 type 3 frames, and 1000 type 4 frames. The company wants to maximize its weekly profit.

TABLE 14.1   **Data for Monet Picture Frame Example**

	Skilled Labor	Metal	Glass	Selling Price
Frame 1	2	4	6	$28.50
Frame 2	1	2	2	$12.50
Frame 3	3	1	1	$29.25
Frame 4	2	2	2	$21.50

Solution

In the traditional algebraic solution method, we first identify the decision variables. In this small problem they are the number of frames of types 1, 2, 3, and 4 to produce. We label these x_1, x_2, x_3, and x_4 (although any other labels would do). Next, we write total profit and the constraints in terms of the x's. Finally, since only nonnegative amounts can be produced, we add explicit constraints to ensure that the x's are nonnegative. The resulting algebraic formulation is shown below:

$$\text{maximize } 6x_1 + 2x_2 + 4x_3 + 3x_4 \quad \text{(profit objective)}$$

$$\text{subject to } 2x_1 + x_2 + 3x_3 + 2x_4 \leq 4000 \quad \text{(labor constraint)}$$

$$4x_1 + 2x_2 + x_3 + 2x_4 \leq 6000 \quad \text{(metal constraint)}$$

$$6x_1 + 2x_2 + x_3 + 2x_4 \leq 10,000 \quad \text{(glass constraint)}$$

$$x_1 \leq 1000 \quad \text{(frame 1 sales constraint)}$$

$$x_2 \leq 2000 \quad \text{(frame 2 sales constraint)}$$

$$x_3 \leq 500 \quad \text{(frame 3 sales constraint)}$$

$$x_4 \leq 1000 \quad \text{(frame 4 sales constraint)}$$

$$x_1, x_2, x_3, x_4 \geq 0 \quad \text{(nonnegativity constraints)}$$

To understand this formulation, consider the profit objective first. The profit from x_1 frames of type 1 is $6x_1$ because each frame contributes $6 to profit. This $6 is calculated as the unit selling price minus the cost of the inputs that go into a single type 1 frame:

$$\text{Unit profit} = 28.50 - [2(8.00) + 4(0.50) + 6(0.75)] = \$6$$

Profits for the other three types of frames are obtained similarly. Their unit profits are $2.00, $4.00, and $3.00, respectively. Then the total profit is the sum of the profits from the four products.

Next, consider the skilled labor constraint. The right-hand side, 4000, is the number of hours available. On the left-hand side, each type 1 frame uses 2 hours of labor, so x_1 units require $2x_1$ hours of labor. Similar statements hold for the other three products, and the total number of labor hours used is the sum over the four products. Then the constraint states that the number of hours used cannot exceed the number of hours available. The constraints for metal and glass are similar. Finally, the maximum sales constraints and the nonnegativity constraints put upper and lower limits on the quantities that can be produced.

For many years all LP problems were formulated this way. Because of this, many commercial LP computer packages are written to accept LP problems in essentially this format. For example, in a popular package called LINDO (for the mainframe or the PC), we would type in almost exactly what is shown above. In the past decade, however, a more intuitive method of expressing LP problems has emerged. This method takes advantage of the power and flexibility of spreadsheets. Actually, LP problems could always be *formulated* on spreadsheets, but now with the addition of Solver add-ins, spreadsheets have the capability of *solving* (that is, optimizing) LP problems as well. Specifically, Microsoft Excel, Lotus 1-2-3, and Quattro Pro all have built-in Solvers, and there is an LP add-in called What's Best! that can be used with all three. All examples in this book will be illustrated with Excel's Solver.[1]

There are many ways to develop an LP spreadsheet model. Everyone has his or her own preferences for arranging the data in the various cells. We will not give any exact

---

[1]This Solver add-in is built into Microsoft Excel, but it has been developed by a third-party software company, Frontline Systems.

prescriptions, but we will present enough examples to help you develop good habits. The common elements in all LP spreadsheet models are the following.

Spreadsheet Elements

1 **Inputs.** All numerical **inputs**—that is, the data needed to form the objective and the constraints—must appear somewhere in the spreadsheet. Although it is not absolutely necessary, our convention is to enclose all inputs in a blue border with shading. We try to put most of the inputs in the upper left section of the spreadsheet. However, we sometimes violate this convention when certain inputs fit more naturally somewhere else.

2 **Changing cells.** Instead of using variable names, such as x's, there is a set of designated cells that play the role of the decision variables. The values in these cells can be changed to optimize the objective. In Excel these cells are called the **changing cells**. To designate these clearly, our convention is to enclose the changing cells within a red border.

3 **Target (objective) cell.** One cell, called the **target cell** or the **objective cell**, contains the value of the objective. Solver systematically varies the values in the changing cells to optimize the value in the target cell. Our convention is to enclose the target cell within a black double-line border.[2]

4 **Constraints.** Excel does not show the constraints directly on the spreadsheet. Instead, we specify constraints in a Solver dialog box. For example, we might designate a set of related constraints by

$$B15:D15<=B16:D16$$

This implies three separate constraints. The value in B15 must be less than or equal to the value in B16, the value in C15 must be less than or equal to the value in C16, and the value in D15 must be less than or equal to the value in D16.

5 **Nonnegativity.** Normally we want the decision variables—that is, the values in the changing cells—to be nonnegative. Depending on the version of Excel, these nonnegativity constraints might need to be specified explicitly. For example, to specify that the values in the range C5:C9 are nonnegative, we include the constraint

$$C5:C9>=0$$

In general, the complete solution of a problem involves three stages. The first stage is to enter all of the inputs, trial values for the changing cells, and formulas relating these in a spreadsheet. We call this *formulating the model*. This stage is the most crucial because it is here that all of the "ingredients" of the model are included and related appropriately. In particular, the spreadsheet *must* include a formula that relates the objective to the changing cells, so that if the values in the changing cells vary, the objective value varies accordingly. Similarly, the spreadsheet must include expressions for the various constraints (usually their left-hand sides) that are related appropriately to the changing cells.

After the model is formulated, we can proceed to the second stage: invoking Solver. At this point, we formally designate the objective cell, the changing cells, and the constraints, and we tell Solver to find the *optimal* solution. If the first stage has been done correctly, the second stage is usually very straightforward.

The third stage is **sensitivity analysis**. In most model formulations of real problems, we make "best guesses" for the numerical inputs to the problem. There is typically some

---

[2]Our red–blue–black color scheme shows up very effectively on a color monitor. The shading (for input cells) and double-line border (for the target cell) are used for clarification on the printed page.

uncertainty about quantities such as unit prices, forecasted demands, and resource availabilities. When we use Solver to solve the problem, we use our best estimates of these quantities to obtain an optimal solution. However, it is then important to see how the optimal solution changes (if at all) as we vary selected inputs.

The spreadsheet in Figure 14.1 illustrates the solution procedure for Monet's product mix problem. (See the file PRODUCTMIX.XLS.) The first stage is to set up the spreadsheet, as explained in step-by-step fashion below.

FIGURE 14.1 **An Initial Solution for Monet's Product Mix Problem**

	A	B	C	D	E	F	G	H
1	Product Mix Problem							
2								
3	Input data							
4	Hourly wage rate	$8.00						
5	Cost per oz of metal	$0.50						
6	Cost per oz of glass	$0.75						
7								
8	Frame type	1	2	3	4	Range names:		
9	Labor hours per frame	2	1	3	2	Available: D21:D23		
10	Metal (oz.) per frame	4	2	1	2	MaxSales: B18:E18		
11	Glass (oz.) per frame	6	2	1	2	Produced: B16:E16		
12	Unit selling price	$28.50	$12.50	$29.25	$21.50	TotProfit: F32		
13						Used: B21:B23		
14	Production plan							
15	Frame type	1	2	3	4			
16	Frames produced	500	800	400	1500			
17		<=	<=	<=	<=			
18	Maximum sales	1000	2000	500	1000			
19								
20	Constraints on inputs	Used		Available				
21	Labor hours	6000	<=	4000				
22	Metal (oz.)	7000	<=	6000				
23	Glass (oz.)	8000	<=	10000				
24								
25	Revenue, cost summary							
26	Frame type	1	2	3	4	Totals		
27	Revenue	$14,250	$10,000	$11,700	$32,250	$68,200		
28	Costs of inputs							
29	Labor	$8,000	$6,400	$9,600	$24,000	$48,000		
30	Metal	$1,000	$800	$200	$1,500	$3,500		
31	Glass	$2,250	$1,200	$300	$2,250	$6,000		
32	Profit	$3,000	$1,600	$1,600	$4,500	$10,700		

Developing the Spreadsheet Model

1 **Inputs.** Enter the various inputs in the ranges B4:B6, B9:E12, B18:E18, and D21:D23.

2 **Production levels.** Enter *any* four values in cells B16:E16. These do *not* have to be the values shown in Figure 14.1. These cells are the changing cells, that is, the cells where the decision variables are placed. Any trial values can be used initially; Solver will eventually find the *optimal* values. Note that the four values shown in Figure 14.1 *cannot* be optimal because they do not satisfy all of the constraints. Specifically, this plan uses more labor hours and metal than are available, and it produces more type 4 frames than can be sold. However, we don't need to worry about satisfying constraints at this point; Solver will take care of this later.

3   Resources used. Enter the formula

$$=SUMPRODUCT(B9:E9,Produced)$$

in cell B21 and copy it to the range B22:B23.[3] These formulas calculate the units of labor, metal, and glass used by the current product mix. The SUMPRODUCT function is especially useful in LP models. Here it means to multiply each value in the range B9:E9 by the corresponding value in the Products range and then sum these products.

4   Revenues, costs, and profits. The area from row 25 down shows the summary of monetary values. Actually, all we need is the total profit in cell F32, but it is useful to calculate the ingredients of this total profit, that is, the revenues and costs associated with each product. To obtain the revenues, enter the formula

$$=B12*B16$$

in cell B27 and copy this to the range C27:E27. For the costs, enter the formula

$$=\$B4*B\$16*B9$$

in cell B29 and copy this to the range B29:E31. (Note how the mixed absolute/relative references enable copying to the entire range.) Then calculate profits for each product by entering the formula

$$=B27-SUM(B29:B31)$$

in cell B32 and copy this to the range C32:E32. Finally, calculate the totals in column F by summing across each row with the SUM function.

The next step is to specify the changing cells, the objective cell, and the constraints in a Solver dialog box and then instruct Solver to find the optimal solution. However, before we do this, it is useful to try a few "guesses" in the changing cells. This has two purposes. First, by entering different sets of values in the changing cells, we can confirm that the formulas in the other cells are working correctly.

The second purpose of trying a few guesses is to provide a better understanding of the model. For example, it is tempting to guess that the frame types with the highest profit margins should be produced to the greatest extent possible. To try this out, begin by entering 0's in the changing cells B16:E16. Obviously, when we produce nothing, we earn zero profit. Next, because frame 1 has the highest profit margin ($6) and its market constraint permits at most 1000 frames, enter 1000 in cell B16. Note that none of the resources are yet used up completely. Therefore, we can make some type 3 frames, the type with the next highest profit margin. Because the type 3 market constraint permits at most 500 frames, enter 500 in cell D16. There is still some availability of each resource. This allows us to make some type 4 frames, the type with the next largest profit margin. However, the most we can make is 250 type 4 frames, because at that point we completely exhaust the available labor hours. The resulting solution appears in Figure 14.2 (page 780). Its corresponding profit is $8750.

We have now produced as much as possible of the three frame types with the three highest profit margins. Does this guarantee that this solution is the best possible product mix? Unfortunately, it does not! The solution in Figure 14.2 is *not* optimal. Even in this small model it is difficult to guess the optimal solution, even when we use a relatively intelligent trial and error procedure. The problem is that a frame type with a high profit margin can use up a lot of the resources and preclude other profitable frames from being produced. So although it is instructive and sometimes enlightening to try guessing the optimal solution, we might never find it. This is where Solver enters the picture.

---

[3]As in previous chapters, we frequently use descriptive range names for selected ranges, shown in the box in the figure. These are not necessary, but they make the model easier to understand and explain.

FIGURE 14.2 Another Possible Solution for Monet's Product Mix Example

	A	B	C	D	E	F	G	H
1	Product Mix Problem							
2								
3	Input data							
4	Hourly wage rate	$8.00						
5	Cost per oz of metal	$0.50						
6	Cost per oz of glass	$0.75						
7								
8	Frame type	1	2	3	4	Range names:		
9	Labor hours per frame	2	1	3	2	Available: D21:D23		
10	Metal (oz.) per frame	4	2	1	2	MaxSales: B18:E18		
11	Glass (oz.) per frame	6	2	1	2	Produced: B16:E16		
12	Unit selling price	$28.50	$12.50	$29.25	$21.50	TotProfit: F32		
13						Used: B21:B23		
14	Production plan							
15	Frame type	1	2	3	4			
16	Frames produced	1000	0	500	250			
17		<=	<=	<=	<=			
18	Maximum sales	1000	2000	500	1000			
19								
20	Constraints on inputs	Used		Available				
21	Labor hours	4000	<=	4000				
22	Metal (oz.)	5000	<=	6000				
23	Glass (oz.)	7000	<=	10000				
24								
25	Revenue, cost summary							
26	Frame type	1	2	3	4	Totals		
27	Revenue	$28,500	$0	$14,625	$5,375	$48,500		
28	Costs of inputs							
29	Labor	$16,000	$0	$12,000	$4,000	$32,000		
30	Metal	$2,000	$0	$250	$250	$2,500		
31	Glass	$4,500	$0	$375	$375	$5,250		
32	Profit	$6,000	$0	$2,000	$750	$8,750		

Using Solver To invoke Excel's Solver, select the Tools/Solver menu item.[4] The dialog box in Figure 14.3 appears. It has three important sections that you must fill in: the target cell, the changing cells, and the constraints. For the product mix problem, we can fill these in by typing cell references or we can point, click, and drag the appropriate ranges in the usual way. Also, if we have named any of the ranges, we can use these range names instead of cell addresses. (If you decide to point, click, and drag, you might need to move the Solver dialog box so that it isn't in the way of the cells you want to select. The Solver in Excel 97 has a great feature for getting the dialog box out of the way while pointing—just click on the right edge of the cell reference box.)

1　**Objective.** Select TotProfit (cell F32) as the target cell, and click on the Maximize button.

2　**Changing cells.** Select the Produced range (B16:E16), the numbers of frames to produce, as the changing cells.

---

[4]Although Solver comes with the Excel package, it is an Excel *add-in*. If there is no Solver menu item under Tools, you will have to add it in. To do this, use the Tools/Add-Ins menu item, then Browse until you find the SOLVER.XLA file (usually under the Program Files\Microsoft Office\Office\Library\Solver directory) and select it. If you can't find the SOLVER.XLA file, it was probably not installed when Office (or Excel) was installed. In that case, you'll have to go back to the Office Setup program and install Solver.

FIGURE 14.3 Solver Dialog Box for Monet's Product Mix Example

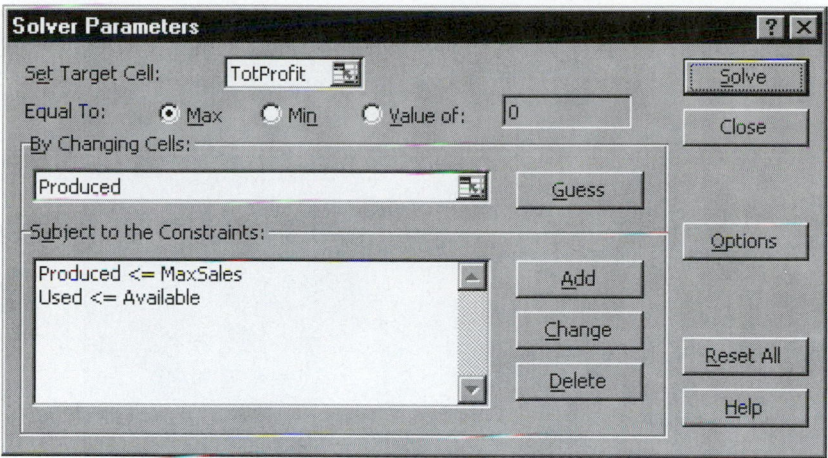

3   **Constraints.** Click on the Add button to add the following constraints:

$$\text{Used} < = \text{Available}$$

$$\text{Produced} < = \text{MaxSales}$$

The first constraint says to use no more of each resource than is available. The second constraint says to produce no more of each product than can be sold.

    Note: The <= signs in column C and row 17 (see Figure 14.1 or 14.2) are not needed in Excel. They are entered simply as *labels* in the spreadsheet and have no effect on any calculations. However, they help to document the model, so we include them in all of the examples. (You are not required to do so when you formulate your own models, but we believe it is a good habit to get into.)

4   **Nonnegativity.** Although negative production quantities obviously make no sense, we must tell Solver *explicitly* to make changing cells nonnegative. There are two ways to do this. First, we can add another constraint as in step 3:

$$\text{Produced} >= 0$$

In fact, before Excel 97, this was the only way to specify nonnegativity constraints. However, with Excel 97's Solver we can click on the Options button in Figure 14.3 and check the Assume Non-Negative box in the resulting dialog box. (See Figure 14.4, page 782.) This automatically ensures that *all* changing cells are nonnegative.

5   **Linear model.** There is one last step before clicking on the Solve button. Solver uses one of several numerical methods to solve various types of problems. The problems discussed in this chapter are all *linear* problems. (We will discuss the properties of linear problems shortly.) Linear problems can be solved most efficiently by the simplex method. To instruct Excel to use this method, we also check the Assume Linear Model in the Solver options dialog box shown in Figure 14.4.

6   **Optimize.** Click on the Solve button.

    At this point, Solver searches through a number of possible solutions until it finds the optimal solution. (You can watch the progress on the lower left of the screen.) When it finishes, it displays the message in Figure 14.5. You can then tell it to return the values in the changing cells to their original (probably nonoptimal) values or retain the optimal values found by Solver. In most cases you will choose the latter. (Actually, this is the message we hope for. However, in some cases Solver is *not* able to find an optimal solution, in which

FIGURE 14.4   Solver Options Dialog Box

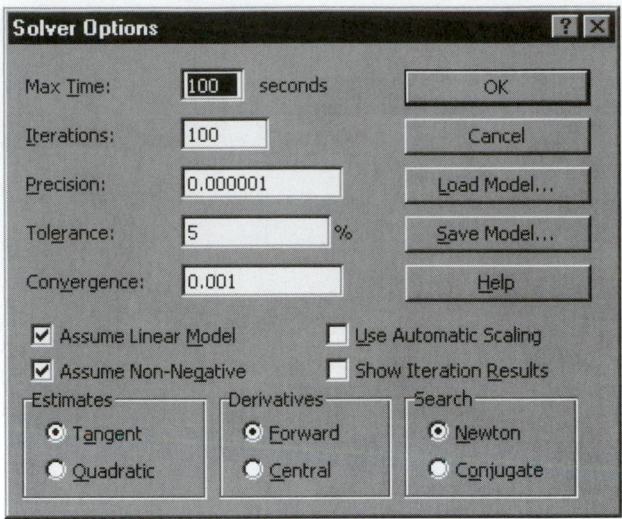

FIGURE 14.5   Solver Message That Optimal Solution Has Been Found

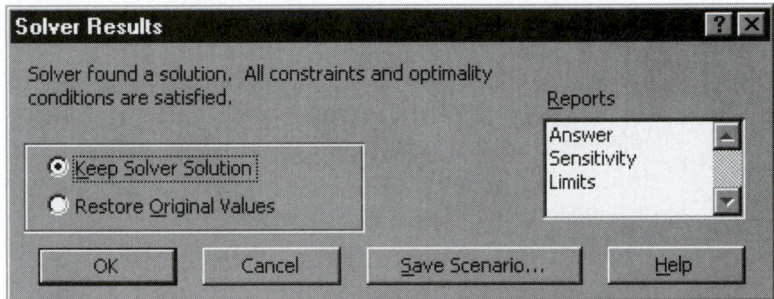

case one of several error messages will appear.) For now, click on the OK button to keep the Solver solution. You should see the solution shown in Figure 14.6.

The optimal plan is to produce 1000 type 1 frames, 800 type 2 frames, 400 type 3 frames, and no type 4 frames. This is close to the production plan from Figure 14.2, but the current plan earns $450 more profit. Also, it uses all of the available labor hours and metal, but only 8000 of the 10,000 ounces of glass available. Finally, in terms of maximum sales, the optimal plan could produce more of frame types 2, 3, and 4 (if there were more skilled labor and/or metal available). This is typical of an LP solution. Some of the constraints are met exactly, that is, as equalities, while others contain a certain amount of "slack."

Experimenting with New Inputs   If we want to experiment with different inputs to this problem—the unit revenues or resource availabilities, for example—we can simply change the inputs and then rerun Solver. The second time we use Solver, we don't have to respecify the target and changing cells or the constraints. Excel remembers all of these settings, and it saves them when we save the file.

As a simple what-if example, consider the modified model in Figure 14.7 on page 784. Here the unit selling price for frame type 4 has increased from $21.50 to $26.50, and all other inputs have remained the same. By making type 4 frames more profitable, we might expect them to enter the optimal mix. This is exactly what happens. The new optimal plan

FIGURE 14.6   Optimal Solution for Monet's Product Mix Example

	A	B	C	D	E	F	G	H
1	Product Mix Problem							
2								
3	Input data							
4	Hourly wage rate	$8.00						
5	Cost per oz of metal	$0.50						
6	Cost per oz of glass	$0.75						
7								
8	Frame type	1	2	3	4	Range names:		
9	Labor hours per frame	2	1	3	2	Available: D21:D23		
10	Metal (oz.) per frame	4	2	1	2	MaxSales: B18:E18		
11	Glass (oz.) per frame	6	2	1	2	Produced: B16:E16		
12	Unit selling price	$28.50	$12.50	$29.25	$21.50	TotProfit: F32		
13						Used: B21:B23		
14	Production plan							
15	Frame type	1	2	3	4			
16	Frames produced	1000	800	400	0			
17		<=	<=	<=	<=			
18	Maximum sales	1000	2000	500	1000			
19								
20	Constraints on inputs	Used		Available				
21	Labor hours	4000	<=	4000				
22	Metal (oz.)	6000	<=	6000				
23	Glass (oz.)	8000	<=	10000				
24								
25	Revenue, cost summary							
26	Frame type	1	2	3	4	Totals		
27	Revenue	$28,500	$10,000	$11,700	$0	$50,200		
28	Costs of inputs							
29	Labor	$16,000	$6,400	$9,600	$0	$32,000		
30	Metal	$2,000	$800	$200	$0	$3,000		
31	Glass	$4,500	$1,200	$300	$0	$6,000		
32	Profit	$6,000	$1,600	$1,600	$0	$9,200		

discontinues production of frame types 2 and 3 and instead calls for production of 1000 units of frame type 4. This increases the total profit to $14,000.

There is one technical note you should be aware of. Because of the way numbers are stored and calculated on a computer, the optimal values in the changing cells and elsewhere can contain small roundoff errors. For example, the value that really appeared in cell E16 (in Figure 14.6) on our PC was 8.731E-09, a very small number (.000000008731). For all practical purposes, this number can be treated as 0, and we have formatted it as such in Figure 14.6. ■

14.4   Sensitivity Analysis and the SolverTable Add-In

Now that we have solved Monet's product mix problem, it might appear that we are finished. But in real LP applications the solution to a *single* model is hardly ever the end of the analysis. It is almost always useful to perform a sensitivity analysis to see how (or if) the optimal solution changes as we change one or more model inputs. We will illustrate a systematic way of doing so in this section.

FIGURE 14.7 Solution to Product Mix Example with New Inputs

	A	B	C	D	E	F	G	H
1	**Product Mix Problem**							
2								
3	**Input data**							
4	Hourly wage rate	$8.00						
5	Cost per oz of metal	$0.50						
6	Cost per oz of glass	$0.75						
7								
8	Frame type	1	2	3	4		**Range names:**	
9	Labor hours per frame	2	1	3	2		Available: D21:D23	
10	Metal (oz.) per frame	4	2	1	2		MaxSales: B18:E18	
11	Glass (oz.) per frame	6	2	1	2		Produced: B16:E16	
12	Unit selling price	$28.50	$12.50	$29.25	$26.50		TotProfit: F32	
13							Used: B21:B23	
14	**Production plan**							
15	Frame type	1	2	3	4			
16	Frames produced	1000	0	0	1000			
17		<=	<=	<=	<=			
18	Maximum sales	1000	2000	500	1000			
19								
20	**Constraints on inputs**	Used		Available				
21	Labor hours	4000	<=	4000				
22	Metal (oz.)	6000	<=	6000				
23	Glass (oz.)	8000	<=	10000				
24								
25	**Revenue, cost summary**							
26	Frame type	1	2	3	4	Totals		
27	Revenue	$28,500	$0	$0	$26,500	$55,000		
28	Costs of inputs							
29	Labor	$16,000	$0	$0	$16,000	$32,000		
30	Metal	$2,000	$0	$0	$1,000	$3,000		
31	Glass	$4,500	$0	$0	$1,500	$6,000		
32	Profit	$6,000	$0	$0	$8,000	$14,000		

The Solver dialog box in Figure 14.5 indicates one possible approach. By checking the Sensitivity Report option, we can obtain a new sheet with a lot of information about the model's sensitivity to various inputs. This report is based on a very well developed theory of sensitivity in LP models. Unfortunately, this report is based on an *algebraic* approach to LP modeling that requires us to adhere to certain conventions. The problem is that there is no real need to adhere to these conventions in spreadsheet modeling. The effect is that Solver's sensitivity report is sometimes very useful and sometimes virtually impossible to unravel. We believe it is more likely to confuse than to enlighten.

Nevertheless, sensitivity analysis is too important to neglect. Therefore, we have written an add-in to Excel called SolverTable that makes sensitivity analysis much more straightforward. This add-in is contained in the file SOLVERTABLE.XLA and is on the CD that comes with this book. To install it, proceed as follows.

Installing SolverTable Add-in

1 Follow the directions in the INSTALL.HTM file to install the SOLVERTABLE.XLA file and associated help files to your hard drive if you have not already done so.

2 With Excel open and any worksheet open, use the Tool/Add-ins menu item.

3 Click on Browse, and then locate the directory where you stored the add-in. Click on the SOLVERTABLE.XLA file, and then click on OK a couple of times to get out of the dialog boxes.

The add-in should now be installed. You can see it as a new menu item, SolverTable, under the Data menu (right above the Data/Table menu item). To uninstall the add-in, use the Tool/Add-ins menu item, uncheck the SolverTable box, and click on OK. Then if you want to reinstall it, you don't need to go through the three-step procedure above. You need only to use the Tools/Add-ins menu item and recheck the SolverTable box.[5]

Using the SolverTable Add-in   The SolverTable add-in was developed to mimic Excel's built-in Data Table feature. Recall that data tables, often called what-if tables, allow you to vary one or two inputs in a spreadsheet model and see how selected outputs change. SolverTable is similar except that now the Solver is rerun for every new input (or pair of inputs). There are two ways it can be used, as described below.

1   **One-way table.** A "one-way" table means that there is a *single* input cell and *any number of* output cells. That is, there can be a single output cell or as many output cells as you like.

2   **Two-way table.** A "two-way" table means that there are *two* inputs that vary and one or more outputs. (You might recall that an Excel two-way data table allows only one output. The SolverTable add-in allows more than one. It creates a separate table for each output as a function of the two inputs.)

We'll illustrate some of the possibilities in the following continuation of the product mix example.

EXAMPLE 14.1 [CONTINUED]

Check how sensitive the optimal profit and the optimal product mix are to (1) changes in the number of labor hours available and (2) the cost per ounce of metal. Then check how sensitive the optimal profit is to simultaneous changes in the hourly labor cost and the total labor hours available.

Solution

We assume that the product mix model has been formulated and optimized (as shown in Figure 14.6) and that the SolverTable add-in has been installed. Then the solution to question (1) is shown in Figure 14.8 on page 786. To obtain this output (the part in the range A37:F48), we use the Data/SolverTable menu item, select a one-way table in the first dialog box, and fill in the second dialog box as shown in Figure 14.9. When we click on OK, Solver solves a separate optimization problem for each of the 11 rows of the table and then reports the requested outputs (frames produced and total profit) in the table. It might take a while, depending on the speed of your PC, but everything is automatic. However, if you want to update this table, by using new labor hour values in column A, say, you must repeat the procedure.

There are several ways to interpret the output from this sensitivity analysis. First, we can look at columns B–E to see how the product mix changes as more labor hours become available. For example, frames of type 4 are finally produced when 4500 labor hours are

---

[5]If the StatPro add-in is still installed—there is still a StatPro menu—it is probably a good idea to uninstall it before running the SolverTable add-in. The calculations will occur more quickly.

FIGURE 14.8 **Sensitivity to Available Labor Hours**

	A	B	C	D	E	F	G
34	Sensitivity of optimal solution to number of labor hours						
35		Frames produced					
36	Labor hours	1	2	3	4	Total profit	Increase
37		$B$16	$C$16	$D$16	$E$16	$F$32	
38	2500	1000	500	0	0	$7,000	
39	2750	1000	750	0	0	$7,500	$500
40	3000	1000	1000	0	0	$8,000	$500
41	3250	1000	950	100	0	$8,300	$300
42	3500	1000	900	200	0	$8,600	$300
43	3750	1000	850	300	0	$8,900	$300
44	4000	1000	800	400	0	$9,200	$300
45	4250	1000	750	500	0	$9,500	$300
46	4500	1000	500	500	250	$9,750	$250
47	4750	1000	250	500	500	$10,000	$250
48	5000	1000	0	500	750	$10,250	$250

FIGURE 14.9 **SolverTable Dialog Box for One-Way Table**

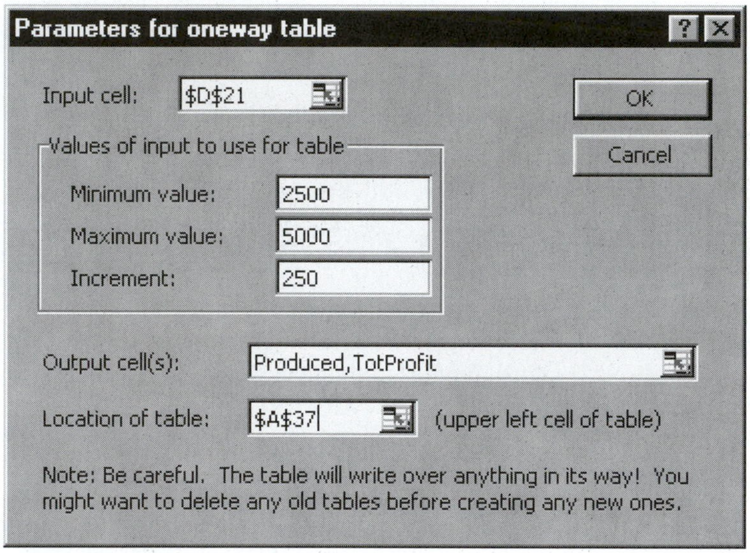

Parameters for oneway table ? ✕

Input cell: $D$21

Values of input to use for table

Minimum value: 2500

Maximum value: 5000

Increment: 250

OK

Cancel

Output cell(s): Produced,TotProfit

Location of table: $A$37 (upper left cell of table)

Note: Be careful. The table will write over anything in its way! You might want to delete any old tables before creating any new ones.

available, and frames of type 2 are discontinued in the final row. Second, we can see how extra labor hours add to the total profit. We show this numerically in column G, where each value is the increase in profit from the previous row. (Column G is not produced by SolverTable; we created it manually.) Note exactly what this increased profit means. For example, when labor hours increase from 2500 to 2750, the model requires that we *pay* $8 apiece for these extra hours (if we use them). But the *net* effect is that profit increases by $500. In other words, the labor cost increases by $2000 [= $8(250)], but this is more than offset by the increase in revenue that comes from having the extra labor hours.

As column G illustrates, it is worthwhile to obtain extra labor hours, even though we have to pay for them, because profit increases. However, the increase in profit per extra labor hour, called the **shadow price** of labor hours, is not constant. We see that it decreases as more labor hours are already owned. An extra 250 labor hours first results in $500 more profit, then $300, and then only $250. This is typical of shadow prices for scarce resources in LP models.

We can also chart the optimal profit values in column F (or any other quantities from a SolverTable output). The line chart shown in Figure 14.10 illustrates how the shadow price (slope of the line) decreases as more labor hours are already owned. (The first decrease in slope is perceptible; the second is hard to see in the chart.)

FIGURE 14.10 **Sensitivity of Optimal Profit to Labor Hours**

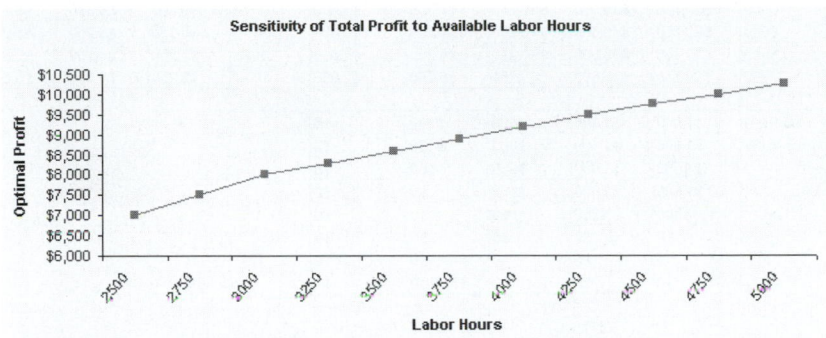

The answer to the sensitivity question (2) is similar and appears in Figure 14.11. We used SolverTable exactly as before; only the input cell and input values differ. Note how the optimal product mix remains unchanged for a cost of metal in the $0.30 to $0.70 range. Within this range, the only thing that changes is the profit, and it decreases only because metal gets more expensive. Outside of this range, however, we change the product mix (and obtain less profit). Intuitively, once metal becomes expensive enough, products that use metal most heavily become less attractive. They will then be produced at lower levels or dropped from the mix altogether.

FIGURE 14.11 **Sensitivity of Optimal Solution to Cost of Metal**

	A	B	C	D	E	F	G
50	Sensitivity of optimal solution to unit cost of metal (per oz.)						
51		Frames produced					
52	Cost (per oz.) of metal	1	2	3	4	Total profit	Decrease
53		$B$16	$C$16	$D$16	$E$16	$F$32	
54	$0.30	1000	800	400	0	$10,400	
55	$0.50	1000	800	400	0	$9,200	$1,200
56	$0.70	1000	800	400	0	$8,000	$1,200
57	$0.90	1000	500	500	0	$6,800	$1,200
58	$1.10	1000	0	500	250	$5,750	$1,050
59	$1.30	1000	0	500	250	$4,750	$1,000

Finally, we answer sensitivity question (3) with a two-way table, as shown in the range A63:F72 of Figure 14.12 (page 788). Now the values of the two inputs, hourly labor cost and labor hours available, are listed along the top and left-hand side, and the address of the single output, total profit, is placed in the upper left cell of the table. To produce this table, we fill SolverTable's second dialog box as shown in Figure 14.13. Now Solver must solve $9(5) = 45$ separate problems, one for each combination of input values, so it can take up to a minute or more. However, the optimal profits are eventually listed in the table. From these, we can see how total profit *decreases* in each row as the hourly labor cost increases

	A	B	C	D	E	F	G	H	I	J	K
61	Sensitivity of optimal profit to changes in labor hours available and hourly labor cost										
62	(Labor costs are along top, labor hours available are along side, profits are in table body)							Decreases as a function of labor cost for			
63	$F$32	6	7	8	9	10					
64	3000	$14,000	$11,000	$8,000	$5,000	$2,000		$3,000	$3,000	$3,000	$3,000
65	3500	$15,600	$12,100	$8,600	$5,100	$2,000		$3,500	$3,500	$3,500	$3,100
66	4000	$17,200	$13,200	$9,200	$5,200	$2,000		$4,000	$4,000	$4,000	$3,200
67	4500	$18,750	$14,250	$9,750	$5,250	$2,000		$4,500	$4,500	$4,500	$3,250
68	5000	$20,250	$15,250	$10,250	$5,250	$2,000		$5,000	$5,000	$5,000	$3,250
69	5500	$20,750	$15,500	$10,250	$5,250	$2,000		$5,250	$5,250	$5,000	$3,250
70	6000	$20,750	$15,500	$10,250	$5,250	$2,000		$5,250	$5,250	$5,000	$3,250
71	6500	$20,750	$15,500	$10,250	$5,250	$2,000		$5,250	$5,250	$5,000	$3,250
72	7000	$20,750	$15,500	$10,250	$5,250	$2,000		$5,250	$5,250	$5,000	$3,250
73											
74	Increases as a function	$1,600	$1,100	$600	$100	$0					
75	of labor hours for each	$1,600	$1,100	$600	$100	$0					
76	fixed labor cost	$1,550	$1,050	$550	$50	$0					
77		$1,500	$1,000	$500	$0	$0					
78		$500	$250	$0	$0	$0					
79		$0	$0	$0	$0	$0					
80		$0	$0	$0	$0	$0					
81		$0	$0	$0	$0	$0					

FIGURE 14.13 SolverTable Dialog Box for Two-Way Table

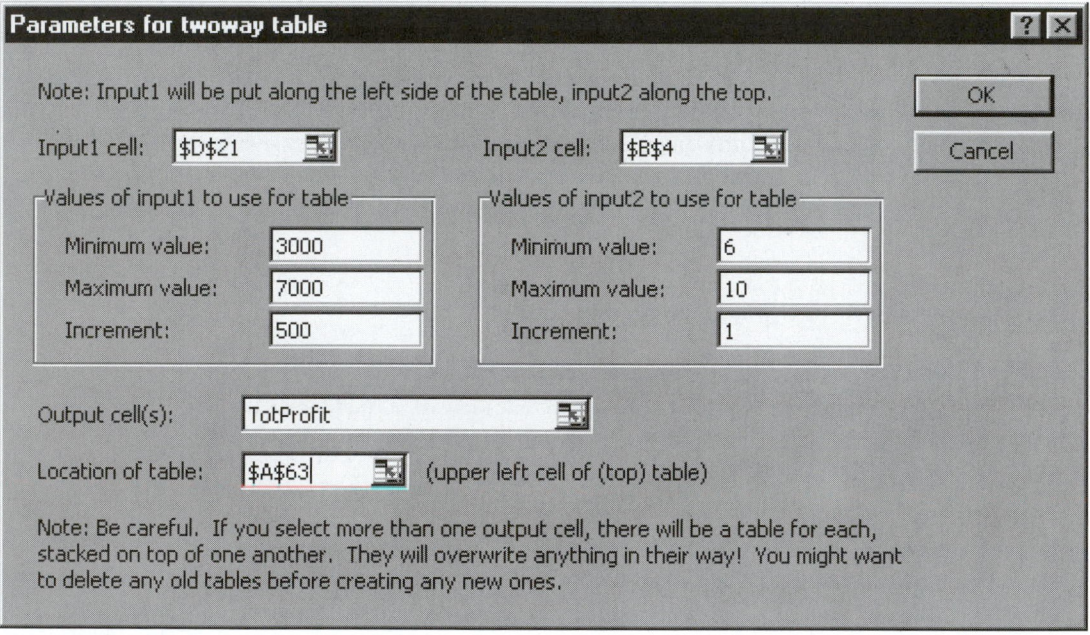

(see the range H64:K72) and how it *increases* in each column as the available labor hours increase (see the range B74:F81). We can also chart the profits in the table. Figure 14.14 shows one possibility.

FIGURE 14.14 **Bar Chart of Optimal Profit**

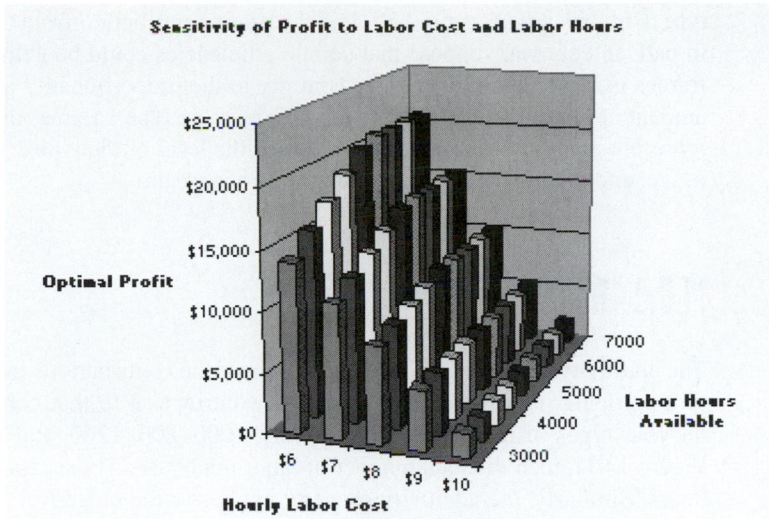

It is always possible to run a sensitivity analysis by changing inputs directly in the spreadsheet model and rerunning Solver. The advantages of the SolverTable add-in, however, are that it allows us to perform a *systematic* sensitivity analysis for any selected inputs and outputs, and it keeps track of the results in a table. Then if we like, we can show these results in graphical form. We will see other applications of this useful add-in in this and the next chapter.

14.5

The Linear Assumptions

L inear programming is an important subset of a larger class of models called **mathematical programming models**.[6] All such models select the levels of various activities that can be performed, subject to a set of constraints, to maximize or minimize an objective such as total profit or total cost. In Monet's product mix example, the activities are the production of the four frame types, and the purpose of the model is to find the levels of these activities that maximize total profit subject to specified constraints.

In terms of this general setup—selecting the optimal levels of activities—there are three important properties that LP models possess that distinguish them from general mathematical programming models: proportionality, additivity, and divisibility. We discuss these properties briefly in this section.

14.5.1 Proportionality

Proportionality means that if the level of any activity is multiplied by a constant factor, then the contribution of this activity to the objective, or to any of the constraints in which the activity is involved, is multiplied by the same factor. For example, suppose that the

---

[6]The word *programming* in linear programming or mathematical programming has nothing to do with computer programming. It originated with the British term *programme*, which is essentially a plan or a schedule of operations.

production of type 1 frames is cut from its optimal value of 1000 (see Figure 14.6) to 500, that is, it is multiplied by 0.5. Then the amounts of labor, metal, and glass consumed by type 1 frames are all cut in half, and the profit contribution from type 1 frames is also cut in half. In contrast, suppose that certain efficiencies could be gained by producing type 1 frames in larger quantities. Then, contrary to the proportionality assumption, the required amount of labor per frame might *decrease* as more type 1 frames are produced. This would represent a *nonlinear* relationship between the level of the type 1 frame activity and labor usage, and it would take us outside of the linear realm.

14.5.2 Additivity

The additivity property implies that the sum of the contributions from the various activities to a particular constraint equals the total contribution to that constraint. For example, if the four types of frames use, respectively, 1000, 800, 1200, and 3000 labor hours (as in Figure 14.1), then the total number of labor hours used is the *sum* of these amounts, 6000 hours. Similarly, the additivity property applies to the objective. That is, the value of the objective is the *sum* of the contributions from the various activities. The additivity property implies that the contribution of any decision variable to the objective or to any constraint is *independent* of the levels of the other decision variables.

14.5.3 Divisibility

The divisibility property simply means that we allow both integer and noninteger levels of the activities. In the product mix example it fortunately turned out that the optimal quantities of frame types 1 through 4 were all integers. However, it is more frequent that the optimal quantities are nonintegers, such as 47.53. In LP models we allow such values. In reality, however, they might not make physical sense. For example, if product 1 is a refrigerator, it makes no sense to make 47.53 refrigerators. (There are products, such as salt measured in pounds, where 47.53 units makes sense, but refrigerators is not one of them!) If we want the levels of some activities to be integer values, then there are two possible approaches: (1) we can solve the LP model without integer constraints, and if the solution turns out to have noninteger values, we can attempt to round them to integer values, or (2) we can explicitly constrain certain changing cells to contain integer values. The latter approach, however, takes us into the realm of *integer programming*, a much more difficult class of problems than LP problems.

Whenever we model a real problem, we usually make some simplifying assumptions. This is certainly the case with LP models. The world is frequently *not* linear, which means that an entirely realistic model will typically violate some or all of the above three properties. However, many successful applications of LP have demonstrated the usefulness of linear models, even if they are only approximations of reality. If we suspect that the violations are serious enough to invalidate a linear model, then we should use an integer or nonlinear model, as we illustrate with several examples in the next chapter.

In terms of Excel's Solver, if the model is linear—that is, if it satisfies the proportionality, additivity, and divisibility properties—then we should check the Assume Linear Model box mentioned earlier. (Recall that it appears in the Solver Options dialog box.) Then Solver will use the simplex method, which is the most efficient method for a linear model, to solve the problem.

Technical Note   In some cases you might think a model is linear, but when you check the Assume Linear Model box, you get a message from Solver that "the conditions for Assume Linear Model are not satisfied." This might indicate a logical error in your formulation, so that the proportionality, additivity, or divisibility conditions are indeed not satisfied. However, it can also indicate that Solver erroneously *thinks* the linearity conditions are not satisfied, and this is typically due to roundoff error in its calculations. If the latter occurs, and you are convinced that the formulation is correct, you can try *not* checking the Assume Linear Model box and see if that works. If it doesn't, consult your instructor. It is possible that the (nonsimplex) algorithm employed by Solver when this box isn't checked simply cannot find the solution to your problem.

In any case, it helps to have a *well-scaled* model. In a well-scaled model, all of the numbers are roughly the same magnitude. If the model contains some very large numbers (100,000 or more, say) and some very small numbers (0.001 or less, say), it is *poorly scaled* for the methods used by Solver, and roundoff error is far more likely to cause problems—not only in Solver's test of the linearity conditions but in all of its algorithms.

If you believe your model is poorly scaled, there are two possible remedies. The first is to check the Use Automatic Scaling box in the Solver Options dialog box (see Figure 14.4). The second option is to redefine the units in which the various quantities are defined. For example, in the Monet model a natural rescaling would be to:

■   Define the changing cells as the number of frames of each type produced *in thousands*.

■   Define maximum sales limitations *in thousands*.

■   Define profit *in thousands of dollars*.

■   Define resource availabilities *in thousands of units* (labor hours or ounces of glass or metal).

If we rescale according to the steps above, the solution in Figure 14.15 (page 792) results. (Actually, all we had to do was rescale the inputs in B18:E18 and D21:D23 and rerun Solver.) Now all of the model quantities are of similar magnitude.

14.6   Graphical Solution Method

Once LP problems are formulated, they are almost always solved numerically with computer software. The amount of computation makes manual calculation prohibitive for realistically sized problems. However, it is instructive to look at a graphical solution procedure for models with only two decision variables. Admittedly, almost no real problems have only two decision variables, but the graphical solution is useful for the insights it provides, even for larger problems.

E X A M P L E   1 4 . 2

To illustrate the graphical approach, we will use a slightly different scaled-down version of Monet's product mix problem. Now there are only two frame types, 1 and 2, and only two scarce resources, labor hours and metal. The algebraic model is given below:

$$\max 2.25x_1 + 2.60x_2 \qquad \text{(profit objective)}$$

$$\text{subject to } 2x_1 + x_2 \le 4000 \quad \text{(labor constraint)}$$

$$x_1 + 2x_2 \le 5000 \quad \text{(metal constraint)}$$

$$x_1, x_2 \ge 0 \quad \text{(nonnegativity constraints)}$$

FIGURE 14.15   Product Mix Problem with Rescaled Values

	A	B	C	D	E	F	G	H
1	**Product Mix Problem**							
2								
3	**Input data**							
4	Hourly wage rate	$8.00						
5	Cost per oz of metal	$0.50						
6	Cost per oz of glass	$0.75						
7								
8	Frame type	1	2	3	4		**Range names:**	
9	Labor hours per frame	2	1	3	2		Available: D21:D23	
10	Metal (oz.) per frame	4	2	1	2		MaxSales: B18:E18	
11	Glass (oz.) per frame	6	2	1	2		Produced: B16:E16	
12	Unit selling price	$28.50	$12.50	$29.25	$21.50		TotProfit: F32	
13							Used: B21:B23	
14	**Production plan**							
15	Frame type	1	2	3	4			
16	Frames produced (1000s)	1.00	0.80	0.40	0.00			
17		<=	<=	<=	<=			
18	Maximum sales (1000s)	1	2	0.5	1			
19								
20	**Constraints on inputs**	Used		Available				
21	Labor hours (1000s)	4.0	<=	4				
22	Metal (1000s of oz.)	6.0	<=	6				
23	Glass (1000s of oz.)	8.0	<=	10				
24								
25	**Revenue, cost summary (all values in $1000s)**							
26	Frame type	1	2	3	4	Totals		
27	Revenue	$28.5	$10.0	$11.7	$0.0	$50.2		
28	Costs of inputs							
29	Labor	$16.0	$6.4	$9.6	$0.0	$32.0		
30	Metal	$2.0	$0.8	$0.2	$0.0	$3.0		
31	Glass	$4.5	$1.2	$0.3	$0.0	$6.0		
32	Profit	$6.0	$1.6	$1.6	$0.0	$9.2		

The objective implies that each type 1 frame contributes a profit of $2.25, whereas each type 2 frame contributes a profit of $2.60. The first constraint is a labor hour constraint. There are 4000 hours available. Each type 1 frame requires 2 labor hours, and each type 2 frame requires 1 labor hour. Similarly, the second constraint is a metal constraint. There are 5000 ounces of metal available. Each type 1 frame requires 1 ounce of metal, and each type 2 frame requires 2 ounces of metal. Find the optimal product mix graphically.

Solution

The idea is to graph the constraints on a two-dimensional graph to see which points (x_1, x_2) satisfy all of the constraints. This set of points is labeled the **feasible region**. Then we see which point in the feasible region provides the largest profit.

The graphical solution appears in Figure 14.16. To produce this graph, we first locate the lines where the constraints hold as equalities. For example, the line for labor hours is $2x_1 + x_2 = 4000$. The easiest way to graph this is to find the two points where it crosses the axes. It crosses the x_1-axis when $x_2 = 0$, that is, at $x_1 = 4000/2 = 2000$. Similarly, it crosses the x_2-axis when $x_1 = 0$, that is, at $x_2 = 4000$. Joining the points $(0, 4000)$ and $(2000, 0)$, we get the line where the labor constraint is satisfied exactly, that is, as an equality. All points below and to the left of this line are also feasible; these are the points where less than the maximum of 4000 labor hours are used. [To see this, try the point $(0, 0)$.

FIGURE 14.16   **Graphical Solution for Monet's Two-Variable Problem**

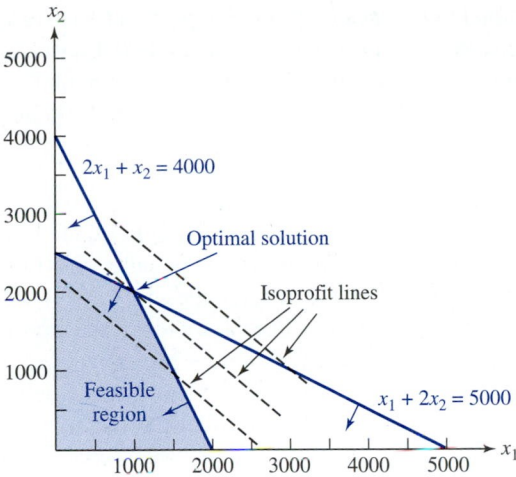

It obviously satisfies the labor hour constraint, so it must be on the feasible side of the line. If (0, 0) did not satisfy the constraint, then the feasible side would be the side *not* including (0, 0).] We indicate the feasible side of the line by the short arrows pointing down to the left from the labor constraint line.

Similarly, the metal constraint line crosses the axes at the points (0, 2500) and (5000, 0), so we join these two points to find the line where all 5000 ounces of metal are used. Then all points below this line, indicated by the short arrows, use less than 5000 ounces of metal. Finally, the points on or below both of these lines constitute the feasible region. These are the points below the heavy lines, as indicated in Figure 14.16. (Of course, the feasible region includes only points to the right of the vertical axis and above the horizontal axis, since negative production quantities are impossible.) You can think of the feasible region as all points on or inside the figure formed by four points: (0, 0), (0, 2500), (2000, 0), and the point where the labor hour and metal constraint lines intersect.

The next step is to bring profit into the picture. This is done by looking at "isoprofit" lines—that is, lines where total profit is a constant. Any such line can be written as

$$2.25x_1 + 2.60x_2 = P$$

where P is a constant profit level. Solving for x_2, we can put this equation in slope–intercept form:

$$x_2 = P/2.60 - (2.25/2.60)x_1$$

This shows that any isoprofit line has slope $-2.25/2.60$, and it crosses the vertical axis at the value $P/2.60$. Three of these isoprofit lines appear in Figure 14.16 as dotted lines. Clearly, as the dotted line moves up and to the right, the profit P increases. So we want to move the dotted line up and to the right until it just barely touches the feasible region. Graphically, we can see that the last feasible point it will touch is the point indicated in the figure, where the labor hour and metal constraint lines cross. (The corresponding isoprofit line is the middle dotted line.) We can then solve two equations in two unknowns to find the coordinates of this point. They are $x_1 = 1000$ and $x_2 = 2000$, with a corresponding profit of $P = \$7450$.

Notice that if the slope of the isoprofit lines were much steeper, then the optimal point would be (2000, 0). On the other hand, if the slope were much *less* steep, the optimal point would be (0, 2500). These statements make intuitive sense. If the isoprofit lines are steep, this is because the unit profit from frame type 1 is large relative to the unit profit from frame type 2. If there is a large enough disparity, Monet will produce only frame type 1 and none of frame type 2. The opposite statement is true if the isoprofit lines are much less steep, inducing Monet to produce only frame type 2 and none of type 1. The crucial point, however, is that only three points can be optimal: (2000, 0), (0, 2500), or (1000, 2000), the three "corner" points (other than (0, 0)) in the feasible region.[7] The best of these depends on the relative slopes of the constraint lines and isoprofit lines in the graph. ■

This graphical approach is virtually never used to solve real problems, but it does provide important insights into LP in general. Namely, all LP problems have feasible regions that can be thought of as multidimensional polygons (figures with straight edges). The only points that can be optimal (except in the case of ties) are the corner points of this polygon. To see which corner point is optimal, we move an isoprofit plane as far as possible in the desired direction (the direction that improves the objective function) until it just barely intersects with the feasible region. The corner point that is touched last is then the optimal solution. The simplex method—the method Excel's Solver uses for LP problems—is really just an efficient method of searching through the thousands (or millions) of corner points that occur in realistic problems.

PROBLEMS

Level A

1   Leary Chemical manufactures three chemicals: A, B, and C. These chemicals are produced via two production processes: 1 and 2. Running process 1 for an hour costs $4 and yields 3 units of A, 1 unit of B, and 1 unit of C. Running process 2 for an hour costs $1 and yields 1 unit of A and 1 unit of B. To meet customer demands, at least 10 units of A, 5 units of B, and 3 units of C must be produced daily.

   a   Use Solver to determine a daily production plan that minimizes the cost of meeting Leary's daily demands.

   b   Confirm graphically that the daily production plan from part a minimizes the cost of meeting Leary's daily demands.

2   Starting with the optimal solution to the previous problem, use the SolverTable add-in to see what happens to the decision variables and the total cost when the hourly processing cost for process 2 increases in increments of $.50. How large must this cost increase be before the decision variables change? What happens when it continues to increase beyond this point?

3   Furnco manufactures desks and chairs. Each desk uses 4 units of wood, and each chair uses 3 units of wood. A desk contributes $40 to profit, and a chair contributes $25. Marketing restrictions require that the number of chairs produced be at least twice the number of desks produced. There are 20 units of wood available.

   a   Use Solver to maximize Furnco's profit.

   b   Confirm graphically that the solution in part a maximizes Furnco's profit.

4   Starting with the optimal solution to the previous problem, use the SolverTable add-in to see what happens to the decision variables and the total profit when the availability of wood varies from 10 to 30 in 1-unit increments. Based on your findings, how much would Furnco be willing to pay for each extra unit of wood over its current 20 units? How much profit would Furnco lose if it lost any of its current 20 units?

5   A farmer in Iowa owns 45 acres of land. She is going to plant each acre with wheat or corn. Each acre planted with wheat yields $200 profit; each with corn yields $300 profit. The labor

[7]This is not quite true. If the slope of the isoprofit lines is *exactly* the same as the slope of one of the constraint lines, then a whole line segment can be optimal. We call this the **multiple optimal solution case**—the case of ties. Even in the case of ties, however, we can still restrict the search for optimal solutions to corner points.

and fertilizer used for each acre are given in the file P14_5.XLS. One hundred workers and 120 tons of fertilizer are available.

a Use Solver to help the farmer maximize the profit from her land.

b Confirm graphically that the solution from part **a** maximizes the farmer's profit from her land.

6 Starting with the optimal solution to the previous problem, use the SolverTable add-in to see what happens to the decision variables and the total profit when the availability of fertilizer varies from 20 tons to 220 tons in 10-ton increments.

a When does the farmer discontinue producing wheat? When does he discontinue producing corn?

b How does the profit change for each 10-ton increment? Make this more obvious by creating a line chart of profit (vertical axis) versus fertilizer availability.

Level B

7 Truckco manufactures two types of trucks, types 1 and 2. Each truck must go through the painting shop and the assembly shop. If the painting shop were completely devoted to painting type 1 trucks, 800 per day could be painted, whereas if the painting shop were completely devoted to painting type 2 trucks, 700 per day could be painted. If the assembly shop were completely devoted to assembling truck 1 engines, 1500 per day could be assembled, and if the assembly shop were completely devoted to assembling truck 2 engines, 1200 per day could be assembled. Each type 1 truck contributes $300 to profit; each type 2 truck contributes $500. Use Solver to maximize Truckco's profit. (*Hint*: Try a graphical procedure first. Then deduce the constraints from the graph.) ■

Infeasibility and Unboundedness

14.7

I n this section we discuss two of the things that can go wrong when we invoke the Solver. Both of these might indicate that there is a mistake in the formulation. Therefore, because mistakes are common in LP formulations, we should be aware of the error messages we might encounter.

14.7.1 Infeasibility

The first problem is infeasibility. If a solution satisfies all of the constraints, we say that it is **feasible**. Among all of the feasible solutions, we are looking for the one that optimizes the objective. Now, it is possible that there are no feasible solutions to the model. There are generally two possible reasons for this: (1) there is a mistake in the formulation (an input entered wrong, such as a $\geq$ instead of a $\leq$) or (2) the problem has been so constrained that there are no solutions that satisfy all of them. In the former case a careful check of the formulation should find the error. In the latter case the modeler might simply have to change, or even eliminate, some of the constraints.

To show how an infeasible problem could occur, suppose in Monet's product mix problem that we incorrectly enter the maximum sales constraints with the wrong inequality: Produced>=MaxSales instead of Produced<=MaxSales. Now Monet must produce *at least* as much as the maximum sales values. If the constraint is changed this way and Solver is then used, the message in Figure 14.17 (page 796) appears, indicating that Solver cannot find a feasible solution. The reason is clear. There is no way, given the resource availabilities,

FIGURE 14.17   Solver Dialog Box Indicating No Feasible Solution

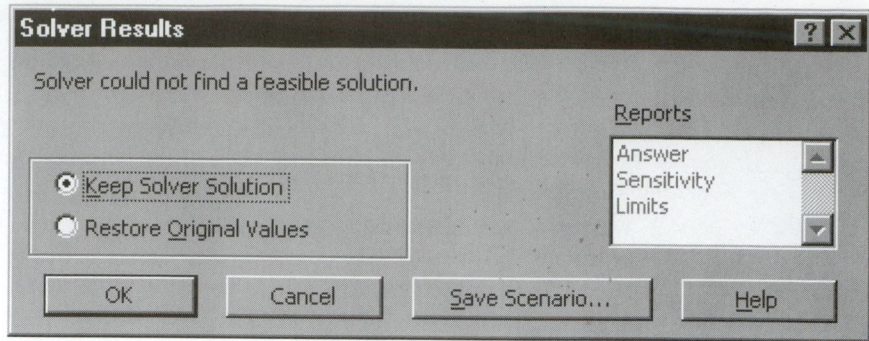

that the company can meet these production constraints. If we are observant, we'll notice the error in the formulation, change the direction of the inequality, and proceed. However, there is no foolproof way of finding the problem when a "no feasible solution" message appears. Careful checking and rethinking are required.

14.7.2 Unboundedness

A second type of problem is **unboundedness**. In this case the model has been formulated in such a way that the objective is unbounded—that is, it can be made as large (or as small, for minimization problems) as we like. If this occurs, we've probably either entered a wrong input or forgotten some constraints. (Or we've found a way to become infinitely rich!) To see how this could occur in the product mix problem, suppose that we enter both the maximum sales constraints and the resource constraints with $\geq$ instead of $\leq$. Now there is no upper bound on how much of each product Monet can make because there is no upper bound on the amount of the resources available. Since each frame is generating a profit, the total profit is unlimited. If these changes in the formulation are made and Solver is then used, the message in Figure 14.18 appears, stating that the target cell does not converge. In other words, the total profit is growing without bound.

FIGURE 14.18   Solver Dialog Box Indicating an Unbounded Solution

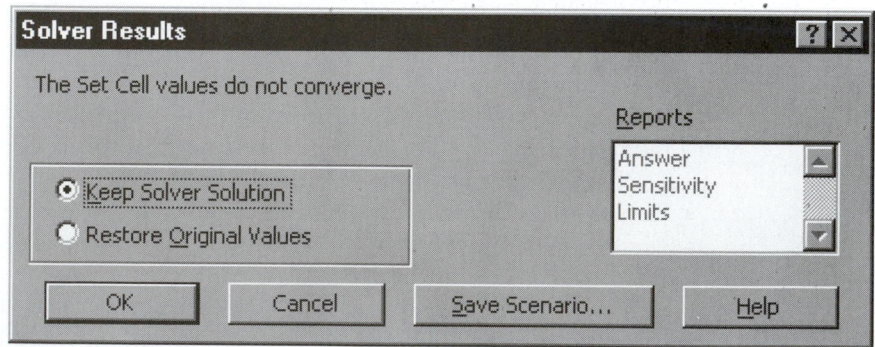

Infeasibility and unboundedness are quite different in a practical sense. It is quite possible for a reasonable model to have no feasible solutions. For example, the people in the marketing department might impose several constraints, the people in the production department might add some more, the people in engineering might add some more, and so on. Together, they might very well constrain the problem so much that there are no feasible solutions. The only way out is for them to change or eliminate some of their constraints. An unboundedness problem is quite different. There is no way a realistic model can have an unbounded solution. If our model does have an unbounded solution, then we must have made a mistake—either we made an input error or we omitted one or more constraints.

14.8 A Multiperiod Production Problem

The product mix example illustrates a typical LP model. However, LP models come in many forms. For variety, we will now illustrate a quite different type of problem that can also be solved with LP. (In the next chapter we will illustrate many other examples, linear and otherwise.) The distinguishing feature of the following problem is that it relates decisions made in several time periods. This type of problem occurs when a company must make a decision now that will have ramifications in the future. The company doesn't want to focus completely on the near future and forget about the long run.

EXAMPLE 14.3

The Pigskin Company produces footballs. Pigskin must decide how many footballs to produce each month. It has decided to use a 6-month planning horizon. The forecasted demands for the next 6 months are 10,000, 15,000, 30,000, 35,000, 25,000, and 10,000. Pigskin wants to meet these demands on time, knowing that it currently has 5000 footballs in inventory and it can use a given month's production to help meet the demand for that month. During each month there is enough production capacity to produce up to 30,000 footballs, and there is enough storage capacity to store up to 10,000 footballs at the end of the month. The forecasted production costs per football for the next 6 months are $12.50, $12.55, $12.70, $12.80, $12.85, and $12.95, respectively. The holding cost per football held in inventory at the end of any month is figured at 5% of the production cost for that month. (This cost includes the cost of storage and also the cost of money tied up in inventory.) The selling price for footballs is not considered relevant to the production decision because it is assumed that all demand will be met exactly when it occurs—at whatever the selling price is. Therefore, Pigskin wants to determine the production schedule that minimizes the total production and holding costs.

Solution

In the traditional algebraic formulation, the decision variables are the production quantities for the 6 months, labeled P_1 through P_6. It is also convenient to let I_1 through I_6 be the corresponding end-of-month inventories. For example, I_3 is the number of footballs left over at the end of month 3. Therefore, the obvious constraints are on production and inventory storage capacities: $P_j \leq 300$ and $I_j \leq 100$ for each month j, $1 \leq j \leq 6$. (*Note*: From here on, to minimize the number of zeros shown, we will express all quantities in hundreds of footballs.)

In addition to these constraints, we need "balance" constraints that relate the P's and I's. In any month the inventory from the previous month plus the current production must equal the current demand plus leftover inventory. If D_j is the forecasted demand for month j, then the balance equation for month j is

$$I_{j-1} + P_j = D_j + I_j$$

The first of these constraints, for month $j = 1$, uses the known beginning inventory, 50, for the previous inventory (the I_{j-1} term). By putting all variables (P's and I's) on the left and all known values on the right (a standard LP convention), these balance equations become

$$P_1 - I_1 = 100 - 50$$

$$I_1 + P_2 - I_2 = 150$$

$$I_2 + P_3 - I_3 = 300$$

$$I_3 + P_4 - I_4 = 350$$

$$I_4 + P_5 - I_5 = 250$$

$$I_5 + P_6 - I_6 = 100 \tag{14.1}$$

As usual, we impose nonnegativity constraints: All P's and I's must be nonnegative. What about meeting demand on time? This requires that in each month the inventory from the preceding month plus the current production must be at least as large as the current demand. But take a look, for example, at the balance equation for month 3. By rearranging it slightly, we can write it as

$$I_3 = I_2 + P_3 - 300$$

Now, the nonnegativity constraint on I_3 implies that the right-hand side of this equation, $I_2 + P_3 - 300$, is also nonnegative. But this implies that demand in month 3 is covered— the beginning inventory in month 3 plus month 3 production is at least 300. Therefore, the nonnegativity constraints on the I's *automatically* guarantee that all demands will be met on time, and no other constraints are needed. Alternatively, we could write directly that $I_2 + P_3 \geq 300$. In words, the amount on hand after production in month 3 is at least as large as the demand in month 3. We'll take advantage of this interpretation in the spreadsheet model.

Finally, the objective is obvious. It is the sum of unit production costs multiplied by P's, plus unit holding costs multiplied by I's.

Developing the Spreadsheet Model The spreadsheet version of Pigskin's production problem appears in Figure 14.19. (See the file PIGSKIN1.XLS.) The main feature that distinguishes this model from the product mix model is that some of the constraints, namely, the balance equations (14.1), are built into the spreadsheet itself by means of formulas. In other words, the only changing cells are the production quantities. The ending inventories shown in row 21 are determined by the production quantities and equations (14.1). To form the spreadsheet in Figure 14.19, we proceed as follows.

1 **Inputs.** Enter the various inputs in the ranges InitInv (B4), HoldPct (B5), B9:G9, ProdCap (B15:G15), Demand (B19:G19), and InvCap (B23:G23).

2 **Production quantities.** Enter *any* six values in the range Produced (B13:G13) as production quantities. As always, you can enter values that you believe are good, maybe even optimal. This is not crucial, however, because Solver will eventually find the optimal production quantities.

FIGURE 14.19   Nonoptimal Solution to Pigskin's Production Problem

	A	B	C	D	E	F	G	H	I
1	Multiperiod Production Problem								
2									
3	Input data								
4	Initial inventory (100s)	50							
5	Holding cost as % of prod cost	5%							
6									
7								Range names:	
8		Month 1	Month 2	Month 3	Month 4	Month 5	Month 6	Demand: B19:G19	
9	Production cost/unit	$12.50	$12.55	$12.70	$12.80	$12.85	$12.95	EndInv: B21:G21	
10								HoldPct: B5	
11	Production plan (all quantities are in 100s of footballs)							InitInv: B4	
12		Month 1	Month 2	Month 3	Month 4	Month 5	Month 6	InvCap: B23:G23	
13	Units produced	150	150	300	300	250	100	OnHand: B17:G17	
14		<=	<=	<=	<=	<=	<=	ProdCap: B15:G15	
15	Production capacity (100s)	300	300	300	300	300	300	Produced: B13:G13	
16								TotCost: H29	
17	On hand after production	200	250	400	400	300	150		
18		>=	>=	>=	>=	>=	>=		
19	Demand	100	150	300	350	250	100		
20									
21	Ending inventory	100	100	100	50	50	50		
22		<=	<=	<=	<=	<=	<=		
23	Storage capacity	100	100	100	100	100	100		
24									
25	Summary of costs (all costs are in hundreds of dollars)								
26		Month 1	Month 2	Month 3	Month 4	Month 5	Month 6	Totals	
27	Total production cost	$1,875.00	$1,882.50	$3,810.00	$3,840.00	$3,212.50	$1,295.00	$15,915.00	
28	Total holding cost	$62.50	$62.75	$63.50	$32.00	$32.13	$32.38	$285.25	
29								$16,200.25	

3   On-hand inventory. Enter the formula

$$=InitInv+B13$$

in cell B17. This calculates the first month on-hand inventory after production. Then enter the "typical" formula

$$=B21+C13$$

for on-hand inventory after production in month 2 in cell C17 and copy it across row 17. In multiperiod problems we often need a slightly different formula for the first period than for all other periods.

4   Ending inventories. Enter the formula

$$=B17-B19$$

for ending inventory in cell B21 and copy it to the range C21:G21. This formula calculates ending inventory in the current month as on-hand inventory before demand minus the demand in that month.

5   Production and holding costs. Enter the formula

$$=B9*B13$$

in cell B27 and copy it across to cell G27 to calculate the monthly production costs. Then enter the formula

$$=HoldPct*B9*B21$$

in cell B28 and copy it across to cell G28 to calculate the monthly holding costs. Note that these are based on monthly ending inventories. Finally, calculate the cost totals in column H by summing.

The logic behind the constraints is now straightforward. All we have to guarantee is that (1) the production quantities are nonnegative and do not exceed the production capacities, (2) the on-hand inventories after production are at least as large as demands, and (3) ending inventories do not exceed storage capacities.

Using Solver   To use Solver, fill out the dialog boxes as follows and then click on Solve.

1   **Model.** Fill out the Solver dialog box as in Figure 14.20. Of course, if we didn't name ranges, we would refer directly to the corresponding cell addresses.

2   **Options.** In the Solver Options dialog box, check the Assume Linear Model and Assume Non-Negative boxes. Note that the latter ensures only that the *changing* cells will be nonnegative. If we wanted to explicitly constrain the ending inventory cells to be nonnegative, we would have to add an extra constraint in Figure 14.20.

FIGURE 14.20   **Solver Settings for Production Example**

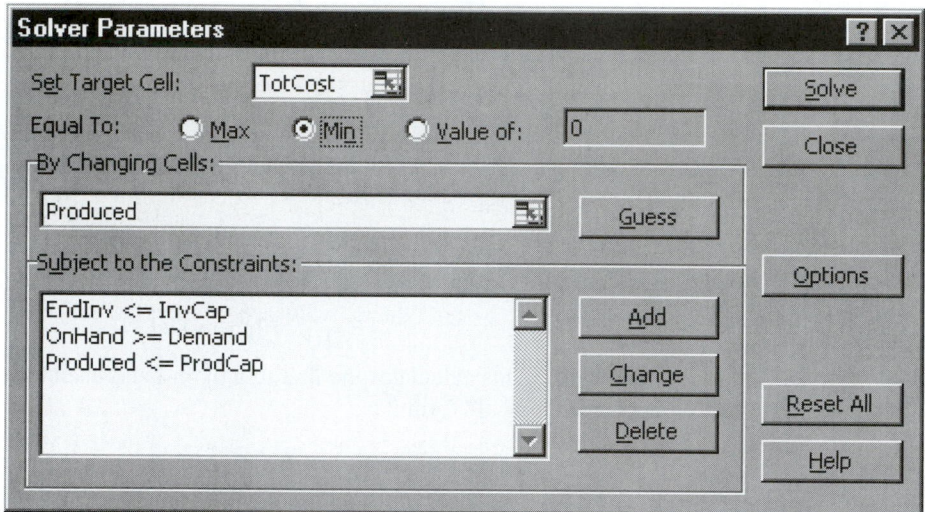

The Solver solution appears in Figure 14.21. This solution is also represented graphically in Figure 14.22. We can interpret the solution by comparing production quantities with demands. (Also, remember that all quantities are in units of 100 footballs.) In month 1 Pigskin should produce just enough to meet month 1 demand (taking into account the initial inventory of 5000). In month 2 it should produce 5000 more footballs than month 2 demand, and then in month 3 it should produce just enough to meet month 3 demand, still carrying the extra 5000 footballs in inventory from month 2 production. In month 4 Pigskin should finally use these 5000 footballs, along with the maximum production amount, 30,000, to meet month 4 demand. Then in months 5 and 6 it should produce exactly enough to meet these months' demands. The total cost is $1,535,563, most of which is production cost. (This is expressed in actual dollars. The value in the spreadsheet is in hundreds of dollars. Also, don't feel sorry for Pigskin, however. Remember that we ignored the selling price. The revenues from these sales should make Pigskin a handsome profit.)

Could you have guessed that this is the optimal solution? Upon some reflection, it makes perfect sense. Because the monthly holding costs are large relative to the differences in monthly production costs, there is little incentive to produce footballs before they are

FIGURE 14.21 **Optimal Solution for Pigskin Production Problem**

	A	B	C	D	E	F	G	H	I
1	**Multiperiod Production Problem**								
2									
3	**Input data**								
4	Initial inventory (100s)	50							
5	Holding cost as % of prod cost	5%							
6									
7								Range names:	
8		Month 1	Month 2	Month 3	Month 4	Month 5	Month 6	Demand: B19:G19	
9	Production cost/unit	$12.50	$12.55	$12.70	$12.80	$12.85	$12.95	EndInv: B21:G21 HoldPct: B5	
10								InitInv: B4	
11	**Production plan (all quantities are in 100s of footballs)**							InvCap: B23:G23	
12		Month 1	Month 2	Month 3	Month 4	Month 5	Month 6	OnHand: B17:G17	
13	Units produced	50	200	300	300	250	100	ProdCap: B15:G15	
14		<=	<=	<=	<=	<=	<=	Produced: B13:G13 TotCost: H29	
15	Production capacity (100s)	300	300	300	300	300	300		
16									
17	On hand after production	100	200	350	350	250	100		
18		>=	>=	>=	>=	>=	>=		
19	Demand	100	150	300	350	250	100		
20									
21	Ending inventory	0	50	50	0	0	0		
22		<=	<=	<=	<=	<=	<=		
23	Storage capacity	100	100	100	100	100	100		
24									
25	**Summary of costs (all costs are in hundreds of dollars)**								
26		Month 1	Month 2	Month 3	Month 4	Month 5	Month 6	Totals	
27	Total production cost	$625.00	$2,510.00	$3,810.00	$3,840.00	$3,212.50	$1,295.00	$15,292.50	
28	Total holding cost	$0.00	$31.38	$31.75	$0.00	$0.00	$0.00	$63.13	
29								$15,355.63	

FIGURE 14.22 **Graphical Representation of Optimal Production Schedule**

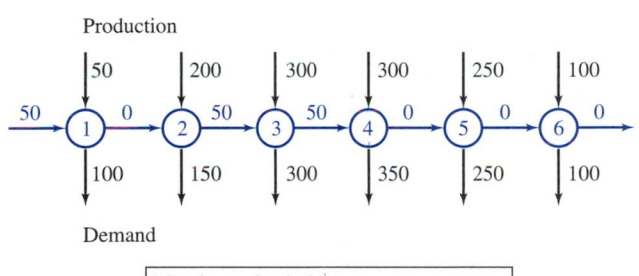

Months are in circles.
Inventory levels are on horizontal arrows.

needed to take advantage of a "cheap" production month. Therefore, Solver tells us to produce footballs in the month in which they are needed—when this is possible. The only exception to this rule is the 20,000 footballs produced during month 2 when only 15,000 are needed. The extra 5000 units produced during month 2 are needed, however, to meet month 4's demand of 35,000, because month 3 production capacity is used entirely to meet month 3 demand. Thus month 3 capacity is not available to meet month 4 demand, and 5000 units of month 2 capacity are used to meet month 4 demand.

Sensitivity Analysis We can again use the SolverTable add-in to perform a sensitivity analysis. We illustrate two possibilities. First, note that the most inventory we ever carry at the end of a month is 50 (5000 footballs), although the storage capacity each month is 100.

Perhaps this is because the holding cost percentage (5%) is fairly large. Would we carry more ending inventory if this holding cost percentage were reduced? Or would we carry even less if it were increased? We check this with the SolverTable output shown in Figure 14.23. Now the only (column) input cell is HoldPct (B5), and the *single* output we keep track of is the maximum ending inventory ever held, which we calculate in cell B32 with the formula

=MAX(EndInv)

in cell B32. As we see, only when the holding cost percentage decreases to 1% do we reach the storage capacity limit. (From this output we can't tell which month or how many months the ending inventory will be at this upper limit.) On the other side, even when the holding cost percentage reaches 10%, we still continue to hold a maximum ending inventory of 50.

FIGURE 14.23 **Sensitivity of Maximum Ending Inventory to Holding Cost Percentage**

	A	B	C	D	E	F
31	Sensitivity of maximum amount of ending inventory to holding cost percentage					
32	Output formula	50				
33						
34	Holding cost percentage	MaxEndInv				
35		$B$32				
36	1%	100				
37	2%	50				
38	3%	50				
39	4%	50				
40	5%	50				
41	6%	50				
42	7%	50				
43	8%	50				
44	9%	50				
45	10%	50				

A second possible sensitivity analysis is suggested by the way the optimal production schedule would probably be implemented. The optimal solution to Pigskin's model specifies the production level for each of the next 6 months. In reality, however, the company might implement the model's recommendation only for the *first* month. Then at the beginning of the second month, it will gather new forecasts for the *next* 6 months, that is, months 2 through 7, solve a new 6-month model, and again implement the model's recommendation for the first of these months, month 2. If it continues in this manner, we say that it is following a 6-month **rolling planning horizon**.

The question then is whether the assumed demands (really, forecasts) toward the end of the planning horizon have much effect on the optimal production quantity in month 1. We would hope not since these forecasts could be quite inaccurate. The two-way table in Figure 14.24 shows how the optimal month 1 production quantity varies with the assumed demands in months 5 and 6. As we see, if the assumed month 5 and 6 demands remain fairly small, the optimal month 1 production quantity remains at 50. This is good news. It means that the optimal production quantity in month 1 is very insensitive to the possibly inaccurate forecasts in months 5 and 6.

Modeling Issue   We assumed that Pigskin is using a 6-month planning horizon. Why 6 months? In multiperiod problems such as this, the company has to make forecasts about the future, such as the level of customer demand. Therefore, the length of the planning horizon is usually the length of time for which the company can make reasonably accurate forecasts. Here, Pigskin evidently believes that it can forecast up to 6 months from now, so it uses a 6-month planning horizon.

FIGURE 14.24 **Sensitivity of Month 1 Production to Demands in Months 5 and 6**

	A	B	C	D	E	F
47	Sensitivity of month 1 production quantity to demands in months 5 and 6					
48	Month 5 demand is along side, month 6 demand is along top					
49	$B$13	100	200	300		
50	100	50	50	50		
51	200	50	50	50		
52	300	50	50	50		

PROBLEMS

Level A

8   A customer requires during the next 4 months, respectively, 50, 65, 100, and 70 units of a commodity, and no backlogging is allowed (that is, the customer's requirements must be met on time). Production costs are $5, $8, $4, and $7 per unit during these months. The storage cost from one month to the next is $2 per unit (assessed on ending inventory). It is estimated that each unit on hand at the end of month 4 could be sold for $6. Determine how to minimize the net cost incurred in meeting the demands for the next 4 months.

9   Starting with the optimal solution to the previous problem, use the SolverTable add-in to see what happens to the decision variables and the total cost when the initial inventory varies from 0 (the implied value in the previous problem) to 100 in 10-unit increments. How much lower would the total cost be if the company started with 10 units in inventory, rather than none? Would this same cost decrease occur for *every* 10-unit increase in initial inventory?

10   A company faces the following demands during the next 3 weeks: week 1, 20 units; week 2, 10 units; week 3, 15 units. The unit production cost during each week is as follows: week 1, $13; week 2, $14; week 3, $15. A holding cost of $2 per unit is assessed against each week's ending inventory. At the beginning of week 1, the company has 5 units on hand. In reality, not all goods produced during a month can be used to meet the current month's demand. To model this fact, we assume that only half of the goods produced during a week can be used to meet the current week's demands. Determine how to minimize the cost of meeting the demand for the next 3 weeks.

11   Revise the model for the previous problem so that the demands are of the form $D_t + k\Delta_t$, where D_t is the original demand (from the previous problem) in month t, k is a factor, and Δ_t is an amount of change in month t. Formulate the model in such a way that you can use the SolverTable add-in to analyze changes in the amounts produced and the total cost when k varies from 0 to 10 in 1-unit increments, for any fixed values of the Δ_t's. For example, try this when $\Delta_1 = 2$, $\Delta_2 = 5$, and $\Delta_3 = 3$. Describe the behavior you observe in the table. Can you find any "reasonable" Δ_t's that induce *positive* production levels in week 3?

12   James Beerd bakes cheesecakes and Black Forest cakes. During any month he can bake at most 65 cakes. The costs per cake and the demands for cakes, which must be met on time, are listed in the file P14_12.XLS. It costs 50 cents to hold a cheesecake and 40 cents to hold a Black Forest cake in inventory for a month. Determine how to minimize the total cost of meeting the next 3 months' demands.

13   Revise the model for the previous problem so that the unit production costs are of the form $c_t(1 + \Delta_t)^k$ in month t, where c_t is the original unit cost (from the previous problem) in month t, Δ_t is an amount of change in month t, and k is an exponent. The c_t's and Δ_t's for cheescakes can differ from those for Black Forest cakes, but k should be the same for both. Formulate the model so that you can use the SolverTable add-in to investigate changes in the production quantities and total cost when k varies from 0 to 4 in 1-unit increments. You can try any reasonable values for the Δ_t's, such as $\Delta_1 = 0.1$, $\Delta_2 = 0.15$, and $\Delta_3 = 0.2$ for cheesecakes, and $\Delta_1 = 0.05$, $\Delta_2 = 0.1$, and $\Delta_3 = 0.15$ for Black Forest cakes. Write a short report on your findings. ■

A Decision Support System

I f your job is to develop an LP spreadsheet model to solve a problem such as Pigskin's production problem, then you will be considered the "expert" in LP. Many people who need to use such models, however, are *not* experts. They might know what the purpose of LP is and what problems it is intended to solve, but they will not know the details. In this case it is necessary to provide these users with a **decision support system** (DSS) that can help them solve problems without having to worry about technical details.

We will not teach you in this book how to build full-scale DSSs, but we will indicate what they look like and what they can do. (We will consider only DSSs built around spreadsheets. There are many other platforms for developing DSSs that we won't consider.) Basically, they contain a spreadsheet model of a problem, such as the one in Figure 14.21. However, the users might never even see this model. Instead, they see a "front end" and a "back end." The front end allows them to select input values for their particular problem. The user interface for this front end can include several features, such as buttons, dialog boxes, toolbars, and menus—the things we are used to seeing in Windows applications. The back end then produces a report that explains the optimal policy in nontechnical terms.

We illustrate a DSS for a slight variation of the Pigskin problem in the file PIGSKIN2.XLS. When you open this file, you'll see that it contains four sheets.[8] The user will see the Control sheet upon opening the file. (See Figure 14.25.) It contains two buttons, one for setting up the problem (getting the user's inputs) and one for solving the problem (running Solver). When you press the Set Up Problem button, you will be asked for a series of inputs: the initial inventory, the number of months in the planning horizon, the forecasted demands for each month, and others. An example appears in Figure 14.26, where you must enter information about the holding costs. These input boxes should be self-explanatory, so that all you need to do is enter the values you want to try. After you have entered all of these inputs, take a look at the Formulation sheet. This sheet contains a spreadsheet model similar to the one we saw earlier in Figure 14.21, but with the inputs you just entered.

FIGURE 14.25 **Control Sheet for Pigskin DSS**

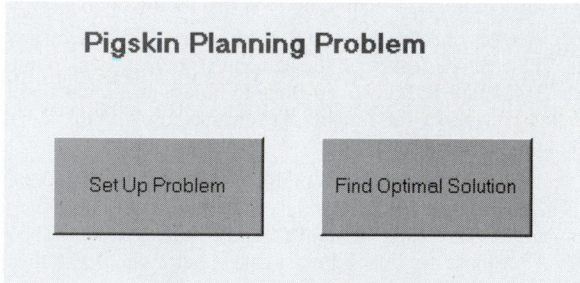

[8]When you open this file, you may encounter an error message about a Sub or Function not defined. Since this application uses Solver in an Excel macro, it must be able to find the SOLVER.XLA file; otherwise, you get an error. If you encounter this error message, click on OK in the error dialog box, then use the Tools/References menu item (which is in the Visual Basic Editor in Excel 97) and check the SOLVER.XLA box. (You may have to "Browse" to find the SOLVER.XLA file. It is usually under the Program Files \ Microsoft Office \ Office \ Library \ Solver directory.) Once this reference is established, the application should work.

FIGURE 14.26   Input Dialog Box for Holding Cost Percentage

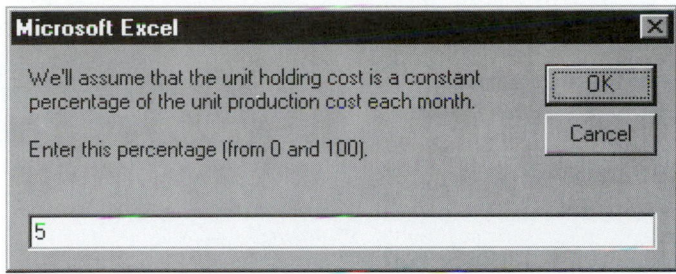

Now go back to the Control sheet and press the Find Optimal Solution button. This automatically sets up the Solver dialog box and runs Solver. There are two cases. First, it is possible that there is no feasible solution to the problem with the inputs you entered. In this case you will see the NoSolution sheet. (See Figure 14.27.) It simply indicates that Solver was unable to find a solution to your problem. In most cases, however, the problem will have a feasible solution. In this case you will see the Report sheet, which summarizes the optimal solution in nontechnical terms. (See Figure 14.28 on page 806, which presents a solution for a 4-month problem.) After studying this report, you are then allowed to click on the Solve Another Problem button, which takes you back to the Control sheet so that you can solve a new problem.

All of this is done automatically by means of the Excel macros. These macros use Microsoft's Visual Basic for Applications (VBA) programming language to automate various tasks. We will not explain any of the details of this language, but you are encouraged to look at the code in the Visual Basic Editor (or the module sheets in Excel 95 or Excel 5) and see if you can get some sense of what it is doing. Of course, in most professional applications the Formulation and programming code would be hidden (and protected) from the end user. These nontechnical people have no need to know the details behind the application (and should not be given access to anything that they could inadvertently damage). They need only enter inputs and look at reports.

14.10   Conclusion

This chapter has provided a good start in LP modeling. We learned how to formulate two simple LP models in spreadsheets, how to use Solver to find their optimal solutions, and how to use the SolverTable add-in to perform sensitivity analyses. We also saw how

FIGURE 14.27   No Solution Sheet for Pigskin Application

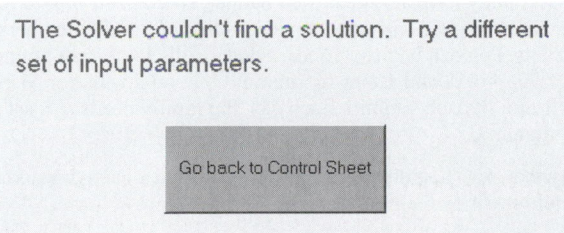

FIGURE 14.28   Report Sheet for Pigskin DSS

Summary of optimal solution

Planning horizon (months)	4
Total production cost	$10,290.77
Total holding cost	$31.25
Total cost	$10,322.02

Solve Another Problem

Monthly schedule (scroll down to see more)

Month 1

Units		Dollars	
Start with	50		
Produce	150	Production cost	$1,875.00
Demand is	150		
End with	50	Holding cost	$31.25

Month 2

Units		Dollars	
Start with	50		
Produce	300	Production cost	$3,825.00
Demand is	350		
End with	0	Holding cost	$0.00

Month 3

Units		Dollars	
Start with	0		
Produce	200	Production cost	$2,601.00
Demand is	200		
End with	0	Holding cost	$0.00

Month 4

Units		Dollars	
Start with	0		
Produce	150	Production cost	$1,989.77
Demand is	150		
End with	0	Holding cost	$0.00

to recognize whether a mathematical programming model satisfies the linear assumptions. In the next chapter we will see a variety of other optimization models, some considerably more complex than those discussed so far, but the three basic steps of model formulation, Solver optimization, and sensitivity analysis will remain the same.

PROBLEMS

Level A

14   Peg and Al Fundy have a limited food budget, so Peg is trying to feed the family as cheaply as possible. However, Peg still wants to make sure her family members meet their daily nutritional requirements. Peg can buy two foods. Food 1 sells for $7 per pound, and each pound contains 3 units of vitamin A and 1 unit of vitamin C. Food 2 sells for $1 per pound, and each pound contains 1 unit of each vitamin. Each day, the family needs at least 12 units of vitamin A and 6 units of vitamin C.

   a   Verify that Peg should purchase 12 units of food 2 each day and thus oversatisfy the vitamin C requirement by 6 units.

b Al has put his foot down and demanded that Peg fulfill the family's daily nutritional requirement exactly by obtaining precisely 12 units of vitamin A and 6 units of vitamin C. The optimal solution to the new problem will involve ingesting less vitamin C, but it will be more expensive. Why?

15 Starting with the optimal solution to the previous problem, use the SolverTable add-in to see what happens to the total cost when the vitamin A and vitamin C requirements both vary (independently) from 3 to 18 in 3-unit increments. That is, form a two-way table. Describe the behavior you observe. In particular, are the changes in total cost the *same* as you look across each row of the table? Are they the same as you look down each column of the table?

16 Bloomington Brewery produces beer and ale. Beer sells for $5 per barrel, and ale sells for $2 per barrel. Producing a barrel of beer requires 5 pounds of corn and 2 pounds of hops. Producing a barrel of ale requires 2 pounds of corn and 1 pound of hops. The brewery has 60 pounds of corn and 25 pounds of hops.

    a Use Solver to maximize Bloomington Brewery's revenue.

    b Confirm graphically that the solution in part **a** maximizes Bloomington Brewery's revenue.

17 Starting with the optimal solution to the previous problem, use the SolverTable add-in to either substantiate or refute the following statements: The availability of corn can decrease by any amount (up to 60 pounds), and each unit decrease will cost Bloomington Brewery the same amount in terms of lost revenue. On the other hand, increases in the availability of corn do *not* have a constant effect on total revenue; the first few extra units have a larger effect than subsequent units.

18 A gourmet cook bakes two types of cake (chocolate and vanilla) to supplement her income. Each chocolate cake can be sold for $12, and each vanilla cake can be sold for $9. Each chocolate cake requires 20 minutes of baking time and uses 4 eggs. Each vanilla cake requires 40 minutes of baking time and uses 1 egg. The baker has 8 hours of baking time and 30 eggs.

    a Use Solver to determine how the cook can maximize her profit.

    b Confirm graphically that the solution in part **a** maximizes the cook's profit.

19 Revise the model for the previous problem so that the baking times for both types of cake can increase by a factor $1 + k$. Formulate the model so that you can use the SolverTable add-in to investigate changes in the numbers of cakes produced and the total profit as k varies from 0 to 0.5 in increments of 0.05. Explain the behavior you observe. In particular, are the changes in optimal profit *linear* with respect to changes in k? If not, indicate how they behave. (*Note*: If you like, you can constrain the numbers of cakes to be integers. However, if you do so, you might run into a problem we observed—Solver states that at least one of the problems has no feasible solution even though they are all clearly feasible.)

20 For a telephone survey, a marketing research group needs to contact at least 150 wives, 120 husbands, 100 single adult males, and 110 single adult females. It costs $2 to make a daytime call and (because of higher labor costs) $5 to make an evening call. The file P14_20.XLS lists the results that can be expected. For example, 30% of all daytime calls are answered by a wife, and 15% of all evening calls are answered by a single male. Because of a limited staff, at most half of all phone calls can be evening calls. Determine how to minimize the cost of completing the survey.

21 Starting with the optimal solution to the previous problem, use the SolverTable add-in to investigate changes in the unit cost of either type of call. Specifically, investigate changes in the cost of a daytime call, with the cost of an evening call fixed, to see when (if ever) *only* daytime calls or *only* evening calls will be made. Then repeat the analysis by changing the cost of an evening call and keeping the cost of a daytime call fixed.

22 Woodco manufactures tables and chairs. Each table and chair must be made entirely out of oak or entirely out of pine. A total of 150 board feet of oak and 210 board feet of pine are available. A table requires either 17 board feet of oak or 30 board feet of pine, and a chair requires either 5 board feet of oak or 13 board feet of pine. Each table can be sold for $40, and each chair for $15. Determine how Woodco can maximize its revenue.

23 Referring to the previous problem, suppose you want to investigate the effects of simultaneous changes in the selling prices of the products. Specifically, you want to see what happens to the total revenue when the selling prices of oak products change by a factor $1 + k_1$ and the selling prices of pine products change by a factor $1 + k_2$. Revise your model from the previous problem so that you can use the SolverTable add-in to investigate changes in total revenue as k_1

and k_2 both vary from -0.3 to 0.3 in increments of 0.1. Would you conclude that total revenue changes *linearly* within this range?

24 Alden Enterprises produces two products. Each product can be produced on either of two machines. The time (in hours) required to produce each product on each machine is shown in the file P14_24.XLS. Each month, 500 hours of time are available on each machine. Each month, customers are willing to buy up to the quantities of each product at the prices also given in the file P14_24.XLS. The company's goal is to maximize the revenue obtained from selling units during the next 2 months. Determine how it can meet this goal. Assume that Alden will not produce any units in either month that it cannot sell in that month.

25 Referring to the previous problem, suppose Alden wants to see what will happen if customer demands for each product in each month simultaneously change by a factor $1 + k$. Revise the model so that you can use the SolverTable add-in to investigate the effect of this change on total revenue as k varies from -0.3 to 0.3 in increments of 0.1. Does revenue change in a linear manner over this range? Can you explain intuitively why it changes in the way it does?

26 There are three factories on the Momiss River: 1, 2, and 3. Each emits two types of pollutants, labeled P1 and P2, into the river. If the waste from each factory is processed, the pollution in the river can be reduced. It costs $15 to process a ton of factory 1 waste, and each ton processed reduces the amount of P1 by 0.10 ton and the amount of P2 by 0.45 ton. It costs $10 to process a ton of factory 2 waste, and each ton processed will reduce the amount of P1 by 0.20 ton and the amount of P2 by 0.25 ton. It costs $20 to process a ton of factory 3 waste, and each ton processed will reduce the amount of P1 by 0.40 ton and the amount of P2 by 0.30 ton. The state wants to reduce the amount of P1 in the river by at least 30 tons and the amount of P2 by at least 40 tons.

a Use Solver to determine how to minimize the cost of reducing pollution by the desired amounts.

b Do you think that the LP assumptions (proportionality, additivity, and divisibility) are reasonable for this problem?

27 Referring to the previous problem, suppose you want to investigate the effects of increases in the minimal reductions required by the state. Specifically, you want to see what happens to the amounts of waste processed at the three factories and the total cost if both requirements (currently 30 and 40 tons, respectively) are increased by the *same* percentage. Revise your model so that you can use the SolverTable add-in to investigate these changes when the percentage increase varies from 10% to 100% in increments of 10%. Do the amounts processed at the three factories and the total cost change in a linear manner?

Level B

28 U.S. Labs manufactures mechanical heart valves from the heart valves of pigs. Different heart operations require valves of different sizes. U.S. Labs purchases pig valves from three different suppliers. The cost and size mix of the valves purchased from each supplier are given in the file P14_28.XLS. Each month, U.S. Labs places an order with each supplier. At least 500 large, 300 medium, and 300 small valves must be purchased each month. Because of limited availability of pig valves, at most 500 valves per month can be purchased from each supplier. Use Solver to determine how U.S. Labs can minimize the cost of acquiring the needed valves.

29 Referring to the previous problem, suppose U.S. Labs wants to investigate the effect on total cost of increasing its minimal purchase requirements each month. Specifically, it wants to see how total cost changes as the minimal purchase requirements of large, medium, and small valves all increase from their values in the previous problem by the *same* percentage. Revise your model so that the SolverTable add-in can be used to investigate these changes when the percentage increase varies from 2% to 20% in increments of 2%. Explain intuitively what happens when this percentage is at least 16%.

30 Sailco Corporation must determine how many sailboats to produce during each of the next four quarters. The demand during each of the next four quarters is as follows: first quarter, 40 sailboats; second quarter, 60 sailboats; third quarter, 75 sailboats; fourth quarter, 25 sailboats. Sailco must meet demands on time. At the beginning of the first quarter, Sailco has an inventory of 10 sailboats. At the beginning of each quarter, Sailco must decide how many sailboats to produce during that quarter. For simplicity, we assume that sailboats manufactured during a quarter can be used to meet demand for that quarter. During each quarter, Sailco can produce up to 40 sailboats with regular-time labor at a total cost of $400 per sailboat. By having employees work overtime during a quarter, Sailco can produce additional sailboats with overtime labor at

a total cost of $450 per sailboat. At the end of each quarter (after production has occurred and the current quarter's demand has been satisfied), a holding cost of $20 per sailboat is incurred. Determine a production schedule to minimize the sum of production and inventory holding costs during the next four quarters.

31 Referring to the previous problem, suppose Sailco wants to see whether any changes in the $20 holding cost per sailboat could induce the company to carry more or less inventory. Revise your model so that the SolverTable add-in can be used to investigate the effects on ending inventory during the 4-month interval of systematic changes in the unit holding cost. (Assume that even though the unit holding cost changes, it is still constant over the 4-month interval.) Are there any (nonnegative) unit holding costs that would induce Sailco to hold *more* inventory than it holds when the holding cost is $20? Are there any unit holding costs that would induce Sailco to hold *less* inventory than it holds when the holding cost is $20?

32 During the next 2 months General Cars must meet (on time) the following demands for trucks and cars: month 1, 400 trucks and 800 cars; month 2, 300 trucks and 300 cars. During each month at most 1000 vehicles can be produced. Each truck uses 2 tons of steel, and each car uses 1 ton of steel. During month 1, steel costs $400 per ton; during month 2, steel costs $600 per ton. At most 2500 tons of steel can be purchased each month. (Steel can be used only during the month in which it is purchased.) At the beginning of month 1, 100 trucks and 200 cars are in inventory. At the end of each month, a holding cost of $150 per vehicle is assessed. Each car gets 20 mpg, and each truck gets 10 mpg. During each month, the vehicles produced by the company must average at least 16 mpg. Determine how to meet the demand and mileage requirements at minimum total cost.

33 Referring to the previous problem, check how sensitive the total cost is to the 16 mpg requirement by using the SolverTable add-in. Specifically, let this requirement vary from 14 mpg to 18 mpg in increments of 0.25 mpg, and write a short report of your results. In your report, explain intuitively what happens when the requirement is greater than 17 mpg.

34 The Deckers Clothing Company produces shirts and pants. Each shirt requires 2 square yards of cloth, and each pair of pants requires 3 square yards of cloth. During the next 2 months the following demands for shirts and pants must be met (on time): month 1, 1000 shirts and 1500 pairs of pants; month 2, 1200 shirts and 1400 pairs of pants. During each month the following resources are available: month 1, 9000 square yards of cloth; month 2, 6000 square yards of cloth. (Cloth that is available during month 1 and is not used can be used during month 2.) During each month it costs $4 to make an article of clothing with regular-time labor and $8 with overtime labor. During each month a total of at most 2500 articles of clothing can be produced with regular-time labor, and an unlimited number of articles of clothing can be produced with overtime labor. At the end of each month, a holding cost of $3 per article of clothing is assessed. Determine how to meet demands for the next 2 months (on time) at minimum cost. Assume that at the beginning of month 1, 100 shirts and 200 pairs of pants are available.

35 Referring to the previous problem, use the SolverTable add-in to investigate the effect on total cost of two *simultaneous* changes. The first change is to allow the ratio of overtime to regular-time production cost (currently $8/$4 = 2) to decrease from 20% to 80% in increments of 20%, while keeping the regular-time cost at $4. The second change is to allow the production capacity *each* month (currently 2500) to decrease from 10% to 50% in increments of 10%. The idea here is that less regular-time capacity is available, but overtime is becoming relatively cheaper. Is the net effect on total cost positive or negative?

36 Each year, Comfy Shoes faces demands (which must be met on time) for pairs of shoes as shown in the file P14_36.XLS. Workers work three consecutive quarters and then receive one quarter off. For example, a worker might work during quarters 3 and 4 of one year and quarter 1 of the next year. During a quarter in which a worker works, he or she can produce up to 500 pairs of shoes. Each worker is paid $5000 per quarter. At the end of each quarter, a holding cost of $10 per pair of shoes is assessed. Determine how to minimize the cost per year (labor plus holding) of meeting the demands for shoes. To simplify matters, assume that at the end of each year, the ending inventory is zero. (*Hint*: You may assume that a given worker will get the *same* quarter off during each year.)

37 Referring to the previous problem, suppose Comfy Shoes can pay a flat fee for a training program that will increase the productivity of all of its workers. Use the SolverTable add-in to see how much the company would be willing to pay for a training program that increases worker productivity from 500 pairs of shoes per quarter to P pairs of shoes per quarter, where P varies from 525 to 700 in increments of 25.

38 A company must meet (on time) the following demands: quarter 1, 3000 units; quarter 2, 2000 units; quarter 3, 4000 units. Each quarter, up to 2700 units can be produced with regular-time labor, at a cost of $40 per unit. During each quarter, an unlimited number of units can be produced with overtime labor, at a cost of $60 per unit. Of all units produced, 20% are unsuitable and cannot be used to meet demand. Also, at the end of each quarter, 10% of all units on hand spoil and cannot be used to meet any future demands. After each quarter's demand is satisfied and spoilage is accounted for, a cost of $15 per unit is assessed against the quarter's ending inventory. Determine how to minimize the total cost of meeting the next 3 quarters' demands. Assume that 1000 usable units are available at the beginning of quarter 1.

39 Referring to the previous problem, the company wants to know how much money it would be worth to decrease the percentage of unsuitable items and/or the percentage of items that spoil. Write a short report that provides relevant information. Base your report on three uses of the SolverTable add-in: one where the percentage of unsuitable items decreases and the percentage of items that spoil stays at 10%; one where the percentage of unsuitable items stays at 20% and the percentage of items that spoil decreases; and one where both percentages decrease. Does the sum of the separate effects on total cost from the first two tables equal the combined effect from the third table? Include an answer to this question in your report.

40 Money manager Boris Milkem deals with French currency (the franc) and American currency (the dollar). At 12 midnight, he can buy francs by paying 0.25 dollar per franc, and he can buy dollars by paying 3 francs per dollar. Assume that both types of transactions take place simultaneously and the only constraint is that Boris must have a nonnegative number of francs and dollars at 12:01 A.M.

   a Formulate a model to maximize the number of dollars Boris can obtain after all transactions are completed. When you run Solver, you should get a "does not converge" message. Has Solver made an error, or is there a logical reason for the message?

   b Use the SolverTable add-in to investigate changes in the decision variables and the objective value when the cost in dollars of purchasing francs varies from 0.30 dollar to 0.50 dollar in increments of a nickel. Explain the behavior you observe in the resulting table. ■

Shelby Shelving is a small company that manufactures two types of shelves for grocery stores. Model S is the standard model, and model LX is a heavy-duty model. Shelves are manufactured in three major steps: stamping, forming, and assembly. In the stamping stage, a large machine is used to stamp (i.e., cut) standard sheets of metal into appropriate sizes. In the forming stage, another machine bends the metal into shape. Assembly involves joining the parts with a combination of soldering and riveting. Shelby's stamping and forming machines work on both models of shelves. Separate assembly departments are used for the final stage of production.

The file SHELBY.XLS contains relevant data for Shelby. (See Figure 14.29.) The hours required on each machine for each unit of product are shown in the range B5:C6 of the AccountingData sheet. For example, the production of one model S shelf requires 0.25 hour on the forming machine. Both the stamping and forming machines can operate for 800 hours each month. The model S assembly department has a monthly capacity of 1900 units. The model LX assembly department has a monthly capacity of only 1400 units. Currently Shelby is producing and selling 400 units of model S and 1400 units of model LX per month.

Model S shelves are sold for $1800, and model LX shelves are sold for $2100. Shelby's operation is fairly small in the industry, and management at Shelby believes it cannot raise prices beyond these levels because of the competition. However, the marketing department feels that Shelby can sell as much as it can produce at these prices. The costs of production are summarized in the AccountingData sheet. As usual, values in blue borders are given, whereas other values are calculated from these.

FIGURE 14.29   Accounting Data for Shelby

	A	B	C	D	E	F	G	H	I
1	Shelby Shelving Data for Current Production Schedule								
2									
3	Machine requirements (hours per unit)					Given monthly overhead cost data			
4		Model S	Model LX				Fixed	Variable S	Variable LX
5	Stamping	0.3	0.3			Stamping	$125,000	$80	$90
6	Forming	0.25	0.5			Forming	$95,000	$120	$170
7						Model S Assembly	$80,000	$165	$0
8		Model S	Model LX			Model LX Assembly	$85,000	$0	$185
9	Current monthly production	400	1400						
10						Standard costs of the shelves -- *based on the current production levels*			
11	Hours spent in departments						Model S	Model LX	
12		Model S	Model LX	Totals		Direct materials	$1,000	$1,200	
13	Stamping	120	420	540		Direct labor:			
14	Forming	100	700	800		Stamping	$35	$35	
15						Forming	$60	$90	
16	Percentages of time spent in departments					Assembly	$80	$85	
17		Model S	Model LX			Total direct labor	$175	$210	
18	Stamping	22.2%	77.8%			Overhead allocation			
19	Forming	12.5%	87.5%			Stamping	$149	$159	
20						Forming	$150	$229	
21						Assembly	$365	$246	
22						Total overhead	$664	$635	
23						Total cost	$1,839	$2,045	

Management at Shelby just met to discuss next month's operating plan. Although the shelves are selling well, the overall profitability of the company is a concern. The plant's engineer suggested that the current production of model S shelves be cut back. According to him, "Model S shelves are sold for $1800 per unit, but our costs are $1839. Even though we're only selling 400 units a month, we're losing money on each one. We should decrease production of model S." The controller disagreed. He said that the problem was the model S assembly department trying to absorb a large overhead with a small production volume. "The model S units are making a contribution to overhead. Even though production doesn't cover all of the fixed costs, we'd be worse off with lower production."

Your job is to complete the formulation of an LP model on the LP sheet (of the SHELBY.XLS file), then run the Solver, and finally make a recommendation to Shelby management, with a short verbal argument supporting the engineer or the controller.

Notes on AccountingData calculations: The fixed overhead is distributed using activity-based costing principles. For example, at current production levels, the forming machine spends 100 hours on model S shelves and 700 hours on model LX shelves. The forming machine is used 800 hours of the month, of which 12.5% of the time is spent on model S shelves and 87.5% is spent on model LX shelves. The $95,000 of fixed overhead in the forming department is distributed as $11,875 (= 95,000 × 0.125) to model S shelves and $83,125 (= 95,000 × 0.875) to model LX shelves. The fixed overhead per unit of output is allocated as $29.69 (= 11,875/400) for model S and $59.38 (= 83,125/1400) for model LX. In the calculation of the standard overhead cost, the fixed and variable costs are added together, so that the overhead cost for the forming department allocated to a model S shelf is $149.69 (= 29.69 + 120, shown rounded up to $150). Similarly, the overhead cost for the forming department allocated to a model LX shelf is $229.38 (= 59.38 + 170, shown rounded down to $229).

Optimization Modeling: Applications

Successful Applications

Many optimization models can be characterized as **logistics problems**—that is, problems of finding the least expensive way to transport products from their origin to their destination. In addition, real logistics problems are often coupled with manufacturing or plant location decisions; the company must decide where to locate its manufacturing plants and what products to produce at each plant. Computer manufacturer Digital Equipment Corporation (DEC) faced such a problem, as reported by Arntzen et al. (1995) in "Global Supply Chain Management at Digital Equipment Corporation." DEC faces a huge global manufacturing and distribution problem with its wide range of products (mainframe computers, minicomputers, PCs, and many types of computer parts and peripherals). It must decide where (or whether) to manufacture these products and how to get them to its customers around the world in the most economical manner.

Until the late 1980s DEC specialized primarily in mainframes and minicomputers, using a manufacturing and distribution system that had proved very successful for over 20 years. But as PCs revolutionized the industry, DEC realized that it had to change—quickly and radically—if it wanted to remain a thriving company. It had too many plants, and too much overhead, and too many groups within DEC were making decisions without central coordination. In 1989 the company began to redesign its supply and delivery network and to reengineer its manufacturing and logistics processes. A key step in these corporate changes was the development of the Global Supply Chain Model (GSCM), an extremely complex linear programming model.[1] Since that time, DEC has used GSCM to perform thousands of optimizations in scores of studies.

The typical models run with GSCM are huge. They generally contain from 2000 to 6000 constraints and from 5000 to 20,000 decision variables. (They are *not* suitable for spreadsheets!) The objective typically minimizes total cost, where total cost includes production costs, inventory holding costs, facility material handling costs, taxes, facility fixed charges, production line fixed costs, transportation costs, and duty costs. The constraints include customer demand requirements, "balance" constraints for production and inventory, limits on the weight of products through the facilities, production capacities, storage capacities, and others.

The GSCM is actually more than an LP model; it is a mixed-integer model with 0–1 (binary) variables for the plant location decisions.

Also, the models become even more complicated because of multiple products, multiple time periods (planning for four consecutive quarters, for example), and the complexities of international trade. Nevertheless, by taking advantage of the special structure of these models and the advanced software that is now available, DEC is able to solve these models routinely.

To illustrate, DEC ran a large study during 1992 to determine the optimal supply chain design for all of DEC's manufacturing. The study recommended an 18-month plan to restructure the manufacturing infrastructure completely to cut costs. Specifically, it recommended that the number of worldwide plants be reduced from 33 to 12, it called for the three basic customer regions (Pacific Rim, Americas, and Europe) to be served primarily by plants within their own regions, and it included a quarter-by-quarter implementation plan. This 18-month plan has since been implemented. By spring 1994 it led to a decrease of $167 million in manufacturing costs (with another $160 million expected by June 1995) and a decrease of over $200 million in logistics costs. This is quite impressive considering that the number of units manufactured and shipped increased dramatically during this same time period. ■

15.1 Introduction

In a survey of Fortune 500 firms, 85% of those responding said that they use linear programming (LP). In this chapter we will discuss some of the LP models that are most often applied to real-world applications. Some typical examples include

- scheduling bank clerks for check encoding
- optimizing the operation of an oil refinery
- planning dairy production at a creamery
- scheduling production of fiberglass products at Owens-Corning Fiberglass
- optimizing a Wall Street firm's bond portfolio

Actually, these problems are just a sampling of the problems we will model in this chapter. There are two basic goals in this chapter. The first is to illustrate some of the many real applications that can take advantage of LP. You'll see that these applications cover a wide range, from oil production to worker scheduling to cash management. The second goal is to increase your facility in modeling LP problems on a spreadsheet. We will present a few principles that will help you model a wide variety of problems. The best way to learn, however, is to see many examples and work through numerous problems. In short, mastering the art of LP spreadsheet modeling takes hard work and practice. You'll have plenty of opportunity to do both with the material in this chapter.

Although a wide variety of problems can be formulated as *linear* programming models, there are some that cannot. Either they require *integer* variables or they are *nonlinear* in their decision variables. We will include examples of integer programming and nonlinear programming models in this chapter, just to give a taste of what's involved. We'll see that the modeling process for these types of problems is not much different than for LP problems. Once the models are formulated, Excel's Solver can be used to solve them. Then SolverTable can be used to perform sensitivity analysis. However, we will point out that these non-LP problems are inherently more difficult to solve. Solver must use more complex algorithms, and it is not always guaranteed to find the correct solution. As long as you are aware of this, you'll see that Excel's Solver provides the power to solve a great variety of realistic business problems.

Although there is a tremendous amount of theory behind the *algorithms* that solve these problems, the modeling process itself is fairly straightforward and is learned best by seeing a lot of examples. Therefore, we will proceed in this chapter by modeling (and then solving) a diverse class of problems that arise in business. The exercises scattered throughout the chapter provide even more examples of how linear programming and its integer and nonlinear extensions can be applied.

All of these models can benefit from sensitivity analysis, either done formally with the SolverTable add-in or informally by changing one of more inputs and rerunning Solver. To keep the chapter from getting too long, we will present only an occasional sensitivity analysis. However, we again stress that in real applications, the development of a model is just part of the overall analysis. It is usually followed by extensive sensitivity analysis.

15.2 Static Workforce Scheduling

M any organizations must determine how to schedule employees to provide adequate service. The following example illustrates how to use LP to schedule employees on a daily basis.

EXAMPLE 15.1

A post office requires different numbers of full-time employees on different days of the week. The number of full-time employees required each day is given in Table 15.1. Union rules state that each full-time employee must work five consecutive days and then receive two days off. For example, an employee who works Monday–Friday must be off on Saturday and Sunday. The post office wants to meet its daily requirements using only full-time employees. Its objective is to minimize the number of full-time employees that must be hired.

TABLE 15.1 **Employee Requirements for Post Office**

	Minimum Employees Required
Monday	17
Tuesday	13
Wednesday	15
Thursday	19
Friday	14
Saturday	16
Sunday	11

Solution

To model this problem in Excel, we must keep track of the following:

- number of employees starting work their 5-day "shift" on each day of the week
- number of employees working each day
- total number of employees

It is important to keep track of the number of employees *starting* their 5-day shift each day, because this is the only way to incorporate the fact that workers work five consecutive days. If you don't believe this, try solving the problem by just keeping track of the number of employees working each day. For example, if you know only that 35 employees work on Monday (and similar numbers for the other days), there is no way to know who is working which five days and whether their shifts are five *consecutive* days.

Developing the Model   The spreadsheet model for this problem appears in Figure 15.1. (See the file POSTAL.XLS.) To form this spreadsheet, proceed as follows.

FIGURE 15.1   **Initial (Nonoptimal) Solution to Post Office Problem**

	A	B	C	D	E	F	G	H
1	**Post Office Scheduling Problem**							
2								
3	Number starting their five-day shift on various days				Range names			
4	Mon	6			Available: B21:H21			
5	Tue	4			MinReqd: B23:H23			
6	Wed	2			Starting: B4:B10			
7	Thu	3			TotEmp: B25			
8	Fri	5						
9	Sat	1						
10	Sun	7						
11								
12	Number working on various days (along top) who started their shift on various days (along side)							
13		Mon	Tue	Wed	Thu	Fri	Sat	Sun
14	Mon	6	6	6	6	6		
15	Tue		4	4	4	4	4	
16	Wed			2	2	2	2	2
17	Thu	3			3	3	3	3
18	Fri	5	5			5	5	5
19	Sat	1	1	1			1	1
20	Sun	7	7	7	7			7
21	Totals	22	23	20	22	20	15	18
22		>=	>=	>=	>=	>=	>=	>=
23	Min required	17	13	15	19	14	16	11
24								
25	Total employees	28						

1   **Daily requirements.** Enter the number of employees needed on each day of the week (from Table 15.1) in the MinReqd range.

2   **Employees starting each day.** Enter *any* trial values for the number of employees starting their 5-day shift on each day of the week in the Starting range. (To save space, we will show only the *optimal* solutions in the spreadsheet figures in this chapter. But don't forget that you can initially enter *any* values in the changing cells.)

3   **Employees on hand each day.** The key to this solution is to realize that the numbers in the Starting range do not represent the number of workers who will show up each day. As an example, the number who show up on Monday are those whose shifts start on either Monday or Thursday–Sunday. A simple way to see who shows up when is to develop a table as in rows 14–20. We link the values in the Starting range to the appropriate places in this table. For example, since 6 workers begin their shift on Monday (and hence work Monday–Friday), we enter the formula

=$B$4

in cell B14 and copy it across to F14. We proceed similarly for the other starting days in rows 15–20. Then we sum *down* each column to obtain the number of workers who work each day in row 21. For example, the formula in cell B21 is

$$=SUM(B14:B20)$$

(Note that the blank cells in cells B15 and B16 are treated as zeros.)

4 **Total employees.** Calculate the total number of employees in cell B25 with the formula

$$=SUM(Starting)$$

(If you were tempted instead to sum the numbers in row 21, you can check that it would be 5 times too large. Do you see why?)

At this point, you might try rearranging the numbers in the Starting range to see if you can "guess" an optimal solution. It's not that easy! Each worker who starts on a given day works the next four days as well, so when you find a solution that meets the minimal requirements for the various days, you typically have many more workers available on some days than are needed.

Using Solver Now that the model has been formulated, the Solver setup is straightforward, as shown in Figure 15.2. We minimize the total number of employees, subject to having enough employees available to meet the minimal daily requirements. We also constrain the changing cells to be nonnegative and check the Assume Linear Model in the Solver Options dialog box.

FIGURE 15.2 **Solver Dialog Box for Post Office Problem**

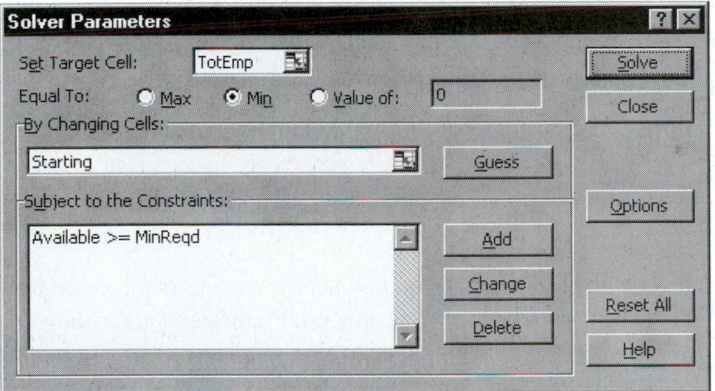

The optimal solution appears in Figure 15.3 (page 820). Note that it requires the number of employees starting work on some days to be a fraction. Assuming that part-time employees are not allowed, this solution is unrealistic. To be realistic, all values in the changing cells should be integers. Fortunately, this can be accomplished quite easily with Solver.

Using Solver with Integer Constraints To require any set of changing cells to be integers, we add an extra constraint in the main Solver dialog box. Now we select "int" instead of <=, =, or >= in the Add Constraint window, as shown in Figure 15.4. With this extra constraint added, the optimal *integer* solution appears in Figure 15.5. It indicates that the post office needs to hire 23 full-time employees, and the Starting range shows how to schedule them.

FIGURE 15.3 **Optimal NonInteger Solution for the Postal Problem**

	A	B	C	D	E	F	G	H
1	**Post Office Scheduling Problem**							
2								
3	Number starting their five-day shift on various days				**Range names**			
4	Mon	6.33			Available: B21:H21			
5	Tue	5.00			MinReqd: B23:H23			
6	Wed	0.33			Starting: B4:B10			
7	Thu	7.33			TotEmp: B25			
8	Fri	0.00						
9	Sat	3.33						
10	Sun	0.00						
11								
12	Number working on various days (along top) who started their shift on various days (along side)							
13		Mon	Tue	Wed	Thu	Fri	Sat	Sun
14	Mon	6.33	6.33	6.33	6.33	6.33		
15	Tue		5.00	5.00	5.00	5.00	5.00	
16	Wed			0.33	0.33	0.33	0.33	0.33
17	Thu	7.33			7.33	7.33	7.33	7.33
18	Fri	0.00	0.00			0.00	0.00	0.00
19	Sat	3.33	3.33	3.33			3.33	3.33
20	Sun	0.00	0.00	0.00	0.00			0.00
21	Totals	17.00	14.67	15.00	19.00	19.00	16.00	11.00
22		>=	>=	>=	>=	>=	>=	>=
23	Min required	17	13	15	19	14	16	11
24								
25	Total employees	22.33						

FIGURE 15.4 **Adding an Integer Constraint**

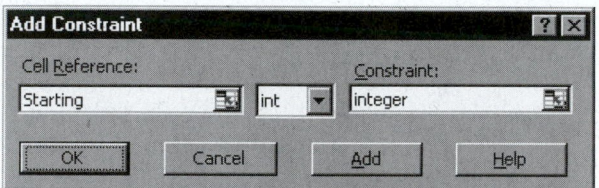

Although the integer requirement is easy to incorporate for this small problem, you should be aware that Solver is now using a different algorithm—not the simplex method—to perform the optimization, and this algorithm can take considerably more time than the simplex algorithm on larger problems. We will discuss other integer-constrained problems and their difficulties later in this chapter.

The solution in Figure 15.5 reveals an interesting aspect common to many optimization problems. Because of the irregular daily requirements and two-consecutive-days-off constraint, no solution can exactly match available workers to daily requirements. All solutions have surplus workers on some days. Sometimes the optimal solution to a modeling problem isn't the "perfect" solution we're looking for, but it's the best possible solution.

There is another interesting aspect to this problem. If you solve this problem on your computer, you may get a *different* solution that is still optimal—that is, it uses a total of 23 employees and meets all constraints. There are at least two optimal solutions to this particular problem, and the one you obtain depends on the *initial* values you use in the changing cells. This is a case of **multiple optimal solutions** and is not at all uncommon in LP models.

FIGURE 15.5 Optimal Integer Solution for the Postal Problem

	A	B	C	D	E	F	G	H
1	**Post Office Scheduling Problem**							
2								
3	Number starting their five-day shift on various days				Range names			
4	Mon	7				Available: B21:H21		
5	Tue	5				MinReqd: B23:H23		
6	Wed	0				Starting: B4:B10		
7	Thu	7				TotEmp: B25		
8	Fri	0						
9	Sat	4						
10	Sun	0						
11								
12	Number working on various days (along top) who started their shift on various days (along side)							
13		Mon	Tue	Wed	Thu	Fri	Sat	Sun
14	Mon	7	7	7	7	7		
15	Tue		5	5	5	5	5	
16	Wed			0	0	0	0	0
17	Thu	7			7	7	7	7
18	Fri	0	0			0	0	0
19	Sat	4	4	4			4	4
20	Sun	0	0	0	0			0
21	Totals	18	16	16	19	19	16	11
22		>=	>=	>=	>=	>=	>=	>=
23	Min required	17	13	15	19	14	16	11
24								
25	Total employees	23						

Our model can easily be expanded to handle part-time employees, the use of overtime, alternative objective functions such as maximizing the number of weekend days off received by employees, and other possibilities. One simple alternative version of the model is illustrated in Figure 15.6 on page 822. (See the file POSTAL1.XLS.) Instead of minimizing the number of workers on the payroll, we now pay a slightly larger wage on the weekend days and minimize the total weekly payroll. The only difference in the spreadsheet model is that the formula for the total weekly payroll in cell B29 is now

=WeekdayRate*SUM(B25:F25)+WeekendRate*SUM(G25:H25)

Perhaps surprisingly, the optimal solution to this problem is the same as when we treated weekends and weekdays equally. However, a closer look shows that it's not so surprising after all. The previous solution in Figure 15.5 has *exactly* as many employees working on Saturday and Sunday as are required. Therefore, regardless of how large the weekend wage rate becomes, we can't decrease the number who work on weekends without violating the minimum requirement constraint. ■

This post office example is called a **static** scheduling problem, because we assume that the post office faces the same situation each week. In reality, demands change over time, workers take vacations in the summer, and so on, so the post office does not face the same situation each week. If we wanted to set up a weekly scheduling model for a supermarket or a fast-food restaurant, the number of variables could be very large and the computer might have difficulty finding an exact solution. In this situation *heuristic* methods can be used to find a good solution to the problem. See Love and Hoey (1990) for an example of how this can be done.

Encoder Scheduling at Ohio National Bank Krajewski et al. (1980) used LP to schedule clerks who process checks at Ohio National Bank. Their model determined the minimum

FIGURE 15.6 Model with Different Wage Rates

	A	B	C	D	E	F	G	H
1	Post Office Scheduling Problem with Differential Wage Rates							
2								
3	Daily wage rate							
4	Weekdays	$96						
5	Weekends	$120						
6								
7	Number starting their five-day shift on various days							
8	Mon	7						
9	Tue	5						
10	Wed	0						
11	Thu	7						
12	Fri	0						
13	Sat	4						
14	Sun	0						
15								
16	Number working on various days (along top) who started their shift on various days (along side)							
17		Mon	Tue	Wed	Thu	Fri	Sat	Sun
18	Mon	7	7	7	7	7		
19	Tue		5	5	5	5	5	
20	Wed			0	0	0	0	0
21	Thu	7			7	7	7	7
22	Fri	0	0			0	0	0
23	Sat	4	4	4			4	4
24	Sun	0	0	0	0			0
25	Totals	18	16	16	19	19	16	11
26		>=	>=	>=	>=	>=	>=	>=
27	Min required	17	13	15	19	14	16	11
28								
29	Total payroll	$11,688						

Range names
Available: B25:H25
MinReqd: B27:H27
Starting: B8:B14
TotPayroll: B29
WeekdayRate: B4
WeekendRate: B5

cost combination of part-time employees, full-time employees, and overtime labor needed to complete the processing of the checks received each day by the end of the workday (10 P.M.). The major input to their model was a forecast of the number of checks arriving at the bank each hour. This forecast was generated with a multiple regression. The major output of the LP was a work schedule. For example, the LP might suggest that 2 full-time employees work daily from 11 A.M. to 8 P.M., 33 part-time employees work every day from 1 P.M. to 6 P.M., and 27 part-time employees work from 6 P.M. to 10 P.M. on Monday, Tuesday, and Friday.

The LP approach to scheduling encoder clerks saved an estimated $80,000 per year in labor costs. The LP approach also resulted in faster processing of the checks. Before LP was used to schedule encoder clerks, the day's checks were rarely processed by the end of the day, whereas after LP was used, the day's checks were processed by the end of the day 98% of the time!

PROBLEMS

Level A

1 In the post office problem (Example 15.1), suppose that each full-time employee works 8 hours per day. Thus, Monday's requirement of 17 workers can be viewed as a requirement of $8(17) = $136. The post office can meet its daily labor requirements by using both full-time and part-time employees. During each week a full-time employee works 8 hours a day for 5 consecutive days, and a part-time employee works 4 hours a day for 5 consecutive days.

A full-time employee costs the post office $15 per hour, whereas a part-time employee (with reduced fringe benefits) costs the post office only $10 per hour. Union requirements limit part-time labor to 25% of weekly labor requirements.

    a Use Solver to minimize the post office's weekly labor costs.

    b Discuss how a change in the part-time labor limitation influences the problem's optimal solution.

2 During each 4-hour period, the Smalltown police force requires the following number of on-duty police officers: 8 from midnight to 4 A.M.; 7 from 4 A.M. to 8 A.M.; 6 from 8 A.M. to noon; 6 from noon to 4 P.M.; 5 from 4 P.M. to 8 P.M.; and 4 from 8 P.M. to midnight. Each police officer works two consecutive 4-hour shifts. Determine how to minimize the number of police officers needed to meet Smalltown's daily requirements.

Level B

3 In the post office problem (Example 15.1), suppose that the post office can force employees to work 1 day of overtime each week. For example, an employee whose regular shift is Monday to Friday can also be required to work on Saturday. Each employee is paid $50 a day for each of the first 5 days worked during a week and $62 for the overtime day (if any). Determine how the post office can minimize the cost of meeting its weekly work requirements.

4 In the post office problem (Example 15.1), suppose the post office has 25 full-time employees and is not allowed to hire or fire any employees. Determine a schedule that maximizes the number of weekend days off received by the employees.

5 A company has daily staffing requirements for two types of jobs, cooks and customer service persons. These are given in the file P15_5.XLS, where each number is the minimal number of workers required for each type of job. To meet these requirements, the company can employ three types of workers: those who cook only, those who can perform customer service only, and those who are able to do both. In each of these three classes, the company can employ only full-time workers. A full-time worker must work 5 consecutive days with 2 days off. The daily pay per worker depends only on the job(s) they are able to perform. Those who are able to perform only one type of work (cook or customer service) earn $40 per day. Those who are able to perform both types of work earn $45 per day. As a matter of policy, the company wants to ensure that at least 15% of its total hours are staffed by "swing workers"—that is, those who can do both types of jobs. The company wants to find a staffing policy that covers the daily work requirements at minimal total cost per week. Use Solver to formulate and solve the company's problem. Your final answer should prescribe (1) how many workers begin their 5-day shift each day of the week, for each of the three worker types, (2) how the swing workers are deployed each day (i.e., cooking or servicing customers), and (3) the company's total weekly payroll. (*Hint*: Don't use integer constraints, at least not initially. They could require a great deal of Solver computing time!) ∎

Blending Models

I n many situations, various inputs must be blended to produce desired outputs. In many of these situations, LP can find the optimal combination of outputs as well as the "mix" of inputs that are used to produce the desired outputs. Some examples of blending models follow.

Inputs	Outputs
Meat, filler, water	Different types of sausage
Various types of oil	Heating oil, gasolines, aviation fuels
Carbon, iron, molybdenum	Different types of steels
Different types of pulp	Different kinds of recycled paper

    The next example illustrates how to model a typical blending problem in Excel. Although this example is small relative to blending problems in real applications, we think you'll agree that it is fairly complex. If you are able to guess the optimal solution, your intuition is much better than ours!

EXAMPLE 15.2

Chandler Oil has 5000 barrels of crude oil 1 and 10,000 barrels of crude oil 2 available. Chandler sells gasoline and heating oil. These products are produced by blending the two crude oils. Each barrel of crude oil 1 has a "quality level" of 10 and each barrel of crude oil 2 has a quality level of 5. Gasoline must have an average quality level of at least 8, whereas heating oil must have an average quality level of at least 6. Gasoline sells for $25 per barrel and heating oil sells for $20 per barrel. The advertising cost to sell one barrel of gasoline is $0.20 and the advertising cost to sell one barrel of heating oil is $0.10. We assume that demand for heating oil and gasoline is unlimited, so that all of Chandler's production can be sold. Chandler wants to maximize its profit.

Solution

To model Chandler's problem, we must keep track of the following:

- the number of barrels of gasoline and heating oil produced (the outputs)
- the number of barrels of each crude oil (the inputs) used to produce each output
- the quality levels of the inputs used to make the outputs
- the total profit earned

Developing the Model　The spreadsheet model for this problem appears in Figure 15.7.[2] (See the file BLENDING.XLS.) To set it up, proceed as follows.

1　**Monetary and quality inputs.** Enter the unit profit contribution and advertising cost for each output in the SellingPrice and UnitAdCost ranges. Enter the quality levels for each crude oil in the QualityLevels range and the quality standards for each output in the range B13:C13.

2　**Inputs blended into each output.** Although it may not be immediately apparent, the quantities Chandler must choose to specify any solution are the barrels of each input used to produce each output. Therefore, enter *any* trial values for these values in the BlendPlan range. For example, the value in cell B17 is the amount of crude oil 1 used to make gasoline and the value in cell C17 is the amount of crude oil 1 used to make heating oil. The BlendPlan range will be the changing cell range.

3　**Inputs used and outputs sold.** Calculate the amount of crude oils 1 and 2 used in the Used range by summing across the rows of the BlendPlan range. Then calculate the amount of gasoline and heating oil sold in the Sold range by summing down the columns of the BlendPlan range.

4　**Quality constraints.** Keeping track of the quality level of gasoline and heating oil is the trickiest part of this model. Begin by calculating for each product the number of "quality points" (QP) in the inputs used to produce the output:

$$QP \text{ in gasoline} = 10(Oil\ 1 \text{ in gasoline}) + 5(Oil\ 2 \text{ in gasoline})$$

$$QP \text{ in heating oil} = 10(Oil\ 1 \text{ in heating oil}) + 5(Oil\ 2 \text{ in heating oil})$$

[2] From here on, to save space we will show the *optimal* solution in the Excel screenshots. However, we will continue to point out that *any* solution—feasible, optimal, or otherwise—can be used initially.

FIGURE 15.7 Blending Model

	A	B	C	D	E	F
1	**Chandler Blending Problem**					
2					**Range names:**	
3	**Monetary inputs**	Gasoline	Heating oil		AdCost: B29	
4	Selling price/barrel	$25.00	$20.00		Available: F17:F18	
5	Advertising cost/barrel	$0.20	$0.10		BlendPlan: B17:C18	
6					Profit: B30	
7	**Quality level per barrel of crudes**				QualityLevels: B8:B9	
8	Crude oil 1	10			QualityObtained: B23:C23	
9	Crude oil 2	5			QualityReqd: B25:C25	
10					Revenue: B28	
11	**Required quality level per barrel of product**				SellingPrice: B4:C4	
12		Gasoline	Heating oil		Sold: B19:C19	
13		8	6		UnitAdCost: B5:C5	
14					Used: D17:D18	
15	**Blending plan (barrels of crudes in each product)**					
16		Gasoline	Heating oil	Barrels used		Barrels available
17	Crude oil 1	3000	2000	5000	<=	5000
18	Crude oil 2	2000	8000	10000	<=	10000
19	Barrels sold	5000	10000			
20						
21	**Constraints on quality**					
22		Gasoline	Heating oil			
23	Quality "points" obtained	40000	60000			
24		>=	>=			
25	Quality "points" required	40000	60000			
26						
27	**Profit summary**					
28	Revenue	$325,000				
29	Advertising cost	$2,000				
30	Profit	$323,000				

For the gasoline produced to have a quality level of at least 8 we must have

$$\text{QP in gasoline} \geq 8(\text{Gasoline sold}) \qquad \textbf{(15.1)}$$

For the heating oil produced to have a quality level of at least 6 we must have

$$\text{QP in heating oil} \geq 6(\text{Heating oil sold}) \qquad \textbf{(15.2)}$$

Inequalities (15.1) and (15.2) are operationalized in the spreadsheet in rows 23–25. First, determine the QP for gasoline in cell B23 with the formula

$$=\text{SUMPRODUCT(B17:B18,QualityLevels)}$$

and copy this to cell C23 to generate the QP for heating oil. Then calculate the required QP for gasoline in cell B25 with the formula

$$=\text{B13*B19}$$

and copy this to cell C25 for heating oil.

5   **Profit.** Calculate the total revenue from both products in the Revenue cell with the formula

$$=\text{SUMPRODUCT(SellingPrice,Sold)}$$

Similarly, calculate the total advertising cost in the AdCost cell with the formula

$$\text{=SUMPRODUCT(UnitAdCost,Sold)}$$

Finally, calculate the profit in the Profit cell with the formula

$$\text{=Revenue-AdCost}$$

Using Solver The Solver dialog box for this blending model appears in Figure 15.8. We maximize profit subject to the quality constraints and using no more of the inputs than are available.[3]

FIGURE 15.8 **Solver Dialog Box for Blending Model**

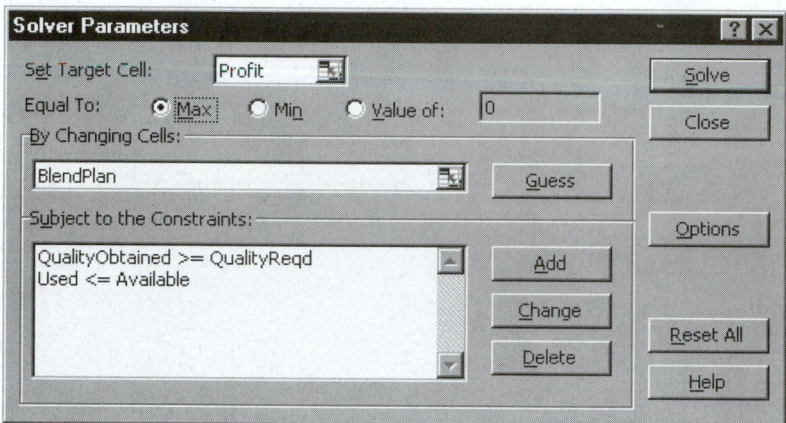

The optimal solution in Figure 15.7 implies that Chandler should make 5000 barrels of gasoline with 3000 barrels of crude oil 1 and 2000 barrels of crude oil 2. It should also make 10,000 barrels of heating oil with 2000 barrels of crude oil 1 and 8000 barrels of crude oil 2. With this blend Chandler will earn a profit of $323,000.

As stated earlier, we believe this problem is sufficiently complex to defy intuition. Clearly, gasoline is more profitable per barrel than heating oil, but given the crude availability and the quality constraints, it turns out that Chandler should sell twice as much heating oil as gasoline. This would have been difficult to guess ahead of time.

Modeling Issues

1 We used inequality (15.1) as the quality constraint for gasoline. It might appear more intuitive to write this in terms of *average* quality points by dividing by Gasoline sold:

$$\text{(QP in gasoline)/(Gasoline sold)} \geq 8 \qquad \textbf{(15.3)}$$

While this is logically correct, we prefer inequality (15.1) for two reasons. First, it is conceivable that no gasoline will be sold. In this case we would be dividing by zero in inequality (15.3), which would cause an error message in Excel. The second reason is that inequality (15.3) is technically *nonlinear*, as Solver will inform you if you check the Assume Linear Model box and attempt to solve. Although Solver is capable

---

[3]Unless we state otherwise, all models in this chapter should have the Assume Linear Model and Assume Non-Negative boxes checked in the Solver Options dialog box. This blending model is no exception.

of handling nonlinearities, we prefer to keep the problem linear when possible. The lesson, therefore, is to "clear denominators" in blending problem constraints.

2   We have assumed that the quality level of a mixture is a *linear* function of the fraction of each input used in the mixture. For example, we have assumed that if gasoline is made with a fraction 3/5 of crude oil 1 and 2/5 of crude oil 2 (as in the optimal solution), then

$$\text{Quality Level for Gasoline} = (3/5)(\text{Quality Level for Oil 1})$$
$$+ (2/5)(\text{Quality Level for Oil 2})$$

If the quality level of the output is not a linear function of the fraction of each input used in the mixture, then we have a *nonlinear* problem. For example, let g_i be the fraction of gasoline made with crude oil i. Suppose that

$$\text{Quality Level for Gasoline} = g_1^{0.5}(\text{Quality Level for Oil 1})$$
$$+ g_2^{0.4}(\text{Quality Level for Oil 2})$$

Then we do not have an LP model. The reason for this is that the quality level of gasoline is not a linear function of g_1 and g_2.

3   In reality, a company using a blending model would run the model periodically (each day, say) and set production on the basis of the current inventory of inputs and the current demand forecasts. Then the forecasts and the input levels would be updated, and the model would be run again to determine the next day's production.

Sensitivity Analysis   One possible sensitivity analysis is to see how a change in the price per barrel of gasoline changes Chandler's optimal product mix. We reason as follows. Since heating oil is easier to make than gasoline (in the sense that a lower quality level is acceptable), it seems unreasonable to consider a case where gasoline would sell for a lower price than heating oil. Therefore, we systematically increase the price of gasoline from $20 (the price of heating oil) and use the SolverTable add-in, as shown in Figure 15.9. Not surprisingly, we find that the product mix (10,000 barrels of heating oil and 5000 barrels of gasoline) remains the same until the price of gasoline increases to some value between $55 and $65. At this point, the optimal solution is to produce all gasoline (approximately 8333 barrels) and no heating oil. Of course, as the gasoline price increases, so does the optimal profit—even when the blending plan stays the same.

FIGURE 15.9   **Sensitivity to Price of Gasoline in the Blending Model**

	A	B	C	D	E
32	Sensitivity of profit and outputs sold to the selling price of gasoline				
33	Price of gasoline	Profit	Gasoline	Heating oil	
34		$323,000	5000	10000	
35	$35	$373,000	5000	10000	
36	$45	$423,000	5000	10000	
37	$55	$473,000	5000	10000	
38	$65	$540,000	8333	0	

Blending at Texaco   Texaco [see DeWitt et al. (1989)] uses a nonlinear programming model (OMEGA) to plan and schedule its blending applications. Its model is nonlinear because blend volatilities and octanes are nonlinear functions of the amount of each input used to produce a particular gasoline.

Blending in the Steel Industry   Fabian (1958) describes a complex LP model that can be used to optimize the production of iron and steel. For each product produced there are several blending constraints. For example, basic pig iron must contain at most 1.5% silicon, at most 0.05% sulphur, between 0.11% and 0.90% phosphorus, between 0.4% and 2% manganese, and between 4.1% and 4.4% carbon.

Blending in the Oil Industry   Many oil companies use LP to optimize their refinery operations. See, for example, Magoulas and Marinos-Kouris (1988) for a description of a blending model that can be used to maximize a refinery's profit.

PROBLEMS

Level A

6   NewAge Pharmaceuticals produces the drug NasaMist from four chemicals. Today the company must produce 1000 pounds of the drug. The three active ingredients in NasaMist are A, B, and C. By weight, at least 8% of NasaMist must consist of A, at least 4% must consist of B, and at least 2% must consist of C. The cost per pound of each chemical and the amount of each active ingredient in 1 pound of each chemical are given in the file P15_6.XLS. It is necessary that at least 100 pounds of chemical 2 be used. Determine the cheapest way of producing today's batch of NasaMist.

7   You have decided to enter the candy business. You are considering producing two types of candies: Slugger candy and Easy Out candy, both of which consist solely of sugar, nuts, and chocolate. At present you have in stock 10,000 ounces of sugar, 2000 ounces of nuts, and 3000 ounces of chocolate. The mixture used to make Easy Out candy must contain at least 20% nuts. The mixture used to make Slugger candy must contain at least 10% nuts and 10% chocolate. Each ounce of Easy Out candy can be sold for $.50, and each ounce of Slugger candy for $.40. Determine how you can maximize your revenue from candy sales.

8   A bank is attempting to determine where its assets should be invested during the current year. At present $500,000 is available for investment in bonds, home loans, auto loans, and personal loans. The annual rate of return on each type of investment is known to be the following: bonds, 10%; home loans, 16%; auto loans, 13%; personal loans, 20%. To ensure that the bank's portfolio is not too risky, the bank's investment manager has placed the following three restrictions on the bank's portfolio:

- The amount invested in personal loans cannot exceed the amount invested in bonds.

- The amount invested in home loans cannot exceed the amount invested in auto loans.

- No more than 25% of the total amount invested may be in personal loans.

    Help the bank maximize the annual return on its investment portfolio.

9   Bullco blends silicon and nitrogen to produce two types of fertilizers. Fertilizer 1 must be at least 40% nitrogen and sells for $70 per pound. Fertilizer 2 must be at least 70% silicon and sells for $40 per pound. Bullco can purchase up to 8000 pounds of nitrogen at $15 per pound and up to 10,000 pounds of silicon at $10 per pound. Assuming that all fertilizer produced can be sold, determine how Bullco can maximize its profit.

10   Hiland's TV-Radio Store must determine how many TVs and radios to keep in stock. A TV requires 10 square feet of floorspace, whereas a radio requires 4 square feet; 5000 square feet of floorspace is available. A TV sale results in an $80 profit, and a radio earns a profit of $20. The store stocks only TVs and radios. Marketing requirements dictate that at least 60% of all appliances in stock be radios. Finally, a TV ties up $200 in capital, and a radio $50. Hiland wants to have at most $60,000 worth of capital tied up at any time. Determine how to maximize Hiland's profit.

11   Linear programming models are used by many Wall Street firms to select a desirable bond portfolio. The following is a simplified version of such a model. Solodrex is considering investing in four bonds; $1 million is available for investment. The expected annual return, the worst-case annual return on each bond, and the "duration" of each bond are given in the file P15_11.XLS. (The duration of a bond is a measure of the bond's sensitivity to interest rates.)

Solodrex wants to maximize the expected return from its bond investments, subject to three constraints:

- The worst-case return of the bond portfolio must be at least 8%.
- The average duration of the portfolio must be at most 6. For example, a portfolio that invests $600,000 in bond 1 and $400,000 in bond 4 has an average duration of

$$[600,000(3) + 400,000(9)]/1,000,000 = 5.4$$

- Because of diversification requirements, at most 40% of the total amount invested can be invested in a single bond.

Determine how Solodrex can maximize the expected return on its investment.

12 Coalco produces coal at three mines and ships it to four customers. The cost per ton of producing coal, the ash and sulfur content (per ton) of the coal, and the production capacity (in tons) for each mine are given in the file P15_12.XLS. The number of tons of coal demanded by each customer and the cost (in dollars) of shipping a ton of coal from a mine to each customer are also given in this file. The total amount of coal shipped must contain at most 6% ash and at most 3.5% sulfur. Show Coalco how to minimize the cost of meeting customer demands.

Level B

13 Sunco Oil manufactures three types of gasoline (gas 1, gas 2, and gas 3). Each type is produced by blending three types of crude oil (crude 1, crude 2, and crude 3). The sales price per barrel of gasoline and the purchase price per barrel of crude oil are given in the file P15_13.XLS. Sunco can purchase up to 5000 barrels of each type of crude oil daily. The three types of gasoline differ in their octane rating and sulfur content. The crude oil blended to form gas 1 must have an average octane rating of at least 10 and contain at most 1% sulfur. The crude oil blended to form gas 2 must have an average octane rating of at least 8 and contain at most 2% sulfur. The crude oil blended to form gas 3 must have an octane rating of at least 6 and contain at most 1% sulfur. The octane rating and the sulfur content of the three types of oil are also given in the file P15_13.XLS. It costs $4 to transform one barrel of oil into one barrel of gasoline, and Sunco's refinery can produce up to 14,000 barrels of gasoline daily. Sunco's customers require the following amounts of each gasoline: gas 1, 3000 barrels per day; gas 2, 2000 barrels per day; gas 3, 1000 barrels per day. The company considers it an obligation to meet these demands.

Sunco also has the option of advertising to stimulate demand for its products. Each dollar spent daily in advertising a particular type of gas increases the daily demand for that type of gas by 10 barrels. For example, if Sunco decides to spend $20 daily in advertising gas 2, the daily demand for gas 2 will increase by 200 barrels. Determine how Sunco can maximize its profit.

14 The owner of Sunco in the previous problem does not believe that our optimal LP solution will maximize the company's daily profit. He reasons, "We have 14,000 barrels of daily refinery capacity, but your optimal solution produces only 13,500 barrels. Therefore, it cannot be maximizing profit." How would you respond?

15 The risk index of an investment can be obtained by taking the absolute values of percentage changes in the value of the investment for each year and averaging them. Suppose you are trying to determine what percentage of your money you should invest in T-bills, gold, and stocks. The file P15_15.XLS lists the annual returns (percentage changes in value) for these investments for the years 1968–1988. Let the risk index of a portfolio be the weighted average of the risk indexes of these investments, where the weights are the fractions of your money assigned to the investments. Suppose that the amount of each investment must be between 20% and 50% of the total invested. You would like the risk index of your portfolio to equal 0.15, and your goal is to maximize the expected return on your portfolio. Determine the maximum expected return on your portfolio, subject to the stated constraints. Use the average return earned by each investment during the years 1968–1988 as your estimate of expected return. ■

Logistics Models

In many situations a company produces products at locations called **supply points** and ships these products to customer locations called **demand points**. Typically, each supply point has a limited capacity that it can ship, and each customer must receive a required quantity of the product. Spreadsheet models can be used to determine the minimum-cost shipping method for satisfying customer demands.

For now we assume that the only possible shipments are those directly from a supply point to a demand point. That is, no shipments between supply points or between demand points are possible. Such a problem is called a **transportation problem**.

EXAMPLE 15.3

Midwest Electric has three electric power plants that supply the power needs of four cities. Each power plant can supply the amounts shown in Table 15.2 (in millions of kilowatt-hours of electricity). The peak power demand (again in millions of kwh) at each city is given in Table 15.3. Finally, the cost (in dollars) of sending 1 million kwh from each plant to each city is given in Table 15.4. Midwest Electric wants to find the lowest-cost method for meeting the demands of the four cities.

TABLE 15.2 **Plant Supplies in Transportation Model**

	Supply
Plant 1	35
Plant 2	50
Plant 3	40

TABLE 15.3 **City Requirements for Transportation Model**

	Demand
City 1	45
City 2	20
City 3	30
City 4	30

TABLE 15.4 **Shipping Costs for Transportation Model**

	City 1	City 2	City 3	City 4
Plant 1	8	6	10	9
Plant 2	9	12	13	7
Plant 3	14	9	16	5

Solution

To set up a spreadsheet model for Midwest Electric's power distribution problem we need to keep track of the following:

- power shipped (in millions of kwh) from each plant to each city
- total power shipped out of each plant
- total power received by each city
- total shipping cost incurred

Developing the Model   The spreadsheet model is shown in Figure 15.10. (See the file TRANSPORT.XLS.) To develop this model, perform the following steps.

1   **Inputs.** Enter the unit shipping costs for each plant to each city in the UnitCost range. Also, enter the capacities of the plants in the Capacity range and the demands for the cities in the Demand range.

2   **Amounts shipped.** Enter *any* trial values for the shipments from each plant to each city in the Shipped range. These are the changing cells.

3   **Shipping totals.** Calculate the amounts shipped out of the various plants in the TotShipped range by summing across rows of the Shipped range. Similarly, calculate the amounts shipped into the various cities in the Received range by summing down columns of the Shipped range.

4   **Total shipping cost.** Calculate the total cost of shipping power from the plants to the cities in the TotCost cell with the formula

$$=SUMPRODUCT(UnitCost,Shipped)$$

This formula simply sums all products of unit shipping costs and amounts shipped.

FIGURE 15.10   **Transportation Model**

	A	B	C	D	E	F	G	H	I
1	Midwest Electric Transportation Problem								
2								Range names:	
3	Unit shipping costs							Capacity: I13:I15	
4				To				Demand: C18:F18	
5			City 1	City 2	City 3	City 4		Received: C16:F16	
6		Plant 1	$8	$6	$10	$9		Shipped: C13:F15	
7	From	Plant 2	$9	$12	$13	$7		TotCost: B20	
8		Plant 3	$14	$9	$16	$5		TotShipped: G13:G15	
9								UnitCost: C6:F8	
10	Shipments								
11				To					
12			City 1	City 2	City 3	City 4	Total shipped		Capacity
13		Plant 1	0	10	25	0	35	<=	35
14	From	Plant 2	45	0	5	0	50	<=	50
15		Plant 3	0	10	0	30	40	<=	40
16		Total received	45	20	30	30			
17			>=	>=	>=	>=			
18		Demand	45	20	30	30			
19									
20	Total cost	$1,020							

Using Solver   The Solver dialog box is quite straightforward, as shown in Figure 15.11 (page 832). We minimize total shipping cost, subject to staying within capacities and meeting demands.

The optimal solution in Figure 15.10 is illustrated graphically in Figure 15.12. A minimum cost of $1020 is incurred by using the shipments listed in this figure. Except for these six routes listed, no other routes are used.

Sensitivity Analysis   In the current model note that total capacity for the plants equals total demand for the cities. Therefore, capacities are all used up, and demands are met

FIGURE 15.11   Solver Dialog Box for Transportation Model

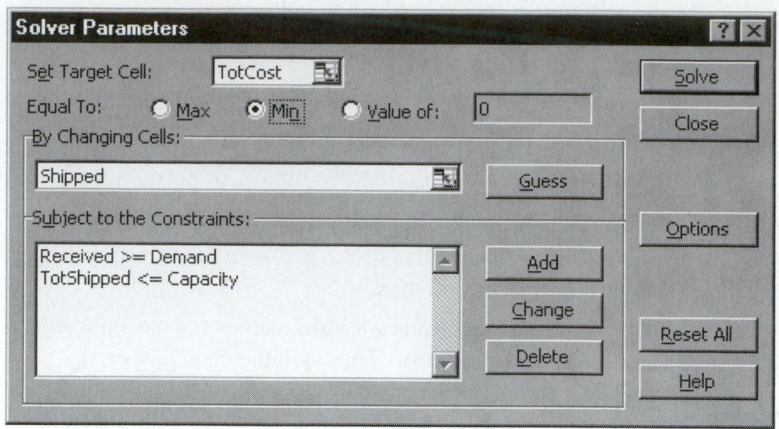

FIGURE 15.12   **Graphical Representation of Optimal Solution**

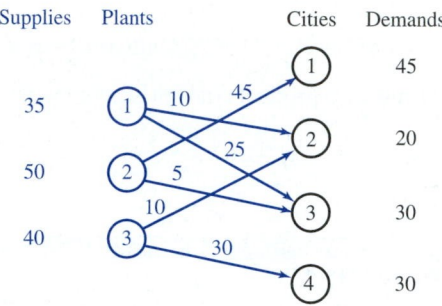

exactly. An interesting sensitivity analysis is to see how total cost decreases if capacities increase. However, instead of increasing a *single* plant's capacity, we'll increase them all at once by the same amount. This presents a problem for SolverTable because it is able to vary at most two inputs simultaneously. However, it is possible to work around this constraint, as shown in Figure 15.13. (See the file TRANSPORT1.XLS.)

The trick is to create a new input in cell C24 (range named ExtraCap), with initial value 0. The Capacity range is then modified to account for this extra capacity. For example, we enter the formula

$$=35+ExtraCap$$

in cell I13 (and similar formulas in I14 and I15). Then we set up the table in rows 27–30, with ExtraCap as the column input cell. When ExtraCap is 10, for example, each plant obtains an extra capacity of 10, and these are reflected in the Capacity range. As we see, the optimal total cost decreases by $15 for each increment of 5 for extra capacity. ■

Modeling Issues

1   If all the supplies and demands for a transportation model are integers, then the optimal Solver solution will automatically have integer-valued shipments.

FIGURE 15.13   Sensitivity of Profit to Increases in Capacity

	A	B	C	D	E	F	G	H	I
10	Shipments								
11					To				
12			City 1	City 2	City 3	City 4	Total shipped		Capacity
13		Plant 1	0	10	25	0	35	<=	35
14	From	Plant 2	45	0	5	0	50	<=	50
15		Plant 3	0	10	0	30	40	<=	40
16		Total received	45	20	30	30			
17			>=	>=	>=	>=			
18		Demand	45	20	30	30			
19									
20	Total cost	$1,020							
21									
22	Sensitivity of total cost to extra capacity at all plants								
23									
24	Extra capacity at each plant		0						
25									
26	Extra capacity	Total cost							
27		$1,020		New range name:					
28	5	$1,005		ExtraCap: C24					
29	10	$990							
30	15	$975							

2   Shipping costs are often nonlinear due to quantity discounts. For example, if it costs $3 per item to ship up to 100 items between cities and $2 per item for each additional item, the proportionality assumption of LP is violated and the transportation model we have developed is not valid. Shipping problems that involve quantity discounts are generally very difficult to solve.

Allocating Electric Power in Norway   The Midwest Electric example is based on Aarvik and Randolph (1975). Their work was used to allocate electric power in Norway. They solved transportation problems having up to 75 supply points and 92 demand points.

15.4.1   The Minimum Cost Network Flow Model

The transportation model is a special case of the **minimum cost network flow model** (MCNFM). In a general sense, this class of problems entails sending "goods" along the arcs of a network at minimal cost when there are capacity restrictions on some or all of the arcs.

There are two basic differences between the transportation model we just discussed and the general MCNFM. First, an MCNFM can have capacity restrictions on some or all of the arcs of the network. Actually, there can also be lower (nonzero) bounds on the arcs. Second, the flows in a general MCNFM don't all necessarily have to be from "left to right," that is, from supply points to demand points. For example, one supplier could ship goods through another supplier's location if it decreases overall shipping costs. In addition, there can be **transshipment** points, where goods neither originate nor end up. Goods are allowed to enter such a location, but they are all shipped out to their eventual destinations.

Figure 15.14 (page 834) illustrates the network setup for a typical MCNFM. The circles (called **nodes**) indicate locations such as cities. The arrows (called **arcs**) indicate roads, rivers, rail lines, and so on, on which goods can be transported. The nodes can be divided into three groups: suppliers, demanders, and transshipment points. We denote these in the figure by S, D, and T. For example, node 3 is a supplier, and it can supply as much as 300. Node 8 is a demander, and it requires at least 200. In contrast, node 5 is a transshipment

FIGURE 15.14 A Typical MCNFM

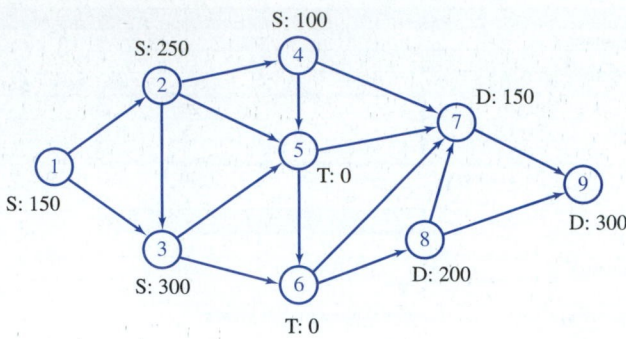

point; goods only flow *through* this node. Note that it is possible for supplier 1 to ship 50 to supplier 3 and for supplier 2 to ship 100 to supplier 3, and then for supplier 3 to ship as much as 450 out to nodes 5 and 6 (even though only 300 *originate* at supplier 3). Therefore, it is more appropriate to refer to the *net* supply at any supply node (and similarly, the *net* demand at a demand node).

To avoid clutter, we haven't shown all of the data on this network. However, it is understood that each arc has an associated unit shipping cost and (possibly) an arc capacity. Then our problem is to get the goods from the suppliers to the demanders at minimal total cost, subject to not violating the arc capacities. When we model this problem, we must also include a **flow balance** constraint for each node. This constraint takes one of three forms, depending on the type of node:

$$\text{Supply node: Flow out} \leq \text{Flow in} + \text{Net supply} \qquad \textbf{(15.4)}$$

$$\text{Demand node: Flow in} \geq \text{Flow out} + \text{Net demand} \qquad \textbf{(15.5)}$$

$$\text{Transshipment node: Flow in} = \text{Flow out} \qquad \textbf{(15.6)}$$

There is nothing mysterious about these constraints. They simply state that we can't supply more than we have, we must meet demands, and nothing can accumulate at transshipment points.[4]

We illustrate a typical MCNFM in the following example.

EXAMPLE 15.4

The RedBrand Company produces tomato products at three plants. These products can be shipped directly to their two customers or they can first be shipped to the company's two warehouses and then to the customers. A network representation of RedBrand's problem appears in Figure 15.15. We see that nodes 1, 2, and 3 represent the plants (suppliers), nodes 4 and 5 represent the warehouses (transshipment points), and nodes 6 and 7 represent the customers (demanders). Note that we allow the possibility of some shipments among plants, among warehouses, and among customers.

---

[4] It is possible that the supply and demand inequalities can be equalities, depending on the context of the problem. For example, a demander might require *exactly* 300 units—no more, no less.

FIGURE 15.15 Network for RedBrand Example

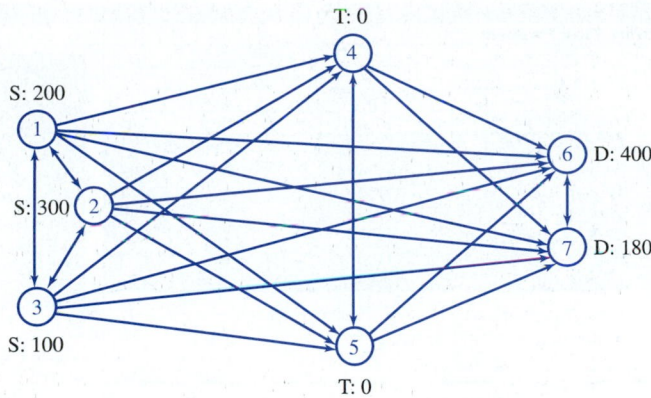

The cost of producing food at each plant is the same, so RedBrand is concerned with minimizing the total shipping cost incurred in meeting customer demands. The production capacity of each plant (in tons per year) and the demand of each customer are shown in Figure 15.15. The cost of shipping a ton of food (in thousands of dollars) between each pair of points is given in Table 15.5, where a dash indicates that RedBrand cannot ship along that arc. We also assume that at most 200 tons of food can be shipped between any two nodes. RedBrand wants to determine a minimum-cost shipping schedule.

TABLE 15.5 Shipping Costs for RedBrand Example

		To Node						
		1	2	3	4	5	6	7
	1	—	5.0	3.0	5.0	5.0	20.0	20.0
	2	9.0	—	9.0	1.0	1.0	8.0	15.0
	3	0.4	8.0	—	1.0	0.5	10.0	12.0
From Node	4	—	—	—	—	1.2	2.0	12.0
	5	—	—	—	0.8	—	2.0	12.0
	6	—	—	—	—	—	—	1.0
	7	—	—	—	—	—	7.0	—

Solution

We need to keep track of the following:

- amount shipped along each arc of the network
- total amount shipped into each node (the inflow)
- total amount shipped out of each node (the outflow)
- total shipping cost.

Developing the Model To set up the spreadsheet model, proceed as follows. (See Figure 15.16, page 836, and the file REDBRAND.XLS. Also, refer to the network in Figure 15.15.)

1 **Unit shipping costs.** Enter the unit shipping costs (in thousands of dollars) in the UnitCosts range. Note that we have entered zero costs for arcs that do not exist in the

FIGURE 15.16   RedBrand MCNFM Model

	A	B	C	D	E	F	G	H	I	J	K
1	RedBrand Minimum Cost Network Flow Problem										
2											
3	Unit shipping costs									Range names:	
4					To					Capacities: C34:I40	
5			Plant 1	Plant 2	Plant 3	Whse 1	Whse 2	Cust 1	Cust 2	CustDemand: H28:I29	
6	From	Plant 1	$0.00	$5.00	$3.00	$5.00	$5.00	$20.00	$20.00	CustNetIn: H27:I27	
7		Plant 2	$9.00	$0.00	$9.00	$1.00	$1.00	$8.00	$15.00	Flows: C17:I23	
8		Plant 3	$0.40	$8.00	$0.00	$1.00	$0.50	$10.00	$12.00	PlantCap: C29:E29	
9		Whse 1	$0.00	$0.00	$0.00	$0.00	$1.20	$2.00	$12.00	PlantNetOut: C27:E27	
10		Whse 2	$0.00	$0.00	$0.00	$0.80	$0.00	$2.00	$12.00	TotCost: B42	
11		Cust 1	$0.00	$0.00	$0.00	$0.00	$0.00	$0.00	$1.00	TotOutflows: J17:J23	
12		Cust 2	$0.00	$0.00	$0.00	$0.00	$0.00	$7.00	$0.00	UnitCosts: C6:I12	
13										WhseNetOut: F27:G27	
14	Shipments										
15					To						
16			Plant 1	Plant 2	Plant 3	Whse 1	Whse 2	Cust 1	Cust 2	Total outflow	
17	From	Plant 1	0	0	180	0	0	0	0	180	
18		Plant 2	0	0	0	120	0	180	0	300	
19		Plant 3	0	0	0	80	200	0	0	280	
20		Whse 1	0	0	0	0	0	200	0	200	
21		Whse 2	0	0	0	0	0	200	0	200	
22		Cust 1	0	0	0	0	0	0	180	180	
23		Cust 2	0	0	0	0	0	0	0	0	
24		Total inflow	0	0	180	200	200	580	180		
25		Total outflow	180	300	280	200	200	180	0		
26											
27		Net outflow/inflow	180	300	100	0	0	400	180		
28			<=	<=	<=	=	=	>=	>=		
29		Capacity/Demand	200	300	100	0	0	400	180		
30											
31	Arc capacities										
32					To						
33			Plant 1	Plant 2	Plant 3	Whse 1	Whse 2	Cust 1	Cust 2		
34	From	Plant 1	0	200	200	200	200	200	200		
35		Plant 2	200	0	200	200	200	200	200		
36		Plant 3	200	200	0	200	200	200	200		
37		Whse 1	0	0	0	0	200	200	200		
38		Whse 2	0	0	0	200	0	200	200		
39		Cust 1	0	0	0	0	0	0	200		
40		Cust 2	0	0	0	0	0	200	0		
41											
42	Total cost	$3,260									

network. Actually, these are irrelevant, because we will set arc capacities for these arcs to zero.

2   **Arc capacities.** Enter the arc capacities in the Capacities range. Note that each capacity is either 200 (for arcs that exist) or 0 (for arcs that don't exist).

3   **Supplies and demands.** Enter the supplies for the three plants in the PlantCap range, and enter the demands for the two customers in the CustDemand range. Also, enter zeros in cells F29 and G29 (to indicate that the warehouses are transshipment nodes).

4   **Amounts shipped.** Enter any trial values for the shipments between nodes in the Flows range. These are the changing cells.

5   **Flows out of and into nodes.** In preparation for the flow balance constraints, calculate the values in the TotOutflows range by summing across rows of the Flows range. Similarly, calculate the total inflows in row 24 by summing down columns of the Flows range.

6   **Transpose flows out of nodes.** We eventually want to compare total outflows to total inflows for the flow balance constraints, and this is tedious if total outflows are in a column and total inflows are in a row. Therefore, it is convenient to transfer the total

outflows to row 25. To do this quickly, highlight the range C25:I25, type the *array* formula

$$=\text{TRANSPOSE(TotOutflows)}$$

and press Ctrl-Shift-Enter. You will notice that the numbers in the *vertical* range J17:J23 have been transposed to the *horizontal* range C25:I25.

7 **Net outflows/inflows.** Now, with the flow balance constraints (15.4)–(15.6) in mind, calculate net outflows or inflows in row 27. Specifically, for the plants calculate the net outflow—that is, total outflow minus total inflow—in each cell of the PlantNetOut range. Do the opposite for the customers; that is, calculate total inflow minus total outflow in each cell of the CustNetIn range. For the warehouses in the WhseNetOut range, you can do it either way (total outflow minus total inflow or vice versa), because these two flows will eventually be constrained to be equal.

8 **Total shipping cost.** Calculate the total shipping cost (in thousands of dollars) in the TotCost cell with the formula

$$=\text{SUMPRODUCT(UnitCosts,Flows)}$$

Using Solver The Solver dialog box should be set up as in Figure 15.17. We want to minimize total shipping costs, subject to the three types of flow balance constraints and the arc capacity constraints.

FIGURE 15.17 **Solver Dialog Box for RedBrand Example**

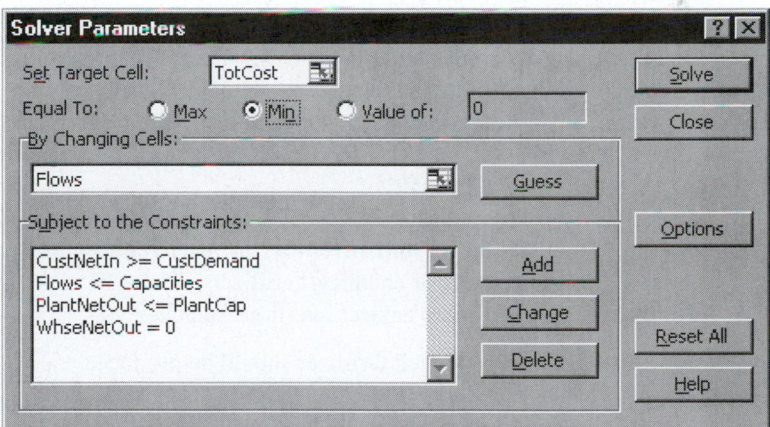

From the optimal solution in Figure 15.16, we see that RedBrand's customer demand can be satisfied with a shipping cost of $3,260,000. This solution appears graphically in Figure 15.18 (page 838). Note in particular that plant 1 produces 180 tons (under capacity) and ships it all to plant 3, not directly to warehouses or customers. Also, note that all shipments from the warehouses go directly to customer 1. Then customer 1 ships 180 tons to customer 2. We purposely chose unit shipping costs to produce this type of behavior (just to show that it can happen). As you can see, the costs of shipping from plant 1 directly to warehouses or customers are relatively large compared to shipping directly to plant 3. Similarly, the costs of shipping from plants or warehouses directly to customer 2 are prohibitive. Therefore, we ship to customer 1 and let customer 1 forward some of its shipment to customer 2.

FIGURE 15.18   Optimal Flows for RedBrand Example

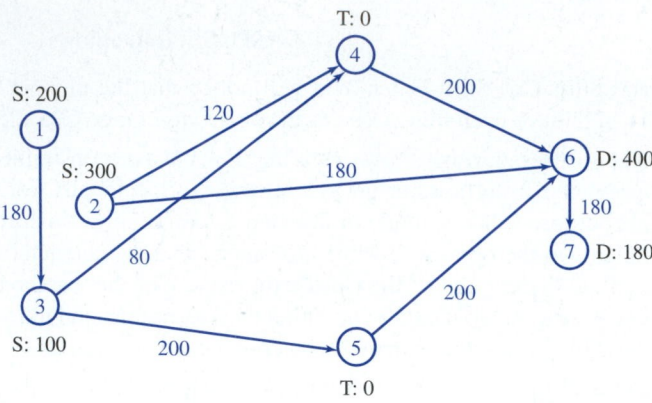

Modeling Issues

1   Spreadsheet Solvers use the simplex method to solve network flow models. However, for these types of models the simplex method can be simplified dramatically. The simplified version of the simplex method, called the **network simplex method**, is much more efficient than the ordinary simplex method. Specialized computer codes have been written to implement the network simplex method, and all large network flow problems are solved by using the network simplex method. This is fortunate because real network models can be extremely large. See Winston (1994) for a discussion of this method.

2   If the given supplies and demands for the nodes are integers and all arc capacities are integers, then the network flow problem will always have an optimal solution for which all flows are integers. Again, this is very fortunate for large problems—we get integer solutions "for free," without having to use an integer programming algorithm.

Production Distribution and Inventory at Agrico and Citgo   Agrico Chemical Company is a large producer of chemical fertilizers. Glover et al. (1979) developed a network flow model to help Agrico answer questions such as

■   How many units of each fertilizer should be produced each month?

■   How should products be shipped to distribution centers and customers?

The key to the Agrico model was to create a **dynamic network**. For each location in a dynamic network, there are nodes representing the location at different points in time. For example, there might be a node for plant 1 at times 1, 2, and 3. A "flow" from the plant 1–time 1 node to the plant 1–time 2 node, for example, corresponds to holding inventory. The Agrico model has saved the company an estimated $8 million annually in holding, production, and distribution costs.

A similar model developed by Klingman et al. (1987) helped Citgo Petroleum to optimize its refinery and distribution operations. This model has saved Citgo over $16 million annually.

PROBLEMS

Level A

16 Transportco supplies goods to three customers, each of whom requires 30 units. The company has two warehouses. In warehouse 1, 40 units are available, and in warehouse 2, 30 units are available. The costs of shipping one unit from each warehouse to each customer are shown in the file P15_16.XLS. There is a penalty for each unsatisfied customer unit of demand—with customer 1 a penalty cost of $90 is incurred; with customer 2, $80; and with customer 3, $110. Determine how to minimize the sum of shortage and shipping costs.

17 Referring to the previous problem, suppose that Transportco can purchase and ship extra units to either warehouse for a total cost of $100 per unit and that all customer demand must be met. Determine how to minimize the sum of purchasing and shipping costs.

18 Steelco manufactures three types of steel at different plants. The time required to manufacture 1 ton of steel (regardless of type) and the costs at each plant are shown in the file P15_18.XLS. Each week, 100 tons of each type of steel (1, 2, and 3) must be produced. Each plant is open 40 hours per week. Determine how to minimize the cost of meeting Steelco's weekly requirements.

19 The Amorco Oil Company controls two oil fields. Field 1 can produce up to 40 million barrels of oil per day, and field 2 can produce up to 50 million barrels of oil per day. At field 1, it costs $3 to extract and refine a barrel of oil; at field 2, the cost is $2. Amorco sells oil to two countries: United Kingdom and Japan. The shipping costs per barrel are shown in the file P15_19.XLS. Each day, the U.K. is willing to buy up to 40 million barrels (at $6 per barrel), and Japan is willing to buy up to 30 million barrels (at $6.50 per barrel). Determine how to maximize Amorco's profit.

20 Touche Young has three auditors. Each can work up to 160 hours during the next month, during which time three projects must be completed. Project 1 takes 130 hours, project 2 takes 140 hours, and project 3 takes 160 hours. The amount per hour that can be billed for assigning each auditor to each project is given in the file P15_20.XLS. Determine how to maximize total billings during the next month by formulating the company's problem as a transportation model.

21 Widgetco manufactures widgets at two factories, one in Memphis and one in Denver. The Memphis factory can produce up to 150 widgets per day, and the Denver factory can produce up to 200 widgets per day. Widgets are shipped by air to customers in Los Angeles and Boston. The customers in each city require 130 widgets per day. Because of the deregulation of air fares, Widgetco believes that it might be cheaper to first fly some widgets to New York or Chicago and then fly them to their final destinations. The costs of flying a widget are shown in the file P15_21.XLS. Determine how to minimize the total cost of shipping the required widgets to the customers.

22 General Ford produces cars at Los Angeles and Detroit and has a warehouse in Atlanta. The company supplies cars to customers in Houston and Tampa. The costs of shipping a car between various points are listed in the file P15_22.XLS, where "NA" means that a shipment is not allowed. Los Angeles can produce up to 1100 cars, and Detroit can produce up to 2900 cars. Houston must receive 2400 cars, and Tampa must receive 1500 cars.

   a Determine how to minimize the cost of meeting demands at Houston and Tampa.

   b Modify the answer to part **a** if shipments between L.A. and Detroit are not allowed.

   c Modify the answer to part **a** if shipments between Houston and Tampa are allowed at a cost of $5 per car.

23 Sunco Oil produces oil at two wells. Well 1 can produce up to 150,000 barrels per day, and well 2 can produce up to 200,000 barrels per day. It is possible to ship oil directly from the wells to Sunco's customers in Los Angeles and New York. Alternatively, Sunco could transport oil to the ports of Mobile and Galveston and then ship it by tanker to New York or Los Angeles. Los Angeles requires 160,000 barrels per day, and New York requires 140,000 barrels per day. The costs of shipping 1000 barrels between various locations are shown in the file P15_23.XLS, where "NA" indicates shipments that are not allowed.

   a Determine how to minimize the transport costs in meeting the oil demands of Los Angeles and New York.

b Assume that before being shipped to Los Angeles or New York, all oil produced at the wells must be refined at either Galveston or Mobile. To refine 1000 barrels of oil costs $12 at Mobile and $10 at Galveston. Assuming that both Mobile and Galveston have infinite refinery capacity, determine how to minimize the daily cost of transporting and refining the oil requirements of Los Angeles and New York.

c Rework part **b** under the assumption that Galveston has a refinery capacity of 150,000 barrels per day and Mobile has a refinery capacity of 180,000 barrels per day.

24 Each year, Data Corporal produces up to 400 computers in Boston and up to 300 computers in Raleigh. Los Angeles customers must receive 400 computers, and 300 computers must be supplied to Austin customers. Producing a computer costs $800 in Boston and $900 in Raleigh. Computers are transported by plane and can be sent through Chicago. The costs of sending a computer between pairs of cities are shown in the file P15_24.XLS.

a Determine how to minimize the total (production plus distribution) cost of meeting Data Corporal's annual demand.

b How would you modify the model in part **a** if at most 200 units could be shipped through Chicago?

Level B

25 Bloomington has two hospitals. Hospital 1 has four ambulances, and hospital 2 has two ambulances. Ambulance service is deemed adequate if there is only a 10% chance that no ambulance will be available when an ambulance call is received by a hospital. The average length of an ambulance service call is 20 minutes. Given this information, queueing theory tells us that hospital 1 can be assigned up to 4.9 calls per hour and that hospital 2 can be assigned up to 1.5 calls per hour. Bloomington has been divided into 12 districts. The average number of calls per hour emanating from each district is given in the file P15_25.XLS. This file also shows the travel time (in minutes) needed to travel from each district to each hospital. The objective is to minimize the average travel time needed to respond to a call. Develop a transportation model to determine the proper assignment of districts to hospitals. (*Hint*: Be careful about defining the supply points!)

26 Oilco has oil fields in San Diego and Los Angeles. The San Diego field can produce up to 500,000 barrels per day, and the Los Angeles field can produce up to 400,000 barrels per day. Oil is sent from the fields to a refinery, either in Dallas or in Houston. (Assume that each refinery has unlimited capacity.) To refine 100,000 barrels costs $700 at Dallas and $900 at Houston. Refined oil is shipped to customers in Chicago and New York. Chicago customers require 400,000 barrels per day, and New York customers require 300,000 barrels per day. The costs of shipping 100,000 barrels of oil (refined or unrefined) between cities are shown in the file P15_26.XLS.

a Determine how to minimize the total cost of meeting all demands.

b If each refinery had a capacity of 380,000 barrels per day, how would you modify the model in part **a**?

27 [Based on Glover et al. (1982)] Braneast Airlines must determine how many airplanes should serve the Boston–New York air corridor and which flights to fly. Braneast can fly any of the daily flights shown in the file P15_27.XLS. The fixed cost of operating an airplane is $800 per day. Determine how to maximize Braneast's daily profit. (*Hint*: Each node in the network represents a city and a time. In addition to arcs representing flights, you must allow for the possibility that an airplane will stay on the ground for an hour or more. You must also ensure that the model includes the fixed cost of operating a plane. To include this cost, the following arcs can be included in the network: from Boston 7 P.M. to Boston 10 A.M. and from New York 7 P.M. to New York 9 A.M.) ∎

Aggregate Planning Models

I n this section we extend the Pigskin production planning model from the previous chapter to more general **aggregate planning models**, where the number of workers available influences the possible production levels. We allow the workforce level to be modified each month through the hiring and firing of workers. We also (eventually) allow demand to be backlogged, that is, demand need not be met on time. The following example illustrates two versions of this model, one without backlogging and one with backlogging.

E X A M P L E   1 5 . 5

During the next 4 months the SureStep Shoe Company must meet (on time) the following demands for pairs of shoes: 3000 in month 1; 5000 in month 2; 2000 in month 3; and 1000 in month 4. At the beginning of month 1, 500 pairs of shoes are in inventory, and SureStep has 100 workers. Each worker is paid $1500 per month and can work up to 160 hours a month before he or she receives overtime. (This amounts to about $9.38 per hour.) A worker can be forced to work up to 20 hours of overtime per month at an overtime rate of $13 per hour. It takes 4 hours of labor and $15 of raw material to produce a pair of shoes. At the beginning of each month, workers can be hired or fired. There are fixed costs of $1600 per worker hired and $2000 per worker fired. At the end of each month, a holding cost of $3 per pair of shoes left in inventory is incurred. The selling price of shoes will stay constant over this 4-month period, so we don't need to incorporate it into the model. (Why not?) Finally, we assume that production in a given month can be used to meet that month's demand. SureStep wants to determine a hiring/firing and production schedule that minimizes its total costs over this 4-month period.

Solution

To model SureStep's problem we need to keep track of the following:

- number of workers hired, fired, and available during each month
- regular-time and overtime hours available and used each month
- production capacity (pairs of shoes) and the production quantities each month
- the inventory levels after production and at the end of each month
- the monthly costs and the total cost

Developing the Spreadsheet Model   The spreadsheet model appears in Figure 15.19 on page 842. (See the file SURESTEP1.XLS.) It can be developed as follows.

1   **Inputs.** Enter the input data in the range B4:B14 (each of these cells has its own range name) and enter the monthly demands in the Demand range.

2   **Production, hiring and firing plan.** Enter *any* trial values for the number of pairs of shoes produced each month in the Produced range, the overtime hours used each month in the OTHrs range, the workers hired each month in the Hired range, and the workers fired each month in the Fired range. These four ranges are the changing cells.

3   **Workers available each month.** In cell B17 enter the initial number of workers available with the formula

=InitWorkers

FIGURE 15.19 SureStep Aggregate Planning Model

	A	B	C	D	E	F
1	**SureStep Aggregate Planning Problem**			Range names:		
2				Demand: B36:E36		
3	**Input data**			Fired: B19:E19		
4	Initial inventory of shoes	500		Hired: B18:E18		
5	Initial number of workers	100		HrsPerPair: B12		
6	Regular hours/worker/month	160		InitInv: B4		
7	Maximum overtime hours/worker/month	20		InitWorkers: B5		
8	Hiring cost/worker	$1,600		MaxOTHrs: B7		
9	Firing cost/worker	$2,000		OnHand: B34:E34		
10	Regular wages/worker/month	$1,500		OTAvailable: B25:E25		
11	Overtime wage rate/hour	$13		OTHrs: B23:E23		
12	Labor hours/pair of shoes	4		OTWageRate: B11		
13	Raw material cost/per of shoes	$15		ProdCap: B32:E32		
14	Holding cost/pair of shoes in inventory/month	$3		Produced: B30:E30		
				RTWageRate: B10		
				StdRTHrs: B6		
				TotCost: F46		
				UnitFireCost: B9		
				UnitHireCost: B8		
				UnitHoldCost: B14		
15				UnitMatCost: B13		
16	**Worker plan**	Month 1	Month 2	Month 3	Month 4	
17	Workers from previous month	100	94	93	50	
18	Workers hired	0	0	0	0	
19	Workers fired	6	1	43	0	
20	Workers available after hiring and firing	94	93	50	50	
21						
22	Regular-time hours available	15040	14880	8000	8000	
23	Overtime labor hours used	0	80	0	0	
24		<=	<=	<=	<=	
25	Maximum overtime labor hours available	1880	1860	1000	1000	
26						
27	Total hours for production	15040	14960	8000	8000	
28						
29	**Production plan**	Month 1	Month 2	Month 3	Month 4	
30	Shoes produced	3760	3740	2000	1000	
31		<=	<=	<=	<=	
32	Production capacity	3760	3740	2000	2000	
33						
34	Inventory after production	4260	5000	2000	1000	
35		>=	>=	>=	>=	
36	Demand	3000	5000	2000	1000	
37	Ending inventory	1260	0	0	0	
38						
39	**Summary of costs**	Month 1	Month 2	Month 3	Month 4	Totals
40	Hiring cost	$0	$0	$0	$0	$0
41	Firing cost	$12,000	$2,000	$86,000	$0	$100,000
42	Regular-time wages	$141,000	$139,500	$75,000	$75,000	$430,500
43	Overtime wages	$0	$1,040	$0	$0	$1,040
44	Raw material cost	$56,400	$56,100	$30,000	$15,000	$157,500
45	Holding cost	$3,780	-$0	-$0	-$0	$3,780
46	Totals	$213,180	$198,640	$191,000	$90,000	$692,820

Since the number of workers available at the beginning of any other month (before hiring or firing) is equal to the number of workers from the previous month, enter the formula

$$=B20$$

in cell C17 and copy it to the range D17:E17. Next, calculate the net number of workers on hand after hiring and firing by entering the formula

$$=B17+B18-B19$$

in cell B20 and copying it across row 20.

4   **Overtime capacity.** Since each available worker can work up to 20 hours of overtime in a month, enter the formula

$$=MaxOTHrs*B20$$

in cell B25 and copy it to the range C25:E25 to calculate the overtime hours capacity for months 2 through 4.

5   **Production capacity.** Since each worker can work 160 regular-time hours per month, calculate the regular-time hours available in month 1 in cell B22 with the formula

$$=StdRTHrs*B20$$

and copy it to the range C22:E22 for the other months. Then calculate the total hours available for production in cell B27 with the formula

$$=SUM(B22:B23)$$

and copy it to the range C27:E27 for the other months. Finally, since it takes 4 hours of labor to make a pair of shoes, enter the formula

$$=B27/HrsPerPair$$

in cell B32 and copy it to the range C32:E32.

6   **Inventories each month.** We include two inventory rows: row 34 for inventory after production has occurred and row 37 for ending inventory, after demand has been taken away. To calculate these, begin by entering the formula

$$=InitInv+B30$$

in cell B34. Then enter the formula

$$=B37+C30$$

in cell C34 and copy it to the range D34:E34. This links the inventory in one month to the ending inventory from the previous month. Next, calculate the ending inventory levels by entering the formula

$$=B34-B36$$

in cell B37 and copying it across row 37.

7   **Costs.** Calculate the various costs in rows 40–45 by multiplying the relevant unit costs in rows 7–14 by the relevant quantities in the body of the spreadsheet. For example, for the holding costs enter the formula

$$=UnitHoldCost*B37$$

in cell B45 and copy it to the range C45:E45. Then calculate the row and column totals in column F and row 46. (Of course, all we really need is the total cost in cell F46, but the breakdown of the costs might be useful to SureStep management.)

Using Solver   The Solver dialog box should appear as shown in Figure 15.20 (page 844). We minimize the total cost, subject to not exceeding the maximum overtime constraint, not exceeding production capacity, and meeting demand on time. We also include integer constraints on the number of workers hired and fired and the production levels of shoes.[5]

Interestingly, SureStep never hires any workers. It even fires a worker in month 2 at the same time that it uses 80 hours of overtime. Evidently, this is cheaper than hiring and *then*

---

[5]This is a rather difficult problem (because of the integer constraints) for Solver, and your solution might differ slightly from ours. To *ensure* that Solver finds the optimal solution in an integer-constrained model, it is a good idea to set the "tolerance" to 0 in the Solver Options dialog box. Otherwise, Solver might stop when it finds a solution that is *close* to optimal.

FIGURE 15.20   Solver Dialog Box for SureStep Model

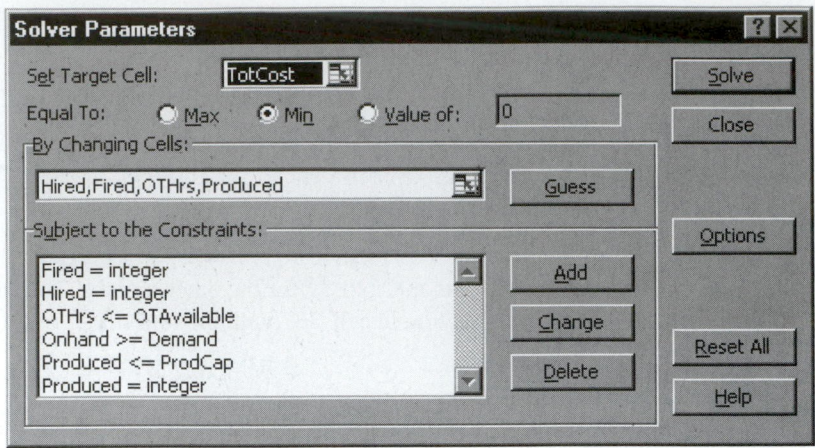

having to fire when demand decreases. Note also that SureStep uses all of its production capacity except in month 4. In that month it has more workers than it needs, but there is a big penalty for firing them and no penalty for letting them sit idle. Finally, the company holds inventory only at the end of month 1. This inventory is then used to help meet month 2 demand.

Model with Backlogging Allowed   In many situations, backlogging is allowed; that is, customer demand can be met later than it occurs. We now show how to modify the SureStep model to include the option of backlogged demand. We assume that at the end of each month a cost of $20 is incurred for each unit of demand (pair of shoes) that remains unsatisfied at the end of the month. This is easily modeled by allowing a month's ending inventory to be negative. For example, if month 1's ending inventory is −10, a shortage cost of $200 (and no holding cost) is incurred. To ensure that SureStep produces any shoes at all, we require that there is eventually enough inventory after month 4's production to cover demand. That way, all demand in the 4-month period will eventually be satisfied.

Modifying the Model   To begin, we enter the per unit monthly shortage cost in cell B15. To take shortages into account, one possibility is to replace the formula currently in cell B45 (see Figure 15.19) with

$$\text{=IF(B37>=0,UnitHoldCost*B37,-UnitShortCost*B37)}$$

While this accurately computes the holding or shortage cost, Solver is unfortunately unable to deal with IF functions accurately, at least when they involve changing cells (either directly or indirectly). Alternatively, we could use the expression

$$\text{=MAX(UnitHoldCost*B37,0)+MAX(0,-UnitShortCost*B37)}$$

instead of the IF expression. However, Solver is also unable to deal appropriately with MAX (or MIN) functions.[6]

We can, however, handle shortages and maintain a linear formulation. The method is illustrated in Figure 15.21. (See the file SURESTEP2.XLS.) We again assume that the number of workers hired and fired each month, as well as the number of pairs of shoes

---

[6] There is a spreadsheet Solver called GeneHunter (1995) that can handle IF, MAX, and MIN functions. GeneHunter uses **genetic algorithms** to solve optimization problems. For most problems genetic algorithms are slower than the algorithms used by Excel's Solver. However, their advantage is that they can handle *any* spreadsheet model.

FIGURE 15.21   SureStep Model with Backlogging Allowed

	A	B	C	D	E	F
1	**SureStep Model with Backlogging**					
2						
3	**Input data**					
4	Initial inventory of shoes	500				
5	Initial number of workers	100				
6	Regular hours/worker/month	160				
7	Maximum overtime hours/worker/month	20				
8	Hiring cost/worker	$1,600				
9	Firing cost/worker	$2,000				
10	Regular wages/worker/month	$1,500				
11	Overtime wage rate/hour	$13				
12	Labor hours/pair of shoes	4				
13	Raw material cost/per of shoes	$15				
14	Holding cost/pair of shoes in inventory/month	$3				
15	Shortage cost/pair of shoes/month	$20				
16						
17	**Worker plan**	Month 1	Month 2	Month 3	Month 4	
18	Workers from previous month	100	94	93	38	
19	Workers hired	0	0	0	0	
20	Workers fired	6	1	55	0	
21	Workers available after hiring and firing	94	93	38	38	
22						
23	Regular-time hours available	15040	14880	6080	6080	
24	Overtime labor hours used	0	0	0	0	
25		<=	<=	<=	<=	
26	Maximum overtime labor hours available	1880	1860	760	760	
27						
28	Total hours for production	15040	14880	6080	6080	
29						
30	**Production plan**	Month 1	Month 2	Month 3	Month 4	
31	Shoes produced	3760	3720	1520	1500	
32		<=	<=	<=	<=	
33	Production capacity	3760	3720	1520	1520	
34						
35	Inventory after production	4260	4980	1500	1000	
36						>=
37	Demand	3000	5000	2000	1000	
38						
39	Excess	1260	0	0	0	
40	Shortage	0	20	500	0	
41	Net (excess minus shortage)	1260	-20	-500	0	
42		=	=	=	=	
43	Ending inventory	1260	-20	-500	0	
44						
45	**Summary of costs**	Month 1	Month 2	Month 3	Month 4	Totals
46	Hiring cost	$0	$0	$0	$0	$0
47	Firing cost	$12,000	$2,000	$110,000	$0	$124,000
48	Regular-time wages	$141,000	$139,500	$57,000	$57,000	$394,500
49	Overtime wages	$0	$0	$0	$0	$0
50	Raw material cost	$56,400	$55,800	$22,800	$22,500	$157,500
51	Holding cost	$3,780	$0	$0	$0	$3,780
52	Shortage cost	$0	$400	$10,000	$0	$10,400
53	Totals	$213,180	$197,700	$199,800	$79,500	$690,180

Additional range names:
Demand4: E37
EndInv: B43:E43
Excess: B39:E39
Net: B41:E41
Onhand4: E35
Shortage: B40:E40
UnitShortCost: B15

produced each month, must be integers. To develop this modified spreadsheet, proceed as follows.

1   Enter shortage cost. Insert a new row below row 14 and enter the shortage cost per pair of shoes per month in cell B15.

2   Rows for amounts held and short. Insert five new rows (which will now be rows 38 through 42) between the Demand and Ending inventory rows. The range B39:E40 will be changing cells. The Excess range in row 39 contains the amounts left in inventory (if any), whereas the Shortage range in row 40 contains the shortages (if any). Enter any values in these ranges.

3 Ending inventory (positive or negative). Here is the key observation. Let E_t be the excess left in inventory at the end of month t, and let S_t be the shortage at the end of month t. Then $E_t = 0$ if $S_t \geq 0$, and $S_t = 0$ if $E_t \geq 0$. So if we allow ending inventory I_t to be negative (meaning that there is a shortage), then for each month we have

$$I_t = E_t - S_t$$

For example, if $I_2 = 6$, then $E_2 = 60$ and $S_2 = 0$, indicating that SureStep has 60 pairs of shoes left over at the end of month 2. But if $I_2 = -30$, then $E_2 = 0$ and $S_2 = 30$, indicating that SureStep has a shortage of 30 pairs of shoes at the end of month 2. To incorporate this into the spreadsheet, enter the formula

$$=B39-B40$$

in cell B41 and copy it across row 41. The trick now is that we have calculated ending inventory in two different ways, in rows 41 and 43. To make sure they match, we'll eventually add a constraint to *force* rows 41 and 43 to be equal.

4 Monthly costs. Insert a new row (which will be row 52) below the holding cost row. Modify the holding cost for month 1 by entering the formula

$$=\text{UnitHoldCost*B39}$$

in cell B51 and copy it across row 51. Calculate the shortage cost for month 1 in cell B52 with the formula

$$=\text{UnitShortCost*B40}$$

and copy it across row 52. (Also, make sure the totals in row 53 and column F are updated to include the shortage costs.)

Using Solver for the Modified Model The modified Solver dialog box appears in Figure 15.22. (Not all of the constraints fit in the window, but the new ones do.) Note the changes: (1) the Excess and Shortage ranges are additional changing cells, (2) the Net range (row 41) is constrained to equal the EndInv range (row 43), and (3) the on-hand inventory after production is required only to be at least as great as demand in month 4, not in all months.

FIGURE 15.22 **Solver Dialog Box for SureStep Model with Backlogging**

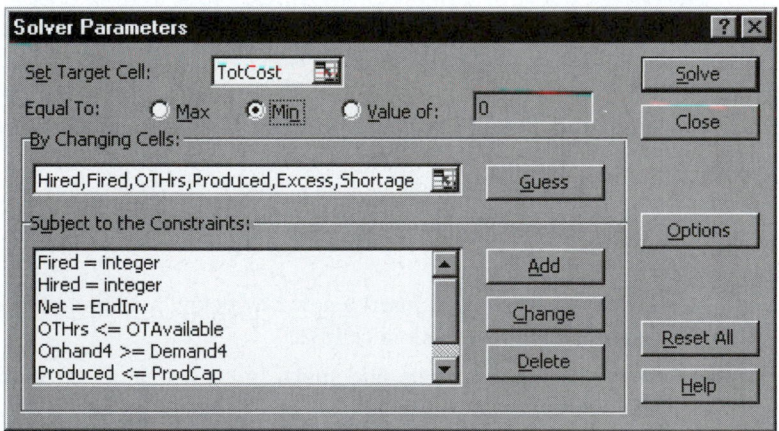

Comparing the optimal solutions in Figures 15.19 and 15.21, we see that SureStep should now fire even more workers in month 3 than before, and it should not use any overtime. The company again holds inventory in month 1, but it incurs shortages in months 2 and 3. Of course, the demands for these customers are eventually satisfied by the end of the 4-month period. The total cost has decreased, but only by $2640. Note that the optimal cost could not possibly *increase*. When we allow more possibilities, as we do when we allow backlogging, the optimal cost can only decrease or stay the same.

Here's a great opportunity to perform a sensitivity analysis on the unit shortage cost. In the no-backlogging model, this cost is essentially infinite, whereas it is now relatively small. The question is how large this cost needs to be before SureStep will not incur any planned shortages. This is a straightforward application of the SolverTable add-in. We leave the details to you.   ■

The Rolling Planning Horizon Approach   In reality, an aggregate planning model is usually implemented via a rolling planning horizon. To illustrate, we assume that SureStep works with a 4-month planning horizon. To implement the SureStep model in the rolling planning horizon context, we view the "demands" as forecasts and solve a 4-month model with these forecasts. However, we implement only the month 1 production and worker scheduling recommendation. Thus (assuming that the number of workers hired and fired in a month must be an integer and backlogging is allowed) SureStep should fire 6 workers and produce 3760 pairs of shoes with regular time labor in month 1. Next, we observe month 1's actual demand. Suppose that it is 2900. Then SureStep begins month 2 with $1360 (= 500 + 3760 - 2900)$ pairs of shoes and 94 workers. We would now enter 1360 in cell B4 and 94 in cell B5 (referring to Figure 15.21). Next, we would replace the demands in the Demand range with the updated forecasts for the *next* 4 months. Finally, we would rerun Solver and use the production levels and hiring and firing recommendations in column B as the production level and workforce policy for month 2.

Modeling Issues

1   Hiring costs include training costs as well as the cost of decreased productivity due to the fact that a new worker must learn his or her job (the "learning curve" effect). Similarly, firing costs include severance costs and costs due to loss of morale.

2   Peterson and Silver (1985) recommend that when demand is seasonal, the planning horizon should extend beyond the next seasonal peak.

3   Beyond a certain point, the cost of using extra overtime hours *increases* because workers become less efficient. We haven't modeled this type of behavior, but it would make the model nonlinear.

Multiproduct Production Scheduling at Owens-Corning Fiberglass   Oliff and Burch (1985) developed an aggregate planning LP model that is used to schedule production of fiberglass products at Owens-Corning Fiberglass. Their model minimizes the sum of direct payroll costs, overtime costs, hiring and firing costs, and inventory holding costs. They also take into account (using integer programming) the cost due to lost production time when a machine changes from making one product to making a different product. Their model saved Owens-Corning over $100,000 annually.

PROBLEMS

Level A

28 Mondo Motorcycles is determining its production schedule for the next four quarters. Demands for motorcycles are forecasted to be 40 in quarter 1; 70 in quarter 2; 50 in quarter 3; 20 in quarter 4. Mondo incurs four types of costs:

- It costs Mondo $400 to manufacture each motorcycle.

- At the end of each quarter, a holding cost of $100 per motorcycle left in inventory is incurred.

- Increasing production from one quarter to the next incurs costs for training employees. It is estimated that a cost of $700 per motorcycle is incurred if production is increased from one quarter to the next.

- Decreasing production from one quarter to the next incurs costs for severance pay, decreasing morale, and so forth. It is estimated that a cost of $600 per motorcycle is incurred if production is decreased from one quarter to the next.

All demands must be met on time, and a quarter's production can be used to meet demand for the current quarter (as well as future quarters). During the quarter immediately preceding quarter 1, 50 Mondos were produced. Assume that at the beginning of quarter 1, no Mondos are in inventory.

a Determine how to minimize Mondo's total cost during the next four quarters.

b Discuss how Mondo's optimal production schedule would be affected by a change in the cost of increasing production from one quarter to the next.

c Discuss how Mondo's optimal production schedule would be affected by a change in the cost of decreasing production from one quarter to the next.

29 Referring to the previous problem, suppose that Mondo no longer must meet demands on time. For each quarter that demand for a motorcycle is not met, a shortage cost of $110 per motorcycle short is assessed. Thus, demand can now be backlogged. All demands must be met, however, by the end of quarter 4. Determine the optimal solution to this modified problem.

30 Shoemakers of America forecasts the following demand for the next 6 months: 5000 pairs in month 1; 6000 pairs in month 2; 5000 pairs in month 3; 9000 pairs in month 4; 6000 pairs in month 5; 5000 pairs in month 6. It takes a shoemaker 15 minutes to produce a pair of shoes. Each shoemaker works 150 hours per month plus up to 40 hours per month of overtime. A shoemaker is paid a regular salary of $2000 per month plus $50 per hour for overtime. At the beginning of each month, Shoemakers can either hire or fire workers. It costs the company $1500 to hire a worker and $1900 to fire a worker. The monthly holding cost per pair of shoes is 3% of the cost of producing a pair of shoes with regular-time labor. The raw materials in a pair of shoes cost $10. At the beginning of month 1, Shoemakers has 13 workers. Determine how to minimize the cost of meeting (on time) the demands of the next 6 months.

Level B

31 Clothco manufactures pants. During each of the next 6 months, Clothco can sell up to the numbers of pants given in the file P15_31.XLS. Demand that is not met during a month is lost—not backlogged. A pair of pants sells for $40, requires 2 hours of labor, and uses $10 of raw material. At the beginning of month 1, Clothco has 4 workers. A worker can sew pants for up to 200 hours per month and is paid $2,000 per month (regardless of how many hours he or she works). At the beginning of each month, workers can be hired or fired. It costs $1500 to hire a worker and $1000 to fire a worker. A holding cost of $5 per pair of pants is assessed against each month's ending inventory. Determine how Clothco can maximize its profit for the next 6 months.

32 During the next 4 quarters Dorian Auto must meet (on time) the following demands for cars: 4000 in quarter 1; 2000 in quarter 2; 5000 in quarter 3; 1000 in quarter 4. At the beginning of quarter 1, there are 300 autos in stock. The company has the capacity to produce at most 3000 cars per quarter. At the beginning of each quarter, the company can change production capacity. It costs $100 to increase quarterly production capacity by 1 unit. For example, it would cost $10,000 to increase capacity from 3000 to 3100. It also costs $50 per quarter to maintain each unit of production capacity (even if it is unused during the current quarter). The variable cost of producing a car is $2000. A holding cost of $150 per car is assessed against each quarter's ending inventory. It is required that at the end of quarter 4, plant capacity must be at least 4000 cars. Determine how to minimize the total cost incurred during the next 4 quarters.

33 Owens-Wheat uses two production lines to produce three types of fiberglass mat. The demand requirements (in tons) for each of the next 4 months are shown in the file P15_33.XLS. If it were dedicated entirely to the production of one product, a line 1 machine could produce either 20 tons of type 1 mat or 30 tons of type 2 mat during a month. Similarly, a line 2 machine could produce either 25 tons of type 2 mat or 28 tons of type 3 mat. It costs $5000 per month to operate a machine on line 1 and $5500 per month to operate a machine on line 2. A cost of $2000 is incurred each time a new machine is purchased, and a cost of $1000 is incurred if a machine is retired from service. At the end of each month Owens would like to have at least 50 tons of each product in inventory. At the beginning of month 1, Owens has five line 1 machines and eight line 2 machines. Assume the per ton cost of holding either product in inventory for 1 month is $5.

a Determine a minimum cost production schedule for the next 4 months.

b There is an important aspect of this situation that cannot be modeled by linear programming. What is it? (*Hint*: If Owens makes product 1 and product 2 on line 1 during a month, is this as efficient as making just product 1 on line 1?) ■

15.6   A Dynamic Financial Model

Often a company must determine the optimal level of investment and/or borrowing at different points in time. In this section we show how LP can be used to model such situations.

E X A M P L E   1 5 . 6

A small toy store, Tyco, projects the monthly cash inflows listed in Table 15.6 (in thousands of dollars) during the year 2000. A negative cash flow means that cash outflows exceed cash inflows to the business—bills exceed revenues. Tyco begins the year with a cash balance of $6500. To pay its bills, Tyco will need to borrow money early in the year. The company can borrow money in two ways. First, it can obtain a long-term 1-year loan and receive the total amount in January. Beginning in February 2000, 1% interest will be charged each month on this loan. The loan must be paid back by the beginning of January 2001. Second, each month Tyco can borrow money from a short-term bank line of credit with a monthly interest rate of 1.5%. All short-term loans must be paid back by the beginning of January 2001. At the end of each month, excess cash earns Tyco 0.4% interest. Tyco wants to maximize its cash on hand at the beginning of January 2001, after paying back all loans. Also, Tyco's policy is to have a cash balance of at least $5000 at the end of each month.

TABLE 15.6   Cash Inflows for Tyco

	Cash Inflow		Cash Inflow
January	−12	July	−7
February	−10	August	−2
March	−8	September	15
April	−10	October	12
May	−4	November	−7
June	5	December	45

Solution

This example is interesting from a modeling point of view. There are different—and probably reasonable—ways to model the problem, and these lead to different solutions. We will describe one possible approach, but depending on the assumptions you make, you could argue for another approach. We make the following timing assumptions.

- Cash at the end of the previous month is carried forward, with interest, to the beginning of the next month.

- At the beginning of each month, short-term loans are paid back with interest and new short-term loans are taken out. The cash balance after these activities must be nonnegative.

- During any month bills are paid and/or revenues are received. The cash balance at the end of the month, after these activities occur, must be at least as large as the minimum cash balance specified by Tyco.

- At the beginning of January 2001, Tyco pays back any outstanding loans with interest. The cash balance after doing so is the amount Tyco wants to maximize.

Developing the Model The spreadsheet model for Tyco's problem appears in Figure 15.23. (See the file TYCO.XLS.) To set up this spreadsheet, proceed as follows.

FIGURE 15.23 Cash Balance Model

	A	B	C	D	E	F	G	H	I	J	K	L	M	N
1	**Tyco cash balance example**													
2														
3	**Assumptions:**													
4	At the beginning of any month, loans are received and loans are paid back with interest - the balance must be nonnegative													
5	At the end of each month, after bills or revenues occur, the balance must be at least some minimal amount								Range names:					
6	The objective is to minimize total interest paid								BalAfterLoan: B26:N26					
7									EndBal: B31:M31					
8	**Inputs**								FinalBal: B39					
9	Monthly rates								InitCash: D15					
10	Long-term loan	1.0%							IntRate: B12					
11	Short-term loan	1.5%							LTLoan: B20					
12	Excess cash	0.4%							LTRate: B10					
13									MinBal: B33:M33					
14	Minimal required cash balance at the end of each month	$5,000							MinCashBal: D14					
15	Cash carried over from December 1999 (with interest)	$6,500							STLoan: B21:M21					
16									STRate: B11					
17	**Financial section**													
18		Jan	Feb	Mar	Apr	May	Jun	Jul	Aug	Sep	Oct	Nov	Dec	Jan
19	Beginning balance	$6,500	$24,944	$14,699	$6,421	$5,020	$5,020	$5,020	$5,020	$5,020	$15,060	$12,303	$5,020	$49,915
20	Long-term loan	$30,344												
21	Short-term loan	$0	$0	$0	$8,882	$13,299	$8,782	$16,197	$18,724	$14,288	$0	$0	$0	
22	Interest on long-term loan	$303	$303	$303	$303	$303	$303	$303	$303	$303	$303	$303	$303	
23	Interest on short-term loan	$0	$0	$0	$133	$199	$132	$243	$281	$214	$0	$0	$0	
24	Long-term interest/payback		$303	$303	$303	$303	$303	$303	$303	$303	$303	$303	$303	$30,648
25	Short-term interest/payback		$0	$0	$0	$9,016	$13,498	$8,914	$16,440	$19,004	$14,502	$0	$0	$0
26	Balance after loan activities	$36,844	$24,640	$14,396	$15,000	$9,000	($0)	$12,000	$7,000	($0)	$254	$12,000	$4,717	$19,267
27		>=	>=	>=	>=	>=	>=	>=	>=	>=	>=	>=	>=	>=
28	Must be nonnegative	$0	$0	$0	$0	$0	$0	$0	$0	$0	$0	$0	$0	$0
29														
30	Cash inflow/outflow	-$12,000	-$10,000	-$8,000	-$10,000	-$4,000	$5,000	-$7,000	-$2,000	$15,000	$12,000	-$7,000	$45,000	
31	Balance at end of month	$24,844	$14,640	$6,396	$5,000	$5,000	$5,000	$5,000	$5,000	$15,000	$12,254	$5,000	$49,717	
32		>=	>=	>=	>=	>=	>=	>=	>=	>=	>=	>=	>=	
33	Minimal balance	$5,000	$5,000	$5,000	$5,000	$5,000	$5,000	$5,000	$5,000	$5,000	$5,000	$5,000	$5,000	
34														
35	Interest on excess cash	$99	$59	$26	$20	$20	$20	$20	$20	$60	$49	$20	$199	
36														
37	**Summary data**													
38	Total interest paid	$4,844												
39	Cash balance in Jan 2001	$19,267												

1 **Inputs.** Enter the relevant interest rates in the range B10:B12, the minimal required cash balance each month in the MinCashBal cell, the initial cash balance in the InitCash cell, and the monthly cash inflows/outflows in the range B30:M30.

2 **Loan amounts.** Enter *any* trial value in the LTLoan cell for the long-term loan, and enter *any* trial values in the STLoan range for the short-term loans.

3 **Beginning cash balance each month.** Row 19 is used to keep track of the cash balance from the previous month. Begin by entering the formula

$$=InitCash$$

in cell B19. Then enter the formula

$$=SUM(B31,B35)$$

in cell C19 (carryover from January to February), and copy it across row 19.

4 **Interest on long-term loan.** Row 22 contains the interest from the long-term loan each month. It is a constant, so enter the formula

$$=LTRate*LTLoan$$

in cell B22 and copy it across row 22.

5 **Interest on short-term loan.** The short-term loan interest amounts vary from month to month, depending on the current short-term loan amount. Enter the formula

$$=STRate*B21$$

in cell B23 and copy it across row 23.

6 **Paybacks (including interest) on loans.** Rows 24 and 25 record the amounts paid back, including the loan amounts and interest. We assume each of these is paid back at the *beginning* of the month it is due. For example, a short-term loan taken out in March, along with its interest, is paid back at the beginning of April. For the long-term loan enter the formula

$$=B22$$

in cell C24 and copy it across to cell M24. Then enter the formula

$$=LTLoan+M20$$

in cell N24 to capture the long-term loan payback plus interest in January 2001. For the short-term loans enter the formula

$$=SUM(B21,B23)$$

in cell C25 and copy it across row 25.

7 **Balance after loan activities.** Row 26 captures the cash balance each month after loan activities but *before* the revenues and bills in row 28. This is the beginning cash balance plus any loans taken out minus any loan/interest paybacks. Therefore, enter the formula

$$=SUM(B19:B21)-SUM(B24:B25)$$

in cell B26 and copy it across row 26. Also, enter 0's in row 28. (These 0's aren't necessary, but they are a good reminder that the values in row 26 must be nonnegative.)

8 **Balance at end of month.** Row 31 captures the cash balance at the end of each month. It is the cash balance in row 26 plus the inflow (or outflow if negative) in row 30. Enter the formula

$$=B26+B30$$

in cell B31 and copy it across row 31. Then enter the formula

$$=MinCashBal$$

in cell B33 and copy it across row 33 to designate the required minimum monthly ending cash balance.

9   **Interest earned on cash balance each month.** Row 35 records the interest earned on the ending cash balance each month. Enter the formula

$$=IntRate*B31$$

in cell B35 and copy it across row 35.

10 **Summary measures.** We want to maximize the cash balance in January 2001, after loans have been paid back, so we record its value in the FinalBal cell (B39) with the formula

$$=N26$$

Tyco might also like to know the total amount of interest it pays throughout the year, so calculate it in cell B38 with the formula

$$=SUM(B22:M23)$$

Using Solver   The Solver dialog box appears in Figure 15.24. Tyco wants to maximize its final cash balance, subject to meeting its end-of-month minimum cash balance each month and also having nonnegative cash after settling its loans each month.

FIGURE 15.24   Solver Dialog Box for Cash Balance Model

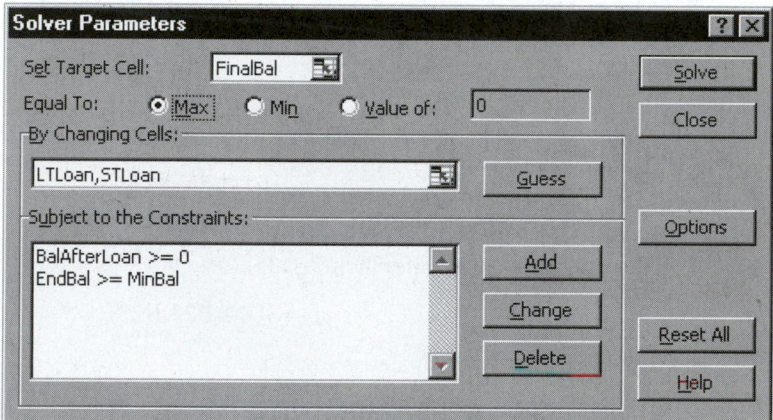

The solution recommends a long-term loan of $30,344 plus short-term loans of various amounts during the six months from April to September. At the beginning of January 2001, Tyco's cash balance will be $19,267, and it will have paid $4,844 in interest.

Sensitivity Analysis   Once this model is built, we can proceed in a number of directions. We can use the SolverTable add-in with inputs such as the interest rates and the minimal required ending cash balance each month. For example, you can check that if the long-term interest rate per month increases to 2%, then *no* long-term loan is taken out, a short-term loan is taken out every month, and the final cash balance in January 2001 decreases to $17,741. Alternatively, if the interest rates remain as they were but the minimal cash balance increases from $5000 to $7500 each month, then the *pattern* of loans is the same as in Figure 15.23, but the loan amounts are slightly different, and the final cash balance decreases to $19,105. That is, this increase in required cash at the end of each month has a surprisingly small effect on the optimal solution.

Another possible change we might consider is a change in the objective. Rather than maximizing the final cash balance in January 2001, we could *minimize* the total amount of interest paid throughout the year, that is, the value in cell B38 of Figure 15.23. All we need to do is change the target cell setting in the Solver dialog box and rerun Solver. The new solution (not shown here but available in the TYCO1.XLS file) is very similar to the original solution, but the loan amounts are modified slightly to achieve a slightly lower total interest (and a slightly lower final cash balance). By the way, the reason these two solutions are slightly different has to do with the interest rate on excess cash. If we set this interest rate equal to 0, you can check that the two solutions are identical. (Can you explain why?)

Finally, we could omit the nonnegativity constraint on the cash balance after loan activities—that is, the BalAfterLoan>=0 constraint. This is simple to do. We highlight this constraint in the Solver dialog box, delete it, and rerun Solver. The corresponding optimal solution (not shown here but available in the TYCO2.XLS file) is again quite close to the original optimal solution. However, we note the following. First, the objective value is *larger* than before ($19,380 versus $19,267). This always occurs when we omit a constraint. A problem with omitted constraints *must* achieve at least as good an objective value as a problem that includes these constraints. Second, we see from Figure 15.23 that the constraints we omitted were binding (that is, held as equalities) only in June and September; all other months had a positive cash balance in row 26. Therefore, we might expect negative cash balances in June and September when the constraints are omitted. This is almost what occurs. June's balance remains at 0, but September's decreases to $-\$10,000$. Of course, this negative cash balance in early September is more than made up by the large inflow in the middle of September, so that by month's end, the cash balance is a positive $5000. ■

Using LP to Optimize Bond Portfolios   Many Wall Street firms buy and sell bonds. Rohn (1987) discusses a bond selection model that maximizes profit from bond purchases and sales subject to constraints that minimize the firm's risk exposure. The method used to model this situation is closely related to the method we used to model the Tyco problem.

PROBLEMS

Level A

34   Finco Investment Corporation must determine an investment strategy for the firm for the next 3 years. At present (time 0), $100,000 is available for investment. Investments A, B, C, D, and E are available. The cash flow associated with investing $1 in each investment is given in the file P15_34.XLS. For example, $1 invested in investment B requires a $1 cash outflow at time 1 and returns $.50 at time 2 and $1 at time 3. To ensure that the company's portfolio is diversified, Finco requires that at most $75,000 be placed in any single investment. In addition to investments A through E, Finco can earn interest at 8% per year by keeping uninvested cash in money market funds. Returns from investments can be reinvested immediately. For example, the positive cash flow received from investment C at time 1 can be reinvested immediately in investment B. Finco cannot borrow funds, so the cash available for investment at any time is limited to cash on hand. Determine how to maximize cash on hand at time 3.

35   At time 0 you have $10,000. Investments A and B are available; their cash flows are shown in the file P15_35.XLS. Assume that any money not invested in A or B earns interest at an annual rate of 8%. Determine how to maximize your cash on hand at time 3.

36 Broker Sonya Wong is currently trying to maximize her profit in the bond market. Four bonds are available for purchase and sale at the bid and ask prices shown in the file P15_36.XLS. Sonya can buy up to 1000 units of each bond at the ask price or sell up to 1000 units of each bond at the bid price. During each of the next 3 years, the person who sells a bond will pay the owner of the bond the cash payments are also shown in the file P15_36.XLS. Sonya's goal is to maximize her revenue from selling bonds less her payment for buying bonds, subject to the constraint that after each year's payments are received, her current cash position (due only to cash payments from bonds and not purchases or sales of bonds) is nonnegative. Note that her current cash position can depend on past coupons and that cash accumulated at the end of each year earns 11.111% annual interest. Determine how to maximize net profit from buying and selling bonds, subject to the constraints previously described. Why do you think we limit the number of units of each bond that can be bought or sold?

37 You are managing a company pension fund. The fund needs to make the payments shown in the file P15_37.XLS (in thousands) on the first day of each year. You are going to finance these payments by buying bonds. Three bonds are available for purchase on January 1, 1995. The price and coupons for each bond are as follows. (All coupon payments are received on January 1 and arrive in time to meet cash demands for the date on which they arrive.)

- Bond 1 costs $980 and yields a $60 coupon in 1996–1999 and a $1060 payment in year 2000.

- Bond 2 costs $970 and yields a $65 coupon in 1996–2005 and a $1065 payment in 2006.

- Bond 3 costs $1050 and yields a $75 coupon in 1996–2008 and a $1075 payment in 2009.

On January 1, 1995, you purchase bonds and then meet your demand of $11,000. During each year your cash on hand earns 4% interest. You must determine the bonds that should be purchased to minimize the January 1, 1995, investment needed to meet the 1995–2009 cash requirements. You may assume that fractional numbers of bonds can be purchased. ■

15.7 Integer Programming Models

In this section we see how some problems can be modeled using 0–1 variables (and possibly other integer variables). A **0–1 variable** is a variable that must equal 0 or 1. Usually a 0–1 variable corresponds to an activity that is or is not undertaken. If the 0–1 variable corresponding to the activity equals 0, then the activity is not undertaken; if it equals 1, the activity is undertaken. A 0–1 variable is also called a **binary variable**.

Optimization models in which some or all of the variables must be integers are known as **integer programming** (IP) models. We have already seen examples in our discussion of scheduling postal workers and aggregate planning at SureStep. In this section we will illustrate some of the "tricks of the trade" that are needed to formulate IP models of complex situations. You should be aware that a spreadsheet Solver typically has a much harder time solving an IP problem than an LP problem! In fact, Solver is unable to solve some IP problems, even when they have an optimal solution. The reason is that these problems are inherently difficult to solve, no matter what software package is used. However, as we will see in this section, our ability to model complex problems increases tremendously when we are able to use IP, particularly with 0–1 variables.

15.7.1 Capital Budgeting Models

Perhaps the simplest IP model is the following capital budgeting example. It perfectly illustrates the "go–no go" nature of many IP models.

EXAMPLE 15.7

The Tatham Company is considering four investments. The cash required for each investment and the net present value (NPV) each investment adds to the firm are given in Table 15.7. The cash available for investment is $14,000. Tatham wants to find the investment policy that maximizes its NPV. The crucial assumption here is that if Tatham wishes to take part in any of these investments, it must go "all the way." It can't, for example, go halfway in investment 1, by investing $2500 and realizing an NPV of $8000. (If partial investments were allowed, we wouldn't need IP; we could use LP.)

TABLE 15.7 Data for Tatham Capital Budgeting Example

	Cash Required	NPV Added
Investment 1	$5,000	$16,000
Investment 2	$7,000	$22,000
Investment 3	$4,000	$12,000
Investment 4	$3,000	$8,000

Solution

The solution of this problem is quite straightforward. Tatham must keep track of

- investments chosen
- total cash required for the chosen investments
- total NPV from the chosen investments

Developing the Model To keep track of which investments are chosen, we use a 0–1 variable for each investment. If a particular investment is chosen, the 0–1 variable for this investment will equal 1; if it is not chosen, the 0–1 variable will equal 0. To form the spreadsheet model, which is shown in Figure 15.25, proceed as follows. (See the file TATHAM.XLS.)

FIGURE 15.25 Tatham Capital Budgeting Model

	A	B	C	D	E	F	G	H
1	Tatham Capital Budgeting Problem							
2								
3			Investment					
4		1	2	3	4			
5	Investment level	0	1	1	1			
6								
7	NPV	$16,000	$22,000	$12,000	$8,000			
8						Total cost		Budget
9	Investment cost	$5,000	$7,000	$4,000	$3,000	$14,000	<=	$14,000
10								
11	Total NPV	$42,000		Range names:				
12				Budget: H9				
13				Cost: B9:E9				
14				Invest: B5:E5				
15				NPV: B7:E7				
16				TotCost: F9				
17				TotNPV: B11				
18								

1   **Inputs.** Enter the NPV for each investment in the NPV range, the cost required by each investment in the Cost range, and the amount of available cash in Budget cell.

2   **0–1 values for investments.** Enter *any* trial 0–1 values for the investments in the Invest range. (Even fractional values such as 0.5 can be entered in these cells. The Solver constraints will eventually force them to be 0 or 1.)

3   **NPV contributions.** Calculate the NPV contributed by the investments in the TotNPV cell with the formula

$$=\text{SUMPRODUCT(Invest,NPV)}$$

Observe that this formula "picks up" the NPV *only* for those investments with 0–1 variables equal to 1.

4   **Cash invested.** Calculate the total cash invested in the TotCost cell with the formula

$$=\text{SUMPRODUCT(Invest,Cost)}$$

Again, this picks up only the costs of the investments with 0–1 variables equal to 1.

Using Solver   The Solver dialog box appears in Figure 15.26. We want to maximize the total NPV, subject to staying within the budget. However, we also need to *constrain* the changing cells to be 0–1. In Excel 97's Solver this is simple, as shown in the dialog box. We add a constraint with Invest in the left-hand box and choose the "bin" option in the middle box. (In previous versions of Solver, we need three separate constraints: one to make the variables integer, one to make them nonnegative, and one to make them less than or equal to 1.)

FIGURE 15.26   Solver Dialog Box for Capital Budgeting Model

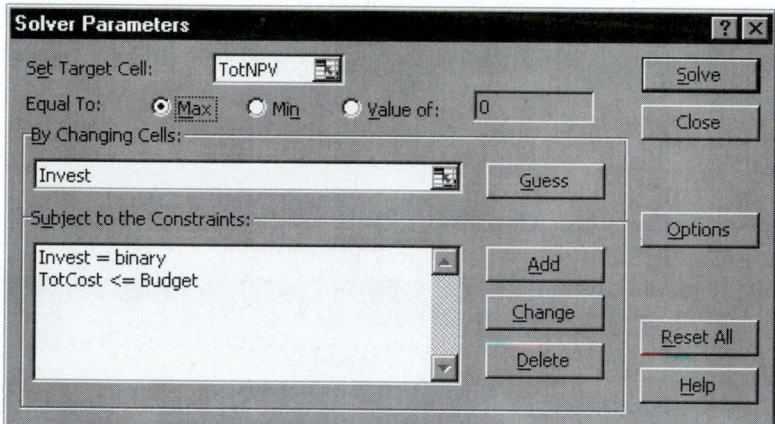

The optimal solution in Figure 15.25 indicates that a maximum NPV of $42,000 can be obtained by selecting investments 2, 3, and 4. These three investments use up all of the available budget.

If we rank Tatham's investments on the basis of NPV per dollar invested, then investment 1 yields $3.20 per dollar invested, investment 2 yields $3.14, investment 3 yields $3.00, and investment 4 yields $2.67. Therefore, investment 1 might be considered the "best" investment, but our optimal solution does not use investment 1 at all! To understand why this is the case, observe that any investment combination that uses investment 1 cannot use more than $12,000 of the budget. (After investment 1, only $9000 remains, and no combination of the remaining three can use more than $7000.) This means that choosing investment 1 forces Tatham to forego investing $9000 of its total budget. On the other hand, the *optimal* investment combination allows Tatham to invest all $14,000 of its budget. This enables Tatham to achieve a higher NPV than it could with any combination that includes investment 1. ■

Modeling Issues

1 The following modifications of the Tatham example can be handled easily:

   ■ Suppose that at most two projects can be selected. In this case we add a constraint that the sum of the 0–1 variables for the four investments is less than or equal to 2, that is, SUM(Invest)<=2. This constraint will be satisfied if 0, 1, or 2 investments are chosen, and it will be violated if 3 or 4 investments are chosen.

   ■ Suppose that if investment 2 is selected, then investment 1 must also be selected. In this case we add a constraint saying that the 0–1 variable for investment 1 is greater than or equal to the 0–1 variable for investment 2, that is, B5>=C5. This constraint rules out the one possibility that is not allowed—namely, where investment 2 is selected but investment 1 is not.

   ■ Suppose that either investment 1 or investment 3 (or both) *must* be selected. In this case we add a constraint that the sum of the 0–1 variables for investments 1 and 3 must be greater than or equal to 1, that is, B5+D5>=1. This rules out the possibility that both of these 0–1 variables is 0 so that neither investment is selected.

2 If Tatham could choose a fractional amount of an investment, then we could maximize its NPV by deleting the integer constraint. The optimal solution to the resulting LP model has a total NPV of $44,000. All of investments 1 and 2 and half of investment 3 are chosen. Note that there is no way to round the changing cell values from this LP solution to obtain the optimal IP solution. Sometimes the solution to an IP *without* the integer constraints bears little resemblance to the optimal IP solution.

3 Any IP involving 0–1 variables with only one constraint is called a **knapsack problem**. Think of the problem faced by a hiker going on an overnight hike. For example, imagine that the hiker's knapsack can hold only 14 pounds, and she must choose which of four available items to take on the hike. The benefit derived from each item is analogous to the NPV of each project, and the "weight" of each item is analogous to the cash required by each investment. The single constraint is analogous to the budget constraint, that is, only 14 pounds can fit in the knapsack. In a knapsack problem the goal is to get the most value in the knapsack without overloading it.

Integer Programming at Monsanto   Monsanto [see Boykin (1985)] used an IP model to determine the settings of its chemical reactors that minimize the annual cost of meeting customer demands. The model is credited with saving Monsanto between $1 and $3 million annually. The model contained a 0–1 variable for each possible setting of each reactor.

Integer Programming in the Steel Industry   Fagersta AB, a Swedish steel company, used an integer programming model [see Westerberg et al. (1977)] to determine the best combination of steel ingots, scrap steel, and alloys to produce different kinds of steel. The model contained a 0–1 variable for each ingot that was available for purchase. The model is credited with reducing Fagersta AB's production costs by 6%.

The Solver Tolerance Option In the Solver Options dialog box there is a **Tolerance** option. Excel's default tolerance is 0.05. To explain the Tolerance option, we must first define the **LP relaxation** of an IP problem. This is the same model as the IP model, except that all integer constraints are omitted. In particular, cells that are originally constrained to be 0 or 1 are allowed, under the LP relaxation, to have any fractional values between 0 and 1. For the capital budgeting example, it is easy to show that the optimal solution to the LP relaxation has an optimal objective value of $44,000, using changing cell values 1, 1, 0.5, and 0. This optimal objective value serves as an initial "best bound" on the optimal integer solution. That is, the optimal objective value for this LP relaxation can only be better, never worse, than the optimal IP objective value.

A tolerance setting of 0.05 means that Solver will stop as soon as it finds a feasible (integer) solution to the IP model that is within 5% of the "best bound." Initially, the optimal objective value of the LP relaxation serves as the best bound. As Solver proceeds to find solutions that satisfy the integer constraints, it keeps updating the best bound. Thus, when Solver stops, it is guaranteed to have an integer solution that is within at least 5% of the "true" optimal integer solution.

The implication is that if we set the tolerance to 0, Solver will (in theory) run until it finds the *optimal* integer solution. So why don't we always use a tolerance setting of 0? The problem is that for many IP models, it can take Solver a long time to find the optimal solution. On the other hand, finding a solution that is *close* to the optimal solution might not be too difficult. Thus, if Solver fails to find an optimal solution to an IP problem, we might be able to find a *near optimal* solution by increasing the tolerance setting.

15.7.2 A Fixed-Cost Model

In many situations a fixed cost is incurred if an activity is undertaken at *any positive* level. This cost is independent of the level of the activity and is known as a **fixed cost** (or fixed charge). Here are three examples of fixed costs:

- Construction of a warehouse incurs a fixed cost that is the same whether the warehouse is used at a low or a high level.

- A cash withdrawal from a bank incurs a fixed cost, independent of the size of the withdrawal, due to the time spent at the bank.

- A machine that is used to produce several products must be set up for the production of each product. No matter how many units of a product the company produces, it incurs the same fixed cost (lost production due to the setup time) for producing the product.

In these examples a fixed cost is incurred if an activity is undertaken at any positive level, whereas zero fixed cost is incurred if the activity is not undertaken at all. Although it might not be obvious, this feature makes the problem inherently *nonlinear*, which means that a straightforward application of LP is not possible. However, the following example illustrates how a clever use of 0–1 variables can result in a *linear* model.

E X A M P L E   1 5 . 8

The Great Threads Company is capable of manufacturing shirts, shorts, and pants. Each type of clothing requires that Great Threads have the appropriate type of machinery available. The machinery needed to manufacture each type of clothing must be rented at the following rates: shirt machinery, $2500 per week; shorts machinery, $3200 per week; pants machinery,

$3000 per week. Each type of clothing requires the amounts of cloth and labor given in Table 15.8. This table also shows the unit variable cost and selling price for each type of clothing. There are 1500 hours and 8000 square yards of cloth available in a given week. The company wants to find a solution that maximizes its weekly profit.

TABLE 15.8 **Data for Great Threads Example**

	Labor Hours	Cloth (sq. yd.)	Sales Price	Unit Variable Cost
Shirts	1.0	4	$30	$17
Shorts	0.8	3	$25	$14
Pants	0.9	4	$35	$22

We first note that the cost of producing x shirts during a week is 0 if $x = 0$, but it is $2500 + 17x$ if $x > 0$. This cost structure violates the proportionality assumption (discussed in the previous chapter) which is needed for a linear model. If proportionality were satisfied, then the cost of making, say, 10 shirts would be double the cost of making 5 shirts. However, because of the fixed cost, the total cost of making 5 shirts is $2585, and the cost of making 10 shirts is only $2670. This violation of proportionality requires us to resort to 0–1 variables to obtain a *linear* model.

Solution

To model the Great Threads problem, we need to keep track of the following:

- number of shirts, shorts, and pants produced
- 0–1 variable for each type of clothing that indicates whether *any* of that type of clothing is produced
- resource usage of labor and cloth
- total profit, which equals revenue from sales minus the cost of renting machines minus the variable cost of producing clothing

We must also ensure that if any of a given type of clothing is produced, then its 0–1 variable equals 1.

Developing the Model   The spreadsheet model, shown in Figure 15.27 (page 860), can now be formulated as follows. (See the file THREADS.XLS.)

1   **Inputs.** Enter the given inputs in the ranges B6:D7, B10:D12, and D23:D24.

2   **0–1 values for shirts, shorts, and pants.** Enter *any* trial values for the 0–1 variables for shirts, shorts, and pants in the ProduceAny range. For example, if you enter a 1 in cell C16, you are implying that some shorts are produced.

3   **Shirts, shorts, and pants produced.** Enter *any* trial values for the number of shirts, shorts, and pants produced in the Produced range.

4   **Labor and cloth used.** Calculate the total amount of labor hours used by entering the formula

$$=SUMPRODUCT(Produced,B6:D6)$$

in cell B23. Then copy this to cell B24 to calculate the amount of cloth used.

5   **Upper limits on production quantities.** Now we come to the tricky part of the formulation. We need to ensure that if any of a given type of clothing is produced, then its 0–1 variable equals 1. This ensures that the model incurs the cost of renting

FIGURE 15.27   Great Threads Fixed Cost Model

	A	B	C	D	E	F	G	H
1	**Great Threads Fixed Cost Clothing Problem**							
2								
3	**Input data**					**Range names:**		
4			**Product**			Available: D23:D24		
5		Shirts	Shorts	Pants		Capacity: B20:D20		
6	Labor hours/unit	1	0.8	0.9		FixedCharges: B12:D12		
7	Cloth (sq. yd.)/unit	4	3	4		FixedCost: B29		
8	Maximum production	1500	1875.00	1666.66667		ProduceAny: B16:D16		
9						Produced: B18:D18		
10	Selling price/unit	$30	$25	$35		Profit: B31		
11	Variable cost/unit	$17	$14	$22		Rev: B27		
12	Fixed charge for equipment	$2,500	$3,200	$3,000		SellingPrice: B10:D10		
13						UnitVarCost: B11:D11		
14	**Production plan**					Used: B23:B24		
15		Shirts	Shorts	Pants		VarCost: B28		
16	Produce any? (1 if yes, 0 if no)	0	0	1				
17								
18	Units produced	0	0	1667				
19		<=	<=	<=				
20	Effective capacity	0	0	1667				
21								
22	**Constraints on resources**	Used		Available				
23	Labor hours	1500	<=	1500				
24	Cloth	6666.6667	<=	8000				
25								
26	**Summary of costs**							
27	Revenue	$58,333						
28	Variable cost	$36,667						
29	Fixed charge for equipment	$3,000						
30								
31	**Profit**	$18,667						

a machine for this type of clothing. We could easily implement these constraints with IF statements. For example, to implement the constraint for shirts, we could enter the following formula in cell B16

$$=IF(B18>0,1,0)$$

Again, however, Excel's Solver is unable to deal with IF functions accurately. Therefore, we instead model the fixed cost constraints as follows:

$$\text{Shirts produced} \leq (\text{Maximum number of shirts that could} \qquad \textbf{(15.7)}$$

$$\text{be produced}) \times (0\text{--}1 \text{ variable for shirts})$$

Of course, there are similar inequalities for shorts and pants.

Here is the logic behind inequality (15.7). If the 0–1 variable for shirts is 0, then the right-hand side of the inequality is 0, which means that the left-hand side must be 0—no shirts can be produced. That is, if the 0–1 variable for shirts is 0, so that no fixed cost for shirts is incurred, then inequality (15.7) does not allow Great Threads to "cheat" and produce a positive number of shirts. On the other hand, if the 0–1 variable for shirts is 1, then the inequality is certainly true (and is essentially redundant). It simply says that the number of shirts produced must be no greater than the *maximum* number that could be produced. Inequality (15.7) rules out the one case we want it to rule out, namely, that Great Threads produces shirts but avoids the fixed cost. However, it will allow the 0–1 variable to be 1 (thus incurring the fixed cost) even if Great Threads plans to produce no shirts. Fortunately, this is not a problem; when Solver maximizes the total profit, it will never obtain such a solution because the total profit could be increased by setting the 0–1 variable equal to 0 instead of 1.

To implement inequality (15.7), we need an upper limit on the number of shirts that could be produced. However, observe that the number of shirts that could be produced is limited by the smaller of

$$\frac{\text{Available labor hours}}{\text{Labor hours per shirt}}$$

and

$$\frac{\text{Available square yards of cloth}}{\text{Square yards of cloth per shirt}}$$

Therefore, the smaller of these can be used as the maximum needed in inequality (15.7). So in cell B8 we calculate an upper limit on the number of shirts that could be produced with the formula

$$=\text{MIN}(\$D\$23/B6,\$D\$24/B7)$$

Then we copy this formula to the range C8:D8 for shorts and pants. For example, we see that at most

$$\min\{(1500/1), \ (8000/4)\} = 1500$$

shirts could be produced.[7]

6 **Effective capacities.** Now we model the fixed cost constraints in the rows 18 to 20. The left-hand sides are already in the Produced range. Generate the right-hand sides of the fixed cost constraints in the Capacity range. Specifically, calculate the right-hand side of inequality (15.7) by entering the formula

$$=\text{B8*B16}$$

in cell B20 and copying it across row 20.

7 **Revenues and costs.** Calculate the total sales revenue in the Rev cell and the total variable cost in the VarCost cell with the formulas

$$=\text{SUMPRODUCT(SellingPrice,Produced)}$$

and

$$=\text{SUMPRODUCT(UnitVarCost,Produced)}$$

Then calculate the total fixed cost in the FixedCost cell with the formula

$$=\text{SUMPRODUCT(FixedCharges,ProduceAny)}$$

Note that this formula picks up the fixed costs only for those products with 0–1 variables equal to 1. Finally, calculate the total profit in the Profit cell with the formula

$$=\text{Rev-VarCost-FixedCost}$$

Using Solver The Solver dialog box appears in Figure 15.28 (page 862). We maximize profit, subject to not using more hours or cloth than is available, and we ensure that production is no greater than effective capacity. The key is that this effective capacity is 0 if we decide not to produce any of a given product.

---

[7]Why not set the maximum number of shirts that could be produced equal to a huge number like 1,000,000? The reason is that Solver works most efficiently when the maximum is as "tight" (that is, as low) as possible.

FIGURE 15.28 Solver Dialog Box for Fixed Charge Model

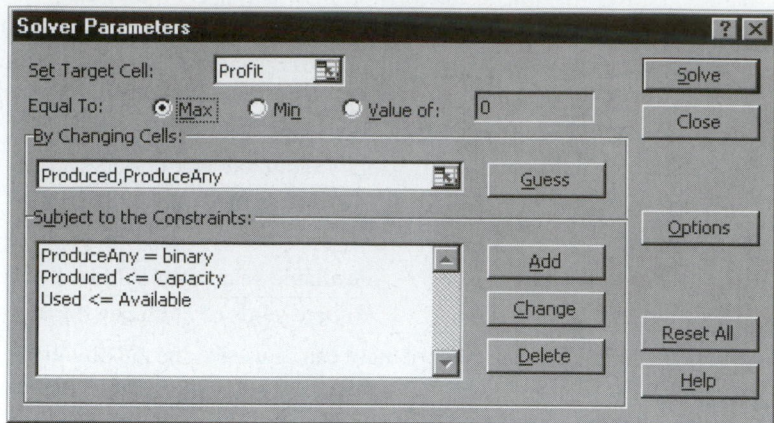

From the optimal solution in Figure 15.27 we see that Great Threads should produce 1667 pairs of pants but no shirts or shorts. The total profit is $18,667. Note that the 0–1 variables for shirts and shorts are both 0, which forces production of these products to be 0. However, the 0–1 variable for pants, the product that is produced, is 1. This ensures that the fixed cost of producing pants is included in the total cost.

It might be helpful to think of this solution as occurring in two stages. In the first stage Solver determines which products to produce—in this case pants only. Then in the second stage Solver specifies how many pairs of pants to produce. Because each pair of pants is profitable (once the fixed cost has been paid), Great Threads makes as many pairs of pants as possible, which is 1667 because of the labor constraint. Of course, these two stages are interrelated, and Solver considers both of them in its solution process.

The Great Threads management might not be very excited about being a pants-only shop. Suppose they want to ensure that at least two types of clothing are produced at positive levels. One approach is to add another constraint, namely, that the sum of the 0–1 values in row 16 is greater than or equal to 2. You can check, however, that when this constraint is added and Solver is rerun, the 0–1 variable for shirts becomes 1, but no shirts are produced! The new constraint forces Great Threads to rent an extra piece of machinery, but it doesn't force them to use it. To force the company to produce some shirts, we would also need to add a constraint on the value in B18, such as B18>=100. Any of these additional constraints will cost Great Threads money, but if (as a matter of policy) they want to produce more than two types of clothing, this is their only option. ■

Locating Distribution Centers   When Dow Consumer Products (a manufacturer of food-care products) acquired the Texize home-care product lines of Morton Thiokol in 1985 to form DowBrands, Inc., the distribution channels of the two organizations remained, for the most part, separate. Each had its own district and regional distribution centers for storing and then shipping products to the customer regions. This led to possible inefficiencies in a business where keeping logistics costs low is the key to survival. Robinson et al. (1993), acting as consultants for DowBrands, modeled the problem as a fixed-cost network problem—which distribution centers to keep open and which routes to use to satisfy which customers with which products. The study was highly successful and convinced DowBrands to close a significant number of distribution centers to reduce costs.

Locating Out-of-State Audit Offices   To increase the collection of state taxes from companies doing business in Texas, the state's auditors must often travel out of state. To reduce the cost associated with these trips, the state of Texas decided to locate auditors at several locations throughout the country. Fitzsimmons and Allen (1983) used a fixed-cost model to help the state of Texas locate out-of-state audit offices.

15.7.3 Set-Covering Models

In a set-covering model, each member of a given set (set 1) must be "covered" by an acceptable member of another set (set 2). The objective in a set-covering problem is to minimize the number of elements in set 2 that are needed to cover all the elements in set 1. For example, set 1 might consist of all the cities in a county and set 2 might consist of the cities in which a fire station is located. A member of set 2 "covers" a city in set 1 if the fire station is located within 10 minutes of the city. The goal is to minimize the number of fire stations needed to cover all cities. Set-covering models have been applied to areas as diverse as airline crew scheduling, truck dispatching, political redistricting, and capital investment. The following is a typical example of a set-covering model.

EXAMPLE 15.9

Western Airlines has decided that it wants to design a "hub" system in the United States. Each hub is used for connecting flights to and from cities within 1000 miles of the hub. Western runs flights between the following cities: Atlanta, Boston, Chicago, Denver, Houston, Los Angeles, New Orleans, New York, Pittsburgh, Salt Lake City, San Francisco, and Seattle. Western wants to determine the smallest number of hubs it will need to cover all of these cities, where a city is "covered" if it is within 1000 miles of at least one hub. Table 15.9 lists which cities are within 1000 miles of other cities.

TABLE 15.9   **Data for Western Set-Covering Example**

	Cities Within 1000 Miles
Atlanta (AT)	AT, CH, HO, NO, NY, PI
Boston (BO)	BO, NY, PI
Chicago (CH)	AT, CH, NY, NO, PI
Denver (DE)	DE, SL
Houston (HO)	AT, HO, NO
Los Angeles (LA)	LA, SL, SF
New Orleans (NO)	AT, CH, HO, NO
New York (NY)	AT, BO, CH, NY, PI
Pittsburgh (PI)	AT, BO, CH, NY, PI
Salt Lake City (SL)	DE, LA, SL, SF, SE
San Francisco (SF)	LA, SL, SF, SE
Seattle (SE)	SL, SF, SE

Solution

The model must keep track of the following:

- the set of cities that each city covers (for example, San Francisco covers Los Angeles, Salt Lake City, San Francisco, and Seattle)
- cities that are selected as hubs
- whether or not each city is covered by a hub
- total number of cities chosen to be hubs

Developing the Model   The spreadsheet model for Western appears in Figure 15.29. (See the file WESTERN.XLS.) It can be developed as follows.

FIGURE 15.29   **Western Set-Covering Model**

	A	B	C	D	E	F	G	H	I	J	K	L	M	N	O	P
1	Western Airlines Set Covering Problem															
2																
3							Potential hub									
4	Cities covered	AT	BO	CH	DE	HO	LA	NO	NY	PI	SL	SF	SE	# covered by		Required
5	AT	1	0	1	0	1	0	1	1	1	0	0	0	2	>=	1
6	BO	0	1	0	0	0	0	0	1	1	0	0	0	1	>=	1
7	CH	1	0	1	0	0	0	1	1	1	0	0	0	1	>=	1
8	DE	0	0	0	1	0	0	0	0	0	1	0	0	1	>=	1
9	HO	1	0	0	0	1	0	1	0	0	0	0	0	1	>=	1
10	LA	0	0	0	0	0	1	0	0	0	1	1	0	1	>=	1
11	NO	1	0	1	0	1	0	1	0	0	0	0	0	1	>=	1
12	NY	1	1	1	0	0	0	0	1	0	0	0	0	1	>=	1
13	PI	1	1	1	0	0	0	0	1	1	0	0	0	1	>=	1
14	SL	0	0	0	1	0	1	0	0	0	1	1	1	1	>=	1
15	SF	0	0	0	0	0	1	0	0	0	1	1	1	1	>=	1
16	SE	0	0	0	0	0	0	0	0	0	1	1	1	1	>=	1
17																
18	Used as hub?	0	0	0	0	1	0	0	1	0	1	0	0			
19																
20	Total hubs	3														
21							Range names:									
22							NCoveredBy: N5:N16									
23							TotHubs: B20									
24							Used: B18:M18									

1   **Inputs.** Enter the information from Table 15.9 about which cities cover which other cities in the range B5:M16. A 1 in a cell indicates that the column city covers the row city, whereas a 0 indicates that the column city does not cover the row city. For example, the three 1's in row 6 indicate that Boston, New York, and Pittsburgh are the only cities within 1000 miles of Boston. Also, enter 1's in the range P5:P16 to indicate that we need at least one hub within 1000 miles of each city.

2   **0–1 values for hub locations.** Enter *any* trial values of 0's or 1's in the Used range to indicate which cities are used as hubs. These are the changing cells.

3   **Cities covered by hubs.** We now determine how many hubs each city is covered by in column N. Calculate the total number of hubs within 1000 miles of Atlanta in cell N5 with the formula

$$=\text{SUMPRODUCT(B5:M5,Used)}$$

and copy this to the rest of the NCoveredBy range. Note that a value in this range can be 2 or greater. This indicates that the city in that row is within 1000 miles of more than one hub.

4   **Number of hubs.** Calculate the total number of hubs used in the TotHubs cell with the formula

$$=\text{SUM(Used)}$$

Using Solver   The Solver dialog box appears in Figure 15.30. We minimize the total number of hubs, subject to covering each city by at least one hub and ensuring that the changing cells are 0–1.

A graphical representation of the optimal solution appears in Figure 15.31, where the double ovals indicate hub locations and the large circles indicate ranges covered by the hubs. (These large circles aren't drawn to scale. In reality, they should be circles of

FIGURE 15.30   **Solver Dialog Box for Set-Covering Model**

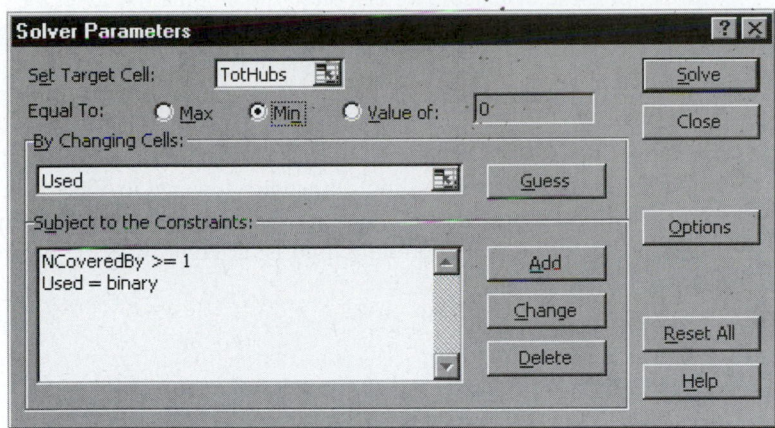

radius 1000 miles centered at the hubs.) Three hubs—in Houston, New York, and Salt Lake City—are needed.[8] Would you have guessed this? The Houston hub covers Houston, Atlanta, and New Orleans. The New York hub covers Atlanta, Pittsburgh, Boston, New York, and Chicago. The Salt Lake City hub covers Denver, Los Angeles, Salt Lake City, San Francisco, and Seattle. Note that Atlanta is the only city covered by two of these hubs; it can be serviced by New York or Houston.

FIGURE 15.31   **Optimal Location of Hubs**

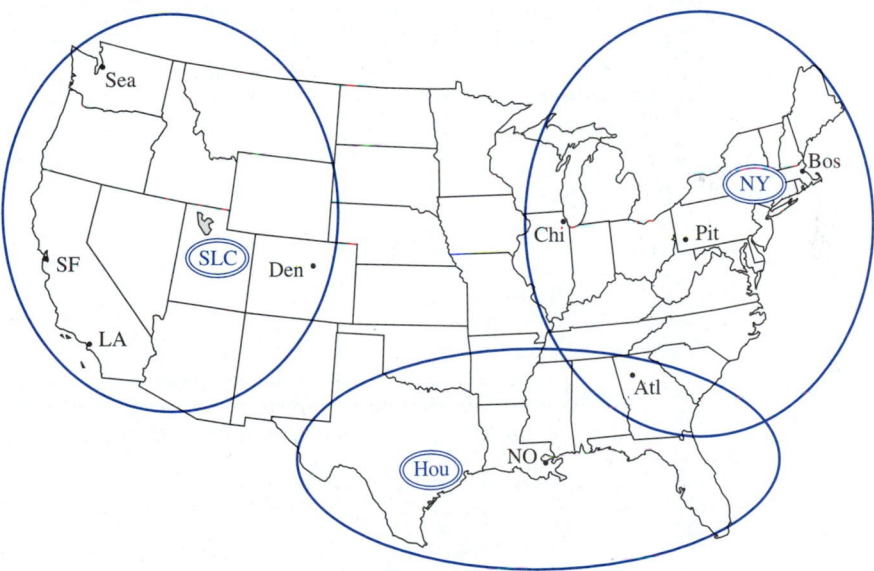

Sensitivity Analysis   An interesting sensitivity analysis for Western's problem is to see how the solution is affected by the mile limit. Currently, a hub can service all cities within 1000 miles of it. What if the limit were 800 or 1200 miles, say? To answer this question,

---

[8]There are other solutions you might obtain, that is, there are multiple optimal solutions, but all require three hubs.

we first need to collect data on actual distances between all of the cities. Once we have a matrix of these distances, we can build the 0–1 matrix, as in the range B5:B16 in Figure 15.29, by using an IF function. The modified model appears in Figure 15.32. (See the file WESTERN1.XLS.) The typical formula in A22 is

$$=IF(A7<=MileLimit,1,0)$$

which is then copied to the rest of the A22:M33 range.[9] The Solver table at the bottom shows the effect of the mile limit. When it is lowered to 800 miles, four hubs are required, but when it is increased to 1100 or 1200, only two hubs are required. By the way, the solution shown for the 1000-mile limit is different from the previous solution, but it still requires three hubs.

FIGURE 15.32 **Sensitivity to Mile Limit**

	A	B	C	D	E	F	G	H	I	J	K	L	M	N	O	P
1	**Western Airlines Set Covering Problem**															
2								Additional range name:								
3	Mile limit	1000						MileLimit: B3								
4																
5	Distance matrix															
6			AT	BO	CH	DE	HO	LA	NO	NY	PI	SL	SF	SE		
7	AT	0	1037	674	1398	789	2182	479	841	687	1878	2496	2618			
8	BO	1037	0	1005	1949	1804	2979	1507	222	574	2343	3095	2976			
9	CH	674	1005	0	1008	1067	2054	912	802	452	1390	2142	2013			
10	DE	1398	1949	1008	0	1019	1059	1273	1771	1411	504	1235	1307			
11	HO	789	1804	1067	1019	0	1538	356	1608	1313	1438	1912	2274			
12	LA	2182	2979	2054	1059	1538	0	1883	2786	2426	715	379	1131			
13	NO	479	1507	912	1273	356	1883	0	1311	1070	1738	2249	2574			
14	NY	841	222	802	1771	1608	2786	1311	0	368	2182	2934	2815			
15	PI	687	574	452	1411	1313	2426	1070	368	0	1826	2578	2465			
16	SL	1878	2343	1390	504	1438	715	1738	2182	1826	0	752	836			
17	SF	2496	3095	2142	1235	1912	379	2249	2934	2578	752	0	808			
18	SE	2618	2976	2013	1307	2274	1131	2574	2815	2465	836	808	0			
19																
20								Potential hub								
21	**Cities covered**	AT	BO	CH	DE	HO	LA	NO	NY	PI	SL	SF	SE	# covered by		Required
22	AT	1	0	1	0	1	0	1	1	1	0	0	0	1	>=	1
23	BO	0	1	0	0	0	0	0	1	1	0	0	0	1	>=	1
24	CH	1	0	1	0	0	0	1	1	1	0	0	0	1	>=	1
25	DE	0	0	0	1	0	0	0	0	0	1	0	0	1	>=	1
26	HO	1	0	0	0	1	0	1	0	0	0	0	0	1	>=	1
27	LA	0	0	0	0	0	1	0	0	0	1	1	0	1	>=	1
28	NO	1	0	1	0	1	0	1	0	0	0	0	0	1	>=	1
29	NY	1	1	1	0	0	0	0	1	1	0	0	0	1	>=	1
30	PI	1	1	1	0	0	0	0	1	1	0	0	0	1	>=	1
31	SL	0	0	0	1	0	1	0	0	0	1	1	1	1	>=	1
32	SF	0	0	0	0	0	1	0	0	0	1	1	1	1	>=	1
33	SE	0	0	0	0	0	0	0	0	0	1	1	1	1	>=	1
34																
35	Used as hub?	0	1	0	0	0	0	1	0	0	1	0	0			
36																
37	Total hubs	3														
38																
39	**Sensitivity of total hubs their locations to the mile limit**															
40								Locations of hubs								
41	Mile limit	AT	BO	CH	DE	HO	LA	NO	NY	PI	SL	SF	SE	Total		
42		0	1	0	0	0	0	1	0	0	1	0	0	3		
43	800	0	0	0	0	1	0	0	0	1	1	0	1	4		
44	900	0	0	0	0	1	0	0	0	1	1	0	0	3		
45	1000	0	1	0	0	0	0	1	0	0	1	0	0	3		
46	1100	0	0	1	0	0	0	0	0	0	0	1	0	2		
47	1200	0	0	1	0	0	0	0	0	0	0	0	1	2		

[9]We've warned a couple of times about using IF functions in relationship to Solver. However, the current use affects only the *inputs* to the problem, not quantities that depend on the changing cells. Therefore, it is permitted.

Station Staffing at Pan Am   Like many other airlines, Pan Am has used management science to determine optimal staffing levels for its support staff (for ticket counters, baggage loading and unloading, mechanical maintenance, and so on). Schindler and Semmel (1993) describe how Pan Am used a set-covering model to determine flexible shifts of full-time and part-time personnel in the United States, Latin and South America, and Europe. The model allowed the company to reduce its deployment of staff by up to 11% in work-hour requirements and suggested how existing staff could be used more efficiently.

Locating Ambulances in Austin, Texas   Eaton et al. (1985) used a set-covering model to determine where emergency medical vehicles should be located in Austin, Texas. They determined the location of emergency medical facilities and vehicles that maximized (with a limited budget) the number of people receiving adequate emergency service. The Eaton model is estimated to have saved Austin over $10 million.

PROBLEMS

Level A

38   Suppose that in the Tatham problem (Example 15.7), each investment requires $2000 during year 2 and only $5000 is available for investment during year 2.

   a   Assuming that available money uninvested at the end of year 1 cannot be used during year 2, what combination of investments maximizes NPV?

   b   Suppose that any uninvested money at the end of year 1 is available for investment in year 2. How does your answer to part **a** change?

39   [Based on Bean et al. (1987)] Boris Milkem's firm owns six assets. The expected sales price (in millions of dollars) for each asset is given in the file P15_39.XLS. For example, if asset 1 is sold in year 2, the firm receives $20 million. To maintain a regular cash flow, Milkem must sell at least $20 million of assets during year 1, at least $30 million worth during year 2, and at least $35 million worth during year 3. Determine how Milkem can maximize his total revenue from assets sold during the next 3 years. In implementing this model, how might the idea of a rolling planning horizon be used?

40   You are given a group of possible investment projects for your company's capital. For each project, you are given the NPV the project would add to the firm, as well as the cash outflow required by each project during each year. Given the information in the file P15_40.XLS, determine the investments that maximize the firm's NPV. The firm has 30 million dollars available during each of the next 5 years. All numbers are in millions of dollars.

41   A manufacturer can sell product 1 at a profit of $2 per unit and product 2 at a profit of $5 per unit. Three units of raw material are needed to manufacture one unit of product 1, and 6 units of raw material are need to manufacture one unit of product 2. A total of 120 units of raw material are available. If any of product 1 is produced, a setup cost of $10 is incurred, and if any of product 2 is produced, a setup cost of $20 is incurred. Determine how to maximize the manufacturer's profit.

42   A company is considering opening warehouses in four cities: New York, Los Angeles, Chicago, and Atlanta. Each warehouse can ship 100 units per week. The weekly fixed cost of keeping each warehouse open is $400 for New York, $500 for Los Angeles, $300 for Chicago, and $150 for Atlanta. Region 1 of the country requires 80 units per week, region 2 requires 70 units per week, and region 3 requires 40 units per week. The costs (including production and shipping costs) of sending one unit from a plant to a region are shown in the file P15_42.XLS. Show how the company can meet weekly demands at minimum cost, subject to the preceding information and the following restrictions:

   ■ If the New York warehouse is opened, then the Los Angeles warehouse must be opened.

   ■ At most two warehouses can be opened.

   ■ Either the Atlanta or the Los Angeles warehouse must be opened.

43   Glueco produces three types of glue on two different production lines. Each line can be utilized by up to seven workers at a time. Workers are paid $500 per week on production line 1 and $900 per week on production line 2. For a week of production it costs $1000 to set up production line 1 and $2000 to set up production line 2. During a week on a production line each worker produces the number of units of glue shown in the file P15_43.XLS. Each week at least 120 units of glue 1, at least 150 units of glue 2, and at least 200 units of glue 3 must be produced. Determine how to minimize the total cost of meeting weekly demands.

44 A product can be produced on four different machines. Each machine has a fixed setup cost, variable production cost per unit processed, and a production capacity, given in the file P15_44.XLS. A total of 2000 units of the product must be produced. Determine how to minimize the total cost.

45 Eastinghouse sells air conditioners. The annual demand for air conditioners in each region of the country is as follows: East, 100,000; South, 150,000; Midwest, 110,000; West, 90,000. Eastinghouse is considering building its air conditioners in four different cities: New York, Atlanta, Chicago, and Los Angeles. The cost of producing an air conditioner in a city and shipping it to a region of the country is given in the file P15_45.XLS. Any factory can produce up to 150,000 air conditioners per year. The annual fixed cost of operating a factory in each city is also given in the file P15_45.XLS. At least 50,000 units of the Midwest demand for air conditioners must come from New York and at least 50,000 units of the Midwest demand must come from Atlanta. Determine how Eastinghouse can minimize the annual cost of meeting demand for air conditioners.

46 [Based on Walker (1974)] The Smalltown Fire Department currently has seven conventional ladder companies and seven alarm boxes. The two closest ladder companies to each alarm box are listed in the file P15_46.XLS. The town council wants to maximize the number of conventional ladder companies that can be replaced with tower ladder companies. Unfortunately, political considerations dictate that a conventional company can be replaced only if, after replacement, at least one of the two closest companies to each alarm box is still a conventional company. Determine how to maximize the number of conventional companies that can be replaced by tower companies.

Level B

47 [Based on Brown et al. (1987)] A Sunco oil delivery truck contains five compartments, holding up to 2700, 2800, 1100, 1800, and 3400 gallons of fuel, respectively. The company must deliver three types of fuel (super, regular, and unleaded) to a customer. The demands, penalty per gallon short, and the maximum allowed shortage are given in the file P15_47.XLS. Each compartment of the truck can carry only one type of gasoline. Determine how to load the truck in a way that minimizes shortage costs.

48 [Based on Bean et al. (1988)] Simon's Mall has 10,000 square feet of space to rent and wants to determine the types of stores that should occupy the mall. The minimum number and maximum number of each type of store (along with the square footage of each type) are given in the file P15_48.XLS. The annual profit made by each type of store depends on how many stores of that type are in the mall. This dependence is also given in the file P15_48.XLS (where all profits are in units of $10,000). For example, if there are two department stores in the mall, each department store will earn $210,000 profit per year. Each store pays 5% of its annual profit as rent to Simon's. Determine how Simon can maximize its rental income from the mall.

49 [Based on Salkin and Lin (1979)] An Ohio company, Clevcinn, consists of three subsidiaries. Each has the respective average payroll, unemployment reserve fund, and estimated payroll given in the file P15_49.XLS. (All figures are in millions of dollars.) Any employer in the state of Ohio whose reserve to average payroll ratio is less than 1 must pay 20% of its estimated payroll in unemployment insurance premiums. Otherwise, if the ratio is at least 1, the employer pays 10%. Clevcinn can aggregate its subsidiaries and label them as separate employers. For example, if subsidiaries 2 and 3 are aggregated, they must pay 20% of their combined payroll in unemployment insurance premiums. Determine which subsidiaries should be aggregated.

50 [Based on Efroymson and Ray (1966)] Breadco Bakeries is a new bakery chain that sells bread to customers throughout the state of Indiana. Breadco is considering building bakeries in three locations: Evansville, Indianapolis, and South Bend. Each bakery can bake up to 900,000 loaves of bread each year. The cost of building a bakery at each site is $5 million in Evansville, $4 million in Indianapolis, and $4.5 million in South Bend. To simplify the problem, we assume that Breadco has only three customers. Their demands each year are 700,000 loaves (customer 1); 400,000 loaves (customer 2); and 300,000 loaves (customer 3). The total cost of baking and shipping a load of bread to a customer is given in the file P15_50.XLS. Assume that future shipping and production costs are discounted at a rate of 11.11% per year. Assume that

once built, a bakery lasts forever. How would you minimize Breadco's total cost of meeting demand, present and future? (*Note*: Although your model is actually linear, the Excel Solver may report that "the conditions for Assume Linear Model are not satisfied" if you do not scale your changing cells and costs in "natural" units. For example, costs can be expressed in units of $1 million or $100,000, and annual shipments can be expressed in units of 100,000 loaves.)

51 [Based on Strong (1989)] In this problem you will use integer programming and the concept of bond duration to show how Wall Street firms can select an optimal bond portfolio. The duration of a bond (or any stream of payments) is defined as follows: Let $C(t)$ be the payment of the bond at time t ($t = 1, 2, \ldots, n$). Let r be the market interest rate. If the time-weighted average of the bond's payments is given by

$$\sum_{t=1}^{n} tC(t)/(1+r)^t$$

and the market price P of the bond is given by

$$P = \sum_{t=1}^{n} C(t)/(1+r)^t$$

then the duration D of the bond is given by

$$D = (1/P)\sum_{t=1}^{n} tC(t)/(1+r)^t$$

The duration of a bond measures the "average" time (in years) at which a randomly chosen $1 of NPV is received. Suppose an insurance company needs to make payments of $20,000 every 6 months for the next 10 years. If the market rate of interest is 10% per year, this stream of payments has an NPV of $251,780 and a duration of 4.47 years. If we want to minimize the sensitivity of the bond portfolio to interest-rate risk (that is, **immunize** the bond portfolio) and still meet our payment obligations, then it has been shown that we should invest $251,780 at the beginning of year 1 in a bond portfolio having a duration equal to the duration of the payment stream.

Suppose that the only cost of owning a bond portfolio is the transaction cost associated with the cost of purchasing the bonds. Let's suppose six bonds are available. The payment streams for these six bonds are given in the file P15_51.XLS. The transaction cost of purchasing any units of bond i equals $500 plus $5 per bond purchased. Thus, purchasing 1 unit of bond 1 costs $505 and purchasing 10 units of bond 1 costs $550. Assume that a fractional number of bond i unit purchases is permissible, but in the interest of diversification, at most 100 units of any bond can be purchased. Treasury bonds can also be purchased (with no transaction cost). A treasury bond costs $980 and has a duration of 0.25 year (90 days). After computing the price and duration for each bond, determine the immunized bond portfolio that incurs the smallest total transaction cost. You may assume that the duration of a portfolio is a weighted average of the durations of the bonds included in the portfolio, where the weight associated with each bond is equal to the money invested in that bond.

52 On Monday morning you have $3000 in cash on hand. For the following 7 days the following cash requirements must be met: Monday, $5000; Tuesday, $6000; Wednesday, $9000; Thursday, $2000; Friday, $7000; Saturday, $2000; Sunday, $3000. At the beginning of each day, you must decide how much money (if any) to withdraw from the bank. It costs $10 to make a withdrawal of any size. You believe that the opportunity cost of having $1 of cash on hand for a year is $0.20. Assume that opportunity costs are incurred on each day's ending balance. Determine how much money you should withdraw from the bank during each of the next 7 days.

53 [Based on Eaton et al. (1985)] Gotham City has been divided into eight districts. The time (in minutes) it takes an ambulance to travel from one district to another is shown in the file P15_53.XLS. The population of each district (in thousands) is as follows: district 1, 40; district 2, 30; district 3, 35; district 4, 20; district 5, 15; district 6, 50; district 7, 45; district 8, 60. Suppose Gotham City has n ambulance locations. Determine the locations of ambulances that maximize the number of people who live within 2 minutes of an ambulance. Do this separately for $n = 1$; $n = 2$; $n = 3$; $n = 4$. ■

Nonlinear Models

I n many optimization problems the objective function and/or the constraints are not linear functions of the decision variables. Such an optimization problem is called a **nonlinear programming problem** (NLP). In this section we will discuss how to use Excel's Solver to find optimal solutions to NLPs. We will then discuss a couple of interesting applications, including the important portfolio optimization model.

15.8.1 Basic Ideas of Nonlinear Optimization

When we solve an LP problem with Solver, we can guarantee that the solution obtained is an optimal solution. When we solve an NLP problem, however, it is very possible that Solver will obtain the wrong answer. For example, if we use Solver to maximize the function in Figure 15.33, it may have difficulty. For the function graphed in this figure, points *A* and *C* are called **local maxima** because the function is larger at *A* and *C* than at nearby points. However, only point *A* actually maximizes the function; it is called the **global maximum**. The problem is that Solver might get "stuck" near point *C*, concluding that *C* maximizes the function, and not find point *A*. Similarly, points *B* and *D* are **local minima** because the function has lower values at *B* and *D* than at nearby points. However, only point *D* is a **global minimum**. If we ask Solver to minimize this function, it might conclude—incorrectly—that point *B* is optimal.

There are mathematical conditions that guarantee the Solver solution is indeed the global maximum (or minimum) we are seeking. However, these conditions are difficult to understand, and they are often difficult to check. A much simpler approach is to run Solver several times, each time with different starting values in the changing cells. In general, if Solver obtains the same optimal solution in all cases, we can be fairly confident—but still not absolutely sure—that we have found the optimal solution to the NLP. On the other hand, if we try different starting values for the changing cells and obtain several different solutions, then we should keep the "best" solution we have found. That is, we should keep the solution with the lowest objective value (for a minimization problem) or the highest objective value (for a maximization problem).

FIGURE 15.33 **Function with Local Maxima and Minima**

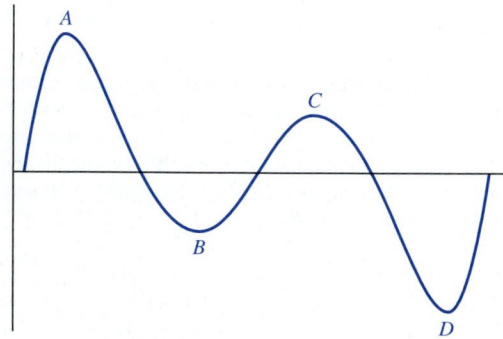

15.8.2 Managerial Economics Applications

Many problems that are discussed in managerial economics are nonlinear but can be solved with Solver. We illustrate one such peak-load pricing example in this section.

E X A M P L E   1 5 . 1 0

Florida Power and Light (FPL) faces demands during both peak-load and off-peak-load times. FPL must determine the price per kilowatt-hour (kwh) to charge during both peak and off-peak periods. The daily demand for power during each period (in kwh) is related to price as follows:

$$D_p = 60 - 0.5P_p + 0.1P_o \qquad \textbf{(15.8)}$$

$$D_o = 40 - P_o + 0.1P_p \qquad \textbf{(15.9)}$$

Here, D_p and P_p are demand and price during peak times, whereas D_o and P_o are demand and price during off-peak times. Note that because of the signs of the coefficients of prices, an increase in the peak-load price *decreases* the demand for power during the peak period but *increases* the demand for power during the off-peak period. Similarly, an increase in the price for the off-peak period decreases the demand for the off-peak period but increases the demand for the peak period. In economic terms, this implies that peak-load power and off-peak power are **substitutes** for one another. It costs FPL $10 per day to maintain 1 kwh of capacity. The company wants to determine a pricing strategy and a capacity level that maximize its daily profit.

Due to the relationships between the demand and price variables, it is not at all obvious what FPL should do. The pricing decisions determine demand, and larger demand requires larger capacity, which costs money. In addition, revenue is price multiplied by demand, so it is not clear whether price should be low or high to increase revenue.

Solution

To solve this problem, we must keep track of the following:

- peak and off-peak prices
- peak and off-peak demands
- peak and off-peak revenues
- capacity (in kwh)
- cost of capacity
- total profit

Developing the Model   The spreadsheet model is shown in Figure 15.34 (page 872). (See the file PEAKLOAD.XLS.) It can be formed as follows.

1 **Inputs.** Enter the constants and coefficients of peak price and off-peak price [from equations (15.8) and (15.9)] in the range B7:D8 and enter the cost per kwh of capacity in UnitCost cell (B10).

2 **Prices and capacity level.** Enter *any* trial prices (per kwh) for peak and off-peak power in the Prices range. Also, enter *any* trial value for the capacity level in the Capacity cell. These are the three values FPL has control over, so they become the changing cells.

FIGURE 15.34   Peak-load Pricing Model

	A	B	C	D	E	F	G
1	Florida Power and Light Peak-Load Pricing Problem						
2							
3	Input data				Range names:		
4					Cap: D18:D19		
5	Coefficients of demand functions				Capacity: D14		
6		Constant	Peak price	Off-peak price	Cost: B23		
7	Peak-load demand	60	-0.5	0.1	Demand: B18:B19		
8	Off-peak demand	40	0.1	-1	Prices: B14:C14		
9					Profit: B24		
10	Cost of capacity/kwh	$10			Rev: B22		
11					UnitCost: B10		
12	Pricing, capacity decisions						
13		Peak price	Off-peak price	Capacity			
14		$70.31	$26.53	27.50			
15							
16	Demands						
17		Demand		Capacity			
18	Peak-load	27.50	<=	27.50			
19	Off-peak	20.50	<=	27.50			
20							
21	Summary of revenues, costs						
22	Revenue	$2,477.30					
23	Cost of capacity	$275.00					
24	Profit	$2,202.30					

3   Demands. The Demand range captures the demands for electricity generated by the pricing strategy. Calculate these by entering the formula

$$=B7+SUMPRODUCT(Prices,C7:D7)$$

in cell B18 and copying it to B19. These formulas operationalize equations (15.8) and (15.9).

4   Link capacity level. Link the capacity level to the Cap range by entering the formula

$$=Capacity$$

in cells D18 and D19. (This step isn't absolutely necessary, but it makes it easier to specify capacity constraints.)

5   Revenue and costs. Calculate the daily revenue in the Rev cell with the formula

$$=B18*B14+B19*C14$$

(Note why the SUMPRODUCT function cannot be used here. Prices are in a row and demands are in a column.) Then calculate the daily cost of operating this level of capacity in the Cost cell with the formula

$$=UnitCost*Capacity$$

Finally, calculate profit as revenue minus cost.

Using Solver   The Solver dialog box appears in Figure 15.35. We maximize profit subject to staying within capacity. However, in the Solver Options dialog box, do *not* check the Assume Linear Model box. This problem is nonlinear. The reason is in the formula for revenue. Prices are multiplied by demands, which are functions of prices. Therefore, revenue essentially includes squares and cross-products of prices, which makes it nonlinear.

FIGURE 15.35 **Solver Dialog Box for Peak-load Pricing Model**

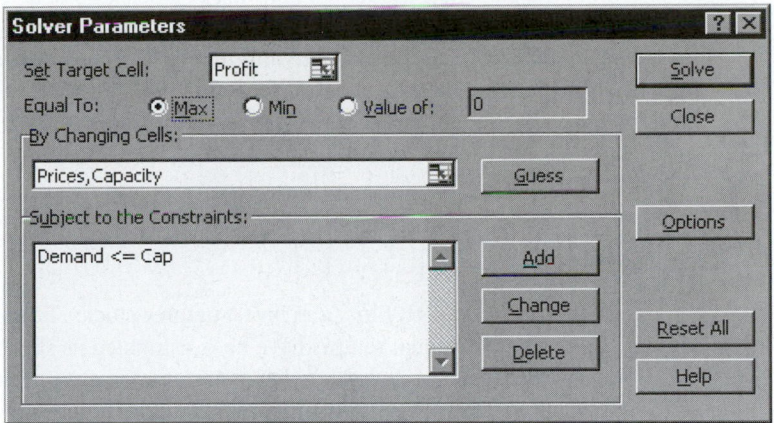

The Solver solution in Figure 15.34 shows that FPL should charge $70.31 per kwh during the peak-load period and $26.53 during the off-peak-load period. These prices generate demands of 27.5 (peak) and 20.5 (off-peak), so that a capacity of 27.5 kwh is needed. The cost of this capacity is $275. When this is subtracted from the revenue of $2477.30, the daily profit becomes $2202.30.

To gain some insight into this solution, let's see what happens if FPL changes the peak-load price slightly from its optimal value of $70.31. If FPL decreases the price to $70, say, you can check that the peak-load demand increases to 27.65 and the off-peak demand decreases to 20.47. The net effect is that revenue increases slightly to $2478.78. However, the peak-load demand is now greater than capacity, so FPL must increase its capacity from 27.50 to 27.65. This costs an extra $1.50, which more than offsets the increase in revenue. A similar chain of effects occurs if FPL increases the peak price to $71. Now peak-load demand decreases, off-peak demand increases, and total revenue decreases. Although FPL can get by with lower capacity, the net effect is slightly less profit.

Is the Solver Solution Optimal? It can be shown (but we will not do so here) that the structure of this model is such that Solver is guaranteed to find the global optimal solution. That is, we know it won't stop at a local maximum. However, you can check this claim by rerunning Solver several times, each time using different starting values for the changing cells. Solver should find the *same* optimal solution in all cases.[10] ∎

15.8.3 Portfolio Optimization

Given a set of investments, how do we find the portfolio that has the minimum variance and yields an acceptable expected return? This question was answered by Harry Markowitz in the 1950s. For his work on this and other investment topics, he received the Nobel Prize in economics in 1991. The ideas discussed in this section are the basis for most models of

---

[10]Actually, we are overstating this slightly. In most nonlinear models—and even in some linear models—Solver will not necessarily find the correct solution if the starting solution is "bad" enough. You should always try to use starting solutions that are in the "right ballpark" whenever possible.

asset allocation used by Wall Street firms. Asset allocation models are used, for example, to determine the percentage of assets to invest in stocks, gold, and Treasury bills.[11]

Most investors have two objectives in forming portfolios: to obtain a large expected return and to obtain a small variance (to minimize risk). The most common way of handling this two-objective problem is to specify a minimal required expected return and then minimize the variance subject to this expected return requirement. The following example shows how we can use Solver to accomplish this.

EXAMPLE 15.11

The investment company RB Flury can invest in three stocks. From past data the means and standard deviations of annual returns have been estimated as shown in Table 15.10 (where we express percentages as decimals). The correlations between the annual returns on the stocks are listed in Table 15.11. RB Flury wants to find a minimum variance portfolio that yields an expected annual return of at least 0.12.

TABLE 15.10 **Estimated Means and Standard Deviations for Investment Example**

	Mean	Standard Deviation
Stock 1	0.14	0.20
Stock 2	0.11	0.15
Stock 3	0.10	0.08

TABLE 15.11 **Estimated Correlations for Investment Example**

Combination	Correlation
Stocks 1 and 2	0.6
Stocks 1 and 3	0.4
Stocks 2 and 3	0.7

Solution

To model RB Flury's problem, we must keep track of the following:

■ fraction of money invested in each stock
■ total fraction of RB Flury's money invested
■ expected annual return of the portfolio
■ variance of the annual portfolio return

Developing the Spreadsheet Model The individual steps are now listed. (See Figure 15.36 and the file PORTFOLIO.XLS.)

1 **Inputs.** Enter the data from Tables 15.10 and 15.11 in the ranges B5:D6 and B10:D12. (Note that the correlation between any stock's return and itself is 1.)

2 **Fractions invested.** Enter *any* trial values in the Invest range for the fractions of RB Flury's money placed in the three investments.

[11]It is a good idea to review the section on weighted sums of random variables at the end of Chapter 4 before covering this section.

FIGURE 15.36 Portfolio Selection Model

	A	B	C	D	E	F	G
1	RB Flury Portfolio Problem						
2							
3	Stock input data				Range names:		
4		Stock 1	Stock 2	Stock 3	ActReturn: B20		
5	Mean return	0.14	0.11	0.1	Invest: B16:D16		
6	StDev of return	0.2	0.15	0.08	MeanReturn: B5:D5		
7					PortVar: B26		
8	Correlations				ReqdReturn: D20		
9		Stock 1	Stock 2	Stock 3	Stdevs: B24:D24		
10	Stock 1	1	0.6	0.4	TotInvest: E16		
11	Stock 2	0.6	1	0.7			
12	Stock 3	0.4	0.7	1			
13							
14	Investment decision						
15		Stock 1	Stock 2	Stock 3	Total		Required
16	Fractions to invest	0.5	0	0.5	1	=	1
17							
18	Expected portfolio return						
19		Actual		Required			
20		0.12	>=	0.12			
21							
22	Standard deviations times fractions invested						
23		Stock 1	Stock 2	Stock 3			
24		0.10	0	0.04			
25							
26	Portfolio variance	0.0148					
27							
28	Portfolio stdev	0.1217					

3 **Total fraction invested.** Calculate the total fraction of money invested in the TotInvest cell by summing across the Invest range. Then enter a 1 in cell G16 to indicate that 100% of the money needs to be invested in the available investments.

4 **Expected annual return.** Calculate the expected annual return in the ActReturn cell with the formula

$$=SUMPRODUCT(Invest,MeanReturn)$$

Then enter the required annual mean return (0.12) in the ReqdReturn cell.

5 **Variance of portfolio return.** In preparation for computing the variance of the portfolio return, calculate for each investment the quantity

(Standard deviation of return) × (Fraction of money invested)

Specifically, enter the formula

$$=B6*B16$$

in cell B24 and copy this across row 24. Now, using the entries in this Stdevs range, calculate the variance of the portfolio return in the PortVar cell with the formula

$$= SUMPRODUCT(Stdevs,Stdevs)$$

$$+2*(B24*C24*C10+B24*D24*D10+C24*D24*D11)$$

The SUMPRODUCT term includes the variance terms from the individual investments. The remainder of this formula includes covariance terms between the investments.[12]

Using Solver   The Solver dialog box appears in Figure 15.37. We minimize the portfolio variance subject to investing 100% of the available money and meeting the minimal required expected return. Again, do *not* check the Assume Linear Model box. This is a nonlinear model because of the squares and cross-products in the variance formula.

FIGURE 15.37   **Solver Dialog Box for Portfolio Selection Model**

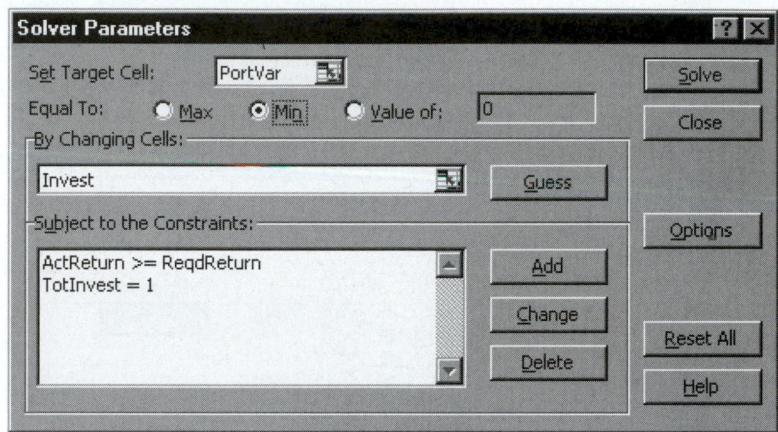

According to the Solver solution in Figure 15.36, this portfolio has a variance of 0.0148 (and a standard deviation of $\sqrt{0.0148} = 0.1217$). RB Flury's optimal portfolio places half of the money in investment 1 and half in investment 3.

Is the Solver Solution Optimal?   It can be shown this portfolio model (and all such models) satisfy conditions that guarantee the optimality of the Solver solution. That is, this Solver solution has the smallest portfolio variance of all portfolios that have a mean return of at least 12%.

Sensitivity Analysis   This model cries out for a sensitivity analysis on the minimal required expected return. Intuitively, as we require higher and higher expected returns, we incur more risk. How much more? We can answer this question easily with the SolverTable add-in, as shown in Figure 15.38. The input is the minimal required expected return, and the single output we keep track of is the optimal portfolio variance. As the table and the accompanying graph indicate, the risk not only increases as the required return increases, but it increases at an increasing rate. Note that for this particular problem, the only interesting values of the required return to examine are those between 0.10 and 0.14. Given the mean returns in row 5 (of Figure 15.36), every portfolio has mean return at least 0.10, and no portfolio can achieve a mean return greater than 0.14.

[12]Again, refer to the end of Chapter 4 for further details.

FIGURE 15.38 **Trade-Off of Risk versus Return in Portfolio Selection Model**

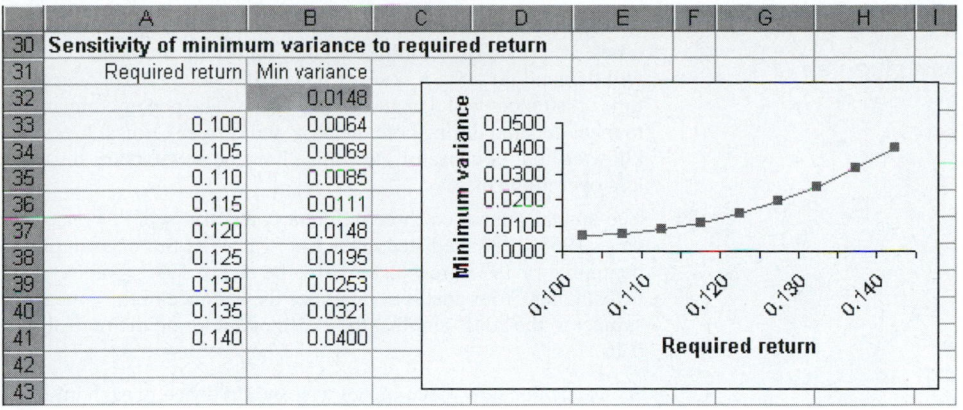

Modeling Issues

1   What does it mean to say that the standard deviation of the annual return from the portfolio is 0.1217? If portfolio returns are normally distributed (which is often a reasonable assumption), then there is (1) a 68% chance that the portfolio return is within one standard deviation of the mean, from -0.0017 to 0.2417, (2) a 95% chance that the portfolio return is within two standard deviations of the mean, from -0.1234 to 0.3634, and (3) a 99.7% chance that the portfolio return is within three standard deviations of the mean, from -0.2451 to 0.4851.

2   If RB Flury is allowed to short a stock, we simply allow the fraction invested in that stock to be negative. That is, we eliminate the nonnegativity constraints on the changing cells.

3   We have equated risk with portfolio variance. Actually, the only part of the variance an investor dislikes is *downside* variance. There are portfolio optimization models that minimize only the downside variance.

PROBLEMS

Level A

54   A total of 160 hours of labor are available each week at $15 per hour. Additional labor can be purchased at $25 per hour. Capital can be purchased in unlimited quantities at a cost of $45 per unit. If K units of capital and L units of labor are available during a week, then $L^{1/2}K^{1/3}$ machines can be produced. Each machine sells for $270. How can the firm maximize its weekly profit?

55   The cost per day of running a hospital is $200,000 + 0.002x^2$ dollars, where x is the number of patients served per day. What number of patients served per day minimizes the cost per patient of running the hospital?

56   Two firms produce widgets. It costs the first firm q_1^2 dollars to produce q_1 widgets and the second firm $0.5q_2^2$ dollars to produce q_2 widgets. If a total of q widgets are produced, consumers will pay $200 - q$ dollars for each widget. If the two manufacturers want to collude in an attempt to maximize the sum of their profits, how many widgets should each company produce? The model for this sort of problem is called a **collusive duopoly model**.

57   A company manufactures two products. If it charges price p_i for product i, it can sell q_i units of product i, where $q_1 = 60 - 3p_1 + p_2$ and $q_2 = 80 - 2p_2 + p_1$. It costs $25 to produce a

unit of product 1 and $72 to produce a unit of product 2. How many units of each product should the company produce, and what prices should it charge, to maximize its profit?

58   [Based on Littlechild (1970)] A power company faces demands during both peak and off-peak times. If a price of p_1 dollars per kilowatt-hour is charged during the peak time, customers will demand $60 - 0.5p_1$ kwh of power. If a price of p_2 dollars is charged during the off-peak time, customers will demand $40 - p_2$ kwh. The power company must have sufficient capacity to meet demand during both the peak and off-peak times. It costs $10 per day to maintain each kilowatt-hour of capacity. Determine how the power company can maximize its daily revenues less operating costs.

59   The annual returns on three different types of assets (T-bonds, stocks, and gold) during the years 1968–1988 are listed in the file P15_59.XLS. For example, $1 invested in T-bonds at the beginning of 1978 grew to $1.07 by the end of 1978. You have $1000 to invest in these three investments. Your goal is to minimize the variance of the annual dollar return of your portfolio, subject to the constraint that the expected return on the portfolio for a 1-year period is at least 0.10.

   a Determine how much money you should invest in each investment.

   b Find an interval such that you are 95% sure that the change in the value of your assets during the next year will be within this interval (assuming normally distributed returns).

   c Find an interval such that you are 95% sure that the percentage annual return on your portfolio will be within this interval (assuming normally distributed returns).

60   Consider three investments. You are given the following means, standard deviations, and correlations for the annual return on these three investments. The means are 0.12, 0.15, and 0.20. The standard deviations are 0.20, 0.30, and 0.40. The correlation between stocks 1 and 2 is 0.65, between stocks 1 and 3 is 0.75, and between stocks 2 and 3 is 0.41. You have $10,000 to invest and can invest no more than half of your money in any single stock. Determine the minimum variance portfolio that yields an expected annual return of at least 0.14.

Level B

61   Each morning during rush hour 10,000 people want to travel from New Jersey to New York City. If a person takes the commuter train, the trip lasts 40 minutes. If x thousand people per morning drive to New York, it takes $20 + 5x$ minutes to make the trip. This problem illustrates a basic fact of life: If people make their decisions individually, they will cause more congestion than need actually occur!

   a Show that if people make their decisions individually, an average of 4000 people will travel by road from New Jersey to New York. Here you should assume that people will divide up between the trains and roads in a way that makes the average travel time by road equal to the travel time by train. When this "equilibrium" occurs, nobody has an incentive to switch from the road to the train or vice versa.

   b Show that the average travel time per person is minimized if 2000 people travel by road.

62   [Based on Grossman and Hart (1983)] A salesperson for Fuller Brush has three options: quit, put forth a low effort level, or put forth a high effort level. Suppose for simplicity that each salesperson will sell either $0, $5000, or $50,000 worth of brushes. The probability of each sales amount depends on the effort level as described in the file P15_62.XLS. If a salesperson is paid w dollars, he or she earns a "benefit" of $\sqrt{w}$ units. In addition, low effort costs the salesperson 0 benefit units, whereas high effort costs 50 benefit units. If a salesperson were to quit Fuller and work elsewhere, he or she could earn a benefit of 20 units. Fuller wants all salespeople to put forth a high effort level. The question is how to minimize the cost of encouraging them to do so. The company cannot observe the level of effort put forth by a salesperson, but it can observe the size of his or her sales. Thus, the wage paid to the salesperson is completely determined by the size of the sale. This means that Fuller must determine w_0, the wage paid for sales of $0; w_{5000}, the wage paid for sales of $5000; and $w_{50,000}$, the wage paid for sales of $50,000. These wages must be set so that the salespeople value the expected benefit from high effort more than quitting and more than low effort. Determine how to minimize the expected cost of ensuring that all salespeople put forth high effort. (This problem is an example of **agency theory**.)

63   Redhound Bus Lines currently owns 700 buses and employs 2200 workers. The company can purchase new buses for $25,000 per bus or sell its current buses for a salvage value of $8000 per bus. The yearly maintenance cost per bus is $1000. Redhound can also hire or fire workers.

The hiring and firing costs per worker are $1000 and $800. The annual wage per worker is $30,000. The fuel cost per thousand gallons is $1100. Redhound must have at least three workers per bus, and each bus can consume at most 10,000 gallons of fuel. (This is figured on a maximum of 100,000 miles traveled at 10 miles per gallon.) The number of vehicle miles, measured in thousands, is a function of the number of buses owned, the number of workers employed, and the fuel consumed (in thousands of gallons). This function is estimated to be

$$\text{Vehicle Miles} = 10.8(\text{Buses}^{0.06})(\text{Workers}^{0.32})(\text{Fuel}^{0.56})$$

Determine how the company can stay within its budget of $80 million per year and maximize the number of vehicle miles driven.

64 Reconsider the RB Flury portfolio example (Example 15.11). Suppose that your goal is to find (among all portfolios that invest all of your money in stocks 1, 2, and 3) the portfolio that minimizes the probability that you will lose money during the next year. Use Solver to find this portfolio. [*Hint*: You may assume that the returns on any portfolio follow a normal distribution. Then the Excel function NORMSDIST(x) will return the probability that a standard normal curve is less than a given number x. For example, NORMSDIST(1) returns 0.84, and NORMSDIST(-1) returns 0.16.]

65 The file P6_65.XLS contains the percentage return on the market for the years 1984–1991 as well as the closing stock price for Ford, Lilly, Kellogg, Merck, and Hewlett-Packard for the same years. Use the approach outlined in Example 15.11 to determine the minimum variance portfolio (of the stocks listed) that yields an expected return of at least 0.22. ■

15.9

Conclusion

In this chapter we have formulated spreadsheet optimization models of many diverse problems. There is no standard procedure that can be used to attack all problems. However, there are several keys to most formulations.

1 First, determine the changing cells. For example, in blending problems it is important to realize that the changing cells are the amounts of inputs used to produce outputs, and in the post office scheduling example, it is important to realize that the changing cells are the number of people who start their 5-day shift each day of the week.

2 Set up the spreadsheet model so that you can easily compute what you wish to maximize or minimize (usually profit or cost). For example, in the aggregate planning model it is a good idea to compute total cost by calculating the monthly cost of the various activities in separate rows and then summing the subtotals.

3 Set up the spreadsheet so that the relationships between the cells in the spreadsheet and the constraints of the problem are readily apparent. For example, in the post office scheduling model it is convenient to compute the number of people working each day of the week adjacent to the minimum required number of people for each day of the week.

4 Optimization models do not always fall into ready-made categories. A problem might involve a combination of the ideas we discussed in the inventory scheduling, blending, and aggregate planning examples. In fact, many real applications are not strictly analogous to any of the models we have discussed. However, the exposure to the models in this chapter should give you the insights you need to solve a wide variety of complex problems.

PROBLEMS

Level A

66. The following investments are available to Finco:

   - Investment 1: For each dollar invested at time 0, Finco receives $0.10 at time 1 and $1.30 at time 2 (where time 0 = now, time 1 = 1 year from now, and so on).

   - Investment 2: For each dollar invested at time 1, Finco receives $1.60 at time 2.

   - Investment 3: For each dollar invested at time 2, Finco receives $1.20 at time 3.

   At any time, leftover cash can be invested in T-bills, which pay 10% per year. At time 0, Finco has $10,000. At most $5000 can be invested in any one of investments 1, 2, or 3. Determine how to maximize Finco's cash on hand at time 3.

67. All steel manufactured by Steelco must meet the following requirements: between 3.2% and 3.5% carbon; between 1.8% and 2.5% silicon; between 0.9% and 1.2% nickel; tensile strength of at least 45,000 pounds per square inch (psi). Steelco manufactures steel by combining two alloys. The cost and properties of each alloy are given in the file P15_67.XLS. Assume that the tensile strength of a mixture of the two alloys can be determined by averaging the tensile strength of the alloys that are mixed together. For example, a 1-ton mixture that is 40% alloy 1 and 60% alloy 2 has a tensile strength of 0.4(42000) + 0.6(50000). Determine how to minimize the cost of producing a ton of steel.

68. Natural Furniture manufactures tables and chairs. Each table and chair must be made entirely out of oak or entirely out of pine. A total of 1500 board feet of oak and 2100 board feet of pine are available. A table requires either 17 board feet of oak or 30 board feet of pine, and a chair requires either 5 board feet of oak or 13 board feet of pine. Each table can be sold for $40, and each chair for $15. Determine how Natural can maximize its revenue.

69. Televco produces TV picture tubes at three plants. Plant 1 can produce up to 50 tubes per week; plant 2, up to 100 tubes per week; and plant 3, up to 50 tubes per week. Tubes are shipped to three customers. The profit earned per tube depends on the site where the tube was produced and on the customer who purchases the tube, as listed in the file P15_69.XLS. Customer 1 is willing to purchase up to 80 tubes per week; customer 2, up to 90; and customer 3, up to 100. Find a shipping and production plan that will maximize Televco's profit.

70. There are three school districts in the town of Busville. The numbers of black and white students in each district are shown in the file P15_70.XLS. The Supreme Court requires the schools in Busville to be racially balanced. Thus, each school must have exactly 300 students, and each school must have the same number of black students. The distances between districts are also shown in the file P15_70.XLS. Determine how to minimize the total distance that students must be bused while still satisfying the Supreme Court's requirements. Assume that a student who remains in his or her own district will not be bused.

71. [Based on Zangwill (1992)] Hallco runs a day shift and a night shift. Regardless of the number of units produced, the only production cost during a shift is a setup cost. It costs $8000 to run the day shift and $4500 to run the night shift. Demand for the next 2 days is as follows: day 1, 2000; night 1, 3000; day 2, 2000; night 2, 3000. It costs $1 per unit to hold a unit in inventory for a shift.

   a Determine a production schedule that minimizes the sum of setup and inventory costs. All demand must be met on time. (*Note*: Not all shifts have to be run.)

   b After listening to a seminar on the virtues of the Japanese theory of production, Hallco has cut its day shift setup cost to $1000 per shift and its night shift setup cost to $3500 per shift. Now determine a production schedule that minimizes the sum of setup and inventory costs. All demand must be met on time. Show that the decrease in setup costs has actually raised the average inventory level.

72. [Based on Fitzsimmons and Allen (1983)] The State of Texas frequently audits companies doing business in Texas. Since these companies often have headquarters located outside the state, auditors must be sent to out-of-state locations. Each year, auditors must make 500 trips to cities in the Northeast, 400 trips to cities in the Midwest, 300 trips to cities in the West, and 400 trips to cities in the South. Texas is considering basing auditors in Chicago, New York, Atlanta, and Los Angeles. The annual cost of basing auditors in any city is $100,000. The cost of sending an auditor from any of these cities to a given region of the country is given in the file P15_72.XLS. Determine how to minimize the annual cost of conducting out-of-state audits.

73 Oilco must determine how many barrels of oil to extract during each of the next two years. If Oilco extracts x_1 million barrels during year 1, each barrel can be sold for $30 - x_1$ dollars. If Oilco extracts x_2 million barrels during year 2, each barrel can be sold for $35 - x_2$ dollars. The cost of extracting x_1 million barrels during year 1 is x_1^2 million dollars, and the cost of extracting x_2 million barrels during year 2 is $2x_2^2$ million dollars. A total of 20 million barrels of oil are available, and at most \$250 million can be spent on extraction. Determine how Oilco can maximize its profit (revenues less costs) for the next 2 years.

Level B

74 During the next 3 months, Steelco faces the following demands for steel: month 1, 100 tons; month 2, 200 tons; month 3, 50 tons. During any month, a worker can produce up to 15 tons of steel. Each worker is paid \$5000 per month. Workers can be hired or fired at a cost of \$3000 per worker fired and \$4000 per worker hired. The cost of holding a ton of steel in inventory for 1 month is \$100. Demand can be backlogged at a cost of \$70 per ton per month. For example, if 1 ton of month 1 demand is met during month 3, a backlogging cost of \$140 is incurred. At the beginning of month 1, Steelco has eight workers. During any month, at most two workers can be hired. All demand must be met by the end of month 3. The raw material used to produce a ton of steel costs \$300. Determine how to minimize Steelco's costs.

75 Gotham City National Bank is open Monday through Friday from 9 A.M. to 5 P.M. From past experience the bank knows that it needs the number of tellers shown in the file P15_75.XLS. Gotham City Bank hires two types of tellers. Full-time tellers work 9 A.M. to 5 P.M. five days a week, with an hour off each day for lunch. The bank determines when a full-time employee takes his or her lunch hour, but each teller must go between noon and 1 P.M. or between 1 P.M. and 2 P.M. Full-time employees are paid (including fringe benefits) \$8 per hour, which includes payment for lunch hour. The bank can also hire part-time tellers. Each part-time teller must work exactly 3 consecutive hours each day. A part-time teller is paid \$5 per hour and receives no fringe benefits. To maintain adequate quality of service, the bank has decided that at most five part-time tellers can be hired. Determine how to meet the bank's teller requirements at minimum cost.

76 [Based on Rothstein (1973)] The Springfield City Police Department employs 30 police officers. Each officer works 5 days per week. The crime rate fluctuates with the day of the week, so the number of police officers required each day depends on the day of the week: Saturday, 28; Sunday, 18; Monday, 18; Tuesday, 24; Wednesday, 25; Thursday, 16; Friday, 21. The police department wants to schedule police officers to minimize the number whose days off are *not* consecutive. Determine how to accomplish this goal.

77 [Based on Charnes and Cooper (1955)] Alex Cornby makes his living buying and selling corn. On January 1 he has 50 tons of corn and \$1000. On the first day of each month Alex can buy corn at the following prices per ton: January, \$300; February, \$350; March, \$400; April, \$500. On the last day of each month Alex can sell corn at the following prices per ton: January, \$250; February, \$400; March, \$350; April, \$550. Alex stores his corn in a warehouse that can hold at most 100 tons of corn. He must be able to pay cash for all corn at the time of purchase. Determine how Alex can maximize his cash on hand at the end of April.

78 [Based on Robichek et al. (1965)] At the beginning of month 1, Finco has \$400 in cash. At the beginning of months 1, 2, 3, and 4, Finco receives certain revenues, after which it pays bills. (See the file P15_78.XLS.) Any money left over can be invested for 1 month at the interest rate of 0.1% per month; for 2 months at 0.5% per month; for 3 months at 1% per month; or for 4 months at 2% per month. Determine an investment strategy that maximizes cash on hand at the beginning of month 5.

79 City 1 produces 500 tons of waste per day, and city 2 produces 400 tons of waste per day. Waste must be incinerated at incinerator 1 or 2, and each incinerator can process up to 500 tons of waste per day. The cost to incinerate waste is \$40 per ton at incinerator 1 and \$30 per ton at incinerator 2. Incineration reduces each ton of waste to 0.2 ton of debris, which must be dumped at one of two landfills. Each landfill can receive at most 200 tons of debris per day. It costs \$3 per mile to transport a ton of material (either debris or waste). Distances (in miles) between locations are shown in the file P15_79.XLS. Determine how to minimize the total cost of disposing of the waste from both cities.

80 [Based on Smith (1965)] Silicon Valley Corporation (Silvco) manufactures transistors. An important aspect of the manufacture of transistors is the melting of the element germanium (a major component of a transistor) in a furnace. Unfortunately, the melting process yields germanium of highly variable quality. There are two methods that can be used to melt germanium. Method 1 costs $50 per transistor, and method 2 costs $70 per transistor. The qualities of germanium obtained by methods 1 and 2 are shown in the file P15_80.XLS. Silvco can refire melted germanium in an attempt to improve its quality. It costs $25 to refire the melted germanium for one transistor. The results of the refiring process are also shown in the file P15_80.XLS. For example, if grade 3 germanium is refired, half of the resulting germanium will be grade 3 and the other half will be grade 4. Silvco has sufficient furnace capacity to melt or refire germanium for at most 20,000 transistors per month. Silvco's monthly demands are for 1000 grade 4 transistors, 2000 grade 3 transistors, 3000 grade 2 transistors, and 3000 grade 1 transistors. Determine how to minimize the cost of producing the needed transistors.

81 The Wild Turkey Company produces two types of turkey cutlets for sale to fast-food restaurants. Each type of cutlet consists of white meat and dark meat. Cutlet 1 sells for $4 per pound and must consist of at least 70% white meat. Cutlet 2 sells for $3 per pound and must consist of at least 60% white meat. At most 50 pounds of cutlet 1 and 30 pounds of cutlet 2 can be sold. The two types of turkey used to manufacture the cutlets are purchased from the GobbleGobble Turkey Farm. Each type 1 turkey costs $10 and yields 5 pounds of white meat and 2 pounds of dark meat. Each type 2 turkey costs $8 and yields 3 pounds of white meat and 3 pounds of dark meat. Determine how to maximize Wild Turkey's profit.

82 The production line employees at Grummins Engine work 4 days a week, 10 hours a day. Each day of the week, the following minimum number of line employees are needed: Monday through Friday, 7 employees; Saturday and Sunday, 3 employees. Grummins employs 11 line employees. Determine how to maximize the number of consecutive days off received by these employees. For example, a worker who gets Sunday, Monday, and Wednesday off receives 2 consecutive days off.

83 [Based on Lanzenauer et al. (1987)] To process income tax forms, the Internal Revenue Service (IRS) first sends each form through the data preparation (DP) department, where information is coded for computer entry. Then the form is sent to data entry (DE), where it is entered into the computer. During the next 3 weeks, the following number of forms will arrive: week 1, 40,000; week 2, 30,000; week 3, 60,000. All employees work 40 hours per week and are paid $500 per week. Data preparation of a form requires 15 minutes, and data entry of a form requires 10 minutes. Each week an employee is assigned to either data entry or data preparation. The IRS must complete processing all forms by the end of week 5 and wants to minimize the cost of accomplishing this goal. Assume that all workers are full-time employees and that the IRS will have the same number of employees each week. Assume all employees are capable of performing data preparation and data entry. Determine how many workers should be working and how the workers should allocate their hours during the next 5 weeks.

84 At the beginning of month 1, GE Capital has 50 million accounts. Of these, 40 million are paid up (0-due), 4 million are 1 month overdue (1-due), 4 million are 2 months overdue (2-due), and 2 million are 3 months overdue (3-due). Once an account is more than 3 months overdue, it is written off as a bad debt. For each overdue account GE Capital can either phone the cardholder, send a letter, or do nothing. A letter requires an average of 0.05 hour of labor, whereas a phone call requires an average of 0.10 hour of labor. Each month 500,000 hours of labor are available. We assume that the average amount of a monthly payment is $30. Thus, if a 2-due account remains 2-due, it means that one month's payment ($30) has been received, and if a 2-due account becomes 0-due, it means that three months' payments ($90) have been received. Thousands of accounts have been examined to estimate the DMMs (Delinquency Movement Matrices) shown in the file P15_84.XLS. Your goal is to determine how to allocate your workforce over the next 4 months to maximize the expected collection revenue received during that time. (*Note*: 0-due accounts are never contacted, which accounts for the lack of 0-due rows in the some of the data.)

85 Powerhouse produces capacitors at three locations: Los Angeles, Chicago, and New York. Capacitors are shipped from these locations to public utilities in five regions of the country: northeast (NE), northwest (NW), midwest (MW), southeast (SE), and southwest (SW). The cost of producing and shipping a capacitor from each plant to each region of the country is given in the file P15_85.XLS. Each plant has an annual production capacity of 100,000 capacitors. Each year, each region of the country must receive the following number of capacitors: NE, 55,000; NW, 50,000; MW, 60,000; SE, 60,000; SW, 45,000. Powerhouse believes that shipping costs are too high, and it is therefore considering building one or two more production plants. Possible sites are Atlanta and Houston. The costs of producing a capacitor and shipping it to each region of the country are also given in the file P15_85.XLS. It costs $3 million (in current dollars) to build a new plant, and operating each plant incurs a fixed cost (in addition to variable shipping and production costs) of $50,000 per year. A plant at Atlanta or Houston will have the capacity to produce 100,000 capacitors per year. Assume that future demand patterns and production costs will remain unchanged. If costs are discounted at a rate of 11.11% per year, how can Powerhouse minimize the present value of all costs associated with meeting current and future demands?

86 Suppose you borrow $1000 at 12% annual interest with 60 monthly payments. Assume equal payments are made at the ends of months 1–60. By entering the function =PMT(.01,60,1000) in Excel, you find directly that the monthly payment is $22.24. However, it is instructive to find this from "first principles"—without the PMT function. Each month you owe an interest payment of 0.01 times the current unpaid balance. The remainder of the monthly payment is used to reduce the unpaid balance. For example, suppose you pay $30 each month. At the beginning of month 1, your unpaid balance is $1000, so $10 of your month 1 payment goes to interest and $20 to paying off the unpaid balance. Then you would begin month 2 with an unpaid balance of $980. Use Solver to determine the monthly payment that will pay off the loan at the end of month 60. (*Hint*: There is no objective to maximize or minimize, but Solver can also be used to solve equations.) ■

This problem deals with strategic planning issues for a large company.[13] The main issue is planning the company's production capacity for the coming year. At issue is the overall level of capacity and the type of capacity—for example, the degree of *flexibility* in the manufacturing system. The main tool used to aid the company's planning process is a mixed integer programming model. A *mixed* integer program has both integer and continuous variables.

Problem Statement   The Giant Motor Company (GMC) produces three lines of cars for the domestic (U.S.) market: Lyras, Libras, and Hydras. The Lyra is a relatively inexpensive subcompact car that appeals mainly to first-time car owners and to households using it as a second car for commuting. The Libra is a sporty compact car that is sleeker, faster, and roomier than the Lyra. Without any options, the Libra costs slightly more than the Lyra; additional options increase the price further. The Hydra is the luxury car of the GMC line. It is significantly more expensive than the Lyra and Libra, and it has the highest profit margin of the three cars.

Retooling Options for Capacity Expansion   Currently GMC has three manufacturing plants in the United States. Each plant is dedicated to producing a single line of cars. In its planning for the coming year, GMC is considering the retooling of its Lyra and/or Libra plants. Retooling either plant would represent a major expense for the company. The retooled plants would have significantly increased production capacities. Although having greater *fixed* costs, the retooled plants would be more efficient and have lower *marginal* production costs—that is, higher *marginal* profit contributions. In addition, the retooled plants would be *flexible*—they would have the capability of producing more than one line of cars.

The characteristics of the current plants and the retooled plants are given in Table 15.12. The retooled Lyra and Libra plants are prefaced by the word *new*. The fixed costs and capacities in Table 15.12 are given on an annual basis. A dash in the profit margin section indicates that the plant cannot manufacture that line of car. For example, the new Lyra plant would be capable of producing both Lyras and Libras but not Hydras. The new Libra plant would be capable of producing any of the three lines of cars. Note,

TABLE 15.12 **Plant Characteristics**

	Lyra	Libra	Hydra	New Lyra	New Libra
Capacity (in 1000s)	1000	800	900	1600	1800
Fixed cost (in $millions)	2000	2000	2600	3400	3700
			Profit Margin by Car Line (in $1000s)		
Lyra	2	—	—	2.5	2.3
Libra	—	3	—	3.0	3.5
Hydra	—	—	5	—	4.8

[13]The idea for this case came from Eppen, Martin, and Schrage, "A Scenario Approach to Capacity Planning." *Operations Research* 37, no. 4 (July–August 1989): 517–527.

however, that the new Libra plant has a slightly lower profit margin for producing Hydras than the Hydra plant. The flexible new Libra plant is capable of producing the luxury Hydra model but is not quite as efficient as the current Hydra plant that is dedicated to Hydra production.

The fixed costs are annual costs that are incurred by GMC independent of the number of cars that are produced by the plant. For the current plant configurations, the fixed costs include property taxes, insurance, payments on the loan that was taken out to construct the plant, and so on. If a plant is retooled, the fixed costs will include the previous fixed costs plus the additional cost of the renovation. The additional renovation cost will be an annual cost representing the cost of the renovation amortized over a long period.

Demand for GMC Cars   Short-term demand forecasts have been very reliable in the past and are expected to be reliable in the future. (Longer-term forecasts are not so accurate.) The demand for GMC cars for the coming year is given in Table 15.13.

TABLE 15.13   **Demand for GMC Cars**

	Demand (in 1000s)
Lyra	1400
Libra	1100
Hydra	800

A quick comparison of plant capacities and demands in Tables 15.12 and 15.13 indicates that GMC is faced with insufficient capacity. Partially offsetting the lack of capacity is the phenomenon of **demand diversion**. If a potential car buyer walks into a GMC dealer showroom wanting to buy a Lyra but the dealer is out of stock, frequently the salesperson can convince the customer to purchase the better Libra car, which is in stock. Unsatisfied demand for the Lyra is said to be *diverted* to the Libra. Only rarely in this situation can the salesperson convince the customer to switch to the luxury Hydra model.

From past experience GMC estimates that 30% of unsatisfied demand for Lyras is diverted to demand for Libras and 5% to demand for Hydras. Similarly, 10% of unsatisfied demand for Libras is diverted to demand for Hydras. For example, if the demand for Lyras is 1,400,000 cars, then the unsatisfied demand will be 400,000 if no capacity is added. Out of this unsatisfied demand, 120,000 (= 400,000 × 0.3) will materialize as demand for Libras, and 20,000 (= 400,000 × 0.05) will materialize as demand for Hydras. Similarly, if the demand for Libras is 1,220,000 cars (1,100,000 original demand plus 120,000 demand diverted from Lyras), then the unsatisfied demand for Lyras would be 420,000 if no capacity is added. Out of this unsatisfied demand, 42,000 (= 420,000 × 0.1) will materialize as demand for Hydras. All other unsatisfied demand is lost to competitors. The pattern of demand diversion is summarized in Table 15.14.

TABLE 15.14   **Demand Diversion Matrix**

	Lyra	Libra	Hydra
Lyra	NA	0.3	0.05
Libra	0	NA	0.10
Hydra	0	0.0	NA

Question GMC wants to decide whether to retool the Lyra and Libra plants. In addition, GMC wants to determine its production plan at each plant in the coming year. Based on the previous data, formulate a mixed integer programming model for solving GMC's production planning–capacity expansion problem for the coming year.

15.2   GMS Stock Hedging

Kate Torelli, a security analyst for LionFund, has identified a gold mining stock (ticker symbol GMS) as a particularly attractive investment. Torelli believes that the company has invested wisely in new mining equipment. Furthermore, the company has recently purchased mining rights on land that has high potential for successful gold extraction. Torelli notes that gold has underperformed the stock market in the last decade and believes that the time is ripe for a large increase in gold prices. In addition, she reasons that conditions in the global monetary system make it likely that investors may once again turn to gold as a safe haven in which to park assets. Finally, supply and demand conditions have improved to the point where there could be significant upward pressure on gold prices.

GMS is a highly leveraged company, so it is quite a risky investment by itself. Torelli is mindful of a passage from the annual report of a competitor, Baupost, which has an extraordinarily successful investment record: "Baupost has managed a decade of consistently profitable results despite, and perhaps in some respect due to, consistent emphasis on the avoidance of downside risk. We have frequently carried both high cash balances and costly market hedges. Our results are particularly satisfying when considered in the light of this sustained risk aversion." She would therefore like to *hedge* the stock purchase—that is, reduce the risk of an investment in GMS stock.

Currently GMS is trading at $100 per share. Torelli has constructed seven scenarios for the price of GMS stock 1 month from now. These scenarios and corresponding probabilities are shown in Table 15.15.

TABLE 15.15   **Scenarios and Probabilities for GMS Stock in 1 Month**

	Scenario 1	Scenario 2	Scenario 3	Scenario 4	Scenario 5	Scenario 6	Scenario 7
Probability	0.05	0.10	0.20	0.30	0.20	0.10	0.05
GMS stock price	150	130	110	100	90	80	70

To hedge an investment in GMS stock, Torelli can invest in other securities whose prices tend to move in the direction opposite to that of GMS stock. In particular, she is considering over-the-counter put options on GMS stock as potential hedging instruments. The value of a put option increases as the price of the underlying stock decreases. For example, consider a put option with a strike price of $100 and a time to expiration of 1 month. This means that the owner of the put has the right to sell GMS stock at $100 per share 1 month in the future. Suppose that the price of GMS falls to $80 at that time. Then the holder of the put option can exercise the option and receive $20 (= 100 − 80). If the price of GMS falls to $70, the option would be worth $30 (= 100 − 70). However, if the price of GMS rises to $100 or more, the option expires worthless.

Torelli called an options trader at a large investment bank for quotes. The prices for three (European-style) put options are shown in Table 15.16. Torelli wishes to invest $10 million in GMS stock and put options.

TABLE 15.16 **Put Option Prices (Today) for GMS Case Study**

	Put Option A	Put Option B	Put Option C
Strike Price	90	100	110
Option Price	$2.20	$6.40	$12.50

Questions

1 Based on Torelli's scenarios, what is the expected return of GMS stock? What is the standard deviation of the return of GMS stock?

2 After a cursory examination of the put option prices, Torelli suspects that a good strategy is to buy one put option A for each share of GMS stock purchased. What are the mean and standard deviation of return for this strategy?

3 Assuming that Torelli's goal is to minimize the standard deviation of the portfolio return, what is the optimal portfolio that invests all $10 million? (For simplicity, assume that fractional numbers of stock shares and put options can be purchased. Assume that the amounts invested in each security must be nonnegative. However, the number of options purchased need *not* equal the number of shares of stock purchased.) What are the expected return and standard deviation of return of this portfolio? How many shares of GMS stock and how many of each put option does this portfolio correspond to?

4 Suppose that short selling is permitted—that is, the nonnegativity restrictions on the portfolio weights are removed. Now what portfolio minimizes the standard deviation of return?

Hint: A good way to attack this problem is to create a table of security returns, as indicated in Table 15.17. Only a few of the table entries are shown. To correctly compute the standard deviation of portfolio return, you will need to incorporate the scenario probabilities. If r_i is the portfolio return in scenario i, and p_i is the probability of scenario i, then the standard deviation of portfolio return is

$$\sqrt{\sum_{i=1}^{7} p_i(r_i - \mu)^2}$$

where $\mu = \sum_{i=1}^{7} p_i r_i$ is the expected portfolio return.

TABLE 15.17 **Table of Security Returns**

	GMS Stock	Put Option A	Put Option B	Put Option C
Scenario 1			−100%	
2	30%			
⋮				
7				220%

Durham Asset Management (DAM) is a small firm with 50 employees that manages the pension funds of small to medium-sized companies.[14] Durham was founded in 1975 and has grown considerably throughout the years. Initially, DAM managed the pension funds of three small companies whose asset values totaled $30 million. By 1991 DAM's funds under management were valued at $2 billion.

James Franklin is a senior vice president at DAM, in charge of managing the equity portion of one of its largest pension funds. Franklin meets on a quarterly basis with company officials who supervise his decisions and oversee his performance. His work is measured on several levels, including both subjective and objective criteria. The subjective criteria include estimates of the quality of research reports. The objective criteria include the actual performance of Franklin's portfolio relative to a customized index of companies in DAM's investment universe. Franklin attempts to "beat" the index not by trying to time market moves, but by investing more heavily in those companies he expects to outperform the customized index and less heavily in those companies he expects to underperform the index.

Franklin has several research analysts who are charged with following the performance of several companies within specific industries. The research analysts prepare reports that analyze the past performance of the companies and prepare projections of future performance. The projections include assessments of the "most likely" or average performance anticipated over the next month.

Franklin analyzes their findings and often asks for additional information or suggests modifications to the analyses. After a period of careful review, the final forecasts for the next month are assembled and summarized. Each month the analysts' forecasts are compared to the actual results. Annual bonuses for the analysts are based in part on the comparison of these numbers.

It is now late December 1991, and the projections for January 1992 are indicated in Table 15.18. The projections have been made for 15 U.S. companies divided into five industry groups. The five industry groups are metals, retail, computer, automotive, and aviation. Franklin would like to use the portfolio optimization approach to see what portfolios it would recommend. He has data containing end-of-month prices for the last two years for each of the companies. The data are contained in the spreadsheet DAM.XLS. Also included in the spreadsheet is information about dividends and stock splits. Using this data James constructs a history of 24 monthly returns for each of the 15 companies.

The past data provide useful information about the volatility (standard deviation) of stock returns. They also give useful information about the degree of association (correlation) of returns between pairs of stocks. However, average returns from the past do not tend to be good predictors of future average returns. Rather than using the raw historical data directly, Franklin creates 24 future return scenarios by adjusting the 24 historical returns. The adjustments are made so that the means of the future scenario returns are consistent with the forecasts from Table 15.18. The adjustments are also made so that the volatilities and correlations of the future scenario returns are the same as in the historical data.

The exact procedure that Franklin uses for developing future scenario returns is described next. Let r_{ij}^0 denote the historical return of security j in month i (for $j = 1, \ldots, 15$ and $i = 1, \ldots, 24$). Suppose that the average historical return of security j is μ_j^0. For security j, denote the forecasted mean return in Table 15.18 by μ_j. (For example, $\mu_1 = 0.6\%$ and

---

[14]Thanks to Ziv Katalan and Aliza Schachter for assistance in developing this case.

TABLE 15.18   Projections for January 1992 for DAM Case Study

Company	Forecasted Mean Return
Aluminum Co. of America (ALCOA)	0.6%
Reynolds Metals	0.9%
Alcan Aluminum, Ltd.	0.8%
Wal-Mart Store, Inc.	1.5%
Sears, Roebuck & Co.	0.8%
Kmart Corporation	1.3%
International Business Machines (IBM)	0.4%
Digital Equipment Corporation (DEC)	1.1%
Hewlett Packard Co. (HP)	0.7%
General Motors Corp. (GM)	1.2%
Ford Motor Co. (FORD)	0.9%
Chrysler Corp.	1.3%
Boeing Co.	0.3%
McDonnell Douglas Corp.	0.2%
United Technologies Corp.	0.7%

$\mu_2 = 0.9\%$, where the index 1 refers to ALCOA and 2 refers to Reynolds Metals.) Franklin creates the future scenario return r_{ij} for security j in scenario i using the following equation:

$$r_{ij} = r_{ij}^0 + \mu_j - \mu_j^0 \tag{15.10}$$

Franklin assumes that any of the scenarios defined by equation (15.10) can occur with equal probability. DAM's policy is never to invest more than 30% of the funds in any one industry group. Franklin measures the risk of a portfolio by its standard deviation of return. He then solves a portfolio optimization model for various minimum levels of mean return to see which portfolios are recommended. After analyzing the trade-off between risk and return, Franklin makes a judgment as to which portfolio to hold for the coming month.

Questions

1   Use the information in the spreadsheet DAM.XLS to create a history of 24 monthly returns for the 15 companies. Compute the historical average return of each stock. In particular, what was the historical return of ALCOA from 12/29/89 to 1/31/90? What was the historical return of Boeing from 5/31/90 to 6/29/90? Explain how you account for dividends and stock splits in computing monthly returns.

2   Develop 24 future scenario returns using equation (15.10). What is the explanation underlying it? In particular, what is the return of ALCOA if scenario 1 occurs? What is the return of Reynolds Metals if scenario 3 occurs?

3   Compute and graph the mean-standard deviation efficient frontier. Compute at least six points on the efficient frontier (including the minimum standard deviation and maximum expected return points). Create a table of results showing the following for each of your points on the efficient frontier: (1) the optimal portfolio weights, (2) mean portfolio return, and (3) standard deviation. (Briefly explain the equations and optimization model used in the spreadsheet.)

16

Simulation Models

Successful Applications

One of the key benefits of simulation methodology is that it allows a company to see how important outputs respond to various scenarios. Each scenario, which is determined by certain inputs and operating policies, can be simulated, and statistics can be collected. By running enough scenarios, the company obtains useful information about which inputs and policies tend to produce the best outputs. This methodology was used in the 1980s by the United States Postal Service (USPS), as described in the article "Management Science in Automating Postal Operations: Facility and Equipment Planning in the United States Postal Service" by Cebry et al. (1992). At the time, the USPS was faced with increasing competitive pressure from a variety of competitors, including other advertising media, alternative retail and delivery companies, and electronic mail. Automation technology was identified as the only way to handle an increase in mail volume, to maintain cost competitiveness, and provide adequate service.

The process of getting mail from the sender to the receiver is an extremely complex one. Mail enters the process as a mixed product—many types of mail addressed in various ways to many geographical regions—and it must be sorted in several stages before it can eventually reach the proper destination. The USPS recognized the need for automated equipment to speed up this process and to save on labor costs. In fact, by the early 1980s it had purchased OCR (optical character recognition) machines that could identify the destination (at least on some mail) and attach a bar code corresponding to the ZIP code to the mail. It had also purchased bar code sensing machines that could read these bar codes and automatically help sort the mail. Part of the cost effectiveness of these new machines relied on heavy use by businesses of the new nine-digit ZIP codes. Unfortunately, businesses were somewhat slow to use the nine-digit codes.

At about this time, the USPS realized that it needed to use management science methods to utilize its existing automation equipment most effectively and to plan appropriately for the future. It hired a consulting company, Kenan Systems Corporation, to help compare automation alternatives. The result was META, a simulation model that quantifies the impacts of changes in mail processing and delivery operations. The META model is very complex, but it can be described briefly as follows.

Mail of various types and of various volumes enters the system and progresses through a number of "links." Each of the links is one step in the overall sorting process that gets the mail from its origin to its final destination. The META model takes as its inputs various mail streams (types of mail with similar characteristics) and routes these streams through the links of the sorting process according to user-specified rules. For example, a rule might specify which mail streams receive highest priority on certain automation equipment at each link. Each set of mail streams and each set of rules corresponds to a single scenario in the simulation model. Given a typical scenario, the model simulates the throughput of the system, the number of errors made, the amount of labor required, and the total cost. These outputs are then compared to identify the best policies for the USPS to implement.

The META model, first developed in 1985, has proved to be extremely useful and versatile. Using this simulation tool, the USPS formulated a corporate automation plan (CAP), which was first released in 1989. By the time CAP was to be fully implemented in 1995, the postal service expected it to save 100,000 work years annually, which translates to over $4 billion. Just as important, by using the model as part of an ongoing planning process, the USPS ensured that it would implement future technologies in a timely and cost-effective manner. ■

16.1 Introduction

A simulation model is a computer model that imitates a real-life situation. It is like other mathematical models, but it explicitly incorporates uncertainty in one or more input quantities. When we run a simulation, we allow these random quantities to take on various values, and we keep track of any resulting output quantities of interest. In this way, we are able to see how the outputs vary as a function of the random inputs.

Simulation models are extremely useful for determining how sensitive a system is to changes in operating conditions. For example, we might simulate the operations of a supermarket. Once the simulation model has been developed, we can then run it (with suitable modifications) to ask a number of what-if questions. For example, if the supermarket experiences a 20% increase in business, what will happen to the average time customers must wait for service?

A great benefit of computer simulation is that it enables us to answer these types of what-if questions *without* actually changing (or building) a physical system. For example, the store might want to experiment with the number of open registers to reduce customer waiting times. Of course, the only way it can physically experiment with more registers than it currently owns is to purchase more equipment. Then if it determines that this equipment is not a good investment—customer waiting times don't decrease appreciably—the company is stuck with expensive equipment it doesn't need. Computer simulation is a much less expensive alternative. It provides the company with an electronic replica of what would happen *if* the new equipment were purchased. Then, if the simulation indicates that the new equipment is worth the cost, the company can be confident that purchasing it is the right decision. Otherwise, it can abandon the idea of the new equipment *before* the equipment has been purchased.

Simulation modeling in a spreadsheet is quite similar to the other modeling applications in this book. We begin with input quantities and then relate these with various spreadsheet formulas to produce outputs of interest. The main difference is that simulation uses *random* numbers to drive the whole process. These are generated with a special function (the RAND function in Excel) that returns a different random number each time it is entered. Each time the spreadsheet recalculates, all of the random numbers change. This gives us the ability to model the logical process once and then use the recalculation feature repeatedly to generate many different scenarios. By collecting the data from these scenarios, we see which outputs are most likely and we see the best-case and worst-case scenarios.

We will illustrate spreadsheet models that can be developed with the basic Excel package. However, because simulation is becoming such an important tool for analyzing real problems, add-ins to Excel are being developed to streamline the process of analyzing simulation models. Therefore, we will also focus on @Risk, one of the most popular simulation add-ins. This add-in not only augments the simulation capabilities of Excel but also enables users to develop models more quickly and easily.

16.2 Random Numbers

All spreadsheet packages are capable of generating random numbers between 0 and 1.[1] These are the "building blocks" of all computer simulations. In Excel, we generate a random number between 0 and 1 by entering the formula

$$=RAND()$$

in any cell. (The pair of parentheses to the right of RAND indicates that this is an Excel function with no arguments. These parentheses *must* be included.) In addition to being between 0 and 1, the numbers created by this command have two properties that make them behave like random numbers:

1   Each time the RAND function is used, any number between 0 and 1 has the same chance of occurring. This means, for example, that approximately 10% of the numbers generated by the RAND function will be between 0.0 and 0.1; 10% of the numbers will be between 0.65 and 0.75; 60% of the numbers will be between 0.20 and 0.80; and so on. Property 1 is often expressed by saying that the random numbers are **uniformly distributed** between 0 and 1.

2   Different random numbers generated by the computer are probabilistically independent. This implies, for instance, that if we generate a random number in cell A5 and know its value, this tells us nothing about the values of any other random numbers generated in the spreadsheet. Therefore, if one call of the RAND function yields a large random number (say, 0.98) in cell A5, then there is still a 50% chance that a number generated by RAND in cell A6 (or any other cell) will yield a value less than 0.50.

To illustrate the RAND function, we generated 500 random numbers by entering this function in cell A4 and copying it to the range A5:A504. Figure 16.1 on page 894 displays the output. (See the file RANDNUM.XLS.) When you try this on your PC, you'll undoubtedly obtain different random numbers. This will happen throughout the chapter and is a characteristic of simulation. No two answers are ever exactly alike. Now try the following. Press the "recalculate" (F9) key. All of the random numbers change. In fact, each time you press the F9 key or do anything to your spreadsheet to effect a recalculation, all of the cells containing the RAND function change.

A histogram of the 500 random numbers for our illustration appears in Figure 16.2. (Again, if you try this on your PC, the shape of your histogram will not be identical to the one shown in Figure 16.2 because it will be based on *different* random numbers.) From

---

[1] Much of the material in this section was covered in Chapter 4, when we first introduced simulation to help explain statistical concepts. However, we will repeat it here for convenience.

FIGURE 16.1 Five Hundred Random Numbers

	A	B	C	D	E
1	**500 random numbers found with RAND() function**				
2	Note: These are formatted to show only 4 decimal places.				
3					
4	Random				
5	0.2547				
6	0.0350				
7	0.4220				
8	0.3278				
9	0.1576				
10	0.7592				
11	0.0175				
12	0.6219				
13	0.6178				
498	0.2900				
499	0.2355				
500	0.3786				
501	0.7235				
502	0.4897				
503	0.0947				
504	0.1558				

FIGURE 16.2 Histogram of the 500 Random Numbers

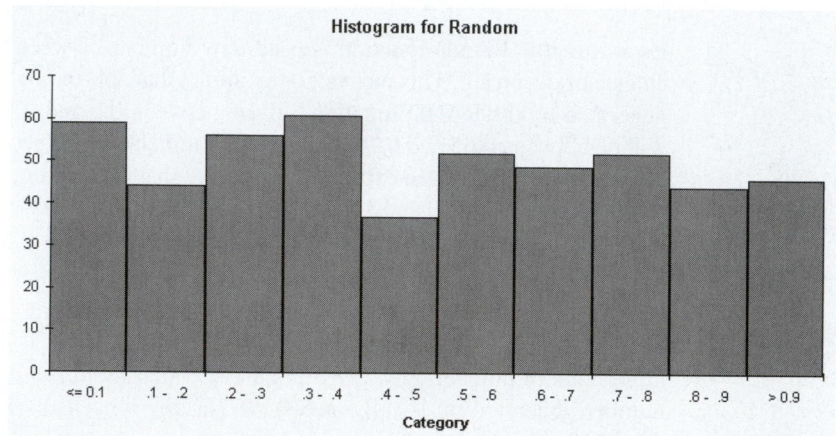

Property 1, we would expect equal numbers of observations in the 10 categories. Although the heights of the bars are *not* exactly equal, the differences are due to chance—not to a faulty random number generator.

Freezing Random Numbers The automatic recalculation of random numbers can be useful sometimes and annoying other times. There are situations where we want the random numbers to stay fixed—that is, we want to "freeze" them at their current values. The following method will do this.

1 **Select range.** Select the range that you want to freeze, such as A5:A504 in Figure 16.1.

2 **Copy.** Use the Copy command to copy this range.

3 **Paste Special with Values option.** With the range still selected, select Paste Special from the Edit menu, choose the Values option, and click on OK. This procedure pastes a copy of the range onto itself, except that the entries are now *numbers*, not *formulas*. Therefore, whenever the spreadsheet recalculates, these numbers will not change.

16.3

Introduction to Spreadsheet Simulation

In this section we show how spreadsheets can be used to perform simulations in which the uncertainty occurs through one or more *discrete* random variables. To illustrate the process, we simulate a simple "newsvendor" problem. This problem occurs when a company (such as a newsvendor) must make a one-time purchase of a product (such as a newspaper) to meet customer demands for a certain period of time. If the company orders too few newspapers, it will lose potential profit by not having enough to satisfy its customers, but if it orders too many, it will have worthless newspapers left over at the end of the day. The following example illustrates this basic problem in a slightly different context.

E X A M P L E   1 6 . 1

In August, Walton Bookstore must decide how many of next year's nature calendars to order. Each calendar costs the bookstore $7.50 and is sold for $10. After February 1 all unsold calendars are returned to the publisher for a refund of $2.50 per calendar. Walton believes that the number of calendars it can sell by February 1 follows the probability distribution shown in Table 16.1. Walton wants to maximize the expected profit from calendar sales.

TABLE 16.1 **Probability Distribution of Demand for Walton Example**

Calendars Demanded	Probability
100	0.30
150	0.20
200	0.30
250	0.15
300	0.05

Solution

For a *fixed* order quantity, we will show how Excel can be used to simulate 50 replications (or any other number of replications). Each replication is an independent replay of the events that occur. To illustrate, suppose we want to estimate the expected profit if Walton orders 200 calendars. Figure 16.3 (page 896) illustrates the results obtained by simulating 50 independent replications for this order quantity.[2] (See the file WALTON1.XLS.) To do this, use the following steps.

---

[2]Note that there are a number of hidden rows in Figure 16.3. This will be the case for many of the spreadsheet figures in this chapter.

FIGURE 16.3 Simulation for Walton Bookstore Example

	A	B	C	D	E	F	G
1	**Simulation of Walton's bookstore**						
2							
3	**Cost data**			**Demand distribution**			
4	Unit cost	$7.50		Probability	Cum Prob	Demand	
5	Unit price	$10.00		0.30	0.00	100	
6	Unit refund	$2.50		0.20	0.30	150	
7				0.30	0.50	200	
8	**Decision variable**			0.15	0.80	250	
9	Order quantity	200		0.05	0.95	300	
10							
11	**Summary measures for simulation below**						
12	Average profit	$222.50		95% confidence interval for expected profit			
13	Stdev of profit	$328.58		Lower limit	$129.12		
14	Minimum profit	($250.00)		Upper limit	$315.88		
15	Maximum profit	$500.00					
16							
17	**Simulation**						
18	Replication	Random number	Demand	Revenue	Cost	Refund	Profit
19	1	0.5279	200	$2,000.00	$1,500.00	$0.00	$500.00
20	2	0.9117	250	$2,000.00	$1,500.00	$0.00	$500.00
21	3	0.5765	200	$2,000.00	$1,500.00	$0.00	$500.00
22	4	0.0251	100	$1,000.00	$1,500.00	$250.00	($250.00)
61	43	0.6565	200	$2,000.00	$1,500.00	$0.00	$500.00
62	44	0.3903	150	$1,500.00	$1,500.00	$125.00	$125.00
63	45	0.1965	100	$1,000.00	$1,500.00	$250.00	($250.00)
64	46	0.3585	150	$1,500.00	$1,500.00	$125.00	$125.00
65	47	0.0231	100	$1,000.00	$1,500.00	$250.00	($250.00)
66	48	0.7556	200	$2,000.00	$1,500.00	$0.00	$500.00
67	49	0.4388	150	$1,500.00	$1,500.00	$125.00	$125.00
68	50	0.8324	250	$2,000.00	$1,500.00	$0.00	$500.00

Range names
Lookup: E5:F9
Profits: G19:G68

1 **Inputs.** Enter the cost data in the range B4:B6, the probability distribution of demand in the range D5:F9, and the proposed order quantity, 200, in cell B9. Pay particular attention to the way the probability distribution is entered. Columns D and F contain the individual probabilities and demand values from Table 16.1. It is also convenient (see step 3 for the reasoning) to have the cumulative probabilities in column E. To obtain these, first enter the value 0 in cell E5. Then enter the formula

$$=D5+E5$$

in cell E6 and copy it to the range E7:E9.

2 **Generate random numbers.** Enter a random number in cell B19 with the formula

$$=RAND()$$

and copy this to the range B19:B68. Then freeze the random numbers in this range as described earlier, that is, with the Copy and Paste Special/Values commands. (*Important note*: From here on, the values in your spreadsheet will differ from those shown here because of different random numbers.)

3 **Generate demands.** The key to the simulation is the generation of the customer demands in the range C19:C68 from the random numbers in column B and the probability distribution of demand. Here's how it works. We divide the interval from 0 to 1 into five segments: from 0.0 to 0.3 (length 0.3), from 0.3 to 0.5 (length 0.2), from 0.5 to 0.8 (length 0.3), from 0.8 to 0.95 (length 0.15), and from 0.95 to 1.0 (length 0.05). These lengths are the probabilities of the various demands. Then we associate a demand with each random number depending on which interval the random number falls in. For example, the random number in cell A19, 0.5279, falls in the third interval, so we associate the third possible demand value, 200, with this random number.

There are two ways to implement this procedure. The first is to use a nested IF statement in cell C19 (and copy it down column C). However, this is quite complex even for a demand distribution with only five values, and it becomes unmanageable for a demand distribution with many possible values. A simpler way is to use the VLOOKUP function. To do this, we create a "lookup table" in the range E5:F9. This table has the cumulative probabilities in column E and the possible demand values in column F. In fact, we entered the cumulative probabilities in column E specifically so that the VLOOKUP command could be used. To generate the simulated demands, first give the range E5:F9 the name Lookup. Then enter the formula

$$=\text{VLOOKUP(B19,Lookup,2)}$$

in cell C19 and copy it to the range C19:C68. For each random number in column B, this function compares the random number to the values in E5:E9 and returns the appropriate demand from F5:F9.

This step is the key to the simulation, so make sure you understand exactly what it entails. The rest is "bookkeeping," as we illustrate in the following steps.

4 **Revenue.** Once the demand is known, the number of calendars sold is the smaller of the demand and the order quantity. For example, if 150 calendars are demanded, 150 will be sold. But if 250 are demanded, only 200 can be sold (because Walton orders only 200). Therefore, to calculate the revenue for the first replication in cell D13, enter the formula

$$=\$\text{B}\$5*\text{MIN(C19,}\$\text{B}\$9)$$

5 **Ordering cost.** The cost of ordering the calendars does not depend on the demand; it is the unit cost multiplied by the number ordered. Calculate this cost in cell E19 with the formula

$$=\$\text{B}\$4*\$\text{B}\$9$$

6 **Refund.** If the order quantity is greater than the demand, there is a refund of \$2.50 for each calendar left over; otherwise, there is no refund. Therefore, enter the total refund for the first replication in cell F19 with the formula

$$=\$\text{B}\$6*\text{MAX(}\$\text{B}\$9-\text{C19,0)}$$

For example, if demand is 150, then 50 calendars are left over, and this MAX is 50, the larger of 50 and 0. However, if demand is 250, then no calendars are left over, and this MAX is 0, the larger of -50 and 0. (This calculation could also be accomplished with an IF function.)

7 **Profit.** Calculate the profit for the first replication in cell G19 with the formula

$$=\text{D19-E19+F19}$$

8 **Copy to other rows.** Do the same bookkeeping for the other 49 replications by copying the range D19:G19 to the range D20:G68.

9 **Summary measures.** Each profit value in column G corresponds to one randomly generated demand. We usually want to see how these vary from one replication to another. First, calculate the average and standard deviation of the 50 profits in cells B12 and B13 with the formulas

$$=\text{AVERAGE(Profits)}$$

and

$$=\text{STDEV(Profits)}$$

Similarly, calculate the smallest and largest of the 50 profits in cells B14 and B15 with the MIN and MAX functions.

10 **Confidence interval for expected profit.** Finally, calculate a 95% confidence interval for the expected profit in cells E13 and E14 with the formulas

$$=AvgProfit-TINV(0.05,49)*StdevProfit/SQRT(50)$$

and

$$=AvgProfit+TINV(0.05,49)*StdevProfit/SQRT(50)$$

At this point it's a good idea to stand back and see what we've accomplished. First, in the body of the simulation, rows 19–68, we randomly generated 50 possible demands and the corresponding profits. Notice that because there are only five possible demand values (100, 150, 200, 250, and 300), there are only five possible profit values: −$250, $125, $500, $500, and $500. Also, notice that for our order quantity, 200, the profit is $500 regardless of whether demand is 200, 250, or 300. A look at the profit values in these rows (including the hidden rows) indicates that there were 14 trials with profit equal to −$250 (demand 100), 9 trials with profit equal to $125 (demand 150), and 27 trials with profit equal to $500 (demand 200, 250, or 300). The average of these 50 profits is $222.50, and their standard deviation is $328.58. (Again, remember that your answers will probably differ from these because your random numbers will differ from those shown in Figure 16.3.)

Typically we want a computer simulation to yield one or more output variables, such as profit, for our analysis. These output variables depend on random inputs, such as demand. Our goal is to estimate probability distributions of the outputs. In the Walton simulation we estimate the probability distribution of profit to be:

$$P(\text{Profit} = -\$250) = 14/50$$
$$P(\text{Profit} = \$125) = 9/50$$
$$P(\text{Profit} = \$500) = 27/50$$

We also estimate the mean of this distribution to be $222.50 and its standard deviation to be $328.58.

It is important to realize that if the entire simulation were run again with different random numbers (such as the ones you might have generated on your PC), the answers would be slightly different. This is the reason for the confidence interval in cells E13 and E14. This interval expresses our uncertainty about the mean of the profit distribution. Our best guess for this mean is the average of the 50 profits we happened to observe. However, because the corresponding confidence interval is very wide, from $129.12 to $315.88, we are not at all sure of the *true* mean of the profit distribution. If we ran this simulation again with different random numbers, the average profit might be quite different from the average profit we observed, $222.50.

A Slightly Different Approach   The above method of calculating cumulative probabilities and then using a lookup table is rather awkward. Therefore, we developed a function that generates random values from a discrete probability distribution in a much easier way. This function, DISCRETE_, is part of the RANDFNS.XLA add-in we included with this book. It is also part of StatPro. So as long as either of these add-ins is loaded, the function will work. Its syntax is

$$=DISCRETE\_(Values, Probs)$$

where *Values* is a range that contains the possible values of the distribution and *Probs* is a range that contains the corresponding probabilities.

An alternative model of Walton's problem that uses this DISCRETE_ function appears in Figure 16.4. The only differences are that (1) there is no cumulative probability column,

	A	B	C	D	E	F	G
1	Simulation of Walton's bookstore						
2							
3	Cost data			Demand distribution			
4	Unit cost	$7.50		Demand	Probability	Range names	
5	Unit price	$10.00		100	0.30	Demands: D5:D9	
6	Unit refund	$2.50		150	0.20	Probs: E5:E9	
7				200	0.30	Profits: G19:G68	
8	Decision variable			250	0.15		
9	Order quantity	200		300	0.05		
10							
11	Summary measures for simulation below						
12	Average profit	$185.00		95% confidence interval for expected profit			
13	Stdev of profit	$315.66		Lower limit	$95.29		
14	Minimum profit	($250.00)		Upper limit	$274.71		
15	Maximum profit	$500.00					
16							
17	Simulation						
18	Replication	Demand	Revenue	Cost	Refund	Profit	
19	1	200	$2,000.00	$1,500.00	$0.00	$500.00	
20	2	100	$1,000.00	$1,500.00	$250.00	($250.00)	
21	3	200	$2,000.00	$1,500.00	$0.00	$500.00	
22	4	150	$1,500.00	$1,500.00	$125.00	$125.00	
61	43	150	$1,500.00	$1,500.00	$125.00	$125.00	
62	44	100	$1,000.00	$1,500.00	$250.00	($250.00)	
63	45	100	$1,000.00	$1,500.00	$250.00	($250.00)	
64	46	250	$2,000.00	$1,500.00	$0.00	$500.00	
65	47	150	$1,500.00	$1,500.00	$125.00	$125.00	
66	48	100	$1,000.00	$1,500.00	$250.00	($250.00)	
67	49	150	$1,500.00	$1,500.00	$125.00	$125.00	
68	50	200	$2,000.00	$1,500.00	$0.00	$500.00	

(2) there is no need for a column of random numbers, and (3) the demands are generated in column B with the DISCRETE_ function. Specifically, the formula in cell B19 is

$$=DISCRETE\_(Demands, Probs)$$

which is copied down column B. The rest of the logic is exactly as before.

Finding the Best Order Quantity   We are not yet finished with the Walton example. So far, we have run the simulation for only a single order quantity, 200. Walton's ultimate goal is to find the *best* order quantity—that is, the order quantity that maximizes the mean profit. We can do this with a data table. Specifically, we can use a data table to rerun the simulation for other order quantities. We show this data table in Figure 16.5 on page 900. (This is still part of the WALTON1.XLS file.)

To form this table, enter the trial order quantities shown in the range A74:A82, enter the formula =B12 in cell B73, and select the data table range, A73:B82. Then use the Data/Table command, specifying that the single (column) input cell is B9 (see Figure 16.3). Finally, construct a bar chart of the average profits in the data table (see Figure 16.6).

Note that an order quantity of 150 appears to maximize the average profit. Its average profit of $270 is slightly higher than the average profits from nearby order quantities and much higher than the profit gained from an order of 225 or more calendars. However, again keep in mind that this is a simulation, so that all of these average profits depend on the particular random numbers generated. If we reran the simulation with different random numbers, it is conceivable that some other order quantity could be best.

FIGURE 16.5 **Data Table for Walton Bookstore Example**

	A	B	C	D
70	**Data table for average profit versus order quantity**			
71				
72	Order quantity	AvgProfit		
73		$222.50		
74	100	$250.00		
75	125	$260.00		
76	150	$270.00		
77	175	$246.25		
78	200	$222.50		
79	225	$146.25		
80	250	$70.00		
81	275	($47.50)		
82	300	($165.00)		

FIGURE 16.6 **Average Profit versus Order Quantity for Walton Example**

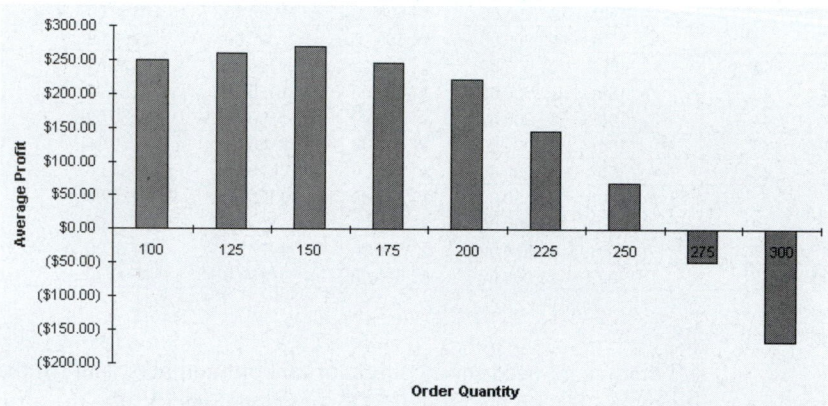

Before concluding this example, we make one other observation. In the Walton simulation we suggested that you freeze the random numbers in column B. If you neglect this step, then every time you press the F9 key, a new set of simulated answers (including those in the data table) will appear. Depending on the speed of your computer, this recalculation can take a long time, even for this relatively small simulation. For larger simulations the recalculation time can be quite large, which is one of the primary reasons you might want to freeze your random numbers right away.[3] However, the drawback is that once the random numbers are frozen, you are stuck with that particular set of random numbers. In most of the rest of this chapter, we will *not* freeze the random numbers. This way we will be able to generate many different scenarios simply by pressing the F9 key.

Using a Data Table to Repeat Simulations The instructions for the spreadsheet in Figure 16.3 indicate one way to build a simulation on a spreadsheet. We construct one row to simulate a typical replication (row 19) and then use the Copy command to perform the other replications in the simulation. This method works fine for "single-row" simulations,

---

[3]Here is a useful Excel tip for speeding up recalculation. Use the Tools/Option command, click on the Calculation tab, click on the Automatic Except Tables option, and click on OK. Now when you enter anything new into your spreadsheet, everything will recalculate in the normal way *except* data tables. Data tables will not recalculate until you intentionally press the F9 key. Data tables can require lots of computing time, so this option can come in very handy.

where all of the elements for a replication fit on one row. Then we can copy this row down to create replications. Most simulations, however, do not fit on a single row. We now illustrate another method, which is more general. It uses a *data table* to generate the replications. Refer to Figure 16.7 and the file WALTON2.XLS.

Through row 19, this method is exactly like the previous method. That is, we use the given data at the top of the spreadsheet to construct a typical "prototype" of the simulation in row 19. However, the next step in this method differs from the previous method. We form a data table in the range A23:B73 to replicate the basic simulation 50 times. In column A we list the replication numbers, 1–50. The formula for the data table in cell B23 is =F19. This copies the profit from the prototype row for use in the data table. Then we use the Data/Table command with *any blank cell* (such as A20) as the column input cell. (No row input cell is necessary.) This tricks Excel into repeating the row 19 calculations 50 times,

FIGURE 16.7 **Simulation with a Data Table for Walton Example**

	A	B	C	D	E	F
1	**Simulation of Walton's bookstore**					
2						
3	**Cost data**			**Demand distribution**		
4	Unit cost	$2.00		Probability	CumProb	Demand
5	Unit price	$4.50		0.30	0.00	100
6	Unit refund	$0.75		0.20	0.30	150
7				0.30	0.50	200
8	**Decision variable**			0.15	0.80	250
9	Order quantity	200		0.05	0.95	300
10						
11	**Summary measures from simulation below**					
12	Average	$323.75		**Range names**		
13	StDev	$158.06		Lookup: E5:F9		
14	Minimum	$125.00		Profits: B24:B73		
15	Maximum	$500.00				
16						
17	**Simulation**					
18	Random number	Demand	Revenue	Cost	Refund	Profit
19	0.8474	250	$900.00	$400.00	$0.00	$500.00
20						
21	**Data table for replications, each shows profit from that replication**					
22	Replication	Profit				
23		$500.00				
24	1	$312.50				
25	2	$125.00				
26	3	$500.00				
27	4	$312.50				
28	5	$500.00				
29	6	$125.00				
30	7	$500.00				
67	44	$312.50				
68	45	$500.00				
69	46	$500.00				
70	47	$500.00				
71	48	$500.00				
72	49	$125.00				
73	50	$125.00				

each time with a new random number. Each time the profit is reported. (If we wanted to see other simulated quantities such as revenue for each replication, we could add extra output columns to the data table.)

To understand why this procedure works, we need to understand how a data table is formed. When we form a data table, Excel takes each value in the left-hand column of the data table (here column A), substitutes it into the cell we designate as the column input cell, recalculates the spreadsheet, and returns the "bottom line" value (or values) we've requested in the top row of the data table (such as average profit). It may seem silly to substitute each replication number from column A into a blank cell such as cell A20, but this method causes the simulation in row 19 to be recalculated with *new* random numbers, which is exactly what we want.

Of course, this means that we should *not* freeze the random number in cell A19 before forming the data table. The whole point of the data table is to use a different random number for each trial, and this will occur only if the random number from the typical trial in row 19 is left unfrozen.

We can carry this method one step further to see how the profit depends on the order quantity. Here we use a *two-way* data table with the replication number along the side and possible order quantities along the top. See Figure 16.8 and the file WALTON3.XLS. Now the data table range is A23:F73, and the driving formula, entered in cell A23, is again =F19. The *column* input cell should again be any blank cell, but the *row* input cell should be B9 (the order quantity). Each cell in the body of the data table shows a simulated profit for a particular trial and a particular order quantity, and each is based on a *different* random number.

By averaging the numbers in each column of the data table (see row 14), we again see that 150 appears to be the best order quantity. It is also helpful to construct a bar chart of these averages, as shown in Figure 16.9. To see whether 150 is always the best order quantity, try pressing the F9 key. (Again, we assume you haven't frozen any random numbers in the spreadsheet.) The entire data table, and hence the averages in row 68 and the corresponding graph, should all change. Keep pressing the F9 key to see whether an order quantity of 150 continues to be the winner!

By now you should appreciate the usefulness of data tables in spreadsheet simulations. They allow you to take a "prototype" simulation and replicate its key results as often as you like. This method makes summary statistics (over the entire group of replications) and corresponding charts easy to obtain. ■

16.4 Simulating from Other Probability Distributions

We have seen that the RAND function is capable of generating numbers that are uniformly distributed between 0 and 1. However, in many situations we want the random numbers to have a probability distribution other than this uniform distribution. For example, it might be more realistic to use a bell-shaped distribution or a skewed distribution.

If the desired distribution is discrete, with a finite (usually small) number of possible values and corresponding probabilities, then we can use the RAND function along with a VLOOKUP function to generate the random numbers. This is exactly what we did in the Walton Bookstore example to generate demands. This method allows us to generate random numbers from any discrete distribution—symmetric, skewed, bimodal, or whatever—simply by setting up the lookup table correctly. We can even simplify this procedure by using the DISCRETE_ function in the StatPro and RandFns add-ins, as discussed above.

	A	B	C	D	E	F
1	**Simulation of Walton's bookstore**					
2						
3	**Cost data**			**Demand distribution**		
4	Unit cost	$7.50		Probability	CumProb	Demand
5	Unit price	$10.00		0.30	0.00	100
6	Unit refund	$2.50		0.20	0.30	150
7				0.30	0.50	200
8	**Decision variable**			0.15	0.80	250
9	Order quantity	200		0.05	0.95	300
10						
11	**Summary measures of simulated profits for each order quantity**					
12				Order quantity		
13		100	150	200	250	300
14	Average profit	$250.00	$255.00	$200.00	$62.50	-$345.00
15	Stdev profit	$0.00	$176.70	$347.18	$430.24	$434.16
16						
17	**Simulation**					
18	Random number	Demand	Revenue	Cost	Refund	Profit
19	0.6669	200	$2,000.00	$1,500.00	$0.00	$500.00
20						
21	**Data table showing profit for replications with various order quantities**					
22	Replication			Order quantity		
23	$500.00	100	150	200	250	300
24	1	$250.00	$375.00	$500.00	($500.00)	$0.00
25	2	$250.00	$375.00	($250.00)	($125.00)	($375.00)
26	3	$250.00	$0.00	($250.00)	$250.00	$0.00
27	4	$250.00	$375.00	$500.00	$250.00	($750.00)
28	5	$250.00	$375.00	$500.00	$250.00	($750.00)
29	6	$250.00	$375.00	($250.00)	($500.00)	$0.00
30	7	$250.00	$375.00	$500.00	($125.00)	($750.00)
67	44	$250.00	$375.00	$500.00	$625.00	$0.00
68	45	$250.00	$375.00	$500.00	$625.00	($750.00)
69	46	$250.00	$375.00	($250.00)	$250.00	($750.00)
70	47	$250.00	$0.00	($250.00)	$250.00	$0.00
71	48	$250.00	$0.00	$500.00	($500.00)	($375.00)
72	49	$250.00	$375.00	$125.00	$625.00	($375.00)
73	50	$250.00	$375.00	$500.00	$625.00	$750.00

FIGURE 16.9 Average Profit versus Order Quantity

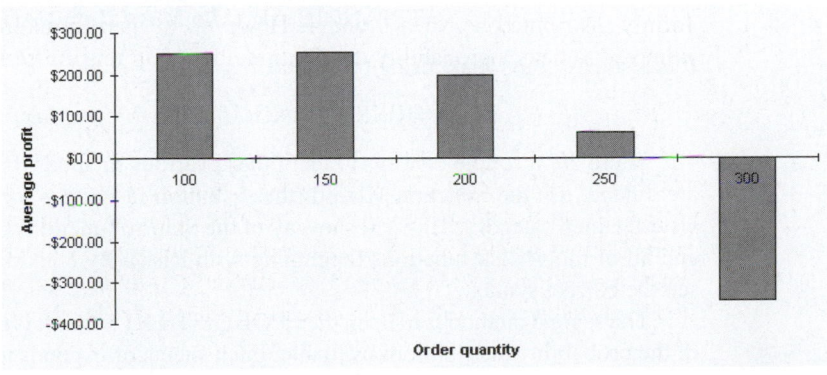

In general, there are many probability distributions we might want to use in simulations. These include some well-known distributions, such as the normal and binomial, and some that are less well known. We then face two issues: Which distribution should we use, and how do we generate random values from it?

We typically choose the distribution on the basis of historical data and/or its shape and general characteristics. Suppose we want to simulate random checkout times at a supermarket. We could gather data on many actual checkout times, create a histogram of these, and try to match this histogram to one of several theoretical distributions. In fact, this is exactly what the Best Fit add-in (part of the Palisade Decision Tools suite) does. We feed it data, and it suggests the best-fitting probability distribution—which we could then use in a simulation model. In the absence of data, we might choose the probability distribution on general considerations. For example, we might choose the normal distribution because of its symmetry and bell shape.

Once we choose a probability distribution, whether it be the normal, binomial, or some other distribution, we need a way to generate random values from this distribution. We offer three ways to do this:

1   Use Excel's built-in functions, along with the RAND function.

2   Use the functions supplied with the StatPro (or RandFns) add-in. All of these functions end with an underscore, as in DISCRETE_.

3   Use the functions supplied with the @Risk add-in. All of these functions begin with RISK, as in RISKDISCRETE.

As an example, suppose we want to generate a normally distributed random value with mean 100 and standard deviation 10. We can get Excel to do this by using the formula

$$=\text{NORMINV(RAND(),100,10)}$$

If the StatPro (or RandFns) add-in is loaded, we can do it by entering the formula

$$=\text{NORMAL\_(100,10)}$$

Finally, if the @Risk add-in is loaded, we can do it by entering the formula

$$=\text{RISKNORMAL(100,10)}$$

These are all equivalent ways of generating a normal random value, but we believe you'll agree that the latter two are easier to remember.

As a second example, suppose we want to generate a random value from the **triangular** distribution shown in Figure 16.10. Here a and b are the lower and upper limits and c is the most likely value. This distribution is often used for times to complete an activity. Then a is the minimum possible time, b is the maximum possible time, and c is the most likely time. There is no easy way to generate this type of random value without an add-in. However, it is easy with StatPro (or RandFns). The syntax is

$$=\text{TRIANGULAR\_}(Min,MostLikely,Max)$$

It is also easy in @Risk, using the syntax

$$=\text{RISKTRIANG}(Min,MostLikely,Max)$$

There are a couple of ways to learn these various methods. First, if any of the add-ins are loaded, use the Function Wizard (the f_x button in Excel's top toolbar), and select the User Defined category. This will show all of the StatPro functions (ending in an underscore) and all of the @Risk functions (beginning with Risk). By clicking on any of these, you'll see the correct syntax.

The second method is to open the PROBDISTS.XLS file. It is essentially a "dictionary" of the probability distributions available. Each sheet corresponds to a different distribution.

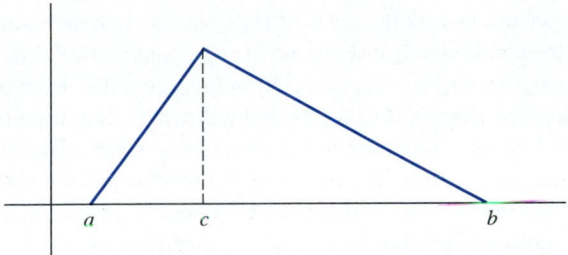

The distributions included are the following: Uniform, Discrete uniform, General discrete, Normal, Binomial, Triangular, Poisson, Exponential, Erlang, and Lognormal.

A typical sheet, for the general discrete distribution we have already discussed, appears in Figure 16.11. It describes the distribution briefly, it lists the parameters of the distribution and whether it is discrete or continuous, and it gives an example of each method for generating values from the distribution. In case any of the add-ins is not loaded (as with @Risk for this example), we get the #NAME? message. However, the syntax for the @Risk function is still apparent. We suggest that you keep this file (or a printout of its contents) handy as you work through this chapter. It will save you from having to memorize a lot of formulas! (Help with the RandFns functions is also available in the RANDFNSHELP.HTM file.)

We illustrate the use of the triangular distribution in the following bidding example. In situations where a company must bid against competitors, simulation can often be used to determine the company's optimal bid. Usually the company does not know what its competitors will bid, but it may have an idea about the *range* of the bids its competitors will choose.

F I G U R E 1 6 . 1 1   **Sample Sheet from the PROBDISTS.XLS File**

	A	B	C	D	E	F	G	H	I
1	**General Discrete Distribution**								
2									
3	Any finite set of possible values with associated probabilities that add to 1								
4									
5	**Parameters**			**Type**		Lookup table required for Excel method			
6	Values	Probabilities		Discrete		CumProb	Values		
7	10	0.1				0	10		
8	15	0.3				0.1	15		
9	20	0.4				0.4	20		
10	25	0.2				0.8	25		
11									
12	**Excel**					**Example**			
13	=VLOOKUP(RAND(),Ltable,2)					25			
14									
15	**StatPro**								
16	=Discrete_(Values,Probs)					10			
17									
18	**@Risk**								
19	=RiskDiscrete(Values,Probs)					#NAME?			

EXAMPLE 16.2

The Rogers Construction Company is trying to decide whether to make a bid on a construction project. Rogers believes it will cost the company $10,000 to complete the project (if it wins the contract), and it will cost $350 to prepare a bid. Four potential competitors are going to bid against Rogers. The lowest bid will win the contract (and the winner will then be given the winning bid amount to complete the project). Based on past history, Rogers believes that each competitor's bid has a triangular distribution with low and high extremes $10,000a$ and $10,000b$ and most likely value $10,000c$, where a, b, and c are given multiples. That is, each competitor's bid is at least a times Rogers' cost, is no more than b times Rogers' cost, and is most likely to be c times Rogers' cost. For this particular example, we use the multiples $a = 1$, $b = 3$, and $c = 1.3$. These four competitors' bids are also assumed to be independent of one another. If Rogers decides to prepare a bid, then its bid amount will be a multiple of $500 in the range from $10,500 to $15,000. The company wants to use simulation to determine which strategy to use to maximize its expected profit.

Solution

A simulation model of Rogers' problem is shown in Figure 16.12. (See the file BIDDING.XLS.) To create this model, proceed as follows.

FIGURE 16.12 **Spreadsheet for Bidding Example**

	A	B	C	D	E
1	**Bidding Problem**				
2					
3	Company's cost to prepare a bid		$350		
4	Company's cost to complete project		$10,000		
5					
6	Competitors' bids - triangularly distributed between a times company's cost				
7	and b times company's cost, with most likely value c times company's cost				
8	a	1			
9	c	1.3			
10	b	3			
11					
12	**Simulation**				
13	Competitor	1	2	3	4
14	Competitor's bid	$20,894.7	$15,555.7	$14,189.8	$18,916.1
15					
16	Outcomes for company				
17	Company's bid	Wins bid?	Company's profit	Range names	
18	No bid		$0	BidCost: C3	
19	$10,500	1	$150	OtherBids: B14:E14	
20	$11,000	1	$650	ProjectCost: C4	
21	$11,500	1	$1,150		
22	$12,000	1	$1,650		
23	$12,500	1	$2,150		
24	$13,000	1	$2,650		
25	$13,500	1	$3,150		
26	$14,000	1	$3,650		
27	$14,500	0	($350)		
28	$15,000	0	($350)		

1 **Inputs.** Enter the cost to prepare the bid and the cost to complete the project in cells C3 and C4. Also, enter the multipliers a, b, and c in the range B8:B10. These multipliers imply that the competitors' bids will be between $10,000 and $30,000, with most likely value $13,000.

2 **Triangular random numbers.** To find the competitors' bids, we need to generate four triangularly distributed random numbers in row 14. To do so, make sure StatPro or RandFns is loaded, and enter the formula

=TRIANGULAR_($B$8*ProjectCost,$B$9*ProjectCost,$B$10*ProjectCost)

in cell B14 and copy it across row 14. For the particular random numbers used in Figure 16.12, we see that competitor 3 has the low competing bid at slightly greater than $14,000.

3 **Possible decisions.** Enter the possible decisions for Rogers in the range A18:A28. This includes the no bid decision.

4 **Does Rogers win the bid?** For each bid Rogers could make, check whether Rogers will win the contract by entering the formula

=IF(A19<=MIN(OtherBids),1,0)

in cell B19 and copying this to the range B20:B28. A "1" in column B signifies that Rogers wins the contract; a "0" signifies that a competitor wins it.

5 **Profits.** Enter $0 in cell C18, because the no bid decision results in no costs and no revenues. For every other decision the profit depends on whether Rogers wins or loses the bid. Therefore in cell C19 enter the formula

=IF(B19=1,A19-ProjectCost,0)-BidCost

and copy it to the range C20:C28. Note that the cost of preparing the bid is outside the IF function. Rogers pays this amount regardless of whether it wins the bid.

The numbers in the range C18:C28 of Figure 16.12 indicate that Rogers would be best—in this particular scenario—to bid $14,000 and make a profit of $3650. In general, if Rogers *knew* the bids of its competitors, it would naturally bid the highest amount that is still less than its competitors' bids. Unfortunately, Rogers doesn't have this information when it makes its decision. So how does it decide on its "optimal" bid?

A reasonable approach is to replicate the simulation many times, keep track of the profit from each possible decision on each replication, average these profits for each possible decision, and choose the decision with the highest average. This is easy to do with a data table, as illustrated in Figure 16.13 (page 908). To create this table, enter replication numbers (1–100) in the range A38:A137, enter the possible decisions (as labels) in the range B36:L36, and enter the formulas from the range C18:C28 in the range B37:L37.

Here is an easy way to enter these labels and formulas. First, select the range B36:L36 and type the *array* formula

=TRANSPOSE(A18:A28)

Enter this in the selected range by pressing Ctrl-Shift-Enter (press all three keys at once). The TRANSPOSE command simply reorients the information from A18:A28 horizontally. Similarly, select the range B37:L37, type the array formula

=TRANSPOSE(C18:C28)

and press Ctrl-Shift-Enter. Finally, to form the data table, select the range A37:L137 and use the Data/Table command with any blank cell as the column input cell and no row input cell.

FIGURE 16.13 Data Table for Bidding Example

	A	B	C	D	E	F	G	H	I	J	K	L
30	Summary measures from data table below											
31		No bid	$10,500	$11,000	$11,500	$12,000	$12,500	$13,000	$13,500	$14,000	$14,500	$15,000
32	Averages	$0	$135	$590	$985	$1,170	$1,275	$1,120	$1,050	$850	$730	$500
33	Stdevs	$0	$86	$239	$472	$858	$1,198	$1,507	$1,723	$1,842	$1,932	$1,888
34												
35	Data table showing profits from various bids											
36	Replication	No bid	$10,500	$11,000	$11,500	$12,000	$12,500	$13,000	$13,500	$14,000	$14,500	$15,000
37		$0	$150	$650	$1,150	$1,650	$2,150	$2,650	$3,150	$3,650	($350)	($350)
38	1	$0	$150	$650	$1,150	$1,650	$2,150	$2,650	$3,150	$3,650	$4,150	($350)
39	2	$0	$150	$650	$1,150	$1,650	$2,150	$2,650	$3,150	$3,650	($350)	($350)
40	3	$0	$150	($350)	($350)	($350)	($350)	($350)	($350)	($350)	($350)	($350)
41	4	$0	$150	$650	$1,150	$1,650	$2,150	$2,650	$3,150	($350)	($350)	($350)
42	5	$0	$150	$650	$1,150	$1,650	($350)	($350)	($350)	($350)	($350)	($350)
43	6	$0	$150	$650	$1,150	$1,650	$2,150	$2,650	($350)	($350)	($350)	($350)
134	97	$0	$150	$650	$1,150	($350)	($350)	($350)	($350)	($350)	($350)	($350)
135	98	$0	$150	$650	$1,150	$1,650	($350)	($350)	($350)	($350)	($350)	($350)
136	99	$0	$150	$650	$1,150	$1,650	$2,150	$2,650	$3,150	($350)	($350)	($350)
137	100	$0	$150	$650	$1,150	$1,650	$2,150	$2,650	$3,150	($350)	($350)	($350)

Once the data table has been formed, the average and standard deviation of the 100 numbers in each column of the data table can be calculated in rows 32 and 33 with the AVERAGE and STDEV functions. Also, bar charts of these averages and standard deviations can be created, as shown in Figures 16.14 and 16.15. As we see from Figure 16.14, a bid amount of $12,500 achieves the largest average profit from these 100 replications. However, we also see from Figure 16.15 that there is more risk (larger standard deviation) associated with larger bids. Because of this risk, Rogers might want to settle for a smaller bid amount such as $12,000.

The numbers in Figure 16.12 and the associated charts are not necessarily the *definitive* answer to Rogers' problem. These numbers are all based on the random numbers that happened to be generated for these 100 replications. To see how things can change, press the F9 key with the BIDDING.XLS file open. After a few seconds, all of the numbers, as well as the corresponding graphs, will change. It is very possible that some bid amount other than $12,500 will achieve the largest average profit. The only way to ensure that a simulation spreadsheet represents *the* definitive solution to a problem is to generate a large number of replications. Unfortunately, the required number of replications varies from problem to problem, so it is difficult to provide clear guidelines in general. All we can suggest is: *the more, the better*!

FIGURE 16.14 Average Profits for Bidding Example

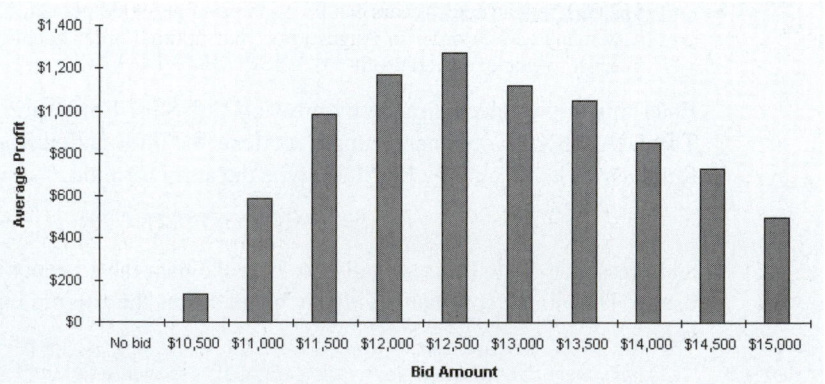

FIGURE 16.15 **Standard Deviations for Bidding Example**

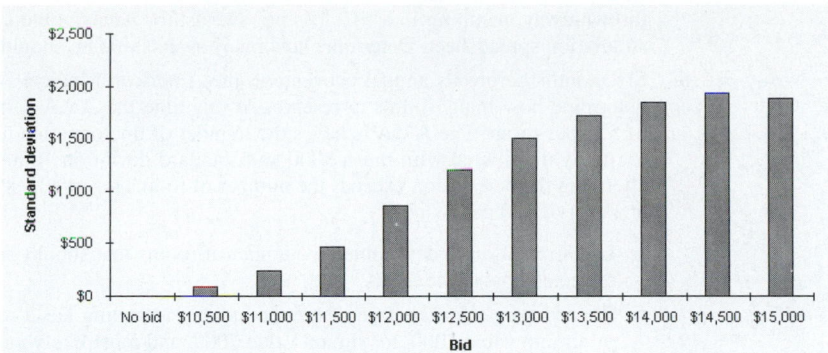

PROBLEMS

Level A

1 Use the RAND function and the Copy command to generate a set of 100 random numbers.

    a What fraction of the random numbers are smaller than 0.5?

    b What fraction of the time is a random number less than 0.5 followed by a random number greater than 0.5?

    c What fraction of the random numbers are larger than 0.8?

    d Freeze these random numbers. However, instead of pasting them over the original random numbers, paste them onto a new range. Then press the F9 (recalculate) key. The original random numbers should change, but the pasted copy should remain the same.

2 We all hate to bring change to a store. By using random numbers, we can eliminate the need for change and give the store and the customer a fair deal.

    a Suppose you buy something for 20¢. How could you use random numbers (built into the cash register system) to decide whether you should pay $1.00 or nothing? This would eliminate the need for change!

    b If you bought something for $9.60, how would you use random numbers to eliminate the need for change?

    c In the long run, why is this method fair to both the store and the customers? Would you personally (as a customer) be willing to abide by such a system?

3 In August 1998, a car dealer is trying to determine how many 1999 cars to order. Each car ordered in August 1998 costs $10,000. The demand for the dealer's 1999 models has the probability distribution shown in the file P16_3.XLS. Each car sells for $15,000. If demand for 1999 cars exceeds the number of cars ordered in August, the dealer must reorder at a cost of $12,000 per car. Excess cars can be disposed of at $9000 per car. Use simulation to determine how many cars to order in August. For your optimal order quantity, find a 95% confidence interval for the expected profit.

4 In the Walton example (Example 16.1), suppose that Walton receives no money for the first 50 excess calendars returned but receives $2.50 for every calendar after the first 50 returned. Does this change the optimal order quantity?

5 A sweatshirt supplier is trying to decide how many sweatshirts to print for the upcoming NCAA basketball championships. The final four teams have emerged from the quarterfinal round, and there is now a week left until the semifinals, which are then followed in a couple of days by the finals. Each sweatshirt costs $10 to produce and sells for $25. However, in 3 weeks, any leftover sweatshirts will be put on sale for half price, $12.50. The supplier assumes that the demand for his sweatshirts during the next 3 weeks, when interest is at its highest, has the distribution shown in the file P16_5.XLS. The residual demand, after the sweatshirts have been put on sale, has the distribution also shown in this file. The supplier, being a profit maximizer, realizes that every sweatshirt sold, even at the sale price, yields a profit. However, he also realizes that any sweatshirts produced but not sold (even at the sale price) must be thrown away, resulting in a $10 loss per sweatshirt. Analyze the supplier's problem with a simulation spreadsheet. Determine how many sweatshirts he should produce.

6 Six months before its annual convention, the American Medical Association (AMA) must determine how many rooms to reserve. At this time the AMA can reserve rooms at a cost of $50 per room. The AMA believes the number of doctors attending the convention will be normally distributed with mean 5000 and standard deviation 1000. If the number of people attending the convention exceeds the number of rooms reserved, extra rooms must be reserved at a cost of $80 per room.

a Use simulation to determine the number of rooms that should be reserved to minimize the expected cost to the AMA.

b Rework part **a** for the case where the number attending has a triangular distribution with minimum value 2000, maximum value 7000, and most likely value 5000.

7 If the number of competitors in the Rogers bidding example (Example 16.2) were to double, how would the optimal bid change?

8 Referring to the Rogers bidding example (Example 16.2), if the average bid for each competitor stayed the same, but their bids exhibited less variability, would the optimal bid increase or decrease? To study this question, assume that each competitor's bid follows each of the following distributions.

a Uniform between 12 and 24

b Uniform between 13 and 16

9 A new edition of our management science textbook will be published 1 year from now. Our publisher currently has 2000 copies on hand and is deciding whether to do another printing before the new edition comes out. The publisher estimates that demand for the book during the next year is governed by the probability distribution in the file P16_9.XLS. A production run incurs a fixed cost of $62,000 plus a variable cost of $10 per book printed. Books are sold for $30 per book. Any demand that cannot be met incurs a penalty cost of $2 per book, due to loss of goodwill. Half of any leftover books can be sold to Barnes and Noble for $3 per book. My publisher is interested in maximizing expected profit. The following print run sizes are under consideration: 0 (no production run), 1000, 2000, 4000, 6000, and 8000. What decision would you recommend? Use simulation with at least 100 replications. For your optimal decision, our publisher can be 90% certain that the actual profit associated with remaining sales of the current edition will be between what two values?

10 It is equally likely that annual unit sales for Widgetco's widgets will be low or high. If sales are low (60,000), the company can sell the product for $10 per unit. If sales are high (100,000), a competitor will enter and Widgetco can sell the product for only $8 per unit. The variable cost per unit has a 25% chance of being $6, a 50% chance of being $7.50, and a 25% chance of being $9. Annual fixed costs are $30,000.

a Use simulation, with at least 400 replications, to estimate Widgetco's expected annual profit.

b Construct a 95% confidence interval for Widgetco's annual expected profit.

c Now suppose that annual unit sales, variable cost, and unit price are equal to their respective expected values—that is, there is no uncertainty. Determine Widgetco's annual profit for this scenario.

d Can you conclude from the results in parts **a** and **c** that the expected profit from a simulation is equal to the profit from the scenario where each input assumes its expected value? Explain.

Level B

11 In the Walton example (Example 16.1), explain why an order quantity other than one of the possible demands cannot maximize the expected profit. (*Hint*: For example, consider an order of 190 calendars. If this maximizes expected profit, then it must yield a higher expected profit than an order of 150 or 100. But then an order of 200 calendars must also yield a larger expected profit than 190 calendars. Why?) ■

Simulating with @Risk

In the rest of this chapter we will use the @Risk simulation add-in, developed by Palisade Corporation. There are two possible advantages of using such an add-in. First, an add-in provides more functionality—we can do more things—than the basic Excel package. We will discuss these extra features shortly. Second, an add-in allows us to perform simulations much more easily than is possible with Excel alone. For example, we typically use data tables in Excel to replicate a simulation. (See the previous bidding example for an illustration.) Then we have to calculate summary statistics, such as averages, standard deviations, and confidence intervals, with built-in Excel functions. If we want graphs to enhance the analysis, we have to create them. In short, we have to perform a number of time-consuming steps for each simulation. Simulation add-ins such as @Risk relieve us of much of this work by performing the typical steps of a simulation automatically.

Although we will concentrate on @Risk in this chapter, it is not the only available simulation add-in for Excel. A worthy competitor is Crystal Ball, developed by Decisioneering. Crystal Ball has most of the same functionality as @Risk. In addition, because of the relative ease of developing "home-grown" applications in Excel with Excel's built-in macro language Visual Basic for Applications, individuals are developing their own simulation add-ins for Excel.

There are three features of @Risk that add to Excel's functionality:

1   @Risk contains a number of functions such as RISKNORMAL and RISKDISCRETE that make it easier to generate observations from the most important probability distributions. We discussed these in the previous section.

2   We can specify any cell or range of cells in the simulation model as **output cells**. When we run the simulation, @Risk automatically keeps statistics (averages and standard deviations, for example) on the values generated in these output cells across the replications. It can also create graphs such as histograms based on these values.

3   @Risk has a special function, the RISKSIMTABLE function, that allows us to run the same simulation several times, using a different value of some key input each time. For example, suppose that we would like to simulate an inventory ordering policy (as in the Walton Bookstore example, Example 16.1). Our ultimate purpose is to compare simulation outputs across a number of possible order quantities such as 1100, 1150, 1200, and 1250. If we use the formula

=RISKSIMTABLE({1100,1150,1200,1250})

the entire simulation will be performed for each of these order quantities separately. Then we can compare their outputs when attempting to choose the "best" order quantity.

In this section we will use two simple examples to illustrate some of @Risk's functionality. Then in later sections we will use @Risk to help solve a number of interesting simulation applications.

E X A M P L E 1 6 . 3

The ABC Company wants to develop a projected monthly income statement for the coming year. However, ABC recognizes that many of the inputs necessary to form this income statement are at best educated guesses. Therefore, it wants to use @Risk to indicate how sensitive important bottom line figures, such as yearly net income after taxes, are to the inputs. The following assumptions are made (where all monetary values are in thousands of dollars).

- January sales are normally distributed with mean 2225 and standard deviation 150.
- The cost of goods in January is uniformly distributed between 870 and 910.
- The marketing cost in January is triangularly distributed with minimum value 90, most likely value 93, and maximum value 96.
- The administrative cost in January is triangularly distributed with minimum value 75, most likely value 78, and maximum value 81.
- The miscellaneous cost in January is triangularly distributed with minimum value 23, most likely value 24, and maximum value 25.
- The tax rate is known to be 33% (no uncertainty).
- The monthly percentage changes in sales and all costs are independent of each other and are all normally distributed with mean 1.5% and standard deviation 1.0%.

These probability distributions reflect ABC's uncertainty about the inputs. Certainly other distributions could have been chosen, but ABC believes that these particular distributions represent the uncertainty in the best way possible.

Solution

The spreadsheet in Figure 16.16 shows ABC's projected income statement for the next 12 months. (See the file ABC.XLS.) The inputs shown at the top of the spreadsheet include projected sales and costs for January, the company's tax rate, and projected monthly percentage changes in sales and costs. For example, the January percentage change in sales (in cell B13) is the percentage change from January to February. The rest of the spreadsheet (in the Income Statement section) is relatively straightforward. The cells in this section use standard Excel formulas that reference the input cells. For example, the formulas in cells B21 and C21 are

$$=B5$$

and

$$=B21*B13$$

This latter formula is then copied across row 21 to generate sales for each month. You should check the other formulas in the Income Statement section to make sure you understand the logic, but since our main interest is seeing how *simulation* works, we will concentrate on this aspect.

Developing the Spreadsheet Model   The main difference between this spreadsheet and the usual type is that probability distributions have been entered in several of the input cells. We enter a particular probability distribution in a cell by using one of @Risk's several functions in that cell. Specifically, we will use the RISKNORMAL, RISKUNIFORM, and RISKTRIANG functions in this example.

1   **January sales.** Enter the distribution of January sales in cell B5 with the formula

$$=RISKNORMAL(2225,150)$$

2   **January cost of goods.** Enter the distribution of the cost of goods in January in cell B6 with the formula

$$=RISKUNIFORM(870,910)$$

FIGURE 16.16 **Simulation Model of ABC Income Statement**

	A	B	C	D	K	L	M	N
1	**Income Statement for ABC Company Using @RISK**							
2								
3	**Inputs (dollar figures in $1000s)**							
4								
5	Sales in January	$2,225						
6	Cost of goods in January	$890						
7	Marketing in January	$93						
8	Administrative in January	$78						
9	Miscellaneous in January	$24						
10	Tax rate	33%						
11								
12	costs	Jan	Feb	Mar	Oct	Nov		
13	Sales	1.5%	1.5%	1.5%	1.5%	1.5%		
14	Cost of goods	1.5%	1.5%	1.5%	1.5%	1.5%		
15	Marketing	1.5%	1.5%	1.5%	1.5%	1.5%		
16	Administrative	1.5%	1.5%	1.5%	1.5%	1.5%		
17	Miscellaneous	1.5%	1.5%	1.5%	1.5%	1.5%		
18								
19	**Income Statement**							
20		Jan	Feb	Mar	Oct	Nov	Dec	Totals
21	Sales	$2,225	$2,258	$2,292	$2,544	$2,582	$2,621	$29,017
22	Cost of goods sold	$890	$903	$917	$1,018	$1,033	$1,048	$11,607
23								
24	Gross margin	$1,335	$1,355	$1,375	$1,526	$1,549	$1,573	$17,410
25								
26	Marketing expense	$93	$94	$96	$106	$108	$110	$1,213
27	Administrative expense	$78	$79	$80	$89	$91	$92	$1,017
28	Miscellaneous expense	$24	$24	$25	$27	$28	$28	$313
29								
30	Total expenses	$195	$198	$201	$223	$226	$230	$2,543
31								
32	Net income before taxes	$1,140	$1,157	$1,174	$1,303	$1,323	$1,343	$14,867
33	Taxes	$376	$382	$388	$430	$437	$443	$4,906
34								
35	Net income after taxes	$764	$775	$787	$873	$886	$900	$9,961
36	Cum net income	$764	$1,539	$2,326	$8,175	$9,061	$9,961	

3 **January marketing cost.** Enter the distribution of the marketing cost in January in cell B7 with the formula

$$=RISKTRIANG(90,93,96)$$

4 **January administrative cost.** Enter the distribution of the administrative cost in January in cell B8 with the formula

$$=RISKTRIANG(75,78,81)$$

5 **January miscellaneous costs.** Enter the distribution of the miscellaneous costs in January in cell B9 with the formula

$$=RISKTRIANG(23,24,25)$$

6 **Tax rate.** Since there is no uncertainty in the tax rate, enter the *value* 33%—not a formula—in cell B10.

7 **Monthly percentage changes.** To generate the monthly percentage changes, enter the formula

$$=\text{RISKNORMAL}(.015,.01)$$

in cell B13 and copy it to the range B13:L17. Although all cells in this range have the same probability distribution, their individual values will be generated independently on each iteration of the simulation. Therefore, these percentage increases will all be different.

Note that *numbers* appear in the spreadsheet in the input cells. The @Risk program indeed keeps track of the formulas entered, but it shows the *means* of these distributions in the input cells, and then it shows the outputs that are based on these means. Therefore, the outputs shown in the spreadsheet reflect one set of input values—the means. However, when @Risk executes, it simulates many different values for the inputs and calculates the corresponding outputs for each set of input values.

Using @Risk   Once we have entered the inputs and the formulas relating these to outputs (specifically, the formulas in the Income Statement section for this example), we must invoke @Risk. This requires the following steps. First, however, note that when we open @Risk, there is a new toolbar. The buttons on this toolbar are used to perform the various @Risk functions. (See Figure 16.17.)

FIGURE 16.17   **Toolbar for @RISK**

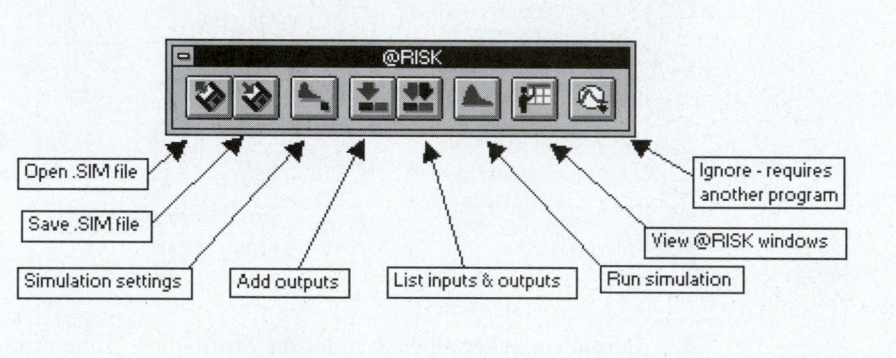

1 **Specify output cell(s).** Specify an output cell or a range of output cells. For this example we specify the "bottom line" output cell N35 (yearly net income after taxes) and the output range B36:M36 (the monthly cumulative net incomes after taxes). As the simulation progresses, @Risk automatically keeps track of the values in these output ranges. To add these cells as output cells, select cell N35 and click on the Add Outputs button (fourth from the left) on the @Risk toolbar. Then select the range B36:M36 and again click on this button.

2 **Specify simulation settings.** We will replicate this simulation 100 times. Therefore, click on the Simulation Settings button (third from the left) and enter 100 in the # Iterations box. (There are many other settings you can make at this stage, but we will accept all of the defaults for now.)

3 **Run the simulation.** To run the simulation, click on the Run button (third from the right). As the simulation runs, you can watch the progress in an @Risk window.

Once the 100 iterations are complete, we see an @Risk screen with a new menu bar, an expanded toolbar, and two windows of summary statistics. From this screen we can see the results of the simulation in both tabular and graphical form. The following results (among others) are available.

■ The upper window (the Results window) shows summary statistics for each of the output cells and (by scrolling down) each of the input cells that contain random distributions. (See Figure 16.18.) For example, we see that the mean value of net income after taxes (averaged over the 100 replications) is $9948.89. The minimum value obtained in any of the replications $5429.72, and the maximum is $13,144.72.

FIGURE 16.18 **Summary Measures for ABC Example**

Cell	Name	Minimum	Mean	Maximum
N35	Net income after taxes / Totals	5429.721	9948.894	13144.72
B36	Cum net income / Jan	432.6693	762.6409	1003.062
C36	Cum net income / Feb	872.3716	1536.848	1992.507
D36	Cum net income / Mar	1310.817	2322.654	3038.049

Simulation #1 of:
Abc.xls
Iterations= 100 Simulations= 1
# Input Variables= 0
# Output Variables= 10
Sampling Type= Latin Hypercube

■ The bottom window (the Summary Statistics window) shows more detailed statistics. To see more of these, click anywhere in this window and click on the maximize button. (See Figure 16.19.) For example, the standard deviation of net income after taxes is $1336. Similarly, the 5th, 50th, and 95th percentiles are $7605, $9973, and

FIGURE 16.19 **Detailed Statistics for ABC Example**

Name	Net income after taxes / Totals	Cum net income / Jan	Cum net income / Feb
Description	Output	Output	Output
Cell	N35	B36	C36
Minimum =	5429.721	432.6693	872.3716
Maximum =	13144.72	1003.062	1992.507
Mean =	9948.894	762.6409	1536.848
Std Deviation =	1335.999	100.2272	200.3495
Variance =	1784894	10045.49	40139.94
Skewness =	-0.2048561	-0.1993058	-0.2052196
Kurtosis =	3.716518	3.292693	3.402062
Errors Calculated =	0	0	0
Mode =	10699.39	775.8262	1691.76
5% Perc =	7604.528	594.3162	1179.537
10% Perc =	8199.541	639.3611	1263.333
15% Perc =	8732.628	660.3975	1339.616
20% Perc =	8862.705	677.313	1362.41
25% Perc =	9198.464	698.4771	1412.671
30% Perc =	9335.539	710.1855	1435.55

$12,146. (These last two values don't appear in Figure 16.19 but they are part of the output.) The 50th percentile is the median; it means that half of the simulated net income values are below it and half are above it. The 5th percentile means that 5% of the simulated net incomes are below it. Similarly, the 95th percentile means that 95% of the simulated net incomes are below it. These percentiles are often useful for estimating the worst and best cases that are likely to occur.

■ To see a histogram of net income after taxes, make sure the Results window is showing and the net income cell is highlighted. Then click on the Graph button on the toolbar. You should see a histogram like the one shown in Figure 16.20. It clearly indicates a bell-shaped distribution around the mean.

FIGURE 16.20 **Histogram for ABC Example**

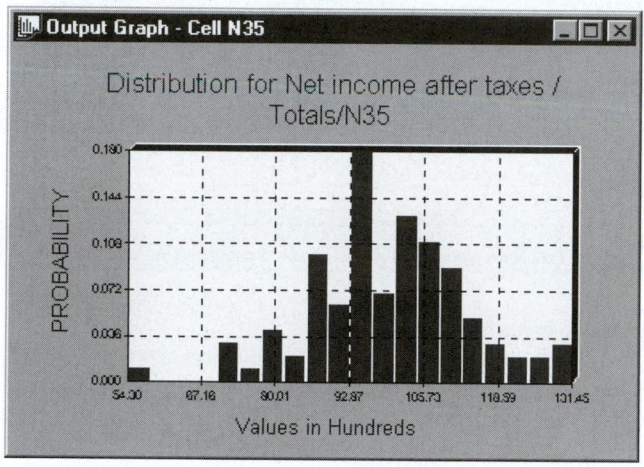

■ If we select an output range, such as B36:M36, that tracks a variable (cumulative net income after taxes) over time, we can then produce a summary chart that shows the time series behavior. To do this, highlight cell B36 in the Results window and click on the Summary button in the toolbar. The graphs shown in Figure 16.21 should appear. In this graph time moves from left to right. The middle line in the graph joins the means for each month. The first band around this line extends to one standard deviation on either side of the mean. The outer bands extend to the 5th and 95th percentiles. The graph clearly indicates the upward trend in cumulative net income, and it also shows how the uncertainty increases as more months are included in the cumulative value.

There are two ways to proceed at this stage. First, we can save the output from the simulation in a .SIM file (a file format readable by @Risk) by clicking on the Save button. Second, we can copy portions of the @Risk output to the clipboard and then paste them into the Excel spreadsheet. To return to the spreadsheet from @Risk, we need to click on the Hide button. Then we can go back to the @Risk output by clicking on the Show button (second from the right) on the @Risk toolbar.

FIGURE 16.21   Summary Chart for ABC Example

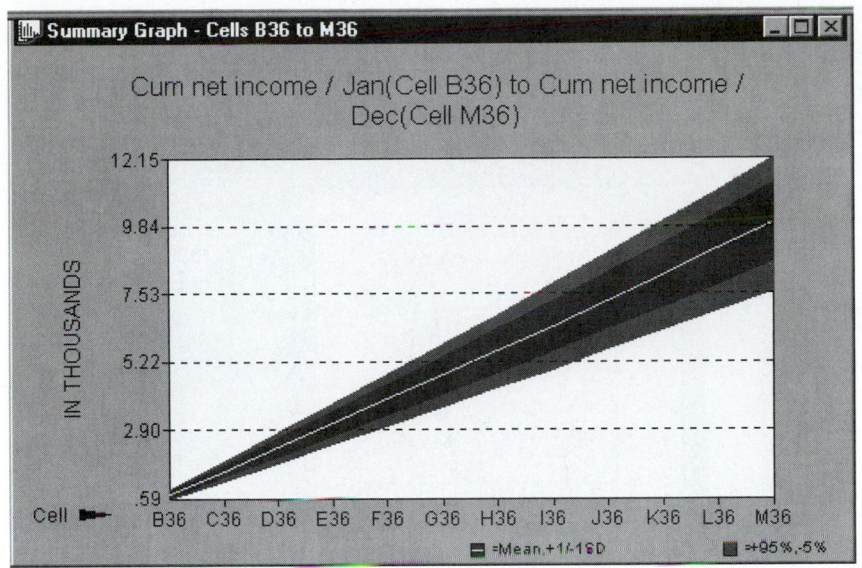

16.5.1 Using RiskView

RiskView is another add-in in the Palisade Decision Tools suite. It is basically a drawing tool that can be used with @Risk (or with Best Fit). Its basic function is to allow us to see a graph of any input probability distribution. When @Risk (or any of the Decision Tools add-ins) is loaded, we see an extra toolbar, as shown in Figure 16.22. Each button on this toolbar corresponds to one of the add-ins in the suite. The right-hand button is for RiskView. To open RiskView when @Risk is already open, we just click on this button.

FIGURE 16.22   Toolbar for Decision Tools Suite

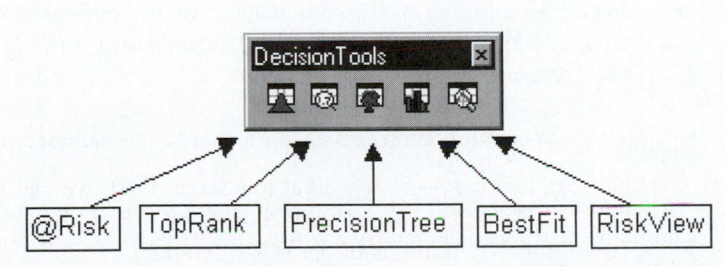

Once RiskView opens we can select any probability distribution and its parameters to see a graph of this distribution. For example, if we want to see the normal distribution of fixed cost in the ABC example, we select Normal from the pulldown list of distributions, enter 2225 and 150 as the mean and standard deviation, and click on the Update Graph button. We immediately see a graph of this normal distribution, as shown in Figure 16.23 on page 918. We invite you to experiment with the other options in RiskView.

FIGURE 16.23 RiskView Graph of a Normal Distribution

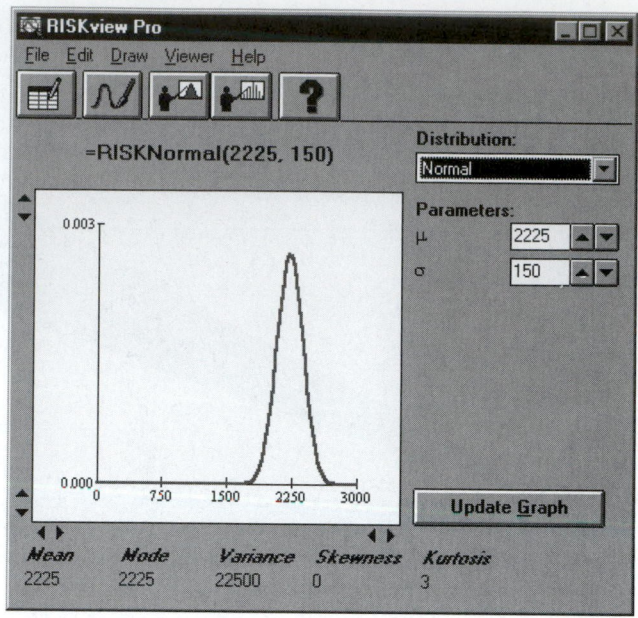

In Example 16.1 we illustrated Excel's simulation capabilities with a version of the newsvendor model. We now analyze this example using @Risk. A comparison of the two approaches clearly indicates the power and ease of @Risk.

EXAMPLE 16.4

Recall that Walton Bookstore buys calendars for $7.50, sells them at the regular price of $10, and gets a refund of $2.50 for all calendars that cannot be sold. We now assume that the probability distribution of demand is continuous, not discrete. Specifically, we assume it is normal with mean 175 and standard deviation 60. (These are very close to the mean and standard deviation of the discrete demand distribution used earlier.) Walton wants to use @Risk to simulate the profits from calendars for five different order quantities: 100, 150, 200, 250, and 300.

Solution

We will take advantage of two @Risk functions to form the spreadsheet model. To simulate a normally distributed demand, we will use the RISKNORMAL function.[4] To run the simulation several times, each with a different order quantity, we will use the RISKSIMTABLE function.

Developing the Spreadsheet Model The spreadsheet model is short and simple. (See Figure 16.24 and the file WALTON4.XLS.) The following steps are required.

---

[4]There is a slight probability that a normally distributed demand could be negative, which wouldn't make any sense. Therefore, you might instead use the RISKTNORMAL function, where T stands for truncated. This function takes four arguments: the mean, the standard deviation, a lower limit, and an upper limit. No values below the lower limit or above the upper limit are allowed.

FIGURE 16.24   Walton Model with Normally Distributed Demands

	A	B	C	D	E	F	G	H	I
1	Simulation of Walton's Bookstore using @RISK								
2									
3	Cost data			Demand distribution			Possible order quantities		
4	Unit cost	$7.50		Normal with:			100		
5	Unit price	$10.00		Mean	175		150		
6	Unit refund	$2.50		St Dev	60		200		
7							250		
8	Decision variable						300		
9	Order quantity	100							
10									
11	Simulated quantities								
12		Demand	Revenue	Cost	Refund	Profit			
13		175.00	$1,000.00	$750.00	$0.00	$250.00			

1 **Inputs.** Enter the monetary inputs in the range B4:B6, the inputs for the demand distribution in the range E5:E6, and the possible order quantities in the range G4:G8.

2 **Possible order quantities.** To indicate that the simulation should be run five times, once with each order quantity, enter the formula

$$=RISKSIMTABLE(G4:G8)$$

in cell B9.[5] (Only the first possible demand, 100, shows in this cell, but all possible demands will eventually be used.)

3 **Simulated demand.** Generate a random demand in cell B13 with the formula

$$=RISKNORMAL(E5,E6)$$

Note that this function requires only two arguments: the mean and standard deviation of demand.

4 **Other simulated quantities.** The logic for the other quantities in row 13 is the same as before for the Walton example, so we won't repeat it here.

Using @Risk   Now that the spreadsheet is set up, you can use the @Risk toolbar buttons (see Figure 16.17) to run the simulation. Proceed as follows.

1 **Specify output cell(s).** The only output we will track in this simulation is profit. Therefore, select cell F13 and click on the Add Outputs button (fourth from the left) to add profit as an output. (Always remember to select the cell or range of cells before clicking on this button because it will add whatever cell is currently selected. However, if you mistakenly add an output, you can click on the List button (fifth from the left), select the mistaken output, and click on delete.)

2 **Specify simulation settings.** Click on the Simulation Setting button (third from the left). The only crucial settings are the number of iterations, which you should set to 100, and the number of simulations, which you should set to 5. These will make @Risk run 100 iterations of the simulation for each of the five possible order quantities.

   The other settings are optional, but you might want to experiment. For example, there are three possible Standard Recalc settings: Expected Value, Monte Carlo, and True EV. If the Monte Carlo option is chosen, all random quantities will change—and the changes will show on the spreadsheet—every time you press Excel's Recalc (F9)

[5] @RISK expects a list of values as the argument for the RISKSIMTABLE function. This list either can be in a range, as it is here, or it can be spelled out explicitly, as in =RISKSIMTABLE({100,150,200,250,300}). Note the required curly brackets.

button. On the other hand, if the Expected Value option is chosen, all random quantities will be replaced by their expected values or, in the case of discrete distributions, the possible value closest to the expected value. In this latter case, if the True EV option is chosen, the exact expected value will be shown. Be aware, however, that these settings affect only what you see on the spreadsheet; they don't affect the way the simulation is run. From now on, all spreadsheets shown in this chapter use the Monte Carlo option—it allows us to see more interesting numbers on the screen!

Another setting you might want to change is the Collect Distributions option. If this box is checked, @Risk will collect statistics on every cell that contains a probability distribution. If there are many of these cells, the amount of memory required could become huge. Therefore, for large problems you might want to uncheck this box.

Finally, if you check the Update Display box, you will see each iteration of the simulation. This is possibly instructive for beginners, but it slows down the simulation considerably. We don't recommend using it. Similarly, you might want to uncheck the Monitor Convergence button. This will also speed up the simulation.

3   **Run the simulation.** Click on the Simulate button (third from the right). This runs the simulation. You can monitor the progress on the lower left-hand corner of your screen.

Once the simulation is completed, you can examine the outputs in graphical or tabular form. Here are a few things to be aware of.

- Sometimes there is no variation in an output variable. Whenever this occurs, @Risk will not let you produce a histogram of the output.

- This example ran five separate simulations, one for each order quantity. You can look at the outputs from these one at a time or all at once. To do either, maximize the Results window. You'll see a couple of buttons in the bottom left-hand corner that allow you to merge the simulations or list them by simulation number. (These two buttons might not quite show unless the Results window is maximized.) See Figure 16.25, which shows the merged summary statistics. This shows, for example, that an order quantity of 150 (simulation #2) produced the largest mean profit. Larger order quantities produced larger best-case profits, but they also produced lower means and lower worst-case profits (actually, losses).

FIGURE 16.25   **Summary Statistics for Walton Example**

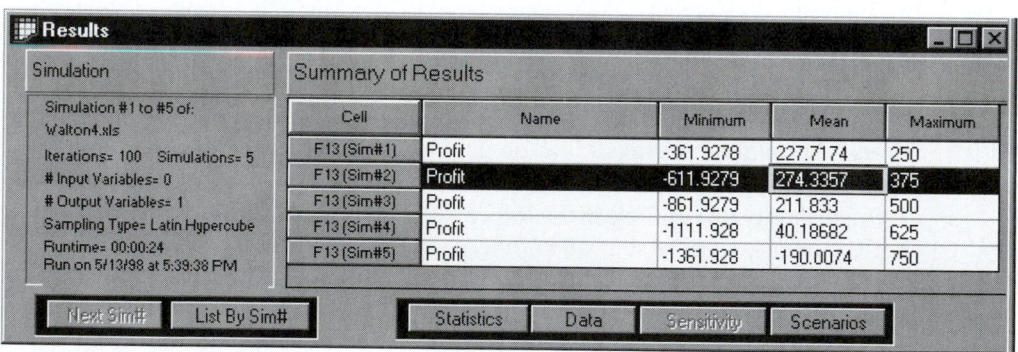

- Two other buttons, Statistics and Data, on the Results window toggle between detailed statistics on outputs and the simulated data. That is, by clicking on Data, we can see the outputs from *each* of the 100 iterations. (See Figure 16.26, which shows results

FIGURE 16.26 Simulated Data for Walton Example

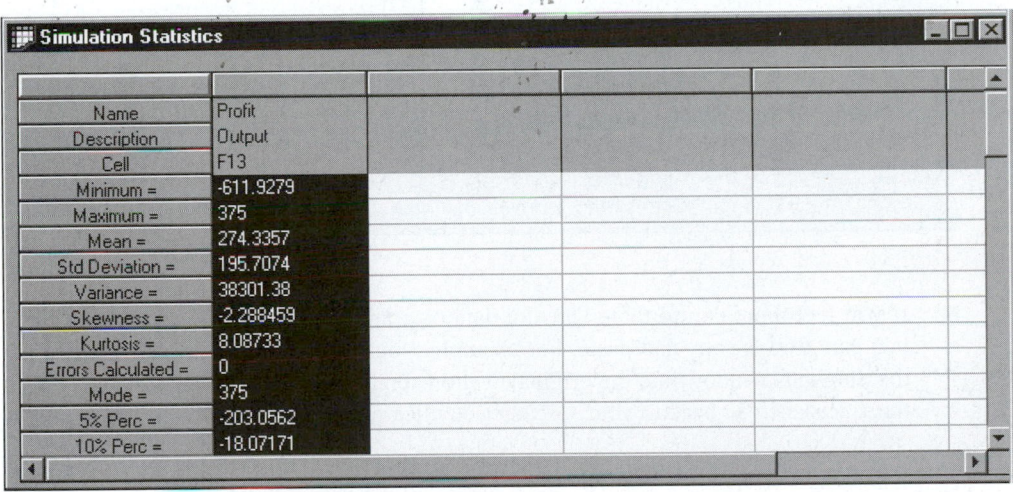

FIGURE 16.26 Simulated Data for Walton Example

Name	Profit			
Description	Output			
Iteration# / Cell	F13			
1	375			
2	152.4512			
3	110.9374			
4	375			
5	41.81592			
6	325.2047			
7	-315.1913			
8	375			

for the first 8 iterations.) In contrast, the Statistics window in Figure 16.27 shows summary statistics only. For example, when the order quantity is 150 (simulation #2), the mean profit is $274.34, the standard deviation is $195.71, the 5th percentile is —$203.06, and the median (50th percentile) and the 95th percentile (not shown in the figure) are both $375.

FIGURE 16.27 Detailed Statistics for Walton Example

Simulation Statistics

Name	Profit			
Description	Output			
Cell	F13			
Minimum =	-611.9279			
Maximum =	375			
Mean =	274.3357			
Std Deviation =	195.7074			
Variance =	38301.38			
Skewness =	-2.288459			
Kurtosis =	8.08733			
Errors Calculated =	0			
Mode =	375			
5% Perc =	-203.0562			
10% Perc =	-18.07171			

■ By selecting any output cell in the Results window and clicking on the Graph button, you can see a histogram of the simulated results. For example, the histogram of profit when the order quantity is 150 appears in Figure 16.28 on page 922. This is perhaps the most revealing output so far. It shows that there is a very high chance that profit will be $375—the maximum possible profit for this order quantity—but there is some chance that profit will be considerably less and even negative. In contrast, the histogram of profit when the order quantity is 250 is much more spread out, as shown in Figure 16.29. (Now that you see the histograms, can you see from the input data why they are like this?)

FIGURE 16.28 **Histogram of Profit with an Order Quantity of 150**

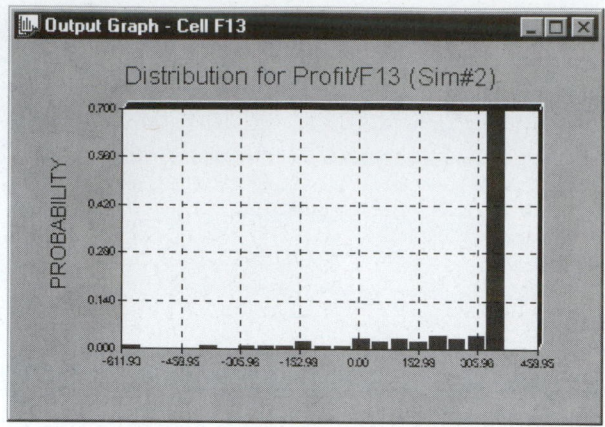

FIGURE 16.29 **Histogram of Profit with an Order Quantity of 250**

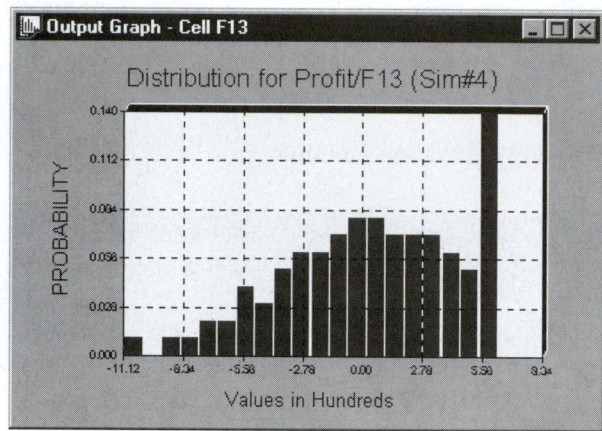

■ If you feel more comfortable viewing data or graphs back in an Excel spreadsheet, you can always copy and paste. For example, you could copy the information from the Statistics window into the original Walton spreadsheet. Remember that to go from the @Risk screen back to your spreadsheet, click on the Hide button.

16.5.2 Using the Graph Type Command

Once we obtain a histogram of a selected output, we can modify the graph in a number of ways. To do so, click with the right mouse button on an open histogram. This brings up a dialog box of graph options. Under the Type options, try selecting the Cumulative Ascending option. The resulting graph (for profit and an order quantity of 200) is shown in Figure 16.30. For any particular profit value (read on the horizontal axis), the height of the bar is the proportion of simulated profits less than or equal to this value. For example, the next-to-last bar on the right indicates that about 60% of the simulated profits are less than or equal to $430. This can be confirmed by looking at the percentiles shown in Figure 16.27. If we instead choose the Cumulative Descending option, the height of any bar above any

FIGURE 16.30 Cumulative Ascending Graph for Walton Example

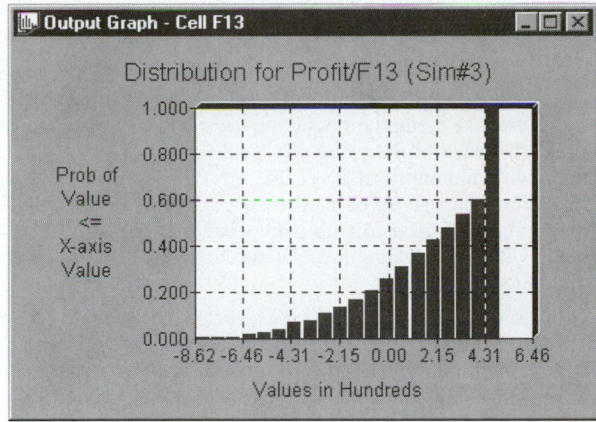

profit value is the proportion of simulated profits greater than this value. There are other graph options you might want to explore, such as changing the scale of the horizontal axis or the title of the graph.

16.5.3 Target Values in the Statistics Output

There is a section of the Simulation Statistics window where we can select target values. This works in two directions. If we enter a dollar value for profit, @Risk will determine the percentage of simulated profits that were less than or equal to this value. Conversely, if we enter a percentage, @Risk will determine the corresponding percentile—that is, the dollar value such that the given percentage of profits were below this value.

To do this, scroll down the Simulation Statistics window until you see the target headings. (See Figure 16.31, which shows results for an order quantity of 200.) For any target #, enter either a value or a percentage in the appropriate cell. @Risk then returns the corresponding value in the other cell. For example, in Figure 16.31 we entered profit values 200 and 300 for targets #1 and #2, and @Risk returned the percentages 62% and 70%. Then for targets #3 and #4, we entered the percentages 5% and 95%, and @Risk returned the profit values −703 and 625.

FIGURE 16.31 Target Values in @Risk

Simulation Statistics				
Name	Profit			
Description	Output			
Cell	[Walton4.xls]Walton!F13			
Target #1 (Value)=	200			
Target #1 (Perc%)=	62%			
Target #2 (Value)=	300			
Target #2 (Perc%)=	70%			
Target #3 (Value)=	-703.056213378906			
Target #3 (Perc%)=	5%			
Target #4 (Value)=	625			
Target #4 (Perc%)=	95%			

PROBLEMS

Level A

12 In the ABC example (Example 16.3), each percentage increase has a normal distribution with mean 1.5% and standard deviation 1.0%, and each is independent of each other. Consider the following alternative method of modeling these changes. The percentage change from January to February (for each of the categories—sales, cost of goods, and so on) has a triangular distribution with minimum value −1.0%, most likely value 1.5%, and maximum value 3.0%. Then the monthly change for each other month is the previous month's change plus an amount that is triangularly distributed with parameters −1.0%, 0%, and 1%. Use @Risk to run the ABC model with these assumptions. Do the simulation results appear to differ very much from the original model's results?

13 In the ABC example (Example 16.3), we selected the range B36:M36 of cumulative net income after taxes as an output range. Using the inputs from the previous problem, select instead the range B35:M35 of monthly net income after taxes as an output range and use @Risk to create a summary chart for this range. Discuss its characteristics and how it differs from the chart of cumulative net income after taxes (in Figure 16.21).

14 In Problem 3, suppose that the demand for cars is normally distributed with mean 100 and standard deviation 15. Use @Risk to determine the "best" order quantity, that is, the one that has the largest expected profit. Using the statistics and/or graphs from @Risk, discuss whether this order quantity would or would not be considered best by the car dealer. (The point is that a decision maker can use more than just *expected* profit in making a decision.)

15 Use @Risk to analyze the sweatshirt sales in Problem 5. Do this for the discrete distributions given in the problem. Then do it for normal distributions. For the normal case, assume that the regular demand is normally distributed with mean 9800 and standard deviation 1300, and that the demand at the reduced price is normally distributed with mean 4800 and standard deviation 1300.

16 Although the normal distribution is a reasonable input distribution in many situations, it does have two potential drawbacks: (1) it allows negative values—even though they may be extremely improbable—and (2) it is a symmetric distribution. Many situations are better modeled with a distribution that allows only positive values and is skewed to the right. Two of these are the gamma and lognormal distributions, and @Risk enables you to generate observations from each of these distributions. The @Risk function for the gamma distribution is RISKGAMMA, and it takes two arguments, as in =RISKGAMMA(3,10). The first argument, which must be positive, determines the shape. A small value produces skewness to the right; a large value produces a more symmetric distribution. The second argument determines the scale. Specifically, the product of it and the first argument equals the mean of the distribution. (The mean above is 30.) Also, the product of the second argument and the square root of the first argument is the standard deviation of the distribution. [Above, it is $\sqrt{3}(10) = 17.32$.] The @Risk function for the lognormal distribution is RISKLOGNORM. It has two arguments, as in =RISKLOGNORM(40,10). These arguments are the mean and standard deviation of the distribution.

Rework the Walton example (Example 16.4) for the following demand distributions. Do the simulated outputs have any different qualitative properties with these skewed distributions than with the normal distribution used in the example?

a Gamma distribution with parameters 2 and 85

b Gamma distribution with parameters 5 and 35

c Lognormal distribution with mean 170 and standard deviation 60

Level B

17 The Mutron Company is thinking of marketing a new drug used to make pigs healthier. At the beginning of the current year, there are 1,000,000 pigs that might use the product. Each pig will use Mutron's drug or a competitor's drug once a year. The number of pigs is forecasted to grow by an average of 5% per year. However, this growth rate is not a sure thing. Mutron assumes that each year's growth rate is an independent draw from a normal distribution, with probability 0.95 that the growth rate will be between 3% and 7%. Assuming it enters the market, Mutron is not sure what its share of the market will be during year 1, so it models this with a triangular distribution. Its worst-case share is 20%, its most likely share is 40%, and its best-case share is

70%. In the absence of any *new* competitors entering this market (in addition to itself), Mutron believes its market share will remain the same in succeeding years. However, there are three potential entrants (in addition to Mutron). At the beginning of each year, each entrant that has not already entered the market has a 40% chance of entering the market. The year after a competitor enters, Mutron's market share will drop by 20% for each *new* competitor who entered. For example, if two competitors enter the market in year 1, Mutron's market share in year 2 will be reduced by 40% from what it would have been with no entrants. Note that if all three entrants have entered, no more entrants will enter. Each unit of the drug sells for $2.20 and incurs a variable cost of $0.40. Profits are discounted by 10% annually.

a Assuming that Mutron enters the market, use simulation to find a 95% confidence interval for its expected net present value (NPV) from the drug.

b Again assuming that Mutron enters the market, it can be 95% certain that its *actual* NPV from the drug is between what two values? ■

16.6 A Financial Planning Model

Many companies use simulation in their capital budgeting and financial planning processes. Simulation can be used to model the uncertainty associated with future cash flows and to answer questions such as the following:

■ What are the estimated mean and variance of a project's net present value (NPV)?

■ What is the estimated probability that a project will have a negative NPV?

■ What are the estimated mean and variance of a company's profit during the next fiscal year?

■ What is the estimated probability that a company will have to borrow more than $2 million during the next year?

The following example illustrates how simulation can be used to compare investment opportunities.

EXAMPLE 16.5

General Ford (GF) Auto Corporation is trying to determine what type of compact car to develop. Two models (model 1 and model 2) are under consideration. Each model is assumed to generate sales for 10 years. To determine which model to build, GF has gathered information about the following quantities through focus groups with the marketing and engineering departments.

■ **Fixed cost of developing car.** This cost is assumed to be normally distributed for each model. The mean and standard deviation for model 1 are $2.5 billion and $0.4 billion; for model 2 they are $2.3 billion and $0.5 billion. The fixed cost is incurred at the beginning of year 1, before any sales are recorded.

■ **Variable production cost.** This cost, which includes all variable production costs required to build a single car, is assumed to be normally distributed for each model during year 1. For model 1 the mean and standard deviation are $8000 and $400; for model 2 they are $7800 and $600. Each year after year 1 the variable production cost is the previous year's variable production cost multiplied by an inflation factor. Each year this inflation factor is assumed to be normally distributed with mean 1.05 (a 5% increase) and standard deviation .015. All production costs are assumed to occur at the ends of the respective years.

- **Sales price.** The sales price in year 1 is already set at $12,000 for model 1 and $11,800 for model 2. After year 1 the sales price will increase by the same inflation factor that drives production costs. Like production costs, revenues from sales are assumed to occur at the ends of the respective years.

- **Demand.** The demand for either model in year 1 is assumed to be normally distributed with mean 100,000. The standard deviation for model 1 is 7500; for model 2 it is 10,000. After year 1 the demand in a given year is assumed to be normally distributed with mean equal to the *actual* demand in the previous year and standard deviation 7500 for model 1 and 10,000 for model 2. For example, if the observed demand in year 3 is 105,000, then the demand distribution in year 4 has mean 105,000. An implication of this assumption is that demands in successive years are not probabilistically independent. If the demand in one year is large, for example, the mean demand for the next year is also large, so that the actual demand for the next year will tend to be large.

- **Production.** In any particular year GF plans to base its production policy on the probability distribution of demand for that year—*before* the actual demand for that year is observed. In particular, if the expected demand in year t is $E(D_t)$ and the standard deviation of demand is σ_t, then GF's policy is to produce $E(D_t) + k\sigma_t$ cars, where k is a multiple that GF will have to select. For example, if it chooses $k = 1$, then its production quantity in any year will be one standard deviation above the expected demand. From the properties of the normal distribution, using $k = 1$ implies that the chances are approximately 5 out of 6 of meeting all demand for the year. (This is because a normal random variable has approximate probability 5/6 of being no more than one standard deviation *above* the mean.) If demand in any year is greater than production, the excess demand is lost. However, if production in any year is greater than demand, GF will sell the excess cars at an end-of-year discount of 30%.

- **Interest rate.** GF plans to use a 10% interest rate to discount future cash flows. This means, for example, that a cash flow of $1 at the beginning of year 1 is equivalent to a cash flow of $1.10 at the end of year 1.

Given these assumptions, GF wants to develop a simulation model that will evaluate its NPV for each model over the 10-year time horizon and suggest which model to build.

Solution

The simulation for model 1 appears in Figures 16.32 and 16.33. (See the file GFAUTO.XLS.) We develop it with the following steps.

1 **Inputs.** Enter the various inputs through row 24. As usual, it is a good practice to enter all of the input values in cells so that they can be referenced in formulas later on. Notice that we have used a value of 1 for the multiplier k in cell H21. This can easily be changed to see the effects of other production policies. (In fact, this might be a good place to use the RISKSIMTABLE function.)

2 **Variable cost inflation factors.** Rows 28–43 contain a single 10-year simulation. The approach is to enter appropriate formulas in columns B and C for years 1 and 2, then copy the year 2 formulas to the columns for the other years, and finally calculate the values in rows 37, 40, 41, and 43. Begin by entering the variable production cost inflation factor relating year 2 to year 1 in cell C28 with the formula

$$\text{=RISKNORMAL(\$B\$17,\$B\$18)}$$

and copy this across to the rest of row 28.

FIGURE 16.32 Inputs for Model 1 of GF Auto Example

	A	B	C	D	E	F	G	H	I	J	K
1	GF Simulation with @RISK for model 1										
2											
3	Input section										
4											
5	Fixed costs (assumed to occur at beginning of year 1)						Demand in year 1				
6	Normal distribution ($ billions)						Normal distribution (1000s of cars)				
7	Mean	2.5					Mean	100			
8	St Dev	0.4					St Dev	7.5			
9											
10	Variable production cost per car in year 1						Demand in other years				
11	Normal distribution ($1000s)						Normal distribution (1000s of cars)				
12	Mean	8					Mean	demand from previous year			
13	St Dev	0.4					St Dev	7.5			
14											
15	Inflation factor						Production policy				
16	Normal distribution						Production each year is mean demand plus a multiple of stdev of demand				
17	Mean	1.05					(for that year). If demand is greater than supply, excess demand is lost.				
18	St Dev	0.015					If the supply is greater than demand, the excess are sold at a discount.				
19											
20	Sales price in year 1						Multiple (k) of st dev used for setting production quantity				
21	No uncertainty ($1000s)	12						1			
22											
23	Interest rate	10%					Year-end discount for leftover cars at the end of the year				
24								30%			

FIGURE 16.33 Simulation for Model 1 of GF Auto Example

	A	B	C	D	E	F	G	H	I	J
29	Simulation section									
30		Nov	Dec	Jan	Feb	Mar	Apr	May	Jun	Jul
31	Actual sales	1200	1280	1440	1200	1520	2080	1920	1520	1040
32										
33	Beginning cash balance			250	337.25	250	250	250	250	
34	Interest on cash balance			1.25	1.69	1.25	1.25	1.25	1.25	
35	Receipts			1296	1360	1312	1568	1936	1872	
36	Fixed costs			250	250	250	250	250	250	
37	Tax, dividend expenses			0	0	150	0	0	100	
38	Material, labor expenses			960	1216	1664	1536	1216	832	
39	Close out previous loan			0	0	17.23	775.66	1002.34	536.40	
40	Cash balance before loan			337.25	232.94	-517.98	-742.41	-281.09	404.85	
41	Loan amount (if any)			0	17.06	767.98	992.41	531.09	0	
42	Final cash balance			337.25	250	250	250	250	404.85	
43										
44	Maximum loan	992.41								

3 Production quantities. The production quantity in year 1 is based on the expected demand and the standard deviation of demand in year 1, so enter the formula

$$=H7+H21*H8$$

in cell B29. For other years the expected demand is the previous year's actual demand, and this is used to calculate the production quantity. Therefore, for year 2 enter the formula

$$=B30+\$H\$21*\$H\$13$$

in cell C29 and copy it across to the rest of row 29.

4 Demands. Generate the demand in year 1 in cell B30 with the formula

$$=RISKNORMAL(H7,H8)$$

As in the previous step, the expected demand in year 2 is the actual demand from year 1, so generate the demand for year 2 in cell C30 with the formula

$$=RISKNORMAL(B30,\$H\$13)$$

Then copy this to the rest of row 30 to generate demands for the other years.

5   **Variable production costs.** Generate the variable production cost for year 1 in cell B31 with the formula

$$=RISKNORMAL(B12,B13)$$

Then use the inflation factor in row 28 to generate the variable production cost for year 2 in cell C31 with the formula

$$=B31*C28$$

and copy this across to the rest of row 31.

6   **Sales prices.** Enter the (nonrandom) sales price for year 1 in cell B32 with the formula

$$=B21$$

Then generate the sales price for year 2 in cell C32 with the formula

$$=B32*C28$$

and copy this across to the rest of row 32.

7   **Production costs.** The production cost for any year is the production quantity multiplied by the variable production cost, so enter the formula

$$=B29*B31$$

in cell B34 and copy it to the rest of row 34. (Note that because the production quantity is in thousands of cars and variable production cost is in thousands of dollars, the resulting product will automatically be in millions of dollars.)

8   **Revenues.** The revenue in any year is calculated in one of two possible ways. If demand is greater than the production quantity, then revenue is the sales price multiplied by the production quantity. Otherwise, if demand is less than the production quantity, then revenue is the sales price multiplied by the demand, plus the discounted sales price multiplied by the number of cars left over. Therefore, calculate the revenue for year 1 in cell B35 with the formula

$$=IF(B29<B30,B32*B29,B32*(B30+(1-\$H\$24)*(B29-B30)))$$

and copy it to the rest of row 35.

9   **Fixed cost.** Generate the fixed cost of developing the car in cell B37 with the formula

$$=RISKNORMAL(B7,B8)*1000$$

Note that the factor of 1000 converts billions of dollars to millions.

10   **NPVs.** Calculate the NPV of all production costs (in millions of dollars) in cell B40 with the formula

$$=NPV(\$B\$23,B34:K34)$$

Then copy this to cell B41 to calculate the NPV of all revenues. Note that the NPV function takes two arguments: the interest rate used for discounting and a stream of cash flows beginning with the flow at the end of year 1.

11   **Total NPV.** Finally, calculate the total NPV in cell B43 with the formula

$$=B41-B37-B40$$

Because the fixed costs occur at the *beginning* of year 1, they are not discounted when calculating total NPV.

To form the analogous spreadsheet for model 2, we can copy this sheet to a new sheet (in the same workbook file) and change the inputs. Here is an easy way to do this. While holding down the Ctrl key, drag the sheet tab of the model 1 sheet to the right. This will create a copy of the original sheet. Then it is a good idea to name these two sheets Model 1 and Model 2. Finally, change the necessary inputs in the model 2 sheet.

Using @Risk   A single simulation can be used to simulate the quantities for each car model.[6] To track the total NPV for each model, select cell B43 from each sheet (separately) as an output cell. The simulated results from 500 iterations definitely favor model 2. The summary of results and simulation statistics shown in Figure 16.34 show that (1) model 2 has a much larger average NPV than model 1 ($684 million versus $481 million), (2) model 2 loses more money in its worst-case outcome than model 1 ($1.67 billion versus $1.34 billion), (3) model 2 has a much better best-case outcome ($3.58 billion versus $2.52 billion), and (4) model 2 has a slightly larger standard deviation of NPVs than model 1 ($870 million versus $611 million).

FIGURE 16.34   **Summary Statistics for GF Auto Example**

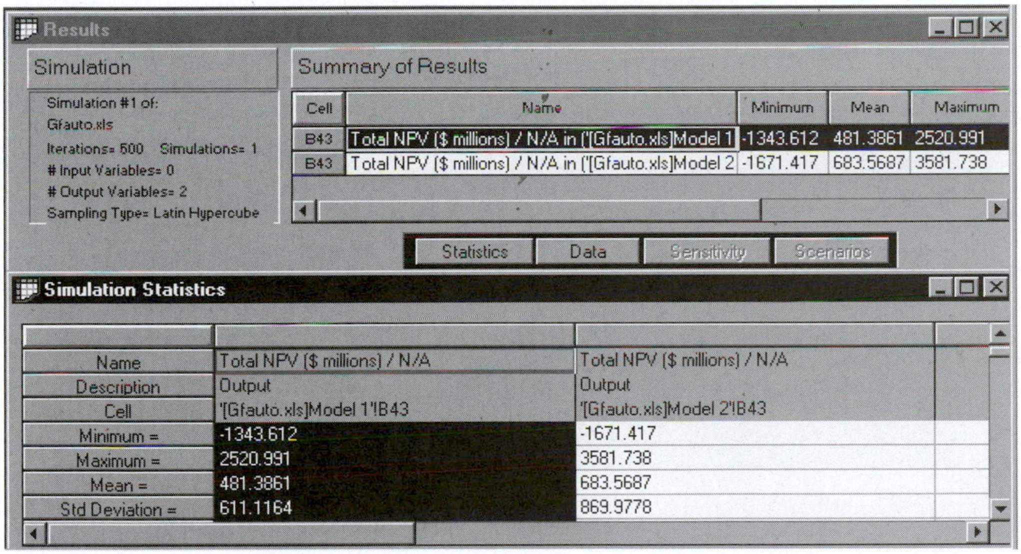

The target values shown in Figure 16.35 (page 930) illustrate model 2's dominance in a slightly different way. Here we entered target values of 0, 1000, 2000, and −1000 for each model. (A value of 1000, for example, corresponds to $1 billion.) The percentages show how many simulated NPVs are below each target value. Looking at the −1000 and 0 targets, we see that model 1 has slightly fewer really large losses and slightly fewer losses of any amount. However, looking at the 1000 and 2000 targets, we see that model 1 has many fewer large gains. In particular, there is less than a 1% chance that model 1 will earn more than $2 billion, whereas the corresponding percentage for model 2 is more than 7%.

[6]From here on, we will not give step-by-step instructions for using @RISK. Remember that it is basically a three-step process: (1) identify the output cell(s), (2) specify the simulation settings, and (3) run the simulation. The first two steps can be done in either order.

FIGURE 16.35   Target Values for GF Auto Example

	Simulation Statistics			
Name	Total NPV ($ millions) / N/A		Total NPV ($ millions) / N/A	
Description	Output		Output	
Cell	'[Gfauto.xls]Model 1'!B43		'[Gfauto.xls]Model 2'!B43	
Target #1 (Value)=	-1000		-1000	
Target #1 (Perc%)=	0.4923548%		1.145869%	
Target #2 (Value)=	0		0	
Target #2 (Perc%)=	22.43202%		23.12455%	
Target #3 (Value)=	1000		1000	
Target #3 (Perc%)=	79.04668%		62.1222%	
Target #4 (Value)=	2000		2000	
Target #4 (Perc%)=	99.21684%		92.48592%	

Finally, histograms for the two models appear in Figures 16.36 and 16.37. (For comparison, it is important to make the scales on the axes the same for each model. This is possible with @Risk's graphical options. We access these by right-clicking on a graph.) The two graphs don't appear to be too different. However, a close look reveals that model 1 has more chances for moderate losses, whereas model 2 has more chances for large gains.

FIGURE 16.36   Histogram of NPV for Model 1

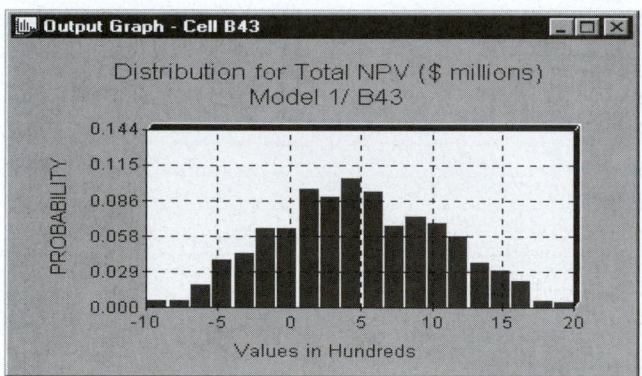

FIGURE 16.37   Histogram of NPV for Model 2

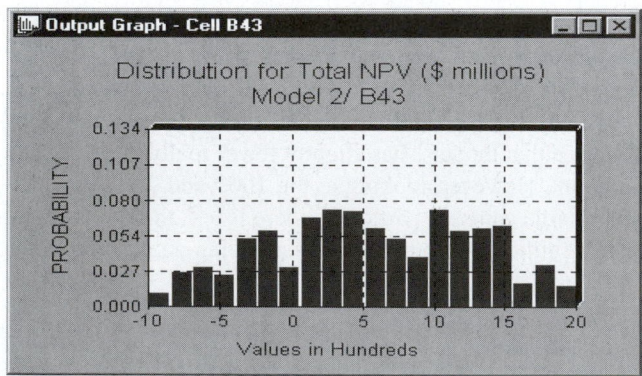

Modeling Issues

1   When we enter two sets of @Risk functions on separate sheets, as we did in this example, @Risk uses different random numbers for the two car models when it runs the simulation. This could give the edge to one model just by chance. That is, one model could obtain a larger mean NPV just because of a relatively lucky set of random numbers. This is one reason we used a larger number of iterations, 200, than before. The larger number of iterations should cancel out the effect of a few lucky or unlucky random numbers.

   In general, when we are performing a comparison among several strategies (two different models, five different ordering policies, and so on), it is better if we can use the same random numbers for each strategy. For example, if we had set up a single spreadsheet for both models and then used the same stream of inflation factors for both models' production and sales prices, this would have subjected both models to more identical conditions. Hence, it would have led to a fairer comparison. Sometimes this synchronization of random numbers is easy to accomplish; other times it is awkward or difficult. In any case, we can partially overcome any chance factor due to different streams of random numbers by running more iterations of the simulation.

2   To compare NPVs for models 1 and 2, we used the NPVs in cell B43 of the respective sheets as the output cells. Another approach would be to calculate the *difference* between these two NPVs in some cell and use the difference as the output cell. Then we could analyze the statistics or the graph of differences to see whether one model is generally favored over the other. A histogram of such differences (NPV for model 2 minus NPV for model 1) appears in Figure 16.38. Although many bars indicate a negative difference (model 1 beats model 2), many more indicate a positive difference.

FIGURE 16.38   **Histogram of Differences in GF Auto Example**

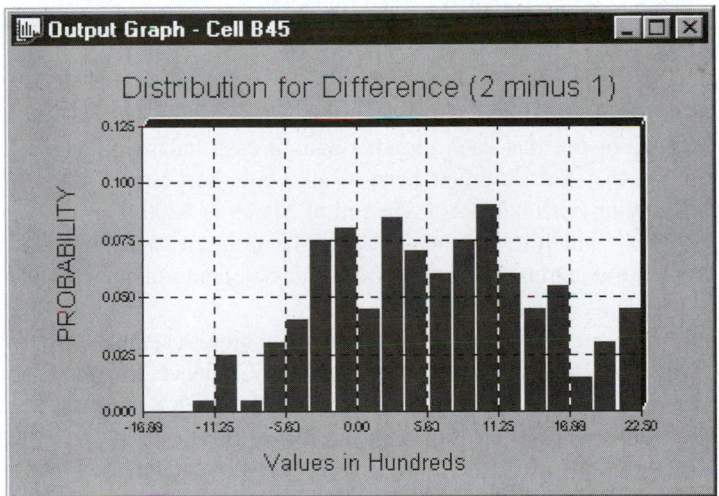

A Cash Balance Model

All companies track their cash balance through time. As specific payments come due, companies may need to take out short-term loans to keep a minimal cash balance. The following example illustrates one such application.

EXAMPLE 16.6

The Entson Company believes that its monthly sales during the period from November 1997 to July 1998 are normally distributed with the means and standard deviations given in Table 16.2. Each month Entson incurs fixed costs of $250,000. In March taxes of $150,000 and in June taxes of $50,000 must be paid. Dividends of $50,000 must also be paid in June. Entson estimates that its receipts in a given month are a weighted sum of sales from the current month, the previous month, and two months ago with weights 0.2, 0.6, and 0.2. In symbols, if R_t and S_t represent receipts and sales in month t, then

$$R_t = 0.2S_{t-2} + 0.6S_{t-1} + 0.2S_t$$

The materials and labor needed to produce a month's sales must be purchased 1 month in advance, and the cost of these averages to 80% of the product's sales. For example, if sales in February are $1,500,000, then the February materials and labor costs are $1,200,000, but these must be paid in January.

TABLE 16.2 **Monthly Sales (in Thousands of Dollars) for Entson**

	Nov.	Dec.	Jan.	Feb.	Mar.	Apr.	May	Jun.	Jul.
Mean	1500	1600	1800	1500	1900	2600	2400	1900	1300
St.dev.	70	75	80	80	100	125	120	90	70

At the beginning of January 1998, Entson has $250,000 in cash. The company would like to ensure that each month's ending cash balance never dips below $250,000. This means that Entson might have to take out short-term (1-month) loans. For example, if the ending cash balance at the end of March is $200,000, Entson will take out a loan for $50,000, which it will then pay back (with interest) 1 month later. The interest rate on a short-term loan is 1% per month. At the beginning of each month, Entson earns interest of 0.5% on its cash balance.

The company would like to use simulation to estimate the maximum loan it will need to take out to meet its desired minimum cash balance. It would also like to see how sensitive the results are to the sales data, shown in Table 16.2. In particular, considering the data in this table as a "base case," it would like to run a simulation in which the means are 20% below the values in the table and another simulation in which the means are 20% above those in the table.

Solution

There is a considerable amount of bookkeeping in this simulation, so it is a good idea to list the events in chronological order that occur each month.

- Beginning cash balance is observed.

- Interest on its beginning cash balance is received.
- Receipts arrive and expenses are paid (including payback of the previous month's loan, if any, with interest).
- Short-term loan is taken out, if necessary.
- Final cash balance is observed, which becomes next month's beginning cash balance.

Developing the Spreadsheet Model The completed spreadsheet appears in Figures 16.39 and 16.40. (See the file CASH.XLS.) It requires the following steps.

FIGURE 16.39 **Inputs for Entson Cash Balance Example**

	A	B	C	D	E	F	G	H	I	J	K
1	Entson Cash Balance Simulation										
2											
3	Input section (all values are in thousands of dollars)										
4	Monthly sales (normal distributions)										
5		Nov	Dec	Jan	Feb	Mar	Apr	May	Jun	Jul	
6	Mean	1500	1600	1800	1500	1900	2600	2400	1900	1300	
7	St Dev	70	75	80	80	100	125	120	90	70	
8											
9	Monthly fixed cost			250	250	250	250	250	250		
10											
11	Tax, dividend expenses			0	0	150	0	0	100		
12											
13	Receipts in any month are of form: A*(sales from 2 months ago)+B*(previous month's sales)+C*(current month's sales), where:										
14		A	B	C							
15		0.2	0.6	0.2							
16											
17	Cost of materials and labor for next month, spent this month, is a percentage of product's sales from next month, where the percentage is:										
18		0.8									
19											
20	Initial cash in Jan	250									
21	Min cash balance	250									
22											
23	Monthly interest rates										
24	Loan interest rate	0.01									
25	Interest rate on cash	0.005									
26											
27	Base level of sales	0.8									

FIGURE 16.40 **Simulation for Entson Cash Balance Example**

	A	B	C	D	E	F	G	H	I	J
29	Simulation section									
30		Nov	Dec	Jan	Feb	Mar	Apr	May	Jun	Jul
31	Actual sales	1200	1280	1440	1200	1520	2080	1920	1520	1040
32										
33	Beginning cash balance			250	337.25	250	250	250	250	
34	Interest on cash balance			1.25	1.69	1.25	1.25	1.25	1.25	
35	Receipts			1296	1360	1312	1568	1936	1872	
36	Fixed costs			250	250	250	250	250	250	
37	Tax, dividend expenses			0	0	150	0	0	100	
38	Material, labor expenses			960	1216	1664	1536	1216	832	
39	Close out previous loan			0	0	17.23	775.66	1002.34	536.40	
40	Cash balance before loan			337.25	232.94	-517.98	-742.41	-281.09	404.85	
41	Loan amount (if any)			0	17.06	767.98	992.41	531.09	0	
42	Final cash balance			337.25	250	250	250	250	404.85	
43										
44	Maximum loan	992.41								

1   **Inputs.** Enter the inputs through row 25. Note that we are going to simulate loans only for the period from January to June. However, we need sales figures in November and December to generate receipts for January and February. Also, we need July sales to generate the material and labor costs paid in June.

2   **Scenarios.** Enter the formula

$$=RISKSIMTABLE(\{.8,1,1.2\})$$

in cell B27. This allows us to run three simulations simultaneously. The middle value, 1, corresponds to the base case. The other two values, .8 and 1.2, correspond to the scenarios in which mean sales are 20% below and 20% above the base case.

3   **Actual sales.** Generate the sales in row 31 by entering the formula

$$=RISKNORMAL(\$B\$27*B6,B7)$$

in cell B31 and copying it to the range C31:J31.

4   **Beginning cash balance.** For January 1998 enter the cash balance with the formula

$$=B20$$

in cell D33. Then for the other months enter the formula

$$=D42$$

in cell E33 and copy it across row 33.

5   **Incomes.** Entson's incomes (interest on cash balance and receipts) are calculated in rows 34 and 35. To calculate these, enter the formulas

$$=D33*\$B\$25$$

and

$$=SUMPRODUCT(\$B\$15:\$D\$15,B31:D31)$$

in cells D34 and D35 and copy them across rows 34 and 35. The latter formula multiplies the fixed weights in row 15 by the relevant sales and adds these products to obtain receipts.

6   **Expenses.** Entson's expenses (fixed costs, taxes and dividends, material and labor costs, and payback of the previous month's loan) are calculated in rows 36–39. Calculate these by entering the formulas

$$=D9$$

$$=D11$$

$$=\$B\$18*E31$$

and

$$=C41*(1+\$B\$24)$$

in cells D36, D37, D38, and D39 and copying these across rows 36–39. (For the loan payback, we are assuming that no loan payback is due in January.)

7   **Cash balance before loan.** Calculate the cash balance before the loan (if any) by entering the formula

$$=SUM(D33:D35)-SUM(D36:D39)$$

in cell D40 and copying it across row 40.

8 Amount of loan. If the value in row 40 is below the minimum cash balance ($250,000), Entson must borrow enough to bring the cash balance up to this minimum. Otherwise, no loan is necessary. Therefore, enter the formula

$$=MAX(\$B\$21-D40,0)$$

in cell D41 and copy it across row 41.

9 Final cash balance. Calculate the final cash balance by entering the formula

$$=SUM(D40:D41)$$

in cell D42 and copying it across row 42.

10 Maximum loan. Calculate the maximum loan from January to June in cell B44 with the formula

$$=MAX(D41:I41)$$

Using @Risk To use @Risk, specify cells B44 and the range D41:I41 as output cells. The latter allows us to see how the loan amounts vary over time. For the settings use 500 iterations and 3 as the number of simulations (one for the base case and one for each of the other two scenarios). The results appear numerically in Figures 16.41 and 16.42 (page 936). The data in Figure 16.41 indicate that for the base case (simulation #2) the maximum loan varied considerably, from a low of $512,247 to a high of $1,401,895. The average was $952,319. The data in Figure 16.42 complement these figures by providing the medians and 5th and 95th percentiles of the maximum loan distribution for each of the scenarios. As you might expect, as sales increase (from the 20%-below scenario to the base case to the 20%-above scenario), the maximum loan tends to decrease. This is due to the increasing receipts that dominate the increasing material and labor costs.

Figures 16.43 and 16.44 illustrate the simulation results graphically. The histogram in Figure 16.43 supports the numerical data in Figure 16.41. The time series graph (using the Summary graph on the D41:I41 output cell range) in Figure 16.44 shows the sequence of loan amounts from January to June. Evidently, the extra tax payment in March typically results in large loans in both March and April.

FIGURE 16.41 **Summary Statistics for Cash Balance Example**

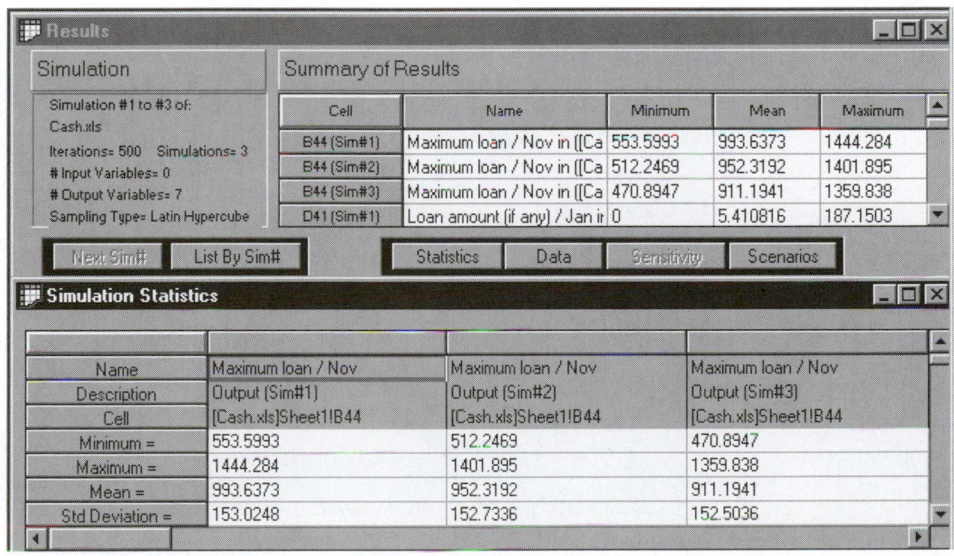

FIGURE 16.42 Target Percentiles for Cash Balance Example

Simulation Statistics

Name	Maximum loan / Nov	Maximum loan / Nov	Maximum loan / Nov
Description	Output (Sim#1)	Output (Sim#2)	Output (Sim#3)
Cell	[Cash.xls]Sheet1!B44	[Cash.xls]Sheet1!B44	[Cash.xls]Sheet1!B44
Target #1 (Value)=	749.66455078125	708.312255859375	671.903930664063
Target #1 (Perc%)=	5%	5%	5%
Target #2 (Value)=	991.59814453125	949.6376953125	909.47119140625
Target #2 (Perc%)=	50%	50%	50%
Target #3 (Value)=	1263.53930664063	1221.75158691406	1180.39916992188
Target #3 (Perc%)=	95%	95%	95%

FIGURE 16.43 Histogram of Maximum Loan in Cash Balance Example

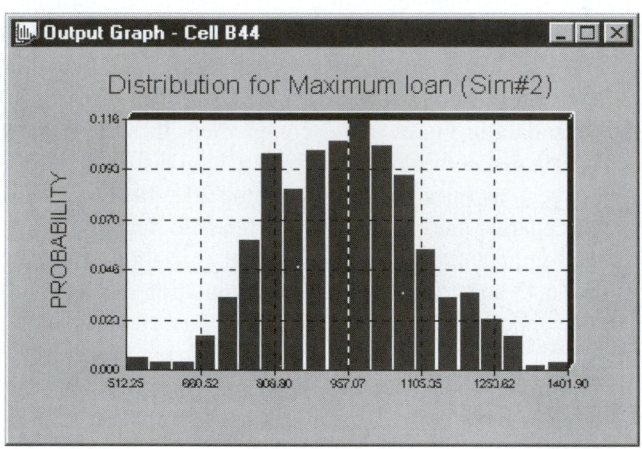

FIGURE 16.44 Time Series of Loan Amounts in Cash Balance Example

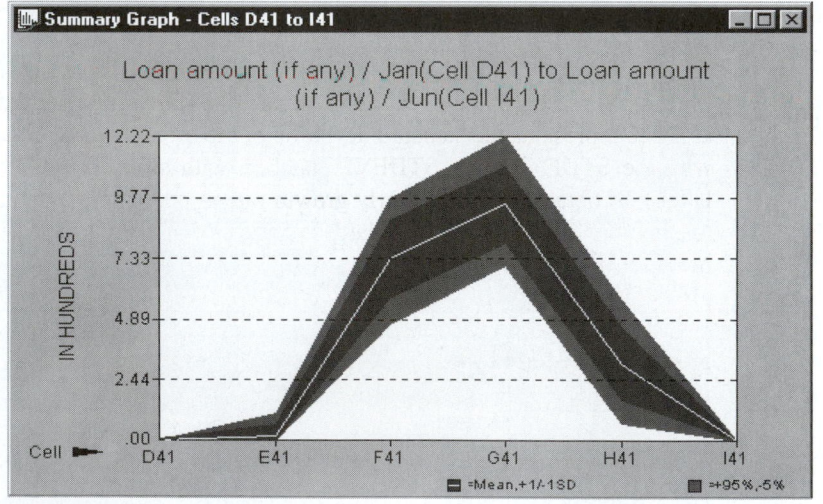

Simulating Stock Prices and Options

I n this section we illustrate how @Risk can be used to simulate stock prices. Then we show how to analyze derivative securities such as call options with @Risk.

16.8.1 Modeling the Price of a Stock

An enormous amount of research has been devoted to discovering the way stock prices change. Although there is not complete agreement on the best model of stock price changes, one popular model states that price changes follow a lognormal distribution. Essentially, this means that the logarithm of a stock's price at any time is a normally distributed random variable. Specifically, the stock price p_t at any time t in the future is related to the current price p_0 by the formula

$$p_t = p_0 \exp[(\mu - .5\sigma^2)t + \sigma Z \sqrt{t}] \qquad \textbf{(16.1)}$$

Here, μ is the mean percentage growth rate of the stock, σ is the standard deviation of the growth rate, Z is a normal random variable with mean 0 and standard deviation 1, and exp is the exponential function (it means to raise the special number $e \simeq 2.718$ to a power and can be implemented in Excel with the EXP function). Both μ and σ are expressed as decimals, such as $\mu = 0.06$ for a 6% mean growth rate, and all quantities are measured with respect to a common unit of time, such as a year.

The spreadsheet in Figure 16.45 (page 938) illustrates how to estimate the parameters μ and σ in equation (16.1) from monthly returns. (See the file STOCKRET.XLS.) We first enter the observed closing prices of the stock in column B. The corresponding monthly returns (percentage changes) are calculated in column C. For example, the formula in cell C6 is

=(B6-B5)/B5

The return of -0.012 corresponds to a decrease of 1.2%. We then add 1 to each return in column C to obtain column D, and we take the natural logarithms of the numbers in column D to obtain column E. For example, the formula in cell E6 is

=LN(D6)

The average of the numbers in column E, obtained in cell E19 with the AVERAGE function, represents the monthly growth rate. Similarly, the standard deviation calculated in cell E20 represents the standard deviation of the monthly growth rate. (It can be calculated with the STDEV or the STDEVP function with slightly different results; we used the latter.) To obtain the mean yearly growth rate in cell E22, we multiply the monthly mean rate by 12. To obtain the standard deviation of the yearly growth rate in cell E23, we multiply the monthly standard deviation by $\sqrt{12}$. Thus, our estimate of the mean yearly growth rate of the stock price is 7.33%. The standard deviation of the growth rate is 9.99%.

Now that we know how analysts find the mean and standard deviation of a stock's growth rate, we use equation (16.1) and simulation to value certain derivative securities.[7]

---

[7]Derivative securities get their name because their value is derived from the value of an underlying security such as a stock. There are many types of derivative securities available in the market; we will discuss only some of the simplest ones.

FIGURE 16.45 Estimating Mean and Standard Deviation of Stock Returns

	A	B	C	D	E
1	Estimating Mean and Standard Deviation of Stock Returns				
2					
3	Historical data				
4	Month	Closing	Return	1+Return	Ln(1+Return)
5	0	$25.00			
6	1	$24.70	-0.01200	0.98800	-0.01207
7	2	$23.70	-0.04049	0.95951	-0.04133
8	3	$22.90	-0.03376	0.96624	-0.03434
9	4	$22.81	-0.00393	0.99607	-0.00394
10	5	$22.89	0.00351	1.00351	0.00350
11	6	$22.56	-0.01442	0.98558	-0.01452
12	7	$23.94	0.06117	1.06117	0.05937
13	8	$24.37	0.01796	1.01796	0.01780
14	9	$24.99	0.02544	1.02544	0.02512
15	10	$26.09	0.04402	1.04402	0.04308
16	11	$26.14	0.00192	1.00192	0.00191
17	12	$26.90	0.02907	1.02907	0.02866
18					
19	Monthly values			Mean	0.61%
20				StDev	2.88%
21					
22	Annual values			Mean	7.33%
23				StDev	9.99%

16.8.2 Valuing a European Call Option

A **European option** on a stock gives the owner of the option the right to buy (if the option is a **call** option) or sell (if the option is a **put** option) one share of a stock on a particular date for a particular price. The price at which an option holder can buy or sell the stock is called the **exercise price** of the option. The date on which the option must be used (or "exercised") is called the **expiration date**.

For example, suppose a stock is currently selling for $50 and you purchase a call option with an exercise price of $56 and a 3-month expiration date. What will you earn from this option? If T represents the expiration date and p_T represents the price of the stock at time T, you will earn $0 if $p_T \leq 56$, and you will earn $(p_T - 56)$ dollars if $p_T > 56$.

Here is the reasoning. If $p_T \leq 56$, you have the option, if you want to use it, of buying a share of stock for *less* than it is worth. This would be disadvantageous, so you would let your option expire—without ever using it. In this case, we say that you're "out of the money." On the other hand, if $p_T > 56$, you can buy a share at the option price of $56, sell it for the current price of p_T, and thereby make a profit of $p_T - 56$ dollars. In this case we say that you're "in the money."

We've left one thing out, however. You must pay for the option in the first place. The question is, what is a fair price for such an option? Because option trading is a multibillion-dollar business, this is an important question! Black and Scholes (1973) were the first to derive a formula for pricing options. Cox et al. (1979) derived a different but equivalent method for pricing options. We will use their model below. It states that the price of an option must be the expected discounted value of the cash flows from an option on a stock having the same standard deviation as the stock on which the option is written and growing at the *risk-free* rate of interest. Here, discounting is done continuously at the risk-free rate. One surprising implication of this result is that the price of the option does *not* depend on the mean growth rate of the stock itself, only on the risk-free rate and the standard deviation of the growth rate of the stock.

In the following example we will use @Risk to estimate the price of a European option.

EXAMPLE 16.7

A share of AnTech stock currently sells for $42. A European call option with an expiration date of 6 months and an exercise price of $40 is available. The stock has an annual standard deviation of 20%. The stock price has tended to increase at a mean rate of 15% per year. The risk-free rate is 10% per year. What is a fair price for this option?

Solution

According to the result of Cox et al. (1979), we need to know the mean of the cash flow from this option, discounted to the present time (time 0), assuming that the stock price increases at the risk-free rate. Therefore, we will simulate many 6-month periods, each time finding the discounted cash flow of the option. The average of these discounted cash flows represents an estimate of the true mean; that is, it estimates the fair price of the option.

Developing the Spreadsheet Model   The spreadsheet model is quite simple, as shown in Figure 16.46. (See the file ANTECH1.XLS.) It can be formed as follows.

1   **Inputs.** Enter the inputs in the range B4:B9. Note that the expiration date is expressed in years. Also, note that we enter the mean growth rate of the stock in cell B6. However, as we discussed above, this value is not used in the model.

FIGURE 16.46   **Spreadsheet Model for AnTech Call Option Example**

	A	B
1	**AnTech Call Option Example**	
2		
3	**Input section**	
4	Current stock price	$42
5	Exercise price	$40
6	Mean annual return	15%
7	StDev of annual return	20%
8	Risk-free rate	10%
9	Option duration (years)	0.5
10		
11	**Simulation section**	
12	Stock price in 6 months (growing at risk-free rate)	$43.714
13	Option cash flow at termination	$3.714
14	Discounted value of option	$3.533

2. **Simulated stock price at expiration date.** Using equation (16.1) with μ equal to the *risk-free* rate, simulate the stock price in 6 months by entering the formula

$$=B4*EXP((B8-.5*B7^2)*B9+B7*RISKNORMAL(0,1)*SQRT(B9))$$

in cell B12.

3. **Cash flow from option.** Calculate the cash flow from the option by entering the formula

$$=MAX(B12-B5,0)$$

in cell B13. This says that if the value in cell B12 is greater than the value in cell B5, we make the difference; otherwise, we make nothing.

4. **Discount the cash flow.** Discount the cash flow in cell B14 with the formula

$$=EXP(-B8*B9)*B13$$

This represents the net present value of the cash flow (if any) realized at the expiration date.

Using @Risk To run @Risk we choose cell B14 as the only output cell, set the number of iterations to 1000, and set the number of simulations to 1. The most important outputs are shown in Figure 16.47. Recall that we are interested in the theoretical mean of the discounted value in cell B14. An estimate of this mean is the average of the 1000 simulated values, namely 4.7584. How accurate is this estimate? We can find an approximate 95% confidence for the true mean by adding and subtracting twice the standard error of the mean, where the standard error is the reported standard deviation (4.957) divided by the square root of the number of iterations. The resulting confidence interval extends approximately from 4.44 to 5.07. Actually, the simulated average is very close to the true price of the option, $4.76, as calculated by financial analysts.

FIGURE 16.47 **Summary Statistics for Valuing Call Option Example**

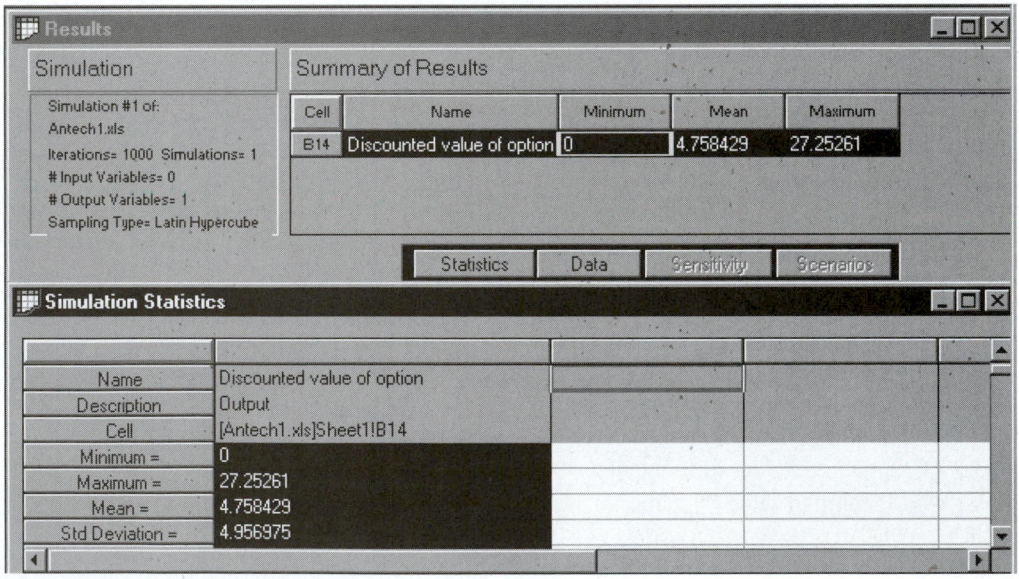

16.8.3 Simulating a Portfolio of the Stock and an Option on the Stock

We now extend this option example. Suppose the investor buys one share of AnTech stock at the current price and an option on this stock, as described in the example, for $4.76. We will use simulation to find the return on the investor's portfolio as of the expiration date. The spreadsheet model appears in Figure 16.48. (See the file ANTECH2.XLS.) Through row 13, it is similar to the spreadsheet in Figure 16.46, so we will describe only the differences.

FIGURE 16.48 **Spreadsheet Model for AnTech Portfolio Example**

	A	B
1	AnTech Portfolio Example	
2		
3	**Input section**	
4	Current stock price	$42
5	Exercise price	$40
6	Mean annual return	15%
7	StDev of annual return	20%
8	Risk-free rate	10%
9	Option duration (years)	0.5
10		
11	**Simulation section**	
12	Stock price in 6 months (growing at stock's rate)	$44.821
13	Option cash flow at termination	$4.821
14		
15	Ending value of portfolio	$49.641
16	Initial cost	$46.76
17	Return from portfolio	6.162%

1 **Simulate stock price at expiration.** In cell B12 we now simulate the stock price when it grows at its *own* growth rate, not the risk-free rate. (The risk-free rate was used only to price the option according to the rule of Cox et al. Now we want to simulate the stock's *actual* price in 6 months.) Therefore, change the formula in cell B12 to

$$=B4*EXP((B6-.5*B7\char94 2)*B9+B7*RISKNORMAL(0,1)*SQRT(B9))$$

2 **Return from portfolio.** The formula in cell B13 is the same as before. However, we don't need the discounted value in cell B14 any longer. Instead, we need the ending value of the portfolio, the cost of the portfolio, and the portfolio's return in the range B15:B17. These can be calculated by entering the formulas

$$=SUM(B12:B13)$$

$$=B4+4.76$$

and

$$=(B15-B16)/B16$$

in cells B15, B16, and B17. The value in cell B17 represents the percentage by which our initial investment has increased.

We again ran 1000 iterations with @Risk, keeping track of the single output cell B17. The outputs are summarized numerically in Figure 16.49 (page 942) and graphically in Figure 16.50. These show the considerable variability in the portfolio's return. Although

FIGURE 16.49 Summary Statistics for Portfolio Example

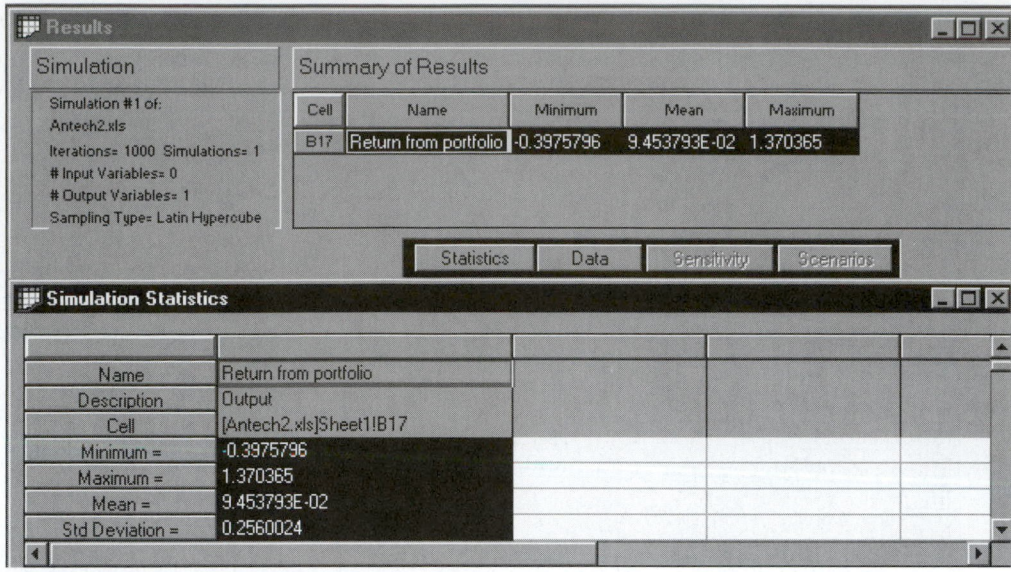

FIGURE 16.50 Histogram for Portfolio Example

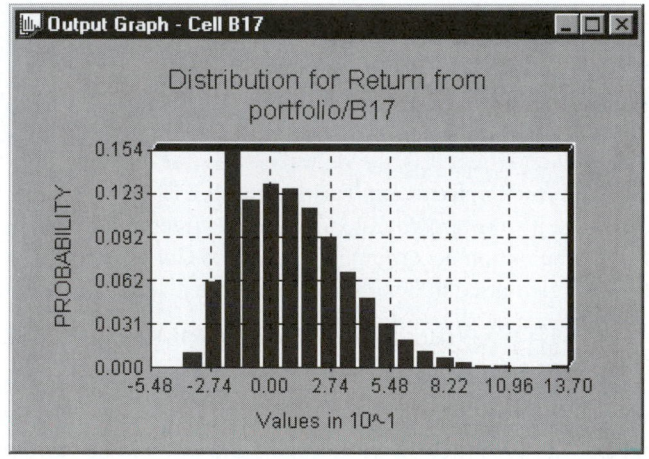

the average return was .094 (a 9.4% gain), the simulated returns varied from a worst-case 40% loss to a best-case 137% gain. Derivative securities are notorious for their variability; this output illustrates why. The best that can be said is that in Figure 16.50, there appears to be more potential for large gains than for large losses.

Modeling Issue If you have any intuition for financial portfolios, you might have noticed that this investor is "putting all her eggs in one basket." If the stock price increases, she gains by owning the share of stock and she also gains from holding the option (since she is more likely to be in the money). However, if the price of the stock decreases, she loses money on her share of stock and her option is worthless. A safer strategy is to **hedge** the bets. She can purchase one share of the stock and purchase a *put* option on the stock. A put option allows her to *sell* a share of stock for the exercise price at the expiration date. With a put option, the investor hopes the stock price will decrease because she can then sell a share at the exercise price and immediately buy it back at the decreased stock price, thus earning a profit. Therefore, a portfolio consisting of a share of stock and a put option on the stock covers the investor in both directions. It has less upside potential, but it decreases the downside risk.

16.8.4 Valuing a More Exotic Call Option

The European call option is rather simple. There are a variety of other derivative securities currently available. In fact, their variety and complexity are what make them attractive—and dangerous!—for the unsuspecting investor. Here we will examine one variation of the basic call option. It is called an **Asian** option. Its payoff depends, not on the price at expiration of the underlying stock, but on the *average* price of the stock over the lifetime of the option. That is, if the exercise price of the option is p_e and the average price of the stock over the lifetime of the option is p_{avg}, then the payoff at the expiration date from the option is the larger of $p_{avg} - p_e$ and 0.

To price an Asian option (or any number of other exotic options), we again need to find the expected discounted value of the payoff from the option, assuming that the stock grows at the risk-free rate. The following example illustrates how to approximate this expected value with simulation.

EXAMPLE 16.8

Consider a stock currently priced at $100 per share. Its mean annual return is 15% and the standard deviation of its annual return is 30%. What is the value of an Asian option that expires in 52 weeks (1 year) with an exercise price of $100? Assume that the risk-free rate is 9%.

Solution

To value this option we will base p_{avg} on the averages of the weekly (simulated) stock prices, assuming that the stock price grows at the risk-free rate. This requires us to generate weekly stock prices from equation (16.1). The key is to interpret p_0 and p_t correctly in equation (16.1). To generate any week's price from the previous week's price, we must identify p_0 with the previous week's price and p_t with the current week's price.

The spreadsheet model appears in Figure 16.51 on page 944. (See the file ASIAN.XLS.) It can be formed as follows.

1 **Inputs.** Enter the inputs in the range B4:B9. (As in the valuation of the European call option, we enter the mean growth rate of the stock in cell B6 even though it won't be used in the simulation.)

2 **Weekly prices.** Enter the initial price (week 0) in cell E5 with the formula

$$=B4$$

Then to generate each weekly price from the previous one, enter the formula

=E5*EXP(($B$8-.5*$B$7^2)*(1/52)+$B$7*RISKNORMAL(0,1)*SQRT(1/52))

in cell E6 and copy it to the range E7:E57. Note that the unit of time is always 1 week (1/52 of a year).

FIGURE 16.51 **Spreadsheet Model for Asian Call Option Example**

	A	B	C	D	E	F	G
1	Asian Call Option Example						
2							
3	Input section			Weekly prices (growing at risk-free rate)			
4	Current stock price	$100		Week	Simulated price		
5	Exercise price	$110		0	$100.00		
6	Mean annual return	15%		1	$100.09		
7	StDev of annual return	30%		2	$100.17		
8	Risk-free rate	9%		3	$100.26		
9	Option duration (years)	1		4	$100.35		
10				5	$100.43		
11	Simulation section			6	$100.52		
12	Average of weekly prices	$102.284		7	$100.61		
13	Option cash flow at termination	$0.000		8	$100.69		
14	Discounted value of option	$0.000		9	$100.78		
15				10	$100.87		
16				11	$100.96		
51				46	$104.06		
52				47	$104.15		
53				48	$104.24		
54				49	$104.33		
55				50	$104.42		
56				51	$104.51		
57				52	$104.60		

3 **Discounted value of option.** Enter the formulas

$$=AVERAGE(E5:E57)$$

$$=MAX(B12-B5,0)$$

and

$$=EXP(-B8*B9)*B13$$

in cells B12, B13, and B14. These are exactly like in the European call option example, except that the payoff in cell B13 is based on the average in cell B12, not on the ending price of the stock.

Using cell B14 as the single output cell, we obtain the summary results in Figure 16.52. It indicates that a good estimate of the value of the option is $4.76, the average value in cell B14 over the 1000 iterations. By going out two standard errors on either side of this estimate, we see that the interval from $4.14 to $5.37 is an approximate 95% confidence interval for the true mean of the distribution—that is, for the value at which the option should be priced. (The actual market price of this particular option turns out to be $4.68.) ∎

PROBLEMS

Level A

18 The current price of HAL computer stock is $280. Its closing price during each of the next 12 months is given in the file P16_18.XLS. Use these data to estimate the annual mean and standard deviation of the return on HAL stock.

19 We are trying to determine the proper capacity level for a new electric car. A unit of capacity gives us the potential to produce one car per year. It costs $10,000 to build a unit of capacity

FIGURE 16.52 **Summary Statistics for Asian Option Example**

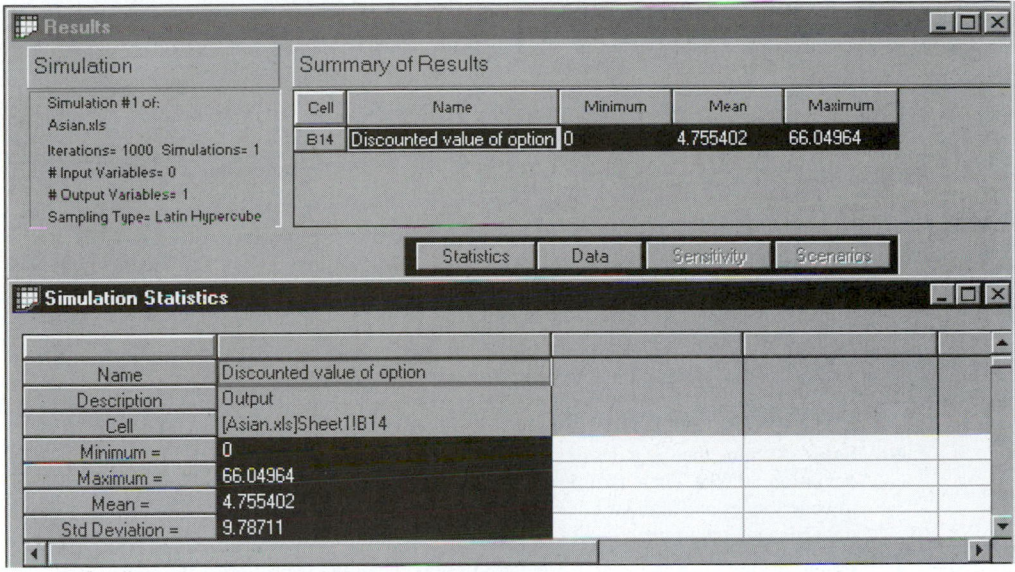

and the cost is charged equally over the next 5 years. It also costs $400 per year to maintain a unit of capacity (whether or not it is used). Each car sells for $14,000 and incurs a variable production cost of $10,000. The annual demand for the electric car during each of the next 5 years is believed to be normally distributed with mean 500,000 and standard deviation 100,000. The demands during different years are assumed to be independent. Profits are discounted at a 10% annual interest rate. We are working with a 5-year planning horizon. Capacity levels of 300,000, 400,000, 500,000, 600,000 and 700,000 are under consideration.

a Assuming we are risk neutral, use simulation to find the optimal capacity level.

b Using the answer to part **a,** we can be 95% certain that the expected discounted 5-year profit is between what two values?

c Using the answer to part **a,** there is a 5% chance that the *actual* discounted profit will exceed what value?

d Using the answer to part **a,** there is a 5% chance that the *actual* discounted profit will be less than what value?

e If we are risk averse, how might the optimal capacity level change?

20 Irwin & Sons is a large brokerage house that does a lot of computerized trading in the stock market. For this problem we'll focus on one particular stock, ABC, that Irwin trades. It follows a "buy low, sell high" strategy, implemented as follows. At the end of any trading day, if the ABC price/share is at least 1% above its ending price from the previous day, Irwin will sell 5% of its ABC shares (rounded to the nearest share). Similarly, if the price/share is at least 1% below its ending price from the previous day, Irwin will add 5% to its portfolio of ABC shares (again rounded to the nearest share). The file P16_20.XLS indicates these trading parameters, as well as the "random walk" model of how ABC's price/share changes from day to day. Although this random walk model of stock prices (which is actually used on Wall Street) is rather complex, you can treat it is a "black box" for all practical purposes and essentially enter the formula described in row 10 in the appropriate cells to simulate ending prices. The positive MPGR implies that the stock price is slowly drifting upward over time, and the fairly large SDGR implies that there are typically a lot of ups and downs in daily closing prices over time. We assume that Irwin starts with 1000 shares of ABC stock in its portfolio, and that the beginning ABC price/share (at the end of day 0) is $50.

a Simulate one sequence of 50 trading days in the range B36:F85. Actually, all you need to do is fill in row 36 and then copy it down.

b Create a time series plot of the shares owned throughout the 50-day trading period and place it on a separate chart sheet called SharesOwned. (This chart should react to new random numbers each time you press the F9 key.)

c Calculate the summary measures requested for this 50-day trading period in the range B88:B92.

d Create a data table to replicate these summary measures 10 times (or more, if you like) in the range B97:F107.

e Using the data in the data table, find the best- and worst-case values requested in cells B110 and B111.

21 Recall from the GF Auto example (Example 16.5) that the company's ordering policy is determined by the factor k, the number of standard deviations above the mean for the production quantity. Rerun the simulation using several different values of k. Is the total NPV very sensitive to this parameter? Which value of k would you recommend that GF Auto use?

22 Dord Motors is considering whether to introduce a new model called the Racer. The profitability of the Racer will depend on the following factors:

■ **Fixed cost of developing the Racer.** The fixed cost is equally likely to be $3 or $5 billion.

■ **Sales.** Assume that year 1 sales is normally distributed with mean 200,000 and standard deviation 50,000. Then assume that year 2 sales is normally distributed with mean equal to year 1 sales and standard deviation 50,000 and that year 3 sales is normally distributed with mean equal to year 2 sales and standard deviation 50,000.

■ **Price.** Assume that the year 1 price is $13,000. Then the year 2 price will be

$$1.05[\text{year 1 price} + 30(\% \text{ diff1})]$$

where % diff1 is the percentage by which actual year 1 sales differ from expected year 1 sales. The 1.05 factor accounts for inflation. For example, if the year 1 sales figure is 180,000, which is 10% below the expected year 1 sales, then the year 2 price will be

$$1.05[13,000 + 30(-10)] = \$13,335$$

Similarly, the year 3 price will be

$$1.05[\text{year 2 price} + 30(\% \text{ diff2})]$$

where % diff2 is the percentage by which actual year 2 sales differ from expected year 2 sales.

■ **Variable cost per car.** The variable cost is equally likely to be $5000, $6000, $7000, or $8000 during year 1 and is assumed to increase by 5% each year.

Your goal is to estimate the NPV of the new car during its first 3 years. Assume that cash flows are discounted at 10%; that is, $1 received now is equivalent to $1.10 received a year from now. Simulate 400 trials and estimate the mean NPV for the first 3 years of sales. Also determine a 95% confidence interval for the mean NPV of the Racer during its first 3 years of operation.

23 Use @Risk to solve the previous problem, but now assume that the fixed cost of developing the Racer is triangularly distributed with minimum, most likely, and maximum values $3, $4, and $5 billion. Also, assume that the variable cost per car in year 1 is triangularly distributed with minimum, most likely, and maximum values $5000, $7000, and $8000.

24 A stock currently sells for $100. The risk-free rate is 12% per year, and the stock's σ is 20%. By considering exercise prices of $90, $100, and $110, show how the value of a call option depends on the option's exercise price. Assume the duration of the option is 1 year.

Level B

25 You have been asked to simulate the cash inflows to a toy company for the next year. Monthly sales are independent random variables. Mean sales for the months January–March and October–December are $80,000, and mean sales for the months April–September are $120,000. The standard deviation for each month's sales is 20% of the month's mean sales. We model the method used to collect monthly sales revenue as follows:

■ During each month a certain fraction of new sales revenue will be collected. All new sales revenue not collected becomes 1 month overdue.

- During each month a certain fraction of 1-month overdue sales revenue is collected. The remainder becomes 2 months overdue.

- During each month a certain fraction of 2-month overdue sales revenue is collected.

- The remainder is written off as bad debt.

You are given the information in the file P16_25.XLS from several past months. Using this information, build a simulation model that generates the total cash inflow for each month. Develop a simple forecasting model and build the error of your forecasting model into the simulation. Assume that there are $120,000 of 1-month-old sales outstanding and $140,000 of 2-month-old sales outstanding at the beginning of January. From the simulation output, you are 95% sure that total cash inflow for the year will be between what two values?

26 Suppose that GM earns a $4000 profit each time a person buys a car. We want to determine how the expected profit earned from a customer depends on the quality of GM's cars. We assume a typical customer will purchase 10 cars during her lifetime. She will purchase a car now (year 1) and then purchase a car every 5 years—during year 6, year 11, and so on. For simplicity, we assume that Toyota is GM's only competitor. We also assume that if the consumer is satisfied with the car she purchases, she will buy her next car from the same company, but if she is not satisfied, she will buy her next car from the other company. Toyota produces cars that satisfy 80% of its customers. Currently, GM produces cars that also satisfy 80% of its customers. Consider a customer whose first car is a GM car. If profits are discounted at 10% annually, use simulation to estimate the value of this customer to GM. Also estimate the value of a customer to GM if it can raise its customer satisfaction rating to 85%; to 90%; to 95%.

27 Suppose an investor has the opportunity to buy the following contract (a stock call option) on March 1. The contract allows him to buy 100 shares of ABC stock at the end of March, April, or May at a guaranteed price of $50 per share. He can exercise this option at most once. For example, if he purchases the stock at the end of March, he cannot purchase more in April or May at the guaranteed price. The current price of the stock is $50. Each month, we assume the stock price either goes up by a dollar, with probability 0.6, or down by a dollar, with probability 0.4. If the investor buys the contract, he is hoping that the stock price will go up. The reasoning is that if he buys the contract, the price goes up to $51, and he buys the stock (that is, he exercises his option) for $50, he can then sell the stock for $51 and make a profit of $1 per share. Of course, if the stock price goes down, he doesn't have to exercise his option; he can just throw the contract away.

Assume that the stock price change each month is normally distributed with mean 0 and standard deviation 2. The investor uses the following strategy. At the end of March, he exercises the option only if the stock price is above $51.50. At the end of April, he exercises the option (assuming he hasn't exercised it yet) only if the price is above $50.75. At the end of May, he exercises the option (assuming he hasn't exercised it yet) only if the price is above $50.00. (This isn't necessarily his best strategy, but it's a reasonable one.) Simulate 250 replications of this strategy and answer the following.

a Estimate the probability that he will exercise his option.

b Estimate his net profit with this strategy. (This doesn't include the price of the contract.)

c Estimate the probability that he will net over $300.

d Estimate the worth of this contract to him.

28 You are considering a 10-year investment project. At present, the expected cash flow each year is $1000. Suppose, however, that each year's cash flow is normally distributed with mean equal to the *previous* year's actual cash flow and standard deviation $100. For example, if the year 1 cash flow is $1200, then the year 2 cash flow is normal with mean $1200 and standard deviation $100, and at the end of year 1, your best guess is that each later year's expected cash flow will be $1200.

a Estimate the expected NPV of this project. Assume that cash flows are discounted at a rate of 10% per year.

b Now assume that the project has an abandonment option. At the end of each year, you can abandon the project for the value given in the file P16_28.XLS. For example, suppose that year 1 cash flow is $400. Then at the end of year 1, you expect cash flow for each remaining year to be $400. This has an NPV of less than $6200, so you should abandon the project and collect $6200 at the end of year 1. Estimate the expected NPV of the project with the abandonment option. How much would you pay for the abandonment option? (*Hints*: You can abandon a project at most once. Thus in year 5, for example, you abandon only if the sum of future expected NPVs is less than the year 5 abandonment value and the project has not yet been abandoned. Also, once you abandon the project, the future cash flows after abandonment should disappear.)

29 Toys Unlimited is developing a new Madonna doll. The company has made the following assumptions:

- It is equally likely that the doll will sell for 2, 4, 6, 8, or 10 years.

- At the beginning of year 1, the potential market for the doll is 1 million. The potential market grows by an average of 5% per year. Toys Unlimited is 95% certain that the growth in the potential market during any year will be between 3% and 7%. It uses a normal distribution to model this.

- The company believes its share of the potential market during year 1 will be at worst 20%, most likely 40%, and at best 50%. It uses a triangular distribution to model this.

- The variable cost of producing a doll during year 1 is equally likely to be any value between $4 and $6. Use a uniform distribution to model this.

- Each year the sales price and variable cost of producing the doll will increase by 5%.

- The fixed cost of developing the doll (which is incurred right away, at time 0) is equally likely to be any value between $4 million and $12 million. Use a uniform distribution to model this.

- Right now there is one competitor in the market. During each year that begins with four or fewer competitors, there is a 20% chance that exactly one new competitor will enter the market.

- To determine year t sales (for $t > 1$), we proceed as follows. Suppose that at the end of year $t - 1$, x competitors are present. Then we assume that during year t, a fraction $0.9 - 0.1x$ of the company's loyal customers (last year's purchasers) will buy a doll during the next year, and a fraction $0.2 - 0.04x$ of people currently in the market who did not purchase a doll last year will purchase a doll from the company this year. We can now generate a prediction for year t sales. Of course, this prediction will not be exactly correct. We assume that it is sure to be accurate within 15%, however. (There are different ways to model this. You may choose any method that is reasonable.)

- Cash flows are discounted at 10% per year.

a Use @Risk to estimate the expected NPV of this project. Also, find a 95% confidence interval for this expected value.

b Use the percentiles in @Risk's output to find an interval such that you are 95% certain that the company's *actual* NPV will be within this interval.

c Explain the difference between the two intervals in parts **a** and **b**.

30 [Based on Benninga (1989)] You are the chief financial officer (CFO) for Carco, a small car rental company. You are trying to get some idea of what Carco's financial and income statements will look like during the current year (year 0) and the next 5 years. The following relationships hold.

- Current assets for each year are a "current assets factor" multiplied by the year's sales, where the current assets factors for different years are independent normal random variables with mean 0.15 and standard deviation 0.02.

- Each year, "fixed assets at cost" equals depreciation plus net fixed assets.

- Accumulated depreciation in year 0 equals $330. For year t ($t \geq 1$), the depreciation equals the accumulated depreciation in year $t - 1$ plus 10% of the fixed assets at cost for year $t - 1$.

- Net fixed assets for year t equals a "net fixed assets factor" multiplied by year t sales, where the net fixed assets factors for different years are independent normal random variables with mean 0.77 and standard deviation 0.04.

- Total assets each year equals net fixed assets plus current assets.

- Current liabilities each year equals a "current liabilities factor" multiplied by the year's sales, where the current liabilities factor for different years are independent normal random variables with mean 0.08 and standard deviation 0.01.

- Long-term debt for year 0 is $280.

- For $t \geq 1$, the long-term debt for year t is the year t debt-equity ratio multiplied by the sum of year t retained earnings and the year t stock. Carco wants to have the following debt-equity ratios in years 1 through 5: 0.48, 0.46, 0.44, 0.42, and 0.40.

- Stock in year 0 is $450. For $t \geq 1$, year t stock equals the sum of year $t - 1$ stock and year t new stock.

- Year 0 retained earnings equals $110. For $t \geq 1$, year t retained earnings is the sum of year $t - 1$ retained earnings and year t retention.

- Each year, total liabilities is the sum of current liabilities, long-term debt, stock, and retained earnings.

- The amount of new stock issued each year must be enough to make total assets equal to total liabilities.

- The interest rate on current debt is 10.5%, and the interest rate on new debt is 9.5%. During each of the next 5 years, 20% of the current $280 in long-term debt must be paid off. Then the *total* amount of new debt during year t is the year t long-term debt minus the amount of initial debt still remaining.

- The new debt for year t equals the *total* new debt for year t minus the *total* new debt for year $t - 1$.

- Year 0 sales equals $1000, and for $t \geq 1$, year t sales equals a "sales factor" multiplied by year $t - 1$ sales, where the sales factors for different years are independent normal random variables with mean 1.1 and standard deviation 0.05. (This does *not* mean that sales during successive years are independent.)

- Year t expense equals an "expense factor" multiplied by year t sales, where the expense factors for different years are independent normal random variables, with mean 0.80 and standard deviation 0.06.

- To calculate yearly interest payments, remember that interest is 10.5% on old debt and 9.5% on new debt.

- Depreciation for year 0 is $0, and for $t \geq 1$, year t depreciation is 10% of the year $t - 1$ fixed assets at cost.

- The before-tax profit each year is the sales minus the sum of expenses, interest payments, and depreciation.

- The tax rate is 47%.

- Dividends each year are 70% of after-tax profits.

- Retention each year is 30% of after-tax profits.

Set up a spreadsheet to model the current year (year 0) and next 5 years of Carco's financial future. Then simulate the firm's future 500 times. Use your output to answer the following questions.

a There is a 5% chance that total new debt will exceed what value?

b On average, total interest payments for the next 5 years will equal what value?

c What is the probability of profit being negative during year 5?

Note: Your spreadsheet is allowed to contain circular references. There are many of these. For example, stock purchased each year depends on long-term debt, and long-term debt depends on stock. To resolve the circular references use the Tools/Options menu item, click on the Calculations tab, check the Iterations box, and enter 20 as the Maximum Number of Iterations. This ensures that the spreadsheet will recalculate itself 20 times, which ensures that the values in the spreadsheet will converge to the correct values.

31 Estimates of Toyco's mean monthly sales for the months October 1997–March 1999 are shown in the file P16_31.XLS. Your goal is to model Toyco's 1997 cash budget given the following assumptions.

- At the beginning of each month, Toyco wants to have a cash balance of at least $20,000, and it will borrow sufficient funds to achieve this goal.

- All sales are for credit; 70% of all payments are collected in the first month after sale, 20% in the second month after sale, and 10% are collected in the third month after sale.

- Inventory at the beginning of each month should equal forecasted sales for the next 3 months.

- Merchandise purchased for sale incurs a cost equal to 75% of sales. On purchases made each month, 70% is paid in the first month after purchase and 30% is paid in the second month after purchase.

- Selling and administrative expenses incurred during a month equal $8500 + 0.09$Sales. These expenses are paid at a rate of 70% during the current month and 30% in the month following.

- If money must be borrowed, it is borrowed month-to-month at a monthly interest rate of 0.7%. Borrowing takes place in multiples of $1000. To model this situation use Excel's CEILING function. For example, CEILING(2500,1000)=3000. Note that you will need an IF statement because CEILING(-500,1000) is not defined. (See Excel's online help for more details about the CEILING function.)

- In February 1999, capital expenditures of $20,000 are incurred. In July and October, capital expenditures of $30,000 are incurred.

- Existing fixed assets are depreciated at $100 per month. Additional capital expenses are depreciated on a straight-line basis at a rate of 1% per month, beginning in the month after the capital expense is incurred.

- Sales for each month has standard deviation 15,000 about the forecasted sales.

a Use your model to predict profit for 1995. How high is profit likely to go? How low?

b To be sure of having enough money to borrow, how large a line of credit will you need for 1997?

c Suppose you could ensure that all accounts receivable would be collected in the month after sale and that beginning inventory for each month could be trimmed to 80% of the next 3 months' forecasted sales. How would this new scenario change your answers to parts **a** and **b**?

32 If you own a stock, buying a put option on the stock will greatly reduce your risk. This is the idea behind **portfolio insurance**. To illustrate, consider a stock (Trumpco) that currently sells for $56 and has $\sigma = 30\%$. Assume the risk-free rate is 8% and you estimate $\mu = 12\%$.

a You own one share of Trumpco. Use simulation to estimate the probability distribution of the percentage return earned on this stock during a 1-year period.

b Now suppose you also buy a put option (for $2.38) on Trumpco. The option has an exercise price of $50 and a 1-year expiration date. Use simulation to estimate the probability distribution of the percentage return on your portfolio over a 1-year period. Can you see why this strategy is called a portfolio insurance strategy?

c Use simulation to show that the put option in part **b** should indeed sell for $2.38.

33 For the data in the previous problem, the following is an example of a **butterfly spread**: Sell two call options with an exercise price of $50; buy one call option with an exercise price of $40 and one call option with an exercise price of $60. Simulate the cash flows from this portfolio.

34 Cryco stock currently sells for $69. The annual growth rate of the stock is 15%, and the stock's annual volatility, σ, is 35%. The risk-free rate is currently 5%. You have bought a 6-month European put option on this stock with an exercise price of $70.

a Use @Risk to value this put option.

b Use @Risk to analyze the distribution of percentage returns (for a 6-month horizon) for the following portfolios:

- Portfolio 1: Own one share of Cryco.
- Portfolio 2: Own one share of Cryco and buy the put described in part **a**.

Which portfolio has the larger expected return? Explain why portfolio 2 is known as portfolio insurance.

35 A "knockout" call option loses all value at the instant the price of the stock drops below a given "knockout level." Determine a fair price for a knockout call option in the following situation:

Current stock price: $20   Knockout price: $19.50
Exercise price: $21   Annual volatility: 40%
Risk-free rate: 10%   Mean growth rate of stock: 12%
Duration of option: 1 month = 21 days (assuming 250 days = 1 year)   ■

A Market Share Model

W e conclude this chapter with a rather complex model of market share behavior. The model is based on the type of competition faced by two dominant brands in an industry, such as Coca Cola and Pepsi. These companies continually attempt to gain market share from one another. However, there are also smaller companies that enter and exit the market. They might be able to gain market share from the giants or vice versa. The following example illustrates one possible model of such behavior. Even though it is reasonably complex, it could be made much more complex by including marketing initiatives (advertising and price cuts, for example) by any of the competitors.

EXAMPLE 16.9

Sweetness and IceT are the two dominant companies in the bottled iced tea market. Each currently possesses 49% of the total iced tea market, with three smaller companies splitting the remaining 2%. At the beginning of any year, a random number of new small companies enter the iced tea market. The actual number of new entries is assumed to be Poisson distributed with mean 1.[8] After the new entries enter the market, there is a random shift in market share among all competitors. Essentially, all competitors lose a random percentage of their market share to other competitors. We will assume that each of these percentages is triangularly distributed with the parameters given in Table 16.3. For example, the percentage of Sweetness's market share lost to IceT has a triangular distribution with minimum value 1%, most likely value 5%, and maximum value 10%. Similarly, the percentage of market share Sweetness will lose to *each* of the small companies has parameters 0.5%, 1%, and 3%. Therefore, the more small companies there are in the market, the more of its market share Sweetness will tend to lose to them.

At the end of each year, each of the small companies has a 50% chance of exiting the iced tea market. Each small company that exits will lose its market share to Sweetness or IceT. The percentage of this market share that goes to Sweetness is triangularly distributed with parameters 40%, 50%, and 60%; the rest goes to IceT. (For simplicity, we assume that none of this market share goes to the remaining small competitors.)

The dominant companies, Sweetness and IceT, want to use simulation to see how their market share is likely to change over the next 10 years.

TABLE 16.3 **Parameters of Lost Market Share Percentages**

	Minimum	Most Likely	Maximum
From Sweetness			
To IceT	1.0%	5%	10%
To each small company	0.5%	1%	3%
From IceT			
To Sweetness	1.0%	5%	10%
To each small company	0.5%	1%	3%
From small companies			
To Sweetness	5.0%	10%	15%
To IceT	5.0%	10%	15%

---

[8]The Poisson distribution is a frequently used discrete distribution. It is discussed briefly at the end of Chapter 5.

Solution

The spreadsheet model is somewhat tedious to develop, but the ideas are straightforward. At the beginning of any year, we observe the market shares of Sweetness, IceT, and the small companies (combined). Next, we simulate the number of new entrants. Then we simulate the shifts in market share during the year. Next, we simulate the number of small companies that exit at the end of the year, and we simulate their market shares that go to Sweetness or IceT. Finally, we tally the total market share at the end of the year for all competitors.

The completed spreadsheet model appears in Figures 16.53 and 16.54. (See the file ICETEA.XLS.) It can be formed with the following steps.

Developing the Spreadsheet Model

1   Inputs. Enter the inputs shown in Figure 16.53.

FIGURE 16.53   Inputs for Iced Tea Example

	A	B	C	D	E
1	**Iced tea market share simulation**				
2					
3	**Input section**				
4					
5	Current market shares of dominant companies				
6	Sweetness	0.49			
7	IceT	0.49			
8					
9	Current data on small companies				
10	Number	3			
11	Combined market share	0.02			
12					
13	Probability any small company will exit industry in any year				
14		0.5			
15					
16	Mean number of new entries in any year (Poisson distributed)				
17		1			
18					
19	Percentage of market share of each exiter that goes to Sweetness -				
20	the rest go to IceT (triangularly distributed)				
21		Minimum	Most likely	Maximum	
22		0.4	0.5	0.6	
23					
24	Percentage of companies' market shares lost to each other and to small companies				
25		Minimum	Most likely	Maximum	
26	Sweetness				
27	to IceT	0.01	0.05	0.1	
28	to each small company	0.005	0.01	0.03	
29	IceT				
30	to Sweetness	0.01	0.05	0.1	
31	to each small company	0.005	0.01	0.03	
32	Small companies				
33	to Sweetness	0.05	0.1	0.15	
34	to IceT	0.05	0.1	0.15	
35					

FIGURE 16.54 Spreadsheet Simulation for Iced Tea Example

	A	B	C	D	E	F	G	H	I	J	K
36	**Simulation section**										
37		Year 1	Year 2	Year 3	Year 4	Year 5	Year 6	Year 7	Year 8	Year 9	Year 10
38	Beginning market shares										
39	Sweetness	0.49	0.4813	0.48779	0.4878	0.4878	0.4878	0.4878	0.4878	0.4878	0.4878
40	IceT	0.49	0.4813	0.48779	0.4878	0.4878	0.4878	0.4878	0.4878	0.4878	0.4878
41	Small companies (combined)	0.02	0.0374	0.02441	0.0244	0.02439	0.02439	0.02439	0.02439	0.02439	0.02439
42											
43	Small companies before and after new entries										
44	Number of smalls before entries	3	2	1	1	1	1	1	1	1	1
45	Number entering at beginning	1	1	1	1	1	1	1	1	1	1
46	Total number of smalls	4	3	2	2	2	2	2	2	2	2
47											
48	Market shares lost during year										
49	Sweetness										
50	to IceT	0.02613	0.02567	0.02602	0.02602	0.02602	0.02602	0.02602	0.02602	0.02602	0.02602
51	to smalls (combined)	0.0294	0.02166	0.01463	0.01463	0.01463	0.01463	0.01463	0.01463	0.01463	0.01463
52	IceT										
53	to Sweetness	0.02613	0.02567	0.02602	0.02602	0.02602	0.02602	0.02602	0.02602	0.02602	0.02602
54	to smalls (combined)	0.0294	0.02166	0.01463	0.01463	0.01463	0.01463	0.01463	0.01463	0.01463	0.01463
55	Small companies										
56	to Sweetness	0.002	0.00374	0.00244	0.00244	0.00244	0.00244	0.00244	0.00244	0.00244	0.00244
57	to IceT	0.002	0.00374	0.00244	0.00244	0.00244	0.00244	0.00244	0.00244	0.00244	0.00244
58											
59	Information on exiters										
60	Market share of smalls before exit	0.0748	0.07324	0.0488	0.04879	0.04878	0.04878	0.04878	0.04878	0.04878	0.04878
61	Number of smalls exiting at end	2	2	1	1	1	1	1	1	1	1
62	Number of smalls remaining	2	1	1	1	1	1	1	1	1	1
63	Combined market share of exiters	0.0374	0.04882	0.0244	0.02439	0.02439	0.02439	0.02439	0.02439	0.02439	0.02439
64											
65	Market shares gained from exiters										
66	to Sweetness	0.0187	0.02441	0.0122	0.0122	0.0122	0.0122	0.0122	0.0122	0.0122	0.0122
67	to IceT	0.0187	0.02441	0.0122	0.0122	0.0122	0.0122	0.0122	0.0122	0.0122	0.0122
68											
69	Market shares at end										
70	Sweetness	0.4813	0.48779	0.4878	0.4878	0.4878	0.4878	0.4878	0.4878	0.4878	0.4878
71	IceT	0.4813	0.48779	0.4878	0.4878	0.4878	0.4878	0.4878	0.4878	0.4878	0.4878
72	Small companies (combined)	0.0374	0.02441	0.0244	0.02439	0.02439	0.02439	0.02439	0.02439	0.02439	0.02439

2 Beginning market shares. For year 1 the beginning market shares are inputs. For example, find the beginning market share for Sweetness in cell B39 with the formula

=B6

For every other year, the beginning market shares are the ending market shares from the previous year. For example, find the beginning market share for Sweetness in year 2 by entering the formula

=B70

in cell C39. Then copy this to the range C39:K41 for all competitors over the remaining years.

3 Entries to the market. In year 1 find the number of small companies before entries, the number of new entries, and the number of small companies after entries by entering the formulas

=B10

=RISKPOISSON($B$17)

and

=SUM(B44:B45)

in cells B44, B45, and B46. Note that the RISKPOISSON function, which takes a single argument, generates the number of new entries in a single year. For year 2 the number of small companies before entries is the remaining number from year 1. Therefore, enter the formula

$$=B62$$

in cell C44. Then copy the formulas in cells C44, B45, and B46 across these rows.

4 **Market shares lost during the year.** Generate the percentage of its market share Sweetness loses to IceT and to the small companies (combined) in year 1 by entering the formulas

$$=B39*RISKTRIANG(\$B\$27,\$C\$27,\$D\$27)$$

and

$$=B39*RISKTRIANG(\$B\$28,\$C\$28,\$D\$28)*B46$$

in cells B50 and B51 and then copy these across rows 50 and 51. Note that the latter of these multiplies the random percentage of market share lost by the number of small companies currently in the market. Next, enter similar formulas in rows 53, 54, 56, and 57 for market share lost by IceT and the small companies. For example, the formula in cell B57 is

$$=B41*RISKTRIANG(\$B\$34,\$C\$34,\$D\$34)$$

5 **Exiters.** Rows 60–63 contain information about small companies before and after exiting. To calculate this information, enter the formulas

$$=SUM(B41,B51,B54)-SUM(B56:B57)$$

$$=IF(B46>0,RISKBINOMIAL(B46,\$B\$14),0)$$

$$=B46-B61$$

and

$$=IF(B46>0,(B61/B46)*B60,0)$$

in cells B60, B61, B62, B63. Then copy these across rows 60–63. The formula in B60 simply tallies the market shares lost and gained for the small companies before exiting takes place. The formula in cell B61 uses the RISKBINOMIAL function to generate the number of small companies that exit. This function takes two arguments: the number of small companies and the probability that any company exits. Because it is not defined if the number of small companies is 0, we need the IF function. Finally, the formula in B63 finds the amount of market share possessed by the exiting companies under the assumption that all small companies have an equal market share. Again, it uses an IF function to take care of the case where there are no remaining small companies—never divide by 0!

6 **Market share gained by exiters.** The assumption of the model is that the market share of the exiters in row 63 is split randomly between Sweetness and IceT. To generate the split, enter the formula

$$=B63*RISKTRIANG(\$B\$22,\$C\$22,\$D\$22)$$

and

$$=B63-B66$$

in cells B66 and B67. Then copy these across rows 66 and 67.

7 **Year-end market shares.** Calculate the year-end market shares of Sweetness, IceT, and the small companies (combined) by entering the formulas

$$=\text{SUM(B39,B53,B56,B66)}-\text{SUM(B50:B51)}$$

$$=\text{SUM(B40,B50,B57,B67)}-\text{SUM(B53:B54)}$$

and

$$=\text{B60-B63}$$

in cells B70, B71, and B72. Then copy these across rows 70–72. If you like, you can check that the year-end market shares sum to 100% for each year, as they should.

Using @Risk There are a number of interesting outputs we can request for this simulation. These include the final market shares after 10 years (cells K70, K71, and K72) and the ranges B70:K70 and B71:K71. The latter allows us to track the time series behavior of the two dominant companies' market shares. Selected outputs are shown numerically and graphically in Figures 16.55–16.59. Figure 16.55 indicates that the final market shares of the two dominant companies in year 10 averaged close to 49%—exactly where they began—but varied considerably, from a low of 37.9% for IceT to a high of 58.0% for Sweetness. Of course, Sweetness and IceT are modeled in exactly the same way in our simulation, so any differences between their outputs can be attributed entirely to chance. The small companies' combined market share averaged to about 2.47% at the end of year 10, but it also varied considerably from a low of 0% (no small companies in the market) to a high of 12.4%.

The histograms for the year 10 ending market share of the dominant companies, shown in Figures 16.56 and 16.57 (page 956), represent behavior we might expect. Namely, they are reasonably bell-shaped around their means. The histogram for small companies shown in Figure 16.58, however, is quite different. We see that there were no small companies left in the market in about 37% of the iterations. When there were small companies remaining, their combined market share was skewed to the right.

FIGURE 16.55 **Summary Statistics for Iced Tea Example**

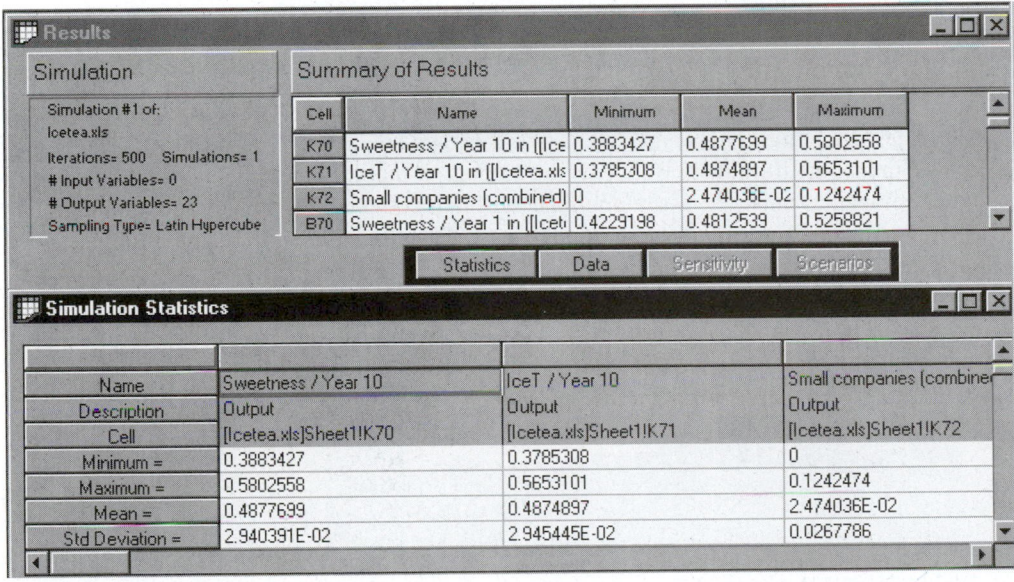

FIGURE 16.56 **Histogram for Sweetness's Ending Year 10 Market Share**

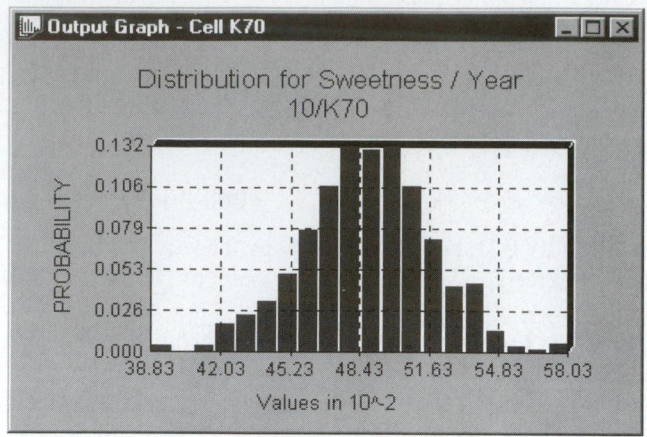

FIGURE 16.57 **Histogram for IceT's Ending Year 10 Market Share**

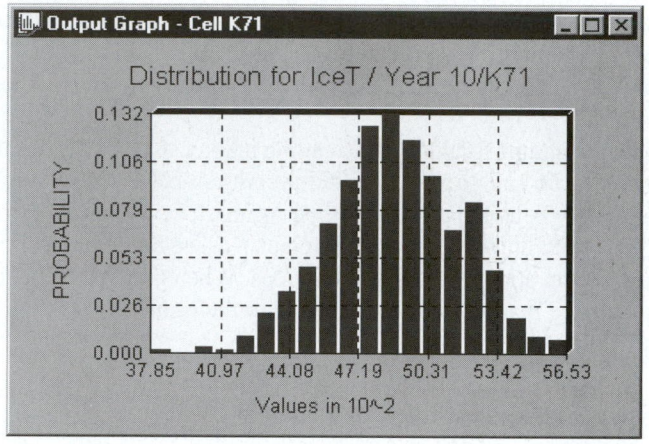

FIGURE 16.58 **Histogram for Small Companies' Ending Year 10 Market Share**

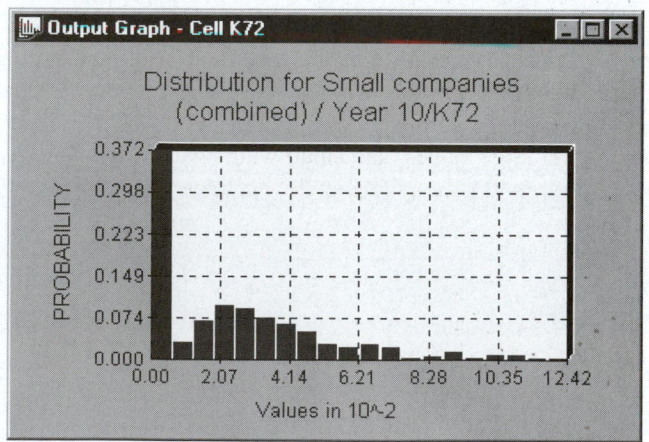

Finally, Figure 16.59 shows time series behavior of Sweetness's ending market share over the 10-year period. (This was produced by using the Summary graph option for cell B70—which is part of the output range B70:K70.) As we see, there is a slight upward trend on average, probably at the expense of the small companies.

As we stated earlier, we could add marketing initiatives such as advertising or price cuts to this simulation model to reflect real-world behavior. The resulting output should be of enormous benefit to the companies involved.

FIGURE 16.59 **Time Series of Sweetness's Ending Market Share**

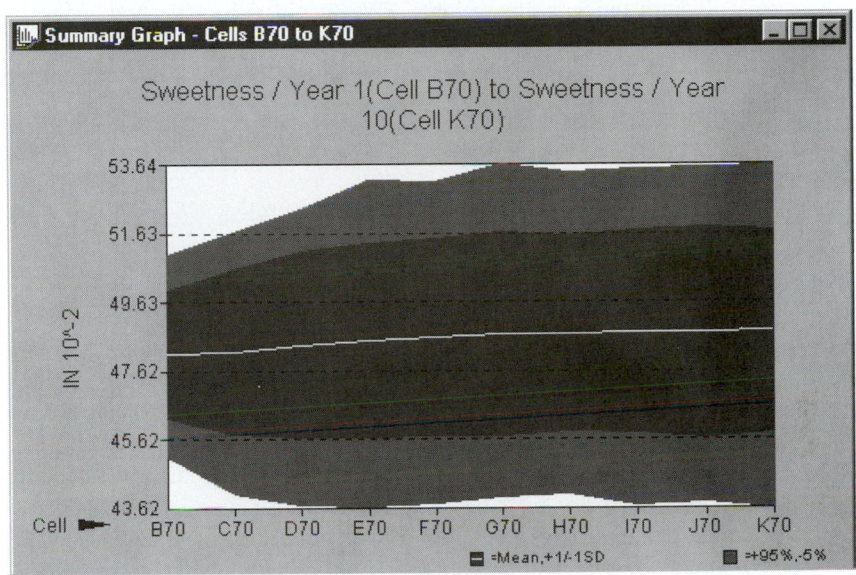

Sweetness / Year 1(Cell B70) to Sweetness / Year 10(Cell K70)

IN 10^-2

53.64
51.63
49.63
47.62
45.62
43.62

Cell ➤ B70 C70 D70 E70 F70 G70 H70 I70 J70 K70

■ =Mean,+/-1SD   ■ =+95%,-5%

16.10

Simulating Correlated Values

Until now, all of the random numbers we have generated with @Risk functions have been probabilistically independent. This means, for example, that if one value is much larger than its mean, the next value is completely unaffected. It is no more likely to be abnormally large or small than if the first value had been average or less than average. Sometimes we don't want to maintain this independence. Instead, we want the random numbers to be correlated in some way. If they are positively correlated, then large values tend to go with large values, and small with small. If they are negatively correlated, then large tend to go with small and small with large. As an example, we might expect daily stock price changes for two companies in the same industry to be positively correlated. If Exxon's price increases, we might expect Amoco's price to increase as well. @Risk allows us to build in this correlated behavior with the RISKCORRMAT function, as illustrated in the following example.[9]

[9]This example is based on the work of Hauser and Gaskin (1984).

EXAMPLE 16.10

There are currently two brands of brownies on the market. The Bisquake Company plans to enter the brownie market with one of two new brands. Each of the existing brands and potential new brands is characterized by three attributes: sweetness (measured on a 1 to 10 scale), chewiness (measured on a 1 to 10 scale), and price per box. These attributes are listed in Table 16.4. Each customer is assumed to choose one of these brands over the others on the basis of a weighted combination of the three attributes. That is, each customer is assumed to calculate a score for each brand as

$$\text{Score} = w_s(\text{Sweetness}) + w_c(\text{Chewiness}) + w_p(\text{Price})$$

where the w's are weights. (We would expect w_s and w_c to be positive because most customers prefer more of these attributes to less, but we would expect w_p to be negative because customers prefer lower prices.) The customer then purchases the brand with the largest score.

TABLE 16.4 **Attributes of Brands in Brownie Example**

	Sweetness	Chewiness	Price
Existing Brand 1	8	6	$3.00
Existing Brand 2	10	7	$3.80
Potential New Brand 1	8	6	$2.00
Potential New Brand 2	10	9	$4.50

Each customer's weights are different, depending on how important sweetness, chewiness, and price are to the customer. However, we might expect these weights to be correlated. For example, we might expect the sweetness and chewiness weights to be positively correlated. If a customer attaches a lot of importance to sweetness, she might also attach a lot of weight to chewiness. We will assume the population of customers assign normally distributed weights with the means and standard deviations shown in Table 16.5. We will also assume that the correlations between these weights are given in Table 16.6. Note that the correlation between a variable and itself is always 1. The other correlations, which are all positive, imply that if a customer puts a large weight on one attribute, he will tend to put a large weight on the other two attributes.

Bisquake wants to use simulation to identify the new brand (from the two possibilities) that is likely to obtain the larger market share.

TABLE 16.5 **Means and Standard Deviations of Weights for Brownie Example**

	Mean	Standard Deviation
Sweetness	5.0	1.0
Chewiness	4.0	0.6
Price	−9.0	2.0

TABLE 16.6 **Correlations Between Weights in Brownie Example**

	Sweetness	Chewiness	Price
Sweetness	1.00	0.80	0.70
Chewiness	0.80	1.00	0.65
Price	0.70	0.65	1.00

Solution

A single iteration of the simulation will simulate the behavior of a single customer. That is, it will generate this customer's weights, find the customer's scores for each of the brands, and see whether the customer prefers new brand 1 or new brand 2 to the existing brands. By performing many iterations, we can simulate the behavior of many customers and approximate the fraction of the entire customer population who would prefer either of the new brands to the existing brands.

Developing the Spreadsheet Model   The relevant spreadsheet appears in Figure 16.60. (See the file BROWNIE.XLS.) It can be formed as follows.

1   **Inputs.** Enter the inputs from Tables 16.4–16.6 in the ranges B6:D7, B11:D13, and B17:D20.

2   **Simulated weights.** @Risk's method of generating correlated random numbers is not very intuitive, but it is quite easy once you see how it works.[10] We want the weights in the range B23:D23 to be normally distributed with the means and standard deviations

FIGURE 16.60   **Spreadsheet Model for Brownie Marketing Example**

	A	B	C	D
1	New Product Decision with Correlated Preferences			
2				
3	Input section			
4	Normal distribution of customers' weights for attributes			
5		Sweetness	Chewiness	Price
6	Mean	5	4	-9
7	StDev	1	0.6	2
8				
9	Correlations between customers' weights for attributes			
10		Sweetness	Chewiness	Price
11	Sweetness	1	0.8	0.7
12	Chewiness	0.8	1	0.65
13	Price	0.7	0.65	1
14				
15	Attributes of existing brands and possible new brands			
16		Sweetness	Chewiness	Price
17	Existing brand 1	8	6	$3.00
18	Existing brand 2	10	7	$3.80
19	New brand 1	8	6	$2.00
20	New brand 2	10	9	$4.50
21				
22	Simulation section			
23	Generated weight	5.00	4.00	-9.00
24				
25	Scores for brands			
26	Existing brand 1	37.00		
27	Existing brand 2	43.80		
28	New brand 1	46.00		
29	New brand 2	45.50		
30				
31	Will either new brand be chosen? (1 if yes, 0 if no)			
32	New brand 1	1		
33	New brand 2	1		

[10]The BINORMAL_ and MULTINORMAL_ functions in StatPro (or RandFns) provide a more intuitive method of simulating correlated normally distributed values.

in the range B6:D7, but we also want them to be correlated. To accomplish this, generate the first weight (for sweetness) in cell B23 with the formula

$$=RISKCORRMAT(B11:D13,1)+RISKNORMAL(B6,B7)$$

This is not really addition. It simply instructs @Risk to generate a normal random number but to correlate it with other potential random numbers, using the correlations in the first column of the correlation range B11:D13. (It uses the *first* column because the second argument of RISKCORRMAT is 1.) Similarly, enter the formulas

$$=RISKCORRMAT(B11:D13,2)+RISKNORMAL(C6,C7)$$

and

$$=RISKCORRMAT(B11:D13,3)+RISKNORMAL(D6,D7)$$

in cells C23 and D23 to generate weights for chewiness and price.

3   **Scores for brands.** Calculate this customer's scores for the four brands in the range B26:B29 by entering the formula

$$=SUMPRODUCT(\$B\$23:\$D\$23,B17:D17)$$

in cell B26 and copying it to the range B27:B29. This formula weights the attributes of each brand with the customer's weights.

4   **Is either new brand chosen?** Either of the new brands will be chosen if its score is larger than the *larger* score of the two existing brands. Therefore, enter the formula

$$=IF(B28>MAX(\$B\$26:\$B\$27),1,0)$$

in cell B32 to check whether new brand 1 is preferred to the existing brands. Then copy it to cell B33 to do the same for new brand 2.

Using @Risk   We set up @Risk in the usual way, choosing cells B32 and B33 as the output cells and setting the number of iterations to 1000 and the number of simulations to 1. The results, shown in Figure 16.61, indicate that 656 of the 1000 simulated customers prefer new brand 1 to the existing brands, whereas 764 prefer new brand 2 to the existing brands. Perhaps this is not *conclusive* evidence that Bisquake should market its brand 2 rather than brand 1 (since brand 2's dominance could possibly be attributed to chance), but it is fairly persuasive.

How do these results depend on the correlation structure we assumed in Table 16.6? First, we note that because price weights are negative, the positive correlation between the sweetness and price weights implies that as a customer puts more weight on sweetness, she puts *less* weight on price—that is, the magnitude of the price weight is smaller. The

FIGURE 16.61   **Summary Statistics for Brownie Example with Positive Correlation**

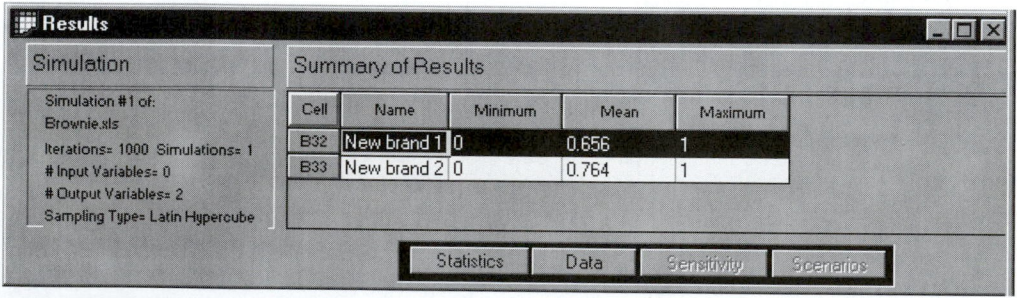

same goes for the relationship between the chewiness and price weights. If we believe these relationships should be reversed, we can simply change the signs of the correlations involving price. We did this, with the results shown in Figure 16.62. New brand 2 is even more dominant in this case.

FIGURE 16.62 **Summary Statistics for Brownie Example with Negative Correlation**

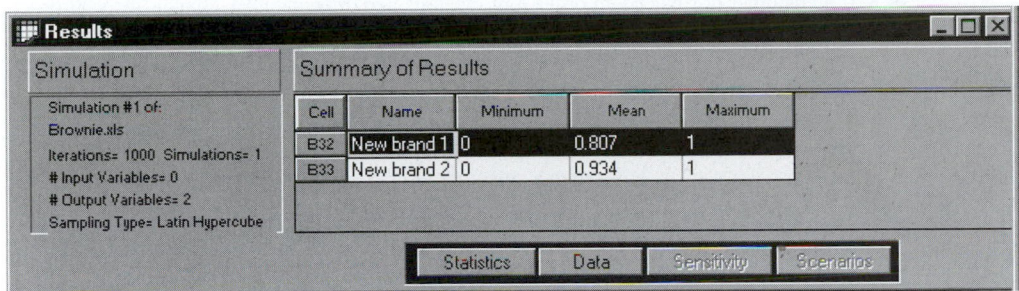

PROBLEMS

Level A

36 Suppose you have invested 25% of your portfolio in four different stocks. The mean and standard deviation of the annual return on each stock are as shown in the file P16_36.XLS. The correlations between the annual returns on the four stocks are also shown in this file. Using simulation, estimate (a) the probability that your portfolio's annual return will exceed 20%, and (b) the probability that your portfolio will lose money during the course of a year.

37 Suppose that the current price of each stock in the previous problem is as follows:

Stock 1: $14	Stock 3: $18
Stock 2: $16	Stock 4: $20

I have just bought an option involving these four stocks. If the price of stock 1 six months from now is $17 or more, the option enables me to buy, if I desire, one share of each stock for $20 six months from now. Otherwise the option is worthless. For example, if the stock prices six months from now are

Stock 1: $18	Stock 3: $21
Stock 2: $19	Stock 4: $22

then I would exercise my option to buy stocks 3 and 4 and receive $(21 - 20) + (22 - 20) = \$3$ in cash flow. How much is this option worth if the risk-free rate is 8%?

38 Suppose that Coke and Pepsi are fighting for the cola market. Each week each person in the market buys one case of Coke or Pepsi. If a person's last purchase was Coke, then this person's next purchase will be Coke with probability 0.9; otherwise, it will be Pepsi. (We are considering only two brands in the market.) Similarly, if a person's last purchase was Pepsi, then this person's next purchase will be Pepsi with probability 0.8; otherwise, it will be Coke. Currently, half of all people purchase Coke and half purchase Pepsi. Simulate one year of sales in the cola market and estimate each company's average weekly market share. Do this by assuming that the total market size is fixed at 100 customers. (*Hint*: Use @Risk's RISKBINOMIAL function.)

39 Seas Beginning sells clothing by mail order. An important question is when to delete a customer from the mailing list. At present, the company does this if a customer fails to order from six consecutive catalogs. It wants to know whether deleting a customer from the list after a customer fails to order from four consecutive catalogs will result in a higher profit per customer. The following data are available:

- If a customer placed an order the last time she received a catalog, then there is a 20% chance she will order from the next catalog.

- If a customer last placed an order one catalog ago, there is a 16% chance she will order from the next catalog she receives.

- If a customer last placed an order two catalogs ago, there is a 12% chance she will order from the next catalog she receives.

- If a customer last placed an order three catalogs ago, there is an 8% chance she will order from the next catalog she receives.

- If a customer last placed an order four catalogs ago, there is a 4% chance she will order from the next catalog she receives.

- If a customer last placed an order five catalogs ago, there is a 2% chance she will order from the next catalog she receives.

- It costs $1 to send a catalog, and the average profit per order is $15. Assume a customer has just placed an order. To maximize expected profit per customer, would Seas Beginning make more money deleting such a customer after six nonorders or four nonorders?

40 [Based on Babich (1992)] Suppose that each week every family in the United States buys a gallon of orange juice from Company A, B, or C. Let p_i be the probability that a gallon produced by company i is of unsatisfactory quality. If the last gallon of juice purchased by a family is satisfactory, then it will purchase a gallon of juice from the same company next week. If the last gallon of juice purchased by a family is unsatisfactory, then the family will purchase a gallon from a competitor next week. Consider a week in which A families have purchased juice A, B families have purchased juice B, and C families have purchased juice C. Assume that families that switch brands during a period are allocated to the remaining brands in a manner that is proportional to the current market shares of the other brands. Thus, if a customer switches from brand A, the probability is $B/(B + C)$ that he will switch to brand B, and the probability is $C/(B + C)$ that he will switch to brand C. Suppose that 1,000,000 gallons of orange juice are purchased each week. Use simulation to answer the following.

a After a year, what will the market share be for each firm? Assume $p_A = 0.10$, $p_B = 0.15$, and $p_C = 0.20$. (*Hint*: You will need to use the RISKBINOMIAL function to see how many people switch from A and then use the RISKBINOMIAL function again to see how many switch from A to B and from A to C.)

b Suppose a 1% increase in market share is worth $10,000 per week to firm A. Firm A believes that it can cut the percentage of unsatisfactory juice cartons in half for a cost of $1 million per year. Is this worthwhile? Again, assume that $p_A = 0.10$, $p_B = 0.15$, and $p_C = 0.20$.

Level B

41 The Business School at State University currently has three parking lots, each containing 155 spaces. Two hundred faculty have been assigned to each lot. On a peak day, an average of 70% of all lot 1 parking sticker holders show up, an average of 72% of all lot 2 parking sticker holders show up, and an average of 74% of all lot 3 parking sticker holders show up.

a Given the current situation, estimate the probability that on a peak day, at least one faculty member with a sticker will be unable to find a spot. Assume that the number who show up at each lot is independent of the number who show up at the other two lots. Can you think of a solution to this problem—faculty unable to park—that does not involve creating more parking spaces?

b Now suppose the number of people who show up at the three lots are correlated, with each correlation equal to 0.9. Does your solution in part **a** work as well? Why or why not?

42 [Based on Hoppensteadt and Peskin (1992)] The following model (the Reed–Frost model) is often used to model the spread of an infectious disease. Suppose that at the beginning of period 1, a population consists of 5 diseased people (called infectives) and 95 healthy people (called susceptibles). During any period, there is a 0.05 chance that a given infective person will encounter a particular susceptible. If an infective encounters a susceptible, there is a 0.5 chance that the susceptible will contract the disease. An infective lives an average of 10 periods with the disease. To model this, we assume that there is a 0.10 probability that an infective dies during a period. Use @Risk to model the evolution of the population over 100 periods. Use your results to answer the following questions.

a What is the probability that the population will die out?

b What is the probability that the disease will die out?

c On average, what percentage of the population becomes infected by the end of period 100?

d Suppose that people use infection "protection" during encounters. The use of protection reduces the chance that a susceptible will contract the disease during a single encounter with an infective from 0.50 to 0.10. Now answer parts **a–c** under the assumption that everyone uses protection. (*Hint*: During any period, there is a probability $0.05(0.50) = 0.025$ that an infective will infect a particular susceptible. Thus the probability that a particular susceptible is *not* infected during a period is $(1 - 0.025)^I$, where I is the number of infectives present at the end of the previous period.) ■

16.11 Using TopRank with @Risk for Powerful Modeling

In this section we will illustrate how another Palisade Decision Tools add-in, TopRank, can be used together with @Risk as a very powerful modeling combination. As we have seen, @Risk introduces uncertainty explicitly into a spreadsheet model. It does so by allowing several inputs to have probability distributions and then simulating random values from these. However, if there are many inputs in a model, it is often a good idea to see which of them have the largest effect on a key output variable. Those that have a relatively minor effect can be treated as nonrandom, with "best guesses" used as their values. We can then focus on the more important input variables and model them, with probability distributions, in an appropriate manner.

TopRank is essentially a what-if tool that allows us to see which of many inputs have the largest effect on an output variable. We first develop a spreadsheet model in the usual way, using best-guess values for all inputs. We then use TopRank to vary each of the inputs through a designated range (while holding the other inputs constant). TopRank reports the corresponding variation of any output we select. We can then see (usually through one of several charts) which inputs are most critical. At this point we could either conclude the analysis or switch to @Risk and model the key inputs with appropriate probability distributions.

This latter strategy is basically what Palisade had in mind when it bundled TopRank and @Risk together. In fact, the Decision Tools toolbar shown in Figure 16.63 allows us to toggle between @Risk and TopRank by clicking on the appropriate button. If TopRank is open and we click on the @Risk button, @Risk takes the place of TopRank. If @Risk is open and we click on the TopRank button, then TopRank takes the place of @Risk.

FIGURE 16.63 **Decision Tools Toolbar**

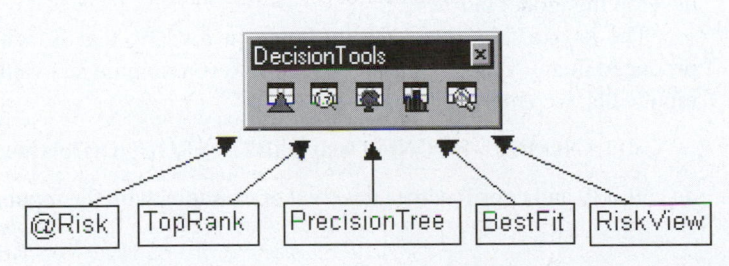

The following example, which will illustrate how TopRank and @Risk can work in tandem, is an extremely important one. Simulation in the business world is often used to analyze potential products. The profitability of a new product is highly uncertain because it depends on many uncertain quantities. Many companies the authors have worked with (including General Motors and Eli Lilly) begin the analysis of every new product by determining the uncertain quantities that might affect the profitability of the product. This analysis is often the deciding factor in whether the product is developed and marketed.

E X A M P L E   1 6 . 1 1

SimTex, a pharmaceutical company, is in the early stages of developing a new drug called Biathnon. As with most new drugs, the future of Biathnon is highly uncertain. For example, its introduction into the market could be delayed, pending tests by the FDA. Also, its market could be diminished by a potential rival product from SimTex's competition. SimTex has identified the following key inputs that will affect Biathnon's future profitability:

- number of years after product is developed until it is produced (due to potential FDA delays)
- number of years for which the product sells
- initial cost incurred in developing the product
- salvage value obtained from equipment after production of the product has been discontinued
- fixed production cost incurred during years in which the product is manufactured
- unit cost of producing the product
- unit price for the product
- initial demand for the product during first year it is sold
- annual percentage growth in demand for the product
- percentage of demand for the product that is lost to the competition
- discount rate used to discount cash flows from the product

These are the inputs to a profitability model for Biathnon. A natural question is how changes in the inputs affect the key output, namely, the NPV of Biathnon over its lifetime. How can SimTex use TopRank and @Risk to analyze this NPV?

Solution

The first step is to develop a profitability model for Biathnon's NPV as a function of the various inputs. For this first step, we use "best guess" values for the inputs. This model appears in Figure 16.64. (See the file SIMTEX1.XLS.[11]) We spell out the particular assumptions in rows 4–10, list the inputs (and give them range names) in rows 13–23, and develop the model in rows 27–38.

The key to this model is the timing in row 29, that is, whether Biathnon is being produced in any year. To allow for general (even noninteger) values in the Delay and Life input cells, we enter the formula

=IF(AND(B27>ROUND(Delay,0),B27<=ROUND(Delay+Life),0),"Yes","No")

in cell B29 and copy it across row 29. For example, with the inputs used in this "base-case"

---

[11]Although we could have developed this entire example in a single Excel file, we split it into three separate files for convenience—one for the base model, one for the TopRank model, and one for the @Risk model.

FIGURE 16.64   Basic Model for SimTex

	A	B	C	D	E	F	G	H	AE	AF
1	**Model of new product by SimTex**									
2										
3	**Assumptions**									
4	Development costs occur at the end of year 0									
5	It takes some years (specified in cell B13) until production begins									
6	Initial demand, fixed costs, variable costs, and revenues begin in this year									
7	The product is produced for the lifetime specified in cell B14									
8	At the end of the product lifetime, the salvage value is obtained									
9	All revenues, costs occur at the ends of the respective years									
10	The NPV is discounted back to the beginning of year 1									
11										
12	**Inputs**					Range names:				
13	Years delayed	2				Delay: B13				
14	Lifetime of product (years)	12				Life: B14				
15	Development cost	$120,000				DevCost: B15				
16	Salvage value	$20,000				SalvVal: B16				
17	Annual fixed cost	$6,000				FixCost: B17				
18	Unit cost	$2				UnitCost: B18				
19	Unit price	$5				UnitPrice: B19				
20	Initial demand	20000				InitDem: B20				
21	Annual demand growth	10%				DemGrowth: B21				
22	Sales lost to competition	20%				PctDemLost: B22				
23	Discount rate	10%				DiscRate: B23				
24										
25	**Financial model (shown for any number of years the product *might* live)**									
26										
27	Year	0	1	2	3	4	5	6	29	30
28	Development cost	$120,000								
29	Is product being produced?	No	No	No	Yes	Yes	Yes	Yes	No	No
30	Fixed cost		$0	$0	$6,000	$6,000	$6,000	$6,000	$0	$0
31	Total demand		0	0	20000	22000	24200	26620	0	0
32	SimTex's demand		0	0	16000	17600	19360	21296	0	0
33	Variable cost		$0	$0	$32,000	$35,200	$38,720	$42,592	$0	$0
34	Revenue		$0	$0	$80,000	$88,000	$96,800	$106,480	$0	$0
35	Salvage value		$0	$0	$0	$0	$0	$0	$0	$0
36	Net profit	-$120,000	$0	$0	$42,000	$46,800	$52,080	$57,888	$0	$0
37										
38	NPV of profit	$284,237								

model, Biathnon is produced only in years 3–14, so these are the only years (from year 1 on) that contribute to NPV. The formulas in the other cells are then straightforward. For year 1 (column C) the formulas in rows 30–36 are

$$=IF(C29=\text{``Yes''},FixCost,0)$$

$$=IF(AND(B29=\text{``No''},C29=\text{``Yes''}),InitDem,IF(C29=\text{``Yes''},B31*(1+DemGrowth),0))$$

$$=IF(C31=0,0,C31*(1-PctDemLost))$$

$$=IF(C32=0,0,C32*UnitCost)$$

$$=IF(C32=0,0,C32*UnitPrice)$$

$$=IF(AND(C29=\text{``Yes''},D29=\text{``No''}),SalvVal,0)$$

and

$$=-C28-C30-C33+C34+C35$$

The second of these formulas (in cell C31) might require some explanation. The first IF checks whether production occurs this year but not the previous year. If so, this must be the first year of production, so that the demand is the initial demand. Otherwise, the second IF checks whether production is still occurring. If so, then demand is the previous year's demand plus the growth percentage. Similarly, the formula for salvage value in cell C35 checks whether production occurs this year but not next year. If so, then this must be the year when the salvage value is obtained. Finally, we calculate the NPV (discounted to the beginning of year 1) in cell B38 with the formula

$$=NPV(DiscRate,C36:AF36)+B36$$

Now that the model has been developed, we could use trial and error (or data tables) to see how the NPV reacts to changes in the inputs. However, TopRank does this easily. Actually, it can be used in a number of ways; we will describe only one of them (although it appears to us to be the most useful).

Using TopRank   To use TopRank, we leave the model alone but change the input section.[12] Instead of entering *constants* in the input cells, we enter TopRank's RISKVARY function. This function has the syntax

$$=RISKVARY(base,minimum,maximum,rangetype,steps,distribution)$$

where:

- *base* is the base case (best guess) for the input
- *minimum* is the smallest possible value for the input
- *maximum* is the largest possible value for the input
- *rangetype* is 0, 1, or 2 and determines the way *minimum* and *maximum* should be entered (even though 0 is the default value, we'll use *rangetype* 2—see the TopRank manual for more details)
- *steps* is the number of values from *minimum* to *maximum* to use for this input
- *distribution* is an optional argument that we will omit

We set up the input section for TopRank as shown in Figure 16.65. (See the file SIMTEX2.XLS.) All entries in columns C–E are *constants* (not formulas). For example, for the development cost in row 15, the base case is $120,000, but we want to examine development costs from 90% to 150% of this base case, that is, from $108,000 to $180,000. We then enter the formula

$$=RISKVARY(D13,C13*D13,E13*D13,2,8)$$

in cell B13 and copy it down to cell B23. This formula tells TopRank to vary this input from its minimum to its maximum in 8 steps. (The next-to-last argument, 2, implies that the second and third arguments are the actual minimum and maximum.)

To use TopRank, we proceed in three steps, very much like in @Risk: (1) use the Change Settings button (see the TopRank toolbar in Figure 16.66) to make various settings; (2) use the Add Output Cells button to select one or more output cells; and (3) use the Run What-if Analysis button to perform the calculations.

For step (1), we suggest changing only one of the default settings. After clicking on the Change Settings button, click on the Input ID tab, and then *uncheck* the Automatically Insert AutoVary Functions box. (Otherwise, TopRank will give you a lot of results you probably don't want.) For step (2), highlight the NPV cell (B38) and click on the Add Output Cells button. Finally, run the analysis in step (3) by clicking on the Run What-if Analysis button. TopRank then varies each input cell from its minimum to maximum, using the number of steps you specified and keeping the *other* inputs at their base levels, and keeps track of all of the NPVs. Like @Risk, it also takes you into its own screen.

---

[12]This discussion assumes TopRank is open within Excel. It can be opened exactly like @Risk, from the Start button of Windows.

FIGURE 16.65   Input Section for TopRank Model

	A	B	C	D	E
12	**Inputs**	Actual	Low	Base	High
13	Years delayed	2	50%	2	300%
14	Lifetime of product (years)	12	50%	12	200%
15	Development cost	$120,000	90%	$120,000	150%
16	Salvage value	$20,000	0%	$20,000	150%
17	Annual fixed cost	$6,000	80%	$6,000	125%
18	Unit cost	2	50%	$2	150%
19	Unit price	5	60%	$5	125%
20	Initial demand	20000	30%	20000	120%
21	Annual demand growth	10%	50%	10%	120%
22	Sales lost to competition	20%	0%	20%	200%
23	Discount rate	10%	60%	10%	200%

FIGURE 16.66   **TopRank Toolbar**

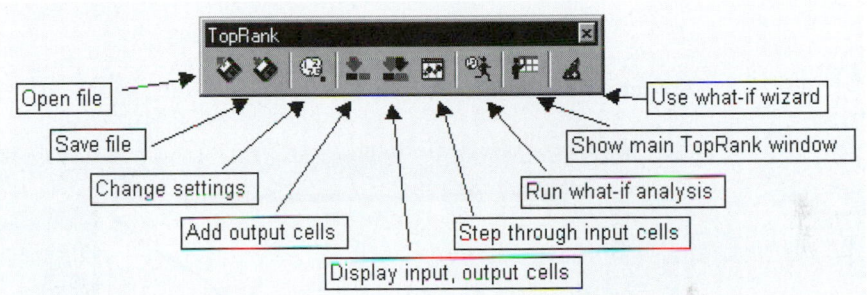

Perhaps the best way to understand the TopRank results is through a tornado chart. (You might recall tornado charts with Precision Tree in Chapter 6.) To create a tornado chart, click on the Graph button in the TopRank screen. You'll get a choice of three chart types: tornado, spider, and sensitivity. Choose the tornado type to get the chart in Figure 16.67 on page 968.[13]

Each bar in the chart indicates the variation in NPV as an individual input varies from its minimum to maximum. For example, NPV decreases by about 70% and increases by about 147% (from its base-case value) when product lifetime varies from its minimum (6 years) to its maximum (24 years). Because the longer bars are always on the top and the shortest are always on the bottom, the inputs at the top of the chart are always the most important ones. In this case the five most important inputs are product lifetime, unit price, initial demand, discount rate, and unit production cost.

Clearly, if SimTex is going to simulate the product's NPV, it should spend most of its time accurately assessing the distributions of these five key inputs. In contrast, the tornado chart indicates that annual fixed cost and salvage value have virtually no effect on NPV. Therefore, little effort should be spent trying to estimate their values accurately—the base-case values will suffice.

Before proceeding to a simulation, we mention the two other chart types available in TopRank: spider charts and sensitivity charts. A spider chart for the SimTex model appears in Figure 16.68. To produce this chart, click on the TopRank Graph button and select the

---

[13]In Office 97, you can paste a TopRank (or @Risk) graph into your worksheet. First, use TopRank's File/Save As menu item to save the graph as a bitmap (.bmp) file. Then get back into Excel, select the Insert/Picture/From File menu item, and select the .bmp file you saved. The downside to this procedure is that bitmap files are *very* large in terms of memory requirements.

FIGURE 16.67   Tornado Chart from TopRank

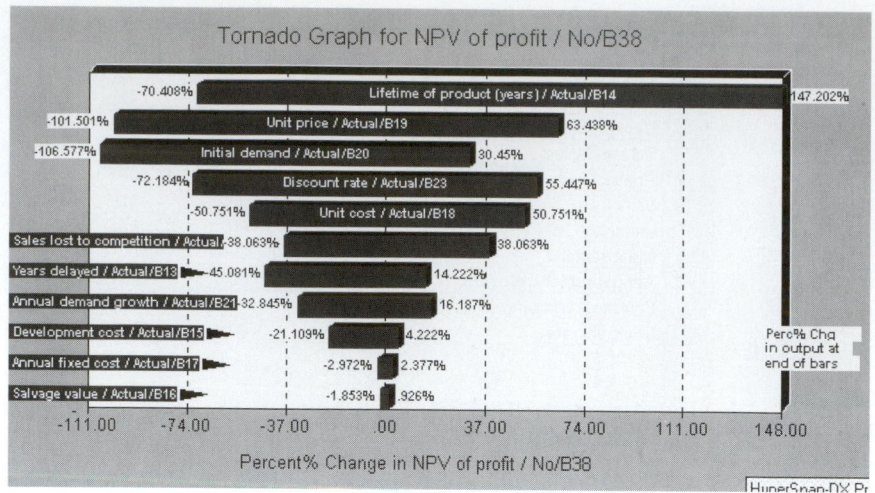

FIGURE 16.68   **Spider Chart for SimTex Model**

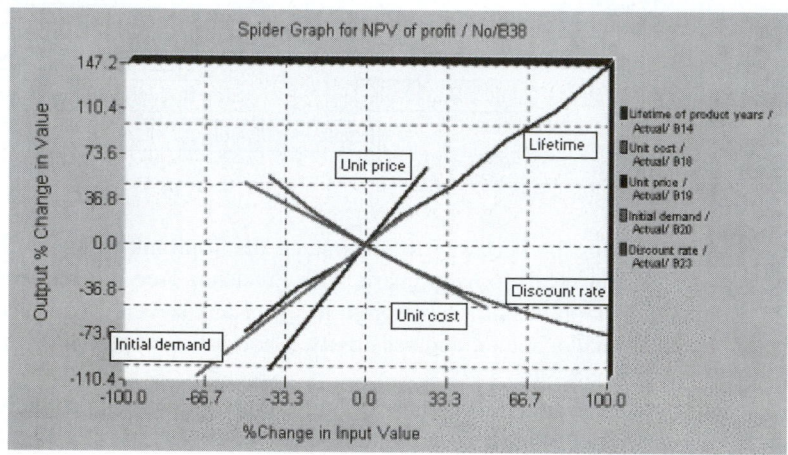

Spider option. Then because the default spider chart shows *all* of the inputs and is quite cluttered, right-click on the chart, choose the Format/Variables to Graph option, and select the five most important inputs from the tornado chart. This chart is fairly straightforward. For each of the five inputs, there is a curve that shows the percentage change in NPV as a function of the percentage change in the input—over the range we specified for the input.

From this spider chart we learn (not surprisingly) that changes in unit price, unit cost, and initial demand result in *linear* changes in NPV. Also, a 1% increase in unit price results in a *larger* percentage increase in NPV than does a 1% percentage increase in initial demand. (Can you see why?). As the discount rate increases, NPV decreases, but the rate of decrease slows; after a while increases in the discount rate cannot decrease NPV much further. Increases in product lifetime appear to increase product NPV in a complex, nonlinear fashion.

The final TopRank chart type, a sensitivity chart, is similar to a spider chart, except that it shows one input only. Also, it shows *actual* values rather than percentage changes. To get a sensitivity chart for any input/output combination, click on the desired input and output in

FIGURE 16.69 **Sensitivity Chart for SimTex Model**

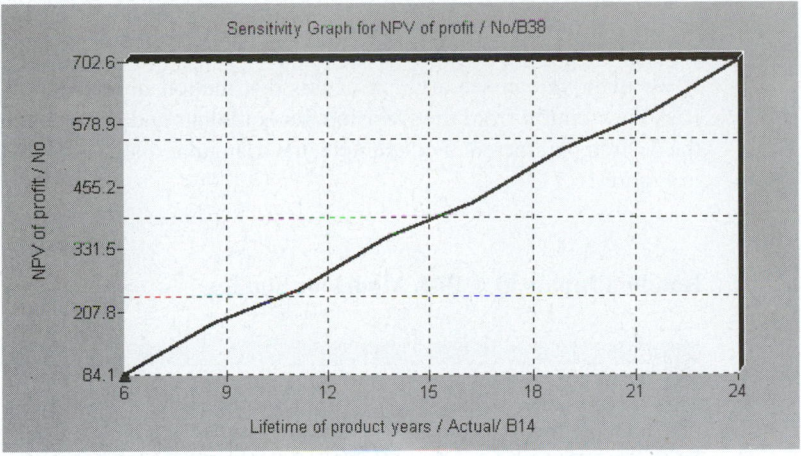

the TopRank Results window, and then click on the Graph button and select the Sensitivity option. For example, a graph of NPV versus product lifetime appears in Figure 16.69.

Running an @RISK Simulation The sensitivity analysis with TopRank has indicated that the five key drivers of NPV are product lifetime, unit price, unit cost, initial product demand, and discount rate. We will now run an @Risk simulation of this model to estimate the distribution of NPV earned from Biathnon. We will keep all inputs other than the five key inputs fixed at their base values, and we will use @Risk functions for the key inputs. Actually, we will use random functions for product lifetime, unit price, unit cost, and initial demand, and we will vary discount rate systematically with the RISKSIMTABLE function.[14]

Which probability distributions should we use to model the product lifetime, unit price, unit cost, and initial demand inputs? There are several ways to proceed in general. First, if we have a lot of historical data on any input, we can use BestFit to fit a distribution to the historical data (as we illustrate at the end of Chapter 5). It is unlikely that SimTex has relevant historical data that would pertain to this *new* product, so we won't pursue this approach. Second, we can use RiskView to examine *shapes* of potential distributions that look like good candidates. Finally, we can choose a *simple* distribution that management has confidence in and assess its parameters.

We choose the latter approach, using the triangular distribution for each of the random inputs. The use of a triangular random variable is common at many companies such as General Motors and Eli Lilly. The triangular distribution is often used because, unlike the normal distribution, it makes no assumption that the distribution of the uncertain quantity is symmetric about the mean or most likely value. In fact, the use of the triangular distribution at GM to model uncertain quantities in the analysis of new products grew directly out of deterministic tornado chart analysis.

To assess a triangular distribution for any input, all we need are minimum, most likely, and maximum values for the input. We use the same values of these that we used in the

---

[14]The discount rate used in a typical new product analysis is usually a corporate rate of 10%–15% and is obtained from the CAPM (Capital Asset Pricing Model). Riskier projects should be discounted at a higher rate than the corporate rate and less risky projects should be discounted at a lower rate than the corporate rate.

TopRank analysis. They are shown in columns E–G of Figure 16.70. Then we enter the usual @Risk formulas in random input cells. For example, the formula in cell B14 is

$$=\text{RISKTRIANG(E14,F14,G14)}$$

If we like, we can see a graph of this distribution in RiskView. We simply click on the RiskView button from the Decision Tools toolbar and select a triangular distribution with the desired parameters. For example, the triangular distribution of product lifetime appears in Figure 16.71.

FIGURE 16.70 **Random Inputs in @Risk Model for SimTex**

	A	B	C	D	E	F	G	H
12	**Inputs**	Actual			Parameters for triangular distributions			
13	Years delayed	2	non-random		Minimum	Most likely	Maximum	
14	Lifetime of product (years)	14.76	triangular		6	12	24	
15	Development cost	$120,000	non-random					
16	Salvage value	$20,000	non-random					
17	Annual fixed cost	$6,000	non-random					
18	Unit cost	$2.20	triangular		$1.00	$2.00	$3.00	
19	Unit price	$5.19	triangular		$3.00	$5.00	$6.25	
20	Initial demand	17947.0	triangular		6000	20000	24000	
21	Annual demand growth	10%	non-random					
22	Sales lost to competition	20%	non-random		Risksimtable values for discount rate			
23	Discount rate	6%	use risksimtable		6%	10%	15%	20%

FIGURE 16.71 **RiskView Graph of Triangular Product Lifetime Distribution**

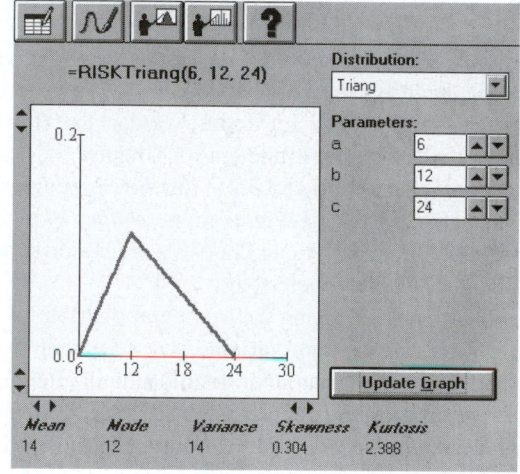

Finally, we model various discount rates in cell B23 with a RISKSIMTABLE function, using the discount rates in the range E23:H23. The formula in cell B23 is

$$=\text{RISKSIMTABLE(E23:H23)}$$

This allows us to try a discount rate appropriate for a less risky project (6%), a project of average risk (10%), and a project of higher risk (15% or 20%).

We now run @Risk in the usual way. In the Settings dialog box, specify 500 iterations and 4 simulations (one for each discount rate). Also, under the Sampling tab of the Settings dialog box, make sure that the Collect Distribution Samples *is* checked. (We'll need it to produce tornado charts.) Then specify the NPV cell as the output cell and run @Risk.

Selected results from the simulation appear in Figure 16.72. (See the file SIM-TEX3.XLS.) For a change, we copied information from the @Risk Simulation Statistics window, pasted it into Excel, and made suitable modifications. We see that if the project is assessed to be less risky than the company's typical project (justifying a 6% discount rate), the project has a mean NPV (often called the risk-adjusted project NPV) of $405,390, whereas if the project is so risky that it deserves a 20% discount rate, the risk-adjusted NPV is only $37,421. Even if the project is extremely risky, it is still worth doing because it has a positive risk-adjusted NPV. The 95% confidence intervals for mean NPV in rows 46 and 47 are calculated directly from the formulas in Chapter 8. For example, the formula in cell B46 (using the number of iterations, 500, as the sample size) is

$$=B42-1.96*B43/SQRT(500)$$

The fact that these confidence intervals are entirely positive is another good reason for SimTex to go ahead with the project.

FIGURE 16.72   **@Risk Results for SimTex Model**

	A	B	C	D	E
40	Selected results from @Risk (500 iterations)				
41	Discount rate	6%	10%	15%	20%
42	Mean =	$405,390	$233,432	$109,165	$37,421
43	Std Deviation =	$286,205	$174,434	$104,168	$68,328
44					
45	95% confidence intervals for mean NPV				
46	Lower limit	$380,303	$218,142	$100,034	$31,432
47	Upper limit	$430,477	$248,721	$118,296	$43,410

Tornado Charts in @Risk   Tornado charts can also be obtained in @RISK, but their interpretation is different than in TopRank. There are two types: correlation and regression. To obtain either, click on the Sensitivity button in @Risk's Results window (nothing happens at first), click on the Graph button in the top toolbar, and select either the correlation or regression option. The correlation and regression charts (for the simulation with a 15% discount rate) appear in Figures 16.73 and 16.74 (page 972).

The correlation tornado chart is easy to interpret. It shows the correlation of each random input in the spreadsheet with the output (NPV). The regression tornado chart is somewhat more challenging to interpret. @Risk takes all 500 iterations as observations and runs a regression using NPV as the response variable and all random inputs as explanatory variables. Actually, it uses the *standardized* values of these variables in the regression and shows the resulting regression coefficients in the tornado chart. Each shows the expected number of standard deviations of change in NPV when any input increases by one of its standard deviations. For example, when unit price increases by one standard deviation (and the other inputs remain constant), we expect NPV to increase by 0.588 standard deviation. In contrast, when unit cost increases by one standard deviation, we expect NPV to *decrease* by 0.365 standard deviation.[15] This is one more way to measure the sensitivity of NPV to changes in the key inputs.

---

[15] The values in the two charts would be identical if there were zero correlations between the input variables. However, a slight amount of correlation between them occurs in the simulation.

FIGURE 16.73 Correlation Tornado Chart from @Risk

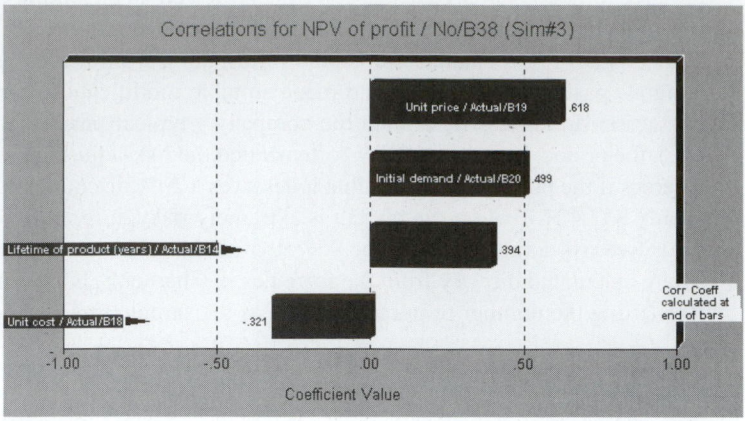

FIGURE 16.74 Regression Tornado Chart from @Risk

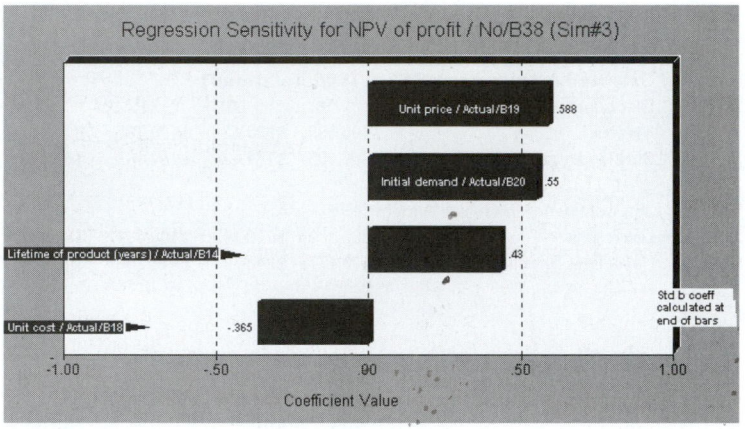

16.12 Conclusion

S imulation has traditionally not received the attention it deserves in quantitative methods courses. The primary reason for this has been the lack of easy-to-use simulation software. Now with Excel's built-in simulation capabilities, plus powerful and affordable add-ins such as @Risk and Crystal Ball, simulation is receiving its rightful emphasis. The world is full of uncertainty, which is what makes simulation so valuable. Simulation models provide important insights that are missing in models that do not incorporate uncertainty. In addition, simulation models are relatively easy to understand and easy to develop. Therefore, we suspect that simulation models will soon be the primary emphasis of most quantitative methods courses—if they aren't already!

PROBLEMS

Level A

43 W. L. Brown, a direct marketer of women's clothing, needs to determine how many telephone operators to schedule during each part of the day. W. L. Brown estimates that the number of phone calls received each hour of a typical 8-hour shift can be described by the probability distribution in the file P16_43.XLS. Each operator can handle 15 calls per hour and costs the company $20 per hour. Each phone call that is not handled is assumed to cost the company $6 in lost profit. Considering the options of employing 6, 8, 10, 11, 13, 14, or 20 operators, use simulation to determine the number of operators that minimizes the expected hourly cost (labor costs plus lost profits).

44 The annual demand for Wozac, a prescription drug manufactured and marketed by the NuFeel Company, is normally distributed with mean 50,000 and standard deviation 12,000. We assume that demand during each of the next 10 years is an independent random draw from this distribution. NuFeel needs to determine how large a Wozac plant to build to maximize its expected profit over the next 10 years. If the company builds a plant that can produce x units of Wozac per year, it will cost $16 for each of these x units. NuFeel will produce only the amount demanded each year, and each unit of Wozac produced will sell for $3.70. Each unit of Wozac produced incurs a variable production cost of $0.20. It costs $0.40 per year to operate a unit of capacity.

    a Among the capacity levels of 30,000, 35,000, 40,000, 45,000, 50,000, 55,000, and 60,000 units per year, which level maximizes expected profit? Use simulation to answer this question.

    b Using the capacity from your answer to part **a**, NuFeel can be 95% certain that expected profit for the 10-year period will be between what two values?

    c Using the capacity from your answer to part **a**, NuFeel can be 95% certain that *actual* profit for the 10-year period will be between what two values?

45 You now have $1000, all of which is invested in a sports team. Each year there is a 60% chance that the value of the team will increase by 60% and a 40% chance that the value of the team will decrease by 60%. Estimate the mean and median value of your investment after 100 years. Explain the large difference between the estimated mean and median.

46 Amanda has 30 years to save for her retirement. At the beginning of each year, she puts $5000 into her retirement account. At any point in time, all of Amanda's retirement funds are tied up in the stock market. Suppose the annual return on stocks follows a normal distribution with mean 12% and standard deviation 25%. What is the probability that at the end of 30 years, Amanda will have reached her goal of having $1,000,000 for retirement? Assume that if Amanda reaches her goal *before* 30 years, she will stop investing. (*Hint*: Each year you should keep track of Amanda's beginning cash position—for year 1, this is $5000—and Amanda's ending cash position. Of course, Amanda's ending cash position for a given year is a function of her beginning cash position and the return on stocks for that year. To estimate the probability that Amanda will meet her goal, use an IF statement that returns 1 if she meets her goal and 0 otherwise.)

47 A *martingale* betting strategy works as follows. We begin with a certain amount of money and repeatedly play a game in which we have a 40% chance of winning any bet. In the first game, we bet $1. From then on, every time we win a bet, we bet $1 the next time. Each time we lose, we double our bet. Currently we have $63. Assume we have unlimited credit, so that we can bet more money than we have. Use simulation to find a 95% confidence interval for the expected profit we will have earned after playing the game 50 times.

48 [Based on Kelly (1956)] You currently have $100. Each week, you can invest any amount of money you currently have in a risky investment. With probability 0.4, the amount you invest is tripled, and with probability 0.6, the amount you invest is lost. Consider the following investment strategies:

    a Each week invest 10% of your money.

    b Each week invest 30% of your money.

    c Each week invest 50% of your money.

Simulate 100 weeks of each strategy 50 times. Which strategy appears to be best? [In general, if you can multiply your investment by M with probability p and lose your investment with probability $q = 1 - p$, you should invest a fraction $[p(M - 1) - q]/(M - 1)$ of your money each week. This strategy maximizes (for a favorable game) the expected growth rate of your fortune and is known as the **Kelly criterion**.]

49 [Based on Marcus (1990)] At one point, the Balboa mutual fund had beaten the Standard and Poor's 500 during 11 of the previous 13 years. People used this as an argument that you can "beat the market." However, is it all that unusual that Balboa beat the market 11 out of 13 times? Consider 50 mutual funds, each of which has a 50% chance of beating the market during a given year. Use simulation to estimate the probability that the "best" of the 50 mutual funds will beat the market in at least 11 out of 13 years. (This probability turns out to exceed 40%, which means that the best mutual fund's beating the market 11 out of 13 years is not an unusual occurrence.)

50 The FailSafe Company operates machines, each of which depends on an important module to perform successfully. This module, in turn, relies on a specific component. If this component fails, the module fails, and the machine fails. To extend the time until component failure, redundancy is built in at the component level. Specifically, 10 identical components are placed "in parallel" in the module. This means that the machine lasts as long as *any* of the 10 components is still functioning. In mathematical terms, if T_i is the time at which component i fails, then the time at which the machine fails is the maximum of T_1 through T_{10}.

    a Assume that each T_i is normally distributed with mean 100 hours and standard deviation 20 hours. Use simulation to find the distribution of the time until machine failure.

    b Now assume that each T_i is lognormally distributed with the same mean and standard deviation as in part **a**. (A lognormal distribution allows only *positive* values, and it is skewed to the right; hence, it is a more realistic distribution for times until failure. It can be generated in @Risk with the RISKLOGNORM function. This function takes two arguments: the mean and the standard deviation.) Repeat the simulation in part **a** with this lognormal distribution. Do you obtain any qualitatively different results?

51 Continuing the previous problem, suppose that the machine has a mission to accomplish. To accomplish this mission, it must survive at least 125 hours. The component times are assumed to be lognormally distributed with mean 100 hours and standard deviation 20 hours. The company must decide how many components to include in parallel so that there is a 95% probability that the machine will accomplish its mission. Use @Risk to help the company make this decision.

52 A ticket from Indianapolis to Orlando on Deleast Airlines sells for $150. The plane can hold 100 people. It costs Deleast $8000 to fly an empty plane. Each person on the plane incurs variable costs of $30 (for food and fuel). If the flight is overbooked, anyone who cannot get a seat receives $300 in compensation. On average, 95% of all people who have a reservation show up for the flight. To maximize expected profit, how many reservations should Deleast book for the flight? (*Hint*: The @Risk function RISKBINOMIAL can be used to simulate the number who show up. It takes two arguments: the number of reservations booked and the probability that any ticketed person shows up.)

53 A Tax Saver Benefit (TSB) plan allows you to put money into an account at the beginning of the calendar year that can be used for medical expenses. This amount is not subject to federal tax (hence the name TSB). As you pay medical expenses during the year, you are reimbursed by the administrator of the TSB until the TSB account is exhausted. From that point on, you must pay your medical expenses out of your own pocket. On the other hand, if you put more money into your TSB than the medical expenses you incur, this extra money is lost to you. Your annual salary is $80,000 and your federal income tax rate is 30%.

    a Assume that your annual medical expense is normally distributed with mean $2000 and standard deviation $500. Build an @Risk model in which the output is the amount of money left to you after paying taxes, putting money in a TSB, and paying any extra medical expenses. Experiment with the amount of money put into the TSB, using a RISKSIMTABLE function.

    b Rework part **a**, but this time assume a gamma distribution (with @Risk's RISKGAMMA function) for your annual medical expenses. Use $\alpha = 16$ and $\beta = 125$ as the two parameters of this distribution. These imply the same mean and standard deviation as in part **a**, but the distribution of medical expenses is now skewed to the right, which is probably more realistic. Using simulation, see whether you should now put more or less money in a TSB than in the symmetric case in part **a**.

54 Lowland Appliance replenishes its stock of color televisions three times a year. Each order takes 1/9 of a year to arrive. The annual demand for the color televisions follows a normal distribution with mean 990 and standard deviation 40. Assume that the cost of holding a television in inventory for a year is $100. Also, assume that Lowland begins with 500 televisions in inventory, the cost of a shortage is $150, and the cost of placing an order is $500.

   a Suppose that whenever inventory is reviewed and the inventory level is x, Lowland orders $480 - x$ TVs. Estimate the average annual cost of such a policy. (Such a policy is called an "order-up-to" policy. The "order-up-to quantity" in this case is 480.)

   b Estimate the average annual cost for each of the following order-up-to quantities: 200, 400, 600, and 800.

55 Assume that all of your job applicants must take a test, and that the scores on this test are normally distributed. The "selection ratio" is the cutoff point you use in your hiring process. For example, a selection ratio of 20% means that you will accept applicants for jobs who rank in the top 20% of all applicants. If you choose a selection ratio of 20%, the average test score of those selected will be 1.40 standard deviations above average. Use simulation to verify this fact, proceeding as follows.

   a Show that if you want to accept only the top 20% of all applicants, you should accept applicants whose test scores are at least 0.84 standard deviation above average. (No simulation is required here. Just use the appropriate Excel normal function.)

   b Now generate 400 test scores from a normal distribution with mean 0 and standard deviation 1. The average test score of those selected is the average of the scores that are at least 0.84. To determine this, use Excel's DAVERAGE function. To do so, put a heading Score in cell A3, generate the 400 test scores in the range A4:A403, and name the range A3:A403 Data. In cells C3 and C4, enter the *labels* Score and >0.84. (The range C3:C4 is called the *criterion* range.) Then calculate the average of all applicants who will be hired by entering the formula =DAVERAGE(Data,"Scores",C3:C4) in any cell. This average should be close to the theoretical average, 1.40. [This formula works as follows. Excel finds all observations in the Data range that satisfy the criterion described in the range C3:C4 (Score>0.84). Then it averages the values in the Score column (the second argment of DAVERAGE) corresponding to these entries. Look in online help for more about Excel's database functions.]

   c What information would you need to determine an "optimal" selection ratio? How could you determine an optimal selection ratio?

Level B

56 We begin year 1 with $500. At the beginning of each year, we put half of our money under our mattress and invest the other half in Whitewater stock. During each year, there is a 50% chance that the Whitewater stock will double, and there is a 50% chance that we will lose half of our investment. To illustrate, if the stock doubles during the first year, we will have $375 under the mattress and $375 invested in Whitewater during year 2. We want to estimate our annual return over a 50-year period. If we end with F dollars, then our annual return is $(F/500)^{1/50} - 1$. For example, if we end with $10,000, our annual return is $20^{1/50} - 1 = 0.062$, or 6.2%. Run 100 replications of an appropriate simulation. Based on the results, we can be 95% certain that our annual return will be between what two values?

57 Truckco produces the OffRoad truck. The company wants to gain information about the discounted profits earned during the next 3 years. During a given year the total number of trucks sold in the United States is

$$500,000 + 50,000\text{GNP} - 40,000\text{INF}$$

where GNP is the percentage increase in gross national product during the year and INF is the percentage increase in the consumer price index (CPI) during the year. During the next 3 years Value Line has made the predictions listed in the file P16_57.XLS. In the past, 95% of Value Line's GNP predictions have been accurate within 6%, and 95% of Value Line's INF predictions have been accurate within 5%. We assume that the actual GNP and INF values are normally distributed each year.

    At the beginning of each year, a number of competitors may enter the trucking business. The probability distribution of the number of new entrants in any year is also given in the file P16_57.XLS. Before competitors join the industry at the beginning of year 1 there are two competitors. During a year that begins with c competitors (after competitors have entered the business, but before any have left), Truckco will have a market share of $0.5(0.9)^c$. For example, if there are $c = 2$ competitors, Truckco's market share will be 40.5%. At the end of each year, there is a 20% chance that any given competitor will leave the industry. The sales price of the truck and production cost per truck are also given in the file P16_57.XLS. Simulate 500 replications of Truckco's profit for the next 3 years.

a Estimate the expected discounted 3-year profit, using a discount rate of 10%. You can use Excel's NPV function here.

b Repeat part **a** if the chance of a competitor exiting increases from 20% to 50%.

58 [Based on Altman (1986)] The Weaver Company, a textile firm, wants to simulate its cash budget for the year 1999. We make the following assumptions. (All cash amounts are in thousands of dollars except where noted for the long-term loan.)

■ Each month, the monthly "base" sales follow a normal distribution with mean of $70,000 and standard deviation $15,000. Then the *actual* sales in any month is the monthly base sales multiplied by a seasonal index for the month. The seasonal indexes are listed in the file P16_58.XLS.

■ Cash sales for a month are 10% of monthly sales.

■ Monthly collections for January and February are each $50,000. For other months, monthly collections are 90% of sales from 2 months ago.

■ Monthly total cash receipts equal cash sales plus monthly collections.

■ Together, labor and material costs are a certain fraction (called the cost factor) of monthly sales. This cost factor, the same for each month of the year, is normally distributed with mean 0.7 and standard deviation 0.03.

■ Monthly cash disbursements include the following:

Monthly labor costs equal the cost factor multiplied by 20% of monthly sales.

Monthly material costs are $33,000 for January. In any other month, they equal the cost factor multiplied by 80% of the previous month's sales.

Monthly operating expenses are 19% of monthly base sales.

The quarterly interest payment in January is $2780. In April, July, and October, it is composed of the interest on the average loan balance for last 3 months, paid at the short-term rate of interest for 3 months, plus 3 months of interest on the $96 million dollar long-term loan, paid at 8.5% annually. The short-term interest rate for the year is normal with mean 14% and standard deviation 1%.

Taxes are paid in January, April, July, and October. Each payment is $4000.

Dividends of $2000 are paid in February, May, August, and November.

Capital expenditures are $4500 in March, $4600 in June, $4800 in September, and $4900 in December.

■ At the beginning of January, there is a cash balance of −$7015. The desired ending cash balance for a given month (after adjusting the loan balance) is 18.8% of monthly sales.

■ Cash evolves as follows:

Beginning cash for month t equals the desired ending cash for month $t − 1$.

End of month cash for month t equals the beginning cash for month t plus the net cash flow for month t.

For all but January, the ending loan balance for month t equals the ending loan balance for month $t − 1$ plus the desired cash for month t minus the end-of-month cash for month t.

For January, the ending loan balance equals the ending January desired cash balance minus the January end-of-month cash.

Simulate Weaver's yearly cash budget 500 times. Find the mean and standard deviation of the firm's total net cash flow for 1999, as well as the mean and standard deviation of the firm's monthly average loan balance for 1999. What is the probability that the firm's 1999 net cash flow will be negative? What is the probability that the firm's ending loan balance will be negative? Note that the monthly net cash flow equals the monthly cash receipts minus the monthly cash disbursements.

59 Computco sells personal computers. The demand for its computers during a month follows a normal distribution, with mean 400 and standard deviation 100. Each time an order is placed, a fixed cost $600 and a variable cost of $1500 per computer are incurred. Computers are sold for $2800. If Computco does not have a computer in stock, the customer buys a computer from a competitor. At the end of each month, a holding cost of $10 per computer is incurred. Orders are placed at the end of each month, and they arrive at the beginning of the next month. Four ordering policies are under consideration:

- Policy 1: Place an order for 900 computers whenever the end-of-month inventory is 50 or less.

- Policy 2: Place an order for 600 computers whenever the end-of-month inventory is 200 or less.

- Policy 3: Place an order for 1000 computers whenever end-of-month inventory is 400 or less.

- Policy 4: Place an order for 1200 computers whenever end-of-month inventory is 500 or less.

Using 500 iterations, determine which ordering policy maximizes expected profit for 2 years. To get a more accurate idea of expected profit, you can credit Computco with a salvage value of $1500 for each computer left at the end of the last month. Assume that 400 computers are in inventory at the beginning of the first month.

60 United Electric (UE) sells refrigerators for $400 with a 1-year warranty. The warranty works as follows. If any part of the refrigerator fails during the first year after purchase, UE replaces the refrigerator for an average cost of $100. As soon as a replacement is made, another 1-year warranty period begins for the customer. If a refrigerator fails outside the warranty period, we assume that the customer immediately purchases another UE refrigerator. Suppose that the amount of time a refrigerator lasts follows a normal distribution with mean 1.8 years and standard deviation 0.3 year.

a Estimate the average profit per year that UE earns from a customer.

b How could the approach of this problem be used to determine the optimal warranty period?

61 Consider a device that requires two batteries to function. If either of these batteries dies, the device won't work. Currently there are two brand new batteries in the device, and there are three extra brand new batteries. Each battery, once it is placed in the device, lasts a random amount of time that is normally distributed with mean 20 hours and standard deviation 5 hours. When any of the batteries in the device dies, it is immediately replaced by an extra (if an extra is still available). Use @Risk to simulate the time the device can last with the batteries currently available.

62 In Problem 50 we assumed that all components in parallel have *independent* times to failure. This might not be realistic. For example, the reason for component failures might be stress from an external force that operates on all components simultaneously. This would induce positive correlation between the component failures times—if one fails early, others are likely to fail early as well. Assume that the times until component failure are lognormally distributed with mean 100 hours and standard deviation 20 hours, as in Problem 50. However, suppose the correlation between any two component failure times is 0.5. Simulate the time until machine failure when there are n components in parallel. Do this for $n = 3$ through $n = 10$. (You can do this with a single simulation if you set up the spreadsheet correctly.) How do the simulated machine times with correlated component failure times compare to those with uncorrelated times?

63 Suppose you buy an electronic device that you operate continuously. The device costs you $100 and carries a 1-year warranty. The warranty states that if the device fails during its first year of use, you get a new device for no cost, and this new device carries exactly the same warranty. However, if it fails after the first year of use, the warranty is of no value. You need this device for the next 6 years. Therefore, any time the device fails outside its warranty period, you must pay $100 for another device of the same kind. (We'll assume that the price does not increase during the 6-year period.) The time until failure for a device is lognormally distributed with mean 1 year and standard deviation 0.5 year. Use @Risk (with its RISKLOGNORM function) to simulate the 6-year period. Include as outputs (1) the total cost, (2) the number of failures during the warranty period, and (3) the number of devices owned during the 6-year period.

64 Rework the previous problem for a case in which the 1-year warranty requires you to pay for the new device even if failure occurs during the warranty period. Specifically, if the device fails at time t, measured relative to the time it went into use, you must pay t multiplied by $100 for a new device. For example, if the device goes into use at the beginning of April and fails 9 months later, you must pay $75. The reasoning is that you got 3/4 of the warranty period for use, so you should pay that fraction of the total cost for the next device. As before, however, if the device fails outside the warranty period, you must pay the full $100 cost for a new device.

65 In the Walton Bookstore example (Example 16.1), we assumed that there is only a single product. Suppose instead that there are two competing products sold by a company. Sales of either product tend to take away sales from the other product. That is, the demands for the two products are negatively correlated. The company first places an order for each product. Then during a period of time, there is demand D_1 for product 1 and demand D_2 for product 2. Each demand is normally distributed with means 1000 and 1200 and standard deviations 250 and 350. However, the correlation between D_1 and D_2 is ρ, where ρ is a negative number between -1 and 0. The unit cost of each product is $7.50, the unit price for each product is $10, and the unit refund for any unit of either product not sold is $2.50. The company must decide how many units of each product to order. Use @Risk to help the company by experimenting with different order quantities.

a Try this for $\rho = -0.3$, $\rho = -0.5$, and $\rho = -0.7$. What recommendation can you give about the "best" order quantities as the demands become more highly correlated (in a negative direction)?

b Rework part **a** when the demands are *positively* correlated, as they might be with products like peanut butter and jelly. Now use $\rho = 0.3$, $\rho = 0.5$, and $\rho = 0.7$ in your simulations.

66 Simulation can be used to illustrate a number of results from statistics that are difficult to understand with nonsimulation arguments. One is the famous central limit theorem, which says that if you sample enough values from *any* population distribution and then average these values, the resulting average will be approximately normally distributed. Illustrate this result by using @Risk with the following population distributions, each of which is very *nonnormal*. Run a separate simulation for each. Specifically, run each simulation with 10 values in each average, and run 1000 replications to simulate 1000 averages. Create a histogram of these averages to see whether it is indeed bell-shaped. Then repeat, using 30 values in each average. Are the histograms based on 10 qualitatively different from those based on 30?

a Discrete with possible values 1 and 2 and probabilities 0.2 and 0.8

b Exponential with mean 1 (use the RISKEXPON function with the single argument 1)

c Triangular with minimum, most likely, and maximum values equal to 1, 9, and 10

67 In statistics, we often use observed data to test a hypothesis about a population or populations. The basic method is that we use the observed data to calculate a test statistic (a single number). If the magnitude of this test statistic is sufficiently large, we reject the "null" hypothesis in favor of the "research" hypothesis. As an example, consider a researcher who believes teenage girls sleep longer than teenage boys on average. She collects observations on $n = 40$ randomly selected girls and $n = 40$ randomly selected boys. (We'll assume that each observation is the average sleep time over several nights for a given person.) The averages are $\overline{X}_1 = 7.9$ hours for the girls and $\overline{X}_2 = 7.6$ hours for the boys. The standard deviation of the 40 observations for girls is $s_1 = 0.5$ hour; for the boys, it is $s_2 = 0.7$ hour. The researcher, consulting her statistics textbook, then calculates the test statistic

$$t = \frac{\overline{X}_1 - \overline{X}_2}{\sqrt{s_1^2/40 + s_2^2/40}} = \frac{7.9 - 7.6}{\sqrt{0.25/40 + 0.49/40}} = 2.206$$

Based on the fact that $t = 2.206$ is "large," she claims that her research hypothesis is confirmed—girls *do* sleep longer than boys.

You are skeptical of this claim, so you check it out by running a simulation. In your simulation you assume that girls and boys have the *same* mean and standard deviation of sleep times in the entire population, say, 7.7 and 0.6. You also assume that the distribution of sleep times is normal. Then you repeatedly simulate 40 observations for girls and 40 observations for boys from this distribution and calculate the above test statistic t. The question is whether the observed test statistic, 2.206, is "extreme." If it is larger than most or all of the t-values you simulate, then the researcher is justified in her claim; otherwise, this large a t-value could have happened just by chance, even if the girls and boys have identical population means. Use @Risk to see which is the case.

68 Chemcon has taken over the production of Wozac from a rival drug company. Chemcon must build a plant to produce Wozac by the beginning of 1997. Once the plant is built, the plant's capacity cannot be changed. Each unit sold brings in $10 in revenue. The fixed cost (in dollars) of producing a plant that can produce x units per year of the drug is given by

$$\text{Fixed cost} = 5{,}000{,}000 + 10x$$

This cost is incurred at the end of 1997. We assume that all cost and sales cash flows are incurred at the end of each year. If a plant of capacity x is built, the variable cost of producing a unit of Wozac is given by

$$\text{Variable cost per unit} = 6 - 0.1(x - 1{,}000{,}000)/100{,}000$$

For example, a plant capacity of 1,100,000 units has a variable cost of $5.90. Each year, a plant operating cost of $1 per unit of capacity is also incurred.

Based on a forecasting sales model from the previous 10 years, Chemcon forecasts that demand in year t, D_t, is related to the demand in the previous year, D_{t-1}, by the equation

$$D_t = 67{,}430 + 0.985D_{t-1} + e_t$$

where e_t is a random term that is normally distributed with mean 0 and standard deviation 29,320. The demand in 1996 was 1,011,000 units. If demand for a year exceeds production capacity, all sales in excess of plant capacity are assumed to be lost. Use simulation to help Chemcon determine a capacity level that will maximize expected discounted profits (using an interest rate of 10%) for the time period 1997–2006.

69   A highly perishable drug spoils after 3 days. A hospital estimates that each day's requirement for the drug is equally likely to be any integer from from 1 to 9 units. Each time an order for the drug is placed, a fixed cost of $200 and a variable purchase cost of $50 per unit are incurred. Orders are placed at the end of each day and arrive at the beginning of the following day. It costs no money to hold the drug in inventory, but a cost of $100 is incurred each time the hospital needs a unit of the drug and does not have any available. The following three policies are under consideration.

- Policy 1: If we end the day with fewer than 5 units, order enough to bring next week's beginning inventory up to 10 units.

- Policy 2: If we end the day with fewer than 3 units, order enough to bring next week's beginning inventory up to 7 units.

- Policy 3: If we end the day with fewer than 8 units, order enough to bring next week's beginning inventory up to 15 units.

Compare these policies with regard to expected daily costs, expected number of units short per day, and expected number of units spoiling each day. Assume that we begin day 1 with 5 units of the drug on hand. (*Hint*: You will need to keep track of the age distribution of the units on hand at the beginning of each week. Assume that the hospital uses a FIFO (first in, first out) inventory policy. The trick is to get formulas that relate the age of each unit of the drug you have at the beginning of the day to the age of each unit you have at the end of the day.)

70   Big Hit Video needs to determine how many copies of a new video to purchase. Assume that the company's goal is to purchase a number of copies that will maximize its expected profit from the video during the next year. Describe how you would use simulation to solve this problem. To simplify matters assume that each time a tape is rented, it is rented for 1 day.

71   Many people who are involved in a small auto accident do not file a claim because they are afraid their premiums will be raised. Suppose that City Farm Insurance has three rates. If you file a claim you are moved to the next higher rate. How might you use simulation to determine whether a particular claim should be filed?

72   Two companies, company A and company B, share practically all of the market share for a product with a large national market. (Coca Cola and Pepsi represent an example.) They compete vigorously with tactics such as advertising blitzes and coupons for reduced prices. Of course, they also try to outguess what the other is going to do. For this problem, we'll take the point of view of company A, which must decide what marketing strategies to take each week. These might be proactive or reactive. A proactive tactic might be to offer 20%-off coupons during a week, regardless of what company B is doing (or has been doing). A reactive tactic might be to offer 20%-off coupons during a week after company B does so. We'll assume that company A can react to company B's actions only in the *following* week (or later). For example, if company B does something in week 20, company A won't learn about this until week 20, so it won't be able to react until week 21 (or later).

Each week the total market share is split between companies A and B. For example, their shares might be 45% and 55%. Using these values for illustration, some of A's 45% might move to B next week, and some of B's 55% might move to A next week. The sizes of these movements are random, but they will depend on actions A and B take during the week. (They might even depend on actions taken in previous weeks. Consider the possible delayed effect of advertising, for example.) You can assume that the net change in company A's market share is normally distributed with mean and standard deviation that depend on current (and possibly previous) actions. You can make this dependence as simple or complex as you like.

The revenues and costs are as follows:

- Each percentage point in market share is worth a certain amount per week in net profit. This is composed of revenue (per percentage point) minus costs (per percentage point).

- An advertising blitz costs a certain amount per week. (For simplicity, we'll assume that each company advertises regularly at some "normal" level. The cost of this is included in the cost per week mentioned above. However, an advertising "blitz" represents something special, and it might be expensive.)

- Instead of, or in addition to, an advertising blitz, either company can issue coupons (at essentially no cost) for a certain percentage off the regular selling price. Then the revenue per percentage point of market share decreases by this coupon percentage.

Remember that we are taking company A's point of view. It can decide each week whether to conduct an advertising blitz, issue coupons, do both, or do neither. These decisions can be based on company B's actions in previous weeks, or company A can ignore company B's decisions. In any case, company B's actions can be generated randomly. To simplify the problem, assume that four fixed probabilities determine company B's actions each week: the probabilities of (1) an advertising blitz, (2) issuing coupons, (3) doing both, or (4) doing neither. (In reality, these probabilities wouldn't be fixed. They would depend on the previous actions of both companies, but this would make the simulation model extremely complex.)

Your job is to develop a strategy for company A that produces a large average weekly profit over the next 2 years, that is, 104 weeks. You can assume any beginning market shares for the two companies at the beginning of week 1. ■

Egress, Inc. is a small company that designs, produces, and sells ski jackets and other coats. The creative design team has labored for weeks over its new design for the coming winter season. It is now time to decide how many ski jackets to produce in this production run. Because of the lead times involved, no other production runs will be possible during the season.

Predicting ski jacket sales months in advance of the selling season can be quite tricky. Egress has been in operation for only 3 years, and its ski jacket designs were quite successful in two of those years. Based on realized sales from the last 3 years, current economic conditions, and professional judgment, 12 Egress employees have independently estimated demand for their new design for the upcoming season. Their estimates are:

14,000	16,000
13,000	8,000
14,000	5,000
14,000	11,000
15,500	8,000
10,500	15,000

To assist in the decision on the number of units for the production run, management has gathered the following data:

Variable production cost per unit (C):	$80
Selling price per unit (S):	$100
Salvage value per unit (V):	$30
Fixed production cost (F):	$100,000

Note that S is the price Egress charges retailers. Any ski jackets that do not sell during the season can be sold by Egress to discounters for V per jacket. F is the fixed cost of plant and equipment. This cost is incurred irrespective of the size of the production run.

Questions

1 Egress management believes that a normal distribution is a reasonable model for the unknown demand in the coming year. What mean (μ) and standard deviation (σ) parameters should Egress use for the demand distribution?

2 Use a spreadsheet to simulate 400 possible outcomes for demand in the coming year. Use the random number seed 5862. Based on these scenarios, what is the expected profit if Egress produces $Q = 7800$ ski jackets? What is the expected profit if Egress produces $Q = 12,000$ ski jackets? What is the standard deviation of profit in these two cases?

3 Based on the same 400 scenarios, how many ski jackets should Egress produce to maximize expected profit? Call this quantity Q^*.

4 Should $Q^* = \mu$ or not? Explain.

5 Create a histogram of profit at the production level Q^*. Create a histogram of profit at the production level $Q = \mu$. What is the probability of a loss greater than $100,000 in each case?

16.2 **The College Fund Investment Decision**

Your next door neighbor, Scott Jansen, has a 12-year-old daughter and he wants to pay the tuition for her first year of college 6 years from now. The tuition for the first year will be $17,500. Scott has gone through his budget and finds that he can invest $200 per month for the next 6 years. Scott has opened accounts at two mutual funds. The first fund follows an investment strategy designed to match the return of the S&P 500. The second fund invests in short-term Treasury bills. Both funds have very low fees.

Scott has decided to follow a strategy in which he contributes a fixed fraction of the $200 to each fund. An adviser from the first fund suggested that each month he invest 80% of the $200 in the S&P 500 fund and the other 20% in the T-bill fund. The adviser explained that the S&P 500 has averaged much larger returns than the T-bill fund. Even though stock returns are risky investments in the short run, the risk would be fairly minimal over the longer 6-year period. An adviser from the second fund recommended just the opposite: invest 20% in the S&P 500 fund and 80% in T-bills, he said. Treasury bills are backed by the U.S. government. If you follow this allocation, he said, your average return will be lower, but at least you will have enough to reach your $17,500 target in 6 years.

Not knowing which adviser to believe, Scott has come to you for help.

Questions

1. The spreadsheet COLLEGE.XLS contains 261 monthly returns of the S&P 500 and Treasury bills from January 1970 through September 1991. Suppose that in each of the next 72 months (6 years), it is equally likely that any of the historical returns will occur. Set up a spreadsheet to simulate the two suggested investment strategies over the 6-year period. Plot the value of each strategy over time for one simulation trial. What was the total value of each strategy after 6 years? Did either of the strategies reach the target?

2. Simulate 200 trials of the two strategies over the 6-year period. Create a histogram of the final fund values. Based on your simulation results, which of the two strategies would you recommend? Why?

3. Suppose that Scott needs to have $19,500 to pay for the first year's tuition. Based on the same simulation results, which of the two strategies would you recommend now? Why?

4. What other real-world factors might be important to consider in designing the simulation and making a recommendation?

16.3 **Ebony Bath Soap**

Management of Ebony, a leading manufacturer of bath soap, is trying to control its inventory costs. The weekly cost of holding one unit of soap in inventory is $30 (one unit is 1000 cases of soap). The marketing department estimates that weekly demand averages 120 units, with a standard deviation of 15 units, and is reasonably well modeled by a normal distribution.

If demand exceeds the amount of soap on hand, those sales are *lost*—that is, there is no backlogging of demand. The production department can produce at one of three levels: 110, 120, or 130 units per week. The cost of changing production from one week to the next is $3000.

Management would like to evaluate the following production policy. If the current inventory is less than $l = 30$ units, then produce 130 units in the next week. If the current inventory is greater than $u = 80$ units, then produce 110 units in the next week. Otherwise, continue at the previous week's production level.

Ebony currently has 60 units of inventory on hand. Last week's production level was 120.

Questions

1. Create a spreadsheet to simulate 52 weeks of operation at Ebony. Graph the inventory of soap over time. What is the total cost (inventory cost plus production change cost) for the 52 weeks?

2. Use a simulation of 200 trials to estimate the average 52-week cost with values of u ranging from 30 to 80 in increments of 10. Keep $l = 30$ for every trial.

3. Calculate the sample mean and standard deviation of the 52-week cost under each policy. Using those results, construct 90% confidence intervals for the average 52-week cost for each value of u. Graph the average 52-week cost versus u. What is the best value of u for $l = 30$?

4. What other production policies might be useful to investigate?

CASE STUDY **16.4   Bond Investment Strategy** . . . .

An investor is considering the purchase of zero-coupon U.S. Treasury bonds. A 30-year zero-coupon bond yielding 8% can be purchased today for $9.94. At the end of 30 years the owner of the bond will receive $100. The yield of the bond is related to its price by the following equation:

$$P = \frac{100}{(1 + y)^t} \qquad \text{(16.2)}$$

where P is the price of the bond, y is the yield of the bond, and t is the maturity of the bond measured in years. Evaluating equation (16.2) for $t = 30$ and $y = 0.08$ gives $P = 9.94$.

The investor is planning to purchase a bond today and sell it 1 year from now. The investor is interested in evaluating the *return* on the investment in the bond. Suppose, for example, that the yield of the bond 1 year from now is 8.5%. Then the price of the bond 1 year later will be $9.39 (= $100/(1 + 0.085)^{29}$). The time remaining to maturity is $t = 29$, since 1 year has passed. The return for the year is −5.54% (= $(9.39 − 9.94)/9.94$).

In addition to the 30-year-maturity zero-coupon bond, the investor is considering the purchase of zero-coupon bonds with maturities of 2, 5, 10, or 20 years. All of the bonds are currently yielding 8.0%. (Bond investors describe this as a *flat yield curve.*) The investor cannot predict the future yields of the bonds with certainty. However, the investor believes that the yield of each bond 1 year from now can be modeled by a normal distribution with a mean of 8% and a standard deviation of 1%.

Questions

1   Suppose that the yields of the five zero-coupon bonds are all 8.5% a year from today. What are the returns of each bond over the period?

2   Using a simulation of 500 trials with a random number seed of 2814, estimate the expected return of each bond over the year. Estimate the standard deviations of the returns. Construct 90% confidence intervals for the expected returns.

3   Comment on the following statement: "The expected yield of the 30-year bond 1 year from today is 8%. At that yield, its price would be $10.73. The return for the year would be 8% (= (10.73 − 9.94)/9.94). Hence, the average return for the bond should be 8% as well. A simulation isn't really necessary. Any difference between 8% and the answer in Question 2 must be due to simulation error."

REFERENCES

Aarvik, O., and P. Randolph. "The Application of Linear Programming to the Determination of Transmission Line Fees in an Electrical Power Network." *Interfaces* 6 (1975): 17–31.

Albright, S. C. "A Statistical Analysis of Hitting Streaks in Baseball." *Journal of the American Statistical Association* 88, no. 424 (1993): 1175–1196.

Altman, E. *Handbook of Corporate Finance*. New York: Wiley, 1986.

Appleton, D., J. French, and M. Vanderpump. "Ignoring a Covariate: An Example of Simpson's Paradox." *The American Statistician* 50 (1996): 340–341.

Armstrong, S. "Forecasting by Extrapolation: Conclusions from 25 Years of Research." *Interfaces* 14, no. 6 (1984): 52–66.

Armstrong, S. *Long-Range Forecasting*. New York: Wiley, 1985.

Armstrong, S. "Research on Forecasting: A Quarter-Century Review, 1960–1984." *Interfaces* 16, no. 1 (1986): 89–103.

Arntzen, B., G. Brown, T. Harrison, and L. Trafton. "Global Supply Chain Management at Digital Equipment Corporation." *Interfaces* 25, no. 1 (1995): 69–93.

Babich, P. "Customer Satisfaction: How Good Is Good Enough?" *Quality Progress* 25 (1992): 65–68.

Balson, W., J. Welsh, and D. Wilson. "Using Decision Analysis and Risk Analysis to Manage Utility Environmental Risk." *Interfaces* 22, no. 6 (1992): 126–139.

Barnett, A. "Genes, Race, IQ, and *The Bell Curve*." *ORMS Today* 22, no. 1 (1994): 18–24.

Bean, J., C. Noon, S. Ryan, and G. Salton. "Selecting Tenants in a Shopping Mall." *Interfaces* 18, no. 2 (1988): 1–10.

Bean, J., C. Noon, and G. Salton. "Asset Divestiture at Homart Development Company." *Interfaces* 17, no. 1 (1987): 48–65.

Benninga, S. *Numerical Methods in Finance*. Cambridge, MA: MIT Press, 1989.

Black, F., and M. Scholes. "The Pricing of Options and Corporate Liabilities." *Journal of Political Economy* 81 (1973): 637–654.

Blyth, C. "On Simpson's Paradox and the Sure-Thing Principle." *Journal of the American Statistical Association* 67 (1972): 364–366.

Borison, A. "Oglethorpe Power Corporation Decides about Investing in a Major Transmission System." *Interfaces* 25, no. 2 (1995): 25–36.

Boykin, R. "Optimizing Chemical Production at Monsanto." *Interfaces* 15, no. 1 (1985): 88–95.

Brigandi, A., D. Dargon, M. Sheehan, and T. Spencer. "AT&T's Call Processing Simulator (CAPS) Operational Design for Inbound Call Centers." *Interfaces* 24, no. 1 (1994): 6–28.

Brinkley, P., D. Stepto, J. Haag, K. Liou, K. Wang, and W. Carr. "Nortel Redefines Factory Information Technology: An OR-Driven Approach." *Interfaces* 28, no. 1 (1988): 37–52.

Brown, G., et al. "Real-Time Wide Area Dispatch of Mobil Tank Trucks." *Interfaces* 17, no. 1 (1987): 107–120.

Cebry, M., A. DeSilva, and F. DiLisio. "Management Science in Automating Postal Operations: Facility and Equipment Planning in the United States Postal Service." *Interfaces* 22, no. 1 (1992): 110–130.

Charnes, A., and L. Cooper. "Generalization of the Warehousing Model." *Operational Research Quarterly* 6 (1955): 131–172.

Cox, J., S. Ross, and M. Rubenstein. "Option Pricing: A Simplified Approach." *Journal of Financial Economics* 7 (1979): 229–263.

Deming, E., *Out of the Crisis*. Cambridge, MA: MIT Center for Advanced Engineering Study, 1986.

DeWitt, C., L. Lasdon, A. Waren, D. Brenner, and S. Melhem. "OMEGA: An Improved Gasoline Blending System for Texaco." *Interfaces* 19, no. 1 (1989): 85–101.

Eaton, D., et al. "Determining Emergency Medical Service Vehicle Deployment in Austin, Texas." *Interfaces* 15, no. 1 (1985): 96–108.

Efroymson, M., and T. Ray. "A Brand-Bound Algorithm for Plant Location." *Operations Research* 14 (1966): 361–368.

Engemann, K., and H. Miller. "Operations Risk Management at a Major Bank." *Interfaces* 22, no. 6 (1992): 140–149.

Eppen, G., K. Martin, and L. Schrage. "A Scenario Approach to Capacity Planning." *Operations Research* 37, no. 4 (1989): 517–527.

Fabian, T. "A Linear Programming Model of Integrated Iron and Steel Production." *Management Science* 4 (1958): 415–449.

Feinstein, C. "Deciding Whether to Test Student Athletes for Drug Use." *Interfaces* 20, no. 3 (1990): 80–87.

Fitzsimmons, J., and L. Allen. "A Warehouse Location Model Helps Texas Comptroller Select Out-of-State Audit Offices." *Interfaces* 13, no. 5 (1983): 40–46.

GeneHunter. Ward Systems Group, Frederick, Maryland, 1995.

Glover, F., G. Jones, D. Karney, D. Klingman, and J. Mote. "An Integrated Production, Distribution, and Inventory System." *Interfaces* 9, no. 5 (1979): 21–35.

Glover, F., et al. "The Passenger-Mix Problem in the Scheduled Airlines." *Interfaces* 12 (1982): 873–880.

Graddy, K. "Do Fast-Food Chains Price Discriminate on the Race and Income Characteristics of an Area?" *Journal of Business & Economic Statistics* 15, no. 4 (1997): 391–401.

Grossman, S., and O. Hart. "An Analysis of the Principal Agent Problem." *Econometrica* 51 (1983): 7–45.

Hauser, J., and S. Gaskin. "Application of the Defender Consumer Model." *Marketing Science* 3, no. 4 (1984): 327–351.

Herrnstein, R., and C. Murray. *The Bell Curve*. New York: The Free Press, 1994.

Hertz, D. "Risk Analysis in Capital Investment." *Harvard Business Review* 42 (Jan.–Feb. 1964): 96–108.

Hess, S. "Swinging on the Branch of a Tree: Project Selection Applications." *Interfaces* 23, no. 6 (1993): 5–12.

Holmer, M. "The Asset-Liability Management Strategy System at Fannie Mae." *Interfaces* 24, no. 3 (1994): 3–21.

Hoppensteadt, F., and C. Peskin. *Mathematics in Medicine and the Life Sciences*. New York: Springer-Verlag, 1992.

Howard, R. "Heathens, Heretics, and Cults: The Religious Spectrum of Decision Aiding." *Interfaces* 22, no. 6 (1992): 15–27.

Huerter, J., and W. Swart. "An Integrated Labor-Management System for Taco Bell," *Interfaces* 28, no. 1 (1998): 75–91.

Kelly, J. "A New Interpretation of Information Rate." *Bell System Technical Journal* 35 (1956): 917–926.

Kimes, S., and J. Fitzsimmons. "Selecting Profitable Hotel Sites at La Quinta Motor Inns. *Interfaces* 20, no. 2 (1990): 12–20.

Kirkwood, C. "An Overview of Methods for Applied Decision Analysis" *Interfaces* 22, no. 6 (1992): 28–39.

Klingman, D., N. Phillips, D. Steiger, and W. Young. "The Successful Deployment of Management Science throughout Citgo Petroleum Corporation." *Interfaces* 17, no. 1 (1987): 4–25.

Krajewski, L., L. Ritzman, and P. McKenzie. "Shift Scheduling in Banking Operations: A Case Application." *Interfaces* 10, no. 2 (1980): 1–8.

Krumm, F., and C. Rolle. "Management and Application of Decision and Risk Analysis in Du Pont." *Interfaces* 22, no. 6 (1992): 84–93.

Lanzenauer, C., E. Harbauer, B. Johnston, and D. Shuttleworth. "RRSP Flood: LP to the Rescue." *Interfaces* 17, no. 4 (1987): 27–40.

Levy, P., and S. Lemeshow. *Sampling of Populations: Methods and Applications.* New York: Wiley, 1991.

Littlechild, S. "Marginal Pricing with Joint Costs." *Economic Journal* 80 (1970): 323–334.

Love, R., and J. Hoey. "Management Science Improves Fast Food Operations." *Interfaces* 20, no. 2 (1990): 21–29.

Magoulas, K., and D. Marinos-Kouris. "Gasoline Blending LP." *Oil and Gas Journal* (July 1988): 44–48.

Marcus, A. "The Magellan Fund and Market Efficiency." *Journal of Portfolio Management* (Fall 1990): 85–88.

Martin, C., D. Dent, and J. Eckhart. "Integrated Production, Distribution, and Inventory Planning at Libbey-Owens-Ford." *Interfaces* 23, no. 3 (1993): 68–78.

McDaniel, S., and L. Kinney. "Ambush Marketing Revisited: An Experimental Study of Perceived Sponsorship Effects on Brand Awareness, Attitude Toward the Brand, and Purchase Intention." *Journal of Promotion Management* 3 (1996): 141–167.

Mellichamp, J., D. Miller, and O. Kwon. "The Southern Company Uses a Probability Model for Cost Justification of Oil Sample Analysis." *Interfaces* 23, no. 3 (1993): 118–124.

Miser, H., "Avoiding the Corrupting Lie of a Poorly Stated Problem." *Interfaces* 23, no. 6 (1993): 114–119.

Morrison, D., and R. Wheat. "Pulling the Goalie Revisited." *Interfaces* 16, no. 6 (1984): 28–34.

Mulvey, J. "Reducing the U.S. Treasury's Taxpayer Data Base by Optimization." *Interfaces* 10 (1980): 101-111.

Norton, R. "A New Tool to Help Managers." *Fortune* (May 30, 1994): 135–140.

Oliff, M., and E. Burch. "Multiproduct Production Scheduling at Owens-Corning Fiberglass." *Interfaces* 15, no. 5 (1985): 25–34.

Pass, S. "Digging for Value in a Mountain of Data." *ORMS Today* 24, no. 5 (1997): 24–28.

Peterson, R., and E. Silver. *Decision Systems for Inventory Management and Production Planning.* 2nd ed. New York: Wiley, 1985.

Press, S. J. "Sample-Audit Tax Assessment for Businesses: What's Fair?" *Journal of Business & Economic Statistics* 13, no. 3 (1995): 357–359.

Ramsey, F., and D. Schafer. *The Statistical Sleuth: A Course in Methods of Data Analysis.* Belmont, CA: Duxbury Press, 1997.

Robichek, A., D. Teichroew, and M. Jones. "Optimal Short-Term Financing Decisions." *Management Science* 12 (1965): 1–36.

Robinson, P., L. Gao, and S. Muggenborg. "Designing an Integrated Distribution System at DowBrands, Inc." *Interfaces* 23, no. 3 (1993): 107–117.

Rohn, E. "A New LP Approach to Bond Portfolio Management." *Journal of Financial and Quantitative Analysis* 22 (1987): 439–467.

Rothstein, M. "Hospital Manpower Shift Scheduling by Mathematical Programming." *Health Services Research* (1973).

Salkin, H., and C. Lin. "Aggregation of Subsidiary Firms for Minimal Unemployment Compensation Payments via Integer Programming." *Management Science* 25 (1979): 405–408.

Schindler, S., and T. Semmel. "Station Staffing at Pan American World Airways." *Interfaces* 23, no. 3 (1993): 91–106.

Schnarrs, S., and J. Bavuso. "Extrapolation Models on Very Short-Term Forecasts." *Journal of Business Research* 14 (1986): 27–36.

Smith, S. "Planning Transistor Production by Linear Programming." *Operations Research* 13 (1965): 132–139.

Stanley, T., and W. Danko. *The Millionaire Next Door.* Atlanta, GA: Longstreet Press, 1996.

Strong, R. "LP Solves Problem: Eases Duration Matching Process." *Pension and Investment Age* 17, no. 26 (1989): 21.

Swart, W., and L. Donno. "Simulation Modeling Improves Operations, Planning and Productivity of Fast-Food Restaurants." *Interfaces* 11, no. 6 (1981): 35–47.

Ulvila, J. "Postal Automation (ZIP+4) Technology: A Decision Analysis." *Interfaces* 17, no. 2 (1987): 1–12.

Volkema, R., "Managing the Process of Formulating the Problem." *Interfaces* 25, no. 3 (1995): 81–87.

Walker, W. "Using the Set Covering Problem to Assign Fire Companies to Firehouses." *Operations Research* 22 (1974): 275–277.

Westbrooke, I. "Simpson's Paradox: An Example in a New Zealand Survey of Jury Composition." *Chance* 11, no. 2 (1998): 40–42.

Westerberg, C., B. Bjorklund, and E. Hultman. "An Application of Mixed Integer Programming in a Swedish Steel Mill." *Interfaces* 7, no. 2 (1977): 39–43.

Winston, W. L. *Operations Research: Applications and Algorithms.* 3rd ed. Belmont, CA: Duxbury Press, 1994.

Zahavi, J. "Franklin Mint's Famous AMOS." *ORMS Today* 22, no. 5 (1995): 18–23.

Zangwill, W. "The Limits of Japanese Production Theory." *Interfaces* 22, no. 5 (1992): 14–25.

Index